WHEELS
for the
WORLD

DOUGLAS BRINKLEY

VIKING

WHEELS

for the

WORLD

HENRY FORD, HIS COMPANY,

AND A CENTURY OF PROGRESS

1903–2003

VIKING
Published by the Penguin Group
Penguin Group (USA) Inc., 375 Hudson Street, New York, New York 10014, U.S.A.
Penguin Books Ltd, 80 Strand, London WC2R 0RL, England
Penguin Books Australia Ltd, 250 Camberwell Road,
Camberwell, Victoria 3124, Australia
Penguin Books Canada Ltd, 10 Alcorn Avenue,
Toronto, Ontario, Canada M4V 3B2
Penguin Books India (P) Ltd, 11 Community Centre, Panchsheel Park,
New Delhi–110 017, India
Penguin Books (N.Z.) Ltd, Cnr Rosedale and Airborne Roads,
Albany, Auckland, New Zealand
Penguin Books (South Africa) (Pty) Ltd, 24 Sturdee Avenue,
Rosebank, Johannesburg 2196, South Africa

Penguin Books Ltd, Registered Offices:
80 Strand, London WC2R 0RL, England

First published in 2003 by Viking Penguin,
a member of Penguin Group (USA) Inc.

10 9 8 7 6 5 4 3 2 1

Ford, Model A, Model T, Mustang, and Thunderbird are trademarks
of Ford Motor Company. Used with permission.

Excerpt from "Maybellene" appears courtesy of Chuck Berry through CMG Worldwide Inc.
(www.cmgworldwide.com).

ILLUSTRATION CREDITS
Insert p. 9 (top): attributed to Edmundson, Tiedtke & Stettler; p. 12 (top): attributed to Nachman;
p. 13: reproduced by permission of the Norman Rockwell Family Agency, Inc.; p. 14 (top): courtesy of Jim Graham. All others courtesy of Ford Motor Company.

LIBRARY OF CONGRESS CATALOGING IN PUBLICATION DATA

Brinkley, Douglas.
    Wheels for the world : Henry Ford, his company, and a century of progress, 1903–2003 /
Douglas Brinkley.
        p.   cm.
    ISBN 0-670-03181-X
    1. Ford, Henry, 1863–1947. 2. Automobile engineers—United States—Biography.
3. Ford Motor Company—History. 4. Automobile industry and trade—History.
5. Industrialists—United States—Biography. I. Title.

TL140.F6 B75 2003
338.7'6292'092—dc21
[B]   2002033066

This book is printed on acid-free paper. ∞

Printed in the United States of America
Set in Fairfield
Designed by Carla Bolte

To U.S. business historian

Ford R. Bryan,

whose knowledge of Ford Motor Company is unsurpassed,

and

to U.S. labor historian Warren Van Tine

of Ohio State University,

the best teacher I ever had,

and

to Stephen E. Ambrose,

friend and mentor

. . . Happy Trails

Every institution is the lengthened shadow of one man.

—Ralph Waldo Emerson

. . . a person educated entirely through books is only half educated. . . . The genius of America is production; and a large percentage of our productive enterprises are headed by men who have come up from the worker's bench.

—William Knudsen

Businessmen go down with their businesses because they like the old way so well they cannot bring themselves to change. One sees them all about—men who do not know that yesterday is past, and who woke up this morning with their last year's ideas.

—Henry Ford

CONTENTS

INTRODUCTION

"I think the wheels were in his head," Margaret Ford Ruddiman explained about her big brother Henry's lifelong mania for tinkering.[1] Indeed, from the early days of his youth, the wheels in Henry Ford's head were turning, in his fascination with farm tools and engines, gadgets and machines, and automobiles. And after that, with business, industry, and society; always, in sum, with how the world, and everything in it, *works*. Some of the flawed notions his mental gears ground out may detract from Ford's legacy as a human being, but even his worst failings cannot lessen the impact of his brightest ideas or of Ford Motor Company, which he founded to express them. Through the company or his own constant activity, the influence of Henry Ford was felt on American history and on human civilization, for good and ill.

The Reverend Samuel S. Marquis, an Episcopalian minister who for many years would head Ford Motor Company's sociological department, wrote of Henry Ford in 1923, "There are in him lights so high and shadows so deep, that I cannot get the whole of him in the proper focus at the same time."[2] W. C. Cowling, the company's sales manager from 1931 to 1937, likewise had trouble penetrating his boss's mercurial temperament. "I think," Cowling explained in reminiscences taped by the Henry Ford Museum and Library in 1951, "Henry Ford's personality was almost ethereal. You might not see him for months, but the spirit of Henry Ford was in that organization always. His personality dominated people whether he said anything or only sat there. He dominated a group because of his personality, not his money, but his personality I can't describe. I think he would have been the same if he'd only had twenty cents."[3]

As I grew up in Perrysburg, Ohio, a suburb of Toledo located on the Maumee River, Henry Ford and his motor company were a part of my life. Every spring, with pronounced regularity, my classmates and I would board a school bus and travel fifty-five miles to the Henry Ford Museum & Greenfield Village for our annual field trip. The collection of buildings in Dearborn is homage to American invention, all of the edifices moved from their original location by Henry Ford. We learned how Thomas Edison invented the lightbulb in his New Jersey laboratory, how George Washington Carver experimented with peanuts in his Alabama institute, and how the Wright brothers transformed their Ohio bicycle shop into an airplane design center. Decades later I still have fond memories of wandering around Greenfield Village, having a try at churning butter, watching a blacksmith make harnesses, and putting around the premises in a chauffeured Model T. Ford's goal was to make history tangible, and so he did. But mostly on these field trips we learned about Henry Ford— the tireless mechanic who put the world on wheels.

The Ford dealership closest to my house growing up was in the town of Maumee, just across the Maumee River from Perrysburg, on a bluff where General William Henry Harrison built a fort during the War of 1812. It was owned by a wonderful man named Will Donaldson, who regaled me with incredible stories about being Henry Ford's chauffeur during the Great Depression. Donaldson, whose father worked for Ford Motor, had graduated from the first high school class sponsored by Henry Ford, held in an old nineteenth-century schoolhouse built in Greenfield Village. Ford, with an eye for young talent, employed Donaldson while still a teenager to drive him around metropolitan Detroit to conduct farm and factory inspections. Together they also drove to Boston, excavated an old fort in Georgia, made soybean burgers for dinner, and rebuilt old Model Ts that had been scrapped in a junkyard. Donaldson once showed me the special pass he had granting access to *any* Ford Motor facility at *any* time. Captivated by his tales, I did a school paper on the unique relationship he fostered with Henry Ford: it was, essentially, my first oral history project.[4]

During those class trips and casual talks with Will Donaldson, the stranger sides of Henry Ford's multifaceted personality naturally escaped my purview. Ford was, to my uninformed mind, the father of the automobile, a tinkerer extraordinaire in the tradition of Benjamin Franklin and Thomas Edison. In fact, Scotch-taped to my bedroom wall, next to autographed pictures of Detroit Tiger All-Stars Mickey Lolich and Al Kaline, was a Norman Rockwell illustration of the young Henry Ford sitting with his father on a Dearborn workbench, taking machines apart and reassembling them. Purchased at a Greenfield Village gift shop, this poster, titled "The Boy Who Put the World on Wheels," had been commissioned by Ford Motor Company in 1953 to help commemorate the company's fiftieth anniversary (it also appeared in *Life* magazine). Eventually, as I entered high school, the Rockwell picture came down, replaced by rock 'n' roll posters of the Allman Brothers and the Grateful Dead, but I did occasionally flip through a book called *Quotations from the*

Unusual Henry Ford. Rereading it twenty-five years later, I found two quotes I had underlined in green felt pen. One read: "I refuse to recognize that there are impossibilities. I cannot discover that anyone knows enough about anything on this earth definitely to say what is and what is not possible." Another one, starred, offered this counsel: "Life, as I see it, is not a location, but a journey. Even the man who feels himself 'settled' is not settled—he is probably sagging back. Everything is in flux, and was meant to be. Life flows. We may live at the same number of the street, but it is never the same man who lives there."[5]

It's not hard to fathom why such cracker-barrel wisdom would appeal to a high schooler. I, like many others, responded to Henry Ford's unfettered optimism. After graduation in the summer of 1978, I abandoned the security of Perrysburg for the Haverfield Hall dormitory at Ohio State University. And my own set of "wheels" became my rolling address, a used, gold 1970 LTD four-door hardtop. From 1960 to 1970, Ford Motor Company had manufactured over 411 different body-styles—the reliable LTD, sadly, ranked as one of the least exciting to a teenager. Yet, brainwashed, perhaps, by those field trips to Dearborn, I was proud to drive a Ford. That car, which bounced like a boat on water, was an extension of myself, my personal sanctuary, my trusty friend, which could take me wherever I wanted to go. Known simply as "the LTD," it remains a part of my college years as surely as Ohio State–Michigan football games, Halloween Harvest balls, and buckets of beer at the Varsity Club just off High Street.

Besides my attachment to the LTD, for which I would change spark plugs, put on new fan belts, and pour transmission fluid, I took a general interest in cars. Nearly every month I would purchase *Car and Driver, Cars & Parts,* and *Road & Track* from the 7-Eleven just a few blocks from my dormitory. Someday I hoped to drive a red Mustang II built on a 96.2-inch wheelbase with a 302-cubic-inch V-8 engine or a vintage Thunderbird convertible, which to my mind had always been much "cooler" than the Chevrolet Corvette. Some people fantasize about a dream home; I always imagined owning my own dream car.

It was as a history major at Ohio State that I learned some of the more surprising facts of Henry Ford's illustrious career. As a student, I developed a particular passion for studies of the U.S. labor movement, thanks in large measure to the best teacher I've ever encountered, Professor Warren Van Tine. With great conviction, Van Tine regaled his class with stories about Woody Guthrie hitchhiking across America with "This Machine Kills Fascists" carved on his six-string guitar, Mother Jones assailing mine owners for poisoning the lungs of babies, and Samuel Gompers championing the Cigar Makers International Union as a prelude to organizing the American Federation of Labor. As I read books by labor historians David Brody, David Montgomery, Nelson Lichtenstein, and others, I was astonished to discover that Henry Ford was considered one of the bad guys, the man who boldly gave workers the "$5 Day" in 1914 only to become the most impassioned anti-union voice in America during the Great Depression. Suddenly, the Henry Ford I had first encountered through the idyllic history at Greenfield Village and at Donaldson Ford, full of Horatio Alger–like pluck and blessed with a genius for machines, was tainted. But one fact was irrefutable: in 1914 his company—Ford Motor—produced and sold more cars than the combined total sold throughout the rest of the world.

After Ohio State, I went on to earn a Ph.D. in U.S. diplomatic history at Georgetown University. On the side, I read whatever I could about the remarkable Henry Ford, thinking that someday I would write a book about him. Two biographies I particularly enjoyed were Roger Burlingame's *Henry Ford* and Carol Gelderman's *Henry Ford: The Wayward Capitalist*. The most informative book ever written about the sage of Dearborn, however, is David L. Lewis's *The Public Image of Henry Ford*. It soon became clear just how elusive the Motor Magnate was. Biographers had long grappled with contradictory accounts of Ford's own verbal accounts and his six ghostwritten memoirs, all of which are laced with anecdotes that don't ring quite true. "I've read everything that I could get my hands on about Henry Ford and I've never agreed with any of them in total," W. C. Cowling once grumbled. "I don't know of anybody that really captured him."[6]

Yet Ford's story hardly needed embellishment: he lived through fascinating times, and did as much as any other individual to make them so. Ford entered the world on July 30, 1863, just under seven months after President Abraham Lincoln's Emancipation Proclamation ended slavery in the United States, and just four years after French engineer Jean-Joseph-Etienne Lenoir built the first practical internal combustion engine, as well as the first vehicle to be powered by one. Although only five hundred of the temperamental Lenoir engines were ever built, they inspired budding engine designers throughout Europe. Even so, Lenoir's achievements were seen as no more than just another couple of sparks in the technological explosion that was redefining Western civilization throughout the last third of the nineteenth century. It was not until Henry Ford's day that the masses would begin to see the possibilities for a "horseless carriage."

Science and engineering burst forth, fueled by the enthusiasm of myriad thinkers and tinkerers in Europe and in North America. In Boston, Scottish-born American inventor Alexander Graham Bell's 1876 patent on the telephone revolutionized human communication. Thomas Alva Edison, the Wizard of Menlo Park, New Jersey, poured out a stream of world-changing inventions, including his 1877 phonograph and his 1879 lightbulb. Slowly but surely, the automobile was coming, too.

In 1878, Germany's Nikolaus August Otto improved on Lenoir's internal combustion engine by using an electric spark to ignite a mixture of coal, gasoline, and air into enough of an explosion inside a cylinder to push a piston and turn a drive wheel. In 1885, Otto's collaborator Gottlieb Daimler developed a gasoline-fueled, high-speed internal combustion engine that could propel a small motorcycle, and, a year later, the first gas-powered four-wheel car. Daimler's work not only predated Henry Ford's by a full decade but provided the basic mechanics for it as well. The pioneering French car manufacturing firm Panhard et Levassor, which issued a catalogue describing its gasoline-fueled automobile line, added to the fundamentals the American inventor would later draw on.[7]

For Henry Ford, being young in an age of prodigious invention meant being alive to share in the bounty of the day's innovations. Even better, he was part of a capitalist nation with an abundant supply of natural resources, the most advanced techniques for extracting them, and the biggest, richest, and least thrifty market of eager consumers in the history of human civilization. In retrospect, Henry Ford's career appears in part to be the product of an uncanny combination of fortuitous circumstances that put a Michigan mechanic of certain obsessive predilections in precisely the right places for him to meet exactly the right people at just the right times. In this way his natural talents were able to express themselves to the fullest.

In his 1855 masterwork *Leaves of Grass,* poet Walt Whitman offered a celebratory hymn to the *doers* in American life, those driven by the urgent potency of the dawn of the twentieth century: "A worship new I sing," Whitman rhapsodized. "You captains, voyagers, explorers, yours / You engineers, you architects, machinists, yours."[8] Indeed, when Henry Ford was growing into manhood, many of America's most durable heroes were bold individualists whose careers had melded science with commerce. Their inventions described their achievements: Eli Whitney's cotton gin, Robert Fulton's steamboat, Cyrus McCormick's reaper, Samuel F. B. Morse's telegraph, Alexander Graham Bell's telephone, John Deere's steel plow. The young Henry Ford aspired to join their ranks.

Populist to his core, Ford preferred fortunes born of production rather than the paper-shuffling kind that benefited only the stock manipulators and financial speculators who contrived them. He disdained men like railroad baron Jay Gould for being greedy "city slickers" helpless in a machine shop, research laboratory, or manufacturing plant. "Did you ever see dishonest calluses on a man's hands?" Ford once asked. "Hardly. When a man's hands are callused and women's hands are worn, you may be sure honesty is there. That's more than you can say about many soft white hands."[9] Ford, like his fellow automotive pioneers, had to either thread every rod and bore every cylinder himself or get an associate to do it. He also had to invent his own ignition system, and he did it all with midnight zeal. Ford saw himself as heir to a tradition of innovation that started with Benjamin Franklin, changing our national character and the world with it. As historian Willis M. West put it, "The American invents as the Greek chiseled, as the Venetian painted, as the modern Italian sings."[10]

Anybody interested in understanding the inventor Henry Ford and his car company must begin by reading historian Allan Nevins's indispensable three-volume study, written between 1954 and 1963. Nevins, working with Frank Ernest Hill, was given unprecedented access to Ford Motor Company Archives. A combination of group biography and business history, the Nevins trilogy profiled such underappreciated figures as James Couzens, Alexander Malcomson, Charles Sorensen, and Percival Perry. Other important books have been written since, but most focused on the Ford family, including a pair that were critically acclaimed: Peter Collier and David Horowitz's *The Fords: An American Epic* and Robert Lacey's *Ford: The Men and the Machine*. But nobody had ever written a comprehensive, single-volume business and social history of Ford Motor Company, and the centennial of its founding on June 16, 1903, suggested the perfect time for such a book.

In addition to my lifelong interest in Henry Ford, and the recognition of the need for a comprehensive Ford Motor Company business and social history, a number of circumstances converged that persuaded me to write *Wheels for the World*. As director of the Eisenhower Center for American Studies at the University of New Orleans, I oversee the largest collection of World War II oral histories in existence. We have tape-recorded and transcribed thousands of first-person recollections of our "citizen soldiers" at D-Day and the Bulge, Iwo Jima and Bataan. Impressed by our collection, William Clay Ford Sr., grandson of Henry Ford and a World War II veteran himself, contacted the center. Did we know that Ford Motor Company had hundreds of oral history "reminiscences" starting with its founding in 1903? Did we realize that in 2003 Ford Motor would be celebrating its centennial? Would we be interested in having access to the company's archive? An offer was made for me—with no strings attached—to pick up where Nevins left off in 1962 and write a fourth volume of the history of Ford Motor. Intrigued, I flew to Dearborn to discuss the possibility.

It was 1997; I had just finished writing *The American Heritage History of the United States* and was looking for a big subject to tackle. No subject could be quite as big as the whole American story, but Ford came surprisingly close. Its rich and influential history sheds light on most major aspects of the twentieth century. In conversations with Bill Ford Jr.—the son of William Clay Ford—who became CEO of the company in 2001, I made it clear that I had no interest in finishing the Nevins project. By its very description that would be a disjointed effort. What did interest me, however, was writing a single-volume business and social history of Ford Motor from 1903 to 2003.

Over the years I've been shocked at how the histories of major corporations have been ignored in high school textbooks and forgotten in university curriculums. Conservatives claim that the trend against corporate history came about because academia is dominated by liberals and leftists who disdain anything that smells of a Fortune 500 company. There is some truth to this argument—but only some. Corporations themselves are also to blame for the fact that they're largely absent from popular history books. By nature, corporations are secretive—afraid of costly lawsuits, upsetting stockholders, or revealing design innovations. They prefer to keep company files closed, cloistered away in some hidden storage facility on the outskirts of town. Most never donate their files to a public archive, where scholars would be free to analyze their achievements and follies. Most companies are overwhelmed with frenetic imperatives to sell this year's product and stimulate future profits. To them, history is often an inconvenience. They prefer glossy, illustrated books that present the company in a flattering Madison Avenue glow, or they opt for dull tomes that outline the facts chronologically, strictly according to the company line.

"What bothers me is that many people who work for our company don't have any idea of our incredible history," Bill Ford Jr. told me over coffee when we first met at his Dearborn office. "We've done a lot of things right and some wrong, but we've survived. We have a great heritage. I don't want to read a candy-coated history that pulls punches. A history of this company should be straight and honest, warts and all." Then he smiled and his eyes grew large. "We'll help you if you include the warts."[11] His comment struck me as a generous, if slightly unusual, attitude for the chairman and CEO of a major corporation. But Bill Ford Jr. is not just another run-of-the-mill executive. He is the great-grandson of Henry Ford, the founder of the company, and was bursting with what some call New Age ideas about the role of automobile manufacturing in the modern world. His pro-environment comments had made him the darling of the Sierra Club and Audubon Society, and he was on the record deploring many aspects of industrialization. He was unafraid, to the dismay of some stockholders, to discuss how petroleum might someday become obsolete, or how hydrogen fuel cells were the wave of the future. When a boiler exploded at the Rouge factory on a sad day in February 1999, killing six plant workers and injuring fourteen, he had received an emergency telephone call. He immediately drove to the site of the accident. Like any volunteer worker, he tried to help the situation the best he could, consoling families and digging through rubble. The *Detroit News* and *Free Press* applauded his actions, deeming him a caring capitalist. "Can you believe we've sunk so low," he asked me shortly after the event, "that when workers get hurt or killed they just assume the company executives won't show up, that we're only worried about law-suits and insurance costs?"[12]

Only time will tell whether Bill Ford Jr. will become a successful chair-man and CEO, but it's difficult not to like him as a person. A history major at Princeton University, Ford not only knows a great deal about his great-grandfather but has carefully studied the career of his uncle Henry Ford II, who took over the company in 1945. As our conversation continued, I was amazed to learn how much Ford Motor Company was planning to do to celebrate its centennial: a yearlong "heritage" media campaign promoting the enduring virtues of the Thunderbird, Mustang, Ford trucks, and other vehicles; a clas-sic auto show on the grounds of Henry Ford II World Center (also known as World Headquarters) in Dearborn with thousands of collectors' cars displayed; a NASCAR race in Brooklyn, Michigan; charity fund-raisers on the Dearborn Proving Grounds Test Track; the production of six new Model Ts; and on and on.[13] He promised that at the next Ford Centennial meeting, he would raise the idea of allowing me free rein from the corporate archives to the company Rolodex, with no strings attached. It sounded good to me: we promised to stay in touch.

Convincing others that I would not be a Trojan horse at World Headquar-ters as the company prepared for its centennial party was not an automatic sell. Objections emerged from numerous corners. How would this sort of "warts and all" history help sell SUVs? Did the company really need to be reminded of Henry Ford's anti-Semitism, Harry Bennett's thuggish anti-unionism, and Lee Iacocca's exploding Pinto on the eve of such an important company oc-casion? Understandably some members of the Ford family feared that what I professed would be a business and social history would end up being another exposé about the debauches of the rich. Eventually, however, Bill Ford Jr. pre-vailed, and I began writing *Wheels for the World,* making numerous research visits to Dearborn over a period of nearly six years.

To help me wade through the mounds of archival material and write *Wheels for the World,* Julie Fenster, a personal friend and historian, was brought onto the book project. We had worked closely together when I was writing *The American Heritage History of the United States,* and the editor of that esteemed magazine, Richard Snow, hired her to write the captions for the illustrations (I was impressed). She had started her career as an editor at *Automobile Quarterly* and was a well-respected expert on cars. When told about my plan to write a history of Ford Motor Company, she immediately hopped on board. She has been my partner on this book, researching obscure facts, helping organize chapter drafts, and offering her shrewd insights into the role the automobile has played in shaping the modern world. Collaborat-ing with her was a joy. Somewhere along the line we decided that once

Wheels for the World was finished, and Ford Motor was put into historical perspective, we would together undertake a centennial history of General Motors, which was founded in 1908, as a companion volume.

In writing *Wheels for the World,* I drew upon hundreds of oral histories; the more recent ones are quoted exclusively here for the first time. There are two main archives connected to Ford Motor Company on which I relied. One is the Benson Ford Research Center at the Henry Ford Museum and Library, which contains more than 25 million pieces of printed and archival source material on the company and related topics. The other is the Ford Motor Company Archives, established in 1951, currently containing approximately 10,000 cubic feet of records, including executive correspondence files, financial records, marketing and public relations materials, production and plant records, company publications, annual reports, photographs, and moving images. The Ford Motor Company Archives, which is not generally open to the public, has entered into a collaborative partnership with the Henry Ford Museum & Greenfield Village to provide access to the historical records of the company. Records will be transferred to the museum when they become available for outside research. I utilized both, but not without the help of some extraordinary assistance. Three Ford Motor Company archivists put untold hours into making this book a reality: Greta Krapac, Cynthia Korolov, and Elizabeth Adkins. Their knowledge of Ford Motor Company and their willingness to track down obscure articles and records were always beyond the call of duty.

As *Wheels for the World* developed, an unexpected change occurred in the way I would write the book. I originally thought that Henry Ford would not loom as large as he does, particularly during the fifty-six years after he died, in 1947. However, on the eve of the centennial, the business philosophy of Henry Ford was still a part of the company. Whether it was his unshakable belief in the importance of company "branding," his maxim that the consumer comes first, or his conviction that progress comes from a cooperative form of rivalry, Ford personified what the company was all about. "Why flounder around waiting for good business?" Ford once asked. "Get the cost down by better management. Get the prices down to the buying power." That is still the company's primary objective. *Wheels for the World,* therefore, tries to trace the enduring force he left to the company he created. It's not just that his only son, Edsel, and then grandson Henry Ford II and great-grandson Bill Ford Jr. have run the company in his wake. It is that at difficult junctures the Ford corporate executive or floor manager sometimes thinks about what the old man would have done. The main reason for Henry Ford's enduring legacy—both within the company and in the business world at large—was perfectly summed up by *Atlantic Monthly* senior editor Jack Beatty, who wrote in *Colossus: How the Corporation Changed America* that, "more than any other inventor, artist, writer or politician, Henry Ford made American dreams come true."[14]

Yet it often surprises people to learn that Henry Ford the "dreammaker" does not appear in the first wave of car inventors celebrated at the Automotive Hall of Fame in Dearborn. Henry Ford did not invent the automobile, but his hometown museum does credit him with putting the "world on wheels." Along the same lines, in 1999 *Fortune* magazine named Ford one of the five "businesspersons of the twentieth century" for creating the affordable Model T and selling more than 15 million of the "people's cars" between 1908 and 1927. *Time* magazine also honored Ford as one of the one hundred most significant industrialists of his time, noting that he changed U.S. labor dynamics by doubling pay for production workers back in 1914.[15] His company's implementation of the moving assembly line the previous year made "Fordism" the most imitated concept in businesses around the world. With the implementation of mass-production methods, including the moving assembly line on the eve of World War I, Henry Ford and his associates set in motion a second industrial revolution. Additionally, it was Ford's opinion—that the *work* should move while the worker stood still—that forever changed the way things are made, and even the way people think.

However, even though Henry Ford—and his motor company's assembly line—developed the means to put a good solid car in the lives of drivers around the world (an industrial miracle if ever there was one), he also sponsored the well-meaning if ridiculous *Peace Ship* expedition during World War I. He created a dense network of spies within his company and fought unionization with intrigue as well as deadly violence. He exhibited an odious anti-Semitism that will always stain his record. Yet he was in his early years an enlightened employer and implemented notably progressive policies for the recruitment of African Americans and the physically challenged in his factories. Henry Ford made one of the world's greatest fortunes partially off the genius of others, but it was he who drew them together and provided the spark of opportunity. All things considered, Henry Ford was a contradiction in virtually every term imaginable. As humorist Will Rogers would note of his industrialist friend, "It will take a hundred years to tell whether he helped us or hurt us, but he certainly didn't leave us where he found us."[16]

As for that disappointing *Peace Ship* voyage, upon returning to the United States three weeks after his vessel's launch, Ford admitted that "I didn't get much peace, but I learned that Russia is going to be a great market for tractors."[17] Indeed, the wheels were always turning.

PART ONE

The Farm Boy

1

Origins

Henry Ford was born on a farm in Springfield Township, Michigan, some ten miles due west of downtown Detroit, an area later incorporated into the larger town of Dearborn. Today it is all a heavily populated suburb of the Motor City with neon-lit boulevards, six-lane highways, and tract upon tract of housing development blocking the view of the flat landscape. In 1863, the year of Ford's birth, however, Dearborn was entirely rural, except for a small cluster of buildings marking the village center. The densely wooded terrain of southern Michigan tilted gently to the east toward a distant horizon, then just beginning to be smudged by the smokestacks rising from Detroit's first generation of factories. Farther still, Great Lakes freighters hauled lumber and raw materials from the state's heavily forested Upper Peninsula down Lake Huron to Lake St. Clair, then down the Detroit River to Lake Erie and the industrial centers of the Northeast. "At the time of the Civil War Detroit was a thriving but still a companionable small city in the home-spun middle west; it had 45,000 inhabitants, and although it had busy docks, shipyards, shops and small factories, it still had the look of its early days, and its base rested squarely on forests, mines, waterways and railroads," historian Bruce Catton wrote in *Michigan: A History.*[1]

When Henry Ford was born, copper was plentiful through the Keweenaw Peninsula in the western part of the state. Even more impressive to fortune seekers were the vast iron ore ranges—Marquette, Menominee, and Gogebic—found in the Upper Peninsula. Reports after the Civil War boasted that Michigan also had major deposits of gypsum, limestone, gravel, and coal.[2] And then, of course, there were the vast hardwood forests, which so impressed Alexis de Tocqueville on his famous 1831 pilgrimage written about in *Journey to America,* where settlements were "infinitely rare" and "cultivated fields seemed to stop all at once."[3] In the 1870s, when Ford was growing up,

Michigan may not have been an outpost as de Tocqueville described, but it was still a frontier in another sense, with its commerce driven eastward and its future looking toward the vast unsettled west. Growing up with such a sweeping perspective on America's wide-open spaces may well have been enough to turn a clever child's imagination to figuring out faster ways to cross those expanses, just to see what lay beyond the rolling plains.

Life down home on the farm sparked Henry Ford's imagination as a boy. It bothered him to see—and to know firsthand—the onerous amount of brutal toil that families performed just to keep their farms self-supporting, much less profitable. It was the potential of machines to ease the lives of farmers that first drew Ford to engineering, and that would continue to inspire his work and focus his business endeavors all his life.[4]

Fortunately for Ford, the village of Springfield Township offered the best of "heartland" life to a teenager with ambition in the latter part of nineteenth-century America. Originally established as a stopping point exactly one day by oxcart from Detroit on the way to Chicago 269 miles off,[5] Ford's township had the daily rhythms of a rural community, but shared little of the cultural parochialism typical of more isolated midwestern farm districts. Bustling Detroit was then, as now, second in size only to Chicago among midwestern cities. And it was near enough to Dearborn to impose its worldly thinking on matters from fashion and entertainment to politics and progress itself. Dearborn was no hick town, and the Ford household ranked among its most sophisticated, as evidenced by the family's subscriptions to several nationally respected newspapers.[6] So while Henry Ford did indeed grow up on a farm, it was hardly the sort of farm to breed a rube. In fact, his father, William Ford, owned one of the region's most prosperous agricultural operations, and in 1876 the well-tended Ford property was selected to represent Dearborn's best in that year's *Illustrated Historical Atlas* of Wayne County.[7]

William Ford had come a long way since leaving Ireland in 1847. At that time he and his family had little choice but to emigrate. They had been evicted from their small stone cottage near the town of Clonakilty in County Cork.[8] At one time, the leased, twenty-three-acre farm had supported as many as ten Fords. Unable to meet the rents, the family left Ireland along with about half of the country's rural population during the devastating potato famine of 1845–1848. Luckily, the Fords had somewhere to call home in America.

William Ford was twenty-one as he crossed the Atlantic in steerage class on a packet ship with his parents, John and Thomasina, two brothers, and four sisters. They were going to join his paternal uncles George and Samuel Ford, who had left for the United States in 1832, journeying across the Erie Canal to settle near Detroit. During the ensuing fifteen years the pioneering brothers sent letter after tantalizing letter extolling the New World's freedoms, as well as the bargain prices at which prime farmland could be had in unspoiled eastern Michigan.[9] As bright as their prospects seemed, however, the Fords suffered a terrible loss en route. During the passage, Thomasina fell ill and died; Henry Ford's grandmother was presumably buried at sea.[10]

The new arrivals, including William Ford, soon made it to Michigan, and built a log cabin on the Ford brothers' property in Springfield Township. A year later, William watched with a twinge of regret as his younger brother Henry headed off with a rucksack, to join the California gold rush.[11] William stayed behind to tend his duty as firstborn son. His father had purchased eighty acres for $200 down in January 1848 from fellow Irish immigrant Henry Maybury, whose family would remain financial angels to the Fords in coming years. The Fords arrived near the start of a period known as the Great Lumber Era in Michigan history; from the 1840s to the 1890s, the state's timber production was over $1 billion—more lucrative than all the gold mined in California at the same time. William caught the spirit of chopping away primeval forest. First he helped to finish clearing his father's acreage. Then he helped to pay off the remaining $150 mortgage on the land by taking a job as a carpenter with the Michigan Central Railroad.[12]

When John Ford retired in 1858, he sold his farm in forty-acre halves to his sons William and Samuel for $600 apiece.[13] The elder son was so proud to be a landowner that he framed his first property tax receipt written for $5.70 in 1859, and hung it on his living room wall.[14] As Margaret Ford Ruddiman would recall of her father, "The great miracle of America seemed to him to be that here was a place where a man could own the land upon which he lived and worked."[15] As a self-respecting Irishman, a people known for marrying late, William didn't think he should court a woman until he could provide for her and the family they might raise. Soon, though, William would be the first Ford in Dearborn prosperous enough to afford a horse-drawn buggy with a top.[16] By then he was also ready to marry.

The ancestry of Henry Ford's mother, Mary Litogot, has always been somewhat mysterious. Born in 1839, she grew up in Wyandotte, Michigan, the only girl among the four children of widowed carpenter William Litogot, who may or may not have been from Belgium; Henry Ford liked to say that his mother's people were Dutch. When Mary was only three, William Litogot died; accounts disagree as to whether it was by falling from a roof or through the ice on the Rouge River.[17] The four orphaned siblings each found a loving home and apparently fared well, particularly Mary, who became the pride and joy of her foster parents, Patrick and Margaret O'Hern. Despite filing no formal adoption papers they always acknowledged her as their daughter.[18]

Patrick O'Hern was from a district in County Cork called Fair Lane—a name that would long be associated with the Ford family and its cars. O'Hern joined the British army and left his home in Fair Lane at about the same time the first Fords had abandoned their bit of Ireland just thirty miles away, and he settled outside Detroit after deserting his unit in Quebec, Canada.[19] In 1850, when Mary Litogot O'Hern was only ten, William Ford signed on as a laborer at her parents' ninety-one-acre Dearborn property,[20] which had been assessed at a then considerable $1,000. In time, the serious-minded young man took note that the little brown-haired girl of the house had grown into a comely, dark-eyed brunette. She returned the attentions of the wiry handy-man with the thick wavy hair and clear gray eyes.[21] On April 25, 1861, when she was twenty-two and he thirty-four, they married.[22]

William Ford continued to work on his wife's family farm, moving into a wood-framed, two-story, seven-room house he and his new father-in-law built on the property. The plain, white-painted dwelling, to which four more rooms would be added over time,[23] was shaded in back by a spreading willow tree and was soon made even prettier by Mary Litogot Ford, who planted ever-greens in front, a pear tree on one side, and an apple orchard on the other.[24] The O'Herns treated William like a son. Within three years they had deeded all their land to him for $1,000, returning half that sum a month later in exchange for a lease allowing the O'Herns to reside on their former property for the rest of their natural lives.[25] A year after that, William Ford made a tidy profit by selling his own original tract, the 40 acres he had bought from his own father for $600 in 1858, for $2,500. With the proceeds he and his wife purchased another 80-acre plot farther west, adding an additional 40 acres to the east for $4,100 in 1867, thus increasing their landholdings to a substantial 211 acres.[26]

The couple's first child, a boy born in 1862, died in infancy; the second was born in an upstairs bedroom in his parents' house on July 30, 1863, and christened Henry Ford. Just four weeks before Henry was born, the Civil War's decisive battle had been fought at Gettysburg, Pennsylvania, ensuring the endurance of the United States as one nation. (As an adult Henry Ford, who fervently believed in reincarnation, claimed that in a previous life he had been a Union soldier who was killed at Gettysburg.) The Ford family had made its own sacrifice for the Union a year before, when Henry's maternal uncle, John Litogot, died in battle at Fredericksburg, Virginia, while serving as a "substitute" for a draftee who had paid Litogot $1,000 to take his place.[27] He was one of 14,000 Michigan men who lost their lives fighting for Abraham Lincoln. Apart from his parents' memory of that sad loss, and his reincarnation theory, the Civil War does not seem to have figured much in Henry Ford's thinking. The great event of the Civil War era, Henry would later say in all seriousness, was that his father invested in a McCormick reaper, which increased productivity of their farm tenfold.[28]

In his later years Henry Ford was nostalgic for the pastoral ideal of the Dearborn of his youth, veritably mandating the truth of his reminiscences by re-creating his hometown as he chose to remember it at his Greenfield Village outdoor history museum. His own sister, Margaret Ford Ruddiman, maintained to the end of her days that her brother's ardent nostalgia, including his autobiography's derring-do tales of remarkable boyhood feats of engineering, was largely the product of rose-colored hindsight.[29] Without question, however, he had an intuitive aptitude for machines. "He never learned to spell, to write a formed hand, to read freely, or to express himself in the simplest written sentence," historian Roger Burlingame explained. "But from the earliest time of which there is a record he was a master of mechanical logic: from a glance at any machine he could understand interdependence of its parts— follow a line of reasoning, however long, through gears, ratchets, cams, and levels."[30]

It remains, of course, both odd and ironic that toward the end of his life Ford would embrace such a sentimentally overblown view of the past, considering that it was his mass-market automobiles that did more than anything else to obliterate the nineteenth-century way of life in the rural United States. By all accounts, Ford as a youth showed nothing but contempt for the slow times in which he was growing up. In that sense, he was at fifteen already an American stereotype—the mechanically ingenious boy, growing up in some dull heartland hamlet, with an obsession for tinkering. Thomas Edison was cut from the same quilt, and as a boy cared little for lessons in reading and writing, wanting only to play with chemicals and clocks. At an early age Ford, like Edison, became almost entirely absorbed in the pursuit of all that he could teach himself about the mechanical arts and physical sciences, from direct observation and hands-on experimentation. And he was fascinated by the transportation revolution taking place in America. In 1873, when Henry was ten, San Francisco introduced its cable car to great fanfare. Even more exciting, in 1887, Richmond, Virginia, installed an electric trolley. The days of the horse-drawn cars were receding, replaced by the electric inter-urban track. The big question was: What next?[31]

Although William Ford managed to pass a love of nature on to his eldest son, the teenage Henry bristled at the supposed charms of his country upbringing and the hard work a rural life entailed.[32] "He didn't like cows at all, and he didn't like horses," Margaret Ford Ruddiman recalled of her big brother.[33] Yet a working farm is a natural laboratory for a tinkerer, especially one with a predilection for efficiency. Fortunately, William Ford, a quiet, hardworking man devoted to the farmwork that made his family so comfortable, with books and toys and trinkets to spare, gave his eldest son free rein to tinker with gadgets to his heart's content.[34] As Margaret remembered, "When we had mechanical or 'wind up' toys given to us at Christmas, we always said, 'Don't let Henry see them! He'll take them apart!'"[35]

And so he did, with both parents' blessings. Although Mary Litogot Ford was a practical and well-organized woman who took pride in keeping an orderly home, she willingly bent her own rules to allow Henry a workbench in the kitchen, so he could fix the other children's toys in any weather, as well as perform more useful domestic repairs.[36] She had a sense of fun. "She made it a good place to be," Ford would recall at age sixty of the mother he adored and the righteous household she maintained.[37]

Henry also remembered Mary Litogot Ford as "of that rarest type, one who so loved her children that she did not care whether they loved her. What I mean by this is that she would do whatever she considered necessary for our welfare even if she thereby lost our good will."[38] To the end of his days, Henry Ford always carried a little blue spiral-bound notebook in his pocket for jotting down aphorisms like those he had learned as a child from his beloved mother.[39]

After he had been one of the world's richest men for quite a while, Ford told an interviewer who asked the secret of his success, "I have tried to live my life as my mother would have wished."[40] It seems telling that in his prosperous years, Henry Ford would prove quite generous to his maternal relations and his wife's family, modestly supportive to his widowed sister Margaret Ford Ruddiman, and virtually oblivious to the fortunes of both his paternal relatives and his two surviving brothers, with whom he had never been at all close.[41]

Another influence on Ford's moral character was the *McGuffey Eclectic Reader* series, which was used in Dearborn's one-room, eight-grade schoolhouse. William H. McGuffey, a professor of moral philosophy at the University of Virginia, preached, among other notions, that bad boys invariably suffered horrible deaths, while good boys grew up to be president.[42] By the time he became president of Ohio University, McGuffey had sold over 122 million copies of his books, mainly to rural schools across America. They taught the fundamentals—like spelling and grammar—and also mini-courses in "Principles of Elocution" and "Lessons in Prose and Poetry." Among the many McGuffey maxims Ford could recite verbatim was a particular favorite of his mother's: "Life will give you many unpleasant tasks to do; your duty will be hard and disagreeable and painful to you at times, but you must do it. You may have pity on others, but you must not pity yourself. Do what you find to do, and what you know you must do, to the best of your ability."[43] Ford, who later reconstructed McGuffey's birthplace, a log cabin from Washington County, Pennsylvania, in Greenfield Village, believed he was the nineteenth-century man most responsible for teaching "industry and morality to America."[44]

Many of those who grew up with Henry Ford have attested that even as a child he displayed the talents, proclivities, and failings that would mark him all his life as that rare combination of gifted inventor, uninhibited dreamer, clever self-creator, and tireless motivator. As a result, he received special treatment from his family even beyond the privileges usually accorded first-born sons, including occupancy of the best-heated bedroom in the house so he could keep warm while tinkering into the wee hours.[45] Although like his five younger siblings—John, Margaret, Jane, William Jr., and Robert—he was expected to perform certain chores, young Henry also enjoyed substantial freedoms, as well as scant pressure to force him into any particular mold. "He was allowed to stay late in bed," Margaret offered by way of example. "There was no particular reason for it, except that he was sleepy. The rest got up and went about their duties, and he stayed in bed. That didn't happen every day, but that was a habit that he formed."[46] As one of his elementary-school mates, Alfred Monnier, put it: "You know that little devil was the laziest bugger on the face of the earth. I worked with him and his father on his father's farm as a hired hand. Henry would work along all right until about ten o'clock in the morning, and then he would go to the house for a drink of water. He would go and get the drink of water, but he would never come back!"[47] In his memoirs, *My Life and Work,* Ford explained away his aversion to labor: "My earliest recollection is that, considering the results, there was too much work on the place." He added, "Even when very young I suspected that much might be done in a better way."[48]

His parents' tolerant child rearing included an open-minded approach to religion as well, despite William Ford's own adherence to the American sect closest to the Anglican Church of his native Ireland,[49] where Protestants made up only 5 percent of the population of overwhelmingly Roman Catholic County Cork.[50] Alfred Monnier's older brother, Edward, who also grew up with the Ford children, remembered seeing the family heading out every Sunday morning to the Christ Episcopal Church of Dearborn in their horse-drawn wagon. William and Mary were always sitting up front and their offspring in the back.[51] Yet the children were allowed and even encouraged to attend services at other churches as often as they wished;[52] after all, their grandfather Patrick O'Hern, who lived with them, was himself a practicing Catholic. In fact, as Edward Monnier recalled, this division of faiths, which might have riven some households, caused not even a ripple at the Fords'.[53] "We were all unprejudiced, because I think our home influence was there," Margaret Ford Ruddiman explained. "We were taught that there was no difference [among believers in different religions]. That was instilled in me, and with my brother it was the same. We felt that one church wasn't the real answer. It was the way you lived and used your training."[54]

Where Henry Ford's later anti-Semitic bigotry came from therefore remains a mystery rooted elsewhere in his life. The common assumption, that he picked up his ignorant prejudices as a boy growing up on a farm in the Midwest, is reductionistic, as well as unjust to William and Mary Litogot Ford, who conscientiously provided their children an ideologically liberal upbringing. One possibility—which historian Neil Baldwin pursues in *Henry Ford and the Jews*—is that young Henry was corrupted, in part, by the offensive anti-Semitic passages that appeared with great frequency in the *McGuffey Eclectic Readers* he was weaned on.[55]

Yet Henry Ford's idyllic childhood, full as it was of privileges, gadgets, ice skating, and playground games, would be marred by the trauma of his mother's death.[56] Twelve days after her eighth childbirth, on March 29, 1876, she died, aged thirty-seven. Henry was not quite thirteen. His rather selfish reaction, typical of an adolescent perhaps, was that "a great wrong had been done to me."[57] Neither the family's daily routines nor the prosperity of their farm faltered as William Ford recruited his twenty-year-old niece, Jane Flaherty, to run the household and care for the children. The fun, however, was gone for the eldest son who had so treasured Mary Litogot Ford's high standards and love of laughter.[58] As he would lament in his autobiography, the consequence of his mother's early demise was that "the house was like a watch without a mainspring."[59]

After Mary Ford died, the household took on the more sedate character of William Ford, whose children remembered him mostly as he spent nearly every night after dinner: lying on a couch in the living room, reading his newspapers.[60] His favorite was the *New York Times*. In fact, their father was by then a leader in the community, variously serving as a churchwarden, on the school board, and at one point on a committee sent to Cleveland to assess that city's installation of electric streetcars and the feasibility of doing the same in Detroit (Ford voted in favor).[61] In 1876, he took it upon himself to visit the Centennial Exposition in Philadelphia, where he saw a huge two-story-high Corliss steam engine on display. While less amusing than his late wife, William Ford proved an understanding father who liked to relax with his children around him, taking them all to the circus whenever it came to town and enjoying the show as much as they did.[62]

Perhaps because Henry was the oldest, he was often aloof from his siblings, spending his free time either at his worktable deconstructing watches or by attending the Saturday dances, church socials, garden parties, husking bees, and other social events Dearborn put on for its young people.[63] Henry was popular and largely contented. All in all, life remained good on the family farm, even if it was hardly the idyll Ford would try to paint it, much later.

———

Despite William's efforts at persuasion, Henry Ford didn't want to become a farmer. The reluctant scion wanted only to get away and leave behind the grain and hay and cattle and sheep and timber and all the work they entailed. He thrilled, however, at hearing his father's stories about seeing the steam engine at the Centennial Exposition. One afternoon in July 1876, not long after

William returned from Philadelphia, Henry claimed he had an epiphany as he headed with his father to Detroit in the family buggy. A wonderful apparition came chugging right at him: a cleverly designed, self-propelled, homemade portable steam engine, the first road machine he had ever seen that could travel under its own power. It was not an especially pretty sight, being basically a "boiler mounted on wheels with a water tank and a coal cart trailing behind."[64] But horses and locomotives had pulled every engine the youngster had encountered before, and "this one had a chain that made a connection between the engine and the rear wheels" that enabled the contraption to move on its own. Nearly half a century later the great industrialist would claim, "I remember that engine as though I had seen it only yesterday."[65] According to his autobiographical account, it was at that moment that Henry Ford resolved to devote the rest of his life to building machines that moved.[66]

Within three years, at age fifteen, Henry quit school, abandoning the option of going to high school and college, the route taken by his best friend, Edsel Ruddiman (whose brother James would later marry Ford's sister Margaret.)[67] On December 1, 1879, Henry headed instead for Detroit and the machines that so captivated him. The youngster's first foray into the urban jungle was not, however, all that bold. "When Henry left the farm for the first time he no doubt had a sense of high adventure," biographer Sidney Olson noted. "Actually he was safe as in church. He had a place to live with a favorite aunt Rebecca Flaherty, whose daughter Jane was looking after William Ford's household. Behind him there was always the security of the farm, with a loving father ready to set him up on acres of his own."[68]

As bustling as Detroit seemed at the time, the Great Lakes port city was just beginning to grow into a major industrial center: its population had increased greatly during the Reconstruction era, numbering 116,000 in 1880 and 205,000 in 1890.[69] The city was teeming with industrial innovations in shipbuilding, steelmaking, chemical manufacturing, metalworking, and mechanics of every description.[70] If one walked for two miles down Jefferson Avenue, a broad street that ran parallel to the Detroit River, one would have found redbrick warehouses, lumberyards, wharf-front tenements, and machine shops in a scene of industrial angst straight out of the pages of Charles Dickens. Residing at the home of his father's oldest sister, young Henry quickly found a position at the Michigan Car Company Works, which built streetcars.[71] He was fired from his first job after only six days; the reason remains a mystery—Ford himself shied from the subject ever after, apart from a few dubious allusions to the effects of his mechanical precocity upon the egos of his more experienced co-workers.[72]

In any case, after that initial failure Henry's father secured an apprenticeship for him at the James Flower & Brothers Machine Shop, which specialized in the design and manufacture of brass and iron machine parts, and with whose owners the elder Ford was well acquainted.[73] If his boy would insist on tinkering for a living, William Ford preferred that he start under the watchful eye of someone known to his family. Henry's apprenticeship at Flower's, however, paid only $2.50 per sixty-hour workweek and his room and board cost a dollar more than that, forcing the young man to supplement his income with a night job repairing clocks and watches for a local jeweler.[74] He hardly minded: Flower & Brothers manufactured all manner of valves, steam whistles, gongs, hydrants, and other waterworks parts, so many that the shop had more specialized machines than men to run them, which opened up plenty of opportunities for a bright novice to familiarize himself with a range of equipment.[75]

Among Henry Ford's fellow apprentices at the Flower & Brothers shop was a ten-year-old named Frederick Strauss, who would go on to work with Ford at a number of enterprises during the next two decades. Eager as they were, the youngsters failed to get much out of their first professional experience. As Strauss later recalled, Flower's "had no apprentice system of any kind. We were just young boys working around the shop." Henry's assigned task, for example, was to operate a very simple milling machine. Although Flower's was fully equipped to take jobs from preliminary engineering and blueprinting straight through to forging and final machining, young Ford saw little of these processes beyond his machine and the cool cellar he and Strauss would disappear to on hot days. "We never had a better foreman in all our lives," Strauss enthused of the boys' oblivious supervisor. "The two of us could do just about as we pleased."[76] This would become a pattern, at least for Ford, of whom Strauss also recalled, "He never was a good worker, but he was a good fellow."[77]

Henry's next job was more serious, if even less remunerative at two dollars a week. It was limited to basic bench machining and provided barely more training than his nine-month apprenticeship at Flower & Brothers had.[78] But his curiosity would not be deterred. As one of his then co-workers would recount to a Detroit newspaper reporter years later, for all his talent at the tasks at hand Ford never worked "too hard"; instead he was forever "wandering about the shop" in his ongoing quest to learn all he could from whatever the more experienced men were doing.[79] Meanwhile, his friend Fred Strauss had started work at a factory across the street, and the two continued pursuing their boyish schemes. "Henry was always wanting to make things," Strauss recalled. "The first time I ever saw him spend any money—he usually got the other fellow to spend it—he bought a set of castings for $1.25." Ford intended to put this purchase into a miniature steam engine; all he lacked was the expert machining to make the thing work. For that he recruited Strauss, who squirreled the rough little castings one by one into his own workplace to finish on his employer's equipment when nobody was looking. As time went on, Strauss and other early companions would be joined by legions of Ford associates with tales of how Henry always wound up giving the orders while others did the work.[80]

As it turned out, the boys never finished their steam engine, not that the failure proved any great disappointment amid all their other projects. Among them, Ford had enlisted Strauss's help in fashioning a measuring device for a boiler (Fred's mother paid a plumber six dollars for the galvanized little model they worked on), in transplanting the workings of one of the Strauss family's clocks into a new and improved eight-day timepiece (the original clock never did get put back together), and in building a boat (which never saw water, and for which Fred's mother again footed the bill).[81] "Henry always had another idea," Strauss explained. "He always wanted to have something else. Every Sunday we started something and never finished it."[82]

Fortunately, at least for the Strauss household, Henry Ford for the moment went back to the land. He returned home to Dearborn in the spring of 1882; since he was nearly twenty, his hometown friends and relatives, chief among them his father, hoped and assumed that "Hank," as he was known then,[83] had gotten the big city out of his system and would settle down to preparing to run the family farm. But the wheels in the young man's head just kept on turning. He agreed to live at home, but insisted on going to work servicing steam engines throughout southern Michigan and northern Ohio as a regional representative for Westinghouse, which had offered him a job on the basis of his mechanical aptitude.[84] Ford had proved his worth with machines when a neighbor named James Gleason asked if he could fix his year-old Westinghouse no. 345, a portable, horse-drawn, 10-horsepower, 225-rpm steam engine the farmer had bought to power his grain separator. Indeed Ford could, and became so enthralled with the efficient little thresher while repairing it that he begged Gleason to let him run the steam engine all that summer, for three dollars a day.[85] And so he spent that summer and the next, living at his family's homestead but working elsewhere and spending most of his free time in the little backyard shop he set up and equipped with a stand-up drill, a foot-powered lathe, and tools of every description, along with a small forge for making more.[86] Thus surrounded by everything he needed for inventing, Ford turned his attentions during the next two winters to building a "farm locomotive" designed to ease what he had always deemed the physical brutality of agricultural life. He had little success at the time.[87]

For the rest of his life Ford would devote considerable effort to perfecting a tractor, an idea germinated by the same farm-bred determination. From the very first, Ford was fueled by the notion that men and women should be spared the harshness and tedium of physical labor, and he was determined to make machines that could do just that.[88] With his own workshop on the farm, he began his tractor experiments early in the 1880s, turning the frame of a wrecked mower into a chassis onto which he rigged his own primitive steam engine, basically a single, carefully hand-cast cylinder fitted with a piston, also of his own design. The resulting contraption sputtered some forty feet, then died.[89] What mattered, of course, was that it had gone at all, as that gave Ford reason to keep experimenting with it, in his unending search for ideal function through form. The pursuit of that grail, that harmony of concept and mechanics that would result in an efficient, smooth-running "farm locomotive," drove Henry Ford all his life, through every one of his endeavors from fixing watches to maintaining steam engines to building better gas-powered cars to founding the world's first mass-market automobile company. His perfectionism centered on improving the fundamentals of vehicle engineering: boosting power without adding weight, connecting engines to drives and wheels to chassis for optimum performance, and inventing the tools that could produce the mechanical advances he had in mind.[90]

Devoting all of his time to mechanical dabbling was typical of Henry Ford, who from childhood to the end of his days nearly always did exactly as he pleased. Yet as self-indulgent as this behavior appeared, then and now, according to the people closest to him Ford's conceit came not so much from egotism as from his single-minded determination to keep charging straight ahead, even if it meant keeping the blinkers on. While it seems doubtful that at twenty he had any idea his future lay in horseless carriages (despite several friends' recollections of some prescient passing references he made in the 1880s),[91] Hank Ford was nonetheless hell-bent after the new, the modern, and the latest technology his age had to offer.

It was just as Henry Ford was growing into manhood that the bicycle craze exploded across America. Popularized in Paris in the 1860s, the bicycle proved a cheap, clean, and efficient mode of transportation. By the 1890s men in knickerbockers and women in bloomers seemed to be pedaling down every country lane and urban thoroughfare.[92] Horses were costly to keep, labor-intensive to maintain, noisy on the cobblestones. A single steed produced several pounds of manure a day, a conduit for flies and life-threatening diseases. Many horses were mistreated by their owners and died of neglect, left to rot in the streets. Bicycles, by contrast, presented virtually no drawbacks or offense to anyone.[93] Many of Europe's bicycle manufacturers, in fact, were slowly venturing into the automobile business: Opel in Germany; Clément, Darracq, and Peugeot in France; and Humber, Morris, and Rover in Great Britain.[94]

Ford, like his European counterparts, adopted many components of the bicycle—its steel-tube framing, ball bearings, chain drive, differential gearing, and pneumatic tires—in his quest to create a car. Ford was not only unafraid of revolutionary change by way of technology, but desperate for it, a passion that afforded him an aura so dynamic, people said one could almost feel him enter a room. That jaunty self-confidence still glints through every photograph of the man (particularly those taken when he was young and handsome), along with his father's fair skin, pale blue eyes, and sharp profile, softened ever so slightly by his mother's fuller and less severe features. Fit and slender all his life, Ford carried himself with a confidence that made him loom larger than his slight five feet eight inches, just as he intended.

Henry fixed steam engines by day and took accounting, typing, mechanical drawing, and general business courses at downtown Detroit's commercial school, Goldsmith, Bryant and Stratton Business University, at night. And he worked on his own inventions when he could. When he was twenty-one, a petite, chestnut-haired young lady of Dearborn's small social circle caught his eye one night at a dance. With help from a mutual friend, he was introduced to the fetching, eighteen-year-old Clara Jane Bryant. Intelligent and sensible as well as pretty, she came, like her admirer, from a prosperous local farm family. The Bryant place lay just five "country" miles from the Ford homestead. Clara's father, the son of a Canadian immigrant, had served in the state legislature. The third-born child and eldest girl, Clara helped take care of a daunting nine siblings.[95] Clara Bryant was "a nice, good-looking girl, a popular and smart girl," Edward Monnier remembered. "She didn't go to many dances, and she didn't have very many beaus in those days that I know of."[96]

Henry Ford told his sister Margaret that he knew within half a minute of meeting the sober-minded Clara Bryant that she was the woman for him.[97] Ignoring his advances at first, before long Clara was piqued by how different he was from all the other, more frivolous young men. She was charmed by his intensity, such as when he demonstrated with genuine enthusiasm his dual-dialed wristwatch. Mutual friends never doubted Ford's chances of winning Bryant over: he was not only as serious and appreciative of pragmatism as she, but a fellow music lover and quite a good dancer, too.[98] Plus, as Edward Monnier recalled, Ford boasted one substantial material advantage: "He had a cutter."[99]

Ford's cutter, a low-slung, cut-down sleigh, was as swift as the horse that drew it over the snow covering the rutted wintry roads of Dearborn. It captured his youthful imagination, and for precisely the same reason his roadsters would prove so appealing to generations of other youths over the coming years. Like the Ford Mustang eighty years later, the 1880s cutter served as a sporty prop for the young at heart, and it attracted girls to boot. Neighbors gauged the relative seriousness of the couple's feelings toward each other by the frequency of Clara Bryant's appearances in Henry Ford's flashy little forest-green sleigh job.[100] The next summer, in addition to going on picnics and buggy rides, the couple secured time together by joining the Bayview Reading Circle, inspired by upstate New York's Chautauqua movement.[101]

Three years after they met, on April 11, 1888, Clara's twenty-second birthday, the two were married in a ceremony held at the Bryants' house. The groom wore a blue suit and the bride a wedding gown she had designed and sewn herself.[102] The Fords settled neatly into an enviable life for young new-lyweds. When they were first engaged in April 1886, William Ford had tried to induce his eldest son to stay down on the farm by offering him the use of the former Moir farm, a heavily wooded, eighty-acre parcel ripe for timber cutting.[103] Henry Ford began paying the taxes on this land in 1887, setting up a portable steam-powered, circular sawmill to produce lumber.[104] After his marriage he took his father up on the full offer and moved with his bride into the property's old farmhouse, which his siblings had spruced up for them as a wedding present. A year later Ford used some of the lumber the tract gener-ated to build a delightful, whimsically balustraded "square house" Clara Ford had designed for them.[105] Thus nestled, the young couple started down the predictable path laid out for them even before William Ford made out his will in 1896, leaving the eighty Moir farm acres to his eldest son.[106]

Within a year or two, however, Henry Ford began making plans to return to work in Detroit, specifically eyeing the Edison Illuminating Company, where he felt certain he could find a job. He deferred to his wife regarding these in-tentions, asking rather than telling her about the proposed move. Henry Ford may have been an impossibly headstrong man, but it was with more than a bow to sentiment that he always maintained Clara was the one person who could make him change his mind. "The Believer," he called her, and her belief in his endeavors remained essential to both his productivity and his happi-ness, not to mention both of their fortunes.

The idea of building a car, Ford later claimed, was inspired by the inge-nious "silent Otto" internal combustion engine, which his former employer, Westinghouse, had sent him to check out at the Otto's first demonstration in Detroit in 1890. The small, light power unit worked on a clever new four-stroke piston system: the first drew an incendiary charge into a cylinder, while the second stroke compressed the charge to spark ignition, expanding the mixture of air and gasoline to drive the piston's third stroke, followed by a fourth to expel the exhaust and start the process again. The engine proved a revelation to Ford. But the firing cycle of an internal combustion engine called for electricity, which he felt he didn't understand well enough. That is why he had applied for a job at the Edison Illuminating Company to begin with—to get a hands-on education.[107]

Clara Bryant Ford readily acquiesced to Henry's desire to return to indus-try in Detroit.[108] With that, the couple exchanged the sturdy square house they had built together for a succession of modest rentals. Margaret Ford Ruddiman later put this first of her sister-in-law's frequent sacrifices into per-spective, explaining that "it was a day-by-day progress. To us, it was just another day."[109] After the couple moved their belongings, with help from Clara's brothers, by hay wagon to a small, ten-dollar-a-month apartment in Detroit in September 1891, Henry Ford bought a subdivided residential lot, presumably to build a house for them, but he sold it two years later.[110] Over the next two decades, as things turned out, Henry and Clara Bryant Ford would move their household into at least ten different rented dwellings before settling down in another house of their own.[111]

The Fords returned to a city falling prey to the economic depression of 1891–1892. A full third of Detroit residents who wanted work couldn't find it. More than 700 of the city's manufacturing concerns were affected, including most of the region's shipbuilding and rail-equipment companies, putting some 25,000 people out of jobs.[112] Before long the Erie Northern Pacific and the Union Pacific Railroads declared bankruptcy. Homeless vagabonds filled the streets looking for bread and shelter. Starving children begged for nickels while working-class women prostituted themselves. Banks began closing with frightening regularity. Honest daily wages were so hard to come by that capitalism was being denounced by dimestore demagogues and ward politicians offering better ways to live.

Henry Ford, however, had no trouble securing the position he desired as a mechanical engineer at the Woodward and Willis Avenue Substation of Detroit's Edison Illuminating Company. He was aggressive, well connected, and fairly well equipped for the mechanical aspects of the job. Detroit Edison provided electricity to about a thousand of the city's residences as well as to some five thousand streetlights. The company operated massive steam generators, and at the age of twenty-eight, Ford was hired by a former Flower & Brothers supervisor to tend one over the twelve-hour night shift. His predecessor had been killed on the job. Undaunted, Ford soon made himself expert at keeping the generator functioning all by himself. This feat attracted enough notice to get him quickly promoted and his salary raised from $40 to $75 a month. Before long he was elevated to chief engineer at the Woodward and Willis Avenue plant, which put him on call at all times at the substantial wage of $1,000 a year.[113]

According to Fred Strauss, to Ford "on call" often meant working on his own projects at the substation, using Edison's equipment to tinker on company time. Along the same lines, through the winter of 1892–1893 Ford taught night classes in machine-shop practice at the Detroit YMCA, for $2.50 per session plus access to the shop's facilities to pursue his own experiments with engine parts.[114]

On November 6, 1893, Clara and Henry's only child was born, a son they named Edsel Bryant Ford after Henry's closest childhood friend, Edsel Ruddiman.[115] A few days later Henry received another raise, to $90 a month, and three weeks after that found himself promoted to chief engineer at the main Edison plant downtown. His new job was located twenty-five blocks from the house he and Clara had rented just that May, precipitating yet another move, one that would prove fortuitous. Their new rental, a brownstone row house at 58 Bagley Avenue, was just three blocks from Detroit Edison and was among the first houses in the city to be wired for electricity. Best of all, it came with a backyard shed that made an ideal workshop, and from it would roll Henry Ford's first gasoline-powered vehicle.[116]

Both Fords later claimed, separately and together, that the reason Henry wanted to return to Detroit in 1891 was to gain the knowledge he needed to build a gasoline-powered motorcar, the fundamentals of which he supposedly sketched out for his wife one night on the back of a piece of sheet music she had been playing on their piano.

Many biographers, along with a number of Ford's colleagues, have expressed doubt that Henry Ford really had narrowed his goals to the creation of a gasoline-powered motor vehicle before moving to Detroit. Not that there would be anything so remarkable in wanting to build a self-propelled vehicle. The dream of a horseless carriage had wafted around throughout the nineteenth century and been realized in Europe in 1885 with the first differential-gear tricycle designed by Carl Benz, an outsize three-wheeler with a small engine turning the rear axle. A vibrant automobile industry was emerging by 1891 in Germany and France, but the United States remained two years away from its very first car ride. That moment finally occurred in September 1893, when the brothers Charles and Frank Duryea drove a gasoline-powered conveyance of their own devising on the streets of Springfield, Massachusetts.[117]

Like the Duryeas, Ford believed at the dawn of the automobile age that the gasoline engine was the most sensible power plant for cars. As much as he revered steam engines he also knew their drawbacks: steam engines took a long time to warm up. As to electrics, the weight of electric batteries made the cars they propelled quite slow.[118]

By Christmas Eve 1893, Ford was ready to test his own inaugural gas engine, a tabletop model made of scraps and looking like nothing so much as a toy cannon mounted on a board.[119] Its principles were simple. He had plugged up one end of a length of gas pipe, left behind by a boiler repairman at the Edison engine room. He then drilled a hole in it and inserted a piece of wire, positioned to make and break contact with the butt end of another wire. This process created a spark that would ignite the mix of air and gasoline inside the cylinder, thereby driving the handmade piston. It took two people to start the engine: one to turn the valve and dribble the gas into the fuel intake hole at the cylinder's firing end, and the other to spin the flywheel, fashioned from a hand wheel off an old lathe, that would draw air and gas into the cylinder, where the spark ignited the mixture.[120] In search of an assistant, Henry carted his creation into the kitchen, where his wife was busy preparing Christmas dinner for the extended Bryant family, coming in from Dearborn for a holiday visit the next afternoon.

Oblivious as ever to such domestic concerns, Henry hooked the wire at the cylinder end into his kitchen's electric power cord, grounded it to a water pipe under the sink, and handed the gas can to Clara. She poured in a few drops of fuel as he spun the flywheel, but nothing happened the first time. On the second attempt the crude little engine coughed to life and then into flames, filling the Ford kitchen with foul-smelling black smoke and making a terrible racket. The Bagley Avenue experiment was a triumph, though, even to Clara. Such a level of forbearance can be explained only by Clara Bryant Ford's deep understanding and appreciation of what her husband was trying to do, and of all they stood to gain from his efforts. As she remarked to her niece Nettie Bryant later that same week, between frequent visits to the shed out back "Henry is making something, and maybe someday I'll tell you."[121]

———

Nobody knows the exact moment Henry Ford locked his sights onto the goal of manufacturing a car propelled by internal combustion, but the joshing at the Night Owl Lunch Wagon records the fact that by the beginning of 1894 he had hitched his own wagon, and reputation, to the star potential of the gasoline-powered automobile. "My first memory of Henry Ford," recalled early associate Lee Curson, "was when I was a newsboy holding down the corner of State Street and Woodward Avenue" in downtown Detroit in 1893 or early 1894. Many of the men on the Edison night shift at the time used to congregate at the dusk-to-daybreak Night Owl Lunch Wagon, an enclosed horse-drawn trolley with stools inside as well as a takeout window. (Ford, whose lunch wagon meal of choice consisted of pie and milk, would later buy the rolling diner and install it at his Greenfield Village outdoor museum.) "I recall that Mr. Ford would come over to the Owl Lunch Wagon," Curson continued, "and those that were sitting around having coffee and doughnuts would always kid Mr. Ford about what he was making now and what he was doing now. They would ask him, 'Have you got a piece of an engine in your pocket, or parts to one of these horseless carriages?'"[122]

By this point Ford had been promoted again and was the highest paid of Detroit Edison's fifty-odd employees, earning a full $100 a month as the downtown plant's chief engineer. His obvious abilities and contagious enthusiasm attracted quite a following among his co-workers. He and a few fellow tinkerers from Detroit Edison rented the basement of an empty storage building across the street and turned it into a machine shop devoted to experimental gasoline engines. Ford was their leader, contributing the ideas and most of the raw materials. His cohorts did most of the actual work.[123] The group's collective talents combined to create workable cylinders fashioned from scrap pipe as well as the idea to use gravity to deliver the fuel into the engine manifold, simply by putting the gas tank on top.[124]

Henry Ford and friends were not the only Detroiters trying to build a realistic, saleable, gas-powered automobile. Oliver Barthel, one of Ford's YMCA night-class students, was working as an assistant to Charles Brady King, a respected, Ivy League–educated independent engineer from California who is still renowned in technical circles as Detroit's true automobile pioneer. As of 1895, King had been making strides toward the production of a viable motorcar for at least two years, and had come far closer to success than Ford. Five years younger than his rival, yet already known for his work in marine engineering, the relentlessly innovative King outdid Ford in that he read everything he could find on automotive engineering. He organized the American Motor League to promote better roads. He even corresponded with would-be carmakers and scientific and technological societies throughout Europe. Henry Ford's reading and contact with other automakers were more sporadic. Barthel, already drawn into Ford's orbit, received a visit from his former YMCA instructor at King's offices one day early in 1896. Ford mentioned to Barthel that he had just popped into John Lauer's well-regarded machine shop in the same building, where he had leafed through a copy of the November 7, 1895, issue of *The American Machinist* magazine. He had become entranced by the first installment of a two-part article detailing the elegantly simple design of an efficient gasoline engine that could be built from commonplace parts with ordinary machine tools.[125] Long afterward, Barthel recalled Ford pointing out the article and declaring, "I want to build one of these."[126]

In fact, Barthel regarded that *American Machinist* article as the spark that set off Ford's obsession with the internal combustion engine, and if it wasn't the main impetus, it certainly pushed him further in that direction. So did the fact that a few months later, on March 6, 1896, Charles King went out for a public ride on St. Antoine Street in his own hand-built motorcar, the first ever seen in Detroit. Nicknamed Tootsie, it was basically a wooden wagon fitted with a four-cylinder engine and it topped out at around five miles per hour.[127] How did King achieve this engineering feat three months before Ford? By one account, two years earlier King had gone to Paris to study the French automotive industry and found its achievements so advanced that he adapted those designs and parts for a new car.[128]

Ford, jealous that King had beaten him in building Detroit's first gasoline-powered car, threw himself into assembling a lighter, speedier, and cheaper car of his own, from the ground up. Where King had money and education, Ford had a more mysterious quality that helped him get things done. As Fred Strauss put it, "Henry had some sort of a magnet. He could draw people to him; that was a funny thing about him."[129] David M. Bell, a Scottish-born blacksmith Ford hired in 1896 to forge his quadricycle's metal parts, remembered: "I never saw Mr. Ford make anything. He was always doing the directing."[130] It was also a necessary talent for a would-be carmaker in the era before camshafts, carburetors, crankshafts, piston rings, push rods, spark plugs, and so many other components essential to the automobile existed, requiring invention and manufacture from scratch.[131]

An idealized Norman Rockwell painting commissioned for Ford Motor Company's fiftieth anniversary in 1953 depicts Henry constructing his first "quadricycle" in 1896. There, in the dimly lit shed behind his Bagley Avenue home with an admiring Clara urging him on, a gleeful Ford beams with hard-earned success. What Rockwell's contrivance fails to portray is the false starts and harsh setbacks with grease-smeared flesh and the ravages of chronic insomnia that resulted from all the long nights spent on the labor of love and vision.[132] Ford toiled and scrounged day and night to build his machine, although in retrospect he would demur that "I cannot say that it was hard work. No work with interest is ever hard."[133]

After a near sleepless forty-eight hours of frenzied tinkering, Ford finally finished his creation early in the morning of June 4, 1896. At approximately 4:00 A.M. he unveiled it, without ceremony and before an audience of only two: his wife, Clara, and his chief assistant on the project, James W. Bishop.[134] Thus it was that the moment passed virtually unnoticed when Henry Ford climbed aboard his first vehicle and prepared to take it for a spin around the dark and rainy streets of Detroit.

It was only then that Ford and Bishop realized the car wouldn't fit through the door of the shed in which they had built it.[135] This lack of foresight, not to mention common sense, seems only a tad less embarrassing by dint of the problem's prevalence among visionary engineers:[136] in 1908, for example, aviation pioneer Glenn Martin would build his first airplane inside an abandoned church, but only when finally he was ready to taxi it out and soar away would it dawn on him that he had no way to get the thing out of the building. Undaunted, Martin opted to "borrow" a bulldozer from a nearby construction site and smash an opening right through one of the church walls.[137] Similarly confounded, Henry Ford chose the same solution: he picked up an axe and knocked a hole through the brick wall and then wheeled out his quadricyle, a light little chassis with four bicycle wheels over which he had fitted the simple gasoline engine.[138]

The proud machinist opened the current from the battery and adjusted the fuel intake by pinching the valve between his thumb and forefinger to serve as a choke. Next, Ford reached into the engine compartment and jerked the flywheel to start it spinning, and as soon as the motor started he clambered up onto the driver's seat. He pulled back the lever to tighten the belt that ran around the rear axle, grasped the tiller, and an instant later a machine built of his own ambition was carrying Henry Ford forward, down Grand River Avenue. With Jim Bishop bicycling ahead to warn off the few carriages and pedestrians on the streets at that hour, Ford made a circle around three main thoroughfares. Only one breakdown on Washington Boulevard marred the trip, caused by a faulty spring that required Ford and Bishop to push the quadricycle over to the Edison plant to fetch a new one.

"We finally had to go to the Edison plant to replace a broken spring on one of the igniters," Bishop recalled. "And when we did, a lot of guests from the old Cadillac Hotel assembled around the car and wondered what kind of infernal machine this thing was, and who was crazy enough to spend a lot of time and money on such a contraption." Ford and Bishop fixed the car and then headed home. They had achieved the experiment's main goal: the vehicle made it full circle back to its starting point under its own power. "We both went to bed for a few winks of sleep," Bishop recalled. "We soon woke up, had a bite of breakfast, which was prepared by Mrs. Ford and then proceeded to the Edison plant to report to work just as if nothing unusual happened."[139] They were, however, bursting with joy. Even landlord William Wreford, after confronting his tenant over the damage done to the wall of his shed, was so impressed by Ford's demonstration of the car that he not only refused payment for the repairs but had the shed's doors widened at his own expense to accommodate the vehicle.[140]

Technically, Ford's inaugural horseless carriage was not a car but indeed a 500-pound quadricycle, so defined by the means through which its two-cylinder, four-horsepower engine drove the back wheels. The transmission consisted of a leather belt connecting the flywheel to a countershaft, a belt tightener serving as the clutch, and a bicycle-style chain to the wheels, the two coordinated through a pulley that delivered the power from the countershaft to turn the rear axle. The resulting conveyance had two driving speeds, no reverse, and no brakes. The driver had to steer from a buggy seat above the engine via a tiller topped by a doorbell button as a horn. Ford's baby carriage trumped King's Tootsie: it could reach about twenty mph.[141]

Throughout that summer Ford kept making improvements to his creation, such as placing water jackets around the engine to keep it from overheating. The car's body, and thus its appearance, mattered far less to him, and remained rather plain and rudimentary. In fact, there was little that was new in either the design or the mechanics of Ford's first effort. Still, the sturdy little vehicle continued to run for several years, and spawned two others after Ford sold the first to an acquaintance for $200 (he would later buy it back from a third party for $60).[142] In the end, the only thing that mattered about Henry Ford's quadricycle was that it worked well enough to keep his mental gears turning toward the development of the modern automobile.[143]

2

Starting Up

By the middle of the summer of 1896, Henry Ford had established himself as a highly regarded Detroit Edison chief engineer earning a handsome $140 a month. That August the company's new president, Alexander Dow, invited the thirty-three-year-old supervisor to accompany him to the Association of Edison Illuminating Companies' seventeenth annual convention, in the Manhattan Beach section of New York City, just a few miles from Coney Island.[1] The junket would prove momentous, as it granted Ford his first direct contact with Thomas Alva Edison, the inventor he had idolized since boyhood for propelling the world out of the gaslight era and into the electric age.[2] Journeying to New York by train, Ford packed a camera so he could have a photographic record of his encounter with greatness.[3]

Edison, born in Ohio but, like Ford, raised in Michigan, had set out on his remarkable career as an inventor in the late 1860s, beginning in telegraphy. He established the world's first industrial research laboratory in 1876 at Menlo Park, New Jersey, an integrated idea factory that was itself one of his most triumphant creations. Two celebrated inventions came in quick succession: the phonograph in 1877 and the lightbulb in 1879. Many others experimented with incandescent lights—William Sawyer, Lewis Latimer, and Hiram Stevens Maxim, to name a few—but it was the ambitious Wizard of Menlo Park who made them work. Edison received 1,093 patents, more than twice as many as any other American even up to the present. All his life he demonstrated a prodigious capacity for work, generally squeezing at least twice as much out of a day as an ordinary person, and on his best days more than most people manage to achieve in a lifetime. "Genius is one per cent inspiration, ninety-nine per cent perspiration," he was fond of saying.[4] Self-taught, Edison scorned both academic theory and social convention. When M. A. Rosanoff joined the West Orange, New Jersey, team in 1903 and calmly asked the great inventor his laboratory rules, Edison erupted with contempt. "Hell, there ain't no rules around here!" he snapped, spitting on the wood-planked floor. "We are tryin' to accomplish somep'n'."[5] Even as he grew famous, Edison's manner remained disarmingly, if calculatedly, down-to-earth. An apostle and avatar of technology, his persona came to hold an unprecedented sway over the nation's industrialists, lawyers, and financiers on matters of progress. The Electric Age, the years roughly between 1880 and 1900, in fact, became known as the Age of Edison, and his legend continued to grow well along into the twentieth century, as he invented such modern marvels as storage batteries, the motion picture camera, and the carbon telephone transmitter. He also pioneered mining and cement production as well as the processes that led to the development of the mimeograph machine. The *New York Times* summed up Edison's monumental achievements in an April 2002 story about his lasting legacy, deeming him "the patron saint of invention itself."[6]

Today it may seem odd that Henry Ford looked upon Edison with the sort of hero worship reserved for pop stars and professional athletes, yet many people, young and old, grew to idolize the dynamic inventor. Growing up, Ford embraced the inventor's belief that "unflinching, unremitting work will accomplish anything."[7] As a teenager he had read newspaper reports about Edison's inaugurating the first permanent electrical generating station on September 4, 1882, on Pearl Street in lower Manhattan, thereby illuminating the offices of the *New York Times* as well as some eighty-five other establishments. Edison himself was on hand to flip the switch. The Pearl Street Station proved the effectiveness of Edison's direct current (DC) system for concentrated geographical areas. This central station concept also became the model for future alternating current (AC) systems, including the Detroit setup at which Henry Ford worked. When Edison predicted in an 1895 newspaper interview that "the horseless vehicle is the coming wonder. It is only a question of time when the carriages and trucks in every large city will be run with motors," Ford knew he was on the right track.[8] The concluding banquet of the 1896 Edison Illuminating Companies convention must have been like an epiphany to him. Through a swirl of parvenus clamoring for Edison's attention, Ford at long last laid eyes upon the "Wizard" who had captivated his imagination for so long. "Edison," Ford explained in his book *Edison as I Know Him* (1930), "was already, to my mind, the greatest man in the world."[9]

While the younger man's recollection of what ensued sounds apocryphal, his account is in fact true. Toward the end of the evening, when the after-dinner conversation bubbling around Edison turned to electric car batteries, Alexander Dow—who refused to allow gasoline on Detroit Edison property—waved toward Ford and chimed in, "There's a young fellow who has made a gas car." Dow proceeded to tell Edison how on a recent afternoon he had heard a "pop, pop, pop" outside his office. Peering out his window he discovered that the racket came from Henry Ford, accompanied by his wife, Clara, and son, Edsel, driving a "carriage without any horses."[10] Edison summoned Henry Ford forward and grilled him about the pistons and ignition cylinders, whereupon Ford sat down and drew his ideas out on the back of a menu. "He asked me no end of details and I sketched everything for him," Ford recalled, "for I have always found that I could convey an idea quicker by sketching it." Edison was impressed. "Young man, that's the thing!" he cried, banging his fist on the table. "You have it. Keep at it. Electric cars must keep near to power stations. The storage battery is too heavy. Steam cars won't do either, for they have a boiler and fire. Your car is self-contained, carries its own power plant, no fire, no boiler, no smoke and no steam. You have the thing. Keep at it!"[11]

Those potent words of encouragement made for a seminal moment in the life of Henry Ford. "That bang on the table"—coming just a little over two months since his first successful quadricyle run—"was worth worlds to me," he exclaimed in *Edison as I Know Him*. The irony was astounding: Edison, the father of electricity, had told him not to bother with an electric car. Ford's mission was recharged. According to historian Ford R. Bryan, who has written extensively on his distant relative Henry Ford, "It was thus burning with as hard a gemlike flame as a filament in one of Mr. Edison's lightbulbs." Ford gushed to his wife upon returning from New York: "You won't be seeing much of me for the next year!"[12] Tenacious disciple that he was, Ford immediately adopted Edison's devotion to hard work, putting one of Edison's lightbulbs to task in his workshop long past every sundown, doing whatever it took to perfect his automobile.

Henry Ford's work ethic and entrepreneurial bent reflected the boom times that saw Detroit's population continue to grow.[13] No U.S. city was expanding faster. When Ford was born Detroit had ranked nineteenth in size; by the turn of the century it had swelled into America's thirteenth largest city, with a population of 285,704. It also boasted the highest percentage of non-English-speaking people in the United States. Having survived the Panic of 1893, it was starting to prosper. The city's main thoroughfare, Woodward Avenue, bustled with sparkling new electric trolleys, and its boatyards hummed under a host of first-rate marine engineers. Taking advantage of northern Michigan's vast natural resources, Detroit was developing into a top producer of iron, copper, and brass, and was the nation's undisputed leader in the manufacture of heating and cooking stoves. Joseph Boyer was one of the many entrepreneurs drawn to the region, moving from St. Louis to Detroit. He became president of the Arithmometric Company, which made adding machines under the Burroughs name. The city's old merchant aristocracy of wholesalers, real estate speculators, railroad executives, and lumber barons continued to over-see Detroit's civic affairs, erecting a $1 million monument on Lower Belle Isle to commemorate their city's bicentennial. The vigor extended even to the national pastime, as professional baseball's Detroit Tigers played to the approval of sold-out crowds at Bennett Park. Life in Detroit represented the cutting edge of a new, improved, exciting urban America.[14] In *A Place for Summer,* historian Richard Bak wrote that Tiger players could be seen "scorching" the grand avenues of Detroit in automobiles "scaring horses and turning young women's heads."[15]

At the start of the twentieth century, therefore, Detroit found itself host to a wide range of enthusiastic entrepreneurs brimming with spirit and hell-bent on success. Among these bold young turks it was the nascent automakers who made the biggest splash. Ever since William Metzger opened the first independent automobile dealership, at 274 Jefferson Avenue in 1898, and then, with hardware dealer Seneca Lewis, cosponsored Detroit's first auto show at the Light Guard Armory, the city had embraced the horseless-carriage craze with a singular zeal. There are a number of logical reasons that Detroit—not New York, Chicago, or some other city—became the vortex of the automobile industry. For one thing, Michigan and Ohio were the business hubs for the bicycle business. By 1900 the bicycle fad was in decline and many manufacturers declared bankruptcy. For those that survived, it was a natural progression to enter the burgeoning horseless-carriage trade. The roster of former Detroit bicycle men who became automobile pioneers includes the Dodge brothers and Barney Oldfield. Detroit had also been a center of carriage manufacturing. But the great timber reserves of northern Michigan were rapidly disappearing, making timber a more expensive raw material. A sterling group of these carriage makers—William C. Durant, Charles Nash, and the Fisher brothers among them—decided the automobile industry had a more lucrative potential. One reason was that iron ore—essential to engine making—was being mined in the Upper Peninsula and was shipped downriver. Because Detroit was located on the Great Lakes waterway, it had grown into a major shipbuilding center. For thirty years workers had been making marine engines, and machine shops were thriving all over town. Most important of all, in 1900 Detroit boasted forty-four millionaires and many of them stood ready to invest in an automotive future.[16]

Harry C. Needham, who occasionally dined with his friends Henry and Clara Ford at Detroit's Family Hotel, where a hearty meal cost just fifteen cents around the turn of the century, recalled the first time he glimpsed Ford's remarkable quadricycle. "I distinctly remember Henry Ford driving up in front of this hotel restaurant where we ate, [in] an automobile made by two pieces of two-by-four with the motor swung in the center and with four bicycle wheels," Needham said. "He sat astride of the motor and operated the motor and drove. If I remember right, he sat on just a board. He sat straddling the motor, and across the front he had a board seat, and Mrs. Ford and Edsel sat on there. Edsel was just two or three years old."[17] Henry Ford had a working car, but what he wanted next, just like the bicycle carriage-wagon makers, as he would soon make clear, was his own car company. And getting that, he knew, would require a great deal more money than he had, and far more hard work than even he could cadge from his friends.

Among the influential Detroiters who took an interest in Ford's early projects was no less than the city's mayor, Democrat William C. Maybury,[18] a future two-term U.S. congressman,[19] whose family had been acquainted with the Fords for many years. It was Maybury, in fact, who shortly after taking office in Detroit in 1897 extended one of Henry Ford's very first "firsts," issuing the would-be carmaker what has long been considered the United States' first driver's license. This license was granted to ward off further complaints about the din Ford's gas-powered buggy made as it putted over the public thoroughfares.[20] Maybury helped out in even more crucial ways once Ford set to building a new vehicle in the basement shop next to the Detroit Edison plant. At the time, Ford had to commission rough metal parts from a blacksmith, who demanded immediate payment for each piece. Thanks to Mayor Maybury, to whom Ford just handed the bills, the smithy never had to wait.[21]

When it became clear that actually producing experimental engines called for more sophisticated machining facilities, Ford decided that the best option would be to create his own shop. Early in 1897, therefore, he found a suitable location and storefront space, in which he installed his old friend Fred Strauss, along with upward of $100 worth of machine tools.[22] Strauss worked on his own projects and some for Henry Ford, at no charge for his labor. "He was always down where I was," Strauss recalled. "Henry never used his hands, to tell the truth. He never came to work until after nine, either. He never could get around in the morning."[23] The escalating expense of trying to build an automobile forced Ford to move his household again in June 1897, this time to cheaper living quarters farther from Detroit Edison. The new quarters did, however, include a barn suitable for use as a home workshop, to which he lured Strauss to help out after his own shop's hours. And Strauss wasn't the only one: in between his light duties at the power plant, Ford kept after a whole phalanx of friends to continue trial-and-error testing of every imaginable machine part, while he kept on advancing his ideas both there at the shop with Strauss and in his backyard barn at home.

Ford completed a second-generation version of his gas-powered vehicle early in 1898. The new model boasted substantial improvements over his inaugural quadricycle, not the least of them cosmetic: with its sleek running boards, shiny brass fixtures, high-rising wheels, and padded two-seat bench,[24] his revamped vehicle looked swank enough to compete with the clean-running, trendy little electric cars then favored by many of those with the wealth and sense of fashion to buy a horseless carriage of any sort.[25] And its performance put it in a league with the robust steam cars of the day.

Steam cars were popularized by the Stanley brothers, identical twins from Newton, Massachusetts. Amateur automakers, they won a race in Cambridge in an 1897 steam-powered car of their own backyard-shed design. They were unlikely heroes, with their derby hats and ramrod posture, yet immediately after the victory the Stanley twins were inundated with more than 200 unsolicited orders for duplicates of their speedy Stanley Steamer. They found themselves sucked into the carmaking business soon thereafter.[26]

Steam-powered automobiles beat their gas and electric rivals on one score in particular: acceleration. With a simple turn of a valve, a steam engine could shoot a vehicle forward fast enough to snap its driver's head back—provided the car had been "fired up" for the half hour or so it took to build enough steam. The noise of the steam under pressure and the sight of the open flame creating it may have made a car look like it was about to blow up, but that didn't happen very often. Besides, through the first dozen years of the American automobile industry, gasoline-powered engines suffered their own drawback when it came to ignition: they required hand-cranking, and anyone trying that on an icy morning might seem wise to opt for a vehicle that would start at the light of a match.

The third choice for the prospective auto buyer at the turn of the twentieth century had even greater appeal for the comfort-minded: an electric car was as easy to start as a toaster, in any weather. Unfortunately, it couldn't go much faster. But speed wasn't a concern for city drivers, since congestion on urban streets designed for carriages made the inability to exceed twenty miles per hour superfluous. Although the range of electric cars was limited as well, they became very popular, particularly with the sort of driver averse to fumes, noise, and the bother of starting the other two types of automotive engines.

Flipping through an old copy of *Horseless Age* or *Motor World* makes it clear that at the turn of the century electric vehicles powered by rechargeable batteries were the most popular with casual motorists, while steam-driven cars got the most respect from auto enthusiasts for their comparative speed on straightaways. Electric vehicles were ideal for in-town errands, liberating women in particular to go where they wanted on their own. Gasoline-powered vehicles came in a sorry third with American consumers, who rightly deemed them dirty, noisy, unreliable, and uncomfortable from the vibration of the firing cylinders. But Henry Ford remained stalwartly behind the internal combustion engine, not so much for what it was in 1898, but for what he knew it could become. Electric and steam engines, he felt, had evolved as far as they could and had nothing more to offer. Most sporting automobile enthusiasts agreed: electric cars were too slow and limited in range. In 1897, in fact, Charles Duryea argued, to the delight of Ford, that bicycles and horses could travel farther in a day than any electric vehicle. "The voices of the male automobilist," historian Michael Brian Schiffer argued in *Taking Charge: The Electric Automobile in America,* "pointing with shrillness to the manifest imperfections of the electric car, drowned out those of its satisfied sometimes female owners."[27] However detrimental its unforeseen consequences would prove to the Earth's environment over time, the internal combustion engine did have advantages that seemed to far outstrip those of both the existing alternatives.

The internal combustion engine had a real believer in financier John D. Rockefeller Sr. With his vast holdings in the Standard Oil Trust, he seemed convinced that the gas-powered automobile would come out on top. He certainly must have hoped so: according to Daniel Yergin's 1992 Pulitzer Prize–winning history *The Prize: The Epic Quest for Oil, Money and Power,* in the 1890s Rockefeller's interests were seriously threatened by the insinuation of electricity into Americans' daily lives. "What kind of future," Yergin proposed, "could Standard Oil—with its massive investment in production, refineries, pipelines, storage facilities, and distribution—look toward if it were to lose its major market, illumination?"[28] The internal combustion gasoline engine, it seems, came along in the nick of time to ensure a bright future for the oil industry. And so it was that Rockefeller, in his youth something of a speed demon behind a team of horses, turned into an internal combustion auto buff noted for taking fast rides in open vehicles, particularly at night.[29] One anecdote held that upon discovering that his family had ordered an electric car for him as a birthday surprise, the outlandishly rich Rockefeller protested: "If it's all the same to you, I'd rather have the money."[30]

In August 1898 Henry Ford was awarded his first patent, albeit in William C. Maybury's name, for a carburetor he had designed the year before.[31] He was unbothered by relinquishing the patent: after all, the Maybury family had been treating the Fords well for many years. Maybury had been Henry's investor and was helping to finance his second car.[32]

Not for long would William Maybury be Ford's only backer, nor would he remain alone in his faith in the upstart automaker. Once Ford secured his first patent, the mayor quickly gathered three similarly eager speculators: notable Detroit businessmen Ellery I. Garfield of the fourteen-branch Fort Wayne Electric Corporation, physician Dr. Benjamin R. Hoyt, and E. A. Leonard of the Standard Life and Accident Insurance Company.[33] They drew up a loose memorandum of agreement whereby the foursome would collectively finance Henry Ford's automotive experiments, each investing $500 "to pay for patents on devices invented by the first party." The deal was that Ford would retain a third of any such patents, the other two thirds going to his investors. The same ratio would apply to the profit from any vehicles actually built and sold by the enterprise. Should any corporation be born of these experiments, the agreement continued, the entity so created would employ Henry Ford "on a fair compensation."[34]

For the moment Ford kept his position at Detroit Edison, although he spent most of his time organizing the new automobile-development shop. This didn't seem to trouble its nominal foreman, Fred Strauss, who was long familiar with Ford's predilections.[35] A year or two later, Strauss would quit a high-paying job at Detroit's established Nageborn machine shop to help his friend out once again, full-time. "I was a darn fool to quit Nageborn's," Strauss admitted long after the fact. "I was getting $16.50 a week there. Of course, Henry didn't know what I was getting. He had a dream. I don't know why I quit, but he had a kind of 'magnet.' He had something over me, anyway."

With a wistful mix of pride and regret, Strauss added: "If he was broke today," speaking then of the richest man in the world, "I would be the first one he would look up. He had a sort of hold over me. My sister used to scold me all the time."[36] Her concerns appeared justified, considering how much work her brother did gratis for Henry Ford.[37] And of course Strauss was hardly the only useful friend over whom Ford exercised that kind of hold. Even on Saturday nights his shop teemed with men he had cajoled into helping build the reputation and fortune of Henry Ford. Yet he deliberately kept them all in the dark about what he, and they, were really up to. Whenever one of Henry's ideas appeared potentially valuable he would meet with attorneys at the law firm of Thomas S. Sprague & Son to seek patent protection.[38]

By the middle of the summer of 1899 Ford had produced another car. This third attempt was bigger, heavier, sturdier, and in every way more polished than his initial quadricycle or its 1898 successor, boasting, among other fresh revisions, a water tank, cylinder jackets, and brakes.[39] On July 29, the *Detroit Journal* ran a long, gushing article about it, boldly headlined "Ford Automobile Has New Features and Is a Novel Machine." Unfortunately, the newspaper story focused on the already superseded design of his year-old second car, although the reporter did get in several glowing references to William C. Maybury and to all the city's new mayor had been doing for Detroit's brilliant young automotive pioneer.[40]

With his patents, patronage, and working prototypes plus the "magnet" of his personality, Henry Ford emerged in 1899 as perhaps the most promising of the nation's many would-be carmakers. Led by Mayor Maybury, some dozen of Detroit's canniest businessmen therefore chose to back Ford in a new enterprise: the Detroit Automobile Company.[41] It had the distinction of being the Motor City's first car manufacturer.[42] The startup firm's original roster of stockholders constituted a who's who of the city's commercial powers at the time, among them Maybury and Ford's other early backers Garfield, Hoyt, and Leonard. Others who jumped on the Ford bandwagon were hardware merchant Clarence A. Black, who had run as the Republican nominee for mayor against Maybury; Dexter Ferry, owner of a large seed company; U.S. Senator Thomas W. Palmer, a former lumberman; and Michigan Savings Bank President George Peck, later head of the Edison Illuminating Company.[43] Also among the charter stockholders, although without paying any money in,[44] was Henry Ford, who was named mechanical superintendent of the new concern at a salary of $150 a month.[45] He was to engineer a line of cars and organize a plant to manufacture them. And most important of all, he was supposed to turn a profit.

Thus it was that on August 5, 1899, the Detroit Automobile Company was formed, backed by financing amounting to $15,000. In fact, five days before its articles of incorporation were filed, the Detroit Automobile Company had been set up and capitalized at $150,000. Only a tenth of that sum, however, was actually paid in cash.[46]

Without regret, Ford left the Edison Illuminating Company on August 15, though it meant turning down a salary offer of $1,900 a year and the title of general superintendent. As a family man, he was leaving an established corporation that had employed him for the past eight years. But it wasn't the automobile business. Although Ford quit ten days after the Detroit Automobile Company was officially established, he had already devoted most of his time to working on its behalf, beginning with his own designs for a gasoline engine.[47] Ford would have to move his family into cheaper quarters yet again, it was true, but at long last he would be making cars full-time and getting paid for it. Later, he would declare that he was "never happier" than in those days between the demonstration of his first quadricycle and the formation of Ford Motor Company. "I was learning something every day," he explained, "and what I was learning was of use to myself and everybody else."[48]

Ford immediately set out to lure the team of the best and brightest he had put together at Detroit Edison. He found only one taker for his risky proposition: electrical wizard Edward S. "Spider" Huff. Of course, Ford also managed to sway the services of Fred Strauss his way once again. When he took his old colleague to see their new workplace, in a rented building on Detroit's Cass Avenue, Strauss reacted with boyish glee. "When we got in there it opened our eyes," he remembered. "It was just perfect for our shop. The place was empty. There wasn't a thing in there except an engine and a boiler and a main line of shaft. The first thing I did was start to get the boiler and engine ready."[49]

On January 12, 1900, the *Detroit Journal* announced that the Detroit Automobile Company would roll out its first delivery truck the next day,[50] basically a high-sitting horseless wagon with a covered two-seat platform jutting out in front.[51] Betraying a talent for public relations, Henry Ford somehow wangled the *Detroit News-Tribune* into running a feature-section front-page article on his truck in its February 4, 1900, edition. The banner headline, "Swifter Than a Race-Horse It Flew over the Icy Streets," was followed by the subhead "Thrilling Trip on the First Detroit-Made Automobile, When Mercury Hovered About Zero."[52] However purple the reporter's ensuing prose, his account of riding shotgun with Henry Ford in his first commercial vehicle proved prophetic: "There has always been at each decisive period in this world's history some voice, some note, that represented for the time being the prevailing power. There was a time when the supreme cry of authority was the lion's roar. Then, came the voice of man. After that, it was the crackle of fire. . . . And now, finally, there was heard in the streets of Detroit the murmur of this newest and most perfect of forces, the automobile, rushing along at the rate of 25 miles an hour."[53]

In reality, Ford's first commercial offering amounted to a rather unimpressive product, entirely mundane but for its place in the history of the automobile industry. It seems that the delivery truck's considerable weight demanded sturdy, carriage-type tires, which Henry Ford personally ordered from the local Columbia Buggy Company. His salesman there, Harvey S. Firestone, would go on to found the Firestone Tire & Rubber Company of Akron, Ohio. Over the next decades Ford would buy tires by the millions from Firestone, and the two titans of American industry would become fast friends as well.[54]

In the wake of the *Detroit News-Tribune*'s glowing assessment, prospects seemed bright for the Detroit Automobile Company, then one of nearly sixty aspiring American auto manufacturing plants.[55] Ford had plans for several vehicles in addition to the successful delivery truck, some dozen of which his shop turned out over the next few months.[56] But all was not well. Unfortunately, the startup company had trouble building more than one vehicle at a time. In fact, Ford had missed both his initial deadline of October 1, 1899, and the extension he wheedled to December 1 to produce even one car.[57] To the profound dismay of his backers, he managed to build only a few more vehicles in his first big-time automaking setup than he had while moonlighting in a shed in his backyard. But Ford simply wasn't used to multiple, much less mass, production: his output the year before the founding of the Detroit Automobile Company had amounted to one and a half cars, and it increased to just seven cars the year after.[58] On an amortized basis, therefore, Ford's investors had paid $1,250 to produce each of the Detroit Automobile Company's twelve vehicles. At a price of $1,000 each, though, the trucks were losing money. What is more, they weren't up to the mechanical superintendent's own standards.[59] By contrast, Ohio's Packard Motor Car Company, which had taken its first step into the car business in April 1899, only a few months before Detroit Automobile, had a solid model to demonstrate by that November and began shipping cars by April 1900. During the next two years 160 Packards would be turned out, and all of them just as quickly sold.[60] The precocious firm moved its operations to Detroit in 1903.[61]

The Detroit Automobile Company began to collapse in November 1900, not even a year and a half after its inception.[62] One of the company's original investors informed another lawyer in Thomas Sprague's office that he and other backers kept hearing how cavalierly Ford was wasting their money, fussing with complex components such as transmissions when superior, preassembled units could be had easily, and cheaply, on the open market.[63] While the company's investors had gotten fed up, the truth was Henry Ford had been frustrated all along. Considering his meager personal stake in its profitability, the way the company was organized offered scant incentive for him to excel. By the same token, however, some of his colleagues attributed the failure to Ford's ineffectual stewardship, the result of the perfectionism that kept him from letting any vehicle out of the factory until it sported every improvement he had conceived up to that moment. As one of his investors opined, "If Mr. Ford has something, he certainly should be willing to put it out. . . . If we wait until it is 'perfect,' we will never see it."[64]

Ford's own patent attorney at Sprague, Prescott Hulbert, visited Detroit Automobile's assembly plant on several occasions and was not impressed. He observed Ford's penchant for perfection firsthand once one delivery wagon was finally complete after a crew of five men had taken an entire week to assemble it. "Henry Ford got into this car," Hulbert recalled, "started it up and drove around the plant dodging all these posts. He drove it around a little bit and then stopped; something was wrong. I can remember that serious look he had. He looked it over and then said, 'Come on, boys, we'll have to pull this to pieces.' So they ripped it apart again."[65] Thus was a week's work lost, for five men.

In November 1900 the company ceased doing business,[66] and the dissolution of the Detroit Automobile Company was formally executed on February 7, 1901.[67] That same year, its most vigorous rival would turn out an impressive 425 merry little, curved-dashboard Oldsmobiles.[68]

In the end, the Detroit Automobile Company failed not so much because Ford took too long to produce a vehicle up to his standards, but because the vehicle he actually produced wasn't very impressive by anyone's standards.[69] The fact is that it was Ford himself who didn't hold up his end of the deal. Detroit Automobile's backers came up with the cash needed to fully outfit the workshop on Cass Avenue with machine tools and men, most of Ford's own choosing. It was understood that these resources would be put toward perfecting a mass-market consumer automobile along the lines of his own third model. It was Ford's demonstration of this car that had persuaded major backers to push for the formation of the company in the first place.[70] But as the loyal Fred Strauss explained, "Henry wasn't ready. He didn't have an automobile design. To get the shop going, Henry gave me some sketches to turn up some axle shaftings. I started machining these axle shaftings to show them we were doing something. It was just to get it going but they didn't belong to anything. We never used them for the automobile. It was just a stall until Henry got a little longer into it."[71]

Unfortunately, Ford just kept stalling, wandering off into the nearby woods, ostensibly to think through some designs, and ordering his staff to ward off the investors. "If they ask for me," he'd instruct, "you tell them that I had to go out of town." Strauss noted Ford's appearances at the shop dwindling to the point that "he might come in every day for about an hour or two."[72] His friend attributed this nonchalance to Ford's dissatisfaction with the size of his own stake, and authority, in the enterprise.

In the end, Ford's backers concluded that their mechanical superintendent had squandered some $86,000 of their funds, a fortune at the time.[73] Ford himself would later insist it was the firm's directors who had badly misread the mass market.[74] He would insist in his autobiography that as far as he could tell, the company's investors had no interest in the development of a better and cheaper car for the good of the American people, "and being without authority other than my engineering position gave me, I found that the new company was not a vehicle for realising my ideas but merely a money-making concern."[75]

Most of the loss from Detroit Auto was absorbed personally by good old William C. Maybury.[76] Unbeknownst to him, much of the money had been spent in an attempt to perfect, of all things, a high-performance race car with no commercial potential whatsoever. To Henry Ford the Detroit Automobile Company had been a laboratory, and car racing a fine means to test vehicles under extreme stress. Unlike most automotive pioneers, including his own backers, Ford realized from the start that the one quality most glaringly lacking in the earliest mass-market cars was speed. Adding it meant discerning even the tiniest operational variances, such as the timing of the gasoline intake and exhaust valves in each cylinder, then refining every engine and drivetrain component to boost the efficiency of each mechanical process, from ignition to combustion to ventilation to steering and all the other minute workings of a car.[77] Ford's eye was always fixed on perfecting every part and thereby the functioning of the whole vehicle.

Despite the debacle of Ford's first enterprise, a handful of his original backers, including Maybury and William H. Murphy, kept their faith in him.[78] They bought the Detroit Automobile Company's assets at a receivership sale in May 1901,[79] rented a smaller portion of the same shop building, and commissioned Henry Ford to keep at whatever it was he'd been doing there.[80]

Best of all, this new arrangement allowed him to hang on to his dream team of technical wizards, who remained as eager as ever to carry out their leader's notions. Several of these men would eventually assume broader roles in the future Ford empire, but in the early days Henry relied on each according to his most conspicuous gifts, and hours of availability. The workaholic Childe Harold Wills, a visionary draftsman, gave Ford time before and after his regular job at the Boyer Machine Company.[81] Designer Oliver Barthel worked in the evenings; quirky, brilliant Edison electrician Spider Huff dropped by whenever he felt like it; and, for hands-on toil, Ford could count on avid moonlighters from nearby machine shops, including lathe operator Ed Verlinden and blacksmith Charlie Mitchell.[82] When Ford insisted there must be a more efficient means of igniting gasoline in a cylinder, it was Spider Huff who came up with ideas for an induction coil (for which he received full credit)[83] as well as a sparking coil encased in porcelain. It was Barthel who arranged for the manufacture of customized insulating casings for the latter. He relied on a member of the only profession skilled in molding and baking porcelain in 1901 Detroit: Dr. W. E. Sandborn, his dentist.[84]

Huff, a Kentuckian, broke with Ford's personal feelings against liquor: he was a hard-living, hard-drinking man. He was also married seven times over the course of his life. So highly did Ford esteem Huff's contributions, though, that no matter how often the volatile hillbilly's penchant for hard drink got him into trouble, Ford would pay the damages, then nurse Huff back to productivity without so much as mentioning any problems with his behavior.[85] Many years later, Ford called in an efficiency expert to assess his company's operations. The anecdote that arose from his visit, and which is believed to be about Spider Huff, has the expert giving Ford a favorable report, with one exception. "It's that man down the corridor," the expert supposedly stated. "Every time I go by his office he's just sitting there with his feet on his desk. He's wasting your money." To this Ford is said to have replied: "That man once had an idea that saved us millions of dollars. At the time, I believe his feet were planted right where they are now."[86]

In each of his early shops Ford established a casual, creative atmosphere loose enough to make the hippest modern dot-com's Foosball room look stodgy. Nobody under Henry Ford dressed for success or anything else but real work, nor cared what time anyone else showed up or went home; after all, most of his employees chose to stick around twice as long as required in regular workplaces. And although formally without portfolio, Ford was still an automaker, and as such he was able to attract the attention of myriad would-be suppliers to the promising new industry. Among those who would prove most daunting down the road was young Alfred P. Sloan Jr., who ran the Hyatt Roller Bearing Company, which solicited Ford's rear-axle bearing business. Sloan, who would one day head General Motors, wrote in his memoirs of a visit he made to Ford's shop around this time. It was the dead of winter when he dropped by the Cass Avenue building, and Sloan noted that when the un-heated second-floor shop grew too cold for Ford and Wills to grip their pencils, they donned boxing gloves and whaled away at each other until their blood flowed fast enough to warm them up, upon which the two men quietly re-turned to analyzing the schematics on their drawing boards.[87]

In 1901, Ford finally completed the race car he had begun under the auspices of the Detroit Automobile Company. It was slender in frame and boasted two cylinders, each a gigantic seven inches around and producing a loud roar.[88] The racer also featured several notable innovations, including, according to *Horseless Age* magazine, "Mr. Ford's patented vaporizer with measuring device, ditto sparking device and a Huff induction coil with a new ribbon buzzer," not to mention "a patented reach and trussed front and rear axles, with equal-izing rods attached to the latter." The patent on this construction had just been issued.

"The vehicle being high-powered is built low," the article continued. "Enough gasoline is carried for a run of 250 miles. A tonneau can be attached to the rear of the body for touring. The weight is 2,200 pounds. Mr. Ford claims to have made a half-mile in 26 seconds and challenges any foreign ma-chine to race him on an American road track."[89]

In reality, Ford had not succumbed to the spreading racing fever. He would always prefer production models to those aimed for the track. What sparked his determination to outrun every other vehicle in the world was a late-budding taste for public renown. From his racing period on, Ford appeared to regard good publicity and solid profits as the balanced sides of his business equation, and would prove that he could win one via the other every time, at least in his professional life.

His situation at home was more private and it was usually more relaxed. The Fords' eight-year-old son, Edsel, was a bright pleasant little boy. As a toddler, Edsel had always seemed delighted by his father's uninhibited silliness during the time they spent together. Ford, always handy with a camera, took many snapshots of his family cavorting together in the early years.[90] But as Clara Bryant Ford wrote in her diary for January 13, 1901, foreshadowing consider-able family unpleasantness to come, "Henry fixed Edsel's old sleigh to take him coasting, but Edsel would not go, said sleigh was no good. He was sent upstairs for punishment for his pride. He was sorry." Of course, six days later she noted that "Henry bought Edsel new coaster," and the day after that, "Henry and Edsel went coasting on the boulevard." Perhaps the only more re-vealing entry in her diary for that year was the one dated April 1: "Tried to fool Henry but could not."[91]

Life was hardly all fun and games for the wife of Henry Ford. As Clara wrote to her brother, Milton Bryant, on December 3, 1901, she and Henry had decided against building a house of their own that year "on account of Henry building the racer," adding that "He could not see to anything else. So we will have to put up with rented homes for a little longer."[92] As her husband later admitted, "What money was left over from living was all spent on experimenting."[93]

Ford hoped the racer would make him the most famous automobilist in the country. The man who held that distinction at the turn of the twentieth century was Alexander Winton, a fiery Scotsman with a fine eye for engineering details. In 1901, Winton was serving as head of his own highly successful namesake car company based in Cleveland. He had a stubborn streak unwavering on one point: his belief that his automobiles were beyond improvement. Once he lashed out at a complaining Winton owner, "If you think you know so much about cars, go and build one yourself!" The dissatisfied customer was one James Ward Packard, who left to found a rather successful automobile company of his own. Winton production cars had attained a certain eminence despite their somewhat stodgy performance on the road, and they certainly ranked near the top of the American automobile market in 1901. This was largely due to Alex Winton's feats of derring-do on the racetrack, which generated the sort of popular publicity that was proving vital to auto sales, even back when cars were still considered novelties in the United States. Winton was the man on whom Henry Ford set his sights, competing against him in one of the most famous races of the day.

As the cliché goes, the more things change, the more they stay the same, so it's not surprising that a century later Ford Motor Company would use every means possible to reach out to the newly ardent, massive NASCAR audience. In 2001 the company appealed to these stock-car racing fans with a full-page advertisement, placed in popular magazines such as *Entertainment Weekly*, proclaiming "the race that changed everything," under a sepia-toned photograph of Henry Ford behind the wheel of his first racer. The text of the ad began: "He wasn't exactly the picture of a race car driver on that mild, partly cloudy October afternoon 100 years ago. And for good reason. He *wasn't* one. Henry Ford was an engineer who saw the automobile as much more than a rich man's toy, and who dreamed of a nation that ran on gasoline instead of oats. He also saw auto racing as a means to jump-start that dream. So, with little preparation and even less caution, he lined up against acclaimed champion Alexander Winton."[94]

The excitement surrounded a twenty-five-mile championship race scheduled for October 10, 1901, on a dirt track in Grosse Pointe Township, not far from Detroit. In the autumn of 1901, the race was on across the Western world to become the first man to drive a car a mile a minute. Four main contenders, each with as much racetrack experience as a driver could have in that infancy of the automobile, were expected to enter the race. The four had been trading the international speed record among them. Henri Fournier, the French daredevil, was the current mile record holder at 1 minute, 14.2 seconds, on 60 horsepower. Pittsburgh's W. N. Murray was to pilot a 70-horsepower speedster, in which he had earlier snatched the mile record. Well-heeled William K. Vanderbilt Jr., the man from whom Murray had taken the record, was said to have paid $15,000 for his fancy, French-built, 40-horsepower "Red Devil," plus another $7,000 in customs duty to import it. And, of course, the imposing Alexander Winton always ensured a big crowd when he raced his renowned, 40-horsepower "Bullet."[95]

The prize for the marquee event at Grosse Pointe was substantial—$1,000 cash, plus a crystal punch bowl, for which a place in Winton's living room supposedly had already been selected.[96] Two of the preliminary races were limited to steam- and electric-powered vehicles, respectively. Much to the disappointment of the swelling crowd, few of the former even made it to the finish, and the best of the latter took more than four minutes to cover a single mile lap.[97] The chance opened up for the gasoline engine to seize the day. However, because the day's first events ran far longer than expected, the championship race was cut back to ten miles.

As it turned out there were only two entrants in the big race. Henri Fournier had opted instead to challenge his own record at a track in New York, while William Vanderbilt had to pull out when his European racer succumbed to mechanical troubles. W. N. Murray scratched his entry when he discovered a leaky cylinder in his engine.[98] The sole entry left to start against Winton's Bullet was an odd-looking race car that had registered only the day before. It was an untested brute to be driven by its actual engineer, Michigan's own Henry Ford.[99] For Ford the presumption of entering a world championship was actually not all that unjustified, considering that some $5,000 in materials had been invested in his car, and far more than that in the time he and his wizards had put into building the thing.[100]

By the same token, devoting every hour to refining the race car had left Ford no time to practice driving it. In fact, he had never even been on a racetrack before, and Grosse Pointe's one-mile dirt oval, recently constructed for horse races, presented such treacherous curves that high wooden fences had been built all the way around it for safety's sake. In the few minutes before the championship race, the dauntless Henry Ford made just two slow practice laps, which couldn't have given him much of a feel for the turns. During the event itself, the devil-may-care Spider Huff would bravely serve as human ballast, perching on the driver's-side running board and gripping handles positioned for him to balance on as he leaned out low and wide to steady the racer around every turn.[101]

Finally the big race was on. Winton shot ahead from the start, his wheels swirling up a cloud of dust as he skidded recklessly around the first turn and sped away. In the early going matters looked grimmer for the challenger with each lap, as Winton's skill allowed him to add to his lead on every curve. Halfway through the race Ford and Huff started to get the hang of it. After the first three miles they lagged by only a fifth of a lap. Once Ford conquered the curves he began steadily gaining on his opponent,[102] much to the delight of the avid Thursday afternoon crowd of nearly seven thousand, which included such future Ford benefactors as coal baron Alexander Y. Malcomson, his assistant James J. Couzens, and champion bicycle racers Tom Cooper and Barney Oldfield.[103]

Then, on the seventh lap, Winton's engine began to smoke, and his car slowed down. Better engineering was about to have its day. Ford quickly closed the gap, passed his struggling competitor, and took the lead to the wild cheers of the partisan hometown crowd.[104] The upstart challenger crossed the finish line an easy first, having covered the ten miles in 13 minutes, 23.8 seconds; no mile a minute, but fast enough to beat Winton.[105] Gracious in victory but pointed on the subject of his car's superiority, Ford told the assembled reporters, "Put Winton in my car and it will beat anything in this country."[106]

Ford's average of just under 45 miles per hour was blistering for 1901.[107] It sounds quaint today only before considering that he achieved it while perched on a flat bench atop an open chassis on unreliable tires, with rudimentary steering. Harry Needham, Ford's old friend from the Family Hotel, somehow insinuated himself into the winner's circle. "I stood very close to Henry Ford," Needham recalled. "I remember distinctly him saying, 'Boy, I'll never do that again. That board fence was right here in front of my face all the time. I was scared to death, and I'll never do that again.'"[108] Indeed, Ford never did race on an oval track again.[109] Once his point was made he didn't have to.

Ford's victory made him the talk of automotive circles. The *Detroit News* gushed that the performance of his two-cylindered entry was so "wonderful" it vaulted Ford to the "front rank of American chauffeurs."[110] Perhaps more important to his future, on November 9, 1901, no less than the august *Scientific American* published a serious article on "Style in Automobiles" in which author Hrolf Wisby declared, "The latest American racing automobile, the Ford, possesses features entitling it to credit as being the most unconventional, if not the most beautiful, design so far produced by American ingenuity.

"It is a model that commends itself strongly to the automobile experts because of the chaste completeness and compactness of its structure," Wisby continued, "a most ingenious arrangement" giving rise to the conclusion that "no matter how we may choose to view this machine, it is an automobile first and last."[111]

For all of the Fords, the victory made for heady times. As Clara Bryant Ford wrote to her brother Milton on December 3, "Henry has been covering himself with glory and dust . . . you should have heard the cheering when he passed Winton. The people went wild." Then, with her usual pragmatism, she added: "That race has advertised him far and wide. And the next thing will be to make some money out of it. I am afraid it will be a hard struggle. You know rich men want it all."[112]

In the wake of Ford's success on the racetrack, William H. Murphy and William C. Maybury, along with a few other backers of the failed Detroit Automobile Company, opted to give the irascible Dearborn engineer another chance. Murphy took the lead in offering to set Ford up in another car company,[113] this one financed with $30,500 in cash on a $60,000 capitalization. Each of six principals—Henry Ford, William H. Murphy, Clarence A. Black, Lem W. Bowen, Mark Hopkins, and Albert E. F. White[114]—received 1,000 shares in the new concern, valued at $10 apiece. Although the new company awarded Ford one sixth of its stock, worth about $10,000, he apparently would receive no salary. But this time there would also be no question who was in charge. The second effort would be called the Henry Ford Company after its designated chief engineer, with Black as president, Murphy as treasurer, and the other shareholders occupying the remaining corporate offices.[115] Articles of incorporation were filed in Detroit within two months of the Grosse Pointe race, on November 20, 1901.[116]

In the eyes of the investors, the goal of the new Henry Ford Company was to produce a lightweight, knockabout car priced for the mass market at about $1,000.[117] To its chief engineer, however, the better course would be to build a four-cylinder race car with an engine so huge it would blow its competitors off the track. In other words, it wasn't long before the same problems that had plagued the Detroit Automobile Company arose. Once again, Ford's interests just didn't jibe with those of the firm he had inspired. And once again because he had a relatively small stake in it, the only way he could see to benefit from the concern was by using it to aggrandize his own reputation, again via racing. "He did not seem inclined to settle down to a small car production plan," recalled Oliver Barthel, who had been hired by the new company full-time as a design engineer. "He talked mostly about wanting to build a larger and faster racing car."[118] As Ford opined in a letter to his brother-in-law Milton Bryant on January 6, 1902, if handled right, "there is a barrel of money in this business. . . . My Company will kick about me following racing but they will get the Advertising and I expect to make $ where I cant [sic] make cents at Manufacturing."[119]

By that all too familiar reasoning, Ford decided to devote both his time and his company's resources to the development of a pair of high-powered racing cars. He designed them in collaboration with star bicycle racer Tom Cooper and longtime associate Harold Wills.[120] The talented Wills could, upon hearing an idea, immediately sketch it as a blueprint on paper.[121]

Much to the distress of the backers, Ford continually refused to stop fiddling with his designs for mass-production cars long enough to start manufacturing some.[122] These clashes of interests became a major source of friction between the chief engineer and the men who paid the bills. His backers' "main idea seemed to be to get the money," Ford would complain in his memoirs.[123]

While Ford was arguing the merits of racing to them, the executives of his namesake company were working to secure the services of a more cooperative, and thus more productive, chief engineer. The savior the moneymen hired to straighten out the Henry Ford Company was Henry M. Leland, a distinguished veteran gunsmith and machine-shop expert so renowned for his uncompromising standards that the instant he entered the automobile industry he became the most respected figure in it.

No youngster, Leland wore a long, narrow beard that had been fashionable among serious gentlemen of the mid-nineteenth century—long before the modern Auto Age of 1901. He was fifty-seven when he threw himself into automaking. A courtly fellow, but with no patience for the second-rate, Leland had been born in Danville, Vermont. By the time he turned eighteen the Civil War had begun. By then, he was an apprentice at Massachusetts's Springfield Arsenal, and he spent America's bloodiest war machining precision metal parts for Springfield's legendary rifles. Afterward he worked at the massive and technologically advanced Samuel Colt factory in Hartford, Connecticut, which produced firearms with interchangeable components. Such innovative machine production of standardized parts had become known as "the American system of manufacturing"; the mass-production assembly-line industrial process it presaged would later be called Fordism.[124]

When Leland grew tired of having a boss in the 1890s, he formed his own company, Leland and Faulconer, a machine and tool manufacturing concern in Detroit specializing in the production of precision bicycle parts and high-quality marine engines. Leland developed processes for tooling machine parts to a tolerance of 1/100,000 of an inch, far more precise than actually necessary for most applications, but an awesome achievement in and of itself.[125]

Then, in 1899, Leland's firm signed a contract to provide transmission gears and other delicate parts for Ransom E. Olds's new "gas buggy."[126] A year later, after a fire consumed the Olds Motor Works—the first factory in the nation designed specifically to manufacture cars[127]—Leland was asked to produce the one-cylinder gasoline engine for the latest, "curved-dash" Oldsmobile. He found it well designed but felt that it could be more efficient if "better made." He was right: simply by refining the machining of its parts, Leland boosted the new Olds engine's horsepower by nearly 25 percent.[128] In 1902 alone, Olds would turn out a staggering 2,500 of the cute little curved-dash Oldsmobiles, the low cost of which made them the first high-production car model in history.[129]

Olds's economical, stripped-down little runabout was not the sort of automobile Henry Leland really wanted to help produce. In fact, Leland refused to adapt in any way to what he scorned as the day's generally lax automaking practices. Instead, he sought to impose the strictest standards of pistol manufacture on the production of first-rate cars. The auto industry had in fact already begun to split between manufacturers of big, powerful luxury models and makers of smaller, lighter, and much cheaper vehicles designed for a potentially much broader market. In 1903, most auto companies were leaning the former way, turning out products with steep prices of $3,000 or even $4,000.

All in all, Henry Leland was a master of the sort of engineering abstractions that went far beyond Henry Ford's trial-and-error approach. And the stage was set for confrontation on another level as well. While Ford remained utterly dependent on his expert workmen, he insisted that they be dependent on him for direction. However, the proudly professional Henry Leland was of no mind to kowtow to a man whom he regarded as an insolent young pup.

When Leland stepped in, Ford was gone—not so much jumping as letting himself be pushed out of his own namesake company just four months after its founding.[130] He took with him a paltry settlement of $900 in cash, the unfinished drawings of his plans for the gigantic new race car, and all rights to the use of his name.[131] In his autobiography, Ford would claim of his forced departure that "in March 1902 I resigned, determined never again to put myself under orders."[132]

Under a new moniker honoring Detroit's founder, Antoine de la Mothe Cadillac, the company went on to not only survive but thrive. In fact, the Cadillac Motor Company enjoyed near instant success under the command of Henry Leland, who substituted his own precisely crafted single-cylinder engine to power a passenger car otherwise based on Ford's designs.[133] The Cadillac name would, of course, continue to symbolize America's highest automotive quality for most of the century after the marque became the top-flight division of the newly founded General Motors Corporation in 1909.[134]

Once again an ex-carmaker, Henry Ford foundered after the split. Not many pioneers in the automobile business had managed to chalk up two notable failures as early as 1902; after all, the industry in America had existed for only three years. And in the aftermath of this latest debacle, Leland's resuscitation of his company under the Cadillac name hardly bolstered Ford's reputation. Yet despite his increasingly notorious volatility, he found a pair of deep-pocketed new associates who cared only for speed. Tom Cooper was a rich, twenty-five-year-old world champion bicycle racer.[135] Barton Peck was even more well heeled, the owner of a Detroit bicycle repair shop and the youngest son of George Peck, the same bank president who had helped fund Ford's first carmaking enterprise.[136] It remains murky exactly what, if any, formal business agreement this new troika operated under, except for their deal that Ford would build two identical race cars and Cooper would own one of them.[137]

What mattered more to Ford was that for the first time he had found financial support from engineering enthusiasts like himself, men who valued experimentation over results and innovation above profit. Revealingly, in his memoirs he spelled out some of the crucial lessons he believed he had learned from the Henry Ford Company's collapse. "Concretely," he declared, "what I most realized about business in that year is this: (1) That finance is given a place ahead of work and therefore tends to kill the work. . . . (2) That thinking first of money instead of work brings on fear of failure and this fear blocks every avenue of business. . . . (3) That the way is clear for anyone who thinks first of service, of doing the work in the best possible way.

"The money influence . . . seemed to be at the bottom of most troubles. . . . I was not free. I could not give full play to my ideas. Everything had to be planned to make money; the last consideration was the work."[138]

The opposite was the case with the new triumvirate of Ford, Cooper, and Peck, who, with the full-time help of Spider Huff and the part-time contributions of Oliver Barthel and Harold Wills, managed to complete the two identical race cars during the summer of 1902.

With an exposed crankcase and no hood or windshield to keep hot engine oil from splashing into the driver's face, Ford's new design measured a monstrous nine feet nine by five feet two, boasted four cylinders as big around as fire logs,[139] and appeared as nothing more than a long wooden wagon with a big hulk of an engine up front. It boasted not only three times the horsepower but twice the engine displacement of the model that Ford had whipped Alexander Winton in the year before.[140] In fact, his new "999" prototype, named for the train that had broken the speed record between New York and Chicago,[141] and its twin "Arrow" may still rank as the ugliest race cars ever to take to a track. Although rated at only 70 horsepower, some Detroit publications gushed that the output of the 999 was actually more like 100 horsepower. As for the ride of his latest model, Ford himself admitted: "I cannot quite describe the sensation. Going over Niagara Falls would have been but a pastime after a ride in one of them."[142]

Toward the end of the summer of 1902, Cooper arranged for a fellow bicycle racer from Ohio to come out to Grosse Pointe to drive the 999. Cooper's untried choice for driver was the brash and dashing twenty-four-year-old Berna Eli "Barney" Oldfield, whose daredevil style on the track and personal panache off it would make him the first real hero of American auto racing. As his biographer, William F. Noonan, put it, he was "a rogue, rule breaker, braggart, sentimentalist, gambler, showman, barroom brawler, dirt-track daredevil, a man without fear."[143] With trademark goggles in place and a bandanna around his neck, Oldfield, who resembled the young Winston Churchill, was a showman extraordinaire. Image aside, later in life Oldfield would reveal that the long black cigars that always jutted from his square jaw were there only to cushion his teeth from the jostling they got bouncing around at high speed in rickety race cars over lumpy dirt tracks. In fact, unlike most of his fellow professional drivers, Oldfield would die in his bed in 1946, after some two thousand races, and twenty-eight years after retiring from the sport.

The first of those races was the October 25, 1902, Manufacturers' Challenge Cup in Grosse Pointe Township, pitting Ford's 999 against three other entrants, including one driven by Alexander Winton.[144] The event would put Barney Oldfield's name in the news for good. The outcome of the race also kept Henry Ford's name in the limelight: with the blue-eyed, mustachioed Oldfield behind the wheel, the 999 won the five-mile contest by a full lap, in the U.S. record-breaking time of 5 minutes, 28 seconds.[145] Throngs of spectators broke down the track fences and carried the brave driver off the course on their shoulders.[146] Later, Oldfield would quip, "Henry Ford said that we made each other. I guess I did the better job of it."[147]

In fact, by the day of Oldfield's first great race, Ford no longer owned the 999, having sold it to Cooper after a deal-ending falling-out between the two partners.[148] As he had always intended to, in his own good time, Ford had begun to turn his attentions to building a car for the common man. Thus, while Oliver Barthel was kept hard at work designing the race cars, Ford had set Harold Wills to work on plans for a new mass-market production car.[149] Of course, Ford had no choice but to seek out the finest technicians if he was to accomplish all he intended; as Barthel explained half a century later: "I never knew Henry Ford to design a car . . . I don't think he could. . . . He even had difficulty in reading a blueprint. . . . Mr. Ford was a cut-and-try engineer."[150]

The medium-cost passenger car Wills was creating under Ford's aegis in the late spring of 1902 offered a radical change from earlier automotive designs. Instead of the horizontal positioning then considered standard in the industry, such as in the Oldsmobile, the new Ford model's two cylinders would be placed vertically. This innovation, which allowed more power to be transmitted to the axle with far less vibration, noise, and engine wear, was a substantial advance in engineering and automotive technology.[151] Naturally, building such an experimental car called for additional funding, and Ford was essentially broke.[152]

So Ford started shopping Wills's new model around in search of fresh investors. Soon he entered into serious talks with avid auto racing fan Alexander

Y. Malcomson, who owned Detroit's biggest coal company. Originally Ford had met the thirty-six-year-old Malcomson while working as night-shift engineer at the Edison Illuminating Company, in which capacity he had visited the supplier's coal yards every few weeks to conduct quality checks. Ford bought his household coal from Malcomson, and also encountered him at his son Edsel's Episcopal Church Sunday school, where he happened to be superintendent.[153]

A short, stocky, muttonchopped, and bumptious self-made entrepreneur, Alexander Y. Malcomson had emigrated from Scotland in 1880, settling in Detroit near other members of his family. In 1894, nearing age thirty, he entered the coal business and soon came to dominate it.[154] Malcomson, nicknamed the Skipper, put his profits into acquisitions that ranged from delivery yards to coal mines and railroad concessions, betraying an appetite for buying concerns much larger than his own, generally on credit stretched to the tattering point.[155] After all, it had been on borrowed nickels that he had begun operating his first, one-horse coal wagon, an endeavor that quickly grew into a fleet of 110 wagons and ten coal yards.[156] Despite, or perhaps because of, his well-deserved reputation for recklessness in Michigan's business circles,[157] Alexander Malcomson would turn out to be the only backer ever to succeed in harnessing Henry Ford's talents. For Malcomson didn't just afford the persistent, if sometimes clownish, dreamer another chance to build cars. He gave the stubborn, avaricious capitalist in Ford a *reason* to build them.

This incentive would be an equal share in any proceeds generated. According to the articles of incorporation drawn up for a $25 fee by Malcomson's Detroit attorneys, John W. Anderson and Horace H. Rackham, and presented on the afternoon of Saturday, August 16, 1902, the partners were to develop a simple, viable, inexpensive model of car.[158] The company would use Malcomson's seed money and existing plans drawn up by Ford and Harold Wills, who estimated they would need some $3,000 to produce a prototype of the passenger vehicle they had in development (it ended up costing around $4,000 to complete).[159] Malcomson and Ford would have equal shares in the Ford race car also then in development, as well as in the inventor's patents and shop facilities.

Malcomson was to put up $500 right away and more cash as needed to produce the commercial-automobile prototype, which would then be put on public display in hopes of attracting enough venture capital to establish a new corporation to manufacture the car in quantity.[160] Stock in that proposed enterprise would be issued with a par value of $100,000. If investors could be found to back the venture with that much paid-in capital,[161] the two original partners would gain equal shares in a 51 percent majority stake in the firm, thereupon to be incorporated as "Ford Motor Company." Both men would sit on the board of directors, Alexander Malcomson with the title of treasurer and Henry Ford with those of vice president and general manager, at a salary of $3,000 a year.[162] Provision was also made for the continued employment of Harold Wills as Ford's top assistant. The partnership agreement made clear that Malcomson would control the company's finances and business dealings, and Ford its technical and manufacturing operations.[163]

By October 1902 Ford had Wills plus ten more employees under him, along with apparently unlimited freedom to do as he pleased in his carmaking. Twice he had wriggled away from situations that might have sucked him down for good; while others may have seen those early failures as crushing blows to Ford, he preferred to maintain that "failure is the opportunity to begin again, more intelligently."[164] And so he intended to do. After all, even though he still had no money to speak of, he had managed to acquire a major stake in a company with his name on it, and of which he would be the real chief engineer.

Yet as Malcomson explained in a letter he sent to Ford, just a few days after the 999's triumph at Grosse Pointe, it was now time for Henry to "hunker down" and come up with the "sample commercial vehicle" he had promised. "Hope you will get everything running in good shape at the shop, so that the work can be pushed at all possible speed," Malcomson wrote. "Our salvation for next Season will be in getting the machine out quickly and placing it on the market early[;] it is pleasing that you have been so successful thus far in getting the right kind of help."[165]

For his part, Alexander Malcomson had made perhaps too fast a start in the automobile industry, scooping up a well-known name and a marketable idea for a car without really thinking through the partnership he was entering into with Henry Ford. According to the coalman's master plan, Ford's new model would be built entirely of components ordered to specification from specialty suppliers; his $3,000 in seed money would finance construction of the prototype that would be shown around to attract more orders. If customers' down payments on ordered cars could be turned around immediately to pay suppliers, then production could begin even without outside investors. After the buyers paid for their cars, the proposed Ford and Malcomson Company could pay its remaining bills from suppliers and emerge from its first model run with a profit, which could then be used to fund a second model run. In Malcomson's fondest reckoning, he and Henry Ford would own the entire enterprise.

By the fall, however, Ford had already overspent his development budget without coming close to completing the prototype. Worse, the coal king was out of ready cash, with nowhere to turn for more. Even his original $3,000 investment hadn't been entirely on the up-and-up. Malcomson was so overextended in the coal business that he dared not let his bankers know he had committed capital to yet another venture. Malcomson entrusted his whip-smart clerk, and coal-yard cashier, James Couzens, a Canadian by birth, with overhauling his companies' operations along more modern management lines, including double-entry bookkeeping.[166] Couzens's taut management would be crucial to Ford Motor Company later, but in 1902 it was Malcomson's optimism that made the next step possible. In November the partners signed the agreement and officially created Ford and Malcomson. It was capitalized with $150,000 divided among 15,000 shares, of which the founders would retain 6,900 shares in exchange for their time, labor, cash investments, and design and patent rights. According to the original plan, they would also purchase another 350 shares for $3,500 in cash. That left a total of 7,750 shares to sell.[167] Whether Henry Ford liked it or not, money and finance were part of the automobile business. Until he had a fortune of his own, he had to depend on the outside capital he so deplored. And this time, with two failures behind him, he had to get along with his backers. Even in the automobile business of 1902, a fourth chance wasn't likely. He had to make the third one count.

3

Founding Ford

When Alex Malcomson was asked early in 1902 whether he worried about shouldering the debt for the components that his new partner was ordering in advance—should the company fail to go into production for any reason, for instance, he would still be liable for the costs—the no-nonsense Scotsman replied with his usual gruff candor: "I haven't got time to worry," he muttered. "I've got a big coal business and I'm working here day and night. I'm just in this, and that's all, I guess."[1]

For Malcomson, it was enough just to be in the promising new automobile industry, to his mind such an epic opportunity that its very potential swept away mundane concerns about finance. He knew he had a tiger by the tail, and all he had to do was hang on to it. Of course, in Malcomson's situation that meant guaranteeing company contracts with money he didn't quite have, then shrugging off the risk. He was hardly alone in that. Thousands of eager capitalists across the country, especially in other burgeoning automobile meccas like Cleveland, Flint, and Indianapolis, were thrilling to the same gamble, as they too launched startup automobile companies in a market suddenly starving for cars. In truth, even those "just in" that market looked certain to rack up quick and enormous profits, provided they could just *stay* in.

For Ford and Malcomson Co. Ltd., the odds of success stretched even longer, as the partnership's beleaguered senior businessman couldn't spare any time to nurture the new venture. Because the infant carmaking concern needed cash even more than experienced management, Malcomson had no choice but to focus entirely on his core coal business. He was in the midst of a successful run, having come to dominate the industry in the eight years since he had brought his "Hotter than Sunshine" coal to eastern Michigan.[2]

Malcomson kept a scrapbook for several years around the turn of the century, chronicling his fast-growing coal firm, along with the rest of his business activities. A bulging volume, it is now housed at the Henry Ford Museum and Library in Dearborn. Along with many articles on shifts in coal prices, no doubt a compelling topic to him at the time, plus a few on local coal-worker fatalities (including the deaths of two men in his own employ), a surprising portion of the newspaper clippings glued so neatly onto the book's pages pertain to firms being taken over by the A.Y. Malcomson Company.

Still more telling, the scrapbook contains a few items only Malcomson himself likely would have cut out to save, including one beginning, "Barney Oldfield in a Ford-Cooper machine at the Fair grounds this afternoon beat the world record for a half-mile track." A handwritten notation next to that clipping identifies its source as the *Detroit Free Press*. All around it are more stories about coal, making the page a mirror of Malcomson's priorities in those early years of the century. Although he remained a coal man through and through—recognizing he had no other choice if he wanted to stay solvent—he simply could not resist the allure of the automobile. And so it was that Alexander Malcomson delegated the management of his new car-manufacturing partnership to his talented thirty-year-old clerk, James Couzens.[3] More important in the long run, Malcomson—so deep in debt he couldn't let his regular bankers know he was investing in yet another risky new enterprise—arranged his carmaking finances with another bank, and put the account in James Couzens's financially pristine name.[4] That was only the beginning of Couzens's monumental contributions to the new company.

The chief asset of Ford and Malcomson Co. Ltd. may have been the accepted perception that, of all the automotive pioneers in Detroit at the time, none knew *more* about cars than Henry Ford. By the same token, there likely weren't many Detroit auto men who knew *less* about cars than James Couzens, who was strictly business from his polished shoes to his derby topper.[5] When Couzens took his first car ride in Alex Malcomson's Winton to prepare for his new duties, he recalled that the boss turned something on the dashboard, explaining that he was changing the mixture. "I thought that he meant he was mixing water with the gasoline," Couzens said, "and I continued to think so for a long time."[6] As just about anybody would know, even back then, oil-derived liquids—including gasoline—simply don't mix with water.

Like the Scottish-born Malcomson and the Irish-American Ford, Couzens came from British stock. He was born in Chatham, Ontario, east of Detroit, on August 26, 1872, the son of English immigrant James Joseph Couzens Sr. and his wife, a Chatham native named Emma Clift Couzens.[7] James Jr. lodged playful complaints with his mother that as a Canadian by birth he could aspire to become neither king of England nor president of the United States.[8]

James Sr., a hard man, had clawed his way up another man's corporate ladder from soap-factory worker to salesman before quitting to start a soap-making firm of his own. He had taken his son along on sales calls throughout Ontario beginning at a very young age to show the boy right and wrong in real business.[9] In time, however, mutual antipathy poisoned the relationship between father and son, to the point that even decades later their relatives remarked how each had deemed the other wanting in virtually every way. Worse, James Couzens Sr. beat his son often and constantly berated him in front of others. Corporal punishment from parents was hardly unusual in the nineteenth century, but even as a child it appears that James Couzens Jr. knew better, reviling his father for trying to break his spirit through brutality and steeling himself from boyhood never to let anyone ever try to do that to him again.

While still small, Couzens began responding to his plight with displays of perfectionism aimed to show his father up. Almost in spite, the boy completed every chore at home and every assignment at school in a glaringly exemplary fashion.[10] The dedication to work that resulted in his character might have been considered a triumph for the hard-knocks school of child rearing, except that the aura of antagonism also caused the youngster to develop a sullen haughtiness that would harden into a thick shell by the time he set out to make his way against the world. In the end, his colleagues in the workplace could neither help but respect James Couzens nor hope to like him. They joked among themselves that when he smiled his annual smile the ice broke up on the five Great Lakes.[11]

At eighteen, the dour youth struck out on his own for Detroit, where he took the job he would keep from 1890 to 1893, checking rail-car inventories for the Michigan Central Railroad[12]—a lowly form of the accounting that would later blossom into one of his greatest business talents. It was in this entry-level capacity that Couzens's tenacious hounding over late coal shipments and overdue payments drew the notice of Alex Malcomson, who hired him to perform the same sort of bulldogging.[13] For all of Malcomson Coal's whirlwind acquisitions and expansion, its headquarters had long remained basically a one-man operation. In truth, Alex Malcomson had never realized how much he needed a right-hand man until he hired James Couzens in 1894 and found a young protégé who would take on any assignment with equanimity, be it sweeping the floor, making sales calls, keeping the books, or haggling with suppliers—and who wouldn't bother the boss again until each job was not only done, but done well.

Malcomson quickly grew dependent on his able clerk, and took care to let Couzens know he was being groomed for an executive position at the dynamic coal house. In time, a close rapport developed between the disparate pair, who despite, or perhaps because of, their occasional fierce arguments often behaved more like father and son than employer and employee.[14] The depth of their mentor-protégé bond may have sprung from genuine warmth on the part of Malcomson combined with Couzens's equally sincere willingness to learn, but something in the filial nature of their relationship loomed ominously. For to James Couzens, and with good reason, a father was not so much a role model to emulate as an impediment to overcome and a villain to vanquish at any cost.

As stern and hard-hearted as Couzens came across to the people he worked with, he was quite another man to those he loved, including Margaret Manning, the hometown girl he returned to Chatham to pursue. Couzens was twenty-six when he and Manning married on August 31, 1898. At the time, he boasted almost four years of steady employment with Alexander Malcomson.[15] The Couzens brood grew to include five children, to whom James Jr. proved a warm, tolerant, and wildly attentive father who delighted in making up cunning games and indulging in other playfulness at home with his family. His kids adored their "Daddy Jim"—but then they didn't have to work with him.

Malcomson's original intent, in late 1902, was that until Ford's new car line went into production—or sooner, if he could spare himself from the coal office—Couzens would watch over the automotive venture, its prospects, and most of all Henry Ford. Couzens had the gravitas for the job, although he was nine years younger than Ford. With his wire-rimmed pince-nez and stern disposition, he seemed to be far deeper into middle age.[16] Eager to justify his employer's trust, Couzens threw himself and his workaholic nature into the launch of the car company. The understanding was that once it was established he and Malcomson would trade places: Couzens would manage the regional coal empire, and Malcomson would run the automotive concern, at least as long as the car craze lasted.[17]

By early 1903, however, Couzens's attitude had already changed and his outlook was broader. He no longer wanted to go back into the small and sooty business of filling Detroit's dank basements with coal. As a logistical exercise, the A.Y. Malcomson Company was merely municipal in reach; an automobile company was national and possibly even international. Whether Couzens had fallen under the spell of the magnetic Henry Ford or had simply recognized that the automobile was destined to be much more than a fad, he soon wanted to remain an automaker.

While Henry Ford seems to have been born with an uncanny understanding of automotive mechanics, and James Couzens with no acumen at all for engineering, the younger man had intuitive abilities that Ford lacked. He was, for example, obsessed with practical matters, a quality that would prove as vital as any of Ford's in the initial success of Ford Motor. To some extent, Couzens's genius was for work itself. Throughout his career, which ended with two terms as a U.S. senator, he proved himself the most tireless and productive man everywhere he worked. In this respect he could not have been more different from Henry Ford, who never displayed the least diligence, preferring to wander through his workplaces, planting ideas, checking progress, and otherwise leading his troops not so much by example as by the abundant sense of momentum he somehow gave off. Even his peculiar absences grew into the inspirational stuff of legend, and the times were not rare when Ford couldn't be found at all, having disappeared to confer with an obscure employee or to tuck himself away to catch a nap. When the company needed direction in matters large or small, though, he was on the spot to give it, more alert than anyone else.

Couzens, by contrast, could invariably be found wherever he was supposed to be, generally engaged in the completion of whatever his common sense dictated was the highest-priority task at hand. His laserlike focus made him an effective leader in his own right—or at least an efficient propeller, in the sense that he was always driving the organization forward, however large it grew, simply by persisting to turn at his own relentless pace, and even if it made him unpopular. "I think it was pretty hard to get along with Mr. Couzens," noted longtime Ford metallurgist John Wandersee. "He expected too much."[18]

So did Henry Ford, of course, and thus a powerfully productive bond was forged between the two men almost immediately.

When Couzens had to report to Malcomson that Ford had overspent the original seed money by 130 percent, he carefully avoided criticizing the engineer. Much as he would have harangued any other party guilty of such an outrageous overrun, in this case he instead set to working feverishly with his boss to secure the supply contracts already in place and to find financing for more, with little success. Alex Malcomson had long since exceeded the level of funding he had agreed to supply as seed money, yet his belief in Ford's potential still didn't wane. On the contrary, the biggest creditor on the books was Dodge Brothers Inc., a firm that supplied major components to automakers and did not make cars of its own. When the Dodge brothers demanded a signed contract for the 250 engines commissioned by the yet unborn Ford car-manufacturing company, Malcomson guaranteed the order personally.[19] Had the venture failed to materialize or its production to keep pace, Malcomson would still have been obliged to pay for the Dodge engines, and would thereby have been left a ruined man. For unbeknownst to the bankers who had fronted the funds to expand his coal business, Malcomson had put its assets openly at risk to start Ford and Malcomson.

The loudest of all the creditors, Horace E. and John F. Dodge,[20] had been raised in near poverty in the town of Niles in western Michigan. John and Horace were born four years apart, in 1864 and 1868, respectively. Those four years were just about the only thing that ever came between them. They were dependent on each other as adults as they had been as constant boyhood companions. When they established their own company in Detroit, John made it a policy not to answer letters addressed to the company only as "Dodge." Any missive that failed to acknowledge the "Brothers" in the name was simply returned.[21]

In the working world, John and Horace would compile precisely the same résumé. "I first met the Dodge brothers while I was working at the Main and Typograph Factory in Windsor, [Ontario]," recalled Walter G. Griffith, later a Ford Motor machinist. The Canadian factory had placed an advertisement for a "floor man," as assembly workers were sometimes known. Griffith worked in a tool crib near the stairway, and remembered that "as I heard two fellows come running up those stairs, I looked out of the window and there were these two young redheads. John was in the lead, as he always was, a leader— Horace tagging along."

The factory superintendent, a man by the name of Piper, looked over to see who was making all of the noise.

"John Dodge," Griffith continued, "who was always spokesman, said, 'We came in answer to the advertisement you had in the *News* for a floor man.'

"'Well,' said Piper, 'We only want one man.'

"John Dodge said, 'We're brothers and we always work together, if you haven't got room for two of us, neither of us will start. That's it!'" Griffith reported, adding, "Piper wheeled around in his chair and said 'Hmmh! Come in Monday morning. Both of you.'"[22]

John and Horace Dodge argued loudly and often, but the brothers presented a united front to the world.[23] They also represented a specific nineteenth-century type of spirit, kicking through life as though it were a frontier to be conquered and all the while enjoying it. Henry Ford was only a year older than John Dodge, but exemplified another of the era's archetypes entirely with his righteousness, independence, and doggedly homespun values.

The burly Dodges were tough in a way Henry Ford most certainly was not. They were strong physical men who were always up for a fight, not for the joy of it, but because in their view of the world, fist fighting was sometimes necessary. Of course, those times nearly always came when the brothers had been indulging their enthusiasm for hard drinking, which was almost every weekend. "The Dodge brothers were certainly inclined to 'paint the town red,'" Griffith said.[24] That did not change much even though the Dodges became rich and adopted social aspirations to match. Throughout their lives John and Horace continued to frequent working-class bars most weekend nights, specifically to get very, very drunk.

No one could dispute that on weekdays the Dodge brothers worked soberly and with brilliant results. John focused on management and Horace on engineering. The machine shop they started in the early 1890s to make bicycle parts had earned a good reputation, which gained a substantial boost in the automotive world with their heroic production efforts on the early Oldsmobile. Dodge Brothers Inc. grew into the largest machine shop in Detroit after the company won the lion's share of Ford Motor's production work. But the Dodges were now making the Ford team nervous. The brothers constantly threatened violence—with their fists—if they weren't paid on time.

Although there was nothing at all unusual about the Dodge brothers' manners and appetites compared with those of many early-twentieth-century industrialists, the Dodges' behavior toward their teetotaling colleague Henry Ford was monstrous. Friendly in a distant way outside of work, they clashed on matters of finance. Ford's compulsion to paint every person near him in business as a monster in one way or another remained his most unappealing trait, especially as seen in the aftermath of the fallings-out that his nature invariably occasioned. Ford could be so attractive, when he wanted to, that few people could see that disfavor was waiting just under the surface. For everyone save his wife, Clara, demonization of the strong and destruction of the weak seemed to be the inevitable end of any close relationship with Henry Ford. This disloyalty would, however, catch up with him eventually.

As the first Model A Fords started to come together in the winter chill of 1903, Malcomson had no choice but to make an earnest effort to sell stock in the company. The capitalization was set at $150,000, of which $100,000 was to be active, with the other $50,000 to be held as treasury stock by the resulting corporation. Henry Ford and Alex Malcomson each took $25,500 worth of this stock, for a total of $51,000 in exchange for their patents, cash, and work to date.[25] The remaining $49,000 was supposed to be paid-in capital. As before, a number of investors familiar with the young auto industry were approached, but not one availed himself of the opportunity to buy into Henry Ford's latest plans to spend money.

The situation grew so dire that even the stolid James Couzens found himself sitting on a curb one day that winter, trying not to cry after an appointment ended with a particularly humiliating rejection of his attempt to sell the stock.[26] The fact was that no objective investor was willing to put money into Ford and Malcomson. Eventually, Malcomson resorted to less objective investors, including every relative and friend he could think of who might take a flier on a risk with such a huge potential payoff. Among the takers were his cousin Vernon Fry, who committed to buy $5,000 worth of stock, and Albert Strelow, a landlord Malcomson had done business with not long before, who also purchased 50 shares for $5,000 and contributed the use of a building as well. Both of the lawyers who drew up the incorporation plan—John W. Anderson and Horace H. Rackham[27]—signed on for 50 shares apiece, too.[28]

Looking out for himself as well as the new company, Couzens told one of the lawyers that he intended "to invest all the money he [could] beg, borrow or steal."[29] That didn't ring quite true. When his mother-in-law surprised him after reading the company's prospectus with an offer of a $15,000 investment loan, Couzens refused to take her up on it. It didn't seem an honorable thing for a son-in-law to do. He did ask for money from his widower father, who laughed him right out of the house. Rosetta Couzens, his schoolteacher sister, however, gave him fully half[30] of her $200 life savings.[31]

Couzen's original intent was to list Rosetta's single $100 share in her own name. Henry Ford, however, objected so strenuously to a woman's being listed as a shareholder in his company that Couzens felt obligated to include her investment in his own stake instead. Ford's reasoning may have been purely chauvinist. However, he couldn't forget how one of the directors of the Detroit Automobile Company had put 100 shares of that firm in his own name, like the other directors, plus another 50 in his wife's name but under his control, thereby according himself a bigger interest in fact.[32] That experience left Ford wary of any investment by a woman, as it could be a cover to stash voting power away for some man; as time went on, matters of ownership and control became obsessive concerns for Henry Ford.

James Couzens added his sister's good-faith $100 to the $400 he could afford to put in on his own, then borrowed $500 in cash from Alex Malcomson and signed a promissory note to the corporation-to-be for $1,500, for a total stock purchase of $2,500.[33] It wasn't much, but it afforded Couzens the interest he wanted in the company to which he would give his all.

Although Malcomson had made himself known as a shrewd and aggressive businessman around Detroit, much of his success came from family connections to investment bankers and other sources of capital. Yet after he went into partnership with Henry Ford to organize a carmaking company, investors grew scarce, connections or not. Perhaps this was because Malcomson had no record in the automobile industry; perhaps it was because Henry Ford did, as the scapegoat for two previous failures. Or perhaps it was because in 1903 the car business just wasn't considered a venue for investment, only for speculation. In any case, Malcomson's usual backers grew much colder than sunshine.

It was by pure coincidence that his cousin, Frank Malcomson, happened to be in the right Detroit tailor's shop being fitted for a suit at the right time to take advantage of an opportunity presented by an overheard remark. In casual conversation, one of the other customers happened to mention that he intended to buy a motorcar. What made the situation so very fortuitous was who made the remark.

Charles H. Bennett, a rich and respectable rifle maker from Plymouth, Michigan, and still a clever mechanic in his own right,[34] would be the only charter investor in Ford Motor Company with no prior financial ties to Alexander Malcomson; ultimately, he would be the most loyal to the coal man.[35] Ambitious even as a teenager, Bennett had begun his career working for his father selling windmills to Michigan farmers, or trying to; in the early 1880s most farmers had not yet become inured to large expenditures for agricultural equipment, as anything they needed they either made themselves or made do without. Undeterred, Bennett continued on a quest for success that eventually led to his control of Plymouth's near bankrupt Daisy Air Rifle Company. As its president, Bennett brought the firm back to life and made a comfortable fortune of his own in the process. More important, at least to him, by 1900 Charles H. Bennett ranked among the leading citizens of his hometown, just fifteen miles west of Detroit.[36] He had learned long before that a good name was worth more than money itself to a man of business; assets, after all, could be earned back.

Those in Bennett's generation—and Ford's—grew up during that Gilded Age when industrial capitalism was pushing harder than ever against the limits of acceptable wealth and ethics in the United States. With the western frontier closing and new global markets opening up, in the last third of the nineteenth century commerce drew many of the brightest and most daring members of society. For the first time, the people doing the most to shape America were not its politicians and soldiers, but the business titans so busily building not only a bold new economy but a wider-minded culture to go with it. Some of these men were truly rapacious and deserved to be despised as robber barons, and many underlined why by adopting the creeds of social Darwinism, which maintained that common laborers should be dismissed as peons incapable of rising above their lack of education and opportunity. Railroad tycoon William H. Vanderbilt summed up the arrogance of his ilk when, after he shut down his trains' New York–Chicago route because of poor ticket sales, a reporter asked him how he could do such a thing as deny the public such vital transportation services. Vanderbilt shot back a phrase that could have served as a motto for the era's tycoons: "The public be damned."[37]

Henry Ford—whose hero forever remained Thomas Edison—nevertheless also learned to admire the master of organization John D. Rockefeller Sr., who created America's most powerful and feared monopoly, Standard Oil. A product of both his times and his intellectual blinders, Ford claimed to believe that the reason Standard Oil was such an unmitigated success was that Rockefeller never abandoned the rustic values he had absorbed as a boy growing up in upstate New York and later in Ohio. In fact, years later Ford sought out the aged Rockefeller and was struck by the old tycoon's strong forehead and bright inquisitive eyes. "As soon as I saw his face," Ford said, "I knew what had made the Standard Oil Company."[38]

On January 10, 1901, about eight years after Rockefeller retired, one major event ensued that helped make the Standard Oil Company boom. The nation's first oil geyser blew its drilling rig 160 feet into the sky over a small knoll just south of Beaumont, Texas. Over the next ten days, a million gallons (more than 12,000 cubic meters) of crude oil shot skyward like Old Faithful before the Spindletop gusher could be brought under control. The following year, over one hundred new oil companies were created in Texas. Fortune seekers poured into southwest Texas by the thousands. Oil prices dropped dramatically to less than five cents a barrel.[39] Spindletop marked the beginnings of the modern petroleum industry. "It was a world of men eager to make their fortunes—oil boomers," David Halberstam wrote in *The Reckoning.* "Men looked at each other and wondered who would become a millionaire by nightfall."[40] Before the Texas well blew, America's output of petroleum products, mostly derived from western Pennsylvania, had been used for lubricating oil and kerosene for lamps. Gasoline was deemed a near worthless by-product that oil drillers used to let run off into the dirt. But with the advent of the horseless carriage, refining gasoline became a bonanza: strike the right vein, and you were set for life. With the discovery of a seemingly unending supply of oil, there was no longer any question what the outcome of the race among electric power, steam, and the gasoline engine would be. The clearest winner was Standard Oil.

For all the damage the greedy lords of Wall Street did to the image of their own profession, it seemed that at the same time every community boasted a local hero at the top of its own business class: someone who made money, certainly, but who made jobs, too, and a good name for a town as a place with a future. These were the captains of commerce whom youngsters growing up in the Gilded Age first learned to admire and sought to emulate.

———

Charles H. Bennett was the upstanding local hero of the business community of Plymouth. And he was proud that southeastern Michigan was starting to garner a reputation as an automobile mecca.[41] Always convivial, Bennett couldn't have imagined, on that fateful visit to a fashionable Detroit menswear shop in the spring of 1903, that merely mentioning that his next errand in the big city that afternoon was to test-drive an Oldsmobile would have such grand consequences. The sporty little two-seat curved-dash Olds was the most popular car in the country—at $450 including mudguards,[42] it accounted for about a quarter of the estimated 12,000 automobiles sold in the United States in 1903.[43] Lightweight to the point that it felt more like driving a buggy than a car, the Olds was easy to operate, as well as cute. Its main drawback was that its single-cylinder engine did chug along rather pokily under what passed for the body curling up around one's feet, and it seldom made it up steep hills. Underpowered but irresistible, the dashing Oldsmobile proved especially appealing to first-time buyers such as Bennett.

As Bennett was leaving the tailor shop, Frank Malcomson stopped him to confess that he had overheard this conversation about the Olds and felt compelled to tell him of a much better car about to go on the market, engineered by Henry Ford in partnership with his own cousin, Alex Malcomson. Bennett had never heard of Ford, but he had seen Malcomson's "Hotter than Sunshine" coal wagons all over Detroit.[44] Intrigued, he told Frank Malcomson that if there was indeed a car on the market better than the curved-dash Olds, he would very much like to check it out.

Upon that promise to give the upstart a fair chance, Frank Malcomson escorted Bennett to the Ford and Malcomson facilities, where Henry Ford was on the spot within an hour with a prototype of his bold new Model A.[45] He invited Bennett to take a test ride in the two-cylinder, eight-horsepower[46] automobile, and the two of them went rumbling off around Detroit in the brisk winter air. "He gave me the usual conversation that a salesman should make," Bennett recalled.[47] In truth, Ford wasn't selling the car, but a stake in his car company.

Impressed enough to forget about visiting the Oldsmobile showroom,[48] Bennett stated his firm desire to buy one of Ford's cars. He liked the Dearborn mechanic's entrepreneurial bent, and asked Henry when this Model A would be on the market and how much it would cost. Ford didn't hazard a guess on either score, but suggested instead that Bennett speak directly with Malcomson. Actually, he didn't just suggest it: he dropped Bennett off at Malcomson's office and disappeared. "He probably had someone else that he was taking for a ride," Bennett supposed.[49]

Malcomson immediately offered Bennett a quarter interest in the car company in return for a cash investment and a place to assemble the vehicles. Their negotiations broke down on Bennett's side, however, when his fellow directors at the Daisy Air Rifle Company balked at the proposal, on the grounds that there was no reason to diversify from air rifles into something as whimsical as the automobile.[50] The deal fared no better on the other side, collapsing the instant Henry Ford learned that an investment from Bennett's company meant his new model might have to be called the Daisy.[51] He was not about to see his latest creation named after either a flower or a gun.

In the end, Bennett personally pledged $5,000 to the new concern,[52] not in cash but in the form of two $2,500 notes, one guaranteed by Alex Malcomson. The company used his credit standing to extend its own purchasing power, since in business then a good name was just as valuable as cash. As it turned out Bennett paid his notes out of the dividends he received from the company's profits a year later. In other words, Charles H. Bennett never put any money at all into Ford's proposition.[53]

Neither, of course, did Henry Ford, at least not in cash.[54] Nearing forty, he wasn't even earning a steady living, officially; under their partnership agreement, neither he nor Malcomson drew any salary. (By some accounts, Ford hired Harold Wills in the autumn of 1902 on the contingency that they split the chief designer's paycheck—so that the co-owner of the company could pay his bills.)[55]

The truth was that Ford was starting over in a treacherous field already crowded with automaking firms. For all anyone knew, the automobile really would be just a fad, as many people believed and more than a few hoped. Because of this uncertainty, many of the mechanics Ford tried to draft to his latest effort declined the opportunity. As family men, they explained, they couldn't risk unemployment and its consequences should the startup company fail.[56] Ford said he understood; he had a wife and child of his own and considered himself a family man first and foremost.

Even with the commitments of Anderson, Bennett, Fry, Rackham, and Strelow added to Couzens's pittance, the new concern was still sorely undercapitalized. So when the Dodge brothers came growling after their overdue remittances that April, Couzens urged Malcomson to propose paying them off in stock. For the brothers it was, of course, a Hobson's choice, as Ford's associates knew full well; by that point the Dodges could either help finance the startup's continuation or suffer losses on their unpaid invoices when the company collapsed. Thanks to the negotiating tactics of Alex Malcomson and Jim Couzens, the Dodges ended up not only taking 35 shares each in exchange for writing off the bills, but also paying in another $1,500 apiece in cash, giving each of them stakes worth $5,000.[57]

Extracting cash from the volatile Dodges certainly had not been a job for the faint of heart, but even smoother steel would be required for the next unpleasant task: going to a banker and owning up to the firm's grim situation. Malcomson and Couzens settled on John Simpson Gray, the president and cofounder of Detroit's German-American Bank, for three reasons: first, the native-born Scot was known to be a very nice fellow and honest to a fault; second, he was seriously rich, having inherited and expanded his father's successful candy company; and third, he was Malcomson's uncle. That said, the sixty-two-year-old Gray was still a banker, and as such was sure to recognize that everything his nephew had done toward starting the car company was ill considered and slapdash. In financial terms, Gray would have been right to think so: Malcomson's nascent enterprise needed a new source of cash in large part because his successful coal company was so overleveraged it could no longer keep paying off its own debt.[58]

Yet Malcomson didn't have to ask for charity, as he had his uncle over the same barrel that had induced the Dodge brothers to take an interest in the car business: if Gray did not supply fresh cash, he would lose the substantial sums he had already advanced to his nephew's coal company. Malcomson knew he could afford to lose this harrowing game of chicken with his creditors only once. But it wouldn't be this time. John S. Gray bought $10,500 worth of stock in the new company—representing 37.5 percent of the cash actually collected—if only to buffer Alex's coal business should this Ford fellow's cars fail to reach the market or flop when they did.[59]

There was only one drawback for Malcomson in his Uncle John's stepping forward with the $10,500 in cash needed to save the struggling operation from collapse: the condition that Gray be made president of the new corporation, and that "if he became dissatisfied with his investment within a year Malcomson would reimburse him." Now it was his nephew who faced the Hobson's choice. But it was only by giving up the top executive spot to John Gray that Ford Motor Company could come into existence—as it did in June 1903, with cash backing amounting to $28,000.

———

Spring was in full late bloom in Detroit midway through June 1903, with temperatures hovering around sixty degrees and gusty northwest winds making it feel even cooler. The city's scrappy Detroit Tigers were on a road trip to play the hapless Washington Senators and local schools were gearing up for graduation ceremonies. The day's top *Detroit News* story detailed a disastrous flood in Teppner, Oregon, that drowned 500 people—nearly half the town's residents, including a Michigan woman who perished with her husband, leaving behind three daughters. In international news, a dispatch from Belgrade confirmed that Serbia's new king would rule in name only—the government would be controlled by the army—and a report from Germany announced that the Socialist Party was likely to gain fifteen seats in the Reichstag in the upcoming election.[60] But there was no mention in the next few days' newspapers, or anywhere else, that at 8:00 P.M. on June 15, a meeting was convened at the Detroit office of A.Y. Malcomson that would change the world forever.[61]

Ten of the twelve prospective stockholders in Ford Motor Company had gathered in an office on Griswold Street to draw up the concern's articles of association, with Horace Rackham serving as chairman. John S. Gray was one of those men who were absent; the launch of the small automaking company was not a pressing concern to an important banker. Henry Ford paced about, hands in his pockets, excited as a schoolboy on his first date. Once the details were hammered out, it was agreed that they would reassemble the next morning at 9:30 A.M. at 68 Moffat Block to sign the official forms required to create a company. That morning James Couzens drafted the mutually accepted articles of association onto the appropriate state form, listing the names of Henry Ford and the eleven other stockholders next to the number of shares for which each had subscribed. Once signed and notarized, these articles were forwarded to the office of Michigan's secretary of state in Lansing. The documents were stamped "received for record" on June 17 and recorded into

Michigan's Record of Corporations no. 53. This notation was then signed by Deputy Secretary of State George Lord, and Ford Motor Company was born.[62]

Although company histories traditionally have given the date of its founding as June 16, 1903, the day its stockholders met in Detroit to fill out the forms, the incorporation actually took effect the next day, when the state received Ford Motor Company's formal articles of association.[63] Whichever date is preferred, the founding of Ford Motor Company ranks among the most significant events in twentieth-century U.S. industrial history.[64] As early as 1952, when the august *Journal of Economic Review* sought a contemporary yardstick for the fabulous profits realized by the founders of the East India Company, which had so enriched the British empire, its editors settled on noting that the imperialists had made fortunes *almost* as spectacular as those of the early stockholders in Ford Motor Company.[65]

One prospective investor learned just how unlucky the number 13 can be: John Gray had talked an associate into putting $500 in the startup until Henry Ford nixed a thirteenth stockholder as potentially bad luck. In 1919, that $500 investment would have been worth $1,750,000 profit.[66]

Upon the conclusion of Ford Motor Company's first formal organizational meeting, Ford offered Couzens a ride home. "What do you think we ought to ask from those fellows?" Ford inquired ostensibly in passing but in fact as a subtle invitation to Couzens to consider his own place in the firm as above that of the coupon clippers who footed the bills. "It is a mistake to make or have too strong attachments, because it weakens your will and character," Ford continued, although Couzens hardly needed such advice.[67]

As agreed, Gray was elected president of the new corporation, largely as a signal to the Detroit business community that the company was on firm financial footing. While Alex Malcomson was made treasurer, the agreement under which his uncle had put in his crucial funding specifically called for him to remain at his coal company, the far more important cash cow as far as Gray was concerned. James Couzens, named secretary and business manager at $2,400 a year, was to look after Ford Motor's organization on a daily basis. Henry Ford was accorded the titles of vice president and general manager in charge of mechanics and production, at an annual salary of $3,600.[68] The remaining stockholders were not expected to participate in the company's operations.[69] An employee at the startup described its management structure in simpler terms: "It was kind of divided up between Mr. Ford taking care of the engineering and shop, and Mr. Couzens taking care of the business."[70] Ten workmen, each hired at a daily wage of $1.50,[71] were expected to assemble fifteen cars a day.[72]

According to Malcomson's original plan, Ford Motor's first cars were intended not to revolutionize a century, but to meet the demands of a single summer; after that, the company could either rest up and make plans for the next summer's selling season or settle up and leave the business, as most of the earliest car manufacturers opted to do. Novelties that they were in the go-go market of 1903, automobiles looked to be as hot a commodity as they ever would be again, and most of those who got into the business were content to take a profit and get out. A few brand names had been established, but most early dealers would sell any car they could acquire, advertising each for its specifications more than its marque. In February 1903, four months before Ford Motor Company was incorporated, William Hughson, founder of Hughson Ford Sales in San Francisco, signed the first Ford franchise agreement. In March, Steve Tenvoorde, a blacksmith and bicycle shop owner, opened the second Ford dealership in St. Cloud, Minnesota, under the auspices of Ford and Malcomson (as of 2003, the Tenvoorde Motor Company is still flourishing).[73]

There were three ways to enter the automobile business in 1903, as there still are today. First, a fledgling company could set up its own machine shop and factory, design its cars' major components on paper, and then produce them in-house. That was the most ambitious course, requiring massive capital expenditures as well as a crack workforce. In return, however, a high-end carmaker such as Packard or Pierce-Arrow could turn out luxury automobiles with unique features while making continual improvements in both design and methods of production. At the other end of the spectrum, a startup company could buy every component, from radiator caps to tailpipes, off the shelf and still assemble a respectable car from them. The resulting low-budget model likely would lack any outstanding appeal, but it would go, and in car-crazed 1903 that was appeal enough. In fact, statistics show that of the three-thousand-odd car companies launched in the United States between 1895 and 1905, the majority put their vehicles together from standard parts manufactured by third parties. Some of them turned out quite good products, including glorified kit cars, such as the initial Auburn, models from Moon, and the Rambler.

The middle route to car production was the one Ford Motor Company took. This approach allowed for the use of some standard, off-the-shelf components, while most distinguishing major parts were built to the specifications of the company's in-house designers. It was the same method employed even more notably at the time to turn out Oldsmobile's popular curved-dash model, with Dodge Brothers making "practically everything but the name plate" for the little runabout, as pioneering motorist Bellamy Partridge overstated it in his history of the American automobile, *Fill'er Up*.[74] (Dodge did not make the body or seats.) Ransom E. Olds may have come up with the bright ideas behind the country's most popular car, but the parts were actually built to spec by others. Similarly, the Dodge Brothers machine shop manufactured the earliest Ford Motor Company automobile engines, delivering the basic power assemblies by horse-drawn wagon to Ford's plant, where they would be completed with the addition of wiring, spark plugs, coils, and dry cells, then lubricated and taken out for road tests fitted onto old chassis kept for the purpose. Once judged satisfactory, the engines would be cleaned and mounted on sparkling new bodies atop pristine wheels, then prepared for shipping.[75]

Much as any engineer might yearn for the comparative luxury of an entire production department in which to execute his every notion—which was the general image competitors had of working conditions at the plush outfits like Cadillac and Pierce-Arrow—the middle way actually relied even more heavily on the abilities of individual draftsmen. At companies like Ford, designers had to envision every precise detail of the specifications that would make their models unique. They had to draw each one flawlessly and oversee all the newly designed parts' manufacturing by outside firms while making sure their own in-house components would fit, and work, with the imported ones. The paperwork itself called for an expert engineering staff to process.

Henry Ford's personal proclivities made matters even tougher. "Mr. Ford, as design engineer," noted Oliver Barthel, "didn't seem to have the idea that things could be designed. He seemed to have the idea that you had to make them by manual methods rather than by sitting down and putting it on a piece of paper. Mr. Ford was a cut-and-try mechanic, if you want to call it that. He wasn't a theoretical man. He couldn't visualize things to put them on paper."[76]

Nor could he actually build them. Frederick Strauss, who was still working for Ford in the first days of Ford Motor Company, observed that "Henry never worked with his hands, either. He could give you advice and he was very smart. He could tell you how things should be done." But Strauss added, "He couldn't read blueprints, nor could he do finish[ed] machine work."[77]

Later, a debate would arise not so much over Ford's skill with blueprints and machine tools but over whether he was a true genius. On the evidence, it seems he could indeed translate his ideas back and forth from mind to metalwork— but as an interim step, blueprints reduced reality to abstraction by *subtracting* one dimension. Ford's genius, if such it was, worked by *adding* a dimension, namely the sense of the *whole* of a machine. He understood that most of his potential customers were mechanically illiterate and that therefore the whole machine had to be simple to operate or they wouldn't buy it—not in the numbers envisioned. What he needed, therefore, was a highly skilled draftsman and design engineer who could draw the trees—including every branch, blossom, and leaf—without seeing the forest. That was Ford's job.

Henry Ford's success had always depended on how much work he could get other people to do in his interests rather than their own. Of all the talented engineers he had encountered through his earlier automotive and racing ventures, the one he had chosen to hire at Ford Motor Company as his right-hand man was Harold Wills, the veteran of the short-lived Henry Ford

Company who had helped design the 999 and Arrow racers while moonlighting from his paying job. Pleasant but direct, Wills was only twenty-five when Ford Motor came into being, but he was already full of enough self-confidence to work with Henry Ford on an equal footing. Wills knew he came from unusually bright stock: his father was a master mechanic who had trained him in basic engineering, and his mother was so keen on Romantic verse that she named her son "Childe Harold" after Lord Byron's poetic hero[78]—although even as a young man Harold Wills commanded such respect that no one ever dared call him Childe to his face.[79]

Before he would give up his day job—as a superintending design engineer at Boyer Machine[80]—to join Henry Ford's latest effort as chief engineer and metallurgist,[81] Wills wanted a piece of the new pie. He was a prime catch for any firm, but Ford didn't have the authority to assign any shares to him outright—so in addition to an attractive salary offer he agreed to forge a separate agreement giving Wills the earnings from twenty of Ford's own shares, amounting to some 10 percent of the founder's holdings in the firm. Again, as one of the company's principals, Ford wouldn't draw a salary of his own until production began.

Wills and his small staff worked the way Henry Ford preferred: tooling parts by hand to create a working model. After that, the model would be continually refined, with Wills drafting blueprints and specification sheets to transmit the ideas to suppliers all over the Midwest and Northeast for actual production.[82] In addition to the parts ordered from Dodge Brothers, a local carriage company received a Ford Motor order for the same number of wooden chassis, at $52 apiece, and the Hartford Rubber Company still another for 2,600 tires, at $40 per set of four.[83]

Landlord and investor Albert Strelow rented a wooden factory building on Detroit's Mack Street (now Mack Avenue) to Ford Motor. After renovations, the shop's main assembly room measured 250 by 50 feet. A day after the company's first directors' meeting, business manager Couzens set up his office in an extension on the first floor, where he could keep an eye on everything that was going on. At first Couzens handled virtually all the administrative tasks by himself, including bookkeeping, sales, and accounts both receivable and payable. His staff consisted of a stenographer and a secretary. Couzens even wrote all of the company's early promotional materials.[84]

Designer Wills, however, would come up with the most lasting Ford promo piece. During the turn-of-the-century advertising boom that helped launch the consumer culture of America, any company that aspired to a national presence had to have a distinguishing logo, with automakers particularly known by their marques. While some firms spent more time fussing over logos than drive trains and deservedly soon wound up gone and forgotten, to this day the best of the early car badges remain recognizable the world over:

Rolls-Royce's rectangular-boxed double R, for example, or the circular shield bearing Alfa Romeo's snake and cross.

Ford Motor Company needed a fine logo, too; it simply would not do in that era just to cast FORD in block letters and screw them on the radiators. So, with his designer's appreciation for the classic and lasting, Harold Wills took out an old printing set he'd used to make calling cards for extra cash as a teenager, and set the letters F-o-r-d in cursive script that included an especially fetching capital F. This logo was old-fashioned even for 1903—but Wills thought it spoke of quality. He drew an oval around the result, and Ford Motor Company had the logo it still uses today. (After a brief post–World War II replacement by block lettering, the original design was brought back in the 1960s under another new corporate identity program and has not been changed since.)[85]

In the more pressing matter of the layout of the first Ford car, Henry Ford displayed his disdain for the single-cylinder engines in favor at the time in runabouts such as seven-horsepower Cadillacs and curved-dash Oldsmobiles. It bothered him that, in 1903, European automakers such as France's Peugeot were already producing cars powered by up to four cylinders, while American automotive engineering lagged behind focusing on such putt-putty little one-cylinder engines.

———

When admirers gushed that as personal transportation the little Olds could do everything a horse could do, Henry Ford responded with the Model A—which could do everything an automobile should do. It accommodated two people, on a bench seat in the open air; had stiff springs, a short wheelbase, and no shock absorbers; and came painted in red.[86] Best of all, it had a two-cylinder, eight-horsepower engine. The power plant was positioned parallel to the seat under a very small hood set lower than the passengers' knees. Behind the seat, the chassis inclined gently back over the rear wheels. The Model A offered the driver relatively simple controls, with two forward gears operated through a foot pedal.[87] All in all, the A offered more power and pep than Ford had to, making it in effect the muscle car of its day.[88] The 1903 Model A weighed a hefty 1,250 pounds, half again as much as the curved-dash Olds, yet the far sturdier Ford runabout could still match the competition's top speed of 30 miles per hour. It cost $750, its only available option being a detachable, bucket-style backseat for $100.[89]

By early summer of 1903 the first Ford was officially in production. With its workforce of only ten assemblers, however, Ford Motor Company got off to a slow start, as most firms do, with cash on hand dwindling to a paltry $223.65 after outlays to employees and suppliers during a bleak initial period when sales still refused to materialize.[90] However dire the situation may have

looked to Henry Ford—and that much worse to James Couzens as he faced
the account books every day—the lean times didn't last long. In fact they
lasted only about a month. On July 15, Ford Motor Company took its first order, from Chicago dentist E. Pfennig for a Model A with tonneau at $850. Af-
ter additional sales plus another cash infusion of $5,000 from Albert Strelow,
within seven weeks the Ford firm boasted a bank balance of $23,000 in
cash.[91]

By the end of the summer of 1903, Ford's Model A had caught on with
buyers in every region of the country. Individuals and dealers alike placed
more and more orders—for each of which Couzens insisted upon payment in
advance—and the pressure at the company shifted to the assembly floor.
"Stop shipping and we go bankrupt," Couzens reminded the vice president
and general manager, Henry Ford.[92]

In an early advertisement that Couzens wrote specifically for *Motor World*
magazine, he touted the Model A as "the most reliable machine in the world,
a two-cylinder car of ample power for the steepest hills and the muddiest
roads, built to stand the severest strains. The same genius which conceived
the world's record maker—the '999'—has made possible the production of a
thoroughly practical car at a moderate price."[93] Interviewed decades later by a
Michigan auto enthusiast, Charles E. Hulse, an illustrator for the first Ford
Motor Company catalogue, remembered Henry Ford's comment upon viewing the artist's draft sketch of the 1903 Model A: "Stretch it out," he said. "It
looks too short." With its mere 72-inch wheelbase, the Model A *was* short,
and Ford recognized right off that sales might be better if the company's ads
made his cars look a little longer and wider than they actually were.[94]

Ford's first automobiles for sale suffered from more serious problems as
well. Design, production, and assembly flaws exaggerated themselves into
malfunctions as soon as the vehicles were delivered, a frustration Couzens
had experienced firsthand when he took an important professional contact for
a test ride, and couldn't get his Model A to scale a gentle hill. Much to his embarrassment, he had to back up and find another way around. Nevertheless,
Couzens understood that the company could not pause to reconsider the design minutiae of its first product. When pressed on the issue of quality control, Couzens told Ford he would approve the dispatch of authorized factory
mechanics to repair any Ford vehicle suffering any kind of mechanical failure.
But to stop production (and shipments) in order to improve the Model A was
simply outside the realm of possibility.[95]

Ford accepted his marching orders from Couzens, and with the help of
Wills and his other trusted employees on the factory floor kept Model As
rolling out of Mack Avenue.[96] As coach and cheerleader for the team, he
would always fondly acknowledge the Herculean effort they put forth. Ford's
style in the workplace made an impression on early Ford Motor Company

worker George Brown. "As far as I can remember, Mr. Ford always wore a business suit," Brown noted. "I can't ever remember Mr. Ford in coveralls, not even when he was working on machines. He'd leave the office and ramble through there [the plant]. He'd make it his business to show a new man how to handle a machine. If he got his hands oily and greasy, that didn't make any difference to him. The fellow would stand there laughing, and he didn't know who Mr. Ford was. He just thought he was some foreman or something like that.

"'Now,' Mr. Ford would say, 'go ahead and try it.' Then, 'No, that ain't the way. You're making hard work out of it! You see that machine?'" The worker would say that he did, according to Brown's account. He continued: "'Well,' Mr. Ford would say, 'that's what they make those machines for, to do the work. You don't want to work hard. When you go home, you don't want to be tired. When you go home to your family, you want to feel good.'" Then, Brown added, "He'd stand there and do half a dozen articles for him and show him how to do them. Finally the man got the swing of it and how to handle it."[97]

––––––––––––

Henry Ford, the fretting perfectionist of previous ventures, had finally started building cars—along with eighty-eight other going U.S. firms, fifteen of them in Detroit, in 1903.[98] Before the end of the year, twenty-seven of these companies would fail, followed by another thirty-seven in 1904.[99] Ford Motor wouldn't be one of them. In the company's first two months, 215 Fords were sold; in its first year, 1,000 vehicles left Mack Avenue, and over its first fifteen months of operation Ford Motor Company built 1,708 cars.[100] By then, the company was so profitable that dividends of more than 100 percent had already been paid out to each investor. There was no money to be lost, only more to be made.[101]

By the beginning of 1904, Henry Ford was happily ensconced at his own company, doing what he had done all his life: collecting talented people around him and inspiring them to even greater efforts. During its first year of operation Ford Motor Company employed 125 workers, including a whole cadre of designers under Ford and Wills tasked with creating new models. The first of these, the Models AC and C, made smooth and predictable improvements upon the Model A, the first simply more powerful and the second an equally sturdy and slightly larger version of the first Ford car.[102]

The first radically different new Ford appeared in September 1904: the Model B, a large, fast, deluxe four-cylinder motorcar the company priced at a startling $2,000.[103] Although it was more than twice the price of the first Model A, European cars made by Darracq, Panhard et Levassor, and Mors were commanding sums three times that. Ford Motor thus joined the many American car manufacturers edging closer to the robust luxury segment of the automotive market. To company directors who had jumped for joy every time a customer ordered the Model A's $100-extra tonneau, selling a car for $2,000 seemed a far easier route to larger and quicker profits. Henry Ford disagreed, but not loudly.

In anticipation of the new model, he had even reverted to an old publicity stunt. During the planning of the pricey Model B, Ford resurrected the four-cylinder engine used in the Arrow racer and modified it to more closely fit the layout of the B. Despite his aversion toward racing, especially after his last harrowing victory over Winton at Grosse Pointe Township, Ford decided to challenge the clock, setting his sights on the speed record. He took his monstrous new-and-improved machine to New Baltimore, located on Michigan's Lake St. Clair, on January 12, 1904. The frozen lake, with the snow brushed away and the underlying ice sprinkled with cinders, would serve as a four-mile straight track. The poster advertising the event proclaimed: "The races will start at 2 o'clock and continue until Mr. Ford lowers the worlds [sic] record. He proposes to make a mile in 36 seconds. Come and see the fun."[104]

Ford had sworn three years earlier never again to race on an oval track, but a straight-line speed contest was different from steering around sharp curves. With Spider Huff as mechanic, Henry Ford and his car performed as promised and broke the land speed record, covering the mile in 36 seconds at an official rate of 91.37 miles per hour. In an unofficial trial a few days before, he had reached 100 miles per hour, or so Ford claimed. In any case, he was quite pleased with his modified racer's performance. He paid Huff a fifty-dollar bonus and warmly accepted the sponsoring Hotel Chesterfield's offer to treat his entire entourage to a muskrat dinner.[105]

The next day's *Detroit Free Press* reported on the jarring the car took from the fissures in the ice. "When I wasn't in the air, I was skidding," Ford said of his assault on the speed record in his autobiography, "but somehow I stayed top side up and on the course, making a record that went all over the world!" That would help put his Model B on the map, but not to the extent that its power could overcome its price. It sold, but not on the scale of other Ford models.

Even if Ford's feat on the ice had not done the Model B much good, it did wonders for Lake St. Clair: sixteen years later Harold Wills would build his own model factory there, making the town of Marysville on the St. Clair River home to the estimable Wills–Sainte Claire motorcar.

Despite a few mechanical problems hardly unusual at the time, Ford Motor products quickly became known for their basic reliability. "The business went along almost as by magic," Henry Ford later recalled of what ensued once his cars gained their reputation for holding up.[106]

Under the circumstances and given the resulting successes, his stockholders might have done well to keep quiet and grow rich while Ford, Couzens, and Wills ran the show. By late 1904, the company was set to transfer operations out of the cramped Mack Avenue factory to a building ten times bigger on Detroit's Piquette Avenue. The first floor alone could accommodate the machine shop, electrical department, and shipping facilities, along with the business offices. The second floor offered plenty of room for Ford, Wills, and their various experimental labs, drafting and design offices, and a second machine shop, while the third floor could be given over to automobile assembly, painting, and finishing, with space left over for storage.[107] Along the top of the factory, on the side facing traffic, a large, white block-lettered sign read, "The Home of the Celebrated Ford Automobile."[108]

The new factory offered a spaciousness sorely lacking at the company's first facilities on Mack Avenue. Even half a century later many Ford Motor employees could still recall their sense of awe at the roominess upon first entering the new building. Mechanic Fred Rockland, the company's chief equipment tester at the time, remembered saying to Henry Ford that he doubted the firm could ever grow to fill all the space. Ford replied, "Let's run it!"—signaling the start of a footrace between the two down the 402-foot length of the building and back. Another employee, Frank Hadas, recalled twelve-year-old Edsel Ford riding his bicycle across the factory's ground floor, weaving in between the posts supporting the upper levels. "There wasn't anything in it practically," Hadas recalled. "He wheeled his bicycle from end to end."[109]

Moving into quarters so much bigger hardly qualified as an extravagance: in 1905, 25 Fords a day were being built by a workforce of nearly 300. Besides, the company's rollout that season of the $2,000 Model B and the $950 Model C combined to bring total annual profits to $200,000—and urgent thoughts of even further expansion.[110] Banker John S. Gray, however, remained unconvinced, insisting that he very much wanted to sell his Ford shares and would, except that he couldn't bear the guilt of passing the risk along to anyone else. Gray sincerely believed the automobile craze was a passing fad and that the average citizen would tire of the work and bother required to operate and maintain a car. In his opinion the giant factory was a wasteful extravagance, a case of Henry Ford's trying to bite off more than he could chew. Alexander Malcomson had no such worries about the permanence of the automobile in American society, but he did fret about the future of Ford Motor Company. In 1905, therefore, he reorganized his coal company into a corporation, selling shares and ceding the management to others. He then declared himself ready to relieve James Couzens and take over the administration of the automotive firm he had done so much to create.[111] But as George Brown described the situation at the plant, "Mr. Couzens was what you'd call 'the man who pulled the trigger.' He was *everything*. Whatever was to go had to pass him."[112]

Malcomson nevertheless submitted a formal proposal to Ford Motor's directors in the summer of 1905 suggesting that James Couzens turn over the management responsibilities. That, after all, amounted to no more than what Couzens himself had agreed to at the founding of the corporation. But things had changed. Two years earlier, Alex Malcomson had earned the right to rule as the beneficent potentate of Ford's fledgling car company by proving himself the only man in the world both willing and able to put up, or put together, the cash to stake Henry Ford. But where Ford, Wills, and Couzens had grown and matured with their company's astounding success, Alexander Malcomson had remained isolated. After two years, when his cash was no longer needed, he seemed less a knight in shining armor and more a country relative, full of swagger but embarrassingly out of step, or so Ford and his new colleagues chose to view him. Loyalty toward others never had been, and never would be, Henry Ford's strong suit.

Malcomson made his situation far worse by overplaying his hand and calling for a vote to fire James Couzens for reneging on his original agreement to cede administrative control.[113] Three of the five directors were outside the company and had known Malcomson for a long time. He thought he could count on their support. But his own elderly uncle, John Gray, voted to keep Couzens, as did John Dodge. John W. Anderson, one of the lawyers, voted with Malcomson. With those four directors' votes thus deadlocked, the decision belonged to Henry Ford.[114]

Like everyone else inside the young company, Ford recognized that there would be no prosperity without James Couzens. The cars may have succeeded on Ford's efforts (and, it must always be added, the talents of Harold Wills), but the company—that vastly more complicated machine that ground out all the accounts and costs, sales and recruitments, schedules and advertising, systems, planning, policies, discipline, and all the other hard, dull work up and down the hierarchy of the firm—was a success because James Couzens had made it one. Henry Ford sided with Couzens when it counted because it was the rational choice to make for the good of Ford Motor Company.

Besides, when Malcomson threw down the gauntlet to Couzens, it had occurred to Henry Ford that he simply no longer liked Alexander Malcomson, and once he acknowledged that he seemed to like himself better. It was a pattern he would follow with just about every professional associate who ever had any real claim on him, as each of his other original shareholders would discover in turn. Over and over again, in his business dealings Ford defined himself by whomever it was he disdained most at the moment, giving him as chilling a capacity for grudges as for disloyalty.

Alex Malcomson, distressed over his inability to assume active management of the company he had made possible, blundered again by announcing plans to start his own car-manufacturing firm, in direct competition with Ford

Motor Company, of which he remained treasurer.[115] Foolish as the gambit was, Malcomson must have drawn some satisfaction from knowing he had the money to invest only because his Ford dividends had been pouring in so regularly and handsomely. Feeling betrayed by the two men he had done so much to help, he no doubt enjoyed the thought that he could use Ford Motor money to show the uppity pups that Alexander Y. Malcomson could not be dismissed so humiliatingly.[116]

He was wrong. In November 1905, Ford and Couzens sidestepped Malcomson by setting up the Ford Manufacturing Company, the function of which would be to build components to be used in Ford Motor Company cars. Because of its rapid expansion in production, Ford Motor really did need a bigger factory to start making its own parts, and to start implementing the vertical integration the company would later take to remarkable lengths. By the end of 1905, not even Dodge Brothers could comfortably accommodate Ford Motor's ravenous need for components all the way up to chassis. But while that may have been the case in production terms, it was not the motivation for the corporate juggling that led to the launch of the Ford Manufacturing Company.

Every stockholder in the new concern was a Ford Motor Company stockholder, but every Ford Motor stockholder was not accorded shares in the Ford Manufacturing Company. Specifically, Alexander Malcomson was left out. Dividends from Ford Motor were simultaneously suspended, cutting off Malcomson's flow of money. The plan, as laid out by Ford and Couzens, was to shift the accounting to let Ford Manufacturing take all the profits associated with the production of Ford vehicles. By design, Ford Motor would be kept at a break-even point.[117]

For the other shareholders, there wouldn't be any real difference: the stock value and dividends from the original company would simply transfer to their Manufacturing shares.[118] For Alexander Malcomson, however, the new setup was Siberian. His dividends were cut out, and his Ford Motor shares became of uncertain value. In addition, at the December 1905 directors' meeting, his old friends demanded his immediate resignation from the board and as treasurer, citing the conflict of interest he had engendered by committing to his own automaking company.

Outraged, Malcomson threatened to sue Ford Motor, whereupon the situation suddenly calmed down, at least to the extent that the other directors tabled their demand for Malcomson to resign his posts. Indeed, the vicious salvos aimed at Malcomson had left some of the shareholders disgusted. Charles H. Bennett, for one, had grown friendly with Malcomson and recognized the value of his energy and vision. In any case, Bennett had not devoted his career to establishing a sterling reputation for business ethics only to become embroiled in any machinations as ugly as those concocted by Ford and

Couzens, especially not in the midst of so much prosperity. "I didn't like getting into a deal," Bennett explained, "where any of the fellows didn't think enough of the rest who had all gone in fairly and squarely, to keep it that way instead of trying to freeze somebody out."[119]

Ultimately, Bennett decided to quit his association with Ford Motor Company. "I wasn't to be frozen out," he averred. "I didn't leave on that account. But I sold out. It never did come out as I thought it would. I felt that in my own community, if it was known that I was in with a crowd of fellows that had frozen out somebody who had gone in there, and fouled his credit, I wouldn't stand quite as high as I would like to stand."[120]

John S. Gray had no such compunctions. When a fellow shareholder later complained to him about the financial shenanigans at the Ford Manufacturing Company, Gray dismissed the entire enterprise as a mere means to a cleverly calculated end. "I have Mr. Ford's promise that when they get things straightened out with Mr. Malcomson," Gray declared, "the Ford Manufacturing Company is to be taken into the Ford Motor Company, just as if it had never existed."

Malcomson considered his options through the first half of 1906, and then, in July, sold his shares. Ford and Couzens maneuvered their way into acquiring them. They also purchased Bennett's stock as well as that of three other shareholders. (Ford Motor Company lore has it that one of those three, landlord Albert Strelow, was spotted in line at the Ford general employment office in the 1920s.) These realignments in the corporation's stock structure, voluntary and otherwise, left Henry Ford with 58.5 percent of the company, up from his original stake of 25.5 percent. Couzens's stake had grown even more markedly, from 2.5 percent to 11 percent. No one else's position had been boosted, although the Dodge brothers and lawyers John Anderson and Horace Rackham each retained their original 5 percent stakes, while John S. Gray kept his 10.5 percent.[121]

According to Bennett, Ford and Couzens were also tempted to "get things straightened out" with Gray, the official president of Ford Motor Company.[122] However, the snappish young cubs felt just enough trepidation around the kindly old lion of Detroit's business circles to hold back from any such moves. Instead, on July 6, 1906, the shift of power took place naturally when Gray died after a brief illness and the stockholders elected Henry Ford to replace him as president of Ford Motor.[123] Gray's shares were to be retained by his estate. With that, Henry Ford was finally satisfied: the company named for him was his and Couzens's to operate however they chose, but for all intents and purposes its ultimate fate belonged to Ford alone.

4

Growing Successes

With majority control of the company in hand, Henry Ford launched one of the modern world's greatest "paradigm shifts" and did so as though he had known he would all along. Even as he witnessed the birth of the automobile industry, Ford understood three things that escaped most others. The first was that the populous but vast United States needed a low-cost car, which meant that it had to be gasoline powered.[1] Second, as historian Richard S. Tedlow explained in his book *Giants of Enterprise,* was that anyone who wanted to manufacture such a car would have to stuggle hard to do so, constantly crossing swords with financial backers clamoring for larger and pricier luxury models. At the same time, a mass-market automaker would have to overcome engineering obstacles to manufacture enough ruggedly dependable yet inexpensive vehicles to turn an acceptable profit. He would, in fact, "have to fight everything and everybody" to make his dream come true. The third point Ford grasped was the importance of establishing both a brand name and consumer loyalty to it, as had been achieved in the 1890s by such enduring concerns as Coca-Cola, Heinz, and Eastman Kodak. Ford had come of age during that era and knew that to succeed, the name "Ford" would have to become publicly synonymous with "automobile."[2] And the man behind the name proved both up to the challenges and eager to take them on. When Ford seized on an idea, he pursued it with single-minded tenacity and a bedrock faith that it could be turned into reality. And more than any other individual, the precocious Ford truly believed from the first that the internal combustion engine would spark a worldwide revolution in transportation.[3]

Historian David L. Lewis may have been correct in remarking that Ford was "a late starter; life for him began at forty,"[4] but in truth the industrialist had been planning his automotive assault on America since he saw his first steam engine as a boy. Ford had never forgotten what dreams had filled him as a youth gazing out across the fields of his family's farm over the empty miles stretching away into the expanses beyond. The world swept open before him and millions of others with wondrousness never quite recaptured after that postbellum era when America was right to feel young again, having conquered its own worst impulses during the Civil War. In the forty years between Henry Ford's birth and that of his motor company in 1903, the world had changed, with any number of terrible beauties born—and still all Henry Ford could see was how much distance lay between people and the places where they wanted to go. Later, as he basked in the spotlight on his world-changing achievements, he would admit in private that "I don't do so much, I just go around lighting fires under other people."[5] That was just as true of a generation of consumers as it was of employees throughout his life.

Ford, of course, was not alone in recognizing that a transportation revolution was afoot. Other entrepreneurs recognized the same outrageous opportunity, though in different ways and to different ends. In October 1902,[6] Henry Leland's Cadillac Motor Company put out the first of the marque's one-cylinder, high-performance cars, charging just $750 for its single-cylinder debut model.[7] On August 1, 1903, a driver in a Packard completed North America's first transcontinental automobile trip, reaching New York City fifty-two days after leaving San Francisco. In a related pursuit, on December 17, 1903, Orville Wright of Dayton, Ohio, became the first human being to fly in an aircraft powered by mechanical means, keeping his 605-pound *Flyer I* aloft for forty yards in the first of many tests at Kill Devil Hill near Kitty Hawk, North Carolina. Mankind's first success at flying, he demurred, was "very modest compared with that of birds."[8]

Orville was wrong. The world was getting smaller faster than ever before, and a large part of Ford's genius lay in recognizing how to take advantage of that fact. He intended to bring the excitement of the latest transportation triumphs to the common man. Moreover, he recognized the importance of doing so not only more quickly but more fully than anyone else. Ford appreciated the marketplace maxim that in the long run quality keeps customers coming back for more.

Ford's timing was perfect: turn-of-the-century American capitalism was ripe for an infusion of fresh tycoons in bold young industries. Since becoming president after the assassination of William McKinley in September 1901, Theodore Roosevelt had been battling the nation's monopoly trusts through the Cabinet-level Department of Commerce and Labor as well as the Federal Bureau of Corporations, the latter tasked with investigating the affairs of big business and making the findings public. It was not lost on those who would be automakers that the president also forged their particular path to success by getting Congress to clamp down on the corruption-riddled railroad industry. The U.S. legislature did just that by passing the Elkins Act, which strengthened the Interstate Commerce Act of 1887 with the requirement that railroads stick to their published rate schedules, as well as the imposition of penalties against any railroad that offered special favors or secret rebates to selected interstate shippers, which likewise would be penalized for accepting any such graft.[9] "In requesting such legislation," historian Edmund Morris wrote in *Theodore Rex,* "Roosevelt was merely echoing a regulatory sentiment that had grown on Capitol Hill during his presidency."[10]

It was also during Theodore Roosevelt's reform-minded administration that state legislatures began passing laws specifically aimed at correcting social problems, by creating state labor boards, for example, and imposing restrictions on child labor. This civic conscientiousness sprang from the American public's growing awareness of the nation's domestic ills, sparked by the realistic urban reporting and powerful journalistic muckraking in bestselling books and mass-circulation periodicals of the day. President Roosevelt summed up the prevailing attitude on September 7, 1903, at the New York State Fair: "We must treat each man on his worth and merits as a man. We must see that each is given a square deal, because he is entitled to no more and should receive no less."[11]

The first decade of the twentieth century thus defined itself as an era not only of good government but of good business practices, and Ford's management grasped the trend from the start. But however sweeping a view Henry Ford commanded of the broader picture, establishing the degree of organizational and financial stability that enables a new company to keep producing more for customers to come back for—in quest of quality and value—remained beyond his vision.

Then as now, of course, it was deft handling of the driest details of corporate finance that determined the success of a startup, especially one as ambitious as Ford Motor Company. Far more than any innovations in product design or efficiencies in manufacturing, it turned out to be clever financial calculations that kept the prices of the earliest Fords down—and down low enough to establish such goodwill among an appreciative public that it would eventually lead to passionate brand loyalty and enormous sales, making the company's handful of bickering stockholders very rich men indeed.

In fact, the first five years after Ford Motor Company's founding proved remarkable less for the firm's obvious success than for what was going on behind the scenes to ready it for still greater triumphs—and much of this preparation, if the part least appreciated today, fell to corporate secretary James Couzens. "J. C. was the entire office management," explained a 1908 article on the early days of the company that was published in the monthly *Ford Times.* "He hired and fired—he kept the books, collected, spent, and saved the cash, established agencies, and dictated policy."[12] Charles E. Sorensen, who began his thirty-nine-year career at Ford Motor in 1905 as a $3-a-day assistant in the pattern department, put the case even more succinctly, calling the firm's first half-decade "the Couzens years."[13]

Within a very short time, Alexander Malcomson's former clerk had not only mastered the intricacies of corporate finance but had also grown to understand the power of fastidious accounting, which in his own way he pushed as hard upon the company as Ford did his precious racing engines. In shaping the firm's financial framework, Couzens concerned himself not so much with the dollars as with the percentage points of the interest rates.

Couzens's boldest accounting initiative was unheard-of in the overcrowded early auto market: he demanded payment in advance from dealers. Whether times were good or bad, under his iron rules any agency seeking to sell Ford Motor products had to front the company a 50 percent down payment on every order. This inflexible policy appeared all the more audacious in an era when car dealers easily could, and did, switch the marques they sold in a heartbeat with little effect on their bottom lines, because no automaker had been around long enough to establish a strong following. But James J. Couzens was neither the bendable sort of executive nor the least bit shy about flexing what very little muscle the young Ford Motor Company had developed by that point. "He was very gruff about it," charter shareholder Charles H. Bennett marveled even years later about Couzens's intransigence on the matter of advance payment. "He'd say, 'That's our policy, and it's that way or nothing.'" Bennett added that most dealers had the same response: "A fellow would come out and he'd say, 'That son of a gun! I'll sell the cars, but if I ever get the chance, I'll bust him in the nose!'"[14]

Yet Couzens's nose went unbusted, for no dealer so much as dared complain about the pay-first policy to the man's face, knowing that such temerity could well lose one the contract to sell Ford cars. In truth, even during its first five years, when the company was enjoying only small-scale success in terms of the number of vehicles it sold, most dealers recognized that in the end Couzens's system worked to their benefit as well: Ford Motor's cars rolled out on schedule and at advantageous prices compared with similar models from manufacturers who assumed the debt incurred in making their products first and getting paid for them later.

Even Charles Bennett, who felt nothing but antipathy for Couzens on a personal level, awarded the de facto chief operating officer full credit for effecting a financing plan that made a profit for the company from every Ford car even before it left the factory. "What man steps in and buys $20,000 or $50,000 worth of goods," Bennett wondered, "and says, 'Here's a check for half of it,' and it wasn't even made? You've got a profit included in that, and not only that, you've got the cash to make it!

"That's what he did," Bennett acknowledged with grudging respect.[15]

And that wasn't all he did. Couzens's unyielding policies also extended

Henry Ford the luxury of five selling seasons of trial-and-error tinkering to correct any minor mistakes in design and manufacturing. Fixing each one of those glitches taught the engineers a lesson, and from that hands-on education Ford and his team would learn just about everything they would need to know to build the all-new model the company labeled T in 1908.

Ford Motor's effort toward developing a truly great nationwide organization was unprecedented. Alexander Winton, then the dean of automakers, even boasted in his ads that his marque had no dealers, and that customers should contact the Winton factory in Cleveland directly. Even those early car manufacturers that did have dealers barely knew who they were, and kept few tabs on their operations. "In those days," wrote automobile historian Floyd Clymer, "a man needed only to buy a manufacturer's car and, if the territory was open, he could have the dealership thrown in."[16] Clymer spoke from experience: from 1904 through 1905 he held the Cadillac, Maxwell, and Reo dealerships in his hometown of Berthoud, Colorado. He was eleven years old at the time.

Over those two years, the "Kid Dealer" sold twenty-six vehicles. He operated out of a room next to his father's office, but the car business was very much Floyd's. One early ad for his Berthoud Auto Company showed the precocious lad striking a pose dignified enough to befit a judge, over the caption "Floyd Clymer—The Kid Agent, Owner and General Manager."[17]

"Ford was not very stout competition then," Clymer recalled, "although in 1905 he built the Model N Roadster at the competitive price of $500. That sum, in crop money or celluloid-collar sales, was almost unheard-of for a four-cylinder car at that time. I had been selling one-cylinder Reos, silent two-cylinder Maxwells, and one-cylinder Cadillacs. But four cylinders for half a thousand, though a considerable sum, was a recognizable bargain that began to make a dent in my sales."[18]

Aggressive pricing and solid quality formed the foundation of Ford Motor's scheme to appeal to prospective car buyers. The third leg of the company's strategic tripod was to keep those already wooed coming back, through good customer relations and particularly the availability of capable service at authorized dealerships. In recruiting local sales representatives, therefore, Ford Motor demanded much higher standards than nearly any other early auto manufacturer, and enforced those standards strictly. Couzens himself interviewed many of the eager applicants for Ford dealerships, weeding out the eleven-year-olds, among myriad others deemed unqualified for both more and less glaring reasons. As writer Robert Lacey explained, "It was Couzens's task to sort through the available hucksters to come up with an aggressive and enterprising sales force whose credit was good enough to pay for vehicles as they received them, cash on the nail."[19] Much thought went into the awarding of the company's prized sales franchises; among other considerations, Couzens's home office calculated projected order figures for dealerships in established cities, based on population as well as sales in comparable locales. In cities regarded as regionally vital, such as Chicago and Atlanta, Ford Motor opted to own and run its dealerships, thereby assuming added responsibilities virtually no other automobile manufacturer dared to take on at the time.

Ford Motor's insistence on maintaining iron-fisted control over its sales outlets grew only in part from Couzens's bulldog instincts. Indeed, however much the firm's stringent rules may have appeared to be the work of the tenacious top bean counter, in fact they were more the brainchild of the supposed casual dreamer Henry Ford, whose edict it was that if anything ever proved wrong with a new Ford, the car had to be fixed immediately at the dealership that sold it. Consequently, Henry Ford had no use for part-time dealers, then common in the industry, who sold cars on the side or out of their homes. He insisted instead on local representation by fully committed outfits that could offer the kind of follow-up services he deemed essential. In his autobiography, Ford delineated some of his requirements of his dealerships, all of them daringly exacting for the time: "A stock of parts sufficient to make prompt replacements. . . . An adequately equipped repair shop. . . . Mechanics who are thoroughly familiar with the construction and operation of Ford cars. . . . Absolute cleanliness throughout every department. . . . A suitable display sign."[20] It was the success of this by-the-book approach to dealer franchising that inspired Ford Motor Company to extend strict and methodical procedures to all its operations, resulting eventually in the world-changing assembly-line system of mass production.[21]

Between Couzens's insistence on salesmanship and Ford's on service, the quality of the company's dealerships shot up alongside their number, which would rise to an astounding 7,000 by 1913. Historian David L. Lewis surmised that by then Ford Motor's sales force likely had grown larger than that of the rest of the automobile industry added together.[22] And the company's chief headhunter was Couzens. He had an incredible knack for handpicking supersalesmen that made Willy Loman seem like a loser: erudite Gaston Plantiff in New York, cunning Louis Black in Philadelphia, gregarious Tom Hay in Chicago, and indispensable Guy Herring in Des Moines, to name a few.[23]

Couzens's demand for cash payment in advance for all orders no doubt went far to motivate the company's dealers to sell their cars as fast as possible, but the pressure from the home office did not end there. An early directive from the home office indicates just how aggressive Couzens's sales methods had become: "A dealer or salesman ought to have the name of every possible automobile buyer in his territory, including all those who have never given the matter a thought. He should then personally solicit by visitation if possible. . . . If territory is too large to permit this, you have too much territory."[24] In other words, anyone fortunate enough to have won a Ford dealership was fully expected to go out and peddle the cars door-to-door. Ludicrous as the mere notion sounds today, dealers actually found buyers in the Fuller Brush way.

––––––––––

Ford Motor rolled out nine different cars between 1903 and the advent of the Model T five years later: Models A, B, AC, C, F, K, N, R, and S. The A, AC, C, and F had two-cylinder engines; the B, N, R, and S four cylinders each; and the Model K a mighty six-cylinder power plant.[25] Most of the models were wildly successful. In October 1903, four months after its formal incorporation, Ford Motor Company returned a dividend of 2 percent to its stockholders, who on November 21 received a second dividend of 10 percent,[26] and in January 1904 still another, of 20 percent. On June 16, 1904, a year after the company came into existence, it paid its initial investors a fourth dividend of a staggering $68,000.[27]

Ford Motor's immediate success looked all the more remarkable coming as it did in a brand-new industry so fraught with failure. In the first eight years of the twentieth century, 502 car-manufacturing firms were launched in the United States alone, and 302 of them either folded or shifted to another line of business.[28] In fact, most of the automobile companies that sprang up before 1905 didn't pay back a single cent to their investors. The majority never even built a single car, either, despite having accepted huge sums of money given in good faith to do so.[29]

In those early years, the automobile's outlandish potential made the business such an easy sell that almost overnight the industry spawned a market that was soon rife with shysters at every level. Demand for cars was soaring, but buyers were for the most part ill equipped to judge such novel products. The arguments made to equally unsophisticated prospective backers of shaky startups centered on how simple a proposition car manufacturing was: all it took, the pitch went, was bolting together some component parts easily bought elsewhere and then selling the assembled results to an eager market. Such bare-boned business plans enabled many would-be automakers to peddle reams of worthless stock certificates, imbued with the promise of cars such as the Eleanor, the Cluts, and the Tuttle, all of which failed to reach production. Companies that actually did manage to build cars were nearly as precarious, often producing models that for some reason never found a niche despite the rapidly swelling market. The dashing, precision-crafted Locomobile, manufactured in Bridgeport, Connecticut, stands as perhaps the most glaring example of a truly fine car that won brief popularity but somehow lacked the staying power to survive the competition in the crowded early automobile market.[30]

Its very unpredictability, of course, made the new industry all the more exciting and attractive to entrepreneurs of all kinds. The individuals who flooded the field at the turn of the century with their blather and blueprints had strikingly little in common beyond a basic enthusiasm for the automobile. (The notable exception was that many started out in the bicycle- or wagon-making business.) The industry itself may have been in its infancy, but for all its aura of derring-do, carmaking was by no means purely a young man's game; many of those who caught the auto bug, such as Cadillac's elder statesman Henry Leland, were established businessmen of a certain age, and with the means to act upon their fervor.

One such enthusiast was Colonel Albert A. Pope of Hartford, Connecticut. He was fifty-four when he entered the auto industry, having accumulated handsome profits for many decades making the nation's most popular bicycle, the Columbia. In 1897, he heeded the investment rumor that the bike was doomed and turned to making cars.[31] Among his brands were the variously viable Columbia, Pope-Hartford, Pope-Robinson, Pope-Toledo, Pope-Tribune, and Pope-Waverley. More for his Pope Manufacturing Company's reputation in the bicycle trade than for owning the nation's best-known auto company as of 1899, Colonel Pope would be the only American car manufacturer listed in the first edition of *Who's Who in America,* published that year.[32]

Another veteran bicycle manufacturer, Thomas B. Jeffery of Kenosha, Wisconsin, was fifty-eight in 1902 when his entry into the auto market, the Rambler, scored as instant a hit as Ford's Model A would a year later. Fifty-year-old industrialist George N. Pierce had been in the birdcage business in Buffalo, New York, when he opted to enter the rather more energetic automotive field in 1896. Pierce thus filed a new incorporation "for the manufacture of bicycles, tricycles, road vehicles and all things appertaining thereto,"[33] most notably the plush road vehicle his startup would eventually produce under the marque Pierce-Arrow. Perhaps the oldest newcomer to the automobile business, Ohio paint company heir John Stoddard, was no less than sixty-seven when he oversaw the design and production of one of America's fastest early cars, the Stoddard-Dayton, in 1904.

Alongside the established U.S. industrialists like Pope, Jeffery, Pierce, and Stoddard who moved horizontally into auto manufacturing in the first decade of the twentieth century stood a number of daring young men with their own driving machines, many still in their twenties and a few even younger than that. Ohio's Frank Stearns, for example, was only seventeen when he built his first car in 1896, the same year thirty-two-year-old Henry Ford assembled his first quadricycle. After college, at age twenty-one, Stearns ran a factory in Cleveland to produce his own marque of automobiles in earnest. Another bright youngster in the burgeoning industry, Harry Knox, opened his own full-scale factory in Springfield, Massachusetts, and started turning out popular cars at the age of twenty-five. Like his fellow prodigy Stearns, Knox enjoyed the advantage of a formal education in engineering, something of a rarity in the early automotive world. Most college men of the time preferred careers in more stable endeavors.

Whatever their ages, the entrepreneurs who surged to the forefront of the auto industry and stayed there long enough to get their names stamped in metal on cars of their own creation came from backgrounds as diverse as their experiences and interests. Some, like Ford, Knox, and Stearns, remained engineers at heart; many of the older auto pioneers distinguished themselves as financiers, while still others came from the ranks of sales and management. And then there were those who were just plain lucky. An unassuming Detroiter named David Dunbar Buick turned out to be one of those fortunate few, if not nearly to the same extent as the men who took advantage of his success.

A onetime James Flower & Brothers Machine Shop apprentice, Buick made a tidy fortune in the bathroom-fittings business before returning to his first love, mechanical design.[34] He was trying to perfect his "Auto-Vim" car engine when he set to assembling an experimental vehicle to house it in 1902. Just as he was about to finish the vehicle, however, he ran out of money. A pair of brothers named Briscoe quickly materialized with a proposal to set up a company to produce Buick's car in quantity. The grateful and desperate engineer agreed to give the brothers all but 0.3 percent of the resulting corporation. Although the terms looked as unfair then as now, without the Briscoes' deal the Buick marque likely would have ended up on the scrap heap of automotive history next to the Eleanor, the Cluts, and the Tuttle. Instead, in 1904 a string of fresh investors propelled Buick—not the man, but the fledgling company founded on his car design—into the capable hands of charismatic financier William Durant, who would carve out the Buick name's prominent and long-held place in the upper echelon of the auto industry.

Whether one came from a bicycle, carriage, coal, or birdcage concern, the consensus within the business world was that the automobile offered boundless opportunities. Naysayers were few from the first and soon grew to sound foolish, as Syracuse University chancellor James Day did in equating buying an automobile with taking up a vice, warning of "young mechanics and clerks and business men . . . mortgaging their homes by the thousand[s] and often losing their positions by their infatuations with this form of pleasure." On the individual level, Day may have been right about cars unleashing "a lack of self-denial" in some young people,[35] but he was certainly wrong when he went on to decry investors' collective $500 million stake in the fledgling U.S.

auto industry as unproductive and a waste of money. In reality, the backers of America's earliest car manufacturers were boosting myriad other firms at the same time, thereby boosting the national economy in broader terms. From the start, automaking established not so much a single industry as an agglomeration of related businesses, many comprising not just a factory or two but wide networks of component and parts suppliers as well. In those early days, therefore, few car companies felt obliged to innovate; technical advances were often left to parts vendors whose very survival depended on mechanical breakthroughs that put the "improved" in the new and improved models purveyed by automakers.

As with most engineering endeavors, progress in the automotive field sprang from the exchange of information. In the early days, the annual automobile show was the industry's favorite forum, where suppliers and automakers met to share news, discuss technical developments, and make deals. One of the early industry's biggest such events, the New York Automobile Show, debuted at the old Madison Square Garden in January 1903. Among those in the throng were Alfred P. Sloan Jr. and his colleague Peter Steenstrup, in attendance to represent their Harrison, New Jersey, company, Hyatt Roller Bearing. They circulated through the two floors at the exhibition, hoping to sell the idea of using Hyatt roller bearings to the automakers in attendance. "Pete and I looked upon these people more or less as adventurers," Sloan wrote in his 1941 memoir, *Adventures of a White-Collar Man*. Yet the convention had an undeniably exciting air. "We could look down on the main-floor crowd," Sloan recalled of his view from the mezzanine, "see each exhibit, discover what the people fancied and likewise observe what was going on in the driving ring. Cars were put through their paces just as if this were a show of horses. It helped sales to show the customers that a car would really run."[36]

That said, when Sloan decided to shop for a car of his own at the auto show, the Massachusetts Institute of Technology–trained engineer showed little of the acumen with which he would later help to build General Motors. Like most first-time buyers in those days, Sloan had little to go on but the appearance of the various models on display. On that basis, he was attracted to one particular model. As he recalled, "Conrad cars were the most tempting-looking automobiles on the floor at the 1903 show." Built in Buffalo, New York, the Conrad was said to be state-of-the-art with all the latest mechanical features. More important to Sloan, it boasted eye-catching body styling, including black patent-leather fenders above the wheels. Nevertheless, while Mr. Conrad himself waxed on and on about the beauty of his car's paint job, the engineer in Sloan tried to open the hood. With some effort he finally managed to pry it off—and discovered that "I was looking at an empty place," as he marveled in his memoir. "There was no engine!"

Then Steenstrup took a look, and asked Conrad what made the car run.

"The truth is," the tyro automaker replied in a vague rush of words, "we haven't really built the engine yet. But the design is right. Mechanical engineers and automobile experts of this country and Europe have pronounced it correct." For some reason even Conrad's sales talk couldn't dissuade Alfred Sloan from buying the car.

When Sloan's new Conrad was delivered, however, it featured a different engine than the one Sloan had been promised. And it wouldn't start. "That was the thing that taught me how to swear," Sloan recalled. His complaints brought Conrad's own son all the way to New Jersey from Buffalo to make repairs, which amounted to stuffing a handkerchief into the carburetor. The car started, upon which the younger Conrad beat a hasty retreat, leaving Sloan with an automobile that just barely worked and then only on occasion, with or without the handkerchief. "I don't think I ever did get a real ride in that car," Sloan reported. "The most we could coax it to run was a few blocks." Before long he sold the shiny new lemon to a friend, who sold it to another friend, who soon after took the thing to an open field and blew it up with a stick of dynamite. "Lots of cars deserved such a fate in the early 1900s," Sloan noted.[37]

Others deserved, and met with, nobler fates. At the same 1903 New York auto show where Sloan burdened himself with the Conrad, the sales manager for Henry Leland's Cadillac Motor Company took orders and down payments for more than 1,000 cars. When delivered, their engines worked and quite well, and by that September forty-eight Cadillac dealers had cropped up around the country.[38]

———

It was also at the 1903 New York Automobile Show that Alfred Sloan, the future president of General Motors, caught a clear-eyed glimpse of Henry Ford, whom Steenstrup knew from Detroit. "A tall, slender man stopped and, after shaking hands with Pete, lifted his derby hat to wipe his forehead," Sloan remembered of the encounter. "After tramping around the show, he was tired. . . . So we three sat and watched the cars go round in the show ring below and talked, for hours I guess. Mr. Ford was tilted back in a chair, his heels caught in the topmost rung, his knees at the level of his chin." Sloan continued his memoir with rather an understatement: "I did not suspect that I was talking with a man who was to take a foremost place among the industrial leaders of all time."[39]

In truth, Henry Ford was not especially distinguished amid the faces at the early auto shows. In his early forties, he was well past the flash of prodigy yet still short of the wisdom of experience. Although he had a fairly solid background in the fundamentals of automotive engineering, his technical capabilities and design talents paled next to those of many other carmaking pioneers around the country. And while Ford often bragged about the car he'd built in 1896, he likely knew he was fibbing when he inaccurately labeled his quadricycle as the first car built in Detroit and the third in the entire United States. In fact, a great many of the early automobile men also had built just such cars in their own backyards, including several well before 1896. This is not to suggest that creating a self-propelled vehicle from scratch around the turn of the twentieth century didn't mark a substantial achievement for anyone who accomplished it; the point is simply that Ford's backyard contraption was hardly unique, and certainly not among the first automobiles ever produced.

In Dearborn, Henry Ford ranked as an automotive genius. In Detroit, he stood among the new industry's leaders. In Michigan, his name was well-known in the business. At the national level, however, among the hundred or so most serious entrepreneurs in the early years of car manufacturing, Ford fell somewhere in the middle of the pack.

Among his contemporaries in the early auto industry, Ford probably had the most in common, in terms of both background and operating approach, with Tom Jeffery, founder of Thomas B. Jeffery Company.[40] Jeffery had grown up in a village not unlike Dearborn in the Devon region of southwestern England, from which he immigrated to Chicago at the age of eighteen. A born tinkerer, like Ford, he entered the bicycle business, and by the 1880s had become a noted figure as a partner and the "mechanical head" of the Chicago firm of Gormully and Jeffery.[41] He entered the automobile industry with his own company in 1902, producing cars as sturdy and well engineered as Ford's. Jeffery named his car the Rambler. Both men's firms made money from the start, perhaps because neither of their founders involved himself in the financial complexities of his concern, unlike the wheeler-dealers heading so many of the other early car manufacturers. Instead, Ford and Jeffery appeared happiest puttering in their factories—the latter invented the clincher rim.[42] In addition, they were equally devoted to maintaining clean and efficient workplaces, which they tended to regard as works in progress, demanding constant improvement.

The two men also shared other personality traits, including a pronounced independence that verged on the asocial. Neither had many close friends, either outside the business world or within it, and both kept their relations with employees friendly but distant. More significant to their respective bottom lines, Thomas Jeffery and Henry Ford shared an uncommon knack for attracting publicity, which the latter accomplished with his strategic dabbling in car racing. Likewise, when one of Jeffery's Rambler test bodies was accidentally rammed into a shed, he seized the moment and sent pictures to the press showing that his chassis had survived without a scratch, while the building was totally ruined. His accompanying press release noted, with Ford-like cheekiness, that "the accident has conclusively shown one thing. . . . We cannot afford to test Rambler clutches against the side of buildings—we need the buildings."[43]

For the first few years the companies Ford and Jeffery founded racked up similar sales records producing similar cars. Had both continued along the same path, Henry Ford likely would be remembered today just the way Thomas Jeffery is: as a very fine carmaker for his times, but a minor figure in the history of the automobile industry. Instead, in 1905 the two manufacturers headed in very different directions, one remaining with his times, and the other changing them forever.

Jeffery chose the natural evolution of building ever bigger and fancier cars, demand for which seemed to be the strongest area of the automobile market. From May 1904 to May 1905, for example, Henry Leland turned out 3,863 of his enlarged Cadillacs, for a grand total of some 8,000 sales by August 1, 1905.[44] Going deluxe appeared to be the most sensible financial strategy for any respected manufacturer, as even the moderately higher prices bigger models could fetch meant more profit per vehicle sold. Concentrating on bigger and better cars held another attraction for a perfectionist like the creator of the Rambler, who couldn't resist the opportunities for fine-tuning entailed in the production of more expensive motor vehicles. And that is where the ways of Thomas Jeffery and Henry Ford parted. The one who would become a titan of industry truly believed that a smaller, cheaper car actually offered the greater potential to achieve higher quality. Experience in the form of a few small failures would soon prove him right, beginning at his own firm.

During 1904, Ford Motor was trying hard to keep up with demand for the Models A and C—and trying even harder to instigate demand for its midsize Model B. An improved stable mate, the Model F, debuted in February 1905. The only truly new design Ford produced that year, the two-cylinder Model F filled the gap in size and price between the company's Models C and B. Weighing 1,400 pounds and riding on an 84-inch wheelbase, the base Model F sold for $1,000, and made its splash with a nondetachable side-entrance tonneau that rendered the car a permanent four-seater. Like the AC and C, the Model F found an interested market, and Ford Motor kept itself very busy manufacturing the peppy little runabouts and selling them at quite a clip.[45] Midway through 1905, just two years after its launch, the company would return its *third* 100 percent dividend to the investors.[46]

To Ford the smart money in the business would be on smaller, less expensive cars of a high enough quality to establish a good image with the broadest public, whose positive word of mouth would spread into more and more sales. As chief engineer, Henry Ford therefore continued to concentrate on streamlining his cars' bodies while at the same time improving their engine performance and overall reliability. The effort paid off again early in 1906, when the company introduced a new four-cylinder car that was nothing like the stout and pricey Model B or even the well-received Models C and F, which basically had just been refined versions of the original Model A.[47] The new, two-seat Model N was a whole new vehicle: lightweight at 1,050 pounds yet sturdy on its 84-inch wheelbase, mechanically advanced with an improved clutch and dual-line brake system, and startlingly inexpensive at a base price of $500, including cowl headlamps and a horn.[48] The Ford catalogue made a virtue of the Model N's lack of other frills, boasting "it is 'just automobile—all automobile.'" Among other things, that meant the top cost extra: $50 for leather, $30 for rubberized canvas.

The stripped-down Model N was an immediate sensation. Unveiled to the public and the rest of the industry at the 1906 New York Automobile Show, Ford Motor's latest creation caused quite a commotion; it hardly seemed possible that the well-constructed four-cylinder car on display could cost so little. "I remember the occasion very distinctly," wrote Connecticut lawyer Bellamy Partridge of the Model N's debut, "because of the number of persons who stopped me on the street the next day or came into my office to ask me if I really believed there was anything to that $500 car."

That day, according to Partridge, "might well have been celebrated as the birthday of the so-called 'low-price market,' for practically all these inquiries came from low-income people, factory employees, artisans, persons who worked with their hands and who never before had dreamed of becoming motorists; for at that time the price of the average car was around $2,137.56. . . . The Model N, though it brought Ford more orders than he could handle, also brought him something far more valuable—the backing and loyalty of the masses."[49]

Customers snapped up the sprightly Model Ns as fast as the factory could turn them out. More than 8,500 of the cars were sold in 1906, making Ford Motor Company the industry's sales leader for the first time. In truth, the contest wasn't even close: the combined sales of runners-up Cadillac and Rambler amounted to only about three quarters of Ford Motor's tally.[50] Given the collaborative nature of the auto business, the company's success quickly spread to its suppliers. In March 1906, for example, Harvey Firestone suddenly found his own firm struggling to keep up with the bounty from his latest sales trip to Ford headquarters: Ford ordered a record 2,000 sets of his most advanced rubber tires for its Model N cars from Firestone's firm, later upping the order by 6,000 more sets[51] and thereby hoisting the Akron tire maker to the top of its industry.[52]

Even with Firestone's improved tires, the Model N did suffer one notable flaw: a terrible ride, even for a two-seat runabout. The car's body looked sleek, but was in fact scrawny. In order to retain the pep for which the manufacturer's products had become known, Ford's engineers couldn't waste a single one of the engine's 15 horsepower carrying added weight in the form of extraneous metalwork. To enable the Model N to reach a top speed of 45 miles per hour, its chassis had to be stripped to the bare bones, which made the vehicle delicate to the point of fragile on the era's mostly unpaved roads. The N sold well because it was fairly fast and extremely cheap, but Henry Ford knew that an improved design could produce a speedy car strong enough to bear four or even five people that would sell even better. He began to focus on proving it.

First, however, he had to endure a setback all the more annoying for its remarkable similarity to the failure of the Model B, and one that occurred for all the same reasons. Despite Henry Ford's strenuous protests, the company gave in and joined the industry's mad dash for horsepower in 1906. Reliability and comfort remained prominent selling points, but it was horsepower that became part of the very names of cars such as the Winton 17, the Cadillac Thirty, and the Elmore 44.[53]

As a result, during the same season in which the swift little Model N made its bow, Ford Motor brought out an ambitious new six-cylinder car as well. "Big Sixes" became all the rage that year, and Ford's 40-horsepower Model K matched the competition on every point that mattered: performance, appearance, and decibels when driven.[54] But even at $2,800 apiece the company lost money on every Model K it sold—the vehicle's design required expensive postproduction engineering, especially on its overburdened two-speed planetary transmission, which meant that each car demanded considerable tinkering just to put it into saleable condition. In fact, the vehicle's enormous engine was better suited to racing than touring, and its innovative transmission was barely adequate for either.[55] A resounding failure, like its fellow disappointment the Model B, the unloved Model K was generally blamed on Alexander Malcomson, who had instigated its production before he left Ford Motor for good in the summer of 1906.

Perhaps the Model K had been doomed from the first as the brainchild of a man Henry Ford had long since disdained and rejected. According to later accounts, its failure rankled Ford forever after, leaving him permanently averse to six-cylinder engines.[56] When he finally agreed to move up from four cylinders, it would be straight to the stalwart Ford V-8.[57]

Ford Motor's new models for 1907, the R and S, were basically the same car as the Model N but for a few improvements to the body and trim. The slightly swanker but equally lightweight two-seater Models R and S also offered upgraded chassis and accessories and, as Henry Ford knew they would, sold as splendidly as their older sibling the Model N, raising Ford Motor's total sales through its first six years to some 16,000 cars.[58]

A large part of the reason for the early success of Ford Motor was its determination to forge a reputation for quality service as well as products. The most remarkable aspect of the company's first five years lay in just how quickly Ford and Couzens built a strong distribution network, leaving other automakers far behind. In fact, the national Ford organization began the shift that made many customers refer to Fords as *Fords* and all others as mere cars. There was a difference according to the common perception, and it started with service. After only five years, Ford's dealership network was actually much stronger than the product lineup it represented. It was capable of far greater things. But then something far greater than anything yet seen in the industry was on its way.

5

Growing Pains

As automobiles in general soared in popularity and Fords in particular gained ever more respect and market share, only one problem nagged at the young company and its dealers—but it was a big one. "When I started to sell Ford cars I found that many of my prospects were afraid to buy a Ford," declared Louis J. Kinietz, who opened his dealership in Medina, New York, in 1907, "on account of the article in the paper saying that if Ford lost his suit with the Selden patent people, they would have to pay the tax on their car or they would lose it."[1] Luckily for Ford Motor Company and its associates, vendors, and customers, Henry Ford had a magic touch for turning lead balloons into golden opportunities, and never displayed it more dazzlingly than in the Selden patent case, which would seal both his own public acclaim and his firm's spectacular fortunes, once and for all.[2]

In the end, the main point the celebrated Selden suit would settle was that Henry Ford was not about to let anything stop him from making good cars for regular people and a fortune for himself in the process. Early on, however, the seemingly interminable patent lawsuit—filed in 1903 and settled in 1911[3]—posed a real threat to the survival not just of Ford Motor Company but of the whole automobile industry. Ford, however, turned out to be the only serious carmaker scrappy enough to refuse to bow to attorney George B. Selden's specious legalities, with the stamina to put up a fight against them in court.[4] Tenacity proved the key to Ford's victory as the case dragged on over a full eight years, in Dickensian *Jarndyce v. Jarndyce* fashion but with far wider-ranging implications.[5] The patent that threatened the entire infant auto industry covered not just the monumental invention but no less than the very *concept* of the gasoline-powered automobile.[6]

The case had its roots in the late 1870s, when George Selden, a young

Rochester, New York, patent attorney, first sketched out his idea for a "road-locomotive." Selden was precociously successful in his profession—the first client of his law practice was George Eastman, seeking counsel on his own first patent, the one that led to the low-cost photographic process that would launch Rochester's Eastman Kodak Company. Nonetheless, Selden practiced law not by choice but under parental pressure to follow in the footsteps of his father, a prominent judge. In truth, the younger Selden was a tinkerer at heart with a particular fascination with self-propelled vehicles. Melding his business and pleasure, in 1879 he applied for a patent on his idea for an "improved road engine" which was powered by a "liquid hydrocarbon engine of the compression type." He had never, however, built a working model of it.[7] That didn't matter: lawyer that he was, Selden's intent apparently was to come up with such precisely vague legal wording for his patent that it would accord him the exclusive right to license—and therefore exact royalty payments from—any and all internal-combustion-driven vehicles to be developed in the United States from the date of the patent's issue to its expiration after the standard seventeen years. If the patent had been issued in 1879, it would have expired in 1896 and been moot in terms of the U.S. automobile industry. That, however, was not Selden's plan.[8]

Once he had submitted his filing to the U.S. government, Selden took advantage of every legal tactic available to delay the application even while holding on to his ingeniously broad claim on the rights to the gas-powered automobile. He kept abreast of advances made by anyone working in the field of gasoline engines or self-propelled vehicles, constantly amending his filing to follow the trends. In this manner Selden managed to nurse his application along over the course of sixteen years, through a whopping one hundred revisions allowed by the U.S. Patent and Trademark Office (USPTO). According to writer William Greenleaf, "During its entire pendency the application was actually handled by the Patent Office for a total of about seven months. For making eight replies to Office actions and paying the final fee, Selden took fifteen years and eleven months."[9]

Founded by inventor-president Thomas Jefferson in 1802, the USPTO awarded over one million patents to American inventors during its first one hundred years. "The Patent System," Abraham Lincoln wrote, "added the fuel of interest to the fire of genius." The difficult mission of the Patent Office was to compensate inventors with a short-term business monopoly while still encouraging competition, which, after all, is the foundation of the free-enterprise system. History tends to remember the triumphant patents that forever changed the world, like Robert Fulton's steamboat or Alexander Graham Bell's telephone. But a visitor to the Patent Office archive—today housed in Pennsylvania, near Pittsburgh—encounters filing cabinets stuffed with clunkers ranging from underwater airplanes to disposable chairs and crustless peanut-butter-and-jelly sandwiches.[10]

Not all inventors, however, have benefited from the patent system Lincoln extolled. Often the USPTO has hastened more legal creativity than technical innovation by allowing wealthy individuals and companies to accumulate thousands of patents, essentially holding the garage tinkers and basement wizards of American romantic lore hostage. In the June 24, 2002, issue of *Forbes ASAP,* Gary L. Reback, the Silicon Valley entrepreneur and attorney who led the assault to break up Microsoft, echoed Henry Ford's complaint against U.S. patent law. "The patent as stimulant to invention has long since given way to the patent as blunt instrument for establishing an innovation stronghold," Reback wrote. "Sometimes the antagonist is a large corporation, short on revenue-generating products but long on royalty-generating patents. On other occasions, an opportunistic 'entrepreneur' who only produces patent applications uses the system's overly broad and undisciplined patent grant to shake down a potential competitor."[11] Henry Ford, known for his ready defiance, was not about to be shaken down by a cunning Genesee River lawyer.

Selden was finally awarded a patent on November 5, 1895. Designated patent number 549,160, it covered every gas-powered vehicle designed since the filing of his application in 1879 and constructed, used, or sold in the United States over the life of the issuance, ending in 1912.[12] To those in the thick of the nascent automobile industry, the patent was absurd. Even Selden harbored some doubts about its viability, as he did nothing for the first four years he held it. He was a passive, patient man. In fact, George Eastman grew so tired of Selden's "lack of aggressiveness" that he fired him in 1897, complaining "we want a fighter." In case of the vehicle patent, Selden was probably waiting for the public to develop enough of a real interest in automobiles to make it impossible for large-scale investors *not* to see the enormous profit potential in their manufacture.[13]

Exactly that happened: in 1899 a cadre of Wall Street financiers became aware of Selden's patent and immediately recognized its outrageous implications. They quickly arranged with Selden to administer his patent under the rubric of the newly reorganized Electric Vehicle Company, in exchange for $10,000 and a fifth of any revenues to be realized.[14] The financiers then set out in pursuit of those revenues, beginning in June 1900 by filing infringement suits against five U.S. auto manufacturers, including the nation's largest at the time, Cleveland's Winton Motor Carriage Company. It was owned by Henry Ford's erstwhile racetrack rival Alexander Winton, who put up a fight against the idea that his company owed royalties to anyone for the right to build a car.[15] After two years of watching the suit wind through the courts, however, Winton had had enough. It was less expensive to settle the case than to pay a team of lawyers to fight it. Once Winton Motor Carriage agreed to remit a small percentage of its sales revenues, the patent-holding corporation turned to the nation's other established carmakers.

As historian Carol Gelderman pointed out, however, "the validity of the Selden patent was implied in any settlement, and Winton's surrender alarmed other leading manufacturers, who banded together to negotiate with the Electric Vehicle Company."[16] The umbrella group thus formed—the Association of Licensed Automobile Manufacturers, or ALAM—began with ten members in 1900 and by 1903 comprised twenty-six of the United States' best-known carmakers. Although few if any ALAM members actually considered the Selden patent valid, the organization they set up to deal with it agreed to pay a 1.25 percent royalty on every gasoline-powered vehicle sold: 0.5 percent would go to the Electric Vehicle Company, 0.25 percent to George Selden, and the remaining 0.5 percent to the ALAM itself. The association named as its top officers two stolid Detroit auto men: Frederic L. Smith, a major investor in Oldsmobile, as president, and Packard general manager Henry B. Joy as secretary-treasurer. Neither had much regard for the cool and standoffish Henry Ford or his new company, deeming both bad risks overall.[17]

The declared intent of the ALAM was not entirely unworthy. The association did operate a patent pool among its members to obviate further lawsuits, so the companies within it shared their proprietary technologies as well as any advances they made. The group's seemingly loftiest purpose was in truth the most suspect: the ALAM made a pledge to raise the standards of the entire U.S. auto industry by granting carmaking licenses only to firms that proved their worthiness by adhering to the association's set codes of ethics and practice. In a process that was more than a little arbitrary, the ALAM consigned to the general category of too "flimsy" for membership any company that did not manufacture its own parts but instead purchased them from suppliers—such as Dodge Brothers. In fact, more than 80 percent of all early automakers fell under that definition of "flimsy," but the ALAM clause regarding "assemblage" operations left open enough loopholes to allow the organization to accept or reject any firm at its discretion. Simply put, the twenty-six charter members of the ALAM feared competition and had the means to squelch it. Their self-interested view was neatly expressed by H. H. Franklin, an ALAM member who headed his own august car company in Syracuse, New York. In 1903 he wrote to the editor of a trade journal in defense of the association's restrictive practices: "The licensees under the patent will surely, as they have a full legal right to do, control the gasoline automobile business," Franklin stated. "It would be impossible for all who have attempted to go into the business to make a success of it. Those already licensed can more than supply the demand."[18]

The crucial shift in attitude engendered by the ALAM centered on the notion that paying the Electric Vehicle Company was not an obligation, but a privilege: only those automakers recognized by the association would be *allowed* to pay the royalty on the Selden patent and thereby gain the privilege of selling gasoline-engine cars in the United States legally. As automotive historian Leslie R. Henry described the situation, the ALAM "exercised monopolistic control over the automobile industry through their power to grant *or to deny* licenses for the manufacture of automobiles."[19] In other words, the ALAM constituted an unofficial trust, or monopoly, hiding behind a U.S. patent at the precise moment of the first decade of the twentieth century that the Justice Department began aggressively busting trusts.

During the first half of 1903 Ford representatives called on ALAM executives to broach the possibility of obtaining a license to manufacture gas-powered cars, but were turned down twice on the grounds that Ford Motor Company did not meet the association's standards,[20] as their firm was a mere "assemblage" operation. The news was meant to sound the death knell for any new carmaker—but Ford Motor wasn't just any startup company. What would later ensue was foreshadowed in the final exchange between the company's executives and ALAM President Frederic Smith at a lunch meeting in a Detroit hotel, a scene recalled by several of those in attendance. As recounted by Theodore MacManus and Norman Beasley in their book *Men, Money and Motors,* it followed Smith's explanation of why Ford Motor was unacceptable for membership in the licensing association.

> "Selden can take his patent and go to hell with it!" roared Couzens.
> Ford, who had been dangling in a chair tilted against the wall, rapped out:
> "Couzens has answered you."
> "You men are foolish," counseled Smith. "The Selden crowd can put you out of business—and will!"
> Couzens laughed unpleasantly. Ford, standing up, pointed a finger at Smith and cried:
> "Let them try it."[21]

They did, and they failed. Henry Ford turned the sort of trick that over time would define him as the most significant figure of America's Automobile Age: he proclaimed that being rejected by the Association of Licensed Automobile Manufacturers was a badge of honor, and therefore just about the best thing that could happen to a fine young automobile company such as his.

The gauntlet was quickly thrown down at Ford's feet. On Sunday, July 26,

1903, an advertisement appeared, four columns wide, in both of Detroit's daily papers, the *News-Tribune* and the *Free Press:*

NOTICE

To Manufacturers, Dealers, Importers, Agents and Users of Gasoline Automobiles

United States Patent No. 549,160 granted to George B. Selden November 5th, 1895, controls broadly all gasoline automobiles, which are accepted as commercially practical. Licenses under this patent have been secured from the owners by the following named manufacturers and importers.

No other manufacturers are authorized to make or sell gasoline automobiles, and any person making, selling or using such machines made or sold by any unlicensed manufacturers or importers will be liable to prosecution for infringement.

Association of Licensed Automobile Manufacturers[22]

It was signed by the ALAM's twenty-six licensed "pioneers of the industry."[23] Two days later, Ford Motor Company took out this rebuttal ad in both Detroit papers:

NOTICE

To Dealers, Importers, Agents and Users of Our Gasoline Automobiles

We will protect you against any prosecution for alleged infringements of patents. The Selden patent does not cover any practicable machine, no practicable machine can be made from it, and never was, so far as we can ascertain. It relates to the form of carriage called a FORE carriage. None of that type have ever been in use; all have been failures. No court in the United States has ever decided in favor of the patent on the merits of the case; all it has ever done was to record a prior agreement between parties. . . .[24]

With less regard for factual accuracy, the advertisement also stated that "Our Mr. Ford made the first Gasoline Automobile in Detroit and the third in the United States."[25] He alleged that he had completed his first car early in 1892, three years before Selden was awarded his patent—and a full four and a half years before he actually finished his first quadricycle. A more precise summation of Ford Motor's position appeared in the form of an open letter from the company's own patent attorney, Ralzemond A. Parker, published in *Motor Age, Horseless Age,* and *Cycle and Automobile Trade Journal* the week of October 1, 1903. Parker's letter read, in part:

So far as our plan of action is concerned for the future it is extremely simple. We intend to manufacture and sell all of the gasoline automobiles of the type that we are constructing that we can. We regard the claims made under the Selden patent as covering the monopoly of such machines as entirely unwarranted and without foundation in fact. We do not, therefore, propose to respect any such claims, and, if the issue is forced upon us, shall defend not only ourselves but our agents and customers to the fullest extent and this, too, without regard to whether or not we join any combination for the purpose of defending against said patent.

In taking this position we cannot conscientiously feel that Mr. Selden ever added anything to the art in which we are engaged. We believe that the art would have been just as far advanced today if Mr. Selden had never been born. That he made no discovery and gave none to the world. If he did, it was a narrow and impracticable one having no value, and that he and his assignees cannot monopolize the entire trade by forcing upon it an unwarrantable construction of his claims by those interested in sustaining them.

It is evident from the foregoing that the association is not a philanthropic institution. It is in the business to make money at the expense of five or six times as many competitors, and that its members have joined together because of some pecuniary benefit in monopolizing the market under cover of the Selden patent, and not because they believe the patent to be impregnable. This is undoubtedly the truth, as is evident, because up to this date, although repeatedly challenged by outsiders and by ourselves, they have brought no action since the association was formed, that we can learn of, against an alleged infringer.[26]

The upshot of all this back-and-forth in the press materialized on October 22, 1903, when the ALAM filed a patent-infringement suit against Ford Motor Company.[27]

But Henry Ford was right: the lawsuit really *was* the best thing that could have happened to him and his company. In fact, to some degree it might be said that the ALAM's suit over the Selden patent *made* Ford, as both the man and his firm won national renown through their long and dauntless fight against the licensing association and the legal maneuvering behind it. To the public, the engineer's intransigent stance pitted a righteous Ford Motor Company against a greedy cabal suspected of monopolistic designs, making Ford actually look *heroic* when his firm persisted in selling its cars in direct contradiction of the ALAM's edict. "The Selden patent is a freak among alleged inventions and is worthless as a patent and device," the new crowned champion of the little man told the *New York Times*. "We are not in the harassing business," Ford proclaimed; "we are making a good product, the best that our factory can turn out, and believe in honest competition in a fair field and so no special favors."[28]

The ALAM immediately resorted to advertisements warning, "If you buy a Ford, you buy a lawsuit."[29] The ALAM's scare tactic had some success dissuading the most timid buyers, but Ford Motor was still selling just about as many cars as it could build. And all the while the company looked brave and dashing for taking its bold stand almost all alone; among American automakers only a few independent concerns, such as Thomas B. Jeffery's Rambler company, slid in behind the Ford suit and continued operating in violation of the dubious Selden patent. Only one other firm in the world, an auto manufacturer based in France, gave Ford Motor's cause any financial support. But according to Henry Ford, the decision to stand up to the ALAM was less a matter of parading his bedrock courage than it was of exercising the good business sense to accept what he estimated at about $1,000 worth of free publicity each week.

Ford's point was well taken, but fighting the suit still couldn't have been any easy decision to make. In the earliest years Ford's legal fees grew into a major expense. It would take eight years for the ALAM's case against Ford Motor to wend its way through the legal process, generating a body of evidence and testimony estimated at five million words of text over the first five years alone.[30] The dispute covered the issue of just how much of Selden's 1879 contraption really applied to the twentieth-century automobiles. Legally it also came down to the simple question of whether Selden's patent covered all gasoline-powered automobiles developed since he had filed his original application in 1879, as the ALAM maintained, or only those created according to Selden's exact design.

Henry Ford's 1904 testimony in the ALAM case launched on a national level the near cult of personality the iconoclastic maverick had always inspired among those who worked with him. And he managed to attain this broader mystique just by being himself. People who knew Henry Ford during his company's early years noticed scant change in his personality even as his firm, his fortune, and his fame grew by leaps and bounds. Around the factory floor he had always been an amiable presence, chatting and joking with even the lowliest workers. At the same time Ford wasn't buddies with anyone at the company, not even his top executives. Yet that had been Ford's way not only back in his own days as a worker, but all his life; even in childhood he had maintained a certain air of detachment from his fellows, always friendly but ever focused elsewhere. Now, as the well-known boss of a booming car company, he remained relaxed and approachable around his employees, asking them questions and offering advice, but only, and strictly, on his own terms. At work, Henry Ford was the one who decided how long a conversation would be, what the subject would be, and whether it would take place at all—just as he had at home as a boy with his family and friends.

Another trait Ford never lost was his playful mean streak. Several early Ford Motor employees recalled this unpleasantly juvenile side of their boss showing up even in his dealings with his own factory workers, who did not exactly enjoy the option of retaliating when he played pranks on them. Engineer Oliver Barthel, who worked at Ford Motor on a freelance basis in 1905, cited one such jest that Ford had another man set up: a car had been rigged to set off a loud, if harmless, explosion in the muffler, when another worker touched an unrelated control on the interior. Perched out of sight to watch his prank play out, Ford found the employee's fright hilarious, guffawing at what he considered his own cleverness in having left nary a trace to suggest his complicity.

"Mr. Ford seemed to have a dual nature," explained Barthel. "One side of his nature I liked very much and I felt that I wanted to be a friend of his. The other side of his nature I just couldn't stand. It bothered me greatly." Barthel—speaking well after joining what he described as a long line of people abused or betrayed by Henry Ford—was hardly alone in noticing the dichotomy between sensitivity and cruelty in Ford's personality. Many of Ford's workers, and all of his executives, had to deal with the same conundrum. "In order to get along with Mr. Ford," Barthel remembered, "you had to have a little mean streak in your system. You had to be tough and mean. Mr. Ford enjoyed that."[31]

As would remain the case with all of Henry Ford's favorite lieutenants through the years, both James J. Couzens and Harold Wills were every bit as tough and prickly as he was. Each boasted the strength of mind and will to stand up to Ford, thereby earning his respect. The fact that the two of them were in the process of creating the company and the cars, respectively, of Ford's dreams probably made them special cases, at least in the early days. Ford was not even necessarily welcome in Wills's creative domain, as the designer did not hesitate to make clear by constructing a private hideaway work space accessible only through a trapdoor—and only to those whom he permitted to enter. Longtime Ford Motor employee George Brown recalled the setup as the maverick Wills arranged it: "In those years," Brown said, "Mr. Wills had his experimental work upstairs in a little two-story brick building at the back of the plant. You had to climb a ladder to get up into it. It had a trap door on top, and if you wanted to get up there, you had to rap on the door. They'd holler, 'What do you want?' You'd tell them your business, and they'd open the trap door. John Wandersee and Wills were working up there all the time."[32]

Yet Henry Ford had no more complaint with Wills's maverick eccentricities than he did with the quirks of James Couzens. All that mattered to Ford Motor's president was that his right-hand men do their jobs brilliantly, and that they did. Indeed, just about every early Ford Motor employee worked a ten-hour day—except for Ford, Couzens, and Wills, who routinely put in twelve to sixteen hours, seven days a week.[33] Bossing the boss around was no offense for anyone who was that committed and who had the expertise and tenacity to work through problems Ford was unable to solve.

As the sums of money coursing through the coffers grew, Couzens began to concentrate ever more of his efforts on making the figures work to the company's advantage. Among other efforts he learned how to use a network of banks all over the country to earn the best interest rates. To take on his former responsibility for sales as he busied himself with administrative matters, Couzens hired the colorful, charming, and incisive Norval Hawkins.

Hawkins's first job at Ford Motor had been selling himself. As everyone in Detroit business circles knew full well, he had been convicted on embezzlement charges in 1894, having taken $8,000 as a cashier at Standard Oil. Hawkins was not a typical ex-con. On the day he emerged from prison, a crowd of old friends was waiting in the street to cheer him on to better things. Hawkins immediately proved himself anew by establishing a successful consulting and accounting business in Detroit before joining Ford Motor as commercial manager. Hired in the autumn of 1907, he used all of 1908 to fine-tune the sales organization Couzens had built. His department's directive was to prepare the company for much larger sales to come.

Norval Hawkins possessed an ideal dual personality for the job. On the one hand, he could play the circus ringmaster, rousing excitement by making Ford's dealers compete with one another like so many trained lions. On the other hand, he was an eagle-eyed accountant, a type so necessary to young firms in expansive industries like automaking. As historians Allan Nevins and Frank Ernest Hill pointed out in *Ford: The Times, the Man, the Company,* Hawkins became obsessed with logistical efficiencies, particularly those achieve by the ways of loading cars and parts into railroad boxcars. He would personally experiment with packing designs for weeks on end until he found the tightest fit.[34] Norval Hawkins shared the Ford vision and understood that small amounts translated into vast savings on the scale of business that his new employer was planning.

———

As workmen scurried about the first two floors of the Ford plant on Piquette Avenue, the team of Couzens and Hawkins might have twenty-five cars to peddle in a good week. Yet something even more significant was happening out of view on the third floor. In a cramped room grandly dubbed the "experimental department," Ford Motor's design engineers were mapping out a new model under the aegis of Henry Ford. "I saw the blackboard sketch in the Experimental Room, which was only about 15 feet by 20 feet in size," said W. Ernest Grimshaw, a workman hired in 1906. "Mr. Joe Galamb and Mr. Julius Haltenberger worked in there. Only people interested in designing were allowed in there."[35] Young Grimshaw managed to get in whenever he was sent upstairs with a message for Ford or one of the others.

"Early in 1907," master draftsman Joseph A. Galamb recalled, "Mr. Ford said to me, 'Joe, I've got an idea to design a new car. Fix a place for yourself on the third floor, way back, a special room. Get your board up there and a blackboard and we'll start working on a new model.'"[36] Many of Ford Motor's third-floor workers remembered the boss explaining his concept for the groundbreaking new car with absolute confidence that it could be done. Their recollections are echoed in a letter Henry Ford had written back in January 1906 to *The Automobile* magazine:

"The greatest need today," Ford wrote, "is a light, low-priced car with an up-to-date engine of ample horsepower, and built of the very best material. One that will go anywhere a car of double the horsepower will; that is in every way an automobile and not a toy; and most important of all, one that will not be a wrecker of tires [worn down from the heavy weight of most cars] and a spoiler of the owner's disposition. It must be powerful enough for American roads and capable of carrying its passengers anywhere that a horse-drawn vehicle will go without the driver being afraid of ruining his car."[37]

Although some reports maintain that the development of the new model began late in 1906, Galamb's account includes the two main points of the story corroborated by nearly every participant in the early effort to create Ford's new car: Henry Ford's direction of the project, and that Ford and the others spent a great deal of time gathered around the latest sketch on the blackboard, staring at it together, pondering it, then discussing it and changing it until some degree of concept, design, and engineering emerged by consensus.

Starting with the Model N as a basis, Ford developed a list of components that he felt could be improved. They included the transmission, the engine, the magneto (which supplied electricity to the spark plugs), and the suspension. Of course, there was not too much left to the Model N, except the dual brake system that would be brought into the new design intact. The half-dozen engineers and assistants in the Experimental Room were capable of designing the new components Henry Ford had vaguely in mind. But something more was required of the new model as well, something beyond nuts and bolts and specs and lines on paper. The car Ford wanted called for science.

"The Models N, R, and S were four-cylinder cars," explained John Wandersee, a mechanic enlisted as an assistant to chief engineer Harold Wills, "and the steel was still too heavy to put a bigger body on; the larger your body and the roomier it is, the heavier your car is, and the harder it is to get more speed. Mr. Ford was always for a light car because it could cut rings around the big cars, so he started the Model T, making it a light car with light parts for a five-passenger car."[38]

In other words, Henry Ford's grand design called for two opposites: large size and light weight, qualities that had not coexisted in automobiles up to that time. "This is where vanadium steel comes in," Wandersee added, vanadium being an element that can be added to steel to form an even stronger, and noticeably lighter, alloy.

While Wills, as chief designer, was continually involved in the practical engineering conducted in the Experimental Room, he often preferred to stay cloistered in his own hideaway laboratory. It surely helped, when avoiding the boss, to be making progress on a problem everyone else was unable to solve— such as how to make big cars light with new metal alloys.

Meanwhile, the Experimental Room grew more crowded than ever as sketches turned into blueprints for parts. In time, those parts were machined and assembled into prototype vehicles for road-testing. Jimmy Smith, a resourceful machinist and designer back then, described Ford Motor Company's experimental department as "a room about 12 feet by 15 feet, big enough to get a car in, milling machines, drill presses, and lathes.

"It was very small," Jimmy Smith added,[39] but what room wouldn't seem small filled with all that, and the dominating blackboard, plus old parts, new parts, possible parts, and a person or two attached to each of them? And there in the middle of it all was Henry Ford, sitting in his "lucky" rocking chair (supposed to have been his mother's), giving advice and staring at the blackboard by turns. In that small room, that great room, together they created the Model T.

"Automobiles have been built too heavy in the past," Henry Ford insisted.[40] He believed that simplicity of design could reduce weight. As it turned out, he was right that simplicity would help, but the real answer as to how to make a lighter car lay more squarely in his using better materials. Ford's insistence—in fact, his obsession—on cutting the new model's weight led Harold Wills to take a careful look at the fundamental material in car manufacture: steel.

Until then few people in Detroit or anywhere else in the American automobile industry had devoted much effort to metallurgy. Steel was considered a commodity that was used in cars just about the way it arrived from the mills of Pennsylvania and Ohio. The more complex parts were forged from costly alloys, but little research was then being done in the United States on steel for use in the structural parts. Wills had some background in metallurgical engineering, and according to several contemporaries was the one who initiated the investigation of substitute alloys at Ford Motor. Nevertheless, Ford himself would later tell the tale that he found a stray piece of vanadium steel in the wreckage of a French race car in Ormand Beach, Florida, and upon picking it up knew instantly that it was the answer to making his ground-breaking Model T. While it is impossible to disprove that any such thing ever happened, given Ford's tendency to rewrite history to his advantage, John Wandersee's more mundane version of the company's exploration into vanadium steel appears more credible: "Wills was the one, as far as I know," he said, "who first got interested in vanadium steel, through J. K. Smith; he was a consulting metallurgical engineer in Pittsburgh."[41] Wills originally inquired about substitute alloys for nickel steel, a composite that was strong but quite expensive. Smith likely suggested vanadium steel, then known only in Europe. At Wills's suggestion, Ford Motor therefore not only conducted tests on the alloy at a specialty mill in Canton, Ohio, but also hired specialists including J. K. Smith to help perfect the processes both of making the steel and of heat-treating parts forged from it for added strength. Within the year between late 1906 and late 1907, Ford Motor Company became the leading force in vanadium steel research in the United States, even taking out patents related to the alloy and its production.

Adding vanadium renders steel stronger, more resistant to corrosion, and lighter than other steel alloys. What's more, vanadium steel was less expensive than alloys with similar properties, and easier to machine as well.

Twenty-five tons of the new steel were delivered to Piquette Avenue for use in test versions of the Model T. Wills next suggested to Henry Ford that the company hire a university-trained metallurgist to develop the steel program further. The project already called for an expert: the process of mixing the compound is tricky in that if the right temperatures are not maintained at the proper times, the result is a lump of vanadium in the middle of a lump of steel. That does not constitute an alloy, or a usable steel.

Wills must have forgotten about Henry Ford's deep-seated prejudice against college-educated employees. (Ford Motor was the one company at which applicants would pretend not to be graduates if they wanted a job badly enough.) Instead of hiring an engineer with a degree, Ford told Wills to make a metallurgist out of John Wandersee, whom Ford had hired as a sweeper at his earlier firm in 1902.[42] The order may have been casual and ornery, but it turned out to be felicitous: Wandersee would go on to a stellar career as Ford Motor's chief metallurgist.

While Wills and Wandersee continued their pioneering work with vanadium steel, the discussions and debates continued on the third floor as the Model T came off the blackboard and into reality. Its creation was very much a group effort. Harold Wills held everyone to a realistic path toward the audacious engineering goals of Henry Ford, who provided the spirit of the enterprise. "I never heard him try to sell a car," an early customer once remarked. "He was trying to sell me the idea."[43] In that respect, Henry Ford probably never did as much "selling" as he had to in the Experimental Room on the third floor of Piquette Avenue. For what he had to sell was his outrageous vision of a car that would be all things to all people—except rich people. The car he wanted to build would be daily transportation for city dwellers, a new kind of workhorse for farmers, and the key to freedom for anyone anywhere left behind by the Automobile Age. As it turned out, Ford's vision would be realized.

With so many suggestions flying around the experimental department, only a few of the advances can be attached to a particular designer. One that can owes to Joe Galamb, who had helped formulate plans for the layout of the whole car and was also made responsible for a new transmission. It took him six months, but his resulting design, which coaxed the old-style planetary transmission into operating more smoothly than it ever had on any other model, would last through the entire production run of the Model T. "Finally, we got the design that was used for 15,000,000 Ford jobs, 15,000,000 Model Ts," Galamb later reflected with fitting pride.[44]

Electrical wizard Spider Huff developed the T's magneto, the electrical component that supplied the spark to the plugs that he and Oliver Barthel had invented back in 1901. Faulty electrical systems in many early cars caused them to stall or run perpetually out of tune. The magneto Huff contributed to the Model T stayed both dry and connected, to the delight of customers who marveled that once their Ts started running, they kept running, a reliability unheard-of in any other car available at that time.

Ford Motor also pioneered a new type of engine for the T, along a design previously considered unworkable: the top part, or head, was removable. The cylinders it protected underneath reflected one other innovation: all four were cast from a single block of metal. These changes made the cylinder block stronger and lighter, yet easier to service. Another design improvement enclosed the motor, transmission, and flywheel (with built-in magneto) together so their lubrication systems could be shared. Wills's introduction of vanadium steel, used in more than 50 percent of the Model T's construction, made it one of the strongest—if not the strongest—car in production in 1908. At about 1,200 pounds, its weight was on a par with that of its rickety predecessor the Model N—but the N was a two-seater. The standard Model T seated five.

The list of improvements continued. Among the most significant were several born of the era's roads conditions—in 1908–1909 more than 80 percent of the byways used by automobiles in the United States were neither paved nor graded. In truth, most "roads" amounted to little more than ruts in the dirt, although conditions were beginning to improve and would continue to do so as the automobile's popularity grew. The Model T was at once ready for both the ruts of the time and the roads that would come. Its frame was built high off the ground, giving the car a clunky silhouette that may not have looked as rakish as that of other cars but that kept the T's belly out of the mud when the wheels fell into holes on poor roads. In addition, the new Ford's suspension offered a near gymnastic flexibility, utilizing a three-point system that let the chassis actually twist. By doing so, as the wheels pulled the car up from a rut they could stay in contact with the ground, where they did much more good than they did flailing in midair. As the joke ran about the man trying to explain why he wanted to be buried in his Model T: "I ain't never seen a hole yet that she couldn't get me outta."

Ford's new creation took account of America's changing road conditions in another, even more auspicious way. The T was the first production model car to feature steering on the left. To traverse roads typically flanked by ditches, drivers keeping to the right preferred the steering on the right. It was the norm in early cars. Drivers could look and see how close their wheels were coming to disaster. On good paved roads free of the ruts and ditches, however, drivers in the United States were better off seated on the left, closer to, and thus better placed to watch out for, oncoming traffic. It was just common sense, but the Model T was the car that proved it. Shortly afterward, just about every other automaker admitted as much and copied Ford's innovation.

In early 1908, some forty Ford Motor workers gathered to help assemble the first test car from the Model T designs. One of the most intense moments came when they wrapped the engine in fifty feet of rope, hoisted it up, and lowered it into the waiting chassis. None of them could have known that the prototype they were building would spawn the most influential consumer product of all time—but they did know they were producing something astonishingly new, different, revolutionary, and right.

For whatever cause, the ropes suddenly started to unravel and the engine began to turn around and around slowly in midair. No one could do anything but watch as the lovingly constructed motor twisted faster and faster out of control. "The motor went into a spin," recalled workman James O'Connor, until "it came down on the floor." Several components broke off completely, with a crack loud enough to split the air.

After a moment of painfully stunned silence, the two factory superintendents on duty launched into a screaming match, blaming each other for the mishap. "I know more about cars than you will ever know!" one roared. In the heat of the moment, according to O'Connor, the other man bellowed the same thing back, a little louder and with the emphasis, "I know more about cars than *you* will ever know!"[45]

More annoyed than angry, Henry Ford coolly stepped forward and shoved both employees toward the door, telling them to get back to their regular jobs.

He was all for healthy competition among workers, but not when it descended to empty bickering. Ford chose to oversee the repairs to the engine himself, staying at the factory as late as the task took. The next day, just seven men and eight feet of rope were allowed around the rebuilt engine, and it only took a couple of minutes to lower it into place.

As for the battling superintendents, O'Connor noted, "I often think about them saying, 'I know more about cars than you do.'" Then he added, "Nobody knew anything about cars."

He may have been right, but at least at Ford Motor Company, they were all learning about cars, and quickly. In that defining year of 1908, the Piquette Avenue factory hummed like a beehive, comparable in intensity of activity to the Manhattan Project that developed the atomic bomb during World War II. Both efforts were multifaceted, yet well coordinated in order to foster the creation of devastatingly practical products. That sort of outcome results only from an insistence on both efficiency and efficacy in every single task. Inspiring it requires a forceful impetus. In the case of the Manhattan Project, there was war for motivation. At Piquette Avenue three and a half decades earlier, there was Henry Ford.

Unlike Harvey Firestone, the tire mogul who amazed his underlings with his ability to do any job at his company, Ford amazed his colleagues with all the things he could not do, or even comprehend. He could not, for example, make or read blueprints, and even though he could work with his hands, he almost never did, except in teaching others.[46] He would not even read his mail, except under duress, as was evidenced on one occasion, reported in the *New York Times,* in December 1910, when baskets were found in Ford's office stuffed with important letters he had never bothered to open. After that, a secretary was assigned to look through Mr. Ford's mail. But even when he was forced to pay attention to a letter, he complained if it went on longer than a page. Far more remarkably, Ford couldn't be bothered with money, either: the story went around the whole factory when the boss absently unfolded a crumpled piece of paper he found in his pocket and it turned out to be a check for $68,000 (equivalent today to about $500,000).[47]

What Henry Ford could do, brilliantly, was lead. It was he who foresaw the growth of the automobile market and pushed his company incessantly toward higher and higher production to meet it. He also, of course, envisioned the product that would take the first and best advantage of that market: the Model T. The great genius Ford displayed in his factory's startup years, however, was a still rarer talent. He managed to imbue the entire Piquette Avenue factory with his own view of the coming world. Although he was known for mumbling and stammering through any sort of public-speaking engagement,[48] Ford had no trouble communicating his grand plans to his employees at Ford Motor, and inspiring them thereby to greater achievements.

"God! He could get anything out of the men because he just talked and would tell them stories," remembered George Brown. "He'd never say, 'I want this done!' He'd say, 'I wonder if we can do it, I wonder.' Well, the men would just break their necks to see if they could do it. They knew what he wanted. They figured it was a coming thing, and they did their best."[49]

Henry Ford had always been personally popular with subordinates, who naturally found themselves looking up to him, but with the creation of the Model T, his combination of a genius's vision and a regular guy's easygoing charm added up to one powerful force of personality. As much as the Model T represented a step up in design for Ford Motor Company—and for the global automobile industry—the effort to create it reflected a leap up for Henry Ford's leadership. For the first time, he found himself extending his talents far beyond his personal reach, inspiring people he would never meet to take part in his endeavors. Ford Motor found myriad ways to grow in the year and a half before the advent of the Model T; after that, so did Henry Ford.

—————

One of the first people to test-drive a Model T, Archie Terrell, returned exhilarated after a long ride over all kinds of roads. "That is a wonderful car," he gushed. "That is *really* a car."[50]

Henry Ford concurred, saying simply, "I think we've got something here."[51] Yet all they had at that juncture early in 1908 was a wonderful car—one, single, wonderful car. At that point Ford himself wondered aloud whether his company would ever build even a tenth Model T. The difference between building test cars and rolling out vehicles by the hundred or even the thousand presented a challenge to the administrators at the Piquette Avenue plant, especially in conjunction with the design work to be done. To put the Model T into actual production, a whole roster of suppliers had to be brought into the process.

Up until its short-lived adventure with the Ford Manufacturing Company, Ford Motor had not been in the business of making parts for its cars; the firm only assembled the products of others. With the launch of Ford Manufacturing as a parallel entity, the firm plunged into the parts-making business. After the manufacturing arm was absorbed into the main company in 1907, Ford Motor continued to make more and more of the various components used in its cars. In fact, this quest for self-sufficiency would not end until well into the 1920s, by which point the company would be not only building its own wooden body frames, for example, but growing its own trees from which to craft them. At the inception of the Model T, however, Ford Motor still depended heavily on outside manufacturers. Some of these suppliers simply followed the Ford designs for specific parts, some made minor refinements, and a few specialty shops actually contributed original engineering for the new model.

The company's myriad suppliers not only had to prove they could produce parts up to the Model T's stringent standards, they also had to convince James Couzens, for one, that they could deliver Ford Motor's orders for large quantities on time. Couzens's strict requirements for vendors made such an impression on Ernest Grimshaw, who worked in Ford's purchasing department when the T was under development, that he could still rattle off the names and products of the firm's major suppliers fifty years later. "The McCord Manufacturing Company made the radiators. Both B.F. Everitt Body Company and C.R. Wilson Body Company made the bodies," Grimshaw said. "Referring to the castings, I believe they came from the Holmes Foundry in Romeo. The A.J. Beaudette Company manufactured tops as well as did the American Top Company in Jackson. The frames came from the Parish and Bingham Company of Cleveland, Ohio. The A.O. Smith Company of Milwaukee, Wisconsin, made the forgings consisting of front axles, front axle spindles, etc. The K.W. Prudden Company in Lansing, Michigan, made the wheels. The John R. Keim Mills of Buffalo, New York, did a lot of our stamping work."[52]

The list could go on. Every manufacturing concern has suppliers, but for Ford Motor at the launch of the Model T, the job of contracting with them was greatly complicated by the huge numbers of units the company wanted. No automobile manufacturer had ever produced 10,000 vehicles in a single year. Many within the industry in fact doubted that Ford would ever find buyers for so many cars at any price; quite a few people regarded the market as saturated. To Henry Ford, by contrast, the Gasoline Era was just beginning. "The automobile," he wrote in January 1906, "is one of the absolute necessities of our later-day civilization."[53] It certainly would be before he was through, but as of 1908, even the concept of the essential "family car" did not yet exist.

In addition to the enormous quantities the firm ordered, contracting out for parts was complicated by the precise machining tolerances the Model T's specifications required. Ford Motor intended to waste no more time coaxing components to fit together—a task for a mallet on occasion back then. In an industry previously unfettered by anything like exacting measurements the typical tolerance for the first Model T parts was to 1/64 of an inch. However exacting that level of precision may have seemed at the time, as one supplier correctly observed: "Pretty soon, they're going to make them a lot closer than that."[54] Of course, as mentioned earlier, Cadillac's engineering chief Henry M. Leland had machined parts to tolerances of 1/100,000 of an inch as early as 1896—in small quantities.

Naturally, Ford Motor's insistence on high quality in vast quantities at low cost put enormous pressure on its suppliers. On another key concern regarding purchase orders, however, Henry Ford made no demands whatever on outside companies; he gave them all the development time they needed to do his jobs right. From the end of 1907 through 1908, Ford Motor imposed no false deadlines to rush the engineers and mechanics at trusted supply houses. So when John R. Keim Mills needed ten months to design a crankcase to specs, it got them. During the development phase of the Model T, Henry Ford made sure that the pace never accelerated enough to become an excuse for mediocrity.

For a time, there was no need to hurry anyway. The Panic of 1907, a short but steep crash on Wall Street, made money scarce and presented Ford Motor with its first real economic crisis. The stock plummet started with the failure of one New York bank that year and soon revealed the desperate condition of many others. It was a case in which the ills and excesses of the New York financial world did real damage to industries all over the United States—a fact that Henry Ford, for one, never forgot.

"You couldn't get a nickel from a bank to save your life," recalled George Brown, who had worked in Ford Motor's accounting department. "In order to get the cash to continue during that little time of depression, Mr. Ford kept building these cars [Model Ns] and shipping them out on what they called sight draft bills of lading, so the dealer had to pay for those cars. . . . Oh boy, what a squeal! What a time the dealers had to get money. They didn't want to lose the dealership, so they did everything, begged, borrowed and stole to pay for those machines."[55] Although the scheme was Couzens's idea, Henry Ford would always remember how it worked. At the same time, in order to stay comfortably afloat Couzens paid suppliers with notes, which amounted to postdated checks. There was a squeal about that from the suppliers, too, but the economic crisis passed within months, before any real damage could be done to the company's business relationships.

Until the nation's full recovery from 1907's "little time of depression," as Brown neatly termed it, Ford Motor's time would be better spent developing a new model rather than trying to launch one, anyway. Thus Henry Ford's patient pacing did not cost the company anything in time lost.

Of all Ford Motor's suppliers, the most important to the firm remained Dodge Brothers. Complicating the situation was the fact that John and Horace Dodge were also shareholders. An attorney would later suggest to Henry Ford that he owed his fortune to the Dodge brothers, repeating a view widely held through the first decade that Ford Motor was in business. "They produced the cars that brought you the money to make you a success," the attorney said—and Henry Ford had no choice but to agree grudgingly.[56]

As independent machinists, John and Horace Dodge might well have worried when Ford Motor began assuming more and more of the actual manufacturing of its cars. As a Ford Motor vice president, however, John Dodge recognized the merits of the increased flexibility in-house manufacturing gave the concern. Throughout the early history of Ford Motor Company, both Dodges voted in support of Henry Ford's seemingly outrageous production increases when others within the organization expressed doubts that the firm could really sell all the cars the founding director proposed to build. In 1906, when the only thing Henry Ford knew about the Model T was that he had a gleam in his eye for a car the likes of which had never been seen before, he started looking for a new factory. He didn't know what this epochal car to be built there would be called. He didn't even know its specific characteristics. But he did know that his company would outgrow the Piquette Avenue plant and need the biggest automobile factory in the world to build his "people's car." With that in mind, Henry Ford began scouting locations, and the man who went with him was John Dodge. Together they would select an expansive parcel in Highland Park in the north part of Detroit, then set to planning the very factory that would push Dodge Brothers right out of the business of making Ford parts.

According to the plans drawn up by Henry Ford and the Dodges, the Highland Park plant would be the biggest building in all of Michigan. To design it, Ford Motor engaged Albert Kahn, considered the leading industrial architect of the day. Consultations with him created yet another chore for the relatively small cadre of executives at Piquette Avenue between 1907 and 1908.

Any concerns the Dodge brothers may have had about the shift toward in-house production at Ford Motor were certainly assuaged by the fortune—the yearly *fortunes*—both men were reaping as Ford stockholders. For the Dodges, annual dividends of over $200,000 each became routine—on an original investment equivalent to $5,000 apiece. Between 1908 and 1910, there was very little one could not buy in Michigan with that kind of income, try as the brothers might to spend it all. Both bought showy houses in neighborhoods formerly reserved for Detroit's established upper class. Horace chose to move with his wife to Grosse Pointe and he bought a yacht, the first of many. Both Dodge families also sent their children to exclusive schools, including Detroit's Liggett School and Connecticut's Choate Academy,[57] with the intent of preparing the next generation of Dodges to take the place in society their fathers' fortunes bought them.

Henry Ford disapproved. He had no use for social climbing or the ostentatious manner in which John and Horace chose to live. Henry and Clara Bryant Ford had stayed in their humble section of town, renting a rowhouse at 332 Hendrie Street until 1905, when ample dividends from Ford Motor enabled the family to move into a house at 145 Harper Avenue. It was roomy though hardly a grand mansion. In 1907 they moved within Detroit once more, this time into a house on Edison Street. Built to their specifications, it reflected the Arts and Crafts style then in vogue and was large enough to require a staff of servants. Even so, the Fords still entertained only a few close friends at a time, and otherwise generally managed to live without much pretension. Henry and Clara considered themselves the only "society" Edsel needed, and were generous parents with their time and attention. Edsel was raised to be polite and unassuming and as a boy remained quite unspoiled by the wealth his family was acquiring. The Ford household did not look to the bright lights of the city for their pleasures, preferring to live in the city as quietly as both Henry and Clara had on their families' Dearborn and Greenfield farms.

What rankled Henry Ford most about John and Horace Dodge, however, was not how they lived, played, or raised their children; it was that both brothers drove Packard cars.[58] Of course, he never could understand why anyone would drive anything but a Ford. Money had nothing to do with it. Ford truly believed that his vehicles were superior and if they made driving possible for the working class there was no reason that they couldn't make it more pleasurable for the rich as well.

———

"The rougher you were with them, the better they ran," marveled one Ford Motor employee who test-drove the first Model Ts early in 1908.[59] Although word of a remarkable new vehicle leaked out, dealers did not formally hear about the new car until that March, when Ford Motor sent out an introductory brochure. The announcement revealed that this Model T had four cylinders, and best of all, the shockingly low price of $850. Even on paper the new car looked exciting—perhaps too much so, for the time being. Some dealers would admit that they hid the advance brochures on the new model in fear that once the public heard about the T, they would never find buyers for their inventories of outmoded Model Ns.

Dealer Louis Kinietz heard about it with the arrival of the brochure. A former Ford factory employee, by then he had struck out on his own as a Ford dealer in New York State. Kinietz literally couldn't wait to see one of the new cars in person. "I got on the train and went to Detroit to see this car," he confessed. "While I was looking at it, Mr. Ford came along, and seeing me he came over where I was, shook hands with me and asked me what I thought of the car. I told him 'I think you have just what you were looking for.'

"He said, 'I know I have.'"[60]

The next step was to let the world know it, too. The first national advertisements for the car, released during the first week of October 1908, did not even mention the name "Model T." Readers of the *Saturday Evening Post* and other such magazines were enticed only to buy "The Ford Four Cylinder, Twenty Horsepower, Five Passenger Touring Car $850.00." That headline was all many customers needed to hear.

The ad was, however, slightly misleading in depicting a Model T all equipped and ready to go. The fact was that for $850 the buyer did not get the top for the car—or the windshield or headlights, either. Of course, the advertised price could have been even lower had the seats and steering wheel been listed as options as well. In reality, nearly every customer ordered a top and a windshield for the car, in addition to several other practically mandatory options, such as a spare tire. Ford Motor's profits, therefore, did not depend on the Model T's base price, but only began there. On top of the starting $850, a customer could easily add $135 for extras, that figure covering a top, windshield, speedometer, headlamps, and a carbide generator to power the last two. Starting in October 1909, all of these options would be included in the car's base price of $950—in effect, a reduction of $35.

The buying public demonstrated a gratifyingly avid interest in the Model T, even though Ford Motor's success with the car built more slowly than its legends might suggest. Orders and inquiries flooded into Piquette Avenue, yet only about 300 Ts came off the line in 1908. Henry Ford took the very first one on a trip to the Upper Peninsula, ostensibly to go hunting but more likely to give the Model T a shakedown. With the start of the auto show season in January, the company began inundating newspapers and magazines with pictures of the Model T and breathless press releases designed to stoke demand. Although generating publicity was only just developing into an art form at Ford Motor, by the time the Model T reached full-scale production at the beginning of 1909, the manufacturer's crack sales infrastructure had already brought in more orders than the company could possibly fulfill. What would prove far tougher than attracting customers in the first full year of production was learning how to handle the onslaught of them. "Dealers, who now came [to the factory] hat in hand, were soon a small army," wrote historian Allan Nevins, "and had to obey orders like one. They were told that they must sell off the earlier models on hand before they could deliver a Model T to a customer, and that they must give evidence of booked sales before even one Model T was shipped to them."[61]

Ford Motor even benefited from a small blizzard of controversy kicked up in January 1909 by an advertising campaign launched by one of its competitors, who insisted that a better car could be made for $1,250 than for twice the money. "The incorrectness of the assertion would seem to be not only obvious," sniffed an editorial in the New York Times, "but irritatingly obvious."[62] Even the paper conceded that it was an arresting thought, though. And at this distance of years, it remains one, for on that very thought rested the future of mass productrion in the automobile industry. A cheap car could not be made cheaply and still succeed. At the same time that people were arguing, even in their own minds, the possibility that a $1,250 car could be better than a $2,500 one, the Model T ads were promising an $850 car that was better than a $2,500 one. Or more: one Ford ad noted after listing the Model T's many features that "few of them or their equal found even in its $5,000 competitors."[63]

And Henry Ford was already talking about reducing the T's price without lowering its quality.

6

Model T Mania

"I will build a motor car for the great multitude," Henry Ford proclaimed to the public by way of announcing the conveyance that would change America, and indeed the world. "It will be so low in price," he declared, "that no man making a good salary will be unable to own one—and enjoy with his family the blessing of hours of pleasure in God's greatest open spaces."[1]

It was quite a sales pitch: at the time of the Model T's introduction on October 1, 1908, city dwellers could not enjoy the Lord's pastoral delights unless they could afford the means to escape. Very few could. Ford, however—a populist businessman whose rural roots informed all of his life's work—was selling not just a car but the dream of a better future to workers, farmers, and others generally forgotten by the Automobile Age. Until the Model T, these neglected consumers considered the auto a toy of the rich, a rarefied mode of transportation too costly for their household budgets. Ford destroyed that erroneous notion. "Brigham Young originated mass production," humorist Will Rogers quipped, "but Ford was the guy who improved upon it. He changed the habits of more people than Caesar, Mussolini, Charlie Chaplin, Clara Bow, Xerxes, Amos 'n' Andy, and Bernard Shaw."[2]

For all its promises of freedom and leisure, the horseless carriage's arrival had left more people behind than it carried along, offering the less fortunate no choice but to watch and yearn as automobiles grew progressively bigger, faster, and more ostentatious—and their well-heeled owners proportionately less accommodating to the safety and sensibilities of their pedestrian fellows. "Unfortunately, our millionaires, and especially their idle and degenerate children, have been flaunting their money in the faces of the poor as if actually wishing to provoke them," warned the *North American Review* in a June 1906 article headlined "An Appeal to Our Millionaires" and bylined "X." Decrying that "the rich prefer to buy immense cars which take almost all of a narrow street or road, and to drive them on all streets, narrow or wide, at such speeds as imperils [sic] the lives and limbs of everybody in their path,"[3] the anonymous author equated the automotive set's arrogance with the hauteur of the Paris aristocracy on the eve of the French Revolution.

The anti-auto mood in the United States prior to the Model T's introduction came short of being that revolutionary, even though the zeitgeist looks remarkably hostile in retrospect. In his account of the Model T era, *Henry Ford and Grass-roots America,* historian Reynold M. Wik cites several instances in which rifles were fired at early motorists to frighten them; in one case, reported in the *Minneapolis Journal* of August 9, 1902, a Minnesotan driving a car was shot in the back by locals opposed to the encroachment of the auto. It was not uncommon in those days for disgruntled citizens, especially in the country, to cover roads with broken glass, chains, or logs, or to dig ditches across thoroughfares in efforts to thwart motorists. "The more stubborn farmers urged that cars be barred on country roads, and such laws were enacted in several counties in Pennsylvania and West Virginia. Extremists went further, urging vigilantes to take matters into their own hands," Wik wrote. "Farmers near Sacramento, California, in 1909 dug ditches across several roads to block traffic and actually trapped thirteen cars."[4]

The automobile faced particularly virulent receptions in rural areas, where farmers feared that the new era would put the horse out of business. "A reckless, blood thirsty, villainous lot of purse-proud crazy trespassers," was how the farm magazine *Breeder's Gazette* described owners of the newfangled machines in 1904.[5] (The depiction may have contained an element of truth: the *North American Review* estimated that more Americans had died in car accidents in the first six months of 1906 than had perished in the entire Spanish-American War.)[6]

Novelist Booth Tarkington took note of this early animus against the automobile in his Pulitzer Prize–winning saga of rapacity and deceit, *The Magnificent Ambersons.* Amid a mix of far less open-minded characters, Tarkington's enthusiastic inventor Eugene Morgan speaks about the force of progress represented by his recent entry into the young car industry. He gushes that "the automobile is going to carry city streets clear out to the county line," and when asked if he thinks cars will "change the face of the land," answers, "They're already doing it . . . and it can't be stopped."

At that, the novel's central character—spoiled, selfish, aggressively idle George Amberson Minafer—replies: "Automobiles are a useless nuisance. . . . They'll never amount to anything but a nuisance. They had no business to be invented." In reality, this was a popular stance in the early auto era, reminiscent of the futile rage of the Luddites, who tried to halt England's Industrial Revolution in the early 1800s. In America, the fear of the changes wrought by the automobile was by no means limited to pompous fools like Tarkington's last and least magnificent Amberson.

Yet Tarkington's forward-looking man of action Eugene Morgan proves more than up to the task of defending the era's rush to modernity and the means that would carry it there. "I'm not sure he's wrong about automobiles," the wiser character gently says of his adversary. "With all their speed forward they may be a step backward in civilization—that is, in spiritual civilization. It may be that they will not add to the beauty of the world, nor to the life of men's souls. I am not sure. But automobiles have come, and they bring a greater change in our life than most of us suspect. They are here, and almost all outward things are going to be different because of what they bring. They are going to alter war, and they are going to alter peace. I think men's minds are going to be changed in subtle ways because of automobiles; just how, though, I could hardly guess. But you can't have the immense outward changes that they will cause without some inward ones, and it may be that George is right, and that the spiritual alteration will be bad for us."[7] (The alteration certainly proves bad for George, who gets run over by a car later in the story.)

Tarkington's fiction hints at his own ambivalence on the question of the real and lasting value of the automobile, although in the end it seems clear that he embraced the revolution. But many other authors and journalists warned of the passenger car's potential to foment mayhem and social insurrection. "Nothing has spread socialistic feeling in this country more than use of the automobile," pronounced one prominent educator, author, and social critic in 1906—Woodrow Wilson, then president of Princeton University. The man who seven years later would occupy the White House sensed in the mood of a nation still plagued by poverty a growing impatience with exaggerated wealth and in particular its ostentatious status symbol, the automobile. "They are a picture of the arrogance of wealth, with all its independence and carelessness," the future president averred.[8] Addressing an audience of North Carolinians the same year, Wilson imagined himself in the place of a father whose child had been struck by a hit-and-run driver. "I am a Southerner and know how to shoot," he told the group. "Would you blame me if I did so under such circumstances?"[9]

Henry Ford had no quarrel with Wilson's sense of outrage at those who abused their sense of privilege. He would, however, oppose the college man's conclusion. The answer, Ford believed, was not, as Wilson argued, to do away with the machines, but with the social dichotomy in their ownership. His thrifty Model T would change minds by fulfilling the promise that, as company billboards declared, "Even You Can Afford a Ford."

To promote its new automobile, Ford Motor Company staged a number of public relations stunts. The most daring pitted two Model Ts against three larger cars in a 4,000-mile race across the country, from New York City to Seattle, beginning June 1, 1909. That was the opening day of the Alaska–Yukon–Pacific Exposition in Seattle and the race was also designed to promote the fair. The automotive event came about thanks to Robert Guggenheim, the publicity-minded, auto-mad twenty-nine-year-old heir to one of America's greatest fortunes. Guggenheim brought his charms to bear on no less than President William Howard Taft, convincing him to open the exposition and start the race. On June 1, at 3:00 P.M. in the East and noon in the West, President Taft pressed a golden telegraph key installed in the White House for the purpose of simultaneously opening the fair and starting the race. His signal was sent via Western Union to New York and Seattle. Upon receiving the presidential decree the mayor of New York City fired the starter pistol, and the great race was on.[10]

While the exposition attracted more publicity from Guggenheim's marquee event than its promoters had dared hope for, it proved an even greater marketing windfall for the fledgling automobile industry. One Ford dealer in the Pacific Northwest recalled that "the unbelievable feat of a motor car attempting to cross roadless plains and mountains to far-off Washington, somewhere in the uncivilized West, inspired newsmen to new heights with their stories of a coming new mode of transportation."[11]

Henry Ford and his company's publicists insisted that their lightweight new car was as reliable and rugged as nearly any passenger vehicle on the market, and believed that a victory in the Transcontinental Contest would prove it. By entering two Model T cars in the race it hoped to outlast the bulkier entries from three established automakers—Shawmut, Acme, and Itala. The lightest of them weighed nearly three times as much as the Model T. Conventional wisdom may have favored the bigger cars, but Ford boasted by far the best transcontinental organization, taking advantage of the services of his dealers' mechanics in practically every crossroads town along the 4,106-mile course, which passed through Chicago, Kansas, and Denver before swinging north through Wyoming and Idaho toward Seattle. The Model Ts were thus expertly overhauled along the way—although race rules specifically forbade the replacement of major components. The owners of Ford Motor's farflung dealerships were keenly aware that a victory would help boost Model T sales all over the country. So, naturally, was its chief executive, who followed the race as closely as the nation's most breathless journalists.

Twenty-two days and fifty-five minutes after leaving New York, the first car crossed the finish line. It was Ford Number Two, and Henry Ford was there to congratulate its two drivers—and himself, of course. It took seventeen more hours for the Shawmut to arrive in Seattle to claim second place, followed several hours later by third-finishing Ford Number One, whose drivers—one of them the company's advertising manager, H. B. Harper—had gotten lost twice along the way, losing a day and a half. "For seven days we wore hip boots and rubber coats while the cars labored through Kansas gumbo and Colorado and Wyoming mud and sand," Harper recalled of the harsh conditions facing his entry upon departing from St. Louis in a thunderstorm. "Nor was it a gentle soothing rain," he continued. "It poured. It hailed, and the hailstones were reported to resemble hens' eggs. Some of you may think you have seen it rain. Had you been with us out of Oakley, Kansas, when the hailstones threatened to demolish the car, or in Wyoming when a cloud burst loose, the ordinary rainfall of good old Detroit would seem as but the falling of the dew."[12] The Acme straggled in a week after the winner, while the Itala never made it past Cheyenne.[13] In the aftermath, the Shawmut team cried foul, complaining that Ford dealers had been overly "helpful" with the company's cars, especially near the end of the race. Ford Motor executives shrugged off the criticism and aggressively advertised their car's achievement, distributing thousands of pamphlets telling "The Story of the Race."[14]

Obligated to investigate Shawmut's complaints, the Transcontinental Contest committee disqualified Ford's winning entry in November 1909, five months after the race was over, concluding, "It was proven to the satisfaction of the committee that Ford Car No. 2 . . . traveled a part of the distance between New York and Seattle with an engine which was substituted in place of the engine stamped in New York by the technical committee of the Automobile Club of America." The Shawmut car was declared the official winner of the Transcontinental Contest, although any good its maker might have derived from the triumph had already become moot. By November the car was no longer in production because the Shawmut company was in the throes of bankruptcy. Meanwhile, demand for the Model T had grown so strong that the company found itself unable to keep up with its own success, which would remain the case for at least the next fifteen years. The Transcontinental Contest revealed how the company was changing in other ways, too. For all James Couzens's constant admonitions about playing by the rules in business dealings, the organization had become ever more accustomed to giving Henry Ford what he wanted—in this case a first-place finish—no matter what. According to one Ford dealer called upon to "help" along the race route, there didn't seem to be any choice in the matter.[15]

Philip Van Doren Stern pointed out in *Tin Lizzie: The Story of the Fabulous Model T Ford* that in 1908 American financier J. P. Morgan offered his outlook on the economy by quoting his father's sage investment advice: "Any man who is a bear on the future of this country will go broke."[16] As Stern observed: "In 1908 the United States had a population of 87,189,392, and more than half its people lived in the country or in very small towns. Gas lighting had been in use for nearly a century; electricity was available in urban areas; the telegraph had been established since long before the Civil War; and the telephone was making rapid headway with 6,437,000 instruments already installed. On the roads at the end of 1908 were about 200,000 automobiles, of which about one third had been produced during the year. Their numbers were increasing steadily, and—except in remote parts of the country—they were no longer a curiosity." Yet most gasoline was still "bought in open cans from hardware dealers," and even though the nation boasted "2,151,570 miles of public roads, only 153,662 miles—hardly more than 7%—were even called 'improved.'"[17]

Morgan was right to encourage bullishness. It was certainly appropriate to the automobile industry. The number of cars registered in the United States grew from some 8,000 in 1900 to nearly half a million in 1910.[18] Motorists were enjoying a brand-new freedom—the freedom to go anywhere they wanted, anytime—and the Model T led the way.[19] The appeal of Ford's "car for the great multitude" lay not merely in its dramatically low cost, but in its durability, ease of driving, and simplicity to maintain. Model Ts were *practical* cars with which people could improve their lives and expand their horizons, as so many owners discovered. One farmer's wife from Rome, Georgia, could have been referring literally as well as figuratively to her family's Model T when she wrote to Henry Ford in 1918, "Your car lifted us out of the mud. It brought joy into our lives."[20]

Women embraced the Model T with as much enthusiasm as men. It was easier to operate than most other gasoline-powered cars, a fact Ford Motor took care to promote. As a company publication explained, "There is no complex shifting of gears to bother the driver. In fact there is very little machinery about the car—none that a woman cannot understand in a few minutes and learn to control with very little practice."[21] Although Clara Ford drove an electric car, her husband's company recognized that women constituted a vast untapped sales market. It published, in fact, a publicity pamphlet titled "The Woman and the Ford" linking the suffragist movement to the Model T. "It has broadened her horizon—increased her pleasures—given new vigor to her body—made neighbors of faraway friends—and multiplied tremendously her range of activity," the Model T pamphlet boasted. "It is a real weapon in the changing order. More than any other—the Ford's is a woman's car."[22]

Stories of women's heroics behind the wheel appeared regularly in the *Ford Times,* the magazine published throughout the Model T era by the automaker and distributed free of charge to its dealers and customers. In 1913, Margaret

Wilfley, the daughter of a Washington, D.C., minister, sent Ford Motor the following account of her first attempt to operate a Model T.

> It has never been our good fortune to own a gasoline car, so I know very little about machines. While walking down a very steep hill here in Washington, the cry of a woman aroused me. Glancing up, I saw a Ford car starting down the hill, with no one at the wheel. A little child was in the front seat, and a woman in the rear one. The child, while climbing about the car had loosened the brake, and the car had started. Several men were standing about, but no one of them seemed to realize the danger. The car by this time was some little distance from me, but I threw down my books and fairly flew after it. Fortunately, one of the doors was open so I easily jumped in, although the car was moving rapidly. At first I could only steer it, but then I struck the right pedal and stopped it. I just wanted to tell you how the simplicity of your machine enabled me to save the two.[23]

Ruth Calkins of Rochester, New York, ignored repeated attempts to dissuade her from making automobile trips without a man to attend to the mechanical matters, touring the northeastern United States and southern Ontario for a month in 1912 with three female friends.[24] Calkins proved a sterling driver, such that even when the car sank nearly to its axles in mud she managed to ease it out with careful cunning rather than the shoulder power of her companions. As Calkins and other women found out, an exhilarating sense of independence could be had behind the wheel of an automobile.[25] "The motor-car has returned the romance of travel," novelist Edith Wharton gushed in her 1908 memoir *A Motor-Flight Through France*. "Freeing us from all the compulsions and contacts of the railway, the bondage to fixed hours and the beaten track, the approach to each town through the area of ugliness created by a railway itself, it has given us back the wonder, the adventure, and the novelty which enlivened the way of our posting grandparents."[26]

If the Model T was the simplest of gas-engine cars to operate, its secret lay with its "planetary" transmission and braking system: both were controlled entirely through pedals on the floor, leaving the driver's hands free for steering. As Robert Lacey, author of *Ford: The Men and the Machine* described it, the car's planetary mechanism was "a primitive sort of automatic gear, worked by three footpedals: a brake, a pedal for forward, and a pedal for reverse. Orchestrating them was an acquired art, rather like playing the organ. . . . But once mastered, all sorts of tricks became available—notably the capacity to shoot straight from forward into reverse, thus making it possible to 'rock' the car out of a pothole."[27] Almost anyone could drive a T for hours without exhaustion, and the little Ford could travel just about anywhere—over paved city streets and rough country roads, up hills, through mud—in all kinds of weather. First, however, the engine had to be started.

Prior to Cadillac's introduction of Charles F. Kettering's electric starter in 1912,[28] all gasoline engines required an initial boost to get them running. When the Model T came on the market, that boost came from man, not machine, through the operation of a crank at the front of the car—not unlike the cord one yanks to start a lawn mower. Some people of smaller stature had trouble, however, working the crank-starter without help. An even graver drawback to using a crank was that it could be downright dangerous. As *American Heritage* magazine editor Richard F. Snow recalled, his father, Richard B. Snow—who once had the honor of playing his violin in front of Henry Ford—used to tell of the time his Model T attacked his brother. According to the elder Mr. Snow, the car "pulled its ugly trick of spinning the starting crank back around when the engine caught and broke his wrist."[29]

The Model T could have had an electric starter after the device was introduced in 1912, but Henry Ford did not want to install the battery needed to power it. Although Ford Motor finally offered a battery-powered electric starter as an option in the mid-1920s, many observers felt that in the interim the Model T lost sales to potential customers—including many in the vehicle's targeted female market—who either could not or did not want to have to exert themselves that much to start a car. In any case, many customers installed starters as aftermarket items.

Across America, the grating, grinding noise a Model T engine made when being coaxed to start up came to serve as an unwelcome extra alarm clock for the neighbors of Ford owners. In the opening scene of his 1922 novel *Babbitt,* for instance, Sinclair Lewis describes the eponymous protagonist waking up in his Zenith, Indiana, bedroom to "the familiar and irritating rattle of someone cranking a Ford: snap-ah-ah, snap-ah-ah. . . . The infernal patient snap-ah-ah— a round flat sound, a shivering cold morning sound, a sound infuriating and inescapable."[30]

In *Ham on Rye,* a semiautobiographical novel of growing up in California in the late 1920s, iconoclastic novelist Charles Bukowski relates his own tale about the shortcomings of the T's crank on a nightmarish Sunday picnic excursion near Los Angeles with his German immigrant father. The elder Bukowski had determined that any orange tree they encountered was fair game for poaching. Having happened upon an orange grove, the two were in the process of filling their large picnic basket with plundered fruit when a tall, angry farmer suddenly arrived on the scene with a shotgun. "Get out of my orchard," the farmer shouted, pointing the shotgun at them and their vehicle and demanding, "Get that god-damned cracker-box started!"[31] The senior Bukowski, overmatched in both bulk and weaponry, began feverishly twisting the Model T's crank—to no avail, for what seemed a very long time. When the engine finally turned over, father and son sped away down a dusty trail, glad to be alive. "I had never seen him drive the car that fast," Charles Bukowski recalled.[32]

The arrival of the Model T in hinterland cities like Omaha and Denver was an event as eagerly anticipated as a Billy Sunday evangelical revival or Buffalo Bill's Wild West Show. Actually selling the new Ford—or any car, for that matter—to the millions of committed horse-and-buggyers who populated the country, however, took both patience and a certain amount of courage. In his wonderfully evocative memoir *Me and the Model T,* Ford dealer Roscoe Sheller of Sunnyside, Washington, wrote of the adventure of selling a Tin Lizzie, as the T was nicknamed, in the American West in 1915, when horses were still the mode of choice and prospective customers had no clue as to how to drive a car. All too many of these tyro test drivers blithely ran past turns and over corners, shouting a loud "Whoa!" instead of applying the brake, and when that didn't work they would jerk the steering wheel in the wrong direction and "freeze to it with the strength of Samson before he had a haircut," Sheller recalled. "I could no more break [the driver's] panic-seized grip than Cleopatra could have tossed an elephant across the Nile."[33]

Teaching an equestrian lot of would-be motorists to drive on the rutted wagon roads of south-central Washington took real fortitude. Sheller's students smashed into everything from ancient sequoias to wooden posts and barbed-wire fences, far too often coming "only inches from a messy death." When such mishaps began to rack up "sickening" repair bills as well as lost sales for his Ford dealership, Sheller adopted a new policy: "I became convinced that it might be wiser to collect full payment for the car *before* attempting driving instructions," he explained in his book. "Then, in case of accident, crumpled fenders, smashed radiators and jack-knifed axles it would be the instructee's responsibility, not mine." Sheller reported that he soon noticed a marked increase in the attentiveness of his clients, remarking, "[The driver's] neck seemed of less importance than damage to his wallet."[34]

The Model T's main selling point was, of course, the low price charged for such a strong, large, and versatile car. The price appeared even more attractive when the scant cost of operating the car was factored into the new Ford's overall value for the dollar. That the Model T could be maintained so inexpensively further fueled the public's raging love affair with the sturdy little runabout. In a period when the *New York Times* was reporting that it cost $1,500 per year to operate an automobile, Model T owners could boast of annual operating expenses less than $100.[35] A well-kept Ford was said to cost about a penny per mile to run—or, as one thrifty fellow noted in the March 1912 *Ford Times,* one fourth of a penny per occupant when his entire family rode along. H. R. Worrall of New Hampton, Iowa, then took his calculations another step, comparing the cost of driving his Model T with that of his former preferred mode of locomotion: walking. Covering a thousand miles on foot cost him $10 in shoes, Worrall figured, but it cost only $7.71 to drive the same distance in his new Model T Torpedo Runabout.[36]

—————

As the swelling numbers of proud new Model T owners learned to master their machines, the old Tin Pan Alley tune "In My Merry Oldsmobile" gave way to singing the praises of Henry Ford's humble new car for the masses, also affectionately dubbed the "flivver" or the "jalopy." Song pluggers and vaudeville troupers began showcasing clever songs such as "The Little Ford Rambled Right Along" (1914) and Jack Frost's "You Can't Afford to Marry, If You Can't Afford a Ford" (1915).[37] The intoxicating feeling that came with driving such a novel vehicle for the first time inspired what might be called "Model T mania," to which even the worldliest sophisticates did not prove immune. Grace Hegger Lewis, widow of 1930 Nobel Prize for Literature recipient Sinclair Lewis, revealed in her memoirs that the greatest thrill of her august husband's life had come when he pulled up in front of their house in his first Model T touring car and inquired of his family, "How about a little ride?"[38] He was so enthralled with his motorcar, in fact, that he penned a highway-romance novel based on the couple's cross-country jaunt in the Model T as newlyweds in 1916. Published in 1919 as *Free Air,* this clever hybrid of the dime store Western and the gothic romance offered Lewis's thinly fictionalized account of his escape with Grace from Minneapolis–St. Paul to Seattle. In it, as the young bride navigates the little car over the deep-rutted roads of rural Minnesota, she describes the pair's automotive adventure as their "voyage into democracy."[39]

The tale of another young bridegroom's seduction by Model T rings stranger than Lewis's fiction. The story goes that Henry A. Wallace, who would later serve as one of Franklin D. Roosevelt's vice presidents, was a promising agricultural engineer when he married his sweetheart in 1914. Most of his acquaintances considered him a sober young man, so it must have come as a surprise when upon exiting his wedding ceremony he made a beeline not for a place to be alone with his bride, but for the Model T his father had given the couple as a wedding present. The bridegroom hopped behind the wheel for what everyone assumed would be a test drive around the block while the bridal party and their guests waited—and waited, and then waited some more. The usually clearheaded Wallace returned in the late afternoon, his wife later recalled, greeting her with a cheery, "Get in—I'd forgotten you!"[40]

Another renowned Model T enthusiast was far better known for his aviation exploits: Charles A. Lindbergh. In his book *Boyhood on the Upper Mississippi,* a collection of retrospective letters he wrote for the Minnesota Historical Society, Lindbergh clearly recalled the day in 1912 when his father had purchased a Ford Model T tourabout, equipped with the "standard foot-pedal gearshift, four cylinder engine, smooth-faced clincher-rim tires, carbide headlights, hand crank, squeeze rubber-bulb horn, folding waterproof cloth top, and quick fasten-on side curtains for rainy days."[41] His mother dubbed the car "Maria" and it was to make a lasting impression on the future aviator. "Before Maria arrived," Lindbergh wrote in 1969, automobiles "seemed almost as separate from our everyday lives as a show up on a stage. The fact that *my* father had bought an automobile was startling and amazing. It took my mother and me a long time to get accustomed to this new member of our family."[42]

Soon enough, the eleven-year-old Lindbergh was piloting Maria at a perilous 25 miles per hour along the unpaved, deeply rutted, and often icy roads of northern Minnesota, in pursuit of groceries in Brainerd or on visits to friends in St. Cloud. "I had become fascinated by automobiles in general and by Maria in particular," he wrote. His account told of lengthy attempts to start up the car in cold weather, of getting her stuck in sand, changing her flat tires, and having to lay tree limbs over mud holes so Maria could make it across. But his most vivid (and prescient) memory was of his father behind the wheel while he stood atop the family Ford's wide running board, hanging on by the struts supporting the car's folding top. "I could pick leaves off branches as we passed, and sometimes when the going was slow, scoop up a stone from the road," the flier recalled, adding, "I liked the wind on my face and through my hair. It was much more fun than riding inside."[43]

The advent of any new vehicle offers the promise of opening up virgin territories for exploration. But the versatility and economy of the Model T made the proposition even more tempting than did other cars of the time, inspiring a new fad: the automobile vacation. Some drivers took to calling the Model T the "Hotel Ford" in tribute to the ease with which travelers could equip the conveyance for camping.[44] The upper half of the car's split windshield, for example, folded down horizontally to create a table—one that could be rendered more elegant by covering it with a cloth to conceal any splattered insects still adhering to the glass.[45]

Elegance certainly seems to have figured into the most celebrated Model T camping trips: those mounted by the founder of Ford Motor himself. These occasional excursions began in 1918 with the professed purpose of affording "vagabonds" Henry Ford, Thomas Edison, Harvey Firestone, and John Burroughs a chance to unwind in the semiwilderness. A renowned naturalist, Burroughs was the relative pauper of the group. "Those who meet Mr. Ford are almost invariably drawn to him," Burroughs wrote in his account of the camping trips in a 1921 book entitled *Under the Maples*. "He is a national figure, and the crowds that flock around the car in which he is riding, as we pause in the towns through which we pass, are not paying their homage merely to a successful car builder, or businessman, but to a beneficent great practical idealist, whose goodwill and spirit of universal helpfulness they have all felt."[46] The self-appointed scribe of these treks, Burroughs was fond of calling them "strenuous holidays." Roughing it, however, hardly describes these rustic outings; the foursome were generally accompanied by a retinue of vehicles driven by chauffeurs and attendants. They used a specially outfitted Model T as a mobile kitchen with a refrigerator to store fresh eggs and ribeye steaks. Their dining table, which sat twenty guests comfortably under a canopy, even hosted presidents Calvin Coolidge and Herbert Hoover on separate occasions.

What's more, as David L. Lewis revealed in *The Public Image of Henry Ford,* this quartet of aging adventurers was everywhere "chaperoned by newsmen and photographers who reported each camper's every move and hung on his every utterance." Ford Motor even sent its own film crew along on the treks to capture history in the making. It was a cunning public relations move. Motion picture theaters all over America soon showed Ford, Edison, Firestone, and Burroughs "engaging in high-kicking, stair-jumping, sprinting, tree-chopping, and tree-climbing contests." And newspaper editors everywhere embraced the adventurers, running bold headlines like "Millions of Dollars Worth of Brains off on a Vacation," "Genius to Sleep Under Stars," "Kings of Industry and Inventor Paid City Visit," and "Henry Ford Demonstrates He's Not Afraid of Work; Repairs His Damaged Car." In his *My Life and Work,* Ford claimed that "the trips were good fun, except that they began to attract too much attention." Yet it was Ford who ordered verbatim reports typed up for him of every related newspaper story from the states traversed by the vagabonds. The Henry Ford Museum and Library, in fact, retains hundreds of clippings documenting the wilderness exploits of this dynamic quartet.[47] These vivid reports, along with detailed itineraries, have been collected by historian Norman Brauer and self-published in a massive tome titled *There to Breathe the Beauty* (1995). There are wonderful photographs of Ford at the 1915 Pan-Pacific Exposition in San Francisco, standing in front of the Firestone Corporation Pittsburgh branch in 1918, and fixing his boots in the Catskill Mountains in 1919, among dozens of others.[48] Studying this archival data on the trips reemphasizes what Ford executive Charles Sorensen wrote in his memoirs about the camping trips: "With squads of newswriters and platoons of cameramen to report and film the posed nature studies of the four eminent campers, these well-equipped excursions were as private and secluded as a Hollywood opening, and Ford appreciated the publicity."[49]

Ford's company was still reaping the benefits of the trips heading into its centennial in 2003. Over jerky, black-and-white newsreel footage of the "vagabond" excursions, Chairman and CEO William Clay Ford Jr. described the trips on a 2002 television commercial, touting his forebears' "invention" of today's ubiquitous sport-utility vehicle. "My two great-grandfathers, Henry Ford and Harvey Firestone, used to take these camping trips every year with Thomas Edison and whoever the president at the time was," Bill Ford Jr. said wryly in the ad. "They called themselves 'the vagabonds.' They sort of invented SUVs. . . . If you think about it, prior to the Model T, most people never traveled more than twenty miles from home in an entire lifetime."[50]

The *Ford Times* chronicled the adventures of many less celebrated Model T wanderers. None were national news, of course. But they were the stuff of banner headlines in hundreds of thousands of individual households all over the world. The publication offered, for example, the story of Mr. and Mrs. Harvey Harper of Phoenix, Arizona, whose 1912 road trip qualified them as pioneers of the family vacation. Setting off from home with their five small children, the couple drove their Ford all the way to the city of Eureka, deep in northern California's ancient redwood country, without ever staying at a hotel. The Harpers conceded in the *Ford Times* that upon arriving in Eureka their trusty Model T was covered with mud, from top to bottom.[51]

In 1910, the company's house organ related the experiences of E. Roger Stearns, a Ford Motor employee who drove from Los Angeles to San Diego—not a terribly difficult trip—and then made the far more harrowing passage through Devil's Canyon to El Centro, California, near the Mexican border. He reported that his Model T handled the tricky mountain roads, rocky canyons, and abundant sand without a single glitch.[52] Had he suffered any problems, of course, Stearns might not have found it so easy to sell ten cars just like his to the El Centro residents who greeted him.

Indeed, the more challenging the terrain, the more Model T owners seemed to relish tackling it to prove their cars' worthiness. *Ford Times* contributor A. B. Foote, for instance, wrapped the tires on his T Roadster with rope, then drove the car up Truckee Summit near Lake Tahoe in the early spring of 1911. Stout towrope and tackle helped rescue Foote's Ford from several deep sinkholes, and at one point he reported, "it was necessary to pull the car across a treacherous mountain stream, by stretching a heavy rope over the water and pulling the car across on pulleys."[53] Nonetheless, Foote and his sturdy Model T accomplished the ascent, to the driver's own admitted amazement.

The *Ford Times* likewise set out to dispel the perception, common in the early Automobile Age, that older motorists might find the vehicles physically difficult to operate. Surely that could not be the case, Ford Motor's internal publication proclaimed in 1912, if "the world's oldest [automobile] owner," Robert Allison—who in 1898 had become the first person to buy a car (a

Duryea) in the United States—could still enjoy driving his Model T at the age of eighty-six.[54]

An astonishing number of those who roved the countryside in a Model T chose to share the exhilaration of the experience in the *Ford Times* or other publications. One of the most compelling of these accounts, down to the last splatter of mud, appeared in the company periodical under the byline of none other than Henry and Clara Ford's only child, Edsel, who drove a Model T runabout from Detroit to Chicago in 1913, when he was nineteen years old. Like any other motorist of the era, the scion of Ford Motor Company had to contend with a vexing dearth of paved roads, decipherable maps, and decent roadside restaurants.

Somewhere past Ypsilanti, Michigan, heading west, Edsel Ford and his un-named companion came to a stop before a good-size creek over which several men were building a bridge. "They said that some wagons and carriages were able to drive through the creek, but all automobiles were compelled to go around several miles through a back way," the young Ford wrote in the company magazine. "We thought that rather than lose so much time, we would try driving through the stream, so we backed up far enough to get a good start, and thought by speeding we could force our way through. But for our wise thoughts we received two wettings. First, when the radiator hit the water it sent a shower all over us, and then by stalling the motor right in the center of the creek, we had to climb out into cold water up to our waists and push for shore. At first the car would not move an inch, but by much tugging and pulling we managed to get near enough to shore so that the crank was up out of water. Then all we had to do was crank for half an hour to get the water out of the carburetor, and finally she started."[55] No one but Edsel Ford would have been allowed to admit in the *Ford Times* that a Model T ever would not start, even if it was underwater at the time.

Whether the townspeople encountered along the way were aware that one of the little car's occupants was Henry Ford's son is not known. Edsel proba-bly did not betray his identity; he was anything but spoiled, and as such prob-ably would not have wanted to attract any special attention because of his family ties. Nevertheless, unwanted attention is exactly what he and his pal attracted in one rural Michigan town when their arrival coincided with that of the afternoon train. "The streets of Paw Paw, like all other towns we passed through the day, were lined with farmers and [horse-drawn] carriages," Edsel Ford wrote, when a loud noise suddenly disturbed the pastoral scene. He continued, "We don't know whether it was the noise of our exhaust or the train, but one or the other scared a horse, who turned around so quickly in the road that he upset the buggy and threw out the two occupants. . . . Well, we did not wait very long in that town, for, as a rule, farmers do not love automo-biles."

After losing their way shortly after that in the deep sand outside South Bend, Indiana, the young travelers opted to follow another motorist to Chicago for the final leg of their journey. "On arriving at the hotel we were very nearly arrested for leaving the car for more than ten minutes in front of the hotel," young Ford concluded. "That was a poor finish for such an enjoyable ride as ours."[56]

America's farmers may have been slow to accept the inevitability of the automobile as an abstraction, but they quickly embraced the Model T, the first vehicle to cater to rural needs. In 1912, *The Farmer* magazine conducted a study of car ownership in Minnesota's agricultural areas for the years 1909 and 1911. The results indicated the rural appeal of the little Ford. The article reported that in 1909, a year after the Model T was introduced, there were 191 Ford cars in towns with populations of 1,000 or fewer; two years later the number of Fords in those areas had grown to 1,187, outdistancing the second-most popular make, the Buick, which had 734 cars in the same region. The magazine's survey also showed that in towns numbering between 10,000 and 20,000 people, Ford ownership had soared anywhere from three to twenty times more than it had been two years earlier.[57]

The Model T's popularity in farm districts owed largely to the car's capacity to render rural life more bearable. Farm living had, of course, never actually jibed with its popular bucolic image as demanding but honest work leavened by an assortment of simple pastoral pleasures. In reality, most farmwork was hard, tedious, and not at all lucrative considering the effort put into it, making the few modern comforts that were available in rural areas unaffordable for most farm families. Even those long accustomed to the everyday hardships of agricultural work couldn't help but envy such amenities of modern city life as electric appliances and telephones. Central heating, indoor plumbing, and hot-water heaters had become standard in all but the poorest urban housing during the Model T's first decade—but not on the farm.

A younger generation of Americans in search of a less hardscrabble existence had therefore begun to abandon their families' farms for jobs in the big city, a choice Henry Ford could certainly understand. "I suspected that much might be done in a better way," Ford explained in his autobiography. "I have followed many a weary mile behind a plow, and I know the drudgery of it."[58]

After Henry Ford grew up and ran as fast and as far away from the farm and its chores as possible, he would do as much as any individual ever has to alleviate that drudgery for others. His company's affordable Model Ts went far to help modernize farming practices as well as rural life overall, for sturdy Ford cars and trucks could be used both for transportation and as tireless iron workhorses. Simply by attaching a belt to the vehicle's crankshaft or rear axle, a farmer gained a power source capable of a multitude of tasks—"grinding grain, sawing wood, filling silos, churning butter, shearing sheep, pumping water, elevating grain, shelling corn, turning grindstones and washing clothes," among others, according to historian Reynold M. Wik, whose own family employed a Model T for all manner of purposes on their South Dakota farm. "In butchering hogs," Wik explained, "the power from a car could be utilized to hoist the pig out of the hot water in the scalding barrel. In the fields, the Model Ts pulled hay rakes, mowers, grain binders, harrows, and hay loaders."[59]

They served in less obvious ways as well. For many rural folk, the isolation of farm life made depression and mental illness common among rural residents. The distance from others—although often only a few miles—denied people regular social interaction. Some farm folk felt fortunate if they were able to flee the confines of their own land more than a few times a year; after all, no humane master would work a team of horses in the fields all day and then hitch the weary beasts up again to take the family out visiting in the evening. An automobile, however, had no such limitations. "Best of all," the *Ford Times* boasted of the Model T, "it has remodeled the social life of the country."[60] One farm woman eagerly recounted how her whole world had opened up since she had acquired her Ford, which allowed her to work in the cornfield in the morning, do housework in the afternoon, and then drive thirty miles into town and back for a band concert at night. The advent of the Model T proved such a spur to rural sociability, in fact, that one farm magazine reported that the cars' presence actually lowered productivity on certain farms where the vehicle was in constant use, all right—primarily for pleasure rides.

The genius in the Model T's design was that the car could be adapted to almost any use, be it as a portable power source around the farm, a delivery van for rural mail carriers, or a traveling salesman's trustworthiest colleague. One man in Seattle turned his into a rolling restaurant.[61] Trainmen fitted their Fords with metal wheels and rode them on the rails. With custom bodies, Model Ts turned into taxis, buses, trucks, fire engines, and police cars. They hauled prisoners and hay, livestock and tourists, and just about anything else people might want to tote about.

Of course, even the proletarian T wasn't *all* serious. Perhaps the most colorful of the car's new uses was for "auto polo," a bizarre sport briefly in vogue around 1913 in which stripped-down Model Ts took the place of polo ponies, their drivers circling around one another while mallet-wielding strikers mounted on each steed's running boards attempted to whack a large ball through a wide goal. Concocted by a Ford dealer in Wichita, Kansas, auto polo flared in popularity and before long was being played before crowds at

New York City's Madison Square Garden.[62] By all accounts, the action was certainly exciting—but unfortunately deadly as well. As players grew more adept and aggressive, rollovers became commonplace. So many people were killed playing auto polo that several states, including New York, passed laws banning it. Ford dealers were urged to discourage it as well on grounds of foolhardiness, and the sport pretty much disappeared after 1915.

Model T racing, on the other hand, developed into a respected specialty on the track, with independent manufacturers offering an array of parts designed to boost the vehicles' performance. Many owners, however, needed nothing more than an open road and another car to get a race going. One driver of a Stafford recalled his duel with a Model T: "He had a half-mile start on me and just when I got within about a hundred yards of him one of my lights jarred out and I had to stop. He'll never get done blowing about beating my Stafford with his little old Ford,"[63] grumped the hard-luck loser, who would go on to win rather bigger races of a different variety, ironically enough setting up his legacy as the very symbol of improbable victory: Harry S Truman.

For others the Model T didn't have to be fast. It was just the cheapest transportation they could find for long-mileage trips. "I sent my wife and daughter home on the train," Ray Kroc, the McDonald's founder, said in 1968, describing a devastating business failure during Florida's real estate boom in the 1920s, "and I drove back to Chicago in a Model T Ford. I left in September 1926. I will never forget that drive as long as I live. I was stone broke, I didn't have an overcoat, a topcoat or a pair of gloves. I drove into Chicago on icy streets. When I got home, I was frozen stiff, disillusioned and broke."[64] The Model T was more than a vehicle; it was a memory.

By the time the Model T phenomenon crested in the early 1920s, the car accounted for two thirds of all the automobiles in the United States, making the name "Ford" virtually synonymous with "car." At large-capacity events such as baseball and football games, stadium parking lots swelled so full of Ts that nobody could find his or her own, even though in its first five years in production the Model T could be had in red, green, gray, or dark blue as well as basic black.[65] The very ubiquity of Ford Motor's "people's car" turned the Model T into comic fodder for all manner of wags, most notably legions of self-satisfied Ford owners. They delighted in needling the swells that their luxury cars no longer enjoyed the exclusive run of the nation's roadways. One such jape went as follows:

Irate Owner [to Chauffeur]: John, pass that pesky Ford. This dust is awful.
Chauffeur: Here we go, sir, but there's not much use; there'll be another one right ahead.[66]

Nor did Ford devotees refrain from tweaking their fellow automobilists for squandering money on vehicles superior to the Model T in price only:

> Two brothers each received a legacy of $2,000. Frank, the haughty one, bought a large six-cylinder luxury car. On the way home, he was passed by his brother Ed, driving a Model T. In the driveway, Frank looked down on his brother's Ford, and said, "Good Lord, Ed, what makes the rattling noise I heard coming out of that thing?"
>
> "That's the $1,500 rolling around in my pocket," said the Ford owner.[67]

The majority of Model T jokes, though, tended to be self-deprecating, often poking fun at the car's notable quirks. Henry Ford didn't mind: he considered any mention of his products free publicity, and knew that for the agile, there's no such thing as bad publicity. He never objected to jests like:

> It's easy to gauge your speed in a Model T. When you go ten miles an hour, your lamps rattle, when you get up to twenty miles an hour, the fenders rattle, at twenty-five miles, the windshield begins to rattle, and when you go faster than that, your bones rattle.[68]

Or:

> A thrifty housewife sent a suitcase full of empty cans to Detroit and received a very nice letter: "Madam, in accordance with your instructions, we are sending you one Ford car, along with eight tin cans which were left over."[69]

Or:

> When you find a Ford hogging the road ahead of you, don't try to skirt around it. Just wait until it strikes a bump and then go right on *under* it.[70]

———

Even as the Model T was attaining its cultlike popularity in the United States, the nation's most successful automaker refused to remain content with simply dominating the U.S. market. Ford Motor had first reached north across the border to try selling its cars in Canada in October 1904—just over one year after the company's founding—by establishing Ford Motor Company of Canada Ltd., based in Walkerville, Ontario. Launching a foreign subsidiary might have seemed an awfully ambitious endeavor for so young a company, but the Canadian market's proximity was simply too tantalizing to resist. Delegated to the purview of Ford executive (and native Ontarian) Gordon McGregor, the Canadian operation was set up in an old redbrick carriage maker building along Riverside Drive in Walkerville. It was an entirely separate corporation that would independently manufacture and distribute Ford cars patterned as closely after the U.S. models as the tougher strictures of Canadian law would permit. However, Canada was only the start for the new subsidiary. "McGregor's first job was to get the infant company off to a good start," writer Angus Munro recalled. "He had traded 51 percent of the shares in the new enterprise for the Ford patent rights and selling privileges to all parts of the British Empire except Great Britain and Ireland." During November 1904 Ford of Canada assembled its first car. A year later it had its first overseas sale—to Calcutta, India.[71]

By the time the Model T came on the scene, Ford Motor Company had operations based in London and Paris as well, with agencies or distribution points in twenty more cities around the world. The company's first overseas assembly plant opened in Manchester, England, in 1911, by which time active Ford dealerships were up and running from St. Petersburg, Russia, to Kuala Lumpur, Malaya, and São Paulo, Brazil. In 1912, Ford Motor was shipping some 300 cars abroad every month—ten times as many as any other U.S. automaker, and enough to create a critical shortage of space on outbound steamships.[72]

With the possible exception of the Singer sewing machine, no U.S.-made mechanical device had ever been so widely distributed around the globe. By 1910 the *Ford Times* could proudly report that the Model T was the very first automobile to be sold not only in Kuala Lumpur but also in Turkey and even in such far-flung island locales as Barbados, Mauritius, and Newfoundland. The article continued: "Naked little urchins on the narrow streets of Bombay dodge the rapidly moving cars. Scantily clothed Ethiopian giants pilot tourist-laden Ford cars through the mining districts of South Africa. The Sphinx, if he [sic] were to speak, would comment on the horseless steed of vanadium steel that so frequently is seen before it. . . . The narrow Jinrikisha roads of the new Japan are being rebuilt so that the pleasures of the American automobile may be enjoyed."[73]

The appeal of the company's products overseas extended beyond the general public. Pancho Villa, the Mexican revolutionary leader pursued by the Wilson administration for crossing the Rio Grande and killing U.S. citizens, used a Model T on his escapes into the mountains of northern Mexico.[74] (That very Model T owned by Villa played itself in a 1934 Hollywood take on the outlaw's exploits, *Viva Villa*. Another early T was used the same year in *The Life of Vergie Winters*, starring Ann Harding.)[75] Famed African missionary Marie Nelson attached a loudspeaker to her Model T to preach the gospel in Angola from her front seat. A Chinese newspaper editor reported that in his country the terms "automobile" and "Model T" had become synonymous.[76] And a Model T Ford wound up the only car among forty-five manufacturers' entries to finish a grueling endurance run sponsored by Russia's Imperial War Department in 1912,[77] when that country's government was considering its first large-scale automobile purchase. (It is indicative of the conditions under which they competed that each car had to be accompanied by a truck carrying supplies, including gasoline.) After the Ford entry finished the course all alone, Czar Nicholas II personally inspected the Model T and later successfully recommended the car to his nation's armed forces.[78] Before long Russian parents took to naming their children Fordson, while across the nation the neologism "Fordize" came to be used to mean "Americanize."[79]

In the many foreign nations where gasoline was prohibitively expensive or hard to find, the Model T endeared itself to consumers by delivering better mileage per gallon than almost any other make of car. In countries suffering road conditions worse than those in the United States, sometimes far worse, the Ford's flexible chassis and high ground clearance proved indispensable; where other cars easily became mired in snow or sand, the Model T's fine balance, light weight, and surprising power kept motorists sturdily on their way. "Nothing on the Kashmir road can compete in any way with the Ford," a Model T owner in India wrote to the *Ford Times* in 1913. "I have had on every occasion four passengers and luggage and I averaged 31 miles to the gallon of gasoline."[80]

The Model T attained its renown, both here and abroad, thanks to Henry Ford's ability to satisfy a far more exigent audience than those who could afford to buy any car: people who could afford to buy only one car. "There is no keener critic than the motorist for whom these vehicles have been constructed," wrote Englishman Alex Gray of the Model T phenomenon. "He cannot afford to waste his substance in riotous experimenting. . . . He wants the cheapest possible car, but he wants to be sure that the last three-penny-piece of his expenditure is coming back to him—with interest, if possible."[81]

It didn't hurt that the Model T's additional virtues held sway with wealthier clients, too. "I own four automobiles," wrote the president of a Brooklyn, New York, iron company in 1909, "costing from fifteen hundred dollars to seven thousand dollars each, and have had more service out of this little Ford Car, which only cost me a thousand dollars, and had less trouble with it, than with any of the other makes."[82] Even some of Ford's harshest critics eventually succumbed to the allure of the company's sensible, hardworking mass-market car and its visionary founder. In 1918, erstwhile auto opponent President Woodrow Wilson not only bought a Model T but also stood among the first politicians to encourage Henry Ford to run for elective office.

Yet the sweep of Ford's influence on the nation a decade after his Model T's introduction hardly required validation from any electorate. His car had opened the American landscape, altered the outlook of consumers everywhere, and forever changed the way automobiles would be manufactured and sold. Even more important, Henry Ford had silenced the fear mongers who cried that the interests of the many would be ground beneath the advancing wheels of full-bore capitalism in the hands of the few. Leading the country in bold new directions even its president could not foresee, Ford would use the T to turn the entire American manufacturing process toward the benefit of the "great multitude." His Model T was only the groundwork for a system that would change the expectations of the American worker.

7

Fordism

The incorporated town of Highland Park, Michigan, is shaped like a cockeyed square and sits within Detroit's city limits about six miles northwest of the heart of downtown. Detroit's main thoroughfare, Woodward Avenue, runs all the way from downtown straight through Highland Park. Other city streets traverse the town, too, but early in the twentieth century most of its landscape was just flat, open space. Before the arrival of Ford Motor, Highland Park boasted a population of 425, plus perhaps that many horses, courtesy of the town's racetrack.[1]

Today, six miles hardly qualifies as a long distance, but in 1906 when Ford Motor chose the racetrack property as the site of its new factory, the company might as well have been going to Toledo or Cleveland or South Bend. What the company craved more than anything else was space—and found it at Highland Park. Henry Ford envisioned a vast building, or a tightly compacted cluster of buildings, that would be laid out to facilitate the production of cars as efficiently as possible. Hauling parts from one building to another, as was being done at the Piquette Avenue plant, struck Ford and his production staff as a tremendous waste of time and manpower. What Ford and his men planned was a factory that would incorporate from its architect's first sketch everything they knew about making cars. An old building would not do. An old style of architecture would not do, either. What Ford Motor required was a factory as progressive as its products. "In 1908 Detroiters watched with amazement the excavations and construction at Highland Park race track," Roger Burlingame wrote in *Henry Ford*. "The idea that anything as big as this could be dedicated to anything as restricted in sales appeal as an automobile seemed pure fantasy to wise, conservative businessmen, and many a head was shaken as the huge buildings went up."[2]

In terms of lasting significance, what Henry Ford and his company did at

Highland Park was not just build the Model T, but plant the seeds for the growth of America's middle class. The strategy behind the effort, a conscious one, ranks as perhaps the most brilliant sales scheme in American history: creating a near universal demand with a pragmatic, high-quality product formerly considered a luxury item. "For all his zaniness," historian Arthur M. Schlesinger Jr. wrote in *The Crisis of the Old Order,* "Ford had a compelling vision of the new age. Modern mass production, he was convinced, had created an economy that was capable of anything; the fact of abundance must therefore revolutionize the philosophy of business. High output, low prices, and high wages must be the new objectives. Only by steadily raising wages and reducing prices could the business community maintain the buying power of the people."[3] The methods developed by Ford Motor Company produced a seismic impact on U.S., and then worldwide, business practices. It was a phenomenon known as "Fordism"[4] and its birthplace was Henry Ford's new manufacturing facility at Highland Park—where scale models would be constructed into reality.

Like many other Detroit companies in need of new buildings, Ford turned to Albert Kahn, who at thirty-eight headed his own bustling downtown architectural firm. The short, barrel-chested Kahn was known for his quiet manners and formal dress, as well as for his gift for state-of-the-art commercial buildings. A technical perfectionist with a sense of deference toward his customers, Kahn once estimated that it took him four or five days just to discuss a building with a client in order to understand exactly what that client had in mind. Drawing a pencil from his vest pocket and sharpening it meticulously while listening to his client,[5] Kahn would then start making the sketches that would turn general ideas into viable structures. Once he got the idea down, he had little further use for abstract discussions; as one colleague observed of him, "Albert Kahn was not a theorist: the 'architecture of tomorrow' had little interest for one so engrossed in creating the architecture of today."[6]

In Albert Kahn—or "AK," as he was called—Henry Ford would find a kindred spirit, at least in some regards. "Today is heralded as the Machine Age— the day of the railroad, the steamboat, the automobile, the airplane and the radio," Kahn declared. "We find beauty in a machine, for the absence of all not absolutely required for the performance of its works."[7]

Kahn was born on March 21, 1869, in Rhauen, Germany (near Frankfurt). His father, a rabbi, brought the family to America when Albert was eleven. Blessed with a gift for drawing, Albert studied art in various Detroit schools before honing the specific skills of his profession at the Mason and Rice architecture firm. When he turned twenty-one he won a $500 traveling scholarship granted by the *American Architect and Building News* and returned to Europe on his own, carefully studying the classical architecture of London, Paris, and Berlin. While in Florence, he found a mentor in Henry Bacon, the future designer of Washington, D.C.'s Lincoln Memorial. No less a figure than esteemed architect Louis Sullivan, in 1893, offered him a position in his firm to replace Frank Lloyd Wright—he turned him down.[8] Once back in Detroit, Kahn pursued his profession with single-minded concentration. Considered a first-rate draftsman, Kahn rose quickly in Detroit's hierarchy of architects.

The earliest designs attributable to Kahn were the whimsically modern wooden porch he created along the entire 660-foot length of the Grand Hotel on Michigan's Mackinac Island and the sturdy Boyer Machine Company plant in Detroit. After starting his own firm in 1902, Kahn received several high-profile commissions, including ones for Temple Beth El on Woodward Avenue, the Conservatory of Detroit's Belle Isle Park, and the Engineering Building at the University of Michigan in Ann Arbor. Although very different in function, all three were designed after classic European styles. Kahn's work on such projects was good, but did not reflect anything but extreme competence. That would change in 1903, when he turned his talents to the specialty that would propel him to the forefront of twentieth-century design: industrial architecture.

That very phrase was practically a contradiction in terms when Kahn received the commission to design a huge new forty-acre factory complex for the Packard Motor Car Company in 1903 on East Grand Boulevard in Detroit. "Kahn the pragmatist did not shy away from the industrial jobs most felt were beneath their dignity," historian Neil Baldwin wrote in *Henry Ford and the Jews*. "All his life he reveled in the common-sense solution of the factory building."[9] Kahn's own sardonic comment was that he had received his first industrial commission only because no truly self-respecting architect would ever agree to create anything so base as a factory. As architectural historian Grant Hildebrand pointed out, however, Packard President Henry B. Joy was a highly sophisticated man who probably recognized Kahn's sensibilities, though "interest alone would not have been quite enough—he would have had to sense ability as well."[10]

The innovative Kahn developed a succession of nine buildings for Packard, but made his definitive leap forward with the tenth. Constructed of poured concrete, reinforced by steel rods, around a highly original arrangement of supporting girders, Kahn's Packard Building no. 10 was open and bright, its sense of spaciousness almost unmarred by interior columns. The building drew attention as a harbinger of a new era in industrial design. Factories would no longer be doomed to the look of "old prison workshops," as one magazine of the day put it before going on to note, "It is most fitting that the automobile industry as the newest great industry of the country should in its new factories add to the strength of the movement toward rational working places."[11]

The automobile industry in general hungered for new and more efficient manufacturing facilities, and with the Packard job in his portfolio Albert Kahn naturally became Detroit's first choice for automotive building design, creating edifices for Hudson and Chalmers, among others. He seemed to relish the challenge of keeping up with the growing scale of the auto industry, and with the need to rethink spaces to suit its ever changing methods. A factory Kahn designed in collaboration with two other firms for the Pierce-Arrow automobile company in Buffalo hinted at this new flexibility in using space. The plant was arranged on a single floor in a carefully logical pattern that fed raw materials into one end and emitted finished cars from the other.

"When Henry Ford took me to the old race course where the Highland Park stands," Kahn recalled in 1929, "and told me what he wanted, I thought he was crazy. No buildings such as he talked of had been known to me. But I designed them according to his ideas." Ford had made some rough sketches, but mostly he talked and Kahn listened, the latter pitching in his own ideas as their mutual enthusiasm for the project grew. The two men quickly forged a partnership of like minds. "Architecture is 90 percent business and 10 percent art," Kahn once proclaimed, as Ford might as well have said of carmaking.[12]

When Ford and Kahn were planning a building together, especially during the meetings that led to Highland Park, they seemed more alike than any other pair of men in Detroit. They shared a part in the genesis of the modern industrial world, yet the two men also had some differences, including the one that Henry Ford, to his lasting shame and discredit, would later use to judge people above all else. This difference was that Albert Kahn was Jewish. The way their relationship thrived, even in the face of Ford's increasingly hateful and public anti-Semitism, would reveal something essential about each of them. They were both, first and foremost, pragmatists. Kahn needed Ford's business and Ford coveted Kahn's skill—the so-called Jewish Question never interfered with their desire to make money. In the coming decades Ford would give Kahn more than one thousand commissions.[13] And Kahn would accept them. He also, to Ford's chagrin, designed over one hundred buildings for General Motors, including the striking Fisher Building. But his loyalty remained with Ford. Hanging on Kahn's office wall all those years was an inscribed photograph of Henry. "To Albert Kahn," it read. "Your best friend is the one who can bring out the best that is in you."[14] (By 1920, however, Kahn, due to Ford's public anti-Semitism, refused to enter a Ford factory.)

Ford and Kahn never worked more closely together than when they were planning the Highland Park plant. They worked in sync, envisioning a bold, dynamic, and much more complex design than had ever been used before. When Henry Ford indicated that he wanted the main building filled with as much natural light as possible, Kahn, assisted by Ford Motor Company engineer Edward Gray, created a unique glass roof and specified massive windows in every wall. The shimmering result inspired the plant's nickname: the Crystal Palace. The main reason Ford wanted so much light inside was not, however, for the cheer of his workers. In his constant quest to eliminate wasted motion in the workplace, he wanted to crowd machines as close together as possible, following the simple logic that it takes less time, energy, and work to move a finished part two feet than ten feet. "You know," Ford pointed out, "when you have lots of light, you can put the machines closer together."[15]

When the Highland Park plant opened on New Year's Day 1910, it covered twelve acres. The main factory was a thin stripe of a building four stories tall, stretching 865 feet along Woodward Avenue.[16] The materials used in the main building—mostly poured concrete and glass, with redbrick accents at the corners—afforded the edifice a clean, modern aspect from the outside. The glass roof featured nearly as many vents as the walls had windows, providing Highland Park's workers fresh air, a nicety few factories in any industry had ever boasted before. Overall, the building's design relied on logic: raw materials were delivered to the top floor, and as they were forged and machined into finished parts made their way down the floors through more than a thousand openings Ford and Kahn had incorporated for chutes, conveyors, and tubes. "To be able to quickly and affordably plan structures of this type, which needed to be flexible enough to accommodate complex and changing industrial activities, Kahn created a new way of working," Sean Ulmer, curator of modern and contemporary art at the University of Michigan, explained in a 2001 retrospective catalogue analyzing Kahn's architectural influence. "At his office in Detroit he created teams of architects who worked directly alongside engineers, cost estimators and construction specialists."[17]

Throughout 1910, parades of Detroiters and international tourists trekked up Woodward Avenue just to look at the result of the combined architectural visions of Henry Ford and Albert Kahn. It was a big building, to be sure. But if the massive edifice had housed a button factory or a stove works, it hardly would have made such a spectacle. The locals drawn to stand in its shadow knew that the Highland Park factory loomed over nothing less than the future of their city. The year before the plant opened, American factories had produced 2 million horse-drawn carriages and 120,000 automobiles. The sprawling Highland Park manufacturing facility restated in brick and mortar what Henry Ford often said in words: "When you substitute a motor driven vehicle for each of these two million wagons and carriages, you get an idea of the automobile of the future."[18] As his company scrambled to produce more than its share of those future automobiles, the town of Highland Park grew tenfold, boasting 4,120 residents one year after the plant opened—just 10 more people than the number employed by Ford Motor Company at its new location.[19] By 1920, Highland Park's population would grow by more than a thousand percent, reaching 46,499 residents.

Frederick J. Haynes, then chairman of the board of Dodge Brothers, toured the Highland Park plant and concluded that no other automobile factory in the nation had a better production setup.[20] Carmakers from around the world came flocking to see the new requisites of their industry in action before their eyes. As Henry Ford delineated them, they were "power, accuracy, economy, continuity, system, speed, and repetition."[21] The company made no effort to keep its mastery of the manufacturing process a secret. As historian David L. Lewis noted, "Responding to the Highland Park plant's widespread publicity, engineering societies, business organizations, and dealer groups visited the plant as early as 1910 to see the 'magic methods' about which they had read and heard."[22]

Guided tours were given gladly at the Crystal Palace, and they represented another difference between Ford Motor Company and most other industrial enterprises of the day. Public relations was yet an unknown art at most companies, which generally forbade visitors from their operating facilities in fear that their ideas and methods might be stolen. Ford Motor had no such concerns. It claimed no secrets and baldly challenged the rest of the business world to try to keep up. More important, the guided tours served as yet another way, perhaps the most effective of all, to spread the Ford message by making an ambassador of every tourist, colleague, or rival who dropped by the new plant. In a single year Highland Park became the technical mecca of the auto industry, and through the next twenty years only one facility would top it: Ford Motor's next great factory, at River Rouge, Michigan. While the River Rouge plant would be even more enormous, neither it nor any other manufacturing facility since would drive the entire industrialized world forward the way Ford Motor's Highland Park plant did between 1910 and 1925.

———

A succession of scientific management theorists wrote copiously about efficiencies in production in the first decades of the twentieth century. The most notable was Frederick Winslow Taylor, a former steel mill foreman who had studied firsthand how to use workers as pieces of a fine-tuned system, void of individuality. With the publication of *The Principles of Scientific Management* in 1911, three years after the introduction of the Model T, Taylor was hailed as the thinking man's Henry Ford. His views on industrial science garnered their widest audience when he made a series of appearances before a congressional committee in the early 1910s to tout his studies of how workers could increase productivity. "Taylor was the first efficiency expert, the original time-and-motion man," biographer Robert Kanigel wrote in *The One Best Way*. "To organized labor, he was a soulless slave driver, out to destroy the workingman's health and rob him of his manhood. To the bosses he was an eccentric and a radical, raising the wages of common laborers by a third, paying college boys to click stopwatches. To him and his friends, he was a misunderstood visionary, possessor of the one best way that, under the banner of science, would confer prosperity on worker and boss alike, abolishing the ancient class hatreds."[23]

Over the decades the rightful legacy of Fredrick Winslow Taylor has been hotly debated. In the third volume of his *U.S.A.* trilogy, *The Big Money* (1936), John Dos Passos took Taylor to task as a callous, coldhearted pragmatist who treated workers like interchangeable units. "He couldn't stand to see an idle lathe or an idle man," Dos Passos wrote. "Production went to his head and thrilled his sleepless nerves like liquor or women on a Saturday night."[24] Whatever one thinks of Taylor, his influence on the way Americans live and do business remains enormous. In fact, Yale University historian David Montgomery, in his seminal *The Fall of the House of Labor* (1987), argues that Taylor's principles of scientific management extended well beyond the assembly line to permeate the way all organizations have been run—not just factories, but corporations, churches, businesses, and every other association in America since the William Howard Taft administration.[25] Business management expert Peter F. Drucker went so far as to write that Taylorism ranks as "the most powerful as well as the most lasting contribution America has made to Western thought since the Federalist Papers."[26]

Both Montgomery and Drucker exaggerated Taylor's importance. While Taylorism served to clarify how human resources could be integrated with modern machinery most profitably, Taylor worked largely according to abstract formulas. Henry Ford, by contrast, pioneered efficiency in the realm in which workers turned raw materials into vehicles before one's very eyes. Ford learned nothing from Taylor; he never read his books nor mentioned him. Ford Motor executives did not debate efficiency-boosting methods with government regulators or in academic journals—the company experimented with them on the floor of the Crystal Palace. As Taylor biographer Robert Kanigel summed up: "The assembly line was indeed a landmark achievement and could probably never have spluttered up from the brain of Frederick Taylor. His defender's assertions to the contrary, he was no revolutionary. Ford, you could argue, was."[27]

The Ford factory at Highland Park was organized to produce finished cars, but it also manufactured more and more of the parts for those cars. Bulk parts were also shipped in boxcars to assembly plants all over the country, where employees turned out finished Model Ts. It was an efficient process, if not nearly quick enough for some customers. "Now and then, the prospective buyers would come in to help build their own cars," recalled Ernest Pedersen, who worked at Ford assembly plants in the Midwest in 1912. "The purchaser would go into the office, pay his money, and get a receipt for the car. Then he would come out and ask which car was going to be his. We would point one out to him and he would go right to work on it. Of course, we inspected that car at the end of the line and drove it around the block to be certain that everything was all right. Then we would show the fellow the right way to crank a Ford, and the proud owner would drive it away." With demand flourishing, Pedersen added that not all of the assembly work was done at factories set up for the purpose. In Sioux City, Iowa, for example, he noted that "we built the cars right at the railroad siding."[28]

As a system, the Highland Park operation was advanced, but not that far removed from Detroit's other well-managed automobile factories. The new plant boasted better machinery than most, and a physical layout considered state-of-the-art, if not revolutionary. The main difference between Highland Park and the rest of the auto plants around town and around the world, however, was that on its opening day, the Ford Motor facility was not finished— and it never would be. No sooner did production start up than the company's executives began prowling the factory floors looking for ways to save time, money, and manpower through further mechanization. It was corporate development through unceasing improvement—and that, in essence, constituted what came to be called Fordism, the restless approach to management that would sweep the industrialized world during the next fifteen years and that has remained the business norm ever since. The basic idea was that the product itself may or may not be improved (in the case of the Model T, it was barely changed during nineteen years of production), but the system behind it must be made better, continuously.

Clarence Hooker, in his book *Life in the Shadow of the Crystal Palace,* cited three types of innovations implemented at Ford Motor Company between 1908 and 1914 that "led the way in revolutionizing industrial production in general and automotive production in particular." The first was the adoption of specialized machinery, followed by the organization of the assembly process to optimize synchronization, and the last was mechanization.[29]

From the outset, Highland Park exhibited the company's commitment to more and better use of machinery. In fact, the plant could be regarded as one enormous machine, turning industrial art into industrial engineering. For Ford Motor, which was just coming through the protracted Selden legal battle, efficient production offered better protection than any patent. In the early days of the Model T, competitors simply could not build so much quality into their cars and sell them at a like price. Later, competitors found that they could not build *any* car for the paltry cost of a Model T. That was Fordism: creating a law unto itself, then going it one better—and then another one.

While the Highland Park plant was under construction, Ford and his immediate associates gave little thought to the Selden patent case brought by the

Association of Licensed Automobile Manufacturers against the company in 1903. By 1909, the struggle had lost its punch and was accepted as a stand-off. By then, the ALAM had received a total of $2 million in royalties, or between $4 and $14 per car, depending on the selling price. Of that, George B. Selden's share amounted to about $600,000—not a penny of it from Ford Motor. Then, on September 16, the long festering case broke into the headlines for the first time in years. A verdict had been reached: Ford Motor Company and its codefendants had lost. The court upheld Selden's patent.

The judge in the case, Charles Hough, had to admit that it was a peculiar story. "No instance is known to me," he noted in his ruling, "of an idea being buried in the Patent Office until the world caught up to it and passed it, and then embodied in a patent only useful for tribute. But patents are granted for inventions. The inventor may use his discovery or he may not, but no one else can use it for seventeen years."[30] The judge could not find any law that had been violated, so Selden won.

"Motor Car Patents Upheld by Court—Whole Industry Affected," ran a headline in the New York Times on page 5. The last line of the accompanying article explained why the verdict was not a big story, but just another small chapter in a long one: the Selden case was bound for a higher court.[31]

While Ford Motor Company intended to appeal, its opponents, the seventy-one members of ALAM, looked poised to control the automobile industry, just as they had six years earlier. Several firms that had been quietly refusing to pay the royalty capitulated in the face of the court ruling. General Motors, only a year old in 1909, was one of the first to come into the fold—a major coup for ALAM, which received $1 million in back royalty payments from that one company alone. As before, the industry group ran advertisements warning prospective customers that owners of unlicensed cars made themselves vulnerable to lawsuits. And just as in 1903, Ford Motor Company retaliated to each of ALAM's threats; newspaper advertisements were tossed back and forth like thunderbolts. These poison-penned rebuttals featured copy written jointly by James Couzens and Ralzemond Parker, Ford Motor's patent attorney.

"This Selden Patent is a freak among alleged inventions and is worthless as a patent and worthless as a device," claimed a Ford Motor ad in February 1910. The tone then turned ominous in a way that could have come only from Couzens: "If the Ford Motor Company cared to resort to such tactics [as the Selden interests were using], it has patents that cover many of the leading features of automobile construction a thousand times more valuable in the automobile industry than Selden's and could also threaten and bring suits against many . . . infringers."[32]

The rhetoric stopped there, just short of becoming incendiary. Ford Motor executives knew they had to be careful to portray their company as the reasonable party in the dispute—and, emphatically, as the friend of the car owner. "Not for a moment, however," the firm's ad thus went on, "had it entered our heads to harass or annoy individual users of licensed product[s] by suing them as infringers of Ford patents." The company repeated its standing offer to indemnify its own customers against lawsuits from ALAM, making its entire asset funds of $12 million available to that cause. Only fifty customers applied for the protection,[33] indicating either widespread respect for Ford's promise or the basic ennui that had grown up around the achingly dull Selden patent case outside the auto industry.

In court, meanwhile, the case remained bogged down in legalistic details for over a year as attorneys on both sides prepared their arguments for the three-judge panel of the U.S. Circuit Court of Appeals in New York. Both James Couzens and Henry Ford went to New York to attend the trial, which lasted just longer than a week in late November 1910.

The panel handed down its decision on January 9, 1911. The judges looked right past the issue of Selden's use or misuse of the patent process. They also ignored the question of whether an invention that had never even been constructed in its own time should receive patent protection. In other words, the appeals court judges ignored every one of the factors that made the Selden patent such a "freak" to Couzens, Parker, and Ford.

Instead, the judges looked only at the intrinsic worth of the patent. To do so, they had to turn back the clock and learn basic journeymen's mechanics circa 1886. At the time Selden filed his patent application, the American-invented Brayton engine was widely accepted as the gasoline power plant of the future. Later Selden would deride the German-designed Otto in his diary, calling it "that damned engine." He turned out to be right to have cursed it. The Brayton may have been a good bet, but it was the Otto engine that would power the U.S. auto industry. According to the judges' ruling, the Selden patent was indeed legally valid; it just didn't happen to cover the modern automobile. "He made the wrong choice," the court ruled regarding George Selden's selection of an engine as drawn on his application. "The defendants," it went on, "neither legally nor morally owe him anything."[34]

Immediately afterward, ALAM made plans to appeal the case to the Supreme Court,[35] while Ford and Couzens made plans to celebrate in New York. Two days later, upon further consideration, the members of ALAM voted to accept the ruling, consoling themselves with the fact that the Selden patent was due to expire in 1912 anyway.[36] Members of the association were even invited to the Ford celebration at Rector's, then among the finest restaurants in the city. Edsel Ford, seventeen at the time, took the train from Detroit to attend, and later recorded in his diary that it was a "grand party, about forty persons present." Many of the dinner speakers gushed over the decision as the beginning of a new era of unrestrained growth for the automobile industry—and that is just what it turned out to be. In truth, the Selden patent meant more when it was revoked than it had ever meant when it was in force. Few companies had been actively inhibited by it during its lifetime, after all—yet every automobile manufacturer felt unbound once it was gone.

For the next year ALAM tried to survive by reconstituting itself as a clearinghouse for automotive industry information. The group dissolved in 1912, however, when its functions were absorbed into another industry association with a more benign history and fewer lingering shadows: the Automobile Association of America, better known as Triple A.

The victory had been expensive for Ford Motor: about $6 profit per car went toward the company's legal expenses. But Henry Ford proclaimed himself delighted to have spent it. After all, the man who once said, "I never made a mistake—and neither did you!" had insisted all along that the favorable publicity the company received as a result of the suit had been well worth whatever the lawyers had charged to handle it. "It appeared that we were the underdog and we had the public's sympathy," Ford observed. "The association [ALAM] had seventy million dollars—we at the beginning had not half that number of thousands. I never had a doubt as to the outcome, but nevertheless it was a sword hanging over our heads that we could as well do without. Prosecuting that suit was probably one of the most shortsighted acts that any group of American business men has ever combined to commit."[37] In the aftermath of the victory, Henry Ford emerged in the public eye as undauntable, independent, and tough, not unlike his cars—and it may have been that the blurring of those images did not come about by coincidence.

———

At the turn of the twentieth century, descriptions of Detroit tended along the lines of "charming" and "quaint." In the decade after 1901, however, the city would change more than it had in the previous half century. One observer compared it to a boom-time mining town: "fast, impulsive and indifferent to the superficial niceties of life."[38] Detroit shot ahead from the dawn of the Automobile Age with astonishing rapidity. The gentle old town's expansive green lawns gave way to widened, paved streets, while sprawling family residences were turned into boardinghouses for the hordes of new workers heading to new jobs at the city's myriad auto factories.[39]

Standing at the corner of Woodward Avenue and Cadillac Square downtown, grand in brick and granite, the Hotel Ponchartrain catered to the old pace of Detroit, but also managed to keep up with the new one. Among the city's institutions, it served as a bridge between that part of Detroit society created with the first French settlement in 1701 and that part born with the first automobile factories in 1901. E. LeRoy Pelletier, a veteran of Detroit's early automobile industry, once took the manager of the hotel aside in the lobby. "If I were you," Pelletier confided, "I would get some red paint, the reddest I could buy, and I would have a great circle drawn in red paint. And within that circle on the floor of the lobby of this hotel, I would have inscribed this legend: 'The Heart of the Auto Industry.'"[40] Most of Detroit's early automobile elite, from Ransom E. Olds to Henry Leland, harbored nostalgia-tinged stories about the legendary hotel. "The Ponchartrain was where motorcar gossip was heard first," Alfred P. Sloan Jr. of General Motors recalled in *Adventures of a White-Collar Man*. "New models customarily had debuts there. . . . Even on ordinary days . . . the table would be covered with sketches: crankshafts, chassis, detail of motors . . . and all sort of mechanisms."[41]

Historian George W. Stark, in his book *City of Destiny*, echoed Sloan's assessment of the Hotel Ponchartrain as a virtual mecca for the burgeoning auto boom. "Men gathered there from the four quarters of the earth," he explained. "It was no uncommon sight to see four or five men carry a heavy piece of machinery into the room, place it on the floor or a table and set it in motion. . . . Everything was shown off in the Ponchartrain bar: tire vulcanizers, rims, valves, brakes, carburetors, magnetos and what not. There, men began to talk a strange new language. Designed as a magnificent playroom, the Ponchartrain bar became a great workroom, too. It was the world's first automotive demonstration room. It was laboratory and countinghouse combined."[42]

It was said that 90 percent of America's automobile business was conducted in the bar of the Hotel Ponchartrain. But that was not true. Statistically, it wasn't even close, simply because Henry Ford could never be found in the bar at the Ponchartrain—and in 1911, the year Highland Park opened, his name was on a full quarter of all the cars sold in the world.[43] Yet Henry Ford remained apart from his peers, if such the other men in his industry could be called. He neither drank nor smoked, so apart from the chance to enjoy the occasional risqué story, the clubby Ponchartrain bar offered little to interest him anyway. Even later, when he was rich beyond the dreams of anyone else in the world, Henry Ford still did not live in the posh areas favored by other automotive millionaires. He did not join their private clubs or share their gilded hobbies, either. Asked once why he did not play golf, Ford replied bluntly that he disliked the sort of ostentatious people who did play the game. (And he was superstitious regarding the sport's inherent danger: the first and only time he teed off at a country club his golf ball hit a young girl in the head.) He once claimed that he would rather repair automobiles in the bowels of Detroit for sixty hours a week than live like a pampered dilettante in Newport or Beverly Hills or Cape Cod.[44] In fact, he did not so much avoid as ignore the camaraderie that other ambitious businessmen relied on, the auto industry having spawned a particularly collegial and even collaborative middle-aged-boys' network of professional associates. The only part of the industry that interested him was Ford Motor, and the only peers he wanted were the fellows he had selected to work for him there.

———

"I never worked for Henry Ford," James Couzens once explained, delicately. "I worked with him."[45] Indeed, the company's own in-house publication proved him right. Each June, the *Ford Times* ran an anniversary article relating and updating the firm's history to that point. In the 1911 edition, the article contained an illustration featuring portraits of Ford and Couzens along with factory photos, all over the telling caption: "Eight years' evolution of the Ford Motor Company and the men who made its immense growth possible."[46]

Of course, both did it with considerable help, and not just from each other. In a dynamic, glamorous young business that was already attracting the best of a generation of production men, Ford Motor was building a team unmatched at the time, and rarely since, in any field. The Ford ideal for an executive bore no resemblance whatever to the iconoclastic Henry Ford but, not surprisingly, looked very much like the profile of James Couzens. These Ford men shared a notable serious-mindedness, keeping them focused on and ever alert for ways to improve the company. Although not necessarily as irascible as James Couzens, like the head manager they came in every day to work, and work hard. At a company that was doubling in size every year, it became ever more of a challenge to find people who would strengthen the team and not merely fill it out.

In 1913, Ford Motor Company purchased one of its suppliers, the John R. Keim steel mills in Buffalo, New York—not for the company itself, or its equipment, but because Henry Ford wanted three of Keim's top managers to work for him. One of them was William S. Knudsen (pronounced *Ka-nood-sen*), a deceptively rumpled, mild-tempered Dane who had immigrated to the United States in 1900 at the age of twenty. Having left behind only vague plans to someday join Denmark's navy, Knudsen had but a rudimentary technical education and spoke no English.[47] He seemed just a skinny, dark-haired Scandinavian, standing six-foot-two with little more to boast of than a prominent nose and a cheerful demeanor. Yet within eight years of taking his first job as a school janitor, Knudsen had risen to general superintendent of the Keim operations, which manufactured steel parts for bicycles. Due to the automobile revolution, however, the bicycle market was in a downward spiral. So with the help of his general manager, William H. Smith, Knudsen struggled to save the company from folding by becoming a supplier of automotive parts. One of their early customers was Henry Ford, who needed frames and axle housings for his Model Ts.[48] From that auspicious beginning in Buffalo, Knudsen would go on to forge one of the most spectacular careers in U.S.

business history, later serving as president of General Motors, and ranking among the ten highest-paid people in the country during the Great Depression. He finished his career overseeing all U.S. wartime production in World War II.

Alex Lumsden, a fellow worker back at the Keim plant, once asked one of the bosses: "How did Knudsen, without the mechanical background, make the headway that he did?"

The reply came in the form of a long story about Knudsen's early days at the firm, concerning his dealings with an employee called John, which Lumsden retold as follows:

Knudsen would come along and say, "John, I want to get these pails for Sears, Roebuck & Company. We've got two gross of pails to make for Sears, Roebuck. Where are they? Why aren't they made?"

John said, "I haven't got any steel."

Knudsen said, "Well, why haven't you?"

John said, "I'll be damned if I know. All I got is eighteen inches wide and what I need is nine inches wide."

Knudsen would say, "Well, John, why don't you take the shears and cut that eighteen inches in two and you'll have nine inches."

He said, "Well, that is exactly what I am doing, Bill."

"No, you're not doing it."

John said, "No, because my shear blades are up in the tool room being sharpened."

"Oh," Knudsen said. Knudsen would walk up the stairs with his long strides and go to the toolmaker and ask him where were the shear blades for John.

He said, "They are in the machine."

"When will they be ready?"

"Oh, maybe in a half an hour."

In twenty-five minutes Knudsen would be there within the time with a wheelbarrow, get the blades and wheel them downstairs and take them over to John and say, "John, here is your shear blades."

"Okay Bill, I'll get them in right away."

Then Knudsen would ask, "When will I get some strips?"

"Oh, in about an hour and a half."

He would be back there within the time with the wheelbarrow to pick up a few pieces.

He said, "Now where will I take these strips to?"

"Take them over to press number so-and-so. Tony so-and-so will blank them for you."

He would take them over there and wait until they got fifteen or twenty all blanked out. Then he would take them up to the Shipping Department and put the tags on them and ship them out. That was another job done. He'd score that off and away he'd go and tackle something else. Continually day after day, hour after hour, that man plodded in that manner.[49]

And in the same way Knudsen got every job done, every time, no matter what and with no surprises—or excuses. In the years when the Model T was taking off, an executive like Knudsen, who found ways to make things happen, on time, without shortcuts, was certain to find a place waiting for him at Ford Motor Company. "You can tell a boy what a pump is," he was fond of saying, "but if he gets a pipe and, by means of a cork on a string, draws water up through that pipe, he really understands what a pump is."[50]

After being "sold" to Henry Ford's carmaking firm along with the rest of the erstwhile John R. Keim Mills, William Knudsen wasn't certain whether to move to Detroit, but he did finally opt to give the auto manufacturer a try— a limited try. When he joined the company, his wife, Clara Euler Knudsen, and their first child remained near her family in Buffalo.[51] Knudsen's first job at Ford Motor proved daunting. The company had built twenty-five new assembly plants around the country, and Bill Knudsen was ordered to leave immediately to oversee the installation of production systems inside fourteen of them. "Don't worry about expenses," he recalled Henry Ford's telling him. "Draw on us for whatever you need." So off he went, and in cities from Boston to Dallas and Atlanta to Seattle, Knudsen found that the company's subsidiary factories had certainly been well constructed—*too* well constructed. Because those same buildings had to be reconfigured to accommodate Ford Motor's carmaking operations, their sturdiness only added to the expense as Knudsen directed contractors to tear through the floors and walls and refit each building. By the time he was through, the assembly plants stood ready, but the bill to get them that way reached $400,000.

Upon his return to Detroit, Knudsen was told to report immediately to James Couzens's office. Company veterans assured him that the only reason Couzens ever asked to see anyone was to give him a good dressing-down. Knudsen left his desk with trepidation, reminding himself that it was Henry Ford who had told him to spend whatever sums it took to organize the regional factories. He steadied himself, then opened Couzens's door, and entered the business manager's office.

"I sent for you, Mr. Knudsen," Couzens declared, "to compliment you on the job you've done."

Knudsen thanked him for the pat on the back and started to leave. Couzens stopped him, saying, "Wait a minute. When we tell anyone what I have just told you, Mr. Knudsen, we accompany it with something substantial." He then handed the younger man an envelope containing a check. Without looking at the amount (which turned out to be $5,000, the equivalent of about $90,000 today), Knudsen assumed it was a loan and assured his perplexed boss that he would return every penny of it. Then he started to leave again. "I wish, Mr. Knudsen, you would wait until I am finished," Couzens interjected with a rare smile before informing his subordinate that, in addition to the free-and-clear bonus check, his salary had been increased by two thirds.[52]

On the spot, Knudsen decided to move to Detroit and remain with Ford Motor, without even consulting his wife back in Buffalo. Clara Knudsen would have little cause to object; her husband would stay at Ford for almost ten years, becoming the most important production manager at the company, not to mention quite a rich man. Bill Knudsen did not have a job title, exactly, but then few people at Ford Motor Company did, beyond those corporate officers required by government regulations to assume defined roles. The corporate culture at Ford held that job descriptions were too confining, in that they told employees as much about what they *didn't* have to do as they did about what was expected of them. The company's officers also discovered that, especially among executives, the absence of job titles fostered a certain insecurity that seemed to increase competition and, therefore, performance. The same kind of thinking, transferred to the factory floor, led to the banning of chairs or seats of any kind. Neither foremen nor anyone else was allowed to sit down. If a worker turned a crate over to make a temporary chair, the odds were good that someone would come along and kick it out from under him.[53]

The test of every rule and procedure at Ford Motor lay in its effect on production. Expense did not matter nearly so much as efficiency in the long run in turning out cars. The $400,000 Bill Knudsen spent to improve the company's regional assembly plants would be regained in earnings born of the upgrades' boosts in productivity; the moments of work wasted by a foreman sneaking a sit-down break could not.

"They think I'm crazy," Henry Ford admitted to Knudsen early on, referring to certain of his shareholders and others in the automobile business who derided his prediction that his company would soon be producing one thousand vehicles per day. "That day will come, sure, and it is not far away," Ford proclaimed. "I am not worried about the market for automobiles. I'm not worried because some of my own backers think I'm crazy. They'll change their minds. What I am worried about is production."[54]

While Detroit's backslappers quaffed cocktails at the Hotel Ponchartrain and talked about looking for the market, the executives at Ford Motor engaged in more profitable pursuits. They were looking for cars: ever more cars, and more ways to produce them to fill the market the *right* cars would create.

Officially, Harold Wills, the guiding hand behind the creation of the Model T, was head of production at Highland Park, although his attention was largely directed toward refining the T during its first few years. Peter E. Martin served as production supervisor, with Charles Sorensen as his assistant. On the factory floors the two men acted practically as equals, Martin handling the machine shop and Sorensen the pattern-making department. "Between the two of them, I'm going to tell you, they were what you could call production men," marveled George Brown. "They got that thing started."[55]

Both men tended toward intimidation, although the thickset, French-Canadian Martin earned a reputation for fair and quite reasonable treatment of employees. The tall, blond, blue-eyed Sorensen, however, had a temper of loud and legendary ferocity to complement his smooth Nordic looks. "People would go away and hide and all that. Even the foremen were scared," recalled foreman James O'Connor of the specter of either Martin or Sorensen on the factory floor. "Sorensen didn't have to threaten a man; they were all afraid of him," he went on. "You would think it was a beast coming through there sometimes. . . . Sometimes he would see a man looking at him and he would fire him."[56]

Yet Charles Sorensen would remain at Ford Motor far longer than any of the other Model T–era executives. And it is possible that no one, not even Henry Ford or James Couzens, loved the company more. As O'Connor noted, the ill-humored production supervisors were only passing along the pressure they themselves were under from management to turn out more cars, faster.

Special foreman Robert A. Shaw, who had developed into Highland Park's in-house troubleshooter on safety matters, told a story that may sum up Sorensen's exacting mind-set best. After Henry Ford had been asked to build an infirmary for men injured on the job, Shaw was summoned to a meeting with the boss that also included Martin and Sorensen.

> Mr. Ford asked me two questions. "So," Mr. Ford said to me, "what would you do, Shaw, if a man cut his finger off with a hatchet?"
>
> From my little scope of experience I said that I thought it was a matter of education. I thought that was a proper answer to give but Mr. Ford said, "No, throw the hatchets out."
>
> I kind of thought that he meant this for an illustration but a few days later in the plant Sorensen asked, "Have you got the hatchets out?"
>
> I said, "No, I think that Mr. Ford meant that as an illustration."
>
> He said, "No, throw them out. You get them out!" I think that Sorensen is the only man who followed individually every word that Mr. Ford spoke, every word.[57]

Several years earlier, in 1909, Henry Ford had published an article under his own byline in the *New York Times* summarizing the system behind his company's success and describing the thinking behind the design of the new Model T plant: "We put $250,000 into machinery for this new car," he wrote, citing an enormous figure for the time, equivalent to the cost of the entire Highland Park building. "The cylinders, for instance, in the little runabout traveled 4,000 feet from the time they entered as rough castings until they reached the assembly room. New machinery for the T has cut down this travel to 400 feet and one man does the work of three."[58]

New and better machinery was in constant development at Ford Motor Company. It was said, in fact, that throughout the long production run of the Model T, at least one new machine or tool was introduced at the factory every single day. Not much of importance may have changed on the T to make it new, improved, or different during its nineteen-year model run, but nothing remained the same about the methods used to produce it. That was the imperative laid down by Henry Ford.

Most of the continual changes to the machinery came out of the tool-design section, headed by Carl Emde. One day, P. E. Martin stopped by and casually, in the course of conversation, gave one of Emde's die makers, Logan Miller, a two-week assignment to walk through the machine shops and look for possible improvements. It was not unusual for Ford Motor's supervisors to pull a bright worker out to join their active quest for betterment. "I had so many ideas that I filled several books," Miller remembered. "These were reviewed by engineering, and there was so much to do with so few experienced tool designers that they didn't have enough time to do it all. Everybody was working for one thing: trying to improve the product at less cost."

On one project, Miller was granted a mere week to make a set of new machines and the dies to go with them. "Well," he said, "you never could say no, because those who did have gone to other places. We just went to work and made it. . . . We had the job running in one week. You didn't say, 'No, I can't do it.' That is the training all of those old-timers had. It was not what it would cost, but how fast you could make it."[59]

Just how fast that was became clear in 1913, when the first assembly line was implemented at Ford Motor Company. The process grew like a vine and eventually spread to all phases of the manufacture of Ford cars, and then through the entire world of heavy industry. There can be no doubt that a powerful revolution occurred at Highland Park—but it was not the assembly line itself that provided the power. Rather, it was the creation of an atmosphere in which improvement was the real product; a better, cheaper Model T followed naturally. Every man on the payroll was invited to contribute ideas, and the good ones were implemented without delay. The good workers were recognized for their contributions, too, and promoted generously. It was not the hiring of so many dedicated workers that fueled the innovations at Highland Park, but the active support of those bright minds that went ahead and did it instead.

It is impossible to say who invented the assembly line, although the contractors hired by Egypt's Pharaoh Cheops to build his Great Pyramid at Giza about 2700 B.C. seem to have been on to the basic idea. By the fifteenth century A.D. the Arsenal shipyard in Venice, using a fully developed assembly line, could outfit the empty shell of a warship in a matter of minutes, largely with matériel made on the premises. A Spanish visitor in 1436 described the shipyard's assembly line operations: "As one enters the gate, there is a great street on either hand with the sea in the middle, and on one side are windows opening out of the houses of the Arsenal, and the same on the other side. And out came a galley towed by a boat and from the windows they handed out to them, from one the cordage, from another the bread, from another the arms, and from another the ballistas and mortars, and so from all sides everything that was required. And when the galley had reached the end of the street, all the men required were on board, together with the complement of oars, and she was fully equipped from end to end."

The Spanish visitor kept count. "In this manner," he continued, "there came out ten galleys fully armed, between the hours of three and nine."[60]

Throughout history, every time the demand for finished products has radically outstripped the best rate of production—but not the supply of raw materials—the potential for the "invention" of the assembly line has sprouted anew. In the early nineteenth century, for example, American clock makers adopted the fundamental process, followed by the nation's gun makers, notably Samuel Colt. Some have argued that Oliver Evans's Delaware flour mill operation or the Westinghouse Airbrake Company was the true progenitor of Fordism.[61] Each time the assembly-line concept had been implemented, however, it had been greeted from the outside as a brutal, almost cruel, and utterly dehumanizing manufacturing system to those who toiled under it.

The inspiration underlying the implementation of the assembly line at Ford Motor Company came, in part, out of a visit a number of Ford workers made to Chicago, where they witnessed the marvel that was the Swift meatpacking plant. It was not exactly an assembly line—a disassembly line would be more like it, in that the pigs were suspended upside down by one heel and moved that way from station to station, at the first of which they were garroted. At each station after that, one particular piece of the animal's anatomy was removed, until nothing was left. However gruesome the scene, anyone who appreciated efficiency could not help but admire the precision timing and coordination each task required to turn a pig into pork for sale. The butchers at the Swift plant never put down their knives and never wasted a movement or a moment.

In 1912 William C. Klann, a Ford Motor foreman, knew that transposing this concept to auto manufacture, however, would call for more than just devising a parts-delivery system. "I went down to Chicago to the slaughterhouse myself," Klann said in a 1955 interview. "I came back and said, 'If they can kill pigs and cows that way, we can build cars that way and build motors that way." Klann then told P. E. Martin about the conveyers in Chicago. The supervisor seemed dubious at first; after all, most people presumed that automaking was simply too complicated an endeavor to be adapted to an assembly-line system.

"If they can do it, we can do it," Klann persisted.

"Well," Martin replied, "see what you can do."[62]

Other Ford Motor employees also claimed to have originated the idea of using an assembly line at Highland Park. Bill Knudsen, for example, told his biographer he had utilized the line back at the Keim bicycle plant and introduced it in the painting process at Ford.[63] Ernest Pedersen likewise thought he had been the first to suggest the assembly line at Ford Motor. It might have been any of these employees, or all of them: experimentation on a small scale was nearly always encouraged at the factory, the prevailing attitude being that it couldn't hurt to give new ideas a chance, whatever their source. In fact, Henry Ford, who is not credited with the origination of the actual line, was certainly responsible for something even more important: the atmosphere that made employees think of constant improvement. Because Henry Ford was in a hurry, the wheels at his company—and throughout the industrialized world—turned even faster.

Ford Motor's first assembly line produced magneto coils—basically spools of wire. Klann broke down the tasks involved in building the coils and arranged them in a specific sequence for the department's workers to follow. The experiment was a success—leaving approximately 1,500 other Model T parts to be incorporated into the assembly-line process. As a start, Klann arranged for the entire magneto flywheel to be built on an assembly line driven by a conveyor. This innovation was the first moving assembly line used at Ford Motor Company, and it reduced production time from 20 minutes per piece (in man-hours) to 13 minutes, 10 seconds.[64]

Next Klann received authorization to set up a conveyor line to assemble crankcases, which weighed 120 pounds apiece. As part of the operation, the men on the line had to clamp the crankcases down as soon as they arrived at each station. Otherwise, as Klann put it, "the whole block could come off and smash a man."

The second day, one did just that when a worker forgot to use the clamp. The falling part broke his leg above the knee. "It was kind of a shock," Klann remembered, "as some of the boys did not want to work on this kind of a conveyor, and they also said that the job was broken up so that instead of one man being responsible for a good bearing job, four men were responsible."[65]

Those twin complaints—about the demeaning effect of the conveyor and the violation of the workman's integrity by the division of labor—would cling to the assembly line wherever it appeared. Until 1913, Ford Motor Company assemblers had been skilled mechanics. The assembly line, however, replaced craftsmanship with sheer systematic toil. As a result, many of Ford's veteran factory workers either jockeyed for promotions or quit the company soon after the lines started to spread. Assembly-line work was for a different type of employee, and they knew it.

The day that crankcase fell on a worker, however, nearly marked the last use of any assembly line at Ford Motor Company. After the accident, James Couzens appeared on the factory floor to see foreman Klann. "He said to me, 'If you are going to just break legs, let's shut this thing off,'" Klann recalled. "After talking for about an hour and showing Mr. Couzens all of the good points about the job and what could be saved on labor and time if the men clamped the cylinders down, he only said, 'Yes, and break all of their legs.'"

Couzens was adamant that Klann take the crankcase conveyer line down. The subordinate tried one last time to save it, protesting, "Look at all the time we save on the job."

"These damn people are breaking legs," remained Couzens's stubborn reply.[66] It is hard to criticize the bottom-line man for valuing worker safety above manufacturing efficiency. To Klann, however, Couzens was acting the villain, and so the foreman worked around the executive's authority, soliciting support for his conveyors from Martin and Sorensen. Within a month, the safety issue had been resolved via better clamps and the addition of a worker to set them as the crankcases came down the conveyor. In the end, the crankcase assembly line would be regarded as the breakthrough proof that even the heaviest parts could be constructed more efficiently on a line.

Once the crankshaft and camshaft assembly lines were also up and running under the new process, more conveyors were installed, at right angles to the first, to allow for more assembly work; stations were then added to incorporate the construction of pistons, rods, and bearing caps. Soon the Ford factory had, as Klann described the setup, "another conveyor coming in from overhead to supply the crankcase at the correct point in the line." Once most of the transmission subassembly process was relegated to the conveyor system, the rear axle was next.

The moving conveyors continued to spread like kudzu throughout the plant, soon enveloping the other subassemblies. Finally the chassis was addressed, and it turned out to be the simplest of all the lines. As soon as the wheels were put on a chassis, it glided along, not unlike a fifteenth-century Venetian galley at the Arsenal, having parts fitted in and onto it at each station along the way. Major parts, especially heavy ones like the engine and radiator, arrived on conveyors from above.

In 1914, Julian Street visited Ford Motor's Highland Park factory as part of the journey across America that resulted in his book *Abroad at Home*. By then, the plant had grown into a complex of eight large buildings and about a dozen satellite shops. Like most visitors, Street was overwhelmed, but more unsettling to him was that he could not understand what he saw going on inside the buildings. He did understand that the men grasped it all perfectly; they could "read" this new language of movement, and Street found that downright frightening.

"Of course there was order in that place, of course there was system—relentless system—terrible 'efficiency,'" Street wrote,

> but to my mind, unaccustomed to such things, the whole room, with its interminable aisles, its whirling shafts and wheels, its forest of roof-supporting posts and flapping, flying, leather belting, its endless rows of writhing machinery, its shrieking, hammering, and clatter, its smell of oil, its autumn haze of smoke, its savage-looking foreign population—to my mind it expressed but one thing and that was delirium. . . .
>
> Fancy a jungle of wheels and belts and weird iron forms—of men, machinery and movement—add to it every kind of sound you can imagine: the sound of a million squirrels chirking, a million monkeys quarreling, a million lions roaring, a million pigs dying, a million elephants smashing through a forest of sheet iron, a million boys whistling on their fingers, a million others coughing with the whooping cough, a million sinners groaning as they are dragged to hell—imagine all of this happening at the very edge of Niagara Falls, with the everlasting roar of the cataract as a perpetual background, and you may acquire a vague conception of that place.[67]

Even more arresting to Street than the noise of the factory was its sudden silence when the lunch break began and all the machines ground to a halt. Some of the men took out brown bags from home and sat down on or around the machines to eat, "like grimy soldiers on a battlefield." Other workers raced for the doors to get a breath of air and a glimpse of sun before returning to the line for the long afternoon.

Ford Motor Company's production nearly doubled every year for a decade after 1913, while the price of a Model T dropped by two thirds. The first experiments with the moving assembly line changed Ford Motor Company—for good and ill—from a fine, successful car company into the greatest industrial enterprise in the world, and from a high-quality workshop into an unskilled-labor mill. Both changes brought about by the moving assembly line also pushed Ford Motor Company beyond the business realm and put it squarely at the vanguard of social upheaval.

"Henry Ford didn't come around and watch us work out these assemblies," William Klann recalled of those days that transformed the company, its workers, and the industrial world.[68] Nevertheless, Ford would later be given credit for creating the assembly line, and what is more, he would take it.

The implementation of the moving assembly line led to huge gains in productivity at Ford Motor Company. It was the start of the era in which efficiency would become the company's most important concern. "The only things we did not do were those things we could not think of," Charles Sorensen observed in his 1956 memoir.[69] Everything, according to Sorensen, had to be tied to the company's capacity to produce ever more vehicles, ever faster. The one problem Ford Motor faced, apparently, was that the factory workers simply were not working hard enough.

John R. Lee, then Ford Motor's head of personnel, admitted that the realization caught everyone at every level of the firm by surprise. "It was along in 1912," he wrote just four years later, "that we began to realize something of the relative value of men, mechanism and material in the threefold phase of manufacturing, so to speak, and we confess that up to this time we had believed that mechanism and material were of the larger importance and that somehow or other the human element, or our men, were [sic] taken care of automatically and needed little or no consideration."[70] Lee, who had come to Ford Motor from Buffalo's Keim factory in 1909 along with Bill Knudsen, may have appeared more sensitive than some of Ford's homegrown executives, although he too could exhibit a chilling scientific detachment, at times referring to the company's workers as "human units."

By the end of 1913, the Highland Park factory employed about 13,000 people, using ever improving machinery in a facility optimized for efficiency. Nevertheless, Ford Motor's productivity per man increased by only 60 percent between 1909, the Piquette Avenue plant's last year, and 1913.[71] A jump in productivity by nearly two thirds may sound impressive, but not in light of the $210 million in capital investments the company made during the same four-year span. Contrasted with its own production forecasts, Ford Motor's worker productivity was not just unimpressive, but dangerous to the future of the enterprise. The situation was no better at other automobile factories, and seemed to be getting worse everywhere; after all, Ford was but one of a half dozen or so large automakers in and around Detroit who were increasing their hiring exponentially.

When Ford Motor Company was founded in 1903, its labor force had reflected the overall population of industrial workers in Detroit: half American-born and half foreign-born. In either case, the most common ethnic background was German, followed by English.[72] German immigrants to the United States were particularly welcome in Detroit: at least a quarter of those who arrived between 1875 and 1910 were skilled mechanics,[73] and an unusually high proportion of the workforce at Ford was composed of first- or second-generation German American craftsmen. Within the next few years, however, while Detroit's existing labor force had long since been tapped, the flow of workers out of the industrialized regions of northwestern Europe dwindled to a trickle. By 1915, for example, more people were immigrating to Germany than were emigrating from it.[74]

Back in the 1890s, 97 percent of immigrants to the United States hailed from Europe, evenly divided between northern and western Europeans, many of whom boasted valuable educations or skills, and eastern, central, and southern Europeans, who were more likely to be either farm workers or entirely unskilled. Two decades later, the ethnic composition of the arrivals had completely changed: only 17.5 percent of U.S. immigrants came from northern and western Europe, 62.1 percent were from other parts of the Continent, and 20.3 percent from elsewhere in the world.[75]

Whatever their national origins, the sheer numbers of immigrants exploded after the turn of the century. More than one million people made their way to America every year between 1906 and 1915.[76] The flood of newcomers from such unfamiliar cultures discomfited many Americans. "Slavonians, Italians, Greeks, Russians and Armenians," declared Wisconsin Congressman Victor L. Berger in a 1914 speech, "have been brought into this country by the million . . . simply because they have a lower standard of living . . . [and] have crowded out the Americans, Germans, Englishmen, and Irishmen."[77] Berger's tocsin echoed a refrain heard throughout the history of the United States, but it built to a crescendo in the 1910s.

Immigration was changing America, in some ways more than ever before or since. The swelling tide of new workers from 1905 to 1915 accelerated the pace of industrialization in the United States. Along with many other industries, auto manufacturers were creating more and more menial jobs through mechanization, almost simultaneously with the shifts in U.S. immigration. As the leading employer in the automobile industry, Ford Motor Company was confronted first and foremost by the myriad opportunities and liabilities inherent in the great immigration wave of the early twentieth century. By 1913, about half of Ford's workers did not understand English, making on-the-job training—the driving force behind much of the progress at Highland Park—difficult at best, and sometimes impossible.

Personnel chief John Lee characterized the hierarchies within each ethnic community as perhaps the most pernicious influences on America's new immigrants. "We have actually found in Detroit petty empires existing," Lee wrote of those who preyed upon the good faith of their less worldly countrymen, who "in some way or other . . . are shipped to Detroit and the knowledge of their coming imparted to someone in our city, to live in quarters selected for them, to buy their merchandise in a market other than [of] their own choosing. . . . Of course, it is to the interest of such men that these foreigners shall know nothing of the English language."[78]

By 1914, 71 percent of the company's workers were foreign-born. Germans no longer topped the statistics, although a notable proportion of men of that extraction had already risen to positions of authority within the organization. Some 21 percent of the workers at Highland Park came from Poland; 16 percent were Russian,[79] followed by much smaller percentages representing twenty other foreign countries, most from eastern and southern Europe: Romanians, Italians, Hungarians, Maltese, and Serbs. Immigrants from even farther-flung homelands also flocked to Highland Park, including Middle Easterners and Japanese, as did many natives of closer neighbors, such as Mexicans.[80]

One unanticipated outcome of Ford Motor's open embrace of foreign-born workers was to make Detroit home to the largest Arab community in the world outside the Middle East.[81] Many Middle Eastern immigrants had not planned to head to Detroit until they heard that Henry Ford's company did not discriminate against Arabs. Word spread quickly, and thus many of the earliest immigrants to the area were Lebanese and Syrians who were hired by Ford and settled around Highland Park to help assemble Model Ts. Ford sociological department archives recently opened at Dearborn's Henry Ford Museum and Library showed 555 Arabic men, classified as Syrians, among the factory's workers in 1916.[82] Bringing their culture with them, this mainly Muslim group (some were Lebanese Christians) established the first Arab mosque in the United States in 1919. Some of these Arab men not only worked at the Ford factory but opened small businesses of their own. Run by their wives and children to serve the workers at Highland Park, a variety of Arab grocery stores, coffee shops, and other enterprises had sprung up as early as the mid-1910s within walking distance of the Model T plant.

"You would get all of these little stores that catered to the Ford employees," remembered Chuck Shamey, the son of Lebanese immigrants. "These little buildings . . . where you buy gloves and you buy work shoes and whatever. . . . The workers would come to the stores and the restaurants and spend their money, and we'd see Ford jackets all the time, and Ford employees coming to get lunches and have dinner." In a very real sense, Highland Park, and later Ford Motor's River Rouge complex, acted as a Michigan-annex Ellis Island for Middle Eastern immigrants. "Ford Motor Company is part of our lives," Shamey explained of the result. "Henry Ford hired all the minorities, and of course they worked so hard. . . . And I think for the most part . . . the Arab immigrants, as hard as they worked, they were grateful for the jobs that they had."[83]

By the same token, members of the two minority groups most reviled by the ignorant and prejudiced in America remained virtually absent from the carmaking business. African Americans were hired at only a few auto factories, most notably Packard, until the labor crunch caused by the First World War. Jews were similarly discouraged from seeking employment in the automobile industry—and they were almost nonexistent at Ford Motor Company.[84]

However troglodyte its own bigotries, Ford Motor, supposed to be the most progressive company on Earth, could still advance only as fast as its most backward employee. Very few low-wage workers, however, had any real inclination to adapt or learn for the good of Highland Park; by and large, they couldn't stand the place. For all the competition for jobs that immigration and periodic economic downturns engendered, carmaking's long hours and tedious toil held little appeal. And employment at Ford Motor Company became even less attractive once the automated assembly line was implemented and the machines started to work the men, instead of the other way around.

"Repetitive labor—the doing of one thing over and over again and always the same way—is a terrifying prospect to a certain kind of mind," as Henry Ford wrote. "It is terrifying to me. I could not possibly do the same thing day in and day out.

"But," he added firmly, "to other minds, perhaps I might say to the majority of minds, repetitive operations hold no terrors. In fact, to some types of minds, thought is absolutely appalling."[85]

Some people thrive on drudgery, he seemed to insist—although his company could not seem to locate those people in 1912–1913, when absenteeism at Highland Park reached 10 percent a day and the annual turnover rate hit 380 percent.[86] Historian Keith Sward wrote, "So great was labor's distaste for the new machine system that toward the close of 1913 every time the company wanted to add 100 men to its factory personnel, it was necessary to hire 963."[87]

Autoworkers showed little loyalty toward any manufacturer and often quit without notice. Sometimes they had good reason, storming out in anger because of a harsh foreman or striking out in pursuit of new skills or better wages. Most of the time, however, "five-day men" quit after a week or so because they just could not bear another day at Highland Park. Ford Motor did make an effort to recognize its loyal employees (for instance, it extended a 10 percent bonus to those who had been with the company for more than three years), but the sort of men drawn to automobile production just did not have the "type of mind," as Henry Ford might have said, to think three years ahead. They were young men for the most part, and whatever their nationality, did most of their thinking about getting drunk on Saturday night and wondering whether to show up for work on Monday. "I pity the poor fellow who is so soft and flabby that he must always have an atmosphere of good feeling around him before he can do his work," Ford once confessed in explaining why he was often indifferent to the morale of workers. "There are such men. And in the end, unless they obtain enough mental and moral hardiness to lift them out of their soft reliance on 'feeling,' they are failures."[88]

In this respect Ford Motor's workers were no different from those at other factories, and that was something the company's executives could not abide. They had assembled the best factory with the largest profits and the greatest potential for more, yet the entire enterprise rested on the output of a shifting horde of poorly motivated workers. Under the circumstances, the factory could only keep pace with the rest of the industry. The unique problem born of Ford's ambition remained: the need to increase production by two times, ten times, perhaps even one hundred times. Production had to keep up with sales—and the cost per car had to go down, always down. For a while, it appeared that Ford Motor's only course would be increased mechanization, as the inherent employment problem was far bigger than any one company. It would just have to be accepted and dealt with as such.

8

The $5 Day

The years immediately prior to World War I were tumultuous times of labor unrest and high unemployment in the United States. For those who had jobs, conditions were very often abysmal. The Commission on Industrial Relations issued a report in 1914 claiming that 35,000 workers were killed in industrial accidents and 700,000 injured during the previous year. Job-related disease was rampant: rheumatism in Wisconsin's beer factories, tuberculosis in West Virginia's coal mines, permanent blindness in Pennsylvania's steel mills—it was as if earning an honest living required the laborer to give up some portion of his or her life. Meanwhile, hourly wages even for skilled workers ran as low as fifteen cents an hour. Amid such sordid conditions unionism and socialism were on the rise. General strikes—including mass picketing and violent clashes with police—were widespread. Class conflict had reached an epidemic state. "The working class and the employing class having nothing in common," said Mother Mary Jones, a furious organizer for the United Mine Workers of America.[1]

Exacerbating the class conflict was the callous way many industrial tycoons lorded their wealth, treating their laborers as uncouth, often rabble to be despised. As Glenn Porter wrote of du Pont in *The Workers' World at Hagley,* "He always had a large bag of dimes and nickels and he threw them up in the air and watched us scramble for them."[2] Jack London, in his 1907 novel *The Iron Heel,* summed up the prevailing ethos of workers ready to challenge the entire capitalist system: "In the face of the facts that modern man lives more wretchedly than the cave-man, and that his producing power is a thousand times greater than that of the cave-man, no other conclusion is possible than that the capitalist class has mismanaged . . . criminally and selfishly mismanaged."[3]

It was against this backdrop of smoldering class warfare that Henry Ford announced that he would pay a five-dollar-a-day wage to his workers. It was the company's most audacious business innovation yet—a true masterstroke. While other automobile makers were drawing lines in the sand, pitting themselves against the workers' rights movement, Ford brought his employees into the family fold. They suddenly *wanted* to work for Ford Motor Company. The announcement was a textbook example of how social problems can become economic opportunities if a company adopts bold, innovative policies. "Ford's action transformed American industrial society," economist Peter Drucker wrote in his *Management: Tasks, Responsibilities, Practices* (1974). "It established the American workingman as fundamentally middle-class."[4]

Stories about how the $5 Day was embraced by the workingman became the stuff of lore. "I heard there was going to be an announcement made that would startle the whole world," James O'Connor, a foreman at Highland Park, recalled of the first week of January 1914.[5] Indeed on January 5, Ford Motor scheduled a small press conference to make the momentous announcement. Only three reporters were invited: one each from Detroit's *Free Press, Journal,* and *News*; the news about to be broken was essentially local, but the company knew it would spread quickly enough once the city papers had it. The invited reporters were shown into the office of James Couzens, then vice president, treasurer, and voice of Ford Motor Company. Henry Ford was also there, as journalist Garet Garrett wrote, "with an air of restless detachment from the business in hand, and stood silently by a window while Mr. Couzens read aloud the statement he wished the reporters to publish."[6]

That announcement, as Couzens read it, began:

> The Ford Motor Company, the greatest and most successful automobile manufacturing company in the world, will, on January 12, inaugurate the greatest revolution in the matter of rewards for its workers ever known to the industrial world.
>
> At one stroke it will reduce the hours of labor from nine to eight, and add to every man's pay a share of the profits of the house. The smallest to be received by a man 22 years old and upwards will be $5 per day. . . . [7]

The reporters were stunned, their pencils frozen in their hands. Ford worker Logan Miller summed up the import more pointedly than Couzens or any of the reporters did that day: "In January 1914," recalled Miller, "it was announced that Ford was going to pay a minimum wage of $5 a day. At that time I was getting $0.32 an hour."[8] This new Ford Motor wage, equivalent to 62.5 cents an hour, amounted to nearly double what the average auto industry worker was earning in those days. The jump sounded even more drastic compared with the median wages paid in other industries—steelworking, for example, at $1.75 per day, or coal mining at around $2.50. The scheme was estimated to cost Ford Motor $10 million during its first year of implementation (the actual cost for that year turned out to be $5,838,929.80), but that was the least of what it meant. The $5 Day, brazen as it was, succeeded in producing what economists would later term "work-discipline."

In earlier eras, even the lowliest factory employees had taken enough pride in their work to discipline themselves, perform well, and thereby keep their jobs. The young automobile industry, and the freewheeling Ford Motor Company in particular, had lost that discipline, and with it the fundamental contract between employer and employee, a relationship based perhaps more than any other on mutual trust and rewards. Without that bond the firm could only spin its wheels, so to speak, making it imperative that Ford Motor find some way to reestablish contact with its labor force and instill work-discipline and motivation within each employee, to prove that workers were not "condemned to slave daily," as Mother Jones put it, for a mere pittance.[9] And it was a way to refute the workers' sentiment, which poet Carl Sandburg promulgated years later in "The People, Yes," that industrialists like Henry Ford preferred machines over humans because a machine "never wastes anybody's time . . . never talks back."[10]

"When Mr. Ford announced that he was going to pay the laboring man in the plant $5 a day, why, he just upset the whole financial situation," recalled George Brown, an office worker at Ford Motor at the time. "As I remember, the newspapers came out and just as much as said that Henry Ford was due for an insane asylum. Why, it was something unheard of to pay a man $5 a day, from $2.34. It was just double the figure. They thought he was crazy."[11]

Many business leaders assailed the $5 Day as an irrational gimmick by a cash-rich company. It infuriated other automakers. Hugh Chalmers, head of the car company bearing his name, complained bitterly that Ford might at least have warned the other firms that its audacious wage announcement was coming. Instead, until the chaos at the Ford employment office calmed down, most of Detroit's other automobile manufacturers suffered high absenteeism and general disruption. Alvan Macauley, the new president at Packard, even called Charles Sorensen at home on the night of the announcement to relate that the news had broken up a board of directors meeting at his own firm. According to Sorensen, Macauley reported that "we all felt like, 'What is the use? We can't compete with an organization like Ford Motor Company.'" Packard, one of America's most respected automakers, enjoyed a solid share of the market for high-price cars, thereby never having to come up against Ford head-on in the showroom. Macauley meant only that Packard could no longer compete with Ford Motor to hire the best workers. "How are we going to avoid paying these wages once you start paying them here in Detroit? We are not running a philanthropic business like you," Sorensen quoted Macauley.[12]

Most large-scale automakers felt the same way—that Ford Motor was in a special situation because it was so profitable, and thus to be resented. After all, it alone could afford such foolishly high wages. Ford Motor had become a "veritable Aladdin's Wonder Lamp proposition," wrote one rival company president petrified by the mere invitation to pick up the gauntlet thrown down by Henry Ford.[13] A *Harper's Weekly* essayist satirized the message the $5 Day gave to Ford employees as follows: "So far as some of you are concerned I have been paying you afterward when each year was over for work I didn't get. Paying you in advance for work I hope to get could not possibly cost me very much more—and could not be any more foolish than that."[14]

When the $5 Day was announced it became Henry Ford's personal property, in the sense that it was widely assumed to be his own idea. A few observers even accused Ford Motor of staging the whole announcement as a publicity stunt—except it wasn't just a stunt, although it certainly attracted publicity, especially for Henry Ford. In the flash of the unveiling of the $5 Day, he became one of the most famous men in the world, better known than his car, even. Already considered "the best friend the working man ever had" for developing the Model T, he suddenly became more than a captain of industry; he was elevated into a social philosopher. Even without the $5 Day, the world would have always remembered the Model T, of course, but the president of the company that built it would likely have remained as anonymous as his peers; Henry Ford would today be a hazy historical figure along the lines of fellow early carmakers John F. Dodge, Walter Chrysler, and Alfred P. Sloan Jr. Instead, in the space of a day, Henry Ford became a folk hero.

Ford, all his life awkward and ill at ease in the company of more than three or four others, found himself perfectly comfortable in the limelight before millions. Turned into a world celebrity overnight with this announcement, he discovered just how much he had to say, once he knew how many people were listening. Every time Ford pulled off the road to offer tramps and hitchhikers a job at Highland Park, it somehow made the Detroit newspapers. The magnanimous persona that formed about him, and which he heartily encouraged, would grow into "the Legend of Henry Ford"—and around this new asset his company would in turn reshape itself.[15]

Ford had always been the resident celebrity within the company. Not only was Ford Motor Company named for him, it had been founded on the reputation of the former race-car driver. After the inauguration of the $5 Day, however, Henry Ford *was* the company. Outsiders soon stopped trying to tell the difference, and his virtues and those of the Model T blurred. Ford proffered his folksy, front-porch opinions on topics for every member of the family. Many of his ideas were surprising in their day, although some have since come into fashion. For example, Ford was vehemently opposed to smoking, an unusual stance for a man of the world to take in 1914. He came to this objection, as he did so many of his extracurricular opinions, because Thomas Edison considered "The Little White Slaver" deadly.[16] "Friend Ford," Edison wrote him from his laboratory in West Orange, New Jersey, three months after the announcement of the $5 Day. "The injurious agent in cigarettes comes principally from the burning paper wrapper. The substance thereby formed is called 'Aerdein.' It has a violent action on the nerve centers, producing degeneration of the cells of the brain, which is quite rapid among boys. Unlike most narcotics this degeneration is permanent and uncontrollable. I employ no person who smokes cigarettes."[17]

Ford also held a dim view of drinking, rarely serving alcohol in his home. He encouraged people to run for pleasure instead, still challenging all comers to a 100-yard dash when he was seventy-five. His recommended eating habits were equally foresighted, insisting on small meals and leaning toward soybean products and vegetarian dishes. On another track, he also expressed his belief in reincarnation, and tried to explain how every person and animal has a "queen cell" that survives from one life to the next. Such notions, whether sage or not, would continue to gush forth from Ford for the next three decades, though how much of this entertaining monologue was genuine, how much a calculated act, and how much a dodge from self-revelation remains in question.

In any case, the $5 Day crystallized the winning formula Ford would use in crafting his image for the rest of his career: the tycoon as overgrown farm boy. Ford, it became known, was uninterested in people of "refinement," with their gravel walks, Harvard ways, and French wines. Before Henry Ford, millionaires looked and acted the part, wearing morning coats, surrounding their families with liveried servants, and shielding themselves from any but the loftiest pursuits and associations. Then as now, money changed people, and what's more, it was *seen* to change them. Henry Ford broke the millionaires' prescribed mold and presented himself as a man unchanged by his self-made fortune. Yet Henry Ford was changed by his money, and by the eerie isolation it brought to his life. He was changed as well by the exaggeration that celebrity brought him. For the sake of headlines, though, he remained that walking contradiction: the millionaire commoner. And where other businessmen shied away from the spotlight, Henry Ford courted the press, fully recognizing that his cracker-barrel ideas made good copy. "Ford, on that day in 1914 when he established a so-called minimum wage of five dollars for eight hours, acquired a halo that transformed him into the perfect target for all the 'realists' and debunkers," Roger Burlingame wrote in *Henry Ford*. "From that moment until long after he was always news."[18]

———————

Ironically, the one thing about which Henry Ford did not have an idea, at least before it was announced on January 5, 1914, was the $5 Day. The plan for the massive raise in employees' wages developed with surprising swiftness during the last few days of 1913 and the first week of 1914—and nearly everyone involved in its creation credited both the idea and the impetus behind its implementation to James Couzens. The one exception was Charles Sorensen, who maintained that he and Ford worked it out by themselves and then presented it to Couzens and the other executives.[19] It is possible that both versions are correct.

Ida Tarbell, the muckraking journalist whose damning 1904 *History of the Standard Oil Company* had led to the successful trust-busting, or breakup, of that firm in 1911, started work on a book about Ford Motor for which she interviewed James Couzens extensively. According to her unfinished manuscript, Couzens was at home reading a magazine "of socialist tendencies" in late December 1913 when the $5 Day germinated in his mind. A reader had sent a letter to the magazine asking a simple question: Why, if the editor believed so fervently in better conditions for workers, did he not pay his own employees more? The editor's response stated that a single small business, such as his magazine, could not change unless every other employer did. "That was an asinine answer!" Couzens exclaimed.

"An idea flashed through his head," Tarbell wrote. "Why shouldn't the Ford Motor Company take a decided lead in paying the highest wages to its workers, thus enabling them to enjoy better living conditions[?]"[20]

The idea of sharing wealth rather than hoarding it fit consistently with Couzens's long held personal philosophy. One of his daughters, Madeleine, had once read an account of Ford Motor's profitability and from it calculated her family's fortune. "Whew, that's a lot of money we have!" she concluded. Her father immediately corrected young Madeleine: the money was not really theirs, he explained, but only trusted to them.[21] In the 1920s, after Couzens left Ford Motor and was elected mayor of Detroit, he instituted a work relief program that became a model for the Roosevelt administration's New Deal initiatives during the Great Depression. At the same time, he donated his own fortune to children's charities in Michigan.

"When you have a team of horses and no work for it," Couzens said to those who argued against his plan to help the unemployed, "you feed it and care for it just the same. Our workmen deserve just as good treatment as our horses."[22] Of course, by the time Couzens made his statement, workhorses had pretty much disappeared from city streets, thanks in part to his efforts at Ford Motor, but everyone understood his point that a society has an obligation to help its least able members share in the general well-being. The initial motivation behind the $5 Day years earlier was that a company, according to Couzens, has the same obligation toward its workers. Exasperated by the hypocrisy in the magazine editor's rationalization, Couzens decided that Ford

Motor should take the dramatic step of sharing profits with its workers not after the fact in year-end bonuses, but in advance, based on reasonable revenue projections. The first person who had to be convinced was Henry Ford.

Ford protested quite accurately, when he first heard Couzens's scheme, that he paid his workers as much as any other employer. It would be on its finer points that the business wizard would have to sell the plan to his cohort—and it would take two days of continuing arguments. The most stinging of these dwelled on the marked increase in union activity in and around the Ford plant during 1913. The Industrial Workers of the World was focusing on the automobile business, having organized an industry-wide strike against Akron, Ohio, tire makers earlier in the year. Although ultimately unsuccessful, the Akron strike had turned violent and disruptive—two things Henry Ford loathed in any sphere. Couzens—who had earned the nickname Old Bear—played upon those fears, grilling Ford: "Do you know that a Russian woman, an anarchist, has been talking to those unemployed men and advocating that you be assassinated?"[23] As the debate continued, Couzens predicted that the announcement of the $5 Day alone would be worth $10 million of advertising. (Surveying the saturation coverage that followed the plan's announcement, two publications in a position to judge—*Printer's Ink* and the *New York Times*—would corroborate Couzens's original estimate.)[24]

Everyone seemed to perceive the $5 Day a little bit differently. To Henry Ford, it was an enormous risk that would turn into the single greatest publicity coup in American business history and the keystone of his lasting legend. To James Couzens, it was an act of defiance and benevolence at the same time, one that would show just how unlike other companies Ford Motor really was. To manager John Lee, the $5 Day would hone a new type of auto worker, one who was relaxed, confident, and motivated—and that, as Lee put it, "is the most powerful economic factor that we can use in the shape of a human being."[25]

Outside Highland Park, however, the most significant impact of the $5 Day lay in its demonstration of how the modern assembly line could be made to work to its full potential. A year earlier, production coordinator Charles Sorensen had prepared a set of figures "compiling production estimates for the next few years," which he showed to a very encouraged Henry Ford.

"I did a lot of night work on this," he wrote in his memoir. "Model T production had virtually doubled each year—34,000 in 1910–11; in 1911–12, it was 78,000 cars. The prospect for 1912–13 was more than 168,000 and by 1920 it should be one million, or beyond the capacity of Highland Park."

That was exactly the kind of talk Ford and Couzens liked to hear.

"As I began building the production figures and costs with varying increasing columns, what caught Mr. Ford's eye particularly was the ever-decreasing costs as volume increased," Sorensen noted. "Finally he said, 'That's enough, Charlie, I have the smell of it now.'"[26] According to Sorensen's figures, the reduced costs, on a per-car basis, realized through increased production could pay for a $5 Day, a $10 Day, or for that matter a $50 Day, depending upon the workers' capacity to keep up with the machinery.

Henry Ford discussed the idea at length with his plant superintendents, most likely after Couzens had posed the plan to him first. Ford may have asked Sorensen to present his findings at that time, without revealing the origin of the idea. Both John Lee and factory floor manager P. E. Martin seemed inclined to think the scheme would prove a huge waste of money. Ford pressed the point, though, and once his lieutenants were sold, however shakily, the company president returned to see his business manager.

For his part, Couzens stayed determined to reach a decision. "If we talk of anything for more than forty-eight hours, we never do it," he observed. Finally, Henry Ford agreed in principle to institute a raise in pay along with reduced hours—but he suggested $3.50 as the daily wage.

"No, it's five or nothing," Couzens declared.

"Then make it four," Ford countered. He was afraid that the bristly, frugal P. E. Martin would not go along with any raise higher than that. But he should have known better than to try to negotiate with James Couzens.

"Five or nothing," remained the moneyman's reply.[27]

George Brown, who worked on Couzens's staff, portrayed the dispute between Ford and Couzens a bit differently. "The only friction that I knew of between Mr. Couzens and Mr. Ford was when the $5 Day went into effect," Brown recalled. "That was what I could really say was the first friction. Mr. Ford figured it was just the men at the machines who were entitled to it. Mr. Couzens couldn't see that. He couldn't see that that was on the level, and he and Mrs. Ford had the same idea, that what's good for one is good for the other. Between the two, they fought Mr. Ford."[28]

In the scant two weeks before the decision would be made to institute the $5 Day, a swirl of influences came to bear on Henry Ford, in addition to the pressure from his wife and his business manager. The decision was an unusual one for him, in that it marked one of the rare occasions that he actually had to act the part of company president. Most matters either originated with Henry Ford, such as his concept for the Highland Park plant, or else could be left to James Couzens to figure out. The $5 Day proposal fell into neither category, which meant Ford had to listen and ponder rather than act, as he usually did, in a manner either dictatorial or oblivious.

"Finally," George Brown said, "Mr. Ford gave in." And as soon as he did, he was given no chance to change his mind. When Horace Rackham, one of the lawyers who had taken a stake in Ford Motor ten years before, happened to stop by the office, Couzens immediately recognized he had a quorum of the board of directors present, and brought the "plan [for] better equalizing the company's earnings between the stockholders and the labor" to a vote. It carried, three to nothing.

Two days later the local news reporters were standing in Couzens's office scribbling, and within hours of that the news was bolting around the world that a major American company was doubling its employees' wages while simultaneously reducing their hours. The same story would make just as big headlines today, but in 1914 its significance went well beyond a windfall for Ford Motor's workers. Up to that bold moment in January, no business had ever nodded to the importance of labor in such a dramatic and costly way. The $5 Day marked, if any one date could, the end of the Gilded Age.

———

As might be expected, the men at Highland Park greeted the news of the across-the-board raise with glee. The lowliest workers seemed the most stunned; even the basest menial laborer was eligible for the $5 minimum daily wage. To those who questioned how a sweeper could possibly be worth that much money, Henry Ford replied, "Why, a sweeper can save five dollars a day in small tools and parts off the floor of the shop."[29] At the other end of the scale, skilled workers would receive somewhat more than the minimum, typically $6 to $7 a day.

Charles C. Krueger, a metal forger, was one of the new $7-a-day men. "Within three weeks, I went from $0.43 an hour to $0.87 an hour," he recalled to the penny, forty-two years later. "I just doubled what I was earning." He went on to point out, "I never heard anyone in the skilled trades mentioning that they resented the fact that the unskilled laborer was getting practically as much as they were. I never heard that," Krueger explained, "because they couldn't go anywhere else and get more than what they were getting."[30]

One worker, a native of Hungary, promptly doubled his personal output of parts for a subassembly. When Highland Park production chief Bill Knudsen asked him how he had managed such a jump, the man replied in broken English: "Mr. Ford pay me two-fifty, he get 250 pieces. Mr. Ford now pay me five dollars a day, he get 500 pieces. I pay him back." His actions, even more than his awkward words, epitomized the response Ford Motor was looking for from the wage increase—even while he spoke to the boss he never lifted his eyes from his work, and kept turning out parts all the while.[31]

The subtlest point of the new wage scale was its being a "profit-sharing" plan, rather than a mere raise. The implication of the term, which was explained many times to the men, was that at its inception the $5 Day would be a one-year experiment in paying workers their share of projected profits in advance. If those profits did not materialize, it was made clear, then the profit-sharing portion of the wage would be withdrawn in 1915, and pay rates would revert to their former levels. As the company expected, employees became used to their early profit shares in a hurry and appreciated the bounty so much they indeed did their part to make sure it kept coming, by boosting their own productivity, practically to a man. Any laggards were very easily replaced—as Ford Motor Company learned almost immediately.

"Well sir, when that announcement was made through the newspapers," George Brown remembered of the $5 Day, "the next day it was a sight there on Manchester Avenue. That place was packed so that a human being couldn't move! It was almost what you'd call a riot. Everybody wanted to work at Ford Motor then at $5 a day, because that was better than doubling a man's wage."[32] In fact, 10,000 men trudged all the way up Woodward Avenue, by foot or streetcar, in Detroit's frigid winter temperatures, to the Ford hiring office on Manchester Avenue, the day after the announcement. While the January 5 revelation had indeed made mention of the company's need for an additional 8,000 men to staff the third shift that would bring twenty-four-hour production to Highland Park, the crush of applicants could not possibly be accommodated. For the moment, the overwhelming response to the wage hike embarrassed Ford Motor, but even that only generated still more publicity, as the response itself became newsworthy. And it did not abate. Trains arrived in Detroit every day carrying men with but one thought in mind: $5 a day.

Couzens and Ford were both in New York City for the 1914 automobile show the second week in January, but they received regular reports from Detroit about the siege. Or at least Couzens did; Henry Ford was himself under siege by reporters, along with a horde of newly minted well-wishers and hero-worshipers. From New York, Couzens issued the order that only those who had resided in Detroit (or adjoining communities) for at least six months were eligible for the $5 Day. Such fine points went lost on the parade of adventurous, desperate, and just plain greedy men who craved Ford Motor's profit-sharing scheme to the point that they could hear nothing else.

On January 12, the date on which the plan officially went into effect, the job-seeking mob grew especially large and agitated, numbering an estimated 12,000 even though the temperature stood near zero. Frustrated and frightened of being left out, the crowd grew thick enough to keep Ford Motor's extant employees from entering the factory. Those workers had to punch their time clocks, however, or risk disciplinary action for being late, not to mention missing out on the new wage themselves. Suddenly, it struck both the current and prospective workers that they were vying for the same, limited number of jobs. Scuffles broke out lasting for two hours.

"It finally got so that even the police couldn't handle it," Brown recalled, "and the servicemen [Ford's own security force] couldn't handle it. They had to call the Highland Fire Department to throw some water on them to try and disperse the crowd. The men started to cut the hoses, so the Fire Department had to stop."[33] No one could blame the men for cutting the hoses. They were being drenched with water on a frigid, windy day. And they still wanted those high-paying jobs. After turning over a few cars and raiding the lunch wagons near their dream employer's premises, the crowd finally dispersed.

During that frantic first week, would-be workers unable to present themselves in person wrote to apply, mostly to Henry Ford himself. Their efforts would have gone for naught even had the president of the firm not been in New York, as he refused to read letters except in dire circumstances. The posted applications and "fan mail" reached an estimated one thousand letters a day after the announcement. The torrent would continue at that pace for more than a decade. Even people with no particular business with Ford Motor Company wrote to its founder as though he were an old friend. This sort of thing just did not happen at other automobile companies—or at any other company, for that matter. "Letters! Letters! Letters!" exclaimed one reporter. "It rains letters. It pours letters."[34] During the first wave of enthusiasm after Ford Motor's revolutionary pledge, the company's mailbags included an unusual proportion of poems, written especially for Henry Ford, to mark the occasion.

Word of the $5 Day spread throughout the South, where fifty years after the Emancipation Proclamation most African Americans were still treated as third-class citizens, toiling for provisions in a sharecropping system that was both segregated and corrupt. Disenfranchised and poor beyond words, many of these African Americans decided to migrate to the North, the Promised Land, where high-paying jobs could be landed in Detroit and discrimination was purportedly almost nonexistent. "Five-dollars a day was what Mr. Ford said, and Negroes came hundreds of miles to line up outside his employment offices," LeRoi Jones (Amiri Baraka) wrote in *Blues People*.[35] These sharecroppers had heard that Ford Motor paid blacks an equal wage and that economic opportunity was a genuine reality. Numerous blues songs, in fact, were written by African Americans around 1914 about "workin' in Mr. Ford's place," where "a man is treated like a man." As Blind Blake sang: "I'm goin' to Detroit, get myself a good job / Tried to stay around here with the starvation mob / I'm goin' to get me a job in Mr. Ford's place, stop these eatless days from starin' me in the face."[36] In mass exodus these African Americans dropped their plows and traveled north of the Mason-Dixon Line in search of a New Jordan. "The name *Ford* became synonymous with northern opportunity," Jones explained, "and the Ford Model T was one of the first automobiles Negroes could purchase—'the poor man's car.'"[37]

Those intent on living the American dream of the $5 Day were as avid as the first Oregon Trail pioneers or the Forty-Niners in the California gold rush, setting out after theirs and willing to leave everything they knew behind. Die maker Logan Miller of Kentucky was among them: a married man, he had been making only half the daily wage Ford Motor proffered. "Years before, my brother had been in Detroit," Miller explained. "He had sent me pictures . . . of the beautiful city of Detroit. From the time I saw those pictures I had a desire to live in Detroit. That, with the idea of the $5 Day, looked very good to me. With what belongings we had, we moved to Detroit. I had the ambition of becoming an employee at Ford Motor Company. I went to Highland Park and asked for a job. I told them I was a die maker. Of course, there were so many men applying for jobs that they had set certain restrictions, such as a man had to be in the city of Detroit six months before they would even consider an applicant." Nevertheless, with his valuable experience and skills, he talked his way into an immediate position at the company.[38]

Unfortunately for some, there was a caveat attached to the promise of Ford's $5 Day. The fine print in the profit-sharing plan was that an employee's personal living situation had to meet certain criteria. The company laid out three basic categories of applicants who would qualify for the higher wage. All others received the standard $2.38 daily wage. The three acceptable categories were:

1. Married men living with and taking good care of their families;
2. Single men over the age of 22 and of proven thrifty habits;
3. Men under 22 years of age and women of any age, who provided the sole support to some next of kin or blood relative.[39]

These vague character descriptions left a great deal of room for subjective judgment. What exactly constituted "taking good care of" a family, and how did one prove "thrifty habits"? The company enlisted a team of thirty investigators charged with ascertaining which employees and applicants fully qualified for the raise, as set out in the guidelines.

C. G. Milner, who applied to work at Ford Motor's Atlanta plant, recalled a somewhat intimidating evaluation process. "At that time, I was boarding in Atlanta," he said later, "and my folks were living out in the suburbs. The fellow making the investigation did not ask me so many questions; he went around asking other people about me. He even talked to my mother and called the lady that was running the boardinghouse. They really checked on everything before you were paid $5 a day."[40]

The company felt obligated, it explained, to ensure that Ford Motor's profits would not merely underwrite local saloons and brothels. Many of the points on which the company judged its employees did indeed encourage them to lead better lives, at least in terms of orderliness. Sobriety was heartily encouraged for all, and particularly for bachelors; husbands and fathers were expected to provide for their dependents, and the company bank encouraged savings with an advantageous rate of return. Although these early expectations and investigations of its employees were well meant, their invasions of workers' privacy stood unprecedented among automobile manufacturers and listed into the troubling realm of social engineering.

"They went out to the home and they had a regular form that they filled out," remembered William F. Pioch, a tool designer. "They picked on your life's history; how you lived, where you went to church, and everything."[41]

The form was based on a letter sent by Ford Motor to its operating offices after the announcement of the $5 Day. It spelled out the matters the company would investigate in relation to all employees below the top tier of management. It read, in part:

> In our investigations here we use the following questions: Are you married? If married, how many dependent upon you? If single, how many dependent upon you and to what extent? Relationship of dependents? Residence of dependents? Married men: do you live with your wives [sic]? Have you ever had domestic troubles? Are your habits good or bad? Have you a bank account? What is the name of the bank and the number of the book? Last employment? Reasons for leaving? Would your home conditions be bettered were your income increased? Would you be willing to follow some systematic plan of saving suggested by the company?[42]

"They went to my home," William Pioch continued. "My wife told them everything. There was nothing to keep from them. Of course, there was a lot of criticism on that. It was kind of a funny idea in a free state."[43]

The Ford Motor investigations, which two years later developed into the company's full-fledged sociological department, were indeed a very funny idea in a free state. Cynics even wondered whether the investigators' home visits and simple but deeply personal questions might not actually be a tactic for discouraging union activity. Whether that was the real reason behind Ford Motor's clean-living rules and monitoring of compliance with them, the suggestion certainly cast a specter. In 1914 and for more than two decades afterward, union-related discussions in automobile factories were generally held in secret, to minimize the risk of immediate dismissal for those involved. Perhaps (it is fair to say) the carmakers' employees gave up their rights to privacy; legally, the mere acceptance by a worker of the profit-sharing covenant with Ford Motor authorized the company to keep close tabs on his or her home life. But that acknowledgment on the part of Ford's workforce was all it took to stifle union activity at Highland Park for a long time to come.

The company's stated motive cannot be dismissed: Ford was paying good money and it had every right to demand a fit, alert, focused, and enthusiastic workforce. Many firms across the business spectrum had learned through experience that workers plagued by debt, drinking, or domestic turmoil simply do not produce at the level of people less distracted by personal worries. When Ford Motor Company expressed its desire for the cream of the crop of employees, it meant the *whole* employee, not merely his or her specific job skills. And so, by using its generous profit-sharing plan to justify keeping only "settled" personnel at Ford, the company successfully honed the effective, reliable workforce it needed.

Interestingly, many of the criteria upon which Ford Motor Company based its extension of the $5 Day to a particular employee presaged the incentives to probity that would be built into the U.S. Federal Income Tax Code, which was emerging during the same period. Like the former, the tax code offered a monetary incentive for people to adopt and maintain stolid lifestyles characterized by home ownership, responsibility toward dependents, and thrift. Ford Motor, in other words, was onto the formula that has since been accepted for encouraging the sort of clean living that leads to a productive workforce or populace. The practice proved that, while it may indeed be impossible to legislate morality, it is quite easy to buy it. As a private concern, however, even in an era of company towns and benevolent paternalism, Ford Motor's intrusive employee investigations skated right up to the line between social engineering and social control.

Because each background check took several months to complete, most Ford Motor Company employees did not see their boost in wages until the middle of 1914, if then. Nevertheless, the impact on the factory floor proved immediate, even among workers still waiting to be vetted. According to John Lee, production in many departments jumped by 50 percent or more. Similarly, overall factory productivity climbed some 15 to 20 percent, starting almost from the date of the announcement. The average daily absenteeism rate dropped from 10 percent to less than 0.5 percent.[44] Turnover—that constant drain on employee morale and factory output—fell equally far and fast, since those who had Ford jobs now wanted to make sure they kept them. Where the personnel office had made 53,000 replacement hirings in 1913, Lee calculated that in 1915 only 2,000 were required, to bolster a total workforce half again larger.

"The $5 Day was the greatest cost-cutting move I ever made," Henry Ford would proclaim. By making the productivity of labor as predictable as that of the machines that set its pace, Ford Motor Company had done no less than redefine industrial capitalism. With its introduction of the mechanized assembly line in 1913, Ford Motor brought the dreaded "speed-up" to the labor force, to the utter delight of manufacturers everywhere. However, being the first concern capable of fully mechanized mass production, Ford Motor Company was also the first to recognize that the whole process would stall flat without the enthusiastic commitment of the workforce. Thus the pioneering company bought that commitment, and perhaps a great deal more, with its groundbreaking $5 Day—to the utter delight of workers everywhere. With that, it was capital's turn to feel intimidated by the Ford revolution.

And a revolution it was, for without the concentrated efforts and abilities of the Ford management team, this twofold advance in industrialized democracy would likely have taken decades to occur. With Ford's aggressiveness, the revolution took just one year. After that, the course was set by which both capital and labor could benefit from the speed-up in production and wages. Prosperous workers begat a prosperous marketplace, which in turn spawned more prosperous companies and in time the result was a new, conspicuously consumer-based economy instigated by Ford Motor and launched spectacularly with the announcement of the $5 Day.

Henry Ford went on to cherish the adulation that resulted. "My idea of heaven," he told a magazine reporter in 1914, "if there is such a place and you can go there, is that the only thing you can take along is goodwill."[45] As historian Roderick Nash explained in *The Nervous Generation: American Thought, 1917–1930*, the $5 Day turned Ford—both the man and the company—overnight into "an international symbol of the new industrialization."[46]

The $5 Day inspired such ardent goodwill that Ford's employees took to wearing it on their sleeves. "Everybody wore their badges on the outside of their coats because they were quite proud to be a Ford man," Charles Krueger explained of the new fashion seen around Detroit. "They didn't wear them inside or where they wouldn't show; they wore them right on the lapel of their coat or on their shirts. Of course, you had to wear them up there to get into the plant, but on Sundays or any other day, these fellows kept their badges on all the time to show everyone that they were Ford men."[47]

PART TWO

The Forward March

9

Alone at the Top

The first ones to grasp the full significance of Ford's $5 Day were the merchants of Detroit, the fourth largest city in the nation and its fastest-growing industrial center. Retailers swiftly cashed in on their own economic miracles by raising prices for clothes, food, rent, and other necessities. Almost overnight, the new wage increase transformed the area around Highland Park into a boomtown.[1] When shopkeepers spied a Ford Motor Company badge, their eyes lit up: Ford employees always had ready money, being paid in cash every two weeks.[2]

Aware that workers were being fleeced at some local shops, Ford Motor Company opened its own store on the Highland Park campus in the summer of 1914. The company store sold only work clothes at first, adding household items and a commissary for foodstuffs later. "You could save anywhere from $3 to $4 on a pair of shoes," remembered George Brown. "Well, that was a big saving. On a work shoe that would probably be $3 downtown, you could buy for $2 out there. They carried A-1 material. It was no shoddy stuff. It was always good material that you bought at great saving too."[3]

Before long, the commissary shops, which eventually numbered eleven, became an integral part of the Ford empire, benefiting employees as well as the company. Soon, the Highland Park store sold some 235,000 pounds of meat a month at lower prices than any competitor in the area, still earning a profit of $262,538.[4]

In 1960, Michigan State University business professors Stanley C. Hollander and Gary A. Marple published a statistical analysis showing how Ford Motor managed to make money even while selling fish, bread, and cheese cheaper than any other outlet in the Great Lakes region. In that study, titled *Henry Ford: Inventor of the Supermarket?*, the professors concluded that Ford Motor's commissary shops were the precursors to the Kroger's, Winn-Dixies, and Wal-Marts of the future, and that Ford had anticipated the new trend toward one-stop shopping a full decade before anyone else. "In many ways, the Ford stores were really *super* supermarkets," Hollander and Marple explained. "A highly routinized form of clerk service was used, instead of the self service and open display of the modern market, but in practically all other respects the Ford commissaries exemplified the modern techniques of mass retailing. The logistics of stock handling and merchandise movement within the stores was developed to a high degree of efficiency."[5]

Ford Motor's sense of responsibility (or paternalism) toward its workforce did not end with its company stores. Concern for the health of employees led Ford Motor to establish an infirmary where careful records were kept on workplace injuries. Soon medical science began to converge with sociology at the Ford factory. Whether motivated by compassion or the ongoing drive for efficiency, the company assiduously traced each injury to its source on the factory floor and sought ways to eliminate dangerous situations. In many of the early accidents, clothing turned out to be the culprit, as neckties got tangled in pulleys or shirtsleeves were caught in presses. Management took note while machines were redesigned so that there were fewer places where clothing could catch, workers were issued a simple dress code with safety in mind, and foremen were instructed to maintain a constant watch for clothing that interfered with particular pieces of equipment.[6]

―――――――

The astounding pace of change at Ford Motor Company in 1914 made it the most glamorous, most widely discussed company in America, if not the world. It was not merely that Ford was trying so many things in so many arenas, nor even that it was succeeding with most of them. What attracted the admiration and envy of outsiders was the brimming confidence Ford Motor exuded. The public's fascination with Henry Ford's maverick role lay in part in his overt image as an iconoclastic, oddly nineteenth-century presence in the twentieth century's most up-to-date business. It seemed that through modern industry Ford had reopened the American frontier. His company was more than a profit-making enterprise; it was a pioneer's domain, where old assumptions about business were cast out in favor of fresh notions. As on any frontier, money did not make for heroes, and Ford Motor had started with very little money. The company did not rely on established connections, either, remaining as stubbornly independent as it had been on the day it was founded. Ford Motor proved that creating a fresh new world out of the industrial domain rested on only two crucial qualities: competence and confidence.

Years later, Henry Ford would underline that point in a discussion about education with a young man who had grown frustrated at what he deemed the industrialist's narrow view of schooling. "These are different times: this is the modern-age," the lad tried to protest.

"Young man," Ford snapped back, "I invented the modern age."[7]

Or at least he drove it along. In truth, by 1900 the United States had already developed into the greatest industrialized country in the world, producing 24 percent of its manufactured goods. By 1913, that share had risen to a full third, with U.S. manufacturing output matching that of European industrial behemoths Britain, France, and Germany combined. Of course, at that point Ford Motor Company was turning out some 200,000 vehicles a year. Thanks to the moving assembly line, the time needed to produce a Model T dropped from 12 hours 8 minutes in 1913 to a remarkable 1 hour 33 minutes only a year later, when the company achieved its founder's long-held goal of making 1,000 cars a day.[8] By then, it produced and sold more vehicles than the next ten U.S. automakers combined.

The next largest American automaker, Willys-Overland of Dayton, Ohio, built about 48,000 cars in 1914 and remained a distant second to Ford Motor Company throughout most of the decade.[9] The 263,210 Model Ts that Ford produced came in a variety of body styles, although the small hood, dashboard, fenders, and, of course, the engine assembly were common to all of them. The bodies themselves, however, were ingeniously and easily interchangeable; one could be lifted off and another bolted in place with basic tools and the help of a few neighbors. Ford Motor Company, like most of its competitors at the time, encouraged its customers to buy at least two different bodies. The enclosed one could be stored in the garage during the summer, when an open touring-car design would be nicer on sunny drives.

Through its first few years of production the Model T had come in different colors according to the body style—red for touring cars, gray for roadsters, and so on. By 1911, the company determined that since it could sell all the cars it could make anyway, using one color of paint would be more efficient in production terms, if more drab for the nation's streets. The color chosen in 1911 was dark Brewster green, with red striping.[10] That choice was subject to change, however, like everything else at Highland Park.

To produce a consistent finish, Brewster green or any other hue of paint required fourteen coats. And each coat had to dry, which could take up to an entire day depending on the humidity. Once a coat was dry, it had to be sanded by hand before the next could be applied. The process of finishing a car body could therefore easily take two weeks.[11] Black paint, as a simpler composition, dried more quickly than colored paint. In fact, to finish a body in black took only about a day and a half, rather than two weeks. By 1914, in consequence, all Model Ts came finished in black paint, and Henry Ford was credited with making the slyly generous offer that "you can have a Model T in any color you want, as long as it's black." Whether Ford actually made the famous quip or not, he was happy to reap the benefit from it or any other little chuckle that promoted his car. The unyielding stance behind the joke smacked of a harsher truth, however—one that would nearly strangle Ford Motor Company. In the mid-1920s, General Motors would counter Ford's obstinance with an aggressive willingness to give its customers anything they wanted, including a whole palette of colors to choose from. But for the time being in 1914, for $500, Model T buyers could not have cared less what their chariots looked like. It was where they could go that mattered.

The advent of the Model T, however, brought with it numerous social problems. With restrictions for operating a motor vehicle practically nonexistent, accidents were epidemic. One fatality hit close to home at Ford Motor. James Couzens gave his elder son, Homer, a Model T for his fourteenth birthday in 1914, back when it was not unusual to see boys that age driving around rural roads like those near the Couzens family's weekend retreat north of Detroit. But that August 8, his T overturned with Homer at the wheel, pinning the boy underneath. James and Margaret Couzens were immediately called to the scene, but by the time they reached the wreckage, their son was dead. James Couzens blamed himself and the car. In the lifelong grief that poisoned him ever after, he never again felt quite the same way he had earlier about Ford Motor Company. According to his biographer, Harry Barnard, "He was haunted by the fact that it was a Ford car—his own product, the foundation of his fortune—in which Homer had died."[12]

Other chinks began to appear in Ford Motor's corporate esprit, too. As the Highland Park plant expanded with the ongoing refinement of its operations, adding buildings every year, one room sat ever more idle, to the point that it began to seem something of a waste of space. That was Henry Ford's office in the administration building, an oblong room of generous proportions, the echo from its emptiness hushed by an enormous oriental rug. A small desk faced out forlornly and quietly from one corner of the otherwise bare office. Even the desk was wasted, though, as Henry Ford was rarely at it, even when he was at the plant. When asked once why he preferred to visit his employees on their turf rather then summon them to his own, Ford replied, "I go to them to save time. . . . I've found that I can leave the other fellow's office a lot quicker than I can get him to leave mine."[13] In the early days, Ford did not consider his real work the kind done in an office. His job, as he saw it, was in the design room or out on the bustling factory floors, and sometimes out on the roads, where Ford often devoted a long part of a day just to test-driving his products. On some days, Henry Ford didn't go to Highland Park at all, choosing to stay at home and work on some pet project all his own. In 1914, for instance, he was frequently off developing a prototype for a new tractor, to be produced by a new manufacturing company he was also working on starting. But with P. E. Martin, Charles Sorensen, and Bill Knudsen overseeing production, Norval Hawkins running sales, and Harold Wills supervising design and engineering, Ford Motor Company did not want for the absence of its boss. An insistence on excellence suffused the company from the top men down through every department, and with James Couzens in charge of it all, supported by John and Horace Dodge, the firm was in no danger of letting anything slide.

The character of Ford Motor's executive team was reflected in that of the company they had pulled out of the ground: bold, tough, and composed no matter the crisis. With the exception of Martin and Sorensen, however, none would remain with the company to the end of the decade. Almost every year after 1914, Henry Ford would watch one of them go, never with any obvious manifestation of regret. Inevitably, this attrition of the old guard would lead to a change in character for the company. But that process had begun long ago, with the change in the character of Henry Ford.

Ford's assumption of his new role as the world's greatest industrialist, first in the press and then at his company, made for a dramatic alteration in his already prickly personality. And while deceptively endearing from a distance, to those close to him the change in Henry Ford was decidedly not for the better.

Other tycoons at Ford's level of success—not that there have been many—clung tenaciously to their trusted partners and executives. Both John D. Rockefeller and Andrew Carnegie pronounced the maintenance of long associations with productive colleagues fundamental to success in business. By the same token, by the time they had reached age fifty-one, as Henry Ford did in 1914, Rockefeller and Carnegie either had retired or were preparing to, each having enjoyed the satisfactions and endured the strain of power for upward of twenty years. At the same age Henry Ford was just getting a taste of what immense power felt like and it did not put him in a mind to retire. Instead, it propelled him to remake himself into the visionary of Highland Park and the people's philosopher of industry—an oxymoron in the case of anyone but Ford. The success of the Model T and the $5 Day had catapulted him above other men at his company who were at least equally responsible for both. And with that boost a terrible change came over Ford. "The whole secret of a successful life is to find out what it is one's destiny to do, and then do it," he would rationalize in his ghostwritten 1929 tome *My Philosophy of Industry*.[14] Implied here was that the acknowledged general no longer wanted to be first among his officers. He wanted to be rid of them.

"To be right means mainly to be in tune with destiny and willing to obey," Ford continued in the words of that book's actual author, technical writer Fay Leone Faurote.[15] "It does not necessarily mean to be agreeable, nor to be agreed with, nor to be popular; it does mean to be useful in the purpose which destiny is trying to achieve in us and through us. If a man is right, he need not fear to stand alone; he is not alone."[16]

The first to go were the Dodge brothers.

———

While Henry Ford's bare room at Highland Park sat idle most of the time, John Dodge's office in nearby Hamtramck bustled with business in 1914. Dodge may have been rough around the edges, but his elegant office was anything but, paneled in oak and lined with leaded-glass bookcases interrupted by a marble fireplace better suited to a castle.[17] The room's furnishings were heavy and strong, like its occupant, and reflected his ducal tastes. His ability to indulge those tastes resulted largely from the enormous profits of Ford Motor Company. With millions of dollars in dividends flowing in, John and his brother, Horace, spent money gobs at a time on their town-size farm, Meadow Brook; on fleets of yachts so powerful they drew the envy of U.S. Navy men; and on donations large enough to keep the Detroit Symphony alive and vibrant.

The relationship between the two companies, so essential to both, was built on a foundation of abiding trust combined with constant argument. As individual charter shareholders, the Dodge brothers collected hefty dividends from Ford Motor, but their own firm did business with the company, too, without any favored status. Indeed, once the two firms' business relationship was firmly cemented, Couzens hammered the Dodges down on automotive part prices with extra vehemence, simply because they supplied so many that any savings per unit would translate into huge savings in actual dollars. Fortunately, Dodge Brothers proved just as aggressive as Ford Motor at reaping the benefits of increased efficiency, and so it managed to keep earning at least a few million dollars a year for each of its founding partners, despite Couzens's price squeeze. Accused early on of taking a usurious sixty-cent profit on a part Ford Motor might have bought elsewhere for much less, John Dodge offered no argument. He was proud of himself, in fact. "Hell," he boasted, "those things don't even cost 60-cents a piece."[18] For ten years, the two companies grew alongside each other like the double barrels in a shotgun: essentially connected, but entirely separate, too.

Not long after John Dodge helped Henry Ford select the Highland Park building site in 1908, he continued to explore Detroit's north side until he decided on a parcel of land for a new 5.1-million-square-foot factory for his own company. Like Ford's Crystal Palace, the new Dodge Brothers facility on Joseph Campeau Street in Hamtramck was designed under the aegis of architect Albert Kahn. It opened at the end of 1910. With a twenty-four-acre complex more in line with the campuslike Packard plant than the linear arrangement of Highland Park, the new Dodge factory consisted of a handful of four-story structures around a center court.[19] Where Ford Motor's plant ranked as the largest auto factory in the world, Dodge Brothers' new head-quarters earned similar bragging rights as the biggest auto-parts factory in the world. Neatly laid out in workstations—and not quite as crowded as High-land Park—the Hamtramck plant was fully equipped to fulfill Dodge's con-tracts for chassis and many other Model T parts in high volumes. Interested observers noted, however, that the new factory looked like more than just a mill for machining car parts. In fact, it had the layout, the equipment, and the space to be much, much more. In many ways the Dodge Brothers factory looked as if it could actually be a full-fledged auto-manufacturing plant.

Every time Ford Motor expanded Highland Park so it could build more of its own parts and reduce its reliance on outside suppliers, Dodge Brothers extended Hamtramck so it could eventually end its reliance on its biggest cus-tomer. These shifts in priorities took place quietly at both companies, thun-derous as their consequences would be. The tension eased for a while in 1912, when John and Horace Dodge went through the motions of negotiating a deal, the most logical one from both points of view: to lease the Hamtramck factory in toto to Ford Motor.[20] By August 1913, however, the Dodge barrel of the dual shotgun was ready to blast away.

"I am tired of being carried around in Henry Ford's vest-pocket," John Dodge finally exploded.[21] As the Ford confederate with the next largest ego, and, in his gruff way, with the most sensitive nature, the elder Dodge would be the first to lose patience with Henry Ford's increasingly peremptory and overbearing attitude. By that summer, he knew that he and his brother could no longer stand to take orders from the ever more autocratic Ford. For the record, John Dodge sent a formal letter to James Couzens resigning his exec-utive post as vice president of Ford Motor as well as his spot on the board of directors. As the possibility of a Ford lease on the Hamtramck factory disap-peared amid the heightened wrath and the first trickle of legal papers, John Dodge also gave Couzens a year's notice that the two companies' current con-tract for parts would be the last between Dodge Brothers and Ford Motor. The Dodges remained stockholders, for the time being, but their involvement in Ford production was through.

At the end of 1913, Henry Ford was busy dealing with the fact that his company had orders for 100,000 more Model Ts than it could produce at its current rate of approximately one car every three minutes.[22] And the pace was accelerating as the market continued to swell. In large part due to the Model T's electrifying effect on the car-buying public, in 1914 the automobile busi-ness was by far the fastest-growing industry in the country. In 1913, it had been the 7th-largest; fifteen years before that, it had ranked a distant 150th. Total production across the country had grown by 28 percent from 1912 to

1913 alone.[23] Even that was but a gust compared with the gales blowing through Ford: in the same year, its production increased by a full 100 percent.[24]

Ford let the Dodges declare their independence without so much as a nod, as he concentrated on his new goals for Highland Park. His dearest wish, he said, was to produce a car a minute[25]—60 per hour, 1,440 per day. Even more audaciously, he also wanted their price tag to fall below $300. Those were his grand objectives and the single-minded Ford had no time for the Dodges, or anyone else focused on anything but helping him to attain them. In fact, he barely looked up from his latest plans to see them go, despite the fact that John and Horace Dodge were the only men in the entire automobile industry who had a more effective understanding of heavy machinery than he did. Perhaps that is why he was not sorry to see them leave. Without the boisterous brothers around, there would be no other voices loud enough to drown him out on the subject nearest to his heart, and the very soul of his business: machines. To retain the best available expertise, tycoons like Carnegie and Rockefeller would have danced jigs if that was what it took to mollify such valuable associates, but that was not Henry Ford's way. He did not have partners, colleagues, or associates, because he did not want them. He stayed loyal only to his own ambitions, as his behavior during World War I would show.

───────

The year 1914, the most important in Ford Motor Company's history, had bitter consequences for the history of the world as the First World War erupted in an outbreak of violence in Sarajevo, Bosnia-Herzegovina, early that summer. The June 28 assassination of Austrian Archduke Franz Ferdinand and his wife gave nations all over Europe nominal justification to settle their tangle of old grudges and new fears on the battlefield. Thus one coalition led by Germany and Austria-Hungary faced off against another comprising the British, French, Italians, and Russians on a full circle of fronts. Insignificant as the changing scene at Highland Park may have looked next to the start of the First World War, the machine-age revolution Ford Motor had fostered in fact played a substantial part in the awful upheaval, economic and social, that roiled Europe to war. A new social tension had developed between "pre-industrialized" societies and modern ones with assembly lines that made automobiles. The momentum of the changes that started at Ford proved unstoppable, in the same inexorable pattern that ended in the massive revolution that led to global war. World War I brought technology to the battlefield.

That same uneasy summer, the Dodge Brothers corporation shook the carmaking industry, and perhaps even Highland Park, a second time. The Dodges did so by declaring their campaign to produce a complete automobile, an exciting new model of their own design. The news was released with genuine enthusiasm and more than a little fanfare at Detroit's Book-Cadillac Hotel, where John Dodge made his way through the formalities in fine fashion. Soon after the grand announcement, he got roaring drunk, adding to the festivities' mood by swinging his cane at the lightbulbs in the chandeliers and wall sconces and smashing them to bits. But nobody really minded—that was just John, a bull who carried his own china shop around with him. Nevertheless, according to *Automobile Topics* magazine, Dodge Brothers' news struck the car industry "like the announcement of a new gold strike—another Comstock Lode or a second Klondike."[26]

Besides, just about everyone in the auto business (and a good many average customers) knew perfectly well that the Dodges had helped build large parts of Henry Ford's cars for years. In fact many industry observers traced the Model T's swift success directly to the brothers—the car may have looked spry like Henry, but it was built tough like Horace and John. While that may have been giving them too much credit, the Dodges had certainly had a major hand in the epic success of Ford's Model T. There turned out to be many people willing to bet that the brothers could repeat the feat. Within days of the announcement of the new Dodge car, 13,741 people applied for dealerships.[27]

The brothers knew that they couldn't take Ford Motor Company head-on with a low-cost utility car like the Model T. Even in 1914, that market was effectively closed to competition, thanks to Ford's unbeatable efficiencies. The Dodges also recognized, however, that while the Model T was creating a vast new class of first-time automobilists, it offered very little room for those customers to trade up later on. Within a few years, those who found themselves tiring of their Model T or with extra money to spend found nothing to move on to at Ford Motor Company. John Dodge may have explained his company's strategy the most succinctly when he predicted, regarding the debut Dodge's prospects, "Think of all the Ford owners who will some day want an automobile!"[28] That did not bother Henry Ford, who as one of America's richest private citizens drove nothing but Model Ts and loved every minute doing so. The new Dodge, though, represented a step up on the same basic theme of a sturdy workhorse of a car, offering 35 horsepower to the Model T's 20. This sleeker new vehicle also boasted a smoother, quieter transmission—and a higher price tag to go with all the improvements, at $780 to the Ford's $450. When production on the first Dodge car started up in November 1914, Henry Ford did not get a true competitor so much as a glimpse at what Ford Motor itself might have built, had an expanded model lineup been among his goals.

In truth, Ford honestly did not seem to care what the Dodge brothers did with their company, or their money. What perturbed him was the way they were still earning Ford dividends—or more to the point, were not earning them. Once John and Horace Dodge stopped contributing actively to his own company's success, he could no longer bear for them to receive funds from Ford Motor Company—more than $1 million in 1913, for example—so all the while, he worked on a plan to make sure that in future Ford dividends helped Ford. And no one else.

━━━━━━━

In the late summer of 1914, Henry Ford conferred with James Couzens about sales and procurement, with Harold Wills about engineering refinements, and with Charles Sorensen and P. E. Martin on manufacturing. Based on what he heard from them, he decided that the company was ready to notch production up to 300,000 Model Ts in the 1914–1915 auto year. "This seemed an enormous amount and nobody thought it could be done, but Mr. Ford figured different," recalled Louis J. Kinietz, the loyal Ford dealer from Medina, New York.[29] The thinking around the factory held that the record-setting goal represented quite a gamble. If that many cars could be made, the company could probably sell them, provided the price was dropped by $50—but, if the price was lowered that far and the sales quota was not met, the company would lose millions of dollars.

"Figuring different" as usual, Henry Ford then announced a bold plan by which his firm could attach the reduced price directly to the increased production with no risk of failure. Banking on his popularity with the American public to attract attention, he personally extended a simple offer to return $50 of the purchase price to each new Model T buyer, if and when the 300,000 sales total was reached. The offer's publicity value, like everything Ford did in the wake of the $5 Day, proved tremendous.

As the orders sailed toward 300,000 (and beyond, by 8,162 cars that season), the Highland Park plant grew to bursting with work for more than 30,000 employees. The mere sight of the factory floor, which was one of the first stops on the factory tours, took visitors' breath away. Newcomers literally gasped when they first beheld the 700,000-square-foot room, crammed with 8,000 different machines.[30] By 1915, most of those machines operated on power transmitted from overhead shafts through long leather belts, "giving the room the appearance of a dense forest," as a tour brochure from that year described it. Even though many of the machines splattered grease and oil all over the place as part of their normal operations, the air on the factory floor was probably cleaner than that many of the workers breathed at home. In the first place, smoking was forbidden on Henry Ford's orders. In the second, the building's state-of-the-art ventilation system replaced the air throughout the vast room five times every hour. Visitors also could not help but be impressed by the spick-and-span sanitation of the Ford Motor machine shops. Every inch of floor was scrubbed to a shine once a week and every surface in the factory polished spotless just as often.[31] Henry Ford held adamant on the point: "Something like seven hundred men are detailed exclusively to keeping the shops clean, the windows washed and all of the paint fresh," he once wrote, adding, "The dark corners which invite expectoration are painted white." The reason for such fastidiousness, he explained, was that "one cannot have morale without cleanliness."[32]

Apparently one could, however, have morale in combination with utter drudgery and extreme stress. After the advent of its assembly line, most of Ford Motor's factory employees were semiskilled workers charged with repeating the same simple task in the complex overall manufacturing process over and over, hour after hour and day after day. Hugh Beynon, a British sociologist, described the high-speed monotony: "The machines were the masters and the men had to keep pace with them."[33]

The company ran a tight ship at Highland Park, but, for the most part, its crew was satisfied (thanks mostly to the $5 Day) and the factory efficient and profitable. Still, something did not seem quite right to Henry Ford. In 1915, therefore, he began to check up on James Couzens. According to the company president's records of this investigation, the treasurer showed up for work only eighty-four times in the first nine months of 1915, fewer than half of the business days over that period. Ford really was in no position to criticize; he wasn't at the plant very often himself that year. But he was the firm's president, and he was Henry Ford. These things made him different.

So while Ford continued to spend as many working days as he liked on his own farm in Dearborn, tinkering with his designs for an inexpensive, lightweight but powerful tractor and mapping out his plans to start a new company to produce it, he began to stew over Couzens's absenteeism. Wherever Henry Ford chose to work, he expected everyone else drawing pay from his company to stay at their desks, drafting tables, or machines, working assiduously to increase profits. Thinking at your desk was allowed at Highland Park—disappearing acts were not. And James Couzens, or so Ford told Charles Sorensen, was losing interest in Ford Motor Company, diverting his energies to getting himself elected governor of Michigan instead. "I have had a clerk kept on him, and he has been at the plant only 184 days during the year," Ford complained to Edwin G. Pipp, then managing editor of the *Detroit News*. "He has been in California and now plans to go to Asheville. I don't believe in absentee control. If Jim is on the job, I'd rather have his judgment than anybody else's on the job. If a man has a job with us, he must stick to it."[34]

For his part, Couzens harbored far darker suspicions about Henry Ford. The mutual animosity grew after the outbreak of World War I, and long before the United States entered the war in April 1917. During this period Henry Ford cast himself as the nation's leading peace advocate, in the manner of Andrew Carnegie, who in 1910 had created his venerable Carnegie Endowment for Peace with U.S. Steel bonds worth $10 million. Admirable as Ford's early stand for pacifism may appear on its face, however, his views carried troubling implications beyond idealistic isolationism in the unsettled years before America entered the war. What's more, it would be those disturbing views that would irredeemably shatter the bond between the two men, Couzens and Ford, without each of whom there would have been no Ford Motor Company.

───────

While Europe was blowing itself to bits in the first two and a half years of World War I, two choices loomed before the United States. One was to stay out of the war entirely, come what may overseas. The other was to side with Britain, France, and their allies. Although there was no chance that America would enter the war on behalf of the German-controlled Central Powers, U.S. neutrality was considered nearly as desirable by German sympathizers. In the swirl of soul-searching and propaganda that pervaded the United States through the first years of the Great War, peace became the cry of Americans of all stripes, from earnest humanists to stubborn isolationists to those quietly siding with Germany. Congresswoman Jeannette Rankin of Montana, the first female member of the U.S. House of Representatives, would later vote against American entry into World War I with the bold declaration: "I want to stand by my country, but I cannot vote for war. I vote No."[35] This was precisely Henry Ford's view immediately after war broke out in 1914.

Ford, who had never been to war, claimed that he had inherited a strong antipathy to it from his mother. Indeed, many Americans of Mary Litogot Ford's generation were staunchly against war in any form or circumstance. In the wake of the Civil War, the United States was understandably at its most pacifist, having suffered the loss of a greater proportion of its citizens than in any conflict before or since. There is no doubt that Henry Ford sincerely agreed with his peace-loving mother's antiwar beliefs. He wanted to create a new and better world through engineering and industry, not to keep impeding progress by fighting over the old one and its archaic concerns.

Ford didn't see the point of killing. While other factory owners through the centuries had benefited from war and often encouraged it, he didn't take that selfish view. His life's work was dedicated to improving human life, not obliterating it. As heartfelt as Ford's pacificism was, though, it was not universally admired. Former President Theodore Roosevelt, who expressed "not merely friendliness, but in many respects a very genuine admiration" for Ford during a speech in Detroit in 1916, also compared him disdainfully to the pacifist Tories of the Revolutionary War and Copperheads of the Civil War: "Men of fine character and upright purpose," he said, "they were against all war and all preparedness for war."[36] The pull for peace has undoubtedly saved millions of lives in the form of wars averted, but specific instances are unfortunately elusive. As Ford would find out, critics found it all too easy to cite pacificist missteps—including his own.

Henry Ford may have been a true peacenik of his time, but there was more to his position than that—and it led back to his ugliest motivation: paranoia.

Over the course of an accelerating campaign for peace in 1915, Ford issued pamphlets and newspaper opinion pieces espousing his peculiarly ignoble form of pacifism. In several of these essays he pointedly blamed New York bankers, and J.P. Morgan and Company in particular, for orchestrating American sympathies behind Britain and France in order to protect a $50 million war loan. In Ford's construct of just about any political or economic occurrence, in fact, New York bankers were usually to be found lurking behind the shadows of ulterior motives. Sometimes, the president of Ford Motor Company sank even lower and named "the Jews" as the culprits behind the war, although he did not explain who exactly "the Jews" were or how they had managed to stir forty-three nations into sending 38 million men into battle.

One of the more strident of Ford's pacifist remarks came in response to the May 7, 1915, sinking of the British cruise ship *Lusitania,* which was torpedoed by a German submarine off the coast of Ireland on its way from New York to England, killing 1,198 people, most of them civilians, including a number of Americans. Before the steamer sailed for Europe, a notice had been placed in New York newspapers by the German government warning citizens of neutral nations, such as the United States, that all Allied ships were potential targets in wartime. That dubious humanitarian act inspired Henry Ford to comment after the awful incident that its victims had been "fools to go on that boat."[37] Insensitive as that was, Ford then went even further in laying out his version of pacifism, stating his firm opinion that all the soldiers in the standing U.S. Army were either "lazy or crazy."

Ford's loopy barbs didn't draw much more notice than his sensitive antiwar comments, but when he made a very public pledge to spend his entire fortune in the pursuit of peace, he stole the headlines from the Great War itself. Continuing on the theme, he promised to burn his factory to the ground before he would turn it over to war production. That made James Couzens furious.

As the United States grappled with the question of entering the war, Canada was already fighting alongside of its mother country, and had been from the first. James Couzens, a native of Canada, sided strongly with the British, in part from national pride but more because it was simply his nature to take the offense in any situation. Where others turned isolationist because of the bloody misery being inflicted on both sides of Europe's battlefields, Couzens favored preparedness and intervention for the very same reason. The carnage had to stop, and he felt that America could help bring it to an end.

The split between Ford and Couzens over America's participation in the

First World War marked the first important disagreement between them in all their years in business together. It also marked the first time Henry Ford's growing public persona would be tested, in terms of its effect on the two partners. It failed on both counts.

George Brown, who worked in Couzens's purchasing department at the time, recalled that the company treasurer's greatest talent probably lay in the finance of manipulation. "I can remember the time where Mr. Couzens used to manipulate funds from one bank in New York to Seattle," Brown averred. "He'd transfer these funds from one bank to the other, and by the time the far bank got it, everything was taken care of. He was a *real* financier, that man!"[38] Couzens, in fact, understood high finance so well he succeeded in opening the Highland Park State Bank, using it for the express purpose of funneling Ford Motor payments to the company's advantage. Thousands of Ford employees also kept their money at the bank, as did Henry Ford. Then, in August 1914, a rumor shot through the nation that there was about to be a run on commercial banks.

The story behind the rumor held that the intricate financial arrangements between various American banks and Europe's Allied governments were verging on collapse. Henry Ford was glad to believe the stories and wanted to withdraw his cash from the Highland Park State Bank, but Couzens assured him that his money was safe where it was. Perhaps *because* Couzens was a master financier, Ford did not believe him. In any case, Ford suddenly ordered that his account be transferred to a savings bank, a safer type of institution under the circumstances. He did not bother to notify Couzens, who fired off a devastating telegram to his boss as soon as he saw the withdrawal order. Dated August 5, 1914, the message read in part: "In these strenuous times, men invariably show the kind of stuff they are made of. We are making arrangements to transfer your money."[39] Couzens felt utterly betrayed, but he had no choice except to follow the order. He remained with Ford Motor for the time, but his long and fruitful friendship with Henry Ford was over forever.

"I remember once when Mr. James Couzens and Mr. Ford came in," recalled Highland Park workman Herman M. Reinhold. "They were going to it hammer and tongs, hands waving and just going to town. I don't know what it was about. It was none of our business and we just kept away from it. They were arguing."[40]

Reinhold did not supply a date for this incident, but it took place in the autumn of 1915. Before then, Ford and Couzens had not been given to heated arguments, and certainly not in front of their employees. By that autumn, though, the frustration on both sides was running high. For one thing, at the beginning of October Ford had ordered that pacifist editorials start appearing in the *Ford Times,* the company magazine that had always been strictly a sales and promotional tool, and strictly under Couzens's control.

By no means was Couzens a war hawk; in fact, he had written a $5,000 check to the League to Enforce Peace, hoping diplomacy would prevail in Europe. Couzens simply could not let Henry Ford use the company publication to voice strange, unsavory, personal opinions, such as "To my mind, the word 'murderer' should be embroidered in red letters across the breast of every soldier."[41] Ford's comments about the *Lusitania*'s sinking and the character of America's soldiers had already cost the company sales. The number did not matter, Couzens maintained. The point was that Ford Motor Company could not reflect its president's political notions, particularly as some of them were potentially offensive to customers and others. Couzens took a stand that might have saved the company from much serious trouble later on, when Henry Ford's increasingly irrational attacks on Jews became associated with Ford Motor to its detriment. Henry Ford, of course, did not see it that way. He considered his political opinions a decided advantage to the company—his company—just as his folksy social views had been in days gone by. His pacifist editorials stayed in the *Ford Times*.[42]

A year earlier, John Dodge had stormed away from Ford Motor with the words "I am tired of being carried around in Henry Ford's vest-pocket." Now it was James Couzens's turn to echo the sentiment, explaining, "I finally decided that I would not be carried along on that kind of a kite," as he walked out of Ford Motor Company for good on October 12, 1915. In a more detailed account of his departure published four days later in the *New York Herald*, Couzens added that his friendship with Henry Ford had "changed of late."

The former vice president of the firm continued, "We started in the automobile business thirteen years ago and it was through my efforts that the Ford Motor Company was built up around one man—Henry Ford. What Mr. Ford has to say is considered by many to be of worldwide importance because his automobile business has been built up to such a gigantic magnitude that he is always in the public eye. I disapprove of his views on unpreparedness and it was such a serious question with me that I decided to break my relations with him."[43]

Couzens never returned to the automobile industry. Within months, he was instead serving as Detroit's police commissioner and combating the thicket of corruption that had spread from the city's law-enforcement department into its courts. His hardboiled investigation was so vociferous and his methods so uncompromising that at one point he was charged with contempt of court and was himself put in jail. Mayor Oscar B. Marx, a close associate of the Dodge brothers, called Couzens "the most unpopular man in Detroit."

With that, Couzens announced that he would run against Marx in the city's next mayoral election, "to find out for myself," as he said afterward, "just how unpopular I was with the people."[44] Couzens won. He was later elected a U.S. senator from Michigan, a liberal Republican with a special dedication to assisting the unemployed and poverty stricken.

Despite his deputy's natural attraction to politics and public service, Henry Ford could have induced Couzens to stay at Ford Motor in 1915 if he had wanted him to. The immediate reasons for the breach, Ford's international politics, could have been painted as inconsequential had he backed off from them for the sake of his company. Ford could not, however, back away from the megalomaniacal, narcissistic attitudes that seemed more and more to define his personality. Because of this streak in Ford, James Couzens's departure was announced in a two-line insertion in the *Ford Times* that made no mention of Couzens's role in the growth of the company. Indeed, it did not go unnoticed around Highland Park that the article featured a large picture of Henry Ford with Harold Wills, the caption describing them as "the two men who have developed the Ford car."[45] Henry Ford, who never had been inclined to put much value on office work, seemed determined to erase Couzens's contributions to his company as soon as they ended. Ford Motor needed to reassure its investors, customers, dealers, and employees that the company would continue to be successful after Couzens's departure. Frank L. Klingensmith was immediately named to take over as treasurer with Couzens's former lieutenant, Norval Hawkins, assuming an even larger role in sales. For the time being, Ford Motor's business offices operated much as before, dispatching matters of accounting, finance, and procurement. But arguably never again in Henry Ford's lifetime would his company's business side hum with the intensity Couzens had brought to it.

The first three members of the "Ford Alumni Association," as the company's top exiles would become known, were by far the most significant losses to Ford Motor. John and Horace Dodge and James Couzens were at least as good at their jobs as anyone else working in the automobile industry in 1914–1915. Expert and aggressive, the three of them could have built a car company out of a bag of dingy towels. When they left, no one remained at Ford Motor who was even close to standing on an equal footing with Henry Ford. And so for a while, at least, the history of the company became as one with the actions, insights, foibles, and impulses of its president.

Ford's debut as the unfettered industrialist-philosopher he fancied himself to be occurred quite suddenly only a month after Couzens left. The grand plan Ford envisioned was a peace expedition to Europe. His partner in working out the details was, oddly enough considering Ford's prejudices, a radical Jewish Hungarian pacifist named Rosika Schwimmer. Portly, squat, and bespectacled, Schwimmer nevertheless exuded a kind of brilliance, and was embraced by leading women's rights activists Carrie Chapman Catt and Jane Addams as a gutsy and effective suffragist. Despite her intelligence, however, Schwimmer maintained a Pollyannaish belief, as many people did at the time, that since there seemed no tangible reason for the war, the opposing sides might find their way to peace if they would just get together and talk out their differences in an atmosphere conducive to negotiations. At best, she was proposing a forum not unlike the modern United Nations. At worst, she was never to be taken seriously. Deemed by President Woodrow Wilson a doctrinaire dilettante trying to move a boulder with a taproom straw, Schwimmer nevertheless quickly became a favorite with the isolationist press in America. What's more, her scheme to enlist a corps of civilians to help broker a truce appealed greatly to Henry Ford when she laid it out for him at a luncheon in November 1915.

Schwimmer was an unlikely ally for Ford in every respect. Not only was she Jewish, she was also an ardent feminist, having earned a reputation before the war as the highest-paid female lecturer on the European continent. The high points of many of her boisterous speeches came in her colorful condemnations of men delivered with a tinge of her ready humor. With the outbreak of World War I, Schwimmer organized the International Congress of Women specifically to find a path to peace, on the theory that the supposedly gentler sex might prove better at finding it.

For his part, Henry Ford believed that women did not belong in business and on a personal level he extended them only a respectful politeness rather than real friendship. That did not hold for Rosika Schwimmer—in this relationship Ford was the follower and she the leader. For all that separated them, Ford and Schwimmer shared not only their commitment to pacifism but a powerful attraction to the limelight, as well as the knack for using it to their advantage. In the 1978 book *The Peace Ship,* Barbara S. Kraft touched on just what it was that Rosika Schwimmer offered to Henry Ford: "She skillfully combined the resourceful techniques of a press agent with her knowledge of European politics, and every organization she touched felt the impact of her intelligence, passion and powerful ambition."[46]

Ford first met with Schwimmer in his office at Highland Park as a courtesy to a fellow pacifist. "His strong, ascetic face reminded me of the portrait of a Greek philosopher I remembered from a rare old book in my parents' library," she would later write of that initial encounter, "and when a humorous twinkle lightened his face, he looked like a wistful but healthy boy. This combination of sage and boy seemed to me always apparent in Mr. Ford." He next invited her, along with fellow pacifist leader Louis P. Lochner of Chicago, to his home in Dearborn for lunch. The enormous Fair Lane estate was not quite complete in November 1915, although the Ford family was comfortably installed in the living quarters. "Mr. Ford was particularly proud to show us two things," recalled Lochner of the visit: "a huge, white-tiled swimming pool and a pipe organ." Ford nevertheless impressed Lochner as surprisingly approachable for a tycoon of his stature, evidencing "a keener sense of the value of publicity and of the way to obtain it" than any other American of his generation.[47] After a lively discussion about the pacifist movement at the Fair Lane lunch, Ford made up his mind: he would leave for New York the very next day to begin a full-time effort to support Schwimmer's International Congress of Women.

Clara Ford tried to discourage her husband from attaching himself to the project, but to no avail. On November 21, Henry Ford was thus in New York City attending yet another pacifist luncheon when Louis Lochner suggested that a special ship take the committee's peace delegates to Europe. "Mr. Ford's imagination was instantly seized with the idea, as was also that of Rosika Schwimmer," Lochner recalled. "I have said that Mr. Ford has a native instinct for publicity. I should add that coupled with this is a keen sense of the dramatic."[48] Both instincts told Ford that with the *Peace Ship,* as it would be called, he could not only rise to action, but what was more, he could be *seen* to rise to action.

No sooner had lunch ended than a stream of steamship agents began arriving in answer to a call to Ford's suite at the Biltmore Hotel, where they gave him price quotes to rent an ocean liner, all the while thinking they were talking to a "Mr. Henry." The Scandinavian American line won the brief bidding contest, and leased Ford all but the already reserved third-class cabin of its *Oscar II.*[49] Among his reasons for choosing it was that the liner was equipped with Marconi radio: the most effective long-range weapon in existence, in Ford's opinion. Preparations for the excursion began in such a giddy rush that few of the organizers stopped to really think about what they were doing. All anyone knew was that a delegation including Henry Ford would leave for Europe on the *Oscar II* early in December in pursuit of global peace. While others scrambled to nail down the details of the undertaking, Ford was left with only one chore, after he put up the cash, the one he considered paramount and did best: announcing his grand plan to the press. Ford himself made dozens of calls to journalists he didn't even know to invite them to a press conference at the Biltmore.

Oswald Garrison Villard, then editor of the *New York Evening Post,* was called away from his breakfast table on November 24 to speak with—to his astonishment—Henry Ford. Villard, himself a well-known pacifist, was invited to help make the announcement. The savvy editor arrived at the Biltmore early and warned Ford that the press was notoriously hostile to the peace movement. "Oh, I always get on very well with the boys," the world's leading industrialist replied. "All you need is a slogan." With that, he suggested: "We'll get the boys home by Christmas." Villard pointed out that that was impossible. So Ford tweaked his slogan into the almost as arrogant "We'll get the boys out of the trenches by Christmas."

"That was the genesis of the famous phrase that went around the world,"

Villard wrote later. "It disheartened me no end for I knew it laid the enterprise open to ridicule; it was already evident to me that he had no clear conception of what it was all about, what the war conditions were, or what he was undertaking. Indeed, it gave me a doubt as to his general intelligence, which was subsequently confirmed more than once."[50]

Henry Ford may actually have considered his *Peace Ship* the best chance to bring an early end to the war. It may even be possible that it *was* the best chance for peace at that miserable juncture of carnage and stalemate during the middle years of the Great War. Where governments had failed, perhaps the *Peace Ship*'s innocence would prevail. After all, Ford had done well with folksiness before, and what could be more down home than an ocean liner full of self-appointed private-citizen peace delegates convinced their good intentions could bring the war to an end. No one has ever been quite sure precisely what Henry Ford hoped to accomplish by launching Schwimmer's odd excursion, not only paying a small fortune to sponsor the voyage but directly participating in it, despite his complete lack of expertise in diplomacy and geopolitics. No doubt Ford truly would have liked to end World War I before America got into it, but even he would later admit that either way the publicity his pacifist cruise generated was well worth the cost to lease *Oscar II*.

At the press conference, Ford struggled to explain his sudden ardor for global peace, at any monetary cost to himself personally. "A man should always try to do the greatest good to the greatest number, shouldn't he?" Ford began, addressing the forty or so curious reporters who had turned out to hear what he was up to now. Ford, who never had been at ease in front of anything like a crowd, stumbled around his point that it was indeed always good to do good, then delivered one of the longest, if most disjointed, speeches of his career, beginning with the slogan he had told Villard about so proudly:

> We're going to try to get the boys out of the trenches by Christmas. I've chartered a ship and some of us are going to Europe. [*Pause*] The main idea is to crush militarism and get the boys out of the trenches. Our object is to stop war for all times, and also preparedness. War is nothing but preparedness. No boy would ever kill a bird if he didn't first have a sling-shot or a gun.[51]

Having run out of words with that little peroration, Ford stepped aside so others could come forward to explain what the *Peace Ship* delegates actually intended to do, which was to set up peace talks in a neutral country and invite representatives of all the belligerent nations to attend.

After a week of preparations, the *Peace Ship* set sail for Europe on December 4. The story of the *Peace Ship* should be considered in light of the considerable bias against the endeavor among those who reported on it. Because most newspaper publishers were against the pacifist movement—war was, after all, very good for circulation—their assigned correspondents ridiculed the excursion mercilessly. In part because of these condescending press accounts, what little serious interest there had been in the effort faded quickly as the *Oscar II* made its way across the Atlantic. Rosika Schwimmer handled all the planning for the intended peace talks, while Henry Ford, ominously, kept more and more to himself. The millionaire industrialist did impress Louis Lochner, anyway, by eating his meals in the third-class dining room while the other delegates vied for tables in first class.

Ford stayed on his *Peace Ship* only as far as its first stop in Christiania, now Oslo, Norway. By that point, he was making a concerted effort to keep away from his fellow delegates, who on the whole turned out to be a volatile bunch of intellectual snobs whose endless blathering the automaker found incomprehensible. In Norway, it became increasingly clear that neither the ship nor its most famous occupant would be enough of an inducement to draw Europe's combatants together. Such deft diplomacy as would have been required, now that the ship was docked, did not seem to be forthcoming from anyone on board. As Allan Nevins would sum up the fiasco, Henry Ford "never regretted having launched the expedition. But he probably recognized that it had been badly managed, and that riding herd on the fantastic individualists who composed the party was a difficult task. He was as lost among them as Schwimmer would have been on the assembly line at Highland Park."[52] After a doctor conveniently confirmed that Henry Ford had suffered a breakdown in his health, the industrialist booked his own passage home, leaving the *Peace Ship* to its mission, which paled even further without him.

The *Peace Ship* delegates tried to struggle on without their sponsor, setting up conference boards in Sweden and then Switzerland, but by the end of a year the endeavor had clearly failed in every way. Rosika Schwimmer, who at one point confided to Louis Lochner that the whole experience was unraveling like a bad fairy tale, retreated from public life once it was over. She took the humiliation so hard she had to check into a sanitarium, suffering a nervous breakdown. "Here was a woman," Lochner wrote, "into whose lap had been thrown as unique an opportunity for securing an exalted place in history as ever came to a member of her sex." That assessment, of course, presumes that the *Peace Ship,* with Henry Ford's financial backing and even his short-lived participation, could have succeeded under the direction of someone other than Schwimmer, which is doubtful.

Henry Ford—the only one who would make it home from the war by Christmas—shook off the derision directed at the *Peace Ship* and went back to Detroit to resume making cars. As cynics liked to point out, he and his company were more famous than ever. And as Ford himself would sum up his adventure in cowboy diplomacy: "I didn't get much peace, but I learned that Russia is going to be a great market for tractors."[53]

10

Making an Impact

The 1915 *Peace Ship* was not Henry Ford's first trip abroad. In 1912, he had taken his wife, Clara, and son, Edsel, to Europe on a summer excursion that included visits to Ford Motor's swiftly growing operations in Britain and France. Everywhere they went, Henry was celebrated as an authentic automotive pioneer, well on his way to one of America's greatest fortunes.[1] The highlight of the trip was a pilgrimage to County Cork, Ireland, where he wandered the countryside in search of his ancestral roots. A story from that trip, possibly apocryphal, has been told over and over again to illustrate Ford's sense of humor, philanthropy, and opportunism. One evening, while the Fords were staying at a hotel in the city of Cork, there was a knock on his door. Henry answered to be greeted by four or five local boosters. "Mr. Ford," they said, "we want to welcome you to Cork City, the home of your father. We're building a hospital and we thought perhaps, in memory of your dad, you'd like to make a donation." Without hesitation, Ford wrote a $5,000 check—it was the right thing to do in memory of all the members of his family who had come from Cork.

At breakfast the following morning, however, he was shocked to see the bold headline in the *Cork Courier:* "Henry Ford Donates $50,000 to Hospital." A few hours later the same civic leaders reappeared at the hotel. "Mr. Ford, we're grateful for the $5,000," they said. "We're sorry about the mistake that the newspaper made, but tomorrow they'll make a front-page correction."

The idea of a retraction struck Ford as a bad public relations move. "Give me my check back," he demanded. They did and he proceeded to rip it up. "What does it cost to build the hospital?" Ford asked, understanding that he had been hoodwinked. In unison the men answered, "Fifty thousand dollars." Without hesitation Ford proceeded to write out a new check, this one for the full sum. "Here, have this in memory of my mother and father, on one condition," he said. "Over the portals of the hospital, I want an inscription. And the inscription is: 'I came among you and you took me in.'"[2] They agreed, and that inscription is today carved in stone on the hospital wall.

Ford found opportunism everywhere on that first trip to Europe. While reporters constantly speculated on his net worth, every monarch from Sweden to Spain wanted a piece of him, some sort of meeting in which to hear about the future from a man who seemed to carry it around in his pocket. No doubt the trip made Ford keenly conscious of his international opportunities, given the eager market he found for a good, affordable family car. As talk of war enveloped Europe two years later, in 1914, it cannot have been lost on him that the gathering winds of war could grow strong enough to blow that robust market away. For a global-minded industrialist, therefore, pacifism equaled pragmatism.

With the *Peace Ship,* however, it looked as though Ford had misread the public mood for the first time. He tried to wave off widespread mockery of the voyage by claiming to welcome it, telling a *New York Tribune* reporter that "the best fertilizer in the world is weeds"[3]—but his assessment rang a bit too cavalier. Had the *Peace Ship* been planned more soberly and publicized less aggressively, it could have been overlooked as the folly of a well-meaning mogul. But the dubious priorities of the whole misadventure left a shadow on Ford Motor Company and that disturbed even some of its most loyal dealers. William P. Young, a lawyer in Pottstown, Pennsylvania, for example, had been so enthusiastic about his own first Model T that he had secured the franchise for his hometown's Ford dealership in 1910. With his teenage son Bill Jr. helping out, the Pottstown agency proved a solid success. "Whenever a new Ford got into a community everybody had a look and a report: 'The darn thing runs all right,'" the elder Young recalled. "Roll one into a given community and soon it was the center of lots of others rolling around it."[4] Young quickly became a disciple of James J. Couzens and a model for the Ford sales practices he represented: "aggressiveness, firmness and with all fairness."[5] Young also admired Henry Ford—up until the moment Ford sailed with that "ridiculous thing," the *Peace Ship.*

"The agency had to listen to the talk and ridicule and defend itself and the company as best it could," Young said of the situation years later. Like many others connected to Ford Motor at the time, he resented the charge being made around business circles that the voyage had been no more than a clever plot to "make everybody in the world think about, concentrate on and want the car or the company name mentioned with the *Peace Ship.* It was discouraging to the agency and many others. . . ."[6]

The Model T juggernaut, however, couldn't be stopped by scattered resentment of the *Peace Ship.* Unfortunately, though, Henry Ford didn't stop connecting his personal opinions with the company name, a tendency that would cause far greater damage just after the war. In 1916, Model T sales in the United States were setting new records and Fords were selling briskly in Asia and South America, far from the European war zone. In the years before the United States entered World War I, the *Ford Times* had often taken on the look of a travel magazine featuring illustrated articles showcasing the Model T in exotic South Pacific island locales, chugging across the Australian outback, and tooling around in remote villages in India. It was a global phenomenon, changing life on the savanna, steppes, or sands, just as it had on the American farm. "In these parts a Ford car is practically always called a 'Famous Ford,'" wrote Clement Hirtzel, a big-game guide from Sutherland, South Africa, who put thirty thousand miles on his T touring Tanganyika's Serengeti Plain. The reason for this fame, Hirtzel believed, was that no other make of car persevered over the rugged terrain. Fords took on the roughest roads and more. "It has yet to be proved what they will not do," he marveled. "The Ford car was never intended to drive a printing press or a flour mill, yet the *East African Standard* newspaper was printed for a week with a Ford car and one of our largest mills was kept running by the back wheels of a Ford when the electric power gave out."[7]

Before World War I, all of the Ford cars for export were made either at Highland Park or at Ford of Canada's factory in industrial Walkerville, Ontario, just across the river from Detroit. Henry Ford was Walkerville's largest stockholder, just as he was in the Detroit company, but as he watched the Canadian company build good cars and loyal markets, he left the operation alone to a surprising extent.[8]

As of 1911, one other facility outside the United States had also been turning out Model Ts: Ford of England's plant in Manchester. At first, that factory was set up only to build cars from parts shipped from Highland Park, the same way assembly sites all over the United States did. Little by little, however, the Manchester plant began to assume manufacturing duties as well, and to depend on British suppliers for bodies and other components. Still, Ford of England, which was organized as a subsidiary of the U.S. Ford Motor Company, was not authorized to export cars anywhere else. The world had already been neatly divided between Ford of Canada and the American company.

Ford of Canada, with robust agencies in India, Australia, South Africa, and other large countries, made a better start than the U.S. company did. On the 1912 European tour, Henry Ford found his company's sales in France perplexingly slow and its agencies in most countries on the Continent sadly disorganized.

Ford sent his personal version of a guided missile, Charles E. Sorensen, to investigate the following year. During that summer of 1913, Sorensen paid visits to Ford sales offices throughout Europe, including the Berlin branch, which he discovered was little more than a garage in an old building far from the city center. When he saw the two Americans responsible for the Berlin office, he let them have it. "I did not feel too proud of this setup and told them we would never go far there," Sorensen recalled.[9] While in Germany he found himself thoroughly impressed, however, by the Krupp Works, a bigger industrial operation than any he had ever seen before. The Krupp family had been making armaments since the sixteenth century, and their factory in Essen had been operating since 1810. Their steel works had been in steady expansion ever since the Franco-Prussian War of 1870–1871, further cementing a fine reputation for expert metalworking. Sorensen wrote that he was "entertained royally" at Krupp, noting among other wonders a room filled with models of advanced firearms and other implements of war, all worked out and ready for production. The room's martial contents harkened back to Henry Ford's belief that to prepare for war was to invite it, but as Sorensen surveyed the Krupp war room, he did not take the implicit threat seriously. At the time, he felt more eager about being able to return his hosts' hospitality, which Ford Motor would do in spades when a group of Krupp executives visited Highland Park early in 1914.

All things considered, Europe seemed the most obvious international market for cars, as customers abounded, along with good roads; so too did competition, nationalism, labor problems, and government restrictions. Nonetheless, the Old World's allure was so strong that neither Charles Sorensen, James Couzens, Henry Ford, nor any other top company executive thought to visit the continent that was developing into the most promising for Ford Motor prior to the First World War: South America.

Ellis Hampton, an urbane, middle-aged sales executive, had been working out of New York as Ford Motor's export manager for less than a year in 1913 when he received the dubious honor of reassignment to South America to open sales branches in the continent's largest countries. Despite South America's large population and the sophistication of some of its cities, no automobile company had ever enjoyed much success there. Among other problems, the political instability in most of its countries made investment risky. As Mira Wilkins and Frank Ernest Hill pointed out in their book *American Business Abroad: Ford on Six Continents,* "Hampton had full authority on behalf of the company. He needed it—to reach New York from Buenos Aires took twenty-one days."[10] Even before Hampton set out, the American consul in Chile warned him that it was a waste of time to try to sell cars in that country; the U.S. Department of Commerce said the same thing about Venezuela, and as for Argentina, it seemed to be hopeless to try selling anything, given that the country was in the throes of an economic panic. Paraguay, Bolivia, and Peru had no roads outside of major cities, and thus nowhere to drive a car *to.* Undeterred, Hampton and his wife dutifully headed down the sea lane to South America, lone emissaries from Ford Motor to the Southern Hemisphere.

As he spent much of his initial year there on trains, the first thing Ellis Hampton discovered was just how huge South America is. It took two to three days to get from one major city to the next: from Buenos Aires, Argentina, to São Paulo, Brazil, for example, or from Montevideo, Uruguay, to Santiago, Chile. However, the travel time was well spent. Hampton succeeded in finding excellent managerial talent across South America. Thus encouraged, he established a branch in downtown Buenos Aires with the help of two locally hired assistants, and then contracted with sales agents all over the rest of Argentina. Next, he signed up agencies in Montevideo and São Paulo. For good measure, Hampton also found good managers and drummed up decent sales orders even in Chile and Venezuela, two countries he had been told were hopeless.

The very fact that most of South America's roads remained in primitive condition, where they existed at all, worked to the advantage of Ford, especially when its rugged little Model T was compared with the European-built cars that dominated the continent's then small automobile market. In the mountains, where paths still grew too narrow for a burro, even a Model T would be of no use, but the sturdy Fords proved capable of conquering more of the ungraded terrain than any other make of vehicle. Within a year Ford Motor's new South American operation had sold nearly 800 Model Ts. By 1917, the Argentine branch alone sold almost 7,000 cars, with sales for the region topping 10,000.

The timing of the company's bold foray into South America could not have been better nor could its decision to ignore pessimistic advice have been any wiser. Ellis Hampton's sales network began operating in 1914 just as war broke out in Europe, choking U.S. exports to England, France, Germany, and Italy. What is more, the war effectively stopped the export of cars from Europe to South America, leaving the field entirely to Americans—and almost entirely to Ford. By 1917, Ford was operating an assembly plant in Argentina and overseeing booming sales branches in Buenos Aires, Montevideo, and São Paulo, and it had sales agents in every country as well as plans for more manufacturing facilities. The effort took its toll, though—Mrs. Hampton wrote to Henry Ford personally, requesting a transfer for her husband so that they could both come home. "Nothing doing," Ford said when he read her letter.[11] Things were going too well with Hampton where he was.

––––––––––

While the outbreak of World War I had a beneficial effect on Ford Motor's fortunes in South America, the situation in England became much more complicated. New car sales continued in both England and France through-out the war (unlike World War II, when automobile production was sus-pended). Vehicle sales in the Allied countries did slow of course, but Ford's added burden was Henry Ford's aggressive pacifism, which proved as offen-sive to most Britons as it had to James Couzens. In America, the issues of war and peace may have been political abstractions; for the Allied nations, they were a matter of survival. Great Britain and the other Allies needed help, and anyone suggesting that the United States withhold it, on whatever pretext, was perceived as unfriendly at best. At worst, Henry Ford appeared to be an enemy of Britain's interests.

Fortunately for the company, Ford of England was in the supremely capa-ble hands of British-born Percival Lea Dewhurst Perry, a man who was noth-ing if not resourceful, and he opened up to the press at every opportunity to explain that Henry Ford's views were his own and had nothing to do with the company's British subsidiary, which was, by the way, employing 2,000 local workers at above-average wages. Perry was living proof of his own belief that Ford opened opportunities and paid off in ways few working-class English-men dared to dream about.[12]

Educated on scholarships, the prim and proper Percival Perry had done well at school but had no connections at a time when a good recommendation was far more valuable than any diploma. With no choice but to struggle his way up the ladder, he began his career in 1896 by taking a menial job at H.J. Lawson's, one of England's earliest automobile dealerships. There the obser-vant Perry recognized, even before the advent of the Model T, that Ford Mo-tor was building better cars at a lower price than any other auto company anywhere. At that time, it took courage even to suggest such a thing in En-gland, as American cars were sneered at as cheap and ugly next to Britain's beautifully crafted automobiles. Cars from the United States were taken about as seriously as Japanese makes would be in America during the 1960s. According to Perry, enthusiasm for Ford Motor "was regarded as a mixture of Quixotism and right down foolishness—when it was regarded at all, which was not often." Nonetheless, Perry gamely helped to organize the first British sales agency for the company's cars in 1904.

"Then commenced a five years' war with the most impregnable prejudice it has ever been the lot of man to run up against," Perry asserted, reveling in his own exaggeration. "The public, its opinions fostered by an anti-American press, could not be induced to vacate their position of insular indifference."[13] The first year sales hit a grand total of twelve. Despite that, Perry remained convinced that Ford Motor had a future in Britain, one so promising he be-came absolutely determined to share in it. He showed this genuine enthusi-asm by visiting Detroit several times entirely of his own accord and at his own expense, sometimes accompanied by his wife, Catherine Meals Perry, who became one of Clara Ford's dearest friends. Indeed, the Perrys were wonderfully attractive people: informed, amusing, and duly sycophantic toward Ford Motor Company and its founder. After Percival Perry convinced Henry Ford of the superiority of English songbirds during the Ford family's tour of his country in 1912, biographer Ford R. Bryan reports, "Perry arranged to send Ford 500 songbirds the following spring, for which Ford provided lavish accommodations on his farm estate at Dearborn."[14] Over the years, the Perrys remained among the very few business associates Henry and Clara Ford saw socially.[15]

Perry's charm was fully matched by his success in establishing Ford cars in England. In 1906, he introduced Ford Model B landaulets as taxicabs in London, whereupon city authorities decreed all such speedy little cabs be painted bright white for safety's sake. Thus rendered all the more noticeable, the Model B's swiftness and reliability soon began to win Londoners over, and the taxis were just the start. In a series of cross-country "reliability trials" staged between 1906 and 1909, Ford entries took gold medals for traveling as far as 1,000 miles without requiring a single mechanical repair. Held in Scotland and Ireland, running up steep hills and through rain-soaked gullies over some of the roughest roads in the British Isles, these reliability trials were specifically designed to make the entrants break down if possible, and the drivers usually did, even when their cars didn't. Perry himself drove a stock Ford Model N in the 1907 Irish trials, a test "of about 1,000 miles," he wrote, "and the Ford made light of them."[16] As the head of Ford of England, Perry oversaw not only sales in Great Britain but also the assembly and bodybuilding plant in Manchester.

With the formal incorporation of Ford Motor Co. (England) Ltd. in 1911, Percival Perry's loyalty was rewarded with the top job of managing director. British sales, although of smaller scale, matched the pace of those in the United States, doubling every year.[17]

Even the greatest British leader of the century had reason to applaud Ford's cars. One day early in 1914, shortly before the outbreak of World War I, First Lord of the Admiralty Winston Churchill arrived by train at the Scottish city of Perth in a panic. He was running desperately late for an appointment with King George V at Balmoral Castle, still some sixty miles away over mountainous terrain. Churchill leapt down to the railroad platform and shouted for the car that was supposed to be waiting for him. "There was much commotion and running about," the *Glasgow Herald* reported, when it became clear that the railway porters couldn't find the First Lord of the Admiralty's car. Churchill, ever a man of action, told his valet to throw his luggage into the back of a Ford taxi, and jumped in after it.

"Where to?" the driver asked.

"Balmoral," Britain's future prime minister replied. At the time, because of the terrain, this was tantamount to telling a New York cabbie to drive to Alaska today. But that driver in Perth in 1914 was game, the little Ford sped through the mountains like nothing, and Winston Churchill made it to his audience with the king on time. As it turned out, the scheduled car had been waiting for him on the other side of the train station the whole time. Perhaps it was more than serendipity that made Churchill opt for the Ford before anyone could locate it though. After all, odds were good that any other car would have broken down over the sixty hard miles to the castle—at least such was the degree of respect the Model T had earned in Britain, according to the *Glasgow Herald*.[18]

In the quest to counteract Henry Ford's pacifist views, Perry would get a crucial boost from another of his boss's pet projects, this one much closer to Ford's area of expertise than international diplomacy. For years, Ford had been dabbling with tractor designs, a pursuit begun with his boyhood determination "to lift farm drudgery off flesh and blood and lay it on steel and motors." In fact, Ford claimed, his "planning of the tractor really antedated that of the motor car."[19] In any case, once pictures of the great automaker driving a prototype in a Michigan cornfield were published in 1907, the idea that Henry Ford might someday produce the populist tractors caught the attention of farmers across the globe. As the years went by, however, Ford failed to solve the engineering problems inherent to an inexpensive, lightweight tractor strong enough to do heavy-duty farmwork. Ford's lifelong ambition to create the ideal tractor would have to wait—until he had the ideal tractor.

In 1915, however, Henry Ford found and shanghaied the right engineer to design a winning tractor. The new man would not be working for Ford Motor. That June, even before blueprints of the tractor existed, Ford organized a new company in Dearborn, Henry Ford & Co., solely to develop a farm tractor on a commercial basis.[20] (It became Henry Ford & Son, Inc., in 1917.)

The engineer Ford chose to design the tractor, at Charles Sorensen's suggestion, was the brilliant Eugene Farkas, who boasted a degree in mechanical engineering from his native Hungary's Royal Joseph Technical University. Flat broke after a year in the Hungarian army and a brief unpaid apprenticeship at a motorcycle factory, Farkas had set out for America in the fall of 1906 knowing, he said, "an estimated seventeen words of English."[21] The neat, well-mannered twenty-five-year-old quickly took the first job that afforded him six months of English lessons, then homed in on his goal of designing cars. His talent led him to jobs with a succession of Detroit automakers. Joe Galamb, a fellow Hungarian, recruited him to Ford Motor, where he assisted in the development of the Model T. In tackling the tractor job, Farkas took general direction from Henry Ford, but came up with most of the innovations on his own.[22] When Ford ordered that the tractor be lightweight, for example, Farkas redesigned it from the ground up to eliminate the need for an underlying frame. The concept was so radical it sparked heated debate even among Ford designers, to whom doing things in new ways was old hat. Indeed, even Henry Ford, the quintessential innovator, blanched at what his new concern's chief engineer was suggesting. But Farkas was able to prove that precise castings could allow the parts of the tractor to fit together so snugly that the heavy connecting bars of a frame were unnecessary. What's more, the frameless design—akin to the single-unit body construction that would become popular in automobiles half a century later—also answered Ford's mandate that the power plant be enclosed to protect it from dirt.

Farkas still had a bright young man's swagger and was working closely enough with Ford to tell the boss straight to his face when he was wrong. Sometimes, though, just communicating with Henry Ford proved harder than changing his mind. Regarding the tractor's transmission, Ford had ordained that it be the same planetary type used on the T. He had also laid out specifications for a T-like drive train to the rear axle. Farkas knew that both would be entirely inefficient in actual use. "Mr. Ford couldn't see that," the engineer recalled. "His idea was that the greater the reduction, the greater the efficiency. Well, that isn't so. Mathematically, he [was] wrong." But as Farkas found out, the laws of mathematics meant little to Henry Ford when he was out to solve an engineering problem. "My high-sounding phrases didn't work at all. There was just no impression," Farkas said, "but finally it came to me. I thought, 'Maybe if I use a non-mathematical expression I can explain it to him.'" After thinking about it for weeks, Farkas finally came up with an image that the company president could understand. "I formulated it this way," Farkas said in a 1954 interview: "that a worm is working under a condition of rolling and sliding, and I said, 'The more rolling the worm does, the higher the efficiency; and the more sliding the worm does, the lower the efficiency.'" The ratio was subsequently altered to reflect Farkas's estimation of the most advantageous setup. In preparing his carefully crafted pitch, Farkas took note that the word to which Henry Ford responded best was "efficiency."[23]

Eugene Farkas quickly became one of Henry Ford's favorite employees, delighting his boss by performing a Hungarian dance at the occasional parties the Fords would throw for the company's engineers.[24] But it was their mutual love of machines that sealed the bond between the two men. "You know," Farkas quoted Ford once telling his wife, Helen Parshall Farkas, "Gene and I are going to run this place. I wish Gene had more boldness. He's too nice a guy to work around here."[25]

Yet work there he did, so well that as of mid-1917 Henry Ford & Son, Inc., had the blueprints for a lightweight, three-speed, 20-horsepower frameless workhorse planned for production both in Dearborn and at a new factory to be erected in his father's home, County Cork, Ireland. Farkas's schematics for the tractor were such works of art they would later be hung in classrooms at Purdue and MIT. Yet Henry Ford still believed the design could be improved, and therefore set no firm schedule for taking Farkas's ingenious tractor into production.

Judging from Ford's first two companies, which failed because he couldn't stop experimenting with cars long enough to actually build any, it seems clear that had it not been for the impatience of his business partners in the early days of Ford Motor, no Ford cars might ever have existed. In the case of the tractor, Henry Ford had no associates pushing him, but, as of April 7, 1917, he had something far more: a genuinely epic public relations opportunity.

———

After the United States formally declared war on Germany on April 6, 1917, Ford of England director Percival Perry, serving part-time as an official with Britain's Food Production Department, lost no time in wiring Henry Ford to request support for accelerated tractor production in England. "Can assure you positively this suggestion is made in national interest," Perry cabled, signing off with a calculated appeal to Ford's sense of drama: "National necessity entirely dependent [on] Mr. Ford's decision."[26]

As an island nation, Great Britain had had to struggle against a German submarine blockade just to feed its people. With many farmers called to war, those who were left behind needed help if they were to produce enough food for the entire nation, as well as an army of millions. Although a Women's Land Army was called up to serve as replacements on the nation's farms, millions of tons of food still had to be imported through seas infested with German U-boats. To the government waging the war, every extra ton of food that could be coaxed from British soil meant that another ton of munitions could be loaded on an inbound ship. Inexpensive, efficient tractors, in quantity, could go far to help boost productivity on farms across Britain, and perhaps even bring new acreage into cultivation.

"In full accord with principle," Henry Ford cabled back to Perry. "Will work night and day."[27]

By that he meant, of course, that Charles Sorensen would work night and day, as Ford assigned his ace production man to facilitate the immediate production of tractors for Great Britain. Within five weeks, Sorensen was touring the south of England to meet with suppliers and distribute specifications for parts. (Remarkably, Sorensen had to send back to the States for only two components: everything but the bolts and screws could be produced to the Ford specs in Britain, and without delay.) British periodicals that had once repudiated Henry Ford's pacifism by refusing to run Ford Motor ads did a sudden about-face, lavishing praise on the American industrialist for sharing his mass-production magic with the Britons manning the home front.

Within another five weeks, however, Sorensen and his team were back in Michigan. As the operations chief explained in his memoir, things had changed overnight, or more accurately over a single afternoon. "By the end of June things were lined up for early production of parts, and I was back in London," Sorensen wrote. "One forenoon an air-raid alert was sounded. I was told this was unusual because the Zeppelins which occasionally dropped bombs on the city always came at night. This raid, however, was a daylight one not by dirigibles but by German planes." The city's undefended financial district was under direct attack, and Sorensen watched it all from a rooftop.[28]

In response to the real fear of German air assaults, Britain's Ministry of Munitions of War shifted its priorities. After determining that its nation's manufacturing facilities had best be devoted to producing aircraft, the British government politely thanked Ford for its initiative regarding tractor production, but declined to allow the company the use of any factory space. The ministry requested that Ford Motor build the tractors in the United States and ship them to England. With an initial order of 6,000, Henry Ford found himself in the tractor business.[29]

In July 1917, Henry Ford & Son was incorporated and took the place of Henry Ford & Co. According to its filing, the new company was to produce tractors, farm implements, and "self-propelling vehicles and mechanisms of every description," a category that included the automobile, significantly.[30] For the time being, at least, the Ford & Son firm, which was wholly owned by Henry, Clara, and Edsel Ford, focused on making tractors alone. The concern's production facilities were situated quite apart from the Highland Park car factory, at Henry Ford's own factory in Dearborn. Separate or not, the efficiency for which Ford Motor Company had become known spread seamlessly to the tractor operation, and in less than a year the British had received all 6,000 of their "Fordson" farm tractors. While their impact on England's food supply was not felt instantaneously, the British government would estimate that before the end of the war, each of Ford's tractors had increased foodstuff production by about 1,000 tons.[31]

Thanks largely to Percival Perry's agility and enthusiasm, Henry Ford had become involved in wartime production before any other major American manufacturer. His initial contribution to the Allied effort, a battalion of farm tractors, was certainly not inconsistent with his well-publicized antipathy toward war of any kind. However, the entry of the United States into the conflict brought even greater pressures to bear upon the automobile magnate who had sworn he would rather burn his factory down than turn it over to war production.[32] Two years before America entered the war, Ford consented to produce ambulance chassis and battle helmets, neither of which were objectionable as weapons of war. Circumstances would soon force him to be less particular.

———

Across Detroit at the Packard Motor Car Company's factory on East Grand Boulevard, thirty-seven-year-old Jesse Vincent had devoted three years to an assignment to design an aircraft engine for possible commercial use. By 1917, Vincent had a pioneering 12-cylinder engine to show for his effort, but with no airplanes in which to test it. Vincent instead tried out his creation in race cars, which blew by anything else on the track, clocking 100 mph in a trial at the Indianapolis Speedway. Vincent's mighty engine was heavy relative to its power output, but it was still far advanced beyond anything already existing in American aviation. When the United States joined the war, the Allies—especially beleaguered France—stated very bluntly what the Yanks could contribute: first, fresh soldiers, and second, airplanes. The French asked for a whopping 22,465 planes. American authorities responded that the United States would produce twice that many.

The very idea was preposterous. Up to 1917, the U.S. aviation industry had turned out a grand total of 700 airplanes. Thirteen other countries had done better than that, and most of them were building much more powerful aircraft than America's favorite flying machine, the Jenny. Just about all the United States had to offer the Allies was Jesse Vincent's new engine; as for its potential in aviation, Vincent's power plant offered little more than promise. It needed more horsepower, less weight, more precise but faster production methods—and testing in actual airplanes.

Above all, Vincent believed that to make his design truly viable it had to have the support of the entire industry, because the United States would never be able to produce a useful wartime engine if its automotive designers, engineers, and manufacturers as well as its aeronautics experts were all working in different directions toward varying ends. Aside from streamlining production, a standardized engine design would allow for easier maintenance in battlefield conditions, where the necessity for an array of different spare parts to differing engine specifications would make repairs both cumbersome and confounding. Not surprisingly, Alvan Macauley, president of Packard Motor Car, concurred with his chief engineer from the outset, and insisted that Vincent go to Washington, D.C., to press the government to designate one engine—his Packard engine—as the standard for the war effort. A former patent attorney, Macauley knew that if Vincent succeeded his company would have to share its technology and give up its head start in the development of a practical airplane engine, but sacrificing the innovation looked like the patriotic thing to do, and the mood of the buying public was growing ever more patriotic. The day's imperative at Packard and across the country was to stop watching the war and start winning it.

On June 4, 1917, Jesse Vincent's design was approved by the U.S. War Department. No longer just a Packard, it was renamed the U.S.A. Standardized Aircraft Engine—in the lingo of domestic propaganda, the "Liberty engine." The success of the Liberty engine program, as Vincent had foreseen, depended on the willingness of rival companies to cooperate with one another. Automakers Cadillac, Dodge, and Pierce-Arrow joined Packard in what soon turned into an engineering melee. Vincent's basic design came under a barrage of some 100 suggested changes every week. Meanwhile, the engine was scheduled to go into production by the end of 1917.

Eventually, the Liberty engine assumed its final form, or forms. Depending on its intended use—from a training plane to a bomber—the standardized engine could be built with four, six, eight, or twelve cylinders. Following European practice, the cylinders worked best when finely bored out of solid steel. Most automobile engines were cast, but to achieve the more precise weight ratios and added strength required for flying, aircraft engines had to be laboriously machined. In a typical automobile engine, a cylinder with a bore (diameter) and stroke (length) of three inches by five inches was regarded as more than ample. In a Liberty airplane engine, the cylinders' bore and stroke had to be five by seven inches. Precision-machined cylinders of that size would take time to produce in bulk quantities, anywhere. For help in solving the problem Vincent turned to Ford Motor Company, whose engineering team had been considered the best in industrial metallurgy ever since Harold Wills introduced vanadium steel in the Model T.

Alex Lumsden, who worked in Ford Motor Company's experimental department when the problem of the Liberty cylinders was addressed, later recalled that Wills had been the one who insisted that the cylinders did not have to be bored. "He conceived the idea that it should be made out of tubing," Lumsden remembered.[33] William Pioch, another experimental department employee at the time, suggested that it was hard to say where the idea came from specifically, but that it emerged from a meeting that included Wills and engineers Carl Emde and John Findlater.[34]

However smart the concept, the devil still lay in the details. Once the tubing was cut to measure, the dilemma became how to close one end of the cylinder. Emde and Findlater built on toolmaker Oliver Hockenberry's idea to cut the tubing at a forty-five-degree angle and then flash-weld it shut. Because Ford Motor gauged the efficacy of every task's performance in terms of "operations," or how many separate efforts were required, Lumsden could not help boasting, "We made the cylinder head complete with the bosses for spark plugs in two operations."[35] Such increased efficiencies were no big deal to those who worked at Ford Motor, where constant improvements were expected, but others on the Liberty engine project could only marvel that the Ford men brought the price per cylinder down from $24.00 to $8.25. Three weeks after Wills, Emde, and Findlater presented their method for making the clipped-tubing cylinder, Ford Motor was asked to manufacture the cylinders for all of the Liberty engines, wherever they were built. Production started in August 1917. By the end of the war the company would deliver 415,377 cylinders.[36] It would also join the team producing completed engines.

Once the United States entered World War I, Henry Ford changed his mind about refusing to produce war matériel. So it was that in November 1917, Ford joined fellow automakers Packard, Lincoln, Buick, Cadillac, and Nordyke & Marmon in a monumental effort to mass-produce Liberty motors for Allied aircraft. At Highland Park, production of Liberty engines would not actually start until May 7, 1918, although Ford Motor was already providing cylinders to all the other factories. The transition from building car engines to building plane engines called for more than just making different parts. Structural tolerances in airplane designs had to come much closer than those in any car engine—even Ford's, which were as precise as any others made.[37]

Henry Ford was not a complete novice in aviation. In 1909, Charles Van Auken, a twenty-year-old sweeper at Mack Avenue, talked his boss into helping him build an experimental Blériot-type monoplane. Ford offered Van Auken two top-flight assistants, design engineers Charles Smith and Harold Hicks; ordered shop employees to make whatever parts the plane needed; and provided a vacant building so his would-be flier could experiment, free of cost to himself. Henry Ford's generosity arose in part from a desire to encourage his own son's engineering interests. Edsel, who was sixteen and aviation-crazed at the time, eagerly spent much of his time outside school at Van Auken's side, helping him redesign a Model T engine for use on one of the first airplanes ever constructed in Detroit. It was ready for testing in just under a year. With sky-high expectations Van Auken took off from a pasture on Ford's Dearborn farm, but never got more than six feet off the ground. Then the crankshaft broke, and within minutes the wind picked the contraption up and smashed it into a tree, leaving Van Auken slightly injured and convincing Henry Ford, at least for the moment, that the airplane business was too dangerous.[38]

But aviation had gotten into the elder Ford's blood. In 1912 he journeyed to Hammondsport, New York, to tour the Curtiss Airplane Factory. Run by the multitalented Glenn H. Curtiss, aviator, businessman, engineer, and motorcycle racer, the company had emerged early on as a leader in the aviation industry. In fact, in 1907, when the Wright brothers, frustrated that the War Department had relegated them to the "crank file," opted to go to Europe to demonstrate their airplane, Curtiss beat them to the punch with the people back home. With unabashed flag-waving, Curtiss made the first public airplane flight in the United States on Independence Day 1908, in an aircraft sponsored by telephone inventor Alexander Graham Bell. Curtiss, bursting with All-American moxie, reminded Ford of himself.

On his visit to the Curtiss factory, Ford encouraged thirty-four-year-old Glenn Curtiss to challenge the Wright brothers' aviation patent in the courts. Ford was convinced that the defeat of the sweeping Wright patent and its chilling effect on U.S. aircraft development would mean as much to the future of flight as his own successful battle to break the Selden patent had meant to automaking.[39] Ford was mistaken. The differences between the Selden case and that of the Wright brothers were great. "The Wright patent covered a brilliant achievement that deserved protection under the law," historian Tom Crouch correctly maintained in *The Bishop's Boys: A Life of Wilbur and Orville Wright.* "Selden had simply found a legal loophole to exploit the system. Henry Ford, however, was unable to distinguish between the two situations, convinced that blanket patents stifled innovation."[40] Ford went so far as to offer Curtiss the services of W. Benton Crisp, his company attorney, who had defeated the Selden patent, with all expenses underwritten; Curtiss accepted the offer. As historian Seth Shulman explained in *Unlocking the Sky: Glenn Hammond Curtiss and the Race to Invent the Airplane,* "The case drove Henry Ford to distraction; he was firm in the belief that patent protections should be used to bring new innovations to market, not to stifle competition."[41]

Despite Ford's long-standing personal enthusiasm for the airplane, some explanation from Ford Motor Company's president appeared necessary regarding why the militant pacifist of 1915 had suddenly remade himself into a peaceable militant whose company was making Liberty engines for the Allied cause in 1917. To justify the switch, Ford offered the astonishing promise that he would "place our factory at the disposal of the United States government and will operate without one cent of profit."[42] When his fellow shareholders pointed out that operating without a profit was unrealistic, and that the government fully expected corporations to earn nominal returns on war contracts, Henry Ford broke ranks. In a move that would cast him with a lasting glow of public goodwill, he then declared that while Ford Motor Company would take a profit on war work, at the insistence of the other shareholders, he would return his 58.5 percent share of it to the U.S. government.

In 1915, as the *Peace Ship* was about to depart New York for Europe, Henry Ford had made a similar pledge, to put up the expenses for a Washington office of the Union Against Militarism, with *New York Evening Post* editor Oswald Villard in charge. "It is worth recording for the light it throws upon Mr. Ford," Villard wrote later, that the union "never received one cent of Ford money. I did my best to collect it. . . ."[43] Even as Villard's associate Louis P. Lochner was writing letter after letter to Highland Park inquiring after the expected $20,000, people all over the world were lionizing Henry Ford for his latest promise not to keep "one cent" of his company's war profits. Very few would check later to see if he kept his word.

William C. Klann, one of many Ford Motor production chiefs pulled off auto work in favor of war work, headed the company's Liberty engine program. "While on this job, I at one time did not go home for three weeks except for a bath," Klann claimed. As competent as any production engineer in Detroit, Klann nonetheless found himself hard-pressed to keep up with the production schedules for—and continual design changes to—the new aircraft engine. He and his team somehow managed to complete their first shipment, but then the U.S. Army stymied efforts to get the finished engines out the door. "We had 200 motors assembled and not one was being shipped," Klann averred. "I asked Mr. [P. E.] Martin, then Mr. C. H. Wills, and then Mr. Henry Ford why we were not shipping these motors if they [the Allies] needed them." No one knew. Finally, Klann asked the Army captain in charge, who casually explained that the engines had to undergo fifty-hour running tests before the government could accept them. Klann completed the tests, but by the time he looked again two weeks later, 442 Liberty engines were lined up awaiting shipment. Upon noticing the dumbfounded Klann, the same Army captain asked as casually as before whether one of the Ford motors had passed the required test in the air. The production chief immediately arranged to have one of the motors installed in a fuselage—only then did he learn that he was required to take the first ride.[44]

The reason for the military's insistence that the chief builder assume the risk carried a sinister cast. Only weeks before, the plane containing the very first working Liberty engine, built by Packard, had crashed "after its pilot began executing an inexplicable series of loops and tailspins culminated by a nosedive into the ground that killed both him and the passenger," according to Stan Grayson in *Packard: A History of the Motor Car and the Company.* "There was talk of sabotage; one man was arrested by Army intelligence, but he was not convicted. [Jesse] Vincent believed the crash was caused by pilot error or mechanical failure."[45]

In any case, the Army officials supervising Ford Motor's Liberty production did not offer William Klann the option of turning the risk of the Ford engine's first air trial over to anyone else. In fact, had Klann known how to fly he would have been expected to take the plane up by himself. As it was, he rode along as the pilot's sole passenger.

"I got dressed up and said, 'Give me all you got, as we want to ship some motors,'" Klann recalled. "When we got up in the air, I got all that I asked for as we flew upside down, rolled over, made nose dives and tail spins. When the motor was just going 90 rpm a minute and only going put, put, put, I stated the motor would stand the test."[46] The next day, P. E. Martin and Harold Wills exploded when they found out that Klann had given in to the Army's pressure to go on the first flight test. But Klann's confidence in his product paid off in getting the shipment of the airplane engines in gear. By the end of the war in November 1918, Ford Motor would deliver 3,940 Liberty engines, ranking third in production behind Lincoln and Packard, which shipped 6,500 each.[47]

Gaining the advantage over Germany in the air was the predominant Allied concern, but not the only one. After the United States took sides with the Allies, Germany's U-boat campaign brought the war to American waters, an immediate threat to all U.S. ships. When the U.S. Navy prepared to take the offensive with a newly designed 204-foot submarine chaser dubbed the "Eagle boat," Ford Motor volunteered to build a prototype at its Highland Park plant. After the first Eagle boat was built and ready for testing, its brilliant engineers had to figure out how to dismantle the craft to get it out of the building so it could be hauled down to the Detroit River.[48] Henry Ford could hardly criticize, since he had made much the same blunder when he was forced to widen the doorway of his Bagley Avenue shed to make way for his quadricycle in 1896. However, the awkward launch of the Eagle prototype was, unfortunately, a portent of more production trouble to come.

Navy officials were impressed with the prototype Eagle boat, as well as with Henry Ford's commitment to build at least 112 more of them within ten and a half months. Among the few people in Washington who remained cool to Ford was Franklin D. Roosevelt, then serving under Josephus Daniels as an assistant secretary of the Navy. Roosevelt's conclusion about Ford was that "until he saw a chance for publicity free of charge, [he] thought a submarine was something to eat."[49] The image of Eagle boats popping off the Ford assembly line did indeed generate many positive articles about Ford Motor Company, especially since the perception was that the boats would be provided to the government practically at cost.

In truth, Ford Motor Company had made rather a good deal for itself, although not an unusual one for government contracts in wartime. The company would willingly apply its engineering expertise to the Allied shipbuilding effort, but the U.S. government agreed to foot the $3.5 million cost of upgrading the firm's facilities to enable the huge increase in production. Some members of Congress questioned the enormous expenditure to put Henry Ford in the shipbuilding business but, as author Robert Lacey explained, "the Navy's own shipyards were overwhelmed with war work, and it was suggested, though not promised, that Ford would buy back the plant when the war was over."[50] The location was carefully selected: Dearborn's River Rouge tract, where Henry Ford would eventually build the largest industrial plant in the world. Without anyone but Henry, Clara, and Edsel knowing it, the federal government unwittingly launched the River Rouge plant when it contracted for the first 100 Eagle boats, at $275,000 each, on January 14, 1918.

Unfortunately, especially given Ford's assurances about meeting production quotas and deadlines, boats share little in common with cars, except in being designed to go from one place to another. Apart from that, their engineering and construction differed so extensively that expertise in building one proved utterly useless when it came to producing the other. (In the 1940s, Henry J. Kaiser, the most efficient shipbuilder on either side in World War II, would learn the same thing. Kaiser could turn out ships even bigger than Eagle boats at the rate of one every eighty hours, yet in his later peacetime try at automaking, he staggered through eight years of production before failing completely.)

Although both cars and boats were made mostly of steel, their metal components were attached differently—where cars were bolted, boats were held together by rivets or through casting—and Ford Motor's workers found it hard to adjust. After a new factory, designed of course by Albert Kahn, was completed at the River Rouge site and an assembly line was set up, Bill Knudsen, designated head of the Eagle boat program, could only watch the entire project stall out time and again as the Ford workmen struggled with the new processes. As they were finally finished, Eagle boats would be launched directly into the river from the new factory building, sliding down the bank on rollers. Each boat made a shakedown cruise via the Detroit River to Lake Erie, executing hairpin turns and other maneuvers meant to break the craft and everything on it, if possible. Clerk George Brown remembered that many of the Highland Park office personnel were invited as a courtesy on the shakedown cruises, but "some of them would come back and stay home a week, seasick!"

Brown also told a story about one of his prewar co-workers who had joined the Army even before the United States declared war so that, as he explained, "I can get a choice." As it turned out, he pulled one of the toughest and least choice assignments: patrolling the docks at Murmansk in northwestern Russia. "He said," Brown recalled of his friend in the service, that "one day there he was on sentry duty and somebody called his attention to smoke on the horizon. They kept watching, anxious to see what boat was coming in. They were all on the alert and had everything ready for a reception regardless of what it was. . . . Finally, they found that three Eagle boats were coming in. When he found out that it was an Eagle, he said, 'George, I just pictured myself sitting at the desk with you. I wished I was back. We were almost freezing to death. . . . What a grand sight it was to see those Eagle boats!'"[51] Boats were often rejected by the U.S. Navy's on-site supervisors, who complained that Ford Motor's workmanship was inconsistent and that the company's own inspections were far too lenient. Although its workforce swelled to 4,380 in July 1918 and peaked at around 8,000 near the end of the year, Ford's riverside factory completed only 60 Eagle boats, most of them after the war was over.[52]

Ford Motor had stumbled badly on the federal contract. Critics presumed that Henry Ford had simply promised too much in agreeing to produce more than 100 Eagle boats in a matter of months. The estimate may indeed have been overambitious. The company was initiating production of tractors and airplane engines at the same time, even while continuing auto output—Model T production was reduced in 1918, but still amounted to 500,000 cars. The shipbuilding fiasco demonstrated that even Fordism had its limits. That was something Henry Ford never quite believed, and his activities during the next decade seemed calculated to show that Fordism in fact had no limits. At the end of World War I, however, the major U.S. industrialist who had sworn he would never accept any war work had taken on one major military project too many.

———

After decades of living in rented homes and apartments, Henry and Clara built a 1,300-acre estate called Fair Lane during World War I; today it's a National Historic Landmark on the campus of the University of Michigan—Dearborn. Named after the area in County Cork where Henry's ancestors had resided, the two-story house designed by architect William Van Tine was built of light-colored Ohio limestone. It resembled a rustic Norman castle, with outer walls one-and-a-half to two feet thick. Hoping to keep Edsel at home Ford had a $30,000 organ, a bowling alley, an immense indoor swimming pool surrounded by heated marble benches, and a game room installed. Edsel himself had suggested that his parents hire Frank Lloyd Wright as the architect, but they were aghast at Wright's daring contemporary designs. The house featured fifty-six rooms and eight fireplaces, some with carving that incorporated Henry Ford's favorite sayings—for example, "Chop your own wood and it will warm you twice" and "Gather ye roses while you may." Like Thomas Jefferson's Monticello in Charlottesville, Virginia, the Fair Lane residence was a monument to Henry Ford's passion for tinkering. In 1914 Thomas Edison, a frequent visitor to the estate, laid the cornerstone of the Powerhouse, which was connected to the main building by a 300-foot underground tunnel. (Later Ford installed a wrought-iron gate in the tunnel as a security precaution. He feared that some crooks might try to kidnap his grandchildren just as they had his friend Charles Lindbergh's baby.)[53]

Using the Rouge River to generate energy, the Fair Lane Powerhouse was the prototype for over thirty waterpower plants constructed by Henry Ford between 1914 and 1944. These water-driven mills, built all over Michigan, were adaptive restorations of nineteenth-century gristmills. The goal was to offer farmers jobs at small plants within their communities. The Powerhouse was Henry Ford's own pride and joy: it housed a twelve-car garage and hydroelectric equipment as well as an actual working laboratory. Ford and a staff of technicians and engineers could often be found in the sparkling laboratory—the top floor of the Powerhouse—plotting and experimenting. Critical design work on many projects was centered at this home laboratory, including the Fordson tractor (1917) and the Gasoline Rail Car (1920). "Uncle Henry's Powerhouse was something to be seen," his nephew Edward L. Bryant enthused, "because it was so clean and efficient and quiet."[54] While the Powerhouse was imposing, the Fords made sure the main house was not too opulent. They disdained the boastful rich of Grosse Pointe and Park Avenue who flaunted wealth in a lavish fashion. "Our house is not a show place but a place to live in and enjoy," Clara noted. "It's a place where you get strength to go on."[55]

The grounds, designed by landscape architect Jens Jensen, were as much a home for the Fords as any room in the house. Clara, a serious gardener and amateur botanist, supervised three greenhouses, extensive general gardens, and tree plantings. The crowning achievement of the grounds was Clara's rose garden, covering more than three acres and ranked with the finest displays, public or private, in the country. She employed twenty gardeners just to care for her ten thousand rose plants. She loved to drive her quiet electric boat on the Rouge River, in back of Fair Lane, to watch wildlife. Most of Fair Lane's acreage, though, was left wild, or very lightly groomed; it was a reserve where Henry Ford never had to be anything but a Dearborn farm boy.[56] "A man who had lived near the Ford estate, Fair Lane, told me he had seen Mr. Ford many times on a summer's morning," recalled a Ford employee named W. Griffith. "He had an old bicycle and would get on it and coast down the hill. He would then push it to the top and coast down again. This he would do several times. Then he would take off his shoes and socks, sit on the edge of the river, and paddle his feet in the water. He would whistle at the birds. Apparently he was a great lover of nature."[57]

The Fords were committed to returning Fair Lane to its natural state, reintroducing deer, raccoons, and rabbits to the property. Henry, in fact, instructed Jensen to return Fair Lane to the way it was when "the Chippewa and Ottawa skied down the banks of the River Rouge."[58] Naturalist John Burroughs said he saw more birds at Fair Lane than at any other natural site in North America—and for good reason. Henry, a board member of the Michigan Audubon Society and the catalyst behind passage of the Migratory Bird Act of 1913, took an active interest in rebuilding bird habitats throughout the estate. When Henry was a youngster, his foster grandfather, Patrick Ahern, had taught him Michigan bird songs, which he learned to imitate. Even before the mansion was finished, hundreds of elaborate birdhouses had been erected at Fair Lane.[59] "You may, in fact, go from one end of the great State of Michigan to another, and you will nowhere find the number of variety of birds that you will see in the same space on the Ford farm," marveled a visitor from the American Game Protective Association.[60] The Fords donated birds, bird-houses, and bird seed to American communities interested in following their lead in the encouragement of saving near extinct songbirds and waterfowl. Because Ford valued privacy—his own and that of the animals—Fair Lane was heavily guarded. The property was located on a small hill overlooking the River Rouge, upriver from the automobile plant: Ford insisted that all of his houses and indeed most of his factories around the world be built on water. In addition to Fair Lane, the Fords maintained winter homes in Ways, Georgia, and Fort Myers, Florida, along with a lodge in northern Michigan.

Clara took a strong hand in decorating the Ford mansions according to a traditional post-Victorian style. The fact that Henry also liked to buy antiques soon became common knowledge among dealers all over the country. Exquisite pieces of furniture, as well as a considerable amount of plain *stuff,* found their way to his Dearborn warehouses. Henry Ford did not necessarily appreciate the aesthetic value of his growing collection, but he felt the strong pull in the power of individual pieces of handiwork—furniture, tools, or even whole buildings—to hold back the clock. For the same reason, he and Clara started a movement to retain folksinging and dancing, before it was forgotten with the passing generations under the din of the new jazz music the Fords abhorred. They insisted on holding square dances at Fair Lane, usually hiring Celtic singers and Appalachian fiddle players on the do-si-do circuit for these old-timey events. Stephen Foster classics like "Beautiful Dreamer" and "My Old Kentucky Home" were played regularly on their magnificent Steinway piano. Although their active program of publishing traditional U.S. folk music became something of a joke around Detroit in the 1920s, they were instrumental in saving an important part of nineteenth-century life in America, one considered precious today.

Throughout World War I Henry Ford, while settling into Fair Lane, caused eyebrows to be raised as he searched for a substitute for gasoline. Conducting agricultural experiments in Dearborn under the auspices of Henry Ford & Son, Inc., he began his quest to have Model Ts and Fordson tractors run on denatured alcohol. Putting John Dailey, who was working in the electrical department at Highland Park, in charge of the alternative fuels project, Ford believed that mashed cornstalks or squeezed German potatoes could get 15 percent more power than petroleum. "Gasoline is going—alcohol is coming," he told a reporter for the *Detroit News* in 1916. "It is coming to stay, too, for it's in unlimited supply. And we might as well get ready for it now. All the world is waiting for a substitute for gasoline. When that is gone, there will be no more gasoline, and long before that time, the prices of gasoline will have risen to a point where it will be too expensive to burn as a motor fuel. The day is not far distant when, for every one of those barrels of gasoline, a barrel of alcohol must be substituted."[61]

Although Ford had built his fortune on gasoline-powered automobiles, he believed its exhaust fumes were having a deleterious effect on the atmosphere. And he didn't care for the bawdy, new oilmen of Texas and Oklahoma who, unlike community-building farmers, drifted around looking for quick riches. If only Model Ts could run on grains or vegetable substances, he reasoned, the farmers could profit instead of Standard Oil. When Michigan prohibited alcohol in 1916, Ford, who didn't drink, saw his opportunity. Although he never joined the Anti-Saloon League of America or tried to close down local pubs, he believed that temperance was a good thing, that whiskey and gin were addictive poisons. But he felt sorry for the sixty Michigan brewers whose operations had folded. He hatched a scheme: that the breweries be converted to making alcohol for cars. "Millions of dollars are invested in these plants," he told the same *Detroit News* reporter. "Economically it would be a shameful waste to have them become idle. But there is no reason why it should become so. Every standard brewing plant can be transformed from a brewery into a distillery for manufacturing denatured alcohol for the use in automobiles or other internal combustion engines."[62]

While American troops were heading to Europe, and his *Peace Ship* was still being lambasted in the press, Ford took a number of trips to effect the development of alcohol fuels. In March 1917 he sailed to Cuba on a yacht, hoping to acquire sugarcane fields and sugar mills, which he could use to make ethanol. Meanwhile, he was warring with the U.S. Internal Revenue Department (as the IRS was then called), which didn't want him operating stills in Michigan. Ford claimed he was trying to manufacture alternative fuels. The U.S. government balked: distilling alcohol, no matter what the purpose, was illegal. Constantly faced with setbacks, the tenacious Ford never gave up on his dream of making oil obsolete. He scouted Florida, one time accompanied by Thomas Edison, looking for the right sugar plantations and farmland. At his forestry operation in Iron Mountain, Michigan, he initiated a program of distilling tons of wood chips. These experiments led to the creation of "briquettes," carbon residue compressed into coal-like squares, which are still used for backyard barbecues all over the world. Stymied by Prohibition statutes and a booming oil lobby that started calling him Crazy "Peace Ship" Henry, for the rest of his life he told whoever asked that gasoline was a transportation agent of the past. Ethanol, or some other clean fuel base in agriculture, was the wave of the future.[63]

———

Henry and Clara Ford's only child, Edsel, lived at home until he married in 1916 at age twenty-two. By then, he had been working at Ford Motor for four years, since graduating from high school in 1912. Edsel Ford had been a good student at the academically rigorous public University School in Detroit, where he acquired a solid grounding through courses in such fundamentals as drafting and basic engineering. In those days, the teenager would drive his Model N to Ford Motor's Piquette Avenue plant after school—willing to lick envelopes or perform any other odd jobs that needed doing. Lazing or throwing money about never counted among Edsel's predilections. Henry and Clara made sure their boy did not become spoiled by the accumulating family fortune. In truth, however, Henry also saw to it that Edsel really had no options, and that the boy knew it. Henry Ford's bias against higher education, for example, left no question that his bright and studious son would not go to Harvard or Yale, much as he may have wanted to.[64] In the 1910s, of course, it was not at all unusual even for the richest scions to enter their family businesses right out of high school. Besides, Edsel took a genuine interest in Ford Motor Company. During his first few years there he worked without complaint in a general capacity around the offices.[65] In his spare moments, he dabbled in various projects with some of the designers, including a six-cylinder version of the Model T.

Edsel Ford shared little in common with the stereotype of the bratty, uncontrollable, and useless millionaire's son. Serious and sensitive, he stayed focused on the job at hand and never wasted time bantering, reading the paper, or tending to his own hobbies. In fact, his workday habits were far more disciplined than his father's. When the young Ford was at the office, he remained at his desk or wherever else he was supposed to be. His even temper, mature deportment, and dedication even lessened the shock of his being named an officer of Ford Motor Company at the tender age of twenty, when James J. Couzens resigned in October 1916. At that time, Frank Klingensmith took over for Couzens as the company's treasurer, and Edsel assumed Klingensmith's corporate position of secretary—as well as overall responsibility for Ford Motor's official correspondence, plus certain aspects of its record keeping. By tackling such large management tasks at such a young age, Edsel Ford refined and expanded his natural organizational abilities.

In fact, it did not go unnoticed for long by the upper management that the boss's son was rapidly developing into a very talented executive. He earned the respect of nearly everyone he worked with—and it was definitely Edsel's way to work *with* people. Where his father was abrupt, Edsel played the diplomat; where Henry Ford was mercurial, his son remained deliberate, and effective.[66]

As an adult, Edsel Ford was slightly shorter, sturdier, and less striking in aspect and energy level than his famous father, but also better mannered, better at sports (being active in skiing, tennis, golf, and squash),[67] better dressed, even dapper, and in time a much better boss than his father ever tried to be. The only real trait the elder and younger Fords shared in equal measure was their love of cars. Yet even that common passion played out differently in the two men, the elder remaining content to rest on the laurels won by his beloved Model T and the younger man eager to try out every model considered advanced in engineering or in the emerging art of automobile styling.

Constrained as he may have felt at times by his father's control over his life, Edsel also enjoyed the extraordinary upside of being Henry Ford's only child. On his twenty-first birthday, for example, his father took him to the family's Detroit bank to show Edsel his present: $1 million, as it looked in gold bullion (equivalent to some $18 million today). The next year, the twenty-two-year-old was named to Ford Motor's board of directors, and the year after that he was appointed secretary of the four-member executive committee that evaluated the company's policy questions and reported its recommendations back to the board to enact.[68] Edsel Ford grew more comfortable in his position at the company, the higher up he climbed.

Edsel was not all business. During the winter of 1915–1916, he signed up for a course of dancing lessons mainly to spend more time in the company of Eleanor Lowthian Clay, niece of the late founder of Detroit's Hudson's department store chain. As tradespeople, the Clay family did not quite rate acceptance into Detroit society, but they came a lot closer than even the richest gas-buggy baron. Demurely fashionable, Eleanor Clay was highly intelligent and independent—as she proved by eschewing a debut—and she shared Edsel's budding interest in the fine arts. Clay even had her own connection to the auto industry: her late uncle, Joseph Lowthian Hudson, had founded not only a prosperous department store but also the thriving auto company named after him. Edsel Ford and Eleanor Clay were married on November 1, 1916, in her uncle's mansion on Detroit's posh E. Boston Boulevard, after which they honeymooned for two months in California and Hawaii.[69] Their first son, Henry II, was born the following September 4.

In August 1917, a month before his son was born, Edsel Ford was drafted, along with some eight million other American men. As Keith Sward noted in *The Legend of Henry Ford,* "Congressman Nicholas Longworth . . . dropped the indelicate slur that of [the] seven persons in the world who were certain to go through the war unscathed, six were the sons of the Kaiser and the seventh was Edsel Ford."[70] Indeed, the way Edsel's eligibility was handled set him far apart from every one of his eight million fellows, and foreshadowed much that would ensue in the son's quiet, lifelong war with his unusually domineering father.

Edsel Ford professed his willingness to serve from the first. The most likely explanation of what happened next is that Henry and Clara forbade him from accepting a commission. A team of Ford lawyers submitted an appeal to the local draft board on Edsel's behalf, basing his case on the indispensability of Henry Ford's only son to a vital war industry. The appeal was rejected and Edsel Ford was "drafted," if only to the extent that he received his classifications.

With that development Henry Ford sent his case—his son's case, that is—directly to President Wilson. Privately, he later told his friend former *Detroit News* editor E. G. Pipp that had Edsel entered the service, "certain interests" unfriendly to Ford would have made sure the industrialist's boy was killed. Ford often relied upon such shrouded references to justify his paranoia.[71]

President Wilson never responded to Henry Ford's appeal. But in the end Edsel's classifications proved enough to keep him out of the service: first as a married man with a child and second because he was indeed working in a war industry, and at an unprecedentedly high administrative level for his years. In truth, only journalists and others ignorant of Edsel Ford's real character called him gutless. Given the fusillades of criticism he faced, "it took more courage for Edsel Ford not to put on a uniform than it would have taken to put on one," as E. G. Pipp explained.[72]

Whatever Edsel's inclination might have been, he bore in his quiet way the brunt of his parents' edict. He did not complain, at least not in public. He did not complicate the situation by spouting any views of his own. And most of all he did not disobey. Edsel Ford never disobeyed, and thus Henry Ford found or created the ideal executive to guide Ford Motor Company through the coming years.

11

Challenging Every Foe

Ford Motor Company continued to produce automobiles during the nineteen months the United States engaged in World War I. In fact the company enjoyed a banner year in 1917, with its introduction of new styling for the Model T. Most noticeably, the T's little snout of an engine compartment grew to be more proportional to the rest of the car, a bow to the day's overall trend toward longer, straighter lines in automobiles. Following another trend, against bright metalwork, the Model T's radiator material changed from brass to steel painted black. More somber, if more modish in wartime, the new T was a hit and Ford Motor's 1917 car sales of 735,017 represented an increase of 50 percent over those of the year before.[1] In addition, the company's introduction of a heavy-duty truck (with the first one-ton chassis) in the summer of 1917 proved perfectly timed to the war effort. Ford trucks joined the caissons rolling through Europe. Model Ts were already there. In fact, specially outfitted Model Ts were the closest thing World War I had to what would become the Jeep: a vehicle that seemed able to do anything, anywhere, in wartime as it had in peace.

The Ford workers who made all of these vehicles represented at least sixty nationalities during the World War I years. Within Ford's factory walls toiled men who, had they never left home, might have been slaughtering one another on some battlefield far from Highland Park: German against Briton, Hungarian against French, Turk against Australian, Croat against Serb, Austrian against Italian, and so forth. Yet despite the peaceful coexistence at Highland Park, "there was a problem where the government suspected German sympathizers were working at Ford," recalled Ernest Grimshaw. "Government men were working right in the operations, possibly on the bench with us, and were constantly alert for sabotage."[2]

Under the intense pressure from the government to retool for war matériel,

Ford Motor Company's production men found themselves working in an atmosphere where every honest mistake was scrutinized as a possible act of Central Powers sabotage. Suspicion even fell on Ford's personal secretary, former banker Ernest G. Liebold, who had been born in northern Michigan but had a German surname and a crisp manner that smacked of the Teutonic to those looking for it. One afternoon during the war, Liebold gave a ride home to a woman who worked in Ford Motor Company's offices, a kindness that did not go unpunished, when the woman reported him to the authorities for having remarked to her in the car, "I think the Germans will quit before they are licked." His innocuous comment, although hardly insightful, was enough to implicate Liebold as a possible German sympathizer, with access to privileged information about the enemy's intentions. The charges annoyed Leibold, but came to nothing.[3]

More disturbing was an effort by powerful outsiders to have the brilliant Carl Emde dismissed from the company. A prolific genius in drafting and tool design, Emde had taken the lead in making a success of Ford Motor Company's Liberty engine project, but his German birth made him an easy target. "Carl Emde and [heavy-manufacturing chief] Charlie Hartner were German and I was German," explained William Klann. "There were a dozen boys on this [Liberty] job that were German, and they [outsiders] claimed the German boys were holding the job back."[4]

The national hysteria against all things German lay at the bottom of the witch-hunt at Ford Motor; Germans were under suspicion in every field. The special attention paid to the company, however, stemmed from another of Henry Ford's personal biases. In 1916, when the United States sent an expedition into Mexico to capture the marauding revolutionary Pancho Villa, Ford had protested the action vehemently. It especially rankled him that while General John Pershing was leading the U.S. troops across the border, the National Guard was called up just in case the military operation escalated. The government had no right, Ford asserted, to send an Army detachment onto foreign soil. That was not an unexpected position coming from a man known to be against war in any form, but Ford did more than express his personal opinion. He stepped over a hostile border of his own, stating as though it were company policy that any Ford Motor worker who left for National Guard service during the Mexican expedition would not be given his job back upon his return. In an editorial the *Chicago Tribune* took exception, labeling Henry Ford an "anarchist" and suggesting that he move his factories to Mexico. "If Ford allows this rule of his shop to stand, he will reveal himself not merely as an ignorant idealist," the newspaper opined, "but as an anarchistic enemy of a nation which protects him in his wealth."[5] Although the *Tribune* allowed Ford to publish a denial that he had threatened to fire National Guardsmen, right-wing *Tribune* publisher Robert R. McCormick refused to retract the charge or to apologize for the name-calling. Ford responded by suing the newspaper for $1 million, his way of making the point that he reserved his right to disagree with the government without necessarily being against it.[6]

The lawsuit was pending throughout America's participation in World War I, not going to trial until May 1919. The majority of Americans may have celebrated Henry Ford for doing his part for the war effort, and especially for promising not to profit from it, but his adversaries remained wary. Many of them were old-line conservatives who deemed him at best a liberal, and at worst a socialist. In any case, Ford was unpredictable, and to some that was enough to raise suspicions against a man with so much power. "I believe Henry Ford is an unscrupulous, rapacious hypocrite," McCormick would complain, "and I think I have his number."[7]

Henry Ford's enemies began to go after him in 1918 as part of a federal investigation into wartime aircraft production. The inquiry had been instigated by an unlikely source: sculptor Gutzon Borglum—later to chisel the Mount Rushmore National Monument in South Dakota—who was thinking of starting an aircraft company in 1918. Partly from selfish motives, Borglum charged the coalition of manufacturers involved in the Liberty engine project with inefficiency and profiteering, and he persuaded his friend President Woodrow Wilson to launch an investigation. The sculptor's complaint fanned the doubts and confusion already surrounding the Liberty project's extreme delays; the United States had, after all, been in the war for a year before production finally began, spawning rumors around the country that there were no new airplane engines, only unearned profits for greedy contractors. To mend the spreading breach in public confidence before it tore apart America's commitment to the war effort, President Wilson launched an inquiry. To head it, he called upon the well-respected Republican he had defeated in the 1916 election, former Supreme Court Justice Charles Evans Hughes.

Among other troubling consequences, the Hughes investigation succeeded in smearing the business reputation of Liberty engine designer Jesse Vincent for having failed to sell his Packard Motor Car stock before entering war work. Because of this oversight Vincent inadvertently "profiteered" all of $55 over the course of the two years he spent making his harrowing efforts on behalf of the nation. Vincent was reprimanded for those ill-gotten gains and was later denied any official citation in recognition of his war work, an honor extended even to his assistants. The choice of the humorless Hughes to head the investigation would have a different implication for Henry Ford, though.[8]

The year 1918 was busy for Ford Motor Company, but even busier for its principal owner. While waging war indirectly on the Central Powers of Europe and directly on certain of his fellow stockholders, Henry Ford still found time to run for Michigan's open U.S. Senate seat. President Wilson had been among the first to encourage Ford to run, while thousands of letters from less exalted well-wishers helped him make up his mind. Neither Ford nor his Republican opponent, Truman H. Newberry, campaigned actively, but the parties behind them turned the 1918 Michigan Senate race into one of the most bitter on record. At the same time that Newberry's backers were scurrying around distorting and exaggerating Henry Ford's positions on both social and wartime issues, Charles Evans Hughes arrived in Detroit to take a close look at the Liberty engine program.

Hughes and his associates toured Highland Park specifically to look for signs that native and ethnic German members of the workforce were deliberately hobbling output. "The day the Hughes Committee came through the plant, we had 100 motors going, all on tests," William Klann remembered. "You couldn't hear yourself think at all for miles around the place with the roar of the motors."[9]

Hughes may have been deafened, but he was not satisfied. Pointedly, he chose to make an example of Carl Emde, casting the German-born tool designer's employment as a loyalty test for Ford Motor Company. "Nothing conclusive could be established against Emde in relation to this work," Hughes admitted, yet "the advisability of removing him from his position of strategic importance was clear to some of the most important men in the management." The Emde case became a cause célèbre at Highland Park. Some Ford Motor executives did side with Hughes and his investigating committee in favoring Emde's removal; their reasoning was that even though he was a naturalized U.S. citizen and even though his work on the Liberty engine was unimpeachable, Emde's position in charge of projects at Ford Motor afforded him access to a full range of industry and military documents that he could, if he chose, copy and send "home" to Germany. Other less jingoistic but more cynical company managers felt that neither Emde's career, nor the principle at stake, was as important as Ford Motor's reputation. To this way of thinking, if the man had even the appearance of a spy to those conducting witch-hunts, then the company would best take the expedient course and fire him, as a demonstration of national loyalty, no matter how brilliant and valuable his work.[10]

"I remember the results of the report that said that the Ford Motor Company was employing enemy aliens in the Design Department," fellow tool designer William F. Pioch said long afterward. "Emde came into a certain amount of criticism because he was a German. I can only tell you that it was just about wrecking the man. He was as loyal as any American that I worked alongside of."[11]

The firestorm over Emde's future at Ford Motor broke out in full force on November 3, 1918, with a vicious Republican ad about Emde in that day's *Detroit Free Press.* The ad called Ford a "Hun-lover" and quoted the Hughes investigation to the effect that Henry Ford was personally shielding Germans at his factory.[12] Henry Ford, of course, was a candidate in the senatorial election to be held two days later, and many of his supporters felt that coincidence had little to do with the timing of the allegations against his chief tool designer. At that juncture, it would have been understandable, if ignoble, for Henry Ford to have traded Carl Emde's career for a Senate seat. Most of his campaign advisers urged him to do just that in view of the number of votes that seemed to depend on it—perhaps enough to win him the election. But no one, of course, had told Hank Ford what to do since Alex Malcomson pushed for him to make the Model K in 1906.

Instead, candidate Ford issued a public statement pointing proudly to Emde's twelve fine years of service to his company as well as to the $345,000 Emde's innovations had saved on the Liberty engine project. Privately, Ford even told Emde that "if they try to hang you they'll have to hang me first."[13] Ford's standing firm behind Emde and the others similarly slurred seemed a rare generous act from an employer.

While Ford often protected his most favored workmen, Emde survived an extremely complicated situation for a different reason: for Ford, leaving the falsely accused "German sympathizer" to twist slowly in the wind would have been tantamount to allowing the same thing to happen to himself, as a so-called anarchist. Anyway, Henry Ford would not admit he was wrong even when he was. He certainly wasn't about to concede defeat when he was right. Winning the election was not worth that much to him.

━━━━━━

The Michigan race had become the talk of the nation the instant Henry Ford filed his candidacy. After all, he had done so at the personal request of the president of the United States.[14] Ford had not only publicly endorsed Wilson's reelection bid in 1916, but even contributed $35,000 to the Democrat's campaign in closely contested California, paying for a last-minute advertising blitz that some pundits credited as the crucial factor in Wilson's 4,000-vote win in that state, and thus in his 23-vote squeak by the Republican Hughes in the electoral college. Nominally Republican, Ford had openly disagreed with the president on some issues in the past, but he became a "Wilson man" in support of the administration's plan to create a League of Nations to ensure global peace in the future.[15] Switching parties wasn't a good political move, though, and Ford seemed to know it, announcing that he would seek the nominations of both major parties.

Solidly Republican Michigan boasted 100,000 more GOP-registered voters than Democrats, and state party leaders had no intention of putting that majority behind any Wilson man, however successful in business. Faced with Ford candidacies in both major-party primaries, Michigan's Republican leaders turned to Yale graduate Truman H. Newberry, a high-profile private investor from Detroit's upper crust who, at fifty-four, was a year younger than

Henry Ford. He was also connected to the dashing automobile industry, having substantially increased his inherited fortune by taking a hefty stake in the Packard Motor Car Company as early as 1902. Most daunting to Ford's senatorial hopes, Newberry had served as secretary of the Navy at the end of Theodore Roosevelt's administration. His brief stint afforded him military credentials so prized in times of war and so glaringly absent in Henry Ford.[16] Newberry beat Ford for the Republican nomination, but Ford easily won the Democratic primary. Then the two met once more in the general election.

Ford ran an old-fashioned campaign: he made no personal appearances, stating clearly from the start that speeches were out of the question. He spent no money, true to his earlier word. "All this campaign spending is bunk," Ford had said during Wilson's 1916 presidential campaign; "I wouldn't give a dollar to any campaign committee"[17]—before bailing out Wilson's California effort. That was more than he would do for his own Senate campaign. Refusing funds from the Democratic Party as well, he instead oversaw the formation of his own nonpartisan Ford for Senator Club.[18] Its total expenditure during both primary races amounted to $335, leaving an unspent surplus of $226.

Truman Newberry's campaign, by contrast, spent $176,568 in the Republican primary alone to beat Ford. His expenditures in the general election were estimated at between $500,000 and $1 million.[19] The Republican machine continually attacked Ford's patriotism in newspaper advertisements, on flyers, and at rallies. *Literary Digest* reported that as election day neared, "everybody supposed to have influence who would take it received his price. It went to individuals, Republicans and Democrats alike, who were thought to be useful; to political, social, industrial and religious organizations; to newspapers, not always in payment for advertising, and to liquidate the expense accounts of persons who never traveled a mile.

"Michigan," the *World* concluded, "was plastered with Newberry money."[20]

Ten days before the election, Newberry received the ringing endorsement of not one but two former U.S. presidents, both writing in *Detroit Saturday Night,* a weekly newspaper in which Newberry had a $6,000 investment.[21] William Howard Taft backed the Republican simply because he hoped the party would recapture the Senate majority Taft had lost along with his presidency. Taft's old adversary, Theodore Roosevelt, gave Ford an even rougher ride. The president of Ford Motor Company, Roosevelt wrote, "would be signally out of place in the American Senate so long as that body is dominated by men who zealously believe in the American ideal."[22] The former commander in chief continued:

> This is the first time in the history of our country in which a candidate for high office has been nominated who has spent enormous sums of money in demoralizing the people of the United States on a matter of vital interest to

their honor and welfare. The expenditure on behalf of pacifism by Mr. Ford in connection with the *Peace Ship* . . . was as thoroughly demoralizing to the conscience of the American people as anything that has ever taken place. The failure of Mr. Ford's son to go into the army at this time, and the approval by the father of the son's refusal, represent exactly what might be expected from the moral disintegration inevitably produced by such pacifist propaganda. . . . It would be a grave misfortune to the country to have Mr. Ford in the Senate when our question of continuing the war or discussing terms of peace may arise, and it would be an equally grave misfortune to have him in any way deal with the problems of reconstruction in this country.[23]

Theodore Roosevelt may have been onto something. Ford's lackluster if not coy campaign only underscored his failure to explain just why he was running. Since he made no public appearances and gave few interviews, none of them revealing, Ford practically invited his opponent to define him. The Newberry team did just that, painting Ford as unpredictable, self-interested, and unpatriotic. His closest associates were left wondering, like Michigan's voters, whether his Senate bid was not just another bizarre publicity stunt. "What do you want to do that for?" Thomas Edison asked his industrialist friend when he heard Ford was running for office. "You can't speak. You wouldn't say a damned word. You'd be mum."[24]

When pressed for his views on the issues of the day, Ford would respond only to letters from voters—one at a time. In these replies, he generally asserted that he would be happy to be a U.S. senator and if elected would "make a real job of it," particularly in the areas that interested him most: supporting the League of Nations as proposed by President Wilson, securing voting rights for women, guiding postwar industry's return to nonmilitary production, and continuing the fight against investment capitalists. Regarding the burning 1918 topic of whether to impose public control over America's telephone, telegraph, and railway systems, Ford advised, "The people should be certain that they are not putting Wall Street tools and stock manipulators into Congress, for Wall Street is already fighting the nation on these questions."[25]

As head of the nation's busiest manufacturing concern, Ford had grown increasingly resentful of financiers who sought to control industry through paper shuffling and manipulation. He was not alone: the American public's antipathy to the machinations of Wall Street was on the rise just as the trust-busting era instigated by Theodore Roosevelt was on the wane in 1918. Had he behaved as though he took his candidacy seriously, Ford might well have put himself in prime position to capitalize on the growing gap between the interests of the populace and the appetites of the investment community. In fact, Ford might well have contributed a powerful voice to the U.S. Senate from 1919 to 1925 and used it to instill a constructive suspicion of high finance that just might have forestalled some of the frenzy that led in different ways to both the 1929 stock market crash and the Great Depression. As it was, business genius or not, Henry Ford did not have what it takes to succeed in politics—beginning with a reason for running.

In an editorial headlined "The Flivver Mind," the conservative journal *The Review* may have hit close to the mark with its arch suggestion that the only reason Henry Ford was running for the U.S. Senate was that he had been asked to. *Nouveau célèbre* as well as newly rich, Ford would agree to any scheme that flattered him, according to *The Review,* be it sailing for peace to Europe, crusading for the welfare of birds, running for high public office, or anything else that appealed first and foremost to his ego.[26] Ford may have summed up his own arrogant naïveté best in May 1916, when he proclaimed to the press: "We want to live in the present, and the only history that is worth a tinker's damn is the history we make today."[27]

Perhaps the most insightful analysis of Henry Ford's political motivation appeared three full years before the Senate campaign. It was written by political and foreign policy reporter Walter Lippmann, who would later go on to Pulitzer Prize–winning celebrity as the *New York Herald-Tribune*'s star columnist. His accomplishments also included helping his friend Woodrow Wilson write the Fourteen Points for achieving world peace in the aftermath of World War I.

In his December 4, 1915, opinion piece, "A Little Child Shall Lead Them," about the *Peace Ship,* which set sail the next day, Lippmann wrote about the political strengths and impossible weaknesses of Henry Ford:

> Mr. Henry Ford's peace trip has aroused violent resentment in America since the day it was announced. Men laugh at it with helpless anger. They regard it as humiliating. They want to break something at the thought of it.
>
> Yet there is hardly one of Mr. Ford's opponents who doesn't long for peace, and hope secretly that America may help bring it about. Something in the protests seems a little too loud. May it not be that we are shouting at Mr. Ford because he has done us the inconvenience of revealing some of the American character a little too boldly? Is our indignation like that of the man making faces at himself in a mirror?
>
> The first fact about Mr. Ford is that he is a very rich man. Whatever he says is therefore sure of a hearing in America. We have always acted instinctively on the theory that golden thoughts flow in a continuous stream from the minds of millionaires. Their ideas about religion, education, morality, and international politics carry weight out of all proportion to their intrinsic importance; and though we have not admitted that riches make wisdom, we have always assumed that they deserve publicity.
>
> This automatic obeisance to wealth is complicated by our notions of

success. We Americans have little faith in special knowledge, and only with the greatest difficulty is the idea being forced upon us that not every man is capable of doing every job. But Mr. Ford belongs to the tradition of self-made men, to that primitive Americanism which has held the theory that a successful manufacturer could turn his hand with equal success to every other occupation. It is this tendency in America which installs untrained rich men at the head of technical bureaus of the government, and permits businessmen to dominate the educational policy of so many universities. Mr. Ford is neither a crank nor a freak; he is merely the logical exponent of American prejudices about wealth and success.

But Mr. Ford reveals more of us than this. He reflects our touching belief that the world is like ourselves. His attitude to the "boys in the trenches" is of a piece with his attitude to the boys in the Ford plant, kindly, fatherly, and certain that Mr. Ford knows what is best. His restless energy and success appear as a jolly meddlesomeness. He gives his boys good wages and holds them to good morals. He is prepared to do likewise for the boys in Flanders and around Monastir. Why shouldn't success in Detroit assure success in front of Baghdad? If Mr. Ford is unable to remember that all men are not made in his own image, it is not strange. Have Americans ever remembered it? Has our attitude towards the old world ever assumed that Europe was anything but a laborious effort to imitate us?

Mr. Ford serves as a reminder of another amiable trait in our character, our belief in the absolute validity of moral judgments. We have never taken much stock in the theory of Socrates that the good man to be really good must really be wise.[28]

Walter Lippmann may have portrayed Henry Ford as the archetype of America's boisterous, overoptimistic hubris at the close of 1915, but in truth the industrialist's extraordinary actions had less to do with nationalism or democratic fervor than with the man's own spectacular and still swelling ego. Three years later, it would manifest again in the traditional way for rich Americans with sharp opinions: with a run for high office.

Longtime Senator Lawrence Sherman of Illinois quipped that election to the U.S. Senate might be precisely what Henry Ford deserved, "for a greater refrigerator for his effervescent brain does not exist." Nothing, Sherman went on, would "cure him better than talking to empty benches." But it was not just Ford the man that the crotchety Republican senator resented, concluding: "And may I say, that I regard the Ford automobile as an international pest."[29]

The generally liberal *New York Times* did not appear to understand Henry Ford any better than the nation's conservative politicians did. The *Times* editorial page had rallied around Ford during the Selden patent case and applauded his initiation of the $5 Day, but expressed bafflement at the industrialist's political ambition. A Ford victory in the Michigan race, in the newspaper's opinion, "would create a vacancy in both the Senate and in the automobile business, and from the latter Mr. Ford cannot be spared."[30] That raised a related question: whether Henry Ford wanted to be spared from his company, whether he could even bear to be away from it, in Washington.

In any case, as election day neared, the Newberry forces stepped up their attacks on Edsel Ford's evasion of military duty. When Ford made no response to the Republican about Carl Emde and other enemy aliens, "the original charge . . . echoed throughout the state in the Monday editions of unfriendly newspapers," noted historian David Lewis. "Consequently, many thousands of voters went to the polls on Tuesday aware of the accusations, but not the defense."[31] Ford's repudiation of the allegations against Emde and other foreign workers at Highland Park ran in most of Michigan's newspapers on election day, but by the time most voters saw it they had already been to the polls. Thus Ford allowed the Newberry camp's last-minute dirty trick to work like a charm.

The race was so close it took three days to produce a final count of the ballots, which showed Truman Newberry beating Ford by 7,567 votes, out of 432,541 cast for the two major-party candidates. The defeated Democrat was stunned, having felt certain from the first that his personal popularity would be enough to turn back any assault on himself or anyone associated with him. Nine days after the election—and five days after the end of World War I—his ego bruised, Henry Ford released a statement declaring himself permanently out of the sort of politics that consisted of "getting down into the ditch and throwing mud." He singled out examples, saying he would not behave like the "two ex-Presidents," Roosevelt and Taft, who had "stopped making faces at each other long enough to get together and take a united wallop at me." The sort of politics that consisted of supporting President Wilson's peace proposals, however, did still interest him, Ford said. Ironically, his postelection proclamation set forth his position more passionately and persuasively than anything he had put out during the campaign.

Most important, his statement made clear how determined Ford was to keep the nation's big-money interests from making themselves the real victors after the war. He warned that, without opposition, they would turn America's industrial strength into a permanent war machine for the politicians and a profit fountain for themselves with nothing for the people.

Making an argument that is still at the center of Congressional debate eight and a half decades later, Ford expressed particular distaste for the amount of money his opponent had spent. "How much was spent in the election to secure that Senatorial seat goodness only knows," Ford's statement cautioned. "If they would spend $176,000 to get one little nomination, they would spend $176 million to [sew up] the country. That is where the danger lies."[32]

Dismissed as a rank amateur in the political arena, a humbled Henry Ford was expected to slink back to his own business, where he belonged. Indeed, he did return to making cars and improving tractors, but it was hardly with his tail between his legs. The richest man in the state of Michigan had never turned sheepish in defeat, no matter how embarrassing things looked from the outside. As far as Ford was concerned the Senate race was a stinging failure—of election oversight. Of course, he was not the first to be disgusted at how easily a statewide election could be bought in America, which is precisely why Michigan had a law on its books in 1918 setting a limit of $3,750 on expenses, except for the purchase of advertising, in Congressional primaries. That was substantially below the $10,000 allowed under federal law at the time. Newberry's campaign committee had clearly broken both the state and U.S. law and was already coming under fire for the outrageous amount it had committed just to gain the Republican nomination. Truman Newberry insisted that there had been no wrongdoing, as he had never spent a penny of his own funds on the race. Using a defense that continues to hobble campaign finance reform to this day, Newberry disingenuously added that he simply could not control what other people did with their money.

That included Henry Ford, as soon became obvious. The vengeful auto tycoon, with the assistance of his cohort Harvey Firestone, hired some one hundred private investigators to scour the state for evidence of electoral fraud. Ford's private eyes spend four months snooping[33] and dug up plenty of dirt—so much, in fact, that no sooner was Truman Newberry seated in the Senate than two separate petitions reached the floor, one demanding a recount in Michigan and the other its freshman senator's expulsion on ethics grounds. Both maneuvers failed, as did similar efforts to shame Newberry into resigning. But Henry Ford had other missions in mind for his battalions of lawyers and private detectives, now that he had tasted the real power they afforded him.

———

For Ford Motor Company, the end of World War I meant a return to full production, and in the case of the Model T, that translated into ever increasing production. To Henry Ford, expansion depended heavily on the freedom to take risks and make expenditures. To him, more than any other businessman, freedom required independence.

Ford's single greatest contribution to the Ford Motor Company may have been his unwavering insistence on constantly increasing production. While everything else about the firm came from the work of many, his was the clarion call for expansion of the factory. The urgent pace of sales undoubtedly encouraged him, as did the sight of out-of-town dealers hanging around the Highland Park lobby in hopes of squeezing a few extra cars out of the factory.

Ford's scheme was based on a well-established formula: increased output allowed for the lower prices, which accounted for the rise in sales. Of course, that combination also drove out competition; by the end of 1914 the Model T had the under-$500 price bracket to itself.[34] What set Ford apart, though, was that year in and year out, he was willing to risk the whole enterprise on production so accelerated it could collapse the entire business in the event of a sharp dip in sales. As David A. Hounshell pointed out in *From American System to Mass Production, 1800–1932,* back in 1914, "exactly one year after the first assembly line experiments at Ford Motor Company, Reginald McIntosh Cleveland wrote an article titled 'How Many Automobiles Can America Buy?'"[35]

Most manufacturers took the question seriously—after all, the traditional course to success dictated expanding in response, and in proportion, to demand. Ford Motor stood alone in boosting production to *anticipate* larger sales—vastly larger sales. Therein lay the inherent risk. If demand dropped, the factory's boosted capacity would look less like a shining monument to Fordism than a crazy company running amok.

Ford didn't worry about that. He was concerned only with bringing down the list price of the T. Everything else would follow from that. Because the potential for increased efficiency and output at Highland Park had been fully tapped, Ford was ready to build a new plant at the River Rouge site. It wouldn't just be bigger than Highland Park, which was already the largest automobile plant in existence. As Ford envisioned it, River Rouge was to be the largest industrial plant of any kind in the world.

Henry Ford's grand plans for the construction of a state-of-the-art smelter (a blast furnace used to meld or refine ores) at River Rouge first percolated in 1916. To finance the plans, Ford Motor Company needed ready cash, which it had in the form of tens of millions of dollars in annual profits. Through its earlier years the company had reserved about half of its net profits to pay shareholder dividends. Starting in 1915, though, the firm switched to a new formula—conveniently supplied by Michigan's corporate laws—that called for a monthly disbursement of 5 percent of corporate capital. What's more, Ford Motor Company opted to base future dividends on a laughably outdated valuation of its assets, listing its nominal capital at $2 million when it was actually fifty times that:[36] the Highland Park factory turned out some $2 million worth of cars in a single workday. Absurdly low as the asset valuation was, the company's resulting dividends were still substantial even by today's standards, amounting in 1919 to about a half million dollars for its top stockholder, Ford himself. Like the backers, Ford had grown used to receiving ten times that amount, but also like the others, he had already banked enough from the previous years' dividends to ensure a fortune several hundred times greater than anyone could have imagined at the company's outset in 1903. Because of the magnitude of their earnings, most of the shareholders had no objections to the new diversion of what would have been more dividends back into the company to fund its further expansion. James Couzens, the second-largest shareholder, could claim to be too busy with his duties as Detroit's police commissioner to pose any opposition, a stance that represented his sister Rosetta Couzens Hauss's holdings, too. Horace Rackham, John Anderson, and the heirs of the late John S. Gray appeared similarly content, leaving only the Dodge brothers to raise a ruckus.

By then, John and Horace Dodge were building a car of their own. The Dodge—something of a big brother to the Model T—was selling extremely well, ranking among America's five best-selling cars since 1915, its first full year in production. "Black Jack" Pershing gave it a lasting endorsement when he used a cavalry of Dodges to chase Pancho Villa (in a Model T) through the steep canyons of Mexico in the same 1916 expedition Henry Ford had so decried. The Dodge Brothers automobile was a continuing success, with its production nipping up and over the 100,000 mark in 1919. But neither it nor any other marque stood in a league with Ford Motor—which sold 521,599 Model Ts that same year.[37]

John and Horace Dodge together held a handsome 10 percent of Ford Motor Company, a stake that had in 1914 alone netted them $1.22 million in dividends[38]—the third seven-figure year in a row—and they wanted those enormous returns to continue for two reasons. First, to keep developing their own car company, they needed as much money as possible. Second, and more important, the Dodge brothers truly believed that Henry Ford was putting Ford Motor's viability at risk by reinvesting so much of its—and thus their—profits in his ambitious plans for River Rouge.

On November 2, 1916, John and Horace Dodge filed a lawsuit against the directors of the Ford Motor Company—Henry Ford, Edsel Ford, Horace Rackham, and Frank Klingensmith—charging that their governance had violated the interests of the stockholders. In particular, the Dodge brothers requested that the Michigan State Circuit Court force the company to distribute three quarters of its profits in dividends, then and in the future, and to stop using the company's money to build the smelting plant or anything else at Henry Ford's personally owned River Rouge site. The Dodge brothers also rejected (at least for purposes of the trial) the $5 Day and price cuts on the Model T, but the first two charges were the fighting points in the rising battle over the future of Ford Motor Company.

As Allan Nevins related, John and Horace Dodge had a valid point regarding the calculation of dividends based on the bogus valuation of Ford Motor's assets at a paltry $2 million. "Indeed," they wrote in *Ford: Expansion and Challenge, 1915–1933*, "the annual report of July 31, 1916, showed that the net profits of the company for the preceding year had been almost $60,000,000, and that its accumulated cash surplus stood at more than $52,000,000. In normal circumstances, a dividend of at least $25,000,000 would have been declared."[39]

When the case finally wound its way into court in June 1917, one of the Dodges' lawyers, William Carpenter, summed up his clients' frustration during an exchange with the circuit court judge. "Mr. Ford," Carpenter said, "has got all the money he needs. His great ambition is to employ as many men as possible and to sell his cars at as low a price as possible without consideration for his duty to his stockholders. When he could have made $60,000,000 to $75,000,000 last year he made only $28,000,000. When all other automobiles were raising their prices, why was it necessary for Mr. Ford to lower his, even had his ambition really been only to maintain his leadership in the automobile world? What he really wanted to do was to become a public benefactor. He wanted glory at the expense of the stockholders.

"We are asking that Mr. Ford run the company to make as large profits as possible," Carpenter continued. "When a business is run only to extend that business and not to make profits it is being run unlawfully."[40] Although many public corporations today, especially in high-growth industries, choose to reinvest all or most of their profits at the expense of shareholder dividends, that practice was unheard-of in the 1910s. Had Henry Ford been in business in the last quarter of the twentieth century, rather than the first quarter, he might not have been compelled to eliminate the outside shareholders. As it was though, in withholding dividends, he was far ahead of his time, and the pressure was on for him to fall into step with the corporate practices of his own day.

The Dodge brothers' suit further argued that building a smelter at River Rouge fell outside Ford Motor's charter. The company had been incorporated for the purpose of manufacturing cars, and after all, under the laws of Michigan the construction of steelmaking equipment such as a smelter came under a different, and quite specific, legal provision. The point was as fundamental to Henry Ford's plans at the time as his emphasis on growth, and the type of plant he wanted to build at River Rouge indicated the direction in which he intended his company to grow. Ford Motor Company, contrary to the trend toward specialization in industry, aimed to subsume the operations of more and more of its suppliers. The idea was eventually to build cars depending entirely on wood, metal, and tires processed from trees, ores, and rubber plants owned by Ford Motor.

―――――

The initial verdict in the lawsuit favored the Dodge brothers on the dividend question but dismissed most of their other claims. Ford Motor was ordered to pay an immediate special dividend totaling $19,275,385, and to alter its dividend policy such that 50 percent of the company's profits would be returned to its shareholders. In addition, the circuit court ruled that construction of the River Rouge smelter would indeed be inconsistent with Ford Motor Company's corporate charter. Naturally, an appeal was filed, which delayed required action until at least 1919.

Then, late in November 1918, Henry Ford dropped a bombshell. He announced that he was resigning as president of Ford Motor at the end of the year. "I am very much interested in the future, not only of my own country but of the whole world," read the official statement released by his office. "I have definite ideas and ideals for the good of all. I intend giving them to the public without having them garbled, distorted and misrepresented." Ford's latest vocation, simply put, was "to become a newspaper publisher."[41] The conduit for his new ambition would be the weekly *Dearborn Independent,* which he had just purchased. Under its previous owners, the *Independent* had been an unremarkable small-town newspaper, but Henry Ford had bigger things in mind for it. "I believe in small beginnings," he continued his statement, "and for that reason we are taking the small home paper and building on that."[42] The general assumption was that Ford was reacting to his recent defeat in the Michigan senatorial race and would use the newspaper as a platform from which to launch the next stage of his political career, perhaps a bid for the White House in 1920.

Whatever Henry Ford may have been leading up to, what he left behind with his resignation were shock waves rippling across the industry. As his replacement he named his twenty-five-year-old son, Edsel, to head the $250 million business. Edsel would remain president for the rest of his life.

Appearances aside, the changeover actually put the firm in the hands, or at least in the name, of a more capable, and certainly more reasonable, executive. The good-natured Edsel Ford was unlike most tycoons' sons his age; the Dodge brothers' scions, for example, could not be bothered with automaking or anything else as serious as business. Horace Dodge Jr. was renowned only for his idle life of boat racing and binge drinking, interrupted when he appeared every so often with a new wife on his arm. Completely the opposite and sober in every way, Edsel Ford took his work as a corporate officer as seriously as he took his new role as a family man. He and Eleanor would eventually have three more children after Henry II: Benson, Josephine, and William.

It would be intriguing to know how Edsel felt as he accepted his new role at the start of 1919. He knew his father's capricious ways as well as anyone, but he must have believed in his new title enough to be genuinely excited at the opportunity before him. He was a car fanatic at the head of a $250 million car company. Life doesn't get much better than that. Unfortunately for Edsel, it does get worse. In any case, the immediate impact of the new roles assumed by father and son was delayed by an extended vacation taken by the entire Ford family to Altadena, California, near Los Angeles, that winter.

Among those in the Fords' new neighborhood was writer Upton Sinclair, whose horrific 1906 novel *The Jungle* had helped improve conditions in the Chicago meatpacking industry. Given his interest in industrial reform, Sinclair was naturally intrigued by Henry Ford and visited him several times in Altadena. Sinclair reported that the Fords—Henry, Clara, Edsel, Eleanor, and Henry II—had leased a surprisingly modest house, where on his first visit the writer found the great industrialist and his son "in the garage, having set up a shop where they could tinker—as Henry had done in the old Bagley Street days before Edsel was born.

"In this place," Sinclair continued, "they had come upon part of an old carburetor, of a make unknown to them. . . . Henry and Edsel were fascinated by the problem of a certain aperture, the purpose of which they could not figure out. They showed it to the author and asked his opinion, but as it happened he was riding a bicycle, and did not know what a carburetor was."[43]

Nevertheless Sinclair managed to engage the elder Ford in an ongoing discussion about the American system of business, a conversation in which the avowed socialist writer suggested that Ford Motor Company would have a better chance to achieve great things if "the people" owned it, albeit with Henry Ford still at the head. That, as it turned out, was exactly what Ford wanted least: anonymous gaggles of people telling him what to do.

On February 7, 1919, the people's judicial system did just that, telling Henry Ford exactly what to do, as the Michigan State Superior Court issued its final ruling on the appeal in *John F. Dodge and Horace E. Dodge v. Ford Motor Company, Henry Ford, et al.* It was a partial reversal, insofar as Ford Motor was newly judged to be within its rights in constructing a smelting plant at River Rouge, but the court upheld the earlier ruling that the company had to pay fair dividends as defined and demanded by the Dodge brothers.[44] Even though the company had already restored a fairly normal dividend for the first two months of 1919, Henry Ford rankled at the court's order that the company pay earlier dividends retroactively. Nevertheless, while the Fords remained in Altadena, company treasurer Frank Klingensmith set about disbursing the $19.3 million due to the stockholders.

"Henry Ford was now fifty-five," Upton Sinclair wrote of him that California winter, "slender, grey-haired, with sensitive features and quick, nervous manner. His long, thin hands were never still, but always playing with something. He was a kind man, unassuming, not changed with his great success. Having had less than a grammar-school education, his speech was full of the peculiarities of the plain folk of the middle west. He had never learned to deal with theories and when confronted with one, he would scuttle back to the facts like a rabbit to its hole.

"What he knew," Sinclair concluded, "he had learned from experience, and if he learned more, it would be in the same manner."[45]

On March 6, Henry Ford announced that he was forming a new automobile company. Refusing to mince words, he admitted he was acting out of disgust with the superior court's decision, which had forced him to disburse Ford Motor's funds against his own best judgment. The news of this new Ford endeavor came as a surprise to the executives and shareholders of Ford Motor Company, who over the next few weeks learned that Henry and Edsel had been up to more than tinkering with old carburetors in that garage in Altadena. Five days later it was Edsel's turn to make an announcement: both he and his father were withdrawing entirely from Ford Motor Company. The younger Ford detailed how this new company would consist of a nationwide network of factories, the first of which would be ready to start operating early in 1920. The product would be a stripped-down, very basic passenger car designed for commuting; the idea was to compete with city streetcars, not with other automobiles. Reporters listened politely, and then asked whether the announcement of the "new" Ford car company was just a ruse to scare Ford Motor's minority shareholders into selling out to Henry Ford. "I know that will be the conclusion," Edsel Ford averred, "but it is not true in the least. We are going to hold our interests in the old company and will not buy a share of anyone's stock, so that charge cannot be borne out."[46]

Elliott G. Stevenson, a member of the Dodge brothers' legal team, pointed out that Henry Ford was forbidden by contract from deserting Ford Motor to start another car company. Still basking in his triumph in the dividend suit, Stevenson may have been hoping for another donnybrook to add to his reputation. Many Ford dealers, though, grew panicky over the possibility of an alternate Ford automobile and the inevitable reduction in their own profits it would bring. Edsel Ford released a careful statement assuring the dealers not to worry, as any new car was years off, and only a possibility anyway. His father, meanwhile, went around promising that the new concern would employ 200,000 men.

Rumors immediately began swirling about the fate of Highland Park. The very notion of Ford Motor Company without a Ford at the helm seemed absurd. The story spread that General Motors was angling to acquire its rival to absorb into its burgeoning collection of auto and parts manufacturing concerns.

GM, itself built like a house of cards upon the shaky base of William Durant's stock manipulations, had supposedly attempted to acquire Ford Motor Company once before. In the autumn of 1909, when General Motors was but a yearling, Durant had devoted his considerable charms to an attempt to persuade Henry Ford and James J. Couzens to part with their stakes in Ford Motor for $8 million. "Couzens was eager to see the sale made," Bernard A. Weisberger wrote in *The Dream Maker*, a biography of William Durant. "At thirty-seven, he had three children, a great deal of money, graying hair, migraine headaches, and an ambition to move onward from the tempests of five years as Ford's chief executive and partial partner."[47] The deal apparently fell through because Durant's Wall Street backers refused to commit cash to the transaction. GM stock was offered instead, but rejected out of hand by Ford and Couzens. By 1919, the idea that GM could even consider buying Ford Motor Company had turned laughable. Durant was so overextended he was in danger of losing his own corporation altogether; in fact, he would be ousted the next year. The rumor that Ford might be available, however, hinted at instability in the company, just as the Fords intended. Investors, of course, tend to shun instability, and by July most of Ford Motor's were ready, if not eager, to sell back their shares. And Henry Ford stood just as ready and eager to buy them.

Shares so closely held would not have been traded on an exchange. Instead, transactions were conducted by the Old Colony Trust Company, a banking firm from Boston, that had been recommended to Edsel Ford by a business acquaintance. Old Colony was on hand to handle negotiations through to each sale. Henry Ford made only one major stipulation: that he would not buy any of the stock unless he could buy all of it. Ford Motor Company had issued a total of 20,000 shares; Henry Ford owned 11,400, Edsel another 300. The remaining 8,300 shares belonged to James Couzens (2,180) and his sister, Rosetta Hauss (20); the John S. Gray estate (2,100); John and Horace Dodge (1,000 each); and the lawyers John Anderson and Horace Rackham (1,000 each). Using the valuation of the company's assets that had emerged in the Dodge brothers suit, each share of Ford Motor Company's stock was judged to be worth $12,500. Those who had put up cash at the firm's founding sixteen years earlier had paid $100 per share.

Anderson and Rackham, who had received a $25 attorney's fee for drawing up Ford Motor's original incorporation papers in 1903, took away $12.5 million apiece in 1919 for the shares they'd each purchased for $5,000 at the company's startup. Albert Strelow, on the other hand, the landlord who turned his two-story Mack Avenue woodworking shop into Ford Motor's first plant, had sold the shares he purchased for $5,000 in 1903 for $25,000 only two years later. Had the rightful father of Ford Motor Company, Alexander Y. Malcomson, held on to his original quarter-interest in the firm, which he instead sold back to Henry Ford for $175,000 in 1906, it would have fetched him more than $63 million in 1919.

Those who held on to their shares did very well indeed. The Dodge brothers could celebrate a windfall of $12.5 million apiece; John Gray's heirs received $26.25 million. James Couzens, by 1919 serving as mayor of Detroit, held out for at least a slightly higher price, mostly as a means to force the Fords to acknowledge his special role in the company's success. He got it, turning his and his sister's stock over in a transaction separate from the Old

Colony deal, at $13,000 a share. Couzens netted some $29.31 million, Rosetta Couzens Hauss a bit above $262,000 on the $100 she had entrusted to her brother when he needed it.

No one, though, had reason to be happier about the big buyout than Henry Ford, who was effectively the sole owner of the Ford Motor Company. According to one report, Henry Ford received the momentous news that all his fellow shareholders had agreed to sell him their interests in Ford Motor just as he entered a courtroom one morning in July to take part in the long simmering libel suit he'd brought against the *Chicago Tribune*. He had probably already heard that the buyout was complete, but the arrival of a telegram bearing the news as he made his way up the steps to the courthouse made for a wonderfully dramatic scene. It was reported the next day in newspapers all over the world. As the stock transactions had been formally executed in his son's name, Henry Ford playfully quipped at the impromptu news conference that sprang up in the courtroom, "Well, if Edsel has bought it, I can't help it."[48]

Once Henry Ford seized complete control of his company, he became the object of yet another wave of public fascination.[49] The cost to take over the company bearing his name came to nearly $106 million, of which Ford was forced to borrow $75 million. In fact, the specter of the loan was the only shadow on his triumph. Prior to that, no record exists of Henry Ford ever having taken out a loan, not even for a mortgage. Even worse, Ford's creditors came from the ranks of the eastern bankers he so despised, among them Chase Securities of New York, Old Colony Trust, and Bond & Goodwin.[50] However, Ford felt certain that repaying even such an enormous sum would prove easy—all he had to do was keep selling Model Ts, something that had never once presented a problem before. In the summer of 1919, however, whispers began to circulate that the nation might be slipping toward a recession. Henry Ford heard the rumors but borrowed the $75 million anyway.

Obviously, Ford insisted on full control over his firm, at any cost. And the prices he was willing to pay were not just financial but professional and even personal. The process of alienation from others that he had begun with his campaign to remove Alex Malcomson, and that had reached its apex with James Couzens's departure, continued with the veritable eviction of the company's outside shareholders. Even more telling, and damaging, Ford accepted the resignation of Harold Wills in March of 1919. Independent and aloof, Wills had from the first set the high standards for engineering by which the Ford factory would long be known. In fact, many of his contemporaries— including, at times, Henry Ford—credited Harold Wills as the real genius behind the Model T. Wills oversaw the original design, as well as every refinement made over the car's first decade, and made sure that mass production never compromised the vehicle's quality. Yet despite the Model T's wild success, over time Wills grew bored. As far back as 1912, in fact, he, Charles Sorensen, and the rest of Ford Motor's engineering department had begun trying to interest Henry Ford in producing a new model, or at least updating and improving the T.

In an attempt to pique their own interest as well as that of their boss, Wills and his engineers had worked overtime to have a whole new Model T ready to show Ford when he and his family returned from their summer-long 1912 European vacation. George Brown happened to be in the garage when Ford came upon the car unexpectedly. He stopped long enough to tell the boss, upon questioning, that the car was planned for production. Brown watched what happened next from a distance.

"He had his hands in his pockets and he walked around that car three or four times," Brown said of Henry Ford, "looking at it very closely. It was a four-door job, and the top was down. Finally, he got to the left-hand side of the car that was facing me and he takes his hands out, gets hold of the door and bang! One jerk and he had it off the hinges! He ripped the door right off!

"He jumped in there, and bang, goes the other door. Bang, goes the windshield. He jumps over the back seat and starts pounding on the top. He rips the top with the heel of his shoe. He wrecked the car as much as he could."[51]

That ended the "new" Ford. The dressing-down that Wills and the others received from Henry Ford soon after ended any inclination to design another, at least for a while. Ford considered the Model T to be perfect in its basic form. While he rejected outright change, he wasn't averse to evolution in the model. Body styles were added or removed and mechanical components refined, all without affecting the unique role of the Model T. "The Universal Car" was an even better idea than before in the aftermath of World War I.

By 1919, Wills had had enough of his boss's stifling control over the expression of his talents and those of his engineering team. What's more, Henry Ford had had enough of paying his chief designer 10 percent of his own dividends, in addition to a salary of $80,000 a year—amounting in toto to some $500,000 annually. Those were the terms of the private arrangement the pair had struck to secure Wills's talents for Ford Motor Company back in 1903, and they made Wills the highest-paid employee at Ford Motor. Ford had long since stopped thinking he got the better end of the bargain so, as historian Keith Sward wrote, "anxious to break off the old relationship by any means short of litigation, Ford resorted to a left-handed tactic. Sometime in 1919, Wills was frozen out of his job. No work passed over his desk. He continued to report for duty, but his functions were pared away as though he were dead. Burly, hard-fisted and already fretting inside his Ford collar, Wills could not abide such treatment."[52]

Indeed, the company's design wizard prickled with as much pride as its president. "I worked under Mr. Wills," explained the metallurgist John Wandersee. "He was all for Mr. Wills, not so much for Ford Motor Company or somebody else.

"That," Wandersee added, "is probably why Mr. Ford let him go."[53] In fact, Wills walked out on his own, but Charles Sorensen, among others, intimated that Henry Ford had gotten fed up with Wills's notorious in-house money-making schemes, most involving the company's enormous metallurgical purchases. Sorensen even alleged in his memoir that Wills had been "financially interested in vanadium," noting that Ford Motor began to phase out the specialty steel in 1919.[54] Wandersee likewise stated, "There is no doubt that Mr. Wills had something to do with steel buying."[55] He further insinuated that Wills had made a habit of advance trading in the stocks of suppliers—notably U.S. Steel—that were about to receive large orders from Ford Motor Company. After a short retirement, Harold Wills started his own automobile company with the help of John R. Lee, another recent expatriate from the Ford executive ranks. The pair was responsible for the Wills–Sainte Claire, one of the sleekest luxury cars of the 1920s.

———

To understand Ford Motor Company, the most important automobile company in the world, one first had to understand Henry Ford. Normally he presented himself through the voices of a cacophony of ghostwriters and journalists, so the public rarely had a chance to hear from him as he was: unfiltered and unvarnished. Even as he (and Edsel) was gaining complete control of the world's largest car company, though, he took the stand in his lawsuit against the *Chicago Tribune*. Ford's testimony would show a side of him the public had never seen before.

Ford's libel suit, argued in the placid hamlet of Mount Clemens, Michigan, charged that the *Chicago Tribune* had injured his reputation when it had called him an "anarchist" in its 1916 editorial. The lawsuit placed the damages to his good name at $1 million. The trial, however, actually had less to do with the *Tribune* and its questionable editorial than it did with the chance for a grand public display of the even more towering and richer, new Henry Ford. For almost two weeks that summer, America's most dazzling industrialist sat in the witness chair and responded to questions probing his character and beliefs. Virtually no line of inquiry was ruled irrelevant, and most major newspapers printed his entire testimony: a rare verbatim interview with the slippery hero of millions.

Dressed in a somber dark suit, Ford arranged himself comfortably in the sturdy wooden chair, casually crossing his legs or stretching them out in front of him. He hardly ever sat up straight, put his feet flat on the floor, or betrayed any other defensive stiffness. After all, he was not the one on trial; he was the plaintiff. As the world was about to learn, he was also a man of remarkably few words.

"What do you know about history? Did you ever read history?" barked the *Tribune*'s defense attorney, Elliott Stevenson, who had also represented the Dodge brothers in their action against Ford nearly three years earlier.

"Quite a lot," Ford responded, in a way that suggested just the opposite.

"Then the *Tribune* editorial calling you an 'ignorant idealist' was true?" Stevenson continued.

"Well, I admit I'm ignorant about some things. I don't know anything about art," Ford replied.

"Don't know much about history?"

"No."

"How can you tell what the future should be in regard to preparedness [for war] if you don't know history?"

"I live in the present," Ford wavered.

"Are you ignorant of the fundamental principles of this government?"

"I suppose it's the Constitution."

"What does 'fundamental principles of government' mean?" Stevenson persisted.

"I don't understand," Ford insisted.

"What is the fundamental principle of government?"

"Just you," Ford replied.

"Is that the only idea you have on it?" the lawyer inquired.

"It's a long subject," said the plaintiff.[56]

Striving to prove that Henry Ford was in fact the "ignorant idealist" the *Tribune* had called him, Stevenson battered the carmaker with general knowledge questions, especially on American history. Thus the nation learned that its leading industrialist had no idea what caused the War of 1812—which had taken place long before he was born, of course—but also that he had only barely heard of the sinking of the U.S. battleship *Maine* off Havana, which had occurred in February 1898, when he was thirty-four. Later questioning led Ford to admit that he did not know much about the Revolutionary War, either, which he proved by identifying Benedict Arnold as a writer, rather than a traitorous Army general. However many junior-high history questions he stumbled over, though, in barbershops and breakfast nooks across the country, Americans leapt to the defense of the automaker. To his fans, all that mattered was how good he was at what he did. As Ford himself was alleged to have boasted, a man didn't have to know who Benedict Arnold was if he could afford to hire people who could tell him.

Had Henry Ford confined himself to making cars, the defense's aggressive attempts to embarrass him would have come across as unseemly and unfair. But the *Chicago Tribune*'s counsel was not questioning a mere automobile manufacturer. Instead, Elliott Stevenson well knew that he was actually vetting the credentials of a self-appointed public educator who had from 1915 to 1917 put his signature to a whole series of nationally distributed newspaper columns, penned by Ford's personally hired "peace secretary" Theodore Delavigne, railing against military preparedness and war.[57] The issue at hand may have been only the *Tribune*'s description of Ford as an "ignorant idealist," but Stevenson's questioning went even further:

"As an educator, you assumed to educate the American people?" the defense attorney asked.

"Assumed to cause them to think," Henry Ford corrected.

"To instruct the American people as to their duties as citizens at the time of a crisis?"

"Instructing the people how they were exploited."

"Do you understand," Stevenson tried to pin his quarry down, "it is the duty of a man that undertakes to educate the people to be educated himself and know what he is talking about?"

"Educated to a certain extent," Ford muttered, unconvincingly.

Stevenson should have hit a nerve. As a cracker-barrel philosopher, Henry Ford could say whatever he liked to his associates, no matter how outrageous, and he often did. What he apparently failed to grasp was that in the vast public arena, where others simply knew more than he did, his personal instincts and experience could not stand up against real knowledge. He may have told a *Chicago Tribune* reporter in May 1916 that "history is more or less bunk," but Ford was wrong about that; a man in his position did indeed have to know history, to be sure that the basis of his opinions held as firm as his potent influence.[58]

Over the course of the trial in Mount Clemens, the public learned many things about the man behind America's favorite automobile. Ford had never broken the law, except traffic tickets for speeding. He rarely read articles past the headlines, and with his income of more than $1 million a year, he had no objection to paying income taxes. "Whatever it is," he said of the tax rate, "the less money I have the less trouble I have." Such quintessentially characteristic homespun Ford assertions kept Henry Ford, for all his millions, close to the heart of the workingman, as did a somewhat more troubling impression he left. Throughout his testimony, Ford was frequently asked by the defense to read various documents aloud. Each time, he demurred, usually protesting that he had forgotten to bring his "spectacles." The suspicion swelled that the great Henry Ford could not, in fact, read. On July 22, Stevenson finally stopped circling the question.

"Mr. Ford," he began delicately. "I have some hesitation, but I think in justice to yourself I shall ask this question: I think the impression has been created by your failure to read some of these things that have been presented to you, that you could not read—do you want to leave it that way?"

"Yes, you can leave it that way," Ford replied. "I am not a fast reader and I have the hay fever and I would make a botch of it."

"Are you willing to have that impression left here?" Stevenson pursued.

"I am not willing to have that impression, but I am not a fast reader," Ford rejoined.

"Can you read at all?"

"I can read," Ford stated.

"Do you want to try it?"

"No, sir."

"You would rather leave that impression?"

"I would rather leave that impression," Ford concluded, and thereby did.

A jury of mainly local farmers listened to the testimony of Henry Ford as it stretched out over day after day. Once the opposing legal teams concluded their closing arguments, the farmers wasted little time finding the *Chicago Tribune* guilty of libel against Henry Ford for having called him an anarchist in print. Whatever items those twelve jurors and the rest of the world had discovered about Henry Ford, evidence of his being an anarchist was not among them. Nevertheless, the court reduced the suggested assessment of damages from the $1 million requested to a symbolic six cents.

The *New York Sun* expressed a certain amusement at the award. "The jury in effect decided that it was not true that he was an anarchist," the newspaper editorialized, "but that calling him such did not injure his reputation to the extent of more than six cents." Across town, the *New York World* dismissed the entire proceeding as so much free advertising for both the *Chicago Tribune* and the auto magnate it had slurred.[59]

Ford's chagrin over the libel case had by 1919 grown moot anyway. Almost a year had passed since World War I ended with the victory of the Allies, thanks to the help of a stable United States, including Henry Ford and his company.

The contentiousness between intellectuals and industrialists, of course, still remains a matter of note, as pundit George F. Will pointed out in his syndicated newspaper column of July 14, 2002. "Many intellectuals disdain the marketplace because markets function nicely without the supervision of intellectuals," Will wrote. "Their disdain is ingratitude: The vulgar (as intellectuals see them) people who make markets productive make the intellectual class sustainable. As [University of Chicago economist] George Stigler (Nobel Prize, 1982) says, 'Since intellectuals are not inexpensive, until the rise of the modern enterprise system, no society could afford many intellectuals. So we professors are much more beholden to Henry Ford than to the foundation which bears his name and spreads his assets.'"[60]

Then, as now, intellectuals were inclined to relegate Henry Ford to his rightful place as an industrial hero. But he wouldn't stay put. Having learned from the court in Mount Clemens that he was entitled to his views, he revved up his plan to disseminate them more widely than ever before. The result was the *Dearborn Independent,* and the books it spawned. With that, Ford the "ignorant idealist" was revealed as the worst kind of ignorant cynic. Perhaps that's what he was all along to those who distrusted his rather antic brand of pacifism.

12

Withstanding the Downturn

The Great War left in its wake a whole rash of problems for every one that it was supposed to have solved. German-born New York financier Otto H. Kahn, who had organized the U.S. railroad system in support of the Allied war effort, referred to the spring of 1919 as "the morning after." For all that had been lost, visionaries like Otto Kahn and Henry Ford could see that a great many opportunities had also opened up.

Had World War I actually been waged over the issue that started it—the struggle for political and economic dominance among Europe's fading empires—then the conflict did indeed end with the signing of the armistice between the Allied and Central Powers on November 11, 1918. In reality, however, the very reasons behind the war shifted in the midst of the fighting, from a clash between blocs of nations to one among the classes within them. In that sense, the Allies' intervention in the Russian Revolution in 1918–1919 must be considered part of the greater war. During those years, Russia's erstwhile Allies—Britain, France, and, to a lesser extent, the United States—turned from their disputes with Germany and Austria-Hungary to the battle in Russia against the establishment of communism. The Allies lost that fight to the Red Army in 1920, and two years later the Soviet Union was officially formed, a mighty federation born of Bolshevism.

To those intent on profiting from the morning after World War I, the sense of power shifting across the globe was as irresistible as the reality of communism was ominous. Thus when a venerable millionaire like Wall Street financier Otto Kahn examined the emerging postwar world, his attention went straight to the plight of the workingman—and to the capital of change for labor conditions, Ford Motor Company. What he and other analysts discovered there filled them with encouragement. For Kahn, Highland Park stood as a bulwark against Bolshevism. "Is there any instance where communistic or even merely cooperative undertakings have produced similar results?" Kahn wondered in an April 1919 speech in Pittsburgh. "Is there any instance where governmental management has produced similar results?"[1]

Probably not. No other enterprise of any kind, in fact, could boast the sort of successes Ford Motor Company attained in every area it entered during the first two decades of the twentieth century. In the hopeful dawn after the horrors of the "war to end all wars," Ford Motor was regarded a shining industrial beacon, showing the way to a world desperately trying to change.

Henry Ford found himself cast as a symbol as well: of the quintessential "self-made man," as Kahn described him, who sanctified capitalism by actively demonstrating what enormous good the very rich could do for the common laborer, such as doubling factory wages while reducing working hours. Yet in the early postwar period Henry Ford revealed his own distrust of capitalism as practiced by bankers such as Otto Kahn. When advised of the classical-school theories of British economists Adam Smith and David Ricardo, and of clergyman-turned-sociologist Thomas Malthus's population studies, Ford scoffed; to him, their Old World version of capitalism centered on the grotesque notion that money was all that mattered, and that capital alone informed economic and social laws. Henry Ford believed otherwise, holding that products and people came first. Money would follow of its own accord. "Gold is the most useless thing in the world," Ford believed. "I am not interested in money but in the things of which money is merely a symbol." And he disdained the idea of savings banks in general. "Money is like an arm or a leg," he often told people; "use it or lose it."[2]

In other words, even as smart a business observer as the admiring Otto Kahn did not really understand Henry Ford or his thinking. Of course, few people ever did, and Ford liked it that way. In one of the little spiral-bound notebooks always kept in his jacket pocket he once scrawled, "I'm going to see that no man comes to know me."[3] Social climbing, gossip, and leisure were antithetical to his nature. "Do your own work, mind your own business and don't engage in controversies," he told a group of young people who wondered if there was a formula to success. "That's the way to get along, and above all else, keep away from lawyers. . . . They are bound to get you in trouble."[4]

Ford refused to believe that the United States won World War I. While victory parades were held in New York and Detroit, Ford talked about the wasted lives of 53,000 American troops who died in combat, not to mention the 63,000 who perished from disease and other causes. He was, however, glad that the Highland Park factory—unlike the many European manufacturers that had been shut down, bombed out, or reassigned to military matériel during the war—had never stopped making Model Ts. Throughout the war years, different body styles were offered as options and various mechanical components refined, but without affecting the basic-black soul that defined the unique role of the T. Now, with the Treaty of Versailles concluded, and a League of Nations ready to help govern the world, Ford Motor Company stood ready with legions of Model Ts to export to every continent. A vast world market lay open to the hardy, affordable little American cars. The few European automakers that did manage to turn out vehicles had little choice but to pick up where they had left off before the war, with massive luxury automobiles and sporty runabouts. Ford, by contrast, offered a reliable utility vehicle so inexpensive it came across almost more as a tool than a car—and thus more as a necessity than a frivolity. Without question, Ford Motor Company came out of World War I the strongest, most important automobile manufacturer in the world.

In 1919 William S. Knudsen made an extensive tour of Ford Motor Company's European operations and recommended the immediate establishment of factories in Spain and his native Denmark, along with an overarching management structure for all of Ford's subsidiaries in Europe. Most of his many suggestions were ignored, a sign that his star was on the wane at Ford Motor. While in Europe, Knudsen paid especially careful attention to the French factory, but prodding its productivity forward proved thorny. At the beginning of the year, French officials flatly refused to let Ford Motor import the metals needed to build its Model Ts.[5] Eventually, that problem was sorted out, but others sprang up to hamper Ford's French operation.

The French did not yearn any less for new cars than consumers in other countries, as indicated by the huge crowds that thronged the Paris Auto Show in 1919. Officials in notoriously xenophobic France simply preferred to support an adaptation of Henry Ford's idea from a domestic manufacturer. At the auto show that year, there were eye-catching Hispano-Suizas, sleek DeDion-Bouton sedans, and American-style Darracq coupes, but it was a tiny French car that drew the most attention: the Citroën 5CV, a stubby but sturdy little job painted in bright yellow and blue. Designed as a low-cost, high-production model, it was unabashedly a Gallic version of the Model T. Its maker, André Citroën, even asked Henry Ford to invest in his company. After all the trouble Ford had gone through to dispose of his own firm's minority shareholders, though, the last thing he wanted was another business partner. Instead he was faced with the next-to-last thing he wanted: a serious competitor. While Citroën would not produce cars in substantial quantities until 1922, the presence of its winning 5CV at the 1919 Paris Auto Show served as apparent confirmation of the rumors floating around Europe that Ford Motor would not keep the low end of the global car market to itself forever. The race was on among several English, French, and Italian firms all making plans to copy the formula behind the startlingly successful Model T.

No American company would even dream of competing directly with Ford in 1919. Those that veered closest were also the quickest to point out the differences. Dodge, for example, made only larger cars intended for, as John Dodge had jibed, "all the Ford owners who will someday want an automobile."[6] Chevrolet—which, thanks to the energy and acumen of Billy Durant, had grown since its founding in 1911 into the United States' second-largest automaker—also priced its products a bit higher than Ford's Model T, promoting the Chevy as a sportier kind of economy car.

American customers after swell, swank, or swift automobiles faced a bounty of choices in 1919. The influence of youthful tastes upon the industry resulted in the sports cars from Stutz and Mercer that looked as if they were speeding for freedom even at a standstill. Styling offered more individualized appeal than ever, with custom coach-builders enjoying the fast-growing business of supplying body work for chassis from Packard, Locomobile, Franklin, and Cadillac. The latest talk of the luxury-car crowd centered on the Lincoln Motor Company, recently launched by Henry M. Leland, Ford's old Detroit Automobile Company rival and later the guiding force at Cadillac. At the age of seventy-four, Leland turned his attention to designing a magnificent new V-8 engine for the first Lincoln model. Even before production began in 1920, the new company logged more than 1,000 orders.

The family car was undergoing a transition in 1919, as closed styles replaced the open tourer as the top choice among buyers. Closed cars had advantages in extreme weather, of course, but for the most part, basic family sedans and coupes were stodgy and dull, and those who could not afford $4,000 or so for a custom-bodied car were pretty much stuck with a plain box on wheels. On the eve of the 1920s the auto market, like most of the wider world around it, craved fresh choices, yet Ford Motor had no immediate incentive to provide them. It was without real competition in the economy car market. Most Model T buyers either could not afford or would not trust any other marque. As a result, the company sold 820,445 cars in the United States in 1919—more than all the rest of America's automakers combined.

The Model T didn't budge from its rather enormous niche, but it did progress—if almost imperceptibly, like the hands of a clock. For the first postwar sales season, the Model T was modernized for greater convenience in two important regards: starting the engine and fixing flat tires. Better late than never, the T finally offered an electric ignition in place of the temperamental hand crank up front. Introduced on Cadillacs a full seven years earlier, the electric starter ranked as perhaps the greatest automobile improvement to that point, especially for drivers in cold climates, which tended to stiffen engines and make them balky. The addition of a push-button starter called for a new electrical system, as previous Fords had no capacity for energy storage. The 1919 Model T thus incorporated a battery for the first time.

Few Ford owners would miss the hand crank, though it did make for a wealth of good stories. James B. Ross of Butler, Pennsylvania, for instance, recalled what ensued when two teenage boys pestered their father into buying a Model T on the premise that they would drive him to work in it every morning. "This chore became tiresome and the boys became lax," Ross explained, "so the old man decided to learn to drive himself, and told his son Louie to pull the car out of the garage for his first lesson. I do not know whether the old man, in getting in, pushed the reverse pedal, but when Louie cranked the car, it promptly backed into the garage and hit the rear wall—whereupon the old man jumped out of the car, shouting, 'See there, Louie. You cranked 'er backwards!'"[7]

But drivers did not master the new electric starter much more smoothly. "One day I pulled up and parked in front of the fraternity house and was met on the lawn by a group of doubting brothers," said one collegian of his Model T. Long frustrated with the car, he had been getting along better with it since employing psychology, so he told his pals. "I've got it licked now," he proclaimed. "I just pat her fender and say, 'Come on, Lizzy, let's go,' and away she goes.

"Their faces got long as they stared past me," the youth continued, "as though they were seeing a ghost. As I wheeled around I heard a familiar clanking and I saw that darn Model T rumbling down the street—alone. . . . If you ever own a Model T, don't rely on your mechanical knowledge. Just get her alone under a shady tree and get acquainted."[8]

The only thing worse than having to crank-start a Model T in bad weather and good clothes was having to fix a flat tire on one in any conditions. Because the T's wheels could not be detached, stranded Ford drivers had to remove the punctured inner tube from inside the tire, patch the leak, squeeze the tube back into place, and then reinflate it, making sure the pressure filled the outer tire just so. The tedious process hardly qualified as fun in a warm, well-equipped garage; out on the road, a flat could ruin even the pleasantest outing. And long after other carmakers had switched to modern detachable wheels—on which flat tires were replaced rim and all, using spares carried for the purpose—the Model T's old-fashioned wheel arrangement remained the bane of Ford owners.

Of course, a great many Model T buyers never thought to clamor for such conveniences. Most customers for the cheapest car on the market had never owned an automobile before. They had no basis for comparison to point up the absence of unfamiliar features. Moreover, a significant portion of Ford Motor's sales were in rural areas, where farm folk used to physical labor and do-it-yourself repairs found no hardship in hand-cranking or roadside maintenance, however messy. At first, therefore, the two major improvements of 1919 were offered as options—the electric starter system for $75 and the detachable rims for $25—that did not affect the base price of the car.[9] Eventually, both became standard features on the Model T as it evolved beyond its original role as the farmer's liberator into the escape mechanism of choice for city dwellers, who apparently preferred their freedom with a certain degree of ease and comfort.

Although the modifications made in 1919 constituted the most substantial redesign in the Model T's entire run, the alterations did not affect Henry Ford's attitude toward the car or its presentation—or, therefore, the overall direction of Ford Motor. Following the company's strategy as he set it out, the T would change little over the years, but its price would change a lot. As the cost dropped from $900 to $440 over only five years,[10] it almost seemed that the price tag was Ford Motor's real product, and the Model T built beneath it.

"When we first reduce the price to a point where, as we think, more sales will result," Henry Ford told writer Garet Garrett, "then we go ahead and try to meet the price. The new price will force the cost down. The more usual way is to calculate the cost and then set the price. That method may be scientific in the narrow sense; it is not scientific in the broad sense.

"What use is it," Ford added, "to know the cost if it tells you that you cannot manufacture at a price at which the article can be sold?"[11]

Ford Motor Company hardly operated in a manner oblivious to costs; on the contrary, its accounting controls were extremely stringent. The philosophy that would drive the company ahead so quickly after World War I, however, came down to setting priorities. When a newly created market, such as that for automobiles in their first quarter century, has not yet been completely tapped, then by definition neither has the potential for increasing the efficiency of manufacturing the product. That is the premise of mass production, and no company understood mass production better than Ford Motor. Even more significant, though, none proved as bold in seizing upon the fact that the economics of high-growth, young businesses worked differently from those in established industries. To play it safe in a predictable market meant, of course, to emphasize manufacturing costs first and to figure out how to sell the products later, thus warding off the direst threat: lost profits. In a fast-growing market, by contrast, the greater threat came from lost sales. For a mass-production manufacturer, therefore, the way to play it *safe* was to emphasize sales first and lower production costs later, thereby avoiding getting outpaced by one's own industry. When Henry Ford insisted that his company would slash the Model T's price in half and by doing so double demand for the car, he was erring on the conservative side. In truth, he believed that halving the price would quadruple the T's sales.

The key was River Rouge, Ford's nascent factory, where Eagle boat production had ceased early in 1919 to no one's regret. As 1920 began, Ford Motor launched all of its efforts into creating the world's largest industrial facility on the 1,100-acre site southwest of Detroit. "Huge raw materials bins were constructed alongside the river, work began on the great power house, coke ovens were built, a blast furnace was fired up, and much of the railroad and transportation was laid out" between the end of World War I and the recession of 1920, historian David A. Hounshell wrote of the beginnings of Ford's River Rouge complex. "But most important, the B building, constructed during the war to mass-produce the Eagle boat, was substantially altered to accommodate a body making plant for the Model T."[12]

Henry Ford threw himself wholeheartedly into planning the River Rouge facility to satisfy his demand for seamlessly efficient operations. "Ford, no verbal or blueprint man, insisted on having scale models of machine tools, conveyors, windows, pillars, and floor space, so that these could be moved around to test ideas about production," wrote Thomas P. Hughes in *American Genesis: A History of the American Genius for Invention*.[13] The most radical innovation dreamed up for River Rouge would have nothing to do with its striking buildings, however. Even as Henry Ford was laying out his general plans for the new plant in the late 1910s, he had also begun buying up northern Michigan timberland and iron ore mines in Minnesota. Having watched the cost of materials soar during the war, Ford determined that his company would never again suffer at the mercy of commodity-market pricing. To keep operating costs down, Ford Motor would depend on its own supplies of raw materials. Henry Ford even bought his own railroad—the Detroit, Toledo & Ironton—to transport supplies into the plant and finished cars out of it.

Ford's grand plan was to make the company completely self-sufficient. Modern business jargon calls the absorption of supply lines "vertical integration." The concept, popular since America's colonial days, had fallen out of favor with the early twentieth century's move toward industrial specialization. By the 1920s, companies in virtually every field tended instead toward "horizontal integration," under which firms extend product lines. The greater emphasis is placed on efficiency of distribution. In a prime example of the horizontal approach, in 1929 cereal maker Postum acquired the Birdseye frozen-foods firm, gelatin giant Jell-O, and various other foodstuff manufacturers. It then merged them all into the new General Foods Corporation. GF made each more profitable by amortizing the costs of getting the products to grocery store shelves all over the country. Had Henry Ford headed Postum, the company's resources might have been plunged instead into a single breakfast cereal, from planting the grains with which to make it to growing the trees for the cardboard packaging. Vertical integration was consistent with Ford Motor's two guiding philosophies: the permanence of the Model T and continually lower pricing for it. More to the point, vertical integration afforded Henry Ford control over nearly every aspect of production. In 1919, however, Henry Ford found himself in the odd position of being in total control, even as he was supposed to be handing over authority to his son.

After Edsel Ford became the president of Ford Motor Company, he groped around for a long time trying to establish his own power base. The first real stab he took at asserting his authority came to worse than naught: it drew the opening salvo in Henry Ford's relentless campaign to humiliate his only heir. Edsel chose his initial battle poorly, firing Charles Sorensen. There was no doubt that the two were incompatible. Where the younger man was unfailingly polite, open in his methods, and rational in his decisions, Sorensen saved his good business manners for Henry Ford alone. He was notorious for his dictatorial treatment of those who served under him; toward executives at his own level his behavior veered between conniving and quietly threatening. Yet Sorensen did not deserve all, or even most, of the blame for his predatory workplace style. That arose from the very nature of the overall Ford Motor approach to management, which encouraged executive insecurity and thrived on the exaggerated dedication that resulted. The lack of formal titles and the competitive spirit may indeed have inspired overachievement, but the company's shark-infested executive suites also turned the art of the power struggle into an essential daily joust for survival—and Charles Sorensen was nothing if not a survivor.

Edsel was probably as intimidated by Sorensen as Sorensen was by the boss's son. The two were nothing alike—gruff vs. suave, rash vs. rational, old-fashioned vs. au courant—and that may well have been the reason they found themselves working together at the top of Ford Motor. They represented the two disparate sides of Henry Ford himself. While the company's guiding spirit retained full confidence in his own ability to maneuver between his various inclinations, he seems to have felt that no one person in the next generation could be trusted to strike a like balance. The veteran production chief, whom Henry Ford had tasked early on with teaching Edsel the ins and outs of automaking, had always made it a point to stay abreast of every rumor that floated anywhere near Highland Park. Thus, when Edsel took the helm at Ford Motor Company, Sorensen already knew perfectly well that his former charge intended to fire him.[14]

Edsel Ford can hardly be faulted for assuming that his elevation to the presidency meant that Ford Motor henceforth would follow his lead. And so it would, of course—just as long as he followed his father's lead, spoken or unspoken. As soon as the young president took office at the beginning of 1919, he dismissed Charles Sorensen as quietly as possible under the circumstances. Edsel was eager to develop executives of his own ilk at Ford Motor Company. He had already begun in a small way. His first recruit had been his brother-in-law, Ernest Kanzler, a Harvard Law School graduate brought to Henry Ford & Son in 1916 to schedule shipments of materials and tractors. Four years later, the talented Kanzler would take over as production manager at Highland Park. His inaugural hire having worked out so brilliantly, Edsel could hardly wait to continue the job of strengthening the management team once he was at the top—and Charles Sorensen was out.

And so Edsel Ford fired Sorensen. Within weeks, however, Sorensen was back, rehired by Henry Ford in direct contradiction of his son's—the company president's—orders. "He promptly put Sorensen back in and told Edsel where to head in," recalled Harold M. Cordell, the elder Ford's assistant secretary through the 1920s. "I think that resulted in a suspension of amicable relations between Edsel and his mother and father; for a good many months they never even spoke to each other."[15] Even after they did resume speaking, the relationship between father and son would never be the same. Edsel's first moment as president presaged everything that would happen to him at Ford Motor Company over the next twenty-four years.

At twenty-six both more capable than and as eager as his youth would suggest, Edsel Ford had justification to feel baffled; after all, his fifty-six-year-old father was supposed to be semiretired in 1919, or so he had promised. When the elder Ford had bought the quaint little *Dearborn Independent* the previous November, he had said he was looking forward to becoming a publisher, and perhaps even a columnist. As much as Edsel Ford may have wished his father would stop meddling at Ford Motor Company, it would not be long before he had even greater reason to wish Henry Ford would focus on *anything* but the *Dearborn Independent*.

Henry Ford, still stinging from his harsh treatment by the media during his *Peace Ship* and U.S. Senate campaigns, not to mention his *Chicago Tribune* lawsuit, had concluded that freedom of the press, as journalist A. J. Liebling would later assert, really does belong to the man who owns one—and so he bought one. Ford already considered himself a wizard at generating good publicity with his ideas on business and industry, and despite his previous media flubs (or because of them), he didn't see why he should not broaden the scope of his musings. The tiny *Dearborn Independent*—circulation 1,000 or so—was to be the seed of a publishing empire dedicated to spreading the philosophy of Henry Ford. The weekly would keep its slim, simple sixteen-page tabloid layout and five-cent price, but its content would turn away from rural news in favor of reaching a national readership.

The newspaper was the primary asset of the Dearborn Publishing Company, of which Henry served as president, his wife as vice president, and his son as secretary-treasurer. Clara and Edsel, however, never had anything to do with the *Independent* beyond appearing on its masthead as corporate officers. To direct the newspaper's content Ford recruited veteran newspaperman E. G. Pipp. A generally liberal-minded egalitarian, Pipp took the job because he admired Ford's populist attitude as well as his generous salary offer. Both men were in fact idealists who believed in Wilson's League of Nations, women's suffrage, Prohibition, and other more and less progressive programs. Pipp felt entirely comfortable with Ford's version of populism when it translated into genuine support for the working class, a stance he found rare and refreshing coming from a major captain of industry. When Ford's populism turned the other way, however, into fierce resentment of the rich and powerful of the American "establishment," even Pipp found his boss's attitude downright ugly.

It was also downright peculiar. Controlling the largest automobile company in the world gave Henry Ford enormous power and an immense fortune that in fact dwarfed those of virtually any of the "rich" folk he so detested. The contradiction appears to have been lost on Ford. He resolutely classed himself apart from his fellow tycoons on the grounds that they were mere exploiters of others' toil, while he actually worked—at least in the loose definition of the term.

Henry Ford could not, of course, write a coherent editorial by himself, despite the fact that he was slated for a weekly column. To begin with, he was a terrible speller. Ford expressed himself in writing only when absolutely necessary, and then only in jotted notes. That was also the way he spoke—in short, staccato sentences. Louis Lochner, who worked closely with Ford throughout the *Peace Ship* effort, quickly picked up on the distinctiveness of Ford's genuine voice. "It is usually easy to tell in any signed statement of Mr. Ford's what words are his own," Lochner explained, "and which have been prepared by someone else. If the sentence is a short, jerky one, it is likely to be Henry Ford's. If it is long and involved, you may be sure that it never left his lips."[16]

In a column under Ford's byline entitled "The American Shop"—chosen at random as a test case—the third sentence runs through ninety-six words and includes four semicolons, so flunks the test. In truth, most of the opinion columns bearing Henry Ford's byline read much more like the work of former *Detroit News* reporter William J. Cameron, for the good reason that they were. Although a longtime alcoholic, Cameron managed to weave Henry Ford's rambling thoughts into capable prose on a weekly deadline. In the beginning, "Mr. Ford's Own Page" read as dully and humorlessly as a stock sermon. Under such soporific headlines as "Managers and Men Are Partners" and "Who Is the Real 'Owner'?," Ford's Cameron-ghosted columns aimed at the hearts and minds of urban workers, while pieces like "Farming—The Food-Raising Industry" and "The Modern City—A Pestiferous Growth" targeted the nation's rural folk. To most readers in every demographic, however, the issues Ford's paper covered seemed passé, its writing listless, and its layout unyieldingly gray. Despite a relaunch with some fanfare, the *Dearborn Independent* struggled to find a readership.

Among Ford's favorite topics during the first year he published the *Dearborn Independent* was investment banking, which he felt concentrated the nation's power in too few hands, and unworthy ones at that. Before the year was out, however, he began to shift his animus away from financiers in general to focus on Jews. At first these bigoted barbs were couched inside columns attacking the global monetary system in broader terms. The articles were not widely read, and so the first of two major questions about Ford's disturbing campaign was why it started at all.

Ford's increasingly vicious anti-Semitism appears to have grown out of his antipathy toward powerful bankers. Yet his ludicrous equation of all Jews with all corrupt financiers, as though the two groups were one and the same, conveniently allowed him to attack both by decrying either as it suited him. Historian Neil Baldwin, in his important *Henry Ford and the Jews,* published in 2001, suggests that the auto magnate's anti-Semitism grew at least in part out of his rural nineteenth-century midwestern upbringing. True enough: the *McGuffey Eclectic Reader* is a case in point. The moralizing *McGuffey Readers* were full of anti-Jewish stereotypes like Shylock, Shakespeare's usurious Merchant of Venice. Quite rightly, Baldwin dismisses such stereotypes as utter nonsense. In 1923, Ford published his autobiography, *My Life and Work,* in which whole pages are devoted to belittling Jews. That same year journalist James M. Miller published *The Amazing Story of Henry Ford.* Based largely on interviews with Ford, it makes clear, without even the slightest qualification, that Ford believed in the spurious tract *The Protocols of the Learned Elders of Zion.*[17]

Richard Hofstadter, in his acclaimed 1955 history *The Age of Reform: From Bryan to F.D.R.,* speculated that Henry Ford's anti-Semitic attitudes arose not from his upbringing at home but from growing up where and when he did with his peculiarly wide-ranging worldview.[18] When the young Henry Ford looked out across the fields of his family's farm, it was not with contentment in the bucolic little universe his parents had created, but with longing and ambition to flee the homestead to go out and do great things in and for the whole wide world. A child like that was bound to pick up more than the average farm boy from the prevailing tenor of his times in the particular place he grew up in, and Ford did.

Hofstadter concluded that Ford's was a "Populist anti-Semitism," which he characterized as a rhetorical style rather than a considered philosophy or a realistic program. He believed that the future captain of industry's anti-Jewish attitudes developed during the 1890s Greenback-Populist movement, which maintained that a corrupt Jewish cabal controlled Wall Street—a belief echoed by other noted Americans, including Reconstruction-era Senator Thaddeus Stevens of Vermont, historian Henry Adams, Detroit radio priest Father Charles Edward Coughlin, and modernist poet Ezra Pound. Most influenced of all, "Coin" Harvey, Thomas Edison's outspoken political adviser, espoused the same views. Even moralizing three-time Democratic presidential candidate William Jennings Bryan, Hofstadter pointed out, fell at one point into a curious dalliance with the vehemently anti-Jewish Ku Klux Klan. "A full history of modern anti-Semitism in the United States would reveal . . . its substantial Populist lineage," Hofstadter wrote. "Henry Ford's notorious anti-Semitism of the 1920s, along with his hatred of 'Wall Street,' were the foibles of the Michigan farm boy who had been liberally exposed to Populist notions."[19]

A number of writers have taken a more psychoanalytical approach to Ford's bigotry against Jews. As far back as 1922, Norman Hapgood, for example, suggested in *Hearst's International* magazine that Ford suffered from a "persecution complex."[20] Perhaps only a genuine neurosis could have explained many of the *Dearborn Independent*'s more lurid charges, such as that Jews had avoided the draft during World War I "so that more gentiles would kill each other." (In fact, a higher percentage of Jews served than the average among subgroups of American males.)

There remains, of course, the possibility that in some regards Henry Ford was just misguided—limited in some aspects of his mental or emotional capacity. In truth, he had already put his lack of intellectual sophistication on display in his testimony at the *Chicago Tribune* libel trial. The characteristically homespun homilies he had Bill Cameron write under his name for the *Dearborn Independent* similarly reflected Ford's disdain for erudition. While other industrialists with an inclination to push society one way or another did so with their wealth through the filter of philanthropic foundations, Henry Ford aimed to reach the masses and take on the world's problems directly. For example, he not only wanted to end global war in a single stroke but actually thought he could do it, and via his mere presence on a boat chartered to Europe for the purpose. Once it became obvious even to him that he could in fact accomplish no such thing, Ford refused to accept that such an undeniable force for good as himself could possibly have been stymied by his own limitations. The only explanation he could fathom focused instead on his naïve notion that a single, powerful, evil counterforce opposed peace for its own nefarious ends: "the Jews," whom Ford concocted into an enemy capable of starting worldwide war as simply as he had fantasized stopping it.

Norman Hapgood concluded that outside of the automotive realm, Henry Ford had the mind of a child. This appears true of the tycoon for both good and ill. On the plus side, Ford certainly evinced a childlike boundless enthusiasm as well as an unshakable optimism that proved inspiring to many of those who worked with and for him. But while boyishness looks charming in a man of a certain age still goading challengers into factory-floor footraces, Henry Ford's imagining monsters under the bed of the industrialized world came across as simply juvenile. Only a mind as limited as a child's needs to make up a bogeyman to help itself deal with its own fears of the harsh real world.[21]

Even before he took over the *Independent,* Henry Ford had taken to substituting "Jews" for any potent, unidentified force he divined in world events. At the same time, he and Clara Ford enjoyed warm friendships with many Jewish families. That inconsistency—that "some of his best friends were Jewish," as it were—is hardly unusual among the prejudiced.

Ford blamed Jews for everything from jazz music to risqué movies, from inflation to world war. That he was irrational is obvious. If his manic sense of prejudice had remained private, it might have been little more than a sign of the paranoia that would affect his whole existence later in life. However, Ford's anti-Semitism was not a private matter, and that fact suggests a second big question: Why was Ford compelled to spread his vitriol through every means at his command?

The power of the press went straight to Henry Ford's head after he bought the *Dearborn Independent.* Anti-Semitic attacks that started out as phrases swelled at his insistence into full-length articles and eventually into whole issues devoted to deploring the phantom international Jewish banking conspiracy he insisted was out to seize control of the global financial system and destroy American manufacturing.

As Ford threw ever more of the *Independent*'s resources into his unsavory attacks, E. G. Pipp quit the newspaper in disgust. By the middle of 1920, six of the eight other original members of its editorial staff had left in protest. Ghostwriter William Cameron remained, however. At first he bristled at the boss's orders to proselytize against "the Jews," but over the course of 1920, drinking ever more heavily, he became a willing cog in the publishing machine Ford actively created to disseminate inflammatory anti-Jewish articles, pamphlets, and books. "I don't think Cameron objected to writing these articles," Ernest Liebold said. "I think he thought he was just engaging in an activity which would require a great deal of research. He went at it."

Liebold, Henry Ford's personal secretary, was in effect the operations manager of the anti-Semitic campaign. He came up with the supposed historical "evidence" behind the tabloid's outlandish accusations, among them that Christopher Columbus's voyage to the Americas in 1492 had been a Jewish plot to conquer the New World. Another of his accomplishments was proving, to Ford's own satisfaction, at least, that Abraham Lincoln had been assassinated by Jews. Unfortunately, the campaign did not end there. In 1920, Liebold took it much further when he came across a copy of a book, translated from Russian, titled *The Protocols of the Learned Elders of Zion.* The volume supposedly contained an ancient, secret transcript of conversations among seven "Learned Elders of Zion" and Freemasons, aimed at teaching their fellow Jews and Masons how to rid human civilization of Christian beliefs and then conquer the world.[22]

Needless to say, Liebold's sacred tome was an utter fabrication. It was actually produced in several editions between 1894 and 1905 by Imperial Russia's secret police in an attempt to stoke anti-Semitism in their own country and to distract its masses from the rising tide of anticzarist feeling. The imperial police did a good enough job dummying up their *Protocols of the Learned Elders of Zion* to make the nonsense vaguely plausible, at least to the uninformed and those who were predisposed to think ill of Jews. To all others, the book's glaring errors put it well beyond even its irrational premise. Experts quickly pronounced the "find" a fake, but gullible, conspiracy-minded people dismissed that assessment as being even more suspect than the supposedly secret text. Among the receptive were William Cameron and Henry Ford, who pored over the volume and apparently believed every word in it. After editing the book for American sensibilities, they serialized it in the *Dearborn Independent* beginning in October 1920, under the running headline "The International Jew." It continued for ninety-one weeks and Ford later published the collected pieces in a widely distributed book of the same title.

"I suggested the name 'The International Jew,'" Ernest Liebold claimed without compunction years later. That title, he explained, reflected his belief that the *Independent*'s anti-Semitic crusade should target solely the mysterious, all-powerful Zionist "elders" whom Henry Ford insisted were maneuvering to control the entire global economy. Liebold argued against excoriating the whole Jewish race, but only out of pragmatism. He thought that the most specific accusations would make the greatest impact and would certainly generate less criticism than a blanket attack on all Jews everywhere. "Ford's answer to that," Liebold later recalled, "was, 'Well, you can't single them out. You have to go after them all. They are all part of the same system.'"[23] And so the *Dearborn Independent* targeted all people of Jewish background everywhere; after all, it was Henry Ford's money, his employees, his newspaper, and thus his message.

Liebold, an able assistant but a man deeply flawed by his prejudices, was just the latest in the long parade of forceful men Henry Ford depended on to amplify and execute his personal inclinations. James Couzens had set the pattern. He was followed by Charles Sorensen and others handpicked for the role of the tough guy who made things work the way Henry Ford, ever acting the nice guy, wanted them to. Although hardly a *tough* guy, like Sorensen, Liebold could certainly play the goon, willing to carry out the dirty chores of the *Independent*'s crusade.

Clara Ford joined Edsel in remonstrating against the anti-Semitic campaign. In September 1923, they both withdrew their names as well as their support for the increasingly unsettling family-owned paper.[24] Unable to muzzle his father via intellectual appeal, Edsel tried to put an end to the publication on the argument that the publishing company had siphoned off some $284,000 in its first year alone, a figure projected to rise to $350,000 annually in the future.[25] Henry Ford would have none of it.

Whatever the motivation, Ford could not be persuaded to stop the *Independent*'s anti-Jewish ravings. What amounted to just a loathsome personal prejudice in like minds became a real danger to Henry Ford himself, to the company that bore his name, and in some sense to the world at large. Nothing illustrates this point more profoundly than the fact that Adolf Hitler was so taken with *The International Jew* that he lamented he couldn't lend a hand with the "Henry Ford for President" movement that took root in 1923. "I wish I could send some of my shock troops to Chicago and other big American cities to help in the elections," Hitler told a *Chicago Tribune* reporter. "We look to Heinrich Ford as the leader of the growing Fascist movement in America. . . . We have just had his anti-Jewish articles translated and published. The book is being circulated in millions throughout Germany."[26]

William Howard Taft loudly voiced his objection to the so-called Sage of Dearborn's insistence on circulating his vicious opinions so widely. The former president had no interest in probing whatever mental aberrations made Ford operate. Taft simply decried his anti-Semitic ignorance and exhorted him to stop spewing it around. "One of the chief causes of suffering and evil in the world today is race hatred," Taft proclaimed in a December 1920 speech in Chicago, "and any man who stimulates that hatred has much to answer for. When he does this by the circulation of unfounded and unjust charges and the arousing of mean and groundless fears, his fault is more to be condemned."[27]

Taft was hardly alone in condemning Henry Ford's glaring fault. But the stubborn industrialist brazenly ignored not only the criticism of the former president and other prominent figures but the considerable outcry from the public, the grumblings of many dealers, and the ardent urgings of his own wife and son. The *Dearborn Independent* kept running its anti-Semitic articles, while Henry Ford remained oblivious that the greatest harm his newspaper was doing was not to "the Jews," but to the Ford Motor Company.

Although Dearborn Publishing remained officially separate from Ford Motor Company, the founder of both saw to it that the newspaper's losses were wiped away within two years by an enormous leap in its circulation. This was occasioned by his order that every Ford Motor dealership had to sell a certain number of subscriptions to the *Independent,* typically 100 annually. Many dealers objected—particularly those who had to pay for most of the subscriptions out of their own pockets to meet the quota—but none refused: a Ford dealership was simply worth too much not to go along. As a result, the *Independent*'s circulation, if not its readership, shot up from just above 70,000 in

1920 to 650,000 by 1924 and to 900,000 as of 1926.[28] Unfortunately for those who made or sold or admired Ford cars, the vicious little tabloid also became inextricably associated with the Ford Motor Company itself.

————

Throughout the first half of 1920 the U.S. economy struggled to stabilize following 1919's zooming inflation. "The nearest we can get to a satisfactory reason for the cost-o'-living situation is that everything is going up because everything else is," an editorial in the *Rochester* (New York) *Times-Union* had opined in August 1919.[29] Leftover inflation from the war years had proceeded unabated since the armistice, prompting a giddy spurt of spending as businesses built up their inventories in the belief that prices would rise even higher. In truth, the economy had begun to overheat. For instance, some two hundred firms jostled for a share of the U.S. car market. The auto industry was banking on increased sales on the basis that returning doughboys would surely want wheels. Faced with an extended period of inflation, however, a lot of veterans and other potential buyers decided to wait for prices to drop. Because the Model T occupied the low end of the automobile market all by itself, Ford Motor Company was, in effect, competing against itself in the form of its own previous sales records. At the beginning of 1920, the T's tallies lagged well behind the pace set in 1919. Despite the sagging sales, the Tin Lizzie's price tag had to stay the same to preserve Ford's business formula. Still, executives at Ford Motor and most other American companies grew only mildly concerned, chalking up the ongoing downturn to the temporary aftereffects of the Great War.

Despite the financial uncertainty of the dim economic situation, many businesspeople were yielding to the temptation of trying to keep up with the accelerating global economy. Investments in new facilities in 1920 outstripped those in any previous year, as well as the next twenty to come.[30] By that summer, though, one financial sector after another began to report reversals. Prices finally reversed, too, with agricultural prices in particular tumbling. As a result, America's farmers—traditionally Ford Motor's core customer base— began declaring bankruptcy in startling numbers: between 1920 and 1921 alone, 450,000 rural families would lose their farms. At the same time, the cash that had flowed all too freely out of the nation's banks throughout 1919 suddenly dried up.

Ford Motor Company sailed into the coming storm dragging three massive obligations, each due in 1921. Late that July, the *New York Times* quoted Henry Ford's summary of his company's predicament: "Back in 1919, we had borrowed $70 million on notes with which to buy out all other interests," meaning the firm's minority shareholders. "Of this we had paid back $37 million, leaving $33 million still to pay and falling due April 18. Then, because of adjustments pending, we still had the final installment of the 1920 income tax to pay, which, with the interest due April 15, made $18 million due the Government. Also, we intended to pay our men their usual bonus on last year's work, which would amount to $7 million more. So all in all, between January 1 and April 18, we had to meet obligations of $58 million."[31]

The trouble was that Ford Motor had only $20 million in cash on hand. Thus in the midst of both a sharp business downturn and its ambitious building program at River Rouge, the company had to come up with an extra $38 million by April 18, 1921.

On September 21, 1920, Henry Ford managed to stop sputtering his peculiar opinions on the pages of his *Dearborn Independent* long enough to speak out on a subject he actually knew something about. On that date, he announced price cuts on all Ford Motor vehicles, ranging from 14 percent on trucks to 31 percent on Model T coupes. "There is a lull in business," he acknowledged. "We are touched by the waiting period that always precedes a reaction; people in every walk of life are waiting for prices to become lower. They realize that it is an unwholesome, unnatural, unrighteous condition of affairs, produced by the war. . . . It is one of the penalties civilization pays for war."[32]

Ford claimed that his company had orders for 146,065 cars and insisted that desperation did not compel the price drops. Rival auto executives countered that he was just whistling in the dark. "So could I make a sworn statement to an order for 4,000 cars in this locality," boasted the New York sales manager for another marque. "But if I tried to deliver those cars tomorrow, three-fourths of them would be returned to me because the dealer or the individual who ordered them hadn't the ready money to pay. Henry Ford is suffering from the same malady that is affecting the health of the rest of us—a sluggish sales market, due to tight money."[33]

For Ford Motor Company, the sickness was a bit more serious. First, the company owed that $58 million that had to be paid within seven months after the price cuts. Second, Henry Ford was not exaggerating when he said that his company was willing to lose money initially because of the price cuts: Ford would indeed be selling vehicles for less than the cost of the materials in them. He was, in fact, betting his company that commodity prices would not remain as high as the postwar inflation had raised them, and that if he lowered his own prices the resulting sales boom he projected would right the whole situation. Ford looked brilliant the day after he announced the price cuts, when his company's New York branch claimed to have sold its entire stock of 500 Model Ts. Unfortunately, the initial surge in unit sales did not last. Yet the Ford factory kept up its usual aggressive pace, turning out cars at peak capacity over three work shifts a day. There was something antic in the way it rushed cars out of the factory, though no customers were waiting. And the production rush was not limited to Highland Park.

"I well remember what happened during Mr. Ford's financial difficulty in the early twenties," said C. G. Milner, assistant superintendent of the Atlanta factory at the time. The plant manager called Milner and the superintendent into an emergency meeting. "He told Mr. McConnell to ship all the parts from our Atlanta branch to Cincinnati, where there was an assembly plant at that time," Milner reported. "To my understanding, parts were shipped from other assembly plants to Cincinnati. All of these parts were assembled into automobiles. The reason they didn't assemble them right where they were was because they didn't have enough parts in any one particular plant to assemble many cars, so they had to ship them all to one plant. Those were rough days."[34]

From the outside, Ford Motor Company still looked like a bastion of prosperity in the dismal economic climate. Nearly every other automaker had either cut back or ceased production altogether. The fact that Model Ts continued to roll out of the Highland Park factory made people take heart—at least things weren't bad *everywhere*. Not even Ford, however, could build cars at a loss forever. In the late autumn of 1920, the company was clearly sliding toward a crisis. Investment bankers circled the firm, keeping note of the mounting financial evidence confirming that Henry Ford was in trouble. Without a full-scale Model T sales riot by the end of the year, he would confront the choice between defaulting on $38 million in debt or heading hat in hand to the banks for help.

It was just at this time, as Ford Motor was facing the direst financial dilemma in its history, that Henry Ford's *Dearborn Independent*—the "Chronicler of the Neglected Truth," according to its slogan—began publishing its "International Jew" series insulting not only Jewish financiers but the banking profession in general. Very shortly thereafter, toward the end of 1920, Americans of every ethnicity and creed began to voice their outrage at the *Independent*'s rants. The only reason the outcry did not ring even louder was that so few people actually read Ford's paper—including many of its paid subscribers, a large number of whom received the weekly involuntarily, as a quota-filling dealership "premium" for having bought a Ford car.

Many of the company's franchisees were mortified by the content of the *Dearborn Independent*. "The Ford dealers took the shock of the Jew articles coming and going," wrote William P. Young, the Pennsylvania dealer who often represented his regional colleagues at corporate meetings in Detroit. "When the Jew articles first appeared we felt the embarrassment keenly and studiously avoided discussion of the subject," Young recalled. "The first reaction of our customers was to regard it as another of those Ford jokes, and they let it go by with comments, 'Oh, he's crazy,' and the like. But as the stuff persisted and we were required to carry in stock and hand out copies and pay subscriptions for customers we began to sense a feeling of disapproval that was affecting the business unfavorably. We lost some business directly and later felt loss of business through influence brought to bear on both Jew and Gentile prospects."

Rather than risk offending actual customers, many dealers resorted to picking names out of the telephone book, with an eye toward foreign-sounding ones whose owners might not be able to read English, with any luck. "And all for what purpose?" Young wondered. "Was it a calculated, ingenious publicity stunt to arouse race and class prejudice with a design to curry favor and cash first from Gentiles and then to be followed by retraction, apology, and passing the buck to regain and hold the business of the Jews? Or was it merely another expression of the arrogance of the later policies, born of the smug possession of hundreds of millions of dollars and complete control of dealer and sales organization to absorb the shock and carry on, in spite of the foolish arrogant stunt?"[35]

Young was writing in a memoir that was privately published in 1931, a few years after he retired as a Ford dealer. In other words, he was entirely independent and could speak his mind. The letters that Henry Ford received from current dealers in the early 1920s, however, ran about thirty-to-one in favor of the campaign in the *Independent*. That did not necessarily reflect the actual sentiments of the franchise body, but only of those dealers willing to put their names to an opinion directed at the head of the company. In any case, Henry Ford probably drew the conclusion from the correspondence that his dealers were behind him. And no doubt, in the atmosphere of prejudice in the early 1920s, a good many were. By autumn 1920, half a year after "The International Jew" columns began, enough people had noticed Henry Ford's crusade to make his anti-Semitism a public issue. The *Dearborn Independent, The Protocols of the Learned Elders of Zion,* and "The International Jew" all entered the day's public lexicon. A minister named John Emerson Roberts gave a speech in Kansas City, lamenting the "absurdity" of such charges as the *Independent's* insistence that a single Jew made all the money generated by American jazz music. "And so," Roberts sighed in conclusion, "I suppose we must reconcile ourselves to the fact that Henry Ford has one—I don't know how many others, but I know one—tremendous defect."[36] Clergymen and other social leaders in nearly every large community in the country spoke out against the auto magnate's diatribes. They weren't the only ones talking about Ford Motor.

─────

During the weeks leading up to Christmas 1920, rumors were swirling through the nation's financial circles that Ford Motor was teetering toward bankruptcy. The scuttlebutt appeared to prove true early in the month, when the company announced that its Highland Park factory would shut down for two weeks beginning on December 23, "for inventory." Business observers around the country expressed concern at the news and skepticism at the excuse given for it. Whispers circulated that Henry Ford had fallen seriously ill. On December 29, not quite midway through the announced shutdown, Ford Motor Company gave credence to the bleakest stories by posting notices that Highland Park would remain closed until February 1 at the earliest.

The New Year did not bring any better news. In fact, it didn't bring any news about Ford Motor Company at all for a few days, as the company's spokesman quit on January 1. Charles Brownell cited his wife's poor health as his reason for leaving, but hardly anyone in the business community believed that a firm's top PR executive would exit at such a dire moment unless he was either disgusted or dismissed. While the meaning of Brownell's departure was still being debated in and around the company, a bigger shock arrived on January 3, 1921: the resignation of vice president and treasurer Frank Klingensmith.

Like the talented executive he had succeeded—James Couzens—Klingensmith had finally had a falling-out with Henry Ford. His struggle with the founder centered on the wisdom of the September price cuts and the company's purchase of the Detroit, Toledo & Ironton railroad, both of which Klingensmith had opposed, as well as the idea of conventional bank financing as the way to shore up Ford Motor's future, a move Klingensmith favored. According to Allan Nevins and Frank Ernest Hill in *Ford: Expansion and Challenge,* the firm's top men drew sides in January 1921 in the struggle over Ford Motor's financial crisis. Charles Sorensen and Ernest Liebold predictably hunkered down in Henry Ford's camp. On the other side, Klingensmith's only ally in his campaign to take the safer course of financing was Edsel Ford— and that may have been a crucial factor in his demise. "Ford wanted no one closer to Edsel than he," as Nevins and Hill put it.[37] The *New York Times,* meanwhile, reported that Klingensmith actually may have left because of Ford's anti-Semitic tirades in the *Dearborn Independent*—or perhaps because one of Ernest Liebold's investigations had turned up the fact that Klingensmith's mother was Jewish.

In any case, the disarray at the top of Ford Motor Company sparked a media frenzy that drew reporters from across the nation to Highland Park, where they found a company in chaos. At one end of the main building, corporate secretary B. J. Craig scurried about denying that either he or William Knudsen had resigned. (He soon proved wrong on the latter score; Knudsen would be out as of April 1, 1921.)[38] At the other end of the building, Edsel Ford was steadfastly refusing to comment on Klingensmith's sudden resignation. Outside his office, meanwhile, about a thousand Ford Motor Company factory workers were staging a noisy demonstration against the shutdown.

The Committee of Ford Workers, as the group called themselves, was not clamoring to get the employees' regular jobs back; what they wanted was the use of the whole factory. As long as Highland Park was closed anyway, the workers' committee was asking to use the factory through the month of January to build cars for themselves. The idea had originated with two members of the General Executive Committee of the American Communist Party, who were in Detroit to monitor the unemployment situation. The pair encouraged the idled auto workers to take Henry Ford up on his "often repeated desire to help the other fellow." The company founder, however, was in no mood to help the other fellow in January 1921, and rejected the committee's appeal. With that, recalled accountant George Brown, "we weren't closed down tight, but we were going down gradually."[39]

Word spread on Wall Street that if the Ford factories ever did open up again, "they would be in new hands."[40] The story circulating among the company's workers held that J. P. Morgan and a parade of assistants had visited Ford's Fair Lane estate late in the month to negotiate a loan. According to an uncorroborated tale, when Morgan mentioned that under the terms of any bailout agreement he would retain the right to approve Klingensmith's replacement as treasurer, Henry Ford was supposed to have jumped to his feet "and told them to get the hell out!"[41]

Although no evidence exists that J. P. Morgan or anyone from his firm visited Henry Ford in January 1921 or at any other time to discuss a loan, the apocryphal tale did capture Ford's thinking at the time. Moreover, New York banker James A. Bower, an old friend, did make the trip to see Henry Ford about possible financing, and even though their talks failed to produce an agreement, Bower never said anything about being treated rudely by the auto magnate.[42] During Ford Motor Company's financial crisis, Ford threw himself back into work. His first move was conventional under the circumstances: he cut costs, looking around his facilities for anything that might be eliminated or converted quickly into cash. In department after department, Henry Ford slashed expenses in two mighty strokes, firing employees by whole sections and then selling off the equipment they had used.

In 1920 L. E. Briggs—who would rise to treasurer of Ford Motor Company twenty-five years later—was working out of the Chicago office as a traveling auditor under chief Louis H. Turrell. That December all of the regional auditors were summoned to Highland Park and reassigned to taking inventories. "There was a feeling of awareness that the company was in a period of financial crisis," Briggs remembered. "There was a great deal of apprehension, because virtually every day, or every few days, purges were going on. Departments were being eliminated overnight." One afternoon, "all of the traveling auditors were called into Mr. Turrell's office," Briggs continued. "In his very benevolent manner, he explained that there was no further need for our services. . . . The next day, the whole Auditing Department was wiped out. Later that same day, as I remember it, Mr. Turrell was fired."[43]

By the time Henry Ford had finished cleaning house, his workforce had shrunk by a quarter, leaving some 15,000 people out of work. "Mr. Ford cut out a tremendous number of telephones, eliminated desks and a lot of clerical help and office help," recalled Norman J. Ahrens, then a young clerk in the purchasing department. "However, despite these changes, the company got increased production," he added.

To convert all this dispensable equipment into cash, Ford Motor Company held a yard sale of sorts. Ahrens said, "I helped sell some of the surplus material: furniture, typewriters, everything else in the line of furniture. . . . We set up our selling room for these items right at the Rouge plant."[44] Among scores of pallets of other items, every pencil sharpener in the plant was put up for sale, on Henry Ford's decree that employees would henceforth trim their nibs with their own penknives. The equipment sale raised $7 million in all.

But office supplies were not the only assets to go. The quest for fast cash grew so desperate that Ford Motor sent B. J. Craig to New York to dispose of the Liberty bonds the company had bought as a patriotic gesture during World War I. These brought in $7.9 million. Next, the firm demanded immediate payment of $6.7 million of accounts receivable.

Finally, Henry Ford set to squeezing cash out of his personal railroad. As Ford Motor owned any raw materials it purchased as soon as they were in the company's possession, those materials represented cash paid in the instant they were loaded into the majority stockholder's boxcars for the trip to Highland Park or River Rouge. Because Henry Ford owned the Detroit, Toledo & Ironton line, moreover, Ford Motor Company could arrange the rail schedules for its factories' maximum benefit—and by doing so cut the average time it took to haul raw materials back and forth from twenty-two days to just fourteen. "Where before we had $88 million tied up in the moving and reserve stocks required to make 93,000 cars a month," Ford boasted of the boost to his firm's operating efficiency since he, Clara, and Edsel had acquired their life-size train set, "now we handle the stock required to make 114,210 cars a month for less than $60 million. Thus, $28 million goes into cash account."[45]

No doubt could remain that Henry Ford indeed had a genius for cost-saving. He also still had a great many ardent fans: during the first week of February, as news of Ford Motor Company's terrible financial straits continued to permeate the city, one Mrs. M. D. Brown of Detroit offered to lend Henry Ford $100—a substantial sum for someone who explained that although she could not afford to help out by buying one of his cars herself, she still wanted to do what she could for Ford in thanks for all he had done for her city. But Ford Motor would not need Mrs. Brown's sweetly tendered $100, or J. P. Morgan's $100 million with all its strings attached.

When the Highland Park factory shut down at the end of December 1920, Ford Motor Company counted 125,000 finished cars in its inventory. Outside observers blanched at the enormous tally and could only conclude that the automaker had run amok, irrationally producing unwanted cars all through the autumn. Veteran Ford employees, however, clearly recognized Henry Ford's canny thinking at work in building the huge inventory of cars. Piles of raw materials, after all, were not saleable. Model Ts, on the other hand, could always be sold, at least in theory. And while Henry Ford himself may not have known exactly where to find customers in the midst of a treacherous depression, he knew a lot of people who did: the 17,000 car salesmen working in the nation's 7,000-odd Ford dealerships.

Dealers across the country suddenly began receiving unordered shipments of Model T cars and Fordson tractors—which, according to the fine print in the company's standard contract, they had to pay for whether they wanted the vehicles or not. To meet the obligation, most of the company's dealers had to turn to their local banks for loans, which meant Ford Motor Company would not have to do likewise. In effect, Henry Ford had foiled the big eastern banks he so despised by getting the cash his company needed to survive from its thousands of country cousins. Between January 1 and April 1, 1921, $24.7 million flowed into Ford Motor's corporate coffers from all over the country.

Nearly every one of the marque's dealerships proved willing to accept its share of undesired vehicles to help bail out the parent company. What irked even the most kindly disposed among them, however, was that at precisely the same time, Ford Motor Company was easing or obliterating its own long-standing rules for dealer conduct. Under the old system created by James Couzens, dealership territories had been sacrosanct. The company's sales franchises were simply not allowed to compete with one another; the rules had always stipulated that each would sell Fords only within its own designated bailiwick, aggressively but without intramural contention. Now Edsel Ford announced that the territorial boundaries had been abolished, that it was every dealer for himself. While the strategy of unleashing car salesmen to go at each other's throats succeeded in boosting sales, the company's less predatory dealers resented the abrupt reversal in tone. They recognized that the shift marked an end to one of the most profitable marketing compacts in the history of manufacturing.

But force-feeding the sales figures worked well enough that Ford Motor Company survived the crisis. As it turned out, the company had the money it needed to meet its debts all along; Henry Ford just had to find it, and quick. That he managed to do so under such intense pressure stands as perhaps his most impressive achievement as a business leader. Thanks to his heroic efforts, by April Ford Motor Company had $87.3 million in cash on hand, far more than enough to cover the $58 million it owed.

Ford Motor Company had been the last American automobile company to buckle under the strains of the depression of 1920–1921, and it was also the first to right itself. In between, the firm helped in no small measure to reverse the inflationary spiral that had made the global economic system so unstable that more than 100,000 businesses were wiped out in that one gloomy year. By March 1921, though, the worst was over. Ford Motor's factory at Highland Park hummed day and night to make up for the lost time, operating at full capacity in three shifts. Thus lit up all night, every night, Henry Ford's plant served in more than one sense as a beacon to guide the industrialized world back to prosperity.

The way it pushed through the grimness between the spring seasons of 1920 and 1921 underlined why Ford Motor deserved its position as the United States' leading industrial enterprise. As for the company's founding spirit, when a *Detroit News* reporter asked Henry Ford what had enabled him to prevail over the depression, he sat straight up and replied: "'Faith is the substance of things hoped for, the evidence of things not seen.'

"You'll find the central idea of the whole thing in the Bible, in Hebrews 11:1," he offered.[46]

<hr>

With the depression of 1920–1921 over, the Model T entered its heyday. As the paraphrase of Sir Isaiah Berlin's famous comparison goes, the fox knows many things, the hedgehog only one: one big one.[47] The prickly Henry Ford certainly knew a big one, indeed one of the biggest ever: his idea for the Model T and its mass production. The trouble only arose when Ford started to fancy himself a fox instead.

In truth, Henry Ford did not need a newspaper, a chartered ship, or even the vast fortune that could afford such trifles to exert the influence upon human society that he seems to have craved—he had the Model T, a car that did more to rework the world than any diplomat or member of the fourth estate ever has. Ford did not invent the wheel, but by putting four of them and a motor under just about anyone who wanted to explore, he offered the reward of a wider world to a whole generation of Model T drivers.

Ford Motor Company's five millionth Model T rolled off the Highland Park assembly line on May 28, 1921, just as the depression was ending and a dozen years after production had begun on the first batch of Tin Lizzies. It would be only three more years before the *ten* millionth T would head out the factory door, on June 4, 1924.[48] Even Americans who were under thirty years old in the early 1920s could remember a time when there had not been a single car on the road anywhere. In their mere three decades, they had seen auto manufacturing evolve from a back-shed hobby into the biggest industry in the United States.[49] They also had watched as Ford's Model T came to epitomize not just American automaking, but the nation's bold new ways of doing business in general. Henry Ford's genius was to surpass putting a cheap car in every garage by putting a pretty good one there at an astonishingly low price.

A 1924 census conducted by Ford Motor Company showed that as Model T number 10 million came off the line, some 8.7 million of its hardy little forebears were still doing yeoman service all over the world.

Ford Motor Company sent its ten millionth T on a hero's tour across the country from New York to San Francisco via the Lincoln Highway, with stops in variously picturesque small towns along the nation's first transcontinental automobile road such as Princeton, New Jersey, and Elko, Nevada. A fully equipped motion picture crew documented the whole journey, celebrating the Model T and the Lincoln Highway both.[50] Mayors in municipalities of every size in every region greeted the car as if it were foreign royalty on a state visit. "Everywhere along the route the sturdy little car bearing the Ford Model T number 10,000,000 is being hailed by enthusiastic crowds while Ford dealers are escorting it from town to town, forming a parade at every place along the line," the *Ford News* reported. "City and state officials are welcoming it and its visit has been made a gala occasion in every community."[51]

The fact that Ford Motor had produced 10 million vehicles and set that many people loose in them boggled many minds, including that of a Harvard University music professor inspired to compose a fourteen-minute fantasia on the achievement. Performed to acclaim on several occasions in 1926 by the likes of the esteemed Boston Symphony and New York Philharmonic Orchestras, F. S. Converse's "Flivver Ten Million" even had Model T sound effects in it—crashes, rattles, and horn blasts the composer had to talk Boston Symphony conductor Serge Koussevitzky into keeping. To Converse, the ten millionth Model T Ford typified "the indomitable spirit of America,"[52] and that included the noise the cars made crashing. And the creator of "Flivver Ten Million" was not the only one who observed how the Model T encapsulated everything the 1920s would be remembered for: prosperity, social freedom, youthful overconfidence, and excess at any age.

Model T sales, phenomenal from the first, swelled into an overwhelming force early in the decade as the car's price continued to drop. Over the course of 1922 alone, the T's price fell from $325 to $319 and then down to $269. The two-seat Model T Runabout, which had gone for $395 in 1919, cost only $260 in 1925, the least that would ever be charged for a new American car.[53] Ford Motor Company neither offered nor encouraged buying on credit, but there was little call for Model T financing anyway: virtually anybody could afford that little. The car's 1925 sticker price amounted to only about one eighth of the average annual income in the United States. At that low a cost, even a halfhearted effort to save up could put a low-wage worker in a new Ford within a year or two.

Other American-built cars continued to sell, of course, but the ever sinking price of the Model T thwarted any thought among other automakers of trying to encroach on the bottom end of the market. In many rural areas, that meant

Ford controlled the entire automobile market. Adolph Derrer of Mt. Carroll, Illinois, had ten adult sons, a remarkable record all by itself, but one that made news in 1922 when all of them had Model T Fords. Dad already owned one. Each of the eleven Derrer Fords was a touring car (the five-passenger convertible that was the most popular of the Model T body styles). Sales of eleven cars in one small town would have been a boon at most American auto companies, but at Ford Motor it was only a peculiarity. The same year, the company's dealer in Palmyra, Nebraska, even put an ad in the local paper offering a $1 reward to anyone who could report the sale of any make of car other than a Ford in his territory.[54]

The Model T had been around for more than a decade, yet it was only just coming into its prime. Two thirds of all the automobiles registered in the United States in 1923–1924 were Fords, and all of them were Tin Lizzies. By the early 1920s, the Model T had attained such vivid brand recognition that nearly every prospective first-car buyer understood the distinction between an automobile and a *Ford*—a flashy commercial product to impress the neighbors or an inexpensive, simple tool for basic transportation.

For most newcomers to car ownership, the Model T represented the first status symbol they had ever acquired. In those days very few Americans ever made a single purchase for as much as $100 except to buy a house. At a few hundred dollars, Ford Motor Company's everyman car introduced a middle ground, and in that sense extended the average American's consumerism to include capital goods. What's more, Henry Ford's mass-market automobile was rapidly turning the United States into the nation of passionate drivers it has remained ever since.

From the start, Henry Ford had been determined to make his car a commodity, consistent in quality and priced to drive right off the dealer's lot on a whim, preferably after the customer succumbed to the allure of a few profit-boosting options. Even people who didn't drive in the first half of the 1920s recognized that the Model Ts chugging down every street in swelling parades had more in common with the recently introduced vacuum cleaner and electric washing machine than they did with the elegant, finely engineered Maxwells and Nashes with which the Lizzies shared the road.

That was precisely how Henry Ford had intended to position his beloved Model T all along. The world did not have to *want* his cars—it had already come to need them. And in the process Ford Motor Company had maneuvered itself into holding a virtual monopoly on America's new household necessity.

13

The Rouge

"Two flies can manufacture 48,876,532,154 new flies in six months," wrote the humorist Luke McLuke. "But they haven't anything on two Ford factories."[1]

The two primary Ford Motor Company factories of the early 1920s, Highland Park in Detroit and River Rouge in Dearborn, produced both finished cars and the parts for satellite factories throughout the world. Overall, the production rate startled the industry by crossing the one-million mark in 1921: 928,750 cars in the United States, 42,860 overseas, and 42,348 in Canada.[2] That figure would rise to 1.8 million Model T cars the next year, but what was especially surprising about the increased production of the early 1920s was that output was growing at a faster rate than hiring. Not only was the number of cars manufactured rising, but that same workforce also made an annual average of 150,000 one-ton trucks, 75,000 tractors, millions of spare parts, and large quantities of by-products that were used by other industries.

More cars and a better-finished product from each worker at a lower cost: Fordism was in full swing. The job cuts of January 1921 had made the company stronger, not weaker. Hourly workers in the factory more than recovered their full numbers, although more than a third of the salaried workers were still gone after a year. In terms of production, the company didn't miss them. Nonetheless, the purge made Ford Motor Company a very different company than it had been. "The elimination of steps and stairs in Ford's organization became distinct, which was a very beneficial thing," recalled Alex Lumsden, a manager in steel production. Financial accounting was reduced to a bare minimum. As the head of a company with assets of more than $536 million in 1923,[3] Henry Ford was relying on year-end bank statements to let him know whether or not the company was making money.

Another unit cut down in 1921 was the sociological department. Formed in 1914 in the wake of the $5 Day, it had grown by 1919 from its original 30 investigators to 150, with about half as many interpreters, keeping records on the lifestyles and spending habits of each of Ford's hourly employees. A remnant of James Couzens's sense of social responsibility, the sociological department also reflected Henry Ford's belief in certain values, including a stable household, steady savings, and cleanliness.

The department was difficult to understand in its own time, and has remained so ever since. In starting it, the company was trying to take care of its own people in the midst of an urban-industrial environment that was brutal on the uninformed employee. Perhaps a worker's home life should have been none of the company's business, yet many Ford employees had serious trouble at home. They were undergoing adjustment to life in the city, life in America, life without family ties. Such pressures and the sharpsters who lurk alongside them preyed on well-paid auto workers. Ford Motor Company was alone among carmakers in exercising an obligation to help its workers adjust. While benefits programs have evolved since, the sociological department was an early example of a company using its strength in support of individual employees. To succeed, it had to navigate a narrow space between the standing indignities of industrial life and charges of invasion of privacy.

The Very Reverend Samuel S. Marquis, former dean of the Episcopal cathedral of Detroit, had been hired to head the sociological department in 1916. He was introduced to Henry Ford by Clara Ford, who was active in the Episcopal Church. Dean Marquis, an energetic and optimistic man, impressed Ford, who took to calling him "Mark." They became friends. "I want you, Mark, to put Jesus Christ in my factory," Ford is supposed to have said in placing Marquis in charge of the department.[4] Like his predecessor, John R. Lee, the clergyman ran the department strictly as a service to employees, and not as a spying operation for management. Marquis did not "put Jesus Christ" into the factory, because he was not a man to proselytize in his position at Ford Motor Company. In spirit, though, Marquis's inclination, following after Henry Ford's, was to help people in trouble. Under his auspices, the department concentrated on difficult cases, especially in the areas of broken families and confused immigrants: "homes of dirt, filth, unsanitary, unkempt and immoral," in the words of an investigator named A. C. Tait.[5] With the promise of increased wages (the $5 Day) for those who complied, the sociological department intervened in fundamental ways: by moving families into satisfactory housing or by insisting that errant husbands break habits such as drinking whiskey and chasing women (at the risk of losing their jobs). It was also empowered to forward the paychecks of irresponsible workers to other members of the household, and it extended loans against future pay.

"I do know this," recalled James O'Connor of his fellow workers at Ford, "that if they weren't taking care of their children and they were divorced, and the husband wasn't paying his alimony and maybe the wife wouldn't bother him, all she had to do was go down to the Sociological Department and they just kept that out of his pay. . . . They took care of a lot of children. I know a lot of people who went down and got the money. It would help restore the home and help keep the children."[6]

Because more than half of the Ford employees were immigrants recently landed in America, the investigators devoted much of their time to settlement work, or "Americanization," as it was called: offering advice ranging from the importance of keeping flies off of food to the way that a worker who started saving money at the age of twenty-two could retire with full pay at the age of fifty.[7] The company supported workers with an organized English-language school and a fully equipped plant hospital. It also placed the corporation's lawyers at the disposal of employees who were in need of advice.

One of the practices investigators particularly discouraged was making purchases on an installment plan. Sharp retailers took advantage of factory workers, especially those coming from rural areas or foreign countries, by offering merchandise on a low down payment, with impossibly high subsequent payments.

An investigator named F. W. Andrews reported on the household of a Russian worker:

> The family consisted of a wife and six children [including a baby]. . . . His home was furnished with two dirty beds (one of which was occupied by the five children who slept crossways in same), a ragged and filthy rug, a rickety old table, and two bottomless chairs (the five children standing up at the table to eat). The wife and children were half clad, thin, pale and hungry looking.

Andrews arranged for a loan from Ford Motor, found a five-room cottage for the family, furnished furniture and clothes—and, he added, "a liberal amount of soap was bought with instructions to use freely." The wife, he was subsequently able to report to Marquis, "is wearing a smile that won't come off."[8]

In addition to owning a home and building a savings account, employees were encouraged to buy a car. Henry Ford officially didn't dictate what kind of car the workers bought. The promise of increased sales if and when 50,000 profit-sharers became Ford customers was not lost on the factory, however.

"If we found a fellow drove a Buick car and he had it parked in our lot," recalled supervisor William Klann, "we'd say, 'Is this your car?'

"'Yes,' the employee would say.

"'Well, you're through working here.'

"'What do you mean?'

"We said, 'Well, you've been late three times in the last two months and we're firing you out.'

"The real reason," Klann explained, "was that he was driving a Buick car.

He was never told that, but anyone who did not drive a Ford car never lasted long after it was found out."[9]

"Lots of them," Thomas Williams recalled of the hourly workers, "were buying motorcycles with sidecars instead of Model Ts as they should have been doing. They'd be brought in and asked why they didn't buy the Model T. Lot of guys resented that, of course, because they thought they should be able to spend their money the way they saw fit."[10]

The sociological department succeeded in its effort to promote thrift, at least among long-term employees. According to company records, the average hourly worker at Ford in 1914 possessed $207.70 in savings and home investment. Those who were still with the company five years later had $2,171.14 on average.[11] Ford, however, was careful not to turn Dearborn into the dreaded company town that ultimately failed in so many other settings. Rather than turning workers into extensions of the factory, Ford Motor Company and its sociological department fostered independence. That was the difference that allowed Dean Marquis to describe his department's approach as "fraternal" rather than "paternal."[12]

In wrestling with an unstable and confused labor force, Ford Motor was hardly alone. Since the beginning of the Industrial Revolution, heavy industry had been endowed with a voracious need for unskilled labor. It also had a natural tendency to take advantage of the common worker, even to the point of abuse. Mass production, by its very nature, exacerbated those conditions, subordinating workers to the machine. The assembly line bound disparate people with nothing stronger than the moving line before them: not language, not background, not culture. There was only the line, advancing at the same incessant speed for each of them, whoever they were. Most other companies surveyed the raw labor force populating their factories in the first quarter of the twentieth century and saw only the group, like a cloud of flies. The management of labor at such places was little more than a calculation of how large the group had to be in order to make it fill the factory predictably. Ford Motor Company was one of the few companies that looked at labor and saw individuals. Critics insisted that Ford's sociological department sought to make those individuals conform to Henry Ford's homespun values, while supporters observed that the guidelines actually only reflected common sense.

The demise of the department reflected as clearly as any other single event the fact that Ford Motor Company in 1921 was not the same company it had been in 1914. The idealism of a young company was gone, replaced by a zeal for efficiency that no longer allowed itself to be distracted by potential in any sphere except the output of automobiles. Charles Sorensen, who emerged during the business crisis of 1920–1921 as the leader of the next generation at Ford, had no particular interest in human development. His attention was trained on the River Rouge plant, and the development of it as a fortress against an unpredictable economy.

In the new atmosphere, the fact that well-adjusted workers were more productive than troubled ones no longer seemed to be worth the bother of hovering over them with a battalion of investigators. H. S. Ablewhite, who resurrected the sociological department during World War II, viewed the demise of the department as a turning point in the company. "Men like Sorensen, P. E. Martin, and various others, they were just more hard-boiled, if you will, and felt the work of the Sociological Department was doing nothing worthwhile and should be done away with," Ablewhite said. "I would pick 1921 as the beginning power of this tough school."[13]

Dean Marquis resigned during the exodus of January 1921, when many seasoned executives left Ford Motor Company. He tangled with Sorensen over the fate of an employee who had been fired for incompetence. Marquis maintained that, according to the company's long-standing policy against the outright dismissal of workers (except for the most egregious offenses), the man should have been transferred. Despite the official policy, Sorensen often fired workers, and Marquis finally took him to task, demanding that Henry Ford decide which of them was right. The timing of the incident worked to Sorensen's benefit. More than anyone, he was fighting the frontline battle to cut costs and to keep Henry Ford from losing control of his company. In addition, he had been the head of Fordson tractor production when it became one of the first Ford commercial operations to move into place at the River Rouge plant and had continued to extend his base of power by ensuring that he remained at the helm of the plant afterward. When Henry Ford backed Sorensen in the decision over the firing, Dean Marquis submitted his resignation. Most of the sociological department was wiped out immediately afterward, leaving a renamed education department with a limited role, including the continuation of English lessons for foreigners.

The highly sensitive Marquis was devastated by what he considered Henry Ford's betrayal. In 1923, he wrote a book called *Henry Ford: An Interpretation,* the first published work openly critical of the folk hero. Marquis was a good writer who made for a bad enemy: his book was scathing in its description of Henry Ford's fading commitment to anything other than making money. "The Ford car is Henry Ford done in steel, and other things," Marquis wrote. "Not a thing of art and beauty, but of utility and strength . . . it keeps going, just as he keeps going contrary to all the laws of labor, commerce and high finance."[14]

Clara Ford was livid about Marquis's book and made inquiries about buying up the entire print run to dispose of it. That wasn't plausible, so she contented herself with refusing to speak to the dean's wife, ever again. Henry, for his part, didn't hold a grudge, though. When "Mark" Marquis was taken ill and receiving free treatment at the Henry Ford Hospital, Ford paid him a personal bedside visit.[15]

———

In 1922–1923, Henry Ford's fortune was calculated at $750 million, though even that figure was low in view of an offer made by John Prentiss to purchase Ford Motor outright for $1 billion. Prentiss, a partner in the Boston securities firm of Hornblower & Weeks, didn't have that amount of money in his pocket; instead, he intended to take Ford public and make a profit on a gigantic stock offering. Prentiss later admitted that he made three attempts to buy Ford Motor between 1919 and 1922. The first time, Henry Ford only laughed at the $1 billion offer. The second time he scoffed at it. And the third time, Prentiss received a telling reply from Edsel: "We are having too much fun to sell out."[16]

The company Henry Ford owned, with Clara and Edsel, earned $119 million after taxes. By one estimate, the Ford fortune increased by $400,000 per day.[17] That made for a rather easy comparison to the factory wage, which had increased to $6 per day in 1919. Ford was not oblivious to the opportunity, or obligation, to share profits, however. Since 1918, the company had offered Ford Investment Certificates, which paid a rate of interest attached to the profitability of the company. The guaranteed minimum was 6 percent at a time when small investors could not hope to receive more than 4 percent at a bank. In good years, those in which Ford earned more than 20 percent on its equity (as in 1923), the rate was much higher.

"It wasn't stock in the Ford Motor Company," explained C. G. Milner, who worked in the Atlanta branch, "but a certificate was issued to you for every dollar you put in and you could invest as much as one-third of your salary each pay day. . . . One year Mr. Ford paid us as much as 18 percent."[18] Milner used his certificate savings to buy his own Ford dealership in Rockmart, Georgia, in 1924.

Despite the raise in pay to $6 per day and the generous savings plan, Ford hourly workers in 1924 were not as well paid as they had been ten years before. The steep inflation during the war and immediately afterward reduced workers' actual income, bringing it in line with that paid by other automakers. The old Ford Motor Company had tried to attract the best workers with the $5 Day and extract more work from them. The company that was reborn in 1921–1922 did things in the opposite order. The factory set the pace and fired those who could not adhere to it.

Nevertheless, in 1922, Ford Motor made another grand gesture in labor relations by instituting a five-day workweek. Formerly, factory employees were expected to show up for eight hours a day, six days per week. The company wanted to give workers more time to relax at home. At the same time, it expected even more effort from them when they were on the job. Ford also wanted to offer employment to a greater number of people—to stabilize its workforce and local economies near its plants worldwide. Ford's announcement of the five-day workweek contradicted the prevailing mood in business circles, which insisted that workers should work longer hours, in part to keep them too busy and tired for union activity. Henry Ford was anti-union, too, but labor leaders praised him, nonetheless. Cigar maker Samuel Gompers, the longtime president of the American Federation of Labor, said of the lightened work schedule, "Mr. Ford will find his new plan as beneficial as he found the introduction of the eight-hour day, both as to quality and quantity of output."[19]

For many, the rebuilding years of 1921–1924 were lean, tough, and exciting. "Extending yourself with all the physical and mental energy that you possessed" was how Alex Lumsden described it.[20]

"In so many places, the politics, so to speak, play such an important part. The end view is lost sight of," recalled Lumsden. "Despite its lack of straight lines in administration," he continued, "the Company by this method of personal contact and association carried out its functions ably."[21]

"You are out there to work," Lumsden added, in what could be a summary of the atmosphere at Ford Motor Company in the early 1920s.

The speed-up that wound up the entire automobile industry during that decade had long been part of the atmosphere at Ford. Foremen became less and less like crew managers and more like mule drivers, shouting at fumblers on the line and exhorting those at their own machines to "Mach schnell . . . putch-putch . . . presto . . . *hurry up!*" In any language, they had to stay on pace.

A joke of the day went:

"How did you happen to lose your job?" the new boss asked an applicant who had been fired from the Ford factory.

"I dropped my monkey wrench one day and by the time I picked it up, I was sixteen cars behind."

The reality was almost that harsh. The work was generally hard and always unceasing. Danger lurked everywhere: oil slicks on the concrete floors, jagged steel or metal, scorching hot motors, and foremen watching your every move. Anthony Harff, a factory worker who worked his way into an office position, arranged for a family friend, an unemployed artist, to start work on the final assembly line at the Ford factory. "First night I picked him up and took him home, he said he was awfully tired," Harff recalled. "He had been underneath the fenders of every car that came down the line, stooped over in a squatty position, and he could hardly straighten up when quitting time came.

"He'd come home at night," Harff said, "and he would sit in a chair and he didn't care whether he ate dinner or not. He just had to sit in an upright position for a while. He was just so tired, and his body ached so that he didn't care whether he moved or not."[22] Harff's friend was unable to return to work after the third day.

The speed-up was everywhere, though. Workers were used to that. The difference at Ford was that it was not merely the men who were hurried, it was the ideas. "Everybody was working for one thing," said toolmaker Logan Miller, "trying to improve the product at less cost." Ideas could come from anywhere and anyone.

At least one new tool was introduced at Ford Motor every single day. Ernest Grimshaw, who worked at the company for more than forty years starting in 1906, recalled that one of the more clever innovations allowed a drill-press operator to drill ten holes at once, where previously he had had to realign the bit ten separate times.[23]

"It was not what it cost, but how fast you could make it," as Logan Miller observed.[24] Henry Ford's most basic philosophy was that the Model T could not be improved, but that the process of making it could. "Time loves to be wasted," Ford was fond of saying. "From time wasted there can be no salvage. It is the easiest of all waste and the hardest to correct because it does not litter the floor."[25] His factories were subject to constant refinement to save extra minutes. To chart the progress scientifically, a time-study department of about eighty men canvassed the factories, recording the number of minutes required to complete each process. They were especially dogged following the installation of a new machine or method.

"We knew if we saved minutes, we saved dollars," explained Anthony Harff.[26]

———

Ford Motor Company's monument to saved minutes was the River Rouge plant. It was not only the most important factory at the company, it was the most important in all of industrial America. Other plants were built or constructed. River Rouge was *created*: a world engineered from a blank sheet of paper, intended to allow the maximum number of operations without wasted time, effort, or cost. At the same time, neighboring processes were not supposed to crowd one another, but rather to benefit each other. "I was with him and Mr. Sorensen one time," engineer William Pioch recalled of Henry Ford in about 1919, "and I was standing by listening to the conversation. He was telling Mr. Sorensen about the way he wanted the plant laid out. He wanted the raw material coming in on one end of the Rouge plant and the finished cars going out on the other end."[27]

At first glance the chosen location for the Rouge—three miles from the Detroit River—seemed ill advised. The River Rouge was in reality just a medium-size stream that led to the Detroit River. Without major dredging and widening, Great Lakes freighters would be unable to journey to Dearborn. Common sense dictated that any new Ford plant be built along the Detroit River. But Ford didn't want to rely on Detroit. He preferred laying down pilings 100 feet deep to create his own deepwater port in Dearborn along the Rouge River. At this site, Ford had ample room to construct buildings and expand when necessary. "I don't like to be in the city," Henry Ford told A. M. Wibel, head of Ford purchasing, who was astounded by how much money his boss was willing to spend on pilings for a Rouge port. "It pins me in. I want to breathe. I want to get out. . . . I want to get an atmosphere where the sun can get in."[28]

American industrialists had seen many impressive factories rise during the new century, but nothing as wholly inclusive as the plant at River Rouge. Just as a university is a collection of colleges, the architect Albert Kahn envisioned the River Rouge as a collection of factories. It had facilities for processing coal equivalent to any in West Virginia or Ohio. Its steel foundry, the largest in the world, was even more modern than those in Pittsburgh or Wheeling. The electric power plant could have serviced a city of 350,000 people. The assembly line was the most mechanized in the automaking industry or any other. In only seven years, from 1919 to 1926, River Rouge grew to include 93 buildings, 75,000 employees, and output of 4,000 cars per day.[29] Even as it made the Highland Park factory obsolete, it accomplished three of Henry Ford's grandest ambitions.

First, River Rouge reduced Ford Motor Company's dependence on outside suppliers. Second, it was designed from the outset to decrease the distance parts and materials had to be moved, especially by manpower. Third, the plant made by-products that could themselves be used or sold. The Ford plant was the envy of industrialists around the world; not because the others wanted to achieve the same things, necessarily, but because it demonstrated that any such goals could be attained through advance planning and unhampered engineering.

"Henry Ford has brought the hand of God and the hand of Man closer together at River Rouge than they have ever been brought in any other undertaking," beamed *Industrial Management* in 1922.[30] One way that Ford Motor unleashed the potential of the engineers, both its own and those working under contract, was by choosing a site for the plant that was not only large, but unencumbered by industrial neighbors.

Dearborn was changing from a farm district to an industrial one, with new buildings occupied by Michigan Bell Telephone, the Pennsylvania Railroad, and Detroit Edison. But it was Ford's tract along the Rouge, near the border with Detroit, that transformed the countryside. "Henry Ford of the Ford Motor Company has put an endorsement on Dearborn unparalleled in the history of city development," said the Reverend J. F. Conley in a speech before the Greater Dearborn Association in 1924.[31] It was the sort of ballyhoo for which civic groups were famous, especially in the 1920s, but, in Dr. Conley's case, it was true. When Ford built the Rouge, Dearborn was no longer a farming village. Some residents resisted the change, of course, but if they wanted to, all of them could profit from it. The old fields and gently sloping hills were fast becoming the capital of progress in the automaking industry. "The influence of the Ford industry is felt throughout the world," observed the *Detroit News*, "but here this influence is concentrated in a development unparalleled in industrial history."[32] Ford Motor went off by itself and built a plant that would by 1924 employ ten times as many people as had lived in Dearborn five years before.

Of course, the reason that factories group themselves together is that they can then take advantage of common transportation carriers. That wasn't necessary for Ford Motor Company. Henry Ford had chosen the site in the first place because of its frontage on the Rouge River, a gateway to the Detroit River and the Great Lakes, which he planned to utilize for most of the plant's transportation needs. While the U.S. government had begun the job of preparing the Rouge River for its new role during World War I, the company spent more than $2 million making it deeper and wider, rendering it navigable for large ships. By 1924, Ford owned two Great Lakes ore carriers, named for Edsel's first two children: the *Henry II* and the *Benson*. In 1925, the first oceangoing ship arrived at the Rouge from Antwerp, Belgium.[33] In addition to the waterway, Ford had his own railroad, the Detroit, Toledo & Ironton, which had been nearly bankrupt when he acquired it. Despite the pessimism of experts, he turned it around and profited by it, moving materials and finished cars to the Ohio River Valley. Workers were paid fairly, and it was considered the cleanest line in America. "Ford loved owning a railroad," historian Carol Gelderman wrote. "Riding tenders on top of the coal was his idea of having fun. Often he instructed his chauffeur to drive until he found a D.T.& I. train to flag down. Ford would get aboard, telling his driver to continue down the highway, always keeping up with the train. Ford would stay perched on the coal for a while, playing the harmonica. Then he would crawl over the coal and into the cab to take over the throttle."[34]

Just as Ford purchased trains and ships as extensions of the River Rouge plant, he also purchased timberland and iron ore mines in northern Michigan and coal mines in West Virginia and Kentucky. He even made a strong bid on the rights to develop power plants and chemical factories at Muscle Shoals, Alabama. Although only the iron mines made a significant contribution to Ford Motor Company production, the fact that the company had its own resources for vital materials made suppliers fear that bloated prices would rile the automaker into increasing the flow of materials from its own holdings. The result was that the Ford Motor mines and its timber operations created an aura of competition out of scale with their actual output. Even when the company purchased raw materials from outside sources, however, it cut costs by shipping them on one of its own carriers.

Moving materials to and from River Rouge was important, but moving them from one building to another around the plant was even more challenging. Many factories used men or trucks to handle goods on-site. That necessitated loading and unloading, two activities that Ford Motor Company wanted to make obsolete. River Rouge depended instead on more than ninety miles of railway track, built in a systemized way around the Highline, a concrete building three-quarters of a mile long and forty feet high. Inside, the Highline had ample room for short-term storage. On the roof were its railway tracks, leading from slips along the river all the way to the heart of the plant. Called the "backbone" of River Rouge, the Highline was a primary reason that the plant ran so smoothly. It could not only deliver materials from its rooftop cars but make room for occasional oversupply.

Transportation inside each building was based on a network of conveyors and cranes that allowed materials to flow in a steady stream where they were needed. Mechanized handling equipment made River Rouge as precise as a Swiss watch—and made it look from an aerial vantage point not unlike the inside of one. A short list of the equipment on hand included conveyors (gravity, spiral, or bucket), moving belts, trolleys, electric vehicles and motor trucks, an array of cranes, moving platforms, cable cars, and electric railways. The secret to saving money at the plant lay in synchronizing the various levels of transportation, since an inconsistent pace in materials handling would cause delays. Anyway, a faster line was a more productive one: more cars meant more money. The fine-tuning served another purpose, as well. A predictable flow of parts and materials—from the source, even in another state, all the way to the line where they were needed—reduced the need for long-term storage. No car company ever made money storing parts, after all. Ford Motor Company obviated the need for a margin of safety in its flow by reducing the margin of error in its transportation at every level.

As manufacturing plants grow, there is nearly always a reduction in the cost of actual production per item. Expansion usually causes other costs, however, including handling, warehousing, and distribution, to swell. Ford Motor Company recognized that tendency in the advance planning for River Rouge. It was a major transportation hub first and only after that was it an assembly plant.

Coal was a prime resource at River Rouge, where forty traincar-loads were used every day. The way coal was used represents the attitude in all matters of those who ran the plant. At most large factories of the day, coal was burned at a power plant to generate power in the form of electricity. Ford, however, installed coke ovens, which refined raw coal into the hot-burning form required in a foundry. At high temperatures in the foundry, the resulting coke gave off coal gas, which was piped to the generating plant, where it was burned to produce electricity. The generating plant, lined in white tile, burned fuel so efficiently that a visiting engineer declared that it was "so cool, quiet and free from vibration that a banquet might be comfortably served either in its boiler room or generator room!"[35]

Just as Ford was one of the only manufacturing companies to have its own coke ovens, it was also one of the few to rely on its own foundry, which was capable of turning out castings in iron, brass, bronze, or aluminum. Covering more than 1.1 million square feet, it received molten steel directly from the plant's blast furnaces and cast it into a variety of parts, including all of the engine blocks used in the Model T. A foundry is a world apart, where metals are heated to the melting point and then poured into molds, a combination of flashing hot temperatures and unexpectedly delicate work. Foundry men must have both brute strength and artistic judgment, because mistakes can be cast right into the metal.

A mere foundry, however enormous, did not fulfill the goal of River Rouge's steel department, which was "raw materials to finished automobile." Between 1924 and 1926, the gaps in the production of usable steel were steadily filled in. In the open-hearth building, as long as a football field and half again as wide, six huge furnaces were heated to 3,200 degrees in order to melt limestone, iron, and other metals to create steel alloy.[36] The blooming mill, another huge building, prepared ingots made in the open hearths for the rolling mill, which occupied yet another large shop.

Underlying all of the buildings, operations, and work at River Rouge was Ford Motor Company's rejection of waste in any form. As it grew, managers looked closely at the residue of its operations, looking for potential products. In 1924, the company investigated uses for the slag left after coal dust was burned in the blast furnaces. The result was a cement factory turning out 2,800 barrels per day.[37] At the same time, 20 million pounds of ammonium sulfate fertilizer, a by-product of coke, were sold each year.[38] In 1925, the company reported overall by-product sales of $11 million, $4 million of which reflected materials formerly considered waste, but converted into a saleable form. A paper mill, for example, was built on the other side of the Rouge River to turn scrap wood into paperboard boxes.[39] When Ford Motor initiated the manufacture of its own windshield glass, it discarded pieces too small for use in a car. Before long, however, the excess glass was saved and sold on the market.[40] While the conversion of by-products into marketable goods was successful on a small scale, the River Rouge plant did not fare well when it strayed too far from automaking. Sidelines such as cast-concrete building materials and structural iron were money losers. The company may have been able to build anything at the new plant, but that didn't mean that it understood how to market everything.

The recognizable process of automaking at River Rouge began in the machine shop, adjacent to the foundry. The parts cast in the foundry were delivered by conveyor to machinists who drilled clean holes and otherwise finished them. To prepare a Model T engine block (known around River Rouge as part T-400) for assembly required forty-three operations in the machine shop.[41] The machines at River Rouge were even closer together than those at Highland Park, leaving only enough space for a man to get by—just barely. And so, statistics on the square footage released by Ford Motor—more than 2 million in 1925—should probably be doubled to be comparable with factories in which a wide aisle separated each bank of machines from the next.

Henry Ford initiated the development of River Rouge as a commercial plant by moving Fordson tractor manufacturing into Building "B." The "B" stood for "boats," since it originally had been the home of the Eagle boat. The "B" building is one third of a mile long and remains the heart of the plant today. Originally, it had two floors, but that was one too many, as far as Henry Ford was concerned. Adamantly opposed to unnecessary effort, especially in moving materials, he argued that a one-story building allowed for the smoothest movement of materials past men and machines. By 1922, when the tractors moved into their own building and automobiles were being built in "B," the top floor was removed and the machines below were organized to flow in a straight line from one end of the building to the other. Because Henry Ford also hated to see men doing any unnecessary lifting, a massive, sliding crane was built into the ceiling. It delivered parts and moved equipment, plucking up broken machines as though they were pebbles.

The body assembly department, a combination of woodwork and metal stamping, occupied one section of the "B" building. The Model T frame was made of hardwood, milled in one of three Ford sawmills in the state of Michigan. In part because of the rejection of waste, and in part because Henry Ford was a bird lover and naturalist, the company pioneered methods that made better use of raw timber so that fewer trees had to be felled. Ford himself insisted that the men who operated the saws at River Rouge should be trained to recognize the optimum way to make cuts by the pattern in the wood and the way it was responding to the blade. More than other hourly workers, the sawyers had the discretion to do their work as they saw fit.

The only thing that River Rouge did not produce was completed Model T Fords. Parts made at River Rouge were shipped to Highland Park just as though it were one of the other assembly branches around the world. Even after every other aspect of production had been moved out of Highland Park, the older factory still turned out the finished cars.

As the new plant rose up and filled out with as many as three major buildings opening *each year* between 1919 and 1926, Ford Motor seemed to divide in spirit into two companies: Highland Park and River Rouge. For several years, they operated on a parallel basis, but in 1924–1925, the Ford universe tilted toward River Rouge. One department after another was closed down at Highland Park and transported by train to the new plant. "You could take, for instance, the Camshaft Department," recalled Anthony Harff. "There were hundreds of machines, and truckload after truckload and carload after carload of machines coming out of that one department to go to the Rouge." After the machines went the employees. And then Ford Motor Company had to make room for their bosses.

P. E. Martin and William Klann were the heads of the Highland Park contingent. Charles Sorensen and Mead Bricker had risen to equivalent positions at River Rouge. When the two facilities began to combine at River Rouge in 1924, "it was just a dog and cat fight," engineer William Pioch recalled.[42] Although the company was in the midst of its most prodigious years, with sales soaring and production becoming more efficient with each passing day, the atmosphere at Ford Motor Company was turning tense and unhappy.

Employees, especially those working in middle management or in the offices, were taken aback at the transition and how fast it occurred. Ford Motor changed from an organization in which people were proud to work to a place where they just tried each and every day not to be fired. At every level, job security disappeared. Dismissals weren't based on necessity, as in the financial crisis at the beginning of the decade. Now as Ford Motor Company was increasing its labor force overall, the firings were part of a power struggle that emanated from the top ranks.

As Highland Park was fading from the scene, Martin still held himself forth as the senior member of the supervisory staff. Sorensen, lord of the stronger facility at River Rouge, used his considerable wile to stifle Martin and leave him behind as Highland Park emptied out. One of the techniques in the battle was to fire managers working under the opposition. The methods of firing seemed calculated to damage morale. A man would arrive for work and find his department moved. If no one would tell him where it was, he finally got the message that he no longer worked for the company. Often, a doomed manager would be told to take a vacation; while he was away, he received a telegram telling him that he'd been terminated. Some managers arrived at work to find their desks destroyed. These new methods were both heartless and irrational—and antithetical to the conditions fostered by Ford Motor Company in the past.

"I remember one time," said Logan Miller, "I came into the tool room and said 'Where did you move my department?' The fellow said, 'I don't know. Stand here; it may come back again!'" Miller survived, but felt no better about the company because of it. "This was the time of the whispered communication," he explained. "You didn't dare say that you heard something unless you knew who the hell you were talking to. I remember down in Pressed Steel, a fellow was standing at the desk in my cage. He was a general foreman from another building and we were talking about the number of people who were being laid off. There was always the question, 'When is your time? Do you think your time is going to be soon?' While we were talking this fellow got a call from the Department of Supervision. He went into the telephone booth . . . came out, shook hands with me, and said, 'Well, they just told me to get out of here.'"[43]

One of those whose fortunes rose in the snarling atmosphere was Harry Bennett, who had joined Ford Motor Company in 1918 as an artist in the art department, his specialty being motion pictures. Though small, Bennett was muscular and conspicuously pugnacious, fond of reminding people that he had experience as a professional boxer. Impressing Henry Ford personally with his tough-speaking ways, Bennett was allowed to carve out a daunting level of responsibility for himself. He had no title in the mid-1920s, but he was ultimately in charge of employment and personnel. By then, he had already organized the "service department" as his personal arm within the factory: an outfit of spies and guards who kept watch on and control over the employees. Bennett was a bright man with noticeable abilities in organization, but he was ignorant of business methods, a fact he sidestepped by gathering innuendo on others and casting himself as Henry Ford's tough-acting right-hand man. Oddly enough, at least a half-dozen men considered themselves "Henry Ford's tough-acting right-hand man," starting with Sorensen, Liebold, and Martin, but the fact that someone as ill equipped as Bennett joined them at the top of Ford Motor Company in such a short time indicates the direction in which the company was headed in the mid-1920s.

While Sorensen was fighting to keep Martin and his loyalists out of River Rouge, he was also part of the struggle with Ernest Kanzler, Edsel Ford's handpicked executive vice president. Kanzler was a rising force at Ford Motor, overseeing production and, to a lesser extent, sales. He handled management tasks easily and was instrumental in the development of River Rouge. No one could erase his power base through mass firings, because his power stemmed from only one man, Edsel Ford. And Edsel considered Ernest Kanzler to be essential at Ford Motor Company. The two men were similar, polished professionals who shared the goal of making Ford Motor's management as modern and progressive as the production facilities at River Rouge. Kanzler, however, possessed a streak of independence; if he believed he was right, he would say so and try to prevail. He wasn't afraid.

Ernest Kanzler was a threat to Sorensen and others who thrived on the lack of formal administration at the company. The two were locked in an ongoing struggle, which worked itself out with Sorensen encouraging Henry Ford to fire Kanzler and Kanzler encouraging Edsel Ford to fire Sorensen. According to Sorensen, both Henry and Clara Ford viewed Kanzler as an outsider who was taking advantage of Edsel and turning him into a pawn. Henry Ford stoked instability in the management ranks and perhaps enjoyed it as long as all of the various combatants were openly sycophantic toward him. But Kanzler was something else: an outsider, truly, and a man unafraid of Henry Ford.

A certain degree of unrest had always circled through the management ranks of Ford Motor Company. Insecurity fostered achievement in Henry Ford's view. The factionalism of the mid-1920s went far beyond that, though. Employees worked in abject fear, and that made many of them pull back and refrain from speaking out with new ideas, lest someone accuse them of complaining. "It was a matter of doing what you were told," said Alex Lumsden. "Instead of having the large viewpoint, you got restricted within yourself."[44] A form of mental paralysis was spreading through the ranks; it may not have been noticeable in the production figures, which were as robust as ever, but it wouldn't stay hidden for long.

The public, for the time being, was sheltered from the intracompany squabbles in the management ranks. The River Rouge complex was garnering glowing accolades in the media and art world as the new citadel of industrial democracy, the American version of the Taj Mahal or Chartres Cathedral. Numerous painters, including Dadaists Francis Picabia and Marcel Duchamp, celebrated automobiles as the aesthetic monuments to the modern world. The French painter Fernand Léger considered the geometric forms found at Michigan factories superior to the ornate palaces scattered across metropolitan Paris or Madrid. The entire new generation of artists, it seemed, wanted to tour the Rouge, the colossus of industrial design, and those who did were awed.

To further enhance the image of the Rouge as industrial and artistic icon, Edsel Ford commissioned the semiabstract painter and photographer Charles Sheeler to capture the essence of "the great American machine"[45] in late 1927. Born in Pennsylvania in 1883, Sheeler had a reputation as one of New York's most influential avant-garde photographers. Critics first lauded him for a series of exquisite photographs of Shaker and Quaker furniture. Sheeler made his living as a commercial photographer working for the Condé Nast publications *Vanity Fair* and *Vogue*. Upon arriving in Dearborn, camera case in hand, he was immediately drawn to the physical beauty of the Rouge. "Every age manifests the nature of its content by some external form of evidence," Sheeler wrote. "In a period such as ours, when only a few isolated individuals give evidence of religious content, some form other than that of the Gothic cathedral must be found for our authentic expression. Since industry predominately concerns the greatest numbers, finding an expression for it concerns the artists."[46] Sheeler was amazed to learn that Henry Ford had hired 5,000 men whose sole job it was to keep the factory buildings spotless. Unlike other industrial sites, there was a brightness to the Rouge, the machines glistened, and the air inside had a comparatively reduced amount of soot. Fresh coats of blue paint were applied whenever a railing or storage tank started chipping. A battalion of janitors with mops and brooms patroled the facility, making sure everything shined.

Overwhelmed by the modern efficiency, cleanliness, and size of the Rouge, Sheeler decided to photograph the "functionalism" of the factory, the geometric perfection of the steel beams and iron pillars and coal heaps. Ignoring a fascinating cast of working-class characters, like the 350-pound German weight lifter or the Lebanese die maker with twenty children, Sheeler instead kept his camera focused on the smokestacks and conveyor belts, the industrial symmetry of the entire Dearborn operation. The approximately thirty-two photographs he took are works of art. His most famous image, *Criss Cross Conveyor No. 6,* housed today in the Museum of Fine Arts in Boston, remains a classic example of industrial design becoming modern art.[47] Sheeler, in fact, was so moved by the Rouge that he also executed a series of paintings and crayon drawings of the complex in which he emphasized the abstract nature of the real world. And, as Edsel Ford had hoped, inviting Sheeler to document the Rouge had a dramatic upside for Ford Motor Company when the February 1928 issue of *Vanity Fair* featured a stunning collection of Sheeler's Rouge photographs. The magazine proclaimed that River Rouge was "the most significant public monument in America, throwing its shadows across the land probably more widely and more intimately than the United States Senate, the Metropolitan Museum of Art, the Statue of Liberty. . . . In a landscape where size, quantity, and speed are the cardinal virtues, it is natural that the largest factory turning out the most cars in the least time should come to have the quality of America's Mecca toward which the pious journey for prayer."[48]

Workers from all over America continually arrived in Dearborn hoping for a job at the famous River Rouge plant. It had become the citadel of the new industrial democracy taking root in America. In correspondence home, workers ignored the polluted river, the hectic pace, the daunting buildings, and the frowning people. They were mesmerized by the possibility of earning an honest hourly wage at the largest industrial facility the world had ever known. It felt good to be working for Henry Ford in the vortex of his automotive empire instead of toiling on some forlorn Iowa farm or isolated Minnesota lumber camp. "I hear they need men at Ford's" is the way the ambitious, redheaded young Walter Reuther of West Virginia told his mother of his new ambition while eating homemade *apfelkuchen.* "I am leaving for Detroit as soon as you can get me packed." Reuther was part of a "suitcase brigade" that migrated to the Detroit area in search of better, more lucrative jobs. For the next five and a half years he worked for Ford Motor Company, first at Highland Park and then at the Rouge complex. "Reuther thrived at the Rouge; both his wages and responsibilities rose steadily," biographer Nelson Lichtenstein wrote of the future union leader. "In 1929 he was classified as an 'A-1 Diemaker Leader,' at $1.40 an hour; still later he exercised the duties, if without the formal title, of a foreman in the B-Building tool and die room, where forty men worked under him. The experience put Reuther at the very apex of the working class; he later bragged that he was among the twenty highest-paid mechanics in the Ford Motor Company."[49]

As Walter Reuther would soon find out, all was not right, however, on the floor of the Rouge. Besides dodging the intrusions of Harry Bennett's service department, workers had to sidestep a minefield of ethnic conflict. The Freemason's order had grown into a powerful clique on the floor. They frowned upon Jews and Catholics and worked to make sure these "undesirables" were denied promotion. In general, the workers of northern European extraction at the Rouge viewed the more recent southern European immigrants as parasites undermining the American way. And it seemed to many workers that foremen were behaving more like gangsters working for the Ford mafia than fair-minded leaders of the rank and file. Given such conditions, the union movement began to percolate under the seemingly smooth production machine at the Rouge. The growing sentiment among the plant's workers in 1927–1928 was summed up by novelist Jack London: "Let us not destroy the wonderful machines that produce efficiently and cheaply, let us control them. Let us profit by their efficiency and cheapness. Let us run them ourselves. That, gentlemen, is socialism."[50] Taking more control, as London pointed out, did not mean workers loathed machines. Many day laborers were as smitten with tools and dies as Henry Ford. In fact, while one side of Walter Reuther's brain was contemplating the proletariat philosophies of Marx and Lenin, the machinist in him marveled at Ford Motor's venture into aviation and he felt lucky to help construct experimental wing sections for planes.[51] Even Henry Ford's detractors knew he was a revolutionary. After all, when Karl Marx began work on *Das Kapital* in the 1850s, the largest manufacturing company around was a cotton mill in Manchester, England, owned by his friend and collaborator Friedrich Engels. The company employed 300 men—the very number Ford Motor Company had hired simply to check employee ID badges upon entering the Rouge. Henry Ford was a force of nature. Those who knew it, and those who survived it, helped him build the River Rouge factory.

14

Lincoln Motor

O nce the mammoth plant at River Rouge was up and running in concert with operations at Highland Park, Ford Motor Company secured an even firmer hold on the "economy" car niche of the global automobile industry. And with more new drivers every year, that was certainly the fat end of the market. During the 1923–1924 sales season Model T Fords accounted for nearly 60 percent of all the automobiles made in the United States. In many ways Ford had begun to look like a monopoly, and that made it a target for corporate reformers.

The state of Mississippi filed suit against Ford Motor Company in 1924, charging it with violating antitrust laws. What seemed to trouble the prosecutors in Jackson most was that Ford's dealership contracts allowed the company to set prices on cars, leaving no room for competition. Moreover, because local Ford dealers were not allowed to sell other makes, the choice of vehicles available to customers in many small towns was limited to one car, the Model T. Several Mississippi lawmakers called for the breakup of Ford Motor Company into competitive units. That alternative might have been taken seriously fifteen years before, but the corporate trend of the early 1920s leaned toward consolidation and newly fashionable bigness. Nevertheless, the agitation in Jackson did present Ford Motor Company in a different light.

"We try not to be a trust," Henry Ford said in response to the Mississippi lawsuit. "We sell our product at the lowest price possible and make it as good as possible." No one could deny that. Yet the result in the marketplace, from Oxford, Mississippi, to Montevideo, Uruguay, was to leave customers on limited budgets no choice but the Ford Model T. Mississippi's antitrust case was dismissed on appeal, but Ford Motor could not so easily dispel the fears that had prompted it. "We're coming into big business," Henry Ford forewarned in May 1925, "and business will grow bigger and bigger. What we are today and

293

what other big businesses are today will look like subsidiary businesses in comparison with what we and the others probably will be fifteen years from now."[1]

The tide had indeed shifted in the automobile industry. While the number of startups had naturally dropped right after the business's infancy at the turn of the century, between 1910 and 1921 the car market boomed, and more firms entered the industry than left it.[2] That second generation included outright sports cars such as Stutz and Kissell, family cars such as Chandler and Saxon, and peppy performance cars including Cord and Chevrolet. A number of the new entries were built by Ford Motor alumni: the Dodge, of course, was the most formidable. Others were the Wills–Sainte Claire, produced by Harold Wills and John Lee, and the Gray, in which former Ford treasurer Frank Klingensmith had an interest.[3] The 1910s saw a U.S. auto industry bursting with big ideas, eager customers, and investors who were all too keenly aware of the vast returns a lucky few had received on their Ford Motor Company stock.

However, the proliferation of automakers ended abruptly with the depression of 1920–1921, which shook Ford Motor and every other company in the business. Nineteen percent of all U.S. car manufacturers went out of business in that single year, and the field's fierce competition continued to claim comers even after the economy came back stronger than ever. Where eighty-eight American automakers operated in 1921, their number shrank to fifty-nine by 1924. Some of the best-known marques folded under the new pressure, including White, National, and Lafayette. Even Winton, America's oldest car company, established in 1897, was defunct as of 1923.

In that treacherous era, two very different Detroit automakers stood out as successes. The first was that enormous and enormously efficient monument to mass production, Ford Motor Company. The second was the Lincoln Motor Company, founded by Henry Leland.

Leland was, of course, the precision engineer who had usurped Henry Ford's place at the Henry Ford Company in 1902, renaming the firm Cadillac.[4] Under Leland, Cadillac attained a reputation for building one of the world's finest luxury cars. All the while, according to many who knew him, Leland could not stop competing on some level with Henry Ford. "Henry M. Leland, tall, whiskered, almost fanatical in some of his utterances, and an engineer with a wide reputation, was opposed to Ford," postulated advertising agency owner Theodore F. MacManus. "Leland, the engineer, was caustic [toward] Ford, the inventor."[5]

In 1904, Henry Leland assumed full management of Cadillac, in association with his son, Wilfred C. Leland, and engineer Ernest Sweet. A Cadillac worker watching the new team approach the factory on their first official day quipped, "Our troubles are over now. . . . Here come the father, son, and holy ghost."[6] All joking aside, the Lelands did occupy a top notch in the hierarchy of Detroit's young automaking industry.

Like Henry Ford, Leland was fortunate to have a son who was a highly competent executive in his own right. And like Edsel, Wilfred was more involved in administration than in engineering or design. He deserves a large measure of the credit for his father's later success. While all of Henry Leland's kin didn't prove as talented, a great number of them seemed to find jobs anyway with the tall, white-bearded old man known around the Cadillac factory floor as "Uncle Henry." Under the Leland regime, the company quickly carved out its own niche among U.S. carmakers. Other luxury automobile manufacturers also established reputations for excellence—Packard, Lozier, Pierce-Arrow, Locomobile, Peerless, and McFarland all built superb machines still coveted by collectors today—but Cadillac led the field. It not only routinely outsold its rivals in the high-priced segment but made the top ten in overall U.S. auto sales every year from 1904 through 1915. After that, thanks in large part to drivers ready to trade up from their Ford Model Ts, the market for low- and medium-priced cars surged ahead and left demand for high-end luxury cars lagging, at least in numbers. But the success of Cadillac transcended mere commerce. The Lelands elevated engineering into an art, pioneering the use of Johansson gauges imported from Sweden in automaking. They managed to lower tolerances in Cadillac components to a thousandth of an inch—mind-boggling for 1907.[7] But that was only the start.

By producing parts with such consistent precision, Cadillac easily attained a goal long sought by automakers around the world: car assembly using interchangeable parts. Before the Lelands succeeded in machining all the parts the same—or at least to within a thousandth of an inch—components had to be adjusted or replaced during assembly; because the parts were not uniform, neither were the cars built from them. At the time the Lelands neglected to publicize the production breakthrough, believing that customers cared more how a car ran than how it was made. Cadillac's English representative knew better. Under the auspices of London's Royal Automobile Club, he arranged a truly daring test of the engineering feat in 1908, wherein three Cadillacs would be dismantled, their 721 parts mixed up and then reassembled into cars—in full public view and without fuss, tinkering, or jimmying.

With paint schemes mismatched here and there, the three reassembled Cadillacs stood in the snow and rain at the Brooklands racetrack near London before a crowd doubtful they would run. The first two cars started on the first crank. The third took two cranks, which was the only cause for complaint as the trio went on to run perfectly over 500 miles. Cadillac's coup may look pallid next to the sixteen-second miracles wrought by race crews in routine pit stops today, but in the first decade of the twentieth century, it was an achieve-

ment that energized and inspired carmakers around the world with the realization that a high-production car could still be a high-quality automobile. As
the auto industry moved forward, Leland's advance became much more than
just a selling point for Cadillacs. After all, Henry Ford could never have pioneered assembly-line automobile production had Leland not developed interchangeable parts first.[8]

Old Henry Leland proclaimed that his finely tuned machines were "made
to run, not just to sell," and he meant it. His top-quality cars gained him such
renown as an auto manufacturer by the First World War that the U.S. Post
Office learned where to deliver the many letters addressed simply to "Henry
Leland, USA." The future head of General Motors, Alfred P. Sloan Jr., then
the young president of the Hyatt Roller Bearing Company, was among his admirers. "He was a generation older than I," Sloan said of Leland, "and I looked
upon him as an elder not only in age but in engineering wisdom. He was a
fine, creative, intelligent person. Quality was his god."[9]

Yet Leland was hardly a popular figure around the factory. Stubborn, demanding, and brutally candid, he not only ruffled feathers but made notable
enemies. Like Henry Ford, he couldn't abide people who didn't share his
views, instances of which he cut to a minimum by running Cadillac as a dic-
tatorship. Employees caught sneaking a cigarette on the job faced summary
discharge; those found drinking alcohol on or off the company's premises
met a similar fate. Character flaws—other people's—loomed as large before
Leland as they did to Henry Ford.[10]

The Cadillac Motor Car Company grew to be prosperous as well as respected, and so did the Lelands. Accordingly, in 1909, William C. Durant appeared with an offer to purchase the company for his new General Motors
Corporation, founded the year before. Buick and Oldsmobile were the first
two cornerstones in what Durant envisioned as a complete automotive consortium. Cadillac would fit in very nicely at the top. The industry consensus at
the time, however, held that GM needed Cadillac far more than the Lelands'
thriving firm needed GM. Billy Durant was nothing if not persuasive, though,
and so was the stock market arithmetic behind his argument. By the end of
the summer of 1909 Wilfred Leland had agreed to sell Cadillac for $4.5 mil-
lion in General Motors stock, the most ever paid for an American automobile
company to that point. Meanwhile, however, Durant was dangling an offer of
$8 million before Henry Ford and James Couzens for their low-end firm.[11]

Ford and Couzens told Durant to come back when he had the $8 million
in cash rather than just stock, and then they could talk. The Lelands, by contrast, had already been swayed to believe in the idea behind General Motors:
separate companies profiting from economies of scale by pooling their technology and purchasing. Only a year after Cadillac joined the growing collection of car and parts makers under the rubric of GM, however, Durant

overextended his resources in the stock market, as was his habit, and lost control of the corporation. A team of New York and Boston bankers swiftly expressed interest in assuming control of General Motors in exchange for an immediate $15 million investment in the enterprise. According to Wilfred Leland, these putative financiers preferred to hold back their cash until they were satisfied that the Lelands would have full responsibility for automotive production not just at Cadillac but throughout the GM roster of companies. Whether the moment of decision played out that dramatically or not, Henry Leland and his son agreed to take on the added responsibilities. They ran GM for the next five years under the bankers' auspices with the help of straight-talking corporate executives such as GM's new president Charles Nash and Buick's rising star manager Walter Chrysler, both of whom would later start car companies of their own. Anchored by the success of the Buick and Cadillac divisions, General Motors turned a fair profit catering to the middle- and upper-tier automobile markets.[12]

Durant was through with neither GM nor the car business in general. Just as Alexander Malcomson had once taken note of Henry Ford because of his exploits on the racetrack, Durant picked out a rough-edged Frenchman named Louis Chevrolet, who was enjoying successful seasons on the track in 1910 and 1911. Durant quickly snapped him up to serve as chief engineer at Durant's new Chevrolet Motor Company. The firm's initial offering, the huge, throaty-rumbling Classic Six, came elaborately outfitted for the wealthy consumer, right down to its whopping $2,150 sticker price. Durant, however, changed his thinking, recognizing that to compete with Ford's Model T, or at least to chase it, he needed to sell lesser Chevrolets in higher volume. A rift ensued. The vainglorious Louis Chevrolet insisted that his name belonged on a big luxury car. In 1913, he sold his stock for next to nothing and returned to France, remaining furious at Durant ever afterward for devaluing his name. It was a terribly costly mistake; Louis Chevrolet soon went broke and could only watch as Durant built the company into a commanding success. Chevrolet died a poor man on June 6, 1941, at the age of sixty-three, in a small Florida apartment. "Like David Dunbar Buick before him," observed James J. Flink in his book *The Automobile Age,* "Louis Chevrolet slipped into personal obscurity while his name became a household word."[13]

In 1916, Durant used his Chevrolet stock to regain control of General Motors, through one of those stock market parries at which he excelled. As head of GM once again, he was as voracious as ever. The abandon with which Durant acquired companies—some of which turned out to be worthless—made even his most loyal lieutenants nervous. As to its skeptics, it frequently drove them away. Charles Nash, a conservative executive who had been perfectly comfortable with the pace and priorities set by the Boston bankers, quit when Durant returned. He lost no time in starting his own company: Nash Motor

Company in Kenosha, Wisconsin (built on the remnants of the old Rambler maker, Thomas B. Jeffery Company). Henry and Wilfred Leland remained at GM, although they were at heart even more conservative than Nash. Inevitably, their strong opinions clashed with Durant's and there was a break, yet it was politics rather than business that led to the final schism.

The Lelands followed the events in the early years of World War I carefully, and hoped that the United States would enter the conflict in aid of the Allies. When America did send troops to France in 1917, Henry Leland, then seventy-three, was determined to do his part. He and his son suggested to Durant that Cadillac begin production of engines for the U.S. government. Yet Billy Durant, like Henry Ford, was a committed pacifist. Besides, 1916 had been a record year for Cadillac, with sales of 18,003 cars, and Durant was not about to give up hard-won momentum.

Refusing to work for a pacifist, Leland wanted to quit GM. The question was, what would he do next? As a twenty-year-old, Henry Leland, still in his native Vermont, had idolized Abraham Lincoln. He made his contribution to the Union cause in the Civil War by making guns in the Arsenal at Springfield, Massachusetts. In 1917, he was compelled to adopt something of the same spirit, traveling to Washington to offer his services as an expert engine maker.[14] He returned with enough encouragement to resign from Cadillac, with Wilfred in tow, and organize a company dedicated to the manufacture of engines. It was called the Lincoln Motor Company, named after his hero and the first president for whom he had ever cast a ballot. Leland had long collected artifacts related to Abraham Lincoln and even had a separate room in which to display them at his home. As head of the new firm, he had a marvelous statue of the Great Emancipator erected in front of the new Lincoln Motor administration building.

The Lelands eventually secured an irrevocable contract for V-12 Liberty engines from the U.S. government, a comfortable basis on which to start their company. Organizing a factory in a rented building on, coincidentally, Lincoln Street in Detroit, the Lelands threw themselves into the development of the Liberty engine. "Quite a few of the Cadillac boys came and that was the beginning of the Lincoln Motor Company," recalled Walter Wagner, one of the high-end GM recruits. "It was a wonderful group made up of practical, long-experienced men. It was natural to start building motors because these men were all motor men."[15]

Wartime restrictions on resources obviated any chance of constructing a factory in the modish steel-and-concrete style pioneered by Albert Kahn, so the Lincoln Motor Company instead installed itself in an old-fashioned building of red brick and wood, suited somehow to its values.[16] Between the factory's opening at the end of August 1917 and the armistice in November

1918, Lincoln built 6,000 of the 7,500 Liberty engines originally ordered by the U.S. government. (For its part, Cadillac reconsidered its pacifist stance and also did a respectable amount of war work.)

As the conflict drew to a close, Lincoln Motor Company was in the same position as a great many of the returning soldiers: no money and nothing to do. During 1919, Henry Leland busied himself with plans for a new car, a glorious culmination to everything he knew about engineering. His standards reached as high as ever, and his latest ambition still higher. "When he made speeches to us he would quiver a little bit and grope for the right kind of words," Walter Wagner remembered of his boss's passion. "He didn't hesitate to stand on the soap box, get the gang of executives together, and just lay it out to them when things weren't going right."[17]

The news that drifted out about Leland's new automobile sparked immense interest among the public. And how could it not, when word was the Lincoln would be the most expensive American car on the market? Indeed, the scuttlebutt leading into the 1920 season held that even the top-of-the-line Packard Twin Six, at $5,500, would fall short in price of the *least* expensive Lincoln, which rumor had it would command a whopping $6,100; at the time a new Ford cost $370. For more than sixteen times as much as a basic Model T, Leland planned to sell an automobile propulsive in power and outlandish in comfort. The inaugural Lincoln "L" series would boast a compact, high-horsepower V-8 engine of a completely new design. The Leland team employed the most advanced engineering of the day, making use of state-of-the-art metal alloys and creating unusual fork-and-blade-type connecting rods. The Leland obsession for quality was such that every engine was run for five hours on a dynamometer, then torn down and examined, then reassembled and tested again before being installed in the L-series chassis. The careful balance of the engine and a sophisticated drive mechanism promised a "vibrationless" ride in the Lincoln. Customers couldn't wait.[18]

The company may as well have been called "Leland" as far as the public was concerned, because the common opinion was that the Lincoln would be a new and improved Cadillac—and everyone who knew cars knew that it was Henry Leland who had set the "standard of excellence" about which Cadillac bragged in its advertising. Investors were just as enthusiastic over the Lelands' steady record in turning profits. When the Lincoln Motor Company was incorporated in January 1920 for the purpose of producing cars, $6.5 million was invested, almost solely on the basis of the Leland name. The 10 percent of the shares offered to the public was snapped up in just three hours.[19] When the first cars were delivered on schedule in September, customers were thrilled with the performance, but there was one thing that Henry Leland forgot: looks count where money and cars meet.

Even Lincoln Motor Company's sales manager, Ralph C. Getsinger, admitted that the new styles looked "suspiciously like pre–World War I Cadillacs."[20] At one point, the dealers organized to visit the Lincoln factory and demand better styling. The person in charge of body styling at Lincoln was Henry Leland's son-in-law, Angus Woodbridge, who had formerly managed a dress shop in Detroit.[21] The Lelands admitted that his work was inadequate and began to solicit designs from independent coach-building companies. The body styling was a problem that could have been remedied during the wave of enthusiasm for the first Lincolns. Unfortunately, that first wave was itself frozen by the depression of 1920–1921. There could not have been a worse time to introduce a new nameplate. In early 1921, desperate for help, Wilfred Leland hired an industrial management consultant from Boston to reorganize the Lincoln operation. The immediate result was predictable: the company's own executives became disenfranchised and many of them quit. The consultant, William H. Ebelhare, was named superintendent of the plant.[22] With that, there was another migration of Lincoln executives—many of those who had come over from Cadillac returned there. Production continued to slow, and within months, the Ebelhare regime was dismissed. The Lincoln factory was in turmoil.

In November 1920, production delays at Lincoln made it impossible for the company to turn cars out on a schedule, angering good customers. As cancellations mounted, economic gloom settled over the country.

Lincoln Motor Company was mired in debt, having purchased its tooling and materials at the height of the postwar inflation; sales of Lincolns fell along with those of every other make. To buy time, the Lelands tried to interest a group of bankers into extending a loan. The group dutifully toured the factory, but concluded that the situation was hopeless; according to their comments afterward, Lincoln had missed its market by initiating sales so late in 1920.[23] If Henry Leland hadn't insisted on devoting a year and a half to planning the new model, there might have been enough momentum to sustain the company through the national reversal. As it was, the factory closed early in 1921, but managed to open again in March.

The bankers were wrong, though—the situation at Lincoln wasn't hopeless when they visited. It only became *truly* hopeless in the fall of 1921, when the U.S. government slapped the tottering company with a bill for $4 million in back taxes. At the time the Lelands were in New York begging for a bridge loan from yet another set of bankers. Upon receiving word of the enormous tax assessment against their company, Henry and Wilfred Leland quietly packed their bags and headed back to Detroit. Making matters worse, a special investigative committee of the House of Representatives looking into irregularities in various World War I defense contracts had begun to home in on Lincoln Motor. Piquing the committee's interest was the finding that Lincoln Motor had been paid for its full order of 7,500 airplane engines, but had delivered only 6,500 of them. Although the government itself had halted further deliveries when the war ended, the fact remained that Lincoln had been paid for motors it had never built. Thanks to the intervention of the man who had defeated Henry Ford, Michigan Senator Truman Newberry, Lincoln Motor evaded a full-scale investigation, even though several members of the House committee maintained that the firm had been overpaid by as much as $9 million.[24] For his part, Ford seems to have had little to say about the problems at Lincoln. He and Henry Leland had an amicable relationship, despite their ugly collision at the Henry Ford Company in 1902, but they were a generation apart. The closest bond between the families was the friendship of Clara Ford and Ottilie M. Leland, Wilfred's wife.[25]

"Say, have you heard about the improvement in the new model Fords?" began a joke of the time. "They're hanging a set of whiskers on all the radiators."

"What's the big idea?"

"It's to make them look more like Lincolns" went the punchline.[26] That joke seemed to be the closest that Ford and Lincoln would ever be.

In November 1921 Lincoln Motor Company had to shut down again while Henry and Wilfred Leland scrambled to find a loan to sustain the enterprise. Without their consent the firm's directors caved in to creditors and filed to place Lincoln under bankruptcy protection. The assets were transferred to a receiver, who began to organize the accounts in anticipation of a sale. In December, the U.S. Internal Revenue Department admitted that it had made an error in calculating the amount Lincoln Motor owed the government in back taxes. Instead of the daunting $4 million bill that had effectively scuttled the automaker, it turned out that only $500,000 was due.[27] For the Lelands it was a bittersweet victory. They might have muddled through the crisis under the more manageable debt. In any case, the new figure gave them fresh hope of realizing their goals for the bankruptcy auction: first, that enough cash would be raised to pay off the company's creditors; second, that the stockholders would be compensated; and third, that they might find some way to remain at Lincoln Motor themselves. To that end, Wilfred Leland called upon Henry Ford at the Fair Lane estate in Dearborn, "entering by the back gate in secrecy," according to Ottilie Leland, "as Ford did not want the negotiations publicly known."[28] The younger Leland presented the case that an infusion of cash would set Lincoln back on the right path, in a much better economic climate. Yet Wilfred Leland left Fair Lane with nothing more concrete than sympathy.

Although the Ford family owned several Cadillacs for formal use, such luxurious cars were at heart antithetical to the soul of Henry Ford's own business. As Ford asserted in his 1923 memoir, at Ford Motor "the key to peak efficiency was high volume." The opposite held true at Lincoln, where 6,000 workers strove to craft a mere 5,000 cars per year, and even then they came up short. At Ford, by contrast, some 150,000 employees turned out 1.8 million Model Ts in 1922. But Clara Ford took an interest in her friend's plight, and lobbied her husband to help the Lelands' ailing concern. His vague response that he would look into the matter did not satisfy her, so she turned to her son Edsel. Although Clara wielded some of the power and a lot of the good sense in the Fair Lane household, the odds of making the acquisition a reality were still long. As natural as the pairing of Ford and Lincoln seems today, during the ascendancy of the utilitarian Model T and the decline of the luxurious Lincoln, the notion that the two could ever meet in anything but a fender bender on some city street seemed preposterous.

Early in January 1922, the judge in the Lincoln Motor bankruptcy case set an auction date for February 4.[29] At the time Lincoln was just one of twenty-eight going U.S. carmakers forced to fold. Henry Ford could not bother himself about all of them, but his wife and son banded together to insist that he examine the situation surrounding Lincoln—and that he consider buying it. The Ford family was close, seeing one another practically every day. However, as in any family, tempers and affections had an ebb and flow. Clara, for example, was said to have been more distant toward Edsel after she found out that he smoked cigarettes—and enjoyed them. That was never quite forgiven, according to family friends. Henry and Edsel, for all of the voids in their relationship at work, had a special camaraderie at home. According to some accounts, Edsel was more easygoing around his father than his mother. That January, however, Clara and Edsel were very much on the same wavelength as they recognized in Lincoln Motor a rare opportunity. Their intervention emphasizes the fact that the ownership of Ford Motor among the three Fords was not merely a gallant gesture on the part of Henry or a clever move by his accountants. The three did share influence, at least occasionally. "Edsel, unlike his father, loved expensive cars of the Lincoln type and it is quite possible that he saw the Lincoln company as a place outside his father's interest where he could exercise some real authority for a change," historian Thomas E. Bonsall surmised. "Whatever the case, Edsel was destined to play a central role in the development of the Lincoln."[30]

Edsel was convinced that the Lincoln was a superb automobile, made by a company with the kinds of flaws, such as cost inefficiency, materials handling, and logistics, that Ford Motor could fix. He surmised that the backing of a $1 billion company couldn't hurt Lincoln's herky-jerky cash flow, either. The question was what tiny Lincoln could do for mighty Ford. The answer was simple and also very, very complex: General Motors.

After the Lelands had left to form their own company in 1917, William

Durant still had an impressive organization, an amalgamation of both car and parts makers. Motivated by his soaring ambition, Durant continued to authorize growth of practically any and every type at the corporation. Aside from plant expansion for the divisions, he gave in to a buying binge, acquiring weak auto companies that added nothing but debt to the corporation. In late 1920, when the economy slowed, GM fell into the same trough that caught every automaker at the time. As with all companies, bad economic times reveal problems in the business, and at GM the depression uncovered huge gaps in the structure of the organization and in the controls used to gauge it. As the price of GM stock tumbled, William Durant was thrown into a personal crisis, since he had borrowed the equivalent of $20 million against his GM stock. To keep him from defaulting and rocking the financial footing of the corporation, two major eastern institutions stepped in and bought him out. The first was J.P. Morgan and Company, the New York bank known as "the corner" in financial circles. The second was the du Pont family, which had taken a position in GM several years before, largely to participate in a business that was fast developing into a good customer for chemicals and paints. After the buyout, Durant was left with stock worth about $3 million, complaining bitterly that the easterners had conspired to snatch control of GM (if so, then he had certainly made it easy for them, with his unnecessary stock market trapeze act).[31] After leaving GM, he almost immediately sold the stock he'd been allotted in order to start yet another multiline car company, Durant Motors. He was not the only entrepreneur in the field: Walter Chrysler was working toward the same goal, as was E. L. Cord of the Auburn Automobile Company in Indiana.[32]

If Henry Ford thought that GM's new pace of success in the medium- and high-priced brackets didn't affect him, Clara and particularly Edsel were not so certain. Ford Motor had to grow beyond flivvers eventually, and Lincoln Motor, a good property for all of its business problems, was a fitting first step. On January 11, 1922, Henry Ford announced that he would make a bid for the company, but only if the Lelands would continue to run it.[33] Sentimentalists hailed the news. Skeptics, including Edwin Pipp, former editor of the *Dearborn Independent,* predicted that it would take only a few months for Henry Ford to prove that he couldn't give anyone autonomy in one of his factories. The Lelands, however, were confident. After all, William Durant had left them alone to operate Cadillac after he bought it for GM in 1909, and so had the Boston bankers. They looked forward to a productive new era under the Ford umbrella.

The price for Lincoln Motor Company was first set at $5 million, but the federal judge monitoring the sale raised the figure to $8 million to protect the creditors. On the morning of February 4, Henry Ford's representative made an initial bid of $8 million for Lincoln at the receiver's sale. Ford was prepared to go to $11 million, but since no other bids came forth, he bought the company for the minimum. "We have built more cars than anyone else," Henry Ford calmly told reporters, "and now we are going to build a better car than anyone else."[34] The signing of the documents took place at the Lincoln administration offices, under the gaze of no less than four portraits of the sixteenth president. A photograph of that compelling ceremony exists today. The founders of the two firms, Henry Ford and Henry Leland, are standing impassively in the back of the room, seeming secondary figures to the merger. The moment belongs to their sons, seated at an elegant table, doing the actual signing. For Wilfred, it is clearly the end of something he felt deep inside of himself: he looks off into space, gloomily. For Edsel, though, it is only the beginning. Clearly full of energy, he looks into the camera with all the youthful authority he could muster.[35]

The rest of the day turned into a celebration at the Lincoln factory, as thousands of cheering employees heard the good news that production would begin again the following Monday. Henry Ford was there, roundly praised for his good deed. He offered no speech, maintaining his usual reticence in public, though his formidable presence couldn't be missed, as a huge banner of his face was unfurled against the exterior of the redbrick factory. "There is not much to say about the sale," he told a reporter, "other than I am extremely happy that I was able to purchase the plant."[36] Edsel Ford was even happier, and confided to a golf companion named J. Bell Moran, "Father made the most popular car in the world; I would like to make the best car in the world."[37]

In the aftermath, the absorption of Lincoln undoubtedly proved to be better for the car than for its creators. Only four months after entering wholeheartedly into the new arrangement, the Lelands found themselves unneeded. Then they were unwelcome, told to leave—fired. The specter of seventy-nine-year-old Henry Leland being escorted from the grounds with his personal belongings in hand was painful for all those who considered him "the Father of the Automobile" in Detroit. It was as though Santa Claus were being deported. Wilfred Leland's wife settled her family's grudge against Henry Ford in her 1958 biography of her husband, co-authored by Minnie Dubbs Millbrook, titled *Master of Precision.* In no uncertain terms the authors claim that Ford had "deliberately set out to cheat and humiliate his family."[38]

Ultimately, the Lelands left Ford Motor under the same circumstances that forced most senior executives out in Henry Ford's heyday. It was a recognizable three-step process. They found their authority countermanded, usually by Charles Sorensen; they then obtained a renewed pledge of loyalty from Henry Ford who invariably promised that things would change; but just as invariably things did not change, and when they grumbled, Ford was through with them. The management style at Ford Motor Company in the 1920s was based on equal parts brute force, calculated manipulation, and recent achievement. The Lelands were weak in each category. Accustomed to presuming authority for himself and his father, Wilfred took to complaining in hopes of regaining their leadership position. They learned the hard way that complaining was almost never effective with Henry Ford. It only inspired his antipathy.

The dismissals reflected badly on Henry Ford, and the Lelands tried shaming him with unfavorable publicity. Their efforts failed: Ford maintained goodwill in an entirely unexpected way. At about the time that Ford bought Lincoln Motor, another creditor was added to the list of businesses and suppliers to whom the company owed money—the U.S. government. After investigating the Congressional charges that Lincoln had been overpaid during the wartime rush to build Liberty engines, a judge ruled that the company return $1.5 million. The figure was less than the $9 million originally bandied about in Washington, but it nonetheless presented an added burden when Lincoln was in receivership. The only asset Lincoln Motor had was the $8 million that Ford had paid to buy the company. Having identified the outstanding obligations, the court paid them off, according to a prescribed priority. Some, like the demand from the government, were paid off in full while others received an equal share of the remaining cash; in Lincoln Motor's case, the company's creditors—businesses that had extended materials or services—received forty-three cents on each dollar of debt. It was tough on the suppliers, but standard in business, and they had no other recourse. After the news sank in, Henry Ford made a bold announcement: he would make up the difference, so that creditors would receive the full amount due. It was a stunning gesture, one that cost the magnate $4 million.[39]

Henry Ford was praised anew, especially in business circles, because he had had no obligation whatsoever to pay off the old Lincoln Motor Company's debts. Perhaps he was interested, as ever, in promoting his image as a humanitarian. Even Henry Ford's most cutting critics gave up trying to find the ulterior motive in the move. Ford had made good.

At about the same time, Ford Motor Company passed through the scrutiny of the same House committee investigating war profits without incurring any fines for overpayment. More telling, though, Ford escaped widespread publicity about his own personal *non*repayment of war profits. Only a few people were rankled by the fact that in 1917, when Henry Ford first pressed his company into the production of war matériel, he made the public and very patriotic promise to return his share of profits on war work. Whenever that promise was recollected, it was cited in admiring terms, with the assumption that Ford had actually sent a check to Washington. Yet when Secretary of the Treasury Andrew Mellon reminded Ford of the promise in 1922, noting that the government had yet to receive any surrendered profits, he was told that the records were still being audited. The audit was never completed to the extent that any profits were returned. There was nothing illegal about that: he didn't actually owe the money he had promised. But Henry Ford was first and foremost a master of publicity, and there was nothing fresh for him to gain by returning war profits—only in promising that he would.

Restitution for the creditors, as fine as that gesture may have been, wasn't enough to placate the Lelands. They maintained that Henry Ford had made a promise to them early on, not only to pay off the creditors but to buy out the shareholders. Henry Leland wanted to rest easy, knowing that no one but himself had been harmed by Lincoln's failure. After leaving the company for good, the Lelands tried through legal means and social pressures to force Henry Ford to buy out 2,400 original stockholders of Lincoln Motor—the second part of the promise they contended that he had made. Ford, however, had no interest in stocks or the people who traded in them, and he considered that most of the people who ended up with Lincoln shares were speculators, hoping to receive a payout from Ford. Considering the rather strange phenomenon that heavy trading in the stock continued right up until the day of the bankruptcy auction, he was probably right. Nonetheless, the Lelands struggled unsuccessfully to make Henry Ford pay. Lincoln's sales manager, Ralph C. Getsinger, remembered a luncheon at which Ford told Henry Leland, "'Mrs. Ford asked me what we were going to do about the stockholders. And,' he said, 'you know what I told her? I told her if they would come out to Dearborn, we'd give them a badge and put them to work.'"[40] In 1931 the Michigan Supreme Court ruled in Ford's favor in this matter.

One year after the last appeal had been lost, Henry Leland died in 1932 at age eighty-nine; seventy years of active work had not tired him as much as had his last four months at Ford Motor. Despite all that he had accomplished in launching both Cadillac and Lincoln, he had to accept that in relation to Henry Ford, he was as helpless as a baby.

The widespread opinion was that after Henry Leland left Lincoln in 1922 the great car would fade from glory. On the contrary, though, Ford's men showed that they did indeed know how to make cars, even luxury ones. True to Ford style, a new atmosphere was instilled into the plant. "The advent of Ford in 1922 put everyone to work in a big way," said Walter Wagner of the Lincoln plant. "We all became very busy. . . . There was money to work with and we had more leeway to accomplish bigger and greater things, such as putting in special machinery, conveyor systems, and modernizing the plant along the pattern of the Ford Motor Company."[41] Edsel Ford was named president of Lincoln, a natural post for the cultivated young man, with his brother-in-law Ernest Kanzler as general manager. In its first year under the Lelands (during a depression), Lincoln Motor had manufactured just over 700 cars. In its first year as a division of Ford, Lincoln output increased to 5,242 cars. The new regime didn't meddle with the mechanical aspects of the car; they wisely resisted tampering with the elegant Leland engineering they had inherited.

The Model L retained the V-8 engine, along with the rest of Leland's innovations.

Edsel was given a free hand as master of Lincoln's destiny and Ford's vast resources; steel mills, research, and all were at his disposal. He also approached coach makers like LeBaron and Fleetwood (before it was acquired by GM) for innovative designs. One of the decisions attributed to Edsel was the use of a racing greyhound dog as the Lincoln's hood ornament. "[Edsel] had exquisite taste and appreciation for really well designed automobiles," designer John Tjaarda recalled. "It was pleasant to work with a man of this caliber, truly a pleasure. Such discernment."[42] Edsel's preoccupation with design and detail demonstrated how different father and son were, for Henry Ford was frank to admit that he neither enjoyed nor understood automotive styling. Coach builder Herman Brunn of Buffalo worked closely with Edsel to produce styles that were much more cohesive than before, with flowing lines, longer hoods, and those cues—a nickel-plated rim on the radiator or a canvas-covered hardtop—that made a car a fashion accessory, something to look good in.[43] In 1927, competing coach builders offered limited-edition coachwork for Lincolns with interior decoration in the style of, for example, ancient Egypt, complete with faux papyrus. Beautiful styling didn't hurt luxury car sales then and hasn't ever since. Automobile enthusiasts even marveled that the Lincoln factory was more refined than the Rouge. "The Ford works have been described as a 'mechanical hell' where the sizzling hot metal finds no peace until it is tortured and assembled into a complete car, to an unceasing chorus of 'hurry, hurry, hurry!'" the *New Zealand Fordist* reported in October 1922. "But the atmosphere of the Lincoln works may be likened to a 'mechanical cathedral' where its builders worship at the altar of accuracy, accuracy, and still more accuracy."[44]

While maintaining or even raising the standard of the Lincoln as an automobile, Ford Motor Company supported it through extensive marketing campaigns that the company could never have afforded under the Lelands. Prospective customers received invitations to the "Lincoln *Salon Petite,*" as it traveled from city to city. At the *salon,* usually staged in a swank hotel, doormen wore livery and salesmen were in tuxedos, while even the cars themselves were surrounded by flowers and fountains. It was a cunning marketing exercise designed to make people with a keen eye for status look past the small blue emblem on the radiator—the one that read, "Ford-built Lincoln." Model T Fords were well built in their own way, but they weren't status symbols among people with $6,000 to spend on a car.[45]

The question naturally arose whether Ford Motor dealers would be expected to sell Lincolns or whether Lincolns should have their own dealer outlets. After much debate the prevailing sentiment was that Lincoln should be separated from Ford salesrooms because "buying a Lincoln at a Ford Agency was like buying expensive jewelry at a five-and-ten store." Model T dealers, whose stock in trade was delivered uncrated, minus body, and stacked twenty-eight to a railroad car, were stunned at the careful manner of a Lincoln delivery: they all had special paper covers, were shipped in closed boxcars, were meticulously washed before drop-off, and an inspector made sure that the paintwork was not even slightly marred or defected. "Very high grade dealers represent Lincoln locally in all parts of this country," a Ford motor advertisement read. "In every important population center there is a Lincoln dealer with experienced men and complete service facilities to match the very high quality and reputation of the car."[46]

The expense alone of delivering the Lincoln to its dealers would have overwhelmed Leland's budget. Without the intervention of Ford Motor Company, Lincoln probably wouldn't have survived. Indeed, during the Great Depression independent luxury carmakers were wiped out at the rate of about one per year: Kissell (1931), Peerless (1932), Marmon (1933), Franklin (1934), Stutz (1935), Duesenberg (1937), Pierce-Arrow (1938). It is a list that might easily have included Lincoln, if the company hadn't procured the patronage of Ford Motor. By the time New York Yankees manager Joe McCarthy presented Babe Ruth with a Lincoln-Zephyr convertible on April 29, 1940, for being "Home Run King," it had earned a reputation as an American "dream machine."[47]

Over the years Lincoln would come to be known as the "car of presidents." Calvin Coolidge, a friend of Henry Ford, placed an order for a 1924 Model L for official use. Herbert Hoover used the same vehicle to travel through America after the onset of the Great Depression. The first Lincoln extensively modified for presidential use was the 1939 "Sunshine Special," a parade car used by Franklin Roosevelt, Harry Truman, and Dwight Eisenhower, respectively. The Lincoln best known in presidential history was the open car in which President John F. Kennedy was assassinated on November 22, 1963. Conspiracy buffs make much of the fact that Abraham Lincoln was shot in the Ford Theatre, while John F. Kennedy was shot in a Lincoln—made by Ford.

That brings up the fact that Henry Ford even one-upped Henry Leland in collecting Abraham Lincoln memorabilia, acquiring the chair in which the sixteenth president was shot while at the theater; Ford paid $2,400 for the chair at a December 1929 auction.[48] Most presidents since Kennedy have continued to use Lincolns: Ford Motor Company has increasingly added state-of-the-art security apparatus, giving the presidential limousines tanklike strength.[49]

From Ford's point of view, Lincoln Motor Company was hardly an immediate success in commercial terms, failing to return steady profits until after World War II. In that case, the argument could be made that Ford should not have entered the production of luxury cars until the late 1940s. However, that misses one of the hidden strengths of the acquisition, and of automobile combines in general. While Ford certainly saved Lincoln, the reverse was also true: Ford Motor Company desperately needed executives versed in something other than building Model Ts. That was rather difficult at a firm where the boss had ripped off the doors of the prototype of another model—and took a hammer to what was left. If Lincoln had been nothing more than a training ground for fresh ideas, it would have been worth $8 million to Ford Motor. It gave an opening to those wanting to dream up new cars and new businesses.

15

———⟨⟩———

Ford Aviation

F rom 1921 to 1926, Ford Motor Company was simultaneously involved
in four pursuits that would have demanded the exclusive attention of
nearly any other company. At Ford, each one seemed to demand priority at the very same time: the exponential increase in Model T sales, the creation of River Rouge as the most advanced and largest industrial site in
the world, the acquisition of Lincoln Motor Company, and the expansion of
Ford overseas into more countries than ever before. Those were only the biggest
of Ford Motor Company's official activities. And then there were Henry Ford's
own pursuits, from historical preservation to improved diet, from the *Dearborn
Independent* to the rebirth of folk dancing. For all that was happening at Ford
in the mid-1920s, though, and for all of the news generated in Dearborn, the
most influential of the company's activities was its commitment to commercial aviation.

Ford Motor Company was the only U.S. automaker to cross into the burgeoning world of commercial aviation during the first decade after World
War I. Packard had flirted with the idea during development of the Liberty
engine, but backed away long before considering actual production. Other
American automakers had also brushed close to the aircraft industry as suppliers during the war, but they found themselves hustling in a fight for their
lives in the automobile industry in the 1920s and couldn't spare any effort for
outward expansion. For its part, General Motors was committed to a presence
in the appliance business, a holdover from Billy Durant's era of acquisition.
Making something simpler than an automobile, such as a refrigerator or
stove, was one thing. Going in the other direction and producing an airplane
required greater resources and a passion for adventure. Henry Ford had both.

Anticipating the importance of commercial aviation, Ford made sure as
early as March 1920 that his certificate to do business in Michigan included

authorization for the Ford Motor Company to manufacture and sell aircraft. In May 1921, Edsel Ford agreed to become a director of the Detroit Aviation Society, but that was at least, in part, an outgrowth of his interest in boating and other sports.[1] Of course, Henry Ford's imposing predilections emanated directly from his cunning as a businessman. In that respect, the airplane industry of the mid-1920s must have been intriguing, even though in business terms, it was nothing at all like the auto industry of 1900. In the early days of the automobile, carmakers sprang up like Topsy, encouraged by the ease of early automaking. Aviation, on the contrary, was actually suffering from a lack of competition in the mid-1920s. The potential seemed enormous, yet none of those hovering on the edge of the industry knew quite how to enter, because the market for new planes was still ill defined. No one could say who the customers would be. American aviation counted only two well-organized companies, the Glenn Martin Company, then in Cleveland, and Curtiss-Wright in Dayton, Ohio. Martin, the biggest airplane manufacturer in the country, had one thousand employees and sales of about $2 million per year, but it was devoted exclusively to military contracts, especially with the Navy.[2]

The companies trying to build planes for civilian use faced various threats. The primary one showed how young the commercial-airplane industry really was: no one was even sure it would come into being. The reason was that many authorities looked past the airplane altogether and placed their faith in dirigibles for civilian transportation. The Navy was at the forefront of dirigible research, with a long lead over the private companies also making experiments. Those rooting for "happy ships," as these airships were then known, placed their hopes behind the Navy's *Shenandoah*, the first dirigible to be constructed in the United States. Because of the low cost of lighter-than-air transportation, the most common opinion was that dirigibles would be used for cargo while airplanes might be reserved for passengers and express mail. In the public perception, airships had distinct advantages over airplanes in that they were docile, slow-moving, and impervious to stunt flying. There was an unfortunate crash of an Italian-made airship, the *Roma,* at Langley Field, Virginia, in 1922, but that was something of a fluke. After a minor part failed, the ship lost its steering and as it drifted lazily to the ground, the hydrogen-filled balloon struck a high-tension wire, bursting into flame. Thirty-three Army officers died in the accident. The Navy's *Shenandoah* was to be filled with nonflammable helium and thus far greater hopes were attached to it.[3]

While the debate over planes and dirigibles limped along, the market remained awash in surplus World War I aircraft: cheap and exciting for the barnstormer, but practically useless for any business more ambitious than fifteen-minute rides at ten dollars, barrel roll included. Outside of the military, the only steady customer for airplanes in the United States was the Post Office's Air Mail Service, which had little choice in who supplied the strong, long-range airplanes it needed. From its inauguration in 1918 through 1924, the Air Mail Service consisted mainly of the transcontinental New York to San Francisco route and was mostly for show. Flying only in daytime, it was not only very expensive to use and maintain, it actually saved little time over the railroads. Airmail pilots had to fly in all weather, on a schedule that was taxing. Of the first forty pilots to sign on with the Air Mail Service in 1918, thirty-one died in plane crashes before 1925.[4] There was no weather service to predict conditions for pilots; rain, sleet, and especially fog were terrifying to even the most steely of them. Maps barely existed and navigation equipment consisted of a compass. If they couldn't see, pilots knew that they were all too likely to steer themselves right into the ground. In addition, a plane had only one engine; if it or anything else failed, the pilot went down with the craft (parachutes were not yet standard equipment). The most dangerous stretch of air in the whole country in those days was the Allegheny region of Pennsylvania, where storms seemed to lie in wait for aircraft, and mountains loomed to finish the flight. Pilots called it the Hell Stretch—like the Bermuda Triangle, but without the sense of mystery. "There were no maps," recalled Ken McGregor, who flew with the Air Mail Service. "I got from place to place with the help of three things. One was the seat of my pants. If it left that of the plane, when the visibility was at a minimum, I was in trouble and could even be upside down. Another was the ability to recognize every town, river, railroad, farm and, yes, outhouse along the route. The third? I had a few drops of homing pigeon in my veins."[5]

In 1925, the Air Mail Service came into its own with the installation of aerial navigation beacons. According to aviation historian Timothy J. O'Callaghan, twenty-four-inch revolving beacons of 7,500,000 candlepower were installed every ten miles across the United States, allowing the planes to fly at night. This enabled the delivery of mail from coast to coast in a bit more than thirty hours, versus the railroads' three-day trip.[6]

The Air Mail Service had a reputation not unlike that of the Pony Express for courage, adventure, and death-defying feats. And yet, in the mid-1920s, the Air Mail Service was eighty times safer than other forms of civilian aviation.[7] The barnstormers who dominated civilian aviation unfortunately gave the field a reputation for plain shoddiness. Estimated in number at about six hundred, they swarmed over the country, introducing the airplane to thousands of intrepid passengers. Foolish antics may have caused some of the fatalities, but even greater danger was caused by the planes themselves. The condition of the aircraft they used could range from brand-new to worn out. In one two-week span in New York State, two barnstorming planes disintegrated in midair. Even new planes could be treacherous. Without government regulation, inept designers were allowed to send people into the air in planes that were little more than death traps. "To be involved in aviation carried the unregulated freedom of owning a horse in the days of the frontier," wrote T. A. Heppenheimer in *Turbulent Skies: The History of Commercial Aviation*. "You flew without a pilot license and with no certificate, even if you intended to carry passengers. The flight schools were similarly unlicensed. . . . For $500 a school might provide lessons, then throw in a leftover Curtiss Jenny as a graduation present."[8]

With little else to go on, the image of commercial aviation in the early 1920s was a combination of barnstorming and airmail flying, and because of that, the industry was in a stall at the very start. The manufacture of better civilian airplanes—assuming that the engineering challenges could be met—required enormous expense in the face of a bleak outlook for selling them. There were no passenger or cargo airlines in the continental United States before 1924. A few entrepreneurs recognized that in principle there was a need for them, but in reality, two things were lacking. First, a sure demand for cargo or passenger services. Second and even more important, commercial airplanes that were affordable yet capable of carrying heavy loads over long distances. Manufacturers awaited customers in the form of airlines, yet the airlines could not form until there was a viable airplane. Flying's reputation for danger didn't help in either case.

The American aviation industry was barely moving, at least as far as private planes were concerned, yet Germany, for all of its postwar problems, was making speedy progress. With the Versailles Treaty's limitation on military expenditure, the Germans had no choice but to pour all of their expertise into commercial craft. Even so, the will to develop commercial aviation was remarkable; within two months of Armistice Day, the first German airline was already organized and offering flights. Although former army planes were used at first, the eventual result was an active aircraft-manufacturing industry and an array of planes. France and Britain also rushed into aviation after World War I. All three countries promoted commercial aviation with government subsidies, some of them as high as 70 percent of industry costs. Subsidies were not a popular notion in the United States, however, and the industry looked to private initiatives.

Both Henry and Edsel believed there were manifold opportunities to make money in flight. The Fords didn't so much enter airplane production as ease into it little by little between 1924 and 1926. The first overture came from a businessman named William Stout. He started lobbying Henry, hoping the industrialist would recognize that commercial aviation was the next logical step in the transportation revolution he had godfathered.[9] Being obsessed with publicizing the Ford name and interested in promoting Dearborn as a capital of progress, Henry was immediately intrigued when Stout approached him about building an airport in his hometown, Dearborn. In fact, southeastern Michigan needed a landing strip. While Mount Clemens, Michigan, happened to have one of the nation's oldest military airports, Selfridge Field, it was located twenty-six miles north of Detroit, a city that had no municipal airport.

Born in Quincy, Illinois, in 1880, Bill Stout had studied engineering at the University of Minnesota. With a fascination for aviation, he covered air meets for the *Chicago Tribune* and founded both the Model Aero Club of Illinois and the magazine *Aviation Age*. He arrived in Michigan in 1914 as an auto engineer and was part of Packard's aviation division during World War I, helping to manage the Liberty engine contract. Partly due to poor vision—he was forbidden by doctors from so much as reading newspapers—Stout was not especially accomplished in design, except in the broadest strokes. He was at his best as a conceptual engineer. The idea behind his own company, which he started in 1922, was based on the use of a composite metal sheet called duralumin—an alloy first developed in Germany before World War I and composed of 92 percent aluminum, 4 percent copper, minor amounts of manganese, magnesium, and sometimes other compounds. Stout believed that duralumin, if attached to a steel frame, would provide a plane with greater strength than "cloth, wood and sticks," as he accurately described standard aircraft construction of the day.[10] The Germans had experimented with all-metal construction, but it was still considered radical in the United States. As head of the Stout Metal Airplane Company, Bill Stout drew on his experience as a journalist, because in fact he was at his best as a booster, a communicator, and a promoter. Skinny and birdlike, he had a knack for simplifying complex points into simple phrases. Stout would be well suited to the atmosphere at Ford. Coincidentally, his factory was on Beaubien Street in Detroit, just down the street from Ford Motor's first building.

The Fords had a small holding of shares in Stout's company—as many Detroit area executives did—but until the idea of an airport came up, they had maintained their distance. Stout's initial contact at the Ford Motor Company was William Mayo, a high-ranking executive who had retained Henry Ford's respect ever since joining the company in 1915. Mayo was not only an astute engineer on matters as small as engine parts or as large as train systems, he had an affable character and often served as a kind of industrial diplomat for the company. He also matched Henry Ford's own expansive vision for Ford Motor. When others failed to grasp the magnitude of the River Rouge plant as Ford imagined it in 1918–1919, Mayo understood the whole concept instantly, as though it were the most natural step possible. Mayo went on to help make sure that it met its potential, overseeing plans as they developed, building by building. The fact that William Mayo was at ease with the future, however large it grew, drew him into the role of liaison between Ford Motor and the aviation industry—as well as between Henry Ford and Bill Stout.

In 1923, when Mayo met Stout, the entrepreneur had just succeeded in producing the nation's first all-steel aircraft, a Navy Torpedo plane. As Stout said, "Mayo was one of the cleverest and most suave salesmen ever, and his fundamental quality was sincerity. So we talked the same language."[11] But in sales it's important to have the right product and in duralumin, Stout did. He was persuasive on the subject, having practically memorized a landmark article in *Aviation* magazine, which spelled out the advantages of the new composition, one of which was that it was easier to work with than steel.[12] Stout intertwined two basic ideas: the urgent need for a commercial airport in the Detroit area and the surefire wonder of duralumin. The implication was that if business leaders in greater Detroit nurtured the struggling field of commercial aircraft, the area might well become the capital of yet another booming industry. Following William Mayo's suggestions, Stout wrote Henry Ford a succinct letter in early 1924, explaining the need for an airfield open to civil aviation and suggesting that a flat tract in Dearborn would be well suited. In April, Henry Ford agreed to underwrite the cost of what he later described as "the finest landing field in the world."[13] Glenn Hoppin, Stout's business manager (and brother-in-law), was present when the possible sites were discussed with Ford.

> Mr. Ford asked a lot of questions. Finally he turned to Mr. Stout and said, "Which one do you think will make the best field?"
>
> Bill said, "Well, I think this one down along Oakwood Boulevard will make the best field, but it will cost the most money."
>
> Mr. Ford replied, "That doesn't make any difference; if that will make the best field, that is the one we will take."
>
> [Ernest] Liebold then spoke up, "Well, Mr. Ford, we have spent some $15,000 putting in sewers and grading streets and getting ready to build the new sub-division in that area along Oakwood Boulevard."
>
> Mr. Ford quickly answered, "Oh, Liebold, maybe it was a sub-division yesterday, but it is a landing field today."[14]

That exchange, as Hoppin remembered it, illuminates why Ford Motor was still an exciting place to work, for all of its clashing personalities. So did the fact that within three days of the conversation, thirty-eight Fordson tractors were rolling onto the site, ready to reshape 719 acres of earth. If their entrance, all in a neat line, seemed staged, that is because it was: Ford movie cameras were on the scene, recording the starting day for use in a promotional film. During six weeks of construction, the only glitch concerned the mature trees on the site. The thought of cutting them down was so painful to Henry Ford that several stands were allowed to remain in place until winter, when they could be transplanted without harm. Although Hoppin was directing operations, Henry Ford was very interested in the new venture, making daily visits to observe progress. The airport's two main grass runways, north-south and east-west, were 3,700 feet long, surrounded by 260 acres of flat ground.[15] More than twenty miles of drain tiles were laid for year-round operation, and although the field was not normally operated at night, it was fully equipped with floodlights to accommodate night landings when necessary. The huge letters F-O-R-D, formed of white stone on the earth and 200 feet from top to bottom, were no mere advertising, but a very necessary welcome to pilots flying 10,000 feet in the air, who often needed to read a sign before they were sure they were at an airport.

The Ford Airport was open to anyone who needed a place to land, and on November 16, 1924, the first plane coasted down the runway. Fittingly, it was Stout's first usable plane, an eight-person all-metal Liberty-engined transport (400 hp, 12 cylinder) filled with 1,500 pounds' worth of cargo—in the form of Stout employees and family members and piloted by Edward Hamilton. Continually pushing municipal pride, William Stout had given the craft a name that was a play on words: *Maiden Detroit* ("Made in Detroit"). The airport was not formally dedicated until January 15, 1925, when large crowds came to see an aerial demonstration of twelve Curtiss fighter planes from the Army's First Pursuit Squadron. Henry Ford, meanwhile, explained his views on aviation quite succinctly to a *New York World* reporter: "The first thing that must be done with aerial navigation is to make it fool-proof. Just now it's 90 percent man and 10 percent plane. That percentage must be turned around. We are not going into the racing business. What the Ford Motor Company means to do is to prove whether commercial flying can be done safely and profitably."[16]

While the Ford Airport welcomed all aircraft, private or military, the whole place seemed to have been created as a gift for the Stout Metal Airplane Company. Both Henry and Edsel Ford, coaxed along by Mayo, had begun to appreciate William Stout. Henry, in particular, often responded to people of Stout's ilk: straightforward, smooth talking, and full of good ideas. For reasons that no one could explain later, Ford Motor even constructed a building on the airport grounds as the new home of the Stout Company. As Stout recalled, it came about when he and Henry Ford were walking around the construction site one summer day. In the course of the conversation, Ford asked what kind of building Stout wanted. Assuming that he would have to finance it himself, Stout went out and made plans with a supply house named Austin. "First thing we knew, they started to build this Austin building," Stout exclaimed, referring to Ford builders. "There was no other word; they just started building a building. One day, somebody called up and said the building was ready, and why didn't we move out."[17]

At least Stout didn't squander his opportunity. In December 1924, he sold the *Maiden Detroit* for $25,000 to the U.S. Post Office, giving a boost to the reputation of all-metal construction. On March 19, 1925, about six months after the company occupied its new factory, its first plane rolled out the door, cleverly named the *Maiden Dearborn*. Called a Stout Air Pullman, the model had room for eight passengers and a price tag of $25,000.[18] It was a triumph for both Stout and Ford Motor. "In my opinion, the greatest single thing I accomplished for aviation was getting Mr. Ford interested in it," Stout later confessed. "From that moment on, Wall Street and the country began to take aviation seriously."[19]

A month before the *Maiden Dearborn* took off from the Ford Airport for the first time, Congress had passed a bill that boosted the prospects for commercial aviation by turning Air Mail flights over to private contractors. Introduced by Pennsylvania Representative Clyde Kelley, the new act was originally designed to help the railroads extend their profitable mail contracts into air service. Many congressmen who voted for the measure, however, recognized that in the end, it would be more far-reaching: the Kelley Air Mail Act would have the effect of subsidizing commercial aviation in America—without the government's giving outright handouts as in Germany, France, and Great Britain.

In response to the Kelley Act, more than fifty airlines scrambled to organize during 1926, preparing to bid for one of the dozens of contracts on the Air Mail routes. All of them had the same idea: to use the mail payments as a guarantee of income so that they could afford aircraft, on which they would then offer cargo or passenger service as soon as possible. Eddie Rickenbacker, the entrepreneurial former war ace, organized one such airline in Florida. Boeing, then building military planes in Washington State, won a mail contract and started an airline subsidiary that would later become United Airlines.[20] Making commercial airplanes only for its own routes at first, Boeing would develop into Ford's strongest competitor in sales to new airlines. Nevertheless, Boeing and other aircraft manufacturers continued to depend most heavily on military contracts. In fact, of the dozen largest aircraft companies in the United States during the 1920s, only Ford would be dedicated exclusively to commercial aviation.[21]

The timing of the Kelley Act was propitious where Ford was concerned, but apparently it wasn't coincidental. While the new law undoubtedly encouraged Ford Motor to continue and even expand its involvement in aviation, most observers credited the Fords with inspiring Congress to pass the new legislation in the first place. Even those who disdained Henry Ford the man knew he had instincts like a fox. The completion of the first Stout Air Pullman in March 1925, and the promise of more to come, was regarded as a burst of success in the aviation world. While Ford Motor Company was simultaneously encouraging a company called the Aircraft Development Corporation, which had a contract to build a dirigible made of duralumin for the Navy, Henry Ford seemed more enthusiastic about attaching his name to the Stout Company. On the day after the completion of the first Stout plane at the Ford facility, Edsel gave a news conference to explain the Fords' role and their interest in aviation. "Since the announcement," he said, referring to the report on the Air Pullman, "the company has had thousands of inquiries." Significantly, he meant that Ford Motor Company had been fielding those thousands of inquiries: it was not only the unpaid patron of the Stout Metal Airplane Company, but the self-appointed sales manager for the firm.

A month later, the Fords started the crucial job of creating a market for Stout's airplanes by initiating the country's first regular commercial airline, carrying cargo every other day between Chicago and Detroit. The service made headlines across the country, as newspapers marveled at the fact that airplanes could actually be run on a schedule. And at Ford, that schedule was taken seriously. "Liebold put a bell on the front of our terminal building operated by a push button in his office," recalled Bill Stout. "When nine o'clock came, Mr. Liebold pushed the button and if Mr. Ford didn't hear the airplane go over within two minutes Jimmy Smith [Ford's general assistant] ran over to see what was the matter."[22] Henry Ford wanted the new airline to be an open experiment, so the details of the operation were available to anyone interested in commercial aviation. A year later, the company reported that the airline, the Air Transportation Service, had started 1,492 flights, and all but 25 were completed as planned. Engine trouble or bad weather caused those few disruptions. The Ford fleet had covered 295,000 miles with a perfect safety record.

After Henry and Edsel watched the takeoff of the inaugural flight of their airline, Edsel made a mundane statement insisting that his family was interested in aviation—but not in making planes. The rumor in Detroit, however, was that Henry Ford wanted Edsel to dominate aircraft manufacture, the same way he himself had long dominated automaking.[23] At the time, Edsel didn't seem to possess any particular fascination with aviation, perhaps because he had never flown. It was among the activities that his father forbade. Edsel was aware that the plane did represent the next revolution in transportation, however, and he wasn't immune to the appeal of what he called "the daily use of airplanes for personal purposes." Other people labeled that idea a "flivver plane," and as 1925 continued, curiosity swelled as to just when Ford would give in to the temptation to start building them.

In fact, Henry Ford vacillated in his interest in aviation. Sometimes he seemed much more excited about building the best airport than anything else. After the runways and hangars had been constructed for the sake of planes, Ford set his engineers to work on what was to become Ford Airport's most famous feature: a 210-foot mast for mooring dirigibles. No mere stick in the ground, it was supposed to be a showcase for Ford Motor's mechanical expertise, as well as a symbol of its commitment to aviation. The final plan called for a tower not unlike those used in NASA's rocket launches fifty years later, a tall iron framework set firmly on four spreading legs. After a dirigible was coupled at the nose to the mast, a built-in elevator would lower it to the ground—a Ford innovation that left other mooring masts in the dark ages.[24] Construction of the mast began in early 1925 and it became a Ford Motor Company priority to complete it by July, when the airport was scheduled to receive a visit from the *Shenandoah*.

Henry Ford was thrilled by the prospect of the celebrated dirigible visiting his airport. After fifty-eight previous flights, the Navy airship would be making a last tune-up tour before attempting the greatest feat ever put before a dirigible (or any other aircraft): a flight over the North Pole. After leaving its home in Lakehurst, New Jersey, the *Shenandoah* was going to visit St. Louis and Minneapolis before landing at Dearborn. Just the sight of the 684-foot monster was said to be one of the glories of the mid-1920s. Henry Ford, who had never consented to a ride in any aircraft, was going to have more than a look— he had accepted an invitation to join the tour on the final leg from Dearborn back to Lakehurst.[25] The publicity would make Ford Airport known even outside the aviation world, framing it in a patriotic context.

Henry Ford's interest in airplanes would ultimately overtake that of dirigibles. One reason was that the airport and the Stout factory had been like an ant farm, something that he could study without getting too close. As with other secondary projects, though, Henry Ford seemed to be waiting for someone close to it to capture his confidence. One person who arrived on the scene at a propitious time was a youth named Harry Brooks, the son of a family friend. Born in 1902 in Southfield, Michigan, Brooks reminded Henry Ford of himself—both were the sons of farmers, mechanically inclined, unassuming yet self-assured. In addition, they were both teetotalers and non-smokers. Brooks embodied a zesty fascination with airplanes, and Ford might have been thinking of him when he said, as he often did, that the art of aviation belonged to the younger generation. As soon as Brooks learned to fly, Ford arranged a job for him testing planes at Stout. Harry Brooks was a gifted pilot, with a sense of fun that made him a popular figure at the factory and in particular with Henry Ford, who called him "Brooksie."

"He was a natural flyer," Stout said of Brooks. "He would do things with an airplane that the old pilots couldn't do. He was just a kid that had practically never flown before. Part of it was nerve or rather lack of nerve. He just had no fear."[26]

Brooks made aviation come alive, but in the end, it took Bill Stout at his most eloquent to finally persuade Henry Ford to make planes. In July 1925, Ford acted upon a conversation he'd started with Bill Stout the previous winter. As Glenn Hoppin related, Ford came through the Beaubien Street factory one day and asked to speak with Stout. "Bill stayed with Mr. Ford and showed him through the plant and explained what we were doing," Hoppin recalled. "Bill talked aviation to Mr. Ford and tried to visualize some of its vast possibilities. Then they went out back of the plant. It was a day in February when the air was sharp but on the south side of the building it was warm in the sun. The two of them sat down on a pile of lumber and were there for two hours. Bill told Mr. Ford his views about aviation. He answered a lot of questions for Mr. Ford and outlined what the possibilities of aviation were and particularly with freight. Freight should come before passengers because you could prove aviation to the public with freight. If you had accidents, you didn't get adverse publicity that you would if people were involved. We could build up a flying record until we got a safety factor in it. We could gain experience in operation and develop and improve better equipment and more reliable engines."[27]

Ford's reply, as Stout later told Glenn Hoppin, was that commercial aviation "is something that somebody has got to put a lot of money behind and make an industry of it. I don't know why the Ford Motor Company shouldn't do just that." Whether Ford uttered those exact words or not, he certainly acted on them over the next eight years. The only problem was that despite having started the Detroit–Chicago air-freight service, Ford wasn't ultimately trying to start an airline, but a production company. Bill Stout would be of less and less use to Ford as the differences between the two goals weighed on daily decisions—decisions requiring expert engineering, not lofty vision.[28]

On July 31, 1925, Ford Motor acquired the Stout Metal Airplane Company for just over $1 million. The biggest car company in the world was finally in the airplane business. "We hope to produce a plane that will be so cheap as to make air service profitable," Henry Ford told the *Literary Digest,* "without government aid."[29] William Mayo, who had been overseeing activity at the airport anyway, became the head of the new aviation division. Stout remained as a well-paid consultant. His chief engineer, George Prudden, was put on the Ford payroll, as were the other employees of the Stout Company. Production of the single-engine Stout planes continued, but a radical new design was under discussion even as the companies merged. The new idea was for a tri-motor plane, with a propeller on the nose and one each on the wings.

_____

As it turned out, the *Shenandoah*'s tour was postponed for two months, so the mooring mast at Ford Airport was finished well in time. Henry Ford may have been looking forward to a close-up of the airship, but the Navy crew was just as excited to examine the innovative mast. The official trip photographer had even been given orders to make a complete photographic record of it. On September 2, 1925, the *Shenandoah* took off from Lakehurst to start its tour. The next day, caught in a sudden storm in western Pennsylvania, along the Hell Stretch, it fought for hours in practically every position except right side up and finally broke into pieces about seventy-five miles east of Columbus, Ohio. Fourteen men died in the disaster, a blow to the Navy and all Americans interested in dirigibles. The Fords backed away from active participation in further research, although they maintained their investment in the Aircraft Development Corporation.

The *Shenandoah* disaster, occurring along the same route that Henry Ford was scheduled to take only a few weeks later, was an emotional issue at the factory. George Prudden, chief engineer at Ford Aviation, traveled to the site of the crash and was pictured in the *Detroit Free Press* gathering information. Upon his return, he was fired. Supposedly, Henry Ford didn't approve of Prudden's name being in the paper. If that account is true, it shows how sensitive the *Shenandoah* incident was at Ford Motor. However, there may have been more to it than that. Prudden's departure allowed for a new direction in the aviation division, under the leadership of a versatile young engineer named Harold Hicks, who moved over from development work on motorboats. Hicks was familiar with airplane design and had an assistant, Tom Towle, with practical experience, as well. With their arrival, creating the next plane at Ford Aviation became an endeavor of *Ford* people.

If Hicks's arrival didn't symbolize the fresh start at Ford Aviation, then the fire that destroyed the Stout factory on Sunday morning, January 17, 1926, certainly did. No one knew the cause, but it wiped out the building, along with Prudden's experimental three-motored plane. Tests with the plane the previous fall had been disappointing. Henry Ford wasted no time on regret over the fire. "Stout, don't look so sad," he said to his chief consultant. "It is the best thing that ever happened to you. It is such an advantage I wouldn't be surprised you set it yourself. Now we can build the type of building and hangar we should have built in the first place."[30] Making it clear that he had never liked the building or the prototype plane, Ford immediately ordered improved versions of each. The replacement building was larger than the original one to accommodate Ford production methods. Designing a new airplane took a little bit longer and did not involve Bill Stout. By then Stout was regarded by Henry Ford and others as little more than a promoter whose ability as a designer had long since been surpassed. While he remained in his consultant's job—at $75,000 per year—he spent his spare time organizing a new service that would eventually grow into Northwest Airlines.

Hicks, Towle, and their team began designing the new plane, called the 4-AT, at Ford Motor's Engineering Laboratory at River Rouge in February 1926. The plane's metal construction and monoplane design (meaning it had single-layered wings) had already been proven successful with the Stout models; to extend capacity, range, and safety, the Fords made the bold commitment to provide three motors. Only six of twenty-eight American commercial plane manufacturers were then listed as building an aircraft with more than one engine, and five of those were one-of-a-kind experimental models. "Multiple engines make flying safer and the life of the plane longer," Edsel Ford explained. "It is not likely that all engines would become impaired at one time, and with one engine in commission a forced landing can be made within an area of 1,000 feet."[31] The key, of course, was the engine. While the company could have ordered aviation engines from Curtiss-Wright or Pratt & Whitney, there didn't seem to be any reason that an organization such as Ford couldn't come up with its own power plant. Henry Ford took a personal interest, laying out broad specifications, as he had in the development of the Model T car, and watching his staff argue over the details on a row of blackboards in the Engineering Lab. "Mr. Ford had a sort of a little couch near the window up there where he'd kind of go to sleep at times," Hicks remembered. "Then he'd wake up and look things over. He kept a pretty close watch on it."[32]

For all of the work that was put into the new eight-cylinder engine, though, it never performed satisfactorily. "It was a very grotesque looking job," Hicks said. "It was a long stroke engine. At that time in internal combustion engine design, long stroke was supposed to be the latest word. Subsequently, it's been found that short stroke with the same piston speed to get high rpm's is quite the way to go."[33] Whatever the reason, the failure of the engine was devastating to Henry Ford. To control costs and quality he had been intent on manufacturing every major component of the airplane, just as he had with his famous car. The necessity to purchase J-4 engines from Curtiss-Wright put a damper on his interest in the Tri-Motor. (Later in the production run, the company used improved J-5 engines, before switching to Pratt & Whitney Hornet engines.) Relying on outside suppliers added to the cost, and although the quality of the J-4s was unimpeachable, Ford Motor was not at liberty to continually refine and improve them, as it was wont to do with any part. The engineering group continued to work on the eight-cylinder engine for two years, but to no avail.

The average airplane in the mid-1920s featured wood and fabric construction, along with one engine turning a propeller in the front. In addition, they usually employed biplane design, which meant that there were two wings on each side connected by wires and struts. Ford's Tri-Motor was different, as the company's airplane catalogue explained: "No one, no matter how skilled, can inspect a piece of wood and tell how strong it is. Spruce should stand 40,000 pounds per square inch: but no one, by examining it, can tell whether it will pull 40,000 pounds or fail at 25,000 pounds. Its flexibility, too, is an unknown quantity; no two pieces will flex alike under strain. Metal, however, is a determinate: it is possible to estimate within 5% of its strength."[34]

Tested on June 11, 1926, only four months after serious design work had begun, the new Tri-Motor was a complete success. Handsome in a pug way, especially with its polished metal exterior, it had a wingspan of 60 feet, a top speed of 110 mph, and a comfortable landing speed of 60 mph. It could carry about eight passengers or 1,200 pounds of cargo.[35] Soon the new planes were sold to fledgling airlines and to the various military branches. At anywhere from $42,000 to $50,000, the Tri-Motor was expensive, but Ford marketed it energetically under the slogan "Look to the Sky." Among the celebrities who purchased the new status symbol was the movie actor Wallace Beery, the star of *Robin Hood* (1922), *The Champ* (1931), and *Grand Hotel* (1932). The Ford Motor Company received widespread accolades for its entry into airplane manufacturing. As the aviation writer H. I. Block explained in the *New York Times* on November 14, 1926, "In spite of all the foreign progress and all the persistent flying since the war by the army, navy and private enterprise, it took the entry of the Fords into the business of building and using airplanes to win the recognition of air transport by the Government."[36]

When Ford sold a Tri-Motor, the plane arrived with a trained pilot, to be employed by the purchaser. Training for at least a month at Ford Airport, the pilot had watched "his" plane through assembly and knew how to fix it as well as how to fly it.[37] The expertise of the pilots undoubtedly added to the reputation of the planes, and Henry Ford was a stickler for aircraft safety, employing only pilots qualified to carry the U.S. mail: men with a good deal more than 500 hours' experience in the air. Ford used his Air Transportation Service as a vehicle for training pilots and airplane mechanics for the new owners of his Tri-Motors. Many of these pilots went on to become leaders in the aviation industry, including Lawrence Fritz, who became an Air Force major general in World War II and an American Airlines vice president afterward.[38]

Even though Ford disdained U.S. government interference in the private sector, he heartily approved of the Air Commerce Act of 1926, which set qualifications for private and commercial pilots and aircraft mechanics. An advertisement for Ford Aviation during the 1920s perfectly summed up Henry Ford's philosophy: "We believe that safety is the foundation on which the success of commercial aviation must be built. In building the Ford tri-motored, all metal transport monoplane, we give first consideration to safety in its design and structure. Speed, comfort, maneuverability, climb, general performance, efficiency—all these have their proper place and receive the consideration they deserve. But in our opinion none of them supercedes safety in importance." Accidents did happen, nevertheless. On May 18, 1926, Ford pilot Ross Kirkpatrick was killed when he crashed in the *Maiden Dearborn* while attempting to land in poor visibility. But overall the record was remarkable. In eight years of manufacturing airplanes and operating the Air Transportation Service, Ford Motor Company suffered only five fatal accidents, a remarkably low tally for that era.[39]

Throughout the new division's early years, Henry Ford consistently gave Edsel credit in interviews for providing the impetus behind Ford Aviation. Because the elder Ford did almost all of the talking and seemed to make the major decisions regarding the airplane program, however, he appeared to be the actual driving force. Employees, for their part, were divided as to which Ford was really behind the department. "In my opinion," chief engineer Harold Hicks said, "Henry Ford was never sold on the airplane. . . . Edsel, of course, was very much sold on the airplane. It was Edsel's interest that really predominated in bringing the Stout Company into the Ford Motor Company. Henry Ford undoubtedly used it for indirect advertising."[40]

William Stout thought just the opposite. "In analyzing who was the more interested in aviation, Edsel or Henry Ford, my analysis was that the old man was most interested, but a little scared," Stout recalled. "He seemed intrigued because of a certain fear of it, and when he subscribed for Edsel, it was from that angle. But when we did see Edsel, he would say, 'Well, Father won't let me fly, so I have no basis to judge whether this is good or not and you have; so go ahead and do what you want.'"[41] On those few occasions when Edsel was allowed to speak for himself, it became clear that the two Fords did not share the same goals. Ever the realist, Edsel grasped that the odds of mass-producing airplanes at a profit were long, so he wanted to focus on practical commercial aircraft such as the Tri-Motor. His ever innovative father was more interested in making an airplane either much larger or smaller than the Tri-Motor and thus so conspicuously different that it would carve out a new niche and become an aviation sales success the way the Model T had among automobiles.

As it turned out, Edsel scored first for Ford Aviation, putting his inherited gift for publicity to the company's advantage via a pet project that shone an international spotlight on the Tri-Motor. Chief of Naval Aviation Admiral William Moffett, who had first met Henry Ford in 1922, wrote to him a few years later to promote the daring cause of Lieutenant Commander Richard Byrd, who was planning his unprecedented trek to the North Pole. "I think that Byrd has the ability and determination to succeed in this undertaking, and I want to assure you that you could make no mistake in putting the utmost confidence in him," Moffett wrote. "He is the kind who enjoys life most when there are difficulties to overcome."[42] Aware that his son had an interest in the Arctic, Henry Ford turned the letter over to Edsel, who seized the moment.

In January 1926, Edsel Ford not only sent Byrd a check for $20,000 but solicited the same amount from John D. Rockefeller Jr., scion of another industrial empire. "The manner in which you have sent this check shows a trust in me which I appreciate deeply and shall try to be worthy of it," Byrd wrote to Edsel. "Nothing quite arouses my sense of responsibility and pleases me so much as an indication such as you have given that you can trust my judgment."[43] The money transformed the Byrd expedition from a pipe dream into a reality and instigated an active correspondence between the explorer and the young man behind Ford Aviation. "Your selection of Wright air-cooled motors is a good one and I believe that this motor is by far the best worked out one of its type at the present time," Edsel Ford would write to Commander

Byrd three years later. "The multi-motored plane is a great boon to safe transportation and I believe eliminates 90% of the hazard, although I doubt that you will be able to find a plane that will stay aloft with one motor running only, under any consideration."[44]

In addition to the funding, Byrd originally hoped to use the new Ford Tri-Motor (or "Tin Goose") to make his polar trip, but the Stout factory fire ended that possibility. He was forced to fly in a German-made Fokker instead, although in tribute to his main financial backer the explorer named it the *Josephine Ford* after Edsel's three-year-old daughter. In return the honored father sent Byrd a Cartier watch, which the commander promised to wear to the Arctic as a symbol of their friendship. "The whole thing would have been impossible without your backing and encouragement," Byrd wrote Edsel in April. "You're the father of this expedition. I owe a great deal to a great many people, but I owe more to you than all the rest put together."[45] The flight finally took place on May 8, 1926. The expedition's success at flying over the actual North Pole is still disputed, but in its own time the feat generated worldwide headlines, if no financial return. To assist once again, Edsel purchased Byrd's celebrated Fokker plane for $30,000 as an acquisition for a planned Henry Ford Museum. As a token of his continuing appreciation, Byrd sent Edsel Ford the flag that had flown over the North Pole.[46]

Thrilled by the Arctic expedition, Edsel threw his money even more enthusiastically behind Byrd's next adventure: a mirror trip to Antarctica to cross the South Pole. This time Edsel provided Byrd $100,000 in cash and equipment, and again persuaded John D. Rockefeller Jr. to match his contribution. For the South Pole trip, Byrd would finally get to use a Ford Tri-Motor, named the *Floyd Bennett* for the pilot of his Arctic excursion, who had died in 1928 trying to rescue two flyers after their plane crashed in Canada. Ford's aviation department took the effects of cold weather and long mileage into consideration in building Byrd's Antarctic airplane. The result featured a thinner skin on the fuselage to reduce weight; a 691-gallon gasoline tank in place of the standard 235-gallon one; skis made of ash and hickory wood for landing on ice; upper wings painted yellow for extra visibility in the event of an emergency landing; and a 525-hp Wright Cyclone engine in the nose instead of the usual 220-hp Wright J-5 Whirlwind, in order to provide more power at higher altitudes. The Ford Tri-Motor airplane completed its history-making 1,600-mile flight over Antarctica on November 30, 1929, two days after taking off and a day after crossing the South Pole. To thank his sponsor, Byrd named several of his newly discovered Antarctic mountain ranges and an island after Edsel Ford and his family. Although Byrd was forced to leave the Ford plane behind at the time of his first jaunt over the South Pole, he went back to retrieve it in 1935 at Edsel Ford's request. Finding the aircraft fairly well preserved in the snow and ice, Byrd brought it back to his home in Long

Island, dismantled it, packed the pieces in twenty-five crates, and shipped them to Dearborn. The *Floyd Bennett* was reconditioned and reassembled for permanent display at the Henry Ford Museum, where it remains today, parked near the *Josephine Ford*.[47]

The voluminous correspondence between Edsel Ford and the explorer, meanwhile, fills many file boxes at Ohio State University's Byrd Polar Research Center in Columbus. Their frequent, detailed missives cover mutual concerns, ranging from food rations, altitude sickness, and media hazards to financial matters and family life. The younger Ford's ardor for Byrd's exploits and the vicarious thrill he found in them come across clearly in his letters encouraging the adventurer to pen his memoirs and plan even more ambitious trips. The year after the North Pole trip, Edsel delighted his buddy "Dick" Byrd by rewarding him with a brand-new Lincoln motorcar. "It gives me a great deal of pride and satisfaction that you are going to drive a Lincoln car," Edsel Ford wrote Byrd, "and I hope that I have not been presumptuous in offering this one to you. I feel very deeply my regard for you and your achievements and it is just one way of trying to express it to you."[48]

─────────

While Edsel was developing the Tri-Motor, and helping prepare for Byrd's first Arctic trip, Henry Ford set his own engineering group to work on a light, midget airplane, nicknamed the Flivver Plane. "We hope to produce a plane that will be so cheap as to make air service profitable, without government aid," Ford informed the *Literary Digest* regarding the Flivver. His statement unmistakably echoed the original ambition of the Model T. And therein lay the Flivver Plane's problem.

The miniplane project had the support of many of Henry Ford's pet employees, including aide-of-all-trades Ray Dahlinger, favorite mechanic Jimmy Smith, and test pilot Harry Brooks—a group Bill Stout took to calling "the back-door gang." Under the project's chief engineer, Otto Koppen, who had a degree in aeronautics from the University of Michigan, the Flivver Plane evolved from a cloud of ideas into a one-seat airplane (although two could squeeze into the cockpit) with a wingspan of about twenty feet. While the first prototype was powered by a three-cylinder Anzani engine, engineer Harold Hicks later took it upon himself to design a 40-horsepower, two-cylinder engine that produced far better results, as it weighed a mere 120 pounds. In tests during the summer of 1926, Hicks's Ford-engine version proved fun to fly and impressive to watch, its minimal extraneous weight allowing it to climb steeply, fly smoothly, and land on just a short strip of runway.

The pilot who made the little plane look good was Harry Brooks, who was as well suited to the sprightly Flivver Plane as Barney Oldfield had been to Ford's 999 race car in 1902. And like Henry Ford's favorite race-car driver of old, Brooks was something of a daredevil. On one occasion, he flew through the open door at one end of the Ford hangar and out through the other end. He also made himself a local legend by landing the Flivver on Woodward Avenue in the Detroit suburb of Birmingham so as not to be late for a luncheon engagement, getting a $500 traffic ticket. It did not deter him from later flying under a bridge and over the contestants plying the Detroit River in a boat race. Although Henry Ford wanted to rescue aviation from just such daredevilry, he never tried to stop Brooks from performing his reckless stunts in the Flivver Plane. Like Ford's own turn-of-the-century car-racing exploits, Brooks's shenanigans might just have been good for business.

When Henry Ford finally took his first ride in an airplane in August 1927, however, it was not in a Flivver Plane, and no common pilot manned the controls. That May, Charles Lindbergh had sealed the promising future of aviation by flying solo across the Atlantic in his tiny *Spirit of St. Louis,* a heroic first that he celebrated with a summerlong tour of the United States. Quite aware that Henry Ford ranked as the most powerful individual in the fledgling American aviation industry, the twenty-five-year-old Lindbergh shrewdly scheduled a stop at the Dearborn airport. At 2:00 P.M. on August 10, the silver *Spirit* executed a few playful turns in the skies above the Ford Motor Company, then landed in front of a small assemblage including Henry and Edsel Ford, William Mayo, Bill Stout, Harry Brooks, and Lindbergh's mother, who lived in Detroit. (In fact, the flyer would later visit her at 1220 West Forest Street, the house in which he was born.) The day after his arrival in Dearborn, however, Lindbergh spent the morning chatting at length with Henry and Edsel Ford before giving a one-man air show to demonstrate the loops and spins the *Spirit of St. Louis* could do. "When he came down," recalled Ford Motor engineer and test driver Al Esper, "Mr. Ford went out to congratulate him and Lindbergh asked him to take a ride. He was put on the spot, and so he just got in the airplane and took off with him."[49]

The only problem with the impromptu invitation was that the *Spirit of St. Louis* had just one seat.[50] But Henry Ford was nothing if not wiry, even at sixty-four, and he gamely squeezed inside the cockpit. As Lindbergh recalled, he "had to sit bent over, on the arm of my pilot seat. But he seemed to enjoy the flight very much."[51] Thus did Henry Ford become the first person ever to fly with Lindbergh in his famous plane after the aviator's transatlantic trip to Paris. The pair cruised over Dearborn for about ten minutes or so, then returned to change Fords and give Edsel a ride. After that, Lindbergh took to the air in a Ford Tri-Motor ferrying a larger party, including Charles Sorensen, P. E. Martin, Mayo, Stout, and Brooks. This time, Henry Ford even took the controls briefly. But while he appeared to enjoy the flight, it failed to fascinate him the way Stout, Brooks, and even Lindbergh had hoped it would. Nevertheless, Charles Lindbergh—who had, after all, learned to drive at age eleven behind the wheel of a Model T[52]—interested Henry Ford enough that the industrialist remained in contact with the dashing young aviator, occasionally broaching possible projects and ways in which they might work together.

Although disappointed that Lindbergh's visit failed to advance their Flivver's cause, the Ford team building the plane refused to give up. To promote it nationally, Harry Brooks had flown it to an endurance record early in 1927, covering 472 miles nonstop. As enthusiastic as ever in the aftermath of the Lindbergh tour, he hoped to reignite the Fords' interest in aviation with another nonstop solo flight, this one from Dearborn to Miami. All went well until a fuel line in the Flivver ruptured, forcing Brooks to set down in Titusville, Florida—200 miles short of Miami, but with a new record in hand, at a distance of 972 miles from Dearborn. Sadly, the final leg of Brooks's trip ended in disaster. On February 25, 1928, his Flivver plane was headed for Miami when it veered off course over the Atlantic Ocean, turned sideways, and crashed just off the coast. The plane was retrieved, but Brooks's body was never recovered. Engineers familiar with the plane advanced several theories as to the cause of the crash, from a broken steering wire to exhaust fumes overtaking the pilot in the cockpit.

The young man's death devastated Henry Ford and he lost all interest in the Flivver. Some employees had always doubted Ford's intention to go ahead with the plane anyway, but even those of the opposite view noted that after the accident the boss would not so much as talk about the aircraft. "After Brooks's death, I know late one night Henry Ford came through the laboratory on his way home," recalled Harold Hicks. "I stopped him and said, 'Mr. Ford, do you want anything more done on the development of this two-cylinder engine?' He said, 'Well, what's it good for?' I said, 'Well, it's good for a Flivver plane.' He said, 'What are they good for?'"

No more Flivver Planes were ever produced, although a replica of Brooks's ill-fated craft was made and flown in 1945. Under William Mayo's management, however, Ford Motor's aviation department would expand to 1,455 workers as it continued to produce a total of 199 Tri-Motor airplanes and to develop new designs. Still, neither Henry nor Edsel Ford played much of a part in Ford Aviation after its first few years. Even in 1927, the company's top decision makers could spare little time for anything but Ford's cars and the troubles that had been brewing behind the success of the Model T. The airport remained active, however, and the Fords eventually hired architect Albert Kahn to design one of the world's first airport hotels. Completed in 1931 to accommodate the overnight travelers passing in ever greater numbers through Ford Airport, Kahn's 179-room colonial-style Dearborn Inn offered a special "Pilot's Row," for airline crews on layovers.

William Stout, who would leave Ford in 1930 to devote himself full-time to his Stout Engineering Laboratory, went on to create a series of unusual machines including the "sky car," a combination airplane and automobile; the "rail plane," a gas-driven railroad car; a collapsible "house trailer"; and a spacious rear-motor vehicle he called the "scarab car." None ever caught the public's imagination, but he had a significant influence on transportation design nonetheless. In 2002 Stout gained the posthumous distinction of being the only airplane designer inducted into the Automotive Hall of Fame.[53]

PART THREE

The Battle Joined

16

Good-bye, Model T; Hello, Model A

No single product in American history has ever changed the United States more or in so short a time as the Model T did in the first quarter of the twentieth century. It didn't start the Automobile Age, but it did start it in the hearts and souls of millions of people who would've been untouched by all the excitement for years or even decades otherwise. The Model T accelerated the advent of the automobile in American society at large by at least ten years, but probably more like a full generation of twenty-five years. There were other cars pouring into the market, of course, but Model Ts, arriving by the millions, gave impetus to the support structure—roads, parking lots, traffic signals, service stations, and so on—that made all other cars more attractive. The Model T, in other words, did not just proliferate—it begat other cars as well. That made it a unique product—or juggernaut—in the twentieth century.

The automotive writer John Keats summed up in *The Insolent Chariots*: "The automobile changed our dress, manners, social customs, vacation habits, the shape of our cities, consumer purchasing patterns, common tastes, and positions in intercourse."[1] Not even the New Deal could claim that. By the 1920s, one of every eight American workers was employed in some automobile-related industry, be it petroleum refining, rubber making, or steel manufacturing. Thanks to the revolution started by Ford Motor Company, most of these laborers made a decent living wage in a five-day, forty-hour workweek. Although 8.1 million passenger cars were registered in the United States by 1920, paved streets were then the exception, not the rule. The dirt roads in or between towns were often rutted or dusty, and sometimes impassable even for the intrepid Ts. Spurred by the rampant popularity of the Model T, however, road construction became one of the principal activities of the U.S. government; as of 1920, building thoroughfares ranked second among public expenditures after education.[2] Michigan's Republican Senator Charles E. Townsend called for a national highway system and a federal highway commission to oversee it. It was a fairly easy political position to take: citizens in every part of the country were clamoring for sleek new roads to match their liberating new vehicles. In addition, states like Colorado and Montana, interested in spurring tourism, were searching for ways to carry more visitors to their parks.[3]

Highways gave birth to the other necessities: the first drive-in restaurant, in Dallas in 1921; the first national road atlas, published by Rand McNally in 1924; the first "mo-tel," in San Luis Obispo, California, in 1925; the first shopping center, in Kansas City, Missouri, in 1925; and the first public parking garage, in Detroit in 1929.[4] "By 1920 the automobile was no longer merely a pleasurable pastime, it was a practical necessity," wrote historian Folke Kihlstedt. "To serve it, an entirely new architectural infrastructure developed."[5] Nowhere did this shift appear more evident than in residential design, in which front parlors and porches gave way to the predominance of the garage. At first they were hidden at the backs of lots, but they slowly began moving up and merging into houses. By the 1940s, some designs even allowed the garage, or carport, to dominate the home's main façade. Thus did automotive housing displace centrally positioned entryways, introducing informality and an auto mentality to middle-class residences. An entirely changed way of life developed around the automobile. When sociologists Robert S. and Helen M. Lynd wrote *Middletown: A Study in Contemporary American Culture* in 1929, they observed that "auto riding tends to replace the traditional call in the family parlor as a way of approach between the unmarried." They also noted that families and neighbors no longer "spend long summer evenings and Saturday afternoons on the porch or in the side yard since the advent of the automobile and the movies. These factors tend to make a decorative yard less urgent; the make of one's car is rivaling the looks of one's place as an evidence of one's 'belonging.'"[6]

Nothing changed the *look* of the American landscape more than the mushrooming of gas stations, seemingly overnight, from coast to coast. Prior to the advent of the Model T, car owners bought their gasoline by the bucketful from hardware stores or street vendors selling fuel from tank carts. Transferring the flammable liquid out in the open was not only messy but hazardous. By the 1920s, enclosed curbside pumps had become commonplace, peddling gasoline under hundreds of brand names, including Texaco, Sinclair, and Gulf. The intense competition inspired gasoline dealers to distinguish their products via easily identifiable stations, prompting rather absurd building-styles to sprout along such popular roadways as U.S. Highway 1 in California, the Dixie Highway along the Gulf Coast, and the Lincoln Highway across the breadth of the country. Some stations were fashioned after quaint English cottages, others were prefabricated in a no-nonsense modernistic style. The 1920s "city beautiful" movement resulted in gas stations that looked like ancient Greek temples or log cabins. Regional influences appeared, with colonial New England and California Spanish mission-style fuel stops.

America's auto boom also brought about a continual need for more safety measures. Every town, it seemed, had its own reckless young Barney Oldfield making a high-octane nuisance of himself—or herself—on public thoroughfares. While the factory version of the Model T was not very fast, with a top-speed of about 40 mph, aftermarket kits and backyard tinkering could easily turn it into a speedster half again as fast. Anyway, there were ways to drive even a slow car too fast, just for kicks, and all the speed demons knew them. William Clay Ford admitted to being such "a dangerous menace," when his grandfather let him drive cars around Dearborn as a child. Once, in fact, his daredevilry got Henry Ford's grandson stopped by the local police. "In Florida where we vacationed there was no age limit to drive," he recalled, "but that didn't fly in Michigan."[7] Driving fast became more popular—and has never lost its thrill for new drivers of each era. "I am careful and I am thrifty," as young Model T owner William Ashdown confessed. "At least I was until I became a motorist." The dangers were no laughing matter, of course. In 1924 more than 23,000 people were killed on highways, with more than 700,000 injured. State and local governments acted swiftly to implement and enforce a multitude of driving, traffic, and safety laws, inaugurating the dreaded speeding ticket, for example.

Yet even the downsides of the automotive revolution—including environmental pollution, car accidents, and traffic congestion—engendered economic and scientific opportunities. One of these would be seized by Detroit police officer William Potts in 1920; his beat afforded him a particularly tiresome view of the chaos and collisions that ensued when bicycles, horse-drawn wagons, and cars all jockeyed to cross the cluttered downtown streets at the same time. Potts adapted a railroad signal and cobbled together red, amber, and green railroad lights into the tricolor traffic signal so familiar today. With the permission of the city police commissioner, Potts installed his automatic light at the corner of Woodward and Michigan Avenues in Detroit. A year later, fifteen more were put up around the metropolitan area; by the end of the decade, every major U.S. city controlled its traffic with tricolor lights. Garrett Morgan of Cleveland, a gifted African American inventor whose parents had been Kentucky slaves, followed up by patenting the modern four-way traffic light now used all over the world.[8]

With every new automobile-inspired innovation, accolades were heaped higher upon Henry Ford for having launched America's car craze. Some of them were deserved, because he had certainly played a role in the success of the T. Some, however, were garnered only because he insisted on snapping up all of the good publicity surrounding Ford Motor Company for himself. Even if Henry Ford's legend was somewhat hollow, the Model T's never was. It was the real thing.

Of all of the many things Ford Motor Company did in the 1920s, a time when it seemed to be everywhere doing everything, the most regrettable was the dismissal of William Knudsen in 1921. In itself, the episode was typical of Ford Motor's executive politics at the time: Knudsen found himself outmaneuvered for the boss's favors, his orders countermanded so often by Charles Sorensen, Henry Ford, or someone else entirely that the situation became untenable for him. Bill Knudsen, as it turned out, brought indispensable talents to Ford Motor Company, on a par with those of James Couzens or Harold Wills. But where their careers at Ford Motor were cut short after years of masterly work, Knudsen had not even reached the peak of his formidable powers when he was fired.

The big Dane's bushy mustache and friendly mien lent him the air of a favorite uncle, but there was much more to him than that. Even the often willfully obtuse Henry Ford had to admit later on that Knudsen was "the best production man in the United States." Ingeniously methodical, Knudsen had laid out and refined Ford Motor Company's factories, approving new processes and working out the logistics to set the work of 100,000 machines streaming smoothly and steadily. He played perhaps *the* integral role in increasing Ford Motor's production from 78,000 cars in 1911, when he joined the company, to more than 1 million cars ten years later.

A writer who once overheard Henry Ford praising Bill Knudsen at a dinner party in Detroit asked the automaker why he had let such an effective executive get away. "That's a fair question," Ford replied. "Mr. Knudsen was too strong for me to handle. You see, this is my business. I built it, and as long as I live, I propose to run it the way I want it run. Mr. Knudsen wanted to run it his way. I woke up one morning to the realization that I was exhausting my energy fighting Mr. Knudsen to get things done the way I wanted them done, instead of fighting the opposition. I let him go, not because he wasn't good, but because he was too good—for me. Now I can concentrate my energies."[9]

Henry Ford was good, too, but not good enough to run his expansive empire without at least a few executives even better than he. The more, in fact, the merrier, but that was not Ford's attitude. His Achilles' heel as a boss was dangerous at any company and nearly suicidal at Ford Motor, and he was increasingly prone to construe his lieutenants' healthy disagreements as personal hostility.

Bill Knudsen's last major assignment at Ford Motor Company was the expansion of production facilities in Europe. Where others, including Henry Ford himself, merely toured Europe's capitals, watching the English branch grow more robust and the French branch grow more frustrating, Knudsen was responsible for selecting sites for new assembly plants. The two factories he launched, at Cadiz, Spain, and at Copenhagen in his homeland of Denmark, were to be long-term successes. As a contingency, Knudsen had planned them for failure as well, leasing equipment and planning operations so that they could collapse with minimal cost if business failed to develop.[10] When Knudsen returned to Detroit in 1920, at what should have been a moment of triumph, he was stunned to find his role had been diminished, not enhanced, by his assignment in Europe. He was used to an abrasive relationship with Charles Sorensen, but now that his rival had achieved a new berth as overseer of the River Rouge domain, the situation became intolerable. "Since I came back from Europe," Knudsen later recalled telling a friend, "I have found that my shop instructions on production matters were countermanded or ignored." In early spring of 1921, Knudsen was preparing to travel to England to oversee operational developments in the branch there when his trip was abruptly canceled.

As of April 1, William Knudsen either tendered his resignation or was flat-out fired. "I can remember when [Henry Ford] let Mr. Knudsen out. Oh, boy, what a time!" recalled George Brown, who worked in the Ford administrative offices. "Mr. Knudsen had everything cleared up and was all set to go when in just a short time, probably a few weeks, he was notified that he wasn't going to Europe; he was all finished. . . . We don't know why he was let out, but if you ever saw a wild man, it was that Mr. Knudsen. When he got the word, he was really upset." According to Brown, the rumor in the office was that Ford and Knudsen had a furious argument in which Knudsen said, "By God, Henry, I'll break you for doing this to me!" Knudsen's later version was slightly different; he said that he resigned from Ford Motor Company specifically so that he would never have to have an argument with Henry Ford; it would have been his first, so he said.

At Ford Motor Company in those rough-and-tumble days, it didn't really matter which; as George Brown had put it, a person was "all finished," either way. And so Bill Knudsen joined the "Ford Alumni Association," the name cynics gave to the long line of able executives who found themselves all finished at Ford. One of them, Frank Klingensmith, asked Knudsen to join the Gray Manufacturing Company, a carmaker that had recently been capitalized by the heirs of Ford Motor founding investor John S. Gray. Knudsen declined, figuring that established automaking firms had momentum and a new company would need massive, almost unlimited, capital in order to persevere against them.[11] Energy and ideas might have been enough to make a small company competitive in the early days, but not in 1921. (The Gray company lasted until 1926.)

In terms of financial strength, the most impressive companies in the auto industry, aside from Ford Motor Company, were Packard and General Motors. Packard made high-end cars and didn't especially need a mass-production man, but Knudsen was intrigued by GM and the new "can-do" spirit building there. With corporate offices in midtown Manhattan, GM was less closely associated with Detroit than the other two companies. The talented Albert Kahn had designed a towering office block for the company on West Grand Boulevard in Detroit, but the manufacturing divisions were spread out in towns all over southeastern Michigan. In that way, and many others, GM was antithetical to Ford Motor, where as many processes as possible were being concentrated behind a single gate at the River Rouge plant.

The aristocratic Pierre S. du Pont, the president of General Motors as of December 1, 1920, represented something new in the auto industry: big business. He had been in the process of retiring from his family's chemical company, looking forward to country pursuits on his Longwood estate, when he was drafted into service at the ailing automaker. An ingenious executive, du Pont firmly believed in those systems and controls that made business as predictable as possible. To tailor his methods to GM, he brought a small cadre of accounting experts to Detroit, but he depended most of all on Alfred P. Sloan Jr., an executive left over from the Billy Durant regime. Sloan may have been a veteran of the old days, but he'd been unhappy all that while. To him, du Pont's bland aura of blue-blooded conservatism was a welcome change from the circus surrounding Durant.

With du Pont's approval, Sloan pruned GM's divisions, so that the gaggle of makes that had been assembled under Durant acquired a sense of direction, one meant to draw a customer upward through the years. Cadillac and Buick were at the top; Oldsmobile and Oakland (to be renamed Pontiac) were in the middle; and, at $795 in 1921, Chevrolet was the lowest-priced GM product. At that price, it wasn't remotely competitive with a new Model T Runabout at $370, but then nothing on the market was. Sloan also reorganized executive positions within the divisions, such that commands came from the upper management only on matters of policy. Decisions regarding the best way to meet the policy were left firmly in the hands of the executives on the scene at each division.

If Sloan had held a mirror up to Ford Motor Company, he could not have created a company plan more exactly the reverse of the proudly unstructured, one-man rule at Dearborn. At Ford, there were still no titles for executives, as well as no organizational chart. "They have all made jobs for themselves," Henry Ford wrote of his executive staff in 1923, "but there are no limits to their jobs. They just work in where they fit best. . . . This may seem haphazard, but it is not. A group of men, wholly intent upon getting work done, have no difficulty in seeing that the work is done. They do not get into trouble about the limits of authority, because they are not thinking of titles."[12]

Ford Motor Company had not always been that way. Under James Couzens, the management had been as rational and well organized as a system of inter-locking offices. A half-dozen years after Couzens left, though, Ford Motor was very much a *shop* and full of struggles. When dealers at a 1922 sales meeting voiced the opinion that the Model T, even then, had run its course, Ford replied, "Well, gentlemen, so far as I can see, the only trouble with the Ford car is—that we can't make them fast enough."[13] That was about all that any-one within Ford Motor Company heard on that topic for the better part of five years to come.

Bill Knudsen was attracted by the suave dynamism that GM was adopting, and he arranged through a friend to meet Alfred Sloan. As a result, Knudsen was invited to join the company in an advisory capacity. Soon afterward, he was offered a job as head of production at Chevrolet. At that point, the future of the division was in doubt, with faltering sales of 61,000, compared with the Model T's 900,000. A consulting firm hired to report on Chevrolet's prospects concluded that no car could compete with the Model T and recommended dissolution. Pierre du Pont was all for that. As Sloan later wrote, noting that the Model T accounted for about 60 percent of the car market to Chevrolet's 6 percent, "With Ford in almost complete possession of the low-price field, it would have been suicidal to compete with him head on. No conceivable amount of capital short of the United States Treasury could have sustained the losses required to take volume away from him at his own game."[14] Nonethe-less, Alfred Sloan argued in favor of retaining Chevrolet in the GM lineup.

Normally, Alfred Sloan might have been expected to follow the advice of experts hired to study a problem; it went hand in hand with the "centralized/decentralized" management he espoused. In the debate over Chevrolet, how-ever, he didn't bother with facts and cold analysis. Rather, he made the emo-tional point that it would be shameful for mighty General Motors to back down from any segment of the market. Rumors at the time intimated that Sloan was reacting to Ford's purchase of Lincoln, considering it a direct as-sault on GM's cash cow, Cadillac. If Ford Motor Company would trod on Cadillac, GM would take on the Model T.[15] But Sloan's reasoning was proba-bly more opportunistic than that. He believed in marketing niches and thought he detected one lurking undiscovered in the low-priced field, just a little above the Model T. With Sloan's support, Chevrolet survived, but only while the policy makers in the New York offices waited for the corporation's engineering star, Charles F. Kettering, to perfect a new air-cooled engine that he promised would revolutionize Chevrolet in one glorious stroke.

Instead, the "copper-cooled," as it was called, required painful delays, time and again. After a year and a half of anticipation, it was launched and then im-mediately abandoned as an unworkable failure—after about one hundred had been sold. All but two of the copper-cooled Chevrolets were gathered back by General Motors and smashed for scrap. One of the survivors had been sold to

Henry Ford, who opted to keep it as a souvenir of the latest attempt to topple the Model T. The president of Chevrolet buckled under the pressure of his failing division and suffered a nervous breakdown. Bill Knudsen was named to take his place.

By then, mid-1923, Sloan had been named president of GM and he had become keenly aware of a new opportunity in the automobile market. As he wrote in his memoir, "Seldom, perhaps at only one other time in the history of the industry—that is, on the occasion of the rise of the Model T after 1908—has the industry changed so radically as it did through the middle twenties. As a challenger to the then established position of Ford, we were favored by change. We had no stake in the old ways of the automobile business; for us, change meant opportunity. We were glad to bend our efforts to go with it and make the most of it."[16]

Sloan described the change he perceived in historical terms: the first era of automobile production was dominated by the luxury carmakers—what he called the "class" market. The second era, he said, was a "mass" market, created and controlled by Ford Motor Company. In the third and final era, which emerged in the mid-1920s, the mass market developed a craving for a bit of class. Mere transportation was no longer enough, and new techniques in the way cars were made, marketed, and financed allowed customers to reach upward, if a car seemed better than anything they could have previously afforded. These were the trends that executives at General Motors exploited, giving it a jump on what Sloan called the "mass-class" era.

Ford's formula throughout these years had been built squarely around price: having developed a universal car, the company fought off competitors by continually driving the price down. At a time when banks didn't yet offer auto loans and customers had to pay cash for car purchases, a lower price did lead to greater sales. It was that simple. But thanks to a GM executive named John J. Raskob, installment buying arrived to energize the automobile industry. Raskob, who knew little about cars but practically everything about the power of money, organized General Motors Acceptance Corporation (GMAC) to offer loans on GM cars. By 1924, one in three cars sold by GM was financed through GMAC. According to a psychology still at work in the marketplace today, customers buying with a loan felt that they could afford a more expensive car than when they had to save the money in advance.

Knudsen soon assigned a rising Chevrolet engineer named Ormand E. Hunt to redesign the Chevrolet with slightly better performance. But what 1925's K model mainly had were good, solid *selling points*: it was longer and stronger than previous models, had a much quieter ride, came in a choice of candy dish colors courtesy of du Pont's Duco paint, and had a built-in Klaxon horn and big-car features on its closed-car models, including automatic windshield wipers and an interior light. Low-cost cars had never before been sold on the basis of looks and amenities—or class. For those also considering a Model T, the appeal of the Chevrolet was simply that it was a modern car, with a gearshift transmission, four-wheel hydraulic brakes, balloon tires, and shock absorbers. The Model T offered none of those, continuing to rely on alternatives introduced in 1908; the base version didn't even offer a self-starter or detachable wheels.[17] By the time factory options and aftermarket accessories had brought a new Ford into line, though, the price was not quite as low as the original list. And that was the gray area in which Sloan was hoping to match the Chevrolet against the Model T.

The emphasis on the closed car was another trend that, according to Sloan, Chevrolet gladly counted in its favor—and cultivated to the hilt. Impervious to weather and relatively quiet, closed cars were the rage of the mass market in the mid-1920s. In addition to everything else, they were a status symbol. Accounting for just 10 percent of sales in 1919, they grew to 34 percent in 1923 and reached 85 percent in 1927.[18] As the battle between the Chevrolet K and the Ford Model T heated up, the clash over the closed car was critical. The heftier K chassis accommodated handsome coachwork. The lighter Model T was not as versatile and its closed models were rudimentary—and certainly didn't offer any of the Chevrolet's comforts.

William Knudsen was tireless in backing up GM's marketing thrust with Chevrolets of ever increasing quantity, as well as steadily improving quality. Every year, he and the sales manager, Richard H. Grant, used one of their own cars to tour a section of the country, visiting dealers in New England, the Deep South, or some other region to stir up enthusiasm and listen to suggestions.[19] Knudsen had no pretensions about his position and made it clear to the dealers and employees that he was only their equal in trying to ensure Chevrolet's success. He became such a relentless zealot on that topic that people assumed that he was living out his grim vow to break Henry Ford. At a company celebration in 1924, following a year in which Chevrolet had doubled its own sales, Knudsen was pressed to say a few words. Suddenly stricken with bad nerves, Knudsen stepped up to the podium at the huge banquet hall of the old Palmer House in Chicago and pointed each hand into the air. "I vant vun for vun," he bellowed, in a Danish accent far thicker than the trace with which he normally spoke. That was his whole speech.

Hardly any of the two thousand Chevrolet dealers present knew what Knudsen meant. Those who did spread the word: he wanted one Chevrolet sale for every Ford sale. Soon the hall was rocked by cheering; it was the first time that GM had admitted publicly that it was really pitting Chevrolet against the Model T. That was bold talk. The previous year, Ford had racked up sales of 1.8 million to Chevrolet's ballyhooed 416,000. "Vun for vun" became a Chevrolet rallying cry.[20]

GM accelerated its loan program with a new innovation that allowed people to trade in a secondhand car and use the proceeds as a down payment. As the value of used cars solidified around the trade-in, Ford was faced with a new enemy, one even worse than anything Sloan or Knudsen could conjure up: its own previous production of Model Ts. The only car that could beat a new Model T was an old Model T at half the price. In the 1910s, when the market was still expanding far beyond Ford's ability to match it and when roads were brutally hard on cars, the used-car market didn't affect new-car sales. By the mid-1920s, though, cars were not necessarily battered and bruised after a year of use. And so sales of 1.8 million Fords in 1923 meant that customers in 1924 had plenty of choice when deciding between a new Model T and a used one.

The same might have been said for Chevrolet sales, but GM gave Chevrolet an important shot of immunity by instituting the model-year change. Improvements were still made throughout production, but additional features—those selling points that turned into bragging points for the customer—began to be saved for autumn, when the new Chevrolet was introduced.

As General Motors mounted its four-pronged marketing attack—installment selling, trade-ins, emphasis on the closed car, and model-year changes—Henry Ford seemed oblivious. Edsel, for one, tried to warn him that the automobile market was changing and leaving the Model T behind. A stubborn Henry Ford simply wouldn't listen. "The Model T is the most perfect car in the world," he insisted. His reasoning was understandable. Model T sales were still increasing. But that was partly because the market for new cars was getting bigger. As Alfred Sloan noted, back in his Manhattan skyscraper overlooking Central Park, Ford's percentage of overall sales was sagging. Chevrolet was winning market share.

"We standardized the customer!" bragged a Ford executive. Chevrolet customized the customer. Black wasn't even one of the colors Chevrolet dealers showed anyone stopping in the showroom, but practically every other color was available. Body styles were vivid and comfortable and after choosing one, the customer could also choose the method of payment. With a GMAC application at the ready, a dealer could close the sale on the spot.

"Colorful and Youthful" read the headline of a Chevrolet ad in 1925, and customers apparently took note, since the Model T was neither. "Bigger and Better" was Chevrolet's motto; every newspaper and magazine advertisement concluded with "Quality at Low Cost." All of the jargon underscored the same comparison, and customers knew that when they looked at an apple red Chevrolet coupe in an ad, they were supposed to compare it with a dowdy black Model T. The sales race took a competitive turn in 1926 as Ford's sales sagged and Chevy's gained strength.

A pragmatic Edsel Ford saw what was coming, as did Alfred Sloan, somewhat more gleefully. And so did seven thousand Ford dealers. "The Model T had run its course," wrote William P. Young, who had a dealership in Pennsylvania. "Every dealer knew it but their reports and recommendations were met with rebuffs and insults. They were told the whole trouble was their lack of salesmanship.

"Price reductions . . . no longer availed to revive the declining Ford business," Young went on. "The policy of makeshift body-changing designs and belated minor improvements no longer satisfied prospective buyers."[21]

Some frustrated dealers were jumping to other manufacturers. Executives were stymied, too, yet no one at Ford Motor was talking about the end of the Model T, not out loud. To do so would have been heresy.

When William Knudsen first arrived at General Motors, he shocked his subordinates the first day—and spread relief through the ranks—by letting it be known that he didn't intend to replace anyone with recruits from Ford. Before long, Knudsen was just as surprised by GM as GM was by him. "Nobody seemed particularly afraid of me," he later told his biographer, Norman Beasley. "If I went up and spoke to anybody, I was answered courteously and frankly. When I looked at the work and asked questions about it, I was given all the information I might ask. It was an entirely different attitude and so striking that I could not help but notice it."

The former Ford man ultimately decided that his old Dearborn company shared most of the same goals Sloan set out at GM, in spreading opportunity and reward equally among the employees. He further concluded, though, that the Ford system was breaking down. He cited four causes: River Rouge had become too large and isolated, Henry Ford was by nature a production man and not an administrator, he had too many responsibilities, and he was taking advice from an undisciplined body of advisers. "Fear was replacing confidence in the Ford organization," Norman Beasley wrote, based on Knudsen's appraisal.[22] The same opinion was voiced by nearly everyone who worked at Ford in the 1920s.

"We very seldom saw the top officials any more," recalled George Brown of the change in the 1920s. "In the old days, we'd see Ford probably every hour or less. After we got out to the Rouge in later years, it was years and years before we saw him. . . . The plant got so large that the old fellows were separated. We didn't have the Ford spirit. It was just like going from a little town into a big city."[23]

The pervasive sense of fear at Ford Motor Company intensified in the mid-1920s with the growing rift between executives, represented on the most basic level by Charles Sorensen of River Rouge and P. E. Martin of Highland Park. "Beginning in 1924, '25 and '26 there was a very decided change in tone and feeling in the Company," said Alex Lumsden, a manager in the steel mill, blaming factionalism for the drop in morale. "That factionalism would be between the Rouge gang and the Highland Park gang. It has been said by the big boss himself—I never heard him say it but we got it from the grapevine and there is always a great danger with a word slipping around through the grapevine—'Oh, that's the Highland Park idea.' The so-called Highland Park gang was treated with contempt and derision."[24]

Sorensen was the head of the River Rouge gang, assisted by Harry Bennett, who was known as "Sorensen's puppy dog."[25] Like Sorensen, Bennett was remorseless where Ford employees were concerned. Both followed orders without question, fired workers without asking the reason, and gathered information within the factory through spying or brute force. They were the men who set the tone at River Rouge.

While Sorensen was advancing the supremacy of River Rouge over Highland Park, he was involved in another, even more personal power struggle. Championed by Edsel Ford, Ernest Kanzler had been named general manager of Ford Motor, and then second vice president. For a period of about eighteen months, he was in fact third in command, behind only Henry Ford and Edsel. Sorensen, who had barely survived his rivalry with Edsel after being fired by the younger Ford in 1919, chafed under Kanzler's authority.

"E. C. Kanzler became vice president in charge of manufacturing and if that wasn't a mess," recalled Logan Miller, who ran the Motor Building at River Rouge. "Kanzler, Martin and C. E. Sorensen were in battles all the time. It was a bitter battle between Kanzler and Sorensen. Did you ever throw a club in the midst of chickens and see how they would scatter? That was generally the picture."[26]

Sorensen insisted that Kanzler didn't belong at Ford Motor and in a sense, he was proved right. "I was there in the formative period," said Sorensen, who had joined in 1906, "and did not find any difficulty in deciding what I should do. I pinned my flag on Henry Ford and that was that, no one could pry me off."[27] Blind loyalty to the founder explained the basis of every one of Sorensen's decisions on the job or in his career. To Sorensen, it was a requisite for leadership at the company. Ernest Kanzler didn't have it.

Kanzler was the last modern executive to work at Ford Motor Company for a long time. He ultimately failed there because he actually questioned Ford policies—out loud. And Sorensen made sure that every instance was repeated back to Henry Ford. By his own admission, Sorensen put a sinister spin on the relationship between Edsel Ford and Ernest Kanzler, telling both Henry and Clara Ford that the outsider was distancing their son from his father. In doing so, he reinforced another image to which the Fords were all too receptive, painting Edsel not as a keen judge of character who was unafraid to hire a dynamic man as a subordinate, but rather as a callow and rather pathetic puppet.

Ernest Kanzler was the better businessman, but Charles Sorensen was the better Ford man. In 1926, Kanzler actually wrote Henry Ford a memo insisting that the company would be better off with a viable alternative to the Model T. "This memorandum is given you so that I can feel that I have dealt honestly and squarely with the responsibility you have given me," Kanzler wrote. "It hurts me to write it because I am afraid it may change your feeling for me, and that you may think me unsympathetic and lacking in confidence in your future plans."[28] It was a brave thing to do, since Kanzler knew full well that Ford was blindly loyal to the car. The six-page memo was effective only in one respect: as solid proof of everything Charles Sorensen had been telling his boss about Kanzler's thirst for power. A few months later, Sorensen had the satisfaction of personally firing Ernest Kanzler. Edsel was no more able to reverse that decision than he'd been able to prevail in his own dismissal of Sorensen seven years before. If anyone came between Henry Ford and his son, it was Charles Sorensen. But it is important to keep in mind that Sorensen's long career was built on the fact that he never did anything that Henry Ford didn't want done.

Kanzler, who was fired not for what he did but for what he said, epitomized the dilemma that hobbled Ford management in the mid-1920s. The company turned out cars at a rate not approached by any other firm. In that, however, it was acting upon a policy launched with the development of the River Rouge plant more than a half-dozen years before. Meanwhile, Henry Ford refused to adopt or even consider new directions for the automobile factory. Absent from active management for long periods while he pursued other interests, he left his subordinates little to do except fight with one another within the inertia at the core of the Ford Motor Company. With no budget for research, no accommodation for development of designs and designers, and no ongoing discussion about the future, the company was in a classic reactionary position: solving management problems only after they came up. The concerns that commanded the most attention were personal and petty.

"When we got to the Rouge plant, everybody had to be literally made over," said P. E. Haglund, a transfer from Highland Park. "They were hard-boiled at the Rouge plant in the twenties and the pressure was terrific. . . . Everybody at the Rouge plant was on edge and jittery. We ran around in circles and didn't know what they were doing. Physically everybody was going like a steam engine, but not mentally. As long as their feet were in motion they were working."[29]

Albert Smith was a popular foreman at River Rouge. "I saw Martin and Sorensen come down to the Motor Building one day and there were two fellows working on their machines," he said. "They were both working but evidently said something to one another and they started to laugh. God, Sorensen got hold of me and he jumped on me. He said, 'What do you think this is? This isn't a laughing matter. This thing's all serious. You take those fellows and lay them off for a week and tell them to wake up.'"[30]

James O'Connor, a seasoned foreman who had recently moved to River Rouge, related a case that showed how a factory could be a beehive of activity and yet be absolutely motionless: "I knew what was going to happen," said O'Connor. "They were all going to be fired, not only me but all the fellows from Highland Park. We didn't make any preparations from one day to the other. I didn't make up any special tools, which I would have done if everything had been peaceable. We knew what was going to happen."[31] In fact, O'Connor was fired merely for being a Highland Park transfer. (He managed to land a machinist's job in another section at Ford Motor and later became a foreman again.)

In 1926, Ford began trying to patch the old flivver for another long ride, introducing a new look in bodywork: longer, lower, and smoother around the hood and front end. Moreover, the company broke its long-standing rule and gave the world Model Ts in a choice of colors. Although only three—black, green, and maroon—were available at first, the concession over colors was a significant indication that Ford Motor no longer had the luxury of dictating terms. That year, Henry Ford even made a personal concession, finally issuing a public apology for his campaign against the Jewish people in the *Dearborn Independent*. Dealers had long complained that his anti-Semitism was losing sales for them. A successful lawsuit by a Jewish businessman libeled in Ford's paper precipitated the apology. The downturn in sales may have humbled him as well and persuaded him to end practices that undoubtedly offended potential customers—of all religions. In any case, Ford kept his word, never disseminating anti-Semitic opinions again.

Still, the damage was already done, as *The International Jew* remained in circulation. In the 1960s, Gerald K. Smith reprinted it in the extremist magazine *The Cross and Flag*. Over the years, other groups, including the John Birch Society, the Arab League, and the Palestine Liberation Organization, continued to print it or promote its lies as factual information.[32]

In the aftermath of the terrorist attacks of September 11, 2001, and the rash of suicide bombings in Israel during the following year, a series of retrospectives on the twisted history of anti-Semitism appeared in magazines and journals. The British writer Christopher Hitchens published a short essay on the subject in *Vanity Fair*. Analyzing the disturbing fact that one third of the Jewish people were annihilated during the twentieth century, Hitchens explained how the anti-Semitic literature of the 1930s led directly into the Holocaust, at least in some quarters. Mentioning Henry Ford, Hitchens wrote that anti-Semitism "has a special appeal to the quasi-educated and the pseudo-intellectual, as well as to the ignorant, who fear modernity and the big city. It is more like a form of mental disorder or collective hallucination."[33]

Over the years, the Ford family, led by Edsel and Eleanor, tried valiantly to make amends for Henry's "disorder." Few gentile families or Fortune 500 companies have done as much since Henry's day to assist Jewish causes. Nonetheless, the family, the company, and the world have been left to cope with the lingering residue of Henry Ford's campaign against the Jews.

———————

The initiatives rushed into place by Ford Motor Company spiked Model T sales, but nothing could hide the fact that the old Lizzie was outdated in a fast-moving market for low-priced cars. Slower, noisier, and trickier to drive than its competitors, it was not even the bargain it had once been. The price of a Ford equipped with features considered standard by 1926 was only 25 percent of the price of a Chevrolet. By then, other automakers were copying GM's success—most notably Chrysler, which was in the process of buying Dodge Brothers. But it was Chevrolet that opened a gaping hole just above the Model T in the market and invested $10 million in a new plant in 1926, to allow for production of 1 million cars in 1927 and accelerate its push toward "vun for vun."

At the end of 1926, rumors swirled through automobile circles that Ford Motor was planning a new model, one that would at the very least replace the gnashing planetary transmission with a gearshift and three forward speeds. It seems the only person who wasn't passing the time speculating about the coming Ford model was Henry Ford, because in fact there was no model in the planning stage. Aside from an eight-cylinder concept chassis, the "X-car," that he'd been noodling with for years, the Model T was still Henry Ford's one and only "perfect car." Even while he insisted that he would keep producing it indefinitely, he began to show signs that he recognized the truth of Alfred Sloan's "mass-class" interpretation of the prevailing market. To writer James Young, he complained, "I sometimes wonder if we have not lost our buying sense and fallen under the spell of salesmanship. The American of a generation ago was a shrewd buyer. He knew values in terms of utility and dollars. But nowadays the American people seem to listen and be sold; that is, they do not buy."[34]

They did not buy Fords. At the beginning of 1927, Chevrolet surged ahead of the Model T in the sales race. At a time when everything seemed to be going Chevrolet's way, even the rumors of a new Ford model—untrue as they might have been—persuaded many loyal Ford customers to wait.[35] Yet, Henry Ford still didn't listen when individuals tried to warn him that the Model T could not go on forever. Sometimes he laughed and sometimes he yawned. When the sales figures slowed from what they had been two years before, however, he had to pay attention. Slowly Henry began to consider a new model, conferring with Edsel on a general layout. After that, he started where he always had, since the very first car he'd built in his own Bagley Avenue garage more than thirty years before. He began with the engine. In February and March, he and a small team honed an enlarged version of the sturdy

Model T engine. Yet the new engine produced only two more units of horse-power than the old.

In April engineer extraordinaire Harold Hicks was summoned from the aviation division. "I was called down to the north end of the big room at the dynamometer section," he remembered.

> There was Sorensen, Martin, and Edsel Ford. They showed me an engine that was running on the blocks. It looked something like the Model T. At least it had four cylinders . . . Sorensen did most of the talking. He said, "Well, Hicks, we've got an engine which is 203 cubic inches." (The Model T was 176, so it was a larger engine than the Model T.) He said, "It is only developing 22 horsepower. You have had a pretty good success in developing power out of engines. If we should give you charge of this development, how much could you get up?" Well, I took the slide rule, that I always carried, out of my pocket and did a few calculations. I said, "I think I can get you 40 horsepower out of this engine." All three of them drew long breaths at that time because they were only getting 22, and they were really in quite a predicament.[36]

Three weeks later, Hicks had the engine back on the dynamometer, with a new carburetor and manifold, among many other changes, and it was putting out 40 horsepower. The new model had an engine. With that, Henry Ford was ready to move forward, to truly advance as a maker of automobiles, for the first time in nineteen years.

The third week of May 1927 was marked by turning points around the world, all of which rated headlines. On May 26, Henry and Edsel Ford drove the fifteen millionth Ford Model T out of their factory. On May 20–21, Charles Lindbergh made his successful solo flight across the Atlantic from Long Island to Paris, opening a new era in flight. And on May 25, Henry Ford announced that he would discontinue the Model T, ending an era in transportation, and in social history as well. Ford's news was as big as Lindbergh's, receiving front-page newspaper coverage around the world. In the announcement, Henry Ford gave his car a thoughtful eulogy. Calling it "a great educator" that had introduced motor power to people everywhere, he said, "It had stamina and power. It was the car that ran before there were good roads to run on. It broke down the barriers of distance in rural sections, brought people of these sections closer together and placed education within the reach of everyone. We are still proud of the Model T Ford car.

"If we were not," he added in a wistful apology for his own procrastination, "we could not have continued to manufacture it so long."[37]

In truth, Ford Motor was broken in 1927, and it would never crest so high again under Henry Ford's aegis as it once had. It would continue manufacturing high-quality cars, but the automotive revolution had shifted into second

gear and General Motors was behind the wheel. "In 1920 Ford had 90 percent of the low-priced car market and was responsible for 54 percent of the
total automotive manufacturing output in the country," Bill Gates of Microsoft noted in 1999, offering a history lesson to future entrepreneurs. "Yet,
by May 1927, technical advances at General Motors and other automotive
companies had forced Henry Ford to take the drastic step of shutting down
his main plant for an entire year to retool for new designs. Today Ford is still a
world leader in automobile production and quality, but it has never gained its
pre-1927 position in the industry. Somebody at Ford saw the changes coming
in the 1920s. An engineer who came up with a new design was fired for his
temerity. The senior leadership wouldn't listen."[38]

Newspaper editorialists and social commentators tried to place the end of
the Model T in perspective, but there was no rush. The Model T may not
have been in command of the automobile market, but it was still in evidence
on every street corner. Eleven million were registered and running as of 1927.
Two out of every three cars on the road were Ts. Not only was the sight of the
Model T ubiquitous, the very sound of it was: more of a bleat than a hum, it
was loud enough to force people to raise their voices whenever one passed
near. Multiplied by a dozen on every block, the Model T gave an insistent
squabble to the background of city life. Its engine had become the soundtrack
for modern America.

A handful of customers blanched at the thought of being without new Ts
and stocked up on them. One man in Ohio laid away a supply and kept driving new Model Ts until 1967.

In "Farewell, My Lovely," a wry yet sentimental tribute to the Model T
penned by *New Yorker* essayist E. B. White in 1936 under the pseudonym
Lee Strout White, the historical importance of flivvers was properly recognized. "There was this about a Model T," he wrote: "the purchaser never regarded his purchase as a complete, finished product. When you bought a
Ford, you figured you had a start—a vibrant, spirited framework, to which
could be screwed an almost limitless assortment of decorative and functional
hardware. Driving away from the agency, hugging the new wheel between
your legs, you were already full of creative worry." Most of the essay, however,
dealt with the void felt when Ford Motor stopped making Tin Lizzies. "The
last Model T," White continued, "was built in 1927 and the car is fading from
what scholars call the American scene—which is an understatement, because to a few million people who grew up with it, the old Ford practically
was the American scene. It was the miracle God had wrought. And it was
patently the sort of thing that could only happen once. Mechanically uncanny, it was like nothing that had ever come to the world before. Flourishing
industries rose and fell with it. As a vehicle it was hard-working, commonplace, heroic; and it often seemed to transmit those qualities to the persons

who rode in it. My own generation identifies it with Youth, with its gaudy, irretrievable excitements."[39]

In the 1930s, novelist John Steinbeck wrote deftly about the Model T. In *The Grapes of Wrath,* the Joad family fled the sorrowful dust bowl of Oklahoma in an overloaded Ford headed down Route 66 to Golden California. Steinbeck actually made a character of a used Model T Ford truck owned by Lee Chong in *Cannery Row,* a grocer who acquired it as compensation for a bill. Dented, caked with mud, without headlights or a license plate, the old truck was an indomitable survivor that never quit chugging along. So what if it didn't have a brake, for as Steinbeck wrote, "when your brake is gone, you can use reverse. . . . And when the low gear band is worn too thin to pull up a steep hill, why you can turn around and back it up."[40]

As the decades wore on, Steinbeck saw the passing of the Model T as the end of American innocence. Deeming the Model T the great romantic icon of his youth, he joked in *Cannery Row* that most babies of his generation were conceived in the front seat. In recognition of the prominent role played by Model Ts in Steinbeck's books, the Ford Motor Company paid the author a small fee to write about his real-life experiences with the Tin Lizzie. The *Ford News* published Steinbeck's short essay, titled "A Model T Named 'IT,'" in its July 1953 issue: "The Model T was not a car as we know them now—it was a person—crotchety and mean, frolicsome and full of jokes—just when you were ready to kill yourself, it would run five miles with no gasoline whatever," he wrote. "I understood IT but as I said before, IT understood me, too: It magnified some of my faults, corrected others. It worked on the sin of impatience; it destroyed the sin of vanity. And it helped to establish an almost Oriental philosophy of acceptance."[41]

At the end of his "sentimental memory" Steinbeck, as if mourning a lost love, pondered the fate of IT, the car that raised him from adolescence to adulthood. "Metal may change its composition through rust or blast furnace, but all atoms remain somewhere, and I have wondered sadly about IT," he wrote. Had it been pushed into the Pacific Ocean? Was it rotting in a San Jose junkyard? Perhaps, he thought, a blast furnace had made it into a bombshell for use in World War II or maybe it was used to make railroad cross ties. "It might be a girder of a bridge, or even something to support a tiny piece of the U.N. building in New York," he concluded. "And just perhaps," he thought, "in the corner of some field, the grass and the yellow mustard may grow taller and greener than elsewhere and if you were to dig down, you might find the red of rust under the roots, and that might be IT, enriching the soil, going home to its mother, the earth." All Steinbeck knew for certain is that he missed his Model T.[42]

Many of Ernest Hemingway's best short stories, such as "Indian Camp" and "Big Two-Hearted River," were drawn from his boyhood experiences in northern Michigan, where his family took their Tin Lizzie on their summer vacations.[43] Driving the Model T through such rugged terrain required thoughtful preparation: two spare tires were attached to the side and a saw was included with the gear, in order to cut tree branches to place beneath the wheels for traction in mud. Since the Model T had no trunk space, luggage was tied to the roof. Ernest's well-organized father kept a trip diary, which included odometer readings, notes on mechanical glitches, and culinary reports. Starting at the southern tip of Lake Michigan, the Hemingways clung to the primitive shoreline roads and headed north, alternating between camping outdoors and staying at inns. Depending on road conditions they covered anywhere from 65 to 137 miles per day. Ernest, the designated grease monkey, was in charge of pulling the choke wire and cranking the car to life, then hopping in beside his father in the front seat to help navigate around potholes.

The summer of 1917 on Wallon Lake was an idyllic memory for Ernest Hemingway, who began working as a reporter for the *Kansas City Star* that fall. With America in World War I, Hemingway enlisted in the Red Cross Ambulance Corps, where he put his mechanical ability to use. Assigned to Italy, he was badly wounded and returned home a hero. With little money, Hemingway continued to tool around in a Model T. The publication of *The Sun Also Rises* (1926) made him famous and modestly wealthy. In 1928, Hemingway and his wife traded in the Model T for a yellow Model A convertible coupe and drove from Arkansas to Key West, Florida.[44] A few years later, flush from the success of *A Farewell to Arms* (1929), Hemingway walked into Trevor & Morris in Key West and traded in his Model A Cabriolet for a Ford V-8 Deluxe Roadster—his dream car. "He declared only a fool wouldn't drive a Ford," manager George Perpall recalled, "and bragged that if I gave him a kit he could build a Model T in a day."[45]

White, Steinbeck, and Hemingway weren't alone. Warm feelings for the Model T were widespread and grew stronger through the years. But in 1927, most customers forgot about the old flivver within minutes of Henry Ford's announcement of its demise. They were fixated on the new model. In fact, the new Ford became a national obsession, fanned (as obsessions often are) by a lack of concrete information. All that Henry Ford would say was that the new Ford would have "speed, style, flexibility and control in traffic."

In 1927, for the first time, Henry Ford began to invest some of the $90,839,000[46] he had as cash on hand, nearly all of it derived from the Model T, to develop its successor, to be called the Model A. At first, Ford hoped to continue production of the Model T while retooling for the A, but the demand simply wasn't there. In early June, the Ford factories shut down and 60,000 workers were laid off. Ford Motor Company quit the 1927 sales race before it could lose out. For the year, its sales would be 480,771. Chevrolet's would be 1,004,398. Knudsen had *two* for "vun." He was aware, however, that Ford was not out for good. It was merely rearming.

To Alfred Sloan, the victory was complete. Though he certainly didn't gloat publicly at the time, he did note in his memoir that with the new model, Ford was still clinging to his old concept—the universal car, perfect and permanent. While Lincoln Motor continued in the luxury range, Ford Motor had nothing to offer in the mid-range, and nothing for the future. Ford still missed the point that strength lay in a variety of models, updated annually to reinforce new sales. Because of that, Sloan could watch the excitement building around the new model dispassionately, dismissing it as "incidental from the long-term point of view."[47]

The Model A may well have come along in the nick of time to preserve the forward momentum of Ford Motor Company. For a while at least, the new car renewed the creative spirit and the can-do attitude that had once pushed the company to achieve more in its short time than any other industrial enterprise in the world. Perhaps that only proved how valuable Henry Ford was as a hands-on manager, who worked best when he worked with his employees. Without the Model A, Henry Ford would have remained isolated as a sadly inconsistent chief of operations. Of even more consequence, the ability of his staff to produce a new automobile would have remained adrift. Ford did not, however, have any engineering genius on his staff, no one of the stuff of Harold Wills. That was a point made by many observers as the Model A came together. Historians Allan Nevins and Frank Ernest Hill in *Ford: Expansion and Challenge* explained, "The fact of the deficiency was true, but the reasons went well beyond personal friction. Nothing is strange or discreditable in the fact that Ford insisted on having engineers who, while capable of original solutions, were willing to subordinate their ideas to his own penetration and originality."[48]

After the engine was generally set, the staff had to design everything else on the car, from chassis, brakes, and transmission to the instrument panel and roofline. Edsel Ford, who had a more active role in the planning of the Model A than he had enjoyed in any other single project at Ford Motor Company, set the length of the car a few inches longer than the Chevrolet K. He insisted that the chassis sit lower to the ground than the Model T, since roads were mostly paved by 1927. Edsel was also instrumental in the campaign for a three-speed transmission. While the Model A would be more comfortable and offer better performance than the Model T, Henry Ford wanted it to be just as sturdy. To that end, a planetary transmission, with less friction and fewer parts, was more dependable in the long run. Up-to-date customers of 1927 didn't care about that, however—they just didn't like the extra effort of operating a planetary drive. Henry Ford toyed with the idea of making the planetary drive operate automatically, with no input from the driver. His subordinates moaned and assured him that there was no time to develop such a thing, and the idea was dropped. He was on the right track, though. To this day, automatic transmissions operate in conjunction with a planetary-type drive. In the end, Henry Ford approved a version of the Lincoln three-speed for the Model A.

To maintain the veil of secrecy crucial to maintaining public interest in the new model, only twelve people at Ford were privy to the entire design as it took shape.[49] That group included Joseph Galamb, who had been lead designer of the Model T, and Eugene Farkas, who concentrated on the chassis and originated unique systems for the four-wheel brakes and the springs. Two of the other engineers were entirely new to Ford: Frank Johnson, who was on loan from Lincoln Motor, where he had been the chief engineer, and Laurence Sheldrick, a recent recruit to the company who refined the Model A engine.

One day, Henry Ford took a Model A off-road, driving it over an open field. By the time he returned, he'd decided to have hydraulic shock absorbers—the same ones used in the Lincoln—installed in the car. Only luxury cars, and the Model A Ford, had hydraulic shocks in 1927; the rest of the industry would eventually follow suit, though.

On another test drive, Harold Hicks and a mechanic had a collision at high speed and they hit the windshield. Nearly all of their serious injuries had been rendered by the jagged glass of the windshield. Because of that, the Model A received another hand-me-down from the Lincoln and became the only car below the luxury class to employ shatterproof safety glass.

The fact is that there was a lot of Lincoln in the little Model A. Edsel Ford used the knowledge gained in his work refreshing the looks of the Lincoln to produce the Model A's irresistible styling. In that department, his father didn't meddle at all, but stood back, genuinely impressed with his son's ability to work with designers and make insightful suggestions of his own. Edsel had a fine understanding of the mechanical side of automobiles, but he was a truly outstanding design director. On the Model A nine body styles were offered, from a snappy roadster to a dignified "Fordor" sedan, complete with a landau roof.

With a viable design ready by July 1927, Henry Ford turned to a task that would be at least as important as the final product itself: working out the production methods. Ford was insistent on one basic point: he wouldn't allow any part of the running chassis to be stamped out of metal. Any piece of steel that could be cut could also be broken. "Everything had to be a forging," explained William Pioch. "Of course, it was quite expensive. There were a lot of stampings on the engine that were to be all forgings. Everything had to be just right. In other words, he wanted a car much better than our competitors' cars."[50] The forgings were complicated to make, but combined with extensive use of an original method of spot welding, they made the Model A one of the most durable cars ever built.

That summer, $80 million worth of machines were installed at River Rouge. In the process, practically every piece of equipment at the huge factory was improved or entirely replaced. The power plant, which had been deemed an industrial marvel when it was capable of producing 125,000 horsepower, was expanded so that it could produce 250,000 hp. For the first time, finished cars would roll off an assembly line at the Rouge; in fact, the Model A was constructed in its entirety there. Old machines were transferred to Highland Park, which was to continue making Model T replacement parts. To implement the tide of changes, employees began to return to work in June, only a month after the layoffs. By October, a full complement of 183,313 people had been recalled to work—in all, 25,000 jobs were lost to improvements in manufacturing methods. Although the animosity between Highland Park transfers and River Rouge veterans was as pronounced as ever, the all-new Model A factory worked: it produced cars.

On October 24, 1927, the *Detroit Times* carried a banner headline: "Ford O.K.'s New Model." The first Model A prototypes generally passed muster with Ford executives, riding comfortably at 50 mph, and 60 mph at top speed. There were minor changes to be made, especially in production methods, and until everything was in order, Henry Ford was in no hurry to introduce the car. Meanwhile, very few people knew what it looked like. In November, production started very slowly and under a general veil of secrecy. Cars were set aside as they came off the line, ready for shipment to key dealerships.

The public had worked itself into a frenzy over the new car. Ford hadn't done a thing to encourage the curiosity, and that is precisely why it resulted. The company didn't hurry the car to market, didn't stoke interest with "teasers" or conduct any campaign more cunning than total silence. Nevertheless, by the beginning of December, 400,000 customers were ready to place orders, sight unseen. On December 2, the company prepared to end their agony by unveiling the Model A at special salons in major cities around the United States.

Riot police had to be called out in Chicago, Detroit, Cleveland, and New York. A crowd estimated in the thousands spent the night outside the New York showroom, waiting for their first glimpse of the car that presumed to replace the Model T. The *New York World* summed up the atmosphere: "The excitement could hardly have been greater had Pah-Pah, the white elephant of Burma, elected to sit for seven days on the flagpole of the Woolworth Building."[51]

No one in the world except Henry Ford could have created such an air of magic and a car that had customers panting at the very words "a new Ford."

17

Model A and Trade Abroad

America was enjoying its pleasures in 1927, welcoming Charles Lindbergh home from his solo flight to Paris, watching Babe Ruth hit homer after homer for the New York Yankees on his way to a record of sixty, and riding the spanking new roller coaster at Coney Island. There was a dizzying abundance in the marketplace. New products offered consumers an astonishing array of choices. Foodstuffs became more brand-oriented than ever before; among the products introduced were Gerber baby food, Borden's homogenized milk, Welch-ade carbonated grape drink, and Hostess cupcakes. The list could go on and on.[1]

As a product introduction, though, the Model A would never be equaled, not in the automobile industry or any other, with the possible exception of the Mustang in 1964. Covered in headlines only a typesize or two smaller than those that would later trumpet the Japanese attack on Pearl Harbor, the introduction of the Model A constituted the biggest news story of the last two months of 1927. Ford fanatics just wanted to see the car, while business investors speculated that a flood of new Fords might energize the sluggish economy of the last two quarters of the year.[2] "The new Ford Car is a wonder," promised an advertisement placed by a Georgia dealer in the *Valdosta Times* on Monday, November 28. "Full details to be given at our show rooms this Friday."[3] Similar ads appeared in local newspapers from Boston to San Diego, yet none of them contained pictures. Details of the new model, including its appearance, were kept entirely secret. A battalion of photographers joined the mobs of the incurably curious lining the overpass leading to the River Rouge plant, hoping to catch sight of the Model A. Various "spy pictures" had been published, but in each case, Ford Motor Company issued denials, claiming that the models depicted were merely experimental. People had no better idea of what the new Ford looked like—it was the national mystery of the day.

On one otherwise quiet day in November, a kind of hysteria rippled through the village of Brighton, Michigan, forty-five miles from Detroit. F. W. O'Brien, the editor of the town paper, hustled outside to see what was causing so many of the townspeople to rush toward the local bank, in such an excited mood. "The new Ford is here," someone shouted. "She's parked just north of the First National Bank!" O'Brien thought it was another Ford joke. A few minutes later, however, he found himself standing with the rest gawking at a snappy two-door ("Tudor") sedan, the first new Ford any of them had seen in nearly twenty years. O'Brien took a series of photographs for his paper, the *Argus*, before a pair of Ford executives came out of a hotel restaurant and casually drove away in the mystery car. "I suppose I could have sold these pictures to some big paper, maybe in Detroit and made a lot of money, but you know a small-town editor of a weekly paper gets just as much satisfaction out of a scoop as the daily-paper men do in the big cities," O'Brien later mused. "Once, anyway, the *Argus* scooped the country."[4]

For once, Ford Motor Company didn't issue any denial, and big papers picked up O'Brien's photographs. The side views showed what looks today like a fairly basic car of the day: black running boards hugging wire wheels, with a pudgy hood and chrome accents around the headlights and radiator. The windows were straight and vertical, but generous enough to make the passenger compartment an airy greenhouse. To the practiced eye of 1927, though, the Model A was indeed eye-catching, because it was so right, and right from the start, like a song that sounds familiar even on the very first hearing. Longer than the Model T, the A carried its extra volume gracefully. It was neither rickety, like the old T, nor bulbous, like so many of its competitors. The secret of the A's appeal was its innate quality of proportion. Few cars before or ever since have been styled with so little excess and so much well-toned versatility.[5] The first Model A came off the Rouge assembly line on October 21—everybody at Ford Motor crossed his fingers that the public would like the new car.

Late in the official debut week of November 28, Ford Motor Company printed an open letter from Henry Ford in more than 2,000 newspapers in the United States. Overall, the advertising budget for the week was estimated at $1.7 million—a hefty commitment from a company that disdained paying for any ads during the Model T's high-momentum days in the early 1920s. Meanwhile, local dealers were writing copious letters to old customers and new prospects, touting the car and the moment. Finally, the day arrived— although at most local dealerships, the only object unveiled at first was a cardboard display. Few showrooms had a "live" Model A; production and distribution would take months to roll actual cars out all over the country. Instead, small town customers were directed to visit one of dozens of "salons" staged in major regional cities. And they did. New York City rated eleven salons, spread among the boroughs. The main showplace was on the corner of Broadway and Fifty-fourth Street, where a sign a half block long was unveiled at daybreak: "The New Ford Is Here." Crowds milled under umbrellas in a cold rain, trying to make out shapes behind plate-glass windows that had been heavily soaped. Precisely at 9:00 A.M., workers inside rubbed the windows clean and New York had its first look at a real-life Model A Ford. An hour later, the doors flung open.

According to Ford Motor's tally, the number of people who attended salons or visited dealerships where the car could be seen reached 10,534,992 . . . on the very first day. "Ten Percent of U.S. Population Sees New Ford First Day of Show," announced the *Ford News*.[6] By the time the special salons closed the following week, 25 *percent* of Americans had gone out of their way to see the car. In Milwaukee, Charlotte, St. Paul, Dallas, Cincinnati, or Fargo, it was the same as people arrived early every day and made mob scenes of city blocks. A Denver newspaper claimed that the city hadn't seen as much excitement since somebody robbed the U.S. Mint. Those among the 75 percent who refused to get in line may have been able to avoid seeing the Model A, but they couldn't avoid noticing that the nation was making a folk holiday out of a product introduction. "I have just come in from looking at your new car on exhibit in Orange," Thomas Edison wrote Henry Ford in early December. "IT is fine. Better than I ever expected."[7]

The *New York World* was one of many newspapers that published editorials trying to explain the Ford phenomenon. The *World* laid it at the feet of "the hundreds of colleges and universities which have now made courses in advertising part of their curricula. We commend the advance advertising of the new model Ford as a piece of work as important and as classic in its own field as, let us say, Spinoza's *Ethics* in the field of philosophy."[8]

Henry Ford was no longer being compared to John Jacob Astor, Cornelius Vanderbilt, or John D. Rockefeller: titans of business. He was a dazzling showman like P. T. Barnum. Whatever the spell cast over the country, it was working. The company counted more than 100,000 orders even before the debut. The salons collected 500,000 more; at the Detroit salon, there was an order every five minutes. Each order required a twenty-five-dollar down payment. One sharp operator went through the lines at the salon on Broadway in New York, collecting the money from eager hands and making notes in an order book. He disappeared moments before someone realized that he had nothing whatever to do with the Ford Motor Company. Selling Model A Fords in 1927–1928 was indeed as easy as taking candy from a baby. If people surrendered to a peculiar fascination with the new Ford, it was because they saw their own evolution reflected in it. Automobilism may have been born with the Model T, but it grew into confident youth with the Model A. And in a sense, so did many of its purchasers.

Customers were intrigued not only by the dapper looks of the new model but by its performance, which had not been a characteristic associated with a Ford product since the brief reign of the Model K in 1906. The Model A's top speed was 65 mph, more than sufficient at a time when 50 mph was the speed limit on the nation's best roads. A Brooklynite named Lewis T. Birch had the distinction of being the first person convicted of speeding in a Model A. His appearance before a judge was front-page news in the *New York Times,* as he protested that he'd gone 32 mph (the citywide limit was 20 mph) only to show a friend how quickly the Ford would accelerate in second gear. Birch received a suspended sentence, but it came with a warning from the judge for all other Model A drivers not to go heavy on the throttle in the new model—he wouldn't be so lenient again.[9]

While a fine-tuned suspension gave the Model A its smooth ride, the very best feature, as far as most customers were concerned, was the price. At $385 (raised to $480 in midyear) for the lowest-priced body-style (the roadster), it was barely more expensive than the last of the Model Ts, which cost $360 in the equivalent style. More important, the Model A cost less than the Chevrolet and was at least as attractive. "The old Ford dript oil into our upturned faces as we lay under it on country roads at midnight," recalled an editorial in the *New York Evening Post* in December 1927. "The new Ford is shown off like a modiste's mannikin to a generation which has lost the joy of getting its hands dirty."

The writer was trying to explain that very personal transition which was affecting all of those who cared about Fords—a swelling number that apparently included more than 25 percent of the nation. Like most of those peering at and into the Model A for the first time at the salons and shows, the editorialist looked beyond its pretty lines to its role as a companion of the road. "The old Ford ruined ten million pairs of overalls," the *Evening Post* writer admitted. "The new Ford is unveiled in hotel ballrooms by salesmen in dinner jackets. The new Ford is new; but it isn't a Ford. . . . It is a remarkable piece of machinery, but it isn't a Ford, because the Ford was an educational institution as well as a machine. The old Ford, the old, black, rusty, cantankerous, obstinate, sputtering Ford, brought wisdom to many fools and made many wise men go raving, tearing mad. This new lily-of-the-valley isn't going to teach us anything. It looks as if it would run indefinitely without complaint, which is all wrong. It is made for serenity and comfort, which is also all wrong. Where is the gas-tank? Out in front where it can be reached. Where is the timer? Up on top where it can no longer bark your knuckles. Where are the brake-bands? In a ridiculously exposed position where their value as trainers of character and refined language is completely lost.

"We are degenerating," the editorial lamented. "We are entering a period of Roman luxury. Back to the pioneer days when we threw sand under the fan belt and tightened the horn with a dime!"[10] The pioneer days, however, were over.

———————

The roar of publicity surrounding the new Ford certainly succeeded in creating demand. Even while the introduction was being hailed as a triumph of consumer enticement, it was turning into a disaster of fulfillment. It seemed to many business analysts that Ford Motor Company was overextended. Besides launching the Model A, the company started constructing a massive new administration building—made of reinforced concrete and faced with white limestone—on the east side of Schaefer Road in Dearborn. Located near the Rouge, the building was 220 feet long, and many of the offices were finished in oak, walnut, and Italian marble.[11] As construction ensued, the River Rouge plant was still learning how to make Model As—a process full of advanced and frustratingly tricky steps. The car's inherent quality, in fact, lay not so much in what it was, but in how it was made, in the generous use of durable steel forgings and the advantage of a new electric welding process.[12] But those and other innovations took time to master. Machines and men had to undergo a long period of adjustment before Model A production ran smoothly. The result was that in 1927–1928, although customers were as eager to buy as dealers were to sell, nearly everyone had to wait.

Cars trickled into the market at the rate of about three hundred per day, but demand was about twenty times higher. For a few months, possession of a Model A was as lofty a status symbol as that of owning a Hispano-Suiza or a Rolls-Royce. The mayor of Lynn, Massachusetts, took delivery of his new Ford in the first wave and announced that he was going to use it in preference to his limousine. Doug (Douglas Fairbanks) naturally wanted one for Mary (Mary Pickford) and asked Edsel Ford to arrange shipment in time for Christmas 1927. He did.[13] Thomas Edison and Will Rogers received early As. And James Couzens, now serving as a progressive Republican senator in Washington, was as curious as everyone else about the car that replaced the Model T. Seeing the Model A at a Washington dealership, he termed it a "daisy" and asked for the honor of buying the first one sold in the capital.[14] He received the thirty-fifth Model A off the line, a gift from his old company.

Movie stars and other celebrities may have been good customers, but by January 1928, when Henry Ford was presiding over a special Ford Industrial Exposition adjunct to the New York Auto Show, there were 600,000 customers waiting for Model As. And interest had yet to subside. On the first day of the Ford exposition, staged at Madison Square Garden, 223,000 people went through the doors. That is twice the number that attend a major state fair today, even on a record-setting day. During the six-day run, more than one million people visited the Ford show. One of those who came was Thomas

Edison. White-haired and failing at eighty, Edison probably attended as a favor to his friend Henry Ford, who would normally have provided him with a private showing. Another man circulated through the show drumming up interest in electing Henry Ford president of the United States. Ford himself had already been quoted during the run of the show, touting Republican Herbert Hoover as his own choice to win the White House in the election of 1928. Nonetheless, the crowds, the publicity, and the energy swirling around Madison Square Garden proved to those carmakers congregating uptown at their auto show that Henry Ford was at the top of his game—or both of his games, making cars and drawing attention.

Competing automakers tried hard to assert themselves. Willys-Overland cut prices on its Whippet by a quarter, so that it could brag that it was underselling Ford. William Durant, who rebounded from his exile from General Motors to form his own automobile conglomerate in the 1920s, advised his dealers not to take orders for his low-priced Star automobiles until they had vehicles in stock or on the way—a direct cut at the thousands of Ford dealers who had absurdly long waiting lists for Model As. "In the new Star Four, I am giving you a bigger and better car than the new Ford," Durant said, echoing the call of the low-price field in January 1928. It was an admission that Ford was back on top. The year before, they had all been chasing Chevrolet.

As for Chevrolet, GM remained defiant, still the mongoose refusing to let go of the snake. Company president Alfred Sloan publicly acknowledged the Model A only in gracious terms, explaining that there would always be room for both Chevrolet and Ford. "But no one believes that Henry Ford is getting chummy with his chief competitor or that General Motors dealers will begin directing prospects to Ford agencies," wryly observed the *Iron Trade Review*.[15] Indeed, Richard Grant, Sloan's vice president for sales, was blunt and emotional in a speech to his dealers during the New York Auto Show. He recalled the way that Chevrolet had finally crippled Ford in 1926, and swept by it with sales of 1 million vehicles the next year, the year Ford Motor Company closed its factory:

> Some people are saying that we became the largest producers of motorcars in the world only because our chief competitor was not producing. That is the alibi they offer. But I want to say that if there had been no stalling, but full production by everybody instead, we would have sold *more* cars than we did! Furthermore, I want to predict that we will be the world's greatest producers in 1928.
>
> But again, there will be an alibi. Some people will say that our chief competitor is not able to produce and deliver cars early in the year because of changes in his plant. Therefore, I go on to 1929. In that year there will be no

alibis. In that year, there will be no alibis and I say the Chevrolet Company will still be the world's largest producer of motor cars.[16]

Grant was right to dismiss 1927 and 1928 (when Chevrolet led) as anomalies in the overall chariot race between the rivals. In 1927, when Ford was barely part of the new-car business, Chevrolet's lead was 1.7 million to Ford's 356,000. The next year, Chevrolet had showrooms full of cars, while Ford did not, and Chevrolet kept a lead of 888,000 to 633,000 (Whippet made a good showing in third that year). But Ford's list of 700,000 standing orders for Model As[17] finally came to fruition and 1929, when both of the leaders were running at top speed, was Ford's year. The Model A rolled out in numbers that topped 1.5 million, while Chevrolet sold about two thirds as many cars. In fact, Ford Motor was selling 34 percent of all the cars sold in America. Perhaps that was not quite as impressive as 1923–1924, when the company controlled two thirds of the market, but by the end of the decade, that market was very different, pressed in from the sides by crafty, well-financed competitors and from the bottom by bargain-priced used cars. Rising above them all, Ford Motor had staged a resounding comeback.

Business observers have long derided the five-month, $250 million shutdown at Ford Motor during 1927. Yet the break allowed the company in general, and Henry Ford in particular, to do something very difficult except from a standstill—change direction. Styling and advertising, both of which had previously been rejected, were heartily embraced afterward. Vertical integration, which had been the conceit of the corporation ten years before, was on the wane.[18]

Probably the most lasting of Ford's many reversed decisions during the Model A changeover related to installment selling. Henry Ford professed to have no use for installment selling during the Model T era, when he held a virtual monopoly in the low-price field. The extension of credit smacked of banking, an institution with which he had never been sympathetic. Installment plans, Ford believed, were "merely a postponement of the day of judgment."[19] However, like Judgment Day, they were inevitable, and in 1924, when Ford Motor Company was introducing its cars into Germany for the first time since the war, it wanted to make an impact and offered cars at one sixth down and the rest in installments.[20] Likewise, Ford gladly turned to installment selling when he needed it in the U.S. market. While the new Model As could compete with Chevys in the showroom, Ford Motor would not beat GM in the dealer's office, where purchase agreements were signed, until it had an answer to GMAC.

To organize a separate entity to offer financing, Edsel Ford worked with a group of Detroit executives led by Ernest Kanzler, who had become an officer with the Guardian Detroit Bank. Under the plan presented to Henry Ford, the car company and the bank would jointly own a new institution called the Universal Credit Corporation, to extend loans to both dealers on new-car inventory and to customers on purchases. "Universal Credit" was an innocuous name, but it was to become a powerful force for Ford Motor Company, presenting hidden accounting advantages pertaining to the depreciation of the cars and the extension of profits over time. More conspicuously, Universal Credit added vitality to sales. The growth in the market no longer lay with driving the price down; that led only to competition with used cars. Customers had to be drawn into buying more new cars more often—and that meant they had to be able to buy them more easily. Through Universal Credit, a person could drive away in a brand-new $550 Model A rumble seat roadster for just $150 down and $12.50 per month. Who wouldn't?

"Even the most experienced can't tell by looking at a car how many payments are to be made on it," Will Rogers noted. In a December 1929 *American Magazine* article, Rogers said of Henry Ford, "He has given us the biggest problem we have in America today and that is, 'Where am I going to park it?'"[21] Will Rogers promoted Henry Ford and the Model A as if he were their paid publicist. And the favor was returned. When a Will Rogers for President movement sprang up in Oklahoma, Ford was one of the few public figures to take it seriously. "The joke of Will Rogers' candidacy for President is that it is no joke," Ford told the press. "It is a serious attempt to restore American common sense to American politics."[22]

Rogers was especially fascinated with Ford's money and how he bandied it about. "It cost him one hundred and fifty million to get America out of one Ford and into another," he concluded in his *American Magazine* article. Ford had done just that—but for that sum he pulled off a marketing coup, successfully replacing a model with two characteristics that were liable to collide in the public mind: the Model T was out-of-date, but it was beloved. Henry Ford managed to replace the T without forsaking it, perhaps because, as everyone knew, no one had loved the "perfect car" more than Henry Ford himself.

The way that Henry Ford operated—the way he made his way through the world, the logic he found within it—baffled people. "I know of no study more absorbing than the Ford psychology," Samuel Marquis wrote in his 1923 book, *Henry Ford: An Interpretation.* Perhaps Clara Ford understood Henry the man. Perhaps Edsel didn't. But no one ever claimed on record to understand that Ford psychology. "My effort," Ford noted, trying to explain himself, "is in the direction of simplicity."[23]

Garet Garrett, a writer from New York, presented himself at the Ford offices for what was to have been a short conversation with the owner in the presence of the company's erstwhile public relations officer, William Cameron. Henry Ford launched into a monologue on the general topic of banking. It went on for more than an hour. "Cameron wearily looked at the clock and said it was time for lunch," Garrett recalled. "Ford led the way; as we were going through the door Cameron held back a little and muttered to me: 'Do you wonder how so much chaff can come out of what you know to be really a fine mill?'

"At the lunch table," Garrett continued, "Ford went on, not from where he had been interrupted but from a new beginning, until soup was served. Then suddenly his tall body stiffened; the expression of his face, which had been very lively, changed to that of a sleepwalker, and he said to no one in particular— to himself, really: 'A-h-h! I'm not thinking about that at all.' With no other word, he rose abruptly, kicked back his chair and walked rapidly away."[24]

By the late 1920s, the workings of Ford's mind were more baffling than ever, simply because he was personally less accessible. While he was hardly a recluse, Ford gave fewer interviews and those he gave were largely granted to familiar, friendly writers, like Samuel Crowther. Under titles such as "If My Business Were Small,"[25] "Why I Believe in Progress,"[26] and "Henry Ford, His Men and His Management," Ford's pronouncements were themselves uniformly familiar and friendly.[27] The old days of scattershot Ford opinions may have been tamed by a controlling circle of advisers, including Charles Sorensen and Harry Bennett, or by age—Ford turned sixty-five in 1928. More likely, though, Ford was ultimately chastened, if not necessarily ashamed, by the lasting hurt of his anti-Semitic campaigning.

From 1903 right up to 1947, the year Henry Ford died, the air around him was usually buzzing with conjecture of one sort or another as each succeeding generation tried to understand how he came to the decisions he did. Thomas Edison, for his part, dismissed Ford's intellect when they first became well acquainted in about 1911, but in the 1920s, when they were much closer, he confessed that he was "afraid of him, for I find him most right where I thought him most wrong."[28] When asked what made Henry Ford tick, Edison handwrote on a note card a succinct analysis: "An even and flowing foundation of energy, a vivid and boundless imagination, a marvelous instinctive knowledge of mechanisms, and a talent for organization. These are the qualities that centre in Mr. Ford."[29]

Although actor Charlie Chaplin is remembered for his film *Modern Times,* in which he lampoons the moving assembly line as inherently monstrous and dehumanizing, he was an admirer of both Henry Ford and the Model T. Chaplin visited the Highland Park plant in October 1923 and was awed by the technological marvel. What he most liked about his Detroit experience, however, was meeting Henry Ford, in whom he found a wicked sense of humor. A few years after his Detroit visit Chaplin wrote, acted, directed, and produced the 1928 film *The Circus*. The movie is about how a well-meaning father decides to take his family on a weekend road trip in his Model T. Instead of joy, the car brings him only headaches. Like a stubborn mule run amok, Chaplin's Tin Lizzie refuses to follow the whims of its owner. Instead of being angry at Chaplin's satire, Henry Ford considered the film an all-time favorite.[30]

In August 1927, Henry Ford crossed back over the gulf between himself and many of the day's most liberal and humane Americans by making a public appeal against the execution of Sacco and Vanzetti. The two Italian immigrants had been convicted of murder in Massachusetts on what many considered insufficient evidence. While some people felt that the trial had been fair, observers from around the world were outraged that the only certain "offenses" committed by Nicola Sacco and Bartolomeo Vanzetti were that they were Italian immigrants, admitted anarchists, and draft dodgers. But that didn't make them murderers. As the execution date drew near, prominent liberals spoke out for the pair, forming a list that included legal scholar Felix Frankfurter, physicist Albert Einstein, reformer Jane Addams, and writers Dorothy Parker, John Dos Passos, and H. G. Wells. "I believe Sacco and Vanzetti should not be executed," Henry Ford said in a public statement that had the sound of his own voice, with his short sentences and direct phrasing. "If there is any doubt about the fairness of their trial, they should have a new trial. But in any event, they should not be killed," he said.[31] Vanzetti wrote Ford a letter of thanks, before he and Sacco were executed that month.

When Henry Ford issued his statement to the Jewish people, Will Rogers wrote, "He's the only millionaire that ever apologized for *anything*." He might have written "billionaire" instead. When Henry Ford was asked at the opening of the auto exposition in New York in 1928 how much he was worth, he turned sharply and replied, "I don't know—and I don't give a damn."[32] Many other people did, however, and in the mid-1920s, word circulated that America had its first billionaire and it was Henry Ford. By other accounts, John D. Rockefeller had amassed $1 billion at the height of his career, but Ford's was the first fortune of that size to be easily recognized in a single property. According to a 1927 survey, the Ford Motor Company was on a list of the ten U.S. companies worth at least $1 billion, either in total assets or market value. U.S. Steel was first on the list, followed by five railroads, AT&T, Standard Oil of New Jersey, General Motors, and Ford Motor. The number of shareholders associated with each of the companies on the list ranged downward from AT&T's 362,000. The average number was 62,000, which included investment trusts and other institutions. Ford Motor claimed a total of 3, and unlike the others, they had personal names: Henry, Clara, and Edsel.

On January 20, 1928, the Ford Administration Building was dedicated with great fanfare. Henry Ford would visit the building, but often just for a couple of hours in a day. Fair Lane had become the epicenter of his social and imaginative life. Henry and Clara lived quietly at the estate, often staying home to listen to the radio and read. Found in Ford's library were numerous volumes, many pertaining to reincarnation, ornithology, and botany. Clara loved Charles Dickens while Henry preferred the works of Ralph Waldo Emerson above all else. They both treasured the poetry of William Wordsworth and Henry Wadsworth Longfellow. The writer and editor Delancey Ferguson visited Fair Lane in 1928 in order to examine a letter from the Scottish poet Robert Burns in Clara's small collection of literary manuscripts. He later recalled his visit in a short piece in *The New Yorker.* "Mr. and Mrs. Ford were sitting in wicker armchairs enjoying the summer evening, like any other American couple with a nice porch to sit on," Ferguson wrote. "[Henry Ford] had on a darkish summer suit and green morocco bedroom slippers. They greeted me cordially, and we chatted for a few minutes. I endeavored to explain why, in editing Burns' letters, it was necessary for me to examine the original manuscripts. They listened politely, much as I would listen to an exposition of quantum physics."

After the three of them went into the library, Clara showed Ferguson the Burns letter, along with several early books she owned. "While this was going on, Henry sat and yawned openly," Ferguson wrote. "Presently, to keep conversation going, I admired the handsome secretary in which the volumes were housed. Henry sat up. 'Are you interested in antiques?' he asked." When the visitor admitted that he was, Henry insisted that he had something to show him. "I thanked my hostess," Ferguson remembered, "and followed my host— still in his green slippers—out the front door and along a path through shrubbery to a vast garage. No servants had been visible since the disappearance of the man who admitted me. Henry loaded me into a Ford coupe—the place was full of Fords—and away we slid."

Inside a cavernous warehouse in the old tractor complex at River Rouge, Ford showed Ferguson his collection. "Explaining that they were not yet arranged for public display," Ferguson continued, "he led me through gallery after gallery, talking steadily. I have a blurred memory of handlooms, wooden Indians, wooden horses, pewter, glass and machinery. In deference to my expressed interest in furniture, I was shown a whole gallery full of fine seventeenth- and eighteenth-century tables, desks, and chests of drawers."[33]

Although Henry Ford was undoubtedly a man of many enthusiasms, the underlying question attached to him in the 1920s concerned his level of intelligence. Business leaders, in particular, were divided over whether Ford was a genius or a dunce, whether his rubelike demeanor was a clever put-on or a troubling sign that he was actually dim-witted. A perfect illustration of this point occurred when a group of the world's top art dealers led by Joseph Duveen pooled together to sell Henry Ford the "hundred greatest paintings in the world." After great debate the dealers selected the various Rembrandts, Turners, and Goyas, among other masterpieces, and had three lavishly illustrated books made, including scholarly text. Armed with these elegant sales tools, the cabal headed to Dearborn, where they were scheduled to meet with Henry Ford at his Fair Lane home.

At first, Ford was wildly excited to meet the art dealers and delighted in the handsome volumes. "Mother, come in and see the lovely pictures these gentlemen have brought," he called to Clara. The Fords pored over the pages. "Yes, we thought you would like them," a beaming Duveen, the spokesman for the group, said. "These are the pictures we feel you should have." All Henry said was that the books must have been costly to publish and handed them back. "But Mr. Ford, we don't expect you to buy these books," a puzzled Duveen explained. "We got them especially for you, to show you the pictures. The books are a present to you." Ford acted bewildered. "Mother, did you hear that?" Ford asked. "These gentlemen are going to *give* these books as a present. Yes, gentlemen, it is extremely nice of you but I really don't see how I can accept a beautiful, expensive present like this from strangers." Duveen was speechless. Was Henry Ford really such a hayseed? Or was he cruelly toying with them? Anxious to close the communication gap Duveen cut to the chase: he explained that the art books had been especially created as a sales catalogue and that they had journeyed to Dearborn believing that Ford would purchase the one hundred masterpieces, thereby becoming an international collector on par with Solomon Guggenheim, Henry Clay Frick, or Detroit's own esteemed Charles Freer. Suddenly Ford's face lost its jovial charm. He turned cold. "But gentlemen," he inquired acidly, "what would I want with the original pictures when the ones right here in these books are so beautiful?" At that the meeting ended. The dealers headed back to New York, books in hand, confused and angry, and with no sale.[34]

Ford *was* a serious collector, as *The New Yorker*'s Delancey Ferguson had learned, but of a different sort. On September 27, 1928, Henry Ford formally dedicated a repository for his artifacts. Greenfield Village, located at the Edison Institute in Dearborn, would be a collection of original buildings moved from all over the country, starting with Thomas Edison's laboratory from New Jersey. Ford's concept, borrowed from the Rockefeller refurbishment of Williamsburg, Virginia, was that people would learn best from exposure to the actual sights and sounds of history. He also established at Greenfield Village an agricultural experiment station, consisting of chemical laboratory and greenhouses, for the express purpose of discovering "industrial uses for farm products." In the coming decades he made powdered milk, grew fields of marijuana in hope of producing plastics, and planted over three hundred types of soybean, all in the name of uniting agriculture and industry.[35]

Today, Greenfield Village occupies eighty-eight acres, dotted with buildings that reflect three hundred years of American life and the more progressive, inventive aspects of its work. That is the outdoor display. The adjoining museum, opened in 1929, has extensive galleries built upon Henry's original collections—one of the most popular artifacts, for example, is the theater chair in which President Lincoln was shot. (A later addition was the Dallas convertible in which President Kennedy was assassinated.) The twin indoor/outdoor museum is visited by more than one million people annually.

Another of Ford's educational endeavors of the 1920s was the development of the Ford Trade School, which offered schooling and occupational training to boys from disadvantaged backgrounds. As at Greenfield Village, Ford's idea was that the students would retain abstract subjects if they applied them in actual work situations. For that reason, two thirds of schooltime was devoted to work, for which students received pay. In 1927, the trade school had 4,500 students and 150 instructors. While Henry Ford took a special interest in the trade school, the Ford Motor Company also organized other institutions in what was known colloquially as "Ford University." An Apprentice School offered a three-year course in one of the factory's specialized fields to men aged eighteen to thirty. Similarly, the Ford Service School offered a two-year course to Ford employees from branches in three dozen foreign countries; they learned the latest methods in manufacturing and assembly.[36]

The trade school, run at a loss, was typical of Henry Ford's philosophy on charity. He rarely donated cash to any endeavor. Indeed, while Andrew Carnegie had set a lofty precedent by giving away more than 90 percent of his fortune through philanthropy, and James Couzens donated $10 million to establish the Children's Fund of Michigan, Henry Ford drew newspaper headlines in 1924 when he made his very first donation to an organization—worth something like $800 million at the time, he gave the YMCA $25,000.[37] It was not that Ford was avaricious when it came to his money. Rather, Ford was an activist and he was also an egotist: he believed that the best way to help people was to move on their behalf in his own way. In the case of his schools and his historical restoration, Henry Ford was creating something new, which was his genius, after all. "Prosperity is not the product of charity but of industry, not of receiving but of producing," Ford used to say. "Money as such has little to do with prosperity, and in itself it does not produce."[38]

If Ford had his own unique sense of philanthropy, and how it should be rendered, he set an admirable example of it through the Henry Ford Hospital, which he founded in 1915 and underwrote throughout the rest of his life. Originally, Ford donated a large sum to the Detroit General Hospital Association, a municipal effort to provide a new public hospital for the city. When he became impatient with delays in starting work, however, he offered to pay back each of the original benefactors and foot the entire tab himself. The offer was immediately accepted.[39] After that Ford was free to do things in his own distinctly timeless style.

With Ernest Liebold overseeing development work, the Ford team studied great hospitals around the country and organized the new hospital, located just north of downtown Detroit, to draw on the best of them. Ford picked up not only ideas but personnel, staffing his new hospital with dozens of esteemed professionals, recruited very heavily from Johns Hopkins in Baltimore. At the Henry Ford Hospital, everyone, rich or poor, paid the same nominal fees for the best care possible. Henry Ford donated $16,525,000 during his lifetime for buildings and equipment, alone. Meeting operational expenses was a separate, continuing obligation. Although the cost of modern medical care forced the hospital to reset its fees in the 1970s, it has maintained its position as one of the finest medical centers in the country, with nationally recognized expertise in the treatment of cancer and heart disease, and in the fields of orthopedics and neuroscience.[40] In addition to caring for patients, Henry Ford Health Systems, as it is now known, has remained true to the founder's desire to build upon progress: it is the sixth-largest employer in the state of Michigan.

Where the hospital complex was concerned, there was no doubt of Henry Ford's generosity. Clara, on the other hand, has traditionally been portrayed as a frugal woman. But in truth she was a behind-the-scenes philanthropist. A devoted suffragist, as was her husband, Clara wanted to improve the strenuous lives of working women. Without fanfare, she donated one third of her taxable income—which came from Ford stock and ownership of other family businesses—to feminist causes. A devout Episcopalian, she also persuaded her husband to build seven nondenominational chapels around America. After the Fords attended religious services at Berry College in Georgia, Clara befriended the founder, Martha Berry, and she embraced the school's educational philosophy of teaching poor children how to earn honest wages. Over a period of time the Fords gave Berry College more than $5 million.[41]

There is no better illustration, in fact, of Henry Ford's philosophy of philanthropy than the reasons behind the donation to Martha Berry. While Ford was leaving Berry College after his first visit, Martha had the temerity to ask him for a dime. "Is that all you want?" Ford asked her, smiling. "I am usually asked for gifts larger than a dime." Handing her the coin, a curious Ford asked what she was going to do with it. "I want to buy ten cents worth of peanuts to plant," she said and Ford nodded that he approved. A few years later, when the Fords returned to the college, Berry brought Henry to see the bounty that his dime had produced—rows and rows of peanut plants. From that moment onward, Ford opened his checkbook to Martha Berry to erect a beautiful gothic stone complex modeled after the architecture at Oxford University.[42] In addition, he built a water reservoir, donated a fleet of trucks, and constructed a brick plant. "I felt Martha Berry," Ford concluded, "could make better use of some of my money than I could myself." Today, due to land donations from Henry Ford, Berry College owns 28,000 acres, making it the largest campus in the United States.[43]

Ford could afford to be generous to Berry College and his other causes. By 1929, the Ford Motor Company was on its way to a record-breaking year. The company's success was primarily due to the Model A, though it still built an array of other vehicles, including heavy- and lightweight trucks. Tri-Motor airplanes, Fordson tractors, and Lincoln motorcars were also part of the Ford offering, despite the fact that none of them were profitable enough to have stood alone without the backing of the corporation.

Starting in 1925, Ford's competition with General Motors no longer stopped at the U.S. border. Both companies were committed to what they perceived as the vast, untapped potential of the European market, which resembled the American market fifteen years before. Dominated by luxury cars, the European industry consisted of too many companies and not enough truly efficient factories. Although firms such as England's Austin and France's Peugeot were selling attractive cars in the low-price field, these vehicles simply cost more than necessary in Europe. The average price of cars sold in America was just over $600 in 1928. In Europe, the average was $1,430.[44] Ford and GM were both convinced that lower prices would stretch the automobile market in Europe.

Automobile ownership was glaringly disproportionate even among industrialized nations, leading the American automakers to the conclusion that progress could certainly be made among the laggards. If the European market grew to match the U.S. ownership rate of one car per every six people, approximately fifteen times as many cars would be sold, as indicated in the table on page 370.

In 1925, GM purchased England's Vauxhall Motors and was in the process of formulating policy for all overseas operations. After a long series of meetings (for which Sloan's organization was famous), the company also purchased a controlling interest in Germany's largest carmaker, Opel, in 1928. GM was not out to build a "universal car" like the Model T. Instead, the policy was to acquire companies in individual countries and build upon their existing reputations.

Ford Motor Company responded by establishing its own policy. Although many of its European operations were long established, they were not making gains with the proper vigor. At first, the launch of the Model A had seemed a natural basis on which to launch a new initiative. In London, the only foreign

Motor Vehicles Registration According to Population (1926)[45]

COUNTRY	NO. OF CARS	BUSES AND TRUCKS	PERSONS PER VEHICLE
ASIA/AUSTRALIA			
Australia	243,055	48,157	20
China	11,200	2,480	31,871
Japan	21,245	11,453	1,789
New Zealand	81,698	14,650	13
EUROPE			
Belgium	50,270	42,443	82
Britain	660,734	242,287	49
France	450,000	285,000	54
Germany	215,150	107,850	1,935
Italy	78,000	36,700	2,642
Netherlands	40,500	15,800	121
Spain	65,000	11,000	286
Sweden	60,300	21,300	74
NORTH AMERICA			
Canada	644,725	74,993	12
Mexico	31,579	6,245	38
United States	17,512,638	2,489,843	6
SOUTH AMERICA			
Argentina	165,000	13,050	54
Brazil	50,000	13,650	481

city to host a salon, newsstand placards were posted throughout the city on the December 2 debut date, reading "All About the New Ford." Thousands of people made their way to a showroom in the Holland Park neighborhood to get a close-up look.

Yet there were complaints throughout the continent that while the new Model A was fetching, it was American through and through: sitting higher up and with greater heft than most European cars in the low-price segment. To assuage customers interested in economy, the company added the Model AF solely for the European market: with a smaller engine, it was subject to lower taxes in most countries and it delivered somewhat better gas mileage than the standard model. Henry Ford was still adamant that it was possible to build a "world car," suited to tastes throughout the world, but with the AF, he admitted for the first time that his company would have to be more supple in its overseas dealings than it had been in the Model T era.

With help from Edsel and from Charles Sorensen, Henry Ford made the decision to formalize the international organization. Ford of Canada would continue to be responsible for the British Empire, except for the British Isles, while Dearborn supplied the rest of the world, except for Europe. The biggest changes occurred in Europe, where individual operations were to be granted new autonomy, and yet develop as a group under the aegis of a recast Ford Motor (England) Ltd. The English company was to be anchored by a vast new factory under construction in Dagenham, east of London on the Thames River. The various European operations would look to Dagenham for production of primary parts, just as the British Commonwealth nations looked to Windsor, Ontario, and the rest of the world looked to Dearborn.

Sir Percival Perry, the man responsible for initially building Ford Motor Company's business in England, had resigned after a bitter quarrel with Bill Knudsen in 1919. He went on to impressive posts in government and business, but always confessed that he considered Ford his rightful home. Henry Ford was just as remorseful; he considered Sir Percival an astute executive, a commodity he needed desperately for his English subsidiary in the late 1920s. In 1928, when Henry Ford invited Perry to resume his former role, it was a relief for them both—and a rare instance when a member of the "Ford Alumni Association" was allowed to return. At the invitation of the Fords, Sir Percival traveled to Dearborn, armed with facts and figures to support his view that Ford's factories in Europe should reflect local investment. As it was, Ford subsidiaries in countries such as Spain and Denmark were typically owned outright by the Ford family or by their corporation.

L. E. Briggs, who had survived a series of cutbacks in Ford Motor's accounting department, was in Europe with a team auditing operations there when Sir Percival's changes were introduced in mid-1928. "I suspect that his idea," Briggs recalled, "involving public participation as it did, was intended to some extent to combat the antagonism that existed in many countries against foreign-owned companies. There was very much of a nationalistic movement going in England at the time. 'Buy British' signs were all over the place. The wider the participation in ownerships, the more it would help, I suppose, in promoting the idea that the companies were locally owned and managed.

"However," Briggs added, "we wished to retain control."[46] When stock was issued in the English company, the Ford Motor Company retained 60 percent of it.

Early in 1929, just as GM was taking control of Opel, Ford Motor Company announced the formation of eight new subsidiaries, in France, Belgium,

Germany, Italy, Spain, Holland, Sweden, and Finland. These units were, in effect, subsidiaries of Ford's English subsidiary. Ford Motor (England) Ltd. would hold 60 percent of the stock in each new Ford while the rest was intended for investors within each respective country.

The news that Ford stock would be available was widely reported in each country, and investors scrambled to participate in the initial public offering. When the English issue was just about to come onto the market late in 1928, Briggs was assigned to Ford's Manchester factory. "The stock was heavily oversubscribed," he recalled. "The fortunate ones . . . merely submitted their applications, which were filled on a quota basis, I assume. In other words, a man may have applied for ten shares and been allotted one. That allotment certificate which he received could be traded. They were being traded at a terrific rate long before the stock was even issued. I don't think anybody could sense the tremendous appeal that the Ford name had."[47] Briggs couldn't: twenty-three years later, he still regretted that he hadn't bought any of the new stock. The English shares shot up in price from £1 to £6 within weeks and were followed by equally exciting offerings in the other countries. For instance, the Belgian shares, scheduled to go on the market at 100 francs, rose before the opening to 540.

The excitement surrounding the Ford issues was gratifying, but Henry Ford was disappointed to learn that the shares, issued mainly in the interest of national pride for the nine nations involved, flooded into American hands as though flowing down a hill. For U.S. investors—who were maniacally interested in stocks in the late 1920s—the foreign shares represented a roundabout way to take part in the ferocious Ford moneymaking machine.

Countries all over the world were eager to take part in the Ford industrial magic—but they did so at their own risk. In Mexico, where the consumer base for automobiles was thin, Ford Motor Company started out slowly. In 1926 it rented a warehouse in Mexico City to build Model Ts, paying workers an astounding $3 a day, far above the going rate. Refusing at first to make a capital investment in the country, Ford insisted that Mexican workers prove they had the mechanical skills to warrant a *real* factory. They did, and in 1932 a ribbon cutting was held for Ford's new Mexico City assembly plant. Before long, it was producing 100 Model Ts a day, even after the car was discontinued in the United States.[48]

After the Rouge complex opened, Henry Ford established an ironclad rule for new international facilities: they had to be built on a river, bay, or lake. This was not just a quirk: Ford believed that waterways were the commercial links to the world. In 1930 he journeyed to the Netherlands to participate in a groundbreaking ceremony for a new factory at Rotterdam—a major port—sponsored by Ford Holland. Throngs of people arrived for the historic event, a brass band played, the mayor was on hand, and newspapers headlined the impending ceremony, treating it as an industrial milestone for the Netherlands. Everybody in Holland, it seemed, wanted to catch a glimpse of the world-famous industrialist. When he arrived, however, he looked perplexed. "Where is the water?" he asked. It was explained to him that the harbor was only a kilometer away. "No water, no plant," Ford snapped, proceeding to leave the site, giving orders to cancel the ceremony. The blueprints for the Rotterdam site were destroyed. Two years later, Henry Ford approved a new factory in Amsterdam—erected on the water.[49]

Even the Soviet Communist Party found Ford Motor irresistible. The five-year plan that Josef Stalin released in 1928 specifically bemoaned the lack of even one automobile factory in the USSR. The whole country boasted only twenty thousand cars. The largest nation on Earth had only a single truck company. While the Soviets had been purchasing Fordson tractors since 1924 and finished cars since 1926, they were intent on building their own automobile industry, and Ford Motor Company was their logical choice for help. Of all the great capitalist companies, Ford Motor was the one based most firmly in engineering (of both vehicles and manufacturing methods) rather than finance. Henry Ford did not sympathize with the Communist doctrine of planned economic development, yet he had an abiding interest in doing business with the Soviets. "People do not stay put," Ford mused about why the Soviet Union was doomed for failure. "That is the trouble with all the framers of Socialistic and Communistic, and all other plans for the ideal regulation of society. They all presume that people will stay put. The reactionary has the same idea. He insists that everyone ought to stay put. Nobody does, and for that I am thankful."[50]

The views Ford expressed in defense of a free-market company (such as Ford Motor) forming a partnership with Communists made a sharp break with Victorian attitudes toward world business. "This system of keeping certain nations dependent on others economically must disappear," he said. "When Russia and China and India and South America come into consuming power, what are you going to do? Surely you don't think that Britain and America will be able to supply them! Surely you don't visualize Britain and America as nothing but vast factories to supply the world! A moment's thought will make clear why the future must see nation after nation taking over its own work of supply. And we ought to be glad to help the work along."[51]

He later put it even more succinctly: "No matter where industry prospers, whether in India, China, or Russia, all the world is bound to catch some good from it."[52]

In the case of the Soviets, Ford Motor Company capped two years of visits and friendly negotiation with a landmark agreement signed in May 1929. It called for Ford Motor to oversee construction of a plant to manufacture Model A cars, in return for a guaranteed order for 72,000 unassembled Fords, along with all spare parts to be required over the following nine years.[53] Since the U.S. government did not then accord diplomatic recognition to the Soviet Union, Ford's new partnership was regarded as a radical departure in some investment and diplomatic circles. But not in big-business ones: a week after the Ford announcement had been digested, the Soviets reported that they had reached similar agreements with fifteen other companies, including E. I. Du Pont de Nemours, RCA, and a half-dozen engineering firms.

Ford Motor Company fulfilled its side of the bargain with determination. By mid-1929, it had dispatched its own cadre of engineers along with a roster of executives that included Sir Percival Perry and Charles Sorensen to launch the world's most complicated industry in a decidedly backward industrial environment. The Soviets planned two Ford factories: a production center on par with Dagenham was to rise in an isolated town called Nizhni Novgorod, located on the banks of the Volga River, while an assembly plant would start operations almost immediately within Moscow's city limits. Privately, Henry Ford believed that the best way to foil communism was to introduce capitalism at its best—a Ford factory, turning out cars for, as it were, the masses. "Ford was convinced," Mira Wilkins and Frank Ernest Hill wrote in *American Business Abroad,* "that what he was doing would alter for the better the attitude of the Russians toward the Western nations. In this he was mistaken."

Writing in 1964, during the standoff of the Cold War, Wilkins and Hill took a dim view of Ford's partnership with the Soviets, who, they wrote, "learned much from Ford, but his aid did not alter in the least their resolve to bring capitalism to an early end. The instruction they received in Dearborn, Nizhni Novgorod, and Moscow assisted them to improve their industry at a faster pace, and today, they are more formidable enemies of Ford's way of life because of the pains he took to teach them. Of course they would have learned in any case, but Ford hastened the process."[54]

John D. Rockefeller often counseled that patience was the most important attribute of any person in business, a fact that encourages the examination of Ford Motor's contract with the USSR in terms of its long-term effects. Communism in the Soviet states was indeed doomed to fall, just as Henry Ford predicted it would. It did not happen in his lifetime, but then World War II intervened and brutalized the course of the Soviet Union's development. (As a matter of fact, Ford Motor's industrial assistance in establishing vehicle production was to prove vital in the Soviet triumph over Nazi Germany on the Eastern Front.) Writing to the U.S. Chamber of Commerce in 1944, Josef Stalin deemed Ford "one of the world's greatest industrialists," adding the hope that "may God preserve him."[55] Never one to praise world leaders, Ford did not return the sentiment—but he did fulfill the Soviet people's desire for his tractors, trucks, and automobiles, just as he did for everyone else. Whether it was more effective in combating communism to starve it behind an Iron

Curtain or spoil it with capitalist temptations was an issue debated in 1929, as well as later years. Just which aspect of the "process" of communism's rise and fall Henry Ford hastened, to use Wilkins and Hill's phrasing, is still open to debate, but he understood the risks and was comfortable taking them: "It makes little difference what theory is back of the real work," he said, "for in the long run facts will control."

Referring to the Soviets, Ford said, "I believe it is my duty to help any people who want to go back to work and become self-supporting."[56]

That very sentiment was due to be tested back home in the most wrenching era the employees of Ford Motor Company would ever face. Between October 24 and 29, 1929, the U.S. stock market fell with a jolt that revealed gaps between perception and reality throughout the American economy. The country was entering a depression, no matter how much Henry Ford tried to deny it at first. Before that depression was through, Ford's workers would know too well the cruelties of the hard times. And so would Henry Ford, as his company became a battleground.

18

Coping with the Great Depression

I n early 1929 Henry Ford published a book entitled *My Philosophy of Industry.* Much like his previous three books, this one, written in collaboration with Fay Leone Faurote, was a hodgepodge of musings about the "Power Age." Modeled after Benjamin Franklin's *Poor Richard's Almanack,* it was actually an uneven mix of advice, predictions, and self-congratulatory pabulum. In his first chapter, "Machinery and the New Messiah," Ford's belief that international businessmen—not governments or religious groups—ran the world came bursting through in print. He envisioned what would be known fifty years later as globalization. "Machinery is accomplishing in the world what man has failed to do by preaching, propaganda or the written word," Ford wrote. "The airplane and the radio know no boundary. They pass over the dotted lines on the map without heed or hindrance. They are binding the world together in a way no other systems can. The [silent] motion picture with its universal language, the airplane with its speed, the radio with its coming international programme—these will soon bring the world to a complete understanding. Thus may be visioned a United States of the World. Ultimately, it will surely come."[1]

If Ford clung to one guiding principle his entire life, it was that technology would bring the world closer together—and even return it to the simplicity of his own rural essence. While economic disaster loomed for the world's industrialized countries Ford saw only golden days ahead. So it was with great optimistic fanfare that in October 1929, with his book selling briskly in stores, and handed out at dealerships, Henry Ford officially opened his monument to both the past and future: the Edison Institute at Greenfield Village.

To salute Thomas Edison, his eighty-two-year-old friend, on the fiftieth anniversary of the invention of the incandescent lamp, Ford invited President Herbert Hoover and Treasury Secretary Andrew Mellon to participate in a grand celebration dubbed Light's Golden Jubilee. Edison journeyed to Dearborn by train with his wife, Mina, and in a touch of the dramatic, got off at the very Smith Creek Station from which he had been ejected as a telegraph operator when he was a boy. Ford had spent $3 million collecting artifacts related to Edison's work, and he lavished $30 million on the institute, a campus that included Greenfield Village as well as a cluster of museum buildings. The centerpiece of the whole place was a reconstruction of Edison's original laboratory from Menlo Park, New Jersey, complete with a yard filled with seven traincar-loads of red New Jersey dirt, for the proper setting.

"Well, you've got this just about ninety-nine and one-half percent perfect," Edison said when he saw it.

"What is the matter with the other one-half percent?" Ford asked.

"Well, we never kept it as clean as this!" Edison said.[2]

A whole roster of leading Americans and world scientists and dignitaries— Owen Young and Gerard Swope of General Electric; Otto Kahn of Kuhn, Loeb; Charles Schwab of Bethlehem Steel; philanthropist John D. Rockefeller Jr.; Nobel laureate Marie Curie; and inventor Orville Wright—gathered in Dearborn to praise the treasured inventor and celebrate technology in general. It was an emotional ceremony as a weary Edison, given an adrenaline shot by doctors, reenacted the moment at which he invented the lightbulb. The ceremony was broadcast live over 140 radio stations and even to shortwave listeners overseas. At the banquet President Hoover was scheduled to salute the work of the genius inventor. Edison almost didn't make it: on the way in he collapsed onto a sofa and cried. He was overwhelmed but summoned his strength, and said a few words to the five hundred people assembled in the museum hall.[3] "The experience makes me realize as never before that Americans are sentimental and this crowning event of Light's Golden Jubilee fills me with gratitude," Edison said. "As to Henry Ford, words are inadequate to express my feelings. I can only say to you that, in the fullest and richest meaning of the term—he is my friend."[4]

There was good reason for Ford's optimism in October 1929, just days before the great stock market crash. Earlier that year America had its first TV broadcast, and continental airline service was established. While Henry Ford boasted about having the world's largest factory at the Rouge, Walter Chrysler was moving into the world's tallest skyscraper in Manhattan. As historian David Kennedy recounts in *Freedom from Fear,* standards of living had soared upward since World War I in the frenetic industrial cities of America: "For urban workers, prosperity was wondrous and real. They had more money than ever before, and they enjoyed an amazing variety of new products on which to spend it: not only automobiles but canned foods, washing machines, refrigerators, synthetic fabrics, telephones, motion pictures (with sound after 1927), and along with the automobile, the most revolutionary of the new technologies—radios."[5] The belief that technology could solve America's woes was widespread. As Kevin Phillips pointed out in *Wealth and Democracy,* law enforcement authorities in Detroit predicted in 1929 that technology was about to make crime nearly obsolete due to radio-equipped cars.[6] Anything, it seemed, was possible in Power Age America, where "progress" was king.

The Wall Street crash might not have affected Henry Ford and his company at all if it had been only a short-lived collapse, one limited to the paper losses of the financial world. Ford, after all, hated Wall Street. He took every available opportunity to deride the whole system of trading shares and the folly of the individual investor who thought that system could be beat. For his own part, Ford certainly didn't suffer any heartache on October 29, 1929— Black Tuesday. He didn't own more than a smattering of stock in any company other than his own and never had. Ford Motor shares didn't crash with the rest, simply because they weren't traded, on that or any other day. However, the crash—which was in reality a series of events that stretched across the period from Wednesday, October 23, through Thursday, October 31— was neither short-lived nor limited.[7] In effect, it was the first telling evidence of an international economy that had tottered out of control. During the Great Depression that resulted, Ford Motor Company was likewise revealed to have problems more serious than anyone would have guessed beforehand.

Most business analysts thought Ford Motor Company was well positioned to lead the industry after Black Tuesday. After all, Ford's major rival, General Motors, was a publicly traded company and it fared very badly in the crash, its shares sliding within weeks of October 29 from a yearly high of 91 to 33. A two-thirds drop was about average for blue-chip stocks during the first few months.[8] Weaker companies simply disappeared. To his credit, Henry Ford wisely refrained from using the occasion of the stock market disaster as a pulpit on which to expand upon his usual antipathy toward Wall Street. Instead, he joined other business magnates, including John D. Rockefeller and J. P. Morgan Jr., in professing complete confidence in the economy. As if to thrust fresh energy into the marketplace Ford Motor Company made price cuts on the booming Model A one week after the crash. The well-publicized cuts were consistent with the company's long-term policy of improving efficiency, setting a new sales threshold, and then sharing the benefits with the customer by reducing prices. Coming during the jolts of uncertainty that followed October 29, the price cuts were intended by the Fords as an irrefutable sign of prosperity. "The company believes that basically, the industry and business of the country are sound," said Edsel Ford. "Every indication is that general business conditions will remain prosperous. We are reducing prices now because we feel that such a step is the best contribution that could be made to assure a continuation of good business throughout the country."[9] Maybe Ford Motor Company couldn't stave off the nation's worst depression, but it was trying.

By early November, the stock market was in a shambles, having obliterated the efforts of several investment houses, including the Morgan banking interests, to establish a bottom by buying large blocks of shares. It was fast becoming apparent that the market was not fit to bounce back. The very real malaises that had been hidden under the surface were suddenly in plain sight at businesses large and small. Overproduction and bloated inventories led to furloughed factories. Unrealistic prices collapsed, leading to deflation at the retail level, while credit defaults flooded markets of all types with used goods at "fire sale" prices. At the vortex of all of the economy's disturbing trends were layoffs and wage cuts. Both accelerated every other negative trend. Andrew Mellon spoke for the conservative business community in general when he offered a prescription for recovery: "Liquidate labor, liquidate stocks, liquidate real estate."[10]

Always the nonconformist, Henry Ford at first refused to countenance either layoffs or wage cuts. He dismissed both as a sign of poor leadership in American business: the knee-jerk reaction of shortsighted executives. Ford Motor Company may have been only the tenth-biggest company in the country, but it was easily the most widely admired. For that reason, Henry Ford was not outlandish in thinking that he and his company could show other businesses a course out of the Depression. While many people were stalled in a state of despair, Henry Ford was anything but, referring to the economy's reversal as "a wholesome thing." A natural contrarian, Ford was able to adopt a seemingly backward viewpoint and make it ring true. Like Mark Twain's Beriah Sellers, hero of *The Gilded Age,* Ford infused commercial optimism into the gloomy first months of the Depression. No economic downturn, he pledged, would stop the technological revolution he championed in *My Philosophy of Industry.*

Ford's optimism made news on November 21, when he attended an emergency conference of industrial titans at the White House, meeting under the rather innocuous name the Committee on Recent Economic Changes. The conclave was hosted by Herbert Hoover but it was meaningless. The image of Henry Ford, Owen Young, former Sears, Roebuck president Julius Rosenwald, Pierre du Pont, and Alfred P. Sloan working together as a capitalist dream team to jump-start the economy was little more than a public relations stunt organized to encourage faith in the stock market.

That afternoon Ford offered his simple philosophy to Hoover: widespread spending power was central to economic momentum. He abhorred business leaders whose chronic pessimism translated into job cuts. Immediately after the White House conference, Ford jumped on his own bandwagon, announcing that he was *raising* the daily minimum wage at all U.S. Ford factories, from $6 to $7. At a time when workers from Pullman porters to M-G-M movie stars were expected to accept pay *cuts* gracefully and even patriotically, the announcement that Ford workers were getting a raise was a thunderbolt. "In this country," Ford explained, "the purchasing power of the people has been practically used up, and still they have not been able to buy all that they must have. I, therefore, suggest the need of increasing the purchasing power of our principal customers—the American people."[11]

The basic idea was the same one that Ford Motor Company had used in 1914, when the $5 Day proved the power of high wages to lead to overall high consumption and increased production. That raise had also proven the power of Ford Motor to act as a catalyst and start a trend in business. During the ensuing fifteen years, Henry Ford had chosen to wield that influence. Most of the time, though, he considered his company an island impervious to outside conditions—and disinterested in them. Before the Depression was through, it would at least succeed in proving that Ford Motor Company was no more an island than any other business in America.

Ford's White House comments to the press were dismissed by *New York Times* financial analyst Alexander Noyes as just another ridiculous example of "that amateur economist's economic eccentricities."[12] However, Ford backed up his optimistic view that his cars would lead the country out of its troubles by announcing a $25 million expansion at the River Rouge plant.

For all the big talk, Ford was quietly hedging his own situation during the last two months of 1929. At the time, the Model A was scheduled to undergo a styling change, with a more assertive radiator and other brightwork, along with a lower profile. Ford Motor Company took advantage of the transition in tooling to quietly curtail production. Nonetheless, 1929 ended as a triumph for the company. Sales were up by 138 percent, with 1.5 million Model As beating out Chevrolet (950,000) and all other makes in the sales race.[13] After losses during the two previous years, due to the awkward changeover from the Model T, Ford Motor Company was profitable again, earning $81 million for the Ford family. That news came as a shock to many rival automakers, who had begun to believe the rumor that Ford was producing the low-price, high-quality Model A with no profit margin.

Everything was not rosy on the Ford balance sheet, however. Unsold inventory at the end of the year was the highest in the company's history. But then, the same thing was true at practically every business in the country. Even with the popular Model A, Ford Motor was in the same situation as other companies. Either fewer cars would have to be made in 1930, or else more would have to be sold. The matter of sales was not entirely up to Ford, though. Dealerships were independent businesses, facing not only the punch of the Depression but an ill-timed cut in the factory's commission rate, from 20 percent to 17.5 percent.[14]

Ford Motor dealers had been used to rough treatment ever since James Couzens left the company. When Fords were selling, a dealership was the best business in town. However, the company made no secret of the fact that the dealerships were expected to pay for the long periods of prosperity by serving as buffers between the company and hard times. Dealers actually considered themselves "oppressed"—independent businesspeople who were pushed and shoved as though they were employees, and low-level ones at that. In the latest phase of the oppression, Ford dealers who had written orders for any share of the 1.5 million Model As sold in 1929 bore the brunt of the late October price reduction: for those who did the math, 90 percent of the price cut had come from the dealers' reduced commission.

Then, in mid-1930, there was talk of yet another Model A price cut. "Some Say Ford Can't Cut Price; Some Say He Shouldn't: He Does," reported a June headline in *Business Week*.[15] To continue the headline: He Had To. In order to operate the River Rouge factory, production had to remain high.

For at least a year after the Wall Street crash, Ford factory workers were the envy of the country. They had jobs and an employer who steadfastly refused to consider layoffs. Ford sales didn't grow in 1930, but they only barely sagged and under the circumstances that was a victory. Henry and Edsel Ford continued to release optimistic opinions. "It's a good thing the recovery is prolonged," Henry Ford fairly beamed in midyear. "Otherwise the people wouldn't profit by the illness." He also boasted that not only wouldn't he cut wages, but he wouldn't purchase supplies from any company that did.

Publicly, Ford Motor Company was trying to pretend that it was immune from the cruel market of 1930–1931. However, the truth not only started to collect, it built up until it was ready to explode.

When a reporter noticed that the company was purchasing more and more parts from outside suppliers, where wages were far lower, Henry Ford was ready with an answer that sidestepped his actual assertions. "We are trying to spread work around," he explained. "The more we can spread manufacture and employment, the more certainly are we making it possible for tens of thousands of people to stay at home and work instead of flocking to Detroit to increase the general problem."[16] The general problem, as Henry Ford put it, was that workers were descending on Detroit, or more specifically on Dearborn. Ford's jovial insistence that the Depression posed no problem to Ford or its workers was not intended as an invitation. It was optimism in its purest form, meant to energize the market. But it was traveling further and further away from reality. People in and around Detroit grew tired of trying to explain that to newly arrived Ford hopefuls, lunch pails in hand, ready to punch a time clock.

In the 1920s, Detroit had risen from the ranks of the American industrial city to become a citadel of modern urban life. Between 1925 and 1929, motorists downtown grew used to having their way blocked by construction cranes as a rash of building projects resulted in a skyline surpassed only by those in New York and Chicago for sheer majesty. In 1929, the vital economic link between Detroit and Windsor, Ontario, was solidified when the old ferry was replaced by the opening of the Ambassador Bridge; a tunnel joined it in 1930. During the 1920s the population of Detroit grew by 58 percent. Even more illuminating, the number of automobile registrations in the metropolitan area grew by 400 percent. As cosmopolitan a city as there was in the United States, outside of New York, Detroit gave people places to go and plenty of things to do—catch a Charlie Chaplin or Greta Garbo movie at the Fox Theater; dine out at the posh Book-Cadillac Hotel, or enjoy amusement park rides at Bob-Lo Park. Detroit was a lively town until the Depression hit. After that, it was never quite the same again, having toppled from the summit of a ride to an even greater extent than any other city.[17]

When Henry Ford promised stable employment and boosted wages, people believed him. That he couldn't pay those high wages and retain every worker in the midst of the Depression was forgivable. Broadcasting the statement, though, was not: so many men flocked to Detroit looking for the $7 Day that conditions there grew dangerous. Civic leaders complained that while Ford's promises had drawn thousands of unemployed men to the city, the company's policy against charitable giving allowed it to evade the responsibility of accommodating them in any way. In 1931, Mayor Frank Murphy struggled valiantly to assist 227,000 unemployed men in his city.[18] Fifteen thousand were homeless, given shelter in a converted body factory nicknamed the "Fisher Lodge." Facing the mass of unemployed in the city, Murphy's assistants variously estimated the number of "Ford cases," or men quietly let go, at between 14 and 36 percent of the total unemployed.

While the mayor surveyed the men waiting for jobs in Detroit, Congress was watching them, too, as it launched an investigation of Communist activities in the city. Charles Sorensen testified on behalf of Ford Motor Company, denying that the Soviet representatives who were attached to the factory as observers were interested in agitation of any kind. If there was any Communist activity in the Ford Motor factories, Sorensen assured the committee that he would know about it. The company had a private police force that kept track of the workers.[19]

The man at the head of that police force, officially called the Ford Service Department, was Harry Bennett, a middle-aged man with piercing blue eyes and thinning hair. Raised in Ann Arbor, he studied at the Detroit Institute of Arts and spent six years in the U.S. Navy, where he saw action in a famous skirmish at Veracruz, Mexico. He made a reputation for himself in the Navy as a lightweight boxing champion, known in the ring as Sailor Reese. As he grew into adulthood, he always wore a bow tie, jaunty suits, and large belt buckles. Originally employed as an artist in the Ford art department, Bennett rose through the ranks to become Henry Ford's private "eyes and ears" at the Rouge complex. The word was out: Bennett could not be fired by anybody but Henry Ford himself. As Ford's chief troubleshooter, running the Ford Service Department, he was in charge of the largest private police force in the world, totaling at its peak 3,000 men.[20] Aside from the boss, Bennett would be the most influential man at Ford Motor Company during the 1930s. "I am," he used to say with a note of seriousness, "Mr. Ford's personal man."[21] He also intimated that he was Ford Motor's broker between the police and gangsters. As a self-styled bodyguard-escort, he carried a gun and often pulled it during arguments. Once William Klann, a production head, was trying to correct Bennett on an annoying mistake. Bennett, whose father had been killed in a brawl, drew a pistol and aimed it at Klann and two associates. Klann admitted that the shock was so great he started crying.[22]

"Bennett had a hand in a lot of things and had a lot of influence," recalled Logan Miller, another production head. "Harry never had anything to do with the operations. That was mostly up to Sorensen. Harry was dealing more with the over-all policies of the Company, especially in labor." Bennett gained his power through the service department. It was charged with not only security at the company, but discipline and espionage as well. Bennett planted men throughout the workforce, listening for any hint of those ideas that frightened Henry Ford most: strikes, unions, and Communist or socialist political activities. To the extent that such ideas were in the air in Detroit in the 1930s, Ford Motor's attitude was typical of other automakers. However, its actions were unusually harsh. "Some years later, I talked with Ringwald," said Logan Miller, "who had been an active union organizer. He told me that they didn't organize the union. He said, 'You fellows did it by your actions and your deeds.'"[23]

One long-standing rule that was symbolic of Ford Motor Company was that no one on the factory floor was allowed to sit down. By the time Bennett was in charge of that and all other company rules, the interpretation was extreme. Even the medical staff knew that they could allow injured workers to have a seat only if the wound specifically involved one of their legs. A gash on the hand had to be dressed while the patient was standing up. If not, a service man was likely to come down hard on the doctor.

"I seen a time here when the foreman couldn't lean against a conveyor or machine when he was looking at anything, watching his men," said Omar Martineau, who was himself a foreman. "He had to stand away from everything."[24] Service men marched through the factory, displaying their guns, sticks, and other weapons and enforcing obscure rules at their whim.

What Henry Ford treasured in Bennett was his quick response to crisis. With friendships in both the Detroit underworld and the FBI, Bennett knew how to put out fires. After Charles Lindbergh's baby was kidnapped, Ford became obsessed with the safety of his grandchildren—Bennett provided the security they needed. Bennett's office was in the basement of the Administration Building at the Rouge. It had a private outside entrance, apparently to accommodate callers with "unofficial" business. But Henry Ford, too, spent a great deal of time there, discussing crimes and even target shooting with .32 caliber pistols. Ford also had a target box in his private garage at Fair Lane. Both Ford and Bennett were good shots. And together they launched a program to hire ex-criminals and athletes.

In overall hiring, Henry Ford was known to favor rehabilitation of convicts. He was also interested in giving employment to blacks and handicapped men.[25] During the 1920s, more than 10,000 African Americans were employed at Ford Motor Company. One reason harkened back to Ford's youth. He believed African Americans deserved a fair chance, that they had constitutional rights, won in the Civil War.

Another reason sprang from his view of the world. African Americans did not then hold any financial power and he did not feel at all threatened by assisting them. In the cause of helping blacks, Ford became friends with the Reverend Robert L. Bradby, pastor of Detroit's oldest religious institution, the Second Baptist Church. They started working in tandem to recruit African Americans with talent and gumption. Before long Reverend Bradby could be seen patrolling the Rouge, making sure no interracial problems developed. Encouraged by his pioneering efforts at integrating the factory floor, Ford soon tapped Father Everard Daniel, a black pastor at St. Matthew's Episcopal Church, to recruit workers for him.

Henry Ford suffered numerous prejudices but "Negrophobia" was not one of them—in fact, he was convinced that African Americans were better workers than most of the white laborers he employed. Over the years historians have pondered why Ford was so comfortable with African American employees. Some claim he used them merely as strikebreakers; others that it stemmed from the conceit of social engineering. The best answer, however, comes from August Meier and Elliott Rudwick in *Black Detroit and the Rise of the U.A.W.* (1979). "In part his hiring of black workers reflected the same philanthropic concern that led him to include in his work force cripples, ex-cons and the blind," these historians wrote. "In Ford's view Negroes, like these other disadvantaged groups, were social outcasts who needed and would appreciate his help."[26] However, the realities of the factory floor and the limits of Ford's largesse dictated that blacks had a clear shot at only the most basic jobs.

Bennett's job was to keep the Rouge workforce of 70,000 as a group of isolated individuals, and not let them create a community. In isolation, the workers, white or black, could be controlled. That was not an atypical goal in

Detroit or any other industrial city in the early 1930s, but no one went about achieving it with the brutish zeal of Harry Bennett. And no one was more despised by workers, distrusted by colleagues, or blindly followed by his own handpicked men. Bennett's influence stamped out the last vestige of the old Ford Motor, a business outfit that operated aboveboard and enjoyed a special loyalty from employees. At a time of instability—whether in the automaking industry or Henry Ford's own psyche—Harry Bennett was the man whom Ford wanted standing between him and his factory workers. Of the many men whom Ford had depended on during his career—Couzens, Liebold, and Sorensen, among them—Bennett was the one he leaned on most consistently, nearly twenty-four hours a day. Historian Keith Sward wrote that Henry Ford regarded Bennett as friend, spokesman, hiring agent, personal body attendant, and captain of the guards. You name it—Bennett filled the bill.[27]

If Ford Motor Company was an unhappy place in 1930, when there was work, it really began to roil in 1931, when vehicle sales dropped a staggering 1 million to less than 500,000. Part of the drop could be attributed to the state of the economy, but Ford's basic market share was also slipping again. Chevrolet was on top in annual sales. Equally as foreboding, Walter Chrysler's new offering, the Plymouth, had risen from its moderately successful debut two years before to take a strong third in the sales race. The Model A, which Henry Ford had marked for a model run of at least ten years, was already flagging. When the A first arrived in showrooms, observers felt that it would occupy its own slot in the automobile industry, being what Alfred Sloan once termed a "static-model utility car." However, the market didn't agree with the predictions. There was no place for a static model, at least not one perceived to be at a standstill compared with the competition. The Model T had been unique. The Model A, which was just as good a car, was not unique: it was one among a gaggle of utility cars. And none of the others were manufactured without running changes year-in and year-out.

Most people in business had been impressed with the way that Chevrolet had caught up to the Model T in the mid-1920s. But *Fortune* magazine and many others were even more impressed with the way Walter Chrysler positioned Plymouth to join the race in 1931. In the midst of the Depression's worst year, the stocky, dark-featured Chrysler sank $2.5 million into a new model that was longer than its rivals, more powerful, and loaded with features. With the introduction of the new Model PA in June, as *Fortune* noted, "the gentleman with the tireless brown eyes left the gentleman with the snappy blue eyes something to think about." For good measure, Chrysler also gave Henry Ford a Plymouth, the third PA off the line, which he personally drove across town to present to his friends Henry and Edsel. In the last half of 1931, the Plymouth was in vogue, while the Model A was becoming more outdated by the minute.

At least the Plymouth had only four cylinders. In 1929, General Motors had introduced its most recent Ford-slayer, a Chevrolet known affectionately as the "Stove-Bolt Six," for its smooth-running six-cylinder engine (and the conspicuously large bolts that held the engine head in place). The Chevrolet was slightly more expensive than the Model A—that fact and the novelty of the new Ford held it back at first. In 1931, however, the Chevrolet's reputation had convinced customers that the premium was worth it. They handed the sales race to Chevrolet.

For Ford Motor Company, 1931 was a disaster. Not only were Chevrolet and Plymouth surging in popularity on their own merits, but Ford was hurting itself. The trouble began early in the year, when rumors began to circulate that the company was planning to counter the vaunted Chevy Six with a low-price, eight-cylinder car. That combination was an oxymoron in 1931—but so attractive to consumers, it was almost an absurdity.

In the early 1930s, the high-price segment of the automobile industry was in the midst of a cylinder contest, in which an eight was respectable but a twelve was a status symbol. And a sixteen-cylinder car, such as those produced by Cadillac and Marmon, was stratospheric. However, low-price cars had been fours for so long that the idea of a similar race in that segment was jarring to old-timers. In any case, the idea that Ford Motor was even considering an eight-cylinder car for people of modest means was the kind of news that could thrill a prospective customer—and ruin the chance of selling the current model. If the flashy new Plymouth and fast Chevy Six didn't make the Model A seem old-fashioned, the specter of an eight-cylinder Ford definitely did.

In an effort to force Model As into the hands of customers, Ford once again used the dealers as a kind of pressure valve. The company announced that the commission rate would increase again; during the course of the year, it was set at 22 percent. No dealer could complain about that. However, fewer and fewer of them could find customers for the Model A. They had better luck making out waiting lists for the new Ford eight.

In 1931, the reality of the Model A's slowing sales hit Dearborn hard. Employment was half what it had been at the end of 1929,[28] and even so, many of those employees were working part-time. "Industry has demonstrated," observed Edsel, "that it can more than supply the demand, which naturally will leave a surplus of labor, and at present nothing appears on the immediate horizon which can absorb this surplus."[29] It was the first admission from the Fords that the Depression had found them, too.

On the principle that there were indeed too many autoworkers for the market conditions, Henry and Clara Ford announced a program of year-round employment for Ford personnel, by which workers could spend the summer working on Ford farms.[30] It was part of Ford's own perception—an unusual one for an industrialist—that in the face of hard times, people should return to the farm and work for themselves. The fact that farm prices were as depressed as most others did not make the plan any less attractive to Ford. It was a humane gesture, but in a sense, it was also part of his own escapist fantasy, during an era that would be well remembered for them: to evade the nightmare that the industrial world had become by 1931, one had only to return to American farm life, circa 1870.

In 1930, the federal Department of Labor completed an extensive study of Ford's Detroit-area labor force. The average annual earnings for those who met the study's criteria—heads of families who had been employed at least 225 days—were $1,694. The average annual expenditure was $1,719; the small difference being taken up by gifts from relatives or low levels of debt. Sixty-one percent lived in one-family houses, 32 percent were in two-family houses, and 7 percent occupied apartments. Thirty-six percent owned radios, a fairly smart luxury, while 5 percent had telephones and 47 percent had cars. The study enumerated every buying decision made by the average Ford family, down to the outlay for asparagus, mackinaws, and books. However, the most telling point in the study was the fact that 59 percent of the families made purchases on the installment plan.[31]

The installment plan makes prosperous times more enjoyable, but it makes hard times much more wretched, as a whole generation of Ford workers was to find out. In that respect, they were not unlike employees in a hundred other industries, except that there was an extra sense of betrayal and confusion among the workers at Ford.

"Fourteen year, I work for Henry Ford," said a foreign-born factory employee named John Boris in 1931. "All kin' jobs . . . millwright, danger jobs; I put in all my young days Henry Ford. Las' July, what you know, he lay me off. When I go out in factory that day I don' believe; I don' believe he do such ting to me."[32] Boris was out of work for nine months before he was visited by an investigator from the company's welfare department. Righting the injustice, the investigator told Boris to report for work the next morning. Because of his seniority, Boris had been making eight dollars a day. He didn't earn that much on his return, nor even the premium of seven dollars that Ford had announced early in the Depression. Workers only received the seven-dollar minimum after sixty days. After sixty-one days, Boris earned it. Two days after that, he was fired and told not to come back again.

The same sort of story was unraveling the lives of good men all over the country, with unemployment hovering at about 14 percent. Yet the situation was different in Dearborn. In some sense, it was personal. Boris hadn't said that he worked for Ford Motor Company, but rather, "I work Henry Ford." The founder had devoted his remarkable talent for publicity to promoting the idea that Ford Motor Company had only one boss, Henry Ford himself. Edsel was the only other Ford executive who was even allowed to grant interviews on a regular basis. Just as a customer could be forgiven for thinking that Henry Ford had personally designed his or her new car and perhaps had built it, an employee like John Boris might easily believe that he was working under a personal covenant with Henry Ford. In fact, Boris acted on that belief, trying unsuccessfully to visit Ford's office in order to straighten out the misunderstanding behind his dismissal.

In April 1931, Ford reiterated the stand he'd taken in 1929: that neither his plant nor any factory that supplied it would cut wages. Ford was adamant on that point, despite the fact that in practice, the wage scale was a farce. Few Ford workers were receiving anything like seven dollars per day for a full week's work. In October, the daily minimum was reduced without fanfare to six dollars. In a sense, it was a kindness for the workers, more of whom could expect more days of steady work at the realistic rate of pay. Even so, the crisis deepened and the Fords couldn't stop it. "If you can tell me," Edsel Ford wrote testily in answer to a letter from the president of a Michigan company, "how we can keep our men employed every day in the week, I would be very glad to know about it. We have had a larger number of employees on our payroll due to large volume in the past, and feel that the most equitable way of handling the present situation is to give the largest possible number of employees work for a limited time, rather than a very few full time."[33]

The situation only worsened for both the company and its employees. In August, the Model A assembly line stopped. The company had all the cars it needed. The line started again temporarily, but shut down for good in October. For the second time in four years, Ford Motor Company was caught short—in the business of building cars, but without a viable car to build.[34]

Adding to Henry Ford's personal misery was the decline of his closest friend and mentor, Thomas Edison. Until Edison's final months, Ford had spent time with him in Fort Myers, which they had developed together as a "garden city." They had worked on ways to create a new synthetic rubber. Ford, along with Harvey Firestone, had persuaded Edison to look for a domestic source of rubber, partly out of entrepreneurial ambition, but also as a way to occupy Edison's time.[35] "To date," Edison told Ford in the midst of the research, "I have examined fifteen thousand plants, trees, and shrubs growing within the United States to discover their possibilities as rubber producers."[36] Edison came up with substitutes, but they were too expensive to be practical. By 1930, Edison was entirely retired.

During 1931, Ford asked for weekly status reports on his friend's deteriorating health. Edison was back in New Jersey, ravaged by diabetes and stomach disorders and in continuous pain. On September 12, Mina Edison had her secretary report to Ford, "There has been no material change in Mr. Edison's condition other than the fact that his strength seems poorer from day to day." When word finally reached him that Edison was near death Ford grew despondent. He said he would have paid any sum for Edison to stay alive. Later in September, he made a hurried trip to New Jersey for a last visit. A month later, the end was near. Desperate, Ford asked the great inventor's son Charles to capture the last breath of Thomas Edison in a test tube for posterity. Thomas Edison died on October 18. (Today, the odd artifact of his last breath is displayed at the Ford Museum in Dearborn.) Henry and Clara made their way to West Orange, New Jersey, where Edison's body remained in an open casket. With Harvey Firestone at his side, the normally impatient Henry Ford listened to an hourlong memorial service, and for the only known time in his life he openly wept. At 10:00 P.M. Eastern time on October 21, many people in the United States dimmed their electric lights for one minute while radio stations observed a minute of silence. Those close to Henry Ford claim he was never quite his old self again after Edison died. He rarely returned to Fort Myers, renting the winter home out and then selling it outright in 1945.[37]

By the beginning of 1932, however, Henry Ford seemed to have gotten over his personal depression to focus on the sorry state of the economy. That February, he didn't merely announce that a new car, the Ford V-8, was ready to enter production. The way he put it, he was pledging his personal fortune to end the Depression: "The American people have made the Ford Motor Company what it is. We have nothing the public did not give us. No surplus exists for personal benefit—every surplus is provided for future use. The future is here and we are going to do our utmost—risk everything, if necessary—to use this surplus which the public, through its dealings with us, has provided, to see if we cannot make what the country needs most—work, jobs!"[38]

Ford intimated that the new model would be introduced within a week or two, and that production at "full capacity" would begin soon after. The news was greeted with high hopes in the national business press, the general attitude being that if anyone could ignite the slumbering economy, it was the Ford Motor Company. However, in Detroit, the news was received with something less than joy. City officials knew that the only certain effect of Ford's pledge was to draw thousands more job seekers to the city. Even closer to the situation, many local autoworkers felt nearly the same frustration at the thought of reemployment under the old Ford rules as they did in being out of work for so long. Those forebodings had been brewing for some workers all winter, and longer than that for others. Under the peculiar hardships of that Depression year in Detroit, Henry Ford's announcement, brimming with goodwill, made things immediately worse.

The employment index in Detroit in late February stood at 69.5 percent. As soon as other automakers heard that Ford Motor was planning to bring out a new model, they closed their own factories. Each wanted to assess the new

Ford before scheduling further production. That added thousands to the ranks of the unemployed and dragged the official index down almost three points, to 66.6, in just one week. For men in need of jobs, the situation was untenable.

Whenever workers in Detroit wanted to march, to demonstrate, or to voice their frustrations in any peaceful way, the city was cooperative, issuing permits and ordering the police to be neutral, if not sympathetic. Mayor Frank Murphy's belief in American democracy was above suspicion (he would later serve as a U.S. Supreme Court justice), yet he developed a very practical policy of tolerance for the many Communist groups at work in the city. As a true reformer, Murphy's feeling was that antagonism would only exacerbate the situation, putting it out of the city's control. "With the election of Mayor Frank Murphy incipient unionists and outright leftists had been accorded the right to demonstrate in the public squares," Keith Sward wrote. "Delegations of the unemployed had been received at City Hall or at various relief depots as a matter of course."[39]

On Sunday, March 6, 1932, a loose-knit Communist group staged a rally in a Detroit hall and called for a peaceful demonstration, the "Ford Hunger March," the next day. On Monday, the demonstrators walked from downtown Detroit to the Rouge plant in Dearborn, and the leaders presented a list of demands on Henry Ford. The demands were:

1. Jobs for all laid-off Ford workers
2. Immediate payment of fifty percent of full wages
3. Seven-hour day without reduction in pay
4. Slowing down of the deadly "speed-up"
5. Two fifteen minute rest periods
6. No discrimination against Negroes as to jobs, relief, medical services
7. Free medical aid in the Ford Hospital for the employed or unemployed workers and their families
8. Five tons of coke or coal for the winter
9. Abolition of service men (spies, police et cetera)
10. No foreclosures on homes of former Ford workers—Ford to assume responsibility for all mortgages until six months after regular full-time re-employment
11. Immediate payment of lump sum of $50 winter relief.[40]

Some of the items did little more than echo the pipe dreams of the men who were tired of being cold and poor. Others were more surprising. For example, Ford Motor Company discriminated to a lesser extent against African Americans than any other automaking company, yet it's clear that some segregation still occurred and it hurt. Since Ford Motor Company was "family owned," and bragged about its theory of high wages and benevolence to workers, these workers wanted to confront Henry and Edsel Ford themselves. The marchers were galled that when Ford Motor had laid off 50,000 to 60,000 employees, Henry Ford seemed utterly indifferent, saying they were "too lazy" to work. And even those workers still employed at the Rouge had grown outraged at the abuses of the company's escalating obsession with surveillance. In all, the demands were nothing more or less than a communication from workers who desperately wanted to be heard. Three thousand of them walked in line to the Detroit-Dearborn boundary on that bitter cold, rainy Monday, March 7.[41] They carried placards that read "We want jobs" and "Come on, Workers, Don't be afraid." They were four abreast, singing, joking, and chanting slogans, as marchers often do.[42] The *Detroit News* described what happened next:

> The marchers stopped. One of their numbers hoisted himself on to a truck. The shivering, watery-eyed men pressed about the truck as closely as they could. The man on the truck—it was Albert Goetz, a Detroit Communist leader—raised his hands for silence and began to speak. "We don't want any violence!" he said sharply. "Remember, all we are going to do is walk to the Ford employment office. No trouble, no fighting. Stay in line. Be orderly." The speaker paused a moment. The crowd was silent. "I understand," he continued, "that the Dearborn police are planning to stop us. Well, we will try to get through somehow. But remember, no trouble."[43]

Perhaps Goetz knew that he was asking the impossible. Directly across the Detroit city line, fifty Dearborn policemen were waiting in formation. They fired tear gas but the wind blew most of it away and the marchers continued on, their gaze fixed on Gate 3 at the Rouge factory. The police retreated to an overpass near the plant and waited there with men from the Ford Service Department. Harry Bennett ordered two high-pressure fire hoses to blast the marchers with freezing water. This only infuriated them. Suddenly, as the marchers approached, Bennett's forces opened fire, killing one man. Among those who were wounded was the photographer for the *New York Times*. Marchers threw stones in return. Part of the march moved off to the side of the road, where a speaker was trying to keep order. At that point, a submachine gun at the gate to the Ford plant opened fire on the crowd. Four people were killed, including a sixteen-year-old newsboy. Nineteen men were seriously wounded, while fifty were grazed. Harry Bennett was the only man opposing the marchers who was seriously wounded—driving into a crowd, he was struck on the head by a rock. The police filled paddy wagons with as many marchers as possible and took them to jail. Six days later, over six thousand people marched down Woodward Avenue to attend the group burial of their fallen comrades—George Bussell, Joe DeBlasio, Coleman Leny, and Joe York—at Woodmere Cemetery, located within view of the smokestacks of the Rouge.[44]

Justifiably, Ford Motor Company and Dearborn police received bad press from the riot. "The Dearborn police are to be condemned for using guns against an unarmed crowd, for viciously bad judgment and for killing four men," the *New York Herald-Tribune* reported. "Such action must arouse resentment among the unemployed everywhere and accentuate class antagonisms so alien to our American life."[45] The *New York Times* report started by criticizing the marchers, yet it concluded more sympathetically: "On the surface it would seem unexplainable that Detroit workers should riot just at the time when the world is being told that industry is reviving. . . . However . . . if 50,000 additional men were put to work in Detroit factories tomorrow, there would not be as many men working as were employed a year ago. Not half the men who were employed in 1929 are working today, yet most of them and their families are still in Detroit, hoping against hope and leading a hand-to-mouth existence."[46]

Whatever worker goodwill Henry Ford garnered from his introduction of the $5 Day back in 1914 was squandered when the fire hoses and submachine gun were unleashed on the so-called Hunger Marchers. His image as the "caring capitalist" dissolved. Upton Sinclair, who had sympathetically embraced Ford a decade earlier, lashed out against his inhumanity in the wake of the Hunger March. In a novel titled *The Flivver King: A Story of Ford-America*, Sinclair claimed that after the fascist response at the Rouge it was fair to say that Ford Motor cars were painted just one color, that of "Fresh Human Blood."[47] In his novel *The Big Money*, John Dos Passos likewise lambasted Ford for his callous, brutal response to the Hunger March: "But when the country on cracked shoes, in frayed trousers, belts tightened over hollow bellies, idle hands cracked and chapped with the cold of that coldest March day of 1932, started marching from Detroit to Dearborn, asking for work and the American Plan, all they could think of at Ford's was machine guns. The country was sound, but they mowed the marchers down. They shot them dead."[48]

The Detroit press staunchly defended the Hunger Marchers in a fashion similar to Sinclair and Dos Passos. "The opposition offered by the Dearborn police evidently changed an orderly demonstration into a riot with death and bloodshed as its toll," the *Detroit Times* reported. "The killing of innocent workmen, innocent of any crime, is a blow directed at the very heart of American institutions."[49]

The consensus was that they were no mob. They were Ford workers. Up to March 7, 1932, that was a difference the company might have been expected to understand. When the machine gun started rattling on that morning, however, a battleground settled in between Ford Motor Company and its workers. That aura of violence wouldn't lift for more than a dozen years. Henry Ford, the man who abhorred war, was willing to wage one against his own men.

19

Model Y: The Ford
Americans Never Knew

As Franklin D. Roosevelt assumed the presidency in 1933, launching his innovative New Deal programs to help pull America out of the Great Depression, the name Henry Ford was still synonymous with prosperity. But there was also a feeling in Europe that his mass production and efficiency concepts were having a corrosive effect on the quality of people's lives. No intellectual captured this fear better than the British polymath Aldous Huxley in his dystopian *Brave New World* (1932)—a phrase that became synonymous with nightmarish technocracy. Written as a parody of H. G. Wells's *Men Like Gods,* Huxley's bleak vision is a place where science has been replaced by the hypertechnological efficiency of Fordism.[1] The regimented supermen of the future in *Brave New World* cross themselves with "the sign of the T" and date all letters "in the year of Our Ford." All calendars begin with the production of the first Model T, and the bible of *Brave New World* is Ford's autobiography *My Life and Work.*[2]

But for all of its cynicism, *Brave New World* was in a sense a dark, left-handed tribute to the achievement of Henry Ford. While Huxley attacked the dehumanizing effect of the assembly line, he saw Ford as a social thinker more powerful than Karl Marx and Sigmund Freud combined. When he visited India later in life, he commented to a friend that he preferred the straightforward, unadorned "refreshing" prose found in *My Life and Work* to the vacuous Hindu spiritual texts he had recently read.[3] And twenty years after penning *Brave New World,* Huxley actually wrote two commissioned travel articles for the *Ford Times.*[4]

The same year as *Brave New World,* a French physician named Louis-Ferdinand Destouches published his first novel under the pseudonym Louis-Ferdinand Céline. *Voyage au Bout de la Nuit (Journey to the End of the Night),* written in a trenchant autobiographical style brimming with arch nihilism and dark humor, was an overnight cause célèbre with French intellectuals. Céline recounted the travails his alter ego, Bardamu, encountered as he traveled the world from 1913 to 1932, helping soldiers in the trenches of World War I, operating a trading post in Africa, and, most memorably, working the assembly line at "Ford's" in Detroit. "It's sickening to see the workers bent over their machines, intent on giving them all possible pleasure, calibrating bolts and more bolts, instead of putting an end once and for all to the stench of oil, the vapour that burns your throat and attacks your eardrums from inside," Céline wrote. "It's not shame that makes them bow their heads. You give in to noise as you give in to war. At the machines you let yourself go with two, three ideas that are wobbling about at the top of your head. And that's the end. From then on everything you look at, everything you touch, is hard. And everything you still manage to remember more or less becomes as rigid as a lion and loses its savor in your thoughts."[5]

Reading Céline is bracing; his prose jars the nerves and speaks to deep human truths. Nobody before, or since, has captured the dehumanizing aspects of Fordism from the worker's viewpoint with such harrowing effect. The protagonist delineates the degradation he experienced seeking employment at Highland Park. "Hardly anybody in that crowd spoke English," he wrote of his fellow applicants. "They eyed each other distrustfully like animals who had often been beaten. They gave off a smell of urinous crotches, like in a hospital. When they spoke to you, you kept away from their mouths, because in there, poor people smell of death." Immigrant workers already employed by Ford warn him not to get "uppity, because if you get uppity, they'll throw you out in two seconds and in two seconds you'll be replaced by one of those mechanical machines he always keeps at hand." As Bardamu starts working the line, he realizes, "We ourselves became machines, our flesh trembled in the furious din, it gripped us around our heads and in our bowels and rose up to the eyes in quick continuous jolts."[6]

———

What Huxley, Céline, and other European intellectuals understood was that, whether you admired his business philosophy or not, Henry Ford was a revolutionizing phenomenon. Nonetheless, Fordism was not bulletproof and Ford Motor Company was in crisis in 1933. Moreover, while Ford Motor's fortunes were collapsing in the United States, its overseas businesses were in no position to make up the difference. Even though economic conditions were not universally weak, the company was failing to take advantage of its global stature. Model A sales were robust in the secondary markets of South America and Asia, but in Europe sales were slower than ever and getting worse. In only its third year, the Model A was under attack in two vital regions.

Domestically, advanced cars from Chrysler and Chevrolet were making the

Ford look like just exactly what it was: one of the nicest cars of the 1920s. By 1932, it was sadly outdated. In Europe, the competition was no less cunning, but it targeted the Model A's engine, which fared very badly under the scheme of taxation used in Britain and other countries. In response, a parade of small cars led by the sprightly Austin Seven revealed the Model A for what it was in Europe: a relaxed American car. That put it out of place in Europe's economy-car market, where the bestsellers were little and light.

After the disastrously abrupt end of the Model T in 1927, the Ford Motor Company was hardly revered for sagacious product planning. In 1930, however, some people within the company thought they saw a similar crisis coming, one that would force the company to abandon its signal belief in the concept of the "universal car." The remarkable Model T, suited to all cultures and any road—or even no road—had effortlessly cultivated an international following. In its own time, it was indeed the universal car, but it left behind a sales pipeline that the Model A couldn't possibly sustain. For the first time, Ford Motor Company could not merely sell into the foreign markets; it was going to have to cater to them.

Sir Percival Perry, chairman of Ford Motor (England) Ltd. (Ford of England), could see that the Model A would never rule European markets the way the Model T once had. Perry had regained his position as Ford's most trusted adviser on European affairs by putting an integrated plan for international growth in place. Only three years after implementation of that strategy, he was stymied. Nonetheless, Perry wasn't easily rattled. Although he understood Ford Motor's capacity for galloping progress, he was also sensitive to the Ford ego and was mindful that his two primary bosses in Dearborn had unshakable faith in the A. Indeed, Perry was hardly allowed to forget it. Edsel Ford wrote to him on October 22, 1930, "You will recall when the Model A was introduced three years ago, we stated we would make more Model A cars than we had made of the Model T. We still intend to do that. In fact we look forward to the day when the thirty millionth Model A will come off the line."[7]

Sir Percival had doubts. He also had two enormous, brand-new factories ready to mass-produce Fords, one in Britain and one in Germany. The plant in Dagenham, England, was the second-largest automobile factory in the world, behind only River Rouge. Covering 491 acres, including 71 acres in plant space, the factory enjoyed the benefit of a half-mile frontage on the Thames.[8] In its versatility, it was modeled on the Rouge, having its own power plant, blast furnaces, and miles of assembly-line space. "Endless vistas of steelwork, under glass roofs so wide that they scarcely intercept the view of the sky, and standing on acre after acre of concrete," marveled a visitor to the new plant in 1931.[9] For Ford Motor Company, the cost of turning a string of old farms into Europe's largest auto factory had soared beyond expectations, well past $10 million. When Dagenham was planned, it was supposed to be the source of completed Model A cars for Britain and other markets, along with parts to be assembled at Ford assembly factories all over the Continent.

One of the European assembly plants was to have been a new Ford factory in Niehl, Germany, on the Rhine near Cologne. The company had considered building a full-scale manufacturing plant there but decided to start more modestly with the assembly facility. However, in 1930, as construction began on the factory, the fragile German economy was falling apart. The Depression hurt Germany, already reeling from massive postwar inflation, more than any other country in Europe. The economy was suddenly overcome by deflation and unemployment rates that hovered around 20 percent. Under pressure from the German government, Ford Motor reverted to its original inclination and recast the Cologne factory as a manufacturing facility, where German hands would create German Fords. The increased cost to Ford Motor was enormous, especially since the company had never had any particular success in the German market. Despite these obstacles, both Percival Perry and Charles Sorensen (who functioned as the head of production worldwide) had high hopes for the new start in Cologne.

As chairman of Ford Motor (England) Ltd.—the Ford subsidiary that oversaw all European business—Perry's job was to set these two new state-of-the-art facilities spinning out new Fords at their promised rate of two per minute. It wouldn't be easy in either place. In Germany, workers had to learn those Ford methods that made industrial miracles everyday events. At Dagenham, which inherited a generation's worth of automaking experience from the first British Ford plant, at Manchester, the pace of production was not the problem. There, the chicken had to come before the egg: cars had to be *sold* at the rate of two per minute before it made sense to produce them at that rate. And that was not quite the case with the Model A.

———

All nations levy a use tax on the automobile, in one way or another. In the United States, the cost was (and still is) a direct assessment, taken as a tax on gasoline. The more gasoline one buys, the more, presumably, one uses the car. In Great Britain, and the many countries that followed its lead, the car itself was taxed annually. The basis for the calculation lay in the horsepower of the engine. However, the horsepower as recognized by Britain's Motor Car Act of 1920 was not the same figure by which manufacturers boast of engine output. The difference between the performance figure (known as "bhp," or brake horsepower) and the British government's Treasury Rating ("fhp," or fiscal horsepower) was confusing to Americans, and it accounted for the preposterous fact that, in England, a Ford Model A was taxed at a higher rate than was a Rolls-Royce.

Fiscal horsepower was derived from a series of calculations based on the number of cylinders in the engine and their bore, or diameter. The Ford Model T had an fhp of 23, while the homegrown British economy car, the Austin, boasted a rating of 7. Affectionately known as the Chummy, mostly because people traveling together in its cramped quarters became just that, the Austin Seven had a 75-inch wheelbase, a full two feet shorter than the Ford. Although rather flimsy, it did boast four-wheel brakes and have an advantageous power-to-weight ratio. A hit in England, the Austin Seven had a hand in launching two of today's leading luxury-car makers: BMW had its origins in the "Dixi," a German version of the Seven built under license from Austin, while Jaguar's founder, William Lyons, made the transition to sports cars during the 1930s from a start building special bodies for Chummies.[10] Austin was carving a strong lead for English automakers, along with copycats Morris and Triumph, in the international economy-car market that Ford had once owned for itself.

The most frustrating aspect of Ford Motor (England) Ltd.'s sagging sales in 1930–1931 is that they couldn't be blamed on the Depression. Britain and especially its automobile industry were lightly touched by the reversals that proved so ruinous elsewhere. In fact, in the waning years of the British Empire, exports supported the home economy. In the healthy auto industry, marques such as Rolls-Royce, Rover, Vauxhall (owned by GM), Riley, Morris (MG), Austin, and Alvis were having good years in the early 1930s, or even gaining market share. In an otherwise upbeat atmosphere for auto sales, the Treasury Ratings, at a cost of £1 per fhp every year, were putting Ford at a real disadvantage. The sheer popularity (and low initial cost) of the Model T managed to overcome it, but to the disappointment of British Ford dealers, the Model A offered no improvement—its Treasury Rating was 24 fhp. Its true output, as measured by the bhp, was 40. Meanwhile, the three-liter Bentley, an 85-bhp rocket, had a Treasury Rating of just 16. In England, the Model A was being classed as, of all things, a luxury car.

The reason was that its cylinders were fat—fat and short. Henry Ford preferred such an arrangement, because in all functions (human or machine) he believed in eliminating unnecessary movement and so, excess wear and tear. The British formula rewarded small-bore engines, regardless of the stroke (the length of the cylinders). As a result, a £100 Ford Model A looked more expensive to customers than a £125 Austin Seven, simply because the difference in Treasury Rating promised to exact a £17 premium on the Ford each and every year. In 1930, Ford tried to patch the problem with the AF, the special export version of the A with narrower cylinders and a reduced fhp of 15— along with reduced performance.

Perry surveyed his eroding business and diplomatically suggested to the Fords that England would require a special Ford. Edsel, who had long studied European automaking, was open to the idea, even though it represented a blow to the Model A's prospects and the investment the company had made in it. By the autumn of 1931, Model A sales in England had fallen to a trickle, even as the great factory at Dagenham struggled to open. Instead of humming with activity, it lay strangely quiet, most of its capacity unused. Officially, the factory began production when a Model AA truck rolled off the line on October 1, but it was a dispirited event, with a cloudy future hanging over the whole enterprise.

Ford Motor (England) Ltd. was losing money at the rate of £1.3 million per year (then the equivalent of $6 million).[11] It wasn't the way that Perry would have wanted to win his point, but the dire situation convinced those in Dearborn that Europe did indeed need its very own Ford. In October, A. R. Smith, general manager of the Dagenham works, arrived in Dearborn to discuss the car that Perry had in mind. Their outline contained four major points: "a small bore engine of about eight horsepower, a ninety-inch wheelbase, a narrow tread, and limited weight"; but the answers were wisely left to the engineers at headquarters.[12]

The horsepower rating of 8 referred to the Treasury Rating, of course. At 90 inches, the wheelbase (or length) would be about a foot shorter than the Model A. More important, the tread (or width) had to be reduced to make the car fit comfortably on narrow country lanes and cobblestone alleys, such as those found throughout Europe. As to the weight, while no Ford authorized by Henry Ford was ever an ounce heavier than it had to be, the Europeans were especially interested in fuel economy, so their Ford would have to be lithe.

On October 19, 1931, Ford Motor Company formally began work on the new car, later called the Model Y. It was a seminal move for the company. Even though few Americans, even those well versed in the lore of Ford, ever heard about the little Y, it would emerge as a product on par with the company's great Model T and Model A cars. With the Model Y, Ford Motor became a truly international company: not merely selling "universal" products overseas, nor overseeing established subsidiaries (as did GM). Instead, Ford made a leap: it stretched to become more than just an automaker to the world, but one *of* the world.

Laurence Sheldrick, a veteran chassis engineer at Ford, took responsibility for the layout of the Y. He was suited to the ticklish job of handling Edsel's project at Henry's company. Harold Hicks once described Sheldrick as "a diplomat; there was no question about it. He got along well not only with Edsel but he got along well with Henry Ford."[13] The new car may have been a rush job, but it was one for which Ford Motor Company was well prepared. Everyone took part in turning it out quickly in order to fill the void at Dagenham. A. R. Smith stayed in Dearborn to oversee development of the new model. On New Year's Day, he was in the engineering lab under the prototype

Model Y chassis, adjusting the brakes, when he heard a voice ask, "Who's under the car?" Smith looked up to see Henry Ford surveying the job.[14]

"Move over," Ford said and climbed under the car to help Smith work on the brakes—holiday or not. Henry Ford watched over progress on the Model Y. In spirit, it represented a continuation of the Model T, even though mechanically, it could be interpreted as a miniaturized Model A. The tough little Y was transportation, plain and simple. Most important, its fhp—and Treasury Rating—was right on target at 8. The car needed only its bodywork and it would be complete. Therein lay a rather profound problem. At Ford, styling was only tepidly acknowledged as a component of automaking.

Over at General Motors, the Art and Color Section (the styling department) was already four years old. Headed by a self-confident young Californian named Harley Earl, it was staffed by over a hundred specialists: artists, engineers, and clay modelers. "They were an active, talkative crowd," recalled GM President Alfred Sloan, "always comparing and pointing to the designs on the blackboards, which, surrounded by black velvet curtains, made the white body lines stand out sharply."[15]

For its part, Ford Motor Company had only Edsel—its lone voice on the importance of styling. The Ford division had no styling staff as of 1931: no chattering designers, no plans, and no inkling that the six years starting in 1932 would be recalled ever after as the flowering of automobile styling. But Edsel could indeed see that styling would be the hallmark of the next era in automaking, and that the Model Y would be the Ford empire's entry point. "While administering the company, Edsel devoted untiring attention to his great love—styling or design, as it is now called," historian David L. Lewis noted in his Edsel Ford Centennial Lecture, delivered in Grosse Pointe in 1993. "It was he, in fact, who brought to the automobile industry the realization that an automobile could be beautiful as well as functional."[16]

———

By 1931, Edsel Ford had been the president of Ford Motor Company for a dozen years. His powers had been compromised in the most public ways by his father. Favorites such as Charles Sorensen and Harry Bennett usurped much of his influence within the company. Yet, as president, Edsel proved to be essential to the survival of the company through its most difficult transition during the 1930s. He did it in his own way: under the circumstances (as he learned early on) his influence was more effective, the less discernible it was.

The shy, modest Edsel turned thirty-eight in 1931. Suave, favoring bespoke suits and custom-made shoes, he had the straight features of his Ford elders and the fine, dark complexion of the Bryants. Although regarded as a more handsome man than his father, he did not have the same commanding presence. Edsel was shorter, standing about five-foot-six, and was merely slim, where his father was wiry, with the coiled energy that the word implies. According to A. J. Lepine, his confidential secretary from 1918 to 1943, Edsel "was an active type and yet, while he wasn't frail, he was not robust in any way. He played tennis, squash, racquettes and golf." As a family man, Edsel also went in for less competitive sports, as Lepine was reminded when he had occasion once to see Edsel's closets at home: "His clothes were always the appropriate thing for each occasion. . . . I saw tobogganing clothes and skiing clothes and stuff like that—sweaters and heavy woolens and things of that sort with stocking caps for winter apparel in bright colors."[17]

In fact, Edsel was frequently named to best-dressed lists, which also included the likes of Fred Astaire, the Prince of Wales, and GM executive Alfred Sloan. However, those men were very public figures, frequently pictured in the press. For a nationally known executive, Edsel Ford was practically a recluse, cooperating over the course of his years at Ford Motor with only two feature articles in national magazines. A dignified sense of privacy was part of Edsel's nature, no doubt, but it was also in keeping with the edict understood by everyone in Dearborn: the spotlight belonged to Henry. "Edsel always recognized the sagacity and ability of Henry Ford properly to time changes and moves which always kept the Ford Motor Company in the public eye and mind," Eugene Lewis recalled in *Motor Memories.* "In other words, while Edsel Ford was the *working* president of the company, the not always shadowy figure of his father was ever in the background—and in the public mind."[18] To survive in his father's lair Edsel shunned publicity, turning down requests for biographical data and for written expressions of opinion. He granted interviews only for compelling business reasons and even banned the use of the pronoun "I" in company statements in which his name appeared. When company publicists requested that Edsel pose for pictures at business functions, his usual reply was "See if you can't get Father to do that. He likes that sort of thing. I don't." Edsel's reputation for shunting newsmen to the elder Ford provoked the *Philadelphia Inquirer* to jibe that his longest statement to the press had been "See Father."[19]

Much has been made over how tough Henry Ford was on his son. He undoubtedly loved Edsel, but stopped short of giving him his full respect. In that gap lay the tragedy of their relationship. Deferential to a fault, Edsel became reticent and shy whenever "Father" (he never used "Dad") entered a room. Often, Edsel would make decisions only to have them overturned by his father. Once, in fact, Edsel had new coke ovens built at Rouge. After only a few days' use, Henry Ford ordered them destroyed. At one executive board meeting Henry Ford slumped out of his seat and shouted, "Edsel, you shut up!" because his son had the temerity to recommend the need for modern hydraulic brakes. Dressing down Edsel became an almost daily routine for

Henry, who wanted his introverted son to be a tough-fisted power broker.[20] To his credit, Edsel refused to be remodeled to meet his father's notions of the perfect son. "The senior Ford never seemed to grasp the fact that his son's differences in personality were a strength, not a failing," historian Thomas E. Bonsall wrote. "Where Edsel was gentle, Henry saw weakness. Where Edsel was imaginative, Henry saw frivolity. Henry spent years trying to make Edsel into a carbon copy of himself instead of letting him be his own man."[21]

One area in which Edsel clearly excelled was as a family man. He and Eleanor Ford remained happily married and were proud of their four children. In 1929 the family had moved into a sixty-room Grosse Pointe Shores mansion. Albert Kahn had designed it in the Cotswold style of rural England in order to downplay its size, with various sections rambling neatly against one another under separate, peaked rooflines. The roof, in fact, was made of slate that had been imported from England, along with the experts to install it. It was a highly personal reflection of the younger Fords and their way of life. But the most significant characteristic of their mansion was that while Henry and Clara lived about ten miles west of Detroit on the Fair Lane estate in Dearborn, Edsel and Eleanor's house was ten miles to the east of the city.[22] At River Rouge, Edsel may have been under his father's eye, but not at home, looking out on 450-square-mile Lake St. Clair. The "Pointes," which consisted of five separate communities—Grosse Pointe Park, Grosse Pointe Farms, Grosse Pointe Shores, Grosse Pointe Woods, and the actual city of Grosse Pointe—were the residential neighborhoods of the well-to-do of Detroit. And Edsel and Eleanor, with their passion for refinement, were right at home. Preserved today and open to the public, their Gatsbyesque estate, located at 1100 Lake Shore Road, is the most vivid reminder left of the man Edsel Ford was, apart from his father.

To bring his general building ideas to fruition, Edsel enlisted a cadre of designers who were at the top of their form, starting with Kahn. The same architect who had developed reinforced concrete into a new look for industrial buildings all over the world was just as facile working in a traditional style. Although the interior of the main house was decorated in an English country atmosphere, with mellow paneling and plasterwork, Edsel engaged Walter Dorwin Teague in the mid-1930s to create streamlined interiors for a three-room redecoration of the house. Jens Jensen, the landscape architect who designed the grounds at Fair Lane, was hired to create the outdoor setting for the house. At the Fords' direction, he cultivated a long tangle of indigenous plants on a peninsula at the north end of the property's 1,000-foot lakefront, making it a wildlife refuge that the family called Bird Island. The children could swim either in the lake or in an indoor pool. Or they could play in the house that Clara Ford had commissioned for Josephine as a seventh-birthday gift. Constructed in two-thirds scale, the playhouse was as complete inside and out as any real house in Detroit.

Edsel's own idea of a playhouse on the estate might have been the garage, which held as many as twenty-seven automobiles. By and large, Edsel was drawn to European cars that matched dazzling performance with stunning looks, Bugattis and Hispano-Suizas among them. His other refuge on the grounds was the boathouse. Since his teenage years, he had been fascinated by fast boats—not an unusual obsession for a boy growing up in the Great Lakes region. At thirty-eight, he was still at it, overseeing the design of speed-boats and taking joy in their appearance and performance in organized races.

Whenever the family convened, it was Edsel who took the photographs and developed them in his own darkroom. As for his father's love of square dancing, Edsel scoffed at it, preferring the fox-trot or Charleston. And often at night while the children were getting ready for bed, he would play George Gershwin on his Steinway piano to unwind. Over the years the family threw parties in the galley, an oblong hangar with great views of the lake; on one occasion, for example, Tommy Dorsey and Frank Sinatra supplied the entertainment.

Henry Ford had once boasted that he wouldn't give five cents for all the art in the world, but Edsel was a serious patron of the arts who believed in making fine painting and sculpture a part of everyday life—for as many people as possible. Edsel, who kept a photograph in his study of John D. Rockefeller entering a Model A, believed that the rich had a social obligation to help the arts flourish. "He was a very gentle person and had this taste for beautiful things," recalled his family member Mrs. Stanley Ruddiman. "The artistic taste was there naturally. Edsel and Eleanor enjoyed and developed that between them."[23] To that end, Edsel served as a trustee of the Detroit Institute of Arts (DIA), and during the Depression underwrote salaries and other major expenses to make sure the museum stayed open. Edsel and Eleanor personally selected the artwork for their own home, an eclectic collection that contained paintings by masters such as van Gogh, Cézanne, and Matisse. A few of the pictures in the house were original Edsel Fords—the company president painted in his spare time and even studied with prominent artists in Michigan. He surrounded himself with fine artwork. "Edsel Ford's office was much different than the average commercial office," A. J. Lepine explained. "He had a couple of paintings by Gilbert Stuart, the colonial painter who made the most famous paintings of Washington." One of the Stuarts in the office was of John Quincy Adams, another was of General Henry Dearborn. Edsel also hung a painting of Alexander Hamilton by John Trumbull.

In 1931, Edsel commissioned the famed Mexican painter Diego Rivera to cover the DIA's large center court with murals depicting the city's workers. In the midst of the Great Depression many wondered why Edsel Ford and museum director Dr. William Valentiner would advance $10,000 to an artist with an anticapitalist tilt to paint a so-called Communist mural. (Edsel would later underwrite an additional $15,000 for unforeseen expenses.) Housing was provided for Rivera at the Wardell Hotel, just across the street from the DIA. A problem, however, ensued when he learned at check-in that Jews weren't allowed to stay in the hotel. Pretending that both he and his wife, Frida Kahlo, were Jewish, Rivera invoked Edsel Ford's name and forced a change in the policy. After Rivera settled in, Edsel gave him a personal tour of the Rouge.[24] "Ford set only one condition," Rivera later wrote: "that in representing the industry of Detroit, I should not limit myself to steel and automobiles but take in chemicals and pharmaceuticals, which were also important in the economy of the city. He wanted to have a full tableau of the industrial life of Detroit."[25]

Diego Rivera spent a month wandering around the Rouge, sketching conveyer belts, talking with workers, and getting to know the processes. A master of detail, Rivera scrutinized machines as if he were Henry Ford himself. How was steel shaped? Who ran the blast furnaces? Where does electricity come from? Rivera asked himself technical questions as he tried to understand the essence of the Rouge—an edifice he considered as magnificent as Aztec and Mayan temples. At last a decision was made. He would paint a series of epic frescoes that would tell the story of Ford Motor Company from all sides of the industrial equation. The series would be called *Detroit Industry* (or *Man and the Machine*). Like Michelangelo about to tackle the Sistine Chapel, Rivera set up scaffolds, hired assistants, and started mixing paints. "I've had to do a lot of preparatory work which has consisted mostly of observation," Rivera wrote his friend Bertram D. Wolfe. "There will be 27 frescoes, which together will form a plastic and thematic unity. I am hoping that this series will be the most complete of my works."[26]

When Rivera finished the murals, only a philistine—or an anti-Communist zealot—could have failed to appreciate their magnificence. Most history books salute Edsel Ford for having the foresight and vision to bring the Mexican master to Woodward Avenue. They also talk about how Rivera painted Edsel's portrait and repeatedly thanked him for being such a gentlemanly sponsor. But Edsel, always in his father's shadow, didn't make much of an impression on Rivera. Even though Edsel squired Rivera all over Detroit, he barely gets mentioned in Rivera's autobiography, *My Art, My Life*. Instead, the single afternoon Rivera spent with Henry Ford fills up a chapter in the book. "Discarding formalities, Ford greeted me with a hearty handshake and then began one of the most intelligent, clever and lively conversations I have ever enjoyed," Rivera wrote. "This amiable genius radiated a kind of luminous atmosphere." He compared Henry Ford in greatness to Karl Marx and Vladimir Lenin—a true revolutionary of the modern age. He endorsed Ford's collection of relics at Greenfield Village as being "organized not only with scientific clarity, but with impeccable, unpretentious good taste." Diego Rivera, the most famous artist Mexico ever produced, felt Ford was his kindred spirit. "I regretted that Henry Ford was a capitalist and one of the richest men on earth," Rivera wrote. "I did not feel free to praise him as long and as loudly as I wanted to, since that would put me under the suspicion of sycophancy, of flattering the rich. Otherwise, I should have attempted to write a book presenting Henry Ford as I saw him, a true poet and artist, and one of the greatest in the world."[27]

Reading this passage, one realizes how difficult it is for the children of the famous to make their own mark. Edsel, trained in the arts, held erudite conversations with Rivera on Cézanne's cubism and Mondrian's minimalism, but still, in the painter's eyes, he was just an industrial prince. What really thrilled Rivera was listening to old Henry Ford tell stories about his Bagley Avenue quadricycle and wax philosophical about how prison convicts were better workers than Harvard graduates. It must have frustrated and baffled Edsel that his father, when so moved, won over everybody with his transparent hayseed charm. For eight months the conscientious Edsel had watched Rivera paint, making sure all his needs were met, and all the heavyset Mexican genius could gush about were the yellowed ballad sheets from Stephen Foster songs that hung on Henry Ford's walls. Resentment, however, never showed in Edsel.

When Rivera's frescoes were unveiled, a firestorm of protest engulfed Detroit. Citizens were livid that the commissioned work was filled with Marxist overtones and exuded sacrilegious smut. In *Dreaming with His Eyes Open: A Life of Diego Rivera*, Patrick Marnham lists just some of the insults hurled at Rivera's work: "anti-American," "defamatory," "an advertising gimmick thought up by Edsel Ford," "communistic," "blasphemous"—the rantings could go on. One city councilman demanded that the frescoes be whitewashed.[28] Publicly insulted as an arbiter of bad taste, Edsel Ford stood by Rivera, simply claiming that he was pleased with the work and would not destroy it. (In contrast, Nelson Rockefeller, who commissioned Rivera the next year to paint a mural in Rockefeller Center in Manhattan, destroyed the work, deeming it a debasement of American capitalism.) Meanwhile, Henry Ford couldn't understand what all the "Diego fuss" was about. He admired the murals for their mechanical exactitude.[29]

Besides his involvement with the DIA, Edsel served as a trustee of the Museum of Modern Art in New York. He was also a director of the Lincoln Highway Association and Shenandoah National Park and he even helped fund Berea College in Kentucky. While most fathers would be proud of a son performing such civic duties, Henry Ford deemed Edsel a "dilettante" and a "Grosse Pointe dandy." Edsel, like a tormented high schooler, found ways to rebel against his dad. His parents were the nation's most vocal opponents of tobacco in the 1920s and 1930s, but Edsel used the lounge room off his of-

fice to smoke—even though cigarettes were banned from all Ford Motor facilities. Henry was also adamant on the subject of liquor, but Edsel was not to
be denied a cocktail when he wanted one. Not that Henry Ford didn't try:
when Edsel was out of town on business, his father was known to travel to
Grosse Pointe Shores to destroy all the bottles in his son's liquor cabinet.[30]

At Ford Motor Company, many managers, from foremen on the line all the
way up to the son of the boss, suffered from an ailment known as "Forditis." It
was a kind of nervous indigestion or exhaustion caused by the friction that set
the pace at Ford Motor. Of course, other companies and other industries have
produced their share of ulcers, but Ford Motor Company—never a relaxed
place—had become a downright unfriendly one in the 1930s. No one suffered a worse case of Forditis than Edsel, on whom the pressures and frustrations of the company devolved most pointedly. "I wondered often how close
Mr. Ford and Edsel really were," said Emil Zoerlein, an engineer at River
Rouge. "I have seen them many times when they were sitting down on a
bench placed along outside the blue room over there [at the engineering fa-
cility]. The two of them sat together on this bench for hours at a time. As I say,
you could tell the nature of the conversation by observing their facial expressions. . . . Edsel always had a worried expression and a painful expression.
Mr. Ford's expression was stern."[31]

If Edsel regularly ducked into his office lounge with his cigarette case to
get through the day, it was understandable. Unfortunately, it was also futile.
Both Forditis and cigarette smoking probably contributed to the quick course
of the gastrointestinal disease that cut his life short a dozen years later, in
1943. "Edsel Ford submerged his own interests to a very remarkable extent,"
observed Stanley Ruddiman. "He said that the Company had been founded
by his father, and that the growth was entirely due to his father's genius and
ability, and those associated with Mr. Ford. Although he was president of the
Company, he did not try to assert his own views. He said he would not do so
as long as his father lived."[32] L. E. Briggs, who worked closely with Edsel,
summed up the sentiments of many: "He was an exceptionally fine gentleman. Rather shy, modest, very polite. I don't think I ever dealt with a more
considerate person than Edsel Ford."[33]

It would be a mistake, a regrettably common one, to let Edsel's quiet ways
in the treacherous game of Ford Motor Company management give the impression that he lost that game, or that his accomplishments were not important ones. He did lose major battles with lesser men and never had the full
power that he deserved, but Edsel's contributions were lasting ones. Indeed,
his career in the 1930s reads as a recitation of practically everything positive,
progressive, and permanent to emerge from Ford Motor Company then, including the resurgence of Lincoln through the Continental nameplate, the
launch of the Mercury division, and the creation of the Ford Foundation.

First, though, there was Edsel's role in the introduction of the Model Y as the first foreign Ford and through it, one quiet step at a time, his establishment of a styling section at Ford Motor Company.

———————

While Larry Sheldrick developed the Model Y chassis under the scrutiny of Henry Ford, Edsel took the initiative in the styling. The new chassis followed the outline of the Model A, but the styling would start from an entirely new page. Edsel was keenly aware that European bodywork, at its best, had little in common with the American look. However, that didn't mean he would commission a styling job from overseas, or even hire a European designer to work in Dearborn. Ford Motor Company wasn't ready for that. Henry Ford, who had no abiding interest in bodywork, did grudgingly admit that handsome styling had helped to make the Model A car a hit after its introduction. He also recognized that, more than anything else, styling had saved Lincoln. To develop new styles for Lincoln, the luxury make known for its sweeping presence on the road, Edsel had taken on the role of *arbiter elegantiae* and learned it well. His contribution, while not creative in the generative sense, required a strong, confident aesthetic appreciation. As a design director, Edsel coaxed original yet workable ideas out of subordinates and watched over myriad details, the sort that creative people sometimes overlook in practical ventures. Moreover, he made the ultimate decisions as to what would continue in development and what would be dropped. "I can judge design, for on that I have had long experience," he said. "But I can only judge."[34]

As a first step toward the establishment of Ford styling, both in spirit and as a new department in the company, Edsel Ford made the decision to assign a single Lincoln Motor employee to create bodywork for the Y. Giving a specialist the job of making a Ford look good was revolutionary for Ford Motor Company. Edsel found his man in E. T. "Bob" Gregorie, a native of Long Island, New York, who had been hired as a draftsman only about a month before. Red-haired and mustachioed, Gregorie was experienced only in boat design. Perhaps because of that, he and Edsel shared a belief in proportion and line—not added-on details—as the basis of good design. In the Model Y, Gregorie let the hood reach all the way back to the windshield, which slanted back, echoing the pitch of the grille and the slots on the side of the hood. The Model Y was as modern for 1932 as the morning news, a small car that looked sturdy and at the same time ready to fly down the road.

Automobile historian Griffith Borgeson questioned whether Gregorie could really have been the author of the influential front-end treatment of the Model Y. "Such immediate and outstanding success for a novice in the field would be most remarkable," Borgeson wrote.[35] He surmised that ideas such as the slanted grille might have been floating around Ford at the time.

Whether the new draftsman was solely responsible for the innovative design, or whether it reflected a continuum of the thinking of others, the Model Y's significance as a design proved the wisdom of Edsel's management of styling.

In February 1932, after only four months of development, Model Y prototypes were on display in European showrooms. At £100, the new Ford was tougher, faster, more versatile, and less expensive than the other bantam cars on sale in England. As soon as the Dagenham plant was tooled for production that October, Model Y cars (or Ford "Eights," as they were often called, in reference to the fhp) started rolling out. They would continue to do so, in other skins, for a remarkable twenty-seven years, breaking even the Model T's record for longevity. Six years later, in recognition for his work at Dagenham, Perry was knighted Baron Perry of Stock Harvard.[36]

Meanwhile, in Germany, the Model Y would be called the Köln (German for Cologne). Due to the inexperience of the workforce there, the launch was delayed until February 1933, when it was formally introduced at the Berlin International Motor Show. For the first few years, Germany's roiling political and economic problems kept Cologne lagging behind its full potential, but at least the factory had a model that fit a country starved for low-price cars.

The Model Y saved Ford's business in Europe. During its first five years, Dagenham produced 135,359 Model Ys, either finished or in the form of parts ready for shipment to assembly plants all over the world. Because of the Y, Ford Motor (England) Ltd. not only survived the worst years of the Depression, but increased its market share. The Model Y also served as a kind of license for the foreign subsidiary, giving it a platform on which to suggest and even develop new models for the needs of the market outside the United States.

In Dearborn, the Y was no less significant, in a different sense. With it, Edsel Ford finally had more than a general vision for Ford styling—he had a person who could translate it into the language of the production automobile. Within a few years, the design motif that he and Bob Gregorie realized on the Y would be imitated on American Fords, and a great many other cars of other makes. The little bantam resolved Ford Motor's worst problems in Europe in 1931–1932 and helped to solve Edsel's worst problem at home in Dearborn.

The employment situation at River Rouge remained difficult throughout the 1930s. Layoffs were regular events, and the complaint was often heard that those with seniority (and higher wage rates) were the first to go. If they were lucky, they were rehired at rookie wages. One of those let go in January 1933 was the young die maker Walter Reuther, who had worked his way up until he was the leader of a forty-man crew.[37] Reuther (pronounced ROOTH-er) had come from a close-knit family in Wheeling, West Virginia.

Both his parents were German born. His father, Valentine, was an ardent social-ist who engaged his five children in nightly debates on a wide range of issues. His mother, Anna, was incisive and highly organized, with unflagging energy. Walter inherited her traits, and his father's politics.

Walter had quit high school to go to work as a metalworker in Wheeling, but he was soon ready to roam. As biographer Nelson Lichtenstein wrote in *The Most Dangerous Man in Detroit:* "For generations, newly minted trades-men, in the old country and the new, had sharpened their skills and discov-ered a broader vision of the world by applying their talents in new workshops, laboring alongside cosmopolitan workmen in distant cities. In the third decade of the twentieth century, there was no place in the world that a young toolmaker could do so to better advantage than Detroit."[38]

Reuther found a job as a skilled workman at the River Rouge. He made the most of his years at Ford, saving his money and earning a high school diploma in his spare time at Fordson High, a local institution closely connected to the Ford family. He later enrolled at City College in Detroit, taking mostly sociol-ogy courses. Young Reuther also started to agitate for a union at Ford Motor Company, a high-risk undertaking but one for which he showed a determined flair. For example, he learned sign language in order to communicate with three workers who could neither hear nor speak. After a particularly bad day in which workers were notified of a five-cent wage cut in the morning and then another in the afternoon, one of the deaf workers gave him a note. "Let's start the Revolution," it read.[39]

Walter Reuther would do just that, later returning to Ford as a labor leader. The redheaded die maker would prove to be more potent than any of the strongmen with whom Henry Ford surrounded himself. He was the only per-son ever to match Henry Ford in stubborn, self-righteous determination, and before he was through, it was his more enlightened vision for the company that would prevail. "There is no greater calling than to serve your fellow men," Reuther was fond of saying, "no greater contribution than to help the weak."[40]

When Walter Reuther was laid off early in 1933 for being a rabble-rouser, he had money in the bank and a yearning to see the world—from the workers' point of view. Refusing to feel dejected, he and his brother, Victor, set off for Europe. They wanted to make Ford vehicles again, this time in the Soviet as-sembly plant in Gorki (as Nizhni Novgorod had been renamed the year be-fore). Victor and Walter sailed from New York for the port of Hamburg in late February 1933. Victor later wrote:

> Walter and I arrived in Germany only three days before the Reichstag was set on fire and Hitler's campaign to take over Germany became an acknowl-edged fact. We were in Berlin by March 1 and saw the smoldering remains of the old parliament [the Reichstag], surrounded by armed guards, the

whole center section gutted and the great glass dome collapsed. Brown-shirted storm troopers were everywhere, hawking special editions of the Nazi-controlled newspapers, which were promoting Goebbels' fabrication about a Communist-Socialist plot to start a civil war, of which this fire was the first signal.

The circus atmosphere around the ruined building—swastika flags flying in the smoke, barkers shouting to the crowd to buy the Nazi papers—would have been ludicrous, if it had not been so tragic.[41]

Adolf Hitler was indeed quick to accuse the Communists of starting the fire that ruined the Reichstag building, the very center and the symbol of Germany's democratic republic. Immediately after the fire, which the Nazis may well have set themselves, Hitler assumed the right to hunt down Communists. At the time, he was trying unsuccessfully to influence the March 5 parliamentary elections that would fill the Reichstag. All he wanted out of those elections was enough support so that the representatives would grant him dictatorial powers. The election didn't go his way, but by the end of March, the fire and his interpretation of it resulted in his receiving such powers.

The fire at the Reichstag marked the end of the old Germany and the start of Adolf Hitler's complete and unlimited power over the country. Valentine Y. Tallberg, the chief engineer of Ford of Germany, was leaving the capital that night. "I was leaving Berlin the night of the Reichstag fire," he later recalled. "I saw the fire from the train, not knowing at that time what it was, of course; we read about it later on. Hitler came to power. . . ."

A native of Sweden, Tallberg had long worked in Detroit and was an American citizen. Moreover, he was regarded as an American by the Germans. Starting in 1928, Tallberg was employed by Ford Motor and assigned to Germany, where he would remain until 1940. "I had traveled all over the country," Tallberg said, "and I saw workers by the thousands all over who were in despair because they didn't have work. It was pitiful to see these men standing around looking for work and not getting any. Immediately after Hitler took power things changed."[42] Strictly from the point of view of the automobile industry, Hitler's economic program opened a new era. But then, regarded from a narrow perspective, the Nazis offered a new start for many fields. Coaxing people into just such a state of myopia was one of their methods.

The German automobile industry did need help in the early 1930s. The economy was so bad that very few Germans could afford the list price of a vehicle. In addition, the tax on automobiles was prohibitive, coming to approximately one sixth the selling price. With stagnated sales, the industry began to lag behind English, French, Italian, and certainly American manufacturers in production methods and even in engineering. The Fords themselves estimated that the German auto industry was fifteen years behind that of the leading countries.[43] Daimler-Benz's Mercedes models were still widely respected (and feared on the racetracks), but other manufacturers flagged—while making due with outdated factories.

Adolf Hitler was well aware of the Ford economic model: cars that people could afford led to people who could afford cars. A few years later, when he was pressing for the creation of a popular-priced German car (the people's car, or *Volkswagen*), he explained it in his own words: "The creation of this car will mean a new mobilization of millions, out of which hundreds of thousands in accordance with the increasing standard of living, will so much easier find their way to better and nicer cars. The Ford car has not placed the high class and expensive American automobiles out of the market; just the opposite, Henry Ford has woken up the big masses of American purchasers whereby the manufacturers of expensive cars have profited to a great extent."[44]

Seeking to wake up masses of German workers, Hitler rescinded the automobile tax. Ford's German production jumped by 100 percent during the first year after that. Other companies revived even more dramatically, and for a short time a sense of euphoria gripped the industry. "We benefited because people started to buy more automobiles," Tallberg explained. "There was a general feeling of optimism in the industry. Oh, you found some that probably looked ahead more than others and said, 'Well, this is not the natural kind of prosperity. This is going to lead to catastrophe later on.' I found many industrialists who thought and spoke that way, back as early as 1933. Of course, it didn't do them any good. They were willing to go along as long as the plant kept going . . . as long as they could keep the men working, they thought, 'Well, what's the use of worrying?'"[45]

Ford-Werke (Ford of Germany) did post a profit for 1933, although it still didn't approach the point at which it could defray Dearborn's investment in the Cologne plant. In fact, over the subsequent nine years, until the Nazis took legal custody of Ford Motor Company's plants and facilities in Germany, the home company received no return on its investment. And, of course, the war years were an utter blank. The lack of return even during the relatively normal business climate of the middle 1930s was due in part to the fact that Ford-Werke was not profitable enough during most years to declare a dividend.[46] And, even when it was, laws strictly precluded removing any such profits from the country.

Ford-Werke continued to cost Dearborn money until the end of the decade. More than that, it remained a source of operating problems. Because of its U.S. ties, it was regarded by the Nazis as an alien company and was subject to special limitations. That was not the case, for example, with Opel, which was considered German, despite its ties to a U.S. parent, General Motors. Ford-Werke was blatantly uncooperative with the government on two key issues in the mid-1930s, further raising animosity.

The general manager of Ford-Werke was Edmund Heine, an executive who would prove to be patently unequal to the complexities before him. However, it was Heine's background that became even more of a liability to the company. Although a native of Germany, Heine had moved to the United States before World War I. In Nazi Germany, a native who had left was even more suspicious than an outright foreigner. Although Ford-Werke accounted for only 5 percent of Germany's automobile sales, it became the target of a slander campaign fueled by competitors and focused on Edmund Heine. The allegations that attached themselves to Ford-Werke were that Heine had gone to America only to make ammunition for use against Germans.[47]

The rumors had an effect, exacerbating the company's problems with its image as a foreign entity. Ford-Werke, with Edmund Heine at the top, was kept off of the German Society of Automotive Engineers' list of certified "German-made" cars, even though the cars rolling off the Cologne assembly line qualified. Without a place on that list, Ford could not hope to sell cars to the government, public institutions, or a great many patriotic Germans.

To competing German automakers, Heine may have loomed as some sort of Yankee, but to Valentine Tallberg, he was "a typical Nazi in the highest degree." Tallberg noted that English was always spoken in the business offices of Ford-Werke, since everyone who worked there either knew the language well or wanted to improve:

> I remember one time I met Heine in the long hallway. . . . I said something to him in English and with a very loud voice that could be heard from one end to another, he said to me in German (but I'll translate it into English), "I want you to remember that we do not speak English here; we speak only German. Just remember that." That may seem like an insignificant thing in itself, but it was a typical thing that happened every day.[48]

Obviously, Heine was under pressure to become a model German. He was not a model executive, though. Pompous and unreasonable, he alienated government authorities. For the same reasons, he annoyed his colleagues at Ford, especially since the business was in dire trouble under his aegis. Sir Percival Perry recommended his dismissal in 1933, but Edsel Ford and Charles Sorensen, the two Ford Motor executives most responsible for turning Ford-Werke around, demurred. They feared that since no likely replacement was at hand, the Nazis would use any transition to impose their own choice upon the company.

"I fully appreciate that Ford policy requires an isolation of political motive from industrial enterprise," acknowledged Perry. However, writing to Edsel Ford about the German situation, he added, "It is impossible to avoid politics. You may, however, rely that I will not be drawn into these matters any more than can be helped."[49]

That was wishful thinking on Perry's part. Once Hitler assumed power, it was not up to others to decide which matters they would be drawn into. In fact, the Ford Motor (England) Ltd. organization would be removed from the Ford-Werke hierarchy in 1934, under extreme pressure.[50] The Nazis did not want Germans taking orders from Englishmen. Two Britons remained, however, in Sir John Thomas Davies and Sir Percival, both of whom served on Ford-Werke's board until the end of the decade.

As a general air of chaos developed at Ford-Werke, Edsel, Charles Sorensen, and others in Dearborn found few people to trust there. Heinrich F. Albert, a director and prominent lawyer, was one source of information. Another European who was held in a measure of trust at Ford headquarters was Prince Louis-Ferdinand, a Prussian and a grandson of Kaiser Wilhelm II, who was then living (like the kaiser) in Holland. Prince Louis-Ferdinand had arrived in Dearborn one day in the late 1920s, requesting not the usual tour-and-lunch-with-the-Fords, but permission to work in the River Rouge plant. The idea of a member of the German royal family working on the line at an auto factory may have been the stuff of a Hollywood movie plot, but Louis-Ferdinand was fascinated by business and, especially, by the possibilities of Ford's brand of mass production. As soon as shares in Ford's European operations went on the market, he took sizable stakes in several of them, including Ford of Germany. He was especially close to Edsel Ford and served as one of his key reporters on affairs across the border in Germany. Henry Ford also liked the workman-prince.

Like many in Europe's aristocracy, Louis-Ferdinand saw nothing particularly alarming in Hitler's dictatorial politics. The regime might make blunders, he once observed, "but at large it has saved the German nation from chaos." By 1934, the prince had become exasperated with Heine's stewardship, as he explained in a letter to Edsel: "The way things are now in Cologne we will be out of business in a year. It is absolutely beneath the dignity of the Ford Motor Company to be satisfied with 5 per cent of the German business, whereas Opel–General Motors sell 50 % of all cars made in Germany.

"Mr. Ford has only two ways to choose with his German plant," Louis-Ferdinand continued, referring to Henry Ford, "to close down or to go ahead in a real Ford way, which means a big way."[51] He advised that Ford Motor placate the Nazis by firing Heine and that it accept Nazi overtures regarding the increase of German workmanship in each car manufactured, the prices to be charged, and the ways that Ford Motor could help Ford-Werke to bolster exports. However, it was not that simple. For Ford Motor in general, and Henry Ford in particular, outside interference in business affairs was anathema.

The same year, Hitler sent an emissary to Cologne to suggest that Ford Motor build a brand-new automobile factory in Hamburg. Moreover, the Führer very much wanted Ford Motor to participate in the manufacture of the Volkswagen people's car. Ford's existing plant in Cologne would not be acceptable because of that city's location near Germany's border with France—in what the government regarded as a danger zone, in case of war. The authorities had already persuaded General Motors to build an Opel plant in central Germany. They also promised that Ford's continuing problems with its foreign status would be dispelled if it cooperated.[52]

Ford Motor did not choose to invest millions more dollars in Germany, however many assurances Hitler's men made of future support, and however many thinly veiled threats they made regarding its continuing status in the country. In trying to explain the parent company's resistance, Heinrich Albert told a group of government representatives from Hamburg, "Mr. Ford is almost a fanatical supporter of the idea that the government should in no way interfere with business, which has to be left up entirely to private initiative."[53] Since, during the Nazi reign, Germany was a land where *everything* was up to the government, Henry Ford did nothing and turned his attention elsewhere. His representatives were left to make the best of the investment that the company already had in Germany.

Henry Ford's anti-Semitism was well-known, and his publications of the early 1920s became, regrettably, a source of continuing inspiration to the Nazis, including Adolf Hitler. Tallberg recalled that every time he returned to Dearborn on business, Henry Ford would take him aside to a corner where they wouldn't be disturbed. Tallberg recalled, "He would say, 'Now tell me, what is taking place in Germany now?' He was particularly interested in what the Nazis were doing and how the Jews were faring over there. I had to tell him quite in detail just what was going on." Tallberg noted that Ford's face did not betray any feelings about what he was hearing, only that he was vitally interested.

"I can remember the time when the Nazis burned all the synagogues in Germany," Tallberg said, referring to the November 9, 1938, *Kristallnacht*. "When I came to Dearborn at that time, I spent a very long time with him because I had to tell him everything, very much in detail. In fact, there was a synagogue not very far away from where we lived. At that time, my boy was about eight or nine years old and you know how kids run around. Well, he came back with a little bit of the Jewish Bible. I don't know if the Jews call it a Bible, or the Old Testament, or what, but he came home with a half-burned one. Mr. Ford wanted to know all about it; so I had to tell him about that too. I had to tell him every little detail of what took place. I had to tell him how the Nazis took the merchandise out of the Jewish stores, dragged it out on the street and let it lay there. They didn't steal it, but they let it lay there on the street. He wanted to know in detail all of those things."[54]

Henry Ford might have been expected to embrace the Nazi regime at the outset, in view of its sinister attitude toward the Jewish race. His company, however, stood aloof from the Third Reich. As the prospects for a Hamburg plant dwindled, the Fords also rejected further overtures to participate in the Volkswagen project, protesting that they believed in natural evolutions, not sudden revolutions "created or stimulated by government measures."[55] At that point Ford Motor had yet another run-in with the Nazis, one that ran entirely counter to Henry Ford's reputation as an anti-Semite.

Edmund Heine was finally dismissed in 1935, as a result of continued warnings from Ford Motor Company auditors that he was fostering a financial disaster. (Heine later relocated to the United States, where he lived during World War II.) His replacement was Erich Diestel, a businessman with no previous experience in the auto field. As Heinrich Albert pointed out, in recommending Diestel, no first-rate German automobile executive would consider working at Ford-Werke because it was out of favor with the authorities. With experience as manager of the Berlin Electric Works, Diestel seemed to have promise, but his administration at Ford was almost immediately rocked by an accusation of a very serious nature in Nazi Germany: he had a Jewish grandfather. That rumor, which turned out to be true, started with a Ford dealer in Hamburg and soon became common knowledge.

Albert soon turned against Diestel, on business grounds and because of the Jewish issue. In 1936, he wrote Edsel Ford an eight-page memo covering the overall situation at Ford-Werke, devoting a full page to the problems caused by Diestel's ancestry. At first, he said, he tried to discuss the matter with Nazi Party officials, but they talked only about how to replace Diestel. "Accordingly the standing of our Company and—directly and indirectly—the sales of our Company, particularly as far as governmental orders are concerned, are endangered," Albert wrote, concluding that Diestel was a liability in difficult times and that he should be replaced.[56] No one in Dearborn agreed.[57] Albert, for his part, promised to work around the situation as best he could.

Charles Sorensen first heard about the charges regarding Diestel from a Ford employee named E. J. Diefenbach, on assignment in Cologne, who took it upon himself to send a warning that there would be repercussions from the German government if a change wasn't made. Sorensen sent Diefenbach's letters back, dismissing the warnings with the comment, "It is a matter that requires no record here."[58] Ford Motor ignored efforts to force a change of management and so Diestel remained the general manager of Ford-Werke. Unfortunately, he was not a very good one at all. In 1938, Sorensen, Perry, and others finally concluded that he did not follow Ford Motor Company procedures and could not continue as an employee. For more than three years, though, Ford Motor Company protected Diestel, surely one of the highest-ranking "Jewish" business figures in Nazi Germany. The reason, once again, was Ford's reluctance to accept orders from any outsider.

Ford Motor did exert its international strength to help Ford-Werke comply with Germany's complicated scheme to increase exports. The parent company stretched itself to send raw materials to Cologne in return for parts and other materials, for which it then had to find a use. Still, German authorities insisted that Ford-Werke was essentially a foreign company. The board had to be recast with a majority of German members, and management had to be entirely homegrown—Sorensen and others were forbidden from issuing direct orders. By the late 1930s, Ford Motor's standing orders were being ignored, including Henry Ford's own edict that his factory not engage in war production.

Valentine Tallberg was the last American to leave Ford-Werke. Just before the Nazis invaded Poland in September 1939, Tallberg received a midday telephone call from an American diplomat, advising him to leave that night. By then, Ford-Werke was building trucks for the German army and there was no reason for an American to be there, anyway. Little by little, the German authorities had won the battle of Ford-Werke, wresting control away from the Fords through regulation, coercion, and covert pressure. In even more subtle ways, they also wrested control of people like Heinrich Albert, who had once been loyal Ford men.

Ford-Werke was a tribulation for Ford Motor from the beginning of the 1930s until the outbreak of World War II. Except for the fact that Ford of Germany would become a valuable asset after the war, it is probable that Henry Ford wished he had never built the factory at Cologne in the first place.

20

For Better and for Worse
in Dearborn

It was during the snowy month of March 1932, not long after the infamous Hunger March, when Henry and Clara Ford spontaneously decided to drive from Dearborn to their winter residence in Fort Myers, Florida. They traveled in a Model A. Ford had his assistant, Frank Campsall, follow him the entire 1,295 miles in a second Model A. Upon arrival, Ford asked James Newton, the young head of development of the Edison Park Community, an investment project in which Ford had a major stake, to arrange an interview with a Miami reporter. Dutifully Newton arrived the next day with the journalist in tow. A genial, happy-go-lucky Henry Ford answered questions while standing on the running board of what was ostensibly the typical Model A that he had just driven all the way from wintry Michigan. Newton also perched on the car. The reporter scribbled furiously as Ford offered up his arsenal of homilies, aphorisms, and parables about the state of American business. When the newspaperman had enough for a story, he departed, taking a bus back to Miami. "As soon as he was gone," Newton recalled, "Ford turned to Campsall and said, 'Should we show Jimmie what he's been sitting on?' I got up and Frank opened up the hood of the Model A. There it was—the new V-8. Ford had wanted to test the engine himself: that was why he had insisted on driving the car from Detroit. He explained they had used the two cars so that if the V-8 engine broke down, they would not have had to take it to a garage and 'spill the beans.' They would just hitch it up to the standard Model A and tow it. The reporter had probably had the biggest scoop of his career within arm's reach, but Ford had kept the news secret, no doubt because he wanted a dramatic occasion to make the announcement."[1]

Two months later, in May, Henry Ford unveiled his latest vehicle—the first Ford to drop the "model" designation. This new car was known bluntly as the "V-8," for the engine that powered it. The only car of the time to offer eight cylinders at an economy price, the V-8 was a sensation, and a bombshell in the hotly contested Ford–Chevy war. It was also a lot of fun to drive and to own—and after a major restyling in 1933, just to look at. Ford Motor had little choice but to rush the V-8 to market. In that respect, it represented the first in a string of decisions forced on the company due to competition during the 1930s. After thirty years of calling its own shots in labor and production, going its own way on finance, taking its time with product introductions (as in the Model A), and generally operating like an outsize colonial blacksmithy, Ford Motor Company had to join the real world of Big Business for the first time during the decade. That real world, as other businesses had long known it, didn't grant the privilege of profit without exerting a distinct influence over company prerogatives. It occurred through a wide array of channels, none of them coordinated or even predictable, but they included turns in the marketplace, government rulings, and the strength of united labor.

Henry Ford tried to hang on to his empire in the 1930s by running it like a tyrant, making his company a place where at least one of the bosses carried a gun and where workers could be fired for so much as laughing on the job. One man dared to sit down on a barrel while he was splicing wires at the River Rouge factory. A boss passing by bellowed, "What are you doing sitting down? You're *fired.*" The man jumped up and replied, "The hell I am! I work for the phone company."[2] Ford Motor would learn that no industrial empire was entirely independent of the labor movement in the 1930s—particularly no automobile manufacturers. After all, Detroit was more affected by the Great Depression than any other American city. Joblessness was a stark reality for 40 percent of Michigan residents. Along the Detroit River, shantytowns sprang up next to garbage heaps. Sanitary conditions deteriorated to the point where rat bites, typhoid fever, and dysentery were commonplace. Quite naturally, Ford Motor, still a powerhouse with 300,000 employees, forty-five plants scattered from Dearborn to Yokohama, and millions of customers, became a prime target of labor's frustrations.[3] Not all of the dissatisfaction, however, emerged from pro-union forces.

Chief among Henry Ford's critics was the demagogic local radio priest, Father Charles Coughlin. Coughlin regularly accused Ford of fomenting the socialist workers' movement by running his company with such autocratic control. Economic despair was widespread, he charged, because Ford and other industrialists were treating workers like soulless units instead of hungry people. When Father Coughlin testified before a Congressional committee on domestic subversion, he suggested that Ford's cold indifference to the plight of American workers was the "greatest force in the movement to internationalize labor throughout the world." Communism was ascending, Coughlin claimed, because the Henry Fords of industry were greedy and irresponsible.[4]

Erskine Caldwell, whose novel *Tobacco Road* was a brutal exposé of life in the rural South, took on the automotive industry in a number of muckraking essays for the *Daily Worker*. A dedicated socialist, Caldwell journeyed to the Detroit area in May 1935 and took aim at Henry Ford, whose name, he wrote, "has been inscribed on the cornerstone of The School of Whoredom." The article that caused the most stir was "The Eight-Finger City," which described how monstrous machines were maiming people, how the streets of Detroit were "littered with fingers, hands, arms, legs and crushed bodies."[5] It was a preposterous image.

Henry Ford paid critics like Father Coughlin and Erskine Caldwell no mind. He believed the way to improve conditions for his workers did not lie in "relief" or "benefits," but in manufacturing the new V-8, which would contribute to economic growth.

There originally was a debate at Ford Motor Company over whether to develop a six- or eight-cylinder engine. "Edsel Ford wanted to make a six, but he knew that his father was opposed to it," recalled staff engineer Emil Zoerlein. "He started to make a six without his father's knowledge. He would switch them over on the line as they were made and say they were truck engines."[6] Henry Ford himself dabbled briefly with ideas for a six, but his heart wasn't in it. Instead, early in 1930, he directed two senior engineers, Carl Schultz and Ray Laird, to begin serious development of an eight-cylinder engine.

Lincoln had introduced a smooth-running V-8 engine in 1929, and while it was too complicated and expensive to use in a Ford, it did renew Henry Ford's faith in the eight, especially in the **V** layout, with two banks of four cylinders each facing each other at a diagonal pitch. In a straight eight, the cylinders make a single line, necessitating a longer hood and a longer crankshaft. Such a configuration interested him no more than the six.

Henry Ford's antipathy toward the six-cylinder engine has been the subject of speculation through the years, just as it was at the company in 1930–1932. "Mr. Ford never liked the 6-cylinder engine because the crank was long and would wind up [get out of sync]," said Jimmy Smith, who was involved in many of Henry Ford's experimental projects. "That's the reason he went to the V-8. He wanted to do away with the long crankshaft. . . . You just can't smooth it out."[7] Another reason for the V-8, however, has been attributed to Ford's natural competitive streak. He loathed the fact that William Knudsen, his former employee, was advertising the Chevy as a "six for the price of four." He took it as a challenge. "I think Mr. Ford was opposed to a six-cylinder car just to be different," suggested Clem Davis, a Ford dealer. "The Chevrolet was a six, and Knudsen was over there. Mr. Ford wanted to have something a little different and better if he could."[8]

Trumping Chevy's six with a V-8 would be a marketing move worthy of Henry Ford at his best. According to Zoerlein, Ford's thinking was that "General Motors had a six, and everybody else had a six, why should Ford have a six?" Also Ford Motor Company realized that it had to give its dealers something exciting to sell in the midst of the Depression. Zoerlein and others, however, have also hinted that Ford's attitude was just another of his inexplicable, incorrigible prejudices. "He experimented with a six way back on his Model K," Zoerlein continued, referring to the 1906 car. "Something went wrong with it. It didn't function right. I assume, knowing him, that that would ruin the thing for him for life. He had a fixed opinion once it had been established."[9]

In late 1930, senior engineers Carl Schultz and Ray Laird started their design work on the V-8 in strict secrecy. To make sure of it, Henry Ford hid them away in the Edison Laboratory, which he had had moved from Fort Myers, Florida, and reconstructed at Greenfield Village. In that historic setting, the engineers worked on a simplified V-8, the first one intended for mass production. With Henry Ford himself and a few handpicked colleagues (including Zoerlein), Schultz and Laird tackled problems like cooling and fuel delivery. There seemed to be no particular hurry. The V-8 was slated to join the Model A, not replace it, as Ford intended to offer customers a choice in models for the first time in decades—in fact, since the days of the Model K. The V-8 showed decent progress during its first year of development, but at the end of 1931, a slight panic swept over Dearborn. The Model A was failing to find customers in sufficient numbers. As word had leaked out that Ford Motor Company was preparing something as compelling as a V-8 car for the general public, customers simply stopped buying the A, rendering it obsolete before its time. Under pressure, Henry Ford had to answer the cry for the new model—his reputation depended on it. He could not extend the product life of the Model A, as he had that of the Model T. The V-8 had taken on an urgent life of its own.

Snatched from the engineers' rooms in January 1932, the V-8 was pressed into a production run that began only three months later. The engine still was not running at peak performance, but Ford Motor Company's engineers doggedly attacked each problem that held it back. "It went into production and we still kept working," said Clem Davis, a member of the group. "There was a lot of work to be done to smooth out the rough spots."[10] It was a far cry from the old Ford way, in which time and expense weren't allowed to encroach on the development process, kept at bay by a wave of Henry Ford's hand.

In 1932, Ford Motor unveiled its lineup, which included both the Model B (a Model A with improved engine power) and the V-8. They looked largely alike, except that the 8 was slightly longer. At $550 it was also $50 more expensive. Customers were fascinated by the Ford V-8. During its debut week, about 5.5 million turned out to see it at special showings across America.

Nevertheless, it was a bad time in which to launch an important new model. Few of those looking could afford to buy a car that year. Beyond consumer reticence about cars in general, there was a rumor that the V-8 engine wasn't reliable: something about the pistons wearing out the cylinders on the downward side of the engine. In fact, early Ford V-8s did develop chronic problems with blown pistons, oil consumption, and overheating. "They came out with it in too much of a hurry," Clem Davis said. "You see, it takes around five years to develop a motor. The sales bogged down. The people were clamoring, and there was so much rumor about this V-8 motor that they were forced to bring it out in 1932. Well, it wasn't ready yet."[11]

Engine unreliability wasn't the only problem with the 1932 V-8—styling was too. The car was not a far toss from the Model A, looking prim and generally upright. Unfortunately, that was the old look in autos. The new look was slanted backward, like something windblown and fast moving. Streamlining hadn't quite arrived, but the slanted look was distinctly part of the transition. The styling on the 1932 V-8 didn't take advantage of the fact that the V-8 was something really new.

It was in 1933 that the V-8 finally made its full impact. Edsel persuaded his father to stretch the V-8's overall length by six inches. He then gave the new dimensions, along with stylists' drawings of the Model Y, to a body designer named Clare Kramer. The result was the Y in concept and detail, expanded to the proportions of the V-8. The slanted grille, hood louvers, and windshield gave a feeling of eagerness to the car. Its fine lines made other styling bits and pieces extraneous. Loath to load a car up with fixes, Edsel Ford was more interested in finding a good silhouette to begin with, and in the second-edition of the V-8, he had just that.

The 1933 V-8 is typically ranked with the best automobile styling of the 1930s—heady praise in a decade known for elegant lines and new ideas in cars. Bob Gregorie, who designed the Model Y, told Henry Dominguez why the 1933–1934 Fords were so successful. "The general proportions of those cars are excellent," he said, while looking at a set of pictures in the mid-1990s. "They are nicely balanced between the front end and the rear end. They have nice detail; everything had a purpose. But most important, the front wheels and the rear wheels are as far fore and aft as possible, and the front axle was ahead of the grille, and that is the base for a good design."[12]

One reason Henry granted Edsel's request to extend the length of the V-8 was that the chassis was being reengineered anyway for 1933. It would be constructed on a sturdy X frame to support the heavy engine more securely than before. In fact, with the new styling and new mechanical components, it was unfortunate that the V-8 had not been held back and introduced afresh as a 1933 model. The '32 sullied its reputation, even if it did generate sales that were certainly needed at the time. However, in 1933 Chrysler forged ahead of Ford in overall corporate sales, with General Motors leading the pack. Given the circumstances *Fortune* declared Henry Ford the "world's worst salesman."[13] Meanwhile, the Model A (or B) was phased out in 1933. As long as parts and customers lasted, it remained nominally in production around the world, but was not officially part of the factory offering after 1934. Unlike the Model T, it left quietly, with no one even noticing, at least at first, that it was gone.

Later, that would change. Appreciation for the Model A was reborn with the collector-car movement after World War II. For a long time, it was the consensus favorite among the world's growing legion of old-car fans. "The Model A was an uncommonly willing car, like a friendly farm dog," wrote Frank Ransome Jr. in *Popular Science* in 1954, noting that it "had the personality of a puppy: it wiggled all over, it wanted to go, it ignored mistreatment."[14] Throughout the 1950s and 1960s, Ford Motor received persistent requests to put the Model A back in production. That didn't happen, but independent parts makers have long reproduced every component, with the result that maintaining a Model A is no more challenging than it is for any late-model used car. The Model A, which didn't last long enough as far as Henry and Edsel Ford were concerned, has had its own last laugh on the market.

By 1934 the Ford V-8 had developed its own legion of enthusiasts. Henry Ford received many letters of unabashed praise for his company's accomplishment from kings, presidents, schoolchildren, and even gangsters. John Dillinger, then Public Enemy No. 1, endorsed the V-8 in a note to Henry Ford on May 16, 1934, written two months before he was killed by arresting officers in Chicago. "Hello Old Pal," Dillinger began his missive. "You have a wonderful car. Been driving it for three weeks. It's a treat to drive one. Your slogan should be: Drive a Ford and watch the other cars fall behind you. I can make any other car take a Ford's dust."[15] A few weeks earlier, Clyde Barrow— he and Bonnie Parker had become the most notorious outlaw couple America had ever produced—also wrote Ford a fan letter. "While I still have got breath in my lungs I will tell you what a dandy car you make," Barrow wrote from Tulsa, Oklahoma. "I have drove Fords exclusively when I could get away with one. For sustained speed and freedom from trouble the Ford has got every other car skinned and even if my business hasn't been strictly legal it don't hurt anything to tell you what a fine car you got in the V-8."[16] He too would soon die from police gunfire, as would Bonnie.

———

Ford Motor Company of the mid-1930s is typically regarded as a dark, almost gothic place, with a shadowy administration, activities shrouded in mystery, and a roster of dubious characters running rampant on the premises. The company was the subject of rumors—for example, that its accounts payable department was so hopelessly disorganized that bills piled up until they were finally paid on the basis of their weight. Ford Motor, once the vortex of futurism in industry, was looking old-fashioned, if not quaint. It was one of America's great business stories—of the generation before. Everyone had heard about the triumph of the Model T, the fabulous rise of its originator, and the gargantuan sense of enterprise at the Rouge, but in the 1930s Ford Motor was settling into a more mundane role. It was no longer the world's biggest automaker. It was only one of the biggest and was navigating the complexities of the car market as one of the pack. Ford undoubtedly suffered in comparison to Walter Chrysler's impressive and relatively new automaking company. It took off, just as Ford was trailing off.[17]

By 1933, Chrysler had given New York City and the world of architecture the Chrysler Building, an art deco masterwork that still looks modern today. Ford, for its part, was adding to the Greenfield Village historical re-creation of the nineteenth century. While there is nothing wrong with history, Ford Motor Company seemed to be wallowing in it, rather than making it. The harshest comparison for Ford Motor Company in the latter 1930s, though, was the one most often made: to General Motors. GM weathered the Depression without a money-losing year. Along with AT&T, Coca-Cola, and a few of the railroads, it was a gleaming example of business progress against the ravages of hard times. Whatever Henry Ford had done to turn his factory floor into a model of efficiency, Alfred Sloan superseded by creating the optimum office environment. Sloan honed management charts until they flowed in only one direction, toward the creation of a motivated workforce. As a result, GM's organization was studied and then copied by thousands of corporations around the world, but no one could copy Ford's organization—there wasn't one. Long into the Alfred Sloan era of business, the combative Henry Ford was still bragging about that. "I don't care how many cars Chevrolet sold last year," Ford exploded at a *Fortune* reporter. "I don't know how many they're selling this year. I don't know how many they may sell next year. And—I don't care."[18]

The Ford Motor Company may have been ripe for sweeping changes, but that was not to be. Instead, in the years before World War II, it underwent transitions in just two respects, both ultimately crucial to its future. One was exciting and creative: the addition of three new car lines to fill out the Ford offering and match it to that of General Motors, from the least expensive Ford to the Deluxe Ford, to the new Mercury, to the Lincoln-Zephyr, to the swanky heights of the Lincoln and the much admired Continental. The new lines were shepherded by Edsel Ford. The other force of change at Ford Motor was the fight for unionization. It made for an uncomfortable interlude in which the company was expected to admit—in which Henry Ford himself was expected to admit—that possibly he didn't know what was best for his workers. There were others who stepped up with distinct ideas about that.

———

Once Walter Reuther left Germany with his brother, Victor, he spent most of 1933 bicycling around Europe. The two young Americans missed very few of the sights, including the great auto factories as well as art museums and monuments. They found that wages for auto workers were lower than those in the United States. At the Morris factory in England, they were told that the reason the factory didn't offer better pay was that more money "would lead to dissipation on the part of the workers."[19] However, working conditions seemed better, since European assembly lines moved less quickly.

That December, the two Reuthers arrived in the USSR, ready to start work in the automobile plant in Gorki. With dies and tools purchased from Ford Motor Company, the Soviets planned to build a Model A: the first automobile completely manufactured in the Soviet Union (previously, Model As had been assembled from parts shipped from the United States). The familiar little car looked like a Ford and ran like one, but it was made by GAZ. And it wasn't a Model A; it was to be known as the MI.

Since few people in the USSR had the technical experience required to manufacture car parts from scratch, skilled auto workers from America were highly valuable commodities. Those who agreed to move to Gorki received generous wages, along with accommodations (and good food) in the special American village attached to the factory. "There are so many striking things here that I dare not attempt to enumerate them all," Walter Reuther wrote in a letter to the *Moscow Daily News,* an English-language publication: "the Red Corner, shop library, the numerous shop meetings where serious problems are discussed, the frank criticism exchanged between the workers and the administration, and the multiplicity of cultural activities connected with shop life.

"I must confess that all these things are foreign to me as one who has received his training in a capitalist auto plant," he added.[20]

Walter Reuther was a longtime socialist, but he never became a Communist, not even when he was working in the USSR. As a socialist, he was committed to workers' rights and the responsibility of society—including businesses—to uphold those rights. However, as he was something of an opportunist himself, he did not believe in a planned economy or in government ownership of capital. Reuther recognized the limitations of the noncompetitive atmosphere at Gorki and the horrors of the police state beyond. At the same time, he reveled in the country's widespread idealism and its sense of hope for every worker. Reuther also had a very good time, as he was usually apt to do, wherever he was. He and Victor went to music events and parties, traveled extensively, and participated in volunteer projects, such as cutting ice or helping with the harvest on local farms.

In 1935, the brothers returned home by way of Asia—"self-appointed social scientists," as Victor said, finishing a three-year, round-the-world tour on workers' wages. Back in Detroit, Walter couldn't find a job. Regardless, he somehow talked his way into membership in Local 86 of the fledgling United Automobile Workers union. In the UAW, he began his life's work.

At that point, no American automobile factory recognized an auto workers' union—neither the UAW nor any of the other organizations that sprang up and then disappeared. The UAW had a better chance than the rest, since it was affiliated with the brand-new Committee for Industrial Organization (reorganized as the Congress of Industrial Organizations in 1938). Gruff John L. Lewis, a former coal miner, founded the CIO in 1935 specifically to focus unionization efforts on mass-production industries. Automaking (in the form of Ford Motor), which had pioneered modern mass production, was a primary object of Lewis's interest. Other targets included the rubber, steel, and electrical industries. Lewis banked heavily on the fact that in the presidential election of 1932, he had thrown strong support to Franklin D. Roosevelt.

At least some of Lewis's faith in the New Deal was rewarded with the passage in 1935 of the National Labor Relations Act, also known as the Wagner Act, which brought a sense of protection to union activities. To most people, it was an affirmation of labor's basic right to organize and to engage in collective bargaining (that is, the union's legal right to represent workers in negotiations with employers). In addition, the Wagner Act provided for the investigation of unfair management practices, including interference with the formation of unions and the refusal to engage in collective bargaining.

With the Wagner Act, labor had the strength of government behind it. With Franklin Roosevelt in office, it also had the sympathy of the president.

Franklin Roosevelt's flagship program for stabilizing the depressed economy, the National Recovery Administration (NRA), contained price and wage controls as well as a provision that forced companies to participate in collective bargaining. Headed by Hugh Johnson, a former cavalry general, the NRA aimed to improve working conditions and abolish unfair trading practices. Henry Ford (who was singularly unimpressed by Roosevelt and his New Deal programs) flatly refused to comply with the NRA and deemed Johnson a "silly dunce." At the time, this was a highly unpopular stance, since businesses all over the country were making a show of optimism and patriotism by displaying the NRA Blue Eagle emblem with its "We Do Our Part" motto. Taking a maverick stance, Ford insisted that forcing his company to follow NRA codes was unconstitutional. "Hell," he snapped when presented with a Blue Eagle sticker. "That Roosevelt Buzzard! I wouldn't put it on a car." Ford grudgingly agreed to adhere to wage and price controls, but nothing, so he said, including the government, could force him to accept collective bargaining at Ford Motor Company. Ford's stand eventually prevailed, when the NRA fell apart in the face of court decisions siding with him about the limitations of government power.[21]

Walter Reuther, arriving back in Detroit simultaneously with the Wagner Act in 1935, entered the labor fight at a propitious time. Using Local 86's entire treasury of five dollars, he traveled to South Bend, Indiana, to attend a UAW convention. Pushing hard, he was elected to the union's executive board. When Local 86 was folded into Local 174, the West Side Local, Reuther was elected president. There were more than 100,000 workers in the territory the West Side Local represented, but it counted fewer than a hundred members.[22]

In 1935–1936, strikes were breaking out in the automaking industry, but not at Ford Motor, Chrysler, or General Motors. All three were headed by men staunchly opposed to the very notion of collective bargaining. Each company took precautions and prepared for walkouts, while trying to win the war of words in the press. For all the big talk, however, there were few people within the Big Three who did not dread the specter of walkouts and pickets, the possibility of scabs (replacement workers), and the aura of violence that traditionally accompanied hard strikes.

In 1935, a new kind of strike occurred in the Firestone plant in Akron, Ohio. It started when the company revised its system for figuring wages. The new system had been formulated by accountants in New York. When the men in the factory complained that they couldn't understand it, the superintendent agreed that he couldn't understand it, either, but nonetheless, they all had to follow it. The men responded by refusing to go home at the end of their shift, thereby insisting that management take their grievance seriously. Because Harvey S. Firestone and his family had a strong tradition of trust in their employees, management did not balk at the factory takeover. They knew that the men would treat the equipment with respect. The sit-down strike was settled after a few days.[23]

The Akron strike was barely reported to the general public, but it caused a stir in labor circles. Not only did it suggest a new philosophical debate, as to whether or not workers actually had property rights in their factories, it offered a unique method of work stoppage. A sit-down strike paralyzed production, yet it was not as confrontational as a walkout—and it didn't leave any room for scabs.

In 1936, Walter Reuther staged a sit-down strike at Kelsey-Hayes, a maker of wheels in Detroit. After the strike ended successfully with recognition of the UAW, the West Side Local grew to 30,000 members. In January 1937, the UAW followed Reuther's lead and organized a massive sit-down strike at a General Motors factory in Flint, Michigan. The strike soon spread through GM's plants and shut down production entirely.

"When the sit-down strikes started," said Secretary of Labor Frances Perkins, "Roosevelt was as much surprised and bewildered by the new technique as anyone else." Most Americans disagreed with the tactic. Even John Lewis considered the sit-down strike immoral, but he stood by the locals who were using it. GM Chairman Alfred P. Sloan was incensed by the strike, absolutely refusing to open negotiations until the plants were evacuated. For more than a month, GM factories were occupied, even as pressure built for the National Guard to forcibly remove the workers. Perkins received Lewis's assurance that the strikers would leave the building as soon as GM's management showed good faith by at least beginning negotiations. For a long time, Sloan refused.

Finally, President Roosevelt placed a personal telephone call to Bill Knudsen, by then GM's president, and asked him to accept Perkins's arrangement. Knudsen, less conservative than Sloan, agreed. After one session between Lewis and Knudsen, the strikers went home, true to their word. As a result of the negotiations, GM recognized the UAW as the collective bargaining agent for those workers who were members and agreed not to discourage other employees from joining.

"From then on, we were on our way," said Victor Reuther of the triumph at General Motors. Chrysler was the next company to receive the UAW's attention and, after a short strike, it came to a settlement as well.

That left Ford Motor Company.

———

"Labor unions are the worst things that ever struck the earth," Henry Ford said in a statement released for publication in April 1937. Unleashing nearly all of his fears at once, he explained why: "Financiers are behind the unions and their object is to kill competition so as to reduce the income of the workers and eventually bring on war."[24]

Such remarks were only one of the many ways that Ford Motor Company sought to dissuade union organizers from so much as looking at River Rouge and the company's other plants. Commenting on what had happened at GM and Chrysler earlier in the year, Henry Ford vowed that his company would never recognize any union.

Henry Ford may have been the only person ever to identify unions as the pawns of financiers, "financiers" being his code for anyone with, in his perception, greater power than he. While that is undoubtedly a peculiar theory, it may be the key to his vitriolic hatred of labor unions. And in further tying the unions to corporate warmongering, Ford may have been making a reference to the du Pont family, whom he often accused of using high finance in order to start wars (and sell ammunition). "Mr. Ford seemed to feel quite strongly that there was a DuPont–Jewish–Roosevelt clique that was more or less tied together. This was pretty deep in him," said engineer Emil Zoerlein.[25] Harry Bennett told Zoerlein that Ford had a persecution complex regarding the three and that "it bothered him all the time." That persecution complex ex-

The Michigan farmhouse in which William and Mary Ford lived with their six children. The oldest child, Henry, was born there on July 30, 1863. This photograph was taken about 1911.

Henry Ford driving his first car in 1905. The vehicle, known as a quadricycle, had had its debut on the streets of Detroit nine years before, on June 4, 1896.

Henry Ford turned the shed behind his home at 58 Bagley Avenue in Detroit into a workshop. It was there, at the age of thirty-two, that he built the quadricycle that launched him as an automaker.

Henry Ford (*standing*) with Barney Oldfield in the driver's seat of the 999 racing car. Oldfield drove the monster racer to a string of records and victories in 1902–1903.

An early Ford Motor Company advertisement showcasing the joy of "auto touring."

An assembly room at Ford's Piquette Avenue plant in 1908, just as Model T production was set to begin. It was spick-and-span, as were all of Henry Ford's factories.

A Model T, fully loaded with Scotsmen, climbs a steep hill in Edinburgh. Owners around the world tested the Model T's strength and agility in similarly imaginative ways, usually without finding its limit.

In 1910, Ford Motor Company opened a flagship factory at Highland Park, Michigan. In this picture, Model T chassis are lined up outside, awaiting bodywork.

Henry Ford in a rare pose: sitting in his Highland Park office. He was far more interested in the busier parts of his factory.

The Highland Park crankshaft assembly room in 1915. What the picture cannot communicate is the cacophonous noise that stunned most visitors to the plant.

James Couzens (*left*) with Henry Ford. Couzens was instrumental in the realization of Ford's business plans from the company's founding until 1916.

Thomas Edison, seated in car, shares a gag with cowboy Henry Ford on one of their periodic camping trips. Even as the two industrialists cemented their friendship exploring the country-side, they helped to popularize automobile camping as a form of vacation.

Charles Lindbergh *(right)* inspects an early Ford airplane, as Henry Ford looks on. Ford Motor Company led the nation in the development of civil aviation in the 1920s.

Workmen polish Ford Model A bodies in a 1929 photograph.

Henry Ford looms over a model of the enormous River Rouge plant in the company of his son, Edsel.

Sir Percival Perry, Henry Ford II, and Edsel Ford. Sir Percival, who started out in life as a penniless young man, linked his fortunes to Ford Motor Company early on. He ended his career as chairman of Ford of Europe and as baron of Stock Harvard.

Union organizers distribute pamphlets outside the River Rouge plant on May 26, 1937. Among those present that day was Walter Reuther, who was a former Ford employee.

Violence broke out as the union men were attacked by factory men allegedly sent for the purpose by Harry Bennett. Union organizers, including Reuther, were badly bloodied in the confrontation, later known as the "Battle of the Overpass."

Henry and Clara Ford.

The second- and third-generation Ford family members. *From left to right:* Edsel and his wife, Eleanor, with their children, Henry II, Benson, Josephine, and William.

The B-24 Liberator, the primary product of the Ford Motor Company facility at Willow Run during World War II.

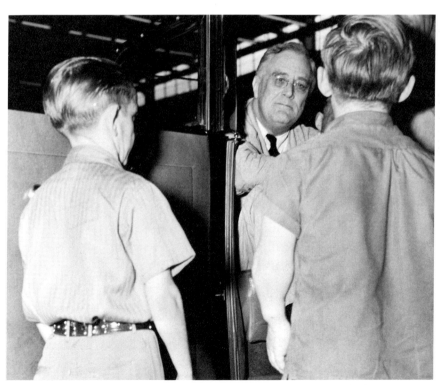

President Franklin D. Roosevelt chats with Ford Motor Company's "little people" during a wartime visit to Willow Run.

Henry Ford.

Henry Ford II with workers at River Rouge in 1945. He had been named president in September of that year. Throughout his career, he made time to walk through any facility he visited, in order to meet employees at every level.

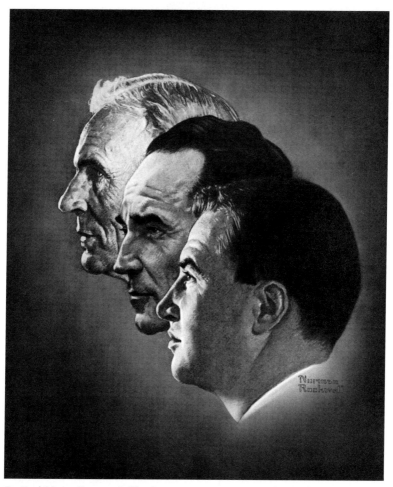

On Ford Motor Company's fiftieth anniversary, Norman Rockwell was commissioned to draw a portrait of the three men who had led it: Henry, Edsel, and Henry II.

A 1955 Thunderbird with an F-100 Super Saber jet. The T-bird gave the dowdy Ford image a strong dose of cool in the mid-1950s.

The Mustang celebrates itself in 1968. Introduced in 1964, it was Ford's most popular car during the decade.

Lee Iacocca was the executive who guided the Mustang through development and received credit for defining the youth market, to which it catered so perfectly.

Philip Caldwell was named president of Ford in 1978 and chairman two years later—in the midst of the company's worst financial crisis. He orchestrated one of the greatest turnarounds in corporate history.

Donald Petersen, who was named president in 1980, set the company on the creative course that led to the introduction of the wildly successful Taurus in 1985.

William Clay Ford Jr. was named chairman of Ford Motor Company in 1999, when he was forty-one, and became its CEO two years later. He was at the helm as the company celebrated its centennial in 2003.

plains how Ford might draw the conclusion that the du Ponts, who owned the single largest stake in GM, were behind the UAW.

"All I know is that Henry Ford did not want the union to get in the Ford Motor Company," said veteran Ford employee Al Esper. "I think that's a very well-known fact. Bennett was the man who was supposed to be stopping them from getting in here. I believe he had full authority from Henry Ford to do that."[26]

By all accounts, Harry Bennett had greater authority at Ford Motor than anyone else except Henry Ford. Charles Sorensen still reigned over production, leaving day-to-day operations to Bennett, but even the bull-tempered Sorensen was wary of encroaching on Bennett's turf. And by the end of the 1930s, Bennett's turf was all of Ford Motor Company in America.

Nominally the head of personnel, Harry Bennett remained in charge of the service department. In 1937, the *New York Times* described the company's security branch as "the largest private army in the world." On Bennett's watch, any employee who was known to be a member of a union—or, worse, who discussed unionization on or off the Ford premises—would be summarily fired. At that, he or she would be getting off easy: the National Labor Relations Board received reports of hundreds of beatings carried out against employees considered sympathetic to union organization.[27] The service department planted men in most departments to listen and watch the other employees. "As I get the picture, none of the top men could make a move without Mr. Bennett knowing about it," said H. S. Abelwhite, who worked under Bennett as the head of the sociological department. "It was nailed down that closely."[28]

Bennett purposely hired tough-looking former athletes—"thugs" was the word used most often. "Plug-uglies" was another. If they couldn't always be on hand to intimidate employees, their reputation would suffice. "I saw the service men around," said a worker named W. Griffith. "In the tool room, in particular, there were a number of ex-pugilists who did very little work. They were *supposed* to be working, but some of them never put on an apron; just walked around there."[29]

Beyond the service department employees, Bennett had an unknown number of "investigators" working for him off the company payroll.[30] No one knew who they were, but they could engage in illegal activities without risking implication of the company. Other auto companies engaged in the same undercover, underhanded methods to repel unions. Bennett went a step further, letting it be known that he had ties to organized crime. That kind of reputation bolstered the aura of omnipotence that Bennett tried so hard to create. With control over every job at Ford and most of the local dealerships, he developed a network of cooperative judges and other politicians in Dearborn and Detroit, and throughout the state of Michigan. "I think we can fairly say that Bennett had the dealerships, in addition to this job patronage, whereby he could arrange for people in the right spot," said Abelwhite.[31]

Bennett's tight control over Ford Motor Company succeeded in forestalling the efforts of the UAW, which approached the "fortress in Dearborn" with trepidation. However, it also made unionization inevitable.

"I didn't have any contact with the service men or the service department," said W. Griffith in a very telling comment, "because I worked honestly and if a man worked honestly and watched his work, he didn't get into trouble. The men resented Harry Bennett."[32]

Had Henry Ford maintained a better atmosphere, something like the one that prevailed before World War I, unionization might have been delayed. As it was, Ford employees were in desperate need of help. "The union was long overdue," observed Abelwhite, "considering the treatment the people received."

The mood at Ford Motor Company was bleak. "Our morale was very high one day and very low the next day," recalled Anthony Harff. "Some of this might seem terribly dark, but after all, someone would come along and lift us up and make us feel good for a few days again."[33] The pressing question among employees during the 1930s was whether Henry Ford knew just how Bennett was running the company. If not, then Ford was still, in effect, on their side: all of them duped together. If, however, Bennett was acting with Ford's acquiescence, then the employees were being betrayed by the man for whom many felt they were working, in a very personal way.

"He was noted to be quite a bully," observed Harff, speaking of Harry Bennett, "and let it be known that he had the backing of Mr. Ford in everything he did. We doubted that sometimes, but we seldom disputed. In many cases, we didn't dare test it."[34]

"There wasn't anything Mr. Ford didn't know about," Emil Zoerlein asserted. "He was perfectly aware of the things Harry Bennett did. I asked him once why he put up with a man like Bennett. . . . He said, 'Well, what's the difference? If I put somebody else in his place, give them a few years, and they'll do the same thing.' Apparently he was just recognizing human frailty in that sense. It was a pretty costly recognition of human frailty."[35]

———

As president of the West Side Local, Walter Reuther nibbled at Ford Motor, staging preliminary strikes at companies that supplied it with parts. At first, Ford refused to make purchases from unionized companies. Before long, that was no longer practical. In mid-1937, Reuther set his sights on the main plant at River Rouge, still the biggest automobile factory in the world, gauged by acreage, workforce, or output. "Unionization of the Ford Motor Company was particularly vital to the defense of the new wage standards and working conditions in the factories organized by Reuther's West Side local," wrote biographer Nelson Lichtenstein. "Even more than Chrysler, Ford established the economic and political environment in which scores of supplier firms operated. It spread anti-union propaganda from its citadel in nearby Dearborn and intimidated tens of thousands of West Side workers who took the Rouge trolley line out Michigan Avenue."[36]

Since most Ford employees knew very little about the UAW, Reuther started his campaign by buying nearly all of the billboard space on the main routes from Detroit to the factory. He then plastered the routes with pro-union messages. To reach the workers directly, Walter Reuther and a UAW colleague named Richard Frankensteen prepared to lead a dispatch of union volunteers to the plant entrance, where they intended to hand out leaflets on May 26, 1937.

The factory was aware of the plan. Edsel Ford had long, intense discussions about it with his father, the younger Ford recognizing that unionization was inevitable in the wake of the Wagner Act. Clara Ford agreed with him, but Henry ignored them both, preferring Harry Bennett's promises to keep the union men and their leaflets away from River Rouge—whatever it took.

Reuther, Frankensteen, and their followers were careful to remain on public property, even as they skirted the River Rouge plant, choosing to approach it by the pedestrian bridge over Miller Road. That was the same overpass that had seen fighting between Ford service men, Dearborn police officers, and unemployed workers during the Hunger March in 1932.

"I was there a couple of minutes," Walter Reuther later said of his arrival on the overpass that day, "and then all of a sudden about 35 or 40 men surrounded us and started to beat us up." Although both Reuther and Frankensteen were badly injured, they eventually made their way to a car on Miller Road. Many other union volunteers, including women in the group, were attacked as well. There was no doubt about what had happened; newspaper photographers captured the beatings on film. The incident, known as the Battle of the Overpass, received terrific publicity—much more than had the tragic Hunger March with its four fatalities. Another difference was the Wagner Act's recognition of workers' rights. In the attacks on the Hunger Marchers, individual members of Ford's staff were guilty. In the beatings on the overpass, Ford Motor Company was at fault.

Edsel Ford was disgusted by the violence, and bitterly disappointed that his father had chosen Bennett's course over his own. Ford Bryan, in his book *Clara,* wrote that the Battle of the Overpass represented just as much of a break for Mrs. Ford: "She could see that Edsel's opinions were being cast aside for those of Bennett, and she exclaimed angrily, 'Who is this man who has so much control over my husband and is ruining my son's life?'"[37] Those same issues would surface again.

In the aftermath of the May 26 battle, Bennett sidestepped the charges against Ford Motor by claiming that all of the assailants had been company employees acting entirely on their own—out of outrage at the idea of a union. Henry Ford, for his part, relented to the degree that union representatives were subsequently allowed to distribute leaflets near River Rouge. Harry Bennett even made a show of opening negotiations with the UAW.

Ford Motor stalled unionization, but by the end of the decade the climate in America had changed dramatically for automobile workers. In 1939 Ford Motor was found guilty of violating the National Labor Relations Act in Detroit. The company appealed the decision but was rebuked by the Circuit Court of Appeals in Cincinnati, and in February 1941 the U.S. Supreme Court refused to review the case.[38] The UAW, with over 300,000 members, was starting to operate from a position of strength.

Just as the effort to organize Ford Motor was gaining a little momentum, the UAW broke apart in factional fighting. The national president, Homer Martin, was right at the center of it. "Dissension," Victor Reuther wrote in his memoir, "the prize that GM had failed to win by employing spies and provocateurs, was delivered to them gratis by Homer Martin."[39] Even after Martin was expelled as president of the UAW, Harry Bennett continued talks with him. In 1940, they actually concluded a deal by which Martin and his new union would represent Ford Motor Company workers. Ford workers rejected the deal, largely because Harry Bennett had included a clause putting his service department at Martin's disposal for discipline within the union ranks. The workers wanted to see less of Bennett's service men, not more.

Early in 1941, the National Labor Relations Board convened meetings specifically to investigate Ford Motor's anti-union activities. Ford "terrorism" was blamed for thirty beatings of union sympathizers, including a nearly fatal attack on a UAW lawyer in Texas. As a result, the company was ordered to affirm on posters within the factory that it was no longer opposed to the UAW. The company was also directed to rehire about a thousand workers fired since 1937 as union sympathizers. Bennett stalled as long as he could and finally responded to the NLRB the only way he knew how. He attended a meeting of a UAW grievance committee and instead of hearing the complaints, angrily fired all eight of the Ford employees serving on the committee.[40]

The UAW was compelled to act. On April 1, 1941, Henry Ford's greatest nightmare came to fruition: the union called for a strike to shut down the Rouge. This time around labor leaders were not going to be caught off-guard by the ferocity of the Dearborn police's tear-gas cannons or Harry Bennett's armed goons. They did, however, have to persuade workers to join the strike—the first one ever staged against Ford Motor Company. At the very outset, Walter Reuther drove to Gate 4 of the Rouge and asked to speak with Bennett, hoping to prevent bloodshed—he was told to get off Ford property. Ready for a showdown, the UAW erected makeshift soup kitchens, medical tents, and communication centers. Handbills urging workers to stay on strike, in order to break the back of the "Capitalist Monolith," were distributed all over the Detroit area. Workers streamed out of the Rouge, and their homes, and headed to the local union hall in Dearborn.[41] No one was sure how the workers would respond. Less than a third were members of the union and all of them knew Henry Ford's attitude toward strikes and strikers. The stakes were high for each individual at the plant. This time around, however, the workers' sense of solidarity was palpable. A union leader later said that the response from Ford's rank and file was "like seeing men who had been half dead come to life." Historian Keith Sward simply characterized the workers' feelings as a "call-to-arms."[42] Predictably, Harry Bennett, speaking on behalf of Ford Motor Company, declared the strike "communistic" and, moreover, an act of treason because the Roosevelt administration had recently initiated orders for war matériel.

In another effort to break the strike, Bennett dispatched Homer Martin to hold "back to work" rallies in the African American community. He was partially successful.[43] Henry Ford had been especially solicitous of black workers over the years, and River Rouge had an unusually high proportion of black workers. About 200 of the employees who refused to strike there were African Americans. NAACP Secretary Walter White flew to Detroit to help persuade those African Americans hunkering down inside the Rouge to leave and join forces with the UAW. In his autobiography, *A Man Called White,* White devotes a chapter to his mediation efforts. Some of those who refused to leave the plant under White's pleading were doing so out of loyalty to the man they considered the least prejudiced employer in Detroit. However, for the first day or two of the strike, the small anti-union force lashed out at the picketers, in a battle that looked altogether too racially divided for Walter Reuther. Hoping to ward off a rift on racial lines, he devoted a great deal of his time to reminding fellow union members that 8,800 of Ford's African American workers had indeed joined the strike.

Still on April 2 the strike took on a racial cast as many African Americans returned to work, crossing the picket line. Hundreds stayed inside the Rouge, armed with six-foot swords and tire irons in case the strikers tried to rush inside the factory. They refused to abandon their workstations.[44] Photographer Milton Brooks of the *Detroit News* was on the scene, making sure his camera was not seen by Ford Motor's goon force, for it surely would have been confiscated. As tensions flared, Brooks hoped to get one memorable shot of the emotions at the Rouge. The opportunity soon presented itself. "I saw a man pick a fight with some of the pickets," Brooks recalled. "He had the wrong of the argument and I could tell from what he said that there would be trouble soon." What Brooks captured for posterity was unforgettable: eight strikers with contorted faces pummeling a so-called scab with billy clubs and fists.

One striker, wearing a UAW cap, his tongue hanging from his mouth in rage, prepares to smash the Ford loyalist in the back. "I took the picture quickly, hid the camera under my coat and ducked into the crowd," Brooks recalled. "A lot of people would have liked to wreck that picture." He won the first Pulitzer Prize for photography for capturing the essence of the brutal clash at the Rouge.[45] The company finally managed to diffuse the situation: in the interest of racial harmony, it encouraged those defending the plant to go home.[46]

The strike continued into May. Charles Sorensen later said that Henry Ford was perfectly willing to close the factory for good, rather than allow the UAW to represent his workers. The strife widened the rift within the Ford family itself. Henry Ford had ordered Edsel to leave the matter entirely to Harry Bennett. But with widespread violence more possible with each passing day, Edsel couldn't remain aloof. He argued with his father in favor of negotiations with the union, and the designation of a date for a union vote. Henry Ford was adamant that Harry Bennett handle the strike—and fight the union to the bitter end. Clara Ford, however, would not allow it. For the first time in her life, she confronted her husband with no turning back, actually threatening to divorce him if he did not settle with the union. Henry Ford apparently couldn't fight her on those terms. He immediately capitulated.[47]

A vote was called for May 26 by which the workers would, with Ford Motor's blessing, choose how they would represent themselves. The anti-union vote came in at only 3 percent. Homer Martin's AFL-sanctioned union received 20,354 votes, while the UAW group in the CIO emerged with 51,886 votes. It was a resounding victory for Walter Reuther. "It's a great victory for the Communist Party, Governor Van Wagoner, and the National Labor Relations Board," a bitter Harry Bennett fumed.[48] However, on June 20, 1941, the Ford Motor Company signed a landmark agreement with the UAW. Henry Ford's last surprise was the contract itself, offering even more liberal terms than the union had requested. Once Henry Ford accepted the idea, he wanted it to be done right, with the result that Ford workers received a much better contract than their counterparts at GM or Chrysler. "In the negotiations the Company granted an almost totally closed union shop, agreed to pay back wages to more than 4,000 workers wrongfully discharged and admitted to a grievance procedure," noted a 2001 book published as a collaboration by the UAW and Ford Motor Company to celebrate the sixtieth anniversary of the agreement. "The Company also agreed to match the highest wage rates in the industry and to deduct union dues from worker's pay. The terms were the most generous in the history of industrial relations."[49]

People who didn't know Henry Ford were perplexed by his transformation. People who did know him were long past being perplexed by him.

Eventually, Henry Ford agreed to meet Walter Reuther to congratulate him as the new voice of automobile workers. "It was one of the most sensible things Harry Bennett ever did when he got UAW into this plant," Ford told him.

"Well, I think so but I didn't think you did," Reuther replied. "How do you figure it?"

"Well, you've been fighting General Motors and the Wall Street crowd. Now you are in here, and we have given you a union shop and more than you got out of them. That puts you on our side, doesn't it? We fight General Motors and Wall Street together, eh?"[50]

21

Mercury

Early in 1935, General Motors was selling six car lines in the United States: starting with the least expensive, these were Chevrolet, Pontiac, Oldsmobile, Buick, LaSalle, and Cadillac. GM executives had devoted inordinate time over the previous dozen years to the precise alignment of those lines and what they called "product policy." The idea of product policy was not only to offer something for every automobile customer, but to carry a motorist from the first thrill of buying a new Chevy, all the way through the family years of an Olds or a Pontiac to either the respectability of a Buick or the flash of a LaSalle and, ultimately, the crowning achievement of owning a Cadillac. Product policy was nothing less than the drive train of General Motors, propelling its long-term success, and so the executive committee engineered the price tags of its cars as carefully as the technical staff engineered any other component of a GM car.[1]

Walter Chrysler followed the GM example closely with five distinct lines, offering the low-price Plymouth, followed by DeSoto, Dodge, and Chrysler; at the top was the Chrysler Imperial, among the best cars in the world. "In 1933, Chrysler had out produced Ford Motor Company for the first time, and after it repeated this accomplishment in 1936, it remained the number two producer in the industry for the next fifteen years," Vincent Curcio wrote in his 2000 biography of Walter Chrysler. "To this day, this is an astounding achievement. The man who started too late had defied all odds and raised his company to the second position in the world in just about a decade. No wonder *Fortune* magazine called its December 30, 1933, issue, devoted completely to Chrysler, 'A Century of Progress, in Ten Years.'"[2]

By contrast, Ford Motor Company was selling just two lines, which were hardly contiguous: the entry-level V-8 and the ultra-swank Lincoln K. With no intermediate option available, customers who were ready to move up from a Ford V-8 after a few years were tacitly directed to go over to the competition for a car that met their needs.

The stubborn Henry Ford wasn't likely to change the composition of his company. For almost thirty years, since the moment he wrested control from Alex Malcomson and the other early stockholders, he considered that the natural course in mass production was concentration on a single product. His purchase of Lincoln seemed initially to bode of expansion into a full line, but that was not to be. Whatever reasons Henry Ford had for buying Lincoln Motor Car, expansion didn't play a part. Leaving the luxury cars mostly to Edsel, Henry Ford devoted himself to the Ford automobile, the sole object of his interest in manufacturing.

The debonair Edsel Ford is remembered today largely for the subservient role he played in his father's life: for the ongoing denigration he endured and the outright persecution that gave Harry Bennett and Charles Sorensen, among others through the years, the right to counteract the decisions of the company's nominal president. Given half a chance in the realm of styling, Edsel brought Ford to the forefront, without bringing ruin down on the company, or even causing any confrontations in Dearborn. Nonetheless, he was the victim of a complicated form of rejection. Henry Ford either couldn't let go of his company or couldn't be bothered to understand his son. He later intimated that by undermining so many of Edsel's prerogatives, he was trying to goad his son into getting angry. Apparently, he longed for Edsel to break out of his shell and show the mustard that had served Ford himself so well in his relations with subordinates. But neither temper nor bluff were in Edsel's nature. It was Henry Ford's misfortune to have a son with natural grace and intelligence instead of selfish conceit, and loyalty instead of spite. However, for the firm as a whole, Edsel's loyalty was a stroke of the very best fortune. It kept him from quitting. By remaining on the job and working through the obstacle course that was his career, he left a legacy on which Ford Motor could later build its future as a full-line automaker. "Poor Edsel," Ford union official Paul Boatin lamented. "Throughout his life he was never given much credit. He had a kind of funny image with workers. There wasn't a hell of a lot of negative stuff written or said about him."[3]

Although widely envied as the young president of Ford and a multimillionaire to boot, Edsel Ford was in a deeper way Ford Motor's everyman. Unlikely as that would have seemed at the start, he spent his working life constantly stifled by the unfair advantages of others. Overruled on many issues and given little credit for good work by others, his was the lot of many modern workers. And surprisingly, just like those whose names are not on the building they work in, Edsel had no recourse, no way out, and no choice but to "like it or lump it." He found a way to prevail, anyway. For all of the internal struggles at Ford Motor and within the Ford family, Edsel would manage to add two new car lines in the second half of the 1930s, along with a model called the Continental, which had something no Ford Motor product had ever had before: star quality.

In 1935, Edsel was forty-two years old and his children were growing into their teens. None of them shared his intense interest in cars, but that didn't concern him or his wife, Eleanor. The youngest son, William, was excelling in sports. The oldest, Henry II, was less distinctive as a youngster: quiet, standoffish, and pudgy. Yet he was a natural leader, according to the younger children, one who didn't have to say much in order to make his influence felt. Edsel, for the most part, indulged his children with the perks of being rich. At the same time, he made them aware that Ford Motor—the source of all privilege—was a family business and that someday they might be called to duty. "Edsel never really questioned the destiny that bound his children to the Ford Motor Company," Peter Collier and David Horowitz wrote in *The Fords: An American Epic*. "The company was like a family religion: it gave meaning to their lives. Whatever doubts he himself had, he never stopped believing."[4]

Every few years, the whole family traveled to Europe. One of the reasons Edsel liked to wander around the European capitals was the same reason today's car fans like to linger for a few hours in Beverly Hills—the chance to see some of the world's most intriguing cars in actual use. Studying a picture of a car in a magazine or advertisement was nothing compared with catching sight of the real thing: a beautiful car in motion, taking a corner or accelerating away from a light. On the Continent, Edsel was exposed to automobiles that he just could not see in America. Years later, Edsel's son William recalled that as a boy, he would sit next to his father and watch him paint European dream cars.[5]

In the mid-1930s, trends in automobile styling started in the custom-body market and eventually filtered to production cars. The United States had its own cadre of about a dozen busy custom coach-builders, with names like Dietrich, Murphy, Brunn, and Waterhouse. While each had a fairly unique look, their work overall was more conservative than that of the most celebrated European coach-builders. For that reason, London and Paris made for better sightseeing for Edsel Ford than Newport or Palm Beach ever could. The Europeans were encouraged to turn their styles into eye-catching art forms, in part because auto shows called *concours d'élégance* were popular between the world wars. Organized to spotlight the latest in styling, *concours* were for ostentatious— and very rich—people. Typically, there were prizes not only for bodywork but for the fashions worn by the motorists. The United States had no such event. Its custom cars, no less than its flivvers, were made for the road and had a practical air about them.[6]

In 1933, however, America's luxury carmakers turned the Century of Progress World's Fair in Chicago into a *concours* of sorts. Ford Motor did not extend itself for auto shows or other exhibits, and so, while Lincoln sent an array of its standard cars, none of them were created just for the fair. The headline grabbers that year in Chicago started with a Packard sedan-limousine, with a body by Dietrich. It was a conventional design except for the hood, which was stretched out to nearly half of the car's 143-inch length. Because the interior appointments were gold-plated, the car was known as the "Golden Packard." Duesenberg, located in nearby Indianapolis, displayed the "Twenty Grand," so called because of its price tag. It had a sleek sedan body by Roll-ston, a Long Island coach-builder.[7] Cadillac sent a racy sedan with a body by Derham. The sensation of the show, though, was the Silver Arrow, built by Pierce-Arrow. The car looked as slippery as a raindrop, with a slanted radiator, front fenders that were incorporated into the hood, and best of all, a roofline that made a gentle slope from the windshield all the way down to the rear bumper. Sadly, only four Silver Arrows were produced. The company was petering out of business and would shut down for good in 1938. However, other automakers feasted on the glimpse of the dawn of streamlined automobile styling that the Silver Arrow presented.

Edsel Ford brought his family to the 1933 World's Fair, and the Silver Arrow undoubtedly made an impact on him. It also made an impact on Chrysler, which beat other high-production companies to streamlining in 1934 by introducing the Airflow, an arresting new design that let the eye follow the upsweep of the wind over the inclining hood. By then, Edsel was bringing along his own supermodern car, based on a very intriguing set of drawings made by John Tjaarda.

Originally from Holland, Tjaarda was employed by Briggs Manufacturing, Ford's major body supplier. Hustling to match the impact of the Century of Progress, Edsel commissioned Briggs to build two prototypes, which then toured the country in a Ford-sponsored "Exhibition of Progress." When the organizers of the Century of Progress made a late decision to reopen their world's fair in 1934, this new car, the Zephyr, took its place in Chicago with the other showstoppers in the Travel and Transportation Building. The exhibitions were a tactic on Edsel's part, intended to ease the idea of a junior Lincoln line on his father, by proving its popularity with the public. However, in order not to rile Henry, the car was described only as a Briggs project, with "no reference to current or future 'Ford' production."[8]

Tjaarda's design, conceived as a rear-engine vehicle, looked remarkably like an enlarged version of the Volkswagen Beetle, a car that would not be introduced as a prototype until 1935. The automobile historian Maurice Hendry has observed that the VW was undoubtedly copied from Tjaarda's Zephyr.[9]

Even before the Zephyr made its positive impact at the Century of Progress, Edsel Ford had become convinced that the Lincoln name needed new life. The division also needed a product with a medium price, since customers for cars like the Lincoln were dwindling. Fewer people could afford them, of course, and as the Depression dragged on, many of the people who could didn't want to be guilty of conspicuous consumption. As a result, Cadillac promoted its lower-price LaSalle and Packard introduced the One-Twenty, both of which shared some of the prestige of their seniors without the aura of damn-the-expense spending. Edsel Ford thought the Zephyr could be a similarly affordable Lincoln.

"I guess the concept of the Lincoln Zephyr was probably the most radical thing that Ford had attempted," Bob Gregorie said of the design. "Inasmuch as it came from an outside source, well, that kind of relieved [Edsel] from a conscience problem."[10] Edsel took the Zephyr to heart, though, and had to wrestle with changes. In the first place, Ford Motor Company was not ready in 1935 to produce a rear-engine car—and never would be, at least through its first one hundred years. The engine had to be in the front. In addition, Edsel wanted to replace the bulbous front end of the original design, and he had his own ideas of how to do it. Mainly, he wanted a pointed front end, vaguely reminiscent of that on the Ford V-8. Both John Tjaarda and Bob Gregorie, who was assigned to the project, tried to talk him out of it, to no avail.[11] "We all tossed in our two cents worth," Gregorie recalled, "but Edsel had already made up his mind."[12]

Introduced as the Lincoln-Zephyr in November 1935, the new car had a 12-cylinder engine—not the same one carried by the Lincoln Ks, but a variation engineered at Ford. The engine had problems through the years, especially in burning oil, but the car was surprisingly light for its size and amazingly strong. It had been developed using an array of equipment and new processes Edsel Ford had quietly instituted in the interest of reducing noise, vibration, and other measurable signs of weak design. Among other things, the younger Ford had ordered that a wind tunnel be built at River Rouge.

The Lincoln-Zephyr was priced at $1,250, well below the factory-bodied Lincoln Ks at $4,000. It hit its mark, with sales of 17,725 vehicles in 1935 and 25,243 the next year. Without robbing significant sales from the old K, the new junior car turned Lincoln from a money loser to a profit center for Ford, and it was a starting point for the most modern look in cars. Moreover, it was a step to filling in the huge gap in the Ford Motor Company line. Edsel Ford was also planning an even more important addition to the lineup, one that would require mass production in the Ford Motor sense of the term.

―――――

It is hard to say whether expanding the lineup or creating an independent styling section was a higher priority for Edsel Ford. In the 1930s, though, as styling became a selling point on par with mechanical engineering, his two goals complemented each other. In February 1935, with the Zephyr on track for production, Edsel Ford felt that the time was right to inaugurate Ford Motor's first design department. In terms of his father's long-standing antipathy toward design, it was a propitious moment. Styling had propelled the flagship Ford V-8 in 1933 and revived it in 1935. But not all of the new styling was homegrown. For example, the 1935 styling update was the contribution of Briggs Manufacturing's design team (specifically Phil Wright, who had been responsible for the Silver Arrow). That update had helped Ford edge out Chevrolet in the sales race for the only time in the decade. Ford—the company and no doubt the founder—was feeling good in 1935.

After losing an estimated $120 million in the years from 1930 to 1933, Ford Motor was healthy again, having notched two profitable years. The role of good styling in the turnaround could not be denied, yet Edsel had had to oversee it under duress, with no full-time staff or advance planning. Remarkably, Edsel's cobbled army had taken on GM's vaunted Art and Color Section (of seventy-five designers) and won its share of battles. To continue the momentum, Edsel knew perfectly well that Ford Motor needed to have a permanent team in place. Styling was fast becoming proprietary for an automaker and he no longer wanted to depend on outsiders, such as Briggs.

What was obvious to Edsel Ford and to the outside world, however, was still dangerous talk inside Ford Motor. Edsel started the new department very quietly by telephoning Bob Gregorie from Florida and asking him to organize a styling section. Gregorie, who had worked with Edsel on the Model Y, later thought it significant that the move was made from afar. "He ordered it to be done without any face-to-face encounter with his father and the others," Gregorie said. Nonetheless, one of those "others," Charles Sorensen, cooperated closely with Gregorie in setting up the styling section. "Sorensen and Gregorie decided to set up the new design department in the southwest corner of the engineering laboratory," wrote Henry Dominguez, "which is an indication that Edsel must have received permission from his father before making the momentous decision."[13]

"In the middle of this design department," recalled Bud Adams, one of the designers, "at the corners of the engineering lab, used to be an area where Henry Ford had taught dancing. Henry Ford was a proponent of folk dancing, and is credited with saving early music and steps, before they were lost with the passing generations. Using the wide floors of the engineering lab, he regularly staged afternoon dances, in which members of his staff were expected to participate.

"The whole floor of this engineering lab," Adams continued, "was a herringbone, teakwood affair that was just beautiful. There was always somebody polishing that thing from one end to the other. When I got in the design department, one of the things that was there, and I think it was a holdover from the dancing days, was this damned stuffed black crow hanging by a wire from the ceiling. Now if anything belonged to Henry Ford, you didn't monkey with it until he told you to. So that old dusty black crow hung up there."[14]

During its first ten years, the design department didn't employ more than two dozen full-time designers, along with a handful of apprentices. Including support staff, the group numbered about fifty. In light of that size, the amount of work completed by the staff is remarkable. With Gregorie as chief designer, the team included Edward A. Martin, who was in charge of drafting, and Walter Kruke, who worked on interior trim. Others were assigned to improve specific auto features: for example, Willys Wagner (bumpers).[15] Years later Gregorie summed up the atmosphere in the design studio as being a "cold-blooded proposition. It was all business—we worked to accomplish profitable results."[16]

The engineering department in general and the body engineers in particular remained skeptical that styling needed to be a full-time vocation. "There was so much political crap going on that they used to drill holes in the partition to spy on [Gregorie]," said Ross Cousins, one of twelve full-time designers in 1938. "They had the watchman at the gate checking him in, checking him out—just so they might be able to get something on him so they could fire him. But they didn't. It was people like Bennett and the top engineer, [Larry] Sheldrick. They'd even come into our department and look in the toilet—look under the doors and see if we were in there too long. We had to almost fight for our existence."[17] Years later, in an interview, Cousins summed up the sentiments of the Ford designers: "Henry didn't like us too well, but Edsel was our godfather and patron saint."[18] This sentiment was echoed by Gene Bordinat, later a vice president at Ford, who was a member of the styling staff in the 1930s. "Well," he said, "we all wore smocks and considered ourselves artistes. The old man thought we were queer."[19]

For 1937, Ford Motor divided its V-8 line, offering a Standard 60-horsepower version and a souped-up 85-horsepower Deluxe. The V-8s borrowed elements from the Zephyr; the availability of a choice actually stoked sales. Edsel thus felt that the time was right to introduce an all-new nameplate to the Ford lineup. Edsel's actions in the 1930s didn't have the immediacy of sweeping, capricious decisions—like those of his father. His accomplishments built on one another in a way that must have been part of a master plan, born of fifteen years living with the empty promise of the Ford Motor presidency.

Edsel Ford had slid the Zephyr into the company almost by sleight of hand, under the auspices of the Lincoln K. The line he was planning next would be all-new. Henry Ford had never been open to such an idea before. But Edsel brought with him a string of successes, and in 1937 he formally suggested a new Ford Motor Company division to nestle between the Deluxe, which cost on average about $750, and the Zephyr, which cost about $1,250. "In other words," Bob Gregorie recalled, "we had to do a Pontiac or a DeSoto deal."[20]

Under pressure from dealers, who were face-to-face with the gap in Ford

Motor's offering, Henry Ford agreed to launch a Pontiac-killer. Both Sorensen and Bennett (who had close ties to a number of dealers) concurred. Another factor in the decision was that the company's return to prosperity in 1935 gave it the working capital to fund the expansion. While Henry Ford was never exactly short of cash, his refusal to borrow money or create debt of any kind made it difficult to commit to spending without having the cash on hand first. With his blessing then, development began in July 1937, in anticipation of a fall 1938 introduction date.

Once Edsel launched the idea, it was entirely his responsibility. He picked the name "Mercury" out of a list of over a hundred possibilities that also included other mythological references, such as the "Athenian," "Hermes," or "Hercules." He bypassed clever possibilities such as the "Zephord," "Cyclops," "Fordocrat," or "Forduke," along with sentimental favorites within his circle, like the "Edison" and the "Dearborn." The fact that Mercury was well-known as the Roman god of speed was considered a good omen; the more obscure fact that Mercury was also the god of commerce may have played a role in the choice, too.[21]

As Sheldrick on the engineering side and Gregorie on the styling side soon began to realize, Edsel wanted the Mercury to be familiar as a Ford product. The quickest description of it was as a "pumped-up Deluxe," four inches longer, 10 more horsepower and about 10 mph faster, at a top speed of 90. "There really wasn't much to the Mercury," Bob Gregorie said. "It was a variation of the Ford. A little more pleasing body lines, and as far as we were concerned, it was just a blown-up Ford in many respects."[22] Gregorie was disappointed that Edsel wouldn't let the design department go further afield with the Mercury. However, for Edsel, that was exactly the point: he was hedging his bet.[23]

"Someone asked me a while back," Gregorie said in 1985, "why they didn't make the front end completely different—a complete breakaway from the traditional Ford-type design. Well, they have to understand when Edsel Ford made up his mind, he wanted something, he wanted it to look like he wanted it to look. He was obstinate as hell."[24]

Edsel's attachment to the Ford aura showed itself in the final nomenclature for the car. To him, the only question was whether it should be called the "Ford-Mercury" or the "Mercury-Ford." Again, he was hedging his bet, lest anyone really believe that the Mercury was a new, untried entity. According to Bob Gregorie, most of the other people working on the project knew that the idea was to hoist Mercury above the Ford level, not anchor it there. From sales to design, he heard the same thing: get the name "Ford" off the Mercury entirely. "Boy," said Gregorie, "that was like a hot poker on Mr. Ford [Edsel]. 'What's wrong with the Ford name? We spent thirty-nine years building it up, and you're telling me it isn't good enough to put on this automobile?'"[25] Only after Edsel attended an auto show and heard the comments of customers circling the car did he agree that the Ford-Mercury had to be the Mercury, all on its own and come what may.

Henry Ford was not particularly enthusiastic about the odds of success for the Mercury, and in any case, he took no interest in it. For several months, he was simply in no condition to do so. In July 1938, Henry Ford suffered a mild stroke. It was dismissed publicly as a bout of the flu, but it curtailed his activity in relation to the Ford line, let alone the more distant Mercury project. "I think the old gentleman left it pretty much to Edsel," said Gregorie.[26] He was speaking of the styling of the car, but the comment was true of the whole project.

Two hand-built Mercury cars, a coupe and a sedan, were test-driven that July. Production soon began at River Rouge and at assembly plants in California, New Jersey, Chicago, Louisville, and Kansas City, Missouri. Within a year, the Mercury was also being made by Ford of Canada and assembled at plants in Mexico, Brazil, France, Romania, Denmark, Belgium, and Holland.[27] The car made its formal debut at the Detroit Auto Show in mid-November. Since all the other new models of the year had already been introduced at previous auto shows, the new Mercury took the spotlight and received more than its share of headlines.

The Mercury cost about $900, giving it space between the V-8 and the Zephyr. "We must not, under any circumstances," said Jack Davis, the general sales manager, "allow the introduction of this new car to absorb any portion of the market which logically belongs to Ford or to Lincoln-Zephyr. This car has been brought out to expand, not to divide, the business which belongs to Ford and Lincoln-Zephyr."[28]

The Mercury would have plenty of competition in the $900 price range, including, among the independents, the Packard's popular-price car, the Six; the Nash Ambassador; the Studebaker Commander; and the Hudson Country Club. General Motors offered the Pontiac Eight, the Oldsmobile Six, and the Buick Special, among others, while Chrysler looked to the Dodge Luxury Liner and the Chrysler Royal Six in the same price span. Mercury didn't have to own the niche, though: it was enough that the new line finally gave Ford a place in it.

Thanks in part to Jack Davis, Ford's auto show presentations were much more impressive in the late 1930s than ever before. At the Ford exhibit in Detroit, a young salesman named Walter Parker devoted a half hour to one customer, a man in sunglasses accompanied by his son. Parker thought he was on his way to a sale when the man interrupted him. "What is your name?" he asked.

"Walter Parker."

"My name is Edsel Ford," his prospect said. "I want you to meet my son, Henry Ford II."[29]

In the first year, Mercury production reached 69,135. On the presumption that few of those sales were robbed from the existing Ford lines (a point debated ever since), it was looked on as an entirely successful launch. "In the end, Ford probably did not care if buyers moving up the ladder saw the 1939 Mercury as a 'big Ford' or as a 'baby Lincoln,'" John A. Gunnell wrote in *Fifty-five Years of Mercury.* "What counted most was that they bought it."[30]

While Henry Ford was totally disinterested in design, he had become obsessive about melding farm and factory together. Committed to recycling, Ford once dumped a bag of chicken bones on the desk of a top Ford Motor research specialist and said, "See what you can do with these." Another time he supervised the delivery of twenty truckloads of cantaloupes to the laboratory, believing they contained properties that were useful for making car components. "Mr. Ford was forty-five years ahead of today's ecologists," observed Joseph Crup, a Ford Motor engineer who once worked as a technician in the research laboratory at Greenfield Village. "He was committed to improving the lot of the farmer, and he was convinced that you should find industrial uses for agriculture crops. He predicted back then that the day would come when automobiles would 'grow' on farms. When he turned his attention to the simple soybean, he found his bumper crop."[31]

Nothing consumed Ford's attention like the soybean, which the Chinese had grown for over five thousand years. Ford knew the history of the highly nutritional bean and had read *Ben Isao Gang Mu,* written by Emperor Shen Nung in 2838 B.C., which explored the soybean's magical properties.[32] Starting in 1932, he cultivated 8,200 acres of soybeans on his farms in Dearborn. Ford wanted to study all of the more than three thousand kinds of soybeans. According to historian Ford R. Bryan, he extracted six tons of soybean oil daily at his Greenfield Village laboratory.[33] He used it to make glycerin, enamels, varnish, waterproof goods, linoleum, soaps, and paints. He enthused that soybeans were low in fat, cholesterol free, and high in protein. "By now," *Fortune* noted in 1933, "he is as much interested in the beans as he is in the V-8."[34] Two soybean-processing facilities were established near the Rouge. Proudly, Ford served soy meals at Fair Lane—celery stuffed with soybean cheese, tomato juice with soybean sauce, apple pie with soybean sauce, and even soybean cookies, coffee, and ice cream. Along the way, he created his own version of tofu. Working closely with Lowell Overly, a process engineer in Ford's metal-stamping division, he designed the first plastic car, made in part with soybeans and hemp. Ford was proud that an axe couldn't dent the trunk lid. And he truly believed that soy could be made into upholstery fiber. "Mr. Ford thought agriculture plastics might become his most significant contribution to society," Overly recalled. "While the famous plastic car was lightweight and could withstand ten times more shock than steel, it just wasn't practical. The plastic took a long time to cure and its brittleness made it difficult to mold on a car frame. Plastic was more expensive than sheet metal, and the formaldehyde used in plastic production made the car smell like a mortuary."[35]

Feeling lonely in his Greenfield Village laboratory, and no longer having Thomas Edison with whom to swap ideas, Ford decided to host the First Dearborn Conference of the National Farm Chemurgical Council in May 1935. Meanwhile, the city of Philadelphia had refused to sell Ford Independence Hall, where the Declaration of Independence was signed, so he constructed an exact replica in Greenfield Village. It was there at the "Clocktower Building" that Henry Ford signed a document known as the "Declaration of Independence upon the Soil." He and the three hundred other agricultural scientists in attendance believed that plants held the secrets to society's woes. Why couldn't soy milk feed the starving in Africa? Couldn't hybrid maize be grown that was wind- and disease-resistant? Was there evidence to show that beet juice could make automobiles run? These were the types of questions asked at the Greenfield Village conference.[36]

The man revered most by these agricultural chemists, however, was not Henry Ford. He was George Washington Carver, the famed head of the Tuskegee Institute. Ford was among his greatest fans. Beginning with letters in 1934 and escalating rapidly in 1937, when Carver visited with Ford at the Dearborn Inn, the two visionaries formed a bond based in their belief in the regenerative properties of the soil. Carver, born a slave in 1864, was once kidnapped by "night riders" and traded for a horse. He grew up to be one of the most important men in the country. When the boll weevil crisis swept across cotton fields in the Deep South in 1906, Carver recommended peanuts as a replacement crop. The humble peanut was as magical to Carver as the soybean was to Ford.[37] "Two of the greatest things that have ever come into my life have come this year," Carver wrote Ford after his Michigan visit. "The first was the meeting of you, and to see the great educational project that you are carrying on in a way that I have never seen demonstrated before."[38]

The two men were genuinely excited that they had discovered each other. Ford embraced the Tuskegee Institute, providing money to cover Carver's laboratory experiments, and even installing an elevator in Dorothy Hall so Carver wouldn't have to climb stairs. Carver returned the favor by spending time at the Ford plantation in Ways, Georgia, helping oversee thousands of acres of crops. When Ford opened a trade school there, specifically to help poor African American children, he named it the George Washington Carver School. "I was with Mr. Ford the entire day," Carver wrote of the school's opening. "I don't think he left me fifteen minutes during the entire day. He rode with me in the car, helped me over rough places, wouldn't let me walk anywhere, and kept people away from me."[39] They were a mutual admiration society.

When World War II started, Ford made his third journey to Tuskegee to try to persuade Carver to move to Dearborn to help him create a synthetic rubber. On July 19, 1942, Carver arrived, to headlines in the *Detroit News* and *Free Press*. He was ensconced in the old Dearborn Water Works Building, which had been reconfigured into a laboratory. Together, he and Ford experimented with sweet potatoes, milkweed, and dandelion. "They shared eccentric genius and enormous mutual respect," Linda O. McMurry wrote in *George Washington Carver: Scientist and Symbol*. "Because of Ford's policy on hiring blacks, for both skilled and unskilled jobs in his automobile plants, Carver, like many other blacks, supported the company's sometimes bloody battle against unionization."[40] Long after both men died, the relationship between Ford Motor and Tuskegee Institute continued. From 1997 to 1999, for example, Ford awarded Carver's school grants worth $4 million.[41]

The attention Henry Ford paid to horticulture was not unusual for a man in his seventies, with time on his hands and money to spare. However, he was not retired from Ford Motor, only distracted enough from it to let some aspects of the administration slip—others were monitored as tightly as ever. While Henry Ford led the company by experimenting with beans and continually telephoning Harry Bennett for reports, Edsel Ford was still trying to make progress on the avenues left open to him.

———

With the advent of the Mercury, Ford Motor could boast that its vehicle lines covered 95 percent of the automobile market.[42] At least in terms of price ranges.

For Edsel Ford, there was still something missing—the excitement he felt about the cars he saw in Europe. There, the best cars were *pure* in spirit, rising to a high point of design with no apparent regard for mundane production considerations. In 1939, Edsel finally had the chance to build the kind of car he would like to buy. The result was the Lincoln Continental, the most admired car of the years just before America entered the war. "That car was art," Bob Gregorie believed. "The eyes never tire of looking at it."[43]

Edsel Ford had been commissioning "one-off" or custom cars built for his own use since he was sixteen. He would come up with the concept and some of the pertinent details and oversee a draftsman who made renderings for production. During the 1930s, Edsel had directed Gregorie in the design of three such specials, all sports cars and all named the "Continental," Edsel's favorite way of saying European . . . and ultra-sophisticated. In late 1938, after a long talk with Edsel, Gregorie conjured up a new idea for one of his boss's personal cars based on the Zephyr chassis. He later boasted that he drew it, with help from his assistant, Ed Martin, in about thirty-five minutes.[44] Edsel instantly loved the drawing, becoming the first of many thousands of people overcome on their first encounter with the marvelously and almost organically simple design.

This Continental was a long car, with pontoon fenders front and back. Its most unique feature was a high trunk line punctuated at its center by the spare tire. This arrangement has been used on other cars since and is known as a "Continental kit." The most seductive aspect of the design, however, was its resolute faith in its own shape and silhouette—that is, it had very few design "elements" to correct the shape or sully it. There was a quiet air of confidence about the Continental—confident enough to *be* quiet—and that quality exuded undeniable strength. It was exactly the type of strength that Edsel Ford displayed in his career.

When the special was completed in March 1939, it was shipped to Edsel, who was vacationing in Hobe Sound, Florida. He drove the car there and at Palm Springs, collecting admiring stares and orders at the rate of about one per mile: two hundred people asked if he would accept a check for a down payment for a car just like his.

Once again using distance diplomatically, Edsel called Dearborn and told Sorensen, Gregorie, and others at River Rouge that he wanted the Continental put in line for production. Because it was a custom body over a fairly standard Zephyr chassis, the job didn't take long and the car went on sale in October. New owners had one trait in common: they liked to be stared at. Otherwise, they wouldn't have survived their first drive in a Continental. Mickey Rooney received the Los Angeles show car as a gift. The popular movie star had become friendly with the Fords while he was on location in Dearborn filming *Young Tom Edison*. Edsel, convinced Rooney was the ideal public spokesperson for the Continental, instructed the Lincoln production manager to build the actor a Lincoln-Zephyr Continental with Lyon blue paint and a "soft and very pliable leather interior, carpet dyed blue to match leather, tan top, radio, and white sidewall tires."[45]

Sales the first model year, 1940, just topped four hundred, each one custom-ordered, at about $2,850 each. Four hundred units in the automobile business was not exactly a heady figure in 1939, yet the Continental made an impact out of proportion to those numbers. Ford had a hit and something to build on in the Lincoln line.

In 1958, twenty years after the introduction of the Continental and fifteen after Edsel Ford's death, a famous car called the Edsel was produced by the Ford Motor Company. The name itself has become synonymous with abject failure in the automotive world: a laughable marketing miss. While it has its defenders to this day, the Edsel was a garish design, full of bits and pieces of molding and chrome, abounding with clunky lines and colliding shapes. In every sense, then, the Edsel was the antithesis of the legacy of its namesake. That his name has been associated with that model is a bitter injustice.

Edsel Ford had no marketing misses in reshaping Ford Motor Company along lines still recognizable more than sixty years later. The Mercury is still the step-up from the Ford. And the Continental, in each of its manifestations, has continued to be understated and sleek, following the sensibilities inherent to the first one. The shame is that people don't think of the Continental as being, in spirit, the real "Edsel."

22

Building Up to War

Henry Ford didn't launch a *Peace Ship* to stop World War II, but he dreamed of doing so—or so he said. Those who read his pacifist pronouncements in the late 1930s would not have predicted that Ford Motor Company would eventually win several Army-Navy "E" citations for exemplary war work and become America's third-largest defense contractor with output worth $5.26 billion (just behind General Motors and Curtiss-Wright), but that is just what it did.[1] Because the prejudices Henry Ford had promulgated in the early 1920s mirrored certain Nazi positions, his actions and statements were closely watched in the years before America formally entered the war. He talked of peace, just as he had before World War I, yet his actions in the interim made people wonder exactly where his sympathies lay.

When new editions and translations of Ford's 1922 *The International Jew* were widely circulated under his name in the mid-1930s, they were presumably unauthorized, yet he refused to speak out against them and was never able to squelch the resurgence.[2] In July 1938, when Ford celebrated his seventy-fifth birthday, he was honored by Adolf Hitler with the Grand Cross of the German Eagle. It was presented to him in Detroit by the German consul. That year was the high season of appeasement, and Germany was working its message of the moment—that it was a civilized nation—by handing out awards to an array of distinguished foreigners in business and government as a show of goodwill. Ford's medal generated anything but goodwill with Hitler's critics in the United States and Great Britain. The Grand Cross was Germany's highest civilian honor, and the sight of Henry Ford posing with it on his breast seemed to redraw the line of admiration that Adolf Hitler had often expressed for the automaker.[3]

Despite a storm of criticism in the United States, Ford refused to give his German Eagle back—in part because it was so controversial. Ford was inclined to stiffen under just such pressure. In addition, he probably kept the medal because doing so rankled his nemesis, Franklin Roosevelt. And he undoubtedly had business reasons to consider. During that same summer of 1938, Ford-Werke was working out a major agreement to produce vehicles for the German government.[4] Ford-Werke badly wanted this contract, and if Henry Ford returned the medal to Hitler, it would have almost certainly punctured the deal—even though Ford-Werke was entirely controlled by Germans by then. The fact that the vehicles in question were troop transports for the German army appeared to be acceptable to him—despite his avowed policy of refusing to manufacture military matériel. Like most others in business and government, Henry Ford thought he could keep the Nazis friendly by staying friendly with them. That course proved to be a tragic failure for all who tried it. "Ford-Werke's in-house publication couldn't have been more fanatically pro-Nazi if Josef Goebbels had edited it," investigative journalist Ken Silverstein reported in a January 24, 2000, cover story in *The Nation*. "The fraternal tie between Ford and the Nazis is perhaps best symbolized by the company's birthday gift to the Fuehrer of 35,000 Reichmarks in April 1939."[5] That "gift" was all but mandatory, and the decision to extend it was entirely made at Ford-Werke, making it another episode in the uncomfortable relationship of the two Fords, one in America and one in Nazi Germany. Ford-Werke may have been, for all practical purposes, an independent company in 1939, but Mr. Ford's name was still on it.

To answer rising suspicions of complicity with Hitler, Henry Ford released statements denying any sympathy with Nazi policies, stating he was a genuine pacifist like Norman Thomas and Oswald Garrison Villard, not a hate monger. He underscored his position by entering into the hottest debate of the autumn of 1938: the American role in the problem faced by Jews fleeing Germany. Ford displayed his talent for making news by professing himself to be in favor of admitting Jewish refugees to the United States.[6] He even offered to employ some of them on Ford farms scattered across Michigan. Most people regarded the position as little more than a pennyweight thrown down in an attempt to balance the very real adversity surrounding Ford's acceptance of the German Eagle. The displaced Jewish refugees would not have been threatening to Ford, whose anti-Semitism had been centered around the fiction that wealthy people within the minority group controlled world events.

A year later, when German tanks poured across the Polish border in September 1939, World War II engulfed Europe, and nations took sides just as they had in 1914. In the face of the Nazis' blatant aggression, hopes for peace probably should have ended, but in the United States, a potent minority still argued very vocally for leaving Germany alone. Some were firmly in favor of Nazi policies and actions. Others were convinced that nothing could beat the German war machine and saw no point in trying. Still others were, like most

Americans at that juncture, simply interested in peace at any cost, hoping that the oceans could still protect the United States from the problems of the rest of the world. Henry Ford's attitude lay somewhere among those reasons. At best, his nonpareil views toward the war were muddled. "War is an orgy of money," he would say, "just as it is an orgy of blood."[7]

In 1940, the German military was the best equipped in the world, the result of a four-year building program during which the rest of Europe found various excuses to sleep. By midsummer, Hitler's armies conquered one nation after another, leaving Britain, ill prepared as it was, alone in the battle for western Europe. To refuse to take sides, as Henry Ford and other "isolationists" were doing, was to accept the status quo: German domination.

Few Americans came right out and supported the German side in 1940–1941. Instead, they joined an organization called the America First Committee, consisting of 800,000 members in approximately 425 chapters, all of which supported the belief that U.S. democracy could best be preserved by keeping out of the European war. There were a number of well-meaning members of the America First Committee, among them Kingman Brewster, who later became president of Yale; famed World War I pilot Eddie Rickenbacker; Chester Bowles, an ad executive who went on to become governor of Connecticut and ambassador to India; Gerald Ford, who later became president of the United States; actress Lillian Gish; and General Robert Wood, chairman of the board of Sears, Roebuck and Company. Two of the most active speakers promoting the America First Committee served in the U.S. Senate: Burton K. Wheeler (D–Montana) and Gerald P. Nye (R–North Dakota). Some members, however, veiled pronounced German bias behind professions of staunch neutrality and American patriotism. The goal for the Nazi sympathizers in the America First Committee was to forestall U.S. intervention in the war until Britain was under German occupation. They presumed that with no landing point in western Europe, the Americans could never mount a successful attack against Germany's burgeoning European empire.[8]

The most famous America Firster was one of the most famous of all Americans: Charles Lindbergh. Blessed with the looks of a matinee idol, accented by a modest demeanor, Lindbergh had been an authentic American hero ever since his 1927 solo transatlantic flight. His marriage in 1929 to Anne Morrow, the elegant daughter of America's ambassador to Mexico, touched romantic hearts everywhere. After the 1932 murder of their firstborn son, the Lindberghs fled newsmen and kooks in December 1935 to seek temporary refuge in Europe. One of Henry Ford's very few close friends, Lindbergh made no secret of the fact that he had more respect for Germany than for any other country in Europe. In 1936, Lindbergh inspected Germany's military aviation program on behalf of the U.S. government, and in August he attended the Olympic Games in Berlin as a guest of Hermann Göring, the head of the

Luftwaffe. Impressed by German industry and society under Adolf Hitler, the Lindberghs considered moving to Germany. "I am absolutely convinced," Roosevelt confided to Secretary of the Treasury Henry Morgenthau Jr., "that Lindbergh is a Nazi." The president was right to keep an eye on Lindbergh; the charismatic flyer posed a threat to his leadership in America's delicate foreign policy. With pronounced regularity, Lindbergh criticized the groups he perceived were leading America into war, charging that they were acting against the country's interests. He expressed doubt that the U.S. military would achieve victory in a war against Germany, which he said had "armies stronger than our own." Outrage erupted following many of Lindbergh's speeches and he was denounced as an anti-Semite. In his hometown of Little Falls, Minnesota, his name was even removed from the town's water tower. Labeled a Nazi sympathizer because of his noninterventionist activities with the America First Committee and mindful that President Roosevelt regarded him as a traitor, Lindbergh responded by resigning his commission in the Army Air Corps Reserves. He also quit the National Advisory Committee for Aeronautics, a direct slap at Franklin Roosevelt and his administration's fledgling attempts to build an air force to meet the German Luftwaffe.[9]

Lindbergh's commitment to America First influenced Henry Ford to join the committee in September 1940. In the years before Pearl Harbor, Ford seemed to feel empowered by Lindbergh's example, especially his testimony before the Senate Foreign Relations Committee against Lend-Lease cooperation with Britain and Soviet Union in their fight against Hitler.[10] The flyer held the view that the United States should negotiate a so-called separate peace with Germany, even if it meant cooperation with the Nazi regime (and yet another incarnation of appeasement). That view—published as Charles Lindbergh's "A Letter to Americans" in Collier's—was endorsed by Henry Ford, who read it as a pacifist manifesto suggesting the Roosevelt administration supply nonmilitary aid to both the Axis powers and the Allies.[11] Along the same lines, Ford sometimes expressed the wish that Germany and Great Britain—two countries he considered war-drunk—annihilate each other.[12]

That was rather a surprising view for a man with customers, colleagues, employees, and factories in both countries. In any case, Ford's views were generally aligned with those of the America First Committee. The officers, anxious to avoid the stigma of anti-Semitism that Ford carried with him, induced Lessing J. Rosenwald, a Jewish director of Sears, Roebuck, to join at the same time. This attempt at window dressing didn't work, since Rosenwald soon quit the committee under pressure from friends. The America First executive committee then voted to shed Ford from the ranks. The minutes of the December 1940 meeting prove that the measure was implemented because Ford had "been unable to give any time or attention to the work of the Committee, and because the Committee could not be sure that from time to time Mr. Ford's views were consistent with the official views of the Committee." The aspiration was that Rosenwald might reconsider his resignation with Ford gone—but he refused. Privately, Rosenwald surmised that Ford never would have been dropped had he made a larger financial gift.[13]

Ford Motor's activities at the other end of the Axis in Japan revolved around an ambitious new assembly plant that had been built in 1936 in Yokohama. Japan was hungry for cars, and production grew to 18,379 vehicles the next year. However, fascism and free enterprise, especially on the part of foreign firms, never mixed, there or anywhere. At the end of 1937, Japan's new government began to restrict Ford production and soon made it clear that the company was no longer welcome in the economic sphere that Japan was planning for itself—and the rest of the region. Dearborn encouraged one of Japan's biggest automakers, Nissan Jidosha Kaisha, to purchase its Japanese assets, but the government closed Ford's operations before any agreement was reached. However, the loss of the Japanese operations was barely noticed at Ford Motor Company headquarters. There, as in most of the United States, attention was focused on Germany in the years before Pearl Harbor.

Henry Ford was not alone among industrialists in choosing to believe that America need not enter the world war—and, furthermore, that until it did, there was no sense in antagonizing the German government. Alfred Sloan, the chairman of General Motors, was also purposefully aloof in 1939–1940, publicly denying that America could get involved in the war. Some of that attitude stemmed from his position on domestic politics. Sloan outdid even Henry Ford in his antipathy toward Franklin D. Roosevelt. Peacetime gave both automobile magnates the luxury of standing against practically anything the New Deal represented—particularly the National Industrial Recovery Act.

When President Roosevelt openly voiced his inclination to aid the Allies and, in particular, the British, who by mid-1940 were fighting the Nazis in western Europe alone, neither Henry Ford nor Alfred Sloan evinced much interest in helping. Both automakers seemed much more afraid of siding with the "socialist" Roosevelt than of underestimating the threat of war with Germany or Japan.[14]

Like Henry Ford, Sloan and several of his top executives were accused of pro-Nazi attitudes.[15] Those isolationist attitudes were complicated by the realities of protecting a major investment in Germany, the thriving Opel subsidiary. However, inasmuch as they were thinking first of themselves and of what was best for their own industries, Ford, Sloan, and similar-minded businessmen were playing straight into the Nazi trap. Narrow self-interest softened populations for conquest more effectively than the thickest barrage of bombs.

In counterpoint to the response of Henry Ford and Alfred Sloan was that of a man who had worked for and who had helped create the legends of both.

William Knudsen had been named president of General Motors in 1937. He had acquired more skills since his years as Ford and then Chevrolet production boss, and could now speak to issues of management, accounting, and marketing in the most modern of American corporations, where every business discipline was treated as a science. In 1940, Knudsen's salary was $300,000, which made him the highest-paid American outside of a Hollywood movie studio.

By May of that year, after a spring in which Norway and Denmark had fallen in quick succession to the Germans, France was teetering on the brink. General George C. Marshall, Army chief of staff, watched the German blitzkrieg roll across the map of Europe and dourly warned that if the United States didn't begin rearming at once, the Germans could land anywhere along the Atlantic coast and continue inland at will. Roosevelt rallied Congress to expand the nation's defenses, including a plan to build the Army and Navy air wings from 500 warplanes to a force of not less than 50,000. In Washington, however, the decision to go ahead with an unprecedented building program quickly revealed a wide gap in the ability of government officials and manufacturers to communicate. Good intentions stalled amid the failure to ask the right questions, understand the answers, and agree to plans. Needing help, Roosevelt asked the legendary Wall Street financier Bernard Baruch, his longtime business adviser, for a list of the three top production men in the country. Baruch replied, "First, Knudsen; second, Knudsen; third, Knudsen."[16]

The president soon called Bill Knudsen and asked him to come to Washington to take a role in the war administration. Knudsen left Detroit the next day. On the way, he stopped in New York to inform Alfred Sloan at the GM headquarters of his intention to lend his services to the national emergency. At the time, the GM chairman didn't yet consider that there was a national crisis. He didn't think there would be a war unless Roosevelt blundered the country into one. The meeting turned acrimonious. Sloan felt that the corporation could make its contribution to the war simply by filling orders from the military; it didn't have to lend its chief officer to Roosevelt. Knudsen, however, didn't back away from his conviction that if the president and the nation needed him, he had to serve.

"They'll make a monkey of you down there in Washington," Sloan said.

"That isn't important," Knudsen recalled saying. "I came to this country with nothing. It has been good to me. Rightly or wrongly, I feel I must go."

Sloan would have none of it. "That's a quixotic way of looking at it," he replied.[17] In the heated pressure of the meeting, the implication was that if Knudsen went, the arrangement would be considered permanent. Bill Knudsen didn't have to think twice. He took his leave of absence in May 1940 and resigned a few months later, never to return.

In Washington, Knudsen spent much of 1940 looking at the confusion in the placement of war orders, asking everyone he met, "Who is the boss?" The usual answer—that Roosevelt was the boss—didn't suffice in terms of accelerating production. Knudsen was a born enemy of useless talk, endless meetings, and wasted time, all of which had a distinct place in the sliding gears of Washington. As a so-called numbers man, Knudsen never stopped fighting the rhetoric he constantly faced on Capitol Hill. At a Senate hearing on a proposed agency that would prioritize the allocation of raw materials, Knudsen was called as a witness. "I'm against it. It just won't work," he said. He was asked to explain why not. "Gentlemen," he said with exasperation, "where I come from, when I say a thing won't work—*it don't work!*"[18]

When in June Knudsen was named director general of the Office of Production Management (OPM), he finally had his answer. He was the boss of the expanding "arsenal of democracy," as the president termed America's manufacturing capacity. Taking a full-time procurement job at practically no pay, Knudsen was one of the first "dollar-a-year men," who formed a bridge between business and government during the war. His job was to translate America's vaunted manufacturing capacity into a reliable stream of wartime matériel—defining projects and separating them into subassemblies, where necessary; assigning major components to appropriate companies or making sure that likely bidders received proposals; overseeing scheduling so that projects converged smoothly into finished products; and assisting in the allocation of resources. Starting practically from a standstill, the challenge was daunting, to say the least. In warplanes, alone, the U.S. military wanted to place orders for about forty different models, in quantities of at least one thousand each. Yet in all of 1940, the United States produced barely three thousand military airplanes of all types. While others were ignoring the war or wishing it away, Knudsen and a cadre of people around Roosevelt were planning for the fight as though it would be the greatest of their lives.

According to Knudsen, jump-starting a construction program for warplanes was the most difficult task. "Everybody liked to look at it," he said of the average airplane design, "and talk saucily about it without knowing a blessed thing about the structure. Of course, the airplane manufacturers had the experience. They knew how to build, but the number of people who talked, without having the faintest idea of the technical problems involved, beggared all description. As a result, I was getting plenty of conversation and not many airplanes."[19]

Starting with World War II, the airplane would enter high-volume production for the first time.[20] With European firms already in high gear, it had a lot of time to make up. Even before Knudsen and his new staff had a chance to sort out the experts from the phonies, the British government approached with a dire order for production of the Rolls-Royce Merlin engine. With no organization yet in place at the OPM offices, Knudsen turned to a firm he knew he could trust: Ford Motor Company. Not only was the company the leader in production technique, but it was unique even among automakers for having built, back in the 1920s, a successful airplane, the Tri-Motor.

The American military, in conjunction with the British government, placed an order with Ford Motor for 9,000 airplane engines, to be built according to the Rolls-Royce design. Charles Sorensen and Edsel Ford negotiated the contract. However, as soon as it was announced in the British press, Henry Ford personally canceled it, insisting, "We are not doing business with the British government or any other foreign government."[21] The reversal was a shock, and the way it was rendered was an obvious slap at the British-American effort to arm against the Nazis.

Actually, Ford Motor Company had previously accepted a contract to build Rolls-Royce engines for French warplanes. Although that contract never came to fruition, due to the fall of France in June 1940, it had given Henry Ford a chance to examine the Rolls-Royce engine. According to Ford Motor aviation historian Tim O'Callaghan, Henry Ford rejected the English contract because in fact he was planning his own, *improved* version of that engine. While that doesn't make up for the fact that the Royal Air Force needed airplane engines desperately and without delay, it does, as O'Callaghan said, "offer a reasonable alternative view of what happened."[22]

In frustration, Bill Knudsen paid a personal visit to Henry Ford, but couldn't persuade him to discuss the British engine deal, let alone change his mind about it. To a direct appeal from Knudsen to reconsider, Ford's face remained a blank. "Do you ever read the poetry of Tennyson?" Ford asked. Knudsen didn't bother to continue the conversation but left without further ado, and without discussing English poetry. He retreated to the summer home he and his family had owned for years on Grosse Isle, south of Detroit. Facing a diplomatic—and strategic—disaster, he called the Packard Motor Car Company. Its president, Alvin Macauley, agreed over the telephone to make good on the Merlin contract.

"Mr. Ford, there'll be a hell of a stink if you don't go through with this job," Knudsen had warned Henry Ford. He was right: the press in North America and Britain criticized the Ford decision as a kind of treachery. A Canadian newspaper called Henry Ford "a menace to democracy." In truth, Ford had already accepted its first contract as part of the wartime mobilization—from the German government. Although Ford-Werke in Cologne was only nominally a Ford Motor Company subsidiary in 1940 and not controlled by Dearborn, it was doing business with the Third Reich, which rubbed salt in the wounds created over the rejection of the Rolls-Royce contract. Officials at Ford of Canada suggested that Henry Ford ameliorate the situation by allowing and even encouraging his Canadian and British subsidiaries to produce war matériel for King George VI's armies. Ford ultimately relented. While that position was equanimous in the strictest sense, since subsidiaries on both sides were allowed to enter war production, it was nonetheless interpreted at the time as Henry Ford's hiding a pro-German bias behind his claims to be a man of peace. Of course, these were the same charges that had been made against him during World War I.

In aeronautics and many other military-related fields, the firm that had pioneered a design was not necessarily in a position to mass-produce it. For that reason, UAW President Walter Reuther developed a proposal, later known as the Reuther Plan, that called for factories in all industries to utilize excess capacity by producing military matériel. The prime attraction of the plan was that American industry could continue its normal production of consumer goods while fulfilling war work. In most cases, the big industries wouldn't be required to tangle themselves up in design work; that had already been done by specialized military contractors. "Reuther's plan would continue civilian auto production but postpone tooling for the 1942 models by six months," historian Nelson Lichtenstein explained in *The Most Dangerous Man in Detroit,* "thereby making available the labor time of as many as fifteen thousand skilled mechanics to build the tools, dies, jigs, and fixtures for the production of an all-metal fighter on a mass-production basis."[23] According to Reuther, his plan would result in production of "500 planes a day," which became its catchphrase. By starting war work immediately, alongside their regular products, factories would avoid the dreaded "conversion," which translated into unremunerative downtime on the factory floor. However, as Reuther acknowledged, industries would have to be tightly coordinated by a joint labor-management council. For that reason, industrialists saw the Reuther Plan as a wartime rendition of the planned economy, just as it was practiced by the Soviet Union. They rejected it as a union power play and scoffed at the idea of "500 planes a day."[24]

In response, Henry Ford made a bold promise that his company could build 1,000 planes a day, "without meddling from the government." Coming from the man who had once built 10,000 Model Ts per day, the promise was worth talking about—and so it was, as an absurd promise that epitomized America's emboldened faith in its own production might. From Henry Ford's point of view, there was nothing outlandish about his promise—if nothing else, it was a well-publicized handle that pulled Ford Motor Company off the sidelines and into the forefront of factories ready, able, and finally willing to accept government contracts for military matériel.

William Knudsen studied the Reuther Plan and came out against it. Although the idea gained many other friends, it was doomed when Knudsen concluded that *"it don't work."* However, under his aegis, and with hundreds of other planners involved, a free-enterprise version of the Reuther Plan emerged in which the OPM shepherded projects forward, largely by letting companies bid on small pieces of an overall job. Typically, the mass-producers took on designs under license from smaller manufacturers. One such example was the production of airplane engines, a high priority in the summer of 1940. Pratt & Whitney, of New Haven, Connecticut, created engines destined for such planes as the P-47 fighter and the C-46 transport.[25] However, as with other small and medium-sized manufacturers of the time, Pratt & Whitney could make them, but not very many and not very quickly. It was up to larger companies to step into the breach and fulfill the orders.

Despite the debacle of Ford's abrupt cancellation of the Rolls-Royce contract, Knudsen offered his old employer the opportunity to manufacture the Pratt & Whitney—it was, after all, an American engine for the U.S. Army. Henry Ford was still edgy about war work. "Don't make it!" he told Sorensen.[26] Eventually, however, Edsel joined with Sorensen and persuaded Henry Ford to cooperate on the all-American project. Instead of attempting to build the 18-cylinder, 2,000-horsepower monsters on the same production lines that accommodated 90-horsepower, automobile V-8s, Ford Motor Company planned a massive new plant at River Rouge. Eventually, the facility would employ 17,000 people, but first the building, with its 31.3 acres in floor space, had to be constructed. This made sense to Charles Sorensen, who was responsible for building it, but the idea enraged labor leaders and others who were impatient for the actual production work to begin immediately in the automobile plant. However, the tooling and other pre-production work for the Pratt & Whitney wouldn't be completed for eleven months. Anyway, Ford Motor didn't do anything in a flimsy or temporary way. Without dawdling, the company went about the business of manufacturing the only way it knew: the airplane engines would be built in a facility that could last fifty years as easily as one year.[27]

On August 8, the war in western Europe started anew with the first ferocious airfight of the Battle of Britain, which pitted a small but cunning British force against an onslaught from the much larger German Luftwaffe. Hundreds of planes on each side took part as the Germans tried to bomb the British into submission. As soon as they controlled the skies, the Nazis planned to invade the British Isles. The Battle of Britain was still raging in October, with the Luftwaffe bombing civilian centers in night raids, when William Knudsen went home to Detroit for a meeting with representatives of the leading automobile and auto-parts firms. While there, Knudsen outlined the major projects awaiting mass production and specifically enlisted the industry's involvement with two bombers, the gargantuan B-17 Flying Fortress and the heavy-duty B-24 Liberator. Knudsen proposed to parcel out the manufacture of each, with sub-assemblies being sent from all over the country to final production plants in centrally located cities. The B-24s, for example, were to be finished at new factories in Fort Worth, Texas, and Tulsa, Oklahoma. As plans developed, Ford Motor Company was asked to participate in the B-24 pool, building various parts. There were enough of them: the B-24, which had been designed by Consolidated Aircraft of San Diego, comprised 101,650 parts.[28] By contrast, the average automobile contained about 15,000.

The Battle of Britain finally petered out with a night raid on October 31. The German Luftwaffe, which Charles Lindbergh and many others had pronounced to be superior to every Allied air force, was vanquished. But since no one could be sure that there wouldn't be another battle in the skies over England, the impetus remained in the United States to build a major air force— and *quickly.*

The B-24 program became an obsession at Ford Motor. However, even though Henry Ford was finally inured to the fact that Ford Motor was in the business of making war matériel, he succeeded in steering his company, in America and in subsidiaries around the world, away from the manufacture of destructive weaponry. In every country except New Zealand, and even including Germany, Ford plants produced only nonlethal items: airplanes, for example, but not the bombs that went with them. It was one legacy, perhaps, of Henry Ford's pacifism. In terms of another predilection, Ford and the quick-tempered Charles Sorensen were not interested in building bits and pieces for others to complete. They wanted to build the entire B-24 plane, maintaining the autonomy of Ford Motor, where every finished product could be traced back to the processes and people responsible for it. For the time being, at least, it accepted a smaller role, as long as it was expandable. At Knudsen's urging, Charles Sorensen and Edsel Ford traveled to San Diego in December 1940 as guests of the Advisory Council for National Defense to visit Consolidated Aircraft and watch B-24s in production there. They were accompanied by Edsel's two eldest sons, Henry II, then twenty-three, and Benson, twenty-one. At the time, a stubborn Henry Ford, uninterested in cooperating with any aviation company, was still telling reporters that a negotiated peace with Germany would be preferable to war. "Willow Run," future Ford Motor CEO Philip Caldwell recalled, referring to the airplane factory that Ford would soon build, "was conceived on the back of an envelope on that flight to San Diego."[29]

In all, Consolidated had built a few dozen B-24s for the U.S. government. Ford Motor Company was already talking about turning out 200 per month. The B-24 was one of the more complicated aircraft of the war, a four-engine propeller plane with a wingspan of 110 feet. It was very fast, with a top speed of 300 mph. Built to carry a crew of six, but often carrying more, it was distinguished by its tail, which did not rise straight up, as might be expected, but out to each side, with oval stabilizers on either tip. Both the rear and the nose were clad in greenhouse windows, for full visibility. The bomber-navigator sat in the nose, with a machine gun at hand, while a gunner sat in the back.[30] The B-24 was an ugly duckling, with its long wings and stubby fuselage, but it was frightening to far-flung enemies: it could fly 3,000 miles without refueling, and it carried up to four tons of bombs.

While in San Diego, Sorensen observed the major aspects of Consolidated's production with disdain, noting in particular the fact that final assembly was not done in a factory building but outside in the California sun. "What I saw reminded me of the way we built cars at Ford thirty-five years earlier," Sorensen recalled in his memoirs. "Here was a custom-made airplane, put together as a tailor would cut and fit a suit of clothes."[31] Intent on contributing to plane manufacture the Ford way, he returned to his hotel room to sketch out a basic layout for Ford's version of a B-24 factory, an undertaking that he later deemed "the biggest challenge of my life." Sorensen determined that Ford Motor Company would build whole planes, not just churn out parts. Henry Ford had never punished anyone for thinking big, and that was the scale on which Sorensen worked out his sketch. As he envisioned it, the new plant would be something like a mile in length, and a quarter mile across, with a full-scale airport attached. In his imagination this was no mere parts factory—it would be the vortex of President Roosevelt's "Arsenal of Democracy."

Blurry eyed from insomnia, Sorensen received Edsel Ford's blessing for the plan over breakfast the next morning. Bill Knudsen was delighted when Sorensen informed him that Ford Motor could provide 540 bombers a month. The president of Consolidated Aviation, however, thought the grandiose scheme ludicrous. He asked Sorensen to "get serious" and urged him to build just 1,000 wing sections for his company. Sorensen's temper flared: "We'll make the complete airplane or nothing."[32]

Knudsen had been expecting an outsize response from Ford Motor Company and so he was enthusiastic about Sorensen's plan to build a whole B-24 factory. The more coordination Ford Motor was willing to take on, the less the OPM would have to do. On March 3, 1941, the company received a $480 million order for 1,200 B-24 "airframe assemblies" (in Ford's case, that translated into practically everything except the engine) and 800 completed planes, along with authorization to build an expansive new facility.[33] By then, a site had already been selected, on a tract of land that Henry Ford had purchased ten years before in Washtenaw County, near the small college town of Ypsilanti. The land, located about twenty-five miles south of Detroit, not far from Ann Arbor, was known as Willow Run. A flat prairie parcel of 975 acres intersected with a willow-lined stream, it was used for soybeans and timber. Ford established Camp Willow Run on the property, a school that instilled the work ethic in sons of dead or disabled World War I veterans. These abandoned youths lived in canvas tents, earned two dollars a day, and shared profits from the corn and tomatoes they grew. This boys' camp folded after two years in operation. With a new global war looming, the idyllic pasture was to become the site of the world's largest factory.

"I went out with Mr. Ford at the start of Willow Run," recalled a construction manager named F. W. "Fritz" Loskowske, speaking of the morning of March 28. The party consisted of Henry Ford, Charles Sorensen, P. E. Martin, Ray Dahlinger, Harry Bennett, "and of course the chauffeurs."

Loskowske continued, "We got out there, and on this corner there was a great big sugar bush, maple bush. The old man thought that was a prize. He hated to see them cut down that tree. . . . Sorensen got out and said, 'We'll put up a *mile* of plant right across here!' Just like that! Everybody looked at Sorensen and thought he didn't know what the hell he was talking about or something." By that afternoon, Loskowske's crews were starting to clear the land.[34] For his part, Sorensen did indeed know what he was talking about. A forty-three-year-old sawmill was brought from Greenfield Village to convert the felled trees to 400,000 board-feet of lumber. "The big circular saw . . . was steam-powered and six feet in diameter," Albert Briggs of Belville, Michigan, recalled. "The logs ran through so fast that the blade got red hot."[35]

On March 5, 1941, the *Detroit Free Press* had published an artist's conception of the new Willow Run plant under the headline "Ford's Warbird Hatchery!"[36] Newspapers around the country repeated the story of Ford's initiative, the $47 million overall cost, and the $11 million that the government was contributing to the new plant (the U.S. government would eventually spend $200 million at Willow Run). The announcement proved to be a much needed boost in morale, since it was the first concrete news of mobilization that the average American could understand: Ford Motor Company had been roused by the talk of war, declaring that once Willow Run was up and running, as the report said, it would emit a B-24 every hour. To Americans, that rate of production seemed enough to vanquish any enemy, anywhere.

Mighty as the planes appeared, there were doubters about the site selection early on. Many people within major industries wondered whether a major factory could be built that quickly on a dirt lane in a meadow. Then there was the issue of an adequate labor force. In June 1940, when France fell and Americans began to take the war seriously, the policy committee of General Motors had begun a study of the potential effects of war production on its own corporation. One of the committee's conclusions was that maintaining full employment would be a primary problem. Because of that, the availability of manpower would be GM's top priority in selecting plant locations.[37] Ford, on the other hand, was more capricious, choosing to build the war effort's biggest factory in a desolate field. While up to 60,000 people would be needed to operate Willow Run, it was located miles from the nearest city, with no transportation, housing, or other accommodation for the fact that all those individuals had to report for work on time, every day. The employment question would haunt the enterprise, but first, the factory had to be built.

By April, the land was completely cleared. The main factory buildings, covering 2.5 million square feet, were constructed by September.[38] Constructing a building was no great trick, however. The greater problem was fitting it out. Creating tooling and specialized machinery for the bomber would take an estimated 6 million man-hours to complete. The dies required for the project alone numbered 11,000.[39] Ford Motor Company farmed out about half of the work to outside firms. Incredibly, the company's 1,800 tool designers turned out three miles' worth of blueprints, a yard wide, every day during most of 1941.[40] On a busy day, working in shifts, they produced five miles' worth of blueprints. Each set then had to be turned into metal by a toolmaker.

Although Willow Run's design was initiated by Albert Kahn, who died in 1943, the finished factory was not so much beautiful as just plain enormous. "While I was going through the plant I had the idea that I was seeing it—but I didn't believe it. I had the impression that it was not happening," said a radio announcer in a live broadcast from the plant. "It has that effect on all of us," said his colleague. "I've been through the plant before, but it leaves me limp each time."[41] The company was determined to bring automobile mass-production techniques to the airplane industry, and so the plant was an outsize version of any Ford Motor production line. From ribbons of aluminum, the bombers took shape, rolling persistently down the main assembly line.

In addition to constructing the B-24 plant at Willow Run, Ford Motor Company was turning out Pratt & Whitney engines and jeeps at River Rouge. Chrysler was involved in production of parts for the B-26 warplane, but its primary focus was on tank production. General Motors predominantly built aircraft engines and subassemblies, but was also manufacturing armament and electrical components. Packard was fulfilling its original contract for Merlin engines and building boat engines, as well. Hudson, Studebaker, and Nash were all engaged primarily in contracts for aeronautical parts, including engines and propellers.[42] By the end of 1940, defense contracts awarded to American automakers totaled $600 million. In the middle of the next year, when the United States began supplying Great Britain and the USSR through the Lend-Lease Act, that figure stood at $2 billion. It was headed for $4 billion at the end of the year.

———

Sitting behind his Dearborn desk on July 25, 1941, Henry Ford was depressed. As a committed pacifist, he abhorred the war talk that was consuming America. He abhorred the fact that Germany had invaded Poland, causing Britain and France to declare war against the Nazis, but he was still convinced that neutrality was the United States' only sane policy. Pressure had cascaded down on him, from the Roosevelt administration and other sources, demanding that he convert his plowshares into swords to help crush the Nazis by mass-producing airplanes. Reluctantly, he was doing just that at Willow Run. The White House, he lamented to associates, was being run by a cabal of immoral fools. Whatever happened to George Washington's staunch warning against foreign entanglements, he wondered? Why did the federal government always try to tell him how to run his company? Wasn't the best foreign policy one of free trade and no military alliances? Jaded from decades of business squabbling, criticisms from the press, and increasing government intervention, Ford's public optimism was tempered by a corrosive private pessimism.[43] There was one ray of light on the international scene, however, that Ford looked on with approval: the rise of Mahatma Gandhi of India. With great interest Ford had kept abreast of Gandhi's unlikely progress.

Disdainful of imperialism, Ford hoped that Gandhi's acts of civil disobedience would persevere, forcing the British out of the subcontinent. He also took great pride in the fact that since 1904, under the aegis of Ford of Canada, and later under Ford of India, his automobiles sold exceedingly well in Bombay and Calcutta.[44] Filled with such pro-Indian sentiments, Ford wrote Gandhi a fan letter. "I want to take this opportunity of sending you a message through Mr. T. A. Raman, to tell you how deeply I admire your life and message," Ford wrote. "You are one of the greatest men the world has ever known. May God help you and guide your lofty work."[45]

Gandhi was delighted and surprised to receive such a generous, personal letter from Henry Ford. It didn't reach him until December 8, one day after the Japanese attack on Pearl Harbor. Fearful that the extension of war spelled doom for mankind, Gandhi embraced the Ford note as a good omen, a declaration of support from the most famous industrialist-pacifist alive. "Gandhi said that he was deeply touched by the message and asked me to convey his regards to Mr. Ford," T. A. Raman, London editor of the United Press of India, later recalled. "I asked him whether I may take back his message in the shape of the simple machine with which Gandhi's name is associated, the spinning wheel. He agreed instantly and sent a secretary and his disciple Madeleine Slade to fetch an old spinning wheel he had used. He autographed it in Hindi and English twice over. While he was writing I said jokingly, 'Ford seems to think that you are the one sensible man in the world!' Gandhi laughed and as he handed it over said with a smile, 'So this goes from one sensible man to another!'"[46]

The spinning wheel, a portable model, had to travel 12,000 miles through submarine-infested waters before Raman personally delivered it to Greenfield Village. "All the way, the blacked-out ship zigzagged and changed course, making the journey from Bombay to New York through Cape Town and Trinidad even longer," Raman recalled. "I got the Captain's special permission to carry the spinning wheel with me into the lifeboat in the event of an emergency."[47] In the darkest days of the Second World War, Henry Ford would often slowly spin the wheel, staring at its spokes, believing that it brought him good luck. Its mechanical simplicity and high moral purpose—making cloth in the interest of self-sufficiency—resonated deeply within him. During the long months when America needed a miracle at Willow Run, Ford would meditate on the symbol of economic independence that Gandhi had sent.[48]

Meanwhile, as Willow Run was gearing up for production, a bittersweet moment occurred for Henry Ford. A Chicago businessman named E. N. Hurley sent Henry Ford a letter that Thomas Edison had written his father during World War I.[49] "You ask, *Where is Ford?* Let me explain," Edison started the missive, trying to explain that his friend's pacifist convictions should not be interpreted as unpatriotic. "Inventors must be poets so they may have imagination. To be commercially successful they must have the practical ability of an Irish contractor foreman and a Jewish broker. These wild children of nature necessarily are a puzzle to a Captain of Industry like yourself. Don't try to understand them."[50] It must have comforted Ford to know that Edison, dead ten years now, had once understood his mercurial attitude. All over America people were once again asking, "Where is Ford?" He knew the answer would come soon—with thousands of B-24s manufactured at Willow Run.

23

—————◦✕◦—————

Willow Run and the B-24 Liberators

"Look Out, Hitler, Here Comes the Flood!" was the title *Popular Science* magazine used on an article about B-24 bomber production at Ford Motor's humungous Willow Run plant in May 1943.[1] By then, the L-shaped factory was to have started full production, with a monthly output of 500 completed planes or airframe assemblies. "Bring the Germans and Japs in to see it," crowed Charles Sorensen; "hell, they'd blow their brains out."[2] Not if they took a closer look behind the hyperbole. In all of 1942, the world's largest factory turned out barely a dozen bombers. The subassemblies were so late that the destination plant in Tulsa had to be shifted to other war work. The Fort Worth plant remained on the B-24 program, but had to operate behind schedule. The *Popular Science* article, in essence, repeated what most Americans knew about Ford's war effort: "Willow Run is America's big all-out attempt to apply the technique of automobile mass production to the rapid manufacture of a four-engine bomber."[3] That sense of bravado was fast becoming a curse on the place, as it circled in a downward spiral in 1942–1943. Far from a production miracle, Willow Run was dragging everyone associated with it into a nightmare. J. H. Kindelberger, president of North American Aviation, resented the fact that the Roosevelt administration had assigned plane contracts to automakers. "You cannot expect blacksmiths," he sniffed, "to learn how to make watches overnight."[4]

Anything that happened in America's wartime industrial mobilization happened in an exaggerated way at Ford Motor Company with its enormous Willow Run plant. Problems, tensions, and the pressures of delay were all greater there than elsewhere. The drama was greater, too, as the Fords faced a family tragedy that had wartime repercussions. However, at Willow Run, the ultimate sense of triumph and a crucial part in the Allied victory would also be as outsized as the plant itself.

In 1941, automakers were enjoying a banner year in vehicle sales, in part due to the very real fear that war would suspend new-car production. However much they produced for the military, cars remained the greater priority. "The U.S. in the past year succeeded in producing five thousand combat planes and five million automobiles," sneered Virginia Senator Harry Byrd in the summer of 1941.[5]

William Knudsen had a lot of things to do in the new Office of Production Management, but the most urgent was antithetical to everything he'd done before in his career. He had to stop the auto industry from making so many cars. In August, the OPM announced an average reduction of 26.5 percent for the remainder of 1941 and 50 percent for the first six months of 1942. Ford Motor Company, which had built 20.2 percent of the nation's vehicles in the 1940 model year, and 18.1 percent the following year, was allotted a production quota equivalent to 18.6 percent of the industry for the '42 model year. Those percentages placed Ford Motor in third place behind the Chrysler Corporation (23.1 percent) and General Motors (44.3). In real terms, though, the cutbacks meant that Ford would be allowed to make only 399,600 cars for the year, about half the number it had made the year before. "It's the not making automobiles," Knudsen said of Henry Ford, "that really stuck in his craw."[6]

The attacks on Pearl Harbor and the Philippines in December 1941 changed the allotments—of course, they changed practically everything as the United States entered a two-front war in Europe and the Pacific. The pressure on American industry, and automaking in particular, increased overnight. Luckily for companies like Ford Motor and GM, the members of the UAW were ready for the war. The UAW boasted 200,000 members in metropolitan Detroit. Many young men enlisted in the armed forces, but those union men who stayed in factories like the Rouge and Willow Run would do their jobs so well that about 25 percent of all Allied war matériel—aircraft engines, artillery shells, bombers, jeeps, machine guns, tanks, and many other products essential to waging modern warfare—would be manufactured in Detroit. Blue-collar workers would transform the "Motor City" into the very epicenter of the "Arsenal of Democracy."[7] As Japan continued its military rampage through the Pacific, the image of Willow Run (or The Run, as workers called the factory) served as a real morale boost. "It is a promise of revenge for Pearl Harbor," the *Detroit Free Press* enthused. "You know when you see Willow Run that in the end we will give it to them good."[8]

The aluminum and other raw materials that entered at one end of the mile-long main building at Willow Run were stamped, stretched, milled, machined, or riveted into parts: in all, 550,000 pieces went into a B-24, not counting the 700,000 rivets. The parts were constructed into subassemblies, which fed into two parallel, final assembly lines. By that point airframes progressed along conveyors, pulled by underground cables. As the planes emerged from the building, they were tested on the adjoining mile-long airstrip.

For all of the effort that went into the planning and construction of a factory so immense, and at the same time so complex, two early mistakes nearly scuttled the whole enterprise. They may have been apparent to experienced production men, but the Ford mystique was such that few outsiders questioned even the company's most unorthodox decisions. Even on the inside, managers were reluctant to question policies handed down from the top: the mystique existed within the company, too. Once inspiring, it became as tight as a straightjacket on the question of Willow Run.

In the first place, the factory probably should not have opted to use steel-cast dies—11,000 of them—in the production of the B-24. Long-lasting but difficult to make, steel dies were appropriate for automobile models. Cars not only had production runs in the hundreds of thousands or even millions, but were subject to relatively few design changes. The B-24, on the other hand, was expected to peak at about 5,000 units per year at Willow Run: a lot for an airplane in 1943, but not much for steel-cast tools and dies. Moreover, the B-24 design used by Ford to set up the new factory had never been tested in combat. Once the United States entered the war, actual experience resulted in a steady stream of design changes. To implement them meant long delays at Willow Run while new steel dies were cast. Because specified improvements took so long to show up in production, the Army took a drastic step in 1942, temporarily suspending the implementation of changes in Ford-made B-24s. Until the process was finally reorganized late in the year, Willow Run B-24s were restricted to use in training.[9]

The decision to use steel-cast dies at Willow Run was Charles Sorensen's. Formerly known as "Cast-Iron Charlie," he was called "Cast-Steel Charlie" at Willow Run in recognition of his pronounced prejudice for the finer metal. His decision regarding the dies, although well intended, proved impractical under the circumstances.

The second problem facing Willow Run was entirely Henry Ford's doing: the location of the plant made finding a wartime workforce extremely difficult. During the Great Depression, automakers had enjoyed a wide choice in hiring, drawing from a ready pool of experienced, reliable workers. That changed once the war started. Within months of Pearl Harbor, it was the workers who had their choice—of factories. A bomber factory located twenty-five miles from downtown Detroit did not tempt many workers away from local plants operated by GM, Packard, Chrysler, Hudson, and even Ford. The *New York Times* noted with alarm on December 5, 1942, that Ford Motor Company was unable to maintain a workforce at Willow Run.[10] Company representatives recruited heavily in rural districts in Michigan, where the choice of jobs wasn't as wide as it was in Detroit. "Some men came all the way from Algonac," recalled Clem Davis, referring to a small town northeast of Detroit. "That's over 100 miles back and forth to Willow Run."[11] A commute that long would have been tough enough in peacetime, but when gas rationing started during the war, it required special permits or careful planning.

After canvassing the Michigan countryside, Ford officials fanned out to towns throughout the upper Midwest, even scouring hollows in Appalachia, looking for labor. Practically any able body would do. So many workers came from the Bluegrass State that Ypsilanti was jokingly referred to as "Ypsitucky." The recruiting drive drew farmhands, store clerks, and others who had never earned as much as an auto worker's wages. "A fellow called me up one day," recalled Tony Harff, who worked in the administration office, "and said we had a fellow out there who came into work that morning and had no shoes on his feet. They didn't know whether to send him out into the plant or not without shoes, but they finally did." Willow Run didn't turn many people down. "The fellow said he never wore shoes in his life," Harff added, "and he wasn't going to start to wear them now, just because he was going to work inside a plant."[12]

The only thing worse than trying to draw workers out to Willow Run was the frustration of trying to keep them there. Ford Motor Company couldn't be faulted for the training it offered inexperienced workers: in fact, its programs were probably too thorough. The company had had long experience in making productive factory workers out of new immigrants, ex-convicts, and the disabled. During the war, it could and did teach factory skills to thousands of neophytes. Unfortunately, a high percentage of workers took what they learned in Willow Run's training programs and immediately secured work in Detroit or another big city.[13] Another problem was that the U.S. government kept drafting workers to join the armed forces in the fight against Germany and Japan. "In January 1943," Harff said of Willow Run, "we hired 1,186 men and lost 1,669. . . . There was a terrific turnover."

Ford Motor Company contributed to the labor problem by refusing to cooperate with the government's efforts to build housing adjacent to the factory. Sorensen was against the plan because he felt the construction, estimated at two years, would drain employees from the plant. Henry Ford was adamantly opposed to a factory village, in some measure because he didn't want to populate a Republican county with voters who would cast ballots along union lines. Eventually, Ford Motor Company did build its own temporary housing complex near the plant. Composed of little more than wooden huts, the workers' quarters didn't invite permanent residency—further contributing to the high turnover. In order to encourage workers to drive in from Detroit, however, good, direct roads to Willow Run were built. In addition, Edsel Ford supported a decentralization plan, under which as much work as possible was shifted to Ford facilities in areas where labor was available. It was something of an echo of the Reuther Plan, instituted on an intracompany basis.

―――――――

In October 1942, a Willow Run worker named Clarence Gabrielson wrote a letter to Henry Ford. After apologizing that "this letter may sound a little subversive," he described the situation surrounding production. "It should be better," he wrote, "and it can be by superiors not passing the buck—take it on the chin, correct your faults and faults of other fellows also. . . . Also inspection is very lax, plant protection is lax. I know it is a new plant but it will stay new as long as things like this exist; also I believe if men were given pep talks every once in a while, it would help; they like to work, some of them, but it don't pan out right. . . . When on production and the B-24E comes out, it will make every man proud to know and see what Willow Run can do when the big fellow and the little fellow get together to beat our common enemy. Well I must close, I believe I'm boring you."[14]

Willow Run probably would have bored Henry Ford. He took only passing interest in the facility, and rarely visited it or conferred with others about it. He did, however, betray his unique sense of perspective. Realizing that history would be made at Willow Run as his company mass-produced Liberators, Henry Ford had the wisdom to commission Charles C. LaCroix to write what became a five-volume study titled "Ford and the War Effort." LaCroix, a native of Prince Albert, Saskatchewan, had started working for Ford in 1925, with stints at the DT&I Railroad and the *Dearborn Independent*. When the war began, he was giving tours at Greenfield Village. Henry Ford approached him about chronicling the story of Willow Run as it unfolded. Ford believed these histories would set the record straight. The volumes LaCroix wrote, now housed at the Benson Ford Research Center of the Henry Ford Museum and Library, are indeed a treasure. With exacting detail and a deep understanding of complex manufacturing issues, LaCroix wrote about Willow Run's airport, hangars, assembly lines, machine shops—everything.[15] There are sections on jettison fuel tanks, the aluminum foundry, wartime advertising, and airplane apprentice school. Although unpublished, "Ford and the War Effort" stands out as the single most important study available on the history of industrial mobilization in metropolitan Detroit during World War II.

As the war work progressed, Henry Ford was embittered in many respects, all too aware of the fact that for the first time, his company had only one customer: the U.S. government. That had not been the case during World War I, when the company continued vehicle production alongside military work. In 1942, the United States was mobilized for war to a far greater extent. New-car sales ended and Ford Motor was, like all other automakers, adjunct to the

U.S. military. Hordes of officers and inspectors descended on Ford plants, especially Willow Run, making demands, inspecting paperwork, and generally examining operations at will. Henry Ford regarded it as a plot to assume control of the company. He was particularly acrimonious toward Bill Knudsen. "All he is here for is to take over our plants," Ford concluded.[16]

Aloof and grumpy, Henry Ford had become a ghost of his former vigorous self. He was, in historian David Kennedy's apt phrase, "a crusty icon of industrialized America."[17] Ford was on the periphery of his company, even while maintaining control, officially, over every scrap of it. The situation wasn't easy to understand, from inside Ford Motor or outside of it. After suffering his minor stroke of 1937, Ford had seemed to make a complete recovery. However, he was ill during much of 1940, sometimes failing to recognize longtime acquaintances. Although his faculties eventually returned, he suffered a second stroke in 1941. Physically, he was all right, but his mind was altered, and he lost many of his well-known attributes. He was rarely relaxed or friendly, in his former, jocular way. His sense of humor gone, he was apt to be hasty and impatient. Much more important, the paranoia that had long driven him to protect the company from unfriendly forces, real or imagined, was unleashed full-force upon the company itself. Ford felt he could trust only one man: "my Harry," as he occasionally called Harry Bennett, to distinguish him from any other "Harry." Bennett, a man who truly believed that violence solved problems, had been a good bulldog to Henry Ford for more than a dozen years, but in 1940, his role began to grow dramatically. As Ford's capacity shrank, Bennett assumed more authoritarian power at the company for himself. "All in all, the Ford-Bennett relationship was a curious mix of impulses practical and emotional, reasoned and instinctive, selfish and unselfish," historians Allan Nevins and Frank Ernest Hill wrote. "The two men respected each other's skills and efficiencies, liked each other's crassness, and saw in each other the strengths needed to cope with a brutal world."[18]

Henry Ford had always aligned himself with strong personalities. His contribution to the business lay in general concepts and a kind of charisma, but that wouldn't have built Ford Motor. He had practically inherited the company from James Couzens in 1919. After that he depended heavily on Charles Sorensen for about twenty years. An unusual sense of dependence on another person was Henry Ford's pattern. It worked because he chose his regents well. Both Couzens and Sorensen were honest men of business, committed to the long-range success of the company. Harry Bennett was not honest. He was not a man of business and was not able to embrace long-range considerations, yet starting with Henry Ford's prolonged illness in 1940, he was the only person, with the exception of Clara Ford, whom the boss felt he could trust. His son, Edsel, was nowhere on the list.

One favorite who was around was Charles Lindbergh, whom Henry Ford hired in March 1942 as a Willow Run test pilot. Because he was deemed persona non grata by the Roosevelt administration, companies like Consolidated Aircraft snubbed Lindbergh. Ford, in kind, snubbed the White House: to him Lindbergh was still the all-American hero. Upon seeing Willow Run, Lindbergh recorded in his diary that the facility was "acres upon acres of machinery and jigs and tarred wood floors and busy workmen . . . a sort of Grand Canyon of the mechanized world."[19] Ford asked Lindbergh to name his salary—he would pay it. The tarnished idol responded that he would accept only what a colonel received in the Air Corps: $666.66 per month.[20]

Before long the Lindberghs, a very wealthy couple, settled into a cozy home in Bloomfield Hills. Lindbergh started work inspecting and test-flying planes at Willow Run. "The government's attempts to stifle Lindbergh's wartime career increased his desire to prove himself a good soldier," biographer A. Scott Berg maintained. "He shifted his high-octane work ethic into an even higher gear, never allowing anybody to accuse him of goldbricking. He usually left for work before daybreak and did not return home until long after dark. He became his own harsh taskmaster, creating assignments for himself when he had exhausted those put before him."[21] So it was that America's two most infamous isolationists, Henry Ford and Charles Lindbergh, teamed up to do whatever they could to make America and Ford Motor first in airplane production. (Although Willow Run was Lindbergh's main base of operation during the war, he twice consulted with General Douglas MacArthur in Brisbane, Australia.)[22] Even when he joined arms in the national effort, however, Ford had his very own way of looking at things. "We have the land and we have the people," he told reporters one day at a Willow Run barbecue. "So don't worry about what's going to happen to America and Americans. There will be a return to the soil and it will be for the better." When pressed to explain how Willow Run, a facility designed to manufacture B-24s, had anything to do with returning to the soil, Ford scoffed at the silliness of the question. "I can visualize a time when almost every family will have a small plane in its backyard. That will merely be another factor in our return to the soil."[23]

———

During one of Henry Ford's bouts of illness, he and Clara were spending the winter at their estate in Ways, Georgia (renamed Richmond Hill in 1941). Henry was not always lucid and his secretary, Frank Campsall, asked Charles Sorensen not to discuss business with him on their frequent telephone calls. Edsel found it best not to call his father at all, for both their sakes. After that, the only person still telephoning from headquarters was Harry Bennett. Finally, Clara became distraught at Bennett's calls and the way his reports riled her husband. Because Bennett had made a comrade of Campsall, she felt helpless to stop the calls at her end. "Mrs. Henry Ford asked Edsel and me to stop Bennett from talking to Ways," Sorensen recalled. "She was distracted. Edsel and I understood. Bennett took the suggestion that he stop talking as a reflection upon himself. He was bound to be negative on anything that Edsel wanted him to do."[24]

In the early 1920s, Edsel had so resented Sorensen's overbearing ways that he used his power as president of the corporation to fire him. He was supported in his decision by Ernest Kanzler. However, in the whipsaw of Ford management during the mid-1920s, Sorensen stayed and it was Kanzler who was fired. Edsel Ford could never understand why his father consistently treated Sorensen with more respect than he paid to his own son. It wasn't warranted. Nonetheless, Edsel learned to work within the situation. Even while eyeing each other warily, the two made a good team: Edsel in the office making the decisions that moved complex projects forward; Charles Sorensen in the plant, bringing grand plans to fruition. Most important, they both dealt effectively with President Roosevelt. Unlike his father, Edsel found the president a smart, genial, tireless patriot. Edsel visited Franklin Roosevelt at Warm Springs, Georgia, in 1928 and made a contribution of $20,000 to build a therapeutic swimming pool at the rehabilitation center FDR established there for polio victims. Edsel truly admired Roosevelt, who did not have the use of his legs, except in the water. To gain a sense of freedom and mobility on land, the president drove a Ford 1936 Phaeton convertible, specially fitted with hand controls. Year in and year out, Edsel's family exchanged birthday greetings, holiday wishes, and special notes of celebration with President and Mrs. Roosevelt. Edsel was convinced that Roosevelt was the true genius behind transforming Detroit overnight into an "arsenal of democracy."[25]

At the beginning of the war, Edsel Ford and Charles Sorensen found themselves more closely allied than ever. In part, they considered that they had to present a united front in the interest of the war effort. The two were largely responsible for building the Willow Run plant in 1941–1942. In addition, they came together in self-defense: as Harry Bennett's two prime targets, they tried to combat his growing influence. But Edsel knew never to turn his back on Sorensen, the master of Machiavellian maneuvers.

To complete the old triumvirate, respectable and serious-minded Ernest Kanzler was on the scene again, after an interlude in banking, working as the field chief of the War Production Board and charged with overseeing Detroit's automobile industry.[26] With that appointment, Henry Ford immediately began his old cant, accusing Edsel of being Kanzler's pawn. The irony was that Henry Ford was now the pawn, Harry Bennett being his sole source for information and thus for opinions.

By that time, Edsel Ford had his own very real problems. His stomach ailment, long suspected of being caused by ulcers, was diagnosed as cancer in January 1942. Some scholars have blamed Henry Ford for Edsel's illness, claiming that his habitual antagonism broke down first his son's nervous system and then his general health. Others have blamed the condition on Edsel's penchant for liquor. Neither is quite correct. Edsel Ford suffered from a rare disorder that had yet to be identified in the 1940s. Now known as Zollinger-Ellison syndrome, it was first described in 1955 by Dr. Robert Zollinger, chairman of the surgery department at Ohio State University Medical School. According to one of his students, Dr. G. Bronn, Zollinger investigated Edsel Ford's case and confirmed that he suffered from the rare syndrome.[27]

Typically found in people between the ages of thirty and sixty (Edsel Ford was then forty-eight), Zollinger-Ellison is caused by the presence of tumors in the stomach, pancreas, or other parts of the upper digestive tract; these tumors secrete a hormone called gastrin, which in turn stimulates the production of the acid that causes ulcers. The resultant ulcers, however, are even more painful than the more common peptic ulcers, and they do not respond to the same methods of treatment. The removal of half of Edsel Ford's stomach in January 1942 was ineffective; the ultimate treatment for Zollinger-Ellison is now recognized as the removal of the entire stomach (a procedure not yet performed in the early 1940s). While external factors can affect any condition, Edsel's disease cannot be traced directly to his problems with his father. He simply had the bad luck to have a serious disease unknown to medicine at that time.

Edsel's debilitation continued after his operation, and during the following year and a half, he couldn't regain his full strength. Others looked at Edsel's gray pallor, emaciated condition, and pained eyes, and recognized that he was a very sick man. Henry Ford insisted that the ailment was self-induced and that if Edsel would follow his advice, eating what he ate, chewing how he chewed, and exercising when he did, the stomach problems would go away. Ford had endowed one of the finest hospitals in the Midwest, named for him and located in Detroit, yet he dismissed and rejected the opinions of the doctors there, who were monitoring Edsel's condition.

Meanwhile, Harry Bennett actively undermined Edsel's work and attacked him personally, spreading his own considered medical opinion, for example, that the reason Edsel vomited so often was that he was a weakling. Charles Sorensen came to Edsel's defense on numerous occasions, either out of basic compassion—a quality surprisingly rare in Edsel's immediate circle at the company—or because he had to stop Bennett's expanding power anywhere he could. "Bennett and Charles E. Sorensen had always been enemies from the start," observed H. S. Abelwhite. "They were both fighting for power. They were both the same type of men, that rough, tough, knock-'em-down, drag-'em-out type of man."[28] For two years, the men charged with running Ford Motor's two enormous local complexes and dozens of satellites and subsidiaries beyond them were distracted from their work and from the world war, engaged in their own death struggle. Henry Ford was fading, a bitter man nearing eighty, fighting all the wrong fights. Bennett joined him in those fights, choosing the path of least resistance in the struggle by helping the boss chip away at whatever was left of Edsel. After twenty years, that abuse was only just beginning to reach its full power. Sorensen was no longer cast-iron or even cast-steel, as the stresses of his work and the struggles just below the surface gave him a variety of ailments; not nearly as serious as Edsel's, they were more in the category of Forditis. He exhibited his usual devotion to Henry and a newfound concern for Edsel, but only as it allowed him to remain pitted against Bennett. "The powers that control the plant," said the *Detroit News* in a critical look at Willow Run in May 1942, "[are] unable to grasp the fact that *we are at war* . . . and to realize that the great, basic purpose of the plant is to help *win*."[29]

On September 18, 1942, Franklin and Eleanor Roosevelt paid an official visit to the Willow Run plant, intended to boost Allied morale by focusing attention on the biggest bomber factory in the world. The United States had fared badly in its first months of military engagement and needed the news that long-distance bombers were about to start pouring out of the Ford plant. Up until the Roosevelts brought their spotlight to Willow Run, people could still believe that was true.

"We went to a lot of trouble in arranging that trip to make sure he saw as much as possible," recalled assistant plant supervisor Logan Miller. "We arranged to have his car driven down between the press lines and through the subassembly area. He saw with his own eyes what was going on."[30]

Henry Ford sat between Eleanor and Franklin in the backseat of an open Lincoln sedan. Edsel sat on a jump seat across from the First Lady, and Charles Sorensen sat across from the president. Sorensen and Edsel explained the processes as the car drove through the plant. There was a lot of explaining to do. "As we moved along," Sorensen recalled, "the president would shout at the top of his voice and point out something that caught his eye. 'Charlie, what is that?' We would stop and I would explain. Mrs. Roosevelt was just as enthusiastic. She would see groups of workers on an operation that interested her. She would call, 'Franklin, look over here!'"[31]

Through the entire trip of an hour and a quarter, Henry Ford didn't say a word. For Sorensen, it was like having guests stop by in the middle of a family fight. "The President and Mrs. Roosevelt were indifferent to him," he noted. "Sitting between the Roosevelts, who were good-sized people, he was almost hidden. He could not enter into the spirit of the event. When I would look at him, he would glare at me furiously. Edsel got the same response." In peacetime, being stuck between the two Roosevelts might have been understandably agonizing for Henry Ford. He couldn't put these feelings aside, not even in war. "Henry Ford hated him," Sorensen said, referring to Roosevelt. "He was furious because Edsel and I were loyal to a cause. We were giving all we had to the cause."

Not long after that, however, word of the factory's problems was out. The Roosevelts' visit was a kind of end to the innocence of the "world's biggest bomber plant." Charles Lindbergh—who refused to even catch a glimpse of the Roosevelts—continued to work countless hours at Willow Run. He found dealing with the entrenched corporate mentality of both Sorensen and Bennett a hassle. His biggest concern was that the Liberators had numerous imperfections, which increased the likelihood of fatal accidents. "I feel quite sure that Ford officials did not realize the mediocrity of the B-24 when they set up such elaborate jigs and machinery for its production," he later noted. "However, even if they had shared my personal estimate of the B-24, I am not sure they would have made any change in their procedure—or that they should have. A very high production of bombers was desired at the earliest possible date."[32]

After Ford Motor Company's exemplary UAW contract expired in January 1942, the company renewed its adversarial relationship with the union. One of the reasons for its disillusionment was that the auto workers' union had been unable to exert complete control over the wartime workforce, with the result that scattered wildcat strikes beset all Ford factories, especially Willow Run. Henry Ford, prone to paranoia, believed that the UAW was conniving to use the war in order to wrest control of the factories, if not of the company itself. He renewed his battle against the union, against the advice of Edsel.

Charles Sorensen was spread too thin in the cause, taking charge of Willow Run, even while overseeing production at River Rouge and Highland Park. He fainted several times on the factory floor from exhaustion, heard ringing in his ears, and began to suffer other signs that his nerves were strained. His health and the dismal output at Willow Run gave Bennett an opportunity to persuade Henry Ford to pull Sorensen out of the bomber factory. Before long, Sorensen was forbidden from so much as setting foot at Willow Run. Although the shift represented a victory for Bennett, Sorensen accepted the fact that he had to step away. At the same time, the Army was applying pressure for a single contact at the head of Willow Run, someone independent of River Rouge operations.[33] Roscoe Smith, the production man then assigned to run Willow Run, "for some reason didn't click there," in the words of one executive.[34]

Smith was replaced by Mead Bricker, a company veteran who had been personally hired by Henry Ford back in 1904 at the Piquette Avenue plant. During a separation from the company, he established himself as one of the outstanding manufacturing executives in the automobile business. He returned to Ford in 1914. As superintendent of the River Rouge plant during the 1920s, Bricker helped raise production to more than 9,000 cars per day, 10,000 on a very good day. "Bricker hadn't been there too long before he was *it* at Willow Run," said Charles Voorhess, a longtime Ford employee. "There's no doubt about it."[35]

At the Ford Administration Building near the River Rouge plant, Harry Bennett was expanding his own responsibilities, with Henry Ford's sanction. While he stayed away from production itself, he did insinuate himself into the delicate situation between Ford Motor Company and the U.S. Army—or, more specifically, between company executives and staff officers charged with overseeing military programs. "He tried to work himself in with the Army representatives that we had out there," said Tony Harff. "It wasn't always successful. I recall a sample of this where he had taken over one of the Army representatives and said that he was going to educate him and bring him around to Ford thinking. As I understand, he made a bum out of this fellow. Shortly after he became a drunkard and he was thrown out of the Army."[36]

When Bennett began to press himself into purchasing, people on both the production side and the finance side of the company were uncomfortable. During World War II, the opportunity for abuses in procurement loomed over every factory, since the production of war matériel required massive orders that were often placed with new suppliers. Bennett allegedly had a labyrinth of deals operating with suppliers, by which he received a consideration for the assurance of Ford Motor's business. However, A. M. Wibel, Ford's director of purchasing, was having none of it. A Ford Motor employee since 1912, he ran one of the most efficient offices in Ford's wartime administration. In the early spring of 1943, Wibel charged Harry Bennett with improper activities in the purchasing program. Bennett, in response, exercised his prerogative as director of personnel to demand Wibel's dismissal. Edsel Ford opposed it vehemently. Wibel's integrity was crucial not only to Ford Motor, but to the trust placed in the company by Army officials. "Virtually all our contracts were on a cost-plus-fixed-fee basis, as distinct from a fixed price," explained L. E. Briggs of the accounting department. "This meant that all of our figures had to be audited in detail. As a consequence, we had several hundred government auditors in here, some of whom represented the Air Forces and some the Ordnance Departments, together with miscellaneous groups."[37] Sloppy work in the purchasing department would invite investigations from the government, slowing up production even more than it was already.

All eyes looked to Henry Ford in the Wibel matter, which came down to a choice between Edsel's instincts and Bennett's. Ford sided with Bennett. Not only was his natural inclination to disagree with Edsel, but he was apt to resist any suggestion that the government should influence his company. Wibel was fired. It was to be the last fight between the father and son.

In April, Edsel told Charles Sorensen that he intended to resign. By then, he was too ill to continue his services anyway. As his condition grew more painful, and his outlook more grim, his father's rejection and cruelty actually grew stronger. Either Henry Ford couldn't accept that his son was dying, or he just didn't care. Both theories have been offered by those close to him. Either way, his monstrous reaction to his son's decline was probably the clearest indication that his mind—the best part of it—was gone.

Charles Sorensen left the only detailed account of the relations between Henry and Edsel Ford in the spring of 1943. His original diary accounts follow; comments he made later about those events follow in italics. It is worth repeating in full, starting with a meeting between Sorensen and Edsel Ford at River Rouge:

> April 15: Edsel came in eleven o'clock. Looks like a sick man to me. I am worried about him. Lunch with him and his father. After lunch we went to Campsall's office. Tonight Henry Ford called me, wants me to see Edsel tomorrow morning and change his attitude on everything in general. Some job.
>
> April 16: To Edsel's office. A serious talk with him about his relations with his father. He was for quitting at once. I convinced him it was wrong. We ended, I believe, with a good understanding. All smiles at lunch. Henry Ford came over to see me, Bennett along. I left for Miami at seven o'clock, glad to be away.
>
> *When Henry Ford called me at home [April 15], I made some notes on what he wanted me to discuss with Edsel. The notes read as follows (I still have the original note and I quote):*
>
> *April 16, 1943*
> *a. Discord over handling labor unions.*
> *b. Wibel and his attitude on Bennett. Says Wibel is through.*
> *c. Bennett in full accord with Henry Ford. Henry Ford will support Bennett against every obstacle. Seeing labor leaders.*
> *d. Bennett's job, no one else's.*
> *e. Change relations with Bennett.*
> *f. Kanzler relationship. Wants it broken up.*
> *g. Regain health by co-operating with Henry Ford.*
> *h. Hope I can be of help.*
> *i. Basis of talk I had with Edsel, April 16, 1943.*
>
> *My first reaction to this after I finished talking to Henry Ford was, "What a brutal thing to do to his son, to send me." But it was evident where all this came from. Bennett had his day. He could never get along with Edsel on any basis. I felt that in a break like this I could be helpful to both father and son. It was the approach I made with Edsel the next morning.*

I explained that I realized that I was on delicate ground. I explained how his father had phoned me, and I showed him my notes. I added that I felt that I could be helpful to him in this disagreement which was apparent to all of us.

If he wished, I would go no further with the matter. I added that it was evident where Henry Ford was getting his ideas. To me, that was not so disturbing as a break between him and his father.

His reply to all this was, "The best thing for me to do is resign. My health will not permit me to go on." He added, "Charlie, I want you to know I appreciate very much what you are trying to do. It is a kindly thing to do and I respect your help." He was in tears.

I sat on a couch with him, and when he calmed down I told him that if he was going to resign, there was only one thing for me to do; that was to resign with him. I would not go on if he was going to resign.

I had enough of people resigning. Any more, and I would let Henry Ford run it himself. I made it clear that if he resigned I would go with him. We discussed our war commitments. I could follow them no matter how tough matters got.

We had the full respect of Washington. Henry Ford had none. I asked him to do only one thing, pull Henry II [then in the Navy] *in, then go away for a real vacation and forget about Bennett.*

Edsel explained to me how he and Wibel had a hot session with Bennett over some supplier who was patronizing Bennett. Edsel told Bennett to stop dealing with any supplier, stick to his union job. He found fault with the way that Bennett was mixing in with the union. I did not know anything about this session. It was plain to see where Henry Ford got his line of Edsel and Wibel.[38]

Six weeks later, Edsel underwent another operation at Henry Ford Hospital in downtown Detroit. Unpasteurized milk from his father's dairy farm had brought an attack of undulant fever, but that was only a small part of the problem. After the operation, the surgeons informed Edsel and Eleanor that the disease had worsened and the hospital could do nothing more for him. Eleanor brought her husband home to Grosse Pointe Shores for the last time. His children gathered around him: Henry II and Benson from the military; Josephine from Texas, where her husband was stationed; and William from his Connecticut prep school. Neither Henry nor Clara could bring themselves to visit. Edsel Ford died at home on May 26, 1943. The family was devastated, but so were all those within the company who were waiting with high hope for the day when Edsel Ford would take over and bring Ford Motor into a new era.

Henry Ford's reaction ranged widely, depending on his mood or the person to whom he was speaking. "If he took Edsel's death very hard, he tried to cover it up," said Charles Voorhess. "I remember him even making statements that everybody should remember that whatever happens is always for the best."[39]

Mrs. Stanley Ruddiman heard a different comment. "Just a few weeks after Edsel had passed on, Mr. Ford wanted so much to talk to someone who would understand how he felt. He asked me to come over to the Museum," she recalled, referring to Henry's collections at Greenfield Village. They walked around the museum. "He said that in life, he and Edsel had not always understood each other and at times could not see eye to eye. He felt now that, before too long, he and Edsel would be together again. He thought there would be better understanding and they could continue working together."[40]

Although Wall Street financiers anticipated that the family would have to sell a major block of Edsel's 41 percent share in the company, in order to settle inheritance taxes, the Fords had found yet another way to keep their huge enterprise from going public. In 1936, Edsel had persuaded his father to establish the Ford Educational and Charity Foundation. Predicated by a division of Ford stock into voting and nonvoting shares, the plan allowed the Fords to keep the management shares, while giving up the others to avoid inheritance tax laws. As a result of the endowment from Edsel's will, the Ford Foundation was well on its way to overseeing the largest endowment of any charitable trust, even while Edsel's heirs avoided a tax bill that might have reached $321 million.

Henry Ford named himself as Edsel's replacement as president of Ford Motor. A few years before, when he was only seventy-five and was still challenging visitors to footraces, just for boasting rights, he might have successfully assumed the responsibilities. Instead, just weeks short of eighty, he was slowing up physically and mentally. His grasp of the complex military contracts before the company was weak, and his commitment to cooperation with the government was tinged with suspicion. When Henry Ford didn't show up at the various Ford plants, however, Harry Bennett usually did, carrying orders from—or purported to be from—the boss.

Army officials watched the situation closely. They needed a version of Ford Motor Company that was growing more effective, not less so. With employment standing at one third of the level that would be required, Willow Run was still running at least six months behind schedule. "The immense plant may go down as an American war catastrophe of mislocation," *Business Week* had noted that March.[41]

War Department officials conferred with Ernest Kanzler about the outlook at Ford Motor Company. They even considered taking control of the company, which would have been within their legal rights. William Knudsen hovered over the plants and detected enough improvement in the operations at

Willow Run to back Mead Bricker's efforts there. River Rouge had never been as much of a problem, building trucks, jeeps, and individual items. Ray Rausch, the general manager there since 1933, was turning out matériel at the steady pace required. However, as a kind of insurance policy on Henry Ford's ability to carry on, Secretary of the Navy Frank Knox sent a letter to Lieutenant Henry Ford II, then stationed at the Great Lakes Naval Training Center, discharging him from his commission. The twenty-five-year-old was needed far more in Dearborn than in the Navy. In terms of management, though, recalling Henry II was for naught. Henry Ford wouldn't allow his grandson so much as a desk in the factory, let alone a job with real responsibility.

During the autumn, Ford Motor chief engineer Larry Sheldrick was fired for no obvious reason, while a roster of other longtime executives resigned under pressure. Finally, the bell tolled for Charles Sorensen. The struggle with the rising power of Harry Bennett prepared the way, but it was probably Sorensen's own mistake that precipitated it. "No one could resent others receiving attention like Henry Ford could," Sorensen said of the day that he had played the genial host for the Roosevelts. "When he was around, the spotlight was for him."[42] Sorensen should have known that ever since James Couzens had first found it expedient to turn Henry Ford into the single spokesperson of the Model T, the cardinal sin for an employee of the Ford Motor Company was receiving publicity. In 1942, Sorensen submitted to an interview and photos for a glowing profile in *Fortune,* entitled "Sorensen of the Rouge." Subtitled with a jaunty heroic description—"Besides making engines, tanks and guns, he is running the biggest bomber factory in the world"—the article mentioned Henry Ford only barely. It was the first of several articles about Sorensen to appear in major publications over the following year.

"I think that articles in the papers referring to Sorensen as the 'wizard of Willow Run' had very much of an effect on his leaving," said Logan Miller. "I heard Mr. Ford say, 'If he wants to get his name in the paper and wants to wear an Army uniform, I'll put him in.'"

Miller added, "I used to live in fear of publicity. The minute a man had his name in the paper, that was just the death warning."[43] Sorensen knew that as well as Miller did. He may, however, have been desperate, hoping that publicity was one way of bolstering his position, in relation to that of the secretive Harry Bennett.

On March 2, 1944, the situation came to a head. Henry Ford gave Charles Sorensen no choice but to resign from the Ford Motor Company. Sorensen wrote in his diary that day, "Campsall called this morning, said Henry Ford felt I should resign—his excuse, I am ambitious to be president of his company."[44]

Anthony Harff recalled him with an epitaph appropriate for Henry Ford's kind of manager: "I think Mr. Sorensen perhaps was a great production man, but probably set his sights a little too high at times. He sometimes made it rough for everybody else."[45] Soon afterward, Sorensen joined the jeep company Willys-Overland as president. Sheldrick also landed on his feet, taking a senior position at General Motors. A. M. Wibel, the former purchasing agent, went to a vice presidency at Nash-Kelvinator.[46]

Under increased pressure from the Army, Willow Run finally turned a corner in 1944. With the old Ford Motor Company bravura, it was finally producing first-rate B-24 Liberators, in line with the original schedule. Mead Bricker, general manager of the bomber plant, deserved a fair share of the credit. Under his brand of tough, logical leadership, the factory reached its potential and then some, going from the back of the pack to the leading edge. Working at Willow Run was a no-nonsense proposition. Music was banned, coffee breaks were nonexistent, and smoking was out of the question. Workers learned the system, and moreover, the system learned to use workers without a great deal of experience, making up for the high turnover rate. By the summer of 1944, Willow Run had produced 5,000 planes and was working at a much faster rate than any other B-24 factory. It was even assigned extra tasks—for example, making spare parts and modifications to older B-24s.

With technique tightening and morale rising, the transformation at Willow Run was dramatic. Inspectors found an average of eight hundred quality problems on each plane in 1942. By 1944, the number of "squawks," as the problems were called, was down to twenty.

One of the employees was Wally Pipp, a former starter for the New York Yankees, whose place at first base was taken one day in 1928 by Lou Gehrig. As is well-known, Pipp never got the position back. At Willow Run, he took on a technical job. "I'm supervising the publication of a manual on all inspection procedures on the B-24 bomber," he told a radio audience in 1943. "I'd like to say that the production results here are nothing short of phenomenal."[47]

One worry Pipp and others had was security at the plant. Willow Run was always on "red alert" status, its employees frisked both on their way in and out of work. If Germany and Japan wanted to defeat the United States, they would have to destroy Detroit's production facilities (or at least slow the factories down). Bomb threats were commonplace, although no device was ever found. Theft was a more commonplace problem. "It was quite an experience," security guard Harvey J. Miller told the *Ann Arbor News* decades after the war. "We had to check everything—look in garbage cans and everywhere."[48]

Then there was constant concern about faulty parts, a theme playwright Arthur Miller wrote about in *All My Sons*, although his story concerned a manufacturer who knowingly sells substandard airplane parts. That was far from the situation at Ford Motor, where the executives wanted to turn out an airplane of unimpeachable quality, but instilling that attitude in tens of thousands of line workers was a constant challenge. "In general," Pipp recalled, "caution and paranoia were part of the daily routine at Willow Run."

To motivate workers, the Willow Run plant newspaper printed accounts from pilots who flew the planes that the factory built. One was called *Yellow Easy* by its crew. "We never coddled that plane," said one of the captains, Richard A. Potter of Toledo. "Other planes would be housed up for the subzero nights with heaters blowing through their engines. But not *Yellow Easy.*" The crew flew the long-range plane out of a base in Italy. "We hit Weiner Neustadt on our third mission," Potter said of a German target. "*Yellow Easy* had one prop sheared completely off—another engine holed by flak, and she struggled home slashed to pieces. Two days later she was ready again and doing her stuff over a target in south France." *Yellow Easy* crashed on its seventieth mission, over Vienna. With the engines on fire and one wing torn in half, it glided gently down, giving all ten men on board time to parachute safely to the ground.[49]

George Sunal, the engineer credited with creating the upper instrument panel in the B-24, recalled the horror of cleaning out cockpits of Liberators that had seen action. "Many were full of bullet holes," he said. "Sometimes we found blood inside, where crew members had been wounded or perhaps killed during combat. It was heartbreaking. And I thought I was doing a lot. You felt you were a part of each plane made. You were at the plant so much, you practically lived there."[50]

A Curtiss-Wright representative who toured Willow Run at the time of the D-Day invasion wrote, "The Ford Willow Run Bomber Plant, flight operations area, with a shop personnel of approximately 420 employees divided into two nine-hour shifts, is delivering to the Army, at present, an average of 13.4 Liberator bombers daily. In light of our own experience this is an impressive record."[51]

Some of the returning Liberators spoke more clearly of victory. Pilots frequently had mascots hand-painted on the fuselage. Cartoon characters and sexy women were favorites. But what cheered the workforce most were the tallies etched near the wings, signifying the number of successful bombing missions completed by a B-24.

The Army Air Force (AAF) launched a propaganda campaign designating the B-24 Liberators the greatest flying machines ever made. They could fly 3,000 miles without refueling, cruised at over 300 miles per hour, and held up to four tons of bombs. What they didn't say was steering the aircraft was brutal on pilots. However heroic the exploits of a plane like the *Yellow Easy*, it was the pilots who made them great. Aside from the dangers inherent to combat, pilots faced a struggle just to fly and land them safely. Warplanes are not designed with the pilot's ease in mind, and the B-24 was no exception. There were no windshield wipers so pilots were forced to stick their heads out the window in bad weather. There was no aisle or bathroom, and few safety features. Pressurization was a real problem, and pilots and crew often had trouble breathing. Chronic dizziness and nausea ensued. Oxygen masks were usually necessary. "Absolutely nothing was done to make it comfortable for the pilot, the co-pilot or the other eight men in the crew, even though most flights lasted for eight hours, sometimes ten or more, seldom less than six," Stephen Ambrose recalled in *Wild Blue: The Men and Boys Who Flew the B-24s over Germany.* "The plane existed and was flown for one purpose only, to carry 500 to 1,000 pound bombs and drop them accurately over enemy targets."[52]

The AAF worked hard to keep the home front informed about America's heroic B-24 airmen. It had novelist John Steinbeck on staff, logging stories of gallantry in the skies over Europe and Asia. He described the new breed of pilot as part of America's tough frontier tradition, men bursting with individualistic pride, heartfelt patriotism, and democratic decency. These free-spirited pilots were, Steinbeck wrote, a combination of "Dan'l Boone and Henry Ford."[53] It was the finest compliment Ford received during the Second World War.

―――

Women constituted a large part of the wartime workforce, the most famous of them all being Willow Run's Rose Monroe, the celebrated "Rosie the Riveter." For a long time, confusion had surrounded the identity of the *real* Rosie, and for good reason. Originally, the U.S. government distributed a poster by J. Howard Miller entitled "We Can Do It!"; it showed a woman in denim overalls flexing her muscles, a bandanna on her head. There was no model for this poster—it was merely a composite symbol of women in the defense industry.[54] Later, illustrator Norman Rockwell painted his own "Rosie the Riveter," using as his model Mary Doyle Keefe of Nashua, New Hampshire—a part-time telephone operator who never riveted anything—for a *Saturday Evening Post* cover (the original artwork fetched an amazing $4.9 million at a Sotheby's auction in May 2002).[55] Meanwhile, the song "Rosie the Riveter," recorded by bandleader Kay Kyser, was inspired by a New Yorker named Rosalind B. Walter. The song was heard all over the world, a big-band-era tribute to women fighting for democracy.[56] Given all the publicity, an effort was undertaken to find a real worker to represent "Rosie" and help promote war bonds. They found her at Willow Run. Actor Walter Pidgeon, known for performances in such films as *Dark Command* and *How Green Was My Valley,* was touring the cavernous factory when he was introduced to an attractive riveter with curly brown hair, almond eyes, a midwestern demeanor, and assembly tools in her hand. "She was just perfect," Pidgeon recalled. "A real honest-to-God, hard-working lady whose name was Rosie." A native of Somerset, Kentucky, Rose

Monroe, a self-labeled tomboy, had had a hardscrabble life. In 1940 her husband was killed in an automobile accident. After Pearl Harbor she joined the home-front effort, accepting employment at Willow Run. With daughters Vicki and Connie in tow, she headed for Ypsilanti, Michigan, in a third-hand Model A, hoping for the best.[57]

Never allergic to hard work, Rose Monroe carried sheet metal, fitted parts, and used jackhammers, all of which made her arms terribly sore. But she never complained. What Rosie wanted most of all to do was to fly. Unfortunately, as a single mother, she was ineligible to join any military or civil aviation programs. (She did earn a pilot's license in the 1950s.) When Pidgeon stumbled upon her, she was doing her job with characteristic diligence. "Mom happened to be at the right place at the right time," her daughter Vicki recalled. All over America, in Pidgeon's famous promotional film, there was Rose Monroe for all to admire, building B-24 bombers that would help crush Hitler's army and Tojo's ships.[58]

In his *The Greatest Generation,* Tom Brokaw profiled another woman at Willow Run: Dorothy Haener. Raised in rural Michigan, Haener was hired by Ford Motor as a B-24 inspector after finishing high school. "A number of my men friends said it wasn't a place for women," Haener recalled. "They said I'd be too nice. I had to fight them." Dedicated to her job, and to the national goal of winning World War II on both fronts, she worked nine-hour days, every day except Sunday. While grateful for employment, Haener was dismayed to find that sexism permeated the factory. Wanting to improve workplace conditions for both women and men, she joined the UAW, becoming what Brokaw called an "eager acolyte" of Walter Reuther. "By the time the war ended," Haener noted, "I was too independent to get married." Instead, she dedicated her life to civil rights and labor causes, befriending Betty Friedan, author of *The Feminine Mystique,* and becoming a founding member of the National Organization for Women.[59]

The most unexpected employees found building B-24s at Willow Run were the "little people," twelve midgets hired because they could crawl into the tight spaces of B-24s under construction. They actually riveted inside wings and inspected rudders. One of the little people, Robert Hardy, even befriended Henry Ford. A native of Wyandotte, Michigan, Hardy had dropped out of high school and joined a New York musical troupe called Rose's Midgets. When World War II started, the twenty-three-year-old Hardy heard through the grapevine that Willow Run needed a dozen "small statured" assembly-line workers. Hardy traveled to Detroit in the only suit he owned and was hired on the spot. "Ford sent me to school," Hardy recalled, "and gave me a course in rivet theory." He joined UAW Local 50 and started inspecting planes. "Henry Ford would visit the line, come over and talk to me, and often would bring celebrities with him," Hardy recalled. "Once, he introduced me to Irving Berlin.

Another time, he brought two young boys and wanted me to show them around to all the work the little people were doing." He was also introduced to Charles Lindbergh, Eddie Rickenbacker, and Henry Wallace.[60]

Besides women and little people, an influx of African Americans found employment in the Ford factories during World War II. The sudden proximity of increased numbers of blacks and whites at work, on public transportation, and in parks kindled bigotry into violence. In February 1943, a white mob attacked several black tenants at the Sojourner Truth housing project in a heavily Polish, north Detroit neighborhood. As tensions escalated afterward, nine whites were killed and thousands of people from both races were injured. Bands of vicious white youths roamed the streets, beating every African American they could catch, and soon the blacks reciprocated. Entire city blocks were destroyed while Mayor Edward Jefferies Jr. and Michigan Governor Harry Kelly were paralyzed by fear and indecision. Kelly even tried to stop federal troops from entering the city in hopes that his state forces could cool the situation. After a week of sporadic rioting, looting, and arson, however, the governor relented and allowed President Roosevelt to send two military police battalions into Detroit. By the time they arrived, however, the uprising had ended. More than 1,800 people had been arrested.[61]

As a constant theme throughout his life Henry Ford tried to help individual African Americans cope with the challenges of being black in America. Besides assisting Tuskegee Institute financially, he embraced a number of local African Americans as if they were family. He gave money to Detroit churches and sent gifts to those African Americans who had stayed loyal to him during the battle over unionization. He also hired runner Jesse Owens, who had won four gold medals at the 1936 Berlin Olympics, to work in the employment division at the Rouge, making sure African Americans were appointed to positions on a basis of equality.[62] After the Detroit riots, even when an issue of racial tension flared up at the Rouge or Willow Run, Ford instinctively took the side of the African Americans. And when white school groups visited Greenfield Village, he would tell them that Booker T. Washington and George Washington Carver were authentic American heroes. "The very uniqueness among American industrialists of Ford's policy towards blacks suggests that beyond self-interest and the importance of successful industrial management lay a genuine philanthropic impulse," August Meier and Elliott Rudwick wrote in *Black Detroit and the Rise of the U.A.W.* "Actually Ford had taken a personal interest in certain individual Negroes, placing them in responsible positions even before instituting the large scale recruitment of blacks late in the war."[63]

———

Of course, Willow Run wasn't the only Ford Motor factory producing matériel during World War II. Gliders were built in the timberland of Ford's installation at Iron Mountain on Michigan's Upper Peninsula. At the River Rouge plant in Dearborn, one of Ford Motor's most successful wartime projects was the quarter-ton 4x4 truck—the jeep. The American Bantam Company had designed the vehicle in 1940, in conjunction with the U.S. Army Quartermaster Corps. Although Ford passed on the initial invitation to bid on building jeeps in quantity, it soon recognized that the little battle car held terrific potential for use in the war and even afterward. Trying to make up for lost time, the company was accused of forcing its way into a contract. "Certain officials of the Defense Commission and the War Department have gone out of their way to favor Ford," wrote I. F. Stone in New York's crusading *PM* magazine.[64] The specter of a giant company shouldering aside the enterprising American Bantam Company ignited a Senate investigation by the oversight committee chaired by Missouri's Harry S. Truman—once a prospective Ford dealer. The findings were not conclusive, but the issue was hot, and so it was no surprise that Bill Knudsen of the OPM recommended that Willys-Overland receive the contract.[65] However, the Army Quartermaster Corps, concerned with receiving as many jeeps as needed, had much more faith in Ford Motor. Through its influence, Ford eventually shared the major portion of the jeep contract with Willys-Overland.

Jeeps, which could go anywhere and then go some more, were ubiquitous in World War II. Early in 1942, boxed jeeps from Dearborn waited on the docks in Rangoon, even as British and American soldiers searched for a way to race north to meet fast-moving Japanese troops. As soon as mechanics could assemble the jeeps, soldiers jumped in and drove north into Burma's jungles and rice paddies to intercept the enemy. That is considered the first time jeeps entered battle, though the Soviets had been using them, through the Lend-Lease program, since 1941.[66]

Soldiers on inspection in Casablanca in 1943 were delighted to see their commander in chief, President Roosevelt, arrive and pass their ranks in the front seat of a jeep. By the time Roosevelt visited Tehran later that year, he brought his own jeep, flying with it in stow. Everyone liked the World War II jeep, at least for short hops. When General and Madame Chiang Kai-shek visited Admiral Louis Mountbatten at his post in India, they wanted a ride in a jeep, and so the three of them went out for a drive. However, the jeep belonged to the men who used it in the roadless fields of battle. In *Tarawa: The Story of a Battle,* Robert Sherrod wrote, "Now, at three minutes past six, the first two American jeeps roll down the pier, towing 37-mm guns. 'If a sign of certain victory were needed,' I note, 'this is it. The jeeps have arrived.'"[67]

Pulled by the government and pushed by the Army, Ford Motor Company ultimately fulfilled its potential, producing war matériel in almost exact proportion to its position in the peacetime economy. In fact, Ford turned in an exemplary record and so did Willow Run, once it was finally on track. "Although some aircraft manufacturers questioned whether the same results could not have been accomplished in less time and at smaller cost," the authors of *The Army Airforces in World War II* concluded, "it seems clear that the Ford experiment was ultimately successful."[68] The greatest progress occurred in 1944, as Ford production finally responded to pragmatic bosses like Mead Bricker, who put it on schedule and kept it there. "Every major wartime production effort of the Ford Motor Company benefited from Mr. Bricker's great manufacturing knowledge and skill," Henry Ford II noted. "In particular the output of 2,000-hp aircraft engines and the unprecedented heavy bomber production at Willow Run were personal triumphs of leadership."[69] The availability of long-range B-24 bombers in large quantities certainly hastened the end of the war in Europe. During the war, Ford Motor produced 8,685 B-24 bombers, 57,851 airplane engines, 277,896 jeeps, 93,217 trucks, 26,954 tank engines, 2,718 tanks and tank destroyers, and so on, down a long list of heavy machinery.[70] Major General James M. Gavin also praised Ford Motor for building 4,291 of the finest motorless gliders ever manufactured in America.[71] Meanwhile, the Lincoln Motor plant contributed by manufacturing 24,929 nacelles (housings) for B-24 bombers.[72]

The production output of the United States has often been credited with turning the tide for the Allies. But when the job was done, production abruptly ended. On April 17, 1945, the AAF and the War Production Board issued a notice of termination. "To the Employees of the Ford Willow Run Plant," it began. "Changing war needs and the rapid collapse of the German Luftwaffe have reduced requirements by the Army Air Forces. Consequently, production will be scaled down progressively and will cease not later than August, 1945."[73]

Hundreds of B-24s were brought back to Willow Run from Europe and disassembled, with the U.S. government stripping them of machine guns, bombs, and photographic equipment. "Oil was run through the engines and gas lines to prevent rusting," historian Timothy J. O'Callaghan wrote in *The Aviation Legacy of Henry and Edsel Ford*. "Hydraulic and brake systems as well as all other moving parts were checked, repaired and coated with suitable preservatives." Although B-24s were among the most recognizable icons of World War II, they quickly became antiquated. Ford Motor Company, for example, shipped almost 500 B-24s for storage in a government facility in New Mexico, where they were eventually destroyed or sold for parts. The frenetic days of Willow Run were over.[74] (Shipbuilder Henry J. Kaiser leased the bomber plant from the U.S. government after the war for $1 million a year in hopes of creating an automobile empire.)[75]

World War II ended in August 1945 with atomic attacks on Hiroshima and Nagasaki. Detroiters congregated along Woodward and Michigan Avenues to celebrate the Japanese surrender with parades and victory rallies. Most industrial companies were eager to return to business in peacetime. Ford Motor Company, however, stood on the edge of oblivion. It couldn't go back to prewar business, like the others; that world was gone with Edsel Ford and Charles Sorensen. It couldn't move forward, either, until someone took over from Henry Ford. It would be either Henry II or Harry Bennett. For Ford Motor Company, the war couldn't end until one last battle was fought.

PART FOUR

The Modern Corporation

24

Peaceful Revolution

Henry Ford II was three years old in 1920, when he had the honor of turning the switch that lit the huge furnace in the first building completed at River Rouge. Propped up in his grandfather's arm, the photograph of the occasion speaks volumes about corporate ascendancy in the Ford family. Although young Henry was given the run of the Ford plants, he rarely took advantage of the opportunity. He just didn't gravitate to the factories the way his grandfather did, making daily rounds like a farmer surveying his barns. Nor did young Henry follow in the footsteps of his father, Edsel, who designed custom cars as a teenager and then had them built by Ford mechanics. Long before the day that little Henry II pulled that lever at the Rouge, it was assumed that he would one day take charge of the Ford Motor Company, yet his elders never pushed him to become an "automobile man." He didn't absorb the daily chatter about frictions and problems at Ford Motor, because his father rarely talked about work when he was home in Grosse Pointe Shores.

That all changed dramatically on a rainy day in September 1945, when Henry Ford II took charge as president of Ford Motor Company: he was twenty-eight years old and the largest organization he had ever managed up to that time was the rowing team at Yale University. Many observers, within the company and outside of it, presumed that he was dangerously underqualified. After all, he had never been properly indoctrinated in Ford Motor ways. Because he was a stranger to the company's glorious past, it was presumed he didn't know a chassis from a tire iron. Some workers regarded him only as a child of the soft-skinned rich. "A few years ago he was a quiet, pleasant, blue-eyed, apple-cheeked young student with a disposition to put off crossing bridges until he got to them," journalist Gilbert Burck wrote in the October 1, 1945, issue of *Life*. "He showed no pronounced aptitude and gave little indication that he had one hidden. The fact that he was in line for control of the world's largest privately owned industrial empire, worth somewhere between a billion or two billion dollars, did not seem to give him pause; after all, not only his able father but his grandfather were very much alive."[1]

That may have been true in 1942, but not in 1945. His father was dead and his grandfather unwell. Although no one who looked at Henry II's résumé would have selected him to take charge of an international automaking firm with 120,000 employees, he would prove to be his grandfather's equal as an industrialist, a leader peculiarly suited to his times and the needs of the company. The first Henry Ford created a company that modernized the world. The second led that company, at long last, into the modern era.

Edsel and Eleanor Ford always sheltered their children from the outside world, in part from a fear of kidnapping. The family guarded its privacy and led a quiet social life in and around Detroit. As grandparents, Henry and Clara Ford found it just as easy to separate their family life from the drama at the business. They enjoyed their grandchildren immeasurably, but as playmates, not apprentices. Henry II, Benson, Josephine, and Billy spent many weekends at Fair Lane, visiting their father's parents. Henry Ford took it upon himself to teach the children how to drive automobiles, bird-watch, and climb trees.[2] "We loved it," Henry II later recalled of his grandparents' Fair Lane estate. "We spent oodles of times out there and we had our own little farm, sixteenth of an acre, whatever it was, and we raised crops. All the farm equipment that we used was built down to child size."[3] At the age of about eight, Henry II made a game with Benson of playing on the runway of the Ford Airport, much to the horror of pilots trying to land. "We also were allowed the run of the whole damn company," Henry II said. "We could run railroads. We could get up in the engines and run them around the Rouge. . . . We used to go in the cashier's cage and dump the payroll on the floor and do all kinds of nutty things." As a boy, Henry II thought the world of his grandparents, particularly Clara Ford. "She was a great entertainer," he recalled. "She had a great wit. She was just fun to be with as well as he was." Meanwhile, every summer Edsel and Eleanor took their children to summer at Seal Harbor, Maine, while the winter holidays were usually spent in Hobe Sound, Florida.[4]

Secure in a life of love and attention, Henry II grew into a well-behaved boy, calm in demeanor and mild in his demands on others. Although he was respectful of his elders, he could be cocky with his friends and classmates. Perhaps most important, his younger siblings, and in particular the sweet-natured Benson, didn't compete with him, but let him take the lead naturally. William Ford, the youngest of the children, would be a star athlete, but Henry II was merely useful on a playing field, taking up football in high school, first at his father's alma mater, Detroit University School. In 1933, he moved away from home, attending Hotchkiss School at Lakeville, Connecticut. His grades were only mediocre, but he wasn't dumb. As the Hotchkiss yearbook put it in the caption under young Henry's picture: "You've got something there if you handle it right."[5] Many young heirs in Henry's position didn't handle very much right, but he was a sensible and very sensitive boy.

While Henry II was probably spoiled as a child, he was no dropout or black sheep when he grew older. Instead, he developed his own way of drifting very quietly through those things that he didn't like—such as Latin classes. He floated quietly through Yale the same way, causing no trouble and claiming no honors. After admitting openly that he hated the engineering major he started as a freshman, he switched to sociology. "I flunked in engineering," he re-called. "The other guys said sociology was a snap course, so I figured that was for me. I flunked it, too."[6] He liked, however, delving into the way people lived their lives—an interest that ran in Henry Ford's family, even more than engineering did. Years later, Henry II's Yale classmates remembered him as a handsome, husky young man who was, at six feet, noticeably taller than either his father or grandfather. He had the bright blue eyes that ran in the Ford family, a small mouth, and full lips, quick to break into a smile. There was about him, however, a faint touch of deviltry—but a likeable amount. "All these people," Henry II said later, speaking of self-proclaimed experts in gen-eral, "are determined to compare me to my grandfather. I am no more like my grandfather than the man in the moon. I am like my mother." According to his longtime friend and biographer Walter Hayes, what he meant by that was that he embodied an upper-class air of detachment, with an emphasis on "order, neatness, punctuality, consideration for servants, truthfulness."[7]

The truthfulness could slip. Just after the last crew race of his senior year, a professor at Yale discovered that young Henry had submitted a term paper written by someone else. Because he made no pretense of being a scholar, the cheating episode was not scandalous. Graduation was close, and he was not so much expelled as simply denied a diploma. Having already gained everything he needed out of Yale, he gathered his bodyguard and his yellow Lincoln-Zephyr and left New Haven without a degree.

That summer, he married Anne McDonnell, a New Yorker he'd been court-ing through his college years. He had met her on a transatlantic crossing of the French liner *Normandie* before his freshman year.[8] Their backgrounds were somewhat similar—Anne's grandfather was Thomas E. Murray, an in-ventor who left a fortune of $50 million, and her father was a financier—but Anne was a Roman Catholic. With only slight disapproval from his elders, Henry II took instruction from Fulton Sheen, the famous radio priest, and adopted the faith. The wedding was held in Southampton, New York, the so-cial event of the year—and Henry II's only notable accomplishment up to the age of twenty-three. The Fords were happy to help him celebrate a bright future, overlooking points that might have brought disapproval in other families—namely, that he'd botched his college graduation and was changing his religion. Edsel, by way of a present, transferred to Henry II 25,000 shares of Ford Motor Company stock, "in recognition of the fact that you are finishing your college career this month, and after being married will join the Ford Motor Company as your future business and also because of the fact that you are at the present time Director of the Company."[9] The new couple honeymooned in Hawaii, just as Henry's father and mother had.

By the time Henry II and Anne settled in Detroit, Benson Ford had also left his college studies at Princeton. The two brothers worked as mechanics at the family company. They expected no special favor on the job, although at night Henry II went home to a swank mansion in Grosse Pointe, unlike most of the other mechanics. He and Anne soon started a family, with two daughters, Charlotte and Anne. They later had a son, Edsel II.

In 1940–1941, Ford Motor was in the midst of the bitter struggle over unionization. New models, including the Continental, were in the showrooms, while the executive ranks were, as ever, roiling. Yet, the eventual heir to the presidency was down in a garage at the Rouge, greasing wheels and replacing motors. "He insisted on doing the dirtiest tasks," *Life* reported, "and resented being treated differently."[10] Henry II liked working in the dynamometer rooms, and experimental shops, where his mentor was veteran engineer Laurence Sheldrick. "He had a terrific appetite for knowledge," Sheldrick recalled, adding that he didn't "pull any punches about getting his hands dirty" or getting his "clothes all messed up."[11] It didn't occur to anyone to invite Henry to meetings or to include him in the process of running Ford Motor. "There was a minimum of parental direction in their choice as to where to start," noted A. J. Lepine, Edsel's secretary, about both boys.[12] In the first place, Ford managers had always risen from the ranks of the workingmen. If banks started top candidates as tellers, and department stores put executive trainees at work behind a cash register, Ford Motor likewise was consistent in its conviction that Henry II should start as a grease monkey.

On a personal level, no one in the family considered that there was any reason to burden the young man with business pressures. By any reckoning, there was plenty of time for him to learn. In 1940, it still appeared that Edsel Ford would reach his retirement age of seventy—in 1963. Under that scenario, Henry II had more than twenty years to prove his mettle and enjoy his youth, which was fortuitous since he didn't exhibit any driving ambition regarding the company. His grandfather may not have made the place conducive to him, any more than he made it to Edsel, but Henry II, in his laconic way, seemed perfectly content to have an easy job in a quiet corner of the River Rouge factory.

Nevertheless, in the spring of 1941, eight months before Pearl Harbor, Henry II suddenly joined the Navy as an ensign. The timing was peculiar, since his first daughter, Charlotte, was born within a month of his enlistment. However, the company's confrontation with the UAW was reaching its ugly climax that spring and Henry II might have entered the service in order to escape the tense atmosphere in Dearborn. Perhaps he was also cognizant of how his father had been ridiculed for avoiding service in World War I. He was first posted to the U.S. Naval Training School in Dearborn, and then assigned to the Great Lakes Naval Training Center near Chicago. He cheerfully accepted his first job as an administrative assistant. The Navy taught him what Ford Motor never had: how to work. "I learned to do what I was told to do when I was told to do it," he said later of his time spent at the Ninth Naval District.[13] As usual, Henry II was admired for his easygoing nature and his lack of pretension, if not for his innate naval abilities.

He was, however, Henry Ford II. That, alone, would make him a commodity of national importance in 1943.

When, after twenty-seven months in uniform, Henry II arrived at the Rouge complex in early August, most of the office workers were on vacation. "Everybody was away, so I picked myself half a desk in somebody's office," he said later. "I didn't even know what all the buildings were for."[14] He wandered around the Rouge on his own, talking to workers and learning the process of automaking. "I am green," he matter-of-factly said, "and I am looking for answers."[15]

Henry Ford took little or no interest in his grandson's presence at River Rouge. At first, he repeated the treatment he'd accorded Edsel: spying on Henry II and sending subordinates with unjustified criticism. The antagonism didn't last long, though. Ford had just turned eighty and was in uncertain health, trying to see the company through the wartime crisis. He was also starting to show distinct signs of senility. Young Henry, with no official title or responsibilities, was not worth his bother.

Charles Sorensen reported that the government was seriously concerned about the two Fords: one past his prime, the other untested. While Sorensen was relaxing in Florida after resigning in 1944, he received an urgent call from Washington. "C. E. Wilson of OPA [Office of Price Administration] wanted me to come back and take over Ford Motor Company for the government," Sorensen wrote in his memoir. "Charlie Wilson's call disturbed me. He said the President insisted upon Henry Ford's removal from the Ford Motor Company and all connection with the war production."[16] Sorensen told Charles Edward Wilson that interfering in the company management during the war effort would not improve anything, but only disrupt production. He may have been right. Ford's operations were too complicated to stop and then start over. In any event, Ford Motor did make the B-24 production program at Willow

Run a success, keeping to its around-the-clock schedules during the last twelve months of the war.

Once World War II was over, though, the Ford family recognized that the transition to peacetime had to be accompanied by a change in management. Just as a precipitous change would have been risky in the midst of the war program, delay immediately afterward would jeopardize the survival of the company.

By late 1945, Henry Ford was no longer well. Early that year, while vacationing in Ways, Georgia, he had suffered another stroke, which left his mind altered. According to Harry Bennett, he was in a "constantly confused state."[17] No one could help but notice that the Henry Ford of the old days was gone forever. "There was a great change in his physical appearance," said Charles Voorhess, who had worked with Ford for decades in the experimental lab. "He had baggy facial features, very pale and much thinner, although he had always been thin enough. . . . He had lost his contented nervous energy and drive."[18] It was as if he had finally resigned himself to his mortality. "He had deteriorated greatly," Voorhess continued, "insofar as discussing his interests or subjects were concerned, excepting some little thing that came along. There was never any more discussion about things. He did so little talking and expressed himself so seldom that it would be difficult to judge if his memory would revert to the earlier period of his life, as is common in older men, or if it stayed pretty much in the present."[19]

Those who spent the most time with Ford, his staff at Fair Lane, felt sorry for him, seeing him as the living embodiment of one of the historical relics he collected at Greenfield Village. "I daresay Mr. Ford showed signs of failing physically and mentally," recalled Rufus Wilson, Ford's full-time chauffeur. "He was forgetful and he knew it, because he remarked about it." Even in illness, Ford had his own perspective on the matter: "He always put it to me," said Wilson, "that he *wanted* to forget. He said, 'I put those things out of my mind so I won't have to worry about them.'"[20]

Henry Ford was suffering from senility. He had good days and bad ones, but by 1945, he could offer almost nothing to the company he had helped to build except signing autographs and presenting himself for photographs. The president in name only, he was utterly dependent upon the ability of Harry Bennett to interpret his intentions. For Bennett, the situation was practically ideal, since Ford would not trust anyone else, least of all Henry II. The situation could have gone on forever, except that Henry Ford himself would not.

With no specific accounting controls, Ford Motor Company was a rich field for pilferers, embezzlers, and other business leeches. All through his career, Henry Ford had preferred to receive reports on his company anecdotally, even through espionage, rather than in the numeric rationale of accounting. Bennett's intelligence-gathering network replaced internal accounting for

Henry Ford. It also allowed Bennett to control the inner workings of the Ford plum, the determination of who made money at Ford—and who made money off of Ford. "I don't have any idea how much he pilfered. I don't know how he did it," Henry II later said of Harry Bennett, "but I'm positive— although I don't have any proof—that he could not have lived the way he did on the salary he had. I'd have called his salary very, very low considering his position with the company. He had had cattle, and he had a house on top of a mountain out west. He stole the place blind either through the dealers or some other fashion. I don't know how the hell he did it, but he did it."[21]

Within the automobile industry, Ford Motor Company was at its weakest at the very juncture when it would need all of its former strength. Every automaker knew that a span of four years with no new vehicles had been agonizing for the car-crazy United States. "Pent-up demand" was the phrase over which automakers were licking their chops in mid-1945. Along with impatient customers, though, the postwar years promised brutal competition. Ford Motor had sagged throughout the 1930s without giving any indication of collapse. However, General Motors and Chrysler were already starting to count it out of the Big Three in the postwar era. They were primed and ready to take huge bites of market share and, if the onetime industry leader faltered, gulps of the Ford empire. Even before the war ended, Ford dealers were under siege from the rapacious Big Two.

Thus, from the perspective of the Ford family, the troubled company, or the outside automobile industry as a whole, time was up for the old-time Ford Motor Company in the summer of 1945. Like many a battered but game Model T, it had survived far beyond its own times. The one-man, one-rule style of management should have given way to the efforts of Edsel Ford and Ernest Kanzler to create a logical hierarchy in the 1920s. It should have been obsolete when the Model T was. Instead, the company banged its way through the 1930s under Henry Ford's unchanging concept of slick production and slack administration.

By World War II, Henry's old Ford Motor Company—the management style he had devised in 1919—was gasping. It persevered until the end of the national crisis. After that, there had to be a new Ford and a new person to drive it. If nothing were done, then Harry Bennett would continue in control, past the point at which a smooth transition could be made. Everyone in the company was afraid of him, both in person and as a mysterious source of an unlimited power to hire, fire, or destroy. At some point in late 1944 or early 1945, Henry Ford went so far as to sign a codicil to his will, stipulating that no one be named president for ten years after his death; during that time the board of directors, with Bennett acting as secretary, would run Ford Motor. Whether Henry II knew about the codicil or not, he was well aware that Bennett was maneuvering to usurp him at the company, just as he had Edsel

Ford. In a flash of anger, Henry II decided to quit, as John Bugas recalled, "and write a letter to every dealer in the country announcing his decision. He was going to tear the whole place to pieces."[22] Henry II soon changed his mind, though, in part because of his father's losing cause in the same battle. Anyone who underestimated the powers that lay within the new man failed to recognize the strength he derived from the memory of his father.

Working his way through various departments at the company during wartime, young Henry looked and listened, without trying to change anything at first. His brother Benson, released from Army duty in the Detroit area, was also gaining some exposure to the workings of the plant. Neither, however, had a position, a mentor, or even a desk. Whenever Henry II did settle into a department and start to make improvements, he found his progress mysteriously stymied: without quite explaining why, subordinates would simply stop cooperating.[23] It was the same treatment Edsel Ford had received and had learned over the course of twenty years to work around, as best he could. Of course, Henry II knew that the source of the countermanded orders was the strange, secretive alliance between his grandfather and Harry Bennett. Perhaps believing Henry II to be as callow as he looked, Bennett tried to form a friendship with his young rival. Both went through the motions of an amicable business relationship, posing for pictures and making respectful comments. But there was nothing but animosity beneath the surface. "I'd say we were excellent actors," Henry II later commented. "Harry Bennett is the dirtiest, lousiest, son-of-a-bitch I ever met in my life."

In 1944, Henry II decided to make a stand. He decided to hire a new sales manager. His choice was John R. Davis, a Ford employee since 1919 and a favorite of Edsel Ford. After a run-in with Bennett, he had been exiled to the West Coast. In typical fashion, Henry II visited Jack Davis personally and asked him to return to Dearborn as head of sales. Davis turned him down. He said, no doubt correctly, that if he bobbed up in Dearborn with a new responsibility, Bennett would more than likely terminate him. Finally, after two days of cajoling, Henry II secured the answer he wanted, but at a high price for added insurance. If Davis were let go, then Henry II promised that he would leave the company, too.

For Henry II, Jack Davis was more than a winning sales manager. Davis was someone he could trust. When young Henry first arrived at River Rouge in 1943, there was no one that he could count on. "You've got to remember," Davis recalled, "that when young Henry came in here the company was not only dying, it was already dead and *rigor mortis* was setting in."[24] Exhibiting even the most common kind of loyalty to the new executive would force an employee to risk his or her own future. Very quietly, Henry II began to gather together a shortlist of men he could confide in, and count on, to share his general view of the future of the company. Davis was one. Mead Bricker became another member of Henry II's circle. The third and most remarkable was John S. Bugas, lawyer and former FBI agent who had been hired as Bennett's right-hand man.

Bugas and Bennett were mismatched from the start. Originally from the wilds of Wyoming, Bugas had been trained throughout his career to replace the chaos of the criminal world with the order of the lawful one. Bennett, on the other hand, reveled in his ability to occupy the murky middle ground between the two. Bugas was uncomfortable with Bennett, whom he saw as a power-mad bully, so he discreetly formed a bond with Henry II; the two would be lifelong friends. But when Bennett realized that Bugas was in the enemy camp, he had his desk moved into the bathroom. That was all in the business day at Ford Motor in 1944.

———

The story that has long circulated is that Clara Ford and Edsel's widow, Eleanor, orchestrated the quiet revolution of September 1945. Henry II later denied it, but the story has some truth, whether actual or apocryphal. Between them, the two women controlled nearly one third of the voting stock of Ford Motor Company.[25] According to the legend, Eleanor and Clara threatened to sell their Ford holdings on Wall Street unless Henry II was named president.

In particular, Eleanor resented Henry Ford and despised Harry Bennett for brutalizing Edsel. If nothing else, every member of Edsel's family felt that the long-term future of Ford Motor should be a nod to the kind of place he would have made it. In the same vein, the short-term shift at the company would serve to bring retribution to those who had turned Edsel Ford into a stranger in his own ranks.

Henry II had his own version of the transition, however. "Davis, Bugas, Bricker and I hatched the whole deal to take over the company," he told interviewer David Lewis in the early 1980s. "We hatched it over at the Detroit Club in one of the private dining rooms. They kept bugging me and saying that the whole place was going down the drain." With the plan in mind, Henry II paid a visit to his ailing grandfather: "I said, 'I think it's about time we did something to clean this place up.' My grandmother was there, and to make the story short, she said, 'Henry, I think young Henry should take over.'"

Henry II continued, "I don't remember whether he said 'yes' or 'no' at that point. The second time I went, she finally said [to the elder Henry], 'Look, you're not well . . . and it's about time somebody got in there.' I couldn't blame Harry Bennett as the main cause of the trouble to my grandfather, because I'd have been hitting too close to home. But I said, 'There are things going on that shouldn't be going on, and I think we've really got to stand up and do some things. I think that I've got to do some things, and I just can't get to you often enough to discuss all the details with you.' I could have gotten to him physically, but I couldn't get to him mentally. The time came, and my grandmother and grandfather were sitting in the house and [Henry the elder] said, 'OK, Henry. You take over. You call the board meeting and I'll write my letter of resignation.' "[26] (Actually, it was his secretary Frank Campsall who wrote it out.)

Under either scenario, Henry II assumed the presidency with something priceless for a man in his position: the complete support of the Ford family—his grandmother, his mother, and his brothers and sister. None of them suggested any course except that Henry II take over and run the company as he saw fit. None second-guessed his ability or piped up with suggestions of others who might be more qualified. Whether the senior women did threaten to sell their shares or not, they would have done that or anything else necessary to give Henry II his own era in the history of the family company. With the family's utter confidence behind him, the younger Henry soon began to look and act like the new president, the real president of Ford Motor.

On the morning of September 21, 1945, the board of directors of the Ford Motor Company met at River Rouge. The directors were Henry, Henry II, and Benson Ford, along with Ford senior executives Harry Bennett, Mead Bricker, B. J. Craig, Ray Rausch, and Frank Campsall. Benson did not attend, because he'd made a vow never to be in the same room with Harry Bennett. Frank Campsall read Henry Ford's letter of resignation. The atmosphere was tense: a showdown that had to remain polite and bend to the rules of order. Some of those present could barely stand it. Ford's letter read, in part, "I feel free to take this step at this time because the crisis period during which I again assumed office has passed."[27]

Before Frank Campsall was even finished reading it, Harry Bennett started to walk out of the room. He knew it was the end for him, too. The others persuaded him to remain until the conclusion of the meeting. Just as Ford's letter suggested, the board named Henry II as his replacement. "After the meeting the other directors went home," Harry Bennett recalled. "I told Henry [II] I wanted to talk with him, and we went into his office. As anyone might have, I felt bitter. I told Henry, 'You're taking over a billion-dollar organization here that you haven't contributed a thing to.' Then I tempered this a little, adding, 'I've tried awfully to like you, and had hoped to part friends.' Henry said the same thing and added, 'I don't know what I'd have done without you. You know you don't have to leave—you can stay here the rest of your life.' But my mind was made up. I had always said that when Mr. Ford left I would go, and I meant it now as I had meant it before."[28]

Henry II's recollection of their private meeting was entirely different, except for the outcome. "I immediately walked out," he recalled, "took Bennett in my office, and fired him. I was frightened to death it would not stick. . . . I was physically scared and mentally scared. Once I was president, he knew it was going to come. There wasn't any way he could avoid it. So I think he just made up his mind that temporarily he'd go along, and then maybe something would change."[29]

Harry Bennett said that he could barely contain his step to a walk on his way out of Ford Motor that last day. "I wanted to get out so fast," he said. "I felt like a man being let out of prison."[30] He had made Ford Motor a prison for so many others, it follows that he was, ultimately, the unhappiest inmate of all.

A lot of things changed during Henry II's first month as president of Ford Motor. More than a dozen of Bennett's close associates were summarily fired along with the "little giant." A thousand more followed: people who did not work for Ford Motor, but for Harry Bennett at Ford Motor. Also fired by Henry II was a holdover from another era: William J. Cameron, the ghost-writer who had put Henry Ford's opinions, including the anti-Semitic ones, on paper. Henry II issued the clear order that everyone at the company was responsible "directly to me," as he put it.[31] Henry II handled each and every dismissal personally. He also found a private hideaway that Ray Rausch had created for his own use, to entertain company and drink.[32] Ford broke down the door with an iron club and then destroyed the lair. Rausch's days at the company were already numbered.

Some of those who were fired in Henry II's purge waited smugly for the elder Henry to restore Harry Bennett and the old balance of power. It was not to be. Henry Ford took little interest in the company after his retirement. With the Bennett regime vanquished, the elder Henry withdrawn, and the worst war in history finally over, Henry II was taking control of the Ford Motor Company in the autumn of 1945.

———

Once the confetti of V-J Day celebrations was swept away and the veterans came home looking for employment, that autumn was a time for pulse taking and inventorying, and Henry II and his chief executives at Ford Motor did just that. The company was worth $1.021 billion.[33] Moreover, it employed 130,000 people in the United States alone. More than half, 75,000 in all, worked at the River Rouge plant in Dearborn. Another 26,000 worked at Ford's thirteen assembly plants: Richmond and Long Beach, California; Dallas; Kansas City, Missouri; Minneapolis; Chicago; Memphis; Louisville; Buffalo; Chester, Pennsylvania; Norfolk, Virginia; Edgewater, New Jersey; and Somerville, Massachusetts.[34] The balance worked at Highland Park and in district offices across the country. When Willow Run closed down at the end of 1945, it reverted to government ownership. Ford cleared out and the four-year adventure there was over.

All of the established automobile companies were flush with cash as the war ended. Ford Motor was among them, with $685 million in the bank and no debt. Ford Motor Company of Canada was healthy, too, with its own subsidiaries operating smoothly in South Africa and New Zealand. Worldwide, Ford Motor maintained its own assembly plants in South America and Central America, but the challenge lay in reestablishing peacetime affiliations with European Ford companies. Ford-Werke had been under Nazi control throughout the war, but upon the liberation of Cologne in March 1945, the German company was administered by military custodians. U.S. commanders immediately authorized the production of trucks, the first one being completed, symbolically, on May 8—V-E Day.[35] Ford of England also sprang back to automobile production, turning out a passenger car on May 25.[36]

Domestically, Ford Motor turned out its first civilian vehicle on July 3, 1945, making it the first of the U.S. companies to put a '46 on the market. The publicity of manufacturing the first postwar automobile was worth millions, but as a design, the new car wasn't much of an achievement—it was nothing more than a '42 Ford, with wooden bumpers, no less, and a plastic rear window, due to lingering shortages of basic materials. Still, the '46 Ford allowed Henry II to launch an effective public relations campaign, boasting that this historic Dearborn company was always "first." Henry II knew that the new model would find customers—anything with four wheels and an engine would be a sellout in the immediate postwar years. However, he recognized that its real purpose was to buy some time, so that the company could originate a truly *new* new car. On many fronts, Henry II had to find ways to keep the company going the next three or four years. The coffers might be full, but the clock was still running down on the future.

As the war ended, nine companies were in the business of making passenger automobiles in the United States: General Motors would account for 38 percent of industry sales in 1946; Chrysler, 26 percent; and Ford, 23 percent.[37] None of the six "independents" made more than 5 percent; Packard, Nash, Hudson, and Studebaker were the established marques, while Crosley and Kaiser-Frazer were newcomers. Crosley entered the market with a bantam car. Kaiser-Frazer was organized by Henry J. Kaiser, who had become nationally famous producing Liberty ships in record times during the war. Kaiser-Frazer was well capitalized, easily raising $50 million through a stock offering—although much more than that would be needed, as it turned out.

All nine of the U.S. carmakers would prosper in 1946–1948, but they each knew that the flood of customers would eventually ebb. The bounty would vanish quickest for the companies with the weakest sales organizations. During the war years, when virtually all car-manufacturing facilities were converted to the production of defense matériel, some car dealerships folded. Others focused on the used-car business and parts and service. Some dealerships converted their shop areas into small manufacturing facilities for war goods. Others simply sold used cars of all sorts, perhaps with an adjacent feed store in rural areas or a grocery store in urban areas.[38] Despite the moratorium on new-car sales, only 10 percent of Ford's dealers had gone out of business during the war.[39] Young Henry's first public speech, in fact, had been in January 1944 before the National Automobile Dealers Association. In that speech he promised that a new, more progressive era between Ford dealers and the parent company was on the way. When he became president of Ford Motor, with World War II over, he would have the opportunity to make good on his word.[40]

In 1945 and 1946, Henry Ford II traveled extensively, visiting dealerships from coast to coast. He wanted to meet dealers personally and wander around their showrooms to hear their concerns. The timing was essential to Ford Motor's survival. He knew that the strong automakers, especially GM and Chrysler, intended to hobble weaker ones by snagging their best dealerships. Ford Motor was especially vulnerable, since the old regime had strained relations with dealers before the war. On his tours, Henry II was certainly personable enough to be welcomed (his grandfather might not have been), but more important, he was so committed to the future that he inspired at least a few years' worth of loyalty from the company's vital dealerships. Henry II was able to reassure dealers from New York to Los Angeles that a new, better Ford would be on the market by 1949. His first success as president was in making sure his Ford dealership network stayed optimistic about the future.[41]

The second-most pressing matter for Henry II was the hardest to ignore. During the war, wildcat strikes—more than seven hundred of them at Ford alone—had crippled production, and labor problems still loomed over the whole industry. Workers were demanding higher wages and better conditions. They complained of the dehumanizing atmosphere at the Rouge and other plants. Henry Miller, the notorious author of *Tropic of Cancer*, captured the prevailing depression found on assembly lines in his 1945 travelogue *The Air-Conditioned Nightmare*. "You wouldn't suspect there was such a thing as a soul if you went to Detroit," Miller wrote. "Everything is too new, too slick, too bright, too ruthless. Souls don't grow in factories. Souls are killed in factories—even the niggardly ones. Detroit can do in a week for the white man what the South couldn't do in a hundred years to the Negro."[42] Miller's bleak blue-collar vision was not far from the truth of postwar Detroit. An executive at GM approached Henry II, smoothly assuming that the new man would join him in a "united front" against wage increases. "You settle your own troubles," Henry II replied gruffly, "I'll take care of mine."[43]

Henry II surprised many people by supporting collective bargaining and proving himself willing to cooperate with unions, though not to capitulate to them. Quite suddenly, he was a leader in the industry in more than just name, showing that a great attribute lay beneath his charms: utter candor. Henry II needed no guile or subterfuge, the machinations of weaker diplomats. He said what he thought simply and quickly, challenging (or affronting) both unions and management in postwar labor disputes.

To act as management's conduit to labor, Henry II appointed John Bugas as the director of industrial relations. Mead Bricker was the head of production. Davis continued to run sales.[44]

Other changes instituted by Henry II took years to develop and implement, although one was immediate. "The first move which I recall," said Logan Miller, "was a policy set up by Mr. Henry Ford II to destroy the fear in men that was borne through a period of years. One thing that he spoke of and was quite concerned about was that he expected every man who was in charge of a group of people to treat them as they would want to be treated themselves. That was pretty hard to understand for some. Some of our supervisors didn't understand that language. . . . The way they could throw their arms, the language used, and belittling people were measurements of accomplishment and success with the old organization."[45] The new atmosphere blew through Ford Motor with Henry II's own personality, based around the humility he exuded and the teamwork on which he depended. "How to treat people is something that is in this new Ford organization," said Harold Hicks, who was, like Miller, a Ford veteran of more than twenty-five years. "They really lean over backwards, perhaps even too far, to make people feel at home and loyal."[46]

Employees, from the top to the bottom, couldn't help responding to the new atmosphere, in which questions were invited and honest answers respected. Outsiders were also amazed at how quickly Ford Motor changed in late 1945. Every reporter had a horror story about trying to pry a story out of Ford in the old days. "Trying to find out what goes on in Ford is like trying to find out what goes on in Russia" was the grouse of one wartime writer.[47] Once a place of secrets and slammed doors, Ford Motor suddenly welcomed reporters, as executives and others were instructed to answer questions as truthfully as possible. The fact that even top executives often didn't have the answers to basic business questions was among the next items that Henry II would address, but his first stroke of true leadership was to brighten the present and thus the future at the Ford Motor Company. "When Mr. Henry Ford II came into the picture, why, we felt our prayers over a number of years had been answered," said Tony Harff, who started with the company before World War I. "We actually prayed, I think, for something like this to happen."[48]

Morale on the assembly lines and in corporate headquarters skyrocketed. "Many employees who were considering leaving the company, including myself, were impressed with the change in employee relations and decided to stay," wrote historian Ford R. Bryan, then an office worker at River Rouge, in an unpublished memoir. "A renaissance was in the making. The old, hard management tactics were being suppressed. . . . Most old-line supervisors had never practiced this relationship, and all were therefore sent to 'charm school'—instruction lessons in how to deal with employees diplomatically."[49]

"He has his grandfather's desire for action. He has his mother's understanding of people," said a friend of Henry II. "He has his father's humanness."[50] Henry II particularly abhorred lies from any employee and, similarly, was careful not to make promises that he couldn't keep. Prompt for any scheduled meeting, he was attentive to the business graces of sending notes of his own composition, often in his own handwriting, for condolences, grievances, or other matters of individual importance for those within the company. Each evening, he drove home in a Ford, Lincoln, or Mercury car taken at random off the line and would complain loudly about defects the next morning.

Hearing of the revolution at Ford Motor, a cadre of U.S. Army Air Force officers with saber-toothed ambitions applied to the company as a group in late 1945. Led by Colonel Charles B. "Tex" Thornton, an aide to Assistant Secretary of War for Air Robert Lovett, the officers had been trained in statistical control and planning as part of a program administered by the Harvard Business School. "Thornton was someone that Lovett immediately liked," journalist David Halberstam wrote in *The Best and the Brightest.* "He came from a small Texas town, was ambitious, bright and pleasantly extroverted; he quickly became one of Lovett's top deputies."[51] Thornton envisioned that the group within the program would stay together to apply in a business setting the methods that had tracked millions of wartime details for the Army Air Corps, the precursor to the Air Force. While Thornton approached nearly a hundred corporations with his unique package deal, he was immediately attracted to the gaping needs at Ford Motor. He carefully composed a telegram and sent it to Henry Ford II personally on October 19, 1945:

> I would like to see you regarding a subject which I believe would be of immediate interest. This concerns a system which has been developed and applied successfully in the management of the Army Air Forces for the past three years. Reference, if desired, Robert A. Lovett, assistant secretary of war for air. Colonel Chas. Thornton.

A day later, Thornton had a reply by telephone. "Could you come to Dearborn?" asked a Ford representative. "Mr. Ford is very much interested."[52] Within weeks, the whole group was hired. It consisted of ten highly educated veterans, ranging in age from twenty-six to thirty-four: Tex Thornton, Robert S. McNamara, Arjay Miller, J. Edward Lundy, Charles Bosworth, Jack Reith, James O. Wright, Ben Davis Mills, Wilbur Andreson, and George Moore. For his part, Henry II was pleased to acquire, in one bold move, a cadre of young executives versed in anything pertinent to control or planning. Seven of the ten, known ever after as the "Whiz Kids," remained in the upper ranks at Ford; two, Robert McNamara and Arjay Miller, eventually rose to the presidency. Initially, the group stayed together, reporting directly to Henry II and making themselves very useful with recommendations for immediate and long-term systems.

"Our work here continues to be hectic, but stimulating," wrote McNamara to a friend early on. "In many ways it reminds me of those early days in the Air Force when there was no information on which to base decisions, no organization pattern and when it seemed as if everyone was running round like chickens with their heads cut off. Ford must be rebuilt from the ground-up. The extent of decay which existed throughout the organization defies description. Channels of communication are poor, controls are lacking, organization is non-existent, planning is unheard of, and the personnel problem is serious beyond belief."[53]

The need was so great that Tex Thornton gave in to the temptation to believe that he was the best one to save Ford Motor. His ambition took over his judgment and he was dismissed after only two years, an outsize ego in a company desperately trying to inculcate teamwork. (Thornton went on to make a conspicuous success for himself as head of Litton Industries.) However intriguing the advent of the actual Whiz Kids, Henry II never viewed them as his top tier of management. They represented only a small percentage of thousands of similarly well educated whizzes who were actively recruited between 1945 and 1955. "The Whiz Kids were really shorthand for saying that Ford Motor was committed to achieving better efficiency," Philip Caldwell recalled. "It was the company's way of saying they had vision."[54] But in hiring the Whiz Kids, Henry demonstrated his inbred capacity for bold leadership. "It was an extraordinary decision for young Ford to make; however, at that bleak moment in his company's history he had nowhere to go but up," Halberstam wrote. "He was reaching beyond the normally closed auto business for a group of non-auto men, whose experience was not in the failure and stupidity of war, but rather in the technology of it, and indeed the technological success of war."[55]

Henry II openly admitted to an obsession with General Motors. When asked to explain his goals for Ford Motor, he would answer in two words, and a grin: "Beat Chevrolet." His desk was generally neat and clear of extraneous papers, but for many years he kept a copy of the GM management chart in a corner where he could see it at a glance. Behind the scenes, Henry II commissioned studies of GM and probably knew more about his rival than did its chairman, Alfred Sloan, or president, Charles Erwin Wilson. Over the years, the two companies had developed in a kind of tandem. When GM underwent its transformation in the early 1920s, it gladly snapped up Ford alumni, including William Knudsen and Norval Hawkins. Others had followed. For the first time, Ford Motor was going to start reversing the flow.

Closely advised by his uncle, Ernest Kanzler, Henry II recruited Ernest Breech to give Ford Motor a sense of organization—something it hadn't had since 1916, when James Couzens got tired of fighting with Henry Ford. Breech was a small, athletic man, with thick black hair and a pencil-thin mustache. In appearance he reminded people of Walt Disney. Born in 1897, he was old enough to be the new chief's father—his older son was one year older than Henry II. Moreover, in background, he shared almost nothing with Henry II.

Breech was raised in Lebanon, Missouri, an isolated Ozark town, where his father was a blacksmith. His mother, educated only through the sixth grade, continually encouraged learning in her four children. After excelling in academics, as well as team sports in high school, Ernie Breech worked his way through two years at Drury College in Springfield, Missouri. One summer, he sold books door-to-door in Missouri villages. With his outgoing personality and self-confidence, he was a success, making more in a day than he made in a week at other jobs. However, he soon quit. With a conscience to match his intellect, it pained him to make sales to people who could ill afford to pay. "Taking this money was like taking candy from a baby," he told his biographer, J. Mel Hickerson, in 1968. "I sold books to one woman who did washing to support her son. Such things preyed on my mind. I did not need money that badly."[56]

Breech left Drury College after his sophomore year in 1917 with the intention of joining the armed services. He never was called up, however. Having gotten married (in anticipation of an enlistment), he left college behind and embarked on a business career in Chicago, taking bookkeeping courses at night. Studying on his own, Breech passed the Illinois state examination for certified public accountants with the highest score registered in 1921. After a series of jobs, he rose to become controller at the Yellow Cab Corporation. By the time it was absorbed by General Motors, Ernie Breech already knew all about GM's accounting procedures; he had copied them in the system he installed at Yellow Cab. For Breech, the merger was a fortuitous career opportunity: his work, which was integral to the deal, was noticed by the top men at GM. Soon, he was installed in the GM corporate offices in New York, working side by side with Donaldson Brown, chairman of the corporation's finance committee; Albert Bradley, vice president for finance; and president Alfred Sloan. Breech would soon regard all of them as personal friends. In 1933, he took control of North American Aviation, a GM division that encompassed three flagging airlines (including TWA), and succeeded in reorganizing it. Four years later, he took the helm at Bendix Aviation, another troubled subsidiary, which made parts for automobiles and airplanes. He did a masterly job, increasing profits from $435,696 in 1938 to $10.6 million in 1940 and $55 million in the last year of the war. He did it in the GM style: installing a workable business organization and then filling it with the right managers.[57]

Inside the automobile industry and outside of it, many observers were aware that Ernie Breech was a superb executive, as precise about numbers as he was intuitive about people. However much talk there was that he was headed for the presidency at GM, Breech felt that he may have missed his chance in 1940, when Charles Wilson was named to replace Bill Knudsen. Wilson was still in place in 1945, when Breech was in his eighth year at Bendix. One of the Bendix board members was Ernest Kanzler, who talked to his nephew, Henry II, about the way that Breech had successfully applied GM organization principles to North American and Bendix.[58] Because Henry II wanted an executive to turn just that same trick at his company, he pursued Breech closely. Breech took the Ford job because, as he said, "I like a good scrap." With a man of the caliber of Breech on board, the challenge of rebuilding Ford Motor instantly turned from dismal to enticing—and definitely quite possible—in the minds of other potential recruits. For almost fifteen years, Henry Ford II and Ernest Breech would work together so harmoniously in the revival of Ford Motor that colleagues gave them nicknames: "the Siamese Twins" and "Nonesuch." After only one year in office, Henry II had already succeeded in turning around Ford Motor, if the crucial aspect of any "reengineering" is putting the right people in place and giving them an atmosphere conducive to success.

But the outlook for the company remained grave. Breech gave his assessment of the place after his first three months in Dearborn. "Our problems seemed almost insuperable," he said. "Things were in a mess. . . . It was August of 1946 and Ford was not ready for the postwar fight. Chrysler and General Motors were ready, we assumed. Studebaker was at the starting line, we knew. But Ford, the proud founder and onetime leader of the industry, was not even ready to get ready."[59]

Some tangible evidence of change was coming into view. New assembly plants at Atlanta and St. Louis were under construction. Highland Park was dedicated to truck, bus, and tractor production. Lincoln and Mercury were combined into a single division, headquartered in Dearborn, and placed under the watch of Benson Ford. The sales department was reorganized around the seven thousand Ford and Lincoln-Mercury dealers. But there was a steep mountain of change to be made beyond that. Ford Motor had to become a new company; fundamentally different from anything it had ever been before. Few people believed it was possible. The closer Breech drew to the situation, the more he thought about the rumor that the Big Three was on the verge of becoming the Surviving Two. He didn't give up, however, and neither did Henry II.

"I was stupid enough to know that [the company] was going to get turned around," said Henry II more than three decades later. "I never questioned that. There was never, never, never a thought in my mind that it wouldn't be turned around."

He continued, "I didn't know how long it would take, but I never questioned that it could be done. And luck was on our side, and God was on our side, and the economy was on our side, and everything else."[60]

25

Death in Dearborn

During the last few years of his life, Henry Ford, cane in hand, went on a drive almost every day with Robert Rankin, one of his ace chauffeurs and a loyal companion. In deference to the boss's innate aversion to traffic signals, Rankin learned routes that avoided them and refined techniques that kept the car moving, at all cost. He was such a skilled driver that he could motor from Dearborn to Grosse Pointe Shores, some twenty miles, without having to stop for a red light.[1] Rankin came to know Henry Ford well. "He never reminisced very much about the early days of the Ford Motor Company," Rankin observed. "Reminisced more about his childhood. In fact, it seemed to me he took the Ford Motor Company in his stride; something that *had* to happen."[2]

The years after World War II were depressing times for the legendary automaker; all of his closest companions—Harvey Firestone, George Washington Carver, and Thomas Edison—were gone. Edsel was gone, too. Henry Ford II once attributed his grandfather's sudden disinterest in the company to failing health and a general malaise about the brutish world of the Atomic Era. "He'd go for a drive every day, and he could walk reasonably well," Henry II recalled. "But he failed in his last three years . . . he gave up."[3] Ford may have given up on most aspects of the outside world, but in his last years, he never tired of looking at the fallow fields of Dearborn, and the landmarks of his younger days. "Mr. Ford was very nostalgic about the old days around here," recalled Clara Snow, a longtime Dearborn resident and friend of the family. "He was always glad and willing to talk to anybody whom he had known back years ago. He was always interested in what had happened in the old days and things that had connection with it. I don't think it was from his own personal angle as from the angle of bringing down to the present generation what the forefathers had had and how they lived and things of that kind which you see in the village and the museum."[4]

More than anybody else, it was Rankin who heard Ford's stories about the virtues of the preindustrial era. "He always knew when we passed the corner of Greenfield and Grand River," Rankin said. "He'd say, 'That's where Mrs. Ford was born.'" One Saturday afternoon, Ford asked to be driven to the square farmhouse that he and Clara had built as newlyweds. He just looked around for a long while. "I've got a lot of money," Ford said, "and I'd give *every* penny of it right now just to be here with Mrs. Ford the same as I was in the old days."[5]

Boredom had never suited Ford. "The unhappiest man on earth," he once told a *Detroit Free Press* reporter, "is the one who has nothing to do."[6] Ford often stopped at the River Rouge complex, but he almost never visited the administration building on Schaefer Road. He did enjoy, however, watching toolmakers and die makers at work. He particularly liked to linger in the experimental department, sometimes chatting with old friends like Charles Voorhess, sometimes just watching the engineers at work. He also visited the sawmill at the plant, talking with the workmen as giant blades turned pine trees into lumber boards. The smell of cut wood always made him content. Whenever Ford visited Greenfield Village, he immediately went to the mammoth engine generator—a castoff from the Highland Park plant—around which he had built the Edison Institute. During the heyday of Model T production, nine such engines had provided the power for the "Crystal Palace." They never ceased to fascinate the old man.

Another frequent stop was a visit with Ray Dahlinger, in either his Dearborn office or his nearby home on the River Rouge. Dahlinger had managed most of Ford's non-automotive projects for more than twenty-five years. He worked for Ford even before that, starting as a driver and construction foreman. A compact man with a high forehead and a shallow chin, Dahlinger was bright, with a pleasant personality. He ran the Ford farms, located throughout southeastern Michigan, in addition to overseeing Greenfield Village and the museum. Ray and his wife, Evangeline, were frequent guests at Fair Lane. Their residence, a substantial colonial (which Ford bought for them), was a second home for him, a place he could visit anytime and be himself, telling stories of the day's work. Over the years, Ford gave the Dahlingers an upper-class lifestyle, with luxury cars, vacation homes, and generous allowances for salary and expenses. "The Dahlingers, husband and wife, were quite ordinary employees of Ford Motor Company until Henry Ford decided to employ them both as personal helpers," historian Ford R. Bryan wrote in *Henry's Lieutenants*. "Their relationship with Henry and Clara Ford extended well beyond that of domestic servants to positions of exceptional influence."[7]

Ford was so fond of spending time with the Dahlingers that rumors circulated suggesting that the vivacious Evangeline was his mistress. The Dahlingers' only son, John (born in 1923), contended in a 1978 book that he was, in fact, the illegitimate son of Henry Ford. The evidence is only circumstantial, revolving around Ford's obvious penchant for spending time with the Dahlingers, Evangeline especially, and his generosity through the years toward John. The conundrum of Henry Ford is that outside of his role in directing Ford Motor, there were exceptions to every rule in his life. He was the master of the modern world—but he longed for the nineteenth-century way of life. He opened his factory to all nationalities and creeds, but he was a maniac on the subject of the Jews. He rejected history but started one of the nation's most important historical museums. He was devoted to Clara, but . . . could he have had an affair? He may have. At any rate, it is perversely satisfying in modern times to think that a man who staunchly held up old-fashioned values was susceptible to ephemeral weaknesses, which is why this alleged affair was easily accepted as fact in several recent biographies. There is no proof, however, or even a supporting trend in his behavior toward women. With Henry Ford, that is crucial, because with him, anything is possible: adultery, certainly. Or even a platonic friendship with a woman. However, Carol Gelderman was one biographer who dismissed the notion that Ford had a dalliance: "As he grew older and devoted more time to the museum and village than to any other enterprise, he spent a portion of every day with Ray, who managed the whole operation, or with Evangeline, who helped locate antiques and old buildings—and never mind what people thought."[8]

In fact, the Dahlingers were not entirely unique in drawing the interest and largesse of Henry Ford. Jack Telnack, a Ford vice president in the 1980s who grew up in the sphere of Ford Motor, cites another example:

> There was a lady living one street away from me in Detroit when I was about four or five. Henry Ford used to come visit her, and so whenever Henry Ford's chauffeur-driven Lincoln would pull up, all the kids in the neighborhood would run up and say, "Hey, Mr. Ford is there!" It turned out that Mrs. Perry was the only black lady living in the neighborhood and her husband worked on Henry Ford's farm before he started the Ford Motor Company and one day they were sawing wood with a two-man saw and Henry Ford said, "This is the way it should be. Blacks and whites should work together, and when I start my company you will have a job in it." Sure enough, when he started the company, Mr. Perry had a job, a white-collar job, and if you check with the Archives, it was written in there that he would have a job for life, and he did. Well, he passed away and Henry Ford always took care of his family—made sure the house was in good repair; he would just take care of them.[9]

The one thing that is certain is that Henry Ford liked old friends best, and as he grew older, they were the only ones who still meant something to him.

For the first two winters after World War II, Henry and Clara Ford left Dearborn behind to spend a few months at their estate in Richmond Hill, Georgia. Acting like a country squire, Ford went on daily rides (in a car) around his thousands of acres, inspecting his property. Other times, he and Robert Rankin meandered in the car through adjoining land. Ford frequently signaled Rankin to stop, so he could talk with farmers they passed on dirt roads. Often he would get out of his car just to scoop up a handful of soil and let it run through his fingers, like a character in a Willa Cather novel.[10] Ernest Liebold, his longtime personal secretary, believed that Henry "judged the kind of people who were around by the condition of their farms."[11] Perhaps Ford saw himself as the local chieftain. Whenever he encountered a moonshine still in the thick underbrush, he would have it smashed. Over the years he saw to it that swamps were drained to prevent malaria and he opened a medical clinic for the poor. And he always carefully eyed the condition of farmland, mulling the crops that were growing or that could be grown. On his own land, he grew soybeans, tung, chia, and perilla, hoping to extract oils from them that could be used in cars. Gum trees covered his property because they were useful in the manufacturing of rayon. The one thing not found at Richmond Hill was any sign of a horse: Ford preferred tractors.

On one occasion at the plantation, Ford played host to James Newton, the young friend who had worked at the Edison Park Community in Fort Myers, Florida. The days Ford had spent in Fort Myers with Edison were among the happiest of his life. Newton, who had gone on to work in Akron, Ohio, as Harvey Firestone's assistant, had something of a father-son relationship with Ford. During the Georgia trip, Newton found Ford in a reflective spirit. "We spent the entire day together, walking and talking," he wrote in his memoir *Uncommon Friends*. "He showed me a different face from the one I was used to."[12]

Often that afternoon, Ford would pause by an old oak stump or some other woodland feature, pull out a pocketknife, and start whittling away at a piece of wood. Ford had refused to attend Harvey Firestone's funeral back in 1938, because emotionally the loss was too much for him. At sixty-nine, Firestone was, in Ford's view, "just too young to die." But Newton had been there, and now Ford wanted to know every last detail of what occurred. Newton obliged, leaving Ford full of follow-up questions. "You said some of his workers were crying when they walked past the casket?" a melancholy Ford asked in what was essentially a monologue to himself. "I wonder whether any of mine will do that at my funeral. Probably not. Bigness and the unions have broken up the closeness there was between boss and worker. Maybe Firestone coped with it better than I have though, I know he was hurt by them, too. Even without unions it's hard to have personal contact with the men any more. The plants have grown so big."[13]

Ford wanted the respect of his original workers. There weren't many of the old-timers left. "You know, Jimmie it's a strange thing," Ford confided in Newton. "I was the one, back in 1914, who doubled the workers' wages to five dollars a day. I upset most of my colleagues, and the bankers."[14]

Even in decline, Ford was, of course, still a powerful titan. His empire consisted of sixty U.S. manufacturing facilities, plus nine in Canada and twenty overseas. He also owned vast agricultural experiment stations in Michigan and Georgia, nearly 500,000 acres of timberland in Michigan and Kentucky, and numerous Great Lakes steamers. Then there were the sixteen coal mines scattered across Appalachia, a glassworks facility . . . the list could go on. The Rouge was still the most talked-about industrial facility in the world. But Henry Ford was lonely, and in some ways an anachronism—a nineteenth-century antique ready for display at Greenfield Village next to a Stephen Foster songbook and a *McGuffey Reader*. The Ford Motor Company didn't need him anymore. And he feared that because of the UAW, his workers saw him as a cruel capitalist billionaire, an obstacle to their enhanced happiness.

From Civil War to Cold War, from horse to automobile, from candlelight to electric light, Henry Ford's eighty-three years spanned an era of fast, sometimes furious change. However, he had done as much as any other individual to shape that change, putting in motion some of the major forces that still affect billions of lives around the world today. "Our great pioneering," Ford once told the *Saturday Evening Post,* "has not been in covered wagons, but in laboratories and workshops and in better ways of living together as a human society."[15] David L. Lewis described the epic proportions of Ford's accomplishments by saying that "the Model T was the log cabin of the motor age."[16] Ford clearly understood the many ways he forced progress to turn its course, in originating the universal car, in using productivity as a means of increasing wealth for all, and in letting the assembly line set the pace of a modern economy. The only thing Henry Ford never understood was the modern world wrought by those changes. He retreated from it, collecting antiques, building a museum, and finally taking long drives through the farmlands of his youth. Tragically, Henry Ford couldn't connect to those people who were themselves products of the modern era he had helped instigate. His own son, Edsel, the quintessential twentieth-century gentleman, had long been a stranger to him. He trusted only old-style men, carried over from the century before.

Although Henry Ford had many days when he couldn't remember faces or events, he was almost always coherent. That is to say, only those close to him recognized that his mind was failing. To a person who had not met him before, he was a mild elderly gentleman, making solicitous conversation and offering old-fashioned advice. Except for strangers, family members, and servants, few people saw Ford during his last months. One of those whom he did not see was the man who had once claimed to be his most loyal ally. After years of constant communication, Harry Bennett spoke to Henry Ford on just one occasion after leaving the company. He then abruptly refused to see Ford or accept any of his frequent telephone calls.[17]

People close to Henry Ford in his last days observed that only children made him truly happy. In December 1946, for example, Henry enjoyed playing Santa Claus at the annual Christmas Party at Greenfield Village. "Mr. Ford loved to do things for children," Clara Snow recalled. "He enjoyed them and he remembered them. He would actually remember the individual child."[18] He also appeared at a company ceremony honoring longtime employees. During the cold, hard winter in Dearborn, however, he took a turn for the worse, and when he and Clara left for Georgia in February 1947, many of his relatives feared that he wouldn't return. But he did come back, and in much better condition than before. He and Clara made the return trip in their private train car, stopping in New York City on the way for a gift-shopping spree in time for Easter. Henry took great pleasure in the selection of special presents for great-grandchildren and others.[19]

On the Fords' first weekend back home at Fair Lane, rainstorms combined with the spring thaw to produce rising waters in the River Rouge—not the factory, but the actual river that ran directly past the Ford estate. The grounds were flooding in places. On Easter Sunday, April 6, John McIntyre, Fair Lane's Scottish-born superintendent, struggled all day with the power plant's generators. With water covering the floor, he found it difficult to keep the generators' fires burning, but managed to produce enough power to keep the lights on in the main house. Worried about a blackout, McIntyre suggested that the Fords spend the evening at the Dearborn Inn. "My gracious, we have fireplaces," Ford laughed.[20] Obliging workers from the estate immediately started tending Fair Lane's numerous fireplaces to keep the house warm. Before long, the telephone lines were down. Charles Voorhess was called to Fair Lane from the automobile factory to help the power plant produce results. While the rains kept falling, however, the water kept rising. With no electricity for cooking on Monday morning, Mrs. Rankin, the chauffeur's wife, came from her own home with an oatmeal breakfast for the Fords.

Later that morning, Voorhess went to the main house and suggested that Henry and Clara go to the Dearborn Inn for their meals. They had lunch there and then, and in the early afternoon, Henry wanted to take a drive around Dearborn to see the effects of the flood. He and Rankin left at 1:30 in the afternoon, the chauffeur choosing the route. The car, a 1942 Ford V-8, was one of the only vehicles on the road, picking its way over the few passable lanes between wet fields and the bloated streams that led to the swirling Rouge River. Ford and Rankin went to the powerhouse at the Edison Institute and then visited Ray Dahlinger in Dearborn.

Henry tried to call Benson from Dahlinger's office, but learned that his grandson was in New York City. He and Rankin went to Greenfield Village before going to the Ford Administration Building on Schaefer Road to visit Henry II. On the way in, Rankin entered through the exit portal. "I'm just showing you how bright he was that day," Rankin explained in an oral history. "I stopped and said, 'Uh-oh, we're going the wrong way,' I noticed it just before. He said, 'Let's go anyway and see what will happen!'"

What happened was that all sorts of people ran over to the car to holler at the driver for going the wrong way—until they saw Henry Ford sitting in the passenger seat. At the last minute, Ford changed his mind about seeing Henry II. Rankin drove out of the parking lot. He made his way down to the dock on the river, where the company's two Great Lakes ships, *Benson* and *Henry II,* were docked. Ford pointed at the latter and said, "That's my yacht." It was an evergreen jest, one that he often liked to make. On the way back to Fair Lane, Rankin passed the Catholic cemetery, where some of Henry's maternal relatives were buried. Henry told a few stories about them and then said that he wanted to visit another cemetery. "The only thing that he said that day was about the little cemetery up on Joy Road," said Rankin. "He wanted to stop there. I guess that was about our last stop on the way coming back. . . . All he had on was what he'd call his 'clodhoppers,' a pair of bedroom slippers. They had all open work and were real comfortable. Of course, he didn't get out of the car." Ford wasn't carrying any money. In his pockets were the simplest bits and pieces, items a boy might carry: a harmonica, a comb, and a pocketknife. "When we stopped at that little Joy Road cemetery," Rankin continued, "he said to me, 'Rankin, this is where I'm going to be buried when I die. In among the rest of my folks here.' He asked me, 'Will you take care of that?'" Rankin said he would, without thinking about it.[21]

On the way home, Ford had Rankin stop at the Fair Lane powerhouse. "Mr. Ford came over with Rankin the chauffeur," Voorhess recalled. "He seemed more lively to me than he had for many months and he said, 'How are you coming?'" Voorhess explained that he had a plan to get the generator running again, and just at that moment, the lights came on.

Voorhess remembered Ford's reaction. "'Well,' he said, "'I'm going up and tell Mrs. Ford that I've been down here and fixed it. That won't make you sore, will it?'" Voorhess said that would be all right.[22]

Rankin continued up to the house and Henry engaged him in a lively conversation about the oatmeal breakfast that Mrs. Rankin had prepared. He said it was the best oatmeal he'd ever tasted. Rankin recalled, "That was about the last he said—that about breakfast—before he got out of the car. That was really quite a shock to me, because he was just like his old self that day."

In the Fair Lane powerhouse, after dinnertime, the water was rising above the generator's fireplaces. John McIntyre hiked up to the main house to warn the butler that the Fords might have to go without lights again that night. McIntyre was standing in the front hall, when Ford spotted him. "Mr. Ford rose from the living room," he said, "and he came into the hallway and shook hands with me. He said, 'Hello, Scottie. Are you having trouble?' He was more like himself that night than I had seen him in eighteen months." Throughout the previous year, Ford had failed to recognize his longtime workman. Inwardly thrilled that the boss was so lucid again, McIntyre warned him that Fair Lane would probably lose power again before the night was out. As McIntyre then recalled, Henry Ford said, "'That's all right, Scottie,' and he tapped me on the shoulder. 'That's all right. I know you will stick by me; you've always done it for years. I never worry about these things.'"[23]

It was 8:50. The house had plenty of heat from the fireplaces, and after McIntyre left, Henry Ford opted to go to bed early. He drank a glass of milk to make him sleep better, but woke up after only a few hours, breathing heavily. Rosa Buhler, a longtime personal servant, woke Clara. "I'm afraid Mr. Ford seems very ill," she whispered. Henry complained to Clara that he didn't feel well. She brought him a glass of water. By then, the electricity was out, and she sent Rosa to tell Robert Rankin to drive off the estate to a telephone and call the doctor.[24]

With his head resting on Clara's shoulder, while she stroked his forehead, Henry Ford struggled for air. All Clara could say was, "Henry, please speak to me," over and over. With great difficulty he folded his hands in a prayer. He died at 11:40 P.M. on April 7, 1947. The cause was listed as a cerebral hemorrhage. On a wall above his bed was a photograph of his beloved mother. The man who had brought the assembly line and the mass-produced automobile to the world would die quietly in a chilly room lit only by oil lamps, a scene reminiscent of his birth in a rural Michigan farmhouse, when Abraham Lincoln was president.

The next day, the news rocketed around the world. In Detroit, the headlines took up most of the top half of the Tuesday newspapers. The Dagenham headquarters in Great Britain immediately announced plans to erect a life-size statue of Henry Ford to remind workers of his leadership. Tributes were issued by leaders from around the globe. So many telegrams arrived in Dearborn for the Ford family that incoming cables had to be rerouted to other cities. Harry Truman, Herbert Hoover, Winston Churchill, and Josef Stalin, among many others, sent words honoring the industrialist.[25] Ford, however, had never particularly understood such politicians, and their predictable tributes showed that they had never really understood him.

On Wednesday, April 9, Ford's body lay in state in Lovett Hall, which was also known as the Recreation Building. It was located next to the Clock Tower, which was the replica of Independence Hall at Greenfield Village. As he had hoped, a steady stream of workers passed to pay their respects in front of the open coffin. They were clad in blue-collar attire: gray overalls, denim jeans, steel-toed boots, and caps, which they clutched in their hands. Union leaders had complaints with the company, and they had once regarded Henry Ford as labor's worst enemy, but they had to respect the man who put the world on wheels. And so they came too. The Detroit News estimated the crowd of mourners at more than 100,000. Two hours after the building opened, a double line a mile long extended out to Oakwood Boulevard.[26] Many people there had memories of Henry Ford, memories lasting only a few instants in most cases. Perhaps that was the only way to understand the late automaker. "I still remember vividly the first time I met Henry Ford," said a local politician in the line. "I was a small boy. My father introduced me to him on Grand Boulevard. I've never forgotten the friendly way he ran his hand through my hair—and I can still point out the exact spot where it happened."[27]

Another man in the line was a coal miner who worked in a West Virginia mine purchased by Henry Ford in the 1920s. He recalled that when Ford visited his newly acquired property, he turned away from the supervisors, all decked out in top hats, and circulated among the miners. Asking why many of them were stooped, Ford learned that the corridors leading through the mine were so low that the workers couldn't stand up while they were inside. He immediately asked for a pair of coveralls and went down in the mine to see for himself. Waiting in line before the funeral bier, the miner remembered how after that visit, the conditions in the mine quickly improved.[28]

On the day of the funeral, Thursday, April 10, flags all over Detroit hung at half-mast. Every Ford Motor plant and showroom around the world was closed, as were nonessential government offices in the Detroit area. Life magazine published an eerie photograph of the assembly line halting production of the 1947 Mercury.[29] In tribute to the last of the original auto pioneers, General Motors, Chrysler, Packard, and all of the other American automobile companies shut their factories down for several minutes of silence at 2:30 P.M., when the funeral service was to begin. The entire state was to pause at that moment, as children in school, motorists on the road, and workers in offices stopped to honor the memory of Henry Ford. "My daughter came home that evening from school," recalled Robert McNamara, then a new executive at Ford Motor. "She had drawn a picture of Ford in his coffin. It was impossible to escape the impact of his death in Michigan."[30] It's estimated that 7 million workers paused to honor Ford. "Nothing like this had ever accompanied the death of an American businessman in the past," historian Richard Tedlow surmised. "Nothing ever will again."[31]

The day was blustery and gray, with remnants of the rainstorms of the previous weekend. People who were at the funeral service at St. Paul's Episcopal Cathedral in Detroit remembered the pall of silence over the large crowd of 20,000 outside the church, and the somber stripes of black lining every sidewalk in the vicinity, made by thousands of umbrellas. A visibly distraught Clara clutched the arm of her grandson Henry II for support as she entered the cathedral. The service was short, read by the Very Reverend Kirk B. O'Ferrall. It was, he said, quite simply the end of an era. The hymn "Victory" was sung followed by a reading of the Lord's Prayer, and with that, the ceremony was over.

Burial was in the Addison Ford Cemetery on Joy Road in Dearborn, which Henry Ford had visited only three days before. The hearse that took his casket to the cemetery was not a Lincoln, but a 1942 Packard—a detail to which Henry Ford would have violently objected. "They lowered the coffin into a hole in the wet, clayey mud," *Time* magazine reported. "The rain came down in buckets, while the police hustled 20,000 sightseers on their way and opened the highway again to traffic. The cars rushed past, filling the night with the smell of gasoline."[32]

Clara Ford—"the Believer"—was devastated by the death of her husband, four days before their fifty-ninth anniversary. As a widow, she would try to remain cheerful, but would periodically fall silent and have to fight back her tears. She lived quietly at Fair Lane until her own death in 1950, at the age of eighty-four.

———

Henry Ford had long been a symbol of the American dream. To anyone in the world outside of Fair Lane, it wasn't the autocratic Ford who was missed. It was the unflinching individuality that he brought to the tumultuous times he lived in, the obstinate way he refused to settle into a pattern but stubbornly remained convinced that anything is possible, at any time and for anyone. For all of the failures and the blunders in his personal opinions, it was the soaring success in the middle of Henry Ford's life—the creation of Ford Motor Company—that was a reflection of what was essential to the man. No one believed more absolutely than he did that an automobile was only an extension of the most old-fashioned man. And few people before him believed more fully in the concept of globalization in business. He considered manufacturing and trading between nations the highest callings of all. The Automotive Hall of Fame in Dearborn correctly states that Henry Ford did not invent the automobile. It notes instead that he is responsible for putting the "world on wheels."

After Ford died, his contributions to society and even to Ford Motor Company continued to kick up a swirl of controversy in academic circles. Starting in the 1910s, with the $5 Day, intellectuals had debated his reputation and the width of the line therein between reality and self-promotion: the so-called Ford Myth.[33] Just as America seems always to devolve into left-wing and right-wing viewpoints, so the attitude toward Ford neatly split as time went on. Everyone worthy of an opinion resented his anti-Semitic campaign. Beyond that, though, liberals lambasted him as an anti-union reactionary and conservatives rejected him as a pacifist maverick. Yet Ford can't be regarded from a partisan point of view, for the very reason that he himself defied both convention and category.

The strongest case against Henry Ford was made in 1958, when esteemed Harvard economist John Kenneth Galbraith published an article called "The Mystery of Henry Ford" in *The Atlantic Monthly*.[34] Without admiration, Galbraith's essay—which was reprinted in his 1960 book *The Liberal Hour* as "Was Henry Ford a Fraud?"—presented Ford's chief characteristics as uncanny luck, superhuman tenacity, and self-advertisement. Other than that, Galbraith contended that Ford was something of a fool, albeit one who had inherited a great company from James Couzens. Such points were convincing as Galbraith presented them, and the essay was widely read and discussed in business schools. If nothing else, Galbraith's revisionist article succeeded in pulling Henry Ford's name out of any discussion of great businesspeople. In a sense, that was long overdue: other people who had helped build the Ford Motor Company deserved far more credit than they'd ever received in Henry Ford's shadow.[35]

Galbraith's principal point was that Henry Ford was *not* a businessman.[36] Usually, that word refers to a person with skills associated with the daily operation of a business, and it is true that Henry Ford didn't have many of those. In fact, he probably couldn't have gotten a job in the administration building of any other company in the world. He wasn't the engineer, the economist, or the production man for the universal automobile. As to his habits, he was generally ignorant of anything outside of a very few topics, and he certainly wasn't a hard worker, putting in fewer hours throughout his career than almost any entrepreneur in any business, large or small. The list of those things that Henry Ford could not do or did not do is a long one. The list of people whose work was indispensable to the building of Ford Motor could also go on and on, but only Henry Ford embodied the spirit of the company.

Galbraith believes quite strongly that in the corporate world the CEO of a company is merely a public relations personality, that a fine-tuned bureaucracy actually runs a big business. This is true for General Motors, but Ford Motor was different. One afternoon back in 1911, for example, Henry Ford was walking through his Highland Park facility. Suddenly a perfectly shined bill drill caught his eye. He smiled and walked over to congratulate the workman responsible for its glow. "Young man, I would hate to see you leave here, but if they ever should let you go, don't worry about another job, because any man that keeps his machine in the fine condition that yours is, is sure to come out on top," Ford told his grateful employee. "That is the best looking machine I ever saw in a big machine room." Word spread throughout the department of Henry Ford's praise. As the *Detroit News* told the story: "A few days later Mr. Ford passed through the same department and the glistening steel fairly blinded him. Every machine in the department was polished until it shone like a diamond. The slap on the back had spread." Because he was the legendary father of the Model T, he commanded both fear and respect.[37]

By making a novelty into a daily necessity, Ford created a template for success that has since been copied by businesses in practically every field. That was leadership. In the business world, Ford exerted an even greater influence, simply by thinking big as no one ever had before. When only a handful of people owned cars, he was already visualizing the day when practically everyone would have one. To him, that day was not far off. At a time when sales of 30,000 Model Ts per year were heroic, he was planning for production of 2,000,000. Henry Ford was a futurist who battled against the tendency of business to rely on precedent and tradition, rather than looking forward to the kind of world that people really want. His reputation continues that fight today. Ford did not bring a great intellect to his company, but he did have the cunning to dominate. More important, he brought imagination to the business world.

Ford's reputation has been haunted by his famous statement that the consumer could have a Model T in any color "so long as it was black." This statement is used to demonstrate that Ford was intractable. But there was logic behind Ford's famous quip: black paint dried more quickly than other hues and he had back orders to fill. When the market wanted Fords in colors, he produced them. He went on to compete head-on with GM, developing the Model A and V-8. When push came to shove, he purchased Lincoln Motor. His experiments with ethanol fuel, soybeans, and plastics were futuristic and farsighted. Contrary to Galbraith's assessment, Henry Ford's mind was never stuck in the moment. He was always looking ahead. "There is subtle danger in a man thinking that he is 'fixed' for life," Ford noted. "It indicates that the next jolt of the wheel of progress is going to fling him off."[38]

Henry Ford was a pioneer in public relations. He recognized the power of brand identity and used motion pictures very early on to spread the Ford image. Ford was adamant that his company cater to the consumer, insisting that service was as important as the original sale. He was also an original thinker in allowing free use of Ford patents. The list could go on and on. It was not blind luck or chronic narcissism that allowed Ford Motor to survive as hundreds of automobile companies folded. It was vision and the courage to act decisively. Henry Ford was the keeper of the flame at the company, projecting and protecting the belief that the Ford car had to be the highest-quality car at the lowest possible price. And it had to be easily recognizable as such. He willed his product to be the best, which is the most important rule of being a businessman. "The place to start manufacturing is with the article," Ford advised. "The factory, the organization, the selling, and the financial plans will shape themselves to the article."[39]

Henry Ford also pioneered in using celebrities to promote his automobiles—a sales gambit widespread today. At Ford Motor Company's World Headquarters, a twelve-story building that opened in Dearborn in 1955 (it was known at first simply as the Central Office Building), there is a voluminous photograph archive in the basement. Whether it's Charlie Chaplin eyeing a Model A, Miss America sitting on the roof of a Ford 8 Sedan, King George VI and his wife, Queen Elizabeth, getting out of a Lincoln, or Guy Lombardo stroking an early Mercury, Henry Ford made sure these luminaries were photographed enjoying his products. He had an international sensibility in this regard. Ford of Spain gave star bullfighters free cars while Ford of England cultivated relationships with soccer standouts. His early career as an auto racer, when he garnered bold headline stories, convinced him that fame—both his own and the borrowing of others'—was a conduit to business success. Besides befriending Thomas Edison, Will Rogers, Charles Lindbergh, Joe Louis, Jesse Owens, George Washington Carver, the Wright brothers, Calvin Coolidge, Eddie Rickenbacker, Barney Oldfield, and Luther Burbank, Ford always made sure a photographer, and often a motion picture crew, recorded for posterity his interaction with these esteemed notables. A picture with any of them, he knew, was worth a small fortune in advertising.[40]

Ultimately, what made Ford great was that he was afraid of neither failure nor going broke. He insisted that in business there were no dead ends, that there is always a way out of a financial jam. Failure, he truly believed, meant a chance to start over again in a more sensible fashion. To Ford, profits weren't financial—they were social. High production numbers were the currency of Ford's life. Often he would send telegrams to Thomas Edison boasting about the newest sales numbers; for example, "Our total world output yesterday of Model A Ford cars was 9,185 which is also our high record of all time," he cabled on June 27, 1929.[41] He laughed at businessmen who worried about having a bad year or making a wrong decision. According to Philip Caldwell, Ford Motor's CEO from 1979 to 1985, there was one business concept Henry Ford never abandoned, one that never let him down: "Pick it up and never put it down, until it's finished."[42]

Nobody ever said that Henry Ford was modeled after anyone else. He was, for better and for worse, an American original. Writing in the February 1937 issue of *Ford News*, he summed up his own historic achievement: "The Ford car blazed the way for the motor industry and started the movement for good roads. It broke down the barriers of time and distance and helped to place education within the reach of all. It gave people more leisure. It helped everyone to do more and better work in less time and enjoy doing it. It did a great deal, I am sure, to promote the growth and progress of the country."[43]

Henry Ford was different for the simple reason that he never tried to be the same as anyone. He was a stubborn patchwork of ideas and enthusiasms, some of them stunning and some dank. All of them were magnified by that twentieth-century force that made the owner of a giant company into a giant, too. To define what Henry Ford *did* may be an elusive problem. To define what Henry Ford *was* is simple—he was an automaker, the man who founded the Automobile Age.

26

Human Engineering

A rumor was swirling around Detroit at the end of World War II, just as Henry II took the reins from his ailing grandfather, that Ford Motor Company didn't figure its debts in the usual way, by adding up the money it owed to creditors. There were either too few employees or too many bills for that method. Instead, workers in the accounting department piled up the company's bills and weighed them. Each pound of paper was figured as a certain amount of money. The most absurd thing about this rumor was that it was true.[1] Ernie Breech, the man Henry Ford II recruited to reorganize the company, later described Ford's financial controls in 1946 as "nonexistent." For the time being, the company had cash on hand, but since the accounts payable apparently weighed more than the accounts receivable, to the tune of $10 million per month, immediate action was needed. Especially during the transition to peacetime production—many companies slipped a bit before they found traction again in 1945–1946—losing money wasn't even the travesty. The real disaster was that Ford Motor had lost track of its own operations and no longer understood them.

Driving himself to work one morning, Breech let the car coast to a stop about a block from the Administration Building outside the Rouge. He felt himself slipping into a funk as he surveyed Ford Motor Company, before his eyes and in his mind. "For the first time in my life, I was overwhelmed," he told his biographer, J. Mel Hickerson. "Not afraid, but badly disturbed." Among many things that faced him were the Ford finances. "Its cash position was barely sufficient to maintain proper bank operating balances," Breech said. "Its financial statements were so elementary that it would take months— yes, years—to install proper accounting methods to obtain any semblance of financial analysis and controls."[2] After the initial jitters subsided, Breech parked the car and did his day's work. Determined but patient, he accepted the fact that, as he had always heard as a boy in the Ozarks, the only way to break up a tall pile of sticks was to start with just one.

Even at its healthiest, Ford Motor was a highly centralized organization—the type of business structure in which decision making is concentrated in one group. Or, in the case of Ford Motor, in one person. Ernie Breech described the pre-1945 situation rather delicately in 1952. "Profit responsibility," he said, "was largely centralized in the chief executive position." As far as old Henry Ford was concerned, the amount of cash on hand at year end reflected the profitability of the entire corporation. "He was old school," Breech reflected. "It was all about accessible cash. He didn't even like money in banks."[3]

With so little information on which to base decisions, executives knew only by intuition whether an individual process was adding to the bottom line or detracting from it. They typically presumed that lower costs in an operation were always favorable for the overall corporate health. That seems logical enough, yet it is not always the case. As a matter of fact, executives at Ford Motor right after the war could not make good operating decisions, except through lucky guesses. An outdated business structure and a dearth of good information were closing inevitably over the company. "With the coming of Mr. Breech," recalled accountant L. E. Briggs, "the whole new program began to unfold, step by step. The first change was in the accounting system." A former accountant himself, Breech sought a clear, detailed, and highly sensitive financial picture. Finding it was another matter. "Breech said he wanted a more complete accounting system," Briggs continued. "We could have done one of two things: we could have either elaborated on the existing Ford accounting system which we all, as accountants, recognized as inadequate in some respects, or we could throw it out in favor of another system. Mr. Breech decided, inasmuch as he was familiar with the General Motors system, that he would prefer to have that installed."[4]

In the General Motors system, accounting in general and cost control in particular were based on narrowly defined profit centers. For example, parts specialists were expected to make money, even when supplying components to GM's own automobile divisions—Bendix (Breech's old domain) could not sell brakes to Buick at so low a price that it lost money and then excuse the deal as being "good for the corporation." What was good for the corporation was allowing managers and top executives to see with clarity the efficiencies and the problems within their own operations. For that reason, Bendix salesmen visited Buick's managers right along with reps from outside vendors; Buick's only loyalty was to its own bottom line.

To carve the Ford mountain into profit centers, Breech enlisted Lewis Crusoe as vice president and director of finance. Crusoe, who had been Breech's second-in-command at Bendix, followed natural lines within the corporation, locking them in with sophisticated accounting principles. He was both me-thodical and unstoppable. Tex Thornton and several of the other Whiz Kids felt as though Crusoe was moving too fast for the good of their own careers, but displaced white-collar workers were not Crusoe's concern. He kept mov-ing through Ford, implementing financial processes and enforcing the disci-pline that made them work.

Changes came quickly in the late 1940s—for the sake of the 1950s and beyond. Neither Henry Ford II nor Ernie Breech—nor anyone else without the elder Henry Ford's instinct—could look into the future without knowing first in hard figures where the Ford Motor Company was in the present. Em-ployees willing to change with the future found job security in Dearborn. Those who were attached to the old system either retired or were fired. L. E. Briggs, who would serve as treasurer starting in 1945, could have been speak-ing for thousands of survivors at Ford when he said in 1951, "I have no brief for the older system except that I just grew up in it. I accepted it as a matter of course. Possibly it's a matter of who ran it. It is rather difficult to readjust yourself to a more methodical approach. I find certain restrictions on my op-erations here that I didn't have before, but I recognize their importance. To sum it up, I feel that everything that has been done is in the way of progress."[5] Management fielded complaints and was open to suggestions—all except one. There was no going back to the Henry Ford era.

Ford Motor Company was no longer dominated by an individual. Like General Motors and all other great corporations, it was run by a bureaucracy. Journalists, who realized that readers identified with individuals, continued to profile Henry II in their reports on the company. He set the new priorities, but beyond that was little more than a spokesperson at the time. John Ken-neth Galbraith, in an unpublished book titled "The Economics of Innocent Fraud," goes so far as to argue that Breech's management, not Henry II, was really running Ford Motor during the late 1940s. "Ford had become a bureau-cracy," Galbraith maintained in a 2002 interview. "The notion of personality was draped all over the organization, but control had passed from owners to management. Henry II simply maintained a public identity and the econo-mists and journalists went along with it. The reality of Ford Motor in the 1950s was that it was a commonplace, somewhat dull, huge corporation. But nobody wanted to read that. You got the attention of people by writing about people. Nobody really wants to hear the drab details about the organization."[6]

Implementing a new accounting system at Ford Motor Company should have been a five-year plan all by itself. Ford Motor, however, didn't have that luxury: everything had to happen at once. Concurrent with the financial reor-ganization, Henry II and Ernie Breech oversaw a resounding decentralization of management. With so much of real importance in flux, leadership was es-sential. According to a sports analogy often used at the time, Henry II was the coach of the new Ford team and Breech was the quarterback, the field manager who made things happen. Asked to comment on Breech's role in the rebirth of Ford Motor, Henry II said in a 1984 interview, "Well, he did it. . . . I don't see how I could say it any more simply. He remade the company. I couldn't have done it. I didn't know enough to do it. I didn't have any idea how to do it."[7]

Under another scenario, Henry II, the scion of the company name and fortune, might have displayed a rather common tragic flaw, in that he would not have *known* what it was that he did not know. Instead of setting the company in the direction of definite goals and then choosing the people to attain those goals, he might have simply gotten in the way. Many family companies have gone to ruin by just such overauthority in a succeeding generation. Henry II was smart enough to admit his ignorance. "He knew how to let others excel," Robert McNamara recalled. "It was a fine quality."[8]

In the newly decentralized organization, Ford Motor's operations were separated along lines that were as distinct as possible, under the circumstances: the Ford and Lincoln-Mercury divisions were the easiest to identify. The decision to combine Mercury with Lincoln—publicly announced on January 30, 1948—was the only surprise. (They would be separated again for two years in the mid-1950s.) Before the 1948 announcement, Mercurys had been aligned more closely with Fords, especially in terms of marketing and dealerships. In fact, the decision even to retain the Lincoln line was also a bit of a surprise within the industry. Lincolns were an expensive luxury, especially for the corporation that was making them. The Continental—the "car for the working millionaire"[9]—still had enough of an aura that used ones sold for almost as much as brand-new models.[10] But the standard Lincoln was only old-fashioned: "a lumbering old bus with an obsolete twelve-cylinder engine," in the opinion of *Fortune,* whose assessment of the whole division was discouraging. "At war's end," the magazine reported, "the only ray of light in the Lincoln picture was the Lincoln Continental, whose tiny volume made it a consistent money loser."[11] Some ray of light.

The rest of the new corporate divisions were less well defined than the two vehicle groups. The Rouge Division consisted of the heavy industrial operations conducted at the main plant, including the production of steel, glass, and tools. All of them had to be "profitable," within the confines of the corporate accounting sheet. The Parts and Equipment Division included ten specialized parts plants owned by the corporation. The General Division was the catchall, including Highland Park's spare parts production, tractor output, and self-standing factories such as a newly built stamping plant in Buffalo. Finally, the corporation's new structure included the Foreign Operations Division, which was a continuation of the old Ford International. The roster of six divisions finalized in 1948 would expand to sixteen three years later, but they represented a start in Ford's modernization.

Each division developed its own purchasing department, was entirely responsible for its own production, and was obligated for its own accounting. Moreover, each prepared its own budgets, a fundamental aspect of charting the future. All of them together made up "Line Operations" at Ford. Like General Motors, the new Ford Motor also encompassed a "Staff" to assist the divisions by assessing progress and supporting the decision-making process, while intervening as little as possible. The two spheres were analogous to the tactical and strategic divisions of Napoleonic military theory. "Under the new system one group does the planning, works out the programs," Henry II told *Business Week* in 1949, referring to the Staff. "Others have the responsibility of seeing that the actual work is done," he added, describing Line Operations.[12]

The Staff consisted of Henry II as president, Ernie Breech as executive vice president, and a small group of executives with general roles in engineering, sales, industrial relations, and so forth. "Assist" was a GM word for the job of the Staff office; at Ford Motor, divisions were never quite that independent, so the role of Staff was more aptly described as "overseeing." As the divisions evolved, Benson Ford took charge of Lincoln-Mercury, defending his father's old turf. The durable Logan Miller was given the Rouge Division. Of the four remaining Ford Motor divisions, three were headed by former GM executives. Lewis Crusoe moved into the top spot at Ford proper. Graeme K. Howard, a graduate of Harvard Business School who had recently ended a twenty-seven-year stay at GM as vice president for European business, took over Foreign Operations.[13] John Dykstra, another GM veteran, was in charge of the General Division. They joined Harold Youngren, who filled a Staff position as vice president of engineering; Youngren had helped develop the Hydra-Matic automatic transmission at General Motors in the mid-1930s. Dozens of other key positions at Ford were also filled by GM recruits.

According to Peter Drucker, who had access to GM offices in 1945–1946 in preparation for his *Concept of the Corporation,* Alfred Sloan didn't resent the frequent Ford raids. Personally, Sloan liked Ernie Breech and Henry II, and respected the memory of his onetime friend, Henry Ford. Less sentimentally, he thought that Ford's survival was essential to maintaining competition in the industry—and that a sense of competition was crucial to staving off government intervention. Free enterprise was always a top priority with Alfred Sloan. With GM in tacit control of large chunks of the auto market and burgeoning with management talent, especially as veterans returned from the war, Sloan could afford to be magnanimous.[14]

"When Henry Ford II," wrote Drucker, "took control and began to turn around his company by raiding GM for managers, Sloan went all out to support him. Everybody else in GM top management was bitter about the colleagues who went over to Ford, the hated competitor. Sloan did everything to enable them to join the Ford team, helped them work out their pensions and profit-sharing plans at GM so as to be able to move without financial loss, and even, I was told, got word to Ernest Breech, a former GM executive . . . , where inside GM he might find hidden top talent for the Ford management team."[15]

In a remarkably short time, Ford Motor Company began to gain momentum. "We've made, we think, an organization out of an aggregation," boasted Breech. The transformation of the ailing company was not lost on all those publications that had been pushed out of the company's business for so many years. Welcomed back, they made a national story out of the new face Henry II was putting on the middle-aged company: *Collier's* called it the "Revolution on the Rouge,"[16] while to *Fortune* it was "The Rebirth of Ford."[17]

In the 1910s, Henry Ford had been the smartest PR man in the country, steering national opinion through hairpin turns that always seemed to lead to his own persona. Henry II couldn't be quite that facile, but he did foster Ford Motor's story in the press with some of the old sense that it was a company apart, one worth rooting for. Ford at its best, as Henry II well knew, was the eternal American story, in metal and muscle. It was wrapped up with the country's ability to regenerate itself, to give a new youth to business, to technology, and even to every citizen.[18]

Cunningly, Henry II was determined to take advantage of the company's invisible assets, including the aura of fascination that surrounded it, even as he helped it shed its old liabilities, notably the fading reputation of its products and methods. To accomplish his ends, Henry II threw open the doors on the company, even when it was still just a work-in-progress. Within the automobile industry and beyond it, people in the postwar world knew that something was going on at Ford Motor. Where trade magazines failed to carry the message from Dearborn, the company published twenty-five magazines of its own, including three directed toward the general public. One of those was the *Ford Times,* which started in 1908 but had not been widely circulated for years. By 1949, it was going out to 1.4 million Ford customers and prospects.[19]

In the midst of the good publicity surrounding the "new" Ford, the company's hourly workers began to regard decentralization with suspicion. At best, it was a disruption. At worst, they considered it a corporate excuse for permanent layoffs. According to one theory circulating within the rank and file in Dearborn, Ford Motor's transformation would eventually result in the closing of the River Rouge plant, its production being "decentralized" to factories all over the country. Engendering the trust of the employees was Henry II's own personal challenge, one of several that only he could accomplish in a company still haunted by the inconsistencies of his namesake. "What people didn't appreciate about Henry II was that he was a careful student of labor relations," said Peter Pestillo, a high-ranking Ford executive in a later era. "He really liked workers. Most CEOs don't."[20] The only question was whether the auto workers would take to Henry II, and the company he was trying to build.

In 1946, Walter Reuther was elected the national president of the United Automobile Workers union. Although he was keenly interested in ensuring that auto workers took part in the postwar era's high standard of living, his first years in office were hampered by infighting in the union. Three groups were at war: his own followers, factions loyal to the previous administration, and a fast-growing Communist wing. Reuther fought hard, especially against the Communists within the UAW. He incurred their wrath in part because they believed that Reuther's stay in the Soviet Union left him with Marxist leanings. Nothing could have been further from the truth, a fact that frustrated the leftists. In addition, the leftist faction had formed links with the mafia, which relied on compliant union stewards to manage a $20-million-per-year gambling business in Detroit-area automobile factories.

The conflict was more than ideological. Between 1947 and 1949, Reuther's enemies made three murder attempts. In the first incident, Reuther was shot through the window of his Detroit home. He was standing with a bowl of peaches in the kitchen and if he hadn't turned the moment before, he almost certainly would have been killed. As it was, he suffered nerve damage that paralyzed one arm. "Those dirty bastards!" he shouted in agony as neighbors came rushing to his aid. "They have to shoot a fellow in the back. They won't come out in the open to fight."[21] Doctors advised Reuther that the damage to his arm was permanent, but after many years of therapy, he regained partial use of it. His brother, Victor, was likewise shot through a living room window thirteen months later. The gunshot hit him in the head, resulting in the loss of his right eye. Finally, on December 20, 1949, a box of dynamite was discovered in the basement of the UAW headquarters building; it had not exploded because of a sudden rainstorm. No one was convicted in the attacks against the Reuthers.[22]

Walter Reuther later voiced his own belief that the violence could be traced to three groups that thought "they could weaken the union if they [got] me out of the way." The first two groups he cited were the Communists within the UAW and the underworld racketeers who wanted access to auto workers. The third was "a small group of diehard employers."[23] Even in the late 1940s, some automobile companies, especially among the parts makers, bitterly resented the union and Walter Reuther's influence.

Reuther would not have included Henry Ford II in that group of anti-union employers. Labor-management relationships were the subject of many of Henry II's speaking engagements. He didn't actually write his own speeches—in fact, one time he looked up from his typescript at a Yale gathering to say, smiling, "I didn't write this, either," referring to the incident that had forced his expulsion from the school years before. The audience joined him in gales of laughter. However, Henry II was the author of the thoughts in his speeches, developing a philosophy around what he called "human engineering." He found that the best place to start was with a basis laid down by the first Henry Ford.

"The job of American Industry—Management and Labor—is to make at lower and lower cost more and better products to sell for lower and lower prices," Henry II said in setting out his ideas on human engineering. With that as the ultimate goal, management was not the boss over labor. Likewise, labor couldn't dominate management. Maintaining that the public was the real boss over both elements of industry, Henry II found a clever way to disarm the head-to-head battering that characterized many labor negotiations. He made it clear that he had no intention of fighting the union simply for the sake of holding his head high as a big-time business executive. "Certainly," he said, "we of the Ford Motor Company have no desire to 'break the Unions,' to turn back the clock to days which sometimes look in retrospect much more attractive than they really were."

The price that Henry II exacted for his fresh take on human engineering was a sense of shared responsibility from the union. He didn't want to play the role of the mean old boss, but he wouldn't allow the union to play Peck's bad boy by taking what it could get without a care in the world. "We don't want to destroy the Unions," he said, continuing with a surprising new idea about the situation.

"We want to strengthen their leadership," Henry II said, "by urging and helping them to assume the responsibilities they must assume if the public interest is to be served." Just as every auto worker longed for stabilized employment, Ford Motor needed a stable labor environment. Working toward that goal was a matter of engineering. Anything less was what he called a "brawl."[24]

In 1947, Ford Motor demonstrated its good faith, putting a pension plan on the negotiating table, even before such a thing was part of the union's bundle of demands. Reuther turned the plan down, in part because it didn't offer the UAW any part in administering the funds. However, two years later, he used the pension demand to push the boundaries of the usual labor contract. Part of his reasoning was that the deflationary situation of the overall economy, in which the price index was falling, made the prospect of a wage increase slight.[25] Pensions represented a more fertile possibility.

Despite Ford's previous offer, the idea of a pension was still considered radical. In American industry, only senior managers could look forward to receiving paychecks after retirement. General Motors, Chrysler, and other automakers had already refused to entertain the idea of a pension plan for auto workers. Reuther prepared his union members for the fight with a series of fiery speeches—with his arm still paralyzed and in a sling from the lingering effects of the gunshot wound. Reuther made his point by noting that GM

President Charles Wilson, who made $516,000 per year, was entitled to a pension, but the average hourly worker, whose pay was equivalent to 0.6 percent of Wilson's, was expected to fend for himself. "If you make $258 an hour, they give it to you," Reuther said of Wilson and his pension. "If you make $1.65 an hour, they say: 'You don't need it, you're not entitled to it, and we are not going to give it to you.'"[26]

When it came time to test the idea of the pension with one of America's automakers, Reuther chose Ford Motor Company. Largely because of Henry II's attitude, Ford was more receptive than other companies to overtures from labor. Moreover, Ford Motor was clawing to regain second place in the industry and was less able to sustain a strike than either GM or Chrysler. Reuther was confident that within the Big Three, Ford represented the thin end of the wedge where labor progress was concerned.

To prepare Dearborn for the fight, the UAW staged a three-and-a-half-week strike over a minor issue in June 1949. Up to that time, Ford had gone eight years without a *major* strike (the 1941 stoppage that led to recognition of the union). More important in terms of timing, the June strike came six weeks before negotiations opened over a new contract with the automaker.[27]

Staking his reputation on the outcome of the Ford talks, Reuther insisted that the company provide a pension plan for all workers with thirty years of service. Director of Industrial Relations John Bugas, who had become one of Henry II's closest advisers, led the Ford team at the table. He had no particular problem with that arrangement. The dilemma was whether or not the pension would be "funded": that is, whether Ford Motor would salt away money each year, in anticipation of future pension payments, or whether it would simply pay its retirees out of current-year profits. Reuther demanded a funded pension plan, which was more secure. He also wanted the UAW to have a hand in administering the monies, a prospect that made other automakers suspect that the pension idea was just an end-run effort by the UAW to gain control of automobile companies and their finances.

After tense negotiations, Ford Motor agreed to the funded plan, believing that the basic idea of the pension would increase loyalty—and therefore stability. Chrysler, which refused to follow suit in agreeing to fund a pension plan, was hit later in 1949 with a three-month strike. Finally, it, too, capitulated to largely the same terms as those at Ford. General Motors followed suit more quietly in 1950.

Ford Motor was the first important American company to adopt a funded pension for its workers.[28] The implementation of the pension plan, for which the company deserves equal credit with Reuther and the UAW, was a turning point in industrial relations. For the first time, hourly workers had a reason to remain with one company and look upon their working life as a career, something into which they invested their time and in return received time, in a sense. For Ford and other automaking firms, it was a long improvement on the situation of the 1910s and '20s, when workers roamed around among Detroit factories on a weekly or even daily basis.

The era of good feeling that existed in Dearborn in 1948–1950 did not stave off the growing suspicion among the rank and file that decentralization would serve to reduce jobs and weaken the workers' position. *Ford Facts,* the publication of Local 600 (representing River Rouge workers), accused Ford Motor of using its reorganization to make "runaway shops" and "runaway jobs."[29] The agitation originated entirely within Local 600; the international union disagreed with the action. Nonetheless, *Ford Facts* gave decentralization a bad name with workers. The company responded with a bright campaign, complete with brochures and upbeat signage, to convince workers that decentralization was not "a scheme to make a ghost town of the Rouge."[30]

The fact was that there had been a reduction at the Rouge, from approximately 80,000 workers to 60,000. Only 5,000 workers were actually laid off; the rest of the jobs fell to the wayside through attrition, but Ford Motor went into the 1950s saddled with its old reputation for gaining efficiency purely through expansion. In the new era, efficiency would come at a higher cost, sometimes at the cost of jobs. Layoffs were especially hard on workers in the midst of the personalized treatment accorded them under the precepts of human engineering.

Henry II and John Bugas recast the employment experience at Ford, starting from the new worker's first interview, a one-on-one talk that replaced the harsh hiring line of old. With indoctrination classes for all employees, rights and responsibilities were clearly understood. In addition, foremen, the first level of management, received continuing training to reduce the level of frustration on both sides of the assembly line. Workers received a checkup on starting at Ford and health care was available around the clock. Continuing education (an idea originally instituted by Henry Ford) became a priority of human engineering and all employees were encouraged to advance at the company. The personnel department even interviewed people who quit, in hopes of ascertaining whether there had been a problem that could be fixed for the next recruit.[31]

Because the themes of Henry II's human engineering have been widely adopted by corporations today, the concepts may seem less striking than they were in the late 1940s. Then, however, they represented a drastic change in the lot of the line worker. Human engineering concepts were credited with reducing Ford's turnover rate by one half within two years. In 1948, when Ford's turnover was 2.9 percent, the average for the nation's manufacturing industry was 4.8 percent. Moreover, wildcat strikes became far less common.

In 1945 (albeit a wartime year, when regulations increased the stress on workers and managers alike), 78,418 man-days were lost to unauthorized strikes at Ford plants. In 1948, only 3,532 days were lost.[32]

The human engineering program, a delayed response to Ford's recognition of the UAW in 1941, represented a second step in the sharing of power and responsibility at the company. The economics of the automobile industry wouldn't allow Ford Motor to command loyalty through astounding pay raises any longer. Wage increases became a union prerogative that no longer even seemed to come from the company. When hourly pay jumped, workers cheered for the union. Ford, in particular, lost a sense of its old identity as the originator of the $5 Day. Henry II developed an entirely new means of connecting Ford Motor to the workforce, but not through paternalism or even the well-meaning social improvement that his grandfather and James Couzens had offered in the 1910s. Certainly, the worker intimidation of Ford Motor in the 1920s and '30s would not have suited the situation or Henry Ford II. Instead, his company's attitude toward labor brought a level of maturity not often seen in the automobile industry before.

At Ford Motor under Henry II, workers were not children and they were not numbers. As far as possible in a company of 120,000, they were given the same respect as the white-collar workforce and even the executive corps. Henry II considered each type of employee a responsible member of the company, to be trusted with straight talk and opportunities for improvement. Henry Ford, the elder, had made men into cogs in the mass-production machine. Henry II called those men by names again. "His blunt, pseudo-candid style, Henry Ford as the common man, appealed to workers on the line," journalist David Halberstam wrote of Henry II in *The Reckoning.* "To them he was independent and free, a man who could tell the other big guys off and sometimes did. At the height of tensions between labor and management, he could walk down a Ford line and still be hailed, worker after worker rushing over to shake his hand."[33]

━━━━━

During the last years of World War II, Ford Motor Company was excited about building a small car for the postwar market. It was to be a four-seat, four-cylinder compact along the lines of a European economy car. Mindful of the pent-up demand lurking in the near future, Ford officials thought that a small car, with a stubby 100-inch wheelbase, would be easy for the company to make and affordable for customers. In the reality of the immediate postwar years, however, Ford Motor soon recognized that neither proved true. No new model was easy to make, in terms of requirements for new tooling and materials. And it would be misguided to push price as a selling point at a time when customers had found ways to afford practically anything that had four wheels and that could be called "new." At Ernie Breech's urging, Henry II dropped the idea of a little car for the domestic market. The design didn't go to waste, though. Ford of France made use of it for its Vedette model, while Dearborn devoted itself to building a prewar Ford with continuing refinements.

The old-new Ford would generate sales for a few years. So did a heavyset version of the prewar Mercury. Even the hand-wrought Lincoln Continental—the sensation of 1940—reappeared in 1946. But the pressure on Ford Motor was for all-new cars, not re-buffed antiques.

The company employed an engineering staff of respectable size, consisting of 2,300 people working under Vice President Hal Youngren. The styling department, however, hadn't really been active since Bob Gregorie left in 1943. Before the department emptied out then, designer Ross Cousins made a sketch of a large, sleek Ford. Gregorie never forgot it, but in the end it would not come to life as a Ford. The car in the drawing featured a fender that was distinct at the front of the car, but almost disappeared as it worked down the side of the car all the way from the headlight to the taillight.[34] It was a bold car, even on paper.

When Bob Gregorie returned to Ford Motor in 1946, he was immediately assigned to create a new Ford and a new Mercury, planned for 1949. New models were always a complex challenge, but never more so than in the midst of the standing start that the postwar years presented. A new Ford could be anything. The 1940–1941 designs were only vague guidelines.

For Gregorie and Youngren and everyone else working on the 1949 Ford, the pressure was especially keen. No Ford model since has been more important to the company; neither the '64 Mustang nor the '86 Taurus had as much riding on it. Henry II made no secret of the fact that he wanted—and the company needed—a car that could beat Chevrolet. If the '49 was greeted with complaints or, worse, boredom, the very future of Ford as an independent concern would be in jeopardy. Ford Motor needed a huge success and nothing less.

"Prosperity" was the buzzword of postwar America. Just as Henry Ford had predicted, blue-collar workers were growing into middle-class consumers. The American dream was to own a suburban house with a car in the garage. By 1947 more than a million veterans had been granted home loans—and they were looking to fill those garages. One afternoon, Walter Reuther was given a tour of the Rouge by a Ford Motor executive and they stopped to study an automated machine. "You know, not one of these machines pays dues to the UAW," the executive said pointedly. Reuther immediately shot back, "And not one of them buys new Ford cars either."[35]

Henry II understood that the easy selling environment of the postwar years was destined to settle down, and the competition, especially from GM, had to heat up. A lot of first-rate people had been drawn to Dearborn for the excitement in the air and the chance to contribute to a new American success story. A '49 flop would start a vicious circle, inducing high-caliber people to lose faith and leave. During Henry II's years as president, he'd proven himself capable in many areas, including reorganization and employee relations. However, he would not actually be an automaker until he had guided a vehicle all the way from planning through production. The '49 would be his chance to carry his mark into the heart of Ford Motor.

The overriding challenge at Ford in the late 1940s was planning. Anticipating a few weeks ahead, let alone several years, is a challenge at any company trying simultaneously to conduct business in the marketplace and re-create itself behind the scenes. With authorization from Henry Ford II, Bob Gregorie was busily developing a Ford design based on Ross Cousins's 1943 drawing. His team also created a more sophisticated version for Mercury, striking in proportion and remarkably beautiful.

Unfortunately, Gregorie hit a snarl in planning, one that practically stopped the clock in the summer of 1946. Looking carefully at the designs, Youngren reported that the 118-inch Ford was too big to produce economically. At the same time, Breech's planning staff calculated that the "big" Ford couldn't be made at a price comparable to that projected for the '49 Chevrolet. The implication of that statement was not lost on Henry II, who immediately rejected the design and told Gregorie to start work on a shorter and lighter model. To hedge his bet, he also commissioned drawings from the freelance studio of George W. Walker in Detroit. Each team had three months to come up with the crucial design.

Walker, a former professional football player, was a decent designer but an ace salesman. Once he built his Detroit company into a busy industrial-design house in the late 1930s, he typically assigned the actual styling to others. For the Ford project, he looked to Dick Caleal, who in turn asked Holden Koto for help. Koto was employed by another car company at the time, but he couldn't resist the challenge and went to Caleal's house each night, where the two designers sculpted a plain but modernistic model car on the kitchen table. Another local designer, Koto's friend Bob Bourke, contributed an idea for the front grille, featuring a chrome bullet-nose in the center. Painted bright blue, the aerodynamic model, submitted by Walker, easily won the competition and was rushed through pre-production. It led to a permanent position for Walker as vice president of styling at Ford. "There was a lot more significance in the 1949 Ford than the fact that it was different," Walker recalled. "It had to be. But more than that, it provided the basic concept of our styling since that time. Practically all cars at that time had bulging sidelines, particularly around the front and rear fenders. We smoothed those lines out and began the movement toward the integration of the fenders and body."[36]

Ford had barely two years in which to turn the little blue model into a full-size automobile pouring out of River Rouge and a dozen assembly plants throughout the country. Meanwhile, however, Gregorie's original entries didn't go to waste. The Cousins-Gregorie Ford became a Mercury. The former Mercury was then bumped up to become a Lincoln. Benson Ford, head of the Lincoln-Mercury Division, had worthwhile cars to work with, especially in the sleek new Mercurys.

The debut of the new Ford lineup on June 8, 1948, was an event as intoxicating as the introduction of the Model A twenty years before. Staged in the grand ballroom of the Waldorf-Astoria in New York City, Ford's glittering six-day showcase cost $500,000. A "49er miner" handed out souvenir nuggets and toy models of the car to gawkers, while a blimp flew over Manhattan with "FORD" lit in neon. A humungous merry-go-round was set up in the ballroom with the new Fords spinning around. Radio broadcaster Fred Allen carried his show from the hotel, asking visitors what they thought of the new Ford.[37] "It was like the good old days of prewar auto shows," marveled *Business Week,* "colorful decorations, company brass in a receiving line at previews, name orchestra playing dance music, sales blurbs over loudspeakers."[38] And just as in those good old days, a new Ford was the talk of the nation, chatter for radio personalities, newspaper columnists, and friendly conversations everywhere.

For half a million dollars, a company like Ford could get people talking, at least for six days. Whether it would last longer than that depended on the car. All of the excitement that June surrounded a car that was, on close inspection, pudgy in profile and rather mild in personality. However, to anyone grown tired of the cars of 1948 and before, the long-awaited Ford was arresting, a break from the past with its fenderless slab sides and gentle lines. It was uncannily sure of itself and completely refreshing in its unfettered way.

"The design was virtually philosophic in its statement of handsome purpose," wrote Strother MacMinn, who taught generations of automobile stylists at the Art Center in Pasadena, California. "With a personality that was all Ford, it was visual evidence of the company's break with its fundamentalist past and its new incarnation as a model business organization."[39] Winning a handful of awards from design groups, the car gave Ford Motor a place at the forefront of the postwar world.

Mechanically, the '49 was also a break with the past, at least with the Ford past, as Hal Youngren and his growing team of engineers rethought the chassis in ways that Henry Ford would never have allowed. As just one example, the '49 featured a solid front axle. The last Ford to use that component also happened to be the last Ford produced before Henry Ford bought the company, the 1906 Model N. The result of the Youngren chassis was a smooth-riding car suited to the highway mode of life becoming common in the United States.

The fact that Ford Motor had a 1949 model on the market excited potential customers, who riffled through paint chips to imagine it in flashy new colors like Fez Red and Miami Cream. Eager to make the '49 Ford attractive to the young-at-heart, the company made a series of convertibles and employed Basil Rathbone, known for his Sherlock Holmes movies, to promote the vehicles.

Sales swelled after Ford's early summer introduction and they didn't stop. The 1949 production model logged total sales of 1,118,740 vehicles—Ford's first million-seller since the 1929 Model A. By some counts, Ford had beaten Chevrolet, although the eighteen-month selling season gave the final tally a boost. Henry II was still looking forward to his first official, uncontested victory. In any case, the competition was neck and neck and would remain so throughout the 1950s, when the race between Ford and Chevrolet took a place in the national folklore.

As World War II receded into the past, normalcy meant to many male consumers a new car. It also meant the freedom to roam. In the postwar era, the demand for better roads hit a feverish peak. Driving around and seeing sites like the Grand Canyon, Yellowstone, and the Everglades became an American obsession. The term "joy ride" became part of the national parlance. In "Brownsville Girl," a nostalgic look at postwar America, Bob Dylan, for example, cowrote lyrics with playwright Sam Shepard about a rendezvous in the Painted Desert with a "platform shoe"–wearing girl driving a "busted down Ford." But the so-called blue highways of America were being replaced by super slabs. In 1940 the first section of the Pennsylvania Turnpike had opened to great fanfare. Americans wanted more superhighways like the famed German autobahns, which could speed motorists along without delays such as red lights and cars turning left. Congress appropriated $1.5 billion in 1944 for the Interstate and Defense Highway Act to improve roads in postwar America, but even that amount was vastly insufficient. At a time when trucking was supplanting the railroad even for long-distance hauling, time was money. Truck convoys needed open roads with smooth surfaces to deliver goods as efficiently as trains.[40]

Beat Generation novelist Jack Kerouac, famous for *On the Road,* kept a detailed diary of the cross-country treks he took in 1948 and 1949. His weekly entries often mentioned the new Ford: for example, "Closed up the house in Denver, went to Frisco in a '49 Ford for $11" or "Then we swerved into a brand new 1949 Ford." Even though Kerouac—whose first wife came from Grosse Pointe—liked the '49 Ford, he harbored nostalgia for the days when the mythic Henry Ford, not Henry Ford II, was alive. He was saddened that Henry Ford and Thomas Edison, two heroes of his youth, were gone, leaving, in his view, only antiseptic Fortune 500 businessmen whose sole goal was getting rich. "Ford and Edison, millionaires, geniuses and contributors to the great American idea of living, were themselves self-abdicating, almost ascetic, extremely spiritual and humble men in the world," Kerouac wrote in his diary, "and everyone knows it. Their aim was not greed and power and wealth, but a 'better way to live'—a thing still to be developed, however, since inferior men always come along to corrupt the uses of great ideas and things."[41]

The emergence of rock 'n' roll in the 1950s would have a big impact on the automobile industry. Always interested in marketing to the youth generation, Ford Motor had an unpaid ambassador in Chuck Berry, who often sang about V-8s. Growing up in segregated St. Louis, Berry refused to ride at the back of the bus. And he drove a Ford. "A used '34 Ford V-8 sedan was my first car," Berry recalled. "It cost me thirty-five dollars, putting ten dollars down. After that it was only five dollars a month. I became popular at school because of my Ford but the key was broken off in the ignition so anybody could run off with it. People sometimes borrowed my car, without asking me, to make-out in."[42] Berry later found himself in the state penitentiary for auto theft. "To me automobiles, freedom and music go hand in hand," Berry reflected. Upon his release he bought a red Ford station wagon, played rhythm and blues clubs in Illinois and Missouri, and eventually made his way to Chess Records in Chicago. It was 1955 and he recorded "Maybellene," with its famous verse:

> As I was motivatin' over the hill,
> I saw Maybellene in a Coupe de Ville,
> A Cadillac a-rollin' on the open road,
> Nothin' will outrun my V-8 Ford,
> The Cadillac doin' 'bout ninety-five,
> She's bumper to bumper, rollin' side by side.
>
> Maybellene, why can't you be true?
> Oh, Maybellene, why can't you be true?
> You done started back doin' the thing you used to do.[43]

"Maybellene" quickly became a top-ten hit and Chuck Berry became one of the founding fathers of rock 'n' roll. In *Rock Folk*, writer Michael Lyndon described best why "Maybellene" was a revolution in popular music: "A beat that made Bill Haley pallid, nutty words like 'motivatin'' and a story about a guy chasing a Cadillac in his beat-up Ford to catch his girl. O the triumph of the 'V-8 Ford' leaving the 'Coupe de Ville' sitting like a 'ton of lead.' But even more, it was the drive of the thing, the two minutes of *rock*, pure manic intensity that sucked you in."[44] Soon Berry wrote other rock hits—"No Money Down," "No Particular Place to Go," and "Too Much Monkey Business"— that portrayed the automobile as an essential factor in American life.[45]

While struggling to get Ford Motor back on its feet and promote the '49 Ford, Henry II launched an unprecedented fund-raising drive for the United Foundation, the forerunner of the United Way. As national chairman of Community Chests of America, Henry II believed that philanthropy worked best when efforts were pooled together. Money could be raised all at once to fund medical, social, educational, and other causes—if the community became directly involved with neighborhoods and companies competing against one another to see who could raise the most money. Big companies writing big checks was just part of the charity equation. Citizens had to get involved, canvassing their neighbors, passing around a donation bucket at football games, ringing doorbells, doing whatever they could in search of donations big and small. Realizing that charity starts at home, Henry II spearheaded the "Michigan Plan" in 1949, uniting 143 separate appeals under one umbrella. It would be known as a "Torch Drive."[46]

So it was that on the evening of October 18 a huge torch was lit on the lawn of Detroit's City Hall. General Mark Clark, who commanded American forces in Italy in World War II, was on hand to pass bouquet-size torches to runners who then sprinted with them to the suburbs.[47] "You in Detroit are fortunate that the leadership necessary for the United Foundation was among you," General Clark told 50,000 spectators. "Citizens of Detroit, I'm happy to launch your Operation Torch."[48] The race for the United Foundation was on. The results were extraordinary. Even as the Ford Motor Corporation made its donation of $310,000, Henry II asked his employees for help. Thousands of Ford–UAW members gave $10 each to the cause—together they raised $940,000. In the Mound Road Plant, 93 percent of the 4,000 employees participated, contributing 142 percent of their quota. Participation by the 13,000 employees in the Rouge Press Steel Plant was 94 percent. Somehow, amid ongoing labor negotiations, Henry II had brought his company together for the cause of helping the needy.

Among other windfalls, it was a public relations bonanza for Ford Motor. The *Detroit Free Press* proclaimed, "Labor Helps Light the Way," while *Life* ran a story titled "Detroit's Torch Lights the Way." In the November 21 issue of *Newsweek,* Henry II, the leader of "the way," was credited with quarterbacking the "largest single contribution of its kind in the history of public-health and welfare fundraising."[49] From 1949 to 2002 Ford Motor Company raised well over $400 million for the United Foundation (Way) Torch Drive. But what was more impressive was that, starting in 1949, the company had created a new procedure to make charitable contributions easier for employees. By checkmarking a single box on a form, workers could have ten, twenty, or one hundred dollars deducted from paychecks to help the United Foundation.[50] This concept was copied by other large corporations, and by the 1960s, payroll deduction had become a regular feature all over America. Having been thrust into his role as head of the world's second-largest auto company, Henry II started early in gaining a broader reputation as a leader in humanitarian endeavors. It was at the core of his perception of human engineering that ideas were even more valuable than dollars in helping people.

27

Fifty Years Old and Still Growing Up

Timing worked in Ford Motor Company's favor during the comeback—or refounding—of the company in the years 1945 to 1953. As Henry Ford II often pointed out, the immediate postwar years offered a long, rich seller's market, during which fundamental problems could be solved even while cars sallied out of showrooms. Ernie Breech thought that it was equally significant that Ford Motor was a private, family-controlled company and could reinvest nearly all of its profits in the solutions to those problems. "We're lucky," he said, "that we didn't have 45,000 stockholders clamoring for us to pay out this money as dividends."[1]

The international situation also unfolded fortuitously in the company's battle for survival. Immediately after World War II, national markets in Europe and the Far East were struggling to move forward economically. "While the rest of the world came out bruised and scarred and nearly destroyed," American veteran Paul Edwards boasted in Studs Terkel's 1984 oral history *"The Good War,"* "we came out with the most unbelievable machinery, tools, manpower and money."[2] The 1944 Bretton Woods conference had established the U.S. currency at a value of $35 per ounce of gold: other nations fixed their rates according to the dollar, in effect recognizing America as the world's central economy. That put a strong wind at Ford's back, but, with the constraints of material shortages and government directives, Ford subsidiaries couldn't realistically expect to advance any more quickly than the markets they served. Until they were rebuilt, intervention from Dearborn wouldn't have much effect—and that was just as well, because at first the home company was in no position to give foreign operations much attention.

The most complicated situation, not surprisingly, was in Germany. In fact, Ford did not receive any direct communication from the Cologne plant from November 1941 until November 1946.[3] Sporadic reports through Ford of

France (France SAF) indicated that the factory had been turned over to the manufacture of military trucks, and so officials in Dearborn were probably not surprised to read in a 1946 report filed by Sir Percival Perry that Ford-Werke had produced approximately 90,000 vehicles for the Nazi army between September 1, 1939, and March 6, 1945.[4] In 1943, the company had formally written off its entire investment in the subsidiary, labeling it a war loss. In accounting and management terms, it no longer owned property in Germany.

Even after the massive Ford-Werke plant in Cologne was brought under Allied control in March 1945 (two months before Germany's complete surrender ended the war in Europe), Ford Motor Company maintained its remove. Allied Occupation authorities were in charge of the factory.

As information regarding wartime Germany filtered out, the extent to which forced and slave labor had been used was especially disturbing. Throughout Nazi-held territories, POWs, foreign nationals, and concentration-camp inmates were funneled into industry, at little or no pay. Like other factories, Ford-Werke depended more and more heavily on forced labor as the German war machine spiraled downward. When the labor force grew from about 4,600 in 1942 to a high of about 5,800 a year later, the increase consisted largely of forced laborers. In keeping with the practice at other essential industries, the Cologne plant was equipped with a rudimentary camp, surrounded by barbed wire, to house forced laborers, most of them eastern European POWs or private citizens.

In 1944, Albert Speer, in his capacity as chairman of the Nazi Armaments Council, authorized the use of concentration-camp inmates in vehicle production. That August, Ford-Werke became home to a small satellite of the Buchenwald concentration camp, housing fewer than fifty men. Sixteen SS (Schutzstaffel) guards were assigned to oversee them. The inmates worked sixty-five-hour weeks, with tiny food allotments and the constant fear of disease, including typhus, which was rampant in Cologne. According to German law, conditions and privileges varied according to the nationality of the worker, but as Germany disintegrated, millions of ordinary Germans faced the same daily lot. "Production at Ford-Werke slowed at the end of the war, in part because of power shortages caused by Allied bombing runs but activity never came to a halt," Ken Silverstein reported in *The Nation*.[5]

Ford-Werke assets had grown by about 13 percent from 1939 to 1945. During that same span, the German company had paid regular dividends, none of which were transmitted to its former stockholders, Ford of England and Ford Motor Company. By the time West Germany's economy untangled itself, including the conversion from reichsmarks to deutsche marks, and the accrued dividends were released to the two Ford entities, they had a value of only about $60,000. In 1954, Ford Motor reentered its investment in Ford-

Werke on the corporate books, using a fair valuation of $557,000.[6] The 1931 plant construction, alone, had cost Henry Ford $1.5 million.

Overall, Ford-Werke had been a money loser for the parent company. Aside from a few decent years in the 1930s, the operation had been a continual drain, both in terms of money and executive energies. No large American company withdrew from Germany on moral grounds in the 1930s, but it would have been especially difficult for Ford to do so, in that it had invested massively in the Cologne plant just two years before Hitler took power in 1933. If not for that state-of-the-art factory and the commitment it represented, there would have been far less to keep Ford connected to the country.

Sixty years later, when questions were raised about the role of foreign business in the Nazi economy, Ford Motor Company took responsibility for having tried to conduct business in Germany in the 1930s. However, it refuted charges, most disturbingly presented by Ken Silverstein, that the company did business with Germany after Pearl Harbor.[7] In 1998, the company commissioned an extensive study, employing forty-five independent researchers in the United States and Europe, to investigate the relationship between Ford Motor and the Nazi regime, as well as that of Ford-Werke and the Nazis; the use of forced labor and the possibility that Ford officials in Dearborn were aware of it at the time; and finally, the financial impact of Ford-Werke's Nazi years on Ford Motor Company. The researchers collected 90,000 pages in an archive and published a summary called *Research Findings About Ford-Werke Under the Nazi Regime*. Simon Reich of the University of Pittsburgh provided an assessment of the source material, concluding, "The evidence provided by the data suggests that there was no complicity on the part of Ford's Dearborn management in assisting the Nazi government's wartime effort."[8]

Lawrence Dowler, associate librarian at Harvard University's Widener Library, also reviewed the findings. Having arrived at the material as a skeptic, he was as impressed with the quality of the research as with Ford's approach to it. "Ford's decision," he wrote, "to 'find the facts' about what happened at Ford-Werke during World War II and make the results of this search accessible to everyone sets a high standard for how corporations, especially global corporations, will now have to respond to inquiries about past policies and practices."[9]

At the end of the war, Ford Motor's situation in Germany was comparable to that of General Motors, which had written off its entire investment in Opel in 1942. Both companies had the opportunity to reassume control of the stock they had owned before the war, but neither could yet assess the condition of its factories there. A year after the war ended, Alfred Sloan still had no interest in resuming GM's business at Opel. He later blamed his attitude on the "emotional impact of the war," as well as the lack of specific information about conditions in Germany.[10] It was not until November 1948 that General Motors finally made the decision to return to Opel.

Dr. Heinrich Albert, who was chairman of Ford-Werke during the war, had written to Edsel Ford in July 1941, just as the Germans were squeezing the Americans completely out of their own company: "As a hardened optimist, I trust I shall live to see the relations between our two countries soon established in a new, favorable and lasting basis."[11] Dr. Albert lived to see that day, but he was not at the center of it. In 1946, British authorities turned down his application to become the custodian of Ford-Werke,[12] probably because his wartime record, which included both co-ownership (with Schmidt) of an arms factory and complicity in an attempt to assassinate Hitler, was too complex to sort out. Instead, Albert was assigned to head Ford's sales operation in Berlin's American and English sectors, a tiny piece of the organization he had once led.

For Ford, the process of returning to production in Germany started with many decisions over which it had no influence. For example, the Allied Control Council appointed Erhard Vitger as custodian (equivalent to managing director) in 1945. Vitger and Robert H. Schmidt had been named comanagers of the company back in 1936, but during the war Schmidt assumed full control. The German authorities did not trust Vitger, a Danish national. Upon the liberation of the plant, Schmidt was removed by the American military on the basis of his cooperation with the Nazis (he was later cleared of complicity and returned to the factory in a technical capacity). Meanwhile, Erhard Vitger operated the factory, under the authority of the Allies, and he oversaw a meeting of the shareholders in December 1947, along with the election of a new board of directors.

In March 1948, while Ford-Werke was still under Allied control, Henry Ford II visited the plant. There was never a question in Dearborn of abandoning the German market, yet a firm course had yet to be set. Attending a board of directors meeting while in Cologne, he encouraged the leaders of the company to design and build a car specifically for the German market.[13] The message was well received by Vitger and the others, especially since the plant was still making only trucks. Five months later, the Allied Control Council was satisfied that Ford-Werke had been "denazified," in the expression of the day, and it relinquished control over the plant. Over the course of the following sixteen months, remaining financial and legal hurdles were cleared and Ford was able to resume control of Ford-Werke.[14]

Germany's first postwar success was the Volkswagen, which was already in production for the civilian market in 1945. Ford Motor had seriously considered buying the Volkswagen company in 1947 but was discouraged by the fact that the company's ownership was still entangled in denazification issues.

Ford also worried that Volkswagen's main manufacturing facility in Wolfsburg was just a few miles from the Soviet occupation zone. In what may have been the greatest miscalculation of his distinguished career, Ernie Breech told Henry II that Volkswagen had no future. "What we're being offered here," Breech told him, "isn't worth a damn."[15] Starting in 1949, however, Ford-Werke reentered the passenger-car market, tooling for production of the popular, prewar Taunus version of the Ford Y.

Ford of France lumbered to its feet after the war, along with the rest of the troubled French automaking industry. Its facilities had been badly bombed during the war, when it made trucks under the management of Ford-Werke. In 1948, overcoming labor and supply problems, Ford of France managed to introduce the brand-new Vedette. Based on Dearborn's postwar small-car design, it was about as popular as any car could be in a country hobbled by government quotas on automobile manufacture. However, even within the many restraints of postwar France, the French company failed to fulfill the potential of either the product or the market, repeating the pattern of a history of fresh starts and new disappointments. In 1947, the managing director, Maurice Dollfus, turned to Dearborn and persuaded Henry II to fund a rebuilding program.[16]

Ford of England's Dagenham manufacturing plant recovered more robustly than either of the other European manufacturing plants. Financially, it was the strongest automaker in Great Britain, where the primary competition still consisted of Morris. In 1947, Morris scored a big hit with the tubby Minor, which was underpowered but cute as a bean. Other low-price cars bursting into Britain's postwar market were the Vauxhall (owned by GM), Austin, and Hillman Minx. Ford sold more cars than any of them.

Making a relatively smooth return to civilian production, Ford of England turned out sturdy Anglias and comfortable Prefects. In 1947, the company produced its first new model since 1939, the Pilot, a spacious five-seater with a powerful V-8. "In an era of austerity and vehicle- and fuel-rationing," wrote the British automotive historian David Burgess-Wise, "the Pilot seemed like totally the wrong car for the times, but its effortless progress endeared it to those who could obtain an extra petrol allowance, like doctors and farmers."[17] And also monarchs—King George VI purchased a Ford Pilot in the popular shooting brake (station wagon) body style.

Ford of Canada, less a subsidiary than a quiet cousin to Ford Motor, made its biggest changes in marketing right after the war. President D. B. Craig was intent on meeting postwar demand with an increased dealer base. The result of heavy recruiting at a time when most companies lost dealers was that the 703 Ford dealers of 1939 were 760 strong in 1945. Even more impressive, a completely new Lincoln-Mercury dealer division had been launched in 1945, and counted 353 showrooms of its own.[18] (Admittedly, some of these "showrooms" consisted of little more than a rack of brochures in a garage, hoping to sell at best one car per month, but the coverage was better than ever before.) Ford of Canada also took the initiative in rebadging its vehicles, adding styling touches to distinguish them from standard U.S. models. Canadian customers had the choice of a Ford or a Meteor, a Mercury or a Monarch. To make things even more confusing, (standard) Ford dealers were allowed to sell Monarchs as a step-up. And (standard) Mercury dealers could offer Meteors as a low-price alternative.

Ford of Canada continued to operate sales offices and assembly plants in nations that had been in the British empire in 1904, when the company was incorporated. Its wholly owned assembly plants were located in Port Eliza-beth, South Africa; Lower Hutt, New Zealand; Geelong, Australia; Singapore; and Bombay, India.[19]

South America, which was considered Ford Motor's own territory, was troubled by political strife. In Argentina, President Juan Peron's regime, with its pro-labor and nationalistic policies, entirely destroyed the Ford business that had once thrived there. In fact, much of Ford's own export business was stagnant after the war; China, another important market, closed with the Communist revolution in 1949. The company operated assembly plants in Havana, Cuba, and Mexico City. Its facilities in Yokohama were still occupied by the U.S. Army in 1947, when William McGinnis, deputy director of the Far East Group, visited Japan. He took a long cab ride out of Yokohama to see whether the Ford plant had even survived. "Drove up front, looked around, all I could see was a broken-down old wooden gate, held together with a chain and a lock, and very, very faint over in one corner was the Ford emblem, it must have been forty years old," he reported. "[The maintenance man] came dottering along with his cane. Went over and told him who I was. Ushered me into his office. Here was a truly wagon-works type of building with a little old stove in the middle, with his chair sitting beside it—and up sitting, so he could look at it, was a picture of the original Henry Ford."[20]

Ford Motor Company had put people in every nation on Earth into auto-mobiles. Moreover, it had created automobile industries in countries that couldn't have developed them on their own. All over the world, customers and employees remained loyal to Ford, but they were having a harder and harder time knowing exactly which Ford deserved their loyalties. Sir Percival Perry's organization plan of 1928 no longer fit a world still stretching and contracting after the worst war it had ever seen.

Once Ernie Breech felt confident enough about the new direction of Ford Motor's domestic operations to cast his eye on Ford International, he became depressed all over again. "One would have great difficulty exaggerating the complete confusion and disorganization that Ford Motor Company faced in its operations overseas—in Canada, too," he recalled later. As Breech examined Ford Motor's relationship with Ford of Canada, he realized that the situation, as reflected by the various types of stock, was sorely out of balance. "We participated in 17.23 percent of the earnings," Breech pointed out. "At the same time, we furnished to Ford of Canada most of their engineering, styling and technical assistance."[21]

The home company's stake in Ford of England disturbed Breech as well. The multitiered structure, by which Ford Motor owned part of the English company, which in turn owned part or all of a dozen other Fords around Europe, seemed unnecessarily convoluted. The same was true of Ford-Werke and Ford of France. There were too many percentages to track, and too little control. Not only couldn't Ford Motor Company coordinate international operations, in some shocking cases it no longer even owned its own trademarks for particular countries. France was one of them. No one abused those rights, but the muddle was nonetheless unacceptable.

In planning reorganization, Breech couldn't follow the General Motors example. GM's foreign operations consisted almost entirely of preexisting companies, such as Vauxhall and Opel, whereas Ford had been built from scratch in every country in which it did business. However, GM controlled the finances, while leaving its individual subsidiaries alone to develop products. In that respect, Ford Motor did need to change, in order to take full advantage of the scope of its international companies. Letting Ford of Canada, Ford of England, and Ford Motor go their separate ways in everything except some shared engineering was only forfeiting the potential of the multinational.

In 1949–1950, Ford Motor embarked on a complex plan to assume majority control of Ford of Canada, as well as Ford of England's stake in each of its subsidiaries. The company inherited minority stockholders with some of the companies, but ultimately it hoped to buy them out. Even as the domestic company was undergoing decentralization—leaving decision making almost entirely within the individual units—the international division was centralizing as quickly as possible. Pulling in its control over factories and sales offices from Egypt to Finland and New Zealand, Dearborn laid the groundwork for a clear chain of command in which it would set the plans and give the general orders. That was exactly the opposite of the original 1928 concept, in which "Ford of" subsidiaries had local shareholders and independent management, while the same Ford model was sold from one end of the world to the other. To complete the switch in policy, the individual "Ford of" subsidiaries would have more discretion over the creation of models unique to particular markets. No longer would there be just one Ford car around the world, but there would be, as soon as possible, just one Ford company.

In the emerging company, world markets were open to all Ford subsidiaries. Ford of Canada no longer "owned" the former British empire. Ford of England no longer "owned" the Middle East. In fact, Dearborn itself completed an important sale directly to the new state of Israel in 1949. With the barriers removed, Ford of England even began to look at the United States as a ripe market for *its* cars.

Most English automakers survived the war without the destruction that devastated other industries. For that reason, the government readily encouraged the industry and hoped that it would spearhead export trade. Donald Healey, the former rally driver who would build a fabulous line of sports cars (using Austin engines), remembered being told that he could have all the steel and other materials that he wanted—if he would bring in U.S. dollars. His Austin-Healeys joined Jaguars, Sunbeams, MGs, Triumphs, and Rolls-Royce cars in that very pursuit. In 1948, Ford of England was in the parade, too, selling good, solid English sedans that looked compact by American standards. The effort, operated through willing Ford dealerships, was only moderately successful.

Ford Motor Company never had any reason to regret its strong commitment to Ford of England, which continued to thrive in the postwar years. A greater surprise, and a welcome one, was the growth of Ford-Werke, after the frustration of the 1920s and '30s—and the tragedies of the war years. Ford of France was the only disappointment of the three European manufacturing centers. To remedy the situation, Ford Motor used its influence in the selection of an executive to replace Maurice Dollfuss. The new director was Jack Reith, an American who had started at Ford as one of the Whiz Kids. With full cooperation from Dearborn, Reith turned the factory around and managed to return good results in the early 1950s.

Many people in Detroit wondered why Ford Motor even bothered with France; GM never had.[22] Conditions there were unpredictable, especially in the 1940s, when Communists were making gains politically. In addition, the French had a particular loyalty to their own cars and carmakers. For outside automakers, France was generally more trouble than it was worth. In 1954, Ernie Breech's master plan came into view when he attended the Paris Auto Show on the lookout for a French company interested in buying his subsidiary.

Breech courted and won Simca, an economy-car maker. As a result of the deal—sometimes called a merger, although Simca made the purchase outright—the French company received all of Ford of France's manufacturing facilities. Everyone was pleased: with the stroke of a pen, Simca became bigger; minority stockholders received a good price for their shares, and those many among them who were loyal to France had the satisfaction of selling out to a familiar marque; Ford got its trademark back and, moreover, it was out of the business of producing French cars under that American name. Its cars continued to sell as well as ever in France, but they were cars built in Cologne, Dagenham, or Detroit.

⸻

To recruit executives of the caliber of Ernest Breech, Lewis Crusoe, and others, Henry Ford II had to be generous, not only with pay but opportunity. "The stick was there," he said of his overall management style. "If the guy did the job, great. I gave him all the responsibility, all the authority, all the pay and emoluments that went with it. Then I let him run with it."[23] Ford Motor went to its main source for top management—General Motors—armed with salary offers that were hard to ignore. However, GM executives were also used to participating in profits, through stock bonuses and options (the right to buy company stock at a low price). GM had pioneered the use of various stock-incentive plans, not only as a basic form of reward, but to encourage executives to think like stockholders. However, Ford Motor Company, privately held, didn't have the ability to make executives into shareholders. Or so the public thought.

In 1947, Henry Ford II initiated a secret stock plan for about three dozen executives. It offered them non-voting shares, which yielded the same dividends received by the only other shareholders: the five members of Edsel Ford's family (his widow, Eleanor, and the four children), Clara Ford, and the Ford Foundation.

The Ford Foundation had been created by Edsel Ford as a legacy in 1936. Looking into the future and the transfer of property through probate, the entire Ford family—including Henry—agreed that the foundation was a clever way to circumvent the U.S. government's so-called wealth tax, which was levied against estates worth over $50 million. To make it work, the family attorney, Clifford Longley, took advantage of a legal loophole.[24] The foundation was to receive the bulk of Henry's estate, which, combined with the endowment from Edsel's estate, resulted in a 95 percent stake in Ford Motor Company.[25] Although its shares were entirely non-voting, they were conservatively valued at just under $493 million. The shares couldn't be sold, but they did generate $25 million of dividends in an average year. Backed by figures like that, the Ford Foundation was by far the richest charity in the country, dwarfing even the Rockefeller Foundation. Yet it had no specific purpose, its charter stipulating only that it would dispense funds "for the public welfare."[26] No sooner had the codicils been signed than the Fords made sure that the new fund gave $115,000 to Henry Ford Hospital and $935,000 to the Edison Institute. But for the most part the foundation remained dormant, giving away only about $1 million a year, until Clara Ford died in 1950.

The job of setting the foundation on a firm course then fell to Henry II. In his typical fashion, he recruited a blue-ribbon committee to study the problem. He specifically sought out H. Rowan Gaither to head it. An attorney in San Francisco, Gaither was the head of the Rand Corporation, a high-level research group associated with the Air Force. Henry II told Gaither, "We want the best thought available in the United States as to how this Foundation can most effectively and intelligently put its resources to work for human welfare."[27] Henry II didn't expect the foundation to promulgate his favorite music or focus on urban problems, for which he had personal sympathies. He was entirely unlike his grandfather in that he did not have his own pet causes to promote. The only exception was that he shared his family's abiding interest in the Henry Ford Hospital, and in 1950 he did see that $13.6 million was approved for a diagnostic clinic there.

Gaither's panel looked at the work of other charitable trusts and at the needs of contemporary society. The final report, issued in October 1950, reflected the thinking of a disillusioned postwar era. That science could accomplish anything seemed to have been proved time and again during the previous century. That humankind had a long way to go, however, had also been proved. The committee concluded that "today's most critical problems are those which are social rather than physical in character—those which arise in man's relation to man rather than in his relation to nature."[28] On the panel's recommendation, the foundation's board of directors voted to dedicate its energies and the Ford family's money toward five areas: world peace, democracy, economic well-being, improved education, and knowledge of human behavior.

Although members of the family sat on the foundation board, they relinquished full control over it: Henry II specifically organized the board to include more outside directors than family members. In that way, the Ford Foundation was to be nonprofit in the purest sense, such that neither the company nor the family could manage it to selfish ends. Its first director was Paul G. Hoffman, whose connection to the automobile industry seemed almost incidental. Hoffman had started his business career before World War I as a car salesman and would end it as chairman of Studebaker. More important to the Ford Foundation, he was just leaving his post as head of the Marshall Plan, having dispensed hundreds of millions of dollars in postwar Europe.[29]

Before accepting $75,000 a year to become president, Hoffman had some conditions. He intended that the Ford Foundation would be independent, even isolated, and he emphasized that point by setting up the headquarters as a think tank for ideas in Pasadena, California, a long way from Dearborn, Michigan. The operating office was to be in New York City. Hoffman was a realist, but he wanted the foundation to be idealistic and ever optimistic in trying to find solutions to society's most hidden, damning problems. When the foundation began its active role in 1950, many reports compared it to the elder Henry Ford's *Peace Ship*—expensive, well-meaning, and naïve. Hoffman's response was a typically candid admission. "We may sail twenty peace ships," he said, "and not a one of them may reach shore." Henry II, who was present, immediately concurred with his sentiment.[30] The foundation was not approaching easy problems and there wouldn't be obvious solutions. "Ford publicly praised his successor as the best man in the order for that job," historian Alan R. Raucher maintained in *Paul G. Hoffman: Architect of Foreign Aid.* "Nevertheless, the trustees failed to define clearly the line between their prerogatives and executive direction. As it turned out, Ford and the trustees could not live with the kind of latitude Hoffman expected. And from the start, at least some of the trustees regarded the move to Pasadena as a mistake."[31] After Hoffman left early on, Rowan Gaither took over the presidency.

―――――

The Ford Foundation's average income of $25 million increased fourfold after Ford's banner year in 1949, when the Ford Division had its first sensational hit since 1928. A boom over at Mercury also contributed to the good results. The next year, while Fords were selling at a 1.1 million-unit clip, 334,000 Mercurys went to new owners.

Intimidating in appearance as well as performance, the 1949–1951 Mercurys are known in collector circles as "James Dean Mercs." In the movie *Rebel Without a Cause* (1955), the actor played a teenager who drove a '49 Mercury, souped up to be even faster than when it was new. The movie either symbolized or incubated a whole generation who believed the only home for a lonely teen was in the driver's seat of a customized family car. The Mercury filled the bill better than any other car of the time.

The standard Mercury was based on Bob Gregorie's sleek design for the 1948 Ford. Noticeably long, with a 118-inch wheelbase (compared with the Ford's 114 inches), the Mercury's styling was as smooth as a sheet in the wind. While most of the original customers liked it just that way, teenagers and others with a hobbyist's knowledge of bodywork looked upon it as a piece of granite just waiting to be sculpted—and then repainted. However the Merc looked, it was surprisingly fast, once it was moving, cruising comfortably at 90 mph. While that was probably too fast for a 1950 car (with 1950 tires), effortless speed was important to car buyers, who were increasingly captivated by limited-access highways. Staring down straightaways, having to pass occasionally, a driver learned to appreciate a reserve of power.

When President Harry Truman wanted a car without the grandeur of his usual Lincoln limousine, he ordered a 1949 Mercury. Stretched to fit a 121-inch wheelbase, his Mercury was turned into a limousine, but a low-key one with cloth seats. Truman used it just one day and then returned it, having learned very quickly that the reason limousines have to be big and grand is to make space in the backseat. The president, who was an average five-foot-nine, felt cramped in his Mercury.[32] The following year, he took delivery of a new Lincoln limousine; it was black with a red interior. With its 145-inch wheelbase,[33] it offered enough legroom for a giraffe.

As a family sedan, a commuter's coupe, or even a teenager's chop-top, however, the Mercury hit the right note. Fifth in sales in the mid-price category in 1946–1951, the Mercury was closing the gap and had at least a shot at third place.[34] Benson Ford, the head of the Lincoln-Mercury Division, worked hard to convince the Ford Motor board of directors that the Mercury had to be different from the standard Ford if it was going to take sales from the likes of Dodge and Olds. Otherwise, its customers would be deciding between buying either a Ford or a Mercury, which would never lead to increased market share for the corporation.

In 1952, Henry II formed a special committee to study Ford Motor Company's lineup, and the ways the corporation could use Mercury to spawn a new line to fill the wide gap below Lincoln. One promising possibility was the 1954 Montclair Sun Valley, which had a see-through plastic top. While its sibling, the Ford Skyliner, had a small transparent panel in the roof, the Sun Valley was clear from front to back. Because the top was tinted green, the big coupe could be ordered in only two eye-catching colors, mint green or yellow. The company dropped the idea of turning the Montclair into a separate line of upscale family cars when the Sun Valley's sales fell to only 1,787 in 1955, its second year. Both the Skyliner and the Sun Valley were hampered by the impression that a greenhouse effect would make the interior hot, despite testing that showed that even in the strong sun, interior temperatures were only 5 percent higher than those of a solid-roofed car.

Talk of a new line was also heard at Lincoln. Ever since the Continental went out of production in 1948, Ford Motor Company had been peppered with letters from loyalists, begging for a revival of "America's most beautiful car." Of course, the company was also getting thousands of letters each year trying to persuade it to resume production of the Model T and the Model A. More than other companies, Ford Motor had built certain automobiles that remained apart in the mind, cars like reveries that needed no improvement. Times might change, but the Model T would always be a great car and many people picked up a pen to tell Henry Ford II just that. Even more correspondents wanted to buy a new 1931 Model A—twenty, thirty, or even forty years after the production run ended for good. Nevertheless, the Continental contingent was taken very seriously in the early 1950s.

The old Continental, which was built for Edsel Ford and then rushed into production, was too costly to build. With that challenge very much in mind, Henry II decided to begin development of a new Continental. He put the project in the hands of William Clay Ford, his youngest brother.

Overall, Lincolns lacked the momentum of the Mercury and Ford lines. Like the Mercury, the 1949 Lincoln (and slightly longer Lincoln Cosmopolitan) offered a new flat-head V-8 engine, part of the freshened running gear engineered by Earl MacPherson, a former GM standout who was recruited to Ford by Ernie Breech. However, the Lincoln was a distant second at a time when Cadillac was in the ascendancy and seemed to represent everything that had made World War II worth winning. Cadillac's styling, with its nascent, P-38 fighter-inspired fins, was daring. The new overhead-valve, high-compression V-8 engine designed for GM by Charles Kettering, the veteran who'd invented the electric starter in 1912, supported all boasting and started the horsepower wars of the 1950s. Refusing to give up, Lincoln came back in 1952 with an overhead-valve V-8 of its own and a luxury car that was actually fun to drive. "Without a doubt, the most outstanding characteristic of the Lincoln is its handling ability," reported *Motor Trend*. "Around sweeping turns at 80 mph, neither rear wheel breaks loose."[35] While Packard gave up market share to both Cadillac and Lincoln, the two American status symbols were matched up and ready to turn on each other.

In 1950, just as Ford Motor Company was picking up the pace of its progress, world events rattled the uneasy peace of the Cold War and, incidentally, up-ended the chances of Ford to pass Chevrolet. Late in the year, the United States joined United Nations forces on the Korean peninsula and intervened in a civil war threatening to become a world war. With the Chinese army amassed on the northern border, no one was quite certain how far the conflict would expand. The United States imposed economic controls on domestic industries, just as it had in World War II. In particular, it set vehicle production limits based on an average from years past. Ford went along willingly, although the price it paid was especially high.

From 1946 to 1949, Ford Motor Company was the nation's third-largest automaker, behind GM and Chrysler. Without the rebuilding program set in motion during those years, it might have remained there, or even sunk out of sight. Instead, during 1949, Ford, with a 21.3 percent market share, was almost exactly tied with Chrysler (21.4 percent). In 1950, Ford's exertions were starting to pay off. It built just over 2 million vehicles, including tractors.[36] However, in the crucial passenger vehicle market, it commanded 24 percent to Chrysler's 17.6 percent. Then the federal government stepped in and cut automobile production by 30 percent for the duration of the war.[37] Using a standard formula, it set Ford's quota where it had been, not where it was headed. As a result, Ford was collared at about 22 percent of the market, and Chrysler caught a break, setting in at about 21 percent. As a result, Ford's pursuit of Chevrolet had to wait.

During the Korean War, Ford Motor Company renewed its defense programs, with little disruption of vehicle production. The company didn't attempt to build bombers from scratch, as in World War II, since America's aeronautics industry had developed into a far better position to do so. However, Ford's Chicago manufacturing plant was dedicated to airplane engines, while a factory in Livonia, Michigan, turned out Patton 48 tanks. The company also made other matériel, including bazooka rockets and wings for the B-47 fighter, in facilities located in Cincinnati and Kansas City.[38]

Meanwhile, the anti-Communist movement reached a feverish pitch at home. On February 9, 1950, Republican Senator Joseph McCarthy of Wisconsin claimed that the State Department was riddled with pro-Soviet spies. His accusations made immediate headlines. "McCarthyism" became synonymous with witch-hunting to the senator's critics, but his defenders maintained that he was a bulwark against Soviet penetration into American politics, culture, and business. A blacklisting of Hollywood stars and literary artists ensued. Henry Ford II found McCarthyism reprehensible. Refusing to adhere to blacklists, Ford Motor Company bravely sponsored an otherwise blacklisted broadcast of a Leonard Bernstein concert on CBS, ignoring letters of protest. It was the first major company to disregard Joseph McCarthy. "They were strong enough and conservative enough," Mark Goodson, the show's producer, recalled, "that nobody could accuse them of anything."[39] In this regard Henry II was as stubborn as his grandfather; nobody, particularly not a rude senator from Wisconsin, told Ford Motor what commercials to make or which entertainers to embrace.

Meanwhile, by 1952, the Korean War had settled into a bitter stalemate. Ford Motor, for its part, grew impatient with the production constraints. "We're proud of our part in the country's defense effort and we're prepared to do anything more that may be required of us in the future," Henry Ford II said in January 1952. "But we're very much concerned right now with the extremely harmful effect of having to cut back civilian production out of all proportion to the amount of defense production actually under way. . . . Our defense sales last year amounted to less than 1 percent of total sales. And yet our normal civilian production was held down almost 25 percent below that of 1950, and in this quarter it will be less than 50 percent of what it was during the peak months of 1950."[40]

Once the production quotas were lifted in 1953, the result was dramatic. In 1954 Ford Motor Company commanded second place in the automobile market, taking 30.5 percent of the market, to Chrysler's 14.4 percent. By then, independent automakers such as Packard and Hudson were sagging ever lower. General Motors, however, also bounded upward when constraints were lifted, taking 49.2 percent of the market—close to the 50 percent mark that was likely to ring antitrust bells at the Justice Department. From its vantage point in second place, Ford turned away from the rest and set its sights back on Chevrolet. According to visitors to Dearborn, "Beat Chevrolet" was all that anyone talked about in the mid-1950s. A reporter from *Business Week* complained lightheartedly, "You hear it so often in the executive suite at the south end of the Ford Administration Building in Dearborn, that you almost expect a brace of good-looking co-eds to pop out of a closet and organize the cheering."[41]

The advent of magazines such as *Motor Trend, Road & Track,* and *Car and Driver* in the first decade after World War II reflected the changing market for automobiles. America had not had a car enthusiast magazine since well before World War I (automobile historians looking for road tests of 1920–1950 American cars have to turn to Britain's *The Automobile* in hopes of finding reviews and statistics). There were three reasons that car magazines came back into vogue, all of which affected the kinds of cars that Ford would build in the 1950s.

First, the magazines that sprang up in 1948–1953 proved that cars had become a hobby, as they had not been since the days of the Mercer Raceabout. More than ever, a sense of personal, even intimate, enticement became part of the automobile business. Car parts no longer had descriptions, they had names: "Touch-o-Matic" overdrive, "Sea-leg Telescopic" shock absorbers, "Soft-Acting" coil springs, and "Safety-Surge" engines. A little extra money for a little something exciting was perfectly acceptable to the automobile buffs. The car magazines were helping define just what was exciting to the hip, modern driver.

Second, the chauffeur was becoming the exception rather than the rule in the luxury car market. People who could afford good cars were driving their own cars. For the first time then, the way that a flagship car felt to drive was even more important than the way it felt to ride in. Magazine road-tests critiqued that feeling in individual cars. Ford Motor had to sell driveability, especially in the Lincoln line, and to manufacture cars that behaved themselves without sacrificing power.

Finally, the sudden popularity of car magazines showed just how competitive the entire automobile industry had become. While no automaking company ever had the chance to snooze, the really snarling matchups of the past—Chevrolet versus the Model T in the mid-1920s; Packard versus Cadillac in the early 1930s—didn't last long. The 1950s produced tight, toe-to-toe competition across the widest spectrum of cars sold in America, and over a long span. Pressing for every point of market share, automakers knew perfectly well that most companies would not survive to see 1960. Engineering breakthroughs might be real or exaggerated, styling advances could be genuine or just garish, and marketing was always full of drumrolls and cymbal crashes, but underneath it all customers had a harder time than ever before choosing between models. Car magazines tried to help; at every possible opportunity, so did automakers.

In terms of self-aggrandizement, Ford Motor Company had the right news story at exactly the right time in 1953. Just as its rebirth seemed a certain success, the company celebrated fifty years in the automobile business. It was not so much a golden anniversary as a golden opportunity to redefine the company, for customers and employees alike. The company produced a film history, *The American Road,* narrated by the actor Raymond Massey. It sponsored a picture book, *Ford at Fifty,* produced by several former editors of *Life.* Privately published, the book was given to customers during the jubilee year. A slightly different version was given to employees. In addition, Ford Motor sponsored a two-hour television show, aired on both NBC and CBS, featuring appearances by Ethel Merman, Mary Martin, and Bing Crosby. Broadcasting legend Edward R. Murrow was the host. In every sphere, the biggest names accepted the invitation to join Ford for the "TV spectacular." The public was invited, as well, specifically in Dearborn, where the Rotunda Building was reopened as a visitors' center.[42]

Originally constructed for the 1933–1934 Chicago Century of Progress World's Fair, the Rotunda was a round tower with serrated edges—like a stack of automotive gears. At 212 feet in diameter and close to twelve stories tall, it was a prime example of late art deco architecture. Filled with Ford-related exhibits, it made for an immensely popular tourist attraction. (Sadly, it burned down in November 1962.)[43] In the exhibits at the Rotunda during the mid-1950s, the emphasis was on safety. For example, in a two-year study in conjunction with the Cornell Medical School, the American College of Surgeons, and the National Safety Council, Ford sought to find out what made driving dangerous and how car design could reduce the number of injuries.[44] Starting in 1956, Ford's cars would reflect the findings with features new in the automobile industry.

Ford Motor Company had plenty to celebrate. One of America's biggest industrial companies, it was first in historical importance. Singer Sewing Machines had organized a world market around a single product; Standard Oil had pioneered efficiencies of scale; American Telephone & Telegraph had conquered technological complexity; General Motors had turned the corporation into a machine that could be tuned for maximum output; and IBM had changed the pace of economic development, making a business of accelerating business. Any of these might have been deemed the most important company in the history of American business as of 1953. But Ford Motor stood outside and beyond the history of business. In the history of people—of the hundreds of millions of individuals whose first experience in buying, driving, or just riding in a car came in a Ford—it was the company with the greatest influence of all time.

The best-received gambit for the fiftieth-anniversary celebration—with the possible exception of the "TV spectacular"—was the hiring of illustrator Norman Rockwell to design a calendar. "We were looking for something to promote the company and at the same time commemorate the fiftieth anniversary," Ben R. Donaldson, director of Ford's institutional advertising, recalled. "We wanted something that would be of service, something that would be kept for a while so a calendar became our choice. At that time as I looked back over the years—of Mr. Ford's early struggles, the Model T and all—it became at once apparent that none other than the 'Rockwellian nostalgic touch' could interpret those fifty years. Thus came about the illustrations that still hang in many of the dealer showrooms across the country." Rockwell even painted a fine, utterly unsentimental group portrait of Henry Ford, Edsel Ford, and Henry Ford II.[45]

While Rockwell's paintings had been commissioned by Henry II, an innovative artist named Robert Rauschenberg finished his own offbeat tribute to the motor company. Born in 1925 in Port Arthur, Texas, Rauschenberg, who studied with German-born artist Josef Albers at Black Mountain College in North Carolina, had long been fascinated with Ford trucks and cars. He liked to "dissect" them, pulling out spark plugs and radiator belts, to use in abstract expressionist paintings, imagist collages, and other conceptual works. Considered the founder of Pop Art, along with Jasper Johns, Rauschenberg thought Ford Motor was a symbol for American culture at large. When he heard it was the company's fiftieth birthday he decided to do something about it. One evening in June 1953 he summoned his friend John Cage, a world-class composer, to his studio. Together they unfurled a twenty-two-foot strip of canvas on the floor. Rauschenberg then carefully applied black paint to all the wheels of an old Model A Ford. Cage then drove across the canvas, leaving tread marks. *Automobile Tire Print* was a sensation at the Rauschenberg retrospective at Chicago's Museum of Contemporary Art.[46]

A subtle aspect of the anniversary of 1953 was that in the midst of the celebration, it was also a leave-taking. For most of the fifty years, Ford Motor *was* Henry Ford. Henry Ford was Ford Motor, too, all by his own design. The reborn company was many, many people. Because the anniversary took place six years after the elder Ford's death—a suitable period of mourning—it gave the company a chance to step out from behind Henry's towering persona. On television, in the picture book, through the documentary, or at the showrooms, Ford Motor was shown as a modern automaking company, where the cars were the stars.

The elder Henry was acknowledged, of course. And his legacy was honored by the company in a way still unique in all of business. As part of the celebration, Ford Motor Company opened an archive for papers related to Henry Ford and his company. The need for it became apparent when family members looked through room after room of Ford's personal belongings after his death. He seemed never to have thrown anything out, from the receipt for the gasoline that powered his first automobile to notebooks and letters from fans. The combination of papers from the family and the business totaled more than 5 million items, in addition to 25,000 photographs. To organize them, Henry II hired archivists of a high academic standard.

The Ford Archives (now housed at the Henry Ford Museum and Library in Dearborn) were a compelling gift from the company in its fiftieth year, both to a past it treated with rare respect and to future researchers and Ford fanatics. Henry II also was a supporter of an oral history project to record the unvarnished recollections of Ford employees from all levels and regions. Administered by specialists trained at Columbia University, it grew to include 338 memoirs of what it was really like to work at Ford.

If the fiftieth-anniversary celebration gave people the general idea that Ford Motor was reborn, the 1954 models gave them solid proof, with a potent new V-8 engine that represented a break with the elder Henry Ford's opinions on the subject. Where Henry Ford had been devoted to the flat-head, long-stroke V-8 he introduced in 1932, the '54 models finally replaced that power plant with an overhead-valve, short-stroke V-8 engine. The basic engineering had been proven on the Lincoln, and when it was combined with the year's reengineered chassis, Fords showed pep they had never had before. The following year, they had styling to match, in an expanding lineup of choices from the most expensive, the Fairlane, to the Customline and the stripped-down Mainline. However, those were just vehicles. The automobile that symbolized the final break with fifty previous years of Ford—the Thunderbird—was yet to be born.

28

Grand Thunderbirds, Tough Trucks, and the Edsel Flop

F oreign makes started to teach Detroit automakers something about the business of selling cars to Americans in the early 1950s. The message was hard to miss as British sports cars were turning heads and capturing the fancy of thousands of drivers. In those days, when Sports Car Club of America amateur races replaced golf courses as the preferred weekend setting for the "in" crowd, Italy's Ferrari was the ultimate dream car. But Ferraris in those years were pure racers, ill behaved on a suburban commute. They were also wildly expensive. English cars offered a fitting compromise between soul-stirring excitement and real-life practicality. Jaguars, Austin-Healeys, Morgans, and other English makes, generally equipped with too little room and too much power, translated those attributes into a combination that seemed to work like a youth tonic on drivers of all ages . . . even American automobile executives.[1]

Chevrolet was the first of the major U.S. automakers to try to copy the trend, introducing the Corvette in 1953. The original two-seat Corvette was snub-nosed, but fetching. Although there was no way to tell from the outside, it had a fiberglass body, the material having been chosen in part because of the scarcity of steel during the Korean War. "The new Chevrolet Corvette has been received with a storm of enthusiastic approval wherever it has been shown," reported the first ad for the new model in Detroit newspapers. It was true. "As the first auto show 'dream car' ever to reach actual production, the Corvette sets a new style for a new field," the ad continued, "the American sports car."[2]

According to a commonly repeated legend, Ford's own sports-car program started in 1951, even before the Corvette debut. The legend came down from a story first told by styling consultant George Walker. In his rendition, Ford Division General Manager Lewis Crusoe was wandering around the Paris Auto Show in 1951, just looking at the exhibits with Walker. Before long,

Crusoe was feeling feverish from gaping at gorgeous European sports cars. Suddenly he'd had enough and he asked Walker why Ford Motor couldn't build a sleek sports car. Walker, being first and foremost an opportunist, said that it could, and that his designers were already working on just such a car. They weren't, but at the first chance, Walker slipped off to a telephone and called his office in Dearborn to place an urgent order for a sports-car design— to be finished before Lewis Crusoe returned home from Paris.

It is a good story, indicating if nothing else the way that every project has to be sold, even within a company. It doesn't seem to be true, however. In fact, at other times, Walker related that the year was 1953, and that his prince-commander was Henry Ford II.[3] In any case, employees who were on the scene in the early 1950s deny that Walker called to instigate any such styling exercise. Furthermore, there isn't a scrap of evidence of a 1951 sports-car de-sign in the corporate archives. Even as an apocryphal story, the tale does suc-ceed in diverting attention away from the Corvette as the inspiration for Ford's own sporting initiative.

Franklin Q. Hershey was hired as director of Ford car and truck styling in 1952. "The project began," he recalled, "when somebody brought a picture of the new Corvette into the Ford studio. We had never even heard of the proj-ect prior to this."[4] Part of Hershey's job was to keep designers occupied with exciting "concept cars," and he immediately set members of his staff to work, imagining a totally new car. It had to be a two-seater that was nonetheless a Ford through and through. After Hershey and Damon Wood, the styling stu-dio director, made basic sketches, a body engineer named William P. Boyer was given responsibility for developing a complete look for the car.

While Boyer was fooling around with ideas in late 1952, Lewis Crusoe wasn't in Paris. He was in Dearborn, looking over market research related to epidemic interest in European sports cars.[5] The numbers of units sold wasn't yet impressive, according to Detroit standards. Sales of all of the imported sports cars together added up to about 12,000 units in the 1952–1953 model year; the worst-selling of Ford's models that year accounted for sales of 128,000. However, the sports-car niche still intrigued Crusoe. For one thing, it was still growing, and he didn't want to miss the chance to be part of it. More important, though, Ford Motor was developing a stepladder of lines and models to match that of General Motors, a superstructure that would carry buyers from their first Mainline to the crowning achievement of Lincoln ownership. The company knew that it still had a way to go. A proposed new Continental would help people over the jump from Mercury to Lincoln. Ex-ecutives including Crusoe were also growing excited about a bigger, fancier Mercury. Looking over his research, Crusoe thought that a new sports car might plug a gap too—keeping upwardly mobile Ford owners in the fold, even as it lassoed MG and Sunbeam owners ready for a slightly bigger roadster.

By December 1952, Crusoe had turned away from the idea. The word was that the sports-car idea was a no-go. Hershey was told to dismantle the team working on the concept.

The next month, Chevrolet formally introduced the Corvette in a spectacular unveiling at the New York Motorama.

On February 9, Ford Motor changed its mind. The corporate Product Planning Committee headed by Henry Ford II issued a letter giving the Ford Division a little less than three months to develop a two-seat car capable of 100 mph.[6] Ford executives who didn't know about the mock-up coming together in Hershey's studio were relieved that the company already had something started.

When the Corvette actually appeared in showrooms in September 1953, it created heavy traffic. Since the Motorama, the company had received tens of thousands of unofficial orders for it, and celebrities like actor John Wayne had pushed their way to the top of the list. Shockingly, though, only 299 customers other than Wayne made good on their orders. The '53 Corvette was a publicity star and a sales flop. Its performance left something to be desired, especially compared with the gold standard of a Jaguar, but that would change.

With its paltry sales figures, the Corvette may not have done much for the bottom line, but it did burnish Chevrolet's image. The fact that an American company could build a sports car, even one with baby fat around the performance figures, amazed and then delighted car buffs in the otherwise stodgy United States. To salvage the initial interest in the car, Chevrolet's Edward Cole assigned Zora Arkus-Duntov, a Belgian-born engineer, to oversee the Corvette program and give the car zing.

Executives at Ford knew that the Corvette had problems, but they were impressed with it nonetheless. They wanted an image change, and a two-seater seemed to be the magic bullet that found its way into the customer's imagination. With the beginnings of an answer to Chevy's little headline stealer, Ford still needed a name for the model it was developing.

In the *ultra*-slick marketing world of the mid-1950s, a catchy, compelling name was as crucial to a car as four wheels. Crusoe extended an open invitation to his staff to submit suggestions; the male-dominated atmosphere of those days is indicated by the fact that the winner was promised a $300 suit.[7] In any case, the prize was a luxury befitting the new car, since suits costing as much as $300 couldn't be found in those days, except through a bespoke tailor. To hedge his bet, Crusoe also solicited a list of names from J. Walter Thompson, Ford's advertising agency. The candidates included Detroiter, Fordster, Hep Cat, Wheelaway, Beaver, Arcturus, El Tigre, Coronado, Apache, Beverly, Eagle, Falcon, Country Club, and Tropicale. Crusoe liked the name Savile.[8]

Alden Giberson, a member of the Ford styling staff, suggested *Thunderbird*. Hershey loved the name and so did Ernie Breech, who had just returned from a golf vacation at a California country club named Thunderbird when he weighed in on the subject. Giberson won himself a new suit. Ford received the best name put on an automobile since the Stutz Bearcat of 1911.

Of course, the Thunderbird was rushed into the marketplace as a 1955 model only because of the challenge laid down by the Corvette. Ironically, though, the Corvette would not even have made it to 1955 if not for the rumor of the new Ford. "There were conversations," Zora Arkus-Duntov said, "about the Corvette being dropped. Then the Thunderbird came out and all of a sudden GM was keeping the Corvette. I think that Ford brought out the competitive spirit in Ed Cole."[9] The first sign was the implementation of a V-8 engine in the '55 Corvette, to match the cylinder count of the Ford.

The two roadsters may have owed each other their very existence, yet they continued down entirely different paths. The Chevrolet division made a long-term commitment to improving the driving characteristics of its nascent sports car, encouraging Arkus-Duntov to turn it into a real weekend racer. Meanwhile, Crusoe pulled the T-bird away from head-on competition with the Corvette as a sports car.

Ford's new two-seater was to be an entirely new kind of a car, for America as well as Europe—a *personal* car. Crusoe invented that term and by it he meant sporty . . . but not sporting. In practical terms, he also meant that the Thunderbird would offer a response to widespread complaints about the Corvette's poor weatherproofing and general comfort level. The most conspicuous concession to comfort was the inclusion of a hardtop for inclement weather. Power accessories and the extensive use of soundproofing materials also gave the Thunderbird a more civilized air.

Styling was to be the greatest concern of all in the new Ford, as Franklin Hershey and his staff embarked on a crash effort to produce an eye-catcher. They succeeded. The result was dapper and distinctly confident-looking with slanted headlights, a wraparound windshield, and a chrome grate on the grille that was undoubtedly borrowed from Ferrari. The engine was a V-8, which might have produced some real zest, except that the effort to make the T-bird comfortable added almost 500 pounds to its original 2,500-pound weight. With a standard transmission, the engine was tuned to produce 193 horsepower; with the optional Ford-o-Matic automatic transmission, it put out 198 hp.

"An outstanding, high-performance personal car with an unusually low silhouette" was how Ford described the T-bird when production began in September 1954. According to the same press release, the new model was "a result of public demand for a distinctly different American-made vehicle combining all-weather passenger car comfort, convenience and safety with top maneuverability."[10]

The new 1955 Thunderbird cost $2,944, compared with $2,909 for the eight-cylinder version of the Corvette. The prices were roughly similar, but the sales story was far from equal. Chevrolet, which had struggled to sell 3,640 Corvettes in 1954, sold a pathetic 700 in 1955.[11] Ford Motor Company sold 14,190 Thunderbirds that year, even more than projected. Sales remained stable over the next two years. Overall, the Ford Division nipped close and almost "beat Chevrolet," accounting for sales of 1.76 million vehicles. Unfortunately Chevrolet's sales surged, too, remaining just out of reach at 1.83 million. That fight was far from over, however.

In 1958, Ford, following its three-year design cycle, would drop the two-seat T-bird and replace it with a four-seat version, part of a long trend for the Thunderbird of becoming bigger and heavier in every new incarnation. Robert McNamara, by then the head of the Ford Division, didn't know a great deal about cars, but he could read the research indicating that the T-bird would appeal to far more customers if it had four seats. Purists who loved the fledgling personal car were anguished, but McNamara and his bean counters were right: the 1958 "square" Thunderbird sold 48,482 units, and the numbers kept climbing from there until total Thunderbird sales went well past the 4 million mark in 1997, when production ended, at least for a while. But it was the original 1955–1957 T-bird that set Ford apart, once and for all, from its humble Model T past. It was downright *vain*.

An enthusiast in Missouri was watching television's *Today* show one day in 1961 when the host, Dave Garroway, called the '55–'57 Thunderbird "an American classic."[12] Word soon spread that the car had been thus anointed only four years after it went out of production. The Missouran was inspired to start the Classic Ford Thunderbird Club and executives in Dearborn took note of the *Today* compliment, periodically mentioning it in press releases.

As a matter of fact, Garroway was not using hyperbole. The first-series Thunderbird was a classic right out of the chute, if "classic" means that it captured the look and the *feel* of a certain time and place: the postwar American good life. Whenever it is that people cruise, rather than drive; when they aren't just sitting in a car, but wearing it like a fashion piece; and when they have money and time to spare, the Thunderbird looks like a brand-new car.

The 1964 model gained pop culture immortality when the Beach Boys recorded the story of a California surfer girl who would have "fun, fun, fun til her daddy takes the T-bird away." The song, which is based on a true incident, was recorded on January 1, 1964, and became an immediate hit single. Brian Wilson, the songwriter, had grown up in Hawthorne, California. His local hangout was a drive-in hamburger joint called Frostie's on Hawthorne Boulevard. One afternoon, he saw a friend pull into the parking lot, cruising in her father's new car. Every man within a one-block area seemed to turn his head in her direction. In a burst of inspiration the twenty-one-year-old Wilson composed the lyrics to "Fun, Fun, Fun," which has done more to enshrine the Thunderbird in automobile history than all of Ford Motor's advertising campaigns combined.[13]

In 1973 a classic 1955 Thunderbird became a star in director George Lucas's *American Graffiti,* a film set in 1962 about a group of California teenagers filled with rebellious spirit, uncertainty, hormonal drive, and hot-rod innocence. (In 1961 President John F. Kennedy had included fifty T-birds in his inaugural procession as a salute to modern automotive style.) In *American Graffiti,* cars weren't just transportation, they were the centerpieces of young people's lives. The most iconic scenes in the film involved a woman in a white Thunderbird. "The film's buried strength shows an innocence in the process of being lost," wrote film critic Roger Ebert, "and as its symbol provides the elusive blonde in the white Thunderbird—the vision of her always glimpsed at the next intersection, the end of the next street."[14]

Trying to capitalize on that "night after," Ford Motor Company began reproducing retro Thunderbirds in 2002. With a starting price of $34,495, the reborn "bird" had a sensational debut, selling out all 25,000 units in just a few months. "We told you the Thunderbird would be back, and here it is," Ford President Jacques Nasser declared at the Detroit Auto Show at its unveiling.[15] Designer J. Mays made the 2002 model ten inches longer than the 1954 original. "Everywhere we drove in our turquoise T-bird, we were quick to collect a crowd," Paul A. Eisenstein wrote in *The Car Connection,* an online journal, after giving it a test ride along California's Highway 1, near Big Sur. "Even those who have no memory of the original convertible seem drawn to gawk and admire its old-is-new lines."[16] The reissue of the Thunderbird is a reminder that vehicles, if they develop a brand loyalty, can always be reintroduced to the marketplace when nostalgia sets in—when they are, in a word, classic.

The T-bird helped Ford sail away from its image as a workingman's car, just as the Corvette yanked Chevrolet away from the aura of a dull car. Those were the failings that the models were intended to fix. The two roadsters, built by two companies competing toe-to-toe and considered similar in many respects, were actually quite different in the eyes of the people who built them.

The Thunderbird is an ideal case study of how Ford Motor rescued itself from peril after World War II: its guiding principle was simply to follow General Motors in as many ways as possible. "There's hardly anything we're doing that GM hasn't done," said J. Emmet Judge, a Ford product planner, in the mid-1950s. "They know their business and a sweet-running business it is. We're just trying to catch up."[17] Before the end of the decade, Ford Motor had caught up, to every possible extent. It was as vigorous a company as GM, with a management roster as deep and products as exciting. The result was that Ford could no longer move forward simply by copying the GM model. A bitter lesson in the form of the Edsel would prove that point and in an indirect way push Ford into a corporate kind of maturity.

By one measure, the company was fifty-five years old in 1958; by another, it was only a thirteen-year-old, having been reborn with Henry Ford II's assumption of the presidency in 1945. Either way, at the end of the 1950s, Ford Motor would have to make its way in the future by proving how *different* it was from General Motors, not how similar it could be if it tried.

At the start of the 1950s, the major impetus at Ford was the development of a lineup to match the marketing juggernaut that GM had constructed out of the Cadillac-Buick-Oldsmobile-Pontiac-Chevrolet lines. While loyal Ford executives were obsessed with "beating Chevrolet," Henry II was privately talking about beating all of General Motors, car for car. As of 1955, Ford Motor was ready to make a try. In staff discussions, the thinking on the subject turned into a kind of game that handicapped each slot in the car market. The standard Ford could, in theory, outsell Chevy, while deluxe Ford models could meet Pontiac. Mercury might take on Oldsmobile, and Lincoln, though it was a distant second in the early 1950s, *could* match Cadillac. Such were the discussions that filled the air in Dearborn.

No matter who was talking, however, and how much imagination was used to plump up the strength of the Ford divisions, one very profitable part of the market was surrendered to GM. It was the upper-medium range of attractive but not ostentatious cars—those that appealed to professionals and families, comfortable, respectable people who wanted a car with exactly the same qualities. In a word, what Ford was missing was a Buick.

In one crucial respect, Ford Motor did have an edge on GM. Trucks, which had been part of the Ford offering since 1905, were something of an afterthought before World War II. That wouldn't be the case in the postwar world. Trucks were destined to become an essential part of the increasing demand for choices in passenger cars. They had a masculine allure that passenger cars lacked. A scene in novelist Joyce Carol Oates's *We Were the Mulvaneys* perfectly captures that allure of Ford trucks. In the novel the narrator's father runs a home-roofing business and uses his Ford pickup both to carry equipment and to advertise. Because he often ventured down unpaved roads his truck was usually splattered with dirt—he liked it that way. "Might as well buy our vehicle mud-colored to begin with," he frequently said, "saves time."[18]

Ford grandly reintroduced its trucks in 1948, along a plan that offered 139 models on eight different platforms matched with one of three different engines. From the super-heavy-duty, three-ton F-8 truck, the models worked down through seven more numbers and a rash of weight ratings to the half-ton F-1 pickup. The F-series, which continues today, became a spectacular success for Ford Motor, inspiring more loyalty than any of its passenger lines. The "Built Ford Tough" F-series anticipated the need for a vehicle that was practical, sturdy, and unpretentious. In the 1960s, it would begin a long run, interrupted only once, as the nation's best-selling truck. By the 1980s, the pickup truck had moved off the farm or construction site and into the hands of many customers who didn't haul anything, and never scuffed the truck bed with anything heavier than a bag of groceries.

In a car world long dominated by horsepower, the pickup truck would come to represent a different kind of strength, a personal statement of ruggedness. If Ford was not catering directly to such future customers with the first F-series light-duty trucks, it was at least starting to attract them, those millions who wanted a truck . . . without needing one. A primary selling point in the light-duty line was the "million-dollar cab," a name that described the cost of developing a truck interior with something of a sedan's amenities, including ventilation and adjustable seating.[19]

The trend continued in the $50 million worth of refinements Ford made in 1953 to its trucks. "There's no mistaking, this is a truck meant for driving," wrote Don Bunn of the '53 model in his book, *Classic Ford F-Series Pickup Trucks, 1948–1956*. "And that's part of the plan. For the first time in truck history, Ford engineers made the driver their most important consideration when designing the F-100 series."[20]

Because hard-bitten farmers hated spending money far more than they liked personal comfort, the standard Ford truck was left as spare as ever, although it was roomier for 1953 and had the addition of small shock absorbers for the seats. However, softies and city slickers could pay extra for the optional "driverized cab," which included a padded ceiling and a quieter ride, armrests, visors, and door locks. The small luxuries that made the F-100 so inviting reveal just how uncomfortable pickup trucks could be when they were, by philosophy and equipment, actually just for work. If you wanted a radio, for example, you had to bring one along. Heaters cost extra. And anyone who wanted air-conditioning in those days could sit outside in the truck bed. Nonetheless, with the F-100 of 1953 the Ford pickup was distinctly moving toward the passenger-car market.

Truck styling had been surprisingly sharp in the 1930s, when showy, art deco sculpture in chromium adorned the grilles on pickups. Appearance once again became a widely discussed selling point with the F-100. Customers couldn't help noticing the low, wide grille, painted light gray in contrast with the body color, which was most often black or red. Overall, the front end was massive and actually out of proportion with the cab and the truck bed trailing rather lamely behind, but customers loved it then—sales jumped from 94,000 in 1952 to 133,000 with the introduction of the F-100—and collectors love it today. The first of the F-100s are considered the most desirable of vintage Ford trucks.

At the other end of the spectrum, the Lincoln was solidifying its reputation around high performance and what was called "roadability." For 1953, Benson Ford, general manager of the Lincoln-Mercury Division, was overseeing a dramatic increase in horsepower, from 160 to 205, making the Lincoln the first American car since the J-Duesenberg to offer more than 200 bhp. Although he was plagued with health problems, Benson enjoyed racing and even drove the pace car for the Indianapolis 500 three times.

If he wanted a place to prove his new grand Lincoln tourer, however, Indiana was not the place: he found it in the very un-Lincoln-like atmosphere of Mexico's roughest backcountry.[21] Benson Ford personally made the decision to support Bill Stroppe, a Southern California racing professional. Stroppe wanted to enter a team of 1953 Lincolns in the 1952 Pan-American Road Race, a long-distance competition in the same category as Europe's glorified Le Mans, Tourist Trophy, Mille Miglia, and Nurburgring races. Run over 1,934 miles of varied terrain in Mexico, the Pan-American was considered the toughest of the quintet.

Remarkably, Stroppe's Lincolns gobbled up the worst of the course as smoothly as they would glide down the New Jersey Turnpike. A driver named Pat Lockwood, driving a Chrysler in the race, described his encounter with a Lincoln driven by Walt Faulkner. "While I was clocking 113 mph," Lockwood said, "Walt Faulkner cruised by in his Lincoln. I dropped in about six feet behind and tried to draft him. I could see his tachometer through his back window—mounted high on the dash cowl—steady on 5,000 rpm . . . 130 mph! What can you do? Next day I was out of the race."[22]

Lincolns finished first, second, third, and fourth in the touring division of the race, the winning car *averaging* 90.98 mph over the rugged course. That time beat most of the Ferraris, Jaguars, and Alfa Romeos entered in the sports-car division as well. After the race, Benson brought the winning drivers to Detroit—not for a parade, but for conferences with the engineering department. No two groups knew the Lincoln better. The discussions about the experience in Mexico resulted in changes implemented on the '54 model.[23] Stroppe's Lincolns repeated their feat in the '53 Pan-American Road Race, finishing in the first four places. In 1954, Lincolns entered by several different teams also dominated the results, but that year, eight people were killed during the running of the race. It was the last Pan-American allowed in Mexico.

Lincoln's participation in the Pan-American race reflected the haunting problem that Ford Motor would face with motor sports over the following two decades. On one hand, the company and its products had a natural affinity for racing. Truly useful engineering ideas emerged from competition. And the advertising certainly didn't hurt. Although Lincoln didn't display the Pan-American results in its own ads, word inevitably circulated that the Lincoln "had beat the European field at its own game." All of that was for the good: for Ford, spectators, and the advancement of the automobile as an invention. On the other hand, the ugly truth was that racing killed people, both observers and participants, and it happened more than just occasionally. Every time there was a bad accident, all of the goodwill was wiped clean and replaced on the part of the public by a gloomy suspicion that car companies were essentially irresponsible and didn't care about anything except selling cars and making money.

Because Ford Motor Company was engaged in an all-out effort to promote safety in its cars during the mid-1950s, racing was especially hard to fit into the picture. It always would be. However, the growing popularity of stock-car racing on the NASCAR circuit gave the company a manageable outlet. Anyway, there was little choice. Chevrolet, Chrysler, and even Hudson were racking up victories that were the talk of the South, where NASCAR fever took hold first. Victories on Sunday translated very distinctly into sales on Monday, especially in the early days of stock-car racing when the entries were by and large *stock* cars—production models that were refined but not substantially altered. Ford Motor entered the fray starting in 1955, cooperating with private racing teams, including one organized by Bill Stroppe to run Mercurys on NASCAR ovals, and hiring Pete DePaolo, a veteran of Indianapolis 500 racing, to oversee a factory stock-car Ford team.

Racing was not, however, the competition that interested Ford Motor most. With Henry Ford II as president, Benson Ford in charge of the Lincoln-Mercury Division, and William Ford Sr. learning the business in charge of a Special Products Division, the brothers were running a hard race of their own. "We do a lot of needling among ourselves," said William Ford. "Of course in the Ford family, everyone thinks he's a stylist. Ben is perhaps the most serious. Henry will give you a hard time on everything and usually does. We are all reasonably opinionated. We agree on policy matters, but when we get into operational matters we disagree quite violently at times. But on one thing we all agree: what we do make, we want to be first with."[24] They seemed to be on their way.

As of October 1954, the Ford Division was running nearly even with Chevrolet in sales. The Thunderbird was the talk of the country's automobile enthusiasts. Mercury was selling well, Lincoln production was increasing. And the first meeting of the Lincoln Continental Owners Club was staged in Greenfield Village.

For a car that had gone out of production only six years before to have a club of devotees was remarkable, especially since the Continental enthusiasts were neither grease monkeys nor hobbyists interested in brass-era horseless carriages. They were upper-middle-class sophisticates adamant in the opinion that the Continental had mastered qualities offered by no other car before or since. It was beautiful but not flashy, as big as an ocean liner and just as smooth, powerful yet easy to drive. The Continental was a quiet conqueror on the road and it was sorely missed.

As part of the regular business, the members of the Lincoln Continental club were scheduled to hear a speech by William Clay Ford. "Ever since 1948, we've been receiving requests that the Continental be resumed," he said, speaking directly to the well-dressed enthusiasts responsible for many of those requests. "Now it gives me great pleasure to announce that we've designed a new Continental and will have a plant for building it. Because of my special interest in this car, I am happy to announce that I will head up this new organization, which will be called the Continental Division."[25] The cheering was loud and long, prolonged by the sheer sense of relief in the air. Of course, the new Continental had been in development for years under William Ford's auspices, but the announcement in his speech made it a certainty in showrooms. It would be introduced in 1955.

For the time being, the Ford version of the GM lineup was coalescing. In addition to Ford and Ford trucks, Mercury, Lincoln, and the haute Continental, the company was also starting research on a Buick beater, to reside between Mercury and Lincoln.

———

In 1954, Ford cars, trucks, and its line of tractors were popular enough to generate $4 billion in sales.[26] The company that the elder Henry Ford had seized for nearly $106 million in 1919 through his buyout of the minority shareholders now had an estimated worth of $3.5 billion.

All of the figures were on Ford's side. Profits, which had been nonexistent in the years immediately before and after World War II, were building steadily, from an estimated $138 million after taxes in 1951 to $200 million in 1954.[27] All the while, Henry II and his team used profits just the way old Henry would have wanted them to—they plowed most of the earnings back into the company. Twenty-eight *new* plants opened at Ford between 1945 and 1955, in such cities as Hapeville, Georgia; Claycomo, Missouri; Louisville, Kentucky; and Wayne, Michigan. They were joined by twenty parts depots and fourteen major office or engineering buildings.[28] Ford was on a renovation jag as well. In all, the company sank $1.4 billion on its manufacturing facilities in the same ten-year span, with the result that in the mid-1950s, Ford Motor was considered the most modernized, automated carmaker in the

United States. Old Henry Ford would have cheered. Ernie Breech, the man responsible for much of the spending spree, was relieved that the Fords took a long-term view when it came to money, and that there were no stockholder groups clamoring for a different policy.

However, the company did have one shareholder clamoring, or at least wondering aloud about the situation. While the Ford Foundation owed its very existence to the largesse of the Ford family—and the exigencies of U.S. tax law—it was increasingly uncomfortable in its role as silent partner in an automobile company. By 1954, H. Rowan Gaither, the foundation president, was concerned that the charity's entire endowment was wrapped up in its ownership of 3,089,908 of the 3,452,900 shares outstanding in Ford Motor. The balance was owned by the Ford family and, in much smaller quantities, by 108 senior employees of the company.

Ford's habit in the postwar years was to distribute about 25 percent of its aftertax profits as dividends—hardly a profligate amount according to the business traditions of the time. However, the Ford Foundation presumed that it could find investments that yielded more income, and as a charity bound to disburse large amounts of money, it made income one of its top priorities. The only consideration held even higher was predictability. The automobile industry, a classic cyclical business, had good years and bad years: that was about all that was truly predictable about it. The Ford Foundation felt that it could make safer projections about income if its capital was spread around widely, with an emphasis on bonds and other investments much "duller" than stock in a car company.

For these perfectly practical reasons, and with no hard feelings, the Ford Foundation indicated that it was ready to sell part of its stake. Since no one person could afford even a fraction of the total holding, the specter of a public sale of stock loomed before Ford Motor Company.

The process of taking the stock of even a small company into the public markets is sensitive and complex. Documents have to be filed in the right order and on time with a host of entities, including the Securities and Exchange Commission, the IRS, and at least one stock exchange. Examiners for those entities have stringent requirements. Even after the way has been cleared, the company has to find an investment banking firm (the underwriter) to assist in this registration process and, upon approval, to distribute the stock, usually through a syndicate of sellers (the brokerages).

Henry II had already made sure that Ford Motor was as prepared as any family-controlled company could be. For years, he had managed the company as if it were a public company, in terms of not only access but accounting procedures, record keeping, and protocol at meetings. "Since I became president," Henry II said, "we have tried to run the company so that anyone who had the right could come in and look at anything we are doing."[29] During his tenure, the company had issued annual reports equivalent to those published by public companies. The only recipients at first were the five stockholding members of the family and directors of the Ford Foundation; later, the company's stockholding executives also received copies.

Nonetheless, the challenge of taking the nation's fourth-largest industrial company public was daunting. The three companies bigger than Ford had been *born* as public companies: General Motors, Standard Oil (New Jersey), and AT&T could never have been built into empires without the public's money. That Ford was so late in joining their ranks was almost as remarkable as the fact that the company itself wouldn't even realize any money from the sale.

Other than the paltry $28,000 seed money raised in 1903, Ford Motor had never needed outside investment. In 1955, it still didn't need money, but it did need the public's trust and common spirit. In Henry Ford's day, a one-owner company could engender confidence and loyalty, depending upon the owner. But Henry II was thinking along different lines. He didn't want people buying his cars simply because he was the president. For the company to survive, it needed an executive, not a front man. The only real way to replace the towering identity of its legendary owner, old Henry Ford, was with hundreds of thousands of owners with other names.

Finding a way to sign them up wouldn't be a simple matter. Overall, planning for the stock issue took two years. The Ford Foundation started by appointing a committee headed by Charles Wilson (not the GM president, but Charles *Edward* Wilson, the former president of General Electric) to investigate possible avenues by which the charity and the company looming behind it could disperse shares. Henry II and the rest of the Ford family maintained a distance and waited to hear what the committee concluded. To effect the sale, any viable plan would convert outstanding stock into new classes. The Wilson committee's initial proposal called for the foundation to sell a portion of its non-voting shares, leaving voting control entirely with the family.

Oddly enough, it was the Ford family who insisted that voting shares also go into the sale. "If you go this road, you might as well go the whole road," explained a spokesman on behalf of the Fords. "When you have strings on it, you fool no one at all."[30] Of course, allowing the public to hold voting shares didn't mean that control left Dearborn—the family opted to retain 40 percent of the voting stock, enough to ensure its decisions would ultimately carry. In May 1955, the Ford Foundation announced that in January 1956 it would offer 15 percent of its holdings in Ford Motor to the public, the biggest single stock issue in the history of U.S. markets.

The news created a sensation. Edward Glassmeyer, vice president at Blyth & Co., the lead underwriter, marveled, "This Ford thing is fantastic. *We've* never seen anything like it, and neither has anybody else. Why, here at Blyth, we've got thousands of letters from people we never heard of before. Lots of the letters seem to be from people who have never invested in stocks in their lives. All of them want Ford, and some enclose checks. We keep the letters on file but, naturally, we return all the checks."[31]

The reason to buy any stock is belief in a company's future, but in the case of Ford Motor Company, much of the pent-up demand seemed to come from people who wanted to buy a piece of Ford's past. A San Francisco Ford dealer who started his agency in 1903 signed up for 250 shares, the most possible according to the limits set in the offering. A seventeen-year-old boy from Ohio wanted five shares, to go with the three Model T Fords he'd collected and restored.[32] In the popular imagination, the story of Ford Motor Company was the greatest business success story in American history; the stock sale seemed to signal that a new chapter was about to begin.

The fate of the previous group of shareholders was well known in 1955: every $1,000 invested in 1903 was worth $2.5 million sixteen years later, and that didn't even count more than $250,000 in dividends. For his part, Henry Ford II tried to warn potential shareholders that it was unrealistic to expect growth on that scale from Ford Motor, circa 1956. He said publicly that many people "are indulging in wishful thinking about their chances for fabulous gains." Ernie Breech issued a warning that Ford Motor shares were "no uranium mine."[33] Deep down, most people must have known that. They still wanted some of the stock.

The greater the number of people who were interested in the stock in the weeks leading up to the offering date in mid-January, the more unrealistic it became to hope for more than a few shares. "Put in for fifty shares and you might get five," said a broker in New York.[34] The Ford Foundation announced that it would increase the number of shares on the block, from 15 percent of its holdings to 22 percent. The extra allotment was intended to alleviate pressure building up before the sale—and make more money for the foundation, of course. This new issue also reflected a split to put even more shares in circulation.

Because of listing requirements, the Ford stock wouldn't be eligible for trading on the New York Stock Exchange until March; that left it to over-the-counter trading in its initial public offering on January 18. On the afternoon of January 17, the selling price for the newly issued shares was officially set at $64.50. People who had put in an order were contacted by their brokers with news of the price and the number of shares the customer had been allotted. Any customer who agreed to that price became, as of the next morning, a newly minted shareholder in Ford Motor Company. Because most of the stewardesses, schoolteachers, and retirees who bought shares intended to keep them, buyers still outnumbered sellers and trading pushed the price up to slightly more than $69 by the first day's close. On Wall Street, old pros talked about the Ford sale as the dawning of a new era, in which "investing in stocks might become as popular as owning a car or a washing machine."[35]

When the smoke cleared, more than 350,000 people owned shares, with an average person holding about 29 shares. That was consistent with the Ford family's plan to make Ford a "people's stock," held by average individuals (and potential car customers). AT&T, the most widely held stock in the 1950s, was the quintessential small-holders' stock, but even its owners were grander than Ford's, having an average holding of 39 shares. General Motors, which was in second place on the most-widely-held list, was a more typical stock, in that it was part of many institutional portfolios and reflected an average holding of 539 shares. In truth, though, the math used to calculate Ford's distribution was symbolic, since it sidestepped the fact that the foundation and the Ford family still owned 79 percent of the shares in the company. The various shareholders watched with dismay, although perhaps not too much surprise, as the excitement surrounding Ford stock quieted down and the share price drooped during the first year from its $64.50 initial-public-offering price to $54.25. "It turned out they were all suckers," said a portfolio manager in New York.[36]

If Ford's new stockholders were out for a quick "killing," then they were indeed suckers. Five years later, in 1961, the stock had recuperated and was nearly double the IPO price. But that is beside the point. The reason many people ordered stock in Ford on January 18, 1956, was not, in the immediate sense, monetary. Likewise, neither was Ford Motor's reason for authorizing the sale. Both sides were party to a historical transition, in which the family in charge of the nation's fourth-largest company acknowledged with uncommon grace that there are reasons, which have nothing to do with money, that a large business in modern times has to have a whole population of owners.

———

While the Thunderbird had shown that Ford Motor Company could build cars with youthful allure and compete in image with the Corvettes, Jaguars, and Austin-Healeys of the road, the arrival of the Continental Mark II in autumn 1955 showed that the company understood an even more rarefied niche, one in which most customers never even looked at price tags. In fact, an exalted price was one of the "selling points" of the new Mark II—at nearly $10,000, it cost at least $3,000 more than the next-most-expensive American car (the Cadillac Eldorado). That had been the idea from the start, as one member of the development team later recalled: "What we had going for us in the Continental Mark II was literally a revival of the Duesenberg concept—a no-holds-barred, all-out luxury car of impeccable design and exquisite taste, amply but not excessively powered—and certain to strip Cadillac of its mantle as the ultimate car in the eyes of Americans."[37]

William Clay Ford, although only thirty, proved to be the ideal manager for the project. He was, in the words of John Reinhart, the chief stylist, "the most enthusiastic guy on earth, though he was also young and a little bashful at the time. But like [industrial designer Raymond] Loewy, he had exquisite taste, and he knew when an idea was 'right.'"[38]

Ford's older brother, Henry II, knew when an idea was wrong. When he saw the renderings of the first design for the Continental, he said, "I wouldn't give a dime for that car," and turned away. To hedge the company's risk in the project—and showing no favoritism for his little brother's feelings—he commissioned four independent design teams to present their own ideas for the new model. The competition was to be judged by Henry II and other members of the company's senior executive staff. William Clay Ford's team, which included Reinhart and Gordon Buehrig (designer of the Cord 810, among other classic cars), went back to work, under enormous pressure. Working late every night and around the clock at times, they produced the design that won the nod.

The team spirit continued all the way through development of the new Continental. As Reinhart later told Richard Langworth of *Automobile Quarterly* magazine, "It was one of those once-in-a-while things, when the men around a car believe in it so implicitly that they'd work at anything for any time to insure its success."[39]

Ford's team refined over the following year a low coupe (fifty-six inches high), with comfortable seating for four. Exquisite in finish and rock-solid in engineering, the new Mark II was understated in design, as though it was aware of all of the road-show excesses of mid-1950s design and chose to remain aloof. The initial response from the public justified the effort behind the new Continental Division and its ultra-sophisticated car. In Cleveland, the waiting list for new Continentals stretched to sixty-seven names—which was impressive for a car that cost five times as much as a standard Ford. In Los Angeles, customers gladly paid a $1,000 premium for a boost to the top of the waiting list. Because the dealer in Syracuse, New York, had no Continental to show—he'd sold every one he received—he arranged to fly interested customers to Detroit for a test drive.[40] No amount of trouble could be too much; dealers received $2,300 for every Continental sold.[41]

The Continental was a fabulous success in its first four months. "I won't sell this car to a man who doesn't belong in it, even if he has the money," huffed a salesman who was making a point about the exclusivity of the car. If he was serious, however, he was confessing to an illegal practice. Anyway, after the first few months, dealers could no longer afford to be choosy. Demand for the Continental wilted. Although the car was everything promised, it was expensive. It was also limited, in that the coupe was the only style available.

Customers rich enough to afford the Continental were likely to be spoiled enough to want a choice in body styles. The actual price paid dropped quickly as the model was heavily discounted.

Even at nearly $10,000, Ford claimed that it lost a thousand dollars on every Mark II. At the typical negotiated price of $8,000, the car was a conspicuous money loser. Had William Clay Ford carried more weight within the company, the division might have been given the opportunity to expand upon the initial reception to the Mark II, with other planned versions, including a convertible and an innovative "berline," with a separate compartment for a chauffeur. To the dismay of fanatics, and the personal disappointment of William Ford, the company had little patience and the Continental was effectively killed in 1957. The name continued, but on a line of Lincolns, not on limited-edition, *true* Continentals. The division also dissolved into the Lincoln-Mercury section.

The Continental Mark II had realized the goal of repeating the impact of the original "Edsel Ford" Continental, introduced in 1940. Each car was ideally suited to its decade, but both were elegant in the way that the early-nineteenth-century arbiter Beau Brummell intended when he said, "If you notice a man's clothes, he isn't well-dressed." Neither the first Continental nor the Mark II tried overtly to draw attention. Yet in their own times and long afterward, they were cars that couldn't be ignored.

By 1955, Ford Motor had proven, twice, that it could *imagine* an exciting car and develop it from scratch. The Thunderbird and the Mark II had been developed by entirely separate entities within the corporation, but in both cases the result was a car that was unique, well constructed, and fetching to look at. The Ford Motor Company of the 1950s could create cars just as well through its endless committee meetings as Henry Ford did with his tight-knit hierarchy.

However, neither the T-bird nor the Continental represented great triumphs for Ford's marketing department. The idea for the T-bird had been thrust upon Ford by the advent of the Corvette, and the Continental arose out of a previous model. In 1955, Ford's Executive Committee authorized a massive marketing effort as a precursor to a new car, a new division, and a whole new niche for Ford Motor Company.

It was a remark from Ford Vice President Lewis Crusoe that crystallized the intention to plunk another division in between Mercury and Lincoln. With the success of Ford and Mercury cars, he complained, "We're growing customers for General Motors."[42] He meant that when people were ready to "trade up" from a Ford, they had little choice but to switch to another make—unless they had enough money to buy a full-scale luxury Lincoln. Ford Motor may have taken 17 percent of the low-medium car market in 1955, but its share of the upper-medium bracket was only 3 percent. Since that upper-medium bracket accounted for half of the cars sold in America, the company had to provide a line to match the market. It had to match Chrysler's Dodge and DeSoto, Packard's Caribbean, and most of all, GM's Oldsmobiles, Pontiacs, and Buicks.

The Special Products Division, which was charged with creating the new car, looked first to its director of planning for market research, David Wallace. He had to define the personality of the new car, based upon the profiles of the people who could be expected to purchase it. With help from the Bureau of Applied Social Research at Columbia University, Wallace canvassed car customers to learn what their perceptions were. The respondents defined the Mercury—then in the midst of its heyday as a strong performance car—as suited to a "dance band leader" or a "race driver."[43] The general perception was that a Mercury owner was no wealthier than a Ford owner, but was more likely to spend money on a speedy car. If that was the prevailing opinion, and the statistics bore it out, then it was no wonder that people who owned Fords didn't gravitate to Mercury as the next step up. It didn't make them look any richer. Such marketing studies showed Ford executives why they were selling only 3 percent of the upper-medium bracket. There weren't all that many dance band leaders or race drivers in the country.

In 1956, Wallace submitted a full report detailing the kind of new car that people seemed to want in the upper-medium range. The car in question was code-named "the E-car," which stood for "experimental car." Wallace wrote:

> The most advantageous personality for the E-car might well be THE SMART CAR FOR THE YOUNGER EXECUTIVE OR PROFESSIONAL FAMILY ON ITS WAY UP.
>
> Smart car: recognition by others of the owner's good style and taste
> Younger: appealing to spirited but responsible adventurers
> Executive or professional: millions pretend to this status, whether they can attain it or not
> Family: not exclusively masculine, a wholesome, "good" role
> On Its Way Up: "The E-car has faith in you, son; we'll help you make it!"[44]

The car being developed to be all those things to just the right people was planned around an all-new but fairly conventional platform. No one could call the interior conventional, however. Drivers could use push buttons to change gears, open the trunk, or adjust the headlights. Once the driver preset a certain speed, the speedometer would flash red to signal when it had been exceeded. The E-car was, like the Continental, planned as a separate division, but it was designed in four separate models. The two largest had boasting rights on engine output for the entire U.S. automobile industry, with 345 bhp.

The most important factor in any new car, however, may well be the styling. With no other input or experiences to go on, a customer is likely to be permanently swayed by the first impression. The E-car, designed by a large staff, was the direct responsibility of Roy A. Brown, a Ford stylist originally from Canada. The result was exactly the opposite of the Continental Mark II, which a *Motor Trend* writer had called "as crisp as Pascal celery." The E-car was anything but crisp. In the same way that a profusion of push-button gadgets had been squeezed into the interior, chrome, lights, and lines crowded practically every surface on the exterior. The front grille, which was wide in the manner of late-1950s cars, had a vertical element, shaped like a narrow shield, in the middle. It was intended to remind observers of the classic radiator shells of the 1930s. Polite people called it the "horse harness." Others called it a toilet seat.

As is altogether too well known, the E-car, later called the Edsel, fizzled. Upon its much ballyhooed debut on September 4, 1957, the car was not well received by the public, failing to find even a fraction of the customers necessary to make it a break-even proposition. There were plenty of reasons offered. The model year, 1958, was a bad season for automobile sales. The car was notorious for bugs and breakdowns. The styling was ungainly and turned off the "smart" people it was supposed to attract. However, the most vehement reason given for the failure of the Edsel was that it was a product of surveys and polls, rather than "seat-of-the-pants" intuition about the business of making cars.

The tragic disappointment surrounding the Edsel was reflected in the search for a suitable name for the car. As with everything else pertaining to it, no effort was spared to find the perfect name. The only specification that Henry Ford II and the rest of his family set at the beginning was that "Edsel" would not be acceptable. With that, a committee at the Special Products Division devised a list of guidelines:

1. The name should be short, so it will display well on dealers' signs.
2. It should have two, or at the most three, syllables to give it cadence.
3. Its sound should be clear and distinct, to aid in radio and television identification.
4. It should start with the letters C, S, J, F or others subject to calligraphic sweep for ornaments and advertisement signatures. Heavy-footed letters as M, W, and K would be out—too rooted.
5. It should not, of course, be prone to obscene double-entendres or jokes. It should not translate into anything objectionable.
6. It should be American; foreign expressions are taboo.[45]

After canvassing strangers at airports and other public places, the Special Products Division enlisted the help of its advertising agency, which sent a representative to Dearborn with a binder containing six thousand names, in alphabetical order and cross-referenced. "But my god," said Richard Krafve, the head of the division, "we don't want six thousand names. We only want one!"[46] That is, one *good* name: everybody in the company cringed when Benson Ford began promoting the name "Drof," which was Ford spelled backward.[47]

The Pulitzer Prize–winning poet Marianne Moore—celebrated for her condensed and precise imagery, in such collections as *Observations* and *The Pangolin and Other Verse*—was even consulted on the basis that she understood language and the modern mood better than anyone else. Moore, a celebrity poet known for wearing a tricorn and black cape at public events, was as dogged in the search as anyone else, writing to the company with dozens of possibilities. Her selections reflected her well-known love of the animal kingdom and natural world. The most conventional name she submitted was Chaparral, but she also tried out Mongoose Civique, Thunder Crester, and Pastelogram. As the project wrapped up, Moore wrote to the division with an afterthought: "May I submit Utopian Turtletop? Do not trouble to answer unless you like it."[48] She did her job: "Turtletop" was an intriguing word. That it wasn't right for the E-car was no disgrace. Nothing, it seems, did fit the new model. Perhaps that was an omen.

Finally, a few dozen of the best candidates were shown to the Ford Executive Committee in the absence of Henry II, who was on vacation in the Bahamas. Among the names on the list—actually, they were written in various scripts on large cards—were several that would show up on later cars from Ford or other companies: Citation, Ranger, and Pacer, among them.

After pondering each of the possibilities, the executive committee was a circle of sighs. Finally, Ernie Breech spoke up. "I don't like the goddam things," he said. "How about we call it Edsel?"

Richard Krafve mentioned Henry II's admonition against using that particular name, and Breech said, tellingly, "Don't worry about that. I'll take care of Henry."[49] Breech did persuade Henry II to authorize "Edsel," which, aside from being his father's name, was a Hebrew word meaning "from the wealthy man's hall." Breech contended that the new car was so certain to be a success, it would be a lasting monument to the late Mr. Ford. Finally Henry II, Benson, William, Josephine, and their mother, Eleanor, agreed that if the executive committee felt strongly about the tribute, they would not stand in the way. The announcement was made public on November 19, 1956. "I am proud and pleased to confirm that the name will be Edsel," Henry II told the press, "in honor of my father who served the last twenty-four years of his life as president of Ford Motor Company." The first Edsel cars were assembled at factories in Louisville, Kentucky; Mahwah, New Jersey; San Jose, California; and Somerville, Massachusetts.[50]

When the new car was placed on sale, the name was cited as one of the primary factors that turned customers off. In the first place, "Edsel" was a thudding, dull-sounding word—it never caught on as a name for people, let alone sedans. Second, it reminded consumers already inclined to be suspicious of big business of the power wielded by the Ford family, then being written about as a "dynasty." Unfairly, customers believed that the name was an overbearing example of the Fords' vanity and the fact that they could name a car any doggone thing they liked. "Citation" would no doubt have helped sell a few more cars. So would "Turtletop," for that matter.

The adventure of giving the E-car a trade name reflected the problem hanging over the entire Edsel project. At the end of the name-selection process, meticulous research was tossed out on a whim. In other areas of the car's development, however, polls and data were followed to a fault. In both situations, Ford Motor demonstrated that it was modern enough to gather the best market research by the best techniques. But it was still unsure exactly how to interpret it and when to use it. "Much of the publicity concerning the Edsel had been bad, citing poor workmanship and poor engineering," John Perrault, president of the International Edsel Club, wrote in 1989. Even so, as he pointed out, there was almost no hope for a rebound. "Had the car been introduced two or three years earlier we might be driving an Edsel today. The economy had a sharp downturn in late 1957 and 1958, leading everyone to stop buying."[51]

The Edsel Division was folded into Lincoln-Mercury in 1958. It had become, in historian Thomas Bonsall's phrase, "the Titanic of automobiles."[52] The following year, on November 19, 1959, the model was quietly discontinued. The numbers produced were 63,110 (1958), 44,891 (1959), and 2,846 (1960). Ford Motor lost over $250 million on the effort. *Time* magazine offered the best obituary of the Ford flop: "The Edsel was a classic case of the wrong car for the wrong market at the wrong time. It also was a prize example of the limitations of market research, with its 'in-depth interviews' and 'motivational mumbo jumbo.'"[53] As John Brooks calculated for a piece in *The New Yorker,* the company could have saved money by giving away 110,810 Mercurys in 1955, instead of trying to build the Edsel. Money aside, if a quarter-billion dollars can be put aside, Brooks left a gentle epitaph for the Edsel and its short history, writing that "maybe it means a time has come when—as in Elizabethan drama but seldom before in American business—failure can have a certain grandeur that success never knows."[54]

Over the decades, Brooks's analysis proved inspired. The Edsel developed a cult following, and status as a pop-culture icon, unimaginable when it was canceled in 1960. "I still believe it was a well-designed car," reflected designer Roy Brown, who went on to lead styling for Ford Motor (England) Ltd. "At least on the '58, trying to find a bad line on that car is a difficult job."[55] Starting in the 1970s, Edsel owners' clubs sprouted up all over the world, celebrating the "biggest loser" in Ford Motor Company history. Many of the Edsel collectors, like Bill Skinner of Fullerton, California, adopted nicknames—he became Edsel Goodwrench. They subscribed to *The Big E* magazine, published five times a year to highlight the lore of the infamous car; attended Edsel conferences; and participated in "Edselcade" auto parades. They also kept track of any movie appearance an Edsel made, typical favorites being *Peggy Sue Got Married,* starring Kathleen Turner and Nicolas Cage, and *Three Fugitives* with comedian Martin Short. James Koch, the proud owner of 250 Edsels, even maintained a dealership in Sacramento as late as 2002, advertising in the local phone book.[56]

Every owner had a story behind the obsession. "It was my mother's first car after her divorce," Thomas Rugg of Rancho Cordova, California, recalled. "I drove it to high school in the early 1960s and was laughed at, made into the butt of jokes. To drive an Edsel was completely unhip. Owners were embarrassed by it, hid it in their garages until nighttime, and then snuck around in the cloak of darkness. But my mother didn't care if it had a stigma; she needed viable transportation." Over the decades Rugg—who is known as "Elroy Edsel" to his friends—took meticulous care of his mother's maroon-and-white car. He believed he "had the last laugh" on his high school tormentors when, in 1995, his Edsel won first place in a national competition. He keeps an archive at his home of various Edsel-inspired material ranging from repair bills and *National Enquirer* reports to Midas muffler ads from the late 1970s boasting that "We Will Never Forget the Edsel."[57]

One Edsel car enthusiast, David McCumber, former features editor of the *San Francisco Examiner,* decided in 1998 to prove that the Edsel was a good, reliable car by embarking on a 10,000-mile journey in one. Leaving his home in Montana, he drove the entire circumference of the United States in his Edsel, getting stares wherever he went. While he was parked outside of Wrigley Field in Chicago, a man walked up to him, thumped his fender, and said, "This muthafucka's in a muthafuckin time warp." McCumber attended the thirtieth-anniversary Edselcade in Dearborn; met a kid in Cocoa Beach, Florida, who offered him $100 for gas money because he was keeping the "Edsel spirit" alive; and struggled constantly with a broken-down fuel pump, getting stranded on Highway 101 in Los Angeles during rush hour. "It was frustrating at times," McCumber admitted, "but my Edsel survived."[58]

With the end of the Edsel in 1960 came the end of Ford's era of imitation of General Motors. After finding that neither the Continental nor the Edsel had inherent staying power, the company concentrated on building cars, rather than divisions. The three all-original models created by the company during the mid-1950s—the T-bird, the Continental Mark II, and the Edsel—

represented the real Ford Motor Company. They also gave the company a direction of its own, the one it would follow in the 1960s. There were lessons even in the failures. The lack of commitment to the Continental Mark II program demonstrated that Ford was still primarily interested in selling Fords. The Edsel, which was also let go, although with better reason, showed that passion is as important as any research in producing a major new model. The Thunderbird wasn't discontinued, but it was bumped up into a four-seat model, with more verve than any standard Ford. Attracting customers in its new configuration, the T-bird gave Ford the answer to its upper-medium-bracket conundrum. Effortlessly, it became THE SMART CAR FOR THE YOUNGER EXECUTIVE OR PROFESSIONAL FAMILY ON ITS WAY UP. In the future, as demonstrated by the 1958 Thunderbird, Ford owners would move up to . . . more Fords.

The adventures of the 1950s proved that Ford Motor was essentially a three-prong car company: Ford–Lincoln–Mercury. More divisions were ultimately extraneous. To that extent, Edsel Ford's legacy could not be improved upon.

29

—— ✵ ——

A Whole New Business

In the mid-1950s, business experts predicted that within a half-dozen years, the Big Three—GM, Ford, and Chrysler—would be the only three. Even in an overall booming market, the number of companies selling cars in America was down to five by 1956. Carmakers that had been in business for a half century crumbled just as easily as the upstarts that had rushed into the postwar market only five or ten years before. "We knew we would spend $50 million in the automobile industry," lamented Henry J. Kaiser in 1955, "but we didn't think it would disappear without a ripple."[1] The automobile market in America had become little more than a joust between GM (50 percent) and Ford (27 percent) that Chrysler (17 percent) sometimes made interesting.[2] "General Motors sold half the cars in the United States from the 1930s through the 1960s because it knew what America wanted: attractive, muscular vehicles and plenty of uncongested highways," historian James M. Rubenstein summarized in *Making and Selling Cars*. "And when the American class structure changed from a broad pyramid of working-class families in the 1920s to a bulge of middle-class families in the 1950s, sales of GM's middle-range Pontiac, Oldsmobile, and Buick models soared."[3]

Hudson, the venerable Detroit company that had turned out family cars since 1909, and Nash Motors, which had produced a solid line of vehicles in Kenosha, Wisconsin, since 1917, were both discontinued in 1957. No one mourned them, no one missed them. By the end, Ford and Chevrolet were each building more than a thousand cars for every single one that Hudson made. The situation was not much better for the remaining two independents: Studebaker-Packard, which was operating at a loss, and American Motors, the quintessential niche player, which had clipped Hudson and Nash from its lineup. "By the 1950s," Maryann Keller wrote in *Rude Awakening*,

"General Motors was a monster, a smug and secure empire." Only Ford Motor Company was posing any real challenge to its profits.[4]

With the collapse of the independents, the Big Three finally dominated the market for cars in America. However, behind the figures, they still didn't control the market—or the customer. If the Hudsons, Packards, Nashes, and Studebakers of the mid-1950s were worn-out names and uninspiring cars, American drivers left them behind and discovered that imported cars offered a whole new world of choices. The craze for foreign sports cars that had started around 1950 became a phenomenon focused on compacts later in the decade. It changed the business of cars in America forever.

The Big Three would help the revolution along, if inadvertently, as a combination of factors compelled Detroit's industry leaders to open doors long locked to outside competition. The anemic carmakers that should have been saved by the moves were past help. However, foreign companies were only just getting started in America and they rushed to take advantage of new cracks in the marketplace.

The nervous mood of big business—very big business—in the 1950s grew out of a dramatic court decision rendered in 1945 in a case filed by the Justice Department against Alcoa, the world's largest aluminum producer, headquartered in Pittsburgh, Pennsylvania. The case ended up in the U.S. Supreme Court. However, one of the liabilities of a company with the scope of Alcoa was that a number of the Supreme Court Justices who should have heard the case recused themselves on the basis of previous contact with the company. Without a quorum of its own, the highest court was forced to delegate the case, assigning it to the Second Circuit Court of Appeals in New York.

The Justice Department's suit, initiated in the New Deal days of 1938, charged that Alcoa was in violation of the antitrust laws solely by virtue of its dominating size. Although Alcoa had not actively pursued anticompetitive practices, the result in the marketplace was the same as if it had: other, much smaller companies simply could not grow. In a surprising verdict still regarded as controversial today, the Second Circuit Court agreed with the Justice Department. Judge Learned Hand, writing for the court, explained that "Congress . . . did not condone 'good trusts' and condemn 'bad' ones; it forbade all. Moreover, in doing so it was not necessarily actuated by economic motives alone. It is possible, because of its indirect social or moral effect, to prefer a system of small producers, each dependent for his success upon his own skill and character, to one in which the great mass of those engaged must accept the direction of the few."[5]

The Alcoa decision meant that giant-size companies had no place to hide: even a business that had grown through honest effort and original ideas could be too big in the eyes of the government. When International Business

Machines (IBM) came under scrutiny, Chairman Thomas Watson was confused and infuriated. He felt that if his company had 95 percent of the market for punch-card machines and nearly as much of the trade in all data-processing equipment, it was only because his thousands of employees had excelled in their jobs.[6] Success was the natural result of high-quality researchers, smart executives, and a hardworking sales force. For four years, Watson fought the government's attempts to vilify IBM, but his son, Thomas Jr., accepted the new reality in business, signing a consent decree in 1956 that committed the company to forsake a number of practices that were perfectly legal for any other firm. "I was determined to settle the suit before it went to trial," the younger Watson later explained. "Settling that case was one of the best moves we ever made, because it cleared the way for IBM to keep expanding at top speed."[7] Although IBM's case didn't reach the trial stage, it was well publicized and represented the ambitions of Attorney General Herbert Brownell, an energetic New Yorker who came to his duties well armed by the Alcoa decision.

The automobile industry was perfectly aware of the disapproving attitude in Washington toward business on a grand scale—"the new legal climate," Alfred Sloan Jr. called it. He attributed it to the "result of interpretations of court decisions later expanded by the Department of Justice."[8] For a while, the Big Three kept as low a profile as they could in the midst of that new legal climate; they were aided in the effort to stay out of the Justice Department's sights by the military's dependence on their contributions to the war in Korea. As the number of automaking companies shrank in the years around 1950, though, independent automakers such as the irrepressible Preston Tucker—who tried to manufacture an innovatively designed rear-engined Tucker Torpedo at a former Dodge aircraft plant in Chicago—loudly accused the Big Three of using political influence to strangle the competition. He was especially critical of Michigan Senator Arthur Vandenberg. Unofficially, Vandenberg was known as "the senator from Detroit" and was well connected to the leading automakers.

However much the independents howled, though, the most damaging criticism of the market position of the Big Three came from their own dealers, who complained that the industry's franchise agreements codified unfair trade practices. The doom of the independents and the seeming serfdom of the dealers eventually found a sympathetic audience in Washington. Joseph C. O'Mahoney, Wyoming's Democratic senator, conducted hearings into the influence of the automobile industry's leaders, General Motors in particular, in late 1955. "It is a plain fact," Senator O'Mahoney concluded at the end of the first week of testimony, "that practically all of the national economy is being dominated by a small number of corporations in almost every major industry . . . so that regulation of commerce is now in the hands of management instead of Congress."[9]

His hearings drew appearances by the top executives of General Motors and Ford, including Henry Ford II, but the investigation caught the attention of the public when dealers spoke for themselves. Actually, O'Mahoney was forced to rely on former dealers, since those still in the business were afraid to speak publicly. Much of the power in any business lies in successful distribution, and in the automobile business, that power was tightly held in Detroit. Dealers were allowed very few of their own decisions, and in the case of a dispute with headquarters, a dealership agreement could be summarily canceled, with only thirty days' notice. Lawmakers heard of a Missouri Buick dealer whose franchise was rescinded in 1954 after he complained too loudly about the number of cars he was given to sell—his father had opened the dealership in 1906, two years before General Motors even existed.

As a result of the O'Mahoney hearings, and almost constant pressure from the Department of Justice, dealership franchise agreements started to change in 1956.[10] In giving up a measure of control over distribution channels, the automakers took the same course chosen by Thomas Watson Jr. at IBM—making amends before antitrust proceedings could start, since no one could say for sure where they might end. Whatever executives in Detroit were saying privately, in public they led the effort to implement substantive changes. For dealers, the most important concession was that they were accorded long-term security for the first time. Automakers could no longer cancel a contract without just cause (and outside arbitration) over the course of a specified term of up to five years. In most respects, the Big Three were models of cooperation and flexibility in responding to the challenge to their authority by O'Mahoney, the dealers, and the Department of Justice. In that respect, the mid-1950s was a unique time in the history of the American automobile in that the prevailing rule was: The bigger the company, the more frightened it was. That is just the kind of inversion that paves the way for a revolution.

For the industry at large, the most significant shift that resulted from the O'Mahoney hearings was the removal, tacitly or explicitly, of clauses forbidding dealers to sell more than one make of automobile. Except in the depth of the Great Depression, when General Motors allowed dealers to double up on nameplates from its own line—typically resulting in a Cadillac–Buick or Buick–Oldsmobile lot—self-respecting car companies insisted on exclusive dealerships, selling only one make.

When the restrictions against dual- or multiline dealerships were suddenly lifted in 1956, the remaining independents saw a window of hope. If high-powered GM or Ford dealers could be induced to double up, a smaller manufacturer would gain access to thousands of outlets and millions of potential customers. Government officials recognized the same possibility; the end of the exclusive dealership was supposed to not only free the dealer from the constraints of the home office, but save room in the market for smaller manufacturers.

By 1956, however, it was too late for the independents to be saved by mere salesmanship or even marketing. Had they had access to the dealerships ten years earlier, more might well have survived. However, by the time strong dealerships did open to outsiders, the Big Three had already institutionalized the annual model change. Customers expected a complete makeover every other year or so, and a full slate of changes and improvements in the interim. Smaller companies once flush with cash in the form of postwar surplus or initial investment capital were strapped by 1956, and none could afford to keep up with the annual model change, which cost a minimum of $50 million, with no guarantee of success. Anyway, many of the independents built mid-price sedans, albeit America's most popular segment, but also its most cruelly competitive.

The timing of the new dealer rules may have been too late to help the independents, but it was perfect for the foreign carmakers trying to turn the novelty appeal of the immediate postwar boomlet into a permanent niche.

In 1955, 58,000 imported cars were sold in the United States. Two years later, the number had surged to 255,000 and it wasn't finished climbing. In 1959, 614,000 foreign cars rolled out of American showrooms.[11] Practically all of the imports were from Europe, where there weren't any companies that didn't need dollars and only a few that didn't join the rush to find them. Germany's Volkswagen was the favorite make, followed at a distance by France's Renault and English Ford. Holland sent the tiny DAF, Italy came in a little late with the Fiat, and Sweden sent its venerable Volvo along with a new auto made by an airplane manufacturer, the Saab. Even Czechoslovakia, then Communist, tried the marketplace with the Skoda, a small convertible with surprisingly glamorous styling. The onslaught came as something of a smorgasbord to American customers used to big, fast, oddly similar cars. The competition among GM, Ford, and Chrysler was undoubtedly cutthroat, but during the 1950s, it succeeded in producing less variety in automobiles, not more.

The imports found their way to established dealerships, which welcomed the chance to sell a little above, or more usually below, Detroit's pricing belt. By the end of the decade, Ford's highest-volume dealership, Courtesy Motors in Chicago, was selling not only Fords but Renaults, Peugeots, and Triumphs, as well.[12]

The imports addressed everything except the middle segment, concentrating on three types of models: economy, luxury, and sports. In 1957–1958, for example, new cars cost anywhere from $1,300 to $13,000. Fords ranged from

$2,200 to $2,500; Mercurys, $2,700 to $4,000; Edsels, $2,600 to $3,650; Lincolns, $4,900 to $5,500; and the Continental Mark III cost $6,000. An English Ford was about $1,750. That made it about $250 less than GM's imported Opels and Victors, but $150 more than the leading economy model, the Volkswagen, at about $1,600.[13]

The VW didn't look anything like anything—animal, vegetable, or automobile—ever seen in America. Without fins, double headlights, or two-tone paint, it was nonetheless an eye-catcher with its rounded silhouette. The company flatly rejected the annual model change and instead made virtues of the timelessness of the VW and the fact that it needed no improvement. In those respects, the VW was the modern version of the Model T, and, like the original "universal car," it helped to open car ownership to people who might not have been able to afford a new car otherwise. American carmakers had neglected that borderline segment of the market, relegating it to the used-car lot. However, given the choice, customers preferred a new car to a used one, and the VW, along with the rest of the economy imports, gave them that choice. But the VW revolution didn't happen overnight. "Despite the mythology that naturally grew up around its success," wrote Phil Patton in *Bug,* "the Bug was hard to sell in the U.S. . . . Little was known about the car except that it had been Hitler's creation."[14] Germany's Beetle did, however, receive glowing reviews in such magazines as *Popular Mechanics* and *Reader's Digest.* Although some of them made their way across the Atlantic in the very early 1950s, the company officially opened the new North American market with Volkswagen of Canada in 1952 and Volkswagen of America in 1955 (its headquarters were first in New York City, then in Englewood, New Jersey). Then, almost overnight, the Volkswagen became the "in" car. By 1970 America had purchased more than 4 million VW Beetles and vans.[15] "The Coke bottle was often said to be the most recognizable shape in the world, the epitome of the single universe product," Patton wrote. "The Bug aspired to equal universality."[16]

Great Britain did not have one blockbuster, like the VW, but with a mob of thirty-five different models, it was the leading source of foreign cars in the United States throughout most of the 1950s.[17] At the forefront were swank Rolls-Royce and Bentley cars that had long been popular in America. Made by the same firm, they had their own dealer network in place. Britain's sports cars, which received more than their share of attention, in the press or on the street, were largely sold through dealerships that specialized in such models. But it was with economy models that the British offering increased in the late 1950s, as makes such as Austin, Hillman, Morris, and Sunbeam looked to hook up with established dealers. By 1958, over half of the British cars sold were handled by multiline dealerships anchored around an American make.[18]

All of the European imports arrived full-born and completely designed, with only minor adjustments for the American market. They had, after all, healthy markets to sell to back home. Japanese automakers, however, did not. With a 40 percent purchase tax on automobiles, very few Japanese citizens could afford a car. Nonetheless, Japan considered itself a manufacturing island, like Great Britain, and regarded the automobile as the most logical product for a country that needed to add value to other people's natural resources in order to turn a living.

After World War II, the American occupation forces in Japan under General Douglas MacArthur restricted automobile production. But the Toyota Company, founded in 1933, knew that ban would eventually be lifted. Eiji Toyoda, son of company founder Kichiro Toyoda, "made a pilgrimage to the great temple of mass production," as he described Ford's River Rouge plant. Young Toyoda's mission to Dearborn was to prepare for the future: he carefully studied the Rouge complex, took detailed notes, analyzed production methods, and then tried to replicate the effort in Tokyo. "Eiji Toyoda told me himself," future chairman of Ford Motor Philip Caldwell recalled, "there was no mystery to the development of Toyota in Japan. He merely came to see the Ford Rouge Plant . . . and then went back to Japan and built the same thing." Toyoda told the story much the same way, but nonetheless, Caldwell's conclusion was off the mark. Toyoda's visit to Dearborn had convinced him that the future lay in manufacturing compact, economical cars under the Toyota brand. The chrome and high-styled fins of the 1950s, he believed, were just a passing phase.[19] In 1955 Toyota built its first model at its new plant; the Crown, as it was called, was the first step in Japan's rise as a leader in automobile assembly.

Toyota and Nissan combined produced 47,100 passenger cars in 1957,[20] and could barely find customers for them. Few countries in the Far East needed cars in bulk and almost no country in Europe would allow Japanese cars onto the market . . . unless they were made at a factory on site. In the summer of 1958, Toyota's Crown Toyopets and Nissan's Datsun Bluebirds arrived in the United States, an open automobile market and a country with a vested interest in Japanese prosperity. Politicians welcomed the cars as an example of Japan's success in capitalism. Car dealers were receptive, too. Even though the Japanese were considered late arrivals in the import rush, they landed just in time to take advantage of the new opportunity for distribution through multiline dealerships. Within two years, nearly all Datsuns were sold at dealerships headlined by a make produced by one of the Big Three. Many Toyotas were linked with established dealerships as well. Toyota even approached Ford Motor in hopes of forming an alliance. The offer wasn't considered seriously in Dearborn. "I think we probably," recalled former Ford CFO Stanley Seneker, "made some strategic errors back in those times by not properly assessing the strength of the Japanese."[21] Ford could be forgiven for the oversight, though. It wasn't a joke at the time that the only problem for the two newcomers was convincing Americans that Japan could manufacture a full-size car, not just a tin toy.

Imports were the talk of the industry in 1957, as the number of cars exported by the United States—still the world's leading auto producer—fell short of the number of the cars imported from overseas. The last time that had happened was in 1905. Most of the growth was built on the economy car, and the only American manufacturer building a car well below the $2,000 threshold in 1958 was the American Motors Corporation, which manufactured the 100-inch wheelbase Rambler and imported the tiny Metropolitan from England.

If places like the Rouge were to survive in a competitive market, they would have to recognize the demand for smaller cars. "It's the suburbanite we want to sell," admitted a marketer at a foreign-car show in New York City. The outward expansion of cities gave rise to two-car families, as well as drivers looking for increased fuel economy. Both enhanced the future of the compact foreign car. "The advent of the small car opens up some interesting speculation on the increase of families owning two or more cars," noted an in-depth analysis of the 1958 car market in the *Conference Board Business Record*. The article explained that in the past, very few families other than those with high incomes owned more than one car. Between 1952 and 1957, however, the percentage of multicar families rose from 4 percent to 10 percent. "The recent availability," noted the article, "of low-cost, low-maintenance vehicles, with adequate service facilities, may have important structural effects on the size of the car market over the next several years."[22]

Because foreign models did seem destined to change the American market, many organizations and publications conducted studies of the cars, the economics, and the people involved with both. The National Automobile Dealers Association (NADA) commissioned a survey in 1959 to determine what kind of Americans were purchasing foreign cars. It found that most were male; only 14 percent were female, below the average for all cars. The specific composite, according to the study, was a thirty-seven-year-old man, five-foot-nine, weighing 166 pounds. Of more importance to automakers, the typical foreign-car buyer was educated (69 percent had attended college), with a good income and a career as an executive or in the professions. Fewer than half said that the import was a second car. The predominant reason given for purchasing an import was "cheaper to operate." The others listed by more than half of the respondents were "easier handling in traffic," "easier to park," "not as much annual depreciation," and "better workmanship."[23] According to those results, price was not the most attractive feature. Customers who simply wanted something different in daily driving looked at imports.

While the variety of models categorized as "imports" made the NADA study inexact—encompassing the owners of Bentleys and VWs alike—the overall impression was that foreign cars were siphoning off a stream of valuable customers, people who were fairly young and still on their way up in terms of income. For the Big Three, the most ominous aspect of the influential study was that an astounding 86 percent of the respondents predicted that they would seek out an imported car as their next vehicle. With sales of imports climbing to 10 percent of the total U.S. market in 1959, that statistic indicated that the fad for small cars was only the thin end of a wedge.

Part of the sport in watching Morgans, Mercedes, Isettas, and Humbers go by on state highways was in wondering how American car companies would match them. At first, the Big Three encouraged customers to buy foreign cars—the ones made by their own European subsidiaries. English Fords had been selling well in America since the late 1940s. GM stepped up its own import program, introducing English Vauxhalls and German Opels, while Chrysler sold Simcas made by its French subsidiary. Studebaker-Packard struck a good deal to sell Mercedes-Benz cars through its dealerships. That addressed the first part of the import revolution—offering customers cars with different ideas, out of the usual American mold.

The second part of the revolution lay in breaking American cars out of that usual mold. In the early 1930s, Ford Motor had been forced to abandon its isolated business path and join the rest of the industry, where car models had to evolve and, more than that, had to answer one another. The Model A, however perfect in its own way, had to change, simply because the Chevys and Plymouths were changing. In a similar way, the entire U.S. automobile industry was forced out of its splendid isolation by the import craze.

For a brief moment from 1953 to 1956, the Big Three had the whole auto business locked down; the independents were down to rags and remnants, but the imports had yet to stake out territory. During that span, lasting from the end of the Korean War to the O'Mahoney hearings, the Big Three brought out passenger cars built on the same assumption, that customers wanted the most horsepower and the finest display of chromium "spaghetti" feasible at the price. As long as that was all that was available, Americans did indeed support the assumption. Isolation, however, was no more realistic for the Big Three than it had been for Henry Ford, a quarter century before.

No sooner did the Big Three become, in essence, the Only Three in America than they found themselves part of a "Big Thirty-five" of international automakers hawking cars in America. Foreign ideas in cars might not have suited everyone in America, but they found the trends that the Big Three overlooked. When American cars shirked on economy in the 1970s, Japanese imports showed them up, and when Detroit's standard of quality slipped in the early 1980s, the contrast of well-constructed imports turned it into a national disgrace. On the lighter side, imports influenced the return of the convertible and the reception of new sports cars in the 1990s. The first tangible proof of the revolution, however, was the decision facing the Big Three, makers of big engines and big cars, over the potential of the compact car in 1957–1958.

———

During a slump year for auto sales in the United States during the 1950s, the Eisenhower administration floated the patriotic slogan "You auto buy now"— meaning products manufactured in the U.S.A. As George Romney, the CEO of American Motors, explained to President Eisenhower, "Consumers are rebelling against the size, the large horsepower, and the excessive styling changes made each year by many auto manufacturers."[24] But there were even deeper problems lurking behind Ike's chipper slogan.

Eisenhower's plea was intended to boost the morale of UAW workers building American-made cars. It didn't work. Detroit factories were noisy parlors of industrial angst. Pollution tainted the air and poisoned the rivers. UAW workers not only wanted more pay—they wanted better lives. UAW President Walter Reuther might have captured the cover of *Time,* and the AFL and CIO might have merged in 1955, but the labor movement was stymied in frustration. Occasionally a significant labor advance was made: for example, when Ford Vice President John Bugas and Walter Reuther created a "supplemental benefits" program in 1955, stipulating that auto workers would not be penalized during periods of unemployment due to conditions beyond their control.[25] For the most part, however, blue-collar assembly-line work was belittled in a postwar culture touting white-collar salaries, higher education through the GI Bill, and the upward mobility of the Organization Man.

Meanwhile, racial discrimination continued to be widespread in Detroit— and the automobile industry was no exception. Just as seamstress Rosa Parks refused to abide by Jim Crow laws and give up her seat on a segregated bus in Montgomery, Alabama, on December 1, 1955, African Americans in Michigan finally said no to what they deemed "institutionalized bigotry" in the auto industry. Groups like the NAACP and the Urban League in Detroit recognized that some advances had been made in job opportunities for African Americans, but they threatened litigation if white favoritism wasn't abolished altogether.

Besides discrimination, poor factory conditions and layoffs were a constant complaint of African American workers. But African Americans found ways to prevail. Take, for example, the unpleasant experiences Berry Gordy, future founder of Motown Records, had when he was first employed at Ford's Wayne assembly plant. A native of Detroit, Gordy had gotten the Ford job thanks to a connection his mother-in-law had with the UAW. In his autobiography, *To Be Loved,* Gordy vividly recalls his first encounter with the world of automobile manufacturing. Like many black rookies, he was assigned to the foundry. "That foundry was hell, a living nightmare," Gordy wrote. "Hot, blowing furnaces, loud clanging noises, dust, smoke and soot everywhere, red molten metal pouring out of huge stoves on conveyor belts. When the bright red liquid steel arrived at my station, it would be cooling down from red hot to black hot. We had to wear large asbestos gloves to keep our hands from burning, while we knocked the new-formed nuts and bolts from their casings with big mallets."[26]

After only one day on the job, Gordy quit. A few months later, desperate for a regular income to support his family, he signed on as an upholstery trimmer at the Lincoln-Mercury plant, earning $86.40 a week. "The minute I walked into the Lincoln-Mercury assembly plant and saw how cool it was—no furnaces, fire or hot metal—I knew this was going to be home for a while," Gordy recalled. "Little did I know when I started how important to my future that assembly line was going to be." What excited him most about his new job was that the tedium of Fordism allowed his mind to wander and he began inventing rhythm-and-blues songs in his head. With the rumblings of machinery pounding as a backbeat, Gordy hummed away, scribbling down pop lyrics and jazz melodies during coffee breaks with the intensity of a man possessed. And the gospel of efficiency Ford Motor practiced helped Gordy to crystallize his concept of opening a recording studio he would call Motown U.S.A. It would be a place where Billboard singles could be mass-produced with the same regularity as Lincoln Continental or Mercury Marquis cars. "At the plant, cars started out as just a frame, pulled along on conveyor belts until they emerged at the end of the line—brand spanking new cars rolling off the line," Gordy wrote. "I wanted the same concept for my company, only with artists and songs and records. I wanted a place where a kid off the street could walk in one door an unknown and come out another a recording artist—a star." Gordy quit Lincoln-Mercury in 1957, established Motown Records in 1959, and had his first stars in Detroit residents like ten-year-old Stevie Wonder, whose song "Fingertips (Part 2)" became a number one hit, and Jackie Wilson, with classics like "Reet Petite" and "Lonely Teardrops." The Motown Sound, as it was called, came to include Marvin Gaye, Smokey Robinson and the Miracles, the Supremes, the Four Tops, the Jackson 5, and the Temptations. While blues music originated on southern plantations as an anguished cry for freedom, Motown had its start at a Lincoln-Mercury factory, where mechanized monotony was transformed by Berry Gordy into some of the most soulful songs ever recorded in the annals of American popular music.[27]

Gordy's *To Be Loved* presented a word picture of the gloomy atmosphere permeating Detroit-area automobile factories in the 1950s, but the most memorable study of the situation was made by Swiss photographer Robert Frank. "Frank captured the dreary angst of Detroit in truly haunting fashion," artist Larry Rivers recalled in an interview. "When I think of Detroit or Ford my mind immediately flashes to his images."[28] Born in Zurich in 1924, Frank immigrated to New York in 1947. Upon arrival he presented his photographic portfolio at *Harper's Bazaar* and was hired on the spot. For five years he worked for the magazine, traveling throughout Latin America and Europe with his trustworthy 35mm Leica cameras. His goal for each photograph, however commonplace the subject, was to give it a deeper narrative meaning. Awarded a Guggenheim fellowship in 1955, Frank decided to document America much as Walker Evans had two decades earlier. He wanted to capture the *real* America, unvarnished and raw to the bone. Inspired by Charles Sheeler's photographs of Ford's River Rouge plant, Frank decided that Detroit would be his first stop on his journey across America.

The pictures Robert Frank took would be published in a 1959 book titled *The Americans,* a matrix of images documenting the daily rhythms of everyday people. Novelist Jack Kerouac wrote in the book's introduction that Frank had "sucked a sad, sweet poem out of America."[29] There was, however, a certain grotesqueness to some of his images: the forlornness of a public beach in Detroit where obesity prevails; a drugstore soda fountain where everybody looks overly anxious for coffee. To Frank, Detroit was the capital of middle-class hard times—some of which he encountered there for himself. When a group of police officers found it strange that he was photographing African Americans at a local juke joint, they frisked him, searched his Ford coupe, and discovered two old license plates in the trunk. That was enough for an arrest. Frank was fingerprinted and tossed into jail as a "suspicious character." The next day, however, he was released. "My night in jail was not so funny as it might have sounded," Frank wrote. "It was depressing and I got scared. I was ready to give up when they let me out."[30]

The next day he resumed his search for *The Americans.* Arriving at River Rouge, Frank was mesmerized by the vastness of the complex. "Ford is an absolutely fantastic place," he wrote his wife. "This one is God's factory and if there is such a thing—I am sure that the devil gave him a helping hand to build what is called Ford's River Rouge Plant."[31] He was fascinated by the dutiful workforce of 60,000, many wearing goggles and overalls, seeming to be bored and dehumanized. For two days, Frank shot photographs of die makers, glass fitters, and machinists. Although many of the workers Frank encountered yelled at him to go away, worried that his images would be used for some nefarious purpose, he wandered around the Rouge foundry taking photos of its gritty and overwhelming essence. In one photograph, for example, the body of a 1955 Ford Fairlane Crown Victoria dangles in midair as a burly worker struggles to land it safely on the floor. Metal sparks spray around the foundry like a plaza fountain as men try to mold steel. If one looks at Frank's Rouge photographs in sequence, one image, *Detroit River Rouge Plant,* stands out. It depicts a man standing serenely on the factory roof while a Ford vehicle drives by. It is a haunting image. "The summer of 1955 was hot and after two days at the River Rouge Plant," he later wrote, "I was told to leave the factory."[32]

Frank didn't stop with factory life, but followed workers home when they clocked out of the Rouge. He struggled to capture the essence of their everyday lives. He took photographs as they attended a strawberry parade, shopped at a roadside stand, or wandered the lonely nighttime streets around city hall. Collectively, the photographs show the pathos of real people trying to achieve the American dream in a hard-edged industrial town. Always, it seems, Frank places the automobile at the center of their lives. "To Frank, the automobile was like the American flag, an object that sustained an enduring iconographic presence in the many photographs he would make in the months ahead," art historian Nancy Watson Barr maintains. "A lurid symbol of American ingenuity, the automobile to Frank was a signifier of all that is meaningful in a society where working class ethos determined a standard of living, a valued lifestyle that symbolized that truth as it stood for America."[33]

The workers Robert Frank encountered were earning on average $5,600 per year—a solid middle-class income for people who needed no particular experience or training, not even a high school diploma. The high wages attracted them and also allowed them to withstand the hard conditions. That was life in an automobile factory. It would be another generation before conditions changed and auto workers were connected to the job with something other than bare wages.

———

To Ford Motor, as well as GM and Chrysler, the popularity of foreign compacts in the late 1950s looked like a temporary fad. In part, that was wishful thinking—none of the Detroit automakers was certain it could build an economical car and still make a profit. European auto workers earned about a fifth the hourly wage of their American counterparts, so the calculation on cost and pricing appeared to be discouraging. In any case, every Detroit automaker was certain of one fact: a company couldn't make as much money on a $1,600 car as on one selling for $2,600, $3,600, or $4,600. If Detroit executives wished that foreign compacts would just go away, the selling season of 1958 didn't make them very happy. Sales were down for everyone in the auto business—with the shining exception of the imports and American Motors' little Ramblers. The more they thrived, the more they humbled the Big Three. At the same time, watching consumer interest in the Edsel wither and die in a matter of months was particularly sobering for Ford Motor, especially since the Edsel had been the most carefully calculated model in Detroit history. The company found that hard to forget. Just in case it was about to calculate itself into yet another mistake, one of omission, it secretly started development of a compact, the Falcon. At the same time, General Motors and Chrysler were also publicly shrugging off the inroads made by the compacts—and in secret GM was designing the Corvair and Chrysler was at work on the Valiant.

When initial planning started on the Falcon, Robert McNamara was vice president of the Ford Division, but soon afterward he was named group executive of all of Ford Motor's car and truck divisions. McNamara was known as the reigning intellectual of the company. "He has the ability," Henry Ford II said at the time, "to keep in his head facts and figures that most of us have to go look up."[34] Much later, Henry II was more specific: "McNamara, like the rest of us, had his failings and he was so damn bright that he couldn't believe anybody else could quite come up to his mental capacities. I think he had a tendency to underestimate the thinking of others. But he made a terrific contribution."[35]

Robert McNamara didn't pretend to be a car fanatic. He was neither an engineer nor an especially enthusiastic driver, but once he had a theme in mind for the Falcon, he began to sound like that original car fan, the elder Henry Ford. His idea was that the Falcon should be light and strong. The reduction of weight would increase fuel economy, and sturdy components would make the car inexpensive to keep.

"On the styling proposition," recalled George Brown, "the styling of the Falcon, it was Bob McNamara's great belief that we should not ornament the car. He felt that it added weight and added costs and took away from gas mileage. We showed, in our research, that the customers would be happy to have a little chrome on the car. . . . But Bob was not about to change the image of the car.

"I think Bob McNamara's concept was right," Brown continued. "Sure, the Falcon would sell in larger volume if it were chromed up, but it would be tapping the same market share we already had. Bob was, I think, dedicated to opening up a new segment of the market—one that was looking for a car as a piece of transportation, durable, reliable and non-stylish."[36]

The order given to the product planners called for a car that weighed 1,500 pounds less than a typical six-seater, that offered 50 percent better fuel economy, and that could be priced at less than $2,000.[37] Development began in July 1957. Weight was the obsession, and engineers congratulated themselves that they ultimately beat the goal of 2,400 pounds by 18 pounds.[38] "We had to make the car feel like a big car," said chief engineer Jack Hooven, "but we had to have the good handling foreign car buyers are always bragging about." Using car-builder's slang, he added, "The car had to be pussy-foot and couldn't have any hash."[39] That meant that unlike foreign compacts, it had to be smooth over bumps and quiet.

The Falcon benefited from a unitized body, which formed most of the structure of the car out of continuous sheet metal, cutting more than 200 parts from the standard process of bolting separate pieces to a framework. Hooven and his staff of about 168 engineers were ingenious in cutting ounces and pounds wherever possible. The door frame, for example, contained just 2 pieces, rather than the 21 found in the standard Ford. Hooven insisted on bumping up the original power plant specification, from four cylinders to six.

Nonetheless, he made up for most of the increased weight by finding ways to cut 120 parts from the basic Ford engine.[40] He also cut 179 pounds from it,[41] in part by using aluminum in place of steel in the pistons and other parts. Henry Ford would have applauded—except for the fact that the engine had six cylinders, a configuration he detested.

For some of those involved in the new model, the Falcon seemed to be a turning point—away from cars infused with personality, in favor of the mundane. "At the time, it seemed an obvious response to the arrival of the small cars from competition," said one-time senior executive Harold Sperlich. "It was a car without much love. There wasn't much passion about it. It was kind of a little car and everything had to be dirt-cheap. The car was always painfully austere . . . didn't have a lot of charm. That speaks to the reluctance with which the companies faced that change in the market. Those were the times."[42]

Ford was preparing to put the Falcon into production as a 1960 model, but the whole program was still an official secret in February 1959. In fact, none of the Big Three wanted to be the first to announce a compact car. For one thing, news of a new model might well cut into sales of '59 cars. Moreover, there was a certain embarrassment attached to one of America's vaunted automakers admitting that the foreigners were right about compact cars. "If our competitors come along with a small car," said Chrysler President Lester Colbert, "we'll come right along with them—but we don't want to be the fair-headed boys and be there first."[43]

Henry Ford II was forced by events to be that fair-haired boy in March 1959. The Ford Foundation wanted to sell two million more shares of its Ford stock, and according to Securities and Exchange Commission regulations, such a sale would have to include disclosure of any expected developments at the company. On the lawyers' advice that the coming Falcon constituted just such a development, Henry II went first. He announced that his company was in the business of building compacts.

After only nineteen months in development, the Falcon was rushed into production. Fortunately, Ford Motor had space waiting. "The introduction of the Falcon was advanced by at least one year," said Ernie Breech, "because we had available the facilities that had been put in place for the Edsel. In a short period of time, these were converted by Del Harder, John Dykstra, and other top production managers to produce the Falcon car. If I were to reveal the profit that the Ford Motor Company made on the first year's production of Falcon cars, one would get some idea of how much was retrieved and recovered from the Edsel experience. A close tragedy was capitalized on and turned into a great asset by an alert group."[44]

Over the spring and summer, details emerged regarding the small cars to be produced by GM and Chrysler. Chevrolet's Corvair was highly original: not only was the engine in the rear of the car, but it was air-cooled. Both characteristics may have been seen on the VW for over a decade, but the Corvair was a total departure from recent American models. During development, the Falcon team heard rumors about Chevy's daring model. "We had heard that General Motors had a rear-engine car," recalled Edmund Baumgartner, "so it was disappointing that we weren't also doing an innovative car, but we did invent new ways of trying to do a more efficient design job."[45] Plymouth's Valiant was distinctively styled with its flaring fenders and a gaping grille. Overall, it was bigger than the other two new compacts and not so spare in the interior. The Corvair seemed to be directed at the driving enthusiast, and the Valiant at the family whose only car had to be a compact car.

The Ford Falcon was the most universal of the trio. The bodywork was not only oddly dapper, but many people considered it downright beautiful. "Best looking Ford since the Thirties," said *Car and Driver,* when the car made its debut in the fall of 1959.[46] The only complaint with the Falcon was its performance, with 0 to 60 mph acceleration listed in some publications at a ghastly 25 seconds. Molasses runs faster than that. The British magazine *The Motor* clocked it at 19.5 seconds, but even at that, the Falcon was still a few seconds slower in getting away from a stop than either of its two main rivals. It was a car for going, but not for going fast.

Road & Track pinpointed the appeal of the new Falcon: "For over twenty-five years the Ford Motor Company has been besieged by the cry, 'Bring back the Model A!' As far as we are concerned the new Falcon 6 is a reasonably close facsimile, at least in terms of what the Model A might have been if it had continued with year-to-year improvements. Automobile design can never stand still, but the basic concept of the new Falcon is pretty much that of the Model A—good, solid, honest transportation."[47]

Good, honest transportation had always been a natural seller for Ford, and the Falcon was a surprise success in its first year, with sales of 435,676.[48] Although some of those sales seemed to have been siphoned from the standard Ford, most were entirely new customers. In the overall industry, the effect of the Big Three's entry into the compact segment was the immediate expansion of the automobile market. People who hadn't bought new cars before were in the showrooms for the first time. Others were signing up for a second car, which was another means of expanding the market. In the new landscape for compacts, the losers were foreign compacts, which sagged in sales for a few years after the introduction of new models from the Big Three. The winner was Ford, which had to shift factory space to keep up with demand for its bestselling Falcon, topping sales of one million after just over two years.

One of those who was not on hand to enjoy the full success of the new model was Ernie Breech, who had been the chairman of the board of Ford Motor Company since 1955. On July 13, 1960, he resigned his active role in the company, retaining a seat on the board and two committee assignments.

Friction had built up between Breech and Henry II, then forty-two and apparently ready to leave his regent behind. Breech downplayed the rumors of arguments and summed up the parting simply and with a broader kind of accuracy: "Henry didn't need me any more," he told friends.[49] He was almost immediately invited to join the management of Trans World Airlines, and was elected chairman of its board of directors in 1961.

Robert McNamara did not last much longer at Ford than Breech, although he left under different circumstances. The executive often blamed since for the Edsel debacle—which he had not planned at all but only inherited, as the head of the car and truck group—McNamara was more accurately recognized as the hero of the Falcon program. In early November 1960, he was named president of Ford Motor Company, the first person not named "Ford" to hold that post since the days of John S. Gray. When McNamara became president, another Whiz Kid nudged upward, too, as Jim Wright took over the car and truck group. Four of the other original Whiz Kid recruits were also in important positions: Arjay Miller was corporate comptroller; J. Edward Lundy was treasurer; Ben D. Mills was vice president of the Lincoln-Mercury Division; and Charles Bosworth was director of purchasing for the Ford Division.

At forty-four, Robert McNamara had been considered to be an obvious choice to take over as president of the world's second-biggest automobile company. He insisted otherwise, however, telling one reporter that the announcement had been "quite surprising, I assure you."[50] What was quite surprising to everyone in Dearborn was that McNamara, after accepting the presidency (with its $500,000 a year salary), didn't even last a month in his new job. The most accurate thumbnail sketch of McNamara during his Ford Motor Company days was written by David Halberstam in *The Best and the Brightest*. "In business philosophy as well as personal life McNamara was a puritan, and the auto business is not the place for a puritan, nor is it necessarily the place for someone who has an abiding faith in man as a rational being committing rational acts."[51]

After the election of John F. Kennedy in November 1960, the president-elect's brother Robert visited McNamara in Dearborn to discuss possible cabinet appointments. In December, McNamara announced that he would leave Ford on January 1, 1961, to prepare for an appointment as the secretary of defense. McNamara remained in that post through both the Kennedy and Johnson administrations, trying to make sense of the Vietnam War, even as he waged it. While his tenure at the Pentagon was problematic, almost entirely because of the way he behaved during the Vietnam War, his legacy at Ford Motor remained as the man who brought the Falcon to fruition and pushed for safety measures in cars.

In the lurch left by McNamara's leaving, Henry II named production ace John Dykstra as president. Dykstra had started his career as a factory worker at GM forty years before. He had been improving the quality of Ford cars for years, with the result that during his time in office, the Ford warranty was extended from the ninety days and 4,000 miles considered generous at the time to one year and 12,000 miles. By today's standards, that doesn't seem very grand, but Ford was the first auto company to offer such a warranty.[52]

For almost sixty years, Ford Motor Company had been a relatively simple machine, for all of its enormity, built to make vehicles. Nearly all profits derived from sales of vehicles or parts. For a short period, the company tried to generate money through its finance arm, Universal Credit, but that effort folded in the middle of the Depression. Beyond that, the furthest it drifted was into the manufacture of farm implements, to complement the tractor business. Later, Korean War defense contracts stretched into a small place in America's permanent military-industrial complex. Such activities were afterthoughts, however.

In the elder Henry Ford's view, the success of the company lay almost entirely in the cost of producing each car. Henry II, who underwent a trial by fire in the late 1940s when Ford Motor was third in the sales race, placed his early emphasis on market share. In that philosophy, the greater the proportion of sales accorded to Ford Motor, the better its competitive position had to be. And competition was the prodding word of the 1950s. In the Model T days, the elder Henry Ford didn't care a snap of the fingers what any other automaker did. However, Henry II had to be an expert on General Motors and to look at his business as a tug-of-war, mostly with GM, for every bruising point of market share.

The tugging would never end, but as Ford Motor Company entered the 1960s, Henry II seemed anxious to find at least a little relief from it. In 1959–1960, his company was stretching out. It reestablished a financing subsidiary, but that was generally still part of the automobile equation. So was the acquisition of two parts businesses, spark plugs and batteries, from Electric Autolite. Although Ford had previously sold replacement parts only through dealerships, it used the Autolite lines in the building of its Motorcraft division to meet the demand for after-market parts from retail stores and mail-order houses. There were farther fields to conquer, though.

In 1956, Ernie Breech had set up the Aeronutronic Division, a small but high-class think tank charged with developing military-electronics projects. It was located in Newport Beach, California, as far as possible from the smokestacks of the River Rouge plant. The profits and prestige in the military-industrial complex now lay not in turning out low-technology weaponry but in the elite science of military electronics. To bolster its position in the growing but complex field, Ford acquired the Philco Corporation in 1961. Philco was mainly known as an appliance company, making radios and televisions, but it also produced transistors and computers and bid on projects in the space program. For the first time, Ford Motor was in the appliance business, but more important, Henry II intended to mate the Aeronutronic Division with Philco in the field of advanced electronics, led by Dearborn's own surplus of management talent.

"We've got to grow," Henry II said in 1961. "The only way we had to grow before was through higher penetration of the car market here [in the United States]. But it's hard to get more than a few points that way now. To get from 30 percent to 35 percent is a Herculean task."[53] (At the time, Ford had 29 percent of the U.S. market for cars, trailing GM's 46 percent.) Ford was looking at new ways to use its prime resources—cash and management talent—and in doing so, it became less of a General Motors copycat than it had been at any time since the war. "Throughout its reconstruction years," wrote Robert Sheehan in *Fortune* in 1962, "Ford gave the impression of being obsessed with G.M.—and G.M., for the most part, was calling the moves, with Ford countering. Today there is evidence of a change in Ford's strategy."[54] In fact, the company's noticeable split away from the GM formula may have been directly related to Henry II's split from Ernie Breech. After Henry Ford II could afford ideas of his own, he may not have wanted to be reminded of the GM archangel he had needed so badly and recruited so resolutely fifteen years before.

Ford was also making a sharp right turn in its international operations. In the late 1920s, the company had sold stock in its various foreign subsidiaries, in part to mollify local governments and customers. Additionally, the juxtaposition of the privately owned Dearborn company and its publicly owned satellites kept the entities separate, which was how the elder Henry Ford wanted it. By the late 1950s, most of the subsidiaries had been absorbed into the larger foreign Ford companies: Ford of Canada, Germany's Ford-Werke, or Ford Motor Company Ltd. in England. During the 1950s, the English Ford company had increased its sales fourfold. Cologne was even more stellar, increasing its sales by eight times and outpacing the growth rate of every other German car company except Volkswagen. The two were still disparate, with VW building more cars by far, but Ford-Werke was moving in the right direction.[55] Management was considerably better than it had been before the war, and the German economic situation, particularly for a company with foreign ties, was infinitely better. Ford of Canada was doing well, too, even though it had stopped exporting on a large scale.[56]

Dearborn owned stakes in each of the three publicly owned foreign Ford firms. By then, however, the American company was also publicly owned. If Germans, Brits, or Canadians wanted to participate in earnings, they could do so the way hundreds of thousands of Americans did, by buying shares of the parent Ford Motor Company. Because separate, publicly owned Ford companies were no longer necessary, Dearborn began to consolidate its international businesses, increasing its holdings in Ford-Werke to 100 percent and

Ford of Canada to 75 percent. That left English Ford, of which the parent owned 54.6 percent.

EnFo, as the Dagenham company was sometimes abbreviated, was one of the most successful car companies in the world under the chairmanship of Sir Patrick Hennessy. When Henry Ford II announced his company's intention to buy out the remaining 45.4 percent, he had plans to make it even more productive: "Our objective is to obtain greater operational flexibility and enable us to coordinate our European and American operations on a worldwide basis."[57]

The fact that Ford Motor was offering a premium of 59 percent on the market price of EnFo shares went a long way toward making stockholders agreeable. To many British politicians, however, the Ford offer smacked of a U.S. plot to take over the British economy. "The Americans have bases in Britain and now they seem quite prepared to take over the whole country," said a member of Parliament in November 1960.[58] Worse, some observers worried that the Ford purchase was a plan to shift more manufacturing to Germany. However, Henry II quickly announced a $196 million investment in the Dagenham plant to convince government officials and nervous unions that Ford was in England for good.

The purchase of Ford-Werke's outstanding shares had been a smoother process. According to a study made before the sale, when Dearborn owned only 52 percent of the Cologne company, most Germans were under the impression that Ford-Werke was an American company anyway. At the same time, they thought Opel, which was wholly owned by GM, was German through and through. The study results made Ford less inclined to buy loyalty with local stock ownership.[59]

For the first time in the history of the company, all Fords were Dearborn's Fords, whether they were manufactured in Argentina, Brazil, Germany, America, or England, or assembled in two dozen more countries. It was a situation that could have led to chaos rather than coordination, but Ford Motor placed its most faithful executive in charge of the International Group. John Bugas, Henry II's early confidant at the company, had helped pull Ford Motor back from the brink in the 1940s, and he cultivated rational progress with labor, as director of Industrial Relations in the 1950s. In 1959, Bugas concentrated all of his efforts on his position as vice president of the International Group.

While Ford was eyeing the growing international appetite for cars, determined to serve it efficiently, developments in Europe were encouraging just such coordination. On March 25, 1957, six nations on the Continent—West Germany, France, Italy, Belgium, Holland, and Luxembourg—formed an economic coalition that eventually developed into today's European Union. The countries came together to sign the Treaty of Rome to establish a customs union with free movement of goods; to dismantle quotas and barriers to trade; and to encourage the free movement of people, services, and capital. Through the Cologne factory, Ford, as a result of the newly launched Common Market, could finally reach markets such as Italy, to which it had had practically no previous exposure due to trade restrictions, as well as France and Belgium, where operations had been disappointing.[60]

With new investment in factory buildings, Ford-Werke was one of the first beneficiaries of the Common Market. Its Taunus model had been a staple since 1939, but was completely redesigned for 1960. The Taunus 17M, a taut and sophisticated four-seater, helped Cologne become an important exporter. It was the first in a string of hits for Ford-Werke.

Ford's International Group would come of age in the 1960s. Before that, Ford Motor Company had been a company weighed down by overseas subsidiaries, which, while they often made money, nearly always presented problems. The reborn International Group became an integrated company, a truly global enterprise with personnel and resources—and ideas—moving from one part of the world to another. Perhaps Dearborn remained the capital of all of the activity, but there was no longer any "over there" to Ford operations. Europe, Asia, South America, Africa, or Australia: under Bugas, those were international operations, but not foreign ones.

The Ford-Chevy sales competition, with all of the excitement it had generated in Detroit, was starting to be left behind at about the same time that the Falcons and Corvairs joined the fray. Around 1960, old-timers were complaining that the automobile market was turning into a "bazaar," too complicated for anyone to follow closely. Where there had once been such a thing as a "standard" Ford and Chevrolet, a basic model, with a few different body styles and perhaps an engine option, there was in 1960–1961 a whole line of models, each with its own catchy name, and each with an array of different bodies and engine options to boot. The Ford line in 1960 included the top-of-the-line Galaxie, followed by the Galaxie Special (Starliner or Sunliner), the Thunderbird, the Fairlane 500, and the Falcon. Ford coined the term "segmented market" for the new scope. By offering a range of models within each Ford franchise, the company bypassed the need for a new division, like those once planned around the Edsel and Continental. Instead, the Ford Division, all by itself, offered something for practically every customer.

Segmentation was one of Robert McNamara's ideas. In 1980, Henry Ford II observed, "I think maybe the whole growth of the automobile industry over the last [twenty] years is due to some thinking of McNamara's with respect to the proliferation of car lines. . . . This sort of thinking has permeated the whole society and has given consumers a broader choice in the marketplace. McNamara was the fellow who started this proliferation in our company."[61]

The market segmentation instituted by McNamara was the natural result of sophisticated market-research techniques that Ford had developed by 1960. Of course research wasn't worth much without good timing and execution—the Edsel had proved that—but throughout the automobile industry, the $50 million gamble over a new model was no longer being left to the instinct of a few savvy managers, men like Walter Chrysler or Henry Ford who never had to wonder what the public might want next. Specific research, combined with analysis, introduced Ford Motor to pockets of like-minded customers and moreover to hidden sides of its usual customers. Market segmentation answered that introduction directly.

"In the sense that the Falcon proved that special niches in the market could be created," McNamara later explained, "as had been done for the two-passenger Thunderbird and as was done by the four-passenger Thunderbird, the Falcon strengthened the view that there were particular segments in the market that could be carved out by one company and at least for a time in which the company would have great competitive advantage. That, I think, led to the conception of the Mustang."[62]

30

Mustang Generation

Well before the youth segment became the driving force of the American retail marketplace, Ford Motor had begun reaching out to teenagers. In October 1957, the firm invited 145 high school journalists from around the country to its annual press preview in Dearborn, footing the expenses for all of them. The 1958 models, memorable for introducing the enlarged, "family-size" Thunderbird, hardly ranked among Ford's sportiest offerings. But the company had no intention of forsaking the next generation of American car buyers. While the teens examined Ford's sensible 1958 lineup of sedans and station wagons, Ford executives studied the youngsters' reactions carefully. "When we sell a car," General Sales Manager Walter J. Cooper candidly informed the high-schoolers, "we have a seven-out-of-ten chance of repeating the sale. We want to sell you teenagers a car."[1] That determination would come roaring into view with the introduction of Ford Motor's most significant postwar offering—the ultra-hip Mustang—in 1964.

The company's interest in the youth market originated with the teen response to Chevrolet's V-8 muscle cars in 1955. Ford had been building its own V-8 models since 1932, but Chevy's high-compression 283-cubic-inch engine reflected the impatience of youth. "The hot one," Chevrolet's ads called its mighty machine, and to this day the 1957 Chevy in particular remains the car most vividly associated with 1950s American teen culture, as iconic as the poodle skirt, the DA greaser haircut, and the drive-in hamburger stand. Although, then as now, few teenagers could afford a new car, their first impressions would eventually influence their buying decisions, and every automaker in Detroit knew it.

The teens of the midfifties represented the "Depression trough" demographic that resulted from a dip in the U.S. birthrate in the 1930s. After World War II, however, the birthrate soared; during the "baby boom" from 1946 through 1957, 76 million babies were born—a bulge that would account for almost a third of the U.S. population in 1980. Many businesses kept a careful eye on the baby boomers as they and their purchasing power grew, but few kept closer watch than Ford Motor Company. And within Ford no executive was taking a keener interest in the rising generation in 1957 than one Lee Iacocca—who at thirty-three was not so much older than the youth that he was tracking. Newly named as director of truck marketing, Iacocca presented a fresh face in Dearborn. He may have arrived only the year before, but it had not taken him long to get noticed.

"I recall how I first knew of Lee," William Clay Ford Sr. said in 1990. "Golf's always been one of my hobbies. [Golf course designer] George Fazio had a dealership just outside of Philadelphia. He said to me one day, 'You've got a great zone manager here in the Philadelphia District. His name is Lee Iacocca.' It was the first time I heard Lee's name. He'd made an impression on a friend of mine that he was a comer. There's no question there is something special about him. He's a hell of an automobile guy."[2]

Lido Anthony Iacocca, born in industrial Allentown, Pennsylvania, on October 15, 1924, was not only an automobile guy but a Ford guy. "My father loved cars," he wrote in his autobiography, *Iacocca*. "In fact, he owned one of the first Model Ts. He was one of the few people in Allentown who knew how to drive, and he was always tinkering with cars and thinking about how to improve them."[3] Nicola Iacocca was an entrepreneur who owned several local businesses, including the Orpheum Wiener House restaurant, two movie theaters, and a car rental agency. He and his wife, Antoinette, had emigrated from southern Italy, but they adapted easily to American ways in east-central Pennsylvania. The Iacocca family, which grew to include son Lee and daughter Delma, remained comfortable, except in the depths of the Depression era.

The Iacoccas were close-knit and hardworking, and while Lee was a sociable schoolboy, he showed no rebellious streak even as a teen. He liked his parents, and they him. His father in particular mixed a loving relationship with high standards: Nicola Iacocca expected good grades, optimism, and an energetic approach to work, plus a sense of fun to boot, and his son came through on all counts. While the Iacoccas faced little if any overt discrimination, as a boy Lee occasionally was aware that among some people, there appeared to be a certain social pecking order, and Italians were not very high in it. Because his parents and many other relatives found financial success in small business, however, Lee Iacocca never considered himself an outsider in Allentown. On the contrary, the community he grew up in—best known for the neighboring Bethlehem Steel Corporation—put him on the path to nearby Lehigh University, nationally respected for its engineering program. "Packard Motor Company had a big laboratory at Lehigh and it's where I trained," Iacocca recalled. "So, I hate to use the cliché but I had the 'gasoline in my veins' early and I loved every minute I was around a car."[4]

Lee Iacocca set his sights on a job at Ford Motor Company when he was still a student at Lehigh. "Even before I graduated," he averred, "I wanted to work for Ford. I drove a beat-up 1938 sixty-horsepower Ford, which is how I got interested in the company." The car was so unreliable that Iacocca concluded, at least in jest, that "those guys need me. . . . Anybody who builds a car this bad can use some help."[5] After going on to earn a master's degree in mechanical engineering at Princeton University, Iacocca took a job at Ford. He left behind his tight family circle and transferred as ardent a devotion to his employer. For the young auto executive, Ford Motor Company was not merely a place to work, but *the* place to do the work by which he would prove himself. For the next thirty years, every one of Lee Iacocca's paychecks would carry the Ford Motor name. He would visit most of the United States and Europe for the first time on company trips. He would revolutionize automotive design and marketing to the enormous profit of the firm, and in doing so would become as famous a Ford man as the scion Henry Ford II, with whom he had virtually nothing in common, except that they had both known since childhood that they wanted to run Ford Motor Company.

In consideration of his two degrees, Iacocca was logically placed as a trainee in engineering. But for all of his dreams of swift success in Dearborn, he didn't last out a year before requesting a transfer. In truth, Lee Iacocca wanted to engineer marketing campaigns, not gearshifts. With an eye to putting his practical business ambitions in motion, he gravitated toward sales, even if it meant quitting his position at Ford Motor's headquarters. After leaving Dearborn, he took a job with a Ford regional office in Chester, Pennsylvania, fifteen miles southwest of Philadelphia.

Iacocca's new job had none of the glamour of life at headquarters: in Chester he was charged with pumping up Ford Motor's fleet sales in the region. Slowly and methodically, he learned what he did not know instinctively about sales, and never looked back. "He was a natural at sales meetings," William Clay Ford Sr. explained. "If he had a point to make, he could be a charmer. He can sell you anything, and back it up with his sales talk, logic, and facts. He reminds me a lot of Bob McNamara in his ability to retain facts, and in the way he can use them. He is an extraordinary salesman, an extraordinary talent."[6] Complementing his sound reasoning and grasp of facts was a sense of irony that translated into a winning sense of humor. It served Iacocca the salesman well, before an audience of one person or millions. Backstage in business, however, he was a much harder man, toughened into arrogance by his own relentless ambition. The fleet sales manager in Chester, Pennsylvania, circa 1949 intended to be a Ford Motor vice president by the time he turned thirty-five.

Iacocca notched his earliest coup by coming up with a sales promotion that helped rescue Ford Motor's sales for the 1956 season. The so-called Iacocca Plan invited customers to buy a new '56 Ford for $56 per month.

Chevrolet may have had the hotter product, but Ford's deal couldn't be beat. After the pitch was copied nationwide, Iacocca was summoned to Dearborn and rose through a series of quick promotions. Robert McNamara's sudden resignation early in 1961 reshuffled the executive ranks, resulting in Lee Iacocca's elevation to vice president in charge of the company's flagship Ford Division. He was thirty-six—a year past his target—but a boy wonder by Detroit standards. Before leaving for Washington, McNamara had given Iacocca some valuable advice, in response to his most recent brainstorm. "Go home tonight," he said, "and put your great idea on paper. If you can't do that, then you haven't really thought it out." From that moment on, Iacocca took a small black notebook with him everywhere he went—not unlike the little blue books the original Henry Ford always carried—and scribbled down every worthy notion that flashed through his mind, even if he was at the dinner table or at a public event.[7] When asked what it was he learned from McNamara, Iacocca answered succinctly: "Discipline."[8]

Later in his career, Iacocca would be accused of surrounding himself with sycophants and cronies at Ford Motor. Indeed, he depended on a circle of close associates from the first. Soon after taking charge of the Ford Division, for instance, Iacocca organized a Thursday evening dinner meeting for what he called the "Fair Lane Committee," made up of selected executives from Ford Motor and its principal advertising agency, J. Walter Thompson. Frank Thomas, who attended the meetings as manager of the Ford account at the agency, recalled that the committee's first goal was to define just exactly what Ford Motor represented as a carmaker and what the company wanted to represent in the future. "Lee was trying to develop and convey a theme," Thomas recalled in 1964. "Now I imagine you can say [with] Chrysler that engineering is its theme, and with GM it's style and general excellence. But what was Ford's? It was the crucial question facing a company that had survived its own life-and-death struggle a dozen years before. Having survived, it was ready to assert itself.

"Was it that Ford stood for basic transportation?" Thomas continued. "Was it the 'lively ones' theme? Was it the safest-car-on-the-road theme? We found we were, as a team, going all over the lot. There were too many stop-and-go projects."[9]

In the 1960s, Ford was undoubtedly established as a brand name, one almost synonymous with the American car. Before Andy Warhol turned Coca-Cola bottles, Campbell's soup cans, and Brillo soap-pad boxes into Pop Art icons, painter James Rosenquist was doing the same for the Ford Motor Company's products. Automobile parts figured in many of Rosenquist's large-scale paintings, reflecting the inspiration of an artist whose first car was a 1937 Model A Ford, followed in 1950 by a highly modified Model A that he bought in Ohio and raced around his home in rural North Dakota at 100 miles an hour.[10] Years later, after he had become one of the hottest pop graphics stars in New York, Rosenquist produced his memorable 1961 triptych canvas, *I Love You with My Ford*. Permanently housed in the Moderna Museet in Stockholm, Sweden, the painting depicts a sleeping woman, orange spaghetti, and the front end of a Ford. "That was my America," Rosenquist once explained. "Ford cars, beautiful women, and orange spaghetti."[11]

To Rosenquist the familiar blue oval of Ford stood for America. Iacocca had a far more sophisticated perception in the early 1960s, however. He found his answer in the cold, hard data that came out of the Ford Division's market research. It presented him with the fact that the U.S. population was growing younger—by the end of 1965, 40 percent of Americans would be under the age of twenty. And the trend would continue through the end of the decade. Alongside the expanding number of young people, the experts predicted an increase in automobile purchases. Each year, according to Ford Motor's market research, one third of Americans aged eighteen to twenty-four bought a new car: more young people meant more car sales. Not only was the population actually getting younger, but the individuals within it had begun adopting more youthful attitudes and tastes. As Americans grew simultaneously richer and better educated, the zeitgeist shifted from a work ethic toward a more avid pursuit of fun. As Dr. Seymour Marshak, a recruit from academia who organized the Ford research, explained, "Everyone knew about the 'war baby' thing, but we had no idea of the extent to which young adults would literally come to dominate in the 1960s."[12]

Older, wealthier customers were also drawn along in the youth movement. They wanted light, lithe cars—not for economy but because they wanted to project a fashionably sporty image. That, of course, represented a sea change in the definition of "status" in the automobile world. In the 1930s, big cars were reserved for the wealthy, and therefore boasted the highest status. In the low-price segments buyers squeezed their families into what felt like gasoline-powered tin cans as the era's posh twelve-foot-long Lincolns and Packards glided by, carrying just one or two people. In the 1950s, Detroit recognized the inner desire for bigger cars, offering road barges even in the lower price categories. Once size had ceased to signify status in automobiles, the industry's snobbier customers sought something new. By the 1960s, the leading edge of the market clamored for sophistication rather than sheer automotive acreage. If well-heeled customers wanted savoir faire, General Motors would give it to them, in cars such as the dapper 1963–1965 Buick Riviera and the flowing 1965–1970 Oldsmobile Toronado.

Under Iacocca, Ford Motor assessed the future somewhat differently. "As early as 1961, it was becoming apparent that the character of our market was experiencing a major upheaval," he said in a 1965 speech. "The first job was to identify what kind of product the new market was restlessly groping for and couldn't find. From exhaustive market research, the picture of a new car—

unlike anything then available—began to take shape. In its broadest outlines, this car had to be distinctly sporty and distinctively styled—preferably with just a dash of foreign flavor. It had to be small and maneuverable, but capable of seating four passengers with room left over for a good-sized trunk. And last but by no means least, the price had to be aimed at the mass market."[13]

The objectives laid out for the new car were ambitious, as was its multi-pronged marketing strategy. The model that would be introduced as the Ford Mustang in April 1964 would be targeted at four disparate audiences: two-car families with a little surplus cash to spend, young drivers with hardly any money at all, women who wanted something easy to maintain, and the sporty set in search of a fun new toy. A single car model was directed at the four previously separate market niches.

Donald N. Frey, head of product planning at the Ford Division, along with project manager Don Petersen, was responsible for the new car's basic specifications. Together they put the exact numbers and measurements to the ideas gurgling from Iacocca's office and handed them over to the engineering and design staffs. In the case of the new car, which would be built on the Falcon platform, the look of the car mattered first and foremost. The first design produced, code-named "T-5," failed to generate much enthusiasm inside the company. As Frey admitted, "Well, it looked just like what it was, a reworked old car . . . that wasn't going to work."[14]

Gene Bordinat, vice president for styling, decided to inject a little competitive spirit into the effort. He assigned the design to three separate teams, one from each of his three main studios: Corporate Projects, Ford Division, and Lincoln-Mercury.[15] Then Bordinat made things more exciting by giving the designers just two weeks in which to produce a clay model. Under normal circumstances it would take twice that long to come up with a model—and that was using a design that had itself taken months to develop.

On the Ford Division team, chief stylist Joe Oros mixed veterans with younger designers, then spent the first few precious days simply talking things out with them. Jack Telnack, who would rise to vice president of styling in the Ford Taurus era of the late 1980s, was one of the "young ones" in the summer of 1962. "I can remember going through the whole exercise for a couple of days with all the designers sitting down and really talking," Telnack recalled. "It was probably one of the most extensive and in-depth formats we'd ever developed for a car."[16]

"Before we started sketching," Oros explained, "we worked up a list of do's and don'ts and tacked it up on the wall. We didn't want the car to look like any other car. It was supposed to be unique."[17] It is easy to describe the result of the Oros team's effort—it was the 1964 Mustang, almost exactly as it would roll out of the factory. The only significant difference between the Ford Division's clay model and the car later produced in the hundreds of thousands appeared in the headlight arrangement. It was, and is, virtually unheard of for a car or any other consumer product to emerge so unaltered from its first prototype. If only to prove their involvement, corporate designers and executives tend to exact a running trail of changes. But in 1962, Ford management was thrilled with the Mustang from the first, as was everyone else who saw the natty new car design. Iacocca, according to Frey, "went ape," he loved it so much.[18] Nevertheless, the Ford Motor Company, as the home of modern market research, wasn't inclined to trust the mere instincts of its own people. Instead, prospective customers were brought in to examine the prototype, while Ford executives pumped them for opinions: Which car company would produce a car that looks like this? How much do you think such a car would cost? What don't you like about it? Would you buy one? What would you use it for?[19]

One such focus group consisted of fifty-two couples with small children and room in the family budget for only one car—"people in other words whom we considered to be the least likely Mustang prospects," as Iacocca put it. He went on:

> Their immediate reaction was that they liked the styling very much, but that the car was completely impractical for them. They said it didn't have enough room for Mommy and Daddy, two kids, the groceries, and where are you going to put the ski equipment?
>
> Then we asked them to estimate the price at which the car would sell. Almost all made guesses of $500 to $1,000 on the high side of our intended selling price.
>
> Then we told them the price—$2,368 f.o.b. Detroit—and a strange thing happened. Without exception, these couples—who had declared the Mustang completely impractical for their uses—walked back over to reappraise the car.
>
> Spontaneously, they began to work out a rationale that would let them decide that the car was practical for them after all. One of the great rationalizations came from a woman. Before she knew the price, she complained that the rear seat would be too small and tight for her kids. But when she found out the price tag, she took another look at the back seat and said, "You know, the compactness of that rear seat could be a real safety factor, because the kids wouldn't bounce around as much in case of a sudden stop."
>
> By this time we were feeling pretty good about the Mustang.[20]

The name Mustang was chosen only after an equally arduous analysis. First, Iacocca sent an advertising executive to the Detroit Public Library to create a list of 6,000 potential names. An early favorite was Torino, the Italian spelling of Turin, because of its sporty European ring. After that a succession of names from the animal kingdom came under consideration, including Cougar, Bronco, Puma, Cheetah, and Colt. Mustang also made the short list, having been used most recently on the Army's deadly P-51 warplane. Because of that, it drew quibbles on the grounds that Ford Motor was out to sell a young people's car, not a World War II fighter plane. But Lee Iacocca didn't see it that way. To his mind the word "Mustang" conjured up images of the idealized American West, where wild horses galloped free across the plains and plateaus. "The name Mustang won," noted the ad executive assigned to compile the original list, "because it had the excitement of the wide open spaces, and was American as hell."[21] The eventual Ford Mustang logo would be adapted from an illustration of a galloping horse in Frederic Remington's *Great Pictures of the Old West.*[22]

Iacocca's primary function as the so-called father of the Mustang lay in persuading Ford Motor's corporate hierarchy to produce it. Of course, he was a master of the grand sales pitch. Even his former boss Robert McNamara, so famously icy and methodical, admitted that he couldn't resist Iacocca's salesmanship. "You're so effective one on one. You could sell anybody anything," he once told his brash subordinate.[23] After that, McNamara made Iacocca submit his arguments in writing.

If any individual could persuade Ford Motor Company to try another bold new product when the company was still sulking over the flop of the Edsel, it was Iacocca. He found that company president Henry Ford II was disposed to go forward with a product directed at the youth market. But what really impressed many top Ford managers was Iacocca's plan to split the model's personality. The reasonable $2,368 base price would be accompanied by more than eighty options, including four different engines and seven transmissions. Depending on a customer's choices, the Mustang could remain an economy car—"the Falcon with a 'skin change,'" as Ford executive Arjay Miller called it[24]—or it could become almost as plush as the company's original Thunderbird. Even more surprising, the Mustang could also be turned into a performance car with enough brute muscle to compete on the racetrack—and to spawn a decade's worth of copycats. "Any list of classic American autos would have to include one in particular: the Mustang," judged the Berkeley Pop Culture Project in its 1991 *Whole Pop Catalog.* "The Mustang began its illustrious history as the original 'pony' car—small, sporty and named after a horse. . . . The great thing about the Mustang was that it came with more than 35 standard items, 40 different options, a zippy engine, and a low price tag to boot! . . . Quoth one Mustang enthusiast at the Ford Motor Company: 'This car is the greatest thing since the Erector set.'"[25]

Because options produced a higher profit margin than the basic vehicles to which they were added, Ford Motor's executives were especially intrigued with the way the Mustang allowed for so much customization. The model received the corporate go-ahead, but nothing about the new Ford would be publicly announced until February 1964, just two months before its launch.[26]

In the meantime, creating the Mustang took precedence as a special project among the Ford Motor employees assigned to move it from blueprints into production. "A piece of everybody who worked on it is in this car," proclaimed Jack Prendergast, Ford's executive engineer for light vehicles, in the spring of 1964. "Our engineers, technicians, mechanics, test drivers—when they didn't think we were raising our baby properly, I heard from them personally."[27]

"The car has 'lived' well with us," Gene Bordinat noted of the styling staff, even before the Mustang went on sale. "If it tires us, the same thing will happen in the marketplace."[28]

Fortunately for Lee Iacocca and Ford Motor Company, the American car-buying public proved as excited about the Mustang as its creators were. It was as if the Mustang's designers had tapped directly into the psyche—and thus directly into the wallets—of the American consumer. Having survived the assassination of President John F. Kennedy the previous November, the nation felt ready in the spring of 1964 to make a fresh start. The U.S. economy was booming and about to get even better; on March 15 the Department of Labor reported that one out of three women in the United States worked outside the home, an increase of 50 percent over the previous fifteen years, to 25 million and growing.[29] President Lyndon B. Johnson had just announced an income tax cut that gave every working American a raise in take-home pay. On the lighter side, the Beatles had just paid their first visit to the United States, to the screaming delight of legions of teens avid to adopt the infectious insouciance of England's Fab Four. Even food makers took note of the changing culture, responding to the keenness for color exhibited by young people by introducing multihued breakfast treats such as Kellogg's Pop-Tarts and General Mills' Lucky Charms cereal.

Actual production of the Mustang began at Ford Motor's massive River Rouge plant on March 9, 1964.[30] At 9:30 P.M. on Thursday, April 16, the company launched a television advertising blitz, unveiling the Mustang in a series of commercials aired simultaneously on all three networks. According to the national Nielsen ratings, 29 million Americans had their first glimpse of the Mustang that evening.

The car officially went on sale the next morning. Across the country, an estimated 4 million people visited Ford showrooms to see the Mustang the first week, eclipsing even the riotous response to the launch of the Model A thirty-six years earlier. And the manufacturer kept up the drumbeat, advertising the Mustang in more than 2,600 newspapers in some 2,200 markets, taking out space in both news sections and in what were then called "the women's pages." "We estimate that we hit 75 percent of all the households in the country through the newspaper medium," reported Frank E. Zimmerman Jr., Ford Motor's general marketing manager.[31]

The 1964 New York World's Fair served as the runway for the Mustang's public rollout, amid speeches, ceremonies, and a spectacular display in the Ford Wonder Rotunda.[32] "Walt Disney cut the ribbon for us," Iacocca recalled. "It couldn't have been a better launch."[33] The chairman of New York's esteemed Tiffany & Company jewelers personally presented Henry Ford II and his company's Mustang the Tiffany Gold Medal Award "for excellence in American design," marking the first time the honor went to an automobile. "I kept one of the originals for myself," Iacocca recalled. "I gave it to my daughter on her thirtieth birthday (she was born the same year as the Mustang came out) and it's a Fairlane engine in a hot convertible, blue with a white top and the pony leather interior, and it's got an automatic transmission—probably the prime car in the Ford stable."[34]

The best advertising, of course, came free of charge in the form of glowing reviews. Alongside Ford Motor Company's own abundant print ads, articles about the Mustang popped up in practically every general-interest magazine; in fact, both *Time* and *Newsweek* featured the car as well as Lee Iacocca on their covers for the week of April 20, 1964. Iacocca recalled in his autobiography that "the twin cover stories had the effect of two giant commercials. After telling its readers that my name 'rhymes with try-a-Coke-ah,' *Time* noted that 'Iacocca has produced more than just another new car. With its long hood and short rear deck, its Ferrari flair and openmouthed air scoop, the Mustang resembles the European racing cars that American sports-car buffs find so appealing. Yet, Iacocca has made the Mustang's design so flexible, its price so reasonable, and its options so numerous that its potential appeal reaches toward two-thirds of all U.S. car buyers. Priced as low as $2,368 and able to accommodate a small family in its four seats, the Mustang seems destined to be a sort of Model A of sports cars—for the masses as well as the buffs.' . . . I couldn't have said it better myself," Iacocca concluded.[35]

Mustangs went on display at fifteen major airport terminals and in the lobbies of more than two hundred Holiday Inns across the country. The promotional blitz ignited powerful interest and did not let up, keeping the car in the public eye for years. "The Mustang was the greatest thing that ever happened to Ford," said Lou Slawson, who worked in the Fleet and Leasing Division. "The first year it came out, the response to that car was phenomenal."[36]

Over the first weekend, the company accepted 22,542 orders. One dealer in Detroit crowed that his parking lot "looked like a foreign car rally."[37] Another in Chicago had to lock the doors of his Mustangs to protect them from all the people who showed up just to sit behind the wheel. A truck driver in Seattle fell so entranced by the sight of his first Mustang in a dealership that he accidentally hit the accelerator and drove right through the showroom window. And when the Mustang made its racetrack debut at a stock-car event in Huntsville, Alabama, a crowd of more than nine thousand motor fans climbed the wall and circled it for an up-close look, delaying the race for an hour. In Garland, Texas, fifteen eager customers all wanted the last Mustang available at the local dealership. An impromptu auction ensued, and the winner slept overnight in his car until his check cleared the next morning.[38]

In thirty days, Ford Motor Company sold 70,000 Mustangs—more than the Thunderbird's total sales over its first three years. By the end of 1964, less than nine months after the model burst upon the scene, a quarter-million Mustangs had been snapped up.[39] Iacocca had prepared for the onslaught of orders; he had taken it upon himself to raise the Mustang's initial production quota to 360,000 units, built both at River Rouge and a plant in San Jose, California. Others looked on the last-minute increase as a gamble. Not Iacocca. "It does little good to look back on a 100,000 sales-year and say, 'If I'd been smart enough to build 200,000, I could have sold them,'" he said. "By that time, you're out on your can."[40] Instead, midway through the model's first year of production, an extra Ford plant in Metuchen, New Jersey, had to be converted to Mustang assembly in order to keep up with demand.[41] As a result, the new model broke the automobile industry's previous first-year-model sales record of 417,174, set by Ford's own Falcon five years earlier. The company celebrated its triumph by lighting up the windows of the Dearborn Central Staff Office Building (later called World Headquarters) on the night of April 17, 1965, to spell out "418,812"—the exact number of Mustangs Ford Motor had sold the first model year.[42]

"Our hot cakes sell like Mustangs!" read a sign in the window of a New York City diner.[43]

From the first, Ford's advertising emphasized the Mustang's double-barreled appeal: it looked far more expensive than it cost, and its sporty design could make anybody look cool. Of course, in a year when America's highest-rated television show was *Bonanza* and among its more acclaimed novels Thomas Berger's *Little Big Man*, it didn't hurt that the car's logo was an icon of the Old West.

Just because the research behind the Mustang happened to have been on target did not mean, however, that Ford Motor Company was finished with its market studies. "The median Mustanger is 31 years old, compared to age 42 for the median purchaser of the regular Ford car," pointed out Product Planning Manager Donald Frey two years and one million vehicles after the car's introduction. "Twenty-eight percent of Mustang buyers are less than 25 years old, while only three percent of Ford buyers are that young." Frey added that 37 percent of Mustang buyers were women.

Among the myriad studies Ford Motor conducted on the Mustang's success was one focused on the car's suitability for romance, for which the company canvassed college students in eight U.S. cities. Somewhat embarrassed when news of the research was publicized, Ford Motor sheepishly released the intelligence that 42 percent of single people preferred bucket seats on a first date, but only 15 percent still wanted them once they were going steady. "Last Saturday night, my boyfriend and I went to the drive-in in his Ford Mustang," a young woman from California wrote to Lee Iacocca. "I must say, sir, that this car is not built for any type of romantic endeavor. Your bucket seats, comfortable for long trips only, cannot sit more than one and a half persons at a single time and as a result one of us has to sit with that sharp edge jabbing us in the derriere."[44] The company made plans to offer a bench seat up front starting with the 1966 model.

Whatever the Mustang meant to more than a million customers, many of them in market niches previously ignored, the car's dazzling success gave its greatest boost to Ford Motor Company. "The Mustang gave the company the first big spiritual lift it ever had since the war," according to W. S. Walla. "When the Mustang came out, Ford had a sport car and a flair that it had been trying to get for a long time. The price was right and the styling was right. It excited everyone—the public, dealers, factory people, even executives."[45]

To put personalities into its sparkling sales statistics, Iacocca's Ford Division took to quoting from the four thousand "love letters" it claimed to have received from Mustang owners in the car's first year. Because the same four or five letters always seemed to be cited—at every opportunity, by a whole gamut of Ford executives—one General Motors manager on hand for such a recitation grumbled that the endorsement sounded like the work of Ford's PR department. The letters were real enough, and certainly glowing: "I'm madly in love with my new Mustang," wrote a Philadelphia mother about what the car meant to her. "For the sake of my brood, I've been dragging a nine-passenger station wagon around for the past fifteen years. For about fourteen years, I've been tired of the whole deal. My Mustang was my key to liberation."[46]

———————

The Mustang first-year production figures proved that the do-it-yourself approach reflected in the wide selection of options had accounted for much of its stellar success. While the car's base list price started at $2,368, its selling price averaged $2,760, according to an April 1965 company press release. More than 80 percent of the first season's Mustangs were ordered with one of the V-8 engines offered for an extra $116 to $181; only radios and whitewall tires ranked as more popular options.[47] The fear that the Mustang would do little more for the company's bottom line than siphon off sales from other Ford models was not borne out. To the contrary, in 1964 and 1965 Ford Motor's overall sales grew by numbers not far off its total Mustang orders. In 1965, for example, Ford's overall sales of 2.4 million cars, some 400,000 units above the previous year's totals, included about 542,000 Mustangs. "If it weren't for this car," noted the industry journal *Steel* that April, "the company might surrender some of its share of the market. But with Mustang's help, Ford should maintain the 26 percent penetration it now holds."[48]

As early as 1964, well before most of the American marketplace caught on to the idea, Iacocca recognized the powerful appeal of popular music to the young-minded consumer. In consequence, Ford Motor Company began sponsoring folk-music concerts to further associate the Mustang with cutting-edge pop culture. But it was a local Detroit recording company that really captured Iacocca's attention: Berry Gordy's Motown Records.

On June 28, 1965, Ford Mustang sponsored "It's What's Happening, Baby," a two-hour prime-time CBS music special featuring Motown and British Invasion acts and hosted by New York disc jockey Murray "the K" Kaufman. Cosponsored by the U.S. government's Office of Economic Opportunity in a bid to encourage America's teens to get summer jobs,[49] the show included performances by Ray Charles, the Dave Clark Five, the Four Tops, Marvin Gaye, Herman's Hermits, Tom Jones, the Supremes, and others, all filmed belting out their best in front of the Mustang assembly line at Ford Motor's River Rouge plant.

The highlight of the program came with Motown stars Martha and the Vandellas doing a rousing rendition of their hit single "Nowhere to Run," which had reached number 9 on the pop charts in mid-March[50] (the B-side was titled "Motoring"). They performed the song dancing around Ford's factory floor in front of bewildered assembly-line workers, making Mustangs all the while. The sponsors of "It's What's Happening, Baby" were apparently oblivious of the irony of three beautiful black women crying, "Nowhere to run, baby, nowhere to hide," for the ostensible pleasure of Ford Motor's regimented workforce in 1964.[51] "The audience of automakers at the filming of the song often had 'nowhere to run' from the tedium of assembly-line work and nowhere to go if automation displaced them from their jobs," noted historian Suzanne E. Smith in *Dancing in the Street: Motown and the Cultural Politics of Detroit.* "The U.S. Office of Economic Opportunity broadcast the show to encourage teenagers to look for part-time summer work but did not offer any long-term solutions to the employment crisis that automation and deindustrialization had produced in cities like Detroit."[52] Lee Iacocca nevertheless deemed the show a landmark television event, while Berry Gordy kept the hits coming off his own assembly line at Motown Records.

The best-known pop music paean to the new Ford was Mack Rice's "Mustang Sally," recorded most memorably by rhythm-and-blues great Wilson Pickett in November 1966. "We got more publicity than we could handle with that song," Iacocca recalled.[53] The lyrics speak for the seductive power of the Ford Mustang:

I bought you a brand new Mustang
'bout nineteen-sixty-five
Now you come 'round, signifying a woman, baby,
you don't wanna let me ride.[54]

Hollywood stars, including Frank Sinatra, Debbie Reynolds, and George Raft, made sure they had Mustangs in the first wave. The Mustang made its greatest splash in the 1968 Steve McQueen action movie *Bullitt,* which boasted a ten-minute stunt-driving sequence through the hilly streets of San Francisco that is still considered the best car chase ever put on film. McQueen's performance aside, the real star of *Bullitt* turned out to be a dark green 1968 Mustang GT Fastback with a 390-cubic-inch V-8 engine. McQueen used it to outrun the bad guys' Dodge Charger. After filming, the original *Bullitt* Mustang had taken such a beating it was consigned to the crusher. Its understudy, however, was bought by an employee of Warner Brothers' editing department, who later advertised it for sale in *Road & Track;* purchased by a New Jersey automobile collector, it was stored in an Ohio hay barn where it resides today. Yet the image of the beefed-up muscle Mustang with McQueen behind the wheel remains so compelling that in 2002, Ford Motor Company took advantage of it by selling a special-edition high-performance model called the Mustang Bullitt.[55] As an enthusiastic Bill Ford Jr. quipped in one of his company's "Ford Heritage" television ads, "That was one of the coolest scenes I'd ever seen in a movie. From that point on, I was hooked. I'm a huge Mustang fan. . . . That's the kind of absolute soul that you can't fake."[56]

Besides pop songs and action movies, Ford Motor enlisted George Barris to customize and product-place Mustangs in popular TV shows. A Hollywood dream maker, with a mechanical bent, Barris souped up Fords that became megahits at international auto shows. Barris first achieved fame by transforming a 1955 Lincoln Futura into the Batmobile, the real star of the *Batman* TV series, which began in 1966. Cleverly, Barris's Batmobile was drenched with whizbang gizmos: a Batphone, antitheft devices, a Batscope, laser power, a remote camera with display screen.[57] "While other kids watched TV to see the stars," comedian and automobile enthusiast Jay Leno recalled, "I watched TV to see the Barris cars."[58]

Barris delivered another famous Ford for the TV show *The Munsters.* One of the sitcom's most popular characters, Grandpa, was a Count Dracula type from Transylvania who drove a scary, hot-rod stagecoach, complete with a footman's seat, Model T radiator, red-plush-velvet upholstery, gas lanterns, and coffin door handles. A 289-cubic-inch Ford Cobra V-8 from a 1966 Mustang GT powered Grandpa's coach. The lead character, Herman Munster, who was seven feet tall and looked like a happy-go-lucky Frankenstein monster, said of the "Munster Koach" that it "got three miles to each gallon of em-balming fluid." Like the Batmobile, the Munster Koach became a megahit at auto shows and county fairs, helping Ford Motor products reach a younger demographic. With Barris's help the TV show soon had another car on the show: a "Drag-u-la."[59] He went on to develop other custom-made Ford cars for Hollywood, most memorably the bright red Mustang convertibles for Sonny and Cher to be used in their movie *Good Times*.[60]

Ford Motor Company had the distinction of giving the youth of the mid-1960s a colorful label: "the Mustang Generation," first used by the *Wall Street Journal* in a headline above a front-page report on advertising to the baby boomers.[61] Before the United States became fully mired in the Vietnam War and the drug counterculture began burdening young people with tragedy, the Mustang represented what the boomers brought to the American market-place: youthfulness, with all of its carefree attitudes and the determination to be different from everybody else. Ford Motor sold more than 3 million Mus-tangs between 1964 and 1973, by which time "improvements" bloated the original model by a foot and more than 650 pounds.

One young member of the Mustang generation would later preside over its rebirth. "My graduation present from high school was a Mustang—a green metallic special paint job," Bill Ford Jr. recalled, speaking of a time when there were no other such Mustangs on the road. "And this baby, with a tan leather interior—it was beautiful, absolutely beautiful. You could see that car coming from a hundred yards. It was a great, great car." Named chairman of his family's company in 1999, Bill Ford Jr. considered the Mus-tang a nameplate brand. "The Mustang brand is unique for our company," he said. "People will say that 'I drive a Ford pickup, or Ford Escort,' but they only say 'I drive a Mustang.'"[62]

PART FIVE

The Turnaround Years

31

Jet Set

In starting on a youth campaign in the early 1960s, Ford Motor Company was following the lead of its chairman, Henry Ford II. He understood, better than anyone, the importance of making cars that appealed to baby boomers and the youth movement in society. Raised in a conservative household, watched over by downright reactionary grandparents, he had married young and had the weight of the corporation dropped on his shoulders when he was only in his late twenties. For fifteen years, Henry II acted far older than his years, putting confidence back in the Ford name through his own dedication to the company. He had few hobbies but liked to travel, taking extensive vacations with his wife, Anne, and their three children. Although known in his inner circle as a "drinking man," Henry II was nonetheless regarded as a steady husband and father in the 1950s. "When I was at Ford," Robert McNamara recalled, "Henry II was too busy to get into trouble. He was learning the ropes and doing a first-rate job at it."[1]

Predictability, directness, and a sense of purpose—all of Henry II's finer attributes were likewise those of the basic Ford car of the late 1950s. At the age of forty-one, however, Henry II abandoned his conservative, stable lifestyle, entering into a transatlantic love affair with the Italian-born Cristina Vettore Austin. He first met her in March 1960 at a dinner honoring Princess Grace of Monaco. Responding to her sprightly insouciance, he spent more and more time in European resorts and social capitals, following her with a kind of desperation, according to observers interviewed by Ford family biographers Peter Collier and David Horowitz.[2] His wife learned of the affair at a cruelly inopportune time, the night before their daughter's 1961 debut, a dazzling party due to receive national press coverage. Over the following two years, Henry II was in turmoil, alternating between his reluctance to abandon his family and his yearning for a different life. He chose the new course, not only out of an emotional attachment for Cristina, but because of the opportunity to break out of Detroit and the constraints he felt there.

Having divorced Anne in 1963, Henry II married Cristina at the Shoreham Hotel in New York City on February 19, 1965. Portrayed as a Cinderella figure by the Italian press, Cristina was pure sparkle. "At that time she was easy to please, invariably punctual, forever asking questions, learning, she said with a laugh, to be Mrs. Henry Ford II," close Ford associate Walter Hayes recalled. "Her tawny hair, green eyes, and high cheekbones made her striking in any company."[3] The 1960s would be different for Ford—the man and the company he led. For Henry II, the fast lane was symbolized by the jet set social world. For the company, it was another kind of jet set, the world of racing. Ford Motor Company had been repressed and even isolated for decades under the elder Henry Ford, turning out cars by the millions, but largely oblivious of the rest of the automobile industry and its more glamorous edges. On one occasion, in early 1935, old Henry authorized a try at the Indianapolis 500, but the result was . . . there was no result, the cars failed to finish and Ford turned his back on racing for good. As it turned out, the company couldn't do the same. After racking up a gaggle of stock-car victories in the 1950s, Ford joined other American automakers in withdrawing from racing in 1957. But in 1962, Ford Motor was back in the game, competing again with a fervor that gripped the whole company. Attacking any type of competition on four wheels, from the drag strips of California to the misty streets of Le Mans, all-out Daytona, and, of course, Indy, Ford was on a mission to prove that it had the stuff to build and race with the best. Even beyond the tally of victories, Ford was proving to itself that it could run with the cool crowd. With racing, the corporate culture changed and Ford's business along with it.

Unlike other big companies, Ford Motor entered into the life of the machine shops and garages that invariably surround racetracks. The company formed alliances with boutique automakers in both Europe and the United States, with the result that a whole generation of independent automobile engineers was nurtured on Ford: its engines, its components, and its unusually accommodating attitude. The second-biggest car company in the world was pulling dozens of tiny auto companies along in its wake in the 1960s—a new phenomenon that gave the auto industry some of its most exciting models.

"We are in the business of selling cars," Ford Division President Lee Iacocca explained. "Racing creates a youthful image for us." That fact constituted one reason that Ford went racing with such a vengeance in the early 1960s.

The other reason was corporate in nature and involved the aggressive development of the global automobile business. As an international language, automobile racing reached car buyers across borders—and quickly. An important victory flashed all over the world in a blink. Not every customer could recite the order of finish at Le Mans or Silverstone, but there weren't many car buyers under the age of thirty in 1962 who didn't know the name Ferrari and that it might just as well have been Italian for "winner." Ford Motor wanted to take that word away from Ferrari.

In fact, Ford Motor Company wanted to take the whole company, sending its imaginative executive Don Frey to Modena, Italy, to try to buy Ferrari Automobili in 1963. Enzo Ferrari, who had founded the company in 1945, would have liked the $12 million that was on the table, but he ultimately turned the offer down. He wanted to run Ferrari and the only way to run it was to own it. "Failure to buy Ferrari," Walter Hayes recalled, "was merely a hiccup and by no means a setback toward the imminent achievement of 'Total Performance.'"[4]

Auto races in America were skyrocketing in popularity and the regional favorites—sports-car racing in the Northeast, drag racing in the West, and stock-car events in the South—had yet to peak. From 1957 to 1962, Ford watched glumly as its archrival, Chevrolet, reaped the benefit of association with race victories, while staying officially on the right side of the overarching Automobile Manufacturers Association (AMA) resolution intended to keep car companies from participating in motor sports. It was well known in the industry that Chevrolet was continuing to support race efforts, but only through dummy divisions within the corporation. Zora Arkus-Duntov, for example, the man who put the guts into the Corvette, was out advising race teams when his job title indicated that he was designing boat engines.[5]

Mindful of the rampant, if secret, race activity, Ford executives were also aware that Chevy was nipping away at Ford's sinking market share. Finally, on June 11, 1962, Henry II couldn't stand it any longer. He announced that Ford was withdrawing from the AMA agreement. "We tried very hard to live with this policy," he said in a written statement. "As time passed, however, some car divisions, including our own, interpreted the resolution more and more freely, with the result that increasing emphasis was placed on speed, horsepower and racing."[6] Brute performance was all right with Ford and its chairman, but from that moment on, it would be out in the open. Henry II had no patience with the hypocrisy involved in the AMA ban. At the same time, Henry Ford II was having his own problems with hypocrisy. A new self-image suited him at that juncture as much as it did his company.

After breaking the AMA ban, Ford Motor Company went a-racing, almost anywhere that it heard the squeal of tires. "In this company," explained Lee Iacocca in September 1963, speaking of the pressure of entering races on a corporate level, "we compare it to a satellite shooting at Cape Canaveral. The chips are down and the world can look on."[7] The company was indeed courting disaster, entering the widest variety of high-caliber competition ever approached by one company. More than a policy, it was a grand boast. Iacocca coined the phrase "Ford Total Performance" for it. However, if the company flopped in even one sphere of racing, the whole program would be a disaster and Ford would be a fumbling giant, a laughingstock.

In February 1963 Ford drivers headed with high hopes to Florida for the Daytona 500, the top event in NASCAR stock-car racing. On arriving, they were dismayed at the buzz on the track that GM (which was still pretending to abide by the AMA ban) had sent a set of special big block engines for the Chevrolets entered in the race. That presented a dilemma, since NASCAR was pledged to ensure that each "stock car" in its races was identical to an actual production car—an effort it has long since abandoned. Chevy's special big block, which hardly qualified as "standard," was nevertheless allowed in the race, to the outrage of Ford fans in the stands and around the country. As it turned out, though, the Chevy engines faltered during the 500.[8] Factory-sponsored Fords finished first and second—and third, fourth, and fifth, too. No other company had ever swept the first five positions at the Daytona 500.

Ford wanted to make sure that the whole world knew about its five-star victory and so it broke the second clause in the old AMA ban and trumpeted the Daytona results in ads on the radio and in 2,800 newspapers.[9] The advertising was even more controversial than Ford's original decision to participate in racing, because many people felt that selling the thrill of speed encouraged reckless driving.[10] Meanwhile, Ford's market share perked up that summer, from a somnolent 22.5 percent early in the year to 26.2 percent during August.[11] And Daytona was only one race: over the course of the whole season, Ford cars won 51 percent of the prize money in NASCAR stock-car events.

America's single favorite automobile race was the Indianapolis 500, a pageant held on Memorial Day weekend, which pitted thirty-three all-out race cars over two hundred laps of a two-and-a-half-mile oval. Over the years the Indy 500 had grown into a patriotic tradition like the Kentucky Derby or the World Series. Ford Motor wanted a piece of that American pie. While driving Indy takes courage and skill, for the drivers the trick is basically to go fast and keep turning left. It is most of all a test of the car builders. It isn't unusual for fewer than ten cars to finish at all, due mainly to breakdowns.

For more than thirty years up to 1962, every Indianapolis 500 race had been won by a car powered by the same engine, tweaked and modernized with the times. The four-cylinder Offenhauser engine dominated in part because the cost of developing a new engine was prohibitive, even to the manufacturer of the Offy, engine specialist Meyer-Drake. Undaunted, Ford Motor assigned veteran engineer A. J. Scussel to develop a new eight-cylinder engine for racing in general and Indianapolis in particular. However, the company chose not to engineer a chassis. Instead, it aligned itself with England's tiny Lotus factory, operated by Colin Chapman, the man considered the best in the field of chassis design. His thought-provoking motto was "Add lightness."

Lotus, founded on an Army discharge grant and a $75 loan from a friend, had earned a stunning reputation in European Formula 1 and 2 racing with its quicksilver racers.

When one of Chapman's lightweight, rear-engine chassis was combined with the new Ford engine in 1963, it was the talk of Indianapolis. Jacques Passino, a Ford employee, recalled the unveiling of the Lotus-Fords just before the first practice runs. "We had two Ford engines in there with all those Offenhausers," Passino said, "and those little old cars rolled out and you could hear this sudden hush—and then a swelling murmur running through the crowd. God! It was wonderful. I grabbed Iacocca by the arm and said in his ear, 'Son of a gun, Lee, you hear that? They're all saying our name. That's what it's all about, man!'" Just the sight of a new Ford racer could get people talking. Iacocca could hardly wait for the cars to start winning.[12]

The Lotus-Fords didn't win in 1963, but they mustered a second-place finish the next year. However, the old Offy crowd was still skeptical. A. J. Foyt and Parnelli Jones dismissed the Lotus-Fords as "funny little cars."[13] Both drivers would change their minds. In 1965, Jones was one of seventeen Indy drivers using Ford engines, and Foyt was asking around for a Ford ride. At the top of the list of Lotus-Ford drivers was Jimmy Clark, the shy Scotsman who was the reigning hero of British racing. To gild the lily Ford imported a pit crew for him as well—at least in a manner of speaking, luring the legendary Wood Brothers crew away from NASCAR. At Indy, where forty-second pit stops were considered speedy, the Wood crew could push Clark's car away after nineteen seconds.[14]

No foreigner had won at Indy since 1916, but Jimmy Clark was certain two weeks before the Memorial Day race that he would cross the finish line first. He loved the Lotus-Ford and knew it was ready. So was he: he won the 500 easily. All of the first four finishers carried Ford engines, and all were rear-engine cars. In two years, Ford had helped revolutionize Indy racing.

And racing revolutionized Ford Motor.

"It was a team effort perhaps unparalleled in the history of the sport," said Don Frey right after the Indianapolis results. "From Henry Ford II on down, we had the entire company behind the campaign to provide a powerplant that would document Ford's long history of leadership in engine manufacturing."[15]

Sales told the score, where it counted at the company. When Iacocca was asked after a speech at the Detroit Athletic Club whether racing helped to sell cars, he replied, "It sure as hell does."[16] A Ford dealer put it more succinctly: "I race on Sunday and sell on Monday. The kids who run my stockers or watch them on Sunday are back at my place of business pricing our products the next day. We reach the sixteen- to twenty-four-year-olds who either buy outright or otherwise influence 40 percent of our sales."[17] "Race on Sunday, Sell on Monday" was used as the title of a Ford brochure about racing.

While it held special meaning at Ford, it also became a catchphrase within the industry. And it translated into other languages, just as well.

In 1965, Ford Motor headed for Le Mans, France. While NASCAR and Indianapolis were as American as apple pie, they didn't matter to international customers for Ford cars.

Two years before, when Don Frey returned from Modena and nervously broke the news to Henry II that the Ferrari deal couldn't be completed, the boss only shrugged. "All right, then," he said. "We'll build our own Le Mans car."[18] A team of Ford engineers immediately started working on it in secret: a car capable of lightning-fast speed, through hairpin turns and over hills, for the span of twenty-four straight hours, round and round an 8.3-mile course in a town in northern France. Another engineering team started work on the same problem in England, led by Roy Lunn, the former chief engineer at Aston Martin. The result in Britain was the Ford GT-40, a low-slung racer (only forty inches high) with an Indy-style 289-cubic-inch engine. The Ford team entered its first Le Mans race in 1964, but was disappointed when the cars developed transmission problems. Afterward, the GT-40 engineering team regrouped as Ford Advanced Vehicles, working in Slough, England, under the direction of John Wyer, a former Aston Martin manager.

Meanwhile, the American arm of the assault on Le Mans was developing a heftier version of the GT car. The group, given the cover name Kar Kraft to maintain secrecy, installed 427-cubic-inch engines in the new racers, called GT Mark IIs. Bringing six entries to Le Mans in 1965, Ford team managers watched as each was stopped by engine problems. No American car had ever won Le Mans, and few people in attendance that day expected that to change in the future. However, Leo C. Beebe, the manager of Ford's racing program, the Special Vehicles Division, scheduled a meeting only four hours after the dispiriting race was over. "I want you to know," he said to the exhausted men he faced, "that this is a victory celebration. We're celebrating our victory in the 1966 race."[19]

Beebe undoubtedly meant every word. "To Ford, winning at Le Mans means as much as landing the first men on the moon means to NASA," wrote Jan Norbye in *Popular Science*.[20] In preparation for the 1966 assault, a new version of the GT Mark II debuted at an endurance race at Daytona. "We don't even know if our *paint* can go twenty-four hours," muttered Beebe just before the start. But in the Florida race the Fords finished first, second, and third—and fifth, for good measure. The whole season was full of such success, but the last test of the season was the important one, Le Mans, in June. As the twenty-four-hour race came to a close, the two leaders were both Fords. They were followed at a distance by another of the Fords. Excited, but prepared for just such a triumph, the team managers ordered the two leaders to slow down so that the finish would feature three Ford GT-40s in a dead heat—for the sake of photographs in publications around the world.[21]

The Le Mans win, together with the string of previous victories that season, gave Ford the World Manufacturers' Championship in 1966.[22] When the company repeated its Le Mans victory in 1967, Henry Ford II was there to see it. In the pits afterward, he partook in the shower of Mumm's '67 champagne that celebrated the win—and the fact that in five years, Ford Motor Company had made it to the top of European racing.

"There is nothing doing against the steamroller of the Americans," Enzo Ferrari wrote in *Autosprint,* an Italian magazine, at the end of the 1966 season.[23] He was referring specifically to the well-financed Ford effort and petulantly threatened to reduce his participation in future racing. Ford, it was true, was spending about $9 million per year on its racing programs,[24] much more than any other manufacturer ever had. However, as team owners have known since the very first automobile races in the 1890s, money alone doesn't buy racing success. Ford brought a generous budget to its race program, but more than that, it brought an organization of effective people. Getting them to move from 0 to 100 percent on racing was a triumph of management, not underwriting.

NASCAR . . . Indy . . . Le Mans. They were only the beginning. The man in charge of the Ford racing octopus, Leo Beebe, fielded ideas from drivers, engineers, and team managers, even while keeping track of a realistic program of car development and race entries. Tall and rangy, with a thin cigar typically jutting out of the corner of his mouth, Beebe stepped up preparation of Fords for drag racing, and simultaneously entered company cars in the far dowdier Mobilgas Economy Run.

A former basketball star at the University of Michigan, Leo Beebe joined Ford in 1946 and had been a useful executive in a variety of spheres—sixteen different jobs, in fact, in nineteen years. In 1957, he was lent to the U.S. government to head a program to relocate 35,000 refugees from the failed Hungarian revolution. His souvenir from that experience was a sign for his desk, "Gondolkozz," which means "think" in Hungarian. Beebe had never even seen an automobile race before he took over Ford's racing program,[25] but that didn't matter. He could judge the people who could judge the cars.

One of the experts that Beebe trusted most was former driver Carroll Shelby. Originally from Texas, Shelby had made his reputation in 1959 by winning Le Mans behind the wheel of an Aston Martin. At the time, no American car had a prayer against the Jaguars, Astons, and Ferraris that dominated road racing. "Call it nationalism, a love for the system of free enterprise or just plain pride," Shelby said, "but getting ridiculed by European racers who rapped the American engineering and car-building know-how . . . got me started." Shelby put his sentiments into a new company, Shelby American, in 1962 and took an idea to Ford Motor. He wanted to match a 289-cubic-inch Ford engine to an A.C. Ace sports-car chassis made in England, and add refinements of his own. When it was through, he'd call it a Cobra. Ford agreed to supply the engines, some of the funding, and as much technical help as Shelby wanted.

In the bargain, Carroll Shelby came away with a car company he never could have started otherwise. Ford got a sports car that could take on the Europeans, bumping off Corvettes along the way, and make the emblem "Powered by Ford" world-famous. Customers queued up on waiting lists for the chance to buy one of the new street-legal rockets. The Shelby aura grew with the addition of the neck-snapping 427-cubic-inch version of the Cobra in 1965. The following year, Shelby American began to turn standard Mustangs into Shelby GT Mustangs, with engineering changes that added about 40 mph to the top speed. They were always white with a blue stripe. Even Carroll Shelby lost track of how many races his Cobras and GTs won. "The image we have established," he said with perfect accuracy, "is that we have the fastest production cars anywhere in the world."[26]

Carroll Shelby wasn't the only carmaker inspired by the potent engines being turned out by Ford Motor Company. Production cars carrying the label "Powered by Ford" kept many small shops humming, especially in Europe.

Shelby's success made him a popular man at Ford. In 1963, his Cobras won the U.S. Road Racing Championship and in the process practically erased the Corvettes from the board. In Europe, Cobras traded victories with Ferrari GTOs in 1964. Just before the last race of the Fédération Internationale de l'Automobile (FIA) season, the Ferrari team was ahead by a small margin in the championship-point standings. Shelby felt that he could make up the amount with a good showing in the final race. Then, according to race historian Alex Gabbard, "Enzo, in a very controversial move, used his political influence to cancel that last race, ensuring that Ferrari would retain the FIA title."[27]

Shelby saw Enzo Ferrari soon afterward and told him, "Someday I'll blow your ass off." That day arrived in the 1965 season, when the Cobra easily won its class in the Manufacturers' Championship, turning back the Ferrari team. Ford didn't entirely vanquish rivals like Ferrari from the racing world, but from 1964 to 1969, it made plenty of room for itself among them. "I don't even have to go to the races down home to see who wins," gloated N. B. Hamric, a Ford-Mercury dealer from Gassaway, West Virginia. "After one of the big races, people come in wanting to see a 'hot one just like the one that won.'"[28]

Dearborn wasn't the only force in the world of Ford racing. Ford Motor (England) Ltd. lent its cooperation—monetary and technical—to Keith Duckworth's idea for a three-liter engine to compete in Formula 1 races. Duckworth was a mechanical engineer from Yorkshire who had previously designed race parts for Lotus. The design was complex, calling for four valves per cylinder, which led to the name Double Four Valve (DFV). Duckworth joined forces with engineer Mike Costin to produce engines under the name Cosworth. The Ford-Cosworth engine, powering a Lotus car, electrified the F1 world by winning its very first race, the Dutch Grand Prix in 1967, with Jimmy Clark at the wheel. It was a triumphant day for both tiny Cosworth and Ford Motor (England) Ltd. Ford-Cosworth DFVs were subsequently used in 257 Grand Prix races, winning 155 of them.[29] Once again, Ferrari was shoved aside, as the Ford-engined cars dominated Formula 1 for almost two decades.

By the end of the 1960s, Ford was beginning to withdraw from active participation in racing. In some cases, it backed away because sanctioning bodies enacted race-car specifications that Ford didn't care to pursue—often, the new specs were erected specifically to contain the powerhouse from Dearborn. In another sense, too, Ford was a victim of its own success. That occurred when success for the company's teams was no longer considered astounding. By 1968–1969, Ford racing victories were just about as common as Saturdays in summertime . . . and when the impact faded, the company was less enthusiastic about footing the bills.

Racing successes certainly continued, as did exciting hybrids. But the decade that had been "powered by Ford" was over. It left a company redefined—and well proven on its own terms of performance and energy. The long season of Ford racing glory left hundreds of moments that race fans and historians still savor. It left names, too, covered in glory: Jimmy Clark, Dan Gurney, A. J. Foyt, Parnelli Jones, Junior Johnson, Cale Yarborough, Mark Donohue, and more.

For Henry Ford II, racing victories were more personal, but for him, that ultimately meant that they were tied up with the success of the company. Right after the first Le Mans victory in 1966, a reporter for *Business Week* wrote perceptively of him, "Not only does he not take defeat easily, he is a member of that international set that treasures fast cars, and his company was about the first to view the world as one auto market, with sales, say, in New Zealand, affected by what goes on in a small town in Northwest France."[30]

In the 1960s, car ownership was growing three times faster in Europe than in the United States.[31] In plain numbers, America, long the world's leading auto market, was absorbing cars at what was thought to be a giddy rate of 7–8 million in the mid-1960s. However, Europe, considered as a whole, was on its way to sales of 10 million cars per year. Some observers compared the European relationship to car ownership with that in the United States in the 1920s: the prevailing question changed from "Why do you have a car?" to "Why don't you have one?"

Ford Motor (England) Ltd. enjoyed a surprising success in the Cortina model, introduced in 1962. At that time, when the parent company was using the Falcon to meet American demand for a family car that was smaller than full-size, Dagenham's Cortina set a new trend in the European market as a family car that was *larger*-than-compact. Sir Patrick Hennessy was the one who had recognized the niche for just such a car and rushed it through design in order to keep his rivals at British Motor Corporation off balance. His directive was for a car with plenty of room—and a low price. A product development manager named Terry Beckett met the challenge, working with a core team of only eight designers.[32] Sir Patrick originally wanted to name the new car the "Caprino." However, a routine check turned up the fact that in Italian "caprino" means "goat manure." Cortina, a less encumbered word, was the replacement.[33] The Cortina, offered in a range of versions, from shooting-brakes (station wagons) to rally cars, became Britain's highest-production car. (Beckett himself would eventually rise to the chairmanship at EnFo.)

Ford Motor (England) Ltd.'s smallest problem during the 1960s was designing attractive cars. Its biggest problem was getting the cars manufactured. Even when all was well, the Dagenham plant couldn't keep up with demand. But the fact is that all was not well for Ford's British operations in the 1960s and early 1970s. Production was plagued by strikes. When Dearborn bought out EnFo's stock in the early 1960s and placed it under the control of the U.S.-based international division, the labor situation at Dagenham suffered. Unions sometimes picked on Ford simply because it had foreign roots. American officials on the scene could neither understand nor accept the prevalence of wildcat strikes in Dagenham, especially since many were at the merest whim of shop stewards. A management consultant familiar with multinational companies concluded that Ford's British factory had "the worst labour relations of any American company in Europe."[34] The government launched several investigations, but to no avail. Ford counted it as a victory when it managed to oust some of the shop stewards it considered the most irritating. However, protracted wrangling between the stewards and the corporation did neither the company nor the average workman any good.

Ford-Werke, in Germany, was a calmer place and built on its strong success with the Taunus. Since the years right after the war, when it struggled to maintain a 4 percent share of domestic auto output, it had quietly increased that share to 18 percent.[35] In 1965, Ford Motor passed General Motors in the international sphere as the biggest automaker in sales outside North America.[36] That would be significant in more than just bragging rights. Ten years later, when American automakers were in the midst of disastrous reversals, it was Ford's foreign operations that sustained it.

As the European automobile market broadened in the late 1960s, Ford Motor was positioned to benefit from the rising tide, but not to take full advantage of it. To Ford-Werke's managing director, John Andrews, the big picture of Ford in Europe revealed a company with 100,000 employees, too many of them employed in counterpoint to one another. The fact that Ford Motor (England) Ltd. and Ford-Werke acted like rivals made no sense to him. He felt that the two needed more direction from the corporation, not less, but that it should come from Europe—not Dearborn. In June 1965, Andrews asked for a meeting with Henry Ford II, who was then visiting Paris with Robert Stevenson, John Bugas's replacement as the head of an international division.

All three were well aware that the Common Market was steadily solidifying. As Germany, France, and Italy began to master a new trait—mutual trust—the tariffs and restrictions that had long hindered trade among countries in Europe dissolved. Increased economic activity didn't follow on a straight line for every industry at once, but nonetheless it followed, irrefutably. The big question of the time was whether Britain would link itself to the six Continental nations that already made up the group (it would, in 1973). In any case, progressive American companies anticipated an increasingly united European economy and prepared for it with centralized operations. Dow Chemical was among the first to transform its transatlantic business into a reflection of the Common Market's open borders. IBM and AT&T were moving gingerly in the same direction. Most other U.S. companies chose not to act at all. In view of Europe's history of strife, they preferred to wait for the Common Market to fall apart.

When John Andrews, a fifty-three-year-old Texan, met Henry Ford II, his idea was to gather all of Ford's business in Europe under one umbrella. Dagenham and Cologne would share engineering, sales, and even manufacturing of new models. Cooperation would also extend to the other thirty-eight Ford plants located in Europe. Andrews's plan had a kind of precedent at Ford. In the late 1920s, Ford Motor (England) Ltd. under Sir Percival Perry had overseen most other operations in Europe. However, in 1965, with the savage battles of World War II within memory for practically every adult, the notion of a single "Ford of Europe" was asking a lot. It asked a lot of the employees of nationalistic entities, to blend and merge. It also asked a lot of Ford Motor Company's leadership. Europe accounted for 25 percent of Ford's total business—almost twice as much as that of General Motors.[37] A conservative management would have waited with hundreds of other U.S. companies, letting the Common Market reach its full effect before reacting to it.

Henry II approved Andrews's plan and set it in motion even before the month was out. The establishment of Ford of Europe would be one of Henry II's most influential decisions as chairman. Working out the details took time of course. (So many trips by so many Ford executives had to be made that Pan-American Airways was induced to schedule a Detroit–Cologne flight.) Nevertheless, within two years, Ford's former international division was a thing of the past. Ford of Europe, Inc., was the new reality, with John Andrews in charge. At the plant level, over the years most American managers were replaced by Europeans.

Most of all, Europeans welcomed the initial decision to put the headquarters for the division in their backyard (GM and Chrysler kept their European headquarters in America). However, the plan to locate it in England stirred resentment on the Continent. A half-dozen ranking executives at Ford-Werke quit over concern that the German arm would once again be controlled by the English one.

One of Ford of Europe's first major moves was to suggest that European customers were prosperous enough to spend a little extra on a stylish car. They admitted they were playing "the Mustang game," as they called it. However, when Ford-Werke joined forces with EnFo to develop the model, they thought of it only as a European sports sedan. Significantly, the car they developed, the Capri, was never described as German or English. It was *European* and, as such, constituted the perfect car to prove the Ford of Europe concept. Built along the same proportions as the Mustang, the Capri was smooth and sophisticated, with a long hood and a short trunk deck. Giving customers a choice of more than two dozen basic configurations of drive train and body style, it was an instant hit all over Europe.

Even under the new structure, most of the individual plants—and certainly the two major ones—remained separate profit centers. Morale seemed to rise, especially in Britain, where local management dealt with labor tensions, easing frustrations on both sides. Nonetheless, the unions continued to challenge Ford in England, to the extent that when the Capri was offered for sale in the United States in 1971, Ford-Werke was given the production order. Because of frequent strikes, Dagenham was passed by; it couldn't be trusted with consistent production.

By the end of the 1960s, sales were on the rise in nearly every country in which Ford of Europe did business. The racing tradition, which was all that much hotter for being only a few years old, coincided neatly with the new impetus. Even France and Italy, both of which had long resisted any influx of Fords, grew into good markets, thanks to the Common Market and the popularity of the little Escort model. The 48-horsepower Escort had been developed by Ford Motor (England) Ltd.—the same company responsible for the 530-horsepower Grand Prix cars everybody was talking about. After sixty-five years in business in Europe, Ford was *in*, at last.

———————

That was just where Henry II wanted it. And himself. In the midst of the "swinging sixties," Henry II emerged as a citizen of the world, on many levels.

The most obvious was that he became known as one of the bright lights of a party that went on and on around the world for those with money—and stamina. His divorce from Anne was a profound disappointment for his mother and other members of the family. In a certain sense, they had lost him. After he and Cristina Austin were married in 1965, they maintained homes in Detroit, New York, and London. To Henry II, the more frivolous the conversation, the more he enjoyed it. One of his two main goals, when he was out in society, was to laugh. Although he was no wit, he could tell a good story. A typical one was elicited when someone at a dinner party asked if he'd known Howard Hughes. According to *Fortune* magazine, which reprinted the anecdote in a profile of Ford, his face lit up. "You know," Henry II said, "back when I was a college kid, I went to a dance one summer out in Southampton. It was a hot night and I was sweating like a pig, so I went into the men's room to freshen up. There was a guy in there with his jacket off and his sleeves pushed up and soap clear up over his elbows. I looked at him, and as I was going out I asked somebody, 'Who the hell is that guy in there taking a shower?'" Henry II couldn't contain his own loud laugh. "That was the only time I ever saw Howard Hughes."[38]

Henry Ford II's second goal when he was relaxing among friends was to hear juicy gossip. He was said to be ravenous for the latest scuttlebutt about who was sleeping with whom, who was on the verge of divorce or other disaster. Whenever Arjay Miller, the president of Ford Motor in the mid-1960s, visited Washington, he made sure to collect a gaggle of good stories to take home to the boss about the imbroglios of the nation's politicians. Henry II's interest in "the latest" was a form of relaxation: an unimportant game in juxtaposition to running the second-biggest industrial company in the world. "All of his faults," explained Sir Patrick Hennessy, "are very human ones. He works hard, and when he relaxes, he wants to have a good time."[39] A fixation with gossip is not unusual among the idle rich. But Henry II didn't qualify as the idle rich. Unlike many in his circle of friends, he was a working man. In the bigger sense, he was dedicated to Ford Motor Company in a way that actually subsumed his personal life. In the narrower, daily sense, Henry II was prepared for the job every day, however late he had been out the night before or how much he had had to drink.

In the late 1960s, when personal style was a line of demarcation between the establishment and the new liberalism, Henry Ford II was the first—and for a long time the only—executive of a major American company to wear his hair at a longer, mod length. At the same time, he let his sideburns grow in. When he was away, he sometimes raised a beard. Nor did Henry II buy into the "generation gap" that made most students take the expression "never trust anyone over the age of thirty" with deadly seriousness. When Henry II hosted a party at a Washington club for cabinet members and congressmen, a group of students arrived at the door, possibly planning an impromptu protest. Instead, they were entertained almost as guests by Henry II, who, according to writer Dan Cordtz, spent "nearly as much time bantering with the students as he spent inside; he even carried out trays of hors d'oeuvres and took a ride on one boy's motorcycle."[40] If a company president did something like that today, he might be regarded as a clever statesman; in the 1960s, Henry II was more likely to be cast as a traitor to his class. He wouldn't have minded that a bit.

All of these things were statements that went hand in hand with Henry II's political views. Even though he was adamantly against the war in Vietnam, he was close to the Johnson White House, mostly because he supported the president's social programs wholeheartedly. Henry II became actively involved in the War on Poverty, and the Ford Motor Company incubated programs in minority hiring and the establishment of satellite factories in blighted neighborhoods. Detroit's problems in race relations and urban decay would eventually challenge him as nothing had since the crisis at Ford Motor after World War II.

While Henry II could be unassuming in person, no one ever pretended that he was easy to understand. At different turns, he was the micro-manager of a monumental business . . . the charmingly shallow good-time guy . . . the social engineer, acting on his own well-researched opinions. In any of these roles, he didn't seem to care if people misunderstood him. Henry Ford II wasn't trying to create a vivid persona. He was trying to live within one.

Henry II worked well with Arjay Miller, who took over as president of Ford Motor from John Dykstra in 1963. The man impatiently waiting in the wings all the while was Executive Vice President Lee Iacocca. He had risen in the company largely through his marketing savvy, and his point of view complemented that of Miller, who had a financial background. However, Iacocca was brash enough to wend his way around Miller, in order to establish a direct line to Chairman Henry Ford II.[41] Meanwhile, Iacocca established his own flying wedge of loyalists within the company. Remarkably, most of them were from the divisional sales office in Chester, Pennsylvania, where he had worked as a recruit in the late 1940s. His onetime boss there, Matthew McLaughlin, was president of Ford Marketing. Others who came to Ford on the Iacocca express from Chester were Theodore H. Mecke Jr. (public relations vice president), John Naughton (vice president and general manager, Ford Division), Bennett Bidwell (vice president and general manager, Lincoln-Mercury), Frank Zimmerman (marketing manager, Ford Division), and William Benton (sales manager, Lincoln-Mercury). Whether they took their orders from the president's office or that of the executive vice president remained to be seen.

Arjay Miller was the son of a Kansas farming couple. Even his name was homespun, derived from his father's first two initials. After a brilliant stint as a student at UCLA and Berkeley, Miller entered the military and then joined Ford as one of the Whiz Kids. He worked in finance and rose to serve as the corporate controller. "The controller's office controlled everybody in finance throughout the company," he later recalled. "Once a year I'd call a controller's conference. All of the controllers from around the world were brought in. They were told two things: first, if you get in trouble with your line boss, you get transferred; but if you get in trouble with me, you get fired! Their job was to blow the whistle if they thought something was wrong."[42]

With something akin to Robert McNamara's capacity for figures and details, Miller also had a genuine love of automobiles. He was president during some of Ford's most exciting years, as the Mustang, racing, and international success all came together. He was also president during the transformation of Henry II, from the crown prince of the company to its undisputed king. Henry II didn't put his fist down on product decisions, but he was increasingly imperious on matters of personnel. Ford Motor Company built its organization on Henry II's passion for recruiting and developing the best people, a process that made Miller proud. "If there's anything I feel good about," he said, "it's the fact that Ford hired so many people while I was there." But eventually Henry II exerted his overt influence. "We lost some good people," Miller admitted, "because he would fall out of love with them and move them out."[43]

In February 1968, it was Miller's turn to move out. The reasons went all the way back to 1921, the year that the elder Henry Ford abruptly fired William Knudsen. A few years later, of course, the Danish-born production ace moved on to Chevrolet and he ended his business career as the president of General Motors. William's son, Semon ("Bunkie"), followed gingerly in his footsteps, always with an eye to becoming president of GM as well. However, in 1968, Bunkie Knudsen was stunned when he was passed over for the top spot. Within the week, Henry II was arranging a clandestine meeting at Bunkie's house, taking care to drive himself in a rented Oldsmobile for cover. As a result of the courtship, Arjay Miller was moved into the new position of vice chairman to make room for Knudsen as president.

While GM staffers professed to be relieved to have the lame duck Knudsen taken off their hands, many outside observers considered him a natural fit for Ford Motor. The company's success was obvious, but somewhat patchy on close inspection. Optimists felt that Knudsen would be just the one to fill in the gaps and make Ford Motor solid and strong throughout—like GM.

"The flow of history is reversed," Henry II said, beaming as he announced the arrival of the new man. "Another Mr. Knudsen, having left General Motors, has been elected president of the company his father helped to build."[44]

One man who was not beaming was Lee Iacocca. He looked back on the fact that he had not only launched the Mustang but fostered improvement in the Lincoln-Mercury lines. He was convinced that if Arjay Miller was out, he was the one who deserved the presidency. Henry II had taken care to call him in and explain in advance of the announcement that he would indeed be president eventually, but that he would benefit from a few more years of "seasoning," a word that the forty-four-year-old Iacocca probably grew to hate. He grudgingly agreed to stay, but didn't reveal what he would do beyond that. "Lee had chewed his way through ten layers of management to get where he was," said a colleague, "and he was determined to chew his way through anyone who was placed above him."[45] Donald Frey, who was second behind Iacocca in line for the presidency, lost patience with the idea of waiting out two administrations. He quit Ford and was soon named president of General Cable Corporation.

Henry Ford II thought he had accomplished a coup in snatching up Bunkie Knudsen, that Ford Motor Company would benefit from a man who understood exactly how GM wrung high profits out of every sales dollar—a statistic in which Ford perennially lagged behind its rival. He plucked Knudsen from the top branches of GM out of the same impulse by which he had once saved his company: an unabashed idolatry of the number one automaker. Twenty-five years later, however, Ford had its own ways. To Arjay Miller, for one, Ford had already surpassed GM in many respects, in particular, financial controls and intracompany pricing. "In my early days at Ford," Miller said, "we copied GM with respect to decentralization and financial controls. Afterwards, we didn't copy anybody."[46] Ford Motor had already outgrown Ernie Breech. In 1968, it might have been too late for another teacher from GM.

Within the corporate walls many Ford loyalists chafed under Knudsen's hands-on management style. According to one rumor running through the company and its dealership network, Knudsen meddled in the appearance of the Thunderbird front end. "He took the Pontiac front end and put it on our T-bird," a dealer from the Midwest grumbled. "We didn't go for that."[47]

One car with which Knudsen had no involvement was the Maverick, coming along for introduction as a 1970 model. A compact car with a relatively jaunty air, it had been an Iacocca project—developed by thousands of Ford employees, but under his aegis. At least, when it was finished, he was very willing to stand next to it, as he had the Mustang, and appear in national magazines as the proud parent. That is what the president of almost any corporation does—setting a direction and taking credit for the result. No one did it better than the first Henry Ford. There was only one difference in the summer of 1969, when the Maverick seemed destined to be a major hit. Lee Iacocca was not the president of Ford Motor Company. But he wasn't about to let the man who was president gain any benefit from the Maverick.

For his part, Bunkie Knudsen deluded himself into thinking that he could work around Iacocca. He may not have realized how far Iacocca's reach extended.[48] If their increasing power struggle came down to a battle of loyalty, the GM big shot was never going to win, not against a man who cultivated that quality in his every relationship, from millions of customers to the person in the next office.

After months of grumbling about Knudsen's meddling, a group of ten ranking executives, not including Lee Iacocca, but definitely including his Chester associates, drew up a list of complaints about his management. Presenting the list to Henry Ford II, they strongly implied that if Bunkie Knudsen didn't leave, they would.[49]

Privately, Henry Ford II was no happier about the autocratic Knudsen than the others were. He had tempered his own management style by overseeing John Dykstra and Arjay Miller. Both were excellent in the job, but low-key, and certainly deferential to Henry II, without being yes-men. Miller, who acknowledged in an interview with David Lewis in 1988 that "Henry was *the* dominant voice,"[50] also knew that honesty engendered the chairman's respect. Sometime after Miller left the presidency, Henry II had a merger plan that he was absolutely determined to see through. He discussed it with Miller, then dean of the Stanford Business School. "I listened to him," Miller recalled, "and said, 'Henry, you can't do it.' I told him what was wrong with the plan. Then he called his wife and said, 'I'm coming home early. Arjay says I can't make the deal.'"[51] The way to work with Henry II was to be direct, let him know everything that was going on, and maintain a constant sense of his special relationship to the company . . . not because his name was on the building, but because he had devoted his whole life, much more than just his career, to it.

To what extent Bunkie Knudsen failed to fit into Ford Motor Company culture, Henry II would never say. However, when faced with a "palace revolt" by top executives, he was easily convinced. On Labor Day, 1969, PR executive Ted Mecke paid a visit to Knudsen at his home, carrying a somber message. According to what he had heard, the president was to be fired the next day. Of course, Mecke was well informed. On September 2, Henry II dropped into Knudsen's office to say that things hadn't worked out. Knudsen, describing himself as "shocked," was out of a job. "I guess I've about run out of auto companies," he said.

It was Lee Iacocca's turn to beam. When reporters asked if he was sad to hear the news of Knudsen's termination, he grinned from ear to ear. "I never said 'no comment' to the press yet, but I'll say it to that one."[52]

Instead of a single corporate president, Ford Motor Company was to be led by a triumvirate of divisional presidents, including Lee Iacocca. It couldn't have been a worse time to let the momentum of the 1960s slide, or to leave employees wondering who was really running the company.

32

Trouble All Around

In May 1967, Henry Ford II and Lee Iacocca were ready to launch a coun-
terattack in the battle against imports in America. After having been
discouraged by the arrival of the Ford Falcon, Chevrolet Corvair, and
Plymouth Valiant early in the decade, and by the zest of the Mustang a few
years later, foreign cars were showing new life, headed toward sales of more
than 1 million units in 1968. An energetic influx from Japan was making itself
apparent, especially on the streets of California, but it was the Volkswagen
Beetle that made the most surprising strides as it became increasingly fashionable among the young and well-educated. "The secret behind Volkswagen's success—which other manufacturers know but do not care to adopt,"
Walter Henry Nelson wrote in *Small Wonder: The Amazing Story of the Volkswagen,* "is a painstaking intensity of design and manufacture."[1]

The VW phenomenon fascinated Ford management, as well it should have.
It represented the very antithesis of the Detroit philosophy on carmaking.
The Volkswagen had no extraneous bodywork, no excess horsepower—nothing, in fact, that appealed to a customer's id. It catered only to transportation
needs. The VW was the outstanding choice for people who hated cars, at
least the way Detroit made and sold them. The fact that the market for it was
actually surging in the mid-1960s was rightly worrisome to Ford. The model
hadn't changed significantly since it had arrived in America fifteen years before. What was changing were the customers.

For the first time ever, status was not the swing factor in the selection of an
automobile. It was being replaced by, of all things, conscience. In the climate
of the mid-1960s, small foreign cars like the VW not only cost less than
American cars to purchase, they took up less space on jammed highways.
Moreover, they didn't pollute as much as their big American cousins. While
carmakers celebrated the auto boom that pushed annual new-car sales over

the 9 million mark, the residents of once idyllic cities like Miami, Phoenix, Denver, and especially Los Angeles watched purple-brown clouds gather and take a permanent place in the skyline. "Smog" was the word of the day and "crisis" was the term coming in the future, at a fast rate of speed. Many Americans knew exactly what the social scientist Lewis Mumford meant when he wrote in 1966, "The great American dream of a nation on wheels, which began with the covered wagon, has come to a dreary terminus."[2] For those who agreed and worried about the social issues collecting around America's guiltless love affair with the automobile, Detroit offered no answers.

By the early 1970s, 70 percent of Americans polled said the environment was the most pressing domestic and international problem—and the automobile industry was the primary culprit. Three fifths of the pollutants dumped into the atmosphere in the United States were attributed to motor vehicle traffic. With the Cuyahoga River on fire in Cleveland from an oil slick and a petroleum spill near Santa Barbara destroying pristine beachfront, the entire concept of the internal combustion engine was called into question. Henry Ford's belief that technology was the "new Messiah" was deemed dangerously misplaced. If one were to judge by the air pollution over Los Angeles, the interstate congestion in Chicago, and the hazardous waste in Houston, the automobile was the "new Satan," destroying Planet Earth at an alarming rate. "Industrial vomit," Alvin Toffler wrote in *Future Shock* (1970), "fills our skies and seas. Pesticides and herbicides filter into our foods. Twisted automobile carcasses, aluminum cans, non-returnable glass bottles and synthetic plastics form immense kitchen middens in our midst as more and more of our detritus resists decay. We do not even begin to know what to do with our radioactive wastes—whether to pump them into the earth, shoot them into outer space or pour them in the oceans. Our technological powers increase, but the side effects and potential hazards also escalate."[3]

Given the environmental crisis at hand, Ford Motor Company became a prime target for criticism. An average-sized car without pollution controls dumped into the atmosphere 520 pounds of hydrocarbons and 90 pounds of nitrogen oxides for every 10,000 miles driven. Although Ford Motor lobbied against it, California law mandated that by 1966 exhaust control devices be placed on all new vehicles to reduce emissions of lead compounds, carbon monoxide, and nitrogen oxide. Soon, national emissions standards were set. And by 1970, with the support of the Nixon administration, several car-related amendments to the Clean Air Act of 1963 were passed.[4] Ford Motor vehemently protested this federal interference into automobile manufacturing, but the writing was on the wall.

Also troubling Ford Motor Company executives was the way their factories, especially the gaping River Rouge plant, were under attack by intellectuals, artists, and environmentalists. Back in the 1920s, the Rouge was profiled in *Vanity Fair* as the shining citadel of clean and efficient industry. In the 1970s, it attracted the attention of *Newsweek* and *Time* as the embodiment of industrial doom. Writing in the prestigious *Iowa Review* in 1978, Detroit-based novelist Joyce Carol Oates summed up the Rouge's new role as the symbol of toxic blight in a poem titled "Ford." It questioned the very concept of Fordism as a philosophy of progress. Oates called the Rouge an "industrial slum," with "porous smoke rising heavy and leaden—pale as a giant's limbs, the sickly air heaving in gusts, sulphuric blooms whipping in the wind." As for the famous logo designed by Harold Wills in 1903, perhaps the best-known company brand in the world after Coca-Cola's, Oates claimed it had become "obscured by filth."[5]

A group of teenagers living in Lincoln Park, just a few miles from the Rouge, formed a rock band known as the MC5 to protest, in part, the destruction of the environment being perpetrated by "Fords," as they called the company. Every day in Lincoln Park, a veil of soot covered picnic tables, houses, and cars. The air reeked of sulfuric chemicals that caused allergies, coughing fits, and eye burn. John Sinclair, MC5 manager and Detroit poet, just kept shaking his head in disgust, saying over and over again "What have we done?" As a citizen of Detroit he was sickened. "The Rouge had so badly polluted the rivers that we couldn't swim in them anymore," Sinclair recalled. "They weren't catching fire like in Cleveland, but they had become poisonous nonetheless." Inspired by the industrial noise that emanated from the Rouge, the band emulated various assembly-line sounds in their live performances, ranging from amp feedback to metallic screeches. "We were looking for a postindustrial future," Sinclair recalls, "where the Fords didn't have all the power."[6]

Ford executives were well aware that a streak of discontent lurked underneath the booming automobile market. The popularity of cheap imports proved it even more blatantly than all of the avant-garde ballads, esoteric essays, and formalist poems put to paper. In response, after years of study, Henry Ford II gave Lee Iacocca the go-ahead to develop a small car, given the code name Delta, for a 1969 launch. Aside from American Motors, which had survived (sometimes quite lushly) by building small cars, Ford Motor was the first American company to commit to its own homemade compact. Chrysler was importing its Colts from Japan. General Motors, which was cashing in on its line of luxury, standard, and intermediate cars, evinced no interest in the compact. The new Delta was to be a genuine compact—not just smaller than gigantic, as the Falcon had been. It was going to be simple, economical, and, because Lee Iacocca was steering its fate, it had to have personality, to boot. Initial work on the Delta, later renamed the Maverick, began in May 1967.

With plans under way for the Maverick, Ford Motor could consider itself responsive to America's changing social fabric, where compact cars were in demand. It was a short moment.

Starting in August 1965, when the Watts section of Los Angeles went up in flames, killing thirty-four rioters, racial tensions were flaring up in nearly every large American city. Detroit's turn came during five bloody days in July 1967.

Instead of pouring money into Detroit's infrastructure, the Big Three stood aside as the capital of American automaking turned into a decrepit ghetto. On June 26, 1967, for example, Ford Motor Company donated $25,000 to the People's Community Civic League of Detroit, for vocational training in the inner city. Benson Ford, who was largely retired from Ford Motor Company because of a heart condition, announced the donation. It was a fine gesture, but not enough to make an impact. At the ceremony, Benson expressed confidence that the civic league could help the unemployed "develop skills and talents into constructive manpower—an essential ingredient for a healthy community."[7] But in 1967, Detroit was anything but a healthy community. Unemployment was dangerously high in the inner city, where the young people needed steady work but were ill prepared for it, due in part to the breakdown of the city school system. Good jobs were going wanting in automobile factories, yet the Ford, Chrysler, and GM plants were inaccessible from Detroit's poorest neighborhoods. So was nearly any sense of opportunity. At least two decades of increasing despair finally drove many residents to frenzy, others to fear, and some to tragedy.

On July 23, 1967, Detroit changed forever as the city's longtime obsession with car models and company trends was relegated to secondary importance. The trouble began close to 4:00 A.M. on that midsummer morning, after the Detroit police went to Twelfth Street and raided an illegal afterhours spot—known in the black community as a "blind pig." A mob quickly formed outside the club, and soon the city's long-simmering racial tensions erupted. First a few bottles and cans were tossed at the police; then the ugliness escalated into looting and arson punctuated by random gunfire. As the massive riots continued, Mayor Jerome Cavanagh asked Governor George Romney, a leading contender for the 1968 Republican presidential nomination, to activate the state's National Guard. In the end, it took nearly five thousand regular U.S. Army troops until July 30 to restore order. Across a six-mile span from Grand River Avenue to Gratiot Avenue, the city "looked like Berlin in 1945," according to the mayor.[8] The disturbances exacted a staggering toll: 43 people were dead; more than 700 were seriously injured; some 5,000 people were left homeless; and 7,231 were under arrest. There had been $50 million in property damages. Rioting, vandalism, and police brutality had brought the Motor City to its knees.

Detroit had become a battleground filled with burned-out tenements and looted stores, shattered church windows, and vandalized cars. One home left standing was surrounded on all sides by debris, as though deposited by a tropical hurricane. Crime was so high in the aftermath of the riot that people were afraid to come out of their homes or cross a street. Detroit became known as the "city of urban despair."

The Detroit riot, the worst in the history of the United States, revealed that the Motor City was not the prosperous, progressive industrial city it had been when Henry Ford was alive. It was literally collapsing into the voids left by fleeing businesses and residents.[9] Out in the suburbs and in the auto factories, life went on as usual during that week in late July; on Gratiot Avenue, however, it looked like World War II. The racial division of Detroit was open and obvious for all to see. Due to the riots, the Detroit Tigers, in contention for the pennant, were forced to cancel a home stand with the Baltimore Orioles. The Tigers' star slugger, Willie Horton, an African American who lived in the city, went to the scene of the riot at one point, hoping to help end it. Meanwhile, Mickey Lolich, the team's best pitcher and a white suburbanite, was called up to serve with his unit of the Michigan Air National Guard, assigned to guard police headquarters downtown.[10]

"What triggered the riot in my opinion," Governor Romney lamented, "to a considerable extent was that between urban renewal and expressways, poor black people were bulldozed out of their homes. They had no place to go in the suburbs because of suburban restrictions." President Lyndon Johnson, disgusted by the burning of Detroit, immediately ordered an investigation. The Kerner Report that resulted concluded that the riots were the fault of Detroit's bigoted, nearly all-white police. There was no sign that black nationalists or civil rights activists planned the eruption. "White racism is essentially responsible for the explosive mixture," the report concluded. For years, Detroit had thought itself immune from such violence. It had a mayor sensitive to ghetto problems and a seemingly sympathetic general populace. However, whatever the good intentions, nothing ever happened in the ghettos to connect them with the booming local economy. Because of that, the solution to the malaise within Detroit's African American community couldn't be solely political.[11]

Two classic accounts of the Detroit riots have been written over the years, one nonfiction, the other fiction. Watching Detroit go up in flames on TV in Connecticut, novelist/journalist John Hersey, best known for his famous 1946 book *Hiroshima*, decided to investigate what happened at the Twelfth Street "blind pig" for himself. Interviewing hundreds of people who participated in the riot, Hersey, in his book *The Algiers Motel Incident*, generally concurred with the Kerner Report. Along the way, he unearthed a startling statistic: although one third of Detroit was African American, the police force was 95 percent white.

While Hersey's book had an immediate impact, and remains a classic example of highly stylized detective work, Detroiter Jeffrey Eugenides, in his 2002 novel *Middlesex*, framed the riot as the defining Cold War moment in the city's history. A brilliant stylist, Eugenides provided an elegant description of the environment around the blind pig: the prostitutes who are "numb to the rawness between their legs"; large African American automobiles without "a single rust spot anywhere"; the screams of "It's the fuzz!" echoing throughout the block; bottles being hurled at cops; and the looting of appliance stores. Written from a first-person perspective, Eugenides's novel came the closest to capturing what it *felt like* to be on the sidelines of the riot—watching as paratroopers from the 82nd and 101st Airborne divisions swarmed over a neighborhood. The tension in his prose is palpable as gunshots cause nerves to jump, and police sirens jolt people into shock. Watching the chaos from a bicycle, the narrator decides that the term "riot" is inappropriate; what he was watching was a "guerrilla uprising," a Second American Revolution. "For three days we didn't bathe or brush our teeth," Eugenides writes. "For three days all the normal rituals of our life were suspended, while half-forgotten rituals, like praying, were renewed." When the smoke from the uprising cleared, he notes, in a mock take on Francis Scott Key's "The Star-Spangled Banner," the Michigan flag was still there. Emblazoned on the flag was *Speramus Meliora; resurget cineribus:* "We hope for better things; it will rise from the ashes."[12] This more positive sentiment, the notion that Detroit-area citizens had an obligation to make amends, propelled Henry II into action.

In his office suite on top of World Headquarters in Dearborn, Henry Ford II was keenly aware of what was happening in Detroit. "Mr. Ford shared with me his strong concern with what to do with Detroit," said Wayne S. Doran, the head of Ford's land development subsidiary. "The riots had just really gotten settled down and a large part of the day was spent talking about the need for corporations or leaders in the communities to demonstrate more effectively their concern and care for the community by doing something physical."[13]

Henry II had inherited the mantle of a company often criticized for not helping Detroit cope with its urban woes. The family's establishment of the Ford Foundation as the world's richest charitable trust had quelled the old cries of selfishness, but the foundation's work was national in scope. Ford Motor had been *born* in Detroit. More to the point, so had Henry Ford II. In August, Ford Motor initiated a new "urban affairs department," charged specifically with presenting a response to the riot in Detroit. More broadly, it was to investigate ways that the company could alleviate racial tensions in the city.[14] The first solution expected from Ford and other area automakers lay in hiring.

It didn't take long for the urban affairs department to identify the hurdles that kept ill-prepared members of the black community permanently at a disadvantage in Ford personnel offices.[15] The first was hidden in the qualifying exams given to every applicant. "We were testing cultural background, not the ability to do a good job," admitted Ford President Arjay Miller.[16] The written tests were suspended immediately after the crisis, and Ford made a public commitment to hire 6,500 workers, primarily from the blighted ghetto.[17] GM and Chrysler promised even higher numbers, more than 12,000 new hires each. However, the challenge of hiring workers from the still waters of the economy was more complex than the companies first realized.

To address the inequality that Henry Ford II considered "the greatest internal crisis since the Civil War,"[18] Ford Motor had to reach out in myriad ways. In the fall of 1967, it opened two recruitment "action centers" in Detroit's ghettos and launched vans as "mobile employment units" that circulated through targeted neighborhoods. Roving recruiters could describe opportunities to residents, accept applications, arrange for physical exams—and offer jobs right on the spot. During the first year of the employment drive, the company hired 5,000 disadvantaged workers through its satellite action centers.[19]

Of course, Ford Motor Company already employed African American workers in its factories, and there were many African American success stories. Mat Dawson Jr., for example, was born in Shreveport, Louisiana, just as the Model T was becoming ubiquitous. Jim Crow ruled the state, so young Dawson ventured north to Detroit in search of equal rights and a decent paycheck. He started working for Ford Motor in 1940 and was still at the job in 2001, one year before his death.[20] Earning a minimum wage operating forklifts at the Rouge, Dawson saved enough money over the decades to become a philanthropist. While others were rioting in 1967 he worked double time daily. Starting in the 1990s, this frugal blue-collar worker established three $100,000 endowed scholarships to Louisiana State University in Shreveport and two donations to Detroit's Wayne State University totaling $400,000. "I like giving back to the kids," Dawson noted. "There is no secret to my making money at Ford. I live modestly, work overtime, invest smartly, and save."[21] After giving away $1 million and appearing on *Oprah,* the unassuming Dawson became an in-house celebrity at Ford, deemed by *USA Today* "the Forklift Philanthropist."[22]

Like other hires, African American workers typically arrived at Ford with experience in some kind of regular work. They understood the fundamental trade-off between a boss and a worker. They could absorb directions. None of that was necessarily true of the "hard-core unemployed." Most of the workers recruited from the inner city had to be indoctrinated to factory work. That process was complicated by the fact that in automaking, the tasks almost invariably involve hard physical labor for the newly hired. At Ford, the turnover on the assembly line was 25 percent per year. "Four hours of work at the plant is about eight hours' worth of work on other jobs," said Berlin Scott, a painter at a Ford truck plant. "A lot of guys take medical leaves to get out of there. They say their shoulder hurts—anything to get off the job."[23] People unused to any regular work schedule would find the pace grueling. In addition, the basic environment of a plant is intimidating: noisy and fast moving.

The auto companies had to learn not only how to hire long-forsaken workers but how to keep them. Special training programs were established for people who arrived with no job skills. In addition, the company invited the mothers of inner-city teens to Dearborn to familiarize them with programs available for students. Progress was made, but no one pretended it was enough.

Shell-shocked by the horror of the Detroit riots, Henry Ford II became an outspoken corporate activist on the subject of racial equality. "Genuinely equal opportunity is, in fact, the most urgent task our nation faces," he said in a speech in November 1967, making the point that those dispossessed on the basis of race or poverty—or both—were right to lash out. "They are understandably angry and impatient to close the gap," Henry II said. "All the measures that show the gap is narrowing also show that it is still very wide. And the narrower the gap becomes, the more outrageous it seems that it should exist at all."[24]

Those were surprising words, coming from the CEO of a Fortune 100 company. As a businessman, Henry Ford II was a liberal, which was extremely unusual in the tumult of the late 1960s. In some quarters, it was also suspect. When Joseph L. Hudson Jr., head of Detroit's largest department store, agreed to serve as chairman of a committee seeking ways to reach out to the black community after the riots, his store received broken credit cards in the mail. White customers—of department-store goods or automobiles—were prone to join the backlash that grew after the black uprising. In today's business climate, an inclusive and socially progressive stand is "politically correct" in corporate America. In 1967, however, mainstream business kept itself at a remove from society's ills, with a blind eye to controversial issues such as racial prejudice. Henry Ford II, the best-known businessman in the country, refused to support the status quo. "He knew he was Henry Ford," said Wayne Doran. "He really wasn't trying to prove very much to anybody of his power or of his importance, he was just sort of rolling along, doing his thing and working hard at trying to be a good leader. And he'd lend his name only to things that he felt were important. He didn't pass his name around for anybody."[25]

Henry Ford II had developed a genuine friendship with President Johnson, whose Great Society programs were helping senior citizens receive health care and African Americans smash Jim Crow laws. Through the years Henry II endorsed candidates of each political party—Dwight Eisenhower, John Kennedy, Hubert Humphrey, Richard Nixon, and Jimmy Carter—but of all the presidents, he was closest to the Democratic Lyndon Johnson. "He was a hell of a nice guy," Henry II said of Johnson. "A lot of people thought he was crude, and all that. Well, he may have been, but that didn't bother me. He was a very nice guy. He was thoughtful; he was pleasant. . . . I was very sorry that he didn't do two things. (a) He didn't understand Vietnam very well, and (b) he was very foolish in his economic outlook because he thought you could have butter and guns at the same time and that wasn't possible."[26] On civil rights issues, though, Henry II backed Johnson entirely. He strongly supported the Civil Rights Acts of 1964 and 1965. In January 1968, they worked together to organize the National Alliance of Businessmen (NAB). As the first chairman, Henry II helped set the group's overall goal, which was to enlist individual businesses to "help turn the hard-core unemployed into productive workers."[27] The group also sought pledges for summer jobs for disadvantaged youth.[28]

In paying attention to those whom Henry II called "people who have been left behind,"[29] the NAB provided a release valve for the frustration building in ghettos across the nation. Closer to home, Henry Ford II set a new standard in his own company by sending a letter to ten thousand Ford Motor managers and foremen. It began:

> Equal opportunity is one of Ford Motor Company's oldest, firmest and most basic policies. The purpose of this letter is to call on each of you to give that policy your full and active support and to put it into practice in new ways and with a new sense of urgency.
>
> Our goal is to do all we realistically can to give people who have been held back by prejudice and poverty a chance to earn a decent life. This goal is entirely consistent with our responsibility to conduct our business soundly and profitably. We cannot provide wider employment opportunities by hiring more people than we need or by keeping people who cannot learn to do their jobs or work with other people. There are, however, many things we can do. . . .[30]

One of the most instantly recognizable things that the company did was to begin using African American celebrities as endorsers, a breakthrough in mainstream advertising. Ford Motor was one of the first companies, if not the first, to employ people of color in national television and print ads. The company rehired Jesse Owens in May 1968. For a major magazine ad, Owens, still in excellent condition thirty-two years after his 1936 Olympic victories, crouched down next to a Ford car as though a foot race were about to start. In the following years, Ford employed comedian Bill Cosby and singer Sammy Davis Jr. as company spokesmen. Most memorably, the company flew heavyweight boxing champion Muhammad Ali to Alaska, where he filmed a commercial surrounded by towering snowdrifts and glaciers. Dressed in a fur-collared parka, Ali had the slogan "Tested Tough" emblazoned across his chest.[31]

Because most of Ford Motor's plants were located in Dearborn and other suburbs, the company provided bus money for new employees, some of whom couldn't afford to commute until the first paycheck or two came in. In fact, Ford Motor had not built a substantial factory in Detroit proper since the earliest years of the century. Even the Highland Park plant was in a separate city; that 1910 plant was being used for storage in the late 1960s. After the riots, however, other companies, in and out of the automobile industry, accelerated the decade-long trend of businesses moving out of Detroit. Nearly all of America's older cities had the same problem at the time: compared with the fresh fields of the suburbs, they were crumbling, crowded, and crime-ridden.

It was the automobile that allowed suburbs like Warren and Birmingham, Ferndale and Troy to expand, of course. And so it was the car, of all things, that brought Detroit, the Motor City, to the brink of ruin.

During the years following the 1967 riot the Detroit arts scene took on a decidedly hard, brutal edge. Motown had become known as the Murder City. Local punk hero Iggy Pop shouted out lyrics of outrage and nihilism from blue-collar barrooms where gloom prevailed. The best fiction writer in metro Detroit, Elmore Leonard, captured the ugly mood created by white flight in such suspense thrillers as *City Primeval,* about a killer cruising down Woodward Avenue looking for his next victim, and 52 *Pickup,* about a Detroit businessman being blackmailed for adultery. In Leonard's novels all roads seemed to lead to the Wayne County Morgue.[32]

The minority hiring spree by Detroit-area automakers in 1967–1968 didn't stop the deterioration of Detroit, but it did alleviate the most violent resentments of the "people left behind" in the African American ghetto. Just months before his assassination in April 1968, Martin Luther King Jr. praised Ford Motor for taking the lead regarding equal rights in the workplace. Through a host of worker improvement programs, some successful, some only well intentioned, there were at least the first glimmerings of hope. Nothing, however, was enough to reverse the overall trend in Detroit. As businesses left, more and more of the city became wrapped in poverty. And then more businesses would leave. After years of trying to encourage the hard-core unemployed in Detroit to come out to Dearborn to work, Ford Motor Company would eventually try to reverse the underlying problem and lead businesses back to the city.

———

As Henry II inventoried the urban crisis in Detroit, with schools being closed for lack of funds and homelessness becoming an epidemic, he grew furious at the Ford Foundation. When the foundation named former Kennedy aide Mc-George Bundy its president in 1966, Henry II was not pleased. He believed Bundy and Robert McNamara had mistakenly led his friend Lyndon Johnson into the Vietnam quagmire. There was something effete and condescending about Bundy, which annoyed Henry II to no end. One of Bundy's first moves as president was to relocate the foundation into a swank headquarters on Manhattan's East Side. Then Bundy started running over budget—to the tune of over $100 million a year—opening foreign offices and making 1,500 new hires. Henry II thought such reckless spending, on foreign countries like India and Brazil, ridiculous. His hometown—Detroit—was on fire and the Ford Foundation told him they couldn't help.[33]

Over the next few years, tensions between Bundy and Henry II continued to boil. Enraged, Henry II started lobbying the foundation's board of trustees in search of capital for Detroit. In 1973 he at last succeeded: the foundation gave $100 million to Henry Ford Hospital. But that proved to only temporarily salve the situation. Sitting in a December 1976 board meeting, tapping his pencil nervously, Henry II grew incendiary with rage. Talk was all about foreign aid while the inner cities of America were rotting away. "I don't think I can stand this much longer," he interrupted. "This place is a madhouse."[34]

A few days later Henry II wrote Chairman of the Board Alexander Heard. To resign saddened him, but to watch the foundation squander resources on foreign projects sickened him to no end. "After thirty-three years I have come to the point where I have said all there is to say. I think it is time for me to step aside, and accordingly, I wish to resign from the Board immediately. The diffuse array of enterprises upon which the Foundation has embarked in recent years is almost a guarantee that few people anywhere will share a common perception of what the Foundation is all about, how its mission serves society."

But then Henry II got to the gist of what was really gnawing at him. Ever since he had been thrown out of Yale, he had developed a disdain, almost as great as his grandfather's, for investment bankers, scholars, and the idle rich. He lived lavishly, he admitted, vacationing on yachts, collecting rare art, and living out of mansions and five-star hotels. But he worked—hard, often sixteen hours a day. He *admired* men with grit, men without airs or affectations. He truly preferred tough negotiations with the UAW compared with catered lunches at the Ford Foundation. "The Foundation exists and thrives on the fruits of our economic system," he scolded in the letter. "The dividends of competitive enterprises make it all possible. A significant portion of the abundance created by U.S. business enables the Foundation and like institutions to carry on their work. In effect the Foundation is a creature of capitalism—a statement that I'm sure would be shocking to many professional staff people in the field of philanthropy. It is hard to discern recognition of this fact in anything the Foundation does."[35]

Ford Motor Company closed out the 1960s by introducing the Maverick. The company was ahead of the rest of the domestic industry with its new compact, but that didn't mean it was out in front of the whole industry. "You try to read the car market," said Lee Iacocca, "and all you can say is 'You dumb foot-draggers—you in Detroit—what took you so long to know imports were going to hit a million?' Now the market is damn well defined, and you know what the market says: 'Give me a hell of a good buy for two grand, will you?'"[36]

Iacocca's import-beating, $2,000 bargain was the Maverick coupe. It went on sale on April 17, 1969—five years to the day after the Mustang's debut and hence Iacocca's lucky date. John Naughton, the general manager of the Ford Division, echoed Iacocca's general reasoning for building a new compact in 1969, but explained it a bit more precisely. "In 1962," he said, "Ford had 36 percent of the small-car market. Last year we had only 8 percent. We feel that we should get 25 percent of this market, at least 400,000 units."[37] He based his math on the fact that in 1968, 1.6 million compacts were sold in the United States. Because the trend indicated that compact sales were still growing fast, Ford's numerical target was feasible. But reaching a quarter of the market share for compacts would involve bumping at least some of the swarming imports out of the way.

To save on tooling costs, the new Maverick was built as a hybrid of other Ford models, containing major components of the Mustang, Fairlane, and Falcon. Only a little longer and wider than the VW Beetle, the benchmark compact, Ford's Maverick had more dash, with fastback styling in keeping with the rest of the Ford line in 1969–1970. To make it funky, in the Flower Power era of nonconformity, Iacocca specified plaid upholstery and exterior paint in unusual colors. Even the names were offbeat: Thanks Vermillion, Hulla-Blue, Freudian Gilt, and Original Cinnamon.

"The Maverick was one of the first 'import fighters,'" said Anthony Fredo, who was in public relations at Ford of Canada.[38] The Maverick may not have vanquished the imports, but it did turn into another hit from the Iacocca camp. On its heels came the even smaller Pinto, a genuine "minicar," which was introduced on September 11, 1970. Iacocca missed his lucky April 17 launch date this time, but then, the Pinto would not be a lucky car. At the start, nonetheless, the Pinto had an aura of success, racking up sales of more than 350,000 in its first year, putting it in the hallowed company of the Falcon and Mustang. Ford Motor believed the Pinto was irresistible and touted it as a "new Model T."[39]

Between the Maverick and the Pinto, Ford sold more than 530,000 compacts in 1970–1971[40]—far more than John Naughton's optimistic projection. It captured 18 percent of the small-car market,[41] which was seven points below Naughton's goal, but the company was at least on the offensive. "Recent surveys indicate four out of every ten Pinto buyers would have bought an import if the Pinto hadn't been available," glowed Henry Ford II.[42]

Flush with success, Lee Iacocca was tapped to become president of the Ford Motor Company at the end of 1970—the sole president, the *real* president, and no longer part of a triumvirate. "Henry came into my office to tell me what he had in mind," Iacocca wrote in his memoirs. "I remember thinking 'This is the greatest Christmas present I've ever had!' We just sat there for a moment or two, he with a cigarette and me with a cigar, and blew smoke at each other."[43]

In 1970, Ford Motor Company, the world's second-largest automaker, produced 4.86 million vehicles. Vehicle sales accounted for 90 percent of corporate revenues (and 93 percent of profits).[44] The Philco electronics subsidiary was a lingering problem, still turning in losses despite its potential. The Autolite parts business was more successful—and too neat a fit with the rest of the company, according to the Federal Trade Commission, which ordered Ford to sell off Autolite or face antitrust charges. International sales were a vital component of the Ford financial picture, accounting for slightly more than a quarter of 1970's total revenues. Overall, the company earned $515 million in profits on nearly $15 billion in sales.

In the United States, where the company held 26.6 percent of the automobile market, 8,000 dealers sold Ford, Mercury, and/or Lincoln cars.[45] By the 1970s, dealership architecture lost much of its individualistic quality; with large plate-glass windows and a towering logo in front, they all exuded a familiar sameness. While distinctive dealerships still existed in downtowns, most had moved to the suburbs, becoming extensions of strip malls and "dysfunction junctions." The sprawl changed the way dealers operated. Instead of trying to be geographically separate from GM or Toyota dealers, Ford dealers preferred "clustering" in a convenient fashion. The basic premise behind clustering was that automobile consumers would visit a handful of showrooms near one another and comparison-shop.

With a half-dozen dealerships in a row on the same suburban strip, it was up to the individual dealer to lure potential customers first with giant signs, fluorescent banners, sticker discounts, and late-night hours. Author Tom Wolfe claimed these giant dealership signs, along with those of fast-food restaurants like Burger King and Dunkin' Donuts, became "the new landmarks of America, the new guideposts, the new way Americans get their bearings."[46] Professional athletes from the National Football League and the National Basketball Association often held autograph sessions at dealerships, promoting the newest models. Local Ford dealers, like their competitors, often used women in sexy cheerleading outfits to advertise their cars. In his classic novel *V,* Thomas Pynchon lampooned the way sex and cars were sold to customers as being interrelated. His seductive character Rachel Outlass, caressing a new automobile, is the star of an unforgettable moment in postwar fiction:

> "You beautiful stud," he heard her say, "I love to touch you." Wha, he thought. "Do you know what I feel when you're out on the road? Alone, just us?" She was running her sponge caressingly over its front bumper. "Your funny responses, darling, that I know so well. The way your brakes pull a little to the left, the way you start to shudder around 5,000 rpm when you're excited. And you burn oil when you're mad at me, don't you? I know."[47]

Few people understood the sizzle that existed between the car and a driver better than Lee Iacocca. At forty-six, he was still rather young for the job of presiding over the world of Ford Motor, but he took in the human face of Ford Motor Company, as it had evolved over the previous decade. Personable and tough, fun but aggressive, Iacocca did not so much arrive at the president's office at Ford as wrap it around himself. He had his cars, his Mustang, his Cougar, his Continental Mark III, his Maverick and Pinto. Whether or not Iacocca deserved as much credit as he received for such bestsellers, there was an unmistakable swagger in an Iacocca Ford. In addition to his cars, he had his people. As Iacocca himself pointed out in his memoir, one of the reasons Bunkie Knudsen had failed to survive at Ford Motor was that "nobody at Ford felt much loyalty to Knudsen, so he was without a power base. As a result, he found himself alone in an alien atmosphere, never really accepted."[48] Iacocca had his power base and it was secure, in the form of the people throughout the ranks who were more loyal to him than to anyone else—even, up to a point, to Henry Ford II.

Iacocca had all the makings of success at Ford Motor. For the first three years of his presidency, the company ran like one of his well-tuned pony cars. In a car market apparently just like that of the booming 1960s, only bigger, Ford Motor stepped up to increasing profits in 1971 and 1972. Underneath, the appetite for automobiles was in flux, however.

The car market was swirling and the reason lay with the small-car segment. It was undoubtedly growing, but no one could be sure that it was permanent. Car buyers and American automakers were out of sync on the subject, as illustrated by an exchange at the 1968 annual stockholders' meeting. Anna Mussioli, a Ford owner and shareholder, stood up to raise a question. "I have just one complaint," she said. "When the Thunderbird came out it was a beautiful sports car. And then you blew it up to the point where it has lost its identity. Now the same thing is happening with the Mustang. . . . Why can't you leave a sports car small? I mean, you keep blowing them up and then starting another little one, blowing that one up and starting another one."

Many car customers had made the same observation. Ford, perhaps even more than other automakers, was guilty of fattening up its best thorough-breds. The reason, of course, was that it was a means of selling more cars. Customers wanted the image of a lithe and peppy sports car while they drove around in a big and comfortable one. Henry Ford II, in responding to Mussioli's comment, hemmed and hawed at first. "I must agree from a personal stand-point that cars could get too big." In fact, big cars were more profitable and that was what he really liked best. However, he said, "that makes it more dif-ficult to maneuver . . . and they no doubt eat up a little bit more gas. . . .

"On the other hand," Henry II continued, getting down to business, "what we try to do is build the kind of car that will sell the most to the general public. Unfortunately, all the public doesn't like the same things and so we have to sort of proliferate."[49] As Henry II seemed to admit—as any automaker knew full well—the desires of the general public were hard to predict. That was about to become more true than ever, with old attitudes about cars unraveling much faster than any American auto company would have believed possible.

By 1972, Ford should have been well positioned, come what might, with a lineup that included five small cars: the newly trimmed-down Mustang II, the Pinto, the near twins the Ford Maverick and the Mercury Comet, and the stylish Capri, which was imported from Ford of Europe. They were sell-ing at a healthy clip, but so were the imports, led by the Japanese Toyota and Nissan-Datsun. Altogether, Americans bought 9.32 million cars in 1972. The proliferation of two-car families had driven the boom of the 1960s. Ten years later, the growing number of three-car families was tracked by Detroit au-tomakers, and at least one small car was generally counted in the mix. In ad-dition, inexpensive small cars replaced used cars for many customers. "The total small-car market now accounts for 38 percent of all sales, up from 22 percent in 1969," observed John Naughton.[50]

The growing impact of Japanese cars and the implementation of safety and antipollution standards should have been the biggest problems facing compa-nies selling cars in the United States, but they were the secondary worries. Instead, in a boom year, production capacity was the prevailing concern. Ford, along with other companies, just couldn't turn out cars fast enough. In 1972, U.S. automakers worked at 103.8 percent of capacity.[51] To pull off that seeming miracle, they were calling in overtime shifts on a consistent basis.

In terms of wages, auto workers had little to complain about. The UAW had driven car companies to share the wealth of the expanding industry in the 1950s and 1960s. An automobile worker, even without a high school diploma or a skill in some trade, could bring home a solid, middle-class income. The man who had fought the longest and hardest to win a high standard of living for the auto worker was nearing the end of his career in 1970. At sixty-two, Walter Reuther had been president of the UAW for almost a quarter century. "We are without question the strongest and most effective industrial union in the world," he told the membership, and he was right. "We have taken on the most powerful corporations in the world . . . and we have prevailed."[52]

In some respects, however, the UAW was no better than the rest of the auto industry. Even though Walter Reuther had been a close personal friend of Martin Luther King Jr. and spoke at the Lincoln Memorial during the 1963 March on Washington, the UAW was almost as rife with racism as the Big Three. Although 30 percent of the UAW membership was African American in 1969, blacks held only 7 percent of the top posts in the union. At that, nevertheless, the UAW was still more open than most unions at the time.

As a leader, Walter Reuther, a bright-burning radical all through his life, had only one problem. He sensed that younger union members regarded him as stodgy. One point that he could put his finger on pertained to overtime—the old guard considered overtime a welcome opportunity to stash away money for the next depression or strike. The younger workers resented it and preferred to stay home as much as possible.

The rank and file at Ford worried that the company would open up new plants in Third World countries, where unions didn't exist and the pay scale was $7 per day. UAW members feared that robots, which had previously performed only a few repetitive tasks, primarily in welding, were becoming ultra-sophisticated. The micro-processor and new computer vision systems were giving robots the ability to handle complex materials, select and distribute parts, and discriminate in the performance of tasks in much the same way as a human being. Many people in the industry were forecasting that by the year 2000, versatile robots would eliminate 37 percent of the jobs in automobile production. It was a concern that Reuther, as president of the UAW, could not dismiss.

On May 9, 1970, Walter Reuther and his wife, May, took a flight on a twin-engine Learjet to northern Michigan, where the UAW had just completed a retreat for its members. It was nighttime and the low clouds and constant rain made it less than ideal for flying. As the leased plane descended, the pilot misjudged and the aircraft hit a cluster of trees, causing a fireball crash that killed everyone onboard. The nation lost a crucial statesman in Walter Reuther. The UAW lost the two people who probably believed in it most. Walter and May Reuther would never be replaced in the movement they helped to start. Four days later, a memorial service was held for them at Detroit's Ford Auditorium. All UAW workers were given the day off. Condolences came pouring in. On behalf of his company, Henry Ford II recognized Reuther as "a central figure in the development of modern industrial history." His death was seen as a closing chapter in that history. Never again would the UAW exert so much influence as when Walter Reuther walked tall.[53]

With the Big Three humming in the early 1970s, the specter of Detroit's deterioration was more conspicuous than ever. The city that had lost 25 percent of its population over the previous twenty years lost three more major employers in 1970–1971 to its suburbs: Kresge, the parent of Kmart; Bendix, the automotive parts supplier; and the American Automobile Association of Michigan. Even William Clay Ford, who had supported the 1968 antiwar presidential campaign of Senator Eugene McCarthy to the point of being considered a potential vice presidential candidate, was tempted to join the "white flight," by taking his Detroit Lions to Pontiac (a move he undertook in 1975). More than ever, the plight of Detroit was tumbling out of control. The *Wall Street Journal* catalogued the city that was being left behind: "boarded-up stores, abandoned houses and a soaring population of hand guns and German shepherds."[54] Uncharacteristically, the newspaper placed the blame on its own constituency. "Business let it happen," it stated bluntly.

Henry Ford II was inclined to agree. "We've got to reverse the trend," he said, referring to the exodus of people, business, energy, and ideas out of Detroit.[55] In 1971, influenced by Max Fisher, a suburban developer, and Bob McCabe, a Detroit business leader, Henry II created a plan for a cluster of new buildings along the riverfront in downtown Detroit called the Renaissance Center. Wayne Doran, head of Ford's land development unit, was involved in the plans from the first. Speaking of Henry II, he later recalled, "he was devastated by those realizations that money was not the solution, but that it had to be personal, it had to be private enterprise, it had to have people who made commitments rather than corporations making the commitments. And that really, as I look back, was the formation of his plans for the Renaissance Center."[56]

The idea was kept secret until a reporter for the *Detroit News* arrived in Henry II's office for an unrelated interview. "The 54-year-old Ford was in his shirt sleeves," wrote *News* reporter Robert Popa, "sitting on the thickly carpeted floor of his office, pointing at a map of downtown Detroit. Outlined on the map were properties which are available and what they're worth.

"An enthusiastic Henry Ford II is something worth seeing," Popa noted. "And Ford *is* enthusiastic about downtown Detroit."[57]

That enthusiasm was contagious in a city desperate for it. After Henry II made a presentation to the City Council about the complex, he received a standing ovation. "Stupendous, magnificent, inspirational," said the mayor.[58] Others, including Lee Iacocca, wondered whether Ford Motor Company should have been dabbling in real estate. The company, however, provided only seed money at first. "There were fifty-one partners in this plan," Henry II later recalled of his adventure in urban renewal. "I held about four meetings out in Dearborn, and everybody came through, including General Motors, when Dick Gerstenberg was its chairman. He decided GM would join and that broke the ice and allowed us to really go ahead. I'm sure we wouldn't have made it without General Motors."[59] Detroit-area businesses supported the idea, which called for construction of a high-rise hotel, deluxe apartments, high-end stores, and state-of-the-art offices on a site overlooking the Detroit River. Each building would offer dramatic views of the Ambassador Bridge, which connected the United States with Canada. Next door was Cobo Arena, where the Detroit Pistons played basketball.

There were some critics, who asked how the gleaming Renaissance towers would help Detroit's racial problems.[60] One man who embodied both the skepticism and the support for the project was the city's next mayor, Coleman Young, elected in 1973. He would serve until 1994, gaining a reputation as a pugnacious politician. Born in 1918, only one year after Henry II, Young started his career in 1936 as a Ford worker at the River Rouge plant. As mayor, Young often worked with Henry II on municipal programs, especially pertaining to the Renaissance Center, but in truth, the political partnership of the two would serve as a historical lesson as to why Detroit has struggled to prosper.

Henry II, a child of privilege, never suffered the worries of poverty for a moment. Everything was handed to him—everything except a sense of true accomplishment, as he worked hard to prove himself worthy of the opportunity granted him at Ford Motor Company. And while he certainly cared a great deal about Detroit, he fled across the moat to Grosse Pointe in the evening, immune from the decay of the "city of urban despair." He was a member of the white elite, while Coleman Young was a man of the assembly line, representative of the blue-collar black neighborhoods of Detroit. "I was never comfortable," Young said, "at the sort of social gatherings frequented by Ford and his fellow industrialists, and on rare occasions when I attended, it only served to remind me that we inhabited different universes.

"I recall one dinner party," Young continued, "when Ford and I were arguing the merits of capital punishment. 'Henry,' I finally said, 'when's the last time someone with your money went to the electric chair?' He was simply the wrong color and the wrong class to understand." In Detroit, in the 1970s and 1980s, however, those were the factions that had to come to understand each other.

The architect of the Renaissance project was John Portman, who had created the Peachtree Center in Atlanta as a shimmering island of high-rise buildings and busy crowds, all in an urban setting. Henry II was openly envious of the way that the Peachtree Center attracted people all through the day, from business workers to those out for the evening, and had transformed Atlanta into a convention town. He believed the Renaissance Center would do the same for Detroit. "You don't go anywhere without a reason," Portman said, in explaining his theme for the Renaissance Center. "You've got to put something in downtown Detroit that makes people *want* to come. You don't make them come."[61] Construction on the glassy new complex began in 1973.

That same year, Ford Motor Company took in $23 billion in revenues, up from $16.4 billion in 1971. Profits were $906 million,[62] a record that would stand for more than a decade. The automobile business is built around cycles, good years and bad ones, but it was about to enter a downturn almost as dizzying for the industry as the Great Depression.

Environmentalists and planners had been talking about an impending "energy crisis" for years. In early 1973, it arrived first in a small way, as gasoline production failed to keep pace with demand, and shortages were reported around the country. Lines in gas stations grew in some cities, while real shortages occurred in Colorado and Kansas. Henry II, concerned that since 1947 America had been importing more petroleum than it produced, was outspoken on the need for a national policy on energy. "I hope to hell New York goes dark for a week," he said of the crisis that May, "then maybe something will happen. People will have more babies, I guess. But I'll tell you something will get done if New York shuts down for a week. I'm not sure if anything else will move it quick enough."[63]

By the end of the year, something came along that affected nearly every American and finally changed the attitude toward energy in America. On Yom Kippur, October 6, the highest of the Jewish high holy days, Syria and Egypt invaded Israel. Stunned by the invasion, Israel appealed to the Nixon administration for help. Without hesitation, the White House authorized an airlift of arms and ammunition to Israel, which helped it drive Egyptian forces back across the Sinai Peninsula to the Suez Canal. The Syrians were also vanquished.

Henry II was vocal in his support of the Israeli victory. In fact, the *Jerusalem Post* later reported that when he was informed that Israel needed trucks to wage the sudden war, "he cleared every Ford truck from showrooms in the country and had them sent to Israel."[64] Perhaps to compensate for his grandfather's anti-Semitism, or simply because he had no prejudice of his own, Henry II had long been an active friend of the Jewish community in America and worldwide. In June 1966, at his direction, Ford Motor had become the first U.S. automaker with formal distribution of its cars in Israel. The countries of the Arab League responded with a boycott of Ford Motor Company products. Coca-Cola, which was also doing business in Israel, was similarly punished by the League, which represented 100 million potential customers. The boycott hurt Ford's profits in the Middle East, but it did at least serve to forge a positive relationship for the company with Jewish American groups. At a press conference in 1975, Henry II was asked when he expected the boycott to lift. "I don't have any idea," he snapped gruffly. "We are not going to change our relationships with Israel to get off the boycott."[65] (The boycott was quietly lifted against Ford Motor Company in 1985.) Despite Ford's antipathy toward the Arab League position, the company continued to cultivate its long-standing relationship with Arabs and Arab Americans in Dearborn, America at large, and abroad.

The tensions in the Middle East affected Ford Motor even more pointedly in the aftermath of the Yom Kippur War. In November 1973, the Organization of Petroleum Exporting Countries (OPEC), a predominantly Arab consortium, punished the United States for its support of Israel in the Yom Kippur War by increasing the cost of oil by 70 percent and refusing to ship oil to America. In December, William Simon, the federal energy czar, asked gasoline stations to enforce a ten-gallon limit on gasoline purchases. Once-crowded highways were practically empty. OPEC succeeded in hindering the pace of American life. Ford Motor even suggested that its own employees leave their cars at home and take the bus to work.[66] "Although it was over in the blink of an eye," journalist Christopher Finch wrote in *Highways to Heaven*, "the 1973 Yom Kippur War between Israel and its neighbors had an impact on the American motorist every bit as dramatic as World War II."[67]

Overnight, "gas guzzlers," in the form of big American sedans and high-performance coupes, went out of style. Customers put their names on waiting lists for little runabouts. The delivery time for a Pinto was five weeks. Certain Toyota models took five months.[68] Meanwhile, customers lost all interest in big cars, which piled up on dealers' lots and at company storage facilities.

Cal Worthington, a dealer known in Southern California for filming eye-catching television ads with a variety of wild animals, operated franchises for Fords, Dodges, and other makes. In the midst of the 1973–1974 oil embargo, he tried hard to cajole his salespeople into selling the big cars. "Men," Worthington shouted, "you all know what we're up against! A subcompact gets 20 mpg against 10 mpg for a standard-size car, but we got to convince 'em that a standard's just as good. Throw some figures at 'em. Tell them that they're three times as likely to be injured in an accident if they're driving a subcompact. Wait a little bit, and then say that with big-car prices down so much, they'd be foolish to sit cramped up in a small car ready to die. . . . Men, get out there and sell those big cars!"[69]

It proved practically impossible, at Worthington or any other dealership. General Motors, firmly associated with the medium- and large-size car, seemed to have the most to lose from the upheaval in the market. During the first months, Ford Motor Company weathered the drought in big-car sales better than either GM or Chrysler by relying on its appealing lineup of small cars. However, the market had changed so drastically that soon all of the U.S.

automakers were affected. Assembly plants started to close, either to alleviate the oversupply or to allow for a changeover to small models. By early 1974, 250,000 auto workers throughout the industry were on layoff.

OPEC ended the oil embargo that March. Gasoline supplies returned nearly to normal and so did people, as they began to wonder whether the whole thing had been anything more than a scheme to raise fuel prices. For a few months, car sales bounced back, but customers remained wary and the last half of the year was a disaster for the U.S. automobile industry. The next year was no better. "I have written off the 1975 model year," said Henry Ford II. At the same time, inflation was raising the price of cars, leading to a malady known at the time as "sticker shock." Those who could avoided auto showrooms altogether. Sales of domestic cars were half what they had been just two years before. Meanwhile, Datsuns, Toyotas, and VWs were surging.

The crisis dazed the Big Three, which had controlled the U.S. auto market and, in the process, carried on the world's longest flirtation with the American car customer. Yet the sense of rejection for U.S. automakers had only just begun. In the mid-1970s, the market was still only toying with Ford, GM, and Chrysler. They knew they were going through a few bad years, but they had yet to accept just how much they had to learn about the business of making automobiles.

33

Financial Crisis

Over at least two generations in America, evolution in the auto industry was neatly regulated by Detroit, through yearly Motoramas and
model introductions. In the 1970s, however, it was beginning to be
dictated from the outside, by the government, the consumer movement, and,
ultimately, competition from Japan. Detroit automobile companies resisted
that basic transition adamantly, if understandably, as they fell from masters of
a universe to servants of a larger system. More territorial than tigers in the
wild, the Big Three wasted valuable years yowling and growling, choosing to
fight the idea of outside influence, resisting the inevitable until it was almost
too late to survive at all. "By 1975 it was, I think, a foregone conclusion that
the Japanese were going to be our competition," Vice President of Car Product
Development Max Jurosek recalled. "By that time we were beginning to recognize the effect that the Japanese carmakers were going to have in the U.S.
market, you could begin to see signs of that transition taking place, and I personally don't think that American business or government responded to that
challenge effectively."[1]

Some of Ford Motor's myriad problems were shared by Chrysler and even by
General Motors, which was in slightly better shape. Three fundamental shifts
turned the business of selling American cars into a hall of mirrors during the
late 1970s: the implementation of government regulations, the encroachment
of Japanese imports, and the vacillations of an unusually fickle customer base.
Underlying all else, the national economic situation—a recession combined
with inflation—didn't help to smooth the way for automakers, for whom no
decision was entirely the right one. John Updike caught the anxieties of the
era perfectly in his novel *Rabbit Is Rich:* "The people are out there getting
frantic, they know the great American ride is ending. Gas lines at ninety-nine

cents a gallon and ninety percent of the stations to be closed for the weekend. People are going wild, their dollars are going rotten."[2]

Ford Motor Company also had its own unique troubles, which put the company into a worse position than it had been in since the end of World War II. While there was no real thought that the company would fail altogether, as was the constant worry about Chrysler, many people predicted that Ford Motor would never be the same again, not as strong, as confident, or as versatile as it had been during most of the postwar years. A clamor ensued for Ford to start investing in the burgeoning world of computers and aerospace. "Outsiders looking at the approaching dilemma of the Ford Motor Company," David Halberstam wrote in *The Reckoning*, "its rising labor costs, its incipient Asian competition, were puzzled that the company did not diversify more, hedging its bets and making itself less dependent on a whimsical, cyclical, and potentially endangered business like auto."[3]

Ford's problems would run deep in the late 1970s, damaging public trust and internal morale. The company was marked with the specter of tragedy related to the Pinto, along with pressing—that is, life-threatening—safety issues on other Ford models. It wrestled with enmity in the ranks of both the workers and the management, represented most vividly for the general public by the abrupt firing of Lee Iacocca as president. In addition, Ford had a hidden problem reminiscent of its downward slide in 1945, when the elder Henry Ford was no longer fit to serve as head of the company. In the late 1970s, Henry II was ailing—"dragging" was the word he used. Henry II in decline was not as detrimental as the first Henry Ford had been, but that didn't help Ford Motor in its struggles.[4]

Given the impending crisis at Ford Motor, Henry II and Lee Iacocca decided to lobby President Richard Nixon. On April 27, 1971, the Dearborn duo visited the White House for a meeting with the "boss" who was gearing up for a reelection bid. The two men at the head of Ford Motor were vitally concerned with the cost of implementing government regulations pertaining to safety. Henry II pressed the point he'd arrived with, that the added expenses for compliance with safety regulations would raise car prices and eventually affect the whole economy. He was part of the old guard in 1971, openly longing for the good old days when safety didn't raise costs. New measures developed in a more natural way, as production allowed. He had never forgotten the dismal response to Robert McNamara's attempt to sell Fords on the basis of safety features in 1956–1957. "We see the price of a Pinto," he told Nixon, "going [up] something like fifty percent in the next three years with inflation part of it, but that's not the big part of it. It's the safety requirements, the emission requirements, the bumper requirements. . . .

"If these prices get so high that people stop buying cars," he said, "they're gonna buy more foreign cars; you're going to have balance-of-payment problems." Of course, the same regulations would apply to foreign-made cars sold in the United States, but overseas factories never ceased to press a price advantage, based largely on the cost of labor.

While Henry II was hoping in general terms for a return to the past, Iacocca was leading a charge focused on the Department of Transportation (DOT), which was setting the safety requirements. He told the president:

> We are in a downhill slide, the likes of which we have never seen in our business. And the Japs are in the wings ready to eat us up alive. So I'm in a position to be saying to [DOT officials], "Would you guys cool it a little bit? You're gonna break us." And they say, "Hold it. People want safety." I say, "Well, what do you mean, they want safety? We get letters. . . . We get about thousands on customer service. You can't get your car fixed. We don't get anything on safety! So again, give us a priority." We cannot carry the load of inflation in wages and safety in a four-year period without breaking our back. It's that simple and that's what we've tried to convey to these people.

Unfortunately, neither Henry II nor Lee Iacocca accepted safety as a high priority, a fact that would loom large in the company's later problems. Cost and competition were their main concerns. Nixon, who taped the meeting, along with all of his other conversations in the Oval Office, welcomed Ford and Iacocca by expressing his opinion that:

> We can't have a completely safe society of safe highways or safe cars and pollution-free and so forth. Or we could have, go back and live like a bunch of damned animals. That won't be too good, either. But I also know that using this issue, and boy this is true. It's true in, in the environmentalists and it's true of the consumerism people. They're a group of people that aren't really one damn bit interested in safety or clean air. What they're interested in is destroying the system. They're enemies of the system.[5]

Nixon's sentiment, although tinged with paranoia, must have put the automakers at ease.

The president promised to look into easing up regulations, but he was statesmanlike enough to indicate that he would have to hear the other side of the argument first. In fact, the visit Ford and Iacocca made to the White House was only one aspect of a constant lobbying campaign conducted by the company in Washington, a city known derisively in Detroit as "twelve square miles surrounded by reality."

The atmosphere of regulation had its beginnings in 1965, when the National Highway Traffic Safety Administration (NHTSA) was created by the federal government. It was a direct outgrowth of the campaign for automotive safety initiated by consumer activist Ralph Nader, who stalked General Motors like a big-game hunter desperate for a kill. Nader was an unusual nemesis for the Big Three. A cerebral, solitary activist with no university affiliation, Nader was fearless in his undaunted pursuit of automobile safety. Deemed a publicity-seeking gadfly by some, in truth Nader was a needed spokesperson for the rights of consumers. Over a period of years, the pressure that Ralph Nader and the NHTSA put on automakers and road engineers successfully reduced the number of traffic deaths. Early on, NHTSA struggled to issue standards that would be meaningful across the wide range of models driven on American roads. One of the first was also the most noticeable, a uniform height for bumpers, to ensure that small cars didn't slide right under bigger ones. At Ford, according to Gene Bordinat, vice president for styling, the new bumper resulted in the inspiration for the restyled 1972 Thunderbird, which attracted customers in droves.[6] Not every regulation was a step in the wrong direction.

Even while the NHTSA was fighting to establish new standards for cars going into production, it learned that its greatest power lay in bringing attention to defective automobiles. And its greatest weapon was the mandatory recall. Where car companies had sometimes voluntarily implemented model repairs over the years, the mandated recall became epidemic in the 1970s. For the first time, automakers had someone checking their handiwork. It wasn't a comfortable feeling, especially since every recall was a blemish on a company's public image. In 1977, 12.9 million cars were recalled on various counts.[7] "There are no standards," said a Ford official rancorously. "Whatever we do, NHTSA and the courts just say we should have done it better."[8]

While GM, in particular, fought the rash of recalls by arguing individual cases in court, the tide was against the automakers. Every recall seemed to inform customers that someone in the auto industry had taken another shortcut.

In addition to the gathering momentum in safety regulation, the 1970 Clean Air Act set limitations on poisonous automobile emissions. The new standards, which were to start taking effect in 1975, were stringent, calling for reductions of up to 97.3 percent in hydrocarbons, carbon monoxide, and nitrogen oxide. In its own way, the Clean Air Act was the ultimate safety regulation, since it undoubtedly reduced the number of people who would have died from respiratory disease in a country fast becoming clogged with smog. However, there was one peculiarity about the new law. At the time that Senator Edmund Muskie of Maine won the fight for the pollution standards on cars, the technology did not yet exist to reduce it. The new law said to Detroit, in effect: either perform an engineering miracle—or go to jail. Even Muskie admitted that he was trying to "force the technology."[9]

Despite the threat, automakers were not averse to the regulations regarding pollution, at least not at first. There was grousing about the deadline for compliance, but not about the overall goal. By 1970, the severity of the problem of filthy air could be seen in any city large enough to produce a rush-hour traffic jam. GM's position was that legislation on the issue of pollution was entirely appropriate, because, while the ultimate result was for the public good, few people would willingly pay extra for a clean-running car. "We knew it had to be done, and it isn't marketable,"[10] explained Dr. Fred Bowditch, GM's director of emissions controls, a $1 billion program. For its part, Ford Motor assigned a staff of 6,500 engineering employees to the emissions problem. Initially, the progress was encouraging, as changes to carburetion and exhaust systems eliminated 90 percent of the overall pollutants. There were, however, two lingering problems.

First, the decrease in emissions resulted in an increase in fuel consumption. That wasn't an easy line to hand customers after the oil embargo of 1973–1974. Second, the same techniques that eased the emission of hydrocarbons and carbon monoxide increased the presence of a third chemical, nitrogen oxide. It was an impasse, and as car companies requested extensions on compliance with the second stage of the Clean Air Act, they were accused of making up excuses for delay, a charge hovering over their response to safety regulations as well. "I've heard about foot-dragging so often, I've begun to think it's part of our corporate name," said an executive at GM.[11]

Lee Iacocca went even further, telling a friendly audience of suppliers in the late days of 1972:

> Although our products sell like hotcakes, we would be kidding ourselves if we didn't recognize that the automobile and the automobile industry are in a lot of people's doghouses. You know what? Some wise guys have even invented a game called "Beat Detroit." Maybe you've heard of it. For eight bucks, you get dice, little car tokens, a game board and a rule book. And, so help me, the object of "Beat Detroit" according to the rule book is "to travel 50,000 miles before you go broke or your car falls apart." If that's a parlor game, I want my kids to play behind the woodshed.
>
> Anyway, what we're seeing is a new kind of national scapegoating in which our huge, seemingly slow-moving industry is not only being blamed for most of our social and economic ills, but is also becoming a barn-door-sized target for the most myopic of our critics.[12]

Sometimes, Washington did go too far. When the Federal Trade Commission heard in 1976 that Ford was offering repairs on known defects—including noisy pistons, for example—only to customers who complained and not to all customers, the agency took the automaker to task. First, the company was warned against offering what were termed "secret warranties." Next, the FTC ordered that Ford, in order to protect itself from claims of false advertising, post large posters in each showroom listing the twenty leading defects to be found on each of its models. Needless to say, the company fought that order with no holds barred, and won its point. Ludicrous as the FTC case may seem, it reflected the new attitude regarding the Big Three and what had once been business as usual. In any case, the FTC mounted only a relatively small assault. Other battles could not be won by Ford Motor, no matter how hard the fight.

Even while Detroit's car companies were facing edicts to build new cars along safety and pollution guidelines, the federal government added rules on fuel consumption. "The motor capital of the U.S. has moved from the Detroit River to the Potomac," complained Henry Ford II.[13] In 1975, the government adopted the Energy Policy and Conservation Act, which took a serious step toward improving the mileage of new cars. Where the onus of energy efficiency had formerly been on consumers, who could choose to buy small cars, the new law moved it directly onto the automakers. According to Corporate Average Fuel Economy (CAFE) standards, each company would be judged on the average gas mileage of its entire fleet of passenger cars. If a company wanted to, it could build gas-guzzling big cars . . . as long as it found a way to lower its overall average by selling a large flock of compacts in the same year.

The CAFE standards mandated that individual companies report averages of at least 18 miles per gallon by 1978 and 27.5 mpg by 1985. Along the way, cars imported by domestic automakers from their overseas subsidiaries or manufacturing partners would no longer count toward the average. In other words, Detroit had to build small cars for itself—and the American driver. In the wake of the CAFE announcement, Ford's average was short by 1.5 miles per gallon. It didn't seem like much, but drawn from a body of more than 2 million cars, it was a hard number to erase. Ford's most fuel-efficient car, the Pinto, brought 30 mpg, which was not a high enough figure to offset the company's full-size fleet. As the deadline closed in, Ford predicted that, if it couldn't comply, it would have to pay $300 million in penalties for every mile per gallon that it fell short.

All car companies were faced with the same regulations—safety, pollution, and CAFE—but the Big Three had a much harder time coping with them than did foreign companies. The Japanese imports, in particular, were designed especially for the American market. So were the domestic models, of course, but they were weighed down with the baggage of tradition. Bill Bourke, Ford's vice president for North American vehicles, was asked in 1977 how Detroit would respond to the interlocking, sometimes conflicting array of orders from Washington. "Our present cars," he said, "evolved over 75 years, during which refinements were made on a year-to-year basis to meet customer preferences. In the next few years a revolution will sweep the industry and its competitive face will be totally changed."[14]

If the government was forcing a revolution on American automakers, the increase of imports from Japan was termed an outright attack. It couldn't be called a *surprise* attack, since the first Toyotas and Datsuns had arrived in the late 1950s. Both of those manufacturers had paused in the mid-1960s, nearly stalling U.S. operations altogether in order to study the situation fully. The first Japanese car tailor-made for American drivers and roads was the Toyota Corona in 1966. With decent performance and a sturdy feel, it was followed by other Japanese cars that made their initial impact in California.

A writer from *Forbes* called the onslaught "an economic Pearl Harbor,"[15] a theme echoed by Ford executive Bennett Bidwell. He looked back on the new competition from Japan during the early 1970s and said, "We were about as well prepared as Kimmell and Short were at Pearl Harbor, even though we had a little more time to see it coming. . . . People came in and bought Mazdas instead of Fords. I don't think any of us really thought that that would ever happen."[16]

Ford employee Arthur Connors saw the foreign onslaught firsthand. As he recalled, it all started with the customers. "When I went to California in 1970 as regional manager," he said, "about the time we brought the Capri in from Germany, people would find when the ship arrivals came and would go down and wait for cars to come out and follow the carload to the dealerships. The people out there just wanted foreign cars. That's the first time I really woke up to it."[17]

By 1975, 18 percent of all new-car sales in America were foreign cars. Of those, one third consisted of European makes, and the rest came from Japan's automakers: Toyota, Nissan-Datsun, Honda, Mazda, and Subaru. Just two years later, in 1977, the market share captured by foreign imports had grown to 21 percent. The Europeans still had the same 6 percent. It was the Japanese share that had jumped, accounting for 15 percent of the U.S. market for cars.

The Japanese cars tended to be high in quality, in part because the companies didn't try to build them to a customer's specifications, or pack each one with a different array of options. Instead, the cars were manufactured from identical build-sheets, which simplified production. It also simplified the purchase for the consumer, who felt less strained by the temptation to add extra features; most were included in a standard price on the average Japanese model. In both respects, the Japanese success repeated Henry Ford's early recipe for the Model T's success. As the Japanese makes found, not all American customers thought of a new car as a fashion item—some looked upon it as a tool of transportation, which was how the elder Henry had started out selling the T.

Japanese compacts received a boost from the emphasis on gas mileage, but the market of the 1970s was not entirely that simple. Even as headlines trumpeted news of the energy crisis, gasoline prices tripled, and lines formed at those stations with gas to sell, some customers still bought big gas guzzlers. The American automobile market was more confused than it had ever been before. "It's a mixed-up market, and anybody who says he fully understands it is crazy," said William Luneburg, president of American Motors, in 1976.[18]

In 1974, Bennett Bidwell introduced the new Lincoln Continental by wondering aloud to reporters if he was "the father of the world's last dinosaur."[19] His pessimism was entirely unfounded, however. The next year, the Continental was sold off of waiting lists.

As Ford temporarily closed down its Metuchen, New Jersey, plant to stop the flow of Pintos and Bobcats, Bill Bourke explained the frustration. "We began converting our big-car plants to small cars following the oil crisis of 1973–74," he said. "The fact is that we are finding it easier to convert plants than to convert buyers."[20]

In truth, Ford Motor had less to complain about than GM in 1977's fickle shift back to big cars. While Ford was the early leader among the Big Three in small-car production, GM made a commitment to "downsize" its entire line in time for 1977. However, that was a big-car year. Like a baseball player eyeing second base from first, GM was caught leaning the wrong way, and its sales suffered. Americans ferreted out full-size cars at Ford, Mercury, and Lincoln dealerships, leading to a good year in Dearborn, during which Ford Motor's profit rate exceeded that of GM—a rare occurrence.

The boost in Ford's profitability was not due to any admirable efficiency drives at the factories. Rather, it stemmed from the company's reluctance to leave full-size cars entirely behind. Where GM made the decision to downsize practically everything in the lineup, Ford couldn't bear to give up its full-size cars entirely. The two rolling living rooms, the LTD and the Mercury Marquis, remained sacred in Dearborn until the end of the decade. Ford had some pretty tempting reasons to protect the big cars—for one thing, they still had sales pop. As one of the last of Detroit's "dinosaurs," the T-bird was the company's bestselling model in 1977. The economics were behind them, too. On a car twice as expensive as a compact, the profit was generally four times as great. Henry Ford II had a great respect for that fact, which he summed up in his oft-repeated expression "minicar, miniprofit." Henry II also held as long as possible to an innate belief that Americans wanted big cars, whatever the passing fads or pressures.

But even if customers had continued to buy the big cars, neither Henry Ford II nor the company he headed had the choice to build them. As Chrysler Executive Vice President Richard K. Brown lamented, "Even if we don't believe in small cars, we have to build them. There's a law."[21] At Ford, as at each car company, a computer system monitored the outflow of vehicles and relayed the up-to-the-minute fleet average. Late in the decade, Ford was living on the edge of disaster, holding back production of the popular Lincoln Mark V with its 12 mpg, while putting 30-mpg compacts on sale and even selling them at a loss in order to eke out the standard CAFE average for the fleet.

It wasn't an easy way to make a buck for any of Detroit's automakers, twisting themselves around government regulations and then trying to reach customers who never seemed to stay in one place. Nevertheless, Ford managed to make money, logging record profits in 1977 and 1978. But its boon was the result of short-term thinking. When the Shah of Iran was deposed by extremists in January 1979, the Middle Eastern oil supply was disrupted once again and gasoline shortages returned to the United States. Japanese automakers benefited, surging to a 20 percent share of the market. General Motors benefited, too. Its big-little "X-cars" (including the Pontiac Phoenix and Chevrolet Citation) met the demand for fuel-efficient cars and gave the corporation a dramatic boost in market share. They also kept GM in the black, while Ford and Chrysler were taking turns setting records for losses.

———

In the late 1970s and 1980s, when the U.S. automaking industry was down and gasping, it did not receive much sympathy. To the contrary, it was scorned for arrogance or sloth in failing to keep up with new trends in automaking. Spoiled by the pace of production in 1971–1973, with customers snapping up record numbers of automobiles, Detroit had resisted the pace of underlying *change* in automaking. The transformation was fundamental for the whole industry, because the most basic issues of what kinds of cars were to be built and how they would operate were no longer left up to the Big Three car companies.

Detroit was going through a revolution, learning to take orders from Washington and trying to make amends with a less complacent type of customer. As a result of the revolution, the Big Three, as a phrase, was no longer a description of the U.S. automobile industry. For the first time since the 1930s, Americans had a wide choice in vehicles. The vanquished places of Reo, Auburn, Hupmobile, and Packard were filled, as the Big Three had grown into a Big Nine, at the very least, with Toyota, Nissan, and Honda moving in to take market share, almost at will, and Mercedes-Benz, BMW, VW, and even Volvo and Saab exerting influence over styling and engineering as never before. For the first time since the 1910s, Ford and GM were only names in the mix.

"Detroit's hegemony in the auto world is waning," *Consumer Reports* observed without regret in 1977.[22] Against this backdrop of industry upheaval, Ford Motor Company fared badly, falling much further than the other American automakers. Back in 1970, it was in better shape than any of the Big Three—not only was it making money, but it was poised to make *more* money in the future. Ford had the head start in making small cars. It had the most appeal to younger buyers. It understood the two- and even three-car family. Faced only with the problems of the outside world, the problems of fuel from the Arab states, regulations from Washington, and competition from Japan,

Ford Motor should have fared better than any other car company. It might even have thrived.

Among the many factors that augured well for Ford in 1970 was its management. In the savvy Henry II and the aggressive Lee Iacocca, Ford Motor had what seemed to be its finest executive tandem since the first Henry Ford and James Couzens. The teaming didn't produce results, however. Instead, it brought out the worst tendencies of each man. And they brought out the worst in Ford Motor during the decade.

Of all of the executives in the postwar era at Ford Motor, Iacocca was unique in promoting himself with much of the sly vigor of the elder Henry Ford. In his two bestselling memoirs—*Iacocca* (1984) and *Talking Straight* (1988)—Iacocca spoke directly to middle-class Americans, not from on high, but very much as the guy next door. He was a corporate maverick, to be sure, but he cultivated the public persona of a man in touch with working-class people who struggled to pay taxes and hospital bills. Just as Henry Ford never tired of telling stories of his humble life on the farm, Iacocca packed his books with reminders that he was the son of Italian immigrants. Both Iacocca and Ford claimed Benjamin Franklin as their special hero.

Taking a page right out of Ford's development of Greenfield Village as an American touchstone with the past, Iacocca served for years as chairman of the Statue of Liberty–Ellis Island Centennial. And just as Ford befriended Edison, Firestone, and other famous people in his own era, Iacocca was close to Joe DiMaggio, Frank Sinatra, and Tom Brokaw, among others. Ford ran for the U.S. Senate and considered a run for the White House; Iacocca also exhibited more than a passing interest in holding public office. In *Talking Straight,* he included no less than three illustrations of bumper stickers that were circulated by others to urge his candidacy. He even added a photograph of New York Governor Mario Cuomo sporting a button reading "Make a Date! Iacocca in '88!"[23]

The most meaningful comparison between Iacocca and the elder Henry Ford lay in the tips for successful business management that poured forth in their respective, ghostwritten books. Iacocca, like a disciple of Ford, claimed that big business should be kept simple, that priorities could be inventoried on a simple 8½-by-11-inch piece of paper. He railed against such Sloanist notions as long-range strategic plans and five-year profit plans—anything that smacked of the bureaucratic. He projected an anti-intellectual stance, mocking Harvard's business school and MIT's management experts, all in the manner of the elder Henry Ford.

Like Ford, Iacocca could be counted on to offer advice on complicated problems that had nothing to do with the manufacture or sale of automobiles. Iacocca offered ideas for ills ranging from the Cold War to the prevalence of suicide and the AIDS epidemic. "Pick a style and stick with it" was Iacocca's ironclad rule of management. Both automakers even dabbled in foodstuffs on the side, Ford promoting soybeans and Iacocca purveying an olive-oil spread.[24] There was one big difference, however, between Lee Iacocca and the man he seemed to emulate, the first Henry Ford. Ford owned a company—Lee Iacocca did not.[25]

Lee Iacocca, the marketing master, offered his own version of what went wrong during his reign at Ford from 1970 to 1978 in his autobiography. The two chapters on the presidency, which are surprisingly brief, reveal little about the big issues facing Ford, but seem distracted by specific points regarding personalities, mostly that of Henry II. In that sense, Iacocca's memoirs of his tenure as president of Ford reflect precisely what it was like—a time when executives were likely to be more concerned with their own maneuverings than with the legions of problems facing the company. Iacocca, given his product successes before his Ford presidency and his heroic resuscitation of Chrysler after it, has often been excused from the failures of Ford Motor in the 1970s. According to his own version, the major decisions were made by Henry II and they were the ones that tripped up the company.

To planners the most frustrating decisions were those that canceled products—and Henry II made many of those in the mid-1970s. During one cost-cutting sweep, two proposed front-wheel-drive models were canceled. Another of the models Henry II quashed was a "van-wagon," which was developed in 1977.[26] Looking exactly like the minivan that became *de rigueur* for families in the late 1980s (and made hundreds of millions of dollars for Chrysler), the pioneering Ford version may have been rejected because it had *too much* good research in support. "We got into a frightful habit in this company," Henry II said after he retired, "of relying too much on surveys. I'm not a big survey man. I think that if you are in the business you ought to know what the hell you want to do and you can't rely on a survey to pull your bacon out of the frying pan."[27]

Iacocca and Ford clashed on many planes. In the midst of the energy crisis, Iacocca's emphasis was on finding another skyrocket success like the Mustang. The more rash he became in looking for the big hit, the more conservative Ford grew in refusing to put his faith, and the company's money, into a miracle model far afield from the rest of the pack. To his ears, front-wheel-drive seemed a gamble and so did the launch of a whole new type of vehicle in the van-wagon. While the company waited, however, he and Iacocca didn't find a middle ground. In fact, they split further and further apart.

Robert Alexander, a longtime Ford executive, was one of Iacocca's closest associates, with no particular sympathies for Henry II. However, he thought that Iacocca was out of control when it came to Henry Ford II. "Lee was really looking for battles," Alexander said. "It was as if Lee was swelled up. He made the victory of [Bunkie] Knudsen where he had taken him out single-handedly.

Maybe he was contemptuous of Mr. Ford, maybe it blinded him where he believed that he could take on anyone."[28]

For more than thirty years with Ford Motor, Iacocca had been focused on moving up at the company. His methods had been based on equal parts in acumen and cunning. If he couldn't drop the raw side of his ambition when he became president, though, the only figure who would know it for sure would be the only man left above him, Henry Ford II. When the distance between the two became so great that Ford stopped trusting Iacocca, rejecting ideas simply because they came from the president's office, Ford Motor stagnated.

Henry Ford II, for his part, said very little about Iacocca in public. From 1980 to 1984, however, he gave a series of interviews to David Lewis, the contents of which were to be sealed until ten years after his death. In those transcripts, rarely published before, Henry II explained what went wrong, from his point of view:

> Iacocca, until the oil embargo, and government regulations got very difficult, was a good executive. But Iacocca . . . let me put it another way. Iacocca was an extremely intelligent product man, a super salesman. It didn't make any difference what he was selling. He was very imaginative, very bright, very quick. But when it finally came down to 1974, '75, he got lost all of a sudden. Completely. He got himself into a blue funk over products. I never developed product lines. That wasn't what I thought my job was. I approved products, but I didn't develop them. I could say no, or I could say yes, or I could suggest ideas. But I didn't do the development work. But then our development work became terrible, and it changed all the time. We never had a good program for any duration. . . .
>
> He thought he was paying proper attention. But he got thoroughly confused in his later years by what the hell to do, and he had a new program every two to three months. The organization was totally discombobulated.[29]

Despite having two of the most effective leaders in the modern history of the automobile industry, Ford Motor was suffering from a total breakdown in leadership by 1975. Iacocca, who thrived on intrigue, used his favorite lieutenants to try to outmaneuver the chairman. Henry II, who was prone to a haughty air of secrecy, periodically fired individuals he regarded as Iacocca's "bagmen."

Ford Motor was operating on borrowed time. It was sagging slowly but surely into the bad habit of goading customers into buying big cars, if at all possible. That was practically enough, until events occurred that showed the terrible weaknesses running through the Ford company.

On August 10, 1978, three teenage girls traveling in a 1973 Pinto on a highway in Indiana were rammed from behind by a van. The collision itself didn't hurt them, but seconds later, their car was engulfed in flames and all three of the girls burned to death. It wasn't the first time a relatively minor accident had turned into a fiery horror in a Pinto. In May 1972, a California woman received fatal injuries when her Pinto exploded into flames after being rear-ended on a San Bernardino highway; her passenger, Richard Grimshaw, survived, but with burns over 90 percent of his body.

Grimshaw's attorney, Mark Robinson, was among the first people outside Ford Motor Company to look into the design of the Pinto. He discovered that Ford had placed the gas tank behind the rear axle, where it would be vulnerable to both initial impact and puncture from bolts on the differential housing, and other sharp objects nearby. In fact, the fuel tank was protected from the back by little more than the sheet metal of the body, six inches' worth of air, and a slim bumper. Furthermore, the filler neck, which led to the gas cap, was situated in such a way that it could easily break off in a collision. With gasoline leaking in the midst of an accident, a conflagration was almost inevitable. That was tragic enough, but Robinson's investigation also uncovered evidence that Ford had known about the Pinto's susceptibility to explosion or fire ever since the model first went on sale.

In October 1970, a "Final Test Report" from the company's Product Development Engineering Office advised that in a rear-end collision at 21.5 mph, the 1971 Pinto "filler pipe pulled out of the fuel tank and the fluid discharged through the outlet. Additional leakage occurred through a puncture in the upper right front surface of the fuel tank which was caused by contact between the fuel tank and a bolt on the differential housing."[30] Subsequent tests in which Pintos were backed into a barrier at slightly lower speeds, ranging from 15.5 to 20.8 mph, resulted in leaks in five of the six cases.[31] Two months after the Pinto was introduced in 1970, engineers submitted a series of design changes to improve the safety of the Pinto fuel tank. All were rejected, as were similar memos on the topic in 1971 and 1972.

In April 1971, a product review meeting at Ford, charged specifically with safety planning, considered the situation surrounding the Pinto's fuel tank and concluded that the contents of the tank could be protected either from the outside, with a polyethylene covering, or from the inside, with a rubber bladder. Its recommendation was to "defer adoption of the 'flak' suit or bladder on all affected cars until 1976 to realize a design cost savings of $20.9 million compared to incorporation in 1974."[32]

A suggested change to prevent fuel from leaking in the Pinto during a rollover was couched in the same language: "Defer adoption of all rollover hardware until 1976 to realize a design cost savings of $10.7 million." The prioritized goal of the safety planning session of the product review meeting was to realize savings, not to protect people riding in Ford cars.

Trade-offs are necessary in any undertaking involving cars. If safety were the only concern, cars would either cost millions of dollars each or have a top speed of only 5 mph. However, as more evidence surfaced in the Pinto case, it only enforced the impression left by the product review meeting memo that cost had been a far more important consideration than safety. Not only didn't the company fix the known problem with the Pinto, it implemented the same fuel tank design on the 1975–1976 Mercury Bobcat.

The first major article in the national press on the Pinto fuel hazards was written by Mark Dowie in the September–October 1977 issue of *Mother Jones.* He asked a person described as a "high-ranking engineer" if anyone had gone to Lee Iacocca, the father of the Pinto, to discuss the car's dangerous flaws. "Hell no," the engineer responded. "That person would have been fired. Safety wasn't a popular subject around Ford in those days. With Lee it was taboo."[33]

Iacocca had his priorities, and near the top was styling. According to Harley Copp, a senior Ford engineer who came out publicly against the company's safety record on the Pinto, the problem was that Iacocca locked in its looks and then told the engineering staff to work within those dimensions. Normally, there would be give-and-take between the styling sections and the engineers. "The car was frozen before the engineers could package all the components," Copp said. "The engineers were left with a minimum amount of space in which to put the spare tire, the fuel tank, the muffler, the suspension, and provide luggage space."[34] At the time of the development of the Pinto, according to Copp, engineers requested permission to place the fuel tank over the rear axle, which would have cut into the amount of luggage space; alternatively, they suggested moving two inches from the long front hood of the car and adding it to the rear deck, giving them the room they needed to properly accommodate the gas tank. Both ideas were rejected.

Between 1970 and 1976, when safety changes were finally made, 1.5 million Pintos fanned out onto American roads. According to what Mark Dowie said were conservative estimates, the Pinto design flaws had caused 500 deaths. An actual count placed the death toll at 59, as of 1978,[35] but the number of deaths was less important than the reason for them.

No one expected the Pinto to be impervious in relatively high-speed collisions. However, in the medium range of about 20 to 35 mph, the Pinto was apt to become a fireball. Since there is nothing flukish about a medium-speed, rear-end collision, any deaths that resulted were too many.

The *Mother Jones* article received a fair amount of attention in consumer circles, but the general public only began to hear of the Pinto's problems in February 1978, when a California jury awarded Richard Grimshaw nearly $128 million—the largest amount ever awarded in a product liability suit up to that time. Most of the assessment was punitive, calculated to take the money that Ford had saved by forgoing the improvements. Although the judge reduced the total award, Ford's lawyers immediately appealed the verdict.

The NHTSA had been inspired by the *Mother Jones* article to commission its own investigation. In tests on ten Pintos, two exploded upon being hit from behind at 35 mph. Eight others leaked sizable amounts of gasoline, either from the tank or from the filler. When the same tests were performed on a comparable model, the Chevrolet Vega, there were no significant leaks. The NHTSA scheduled a public hearing for June 14, 1978, to air its concerns, but Ford Motor finally relented, voluntarily recalling all 1.9 million of its 1971–1976 Pintos and 1975–1976 Bobcats.[36] Dealers would cover the tank with the flak suit and install a longer filler pipe, at no charge.

Two days after Ford's announcement, the CBS television show *60 Minutes* covered the problems with the Pinto fuel tank and Ford's strangely apathetic attitude toward them. With that, the Pinto became a national scandal. Some Pintos began to sport bumper stickers reading "Hit me and we blow up together!"

Two months later, the Ehrlich girls in Indiana went out for their ride, apparently oblivious of the danger posed by the Pinto (the family would receive a recall notice on the car in February 1979). They were burned to death in what should have been a minor accident. The prosecutor in Elkhart County, Michael Cosentino, was enraged by the senseless accident. He familiarized himself with the background on the Pinto and then brought the case to a grand jury, which returned indictments against Ford on three counts of reckless homicide.[37] A corporation had never been charged with murder before: another first for the strange, sad case of the Ford Pinto.

When push came to shove, Henry Ford II, the modern executive who transformed Ford Motor into a public corporation in 1956, behaved like the head of a small family firm. Henry II oversaw the selection of legal counsel himself and authorized a war chest of several million dollars. A team of ten lawyers from Chicago supported lead defense attorney James Neal, who received $1 million just for his efforts. On the other side, Elkhart County made a special appropriation of $20,000 to fund its prosecution.

All of Ford's legal fees were well spent. Neal and his team seemed to control the trial, eliciting the willing cooperation of the judge. Neal methodically succeeded in having most of the prosecution's evidence and even the testimony of some of its key witnesses disallowed. He claimed that the Pinto fuel-tank design was identical to that of many other compacts of the time, and that once a recall became necessary, the company had done everything possible to comply. While jury members were inclined to regard the Pinto as "a reckless auto," in the words of the foreman, a retired farmer, there was simply not enough evidence presented in the courtroom to convict.[38] Ford was found innocent.

Back in California, the state Court of Appeals, which had access to all of the available material concerning the Pinto, upheld Richard Grimshaw's victory over Ford and a $6.6 million award. According to the decision, "Ford's institutional mentality was shown to be one of callous indifference to public safety. There was substantial evidence that Ford's conduct constituted 'conscious disregard' of the probability of injury to members of the consuming public."[39] Nothing worse could have been said of an automaker.

Pinto sales plummeted, but that was not the end of Ford's safety scandals. During the 1970s, Ford cars that were equipped with automatic transmissions were regularly blamed for slipping from park into reverse without warning. From 1969 to 1979, at least 128 deaths and 1,700 injuries were blamed on the defect.[40] For years, Ford replied to the charge by accusing drivers of negligence. Meanwhile, it was slapped with 240 lawsuits stemming from the transmission problem.

To answer the allegations, Ford Motor Company hired former Secretary of Transportation William Coleman Jr. While the NHTSA threatened to require recalls of all 16 million affected Fords, the company adamantly denied that there was anything inherently wrong with its transmission. Neither side seemed likely to back down.

In 1981, a compromise was accepted, grudgingly, by the DOT. Ford Motor offered to send the owner of every car in question a package of educational materials including stickers for the dash reminding drivers to put the gearshift firmly in park, set the hand brake, and turn the car off before getting out of the car. With the car off and the brake on, a transmission couldn't have much effect, whether it was defective or not.[41]

The Ford name was becoming associated in the public mind with unsafe automobiles—and a reluctance to put the consumer first. According to a survey, 36 percent of the public thought of Fords as dangerous. Only 6 percent thought of GM cars in the same light and an even lower percentage had a problem with Chryslers. Henry Ford II had established a culture in which safety was resisted, at least as a public issue, as though no one could *force* Ford Motor to produce safe cars. That grew into a culture under Iacocca in which safety was a concern, but not a high priority. If Lee Iacocca deserves credit as the man responsible for the Mustang, in spirit if not in every detail, he also has to be burdened with the legacy of the Pinto, another vehicle of which he was once proud.

The culture at Ford Motor in the 1970s was fixated on cost, profit, and money. Short-term results propel ambitious people, like Lee Iacocca, forward. They also tend to please large stockholders, like Henry Ford II. By the mid-1970s, the two of them were making a daily sport of pointing out their respective differences, but in looking too closely at the quarterly results, they may have had more in common than was good for the company.

In 1976, Henry Ford II was diagnosed with angina pectoris, a painful heart condition. At fifty-eight, he already knew all about angina, which had affected other members of his family, including his brother Benson, who died of a heart attack. Even without the hereditary factor, Henry II's lifestyle must have put a strain on his health. For most of his life he had smoked heavily, and for more than twenty years he'd been known to drink to excess. He disdained exercise, traveled at a hectic pace all over the world, and held a stressful job. In addition, his personal life was in turmoil. He and Cristina separated early in 1976, long after realizing that they had practically nothing in common—but not very long at all after Cristina realized that Henry had a steady girlfriend, thirty-seven-year-old Kathy DuRoss. After the separation, Ford moved out of the house and lived in a suite attached to his office in Dearborn.

Gossip swirled around Henry Ford II. He was a full-time playboy and a full-time automobile executive, yet he often confessed that he felt lonely. One of his oldest friends, John Bugas, explained the pattern of Henry II's business associations and personal relationships: "He falls in and out of love with both men and women. Usually it lasts a few years. Never more than six. For a time they can do no wrong. And then comes the time when they can do no right."[42] Cristina's allotted time was over. Then Henry II became ill and faced the fact that he could not hope to remain at his company for more than a few more years. When he made plans based upon that fact, Lee Iacocca's time was over, too.

"I had to get out," Henry II later recalled, referring to the responsibility of running the company. "I didn't have any choice. I had to get out. I was dragging. I was not doing anybody any good, including myself."

In terms of grooming a successor, Henry II continued, "I couldn't see Iacocca, but even if I'd not had to get out, I probably wouldn't have been able to keep him. He was just not my cup of tea."[43]

Another factor that put Iacocca permanently out of favor was the death of Henry II's mother, Eleanor, on October 19, 1976. Through the years, Iacocca had been able to count Edsel's widow as an ally who often stepped in to smooth arguments between the chairman and president of Ford Motor. Iacocca, in his memoirs, went so far as to say of Eleanor and Henry II that she "kept him somewhat in line. But when she died in 1976, his whole world came tumbling down."[44]

After 1976, Henry II quietly took responsibilities away from Iacocca. He continued that effort on an official basis in 1977 by creating a new hierarchy at the company, establishing an "office of the chief executive," by which he would share his duties with Lee Iacocca and Philip Caldwell, who was named vice chairman. However, Henry II "had an extra vote."[45] Henry II pointedly expressed a desire to place the company in capable hands until another member of his family could take over. At the time, his own son, Edsel II, was just twenty-eight and working as a company executive in Australia. Early in 1978, Caldwell was given another title, deputy chief executive officer. With that, Iacocca was told to report to Caldwell.

Over his quarter century at Ford, Philip Caldwell had become known for his minute examination of every problem put before him. Caldwell even thrived as president of the troubled Philco electronics division. He served as head of Ford of Europe, and then all of the company's operations outside of the United States, before Henry II tapped him for the office of the chief executive. In personality, Philip Caldwell was the antithesis of Lee Iacocca. Self-contained, deliberate, and generally oblivious of the emotions of others, Caldwell was the tortoise to Iacocca's hare.

Selecting Philip Caldwell as vice chairman added insult to injury for Lee Iacocca, who actually inquired about a job running International Paper before deciding to stay on at Ford Motor. He may have thought he still had some hope in what had become an open struggle against Henry II.

Henry Ford II distrusted Lee Iacocca. In 1975, he had even authorized $1.5 million of the company's money to conduct an investigation of the president, his business and private life. Nothing of any interest was discovered. In the summer of 1978, Iacocca took a treacherous gamble, contacting members of the board of directors, looking for support in a showdown with Henry II. In doing so, Iacocca made the mistake of giving his boss hard evidence that he couldn't be trusted.

Henry II had the excuse he needed. On July 13, 1978, Lee Iacocca was called into the chairman's office and fired. Reporters were quick to point out that he thus joined a long and honorable list of former Ford favorites who never made it to retirement age at the company: James Couzens, Charles Sorensen, Ernie Breech, and Bunkie Knudsen, among them. Many people liked the poetic justice about Iacocca, who had grinned like a bandit on the occasion of Knudsen's surprise firing, facing the same fate only nine years later. "For a time Iacocca was overwhelmed by his bitterness," David Halberstam wrote in *The Reckoning.* "The firing was the final mortification. It was as if the last few years Henry Ford had confirmed all Iacocca's darkest suspicions, that despite his immense salary, his lavish perks, his title of president, he was the employee, the crude little Italian who worked for and had been tolerated by the WASP owner."[46]

Within the company, there was as much relief as regret at the firing. Even Iacocca fans such as Bill Bourke recognized that a parting had probably been inevitable. "There might be quieter ways of doing it," Bourke said of the news. "Other people set off firecrackers. We drop atomic bombs."[47] For two days in a row, the story was carried on page one of the *New York Times.* Eventually Iacocca grew relieved. "Thank God all the bullshit is over," he confided to a friend.[48]

Iacocca left Ford Motor a very different company than he had found it—more spirited and nimble in the way that it created cars. If he was a salesman first, as Henry II said, he sold Ford on a new image for itself, as a marketplace of bold ideas. But most of Iacocca's best work took place when he was a product man in the 1960s. As president in the 1970s, he didn't improve production quality or union relations. Inexplicably, product development also declined. Overall, the company was resisting the very trends it ought to have used to catapult itself forward. Lee Iacocca was not the right man to head Ford Motor Company.

Neither was Henry Ford II. The chairman was having his own problems by 1978. He was accused of being bored with the automobile business, of being overly pessimistic and unenthusiastic. Whatever the exact nature of his "dragging," he was certainly a more distant figure than he had been before. One executive went so far as to say that he "seemed slower" in the mental sense.[49] The one thing that Henry did know was that he had to retire. He felt obligated to wait until a verdict was returned in the Pinto homicide case in Indiana. At a board meeting in March 1980, just after the not-guilty verdict was returned, directors gave a hearty cheer for Henry II, who formally retired as CEO, while remaining chairman of the board of directors. Philip Caldwell, who had taken Iacocca's place as president, moved up to become CEO. Donald Petersen, a popular executive around Ford and a committed automobile buff, took over the presidency.

Even as the cheering was ringing through the boardroom, however, Ford Motor was losing money at a record pace. Sales had tumbled worldwide. The market demanded new kinds of cars, but the company was running out of cash with which to tool up. Costs were nearly out of control. The Japanese cars were still coming in droves, and, according to DOT figures, their unit cost was at least $1,000 less than that of the average U.S. car. Those were only small problems, though, and so was the company's staggering loss of $1.4 billion for the year. Even people who assumed that Ford would survive its financial problems doubted that it, or any American company, could make a car to the high standards of a Japanese or German car. The assumption was that sheer salesmanship would allow the Big Three to survive. But for Ford, the days of sheer salesmanship were over. The big problem facing the company in 1980 was remembering how to unleash its talents.

Although Ford Motor was struggling, as Ronald Reagan became president, Chrysler was in even worse shape. Investors began murmuring about a merger. Early in 1981, representatives of Salomon Brothers, the New York investment bank, quietly arrived in Dearborn to propose a merger of the Chrysler Corporation and Ford Motor Company. They had been authorized to do so by the Chrysler management. The merger they described would be a very big deal: Ford was the third-largest industrial company in the United

States and Chrysler was number ten. The motivation on Chrysler's part, however, wasn't the opportunity to grow, but the mere chance to survive. The year before, Chrysler had posted the worst results in U.S. corporate history, with a net loss of $1.7 billion. In fact, the last thing that Ford stockholders needed in 1981 was another ailing car company. The one they already owned presented challenges enough. Ford Motor had posted its own loss of $1.4 billion in 1980, a staggering figure that would have stood as the record if not for Chrysler's report. The Ford board of directors discussed the merger proposal extensively, before rejecting it on the basis that it was "not in the best interest of Ford or its stockholders."[50] They were determined to either sink or swim on their own.

34

The Quality Crisis

W hen Henry Ford II retired in 1980, no one knew for sure how much influence he would continue to exert over Ford Motor Company. Although he was no longer CEO, he still represented the Ford family, which owned nearly 40 percent of the voting stock. More important, he was still Henry Ford II. For thirty-four years that simple fact had meant that he was the boss at Ford Motor Company. According to a story that circulated through press accounts, Henry II had won tough arguments at work in Dearborn simply by reminding his adversaries whose name was on the outside of World Headquarters. He later denied that he had ever stooped to such a ploy. But anyway, he didn't have to. He was Henry Ford II. The circle of power at Ford Motor always ended with him, and many people anticipated that nothing would alter that. "If you think Henry II was the man in Dearborn, you should have seen what it was like when he traveled in Europe," Lee Iacocca recalled. "He always had access to the top people, even kings and queens."[1] As the *Detroit News* noted, Henry Ford II not only dominated his own company, he "dominated the public's perception of the U.S. auto industry."[2]

For all of the work Henry Ford II put in as the head of the company from September 21, 1945, to March 13, 1980, for all of the twelve-hour days and tightly scheduled business trips, the studious preparation and tedious meetings, his two most important decisions were the ones with which he began and ended his career. First, the hiring of Ernest Breech in 1946. Second, the selection of Philip Caldwell and Donald Petersen to take over in 1980. Henry II was not always right in the men he chose for top positions. He was certainly not always right in the men he fired. However, Henry II did manage to come up with the right names when the company needed them most.

Neither Caldwell nor Petersen was selected out of friendship; Henry had an ironclad policy of steering clear of overt cronyism with colleagues. (The one notable exception to that rule was John Bugas, with whom Henry II enjoyed a close friendship; nonetheless Bugas was passed over for the presidency in the mid-1960s.) Nor were Caldwell and Petersen members of any old-boy network. Both men came from similar backgrounds, having been raised in humble, unpretentious households where hard work and personal integrity were instilled.

Philip Caldwell hailed from South Charleston, Ohio. He attended a small school called Muskingum College in New Concord. He then went to Harvard Business School on a scholarship. He thrived there and he further developed his organizational skills in the U.S. Navy, serving on Admiral Chester Nimitz's advanced planning staff during World War II. It was in this important post that he learned the "art of procurement," making sure that the necessities of war were delivered to American battleships in the Pacific. "Failure could have resulted in thousands of Allied casualties," *Fortune* magazine noted in a profile. "Unstinting attention to detail enabled Caldwell's team to succeed."[3] Imbued with a penchant for cars and trucks, Caldwell joined the corporate world with Ford Motor in 1953. Colleagues saw him as a smart, dapper man with a squat physique who worked overtime for fun. He was a consummate professional, and his commitment to Ford Motor was tangible. By the time he was CEO, his hair was silvery and thinning, but he still walked with the gait of a young executive. "A lot of top people at Ford, like him, were short men with huge, resonant voices," recalled Paul Weaver, who worked in public affairs, speaking of Caldwell's baritone.[4] When Caldwell spoke, employees listened.

Donald Petersen was born on September 4, 1926, in Pipestone, Minnesota. He grew up in a close-knit family, which moved to California. "Although my own family didn't have much money when I was growing up," he later recalled, "my parents always praised me, especially for what I accomplished at school."[5] His father told him to aim for college, promising that they would find the tuition money somehow. As it turned out, the Navy paid for most of Petersen's undergraduate schooling. After enlisting during World War II, he earned a bachelor's degree from the University of Washington as part of his training. Later, Petersen went to Stanford University for an MBA and served as an officer in the Marine Corps. He then joined Ford Motor Company. Petersen garnered accolades in the 1960s when, as car planning manager, he helped launch the Mustang. He also ran the lucrative truck operations section from 1971 to 1975.

Like thousands of others at Ford in the postwar years, Caldwell and Petersen each worked steadily up a ladder of various positions, without any shortcuts. If Henry II had the final vote on naming Ford's leaders through the years, at least he cultivated his ranks as a meritocracy.

When Philip Caldwell was named CEO in 1980, he made history. For the first time, no member of the Ford family was actively involved in the top management decisions. William Ford Sr. remained in an advisory capacity as vice chairman, but both he and his brother, Henry II, left Caldwell alone to handle the company's problems. And Caldwell was faced with several of the biggest. "There is no doubt about it," former Ford executive Harold "Red" Poling recalled. "He had his hands full."[6]

Ford Motor not only was ailing financially but had lost its way—its reason for being. Those two characteristics were undoubtedly connected. For at least ten years leading up to 1980, Ford was a company obsessed with profits to the exclusion of practically all else. Cars were made in factories regarded as "war zones" by the people who worked in them. Dearborn had impressed plant managers around the country that it was more important to meet production quotas than to maintain quality standards. Line workers received the underlying message. "If something wasn't right," said an assembler at Ford's Louisville plant, "we'd let it go and hoped the inspector caught it. We didn't care a lot. If I hollered too often, I'd be taken to labor relations for not doing my job."[7] The situation was not much different at Ford's other plants. One worker in Michigan remembered seeing a truck go down the line with both an automatic transmission and a clutch. Carelessness like that wouldn't have happened in Japan.

The low priority on quality at Ford was pushed down from the top. However, when the competition from imports caught up to the American automobile industry, it didn't take long for that message to rise back up through the same ranks. In 1980, executives were actually ashamed of the cars they were expected to sell. "I didn't want my friends and neighbors to buy one of our cars," admitted Ford's executive director of marketing, a man who should have been pushing for everyone to buy one of the company's cars. "I didn't want to hear their complaints."[8]

Paul Weaver made the point that since Ford executives received new cars as a matter of course, three times a year, none of them were staying abreast of what it was like to shop for a car or negotiate a price. Moreover, he wrote, "no one ever expressed any enthusiasm for cars that I detected." If the executives Weaver met weren't car types, they were equally uninterested in customers, blue-collar workers, and shareholders. "What did interest my colleagues at Ford," he wrote, "what we talked about obsessively in meetings where company statements on policy issues were drafted—was the company's position in the auto industry."[9] At a company where the employees were uninterested in the product, the customers, the workers, and the shareholders, it is not surprising that after a while, the position in the industry wasn't really worth talking about at all.

For years, Ford Motor had fought for market share from a fairly secure perch in the mid-20s, by percentage. GM sold about twice as many of America's cars; Chrysler, where Iacocca soon landed, about half as many. In 1980, however, Ford's market share was down to 16 percent. Observers speculated that Chrysler—even though it was a ward of the federal government—was in a position to surpass Ford. The legacy from the 1970s was that Ford built cars rated as the worst in the Big Three.[10] And even the best of the Big Three could no longer keep up with the Japanese or the Germans.

During the heyday of the first Henry Ford, the company was focused on a mission to put the world on wheels, to make automobiles affordable and practical for nearly everyone. Every decision the company made—from building only one model, the venerable T, to paying Detroit's best wages in an attempt to increase production—flowed naturally from that one goal. In a sense, company executives didn't set the policies; the goal of supplying the world with a universal car did. In Ford Motor's second great era, begun under Henry II and Ernest Breech, the mission was modernization. While Ford at first mimicked GM's notion of starting consumers with a used Chevy and having them end up in a Cadillac hearse, it later became a fountain of original ideas, challenging its larger competitor for front-runner status. In the 1950s and 1960s, innovations at Ford had the best chance of being accepted if they showed the glimmers of the modern world: aggressiveness, youth, speed, or high technology.

When that initiative petered out, government regulations and internal bickering kept management from implementing a new theme. Bad decisions and then bad times followed. By the time Ford came face-to-face with disaster in 1980, it had no compelling corporate goal.

The job of finding a new direction for Ford Motor Company fell squarely on the shoulders of Philip Caldwell. Although some critics felt that he was slow to take action in the midst of Ford's crisis, Caldwell made an immediate change in the atmosphere around headquarters, simply by dint of his personality. Unlike many of his predecessors in the executive suite, he didn't drink or smoke. And unlike practically all of them, he didn't swear. Caldwell was as careful in business as he was in handling himself. He didn't wax enthusiastic about fast cars or new sales programs or futuristic ideas of any kind. He was concerned about only one thing: the right decision. The difference was the source of frustration for other executives. One described the Ford CEO as "someone who liked to go to bed at night still thinking he had not made his first mistake."[11]

Caldwell approached decisions with dogged research and relentless discussion—and he expected the same from subordinates. Caldwell had no use for hunches. "The company could have pulled in its horns, hunkered down and waited for a miracle," Caldwell later noted. "But that would have given away Ford's future."[12]

What some of the junior executives may have failed to recognize, after becoming used to the gut reactions and instant answers of the Iacocca administration, was that in 1980 Ford Motor could not afford any more mistakes. Each day that passed without the CEO having made one was a gift in the fight to survive as a major automaker. "We were broke," longtime Ford executive Pete Pestillo recalled. "Just stabilizing the situation was an accomplishment."[13] A company that is losing more than $1 billion each year is faced with harsh choices. It can watch cash reserves slip away, cut costs drastically, or borrow money at high, short-term rates. To survive, Ford Motor had to do all three. In 1978, when Henry Ford II was clutched by conservatism, Ford Motor was sitting on an unusually large amount of cash—$4 billion.[14] Much of that was gone by 1980 and the company still had to borrow $2.5 billion. To make matters worse, the rates it paid on its debt edged to the upward side of prime as its credit rating was slashed by Standard & Poor's.

To stop the bleeding, Caldwell authorized cost reductions of $4 billion in just over two years. On that side of the ledger, he depended on the services of Red Poling, the vice president of North American Automotive Operations. Costs were out of control in that division, due in part to the drive to comply with regulations and in part to management's lack of policy. It takes tough decisions to trim corporate fat—while leaving the muscle. Red Poling, whose background was in finance, was charged with making the reductions. Poling was the man for the job, according to Petersen. "He eats up factual information, computes it, stores it, and then applies it to various actions," Petersen stated in his memoir, *A Better Idea*. "He concentrates on the numbers—charts, statistics, and so on—instead of written material. . . . He can challenge the daylights out of people on facts and financial details."[15]

Layoffs and plant closings lowered Ford's overall costs, but the greater concern was its per-unit cost. The cars that were coming off the line had higher built-in costs than those of practically any other vehicles on sale in America. (Maybe Ferraris or Rolls-Royces cost more to build, but Ford wasn't competing with them.) While Poling looked for savings in overhead, which affected the white-collar sections of the company, he also asked suppliers for across-the-board price cuts of 1.5 percent. He couldn't, however, ask the UAW for relief from the standing wage agreements that made Ford cars cost $200 more to build than equivalent Chrysler vehicles. Ford was locked into its labor contract. Moreover, it also seemed to be locked into decades of animosity with the union, as well as its own factory workers.

While Poling was trimming $4 billion from the company's accounts payable, the corporate president, Donald Petersen, was leading an effort to add $3 billion to the same column, through the regeneration of Ford Motor Company. Even while the company was cutting production of cars left over from the bad old days, it was launching production of a new generation of cars, due out in 1982–1983.

The cars the company had slated for the future didn't look at all like Fords, which smacked of GM's boxy cars, anyway. The new models were edgeless, with rounded corners and a soft flow to the silhouette. Chrome protrusions were reduced to a minimum. "Instead of building silver boxes, we're building silver bullets," explained Robert Zokas, a design director at Ford.[16] The "aero" look, as it was called, actually did use aerodynamics to cut wind resistance and so improve gas mileage. But it was the effect on customers that interested Ford most. "It's a bit of a job turning people around," said Jack Telnack, vice president for styling, "but our president, Mr. Petersen, knows the way I feel about design and the kind of look I'm trying to achieve and he's supporting me 100 percent. I am absolutely convinced people are ready for this. We've underestimated the American public."[17]

Telnack had been head of styling for Ford of Europe and was banking on his conviction that Americans would respond to the sophisticated styling prevalent there. It was indeed a gamble, though. At other auto companies, Ford's aero look was disparaged as the "jelly-bean" look—too radical and yet too understated for the singularly overstated American driver. Henry Ford II agreed with that assessment. In the planning stage, he came out against the aero look.[18] However, he didn't try to squelch it, as he might have five years before. He let Caldwell make the final call. As a matter of fact, Henry II remained on the sidelines, to the surprise of many people in Detroit. "I think Phil's extremely well suited for his job," Henry II said in 1982, "and is doing an outstanding job. I don't know of anybody else who could do it as well as he's doing."[19] Not even, apparently, Henry Ford II.

The look of the coming generation of Fords was only one consideration in the resuscitation of the company. The new styling generated talk in car magazines and even a little respect for Ford's daring, but the aero look was only skin-deep. Ford cars had to be just as radically transformed underneath if they were to sell in healthy numbers. They needed to be well engineered, carefully built, and reliable—because the Japanese and German cars were. While cost cutting and building bold cars were factors in the attempt to start Ford moving forward again, they didn't constitute the mission that would turn Ford into a new company under Philip Caldwell. As the automaker entered its third well-defined era, its imperative would have to be something as real and far-reaching as its earlier goals had been, so that it would, like them, take on a life of its own.

"Quality is the number one objective of the Ford Motor Company," Caldwell announced at the very first board of directors meeting over which he presided.[20] Normally, that is the kind of comment made all too easily by a corporate chairman. As the equivalent of a political campaign promise to lower taxes or improve education, it is nice to hear, but just as typically forgotten in the aftermath.

Caldwell's assertion was especially striking, however, because Ford's passenger-car production in 1980 was so far out of sync with the philosophies and processes that ensured consistent quality. For Ford to boast about quality as its goal was either intrepid or pathetic. The people who would ultimately decide which were the workers who built the cars on Ford assembly lines. They were the ones Caldwell's team had to convince.

"Every management team that is trying to change a company's culture," wrote Don Petersen, "runs into skeptics who say, 'Okay, you say that "Quality is Job One." But we're so financially driven and so cost-conscious, we'll believe you only when we see you putting quality ahead of cost.' In order to overcome this kind of skepticism, the company has to prove that it will practice what it preaches."[21]

Caldwell, Petersen, and Poling lost no time in showing just how serious they were about raising production standards. In 1980, during their first summer in charge, when the company was losing money at a record clip, two stunning decisions proved just where quality lay in their priorities.

At the time, Ford was faced with the choice of closing either an outdated factory in Norfolk, Virginia, or a fairly new one in Mahwah, New Jersey. If saving money—the usual basis for making a selection—were the only factor, then the Norfolk plant would have been finished. "But the Norfolk plant was putting out quality products," recalled Donald Petersen, "and employee relations were excellent. The Mahwah plant was relatively new, but the employees there weren't working together well, and their quality record was not good. Red Poling, who was in charge of Ford's North American operations, strongly desired to keep Norfolk open, because it was a plant in which quality was the top priority. To the surprise of many people, the company accepted Poling's recommendation. This sent a simple message: from that day on, the plants with the worst quality records would be the first to go."[22]

During that same summer, Poling was involved with an even bigger decision. At the time, with the market clamoring for small cars, Ford Motor was poised to begin U.S. production of the Escort, a compact with design roots in Europe. The company needed the Escort desperately—dealers wanted something new to create showroom traffic and financial officers were looking for the cash flow to be generated by the high-volume car. Moreover, Ford was constantly straining to meet the government's CAFE gas-mileage goals, and the lightweight Escort was sure to raise its fleet's average fuel economy. "Job One," the industry's name for the first vehicle to roll down a new-model production line, was hotly anticipated in mid-June 1980. Then Poling received word from plant officials that the process of building the Escort still had kinks, which were bound to show up as defects on finished cars. In the past, improvements would have been made on the fly, and production would have begun on schedule.

"I decided to delay 'Job One,'" Poling said of the crucial Escort startup. "We delayed 'Job One' for a month, at a time when the company could sell every small car it could produce. We were losing huge sums of money, and we needed the profits that we could get from those small cars. But it was the right thing to do; we needed to make sure the product was right. *That* sent a very strong signal throughout North America that we were serious about quality."[23]

The message coming from top executives was strong enough, but it only laid the groundwork for a new atmosphere. No one pretended that the rank and file would be an easy group to inspire. In the first place, communication between labor and management at any U.S. automobile factory was practically nonexistent in 1980. Building cars had reached a kind of perfection as a dehumanizing institution. It was not that the workers became part of the machinery, as early social critics observed with a kind of terror, looking at assembly lines. That was accepted as part of the craft of building cars: blending people and complex tools. By and large, workers regarded that as a necessary part of the work. What wasn't necessary, although it was just as real and unceasing as the conveyers, was the systematized refusal to recognize the auto worker as a person, a human being with a mind.

"It was dog-eat-dog," recalled Jeff Cooper, a Ford worker in Michigan. "You came in, you hated your foreman, your foreman hated you, you did your job, and you hoped they didn't mess with you. They used to write you up for stupid things. The foreman would tell you to go somewhere and you would go get a drink of water on the way and he would write you up for not following a direct order."[24]

In the adversarial climate, workers took orders and were rarely allowed to respond with comments about their work. It's safe to say that they were never encouraged to do so. Outright complaints were piped through the union to management, by way of committeemen. And so, the individual auto worker was completely invisible to management. At Ford Motor Company, which had a harsh reputation as an employer, the gulf was even wider. Philip Caldwell could make all the comments he liked about quality, but there was no way to force those sentiments onto the hundreds of thousands of assembly-line workers, each one of whom was making dozens of decisions per day that affected ultimate build-quality.

Before quality could improve, Ford Motor had to find its workers in the corporate fabric. It had to cut through long-standing traditions of ignoring them and discover ways to communicate with them. And if the company wanted to fulfill the mission of its third era, if it wanted to build high-quality cars, it had to put itself and its auto workers on the same side of the battle. In the process, it would have to knock down sixty years of animosity. The key to Ford's survival as a major corporation did not lie with Red Poling's knack for cutting costs, Don Petersen's talent for bringing forth aggressive new cars, or Philip Caldwell's ability to steer a steady course through financial whirlpools. The future of the company depended on the individuals who built the cars.

Likewise, the workers' own future in the business of manufacturing cars depended on the condition of Ford Motor Company as never before. In 1980–1981, with sales dropping and more than a third of Ford's labor force on layoff, the workers had strong reasons to cooperate with management. Although everyone in the domestic auto industry was in trouble, the numbers were stacked even higher against the American auto worker than against the automaking companies. The reason was that the Big Three had the option of importing cars to sell in the United States. In 1980, Japanese companies paid auto workers, on average, the equivalent of $10.78 per hour. Ford was paying just over $20.[25] That wasn't even the worst of it. At Ford and other U.S. auto companies, labor costs were rising by at least 10 percent per year, while in Japan, wages were going up by only 7 percent. That foreshadowed an ever-increasing disparity in the future.

Nearly every individual nickel in the workers' $20 wage package had been won in a separate struggle by the United Auto Workers. In the days when the American companies competed only against one another, generally prosperous times for the Big Three, $20 was not too much money. In the 1980s, however, when the American auto worker was considered an endangered species, the wage rate became the prevailing issue of international competition.

The future of both Ford Motor Company and the workers in its factories depended on the leadership of the UAW. The union could hold firm to its hard-won concessions, accepting the risk of losing jobs to overseas factories. The reasoning behind that position could be based in optimism (that the overall car market would improve enough by the mid-1980s to return U.S. automakers to their former prosperity) or in pessimism (on the basis that industries such as the textile trade had proven that it was impossible to compete with the wages paid to foreign workers, so auto workers might as well hang on to their good wages as long as possible).

Fraser knew that the pressure was building in 1980–1981 for the auto workers to give back some of what they had won, whether in wages, in benefits, or in control over factory conditions. The union had a contract at Ford that didn't expire until September 1982, but without a replacement contract, according to the talk around Detroit, Ford's hope of turnaround would be drastically hampered. Some of the company would almost certainly have to be sacrificed.

Even if Fraser believed the auto companies' dire warnings, pockets of the UAW membership were extremely skeptical, and that was enough to make any smart union president wary. "From a bargainer's point of view, who knows whether or not they're bluffing," Fraser said of Ford negotiators late in 1981. "Even if we were willing to go to the bargaining table, our opposition [other factions in the union] would make the case that the economic climate is so bad, so poisoned, that no matter what we do, it won't help business."[26]

To negotiate with the UAW, Ford Motor named a new type of executive for the post of vice president of employee relations. Peter J. Pestillo was a Connecticut lawyer with very little experience in Detroit-style union negotiations. Nonetheless, he had a national reputation in the field of employee relations, and Philip Caldwell had personally recruited him. Fresh to the field, Pestillo wasn't burdened with the tough talk and strong-arm attitude of Ford's former approach to unions. At the same time, he was anything but naïve and could hold his own with anyone, point by point, but in his own soft-spoken way. "We respected workers," Pestillo recalled. "It was not a phony sentiment."[27]

On the other side of the bargaining table, the UAW appointed Don Ephlin in 1980 to take charge of union activities at Ford Motor. Ephlin brought a fresh attitude that was unique at the time: he actively looked for ways to draw the union and the company management closer together, under common goals. A sensitive listener and quiet conversationalist, Ephlin was as utterly rational as Pete Pestillo. Together, the two of them made a cartoon out of the many fist-pounding, threat-making, vituperative negotiators who had preceded them through the years. However, the deeds, not the words, were of more interest to the people in Ford's management and labor force whose fate would hinge on the accomplishments of Ephlin and Pestillo.

In the early 1980s, an auto worker earned a high wage, an upper-middle-class living for those with seniority. Automobile workers typically owned their homes and had a new car or two. Dee Mueller, who began working at a Ford truck plant near Detroit in 1978, had previously been a waitress. "The year before I started at the plant," she told Richard Feldman for the book *End of the Line,* "I'd made maybe $5,000. I made $32,000 the first year at the plant. That was exciting to me. The more I made, the more I liked it." However, later in her interview, she admitted that she had to listen to popular music on a stereo to get through the job. "No matter how tired I get, how sore my muscles are, how much my fingers ache, if I hear a good song, nothing bothers me."[28]

The majority of auto workers, though, hated the very thought of their jobs. Tony Hamilton, who worked at Ford's Louisville assembly plant, said that he felt physically sick every time he arrived for work. "I'd sit in the parking lot and think of some excuse I would tell my wife for not working that day," he said.[29] The labor problem facing Ford was complex. Something was hindering auto workers from doing their best. High wages alone could not break through.

On January 15, 1982, Pestillo presented a plan to Ephlin, outlining a new labor contract to replace the existing one. It was a bold move, one that might have been greeted with laughter or umbrage at almost any other point in the forty-one-year history of Ford-UAW relations. However, the cold fact was that the 1979 contract was already sorely outdated. A new agreement could meet rising concerns on both sides, in the face of the crisis in the auto industry. Using that possibility as the wind at their backs, Pestillo and Ephlin met nearly every day for three weeks before announcing a historic breakthrough.

The new contract was the first ever to reduce the overall package for UAW workers at Ford Motor. But Ford workers liked another stipulation: the company would not ship any manufacturing jobs overseas or to other sources. In another measure extending job security, in the event of layoffs, Ford offered guaranteed income to workers with fifteen years of service. Rushed through the approval process, the new pact was approved by a three-to-one margin in rank-and-file voting.[30] Don Ephlin said that the new contract "reassures our people who have been living on the edge of disaster."[31]

It did the same for Ford Motor. The company received concessions that contained wages and reduced vacation days; it stood to save as much as $1 billion due to the agreement.

One clause that stayed in the background of the hoopla surrounding the new contract provided for profit sharing for production workers. At the time, the notion of Ford's making a profit substantial enough to activate the profit-sharing plan seemed remote. Later in the decade, however, that clause would have a signal effect on the attitude of union workers toward the Ford Motor Company.

In February 1982, when the new contract went into effect, 104,700 UAW members still had jobs in Ford factories. More than half as many, 54,830, were on indefinite layoff, with scant hope of returning. Another 11,450 were on temporary layoff. Few people thought that Ford would ever employ 160,000 auto workers in North America again. The overriding goal was to protect the jobs that were left, while there was still time. "We're chasing after thirty years of mistrust," Pete Pestillo had said in the new atmosphere created by the ratification of the contract. "There are people in both camps who need teaching that there really is a very favorable end product of avoiding conflict."[32]

The sense of conflict ran deep within the factories. People at the company, long cut off from each other—even when they worked side by side—had to start listening to one another. "I visited several plants," said Red Poling, "and asked to meet with the union leadership as well as the plant management. Doing so was a major deviation, because the executive vice president of North America [Automotive Operations] just didn't meet with the union leaders. I did. I told them that it was the perception of the American public that we couldn't produce quality products in the United States to compete with the Japanese, and unless we changed that perception as well as the reality, there was no future for any of us. We needed their suggestions and their help. They were the people who knew best what to do to improve quality.

They were the people who were working on the products day in, day out. The response I received at two of the plants that I visited was, 'Is this another of those programs, or are you really serious?' I replied, 'We're really serious, as long as I'm around.' So we got a cooperative effort going with our employees in improving quality."[33]

One of the most tangible ways that Ford proved its commitment to quality, even over quantity (the traditional impetus of the automobile factory), was through the installation of a "stop button" at every worker station in most factories. If there was a problem, the company wanted it solved immediately, and not merely passed along in hopes that someone else would catch it later and correct it. According to some line workers, foremen found ways to punish people who used the stop button, even though it typically held up production for only about thirty seconds. As far as the company's top management was concerned, however, stopping the line was more acceptable than sending out a bad car. At one plant, the stop button was credited with reducing quality "concerns," as the company called defects, from an average of seventeen per car to less than one.[34]

To elicit the suggestions and help of the assembly-line worker, Ford had a program in place called Employee Involvement (EI), which provided a forum for moderated discussions of complaints and ideas. Operated independently within each factory that wanted it, EI brought management, engineering, and line workers together—voluntarily, but on company time. At first, EI typically dealt with problems of personal comfort, such as cleanliness, around the plant. Once workers gained confidence, they started suggesting ways to improve production at their own stations. Even while those ideas kept coming, the EI committee would often select recurring problems for study and discussion by a special team.

In Ford's Sharonville, Ohio, plant, workers grew tired of compensating for the poor quality of parts from a certain supplier. With management approval, and even applause, EI took the lead in warning the vendor to raise the standards within two weeks or lose the Sharonville account. In the old days, an order like that couldn't have come from the factory floor; now, at a time when each production plant was being held accountable for the quality of the vehicles (or subassemblies) it sent out the door, the workers didn't just install a part they knew to be bad and then forget about it. At Sharonville, workers got angry, and management considered that a healthy sign. "EI people won't run junk" was the way one Sharonville assembler put it. Two weeks later, the vendor had made no improvements and its parts were no longer accepted at the Sharonville factory. Two months after that, the vendor's salespeople were back, humbly describing the changes made in production techniques, in order to improve the standards for Ford parts.[35]

The longtime manager of the Sharonville plant, Thomas McCaffrey, had once been at odds with workers, in the time-honored way at Ford. "Yeah, the threat of shutting down the plant was a motivating factor for all of us," he said. "But in my opinion, the 'religion' was always there. We never opened the doors for them. I don't think the people changed. I think we gave them the opportunity to use their talents and to dedicate themselves to doing a good job. We also began treating them differently—with respect—as opposed to the traditional way we ran our business from the top down: 'Do it, damn it, I'm the boss.' We just opened the doors and when you open the doors, those people want to do a good job."[36]

At the Louisville assembly factory, employees and management, having tired of the state of war that long existed there, developed their own avenues of detente. In 1980, Don Ephlin and Pete Pestillo visited the plant to recommend the implementation of EI. The company was so impressed with the reception of the program, as well as the sharp rise in overall quality standards, that it chose to share early designs for future vehicles (a new Ranger truck and the Bronco II) with the auto workers who would one day be expected to build them.

As surprising as it now seems that workers had never been consulted on matters of production, it seems just as inexplicable that assemblers were never before shown blueprints of coming designs. The Louisville labor force came forward with more than 540 suggestions that were eventually utilized in the Ranger and the Bronco.[37]

Of the ninety-one plants owned by Ford Motor Company, eighty-six operated EI programs by 1984. In another time and under other circumstances, the UAW would probably not have allowed the company to bypass its own system for filtering workers' comments and presenting them to management. If EI deserved some of the credit for the dramatic improvement of build-quality in Ford cars during the early 1980s, the union should be recognized for giving it a chance in the first place.

"It's democracy in the workplace," said the head of the local at Ford's Rawsonville, Michigan, plant. "It makes the people more aware of their own self-worth and intelligence and it makes them better union members."[38] That was one view of EI. There were others.

"Employee Involvement is for the company," said Hillory Weber, who had been working at Ford plants in Michigan since 1953. "It's to eliminate manpower. EI is educating the company about things that you're capable of doing that the company didn't know about. If you tell them how to do a man's job faster or better, that's taking the job away from him."[39]

Part of the company's goal was undoubtedly to dispel the attitude, which might be called solidarity, that protecting jobs for auto workers was far more important than improving efficiency or even quality for the company. To those who believed that the UAW existed to make work, EI was a threat. It was a bitter turn for many who had fought the good fight through the years, but the UAW was changing with the times and it supported EI. It was not going to risk 100,000 core jobs for the sake of 25,000 or 30,000 extraneous ones. To some workers, that translated into a victory for the company.

"I don't understand that way of thinking," responded plant worker Jeff Cooper, "because we are the company."[40]

That was the new idea at Ford Motor.

———

While the pursuit of quality developed into a full-fledged corporate culture, Ford still had to survive financially. It did so in large part through strength in two areas: international operations and trucks.

While Americans struggled with high gasoline prices and rigorous foreign competition during the 1970s and early 1980s, drivers in most overseas markets were already used to both. Ford's sales around the world surged on the basis of the Fiesta, an economy car introduced in 1976. The company's first front-wheel-drive car, the compact Fiesta encompassed ideas from company outposts on practically every continent. It was developed over the course of almost three years in the early 1970s, at a cost to the company of $600,000 per day, under the watch of the man who was then chairman of Ford of Europe: Philip Caldwell.

A tremendous hit, the Fiesta was manufactured from parts made at Ford plants throughout Europe. It was assembled at Cologne, Dagenham, and Ford's newest automobile manufacturing plant in Valencia, Spain. At the same time that the little compact was helping boost Ford to first place in sales in Europe, Ford developed a reputation for advanced design, especially in Germany.

Although American vehicle operations were sinking into a quagmire in the late 1970s, Ford of Europe was an exciting place to be, where cars were actually still fun to make. Sales were so strong that subsidiaries were not only sending a portion of profits back to Dearborn, but extending loans to the home office, as well.

Most of the same things could be said for the truck division in the United States. Don Petersen, who had been appointed general manager in 1971, explained the dubious privilege of working there at the time: "The truck division was traditionally where they sent you if you weren't on the fast track. The car division was the glamour side of the business. . . . The atmosphere [in trucks] was positive because these people had come to know one another well and had found they liked working on trucks.

"In my four years in the truck division," Petersen continued, "I discovered that any organization can function better if people work together with a common goal of serving the customer instead of playing political games."[41]

Looked at from another point of view, Petersen, Caldwell, and other executives once relegated to trucks were given the opportunity to develop a management style in isolation from the passenger-car division, which was generally chasing its tail. In 1982, Ford historian David Lewis asked Henry II why the truck division had been so successful during the 1970s. "I think the whole answer is that the truck business has been left alone. Top management hasn't interfered," Henry II laughed, "to the extent that it has on passenger cars. We've had a series of good managers in our truck business, and they've more or less been free to manage."[42]

In 1968, Ford passed Chevrolet as the bestselling truck in the United States, and it has stayed in first place with only one interruption ever since. Leading the industry in truck sales was to become a stupendous asset, especially as the market for trucks continued to grow on several fronts. Full-size pickup trucks weren't staying down on the farm, but were perceived as bargain-price everyday vehicles for more urban drivers. In addition, Ford copied the Japanese introduction of the small truck, with the Ranger. All along the way, the company developed the market for sports-utility vehicles, with the Bronco, and produced another solid hit with its Econoline vans.

By the late 1970s, trucks accounted for more than a third of Ford's vehicle sales in the United States—and almost half of the company's profits.[43] In the bleak years when there were no profits in cars for the company, Ford trucks proved just how strong they really were by helping to hold up the company's sagging ledgers. The bean counters at Ford learned to appreciate trucks, which were more resistant to foreign competition than passenger cars. That was partly because Ford's trucks were well made and couldn't be easily dismissed on account of quality. Second, customers tended to prefer domestic truck brands; many businesses that bought trucks wanted to be seen "buying American." Third, truck customers didn't dicker over the price or demand discounts to the extent that car customers did, so the profit margin on trucks was substantial.

In the early 1980s, when Ford's passenger-car lines were trying to rebound from a market share of 16.6 percent, the company's trucks commanded a 40 percent market share. "What's been holding Ford together is trucks," said Mac Gordon, an analyst who published a newsletter about the automobile industry.[44]

From 1980 to 1982, Ford Motor lost both money and respect in the industrial world. Widely considered an outdated company, it seemed that Ford had been left behind in the rush to imports. Certainly, there were still people around who bought Ford cars, but it seemed that no one was *talking* about Fords. No excitement emanated out of Dearborn, only a kind of shame. Edsel Ford II, the son of Henry II, was in his thirties then, working in product planning. With his father's gift for candor, he observed, "People thought we built boring cars."[45] That was when the company had no choice but to carry over plans put in place in the 1970s.

Ford Motor quietly changed its ways during these three years. The transformation wasn't necessarily apparent to the outside world, but within the company morale was growing. "I don't think we can become the biggest," said Red Poling. "But I think we can become the best."[46] In 1983, the company was ready to show how. It sprang five aero-styled models, including the Tempo and Topaz, onto the market. As with the Ranger and Bronco II, the Tempo models were developed for production with input from line workers. The rounded styling of the models attracted attention, and the solid ride they offered on the road closed many a deal. Helped along by Japan's self-imposed quotas on automobile exports, Ford's new models sold even better than projected, and Dearborn almost immediately gained back 2 percentage points of its lost market share.

When the company reported its financial results for 1983, the business world was stunned—Ford Motor posted *earnings* of $1.8 billion. It was not only a surprise end to the streak of three bad years, but the biggest profit ever reported in Dearborn. "Certainly, 1983 has been a godsend," Philip Caldwell said, "compared to 1982 and previous years." He thought 1984 might turn out to be even better and he was right, as Ford earned $3 billion that year. Caldwell's combination of cost cuts had lowered the break-even point for vehicles by an astonishing 40 percent. In 1979, the automaker had to sell 3.5 million cars and trucks before it turned a profit. By 1983, that number was down to 2.5 million. And that made it very possible to earn a profit. Caldwell's emphasis on quality made it almost a certainty.

Ford proudly released statistical research on quality that showed it had gone from worst to first within the Big Three; from that point on, it was aiming to outstrip the imports, especially those from Japan. Fear of the Japanese and the loss of jobs had helped inspire Ford auto workers to make the start on quality. However, when profit-sharing checks of $400 were distributed to factory workers on the basis of the 1983 results, followed by $2,000 the next year, the company gained 100,000 full-fledged partners in the drive for quality. The improvements that workers were making, they were finally making for themselves.

Patrick Bedard wrote in a column for *Car and Driver* in the summer of 1985, "Near as I can tell, cars all have pretty much the same stuff: paint on the top, wheels on the bottom, seats on the inside, taillights on the outside and on like that. . . .

"About two years ago," Bedard continued, "I noticed that some cars were different. They were missing something. They didn't sound like a Yuban can of lock washers when I drove them down the road. They were quiet, like bananas. And every time I found myself in a car like that and looked down to see what I was driving, there was a blue Ford oval."[47]

And that was four months before the introduction of the Taurus, the car that would put not only Ford Motor but the whole American automobile industry back in front.

35

Team Taurus

In the 1980s, while GM was suffering from a bout of inertia and Chrysler was congratulating itself simply for surviving, the success of Ford Motor Company meant something important, not just within the automobile industry but to U.S. business as a whole. For years, Americans had been fed a diet of dismal news on the theme that the nation's manufacturing expertise was crumbling and that the future belonged to the service sector. For a while, it seemed that there was nothing the American worker could do right—and nothing the Japanese worker did wrong. With the robust return of Ford, however, even the most cynical observers had to admit that the United States still knew its business. Remarkably, a blue-collar company from a Rust Belt city turned into a model for the modern economy. "I found the decade of the 1980s extremely satisfying," recalled Don Petersen, who succeeded Philip Caldwell as CEO in 1985. "The policy steps that President Ronald Reagan took allowed us to excel again as a company. He brought inflation down and cut taxes so working people could afford family sedans again."[1]

The car that brought Ford's message to the streets was the Taurus, the most significant American car of the 1980s. At its launch in late 1985, the Taurus (with its sibling, the Mercury Sable) surprised the market simply by standing as a statement of competence and, more than that, of self-confidence. The notion of a high-quality American model was downright startling back then, but in making it a reality, Ford pried open a door that had slammed shut for many customers in the early 1980s. For the company, the Taurus had been an enormous risk. "Had the Taurus not worked," Philip Caldwell said, "we would have been finished as a company. It would have been a desperate situation."[2]

The Taurus/Sable represented a complete departure from previous Big Three cars. First, there was the styling, which was rounded, flush, and avant-garde to a degree that Ford had not projected since Edsel Ford was spotted driving around Florida in the original Lincoln Continental. Styling, as such, wasn't new as a selling point, but it was where the Taurus left Detroit behind. Instead of making its splash through the traditional American method of troweling cubic inches onto the engine, it offered hundreds of details throughout, reflecting thorough planning and fine build-quality: for example, a wide-open door could be shut with the force of a single pinkie; moreover, it latched easily . . . and it made a satisfying *clunk* when it did.

The Taurus left behind the days when owners might brag about the number of cylinders, even while learning to ignore phantom rattles. The boasting it inspired concerned something that didn't show up on a window sticker: a solid feel. It may have been the first American car sold on a long list of subtleties. "If we were to describe the Taurus's design in a word, the word is thoughtful," noted *Consumer Reports* in May 1986. "The automaker clearly studied the features of the world's cars and chose the best for its Taurus/Sable."[3]

The introduction of the Taurus affected the entire domestic automobile market, marking a distinct change in the general attitude toward American cars. No longer could they be dismissed out of hand, with an approving nod toward Japan or Europe. The Taurus/Sable was nothing less than a sure sign that Detroit was coming back.

The Taurus era at Ford Motor Company began with a visit that Don Petersen paid to Jack Telnack in the North American Automotive Operations design studio shortly after he became president in 1980. Telnack, a lean, dapper man, had a natural ebullience that complemented Petersen's more quiet but equally amiable nature. Working every day in the design studio, located behind the Henry Ford Museum and Library, Jack Telnack was not far from home—in any sense. Born at the Henry Ford Hospital in 1937, he grew up in Dearborn and his father once worked at the River Rouge plant. Cars, and especially Fords, would be his life's work. "When I was in high school, I fell in love with the 1941 Lincoln Continental but I couldn't afford one and neither could my father," Telnack recalled, referring to the early 1950s. "I remember showing him the car and saying, 'Dad, buy one.' I fell in love with a burgundy one with a tan convertible top on it. Well, he bought a burgundy Ford instead of a Lincoln. I'll never forget it. But I wasn't satisfied. When I turned sixteen, my first car was a '41 Mercury convertible—twelve years old at the time. I bought myself a welding torch and cut the body off the frame and channeled it. I dropped it six inches on the frame and tried to get it to look like a Lincoln Continental." After studying at the Art Center College of Design in Pasadena on a Ford scholarship, Telnack returned to Dearborn at the age of twenty-one to start work as a designer. "The first person I worked for at the Ford studios in 1948 was designer Alex Tremulis," Telnack recalled. "He had designed many cars before he came to Ford, including Duesenbergs and the first Tucker. He was really a strong advocate of aerodynamic design, even back then." Telnack's star rose quickly, catching the attention of Philip Caldwell and Don Petersen. He contributed to the Mustang, Maverick, and Pinto models before taking assignments in Australia and Europe. "In Europe," he recalled, "we were doing the first slant-backed front end in any Ford product, any place in the world. My direction at the time was 'Always do vertical front ends.'"[4]

By the time Telnack returned to Dearborn in 1976, he was a manager and no longer a designer per se. He was the arbiter, who moved the staff toward certain broad ideas. That wasn't easy in 1980, when he was in charge of the 550 people who created styling for Ford's U.S. passenger cars. "The whole design approach at that time was to fill out the cube," he later explained, perhaps indicating why the Ford Fairmont was known in enthusiast circles as the "Squaremont."

"You'd just try to make the car as wide as you could," Telnack said. "There was no taper either in the side view or the plan [overhead] view."[5] Future Thunderbirds and Cougars in the forms of overembellished blocks were the designs he was pointing out when Don Petersen asked a blunt and now legendary question: "Are you really happy with what you're doing here?"

Telnack had a ready answer. "No," he said.[6]

Petersen replied, according to Telnack, "'Well, if that isn't what you like, what would you like to do?' I said, 'Give me a couple of weeks and I'll show you.'"[7]

Philadelphia Inquirer reporter Mary Walton, in her 1997 book *Car*, described the famed Ford Motor Design Center as Telnack went to work. "From the outside it was an undistinguished low-slung redbrick building without windows," Walton wrote. "Within, it was larger than life, with dimensions sized to cars, not people. The corridors were fifteen feet wide so cars and trucks could drive through them. There was a huge domed showroom equipped with eight turntables and a sound-and-light system for mini auto shows; on the walls of the showroom lobby were full-length portraits of Edsel Ford with son William Clay Ford."[8]

At the design center Jack Telnack gathered sketches his staff had made on the sly, enthusiastically depicting Thunderbirds with shape, rather than geometry. Once Petersen had seen them, he took steps to liberate the designers. They no longer had to follow the industry formula, which was then set by GM, or even continue with any preset "Ford" themes. In effect, the staff was forbidden to do only one thing: continuing to turn out cubes. "We just had to get the basic thinking and implementing back in the hands of our professional people," recalled Petersen. "There had been so many superimposed requirements, so many ideas about what sorts of things had to be accomplished, that bit by bit it had choked off their initiative and creativity. And so part of what I tried to do was encourage the technical people and the design people to go ahead and express what it was that they thought we ought to be doing."[9]

In a sense, Petersen was doing the same thing with the professional staff that he was actively trying to do with the wage earners: pay them for being much more than robots. He wanted 100 percent of what they had to offer in terms of ideas about Ford cars. His boss, Philip Caldwell, was in agreement. Whenever the CEO visited the studios, Telnack recalled, he emphasized that the company could not build a new foundation on old designs. "We're shaping a new corporation here," Caldwell would say. "We have to make a strong statement with our products. I really want you guys to show me something different."[10]

The result was aerodynamic styling, which was so arresting that Red Poling, chief of North American Automotive Operations, had to think about ways to let customers grow accustomed to it. In 1980, Poling laid out a program that would give Ford Motor a predominantly new, aerodynamic lineup by the middle of the decade. Starting with the well-received 1983 Thunderbird, and then the Continental Mark VII and the Tempo/Topaz in following years, the market embraced the aero look in stages. It was so different in its time, however, that even the designers were apt to lose their nerve. "We had to force the designers to keep their hands off the '83 Bird once it was done," Telnack said. "There was a real temptation to go back and start putting in all those traditional clues that we felt comfortable with."[11] However, simplicity was the key to Ford's aero look, and part of Telnack's role was making that reminder from time to time.

The stylists weren't the only ones charged with creating a car in a new way—one that they actually *liked*. Early in the development of the Taurus, Ford Motor Company undertook an expansive study. According to Addison Guthrie, chief engineer for luxury and midsize cars, the company purchased "all the cars in the world that we thought had some neat features one way or another."[12] The total number was more than fifty.[13] Only a few were made by Ford or its international subsidiaries; the rest came from elsewhere, including Audi, Saab, Honda, Chevrolet, Opel (GM's German subsidiary), and Toyota.

Known as the Best-in-Class program, it was nothing if not a well-organized effort. Hundreds of Ford planners, engineers, suppliers, assembly workers, and others participated, separating into "juries" and judging the cars on very distinct points. Ford cars only occasionally won. At the Best-in-Class clinics, it was by no means impolitic to praise competitors' cars. In Ford's opinion, for example, the Toyota Cressida had the "best front armrest comfort." The Opel Senator had the best armrest comfort in the backseat. The Nissan Maxima won in the category of "best oil filter accessibility." The Audi 100 took the honors in "best accelerator pedal feel."[14] The list went on through more than 400 such minute factors. The Audi 100 happened to win Best-in-Class in more categories than any other model, but that didn't matter. The test was all about specifics.

The Best-in-Class program put the emphasis on the small factors so long overlooked in American automaking. While very few people buy a car on the basis of the comfort level of the front seat armrests, excellence in 400 such nuances drove Ford toward a cohesion of standards in the new Taurus. Through widespread participation in the clinics, employees and suppliers knew that nothing was insignificant on the Taurus. As a result, the company later boasted that the completed Taurus/Sable would have won Best-in-Class in 80 percent of the categories. (A perfect score was impossible because excellence in certain categories necessitated some sort of compromise in others.)

The overriding theme of the Taurus lay in looking at the car from the customer's point of view. At the time, that was a lost art in Detroit, but one that company executives were determined to revive. At ten distinct points during the Taurus's five-year incubation period, Ford researchers surveyed consumers and listened to panels as part of the most extensive research program ever organized around a single model.[15]

The research program was launched from on high with the stroke of a pen. A far greater challenge for Ford management lay in convincing employees to constantly approach the new models from the customer's point of view. According to Al Guthrie, "Mr. Caldwell would continually ask . . . 'Why should I buy a Taurus?' That got us making doggone sure that the car was going to be customer-oriented."[16] In addition to making the new model appealing to the customer (as either driver or passenger), attention was paid to making it accessible to home mechanics. Dipsticks and other service points under the hood were color-coded, and whenever possible, maintenance parts were designed to be replaced without tools.[17]

The Taurus charted as much new ground in organization as it did in attitude. On previous models, departments worked in isolation from one another: product planners, engineers, designers, production managers, suppliers, plant employees, marketers, and the sales force were like stages on an assembly line that created new models. In "Team Taurus," expertise from each area was available simultaneously. It put a strain on scheduling and communications, but had the benefit of allowing employees to solve problems sooner, rather than later, and make suggestions while they were still viable. The man overseeing it all was Lewis Veraldi, the vice president for vehicle development and the captain of Team Taurus.

Like Jack Telnack, who joked that he was born with a blue oval on his chest, Lew Veraldi had roots with Ford Motor going back even before he was hired by the company. As a teenager in the mid-1940s, he studied at the Henry Ford Trade School in Dearborn. After a stint in the Army, he took a job as a file clerk in Ford's engineering department. By the end of the 1950s, he was known as a clever chassis engineer, but as he worked his way up in the ranks, his focus shifted to responsibilities in manufacturing. Veraldi's specialty was straddling engineering and manufacturing. The two made a natural pair in Veraldi's mind, but he was practically the only one around who thought so. "I went from the design engineering to the manufacturing end of the business," he said. "Traditionally, when you engineer a car, you design it, you release it and you give the drawing to the manufacturer and say, 'Here, go make it.' It was always a sequential process: you did everything in segments. Every time you handed off a design or released a drawing the next area down the stream always had trouble with it."[18] Eventually Veraldi came to resent what he called "this segmentation, this sequential effect" as a wholly unnecessary burden.

Veraldi was assigned to Ford of Europe in the 1970s to oversee the development of the Fiesta. Segmentation was not only problematical there, it was downright treacherous, as design engineers were banned from setting foot in assembly plants. Veraldi found ways to bridge the gaps between the two feuding departments. Once he returned to Dearborn and took responsibility for shepherding the Taurus, he extended the development team to include a representative from every aspect of automaking. It was a far cry from the system that had produced the Pinto by "freezing" the general dimensions and then denying engineers the chance to make adjustments.

Team Taurus was in the enviable, if daunting, position of having a blank page on which to work: the engine, the chassis, and other components were to be custom-designed just for the new model. The alternative, building the car out of parts left over from other Fords, was far more cost-effective—and for a company quaking under record losses, that was a tempting route. However, Caldwell, Petersen, and Poling had convinced the board of directors that the only way to build a new corporation was by starting from scratch, at least in the case of the midsize Taurus, which was slated to take the place of the larger LTD as the "standard" Ford car. The board agreed, authorizing a $3.25 billion spending program. As Lew Veraldi put it, with only slight exaggeration, "We decided we had better do something far-reaching—or go out of business."[19]

Based on customer input, one of the earliest decisions regarding the new model was to make it a front-wheel-drive car, Ford's first in the midsize range. That decision underscored the fact that the Taurus was to be all-new. "There was really very little that we could hope to use or carryover," recalled John Risk, director of product planning. "Sure, we had targets in terms of cost, weight, and particularly profit. But I can't recall any instance where we were compromised by not being able to execute the best design that we felt was possible by one of our target levels in terms of cost or whatever."[20]

As a matter of fact, the Taurus and Sable were originally planned as smallish cars, in anticipation of gasoline prices of $3 or more per gallon. However, when fuel prices stabilized at about $1.25, the new models had room to grow. Due to the flexibility offered by the Team Taurus structure, the shift was made without much ado. One aspect of Team Taurus that is baffling in retrospect is that it brought together interior and exterior stylists for the first time. Amazingly, designers on previous models had been largely oblivious of each other's work. The designer in charge of the Taurus/Sable interiors was Mimi Vandermolen, a Hollander by birth who was raised in Canada. A car fanatic since childhood, she studied industrial design at college and then joined Ford Motor in 1970.[21] (It was the first company that hadn't asked her whether she could type.)[22] Ford wanted Vandermolen as a designer, first of Philco products and soon afterward of Ford cars, including some work on the Mustang in the 1970s. Overseeing the Taurus interior, she became a disciple of the emerging art of ergonomics: making sure that every control was easily at hand, and that it felt *right* to the touch.

Vandermolen's team devoted most of one year to the part of the car that affects customers more directly than any other: the seats. Like the interior as a whole, the seats were intended to be roomy. "I wanted seats you can sit in for ten hours straight," Vandermolen explained. "If you're uncomfortable on long trips, no matter how great everything else is, you're unhappy."[23]

By the 1980s, no one rose high in the ranks of Ford Motor Company without first gaining experience overseas, especially at Ford of Europe. Red Poling, for example, had worked for Ford of Europe from 1972 to 1979. "Japanese cars were making inroads in Europe during those years," Poling remembered. "You could see that they would soon flood the American market."[24] Lew Veraldi, for his part, had never even been to Europe before he was assigned to work there. All of the executives who guided the Taurus understood something about European cars, and how they differed from American Fords. Petersen, in particular, was adamant that compared with the average European vehicle, American cars "had a numbness to them, a lack of association for the driver with the automobile."[25] As the ultimate product planner of the Taurus, he wanted Veraldi's engineers to produce a car that was intriguing to drive, just as he wanted Telnack's designers to produce one that was intriguing to see. The engineering of the new model, often overlooked because of the unique styling, was as much a departure from old Detroit ways as the bodywork.

Ten years after the first gas crisis, Ford and other automakers were employing computer technology and other innovations to coax more power from an engine, even while it burned less gas. The 1986 Taurus was 1,600 pounds lighter than its 1970s predecessor, the LTD, while delivering only slightly less horsepower from an engine one half as big. In other words, the power-to-weight ratio was even better on the Taurus than on the big-engined LTD. Similarly, the Taurus was fifteen inches shorter and nine inches narrower than the LTD, yet it had a comparably roomy interior, due in large measure to the adoption of front-wheel drive. As a result, the Taurus's gas mileage was 60 percent higher than that of the LTD[26]—this was a crucial achievement for

Ford Motor, which had lost its struggle to meet CAFE standards in 1985,[27] the year before the Taurus had an impact on the fleet average.

The most noticeable result of the Taurus's blank-page engineering was in the steering and suspension. The new model went exactly where it was pointed, and not just generally in the right direction. That was something very new to American cars, which were designed to shield the driver as much as possible from the feel of the road. However, some sensation from the steering wheel, and a general connection to the terrain beneath the tires, actually made driving easier, as import buyers were finding out in droves during the early 1980s. The scrutiny of the Taurus suspension made it a car with, as one reviewer later wrote, "rather amazing handling. . . . Even the best German sedans are not better than this."[28]

The Taurus might be summed up as Ford's attempt to build a European car, using Japanese-style manufacturing methods, for the American market. "Our goal was twofold," Poling recalled. "Quality followed by cost was what caused the company's resurgence."[29]

The styling of the Taurus never again seemed as modern as it did when it was first unveiled during pre-production in 1985, but that is only because it was so successful in ushering in a new era. The flush windows and lights, integral bumpers, and rounded, unadorned bodywork anticipated ever more organic shapes from other automakers for years to come. The only other 1986 model to set the same pace of change, and with much the same style, was the Audi 5000. Telnack insisted that despite similarities, especially in the flush window treatment, the Ford was created without influence from the German car. To CEO Don Petersen the Taurus had what he called the "greenhouse effect," a smooth external design that exuded clean comfort and Japanese-like efficiency.[30]

However, there was a crisis early on—or at least, what seemed to have been a crisis. When the body styling was nearly finished, customer surveys revealed that many people rejected it as being "too different." At Chrysler, CEO Lee Iacocca saw a prototype and scoffed, "It looks like a potato." A high-ranking GM executive deemed the Taurus "that jelly bean." Rejection didn't spook Jack Telnack at all, though. "We wanted customers to feel a little bit uncomfortable with the design," he said,[31] explaining that when a certain percentage of people—not too many, but not too few—regard a car as exotic, the style has a good chance of remaining modern for years. "These critics were still sticking to their hard-box designs, and all I said at the time of the Taurus was 'Look out, competition, you won't have any choice. You'll have to follow it.'"[32]

The first plant selected for final assembly of the Taurus was in Atlanta. Chicago was selected soon after. Remarkably, both factories were originally built to produce Model Ts. Rather than construct new buildings, Ford's plan was to renovate old plants by increasing the use of computer technology, robots, and overall automation. Although the Taurus was designed with efficient assembly in mind—it had 1,700 fewer parts than the LTD[33]—the emphasis on quality delayed the original Job One production date three times during 1985.

Once the design work was finished, the headquarters of Team Taurus moved from Detroit to Atlanta. Petersen was often there and he used to wander around the assembly plant asking workers for productivity suggestions. "The people on the line kept saying, 'Why can't you leave the damn doors off the body until the very end? They get in our way.' It was a good question and it led to door assembly lines, which ran in conjunction with the main assembly line. It's amazing that we had never thought of that in Dearborn." One oldtime UAW worker suggested to the new CEO that the factory use a uniform screw for all Taurus parts instead of twenty-five different sizes, which inevitably caused confusion on the assembly line. "We really were a team," Petersen recalled. "Now thousands of Ford employees claim they helped create the Taurus. There is no one person who should get credited for the success."[34]

Job One was completed in November 1985, and the Taurus was finally a reality. To celebrate, Ford Motor held a week-long series of parades and media events in Atlanta. Due in part to the efficiencies of the team approach, the cost of developing the new vehicle was actually under budget, at $2.9 billion.[35] Still, that was enough of a gamble for Ford Motor, which had no room in its fortunes for a failure. Nonetheless, the company had to wait a month to find out whether paying customers would accept the Taurus. Having missed the traditional autumn season for model introductions, Ford had no choice but to wait out the Christmas holiday. But not by much: the Taurus and Sable were scheduled for launch on December 26. Most dealers accumulated cars in stock before then but were forbidden to actually sell them until the day after Christmas.[36]

Meanwhile car magazines ran glowing reviews, based on hand-built prototypes supplied by the factory. "This Ford repudiates everything LTD ever stood for," *Car and Driver* marveled in its October issue, as though that were the highest form of praise. The article then ran through a point-by-point analysis of why, in its words, "this family hauler is easily the gutsiest car of our time.

"A full road test will be in your mailbox as soon as real cars are available," the *Car and Driver* review concluded, referring to the long-awaited factory-built Tauruses. "If you buy something else in the meantime, don't say we didn't warn you."[37]

"It stands out in the material landscape," *Business Week* claimed in a glowing cover story. "The sleek, elegant lines of a liquid black automobile as it slips around a curve. The difference is design, that elusive blend of form and function, quality and style, art and engineering. Was this product created in famous design studios of Paris, Munich, Milan or Turin? No. The car is a Ford Sable from Detroit."[38]

Ford was hoping for sales of about 500,000 Tauruses and Sables per year. By December 26, the company already had a gratifying 103,000 orders in hand. In an understated, button-down, 1980s way, the excitement surrounding the Taurus was reminiscent of Ford's best new-model introductions from the Model A to the Mustang. Perhaps the police didn't have to be called, as they were in 1928, and Wilson Pickett didn't sing about Taurus Sally taking a joyride, but more than half of the American public knew about the new Fords, according to a survey, and showrooms were crowded that first week after Christmas. Fred Griffith, who hosted a television show in Cleveland, went on the air to show off his new Taurus, bought after twenty years of driving imported cars. "It goes around corners like it's on rails," he told his audience, "something I've never been able to say about an American car before."[39]

Along with the two-month backlog on orders, the sweetest sign for Ford that the Taurus/Sable was a success came in the response of competitors. GM, the old master, got in line behind the new Taurus, immediately making changes to its models in an attempt to give them the modern look of the new Fords, but little could be done in the short term. One designer at GM's tech center in Warren, Michigan, estimated that the Taurus gave Ford a two-year head start in styling.[40] Meanwhile, Ford dealers everywhere had cause for celebration. "It was extremely exciting," salesman Gil Trainor of Don Bohn Ford in Harvey, Louisiana, recalled. "You have to use all the psychology in the world to figure out what the public wants. The Taurus was it. Its major selling point was that it was a midsize car with a front-wheel drive."[41] Jim Click of Tuttle-Click's Automobile Group in Tucson, Arizona, was more succinct: "It revitalized our entire business. It was a wild, wild success."[42]

After production finally managed to catch up to demand in 1987, the Taurus was the most popular car in the United States,[43] a position it would occupy often over the following dozen years. For all of the attention paid to quality, however, early on the Taurus/Sable had reliability problems, which Ford tried to answer through immediate repairs where necessary. Within three years, improvements had been made. With the approval of the Better Business Bureau, Ford was able to claim that the Taurus and Sable were "the best-built cars in America, from 1981–89."[44]

And, in fact, the company was claiming more than that. In a 1989 interview, Red Poling offered that Ford was a "major contributor" to the "tremendous improvement in morale" that blossomed nationwide during the Reagan years.[45] Philip Caldwell saw the situation the same way. "The company was in desperate shape at the end of the 1970s," he recalled. "The situation was sad. We had terrible quality problems. But by the time Reagan left office we were on top. Both Ford and the economy were booming."[46] The Ford turnaround, the top executives believed, was symbolic of the decade in which America put the dreaded days of Vietnam and Watergate behind it and won the Cold War. "Any way you slice it," Petersen noted years later, "there was no more exciting automobile company to work for in the 1980s than Ford."[47]

Apparently Ronald Reagan felt the same way. On April 11, 1984, he arrived at the Ford Claycomo Assembly Plant in Kansas City, Missouri, to deliver a stump speech. It was a fitting working-class venue at which to celebrate economic rebirth. When Ford Motor Company built its initial factory in Kansas City in 1906, it was the first branch assembly facility in the automobile industry. In 1957 Ford sold it, but later opened a new factory in the city. It grew to cover over 4.5 million square feet and employ over 5,000 workers in the manufacture of Tempo/Topaz cars and F-series trucks. With a giant Ford banner behind him, Reagan took to the podium as UAW workers cheered. Wearing a Ford baseball cap given to him by Philip Caldwell, Reagan talked about the greatness of Ford Motor Company. "There was a time when Claycomo nearly had to shut down," Reagan intoned. "But today almost 5,000 people are working two ten-hour shifts, producing 86 cars and trucks an hour, 1,600 a day. You're continuing a Ford tradition that began here in Kansas City in 1906 with nearly 7 million cars built in all. And whatever you may have heard about my age, I wasn't here at the time. But you're not getting older, you're getting better."[48] After the speech he dined with UAW workers in the cafeteria.[49] It was a day Caldwell would never forget. "The workers were Democratic," Caldwell recalled. "But Reagan won them over. One chap kept saying 'I don't believe it' over and over again. Then he started saying loudly 'What will I tell my mother?' in rote fashion. Finally, Reagan answered him: 'Tell her I voted for FDR four times before I became a Republican.'"[50]

———

At the beginning of 1985, before the introduction of the Taurus, Philip Caldwell reached the mandatory retirement age of sixty-five. He had been at the helm only a few years, but he left a very different company from the one he had found, transformed and invigorated. The $4.8 billion that Ford Motor earned in 1983–1984 more than made up for the $4.4 billion it had lost the preceding four years.[51] Moreover, Ford was as bold as it had ever been before. In dismantling the remnants of the star system at Ford, and in placing a new emphasis on team spirit and individual contribution, it was hard to tell where Philip Caldwell left off and Donald Petersen began. Both believed firmly in the need to set fundamental goals and then achieve them through the widespread involvement of the workforce.

When Caldwell retired, Petersen, at the age of fifty-eight, took his place as chairman and CEO, while Red Poling moved into the president's office. It was the first time in the history of Ford Motor Company that there had been a peaceful transition of power. No one had to be fired, squeezed out, or forced to resign. No one had to get sick or die, either. After eighty-two years in business, Ford Motor had finally learned that power could be passed without an accompanying war. "Grown-ups understood that sometimes you have to let go," Caldwell recalled. "What was essential was that the company move forward in a spirited, hassle-free way."[52]

For Henry Ford II, the orderly transition of power was an important aspect of the legacy he often said he hoped to leave at the company. He wanted to be remembered for developing a solid organization, not so much in terms of specific people, but in the executive structure. "He cared about the company as an institution," longtime Ford executive Peter Pestillo said of Henry II. "He truly was a man without pretense. He thought of everybody who worked for his company—management and labor—as equals."[53]

In retirement, Henry II spent time with his third wife, Kathy, at homes in Florida and rural England. He traveled extensively to visit Ford plants around the world in a kind of ongoing farewell tour. Due to his lifelong commitment to Israel, and minority rights overall, the Anti-Defamation League of B'nai B'rith gave Henry Ford II its American Heritage Award in 1980. The awards ceremony was held at New York's Waldorf-Astoria Hotel, with CBS News anchor Walter Cronkite hosting the presentation in a *This Is Your Life* format. Adjacent to the ballroom, in a reception area, a 1913 Model T was showcased, signifying the year that the ADL was founded "to end the defamation of the Jewish people and to secure justice and fair treatment for all citizens alike." A long list of friends and acquaintances heaped praise on Henry II, including Marian Sulzberger Heiskell of the New York Times Company, Maxwell E. Greenberg of the ADL, New York Governor Hugh Carey, and Rabbi Ronald Sobel of New York City's Temple Emanu-El.[54]

Reaching out to those dealt real harm by his grandfather's vitriol was one of the finest legacies of Henry Ford II's life and work. Philip Slomovitz, editor of the *Jewish News* in Detroit, was a reporter at the *Detroit News* in the 1920s, when the elder Henry Ford was making his attack on Jews in the *Dearborn Independent*. "Henry Ford II has done a great deal to atone for the sins of his grandfather," he said. Richard Lobenthal of the Anti-Defamation League in Detroit noted, "Every Jew I know who knew him told me on the basis of their personal, long-standing relationship with Henry II that he didn't have an anti-Semitic bone in his body." Henry II was still known in Israel as the industrialist who boldly stood up to the Arab boycott, and ultimately triumphed over it. By July 1987 Ford had created dealerships in seven Middle Eastern nations, including Saudi Arabia, Jordan, and Kuwait.[55]

Two years after the change in Ford's leadership and one year after the introduction of the Taurus, Henry Ford II contracted pneumonia, possibly as a result of being infected with Legionnaires' disease while traveling in Europe.[56] On September 29, 1987, less than a month after his seventieth birthday and after two weeks of treatment at the Henry Ford Hospital, he died. (It was exactly thirty-seven years to the day since his grandmother Clara Ford had passed away.) Seemingly unafraid of death, he approached it very quietly, though during his last few days he was heavily sedated. Under headlines such as "Detroit Loses a Legend," "The Last Tycoon," and "Auto Industry Giant," newspapers all over the world published lead obituaries about Henry II, trying to recount the life of a man who had been a knight-errant in his youth, saving a company and 100,000 workers from ruin. Later in life, he caught up with the carefree days he'd missed in his twenties. "A complex man known for his blunt talk and common tastes as well as his flamboyant life-style and unabashed indulgence, Ford leaves a legacy of industrial renaissance at the company that bears his name and reputation for dogged, if less successful, struggle on behalf of the city of his birth," the *Detroit Free Press* summarized in a ten-page obituary.[57] As Mayor Coleman Young ordered Detroit's flags flown at half-mast, tributes came pouring in from all corners. General Motors Chairman Roger Smith praised his leadership in labor relations, Chrysler Chairman Lee Iacocca talked about his hyperkinetic work ethic, and President Reagan lamented that the auto industry had lost a giant.[58] Even consumer activists Ralph Nader and Joan Claybrook praised him for his uncompromising candor. Edsel Ford II, who was then sales manager for the Lincoln-Mercury Division, honored the least well known side of Henry II's famously complex personality in announcing his father's death: "He was also a loving husband, father and grandfather," Edsel said in his remarks. "I know he cared for his wife, Kathy, as well as my sisters and myself. I also know that he held a very special place in his heart for his grandchildren."[59]

Two years before, when a television interviewer asked Henry II to comment on the odds of Edsel II becoming chairman someday, he almost inadvertently described his own life, as he perceived it: "If you want to take on this job of wanting to go all the way in the Ford Motor Co., you've got to marry the Ford Motor Company. There's nothing else in between, and it's a tough job. It's very time-consuming and it's a dedicated kind of a proposition. You've got to give up all the other things and really make that your number one, and some people don't want to do that."

"Did you?" the interviewer pressed.

"I did," he said.

"Marry the company?"

"That's right," Henry II said.[60]

According to Henry II's videotaped instructions, a private service was held at the same St. Paul's Episcopal Cathedral where the first Henry Ford's funeral had been held forty years before. A few days later, a memorial service celebrated the life of the automaker, closing with his favorite song, "When the Saints Go Marching In," played by the Preservation Hall Jazz Band of New Orleans. (He once had Nat "King" Cole sing the song at the debut party of one of his daughters.) Ford factories around the world observed three minutes of silence on the day of the memorial service, and flags at Ford factories and other Detroit-area businesses were flown at half-mast. *Newsweek* reporter Jim Jones explained Henry II the best when he said he was "American royalty who wanted no part of it."[61] "He had made friends all over the world," his daughter Anne Ford recalled. "For decades he'd get home at 8:00 at night and take over for a few hours. He was married to the company. He'd be up at 6:00 A.M. rushing off to work again. He used to say he wasn't smart, but he had street smarts and people liked him."[62]

Stories about Henry Ford II's colorful life filled the pages of the Detroit newspapers after his death. Ford Foundation executive Fred Friendly saw him as a "man etched with candor," while gossip columnist Liz Smith considered his behavior "vulgar." John Bugas, a good friend and Ford executive for three decades, conceded that Henry II was difficult, that he "seethed and stayed sore for a long time." His close business associate Max Fisher believed that Ford just couldn't "stand a phony," that he could "spot them a mile away." But the most historically important tribute came from retired UAW President Douglas Fraser, who had once maligned a GM chairman as a "horse's ass." His views on Henry II couldn't have been more different. "He was more of a maverick—in the best sense of the word—than other corporate leaders," Fraser believed. "Very early on he was interested in community affairs. He worked with Walter Reuther when you couldn't find other executives."[63] According to Fraser, Henry II was a true Democrat who signed on to all of the Great Society programs, fund-raising for leading Michigan politicians seeking office as Democrats. "Hundreds of thousands of Ford men and women and dealers throughout the world remember the day that Henry Ford II visited their plant or office or laboratories," Ford Motor Chairman Donald Petersen told a reporter. "For nearly four decades Mr. Ford was Ford Motor."[64]

Since Henry II had not been active in management for seven years, his death had no effect on operations. All through 1986, for example, he missed corporate board meetings with stark regularity.[65] Nevertheless, his death closed out an imperious era at Ford Motor, one that had started with the first Henry Ford more than seven decades before. During that time, the two Henrys ruled with only as much opposition as they cared to entertain. In the elder Henry's case, that was not much, at all. In Henry II's case, there was a point at which he could not entertain opposition, either. Only he knew precisely when that point happened to be. During the company's first seventy-seven years, the name "Henry Ford" constituted a kind of title all by itself, giving an extra vote of intimidating seniority to the two powerful personalities who carried it. With the death of Henry II, however, a traditional and mysterious sense of privilege vanished from Ford Motor. It was a public company, just like any other.

Without question, the death of Henry Ford II left a void in the automotive industry. He was, for the most part, an old-fashioned industrialist who operated on gut instinct and with quotable candor. (When a reporter once asked what it was like competing with General Motors, he snapped, "Like trying to screw an elephant.")[66] Daily, when confronted with problems, he met them head-on, refusing to ever be perceived as a shrinking violet. On one occasion, he launched into a diatribe against the idiocy of polls and surveys. "A lot of people in the past, maybe even today, tend to say, well, this is what the survey says, and thereby relieve themselves of making a decision. I think that's bunk. If people don't think they know what the public is going to want they shouldn't be in the job."[67]

Everybody understood one thing about Henry Ford II: he had been head of the company by the right of primogeniture. "He always had been an industrial prince," David Halberstam wrote in an exclusive obituary for the *Detroit Free Press*. "With the possible exception of Nelson and David Rockefeller and Averell Harriman, no such public figure was raised in such splendor."[68] But all the artful obituaries so carefully collected at the Henry Ford Museum and Library at Greenfield Village don't tell the real story of Henry Ford II. Although the former vice chairman of Ford of Europe, Walter Hayes, wrote a useful reflection on Henry Ford II titled *Henry* in 1990, and Victor Lasky produced the biography *Never Complain, Never Explain,* there will probably never be a fully detailed book about Henry II—and for good reason. When historian David L. Lewis was interviewing Henry II during the early 1980s, he asked where his personal papers would be housed. "I'm presently destroying all my files because I don't want to have anybody get into any of my personal files." Lewis was stunned. "Say it isn't so," he pleaded. Henry II was perfectly serious. Pointing to the shredder in his office he reiterated that he was destroying "the whole goddamn thing," and was "having more fun than hell" doing it. Consequently, the best sources for understanding Henry II have been oral histories and newspaper clippings. The paper trail is thin, at best.[69]

At the time of Henry II's death, the Ford family still owned or controlled all of the Ford Class B stock (which represented 40 percent of the voting stock), although the shares were spreading out. Josephine Ford and William Clay Ford, the two remaining members of the third generation (Henry and Clara's grandchildren), owned the largest stakes, while more than a dozen members of the fourth generation were also vested in the family fortune by 1987. The cousins, as the fourth generation was sometimes called, were far-flung geographically and in terms of their interests; most had nothing to do with the automobile business. One of Henry II's daughters, Charlotte, made a mark as a writer and authority on etiquette. (Her daughter, Elena—from her first marriage, to Greek shipping tycoon Stavros Niarchos—was an executive at Lincoln-Mercury in the early 2000s.) His other daughter, Anne, lived in the New York City area and was married to WNBC television newsman Chuck Scarborough. (She had previously been married to restaurateur Giancarlo Uzielli and had two children with him—Alessandro and Allegra.)

Predictably, the *Detroit Free Press* ran a story following Henry II's death titled "Is There a Ford in Company's Future?" As the article pointed out, four of the Ford cousins were working at the car company at the time. Walter Buhl Ford III (Josephine's son), the oldest of them, worked as an advertising specialist, but did not seem to have ambitions in general management. Benson Ford Jr. was a customer-relations representative in Ford Parts and Service Division. But the two rising stars, the newspaper maintained, were Edsel Ford II and William Clay Ford Jr.[70]

Born on December 27, 1948, Edsel Ford II graduated from Babson College, a business school near Boston. He was no better as a student than his father, Henry II, had been, but like his father, he took immediately to his work at Ford Motor, where he started in 1973. Known as an amiable young man with a wide grin, Edsel made his mark in various sales departments in the company. He later took charge of marketing for Lincoln-Mercury during the launch of the Sable. "I sometimes feel like I've been working for Ford Motor since I was born," Edsel II once said, without a trace of resentment. He understood the respect—and curiosity—many people held for the Ford family. However, when the spotlight landed on the cousins, he was somewhat abashed. The unending interest, he said, "is due to what my great-grandfather did, and what my father has done for the automobile industry and for Detroit. . . . The great-grandchildren, jeez, we're just trying to do a job."[71]

Born on May 3, 1957, Bill Ford Jr. was another cousin just trying to do a job at the company in 1987. But, by all accounts, the expectations for Bill Ford Jr. to rise to the top were commonplace around World Headquarters during the Taurus era. The only concern some executives had was that he loved sports, history, and the wilderness more than manufacturing cars. Growing up in Grosse Pointe, Bill played soccer and hockey as a youth. He was also captain of the football team at Hotchkiss, the prep school he attended. "I kind of grew up out of the spotlight and had a real normal childhood," Bill Ford Jr. recalled. "Even though I grew up in a wealthy suburb like Grosse Pointe, my parents put me in Little League in St. Clair Shores, which is a much more blue-collar town. All my teammates, whether it was in football or hockey or baseball, were all guys who never went to college." What set him apart from other boys his age, besides being a Ford, was his intense infatuation with American history, particularly Abraham Lincoln, Thomas Edison, the Plains Indians, and his own ancestor, Henry Ford. His parents refused to spoil him, making him work summers for spending money. "My biggest memory of Greenfield Village growing up was that I worked as a gardener there one summer during high school and was spraying plants," he recalled decades later. "They gave me the sprayer to fertilize the plants with this blue stuff, and somebody called my name and I turned and nailed this lady in this white dress. I had to use my entire summer's earnings to buy her a new one."[72]

When it came time for choosing a college to attend, Bill Jr. decided on Princeton University. Originally a political science major, he later switched to history. His senior thesis was titled "Henry Ford and Labor: A Reappraisal."[73] It's a work he was not particularly proud of. "My thesis was a disaster," he laughed in a 1999 interview. "It's so embarrassing and the problem is it's on the public record. I wrote the thing in six days." What's fascinating about reading this thesis, however, was how attuned he was to the history of his great-grandfather as an industrial philosopher. Leading a normal college life, Bill Jr. was also studying the work of Henry Ford, learning lessons that would serve him well when he entered the business world. His favorite Ford maxim became "People Before Profits," and years later it grew into his motto. "His philosophy was you take care of your people and your profits will flow from that," he said of his great-grandfather, "and again I think that's a notion we've gotten away from as an industry and a company. I mean you're only as good as your people. It's the only sustainable advantage any company has. And if you don't treat them like they are the most important thing then you're not going to win long-term. That's something I think about *all* the time."[74]

After graduating from Princeton in 1979, Bill Jr. started working at Ford Motor Company as a product planner. He eventually gained experience in a wide array of posts in finance, sales, and manufacturing. The job he was most proud of, however, reflected back to his Princeton thesis: in 1982 he served on the company's national bargaining team in their breakthrough labor talks with the UAW. He then began an Alfred P. Sloan Fellowship at the Massachusetts Institute of Technology. "Because MIT was heavily quantitative, and I was a liberal arts grad, I think I really needed to shore up the quantitative side of my skills," Bill Jr. recalled. "I was terrified, because I was one of only two nonengineers in my class at MIT. And it worked out fine; I found out I had some kind of aptitude. I thought I was going to flunk out. Actually, fear is a great motivation. I worked really hard and actually did real well." Bill Jr. had gotten married just two weeks before the MIT program started. He and his wife, Lisa, rented a brownstone in Boston's Back Bay and started their life together. "It was a pretty wild year," he recalled. "I completed a two-year program in fifteen months."[75]

On January 14, 1988, Bill Ford Jr. became a member of the board of directors. His primary boss throughout the late 1980s was Don Petersen. "I used to send him from department to department for experience," Petersen recalled.

"I thought he was the most likely fourth-generation Ford to rise to the top. Not that he had any remarkable skill. What he had was a fine manner. He never became fully knowledgeable of any particular aspect of the company. But he was naturally bright and that can compensate for a lot."[76]

The four Fords carrying on the legacy at their family's company were the subject of constant speculation in Detroit newspapers, in terms of which of them might become chairman someday. For the time being, however, as Henry II was laid to rest, they were just another four employees at Ford Motor, charged like all the others with looking for ways to produce better cars. That was the inherited legacy of the Taurus era.

———————

Ford Motor Company's rebirth in the 1980s represented the greatest turnaround in all of business history. In terms of raw finance, the company shifted from setting a national record for losses to earning more money than any other automaker worldwide. Internally, it changed the way its employees worked together, and in doing so, it pulled off a turnaround of an even more difficult sort. Many companies through the years had sunk low, just as Ford had at the beginning of the decade. Certainly thousands of firms in the automobile business during the twentieth century had collapsed in finance, product development, and morale, just as Ford had. But none managed to bounce up as high afterward. The story of Chrysler Corporation's return to profitability contained more drama, especially in the image of Chairman Lee Iacocca repaying federally sponsored loans ahead of schedule, but in truth, Ford's resurgence took it much further.

After starting in a harrowing tie with Chrysler as the sickliest of America's major corporations, Ford Motor emerged by the end of the decade as the leader of the entire automobile industry, earning more money than General Motors in 1987. It hadn't managed that since the Model T days of 1924. In 1988, Ford Motor came close to earning more than GM and Chrysler *combined*. The success of Ford Motor was impossible to ignore. Its stock was a newfound darling on Wall Street, rising by more than thirteen times from 1980 to 1989, and business publications vied to drape Ford's leaders with honors. Company executives practically had a lock on *Automotive Industries'* Man of the Year award, taking it five times from 1982 to 1989. In *Fortune*, Philip Caldwell was labeled "Mr. Turnaround." The same magazine's poll of CEOs voted Donald Petersen the nation's most effective CEO in 1988.

What the business writers didn't notice, customers did. Over the course of the decade, Ford improved quality to the point where its cars could be compared to those of Japanese automakers: faint praise, perhaps, in an industry known for its superlatives, but ten years earlier, the two were going in drastically different directions. On California freeways, where Ford had been fading into extinction a few years before, the company claimed two of the state's three bestselling passenger cars in the middle of the decade, in the Thunderbird and the Fiesta. If Ford cars weren't yet out in front of Toyotas, Nissans, and Hondas, at least the gap was closing fast. "We were catching up to the Japanese in every regard," Don Petersen recalled. "And in every aspect we were better than General Motors."[77]

36

New Horses

T he last half of the 1980s was the good old days for Ford Motor Company. Starting in 1982, customers had been barraged by the company's jingles "Have you driven a Ford—lately?" and "At Ford Quality
Is Job 1," and they responded to them, raising Ford's market share to 22.3 percent by the end of the decade.[1] Ford cars were not only selling, they were out-
selling those of Chevrolet—by a lot—in 1988 and 1989.[2] Ford hadn't handed
Chevy such a sound thrashing since the 1920s. In Ford factories, productivity
was up and costs were down.[3] To build a Taurus/Sable, for example, Chicago
and Atlanta assembly-line workers took 24 man-hours, two-thirds the time required at GM or Chrysler plants for similar models.[4] The result of popular
models and efficient manufacturing was practically inevitable: Ford Motor
earned enormous profits. "The company was now getting out and around the
country in a way that neither it nor any other had ever done before," wrote Alton F. Doody and Ron Bingaman in *Reinventing the Wheels: Ford's Spectacular Comeback.*[5] Rather than a jingle, Ford's theme song could have been "On
the Road Again," a Willie Nelson hit that was emanating from many a car radio at the time.

In 1986, Ford Motor Company reported record profits of $3.29 billion,
more than those at General Motors, which was twice as big in terms of assets.
Part of the story, of course, was GM's problematical downturn. "Never in my
wildest imagination," Philip Caldwell recalled, "could I have foreseen how
badly GM would stumble."[6] Texas industrialist Ross Perot, a maverick once
closely affiliated with GM, said, "The company's problem is not a lack of
money, but a lack of ideas and priorities."[7] Both items were in strong supply at
Ford Motor.

When Ford beat GM, it grabbed headlines in business pages around the
country. Reporters in Detroit sought out former Ford top executive Robert

McNamara and asked him to comment. "In my dreams," McNamara said, beaming, "I pictured Ford topping GM, but outside of dreamland, it was hard to visualize. GM had—and still has—such a tremendous advantage in market share, economies of scale and marketing that are hard to overcome. Ford has done it and should be congratulated."[8]

Ford's financial feats kept coming. During some fiscal quarters, it earned more than GM, Chrysler, and American Motors put together. In 1987, the company actually earned more than all European and Japanese automakers combined.[9] Turning in record profits and once more beating GM in 1988, Ford Motor Company was indisputably the most profitable automaker in the world. Investors took note and the price of Ford stock rose sharply during the 1980s. CEO Don Petersen was the man of the hour, toasted at gatherings and featured on the covers of *Fortune* and *Forbes*. Yet he capped his fabulous era at Ford by resigning abruptly in November 1990—more than a year ahead of schedule. "I had done what I had set out to do," Petersen recalled of his tenure. "It was the proper time to turn over the reins."[10]

Ironically, the immediate reason for his hastened departure revolved around the advance planning for that very retirement. Ford's board of directors, which devoted a great deal of time to talk of succession in the executive ranks, didn't back Petersen's preference that Allan Gilmour succeed him as CEO in 1992. A Vermont native, Gilmour was a well-respected and articulate automobile man with degrees from Harvard and the University of Michigan. However, his experience was limited to staff positions at headquarters, such as president of Ford Motor Credit Company and president of the Ford Automotive Group. He'd never proven himself out in the field, where the cars came together or where they were pushed out the doors of showrooms. A no-nonsense cost cutter, Gilmour was also openly gay, which made him a rarity in the highest ranks of corporate America.[11] The board's choice was Red Poling, who was already serving as president but would soon be approaching retirement age. To pave the way for a productive line of succession, the sixty-three-year-old Petersen stepped aside and let Poling get started. "There was nothing strange about my resignation," Petersen recalled. "My wife and I wanted to return to California. We loved the West. And my heart was ailing. I couldn't have left on better terms."[12]

Petersen, more of a product guy, and Poling, a bean counter, had had their disagreements, but they had worked together for years and so the transition was seamless. There was going to be a difference, however, in management style. "Red was no fun," said Philip Caldwell, who was himself not widely known for insouciance. "He was all straight-faced and number crunching."[13]

Poling did betray a sense of humor about that number crunching, however—when it went right. He counted his happiest day at Ford Motor Company as the one in 1983 when executives realized that the company would turn a profit, after years of losses. On that day, with champagne being poured, his nickname was temporarily changed; he was no longer "Red" but "Black" Poling.[14]

In reality, besides his health concerns, the underlying reason for Petersen's early exit grew out of his relationship with the Ford family, holders of an immutable 40 percent stake in the voting stock. Petersen, who owed his role in the chairman's office to Henry Ford II, had neglected the family lion in his final years. He claimed that he didn't want to burden Henry II with business problems, but Henry II didn't see it that way. The problem that upset him and others in the family most of all was that Don Petersen hindered the ambitious young cousins, Edsel II and Bill Jr., from taking influential positions in the company or on the board of directors (on which they both held seats). "I've made it clear on one or two occasions to Mr. Petersen," said Edsel II ruefully, "that it does seem a bit odd to me that there are three classes of directors: inside, outside, and Billy and me."[15] Even those family members who were not actually working at the company, including Henry II's daughters, Charlotte and Anne, were intent on seeing Fords rise to the top. Because the so-called fourth generation was so agitated, the family's view of Petersen only dimmed more after Henry II died. And without the support of the Fords, he certainly was not discouraged from retiring early, however halcyon the times.

At the end of the 1980s, Ford Motor Company was awash in two commodities—money and worries about the future. Just when the company was enjoying its unexpected leap into star status, a rumor began to circulate that within five years, Toyota would surge and take Ford's spot as the number two automaker in the world in terms of sales. The rumor played into Ford Motor's worst fears. The dread of just such a tumble, whether from competition or a business downturn, colored strategic planning at Ford and was most apparent in the attitude toward cash on hand, which piled up after years of high profits and conservative management. Amounting to about $10 billion in 1990, the money had to be spent. Depending on just how it was used, Ford would be a much different company afterward.

As the money continued to accumulate, there was murmuring from some investors that the company should use it to buy back stock, which would increase the value of the shares left outstanding. In Ford's case, a buyback constituted little more than an indirect way of handing the extra loot over to the stockholders. However, the Ford family, with its $2 billion stake, was against that idea, being more interested in the long-term future of the company than in plumping individual portfolios. In the end, only about one fifth of the company's cash was allocated for buybacks.[16] The rest was aimed squarely at the company's future.

Under Petersen, Ford had reduced costs in the 1980s by sticking to a notably conservative manufacturing outlook, refusing to be tempted into creating too many cars, or worse yet, excess production capacity. Companies have no choice in the face of slow sales (which are always on the horizon in the cyclical automobile business) but to carry empty factories, and laid-off employees, at considerable expense. For that reason, Ford had no interest in spending any of its nest egg on new factories. Instead, the company devoted a respectable amount of money to improvements in existing factories, including the busy truck plant in Louisville, and the Taurus facilities in Chicago and Atlanta. Nonetheless, the total outlay on upgrades also barely put a dent in the $10 billion.

For most manufacturing companies, banking seems a much brighter, cleaner business. Ford had special reasons to be drawn to finance. Ford Motor Credit was a bustling profit center for the company throughout the 1980s. Under the aegis of an affable former economics professor named James W. Ford (no relation to the Ford family), it grew a long way past making automobile loans. In 1985, it bought a bank, First Nationwide, that soon made its own acquisitions to grow into the sixth-largest savings-and-loan in the United States. In 1988, the year James Ford retired, his credit division generated $679 million, or one fifth of the overall company profits.[17] Four years later, the renamed Ford Financial Services Group made an enormous purchase, paying $2.7 billion for the Associates Corporation, a finance company based in Dallas. Associates made commercial loans, but was particularly strong in home-equity lending. From there, Ford Motor pushed into consumer credit; by the early 1990s, Associates began issuing "Ford" credit cards, affiliated with either Visa or MasterCard. Home equity and consumer credit were each tricky areas, but at least they didn't follow the same pattern as the automobile business. "There's nothing Ford can do about the cyclicality of the auto business," explained George V. Brown III, a strategic planner with the Financial Services Group, "but there is something we can do about the cyclicality of the company's earnings."[18]

The same fear of vulnerability was rampant among Ford executives everywhere, and would remain so for over a decade. Aside from finance and automobiles, the company tried to acquire Hughes Aircraft in 1984, but was ferociously outbid by General Motors. Ford did purchase a controlling interest in Hertz in 1987 for $1.3 billion. The leader in car rentals, Hertz conducted business in approximately 1,900 locations in America and 5,100 worldwide. "My board was pressing me to diversify," CEO Donald Petersen recalled. "There weren't many ways to do it right. Hertz, in my opinion, was the perfect fit. It was a good way to get a Ford product into the hands of Americans. The hope was they'd like our product and want to buy one for themselves."[19]

Historical antecedents showed that Ford Motor was ideally suited to become Hertz's corporate parent. The rental company got its start in 1918, when twenty-two-year-old Walter L. Jacobs, a racing enthusiast, opened a car rental agency in Chicago with a fleet of a dozen Model T Fords. An excellent mechanic, Jacobs maintained the cars himself, at least at first. Within five years, he had expanded and his company was averaging $1 million in annual profits. That's when John Hertz, chairman of Yellow Cab and Yellow Truck and Coach Manufacturing, bought him out. When Hertz sold those two main businesses to GM in 1925, Hertz Drive-Ur-Self, as it was called, went along.[20] John Hertz stayed on (as did his young accountant, Ernie Breech) and the company flourished. When Midway Airport opened in Chicago, there was a Hertz office to serve it. By World War II, the name Hertz was synonymous with the rent-a-car business. However, GM spun it off in 1953, when it was worried about antitrust violations.

At the time that Ford bought its stake in Hertz, automakers were generally convinced that in order to retain sales to car rental companies, they had to own them outright. On that basis, Ford reeled in Hertz, while the other members of the Big Three absorbed other rent-a-car companies. However, GM and Chrysler soon regretted the whole strategy, as they realized that they lost more money trying to run rental agencies than they earned by locking in fleet sales. Both sold out. Ford Motor, however, thrived in the car rental business and considered Hertz a permanent adjunct, making it a wholly owned subsidiary in 1994.

Ford Motor's overall strategy of acquisition, started under Red Poling and Donald Petersen, continued well into the 1990s. By then, though, the acquisitions were much more than mere lines on the ledger. For those on the outside, they were the most obvious evidence of a fundamental shift in the philosophy of Ford Motor Company.

Globalization, the ultimate defensive tactic, became the guiding principle of Ford's major outlays in the crucial years from 1987 to 1999. It was the culmination of a theme that started only one year after the company made its first automobile, and Henry Ford first started to sell cars across the border in Ontario, eventually joining with local businesspeople there to build and sell more. Ninety years later, however, after at least six different incarnations, Ford's "international" operations disappeared, in effect, to be replaced by one company sending ideas and cars throughout the world.

Strategies aside, Ford's position in the mid-1980s was akin to that of a car fanatic let loose on automobile row with a blank check. Practically every automobile company was available, or seemed to be, giving rise to rumors that Ford was on the verge of buying firms as disparate as BMW and Toyota, Fiat and Aston Martin.

For small- and medium-size companies, Ford's sheer heft translated into security. The common assumption in the late 1980s was that the automobile world was headed toward consolidation into a grand total of six companies: two based in Asia, two in Europe, and two in America. With talk like that in the air, even prima-donna firms that once insisted upon their independence were starting to look around. Those that tried to go it alone were presumed to be doomed. A proposed deal with Italy's biggest automaker, Fiat, seemed like a good fit, handing Ford a boost on the European continent and giving Fiat what a Ford alliance would offer any company: the many assets of the second-biggest automobile company in the world.

However, the Fiat deal fell apart soon after talks began. Chairman Giovanni Agnelli was proud of Fiat's position as Italy's automotive leader and he couldn't bring himself to cede its autonomy to Dearborn. Joint management was patently unworkable and so Ford walked away. The company next expressed interest in Britain's Austin Rover, then a government-owned conglomerate. However, despite the fact that Ford had been making cars in England longer than Austin and almost as long as Rover, the British public balked at the idea of a "foreign" company taking over such a large chunk of its automaking tradition. After Ford was turned away, Austin Rover was broken up into complementary parts, including Jaguar and the Rover Group, which became public companies.

Alfa Romeo, founded in 1908, had a warm reputation for building sports cars, but in the late 1980s its lineup was actually laden down with sedans; good cars but not great ones. By 1986, it hadn't made money—or a decent sports car, for that matter—in thirteen years. Alfa, owned by the Italian government, came up for sale late that year and Ford Motor was an ardent suitor, on the very verge of buying it, when at the last possible minute Chairman Agnelli of Fiat met with the prime minister and persuaded him not to allow an interloper to snatch Alfa away.[21] Next, Agnelli turned his powers of persuasion on the general public in Italy, which took up the nationalist cause, and Ford Motor, openly disappointed, lost the deal. By no coincidence, Fiat subsequently bought Alfa Romeo, but has done little with it since. As an industry analyst explained at the time, "It was a blocking move."[22]

In 1987, Ford Motor finally managed to buy a car company, small but potent Aston Martin of Newport Pagnell, England. Aston Martin was a household word signifying "superb sports car," despite the fact that few people had ever seen one. They were as rarefied as Fords were ubiquitous. In the 1980s, Aston was making brawny sports models as well as ultra-expensive sedans under the Lagonda name. Its production output was five cars per week. Ford Motor built that many cars in five minutes.[23]

The handmade cars were undoubtedly imbued with a strong mystique. One of Aston Martin's greatest glory days occurred in 1959, when a DBR-1 won the twenty-four-hour Le Mans race. It received a bigger boost in reputation in 1964 when Sean Connery, playing James Bond in *Goldfinger,* drove an Aston Martin DB5 around the scenic roads of Europe. "What the first Bond movie did was a phenomenon," noted company historian Roger Stowers. "Absolutely unique. In one week we became one of the most famous motorcar companies in the world."[24] Saudi Arabian sheiks, Wall Street brokers, and Hollywood movie stars all clamored to own an Aston Martin. Cass Elliott of the Mamas and the Papas walked into a Los Angeles dealership, barefoot and dressed like a hippie, to plunk down cash for a DB5. Beatle Paul McCartney used his Aston Martin as a portable sound studio, composing "Hey Jude" while driving around the English countryside in it.

As they say in England, the price of an Aston is equivalent to that of a house, and few people could afford both. The company sold its cars the way a tailor fitted a suit: each vehicle was bespoke. Aston Martins, like Morgans and top-of-the-line Rolls-Royces—but unlike any American cars—completely bypassed Henry Ford's rules of mass production. The Aston Martin factory was a step back in time. Highly trained craftsmen in leather aprons assembled the cars out of hand-hammered pieces. The bodies received twenty coats of paint, hand-rubbed between each application, where most cars are finished after two coats. Customers were given a wide choice of colors, upholstery, and options, but certain traditions were upheld: for example, an Aston Martin should never be painted white or red. (It isn't good form to ask why not.) At Aston Martin, engines were "signed" by the chief mechanics who produced them. Some customers will buy only an Aston with a Terry Durston engine, for example. Prince Charles insisted on a V-8 built by Don Osborne. Aficionados claim that they can tell the difference simply by the sound. Before any car was released to the customer, it was not merely inspected, it was audited. "I audit three cars a week," said David Kitchener, who held the revered title of final vehicle auditor. "I go through the car with a fine-tooth comb looking for tics." Kitchener is so meticulous that he has never scored a car higher than 90 (out of 100) on its first review.[25]

For Ford, Aston Martin didn't seem like a revolutionary acquisition. The company only paid $33 million for a majority stake in it—pocket change in the general scheme of its business. However, for the first time since Clara Ford pushed for the purchase of Lincoln Motor in 1921, Ford Motor Company had admitted that an outside automaker was worthy of its affection. And for the first time since Edsel created the Mercury Division in 1938, the company gained a new sibling.

To the complete surprise of sports-car fans, Ford didn't ruin Aston Martin. It didn't order the panel beaters in Newport Pagnell to build a hatchback. It didn't steal the name and use it on a two-tone Mercury Marquis. Instead, Ford gave Aston the money with which to develop new models and the support to help sell more of them. As a result, production went up from 200 per year to 700—a remarkable increase, even if the world has yet to be inundated with Aston Martins. In 2002 Aston Martin embarked on a program to produce 5,000 cars annually by 2005. To sell them, seventeen new dealerships would be created worldwide, fourteen of them in the United States.[26] "Ford guessed right," Csaba Csere, editor in chief of *Car and Driver* magazine, noted. "As they looked forward, they could see that the super exclusive market had room for growth and that the powerful images of the brand would be valuable."[27]

However, Ford's sensitive treatment of Aston Martin didn't impress Jaguar, for one, which spurned advances from Dearborn later in 1987. Jaguar had been founded as a body company in the 1920s, which may explain why the cars it began to produce in the 1930s have always been, if nothing else, exceedingly beautiful to look at. Illustrator Gordon Crosby of *Autocar* magazine was commissioned to create a mascot for the car in the 1930s. His "leaping cat" hood ornament was powerful and mysterious, like a jaguar in the wild, and it has become one of the most recognized symbols in the history of automobiles. The image suited the cars, which were truly exciting through the years. Wolfgang Reitzle, a former Ford executive, said that Jaguars were built with "emotional engineering."[28] After World War II, the company moved into a series of former aviation buildings on Brown's Lane in Coventry, England, an address famous ever since among car fans. Jaguar was renowned for its sports cars, but its passenger cars were consistently popular as well, lined with burl wood, leather, and a general air of good living.

The match between Ford Motor Company and Jaguar should have been perfect from the start; each company genuinely seemed to need the other. Jaguar, requiring new capital for future models, couldn't go it alone. And while Ford had built a fine tradition with Lincoln, that was no longer enough in a luxury segment that was divided between the demand for large, soft-riding American cars and European makes with more distinctive performance. Mercedes-Benz and Jaguar had pioneered the segment, drawing customers up from entry-level foreign cars, or over from Lincoln and Cadillac. By the 1980s, BMW was in the mix. Ford wanted to be in it, too. So did Nissan and Toyota, but they actually did something about it, developing the Infiniti and Lexus models, respectively, for introduction late in the decade.

The two Japanese companies spent an average of $500 million, but in the end, they had something no American automaker had: a European-style luxury car. GM responded by infusing money into Cadillac to create models that leaned ever more sharply across the Atlantic. Ford, for its part, took a shortcut. It went shopping in Coventry.

In Coventry, Jaguar was even more rattled than Ford by the advent of the Lexus and Infiniti. Losing money, it was barely hanging on to a sales plateau of 50,000 cars per year. Not all of Jaguar's problems were due to the Japanese influx, however. At a time when other cars were improving in performance, Jaguar had stagnated. It possessed both the ideas and the expertise to leap ahead of the others in engineering, but not the money to produce break-through models. Jaguar was flagging, yet it was still a unique company. The generally accepted opinion in America was that for an everyday car, nothing exuded more class than a Jag. The people who drove them, however, did have to have a little patience with their idiosyncrasies: climate controls that either baked passengers into a sweat or else left them shivering; radios with opinions of their own about what to play, if anything; and repair costs that were illogi-cal at best, with simple parts often costing more than complex ones. A legion of fans didn't mind a bit. The executive offices at Brown's Lane were lined with photographs of Jaguars being used by celebrities ranging from Clark Gable to Roy Orbison. Queen Elizabeth rode in Jaguars or Daimlers, all of which were painted a special color, Sandringham Claret, allowed for no other customers.[29]

According to the contingencies put in place by the British government dur-ing Jaguar's 1985 privatization, foreign companies could not own more than 15 percent of the firm's stock until 1990. When Ford Motor made its second approach in 1989 by buying a 15 percent stake, Jaguar balked, as executives recognized that Ford ultimately had acquisition in mind. Sir Peter Egan, the chairman, wanted his company to remain independent. With that in mind, he had already solicited interest from GM in taking a minority interest in the company—just enough to help, but not enough to dominate. Ford didn't know about that secret arrangement; instead, it was anticipating trouble from the British public. However, the all-England fervor that had scuttled Ford's Austin Rover deal in 1985 had completely dissipated. A gloomy realism had taken its place.

"There is a motor industry in Britain, rather than a British motor industry," said Garel Rhys, a professor at the Cardiff Business School in Wales, as well as an adviser to the House of Commons Committee on Trade and Industry.[30] Ford Motor representatives dutifully visited members of that committee, along with other politicians and labor officials, stressing the company's "very long history of commitment to the United Kingdom." The Ford contingent found that the British public wasn't at all averse to the takeover. But mean-while Egan firmed up his plan to turn GM into a white knight that would save Jaguar from the clutches of Ford.

GM accepted his invitation to buy shares in order to head off Ford and bidding between the two companies seemed ready to begin in October 1989. Ford calculated that the buildings and other hard assets were worth $500 mil-lion.[31] Even that figure was generous. As one executive put it, "There is noth-ing wrong with Jaguar that running a bulldozer through Brown's Lane wouldn't cure." In any case, the next calculation tried to put a value on

Jaguar's reputation. Overall, Ford decided that in consideration of the Jaguar name, it was willing to pay Jaguar's stockholders $2 billion, at the most. As with many an individual who attends an auction, however, Ford's resolve on the issue of price was not as strong as its desire to win the bidding. On November 2, Ford suddenly boosted its offer to $2.52 billion. GM dropped out, insisting in an official statement that Jaguar was worth "very significantly below" that price.[32]

In a backhanded way, Alex Trotman, the former head of Ford of Europe and Ford Motor's chairman in the mid-1990s, later admitted that the price probably had been too steep. He told *Forbes* magazine in 1995 that, given the chance, Ford would buy Jaguar again, "but if I had to buy my own house again, I'd try and beat the price."[33]

Not only had Ford paid top dollar for a company that needed an injection of at least $1.5 billion just to survive, it also had to agree to preserve Jaguar's independence, according it a separate board of directors, financial structure, and dealer network. Ford defended the Jaguar acquisition by predicting that the luxury market would only continue to expand in the 1990s as baby boomers reached their fifties and sixties. Plain, raw emotion played a part in the acquisition, too, and helped justify the price. More than one observer noted that Ford Motor executives had displayed a penchant for Europe in general, and England in particular, ever since Edsel Ford's day. On that basis, it was no surprise that they wanted to own Jaguar. "Part of it could be that they all just love Jaguars," said David Cole, an analyst at the University of Michigan. "Now it will be legit for them to drive one!"[34]

Within two years, Ford Motor installed an Englishman named Nicholas Scheele (pronounced *Shay-lah*) as president and CEO of Jaguar. "Clearly," he said, "Jaguar at the time of acquisition had a limited product range and a fairly mature product range, to be kind."[35] While Jaguar developed new models, Scheele and his management team cut costs, making Jaguar profitable again by inducing fewer auto workers to build more cars. "I was criticized for grossly overpaying for Jaguar," Don Petersen later reflected. "But I don't think that is so. We had never gotten anywhere with luxury cars in Europe. Our Grenada and Lincolns went nowhere. With one check we corrected that."[36]

For its next major acquisition, Ford Motor Company increased its stake in Mazda, Japan's fifth-largest automaker and a company with which it already had a long association. In 1984, Ford and Mazda had joined forces to build a $500 million plant in Mexico, initially for the production of compact Tracers.[37] In addition, the two companies had joint ventures in Michigan and Japan, and owned a joint stake in Kia, a Korean carmaker.[38] Petersen was the driving force behind increasing Ford Motor's share of Mazda throughout the 1980s. "We needed a beachhead in the Asian market," he recalled. "And, even more importantly, Mazda had terrific experience with front-wheel-drive technology. They were on the cutting edge—we needed their R&D. As a brand name, however, Mazda was irrelevant. It did have the cachet of manufacturing a high-quality car."[39] After Petersen retired in 1990, the symbiosis between the two companies continued. However, after barely surviving years of huge losses, Mazda was finally faced with the necessity of ceding control to an outsider. Ford Motor was the friendliest of the outsiders, so, in April 1996, it bought a controlling interest and installed one of its typically well-traveled executives, Henry D. G. Wallace, as president. "This is major," commented Bob Neff, head of the American Chamber of Commerce in Japan. "For a Japanese company to be acquired by a foreign company is basically unheard-of."[40]

In 1999, Ford Motor Company followed up its acquisition of Jaguar by purchasing the passenger-car division of Volvo. The Swedish company, which is also a major producer of trucks and heavy equipment, wanted to split off the car business and, since GM had recently purchased Saab, it perceived Ford Motor as a suitable match. The Volvo had a distinctive niche, around the world, as an unpretentious car typically driven by upscale customers. The company sold about 80,000 cars in the United States each year and 185,000 in Europe. After heated negotiations over price, Ford Motor acquired Volvo's car division for $6.47 billion, down from the original asking price of $7.5 billion. Ford didn't really have to dicker: by that point, after yet another decade of healthy profits, its cash reserves had risen to $22 billion.[41]

A year later, Ford Motor Company closed out its spate of automotive acquisitions right where it began, with Rover. The seller was BMW, which had purchased the Rover Group in 1994. At that time, Rover was a weak, outdated company, but one with two jewels—both very tiny, in the general scheme of international automaking. Its Range Rover was a surprise success, practically inventing the luxury four-wheel-drive market. And the peppy Mini, a remnant of the Swinging Sixties, was as strong and youthful as ever. Neither of those vehicles was exactly priceless, however, and they were enhanced very little by Rover's accompanying line of passenger vehicles, yet BMW could not be dissuaded from making the acquisition. The Bavarians paid $1.2 billion for Rover and then shoveled a whopping $5 billion more into it to keep it afloat. Around BMW, Rover was known as "the English patient," after the hopelessly ill character in the novel and movie of that title.[42] When BMW finally tired of tending the patient, it sold off practically everything except the Mini. Ford took over Land Rover (including Range Rover) for $3 billion.

Land Rover's four-wheel-drive SUVs were regarded as the toughest civilian vehicles around, practically *de rigueur* on an African safari or an exploration of the Australian outback. During its first fifty-three years in business, Land Rover, headquartered in Graydon, England, produced only eight different models. In 1999, the year before the acquisition, the company sold a record 177,800 vehicles.[43]

Although Land Rovers were rigorously tested on an engineering basis, production problems had led to a slackening reputation for quality at the time of the Ford acquisition.[44] According to the scenario established elsewhere, Ford could lend production expertise, without tampering too much otherwise. Former Aston Martin CEO Bob Dover, who moved to Land Rover, recalled, "When Land Rover was acquired by Ford Motor, people said, 'Well, they did a good job of leaving Jaguar alone and not messing things up. It should be okay for us.'"[45]

Adding new names to a roster of car lines was not especially difficult, not for a cash-rich company. However, even as Ford Motor brought in Aston Martin, Jaguar, Mazda, Volvo, and Land Rover, it was simultaneously looking inward. The goal was to rethink the alignment of the three key dimensions of its business world: automobile, sales regions throughout the world, and job functions (such as engineering). Those dimensions were no longer going to fit together according to traditional thinking, nor would they separate along artificial demarcations. Ford ideas and Ford people had to circulate uninhibited by regional geography. The cars, of course, had to follow. That change in perception, an impetus known as "Ford 2000," originated with Alex Trotman, a native of Scotland who was named chairman of Ford Motor in November 1993, when Red Poling's retirement took effect.

Trotman, a wiry man with dark hair and a pencil-thin mustache, had a formal air—not the reserve of a man like Philip Caldwell, but the crispness of a military officer. That was fitting, since Trotman had been a navigator in the Royal Air Force before joining Ford of England in the 1960s. He eventually ran Ford of Europe, before moving to the executive suite in Dearborn, where he was named president on January 1, 1993. Before the year was out, Trotman had hopscotched over Allan Gilmour, then vice chairman, to become the new chairman.

Alex Trotman was undoubtedly a visionary. He was also a diplomat, and as president, he had periodically invited members of the Ford family to visit, talk, and see the latest cars. He also kept a photograph of Henry II on the bookshelf in his office. "To me," he explained, while standing near his desk, "Mr. Ford is still sitting in that chair sometimes. In many ways, I still think this is his office."[46] In any case, the Ford family placed its confidence in Alex Trotman. As chairman, he instituted Ford 2000 with sweeping changes in the way that Ford cars were developed. Along the way, he eliminated three old warhorses: North American Automotive Operations, European Automotive Operations, and Automotive Components Group. They were replaced by one umbrella group, Ford Automotive Operations, encompassing two continents, later to be joined by Latin American and Asia-Pacific operations. In addition,

Ford 2000 called for five engineering centers, developing cars for world markets according to model type. Four of them were to be located in Dearborn, creating basic designs, or "platforms," as they are known, for full-size front-wheel-drive cars, rear-wheel-drive cars, SUVs and pickup trucks, and commercial trucks. The fifth center would be located in Europe, developing primarily small cars.

Ford 2000 was intended to make the company more efficient and better able to compete with Toyota and GM in the fast-growing markets outside Europe and North America. Erasing borders and learning to think in terms of common parts, if not whole platforms, was crucial. However, critics complained that Ford was trying to create a line of thinly disguised "world cars." If that was the case, the company was at cross-purposes, since it was then in the process of acquiring companies that made some of the most distinctive cars around. Either Ford was wasting its money trying to homogenize the automobile design process or, if all it wanted was another kind of Lincoln, it was wasting its money buying Jaguar. However, this criticism was invalid: what Trotman was actually interested in building was not a world car, but a world car-company, one that never stopped looking for the economies available to it.

Due to Ford's global efforts, by the mid-1990s it ranked as the bestselling make in Europe and in Australia.[47] In the United States, Ford Motor counted five of the ten top-selling cars as its own by 1993.[48] By 1995, the company's share of the domestic vehicle market was 25.6 percent,[49] up from 19.3 percent fourteen years before. In the United States, customers were fixated on three Ford models. The F-150 pickup continued to lead in the truck segment, as it had since the 1970s. The Taurus was the leader among all passenger models, bumping the Honda Accord to second place in 1992.[50] It remained number one through 1996.[51] To complete the trio of bestsellers, in 1990 Ford introduced the Explorer, which shot to first place in the newly invigorated SUV segment.

As the *Wall Street Journal* observed in 1994, "The luxury car of the 1990s is a truck."[52] While sales of pickup trucks were soaring, an even more impressive jump was made in the SUV segment. In the 1980s SUVs such as the Jeep Cherokee and the Chevy Suburban were a short throw from the trucks on which they were based, with the result that they were powerful enough to haul trailers, but barnlike both in driving characteristics and interior appointments. Typically, they appealed to gentleman farmers who needed to haul horses to shows or hobbyists taking antique cars to meets. In 1990, however, the market made a sharp turn, as SUVs became more civilized, even as customers became more rugged. "The answer to why SUVs became so popular is simple," observed Lee Iacocca. "The baby boomers who had bought the Mustangs grew up. Twenty years had passed. They got married, had two kids, and moved to the suburbs. In came the world of SUVs. Basically women and mothers like the command positions, they like sitting high up. Dealers are selling weight, they're selling 'put a lot of iron around you' for safety reasons. So what if you only get eight miles per gallon and your SUV pollutes like hell? Your children are safe. People think they're going to drive it to the wilderness. In truth, they drive it to the shopping center."[53]

In the 1990s, men and women, rich people and poor, country folk, suburbanites, and city dwellers were becoming homogeneous in their tastes. Everybody, it seemed, wore dungarees, ate fast food, had cable television, and generally believed that to be tough was to look cool. The SUV fit the bill, as a vehicle that was as strong and versatile as its customers hoped to be. Because SUVs were classified as "light trucks," they were not governed by federal regulations for fuel consumption, with the result that they offered full-size comforts to a generation tired of downsizing. The big surprise, however, was not merely that SUVs were ready to grow in popularity in 1990, but that they even had the pull to displace luxury cars. Younger buyers—and those who wanted to look young behind the wheel—found it easy to bypass the luxury sedan and even the sports car in favor of an entirely new means of conspicuous consumption: the fully loaded "sport ute."[54] Trendsetters, including sports stars, entertainers, and California drivers in general, all helped to put SUVs in the spotlight. As the fad rolled out over the whole country, the SUV and the pickup combined to lead the light-truck segment to first place in total sales, outpacing passenger-car sales starting in 1990.[55] Ford Motor's timing couldn't possibly have been better.

Ford started planning the Explorer in 1986, when Ed Hagenlocker, vice president and general manager of Truck Operations, launched an effort to create a four-door, four-wheel-drive, fairly compact SUV. Unlike other vehicles in that category, which were merely stretched from two doors to four, the Explorer was designed from the first to accommodate a crowd. The backseat was as easy to get to as the front seat, which couldn't be said of the Toyota 4runner or the Jeep Cherokee. In addition, the Ford was snappy looking, inside and out, and had a sedanlike finish on the inside. It seemed to be the first SUV to know that it wouldn't always be used out in the rough. None of the Explorer's characteristics were particularly dramatic, yet it inspired confidence, as had no other SUV before it. "The people in the company who have seen the vehicle are really excited," said product planner Roger Schebor, before the launch at the end of 1990. "Even the people in Louisville [the production plant] are really pumped up, they're looking forward to building it. The dealers can't wait to get their hands on it. And when we do our driving evaluations on the road, the vehicles attract a lot of attention."[56]

The Explorer either created or met a phenomenal surge in SUV sales.

While its predecessor, the Bronco II, had accounted for sales of 109,000 in 1989, the Explorer was up to 250,000 by 1992, and it was still climbing. Because of the popularity of the Explorer, the F-150, and minivan models, Ford Motor Company remained an industry leader.[57] That was fine with management: trucks, minivans, and especially SUVs had an even higher profit margin than luxury cars, and they didn't require the same heavy advertising.

Ford Motor Company was in robust condition as Alex Trotman prepared to retire in 1998. Over fifteen years, most of them very good ones, it had risen to become number one among the Big Three not only in profits, but in the esteem of most observers. GM was still bigger, but Ford generated more excitement and was more at home in the far reaches of the world. In a bold move spearheaded by Wolfgang Reitzle, Ford even relocated headquarters of its Lincoln-Mercury Division from Dearborn to an ultra-modern industrial park in Irvine, California. The company wanted to showcase Lincoln as an international luxury brand by integrating it with Land Rover, Aston Martin, Jaguar, and Volvo as part of its Premier Automotive Group (PAG). PAG's North American headquarters in Irvine was a state-of-the-art operation, including video teleconferencing facilities, vehicle displays, and offices for more than 150 employees. "Our choice of Southern California is significant," Ford's vice president and general manager of Lincoln-Mercury, Mark Hutchins, proclaimed at the July 14, 1998, opening of the division's world headquarters in Irvine. "Around the world, California is known as a creative epicenter. Cultural trends and automotive ideas often start here. We intend to absorb all that California offers."[58] The other reason for relocating, which Hutchins didn't allude to, was that California was the number one market in the world for luxury vehicles.[59] Lincoln, it was thought, would thrive there. As the question of succession arose, however, the company was not so very global. It returned to its Michigan heritage. Once again, the time had come for the Ford family to have its say at Ford Motor.

37

Momentum

Three years before its hundredth birthday, Ford Motor Company was feeling fine—perhaps too fine. As humankind prepared to celebrate the dawn of a new millennium, the company's founder, Henry Ford, was named Businessman of the Century in a popular poll, which also judged his Model T the Car of the Century. More to the point, at the beginning of 2000 Ford Motor was on the verge of overtaking General Motors as the number one automaker in the world, having restored its reputation for product quality, operating efficiency, and overall innovation, not to mention profitability. Between 1997 and 2000, Ford Motor had earned a staggering $39 billion.[1] Such bulging coffers suggested the company had money to burn—which is exactly what it appears to have done with it.

The go-go days didn't even last halfway through 2000, when the same company that had been so flush the year before suddenly found itself strapped for not only fresh products but operating cash. Its edge in auto manufacturing vanished. The morale of its executive and professional staff, not to mention the rest of its 350,000 employees, had also evaporated. Even Ford Motor Company's reputation had fallen into serious doubt, thanks largely to a series of problems with Firestone tires installed on Ford vehicles. "We found ourselves in a hole," Bill Ford Jr. said of the situation. "The question was how did one get there and how do we pull ourselves out?"[2]

Ford Motor's downturn resulted from a confluence of bad luck, faulty analysis, and a ruinous hubris. The latter grew out of a characteristic that had defined Ford Motor since its founding. Over the years the company had in fact grown in good times and persevered through bad times by institutionalized pride and the spirit of self-confidence laid down by its founders.

From its prickly beginnings, Ford Motor Company had been given a distinct attitude by Henry Ford and his equally intransigent colleagues, including financial manager James Couzens, design chief Harold Wills, and production whiz Charles E. Sorensen. Ford Motor had always depended on the can-do spirit of its employees and the innovations that their enthusiasm inspired. What Henry Ford grasped in 1903 was that cars possessed limitless potential; what Ford Motor continued to understand, over the decades, was how cars would remain relevant and even inspiring. Henry Ford started the momentum, while great automobiles like the Model T, the Model A, and the Mustang gave it a firm direction. The Ford momentum was given strength by the standards of the company's past and a crisp pace by ways of doing things and making judgments, passed down from the successes—and failures—of a hundred years. "The family always hung in there," Lee Iacocca noted of the Fords' ability to rebound from economic downturns. "The company will be around for a long, long time because the family never throws in the towel."[3]

For Ford Motor Company to sputter and stall in 2000–2001 may have been shocking, even to experienced observers like Lee Iacocca. What wasn't surprising, however, were the methods the company used to try to right itself. Lessons of survival were to be found in the most insistent part of the Ford momentum. The drastic ups and downs of the final four years in Ford's first century made them not only a microcosm of the whole long history of the company, but a reminder of how powerful that history can still be. As Ford started to stumble, the people at World Headquarters turned to their heritage to help chart a course for the future. In the annals of the past lay reminders of the tenacious attitude and even the creative arrogance that made the company what it was.

By the end of 1998, Alex Trotman, the architect of Ford's success during the 1990s, had been knighted by the Queen in his British homeland. Continuing the royal theme but in a sarcastic light, he had taken to calling Bill Ford Jr. "Prince William," and was unenthusiastic about the prospect of any of the Ford cousins taking over leadership of the company. Trotman accepted the role of the Fords in the ownership of the company, but he didn't like limiting the choice of a new chairman to members of a single family.

Bill Ford Jr. was unquestionably the leading candidate within that family. Edsel II had retired as president of Ford Credit in 1998, ceding the fast lane, at least for the time being, to his cousin.[4] At the time, Bill Ford Jr. was no longer working for the company either, but his early exit had been a point of order, rather than preference. When he was named to the powerful position of chairman of the finance committee on Ford's board of directors, he knew he could not keep a role in day-to-day operations. For that reason, he left Ford Motor to manage his father's professional football franchise.

The Detroit Lions, who played in Pontiac, were frustrating as a team. Although well stocked with stars, including the running back Barry Sanders, they rarely put together a winning season, let alone a drive for the championship. While Bill Ford Jr. couldn't change that, he did replace head coach Wayne Fontes soon after taking over in 1995. He could, however, make a direct difference in the Lions as a business proposition, actively marketing the team rather than simply opening the stadium doors and waiting for fans to arrive on their own. He put the Lions on the Internet before some teams had even heard of it. He also reversed his father's 1976 move to the suburbs by orchestrating the development of a 65,000-seat, $500 million stadium in downtown Detroit. Under construction for almost three years, Ford Field would open in time for the 2002 season.[5]

Running the Lions for three years, Bill Ford Jr. showed that he could hold his own against them all in an extremely competitive, pressured business. As the largest management job he'd handled up to that time, the Lions franchise was a proving ground. While the Ford family was absolutely determined that Bill Ford Jr. serve as the next chairman of Ford Motor, he was ambivalent. At any rate, he was not driven to it out of personal ambition. "It was wonderful running the Lions," he recalled. "And I always wanted to help Ford Motor out. But I wasn't interested in making a lot of money. I had way more than enough. I did care what happened at Ford because it was our family business."[6]

Bill Ford Jr. was respected inside and outside the family for his quick, intuitive intelligence. He was honest to a fault, sincerity being one of his outstanding qualities. He was also idealistic, drawn to noble causes and altruistic pursuits that cynics might reject. He was especially passionate about the defense of the environment and seemed happiest spending time with his family swimming in upper Michigan, fly-fishing in Alaska, or skiing in Colorado. As Bill Ford Jr. drew nearer to the leadership of Ford Motor, however, those many people prejudiced against the children of billionaires found it hard to believe that he was likely to be the least selfish or spoiled person in any gathering. They derided his green proclivities as tree-hugging nonsense. Those who believed that a business leader had to be saber-toothed and egomaniacal were equally disoriented. Bill Ford Jr. was a good guy, a nice guy—and in 1999, that made him the latest in a line of highly original leaders at Ford Motor. "Most guys who take this on had career-long ambitions and come to the job rubbing their hands together," a top Ford executive recalled. "But this guy came with his hands over his eyes, saying, 'Why me, why me, why now?'"[7]

The fact that Bill Ford Jr. had his own style, and didn't much care to live up to anyone else's idea of the "modern businessman," put him in a league with only one other man, his great-grandfather, Henry Ford. The elder Ford didn't fit a mold—he didn't have to and neither did Bill Ford Jr. The family, including Bill Sr. and Henry II's daughters, Charlotte and Anne, were intent on seeing him named chairman of Ford Motor in order to ensure a long-range point of view at the company. They knew that with his strong sense of family values, he was the right person for that job. "He is very humane and down-to-earth," his cousin Anne Ford noted. "There is nobody who has met him who doesn't immediately like him. All of us in the family are his biggest boosters."[8]

However, Bill Ford Jr.'s innate tact and friendly manner made most outsiders wonder if he had the backbone for the top job. He was dogged by what *Time* magazine called "his reputation for being overly diplomatic—read mousy."[9] In that respect, he was in the same position his grandfather, Edsel Ford, had once been in. Both were damned by the assumption that a considerate personality means a lack of forcefulness. Confined to Ford Motor his entire career, Edsel never had the chance to get out from under that assumption. In a similar way, Bill Ford Jr. was also relegated to peripheral roles during his first stint with the company, making a success of each assignment, yet denied any important role at the core of the company. As head of the Lions, he finally showed his mettle, holding his own line in tough negotiations on a number of fronts.

In the summer of 1998, the board of directors agreed with the family that Bill Ford Jr. was ready. "It's not exactly a shocking revelation," *Ward's Auto World* commented when the deed was finally done, "but William C. Ford Jr. will succeed Alex Trotman as chairman of the family's main business."[10] Bill Ford Jr. took office as of January 1, 1999, nineteen years and four chairmen after Henry II formally retired. There was undoubtedly a fascination surrounding the idea that a Ford was once again in charge: that even in a corporate world short of the divine right of kings, the transition of power was a family matter. There were other examples among Bill Ford Jr.'s contemporaries. At the St. Louis headquarters of Anheuser-Busch, brewers of Budweiser beer, August Busch IV was named president in 2002.[11] Jamie Houghton, CEO at Corning, was the fifth-generation representative of the founding Houghton clan. S.C. Johnson & Son, the waxmaker, was privately held and so easier to control, but in 2001, it named a new chairman in Dr. Fisk Johnson, the great-great-grandson of the founder.[12] None of those companies, however, nor practically any other, was as large or as storied as Ford Motor.

At forty-one, Bill Ford Jr. was young for the job of running a ranking industrial company, but not for the overall world of business in the late 1990s. Compared with the wunderkinder in their twenties who headed high-tech companies and made billions of dollars overnight, Bill Ford was an old man. However, he was still a good fifteen years younger than Trotman, Poling, Petersen, or Caldwell had been when he took the chairmanship at Ford Motor Company. "You must realize," Bill Ford Jr. said, when asked about his age, "that even though I'm forty-one, this has been part of my life since the day I was born."[13] It had been the same with his uncle, Henry Ford II, who had known even as a child that his only place would be at Ford Motor. Henry II had also taken the helm early, becoming president at twenty-eight; he established the idea of a management tandem, hiring the highly experienced Ernest Breech for his organizational skills. Bill Ford Jr. was well aware of his position as the latest Ford to head the company. "Everything that I have in life is due to this company and what Henry Ford and his descendants did for me and my family," he said, explaining his sense of commitment. "While I'm certainly cognizant of what they did, and even very mindful of what H.F. II did in the position he found himself in, I am also very mindful of the fact that I'm different and the times are different."[14]

Nonetheless, the board took a page from Henry II's book, appointing Jacques "Jac" Nasser, a veteran Ford executive, as president and CEO to work alongside Bill Ford Jr. Nasser, fifty-two, was a native of Lebanon, who had grown up in Australia. As a child, he had hidden his lunchbox from the other children at school, because his food was Middle Eastern, and tagged him as the same. Some people theorized that, as the child of immigrants, Nasser developed an affinity for minorities in any society, a trait that would affect his hiring practices while CEO at Ford. The Nassers were a business-oriented family; the father encouraged his children to make money at an early age. Jacques and his brother began repairing bicycles and selling coffee for extra cash before they graduated from high school. Jacques entered the Royal Melbourne Institute of Technology, hoping to become an engineer. "They put us all in front of a big board," Nasser recalled. "I couldn't draw a straight line. I called my professor over and told him I'd be the world's worst engineer."[15] He graduated instead with a degree in international business. While at school he had made money by purchasing vintage automobiles at auction, fixing them, and reselling them at a profit. "He chose automotive for his career because he wanted a global industry," Marjorie Sorge noted in a cover story on Nasser for *Automotive Industries.*[16]

After joining Ford of Australia in 1968 as a financial analyst, Nasser purposefully developed a reputation as a globetrotter. During thirty-two years at Ford Motor Company, he worked his way up on the financial side, with stops along the way as director–vice president of finance administration for Australia, manager of Ford's joint ventures with Volkswagen in Brazil and Argentina, and head of Ford's Hermosillo (Mexico) assembly plant. By the early 1990s, he was in Dearborn as head of Ford Automotive Operations. Nasser was known as an unrepentant cost cutter, which impressed the board of directors. Even though the company bank accounts were bulging with record profits, the directors were attracted to the idea that as president Nasser would provide the fiscal discipline to counterbalance any inexperience Bill Ford Jr. might display. As it turned out, however, 1999–2000 would not be an era known for corporate discipline—not at Ford Motor Company, not anywhere.

The bubble of 1999–2000 was something like a reverse panic in American business. The great fear was *not* to be left holding shares, as in a normal business storm, but rather to be left without two big fistfuls of investments. Practically everyone was drawn to the chase for opportunity, and Jac Nasser was no exception. His discipline dissipated. Nasser admired the way that Jack Welch had turned the emphasis at General Electric from manufacturing to financial services. While he did not intend to copy GE entirely, he did believe that Ford Motor could expand into the realm of services. What was more, he believed that if the company did not take advantage of new opportunities, it would be lost for good, left behind in the "old economy."[17] There was no uglier term in 1999 than "old economy." As Michael Lewis explained in his book *The New New Thing,* an exploration of the boomtown mentality of the Silicon Valley, businesspeople worried every day that they were losing out to the latest technology. Detroit was no different from San Jose.[18]

Within six months, Nasser had replaced a number of long-serving marketing executives with a group of conspicuously young non-Ford vice presidents. They were there specifically to help Nasser turn Ford from a company built around cars to one built around consumers. "His arrival at Ford," *Business Week* noted, "signaled Nasser's determination to turn Dearborn into a sort of Camelot for car mavericks."[19] Once a suitably savvy team was in place, the company went on another acquisitions binge, but it wasn't buying auto companies—it wanted a place in the Internet revolution.

Through the free, unregulated, and seemingly limitless reaches of cyberspace, Thomas Jefferson's ideal of a truly open marketplace of ideas began to be realized heading into the year 2000. In a startlingly short time, virtually every large-scale business concern worldwide would establish a presence on the Internet, hell-bent to make the most of it. Caught up in the fever, between January 1999 and January 2000, Ford launched three interactive Web sites aimed at customers, in addition to expanding its own corporate site.[20] It also formed partnerships on a wide array of projects with the likes of Microsoft, Yahoo!, Trilogy Software, Oracle, TeleTech Holdings, Vehix.com, iVillage.com, and Bolt.com. It made an investment in Carclub.com and signed on as a founding sponsor of the Digital Entertainment Network, which catered to teenagers.[21]

"We're forming Internet joint ventures left and right," Bill Ford Jr. admitted in December 1999. "The good news is that every time I meet with John Chambers from Cisco, Scott McNealy from Sun, Steve Ballmer from Microsoft—we meet with them all the time and everybody tells us we are way ahead of anybody else in the [auto] industry as far as the Internet is concerned."[22]

Nasser concurred in an interview conducted two months later. "This is so fast-moving, and things are changing so rapidly," he said, "that we prefer not to telegraph what our intentions are. But when you look at what Ford Motor

Co. has embarked on in our complete Internet strategy over the last year or so, I think we are in the lead in terms of the Internet and how e-commerce relates to the rest of our business."[23] He would not have wanted to be anywhere else. However, not everyone at Ford Motor was convinced that Jac Nasser was moving in the right direction. In any case, many worried that he was moving far too fast. To help make converts of those inside the company, Nasser formed yet another set of partnerships, with UUNet, Hewlett-Packard, and PeoplePC, to give every Ford Motor employee the use of a home computer, with Internet access, all for a nominal fee of $5 per month.

One person who applauded Nasser's sudden foray into high tech was Michael Dell, founder of Dell Computer. "I don't think he has any choice," Dell said. "If it were me, I'd be driven by the fear that if I didn't do it, somebody else would."[24] Nasser's strategy entailed more than merely establishing a presence on the Web. He wanted to exploit the potential of e-commerce on as many fronts as possible. With the value of Internet companies soaring, Nasser presumed that Ford Motor could eventually spin off its Web-based businesses, reaping huge profits even as the company advanced with the latest technology.

"The point is," Bill Ford Jr. explained, "the very way we interact with customers is very different than the old model. And the Internet plays a very big part in that. It's going to be exciting. What we have, which is tremendous, which nobody else has, is customers. All these Silicon Valley startups, they've got all these great ideas, but they don't have any customers. We've got the biggest customer base in the world. And they're dying to hook up with us."[25]

Spreading out over the Internet was not the only way that Ford Motor was transformed under Jac Nasser. He also presided over acquisitions that put the company into service-oriented businesses, some of them only vaguely related to the automobile business. The company bought a chain of repair shops in Great Britain, a concierge service, a company that sold extended warranties, and a recycling firm. In one of the few moves that did relate directly to Ford's lineup of automobiles, Nasser had been the driving force behind the establishment of the Premier Automotive Group, the wing that included Lincoln, Jaguar, Aston Martin, Volvo, and Land Rover. As CEO, he continued to support it and its glamorous components. They were center stage at the company—literally. "Ford Motor Co. brought an impressive stable of brands to the Frankfurt Auto Show last month: Jaguars, Volvos, Mazdas, even Aston Martins," *Business Week* noted on October 11, 1999. "Just one thing seemed to be missing: Fords. Cars carrying the trademark oval huddled in a corner of Ford's exhibition space, next to the espresso bar and the free food."[26]

Testing the equities market, Ford Motor spun off its automotive parts business, having developed it as a wholesale operation over the previous forty years. To promote the idea that the new entity was separating from Ford Mo-

tor, it was renamed Visteon. At birth, it was the second-largest radio manufacturer in the world—and was number one in Europe. It was also the world
leader in passive concealed antenna systems.[27] It became completely independent as of June 2000, taking about 77,000 employees, including one of
Ford's brightest, Peter Pestillo, the longtime vice president for labor relations
who became CEO.[28] "I never, ever wanted to be CEO of anything," Pestillo
recalled. "Suddenly I found myself one."[29] On June 29, the day that Visteon
shares started trading, he rang the bell at the New York Stock Exchange; with
annual revenue of $19 billion,[30] Visteon was already eighty-seventh on the
Standard & Poor's index of the largest publicly traded companies.[31] Nonetheless, more than three quarters of its business was conducted with Ford Motor,
a master-servant relationship that would be difficult to sort out immediately
after the divestiture. In fact, Visteon's independence was hardest for Ford
Motor to accept, as it continued to expect something akin to "most favored
nation" status, especially in the matter of pricing.

When Jac Nasser spoke about his vision for Ford Motor as a global company, with a leadership role in technology, he could be inspiring. Jeremy Cato,
a Canadian journalist, described a talk Nasser gave in 1999:

> One evening at the Tokyo Motor Show, I attended a small Ford reception
> for foreign journalists and auto analysts. Nasser and all of Ford's senior
> brass were there, with Nasser acting as host. He capped the night with an
> unscripted and thoroughly impassioned speech about his vision for Ford in
> the 21st century. He talked about how Ford needed to make great cars and
> trucks, but also the role of corporate responsibility to the environment and
> to local economies and the people who work in them. My wife, who had
> come with me to visit her nephew teaching English in Tokyo, turned to me
> and said, "Wow, he's good. I could work for that guy."[32]

Too few Ford Motor Company employees saw that side of Jac Nasser. Instead, they saw the man they nicknamed "Jac the Knife." One of the ways he
cut costs was by removing senior managers and engineers with little room or
interest in advancement. While the general idea was to eliminate deadwood,
the program had the unfortunate effect of institutionalizing the Peter Principle, which holds that people in business are promoted until they reach a job
they can't quite do. In the Ford program, people who were perfectly comfortable in their jobs, with no desire to move up, were laid off or invited to leave
via a buyout. Because many of the longtime workers were white males, the
whole program was regarded by some as a ploy to reconstitute the makeup of
the workforce, by replacing middle-aged white men with a more diverse
crowd.[33] Several major lawsuits resulted.

Nasser was also the champion of an evaluation system known as "10-80-
10," that targeted the company's top 20,000 managers and white-collar work-

ers. Based on a curve, it took raises, bonuses, and other perks away from employees rated in the bottom 10 percent, giving them instead to those in the top 10 percent. The middle 80 also received some of the plunder. Although the system seemed fair, it created raw nerves throughout the company. Employees felt as though they were competing against each other, not working as a team.

Feelings were also stretched to the limit in the dealership ranks. Not only did franchisees look dimly on Ford's budding attempts to sell cars through the Internet, they felt threatened by experiments with company-owned superdealerships.[34] Known as the "Auto Collection," the idea was to consolidate many of the Ford outlets in a certain area, by absorbing dealerships in exchange for an investment position in a new umbrella sales organization. The new entities were retail stores, in the sense that the best price was posted on each car and was nonnegotiable (except inasmuch as trade-ins offered room for dickering). The first Auto Collections appeared in Rochester, San Diego, Tulsa, Oklahoma City, and Salt Lake City.[35] The concept eliminated the dealer's role as an independent businessperson.

For all the changes Nasser tried to bring during his first year as CEO, Ford Motor seemed to march on as before when it came to making money. By the spring of 2000, the company had cash reserves of $25 billion, a fact that maddened investors. To appease the more vociferous of them, the company offered a $5.7 billion premium to shareholders, returned in the form of either cash or more common stock. The Ford family demonstrated its loyalty by choosing shares, then valued at about $28 apiece.[36] Cash would have been the smarter choice; Ford Motor shares were going for a paltry $8 twenty months later.

The twelve months ending in May 2001 were the most treacherous and *the* worst year in the company's history. It seemed that everything that could go wrong did, including management upheaval, employee demoralization, and a drastic profit reversal. But that was not the worst of it. A crown jewel in the company's lineup, the Explorer—a model that generated two thirds of the corporation's profits—stood at the center of the most extensive and widely publicized automotive safety recall of all time. That was only the start of the debacle.

When the Ford Explorer was being planned in 1986, according to Roger Schebor, manager of program planning for light trucks, "Firestone was brought into the program early on to do all the tire development."[37] Of course, Firestone had been involved in the creation of many Ford models, ever since Henry Ford and Harvey Firestone formed a fast friendship in 1896. By 1906 Ford, convinced that Firestone made the best tires, ordered 2,000 sets. By the

1920s, Firestone supplied 65 percent of the tires on Ford vehicles.[38] The dynasties were brought even closer together when Harvey's granddaughter Martha Firestone married Henry's grandson William Clay Ford in 1947. Long after Henry Ford and Harvey Firestone were gone from the scene, their companies remained as friendly as ever. A Ford without Firestone tires was the exception, over billions of miles.

That road came to an end in February 2000, when reports on a local TV station in Houston led to an investigation by the National Highway Transportation Safety Administration of the danger that tires installed on Explorers were prone to disintegrate at high speed and in hot weather. In May, after an initial survey, the NHTSA linked the deficiency to thirty-three accidents and four deaths.[39] That toll would rise with further research, but it was enough to launch a full investigation at the safety agency. Over the summer, headlines—and panic—increased. Meanwhile, early research into the problem at Ford Motor was hampered by Firestone's refusal to release data that it had collected regarding both the tires in question and accidents related to them.[40]

The problem was not entirely a surprise to Ford Motor, which in March 1999 had tried to influence Firestone to launch a recall of certain types of tires installed on Explorers that were used in Saudi Arabia. Ford based its concerns on reports of tire failures (and subsequent vehicle rollovers) that had occurred there. According to a memo that summarized a meeting at Ford with a representative from the tire maker, "Firestone Legal has some major reservations about the plan to notify customers and offer them an option. First, they feel that the U.S. D.O.T. will have to be notified of the program, since the same product is sold in the U.S. . . . They believe the best course of action for the vehicles already in the market is to handle the tire issues on a case-by-case basis."[41] Sweeping the problem under the rug was not good enough for Ford Motor.

By long tradition, a carmaker was legally responsible for every part on a car it sold, except for the tires, which were covered by the supplier. Regarding the defective tires, Ford was in the uncomfortable position of feeling ethically responsible, although it was not legally obligated. On its own, the company initiated an offer to replace the suspect Firestones, but only in the Middle East.[42] Unfortunately, those early concerns do not seem to have been circulated through the company. When the story broke in the United States a year later, Ford's top executives were apparently hearing it for the first time.

In early 2000, Firestone was still inclined to struggle against the impact of the recall. A subsidiary of Bridgestone, a Japanese tire maker, since 1988, Firestone seemed to be out of sync with the priorities of the American consumer in a panic situation. As companies from Johnson & Johnson to Jack in the Box had learned in similar circumstances, frightened customers require full disclosure and total support; all thoughts of profitability have to be suspended in the cause. In the absence of firm information, Explorer/Firestone customers were, at best, confused. Many were downright terrified. A dealer in Garland, Texas, reported that his Explorer customers were "scared to drive."[43]

In early August, the situation came to a head. Under an order from the NHTSA, Firestone finally announced a recall of 6.5 million tires; four different types, all used on Ford Explorers, were covered. However, despite the high emotions on the issue, Firestone waited almost a week before announcing the recall and it refused at first to reimburse drivers who replaced their Firestones with tires of other brands.[44] Ford dealers were immediately inundated by customers demanding replacements, and both companies had to scour the world for suitable tires. Bridgestone/Firestone even flew tires in from Japan, at great expense. In order to free suitable tires, Ford Motor closed down three Explorer and Ranger factories and redirected their supplies.[45]

When the NHTSA strongly suggested early in September that the recall be expanded to include other kinds of tires, Firestone refused. In a continuing effort to lay off the blame, it also began to implicate Ford, insisting that either the Explorer was inherently prone to rollovers, or the automobile manufacturer had recommended a tire pressure so low that the rubber was more apt to heat up and shred.

Even as the NHTSA figures on the number of people killed in Firestone/Explorer accidents grew past 140, Ford Motor tried hard to take a proactive approach to its customers. Jac Nasser appeared in a pair of sobering television commercials, which started airing within weeks of the recall. They explained as clearly as possible what was happening in the recall and how Ford Motor was responding. "Millions of families have placed their faith and trust in the Ford Explorer," Nasser said in one of the spots. "And government data shows that, for the last ten years, Explorer is one of the safest SUVs. In fact, my family has three Explorers."[46] Nasser tried to make himself available to answer questions about the recall, even inviting customers who couldn't find replacement tires to call his office—a gesture credited with causing pandemonium on the switchboards at World Headquarters, but also with expediting the completion of the recall. However, when Arizona Republican Senator John McCain called on Nasser to testify before the Senate Commerce Committee, the Ford CEO demurred at first. He didn't want to appear on any panel with representatives of Bridgestone/Firestone. He was already adamant about isolating Ford from the tire company.[47]

More than Ford Motor Company might have wished, it was drawn into a brawl with Firestone, continually forced to deny any insinuation that the Explorer was at fault for the accidents. The two companies traded barbs and mountains of evidence at press conferences, before Congressional committees, in NHTSA sessions, and anywhere else that one or the other could gain an audience. At the end of the year, each side was issuing reports analyzing the problem. Both concluded that production methods and design flaws in the tires made them prone to failure, but Firestone continued to blame Ford for recommending low pressure for the tires, while specifying high vehicle load (weight) allowances.

With the introduction of a new Explorer model scheduled for early 2001, Ford Motor wanted most of all to settle the safety issue—and put the public relations maelstrom to rest. The recall had already cost the company $500 million.[48] To show that it was doing business differently, Ford extended its new-car warranty to include tires. By doing so, it let the customer know that it would take responsibility for every aspect of its cars. Moreover, including tires in the warranty allowed Ford to insist that its tire suppliers share all data regarding complaints or problems.[49] It would not have to request data, as in the Firestone debacle, and wait in frustration for it to be delivered.

Remarkably, Ford Explorer sales didn't miss a beat due to the recall, except inasmuch as supplies were decreased by the bottleneck involving the tires. The model was the bestselling SUV in the United States for the tenth straight year, breaking its own record with sales of 445,157. In January 2001, the new Explorer arrived in showrooms and took off, as popular a model as ever despite a slowing economy. However, the problems with Bridgestone/Firestone and its tires would surface again in 2001, even more ferociously than before.

Research supplied by public-interest groups augmented an NHTSA advisory by warning that various kinds of Firestone tires installed on Explorers and on Ford trucks were still a source of danger from disintegration. Ford Motor, struggling to maintain a heated sales pace for the Explorer in the face of an economic downturn, was not about to let the Firestone stain spread to its all-around bestselling vehicle, the F-150 pickup—or to any other model, for that matter. Ford representatives, including Carlos Mazzorin, group vice president for global purchasing, traveled to Firestone's headquarters in Nashville, in hopes of negotiating a voluntary recall. None was forthcoming, as the tire maker continued to imply that its tires were fine and the only problem was with Ford's vehicles. The four-hour meeting, held on May 21, ended when Firestone president John Lampe pulled a letter from his briefcase. Handing it to Mazzorin, he said, very simply, "I'm sorry to have to do this, but at this point we've got to break our relationship with you."[50] The letter categorically ended all business between Firestone and Ford Motor. It was a shocking move, but Ford Motor didn't flinch.

The next day, Ford announced that it was recalling every last Firestone tire still equipped on its Explorer and truck vehicles—13 million tires in all. The cost was calculated at $2.1 billion, but it was worth it for Ford to know that it was not going to suffer any further damage as a result of Firestone tires. While Ford research indicated that the Firestones remaining on its light trucks and SUVs were three times as likely to disintegrate as other tires, government officials were unconvinced that the problem was quite that serious. It may have been true, as Firestone's John Lampe gloated, that Ford was replacing "good tires with good tires,"[51] but the automaker didn't want to take any chances. It was finished with Firestone.

Firestone continued the grudge match a few weeks later by formally asking the NHTSA to investigate the Ford Explorer for defects that made it susceptible to rollover. Once again, industry observers were shocked by the depths to which Ford and Firestone had sunk. No one could recollect another instance of one company asking the government group to go after another.[52]

In the face of these developments, journalists looked beyond the figures and even the impact on safety. The bigger story, it seemed, was the breakup of America's oldest business chums. Dozens of articles appeared mourning the end of a business friendship that had lasted nearly one hundred years. Henry Ford and Harvey Firestone were remembered, and inevitably, Bill Ford Jr. was asked to comment. He was, after all, as much a Firestone as he was a Ford; his mother was Harvey's granddaughter. "This decision is a painful one for me personally," he said, regarding the recall that effectively erased the name Firestone from Ford's most popular vehicles. "To see all this taking place is deeply disturbing."[53]

In a sense, however, Bill Ford Jr. symbolized the reason that the break was inevitable. He had no connection to Firestone Tire & Rubber. He worked for Ford Motor and, like every descendant of Henry Ford, was still connected through family ownership to the company. Firestone, though a publicly held company from the beginning, had once been just as much of a family enterprise; Harvey Firestone Jr. was president for an even longer term than his father, and Harvey III took charge until the 1960s. However, by the time Bridgestone bought it out in 1988, few family members still owned stock and those who did had no particular influence. It was a typical evolution, as family members moved on to value other pursuits. And Firestone Tire & Rubber moved on, too, transferring its headquarters from its original hometown of Akron to Tennessee. Ford Motor, however, stayed in Dearborn and kept hold of the Fords. No matter which company was right or wrong in the tire controversy, it might have been worked out if there was still more of *Firestone* in Bridgestone/Firestone. As it was, the 2001 breakup seemed an afterthought for two companies that had grown distant many years before.

Investigations into the cause of the accidents continued long after the public scandals of 2000–2001. Several theories were advanced, including one maintaining that neither Ford nor Firestone had produced culpable products, but that all SUVs were susceptible to tire strain and subsequent rollover. However, the tire problems cost Ford Motor Company at least $3 billion. More than that, they cost the lives of 271 Ford customers.[54] Although the NHTSA eventually exonerated Ford, concluding that the design of the Ford

Explorer was not to blame for the accidents, the entire episode cast a pall over the headquarters. Within the company, there were whisperings that the kind of senior engineers and solid middle managers purged as "low potential" were just the types who might have spotted the Firestone problem early on, before it became a full-blown disaster. "I remember around Christmas 1996," said a technical specialist named Craig Toepfer, "they got rid of so many senior engineers and guys with test-operations experience. You knew it was going on because the billboards at work were filled with retiree party announcements. Those older guys were the ones who we relied on to catch quality problems."[55]

Overall, Ford's hard-won standards in both quality and productivity were seen to be slipping in 2001. There was a sense that the company was involved in so many ventures—the Internet, automobile repair, and other services—that it was overlooking just how hard it is to build and market a successful automobile. While the Firestone tire debacle didn't reflect anything in particular that Ford had done wrong, it was a humbling experience nonetheless. It reminded the company that its attention had to be directed, full-time, to the cars its customers would drive. As one result of the Firestone debacle, Ford equipped its new Windstar minivans with a state-of-the-art tire-monitoring system. If a tire pressure was low, the Windstar dashboard would light up with an image of a radial tire with an exclamation mark in the middle. The owner's manual, however, warned that this new tire-monitoring system was not 100 percent foolproof.[56]

While Ford Motor Company was working through its exploding tire woes, it still managed to launch a number of exciting new vehicles, which reminded investors and consumers alike why it ranked as the fourth-largest U.S. corporation (behind Wal-Mart, Exxon Mobil, and General Motors).[57] In 1999, for example, Ford partnered with Harley-Davidson to produce a special-edition F-150 Supercrew truck. Offered in a limited quantity, it was typically painted "dark shadow gray," with the famed Harley-Davidson bar-and-shield logo on the grille, rear quarter panel, and hubcaps. At the launch, the two companies highlighted their shared history, each having been founded in 1903. "A strategic alliance between the Ford Motor Company and Harley-Davidson makes mutual historic and business sense," noted Gurminder Bedi, vice president of the Ford Truck Vehicle Center. "Our common heritage as American motor vehicles manufacturers and our common centennials of 2003 were just too good to pass up as a natural business opportunity."[58] The Harley-Davidson F-150 was manufactured at Ford's truck plant in Oakville, Ontario. Under the hood, 340 hp blasted out from a supercharged 5.4-liter Triton V-8 engine with 425 pound-feet of torque—with the pedal to the metal, it sounded like a gang of Hells Angels roaring up a hill. "What can I say?" wrote Laura Ricks, automotive editor of the *New Orleans Times-Picayune,* after test-driving one. "Think of Vin Diesel or maybe The Rock on steroids, a pan of frosted brownies and six cups of Colombian dark-roasted double espresso and you've got the picture."[59]

Base-priced at $35,750, the F-150 Supercrew sold well to hard-core bikers, like those who converged on Sturgis, South Dakota, every summer. It was there, in August 1999, with the Black Hills forming a backdrop, that Ford and Harley introduced the new truck. The throaty F-150 Supercrew's appeal spread beyond the biker crowd, however, encompassing even urban professionals who yearned for a Harley-Davidson's "brute power" but shied from going as far as to buy a motorcycle. "I'm a little too conservative to get a Harley bike," admitted Louisiana dentist Emmett Zimmerman when he bought his F-150 Supercrew. "This is my way of getting a Harley."[60]

Ever since Ford Motor introduced its all-new post–World War II F-1 pickups in January 1948, the Truck Division had been the company's steadiest cash cow. From 1981 to 1997, for example, the F-series outsold every other vehicle—car or truck—in North America. Starting in 1976, when it regained its lead over Chevrolet in truck sales, it outsold every other truck in the United States for a quarter century. The eight F-Series assembly plants scattered around North and South America were among the most productive industrial facilities in the world. And the Ford Truck Proving Grounds in the Arizona desert, where F-series vehicles were put through their drills on a track filled with obstacles, had grown into a legendary endurance facility. The names of those obstacles reflected the harrowing challenges they represented: Sandwash, Twist Ditch, Translator Hill, Power Hop Hill, and Mudbath. "We give our F-150s a thorough beating beyond anything customers will put them through," Bedi noted. "Before a customer puts his new F-150 to work we've been hard at work putting more than five million miles of durability, development and evaluation testing on prototypes to ensure they have earned the 'Ford Tough' label."[61] At the January 2003 North American Auto Show in Detroit, the newly designed F-150 garnered the most enthusiastic media attention—in part because for the first time some models had an automatic gearshift installed between the seats, instead of being ensconced on the steering column.[62]

As Ford Motor headed toward its centennial, the company turned to past brands to boost profits and invigorate its sense of identity. The relaunch of the Thunderbird in 2002 was a solid hit with customers. The company manufactured only 25,000 of the hardtop convertibles, which sold out in just a few months. Automobile critics around the world praised the retro Thunderbird for its high-quality components and eye-catching design. "Its weight (3,775 pounds) keeps it from being a true sports car," *Auto Guide* noted. "Yet this new T-Bird is a pleasure to drive, even on secondary roads." The Automobile

Association of America summed up why the new T-bird was so successful by naming it "Cool Car" of the year.[63]

Mercury tried to capitalize on its own heritage in June 2002, when the 2003 Marauder appeared in showrooms. Modeled after the 1963 Marauder, a widely admired race/muscle car, the new version was intended to inject excitement in Ford Motor's dullest division. There was nothing unusual about looking backward for ideas to polish a brand name. At the time the Marauder was launched, Nissan was about to reintroduce the Z car; Chrysler, the 300M sedan; and Pontiac, the GTO. But there was something desperate about the Marauder. At the time the Marauder appeared in showrooms, Mercury sales had dropped 22.8 percent over the previous year. The word most attached to Mercury was "staid," and the hope was that the Marauder, along with the new Mercury Mountaineer, a handsome SUV, would make Mercury relevant again. While both the Marauder and Mountaineer were very well received, Ford still had to deny rumors on the eve of the centennial that it intended to discontinue the entire division.

New models proved important, but the best news for Ford Motor following the Firestone tire flap was that the Explorer continued to sell well. Automotive experts were astonished by its resilience. Somehow customers forgot images from previous years, of mangled Explorers and shredded tires, and continued to buy the vehicle in astounding numbers. Ford sold 51,021 Explorers in August 2002, breaking all records for SUV sales in a single month. Even George Pipas, Ford's leading sales analyst, was stunned. "If ever there was a comeback kid," he told the Detroit News, "it's the Explorer."[64]

Why did the Explorer survive the Firestone crisis? Analysts across America offered varied explanations. Some felt that like Johnson & Johnson's Tylenol, bottles of which had been poisoned in Chicago-area stores in the early 1980s, the Explorer was too well established just to fade away. There was also Ford's follow-up offer of zero percent financing. But the main reason was one that old Henry Ford would have understood: brand loyalty. More than four million people owned Explorers and were happy with them. They were ready to buy the redesigned Explorer and to trust Ford Motor Company that the tire problems were over. Mark Truby of the Detroit News summed up the Explorer's unique position when he wrote that it was "nearly unheard-of for a consumer product to pass through a blizzard of negative publicity and safety questions virtually unscathed."[65] As for those recalled Firestone tires, Bill Ford Jr. had truckloads of them ground up and spread beneath the turf at Ford Field and underneath a highway in New Mexico, as part of his campaign against wasting resources.[66]

As it became more apparent that Ford Motor was going in the wrong direction in 2000–2001, or at any rate in too many directions at once, people within the company, along with the family, began to feel as though they had heard too much from Jac Nasser, who was loaded with operational responsibility as both CEO and president, and not enough from Bill Ford Jr., left in the background as chairman.

The one issue on which Bill Ford Jr. was making an impact in the corporation at that time was the environment. He believed that eco-efficiency was the wave of the future, and that to be competitive Ford Motor Company had to manufacture high-tech, environmentally friendly vehicles. He made speeches on a topic he had thoroughly researched: the need to phase out the internal combustion engine in favor of hydrogen fuel cells. Bill Jr. tried to encourage a new "green attitude" at Ford and in the wider auto industry. A major new vehicle assembly plant at River Rouge, for example, was designed to be part of the natural landscape, not an industrial blight on it; the roof of the 1.1-million-square-foot assembly plant was insulated with sedum, a type of ground cover. Ford persuaded the board to allocate $2 billion to recast the entire River Rouge plant as the site of a new kind of industrial revolution: a green one, quite literally, with space for meadows, in addition to high-tech methods of reducing pollution, inside the plant and out. He wanted nothing less than to transform Ford Motor's great twentieth-century icon into a new model of clean, eco-efficient sustainable manufacturing. "I would like the Rouge again to be the most copied and studied industrial complex in the world," Bill Ford Jr. said. "My great-grandfather would have thought this was fantastic."[67]

Henry Ford had Albert Kahn to design his factories of tomorrow, and Bill Ford Jr. embraced the vision of the brilliant architect William McDonough, whose home base was Charlottesville, Virginia. Under Ford's visionary leadership, the Rouge complex would be transformed into a green oasis with twenty-two acres of wetlands, grass boulevards, bird sanctuaries, and pollution-free canals.[68] "All the air will be filtered and clean so you'll be in a beautiful space with daylight and fresh air and good food," McDonough enthused. "And up over workers' heads will be birds chirping. That's a whole different view of industrial manufacturing."[69] The River Rouge, considered one of the dirtiest waterways in America, would be brought back to life, safe enough to swim in. (Over $535 million in federal grants had been allocated by 2003 to help Ford Motor clean up the river.) The factory, meanwhile, would have solar panels and ivy covering its sides to manufacture oxygen and cool the massive edifice. Ford believed this new eco-efficient facility would help increase vehicle production, reduce air and water pollution, and make life better for his employees.[70]

Henry Ford, like his great-grandson, had hated wasting resources. He advocated recycling and promoted corn-derived ethanol as a fuel. Ford wrote in 1926, "You must get the most out of time."[71] Both men felt nature regenerated the human psyche. While the old man read works by naturalist John

Burroughs, his great-grandson absorbed such environmental classics as Rachel Carson's *Silent Spring* and Edward Abbey's *Desert Solitaire*. So Bill Ford Jr.'s Thoreauvian environmentalism was, in a sense, a family tradition.

On the environmental front Bill Ford Jr. found an unexpected ally in Lee Iacocca, who had retired to Bel Air, California, to head an electric bike and car company, the eponymous Lido Motors. "The car's a wonderful thing," Iacocca noted; "it gave people mobility, it created jobs, but it had a couple of ugly side effects called pollution and congestion." While at Ford Motor, Iacocca had given the head of scientific laboratories, Mike Barrons, millions of dollars a year to explore the possibility of an electric car. Even after Iacocca moved to Chrysler, the company continued to build electric vehicles, eventually producing the Th!nk car line in conjunction with a Norwegian firm. While the Th!nk program had flopped, largely on technical grounds, Iacocca still believed that Bill Ford Jr. was pioneering along the right path. "Billy is right on all accounts. The technology *is* available so it's only right to slowly introduce it to the new generation and show them how quiet and nonpolluting it is."[72]

Bill Ford Jr.'s environmentalist stance made him a media darling. *Newsweek* featured him on its cover, applauding his efforts to talk about the health hazards of auto emissions and the dangers of global warming. The *New York Times* regarded him as the embodiment of Detroit's new turnaround. But just as environmental groups and the media hoisted him to stardom, they also stood ready to rip him down. He made a great splash in January 2001 at the Los Angeles Auto Show when he unveiled Ford Motor's Escape HEV (hybrid electric vehicle) designed to be one of the cleanest, most fuel-efficient SUVs manufactured anywhere. "Whether in the city or off the beaten path, the new Ford Escape has been designed to leave a light footprint on the environment," Jim O'Connor, president of the Ford Division, declared. "For a new generation of smart SUV owners, it is a demonstration that environmental compatibility can be a lot of fun."[73] The Los Angeles show was the last time Bill Jr. got great press on the environment, though. Soon he began to feel quite misunderstood, as he came under attack as a "hypocrite,"[74] blamed for every gas-guzzling SUV sold by Ford and every hydrocarbon released by a Ford car into the air. Angry environmentalists wanted Ford to sell only pocket-sized Escapes, not hefty Navigators, Explorers, and Expeditions.

The Sierra Club went after him with a determined vengeance. "We've focused our attack on Bill," Daniel Becker, director of the Sierra Club's Global Warming and Energy Program, explained, "because he knows better than to run ads against the CAFE standards and keep pushing SUVs on consumers. He is an irresponsible corporate executive and phony environmentalist."[75] The Sierra Club's logic was that Bill Ford Jr. would become the environmental leader of the Big Three and truly live up to his conservationist values only if it exposed the disparity between his words and actions. He was being made an example because he was one of them.

Yet Bill Jr. had never claimed to be a single-minded environmentalist. He had always described himself as "an environmentalist/industrialist," interested in leading his company and the rest of the field in a new direction, not in changing Ford Motor in one fell swoop. "I think being painted as an environmentalist in some ways hurts me," he said, "because people think I'm a one-dimensional person. And they also think that therefore, by definition, I don't care about the shareholder, the customer. The environment really to me is just one more piece of the puzzle."[76]

People inside Ford Motor Company were sometimes uncertain as to Bill Ford Jr.'s priorities regarding the environment. Nevertheless, he was certainly a popular figure there, with an easygoing, jocular manner around employees at all levels. As chairman of the board of directors, he was instrumental in long-term planning and, specifically, in overseeing where and how the company spent its money. However, as the board, the family, and a great many people who worked at Ford Motor felt more and more strongly that the company was unraveling, Bill Ford Jr. found that he had no leverage with which to effect changes. In fact, he was not included in operational decisions or even in briefings on issues of the day. Jac Nasser, a one-man band of a leader at Ford Motor, was leaving his boss out. Perhaps if the business had been going well, no one would have minded. In March 2001, Ford Motor had come close to overtaking GM as the world's leading automaker, on the basis of sales and market capitalization,[77] but everything receded from that point on: profits, sales, and even dividends. Barely more than a year after the company distributed a special dividend to shareholders, it was forced to lower the regular one. Things were not going well.

Something had to be done and it was Bill Ford Jr.'s turn to do it. The man some had thought too "mousy" to wield power had to act. "I have the responsibility for 350,000 people here," he once explained, "and I have to make the right decisions for them and their families and their future—and that really then makes it relatively easy to be tough. Because the alternative to that is to be soft and let it drift, and that's a sure way to ruin."[78]

Interestingly, it was just around this time that Ford Motor Company began winning plaudits in the press for initiating a number of costly new cradle-to-grave employee-benefit programs. Under the headline "Family Is Job One," for instance, in May 2001 *Time* noted: "Corporate child care is hardly a new concept, but the Ford Motor Co. is promising to take this benefit to a new level. The company will offer an ambitious range of subsidized services that include 24-hr. on-site child care, summer camp and tutoring for middle schoolers, recreation and SAT prep for teens as well as financial planning for retirees and assistance to shut-in seniors. Beginning this fall and working closely with the UAW, Ford will roll out the red carpet for employees at 31 family service and learning centers over the next two years."[79]

Not since the days of Henry Ford's company stores and the early, humanitarian Sociology Department had an American automaker committed to such an extensive employee-support plan. Industry observers saw the hand of Bill Ford Jr. in such developments. At least at intervals, it seemed Ford Motor needed an actual Ford at the top to stoke the internal enthusiasm the company had always relied upon.

Beginning with a February 6, 2001, *New York Times* article headlined "Ford Heir Struggles for Control," the press speculated that Jacques Nasser's days were numbered. Bill Jr., as chairman, did not feel the CEO was in a position to provide the leadership that the company needed, and on October 30, 2001, he said as much to Nasser in a three-hour meeting that ended with Nasser's resignation. Bill Ford Jr. became CEO, while also remaining chairman. In a speech the next day at World Headquarters in Dearborn, he explained his vision in terms that every Ford employee could understand—in that era or any other. "We need," he said, "to get our focus back on the basics of our business—building great cars and trucks."[80] From that moment onward the slogan at World Headquarters was "Back to Basics."

Having been watching their stock portfolio dwindle, the Ford family was ecstatic about purging the company of Jacques Nasser. "The company, dealers, and family would have been better off if Bill assumed the CEO job earlier," Anne Ford believed. "We all saw that *that man* was bringing the company to ruin."[81]

It is not hard to sum up Nasser's tenure at Ford Motor Company: he failed to reinvent the company, as he so ambitiously had hoped to do. Moreover, he let the core business of automaking drift. While he cleaned out his desk at corporate headquarters, the business world was aghast that Ford Motor Company had lost $5.5 billion in 2001 on his watch. History will no doubt remember him as the Ford Motor CEO who dealt with the Firestone tire problem as well as could be expected. However, under his reign, some of Ford's most promising managerial talent was driven out to make room for his disciples from outside the auto industry. "Talk to just about anyone in the industry, particularly in Detroit," Daniel Howes wrote in the *Detroit News* a few days after Nasser's dismissal, "and they'll shake their heads in amazement at how quickly Ford under Nasser went from world-beater to doormat."[82] Time may well credit Nasser for bringing Land Rover and Volvo into the Ford family, but at the moment of his firing the only thing credited to him was his own ambition. "Most analysts say that while Mr. Nasser was broadening Ford's reach, he did not do enough to keep its core business competitive," Danny Hakim wrote in the *New York Times* a year later, evaluating his legacy. "The pace of product development stagnated, quality rankings slumped and Ford's cost structure made General Motors look svelte by comparison. Beyond that, Mr. Nasser's style alienated many of the company's leading constituencies—from dealer groups who resented the company's incursion into dealerships to white-collar workers who objected to a new corporate grading system."[83]

To Bill Ford Jr.'s credit, he fired Nasser decisively, when it became necessary. He and the rest of the board realized that Nasser was addicted to spending money—the company's money, more specifically. His ability to burn through billions was unprecedented in the annals of American business history. (After taking a year off, Nasser was hired by Bank One's leverage buyout arm, which made him nonexecutive chairman of Polaroid.)[84]

The mess left behind was for Bill Jr. to clean up. At a similar crisis point, Henry Ford II had recruited Ernie Breech and other highly experienced auto executives to help him reorganize the corporation. He also brought in the Whiz Kids. Bill Ford Jr., after ridding the company of Nasser's followers, was prepared to do the same as the centennial approached. He turned to a cabal of seasoned automobile executives—the so-called Old Wizards—to help him save Ford Motor.

Most of the Wizards had distinguished careers in selling vehicles in Europe, and many were from Great Britain. They were pros who knew the industry better than anyone else around. Nick Scheele, who had performed a miracle during the 1990s in making Jaguar profitable, became chief operating officer. With the relaxed personality of an English country gentleman, Scheele tackled his job as second-in-command with the same focus that had made a success of his management at Jaguar. His theme then, and later for Ford Motor as a whole, was building excellent cars. While the company was involved in other pursuits, automaking was the identity that bound everything else together, in his eyes. When asked about his vision for Ford Motor in a TV interview, Scheele responded, "I think Ford, really, you've got to look backwards before you look forward. We are now ninety-eight years old. Founded in June of 1903. We're close to the end of our first century. We're looking forward to build[ing] Ford into the next century. And to do that, you can only do it with commitment from everybody who works with and for us. . . . We need to work for the next century with fantastic product."[85]

Englishman David W. Thursfield was already serving as CEO of Ford of Europe when he was called to World Headquarters to become group vice president of international operations. Because the company's profitability had changed so quickly, with a loss for 2001 after years of good earnings, recognized finance experts were given a strong role in Bill Ford Jr.'s revamped executive suite. One was Carl Reichardt, formerly chairman of the Wells Fargo Bank. Another would be Allan Gilmour, the former Ford vice chairman, who had retired in 1995; in 2002, at sixty-seven, he became chief financial officer.

Under Bill Ford Jr., Ford Motor Company simplified itself. It did away with programs that distracted those associated with the company from focusing on building or selling cars. It almost immediately divested itself of most of the consumer- and Internet-based businesses that were supposed to turn it into a service company. The Auto Collection superdealerships were dismantled, to the relief of dealers. And employees were equally happy, by and large, to see the 10-80-10 evaluation plan canceled.

"Most of the people joined this company," Bill Ford Jr. said about a year after becoming CEO, "because they love cars and trucks. And the fact that we are now rededicating ourselves to building fantastic cars and trucks is something that really is firing up the troops."[86]

Becoming a simpler operation, however, meant Ford Motor Company also had to become a smaller company. Early in 2002, three months after taking on the role of CEO, Bill Ford Jr. announced a massive worldwide restructuring that would eliminate four models, including the venerable Lincoln Continental, five plants, and 35,000 jobs—10 percent of the company's workforce.

For years, it had been Ford Motor Company's little secret that it could produce many more cars than it actually did, turning out about 4.8 million annually in North America, even though the firm had the facilities and manpower to build some 5.7 million units per year. In truth, the company had been making so much money that it could afford this luxury of reserve production capacity 20 percent above marketable output. Plant closings in the midst of such prosperity, however sensible, would have spawned serious problems with both the UAW and local governments. Anyway, compared with that of other automakers, Ford's production capacity was downright lean. By 2002, however, Ford Motor's fortunes had taken a downturn, leaving the firm no choice but to make some unpopular decisions. The consequences included shutting down a Ranger plant in Edison, New Jersey; engine-parts manufacturing facilities in Cleveland and Dearborn; and an Explorer plant in St. Louis. Industry observers blanched most at the last, deducing from the St. Louis closing that the company had reason to doubt the vigor of Explorer sales projections for the future—speculation that proved untrue.

"We realize that some of the things that must be done will be painful," Bill Ford Jr. admitted in announcing his firm's restructuring. Then he added, "I can't begin to describe how sorry I am."[87]

On that day and for many others to come, Bill Ford Jr. had to face the downside of inheriting the helm of Ford Motor Company. Along with the corporate perks and power, he was forced to get used to performing "a high-wire act without a net." He reflected, "Everything I do as CEO—and I have learned this kind of the hard way, in the first six months on the job—every decision upsets somebody. And so all you can do is just stay true to your principles and do what you think is the right thing, and let the chips fall where they may."[88]

Predictably the news of Ford Motor's plant closings did not sit well with the UAW. On November 1, 1999, the company had brokered a three-year labor agreement with the union in which job security protections under its Guaranteed Employment Numbers program had been substantially increased. At the time, Ford's chief negotiator, Vice President Ron Gettelfinger, had declared, "I am confident that this contract will provide the UAW active and retired workers and their families unprecedented job and economic security."[89] Union President Stephen P. Yokich likewise pronounced the accord a milestone. It was reached, however, before Ford Motor began closing plants and laying off workers by the thousands. In truth, the UAW was itself in a downward spiral at the dawn of the twenty-first century. Over Labor Day weekend 2002, for instance, the Sunday edition of the joint *Detroit News and Free Press* ran a story headlined "Unions Fight to Maintain Relevance." With national news reports of layoff notices piling up, corporate accounting scandals spreading, and the economy sagging, the UAW was hurting, alongside the rest of America's labor organizations and those they represented.[90] Many of the new factories operated in the United States by foreign automakers were nonunion, and as their numbers grew, auto union membership dropped by more than half nationwide, from 1.5 million in 1979 to fewer than 700,000 in 2001. Younger workers, uninterested in union benefit plans, simply saw less reason to pay UAW dues, if they could get away with it by working at nonunion shops.

Organized or not, however, all the firm's employees were left to wonder why erstwhile CEO Jacques Nasser garnered $17.8 million for his services in 2001, the same year he was ousted from the company. The math never could make sense to the average assembly-line worker. Why should Nasser or any other employee get a 35 percent raise over his 2000 compensation during a year in which the company reported a $5.5 billion loss? The answer looked as clear as the corporate calculations were murky: like most CEOs of major U.S. concerns, Jacques Nasser had been grossly overpaid.[91]

Acknowledging the laborers' resentment, Bill Ford Jr. made a point of refusing any salary or bonus compensation other than stock options. "If we do get it right, I'll get paid very well on these stock options," he said. "If we don't, I won't get paid. That's a risk I'm willing to take."[92] Actually, paying executives in stock options and thus encouraging them to manage for the sake of the share price had led to many of the corporate scandals of 2001–2002. However, Bill Ford Jr. was not much concerned with enlarging his personal fortune, and his refusal of a regular salary went far to ingratiate him with his company's rank and file. His personal popularity deepened as he made a habit of dropping in at the Rouge plant to talk with workers candidly in a style not unlike that of his uncle Henry Ford II and his illustrious great-grandfather. Thus, as its centennial neared, despite the rash of plant closings, Ford Motor enjoyed better labor relations than either GM or DaimlerChrysler. Clearly, Bill Ford Jr. seemed intent on keeping it that way—and on keeping the public's favor, too.

Neither would prove easy in the opening years of the twenty-first century, as grim financial news continued to churn out of Dearborn and Ford Motor's stock sank into single digits. True to his heritage, Bill Ford Jr. did his best to put a brave face on the situation. In the Ford Motor Corporate Citizenship Report, released after a four-month delay, the corporation showcased the improvement of the fuel economy of its SUVs by 7 percent over its previous models. The effort backfired, however, as conservation groups interpreted the report as the company's signal that it was abandoning any serious commitment to protecting the environment. A defensive Ford Motor countered that the company was not finished: it would boost fuel efficiency in its 2005 SUVs by a full 25 percent.[93]

One area in which Bill Ford Jr. put his alternative-fuels campaign into action was with the partnership he forged with the National Park Foundation and the National Park Service. Together they started replacing old tour buses that ran on gasoline with vehicles propelled by clean propane fuel. In Montana's Glacier National Park, for example, Bill Ford Jr. had the venerable 1930s open-air tour buses converted to run on clean fuel. In March 2001 these historic buses once again climbed across the Continental Divide amid towering cliffs and glacial summits offering sightseers majestic views—and they weren't putting pollutants in the atmosphere.[94]

As always, there was also good news coming from the Truck Division. Explorers continued to be the bestselling SUVs. It was with great joy that COO Nick Scheele, accompanied by UAW-Ford President Gerald Bantom, visited the Louisville, Kentucky, Assembly Plant in September 2002 to watch the five-millionth Explorer roll off the line. The purchasers were Patrick and Donna Barry of Louisville, who had gone to purchase their fourth Explorer and were told that it was the five millionth, a black Explorer XLT with the sport package. Workers cheered, the Barrys beamed, and the plant manager, John Tankesleg, declared the Explorer a "star."[95]

But the five-millionth Explorer was a rare high note in an off year when the bad news just kept coming. Jaguar suffered operating losses of nearly $200 million; workers in divisions worldwide howled over the plant shutdowns; and the company's bond rating, a measure of its creditworthiness, tumbled to near-junk status.[96] Moreover, immediate competition loomed on every front: General Motors was waging an effective price war, offering no-money-down financing packages on its cars; DaimlerChrysler kept winning good press as the "industry's latest comeback" story; and Toyota and Nissan continued to gain ground in the truck market.

Business was so bad at Lincoln-Mercury that the division was forced to move its headquarters back to Dearborn from its ostensibly more glamorous outpost in Irvine, California.[97] Perhaps most disturbing of all, Ford's would-be modern-day Model T—the low-cost Ford Focus, first introduced in 1999—

went through no fewer than eleven safety recalls over a couple of years. Designed largely in Europe, the Focus offered nifty styling and handling, but from its inception the inexpensive little car had drawn complaints about faulty wiring and even engine fires. *New York Times* Detroit bureau reporter Danny Hakim went so far as to call the Ford Focus the "most error-prone car in the industry."[98]

Consequently, while GM's share value rose, Ford Motor's took a swan dive. In 2002 overall sales fell 8.8 percent. Between May and October 2002, Ford stock fell an astounding 60 percent. On October 10, a share in Ford Motor traded at $7.60, down from $23 just fourteen months earlier. "I never thought I'd see the day when a share of Ford stock was under $8," noted Lee Iacocca. "It's unbelievable—but it will come back."[99]

Anxious to put a good face on the dire situation, Allan Gilmour recommended that investors just "ignore" Ford Motor Company's falling stock, viewing it as a temporary dip and not a sign that the company was headed toward bankruptcy. "It's been a terrible stock market, not only for Ford but for many other companies as well," Gilmour maintained in October 2002. "Within the last week or two, something like 800 companies on the stock exchange reached their low for the last fifty-two weeks, so everything is way, way down, and we've obviously been way, way down, also." Conscious that since the September 11, 2001, terrorist attacks, American consumer confidence had diminished, Gilmour insisted that Ford Motor had "good plans and good execution" slated for the future. As a blue-chip stock, Ford Motor Company, he insisted, was always a winning bet.[100]

Following writer Norman Mailer's dictum that "only in movement does man have a chance," in October 2002 Bill Ford Jr. began barnstorming the country with chief financial officer Allan Gilmour at his side, meeting business leaders from Boston to San Francisco to spread their optimism about the firm's future. Ford Motor Company had been down before, the executives assured skeptics, yet it had always soared from the ashes and would again. Their motto was "A resurgence is under way." Although the goodwill tour won plaudits, the junket did nothing to solve Ford Motor's pressing financial dilemmas. As Norihiko Shirouzu wrote in the *Wall Street Journal,* any way you sliced it, Ford Motor was "beleaguered."[101]

It is said that blood will win out, and in 2002 the future of Ford Motor Company depended on the truth of that adage. In the century before, on a surprising number of occasions, only the forceful persona of founder Henry Ford had rescued the company from certain ruin—usually through his sheer will, combined with his near infallible powers of coercion. In the second year of the twenty-first century, the same feat fell to his great-grandson. Bill Ford Jr. had long tried to downplay what he called the "cult of personality" surrounding his position in the company, however. Although he had been asked several times to appear in Ford Motor's advertising for the good of the firm, he demurred. "No one else in business can say their chairman and CEO is the great-grandson," explained Nick Scheele, one of those who pushed the idea.[102] Finally, early in 2002, after marketing executives presented Bill Ford Jr. with hard research that proved how much his name meant to Ford Motor, he did star in some TV commercials. "It can help the company," Bill Jr. noted. "That's why I decided to do it. The research told us that the heritage of the company was something very strong and something we didn't play to enough."[103]

Like his great-grandfather, however, Bill Ford Jr. agreed to give up his relative anonymity only on his own terms. "They had a number of staged things for me," he said. "They wanted me to say certain things about certain products and I said no, because I don't feel that way. I don't want to do anything in the ads that isn't real and isn't part of my life."[104] In the end, the CEO simply spoke into a camera in his shirtsleeves for a couple of hours on the aspects of Ford Motor Company that meant the most to him, including the daunting legacy of the first Henry Ford. The resulting video was then edited into a series of "No Boundaries" commercials, some featuring vintage film and sleekly produced state-of-the-art footage of the latest Ford models in action.[105]

Bill Ford Jr.'s well-received, up-close-and-personal "No Boundaries" ads were only a start toward winching his family's firm from its mire of troubles. Ford Motor began looking more closely at its entire history in preparation for the company's centennial celebration in June 2003. The timing would prove fortunate. Recalling Ford Motor's grand heritage served to remind customers and employees alike that their investment lay in an enterprise that had survived hard times before and had a track record of emerging from them triumphant. And each time the company had pulled itself out with a combination of innovation and improvement.

Even before airing Bill Jr.'s ad campaign, the company had begun running print advertisements underlining its century-long commitment to high corporate standards and principles. One ad that appeared in national magazines in the summer of 2001, headlined "the goal is not to meet expectations, but to define new ones," included a black-and-white photo showing race-car driver Jimmy Clark and owner Colin Chapman after notching Ford Motor's first victory at Indianapolis in 1965 in a "Lotus powered by Ford" car; the caption noted the win "was also the first for a rear-engine chassis." The text of the ad made the point unmistakable: "At Ford, our goal is to stay on the cutting edge by constantly thinking ahead. . . . It's all part of a winning attitude that's at the very core of Ford Racing" as exemplified by Clark and Chapman, "whose spirit and passion broke new ground in competitive motorsports. It's this same forward-thinking attitude that shapes our products as we move into the new century." The tag line read "We Race. You Win."[106]

A year later, Ford Motor would introduce its 2003 Roush Mustang 360R, described in the *New York Post* as a "serious wheel-spinner and head-turner with the balance of an Olympics gymnast and a price tag of $39,995." The sleek new speedster bore the name of NASCAR design-engineering star Jack Roush, identified by auto reviewer Russ Devault as "Ford's go-to guy now that Cobra-creator Carroll Shelby is more legend than performance practitioner." After waxing near passionate over the blazing new Mustang, the paper reported a feature even more exciting for its manufacturer than the car's 360-horsepower engine: its "recognition factor." "It stumped some," the reviewer wrote of people who witnessed his test drive, "but a surprising number of middle-aged males and teen-age females correctly and immediately identified the 360R as a Roush Mustang."[107] This was the kind of brand recognition Henry Ford himself had risked his neck to get even before he founded Ford Motor.

Another racing-linked full-page ad appeared in *USA Today* to invite the public to the Ford Racing Centennial Festival at Greenfield Village in October 2002, featuring nearly 200 cars and a host of Ford Racing's star drivers and designers. The ad, like the festival, again emphasized the company's traditions and surviving power, noting of the original Henry Ford's historic victory over Alexander Winton exactly a century before that "he wasn't exactly the picture of a race car driver. . . . And for good reason. He wasn't one. Henry Ford was an engineer who saw the automobile as much more than a rich man's toy, and who dreamed of a nation that ran on gasoline instead of oats. He also saw auto racing as a means to jump-start that dream. . . . And while America has changed profoundly since 'the race,' the passion with which we race, research and build vehicles, a passion inherited from Henry Ford himself, remains *un*changed."[108]

Again, the point was unmistakable—especially coming just two weeks before the founding Ford's great-grandson would take over the corporate driver's seat as chairman and CEO. Like his most illustrious forebear, Bill Ford Jr. seemed to have an intuitive grasp of how to use his name to his firm's best advantage exactly when it was needed. And like his great-grandfather, who first afforded wheels for the world, Bill Ford Jr. appeared intent on putting his company's focus back on the tactic that underscored so much of its century-long success: giving customers what they wanted.

Thus were born Kathy and Lewis, to whom in 2002 Ford Motor Company pinned a substantial chunk of its future. Kathy, thirty-nine, was a white part-time speech pathologist and Humane Society volunteer married to Joe, a civil engineer with whom she has two children, ages six and ten, and one large dog. She graduated from Syracuse University and plays in a weekly volleyball league. Lewis, forty-one, is a black First National Bank branch manager in Charlotte, a gym regular, and a weekend home-renovation enthusiast married to Anne, a real estate agent with whom he has two children, ages fourteen and seventeen. The elder, Jennifer, is a freshman at the University of North Carolina; the couple's son looks forward to getting his learner's permit. The most interesting aspect of these detailed backgrounds is Kathy and Lewis do not exist, except in the analyses of the Ford Motor marketing department.[109]

Early in 2001, in a number of cities nationwide, Ford Motor commissioned "customer immersion" market research on both its own recent buyers and those of its rivals to pinpoint precisely what the modern public wanted from and in their cars. "Surveyors practically moved in with families," Greg Schneider reported in the *Washington Post*, "to see not just how they drove but how they lived, so the cars could be put into a larger context. The surveyors would show up at 8 A.M. and hang around through dinner, snooping in refrigerators, riding along to soccer practice or the grocery store."[110] The data thus gleaned were then meticulously pored over and parsed by the marketing staff as well as by executives and staffers throughout the corporation. The resulting analyses begat Kathy and Lewis—and the new Fords designed just for them.

For Kathy, the company designed a gas-electric hybrid; for Lewis, a European-style sedan. Perhaps most telling about Ford Motor's turn-of-the-century, soft-science market-research approach to its new designs, however, were the hard-science engineering and manufacturing redesigns that accompanied its 2001–2002 customer studies. Just as the significance of the Model T—revolutionary as it was in itself—pales compared with Ford Motor's pioneering efforts in the assembly-line mass-production methods that made the car ubiquitous, what may prove most lastingly profitable about Kathy's and Lewis's cars, the Freestyle and the Five Hundred, is that they will use the same frame and be built at the same plant in Chicago, reconfigured for the purpose from Taurus production. In other words, if it turns out that there are more Lewises than Kathys looking to buy new cars, Ford Motor can immediately start turning out more Five Hundreds than Freestyles at their Chicago plant—until a time when the market shifts again. "The Freestyle and its cousin, the Ford Five Hundred, are just two of the breakthrough products we'll be introducing in the coming years," Ford Division President Steve Lyons announced at the October 2002 Las Vegas dealers meeting. "In 2002, we focused on the SUV lineup. In 2003, we'll introduce the next generation of the world's best selling vehicle the Ford F-Series and a redesigned version of the minivan safety leader, the Ford Windstar. The year 2004 will be the year of the car, the Freestyle, Five Hundred and our production version of the GT40 concept. And that's only part of the story. There's much more to come."[111]

That kind of adaptive thinking—the wheels always spinning—has been the hallmark of Ford Motor Company in its best times. "There's a sense of urgency here now," Bill Ford Jr. acknowledged in the second half of 2002, "and it's my job to make sure it stays there."[112] The same sense of urgency has driven Ford Motor Company ahead for a century.

Epilogue

Sitting at a small glass table in his Ford Motor Company office twelve floors above Dearborn, forty-five-year-old Bill Ford Jr. looks far too young to be running the fourth-largest company in the world. A black belt in the martial art of tae kwon do le, he looks fit enough to start at shortstop for the Detroit Tigers. Considering the two years Ford Motor Company has just had, he had better be in shape, as it's likely to take quite some energy and effort to reverse the downward spiral left by the debilitating Nasser era. The good news for Ford Motor Company is that something about Bill Ford Jr. promises he's up to the job.

Manifesting his distaste for nonbiodegradable materials, the curtains, carpeting, and upholstery in Bill Ford Jr.'s office are all made of hemp. An acoustic guitar rests in his office corner just in case he wants to strum a Neil Young or Eagles song at lunch. There is an air of nonchalant enthusiasm about Bill Jr., a man clearly comfortable in his own skin. Unlike the bulk of corporate titans, he prefers to drive himself to work, from his home in Ann Arbor thirty miles away—usually behind the wheel of his favorite car. It's a Ford Motor product, of course, but not necessarily a top-line Jaguar, Volvo, or Lincoln. "If I had just one vehicle for the rest of my life it would be a Mustang convertible with a good sound system," Ford says with a smile of the car he chooses to commute in, top-down if the weather permits. "I've always had a soft spot for Mustangs. They're certainly not the most expensive sports car you can have," he admits. "Certainly not the most refined sports car you can have. But to me, they're the essence of American driving; they're the quintessential American car."[1]

Bill Ford Jr. is all about "quintessential American cars." To help Ford Motor Company promote its centennial, he had six jet-black Model Ts powered by 22.5-horsepower engines built in a garage in western Wayne County to add to Greenfield Village. About 15 million Ts were built between 1908 and 1927, but only 250,000 have survived. So Bill Ford Jr.—in a burst of nostalgia—had Ford workers build new Ts for the first time since Calvin Coolidge was president.[2] The man loves his heritage. In fact, we are meeting to discuss not just Model Ts but Ford Motor Company's centennial in general, which is only months away. There is a digital countdown clock at World Headquarters, which ticks off the seconds left until June 16, 2003, creating both excitement and nervousness throughout the building.

Writing *Wheels for the World,* I was constantly amazed at how large a shadow the original Henry Ford still casts on his company. Outside of Bill Ford Jr.'s office, for instance, are blowups of Henry Ford in his quadricycle, Henry Ford sitting with Edison, and Henry Ford studying the Rouge facility with Edsel. Given his omnipresence, I asked his great-grandson how often he thinks about the company's founder. "You know, it's interesting," he responded. "On the one hand I admire him greatly. I've studied him a lot and I feel like I know him quite well. On the other hand I don't want to be captive to somebody else's vision. And while I certainly would never repudiate his vision or turn my back on it, lives are different and the world is different, and I don't ever want to be looking backward. I want to be looking forward." Pouring a glass of water, he went on to explain that the *real* lesson of Henry Ford, the one that he constantly draws upon for inspiration, was his ability to imagine the future. "I think he was a real visionary," he offered, "and I certainly owe everything I have in my life to him and to his vision. And I never lose sight of that."[3]

As we started discussing the philosophy of Henry Ford in more depth, Bill Jr. grew animated, talking about the $5 Day, the "vagabond" trips, the soybean farming, and the ethanol experiments. "In terms of his philosophy," he explained, "I've embraced the whole notion that he was incredibly inquisitive and never took no for an answer and hated to be told he couldn't do something. That is also the way I feel. We're only limited by our imagination. I'm not suggesting, however, we go running around like chickens with our heads cut off and try to do a little of this and a little of that. But I do think that the conventional thinking isn't appropriate for where the automobile industry stands today. Just look out the window and you can see how he changed the world. And guess what. It's still changing."[4]

From this bird's-eye view in Dearborn, I could indeed see the world Henry Ford created: freeways congested with cars, billboards selling goods to distracted drivers, towering gas station signs, factories humming with work, shopping malls surrounded by a sea of vehicles, and suburban tract developments. You could also see Henry Ford Community College, Fordson High School, Henry Ford Hospital, and Henry Ford Centennial Library among the dozens of nearby landmarks that bear his name. These are all modern tributes to Henry Ford's fertile imagination. No question about it—the societal changes that Henry Ford wrought are still with us. And his ghost, or at least the foot-prints he left behind, can still be found all over metropolitan Detroit if you look hard enough.

Over the years Detroit has often paid tribute to the legacy of Henry Ford and the early days of the automobile. You can stand, for example, in front of the Michigan Building, a downtown office tower, and read a plaque that says "Birthplace of the Ford Automobile." This is 58 Bagley Avenue, the exact spot where Henry Ford and Jim Bishop built the quadricycle in the brick shed out back (the original workshop is at Greenfield Village). In front of the Detroit Edison Building is a bust of Alexander Dow, Ford's boss at Detroit Edison from 1893 to 1899, with an inscription that reads "Engineer, Scholar, Citizen." Nearby is the Detroit Club, where Henry Ford had coat hook no. 1 and Henry Ford II plotted to usurp Harry Bennett at the company in 1945. At the UAW-Ford National Programs Center along the Detroit River is a life-size statue of Henry Ford II reaching across a table to shake Walter Reuther's hand (before moving to Grosse Pointe Shores, Edsel and Eleanor Ford had a home on that site).

Most people never see these plaques and statues. They're more apt to encounter the Ford legacy at the Motor City Casino, located in central Detroit on Grand River Avenue and decorated with large photographs of Henry Ford, Highland Park, and the Rouge. The old Dodge Brothers machine shop is now occupied by Niki's Pizza. Albert Kahn's architectural gems are everywhere, but the Fisher Building, with its ornate ceilings and frescoes is the most impressive. Across the street from the Fisher is the old General Motors head-quarters; the corporation moved in 1999 to the Renaissance Center.

A retired professor of anatomy named Dr. Jerald Mitchell now lives at 140 Edison Street, the home of Henry and Clara Ford from 1908 to 1915. James Couzens, who died in 1936, lived only a few blocks away. His grandson, Ted Roney, is now a car salesman at Roy O'Brien Ford in St. Clair Shores. Just down the road is also the Hudson Mansion, where Edsel and Eleanor were married in 1916. They are buried in Woodlawn Cemetery, next to a pond teeming with ducks and geese. Many Ford Motor executives are buried at Woodlawn, including Ernest Kanzler, James Couzens, John Gray, and C. Harold Wills.

At the time of Ford Motor Company's centennial the Great Lakes continued to be the most underappreciated material resource in North America. Over 65 million people—slightly less than one third of the combined U.S.-Canadian population—reside along the five lakes. And more tonnage of freight goes through the Detroit River than through the Panama and Suez Canals combined. From Belle Isle, the city park located in the Detroit River, you can still get a wonderful view of Ford Motor's Walkerville factory in Canada, its smokestacks the most noticeable high-rise structure along the bank.

Of all the Ford haunts in Detroit, none is more eerie than the old Highland Park plant, birthplace of the moving assembly line and the $5 Day. In 1928 Ford Motor shifted the production to the River Rouge plant in Dearborn, limiting Highland Park to truck and tractor manufacturing. Albert Kahn's "Crystal Palace" slowly aged into a dreary, desolate, abandoned ruin. Although it is now owned by Woolward-Manchester Properties, Ford Motor still stores boxes of legal records in the massive U-shaped redbrick structure. Windows are smashed, weeds sprout up like forlorn sea oats, and an old rusted flagpole juts into the air. It's a monument now to rust and decay. Seagulls and pigeons swirl around looking for food and roosting spots. But the premises can still offer clues to the glory days. If you strain your eyes, you can read a faded sign: "All Ford Models." Gray plywood boards cover holes in the structure, making it difficult to peer inside. Behind the abandoned factory, on Dearborn Road, an old Ford security booth survives, the blue oval still easily recognizable. "Keep Out—Private Property" signs are posted everywhere. High fences with barbed wire along the top make the entire facility seem like a state penitentiary where true-life stories are best forgotten. Even the historic marker in front is tilted sideways, bent over as if a strong northern wind would knock it down.

There is life, however, just a block from the closed factory at Model T Plaza. Cars of every kind—including new Thunderbirds, old Crown Victorias, ageless Broncos, and dented Escorts—fill the football-field-length parking lot. Few who shop at the Hollywood Video or Foot Locker or Payless ShoeSource in this strip mall have the faintest idea that the hulking Crystal Palace next door was once the vortex of the industrial world. Inside the Farmer Jack grocery store, however, next to the lines of shopping carts at the entrance, there are reminders: first, a blown-up photograph of Highland Park taken in August 1913. And there, placed under glass is Model T number 164133, built on July 13, 1913. It's a rare survivor from a long-ago era, Henry Ford's commonplace car presented as a modern-day antique. At the Highland Park library you can find an old conveyor belt from the factory.

Although one can still drive along the Rouge River on Hines Road and find patches of unspoiled wilderness, Dearborn, a city of 100,000, has become a crowded suburb brimming with shopping malls, apartment complexes, and automotive parts operations. Everywhere surrounding Henry Ford's Fair Lane estate, a pastoral oasis amid sprawl, are incontrovertible signs that the automobile revolution has marred the landscape. Traffic congestion, stoplights on every corner, huge six-laned avenues, the interstate that bisects the town, drive-in fast-food huts, twenty-four-hour mini-markets—Dearborn is undistinguishable from other midsize American cities. The only difference is—and it is a major one—the word "Ford" looming everywhere.

The ethnic makeup of Dearborn has changed considerably over the years. Ever since Henry Ford's $5 Day, Middle Eastern immigrants have been settling around the Rouge, opening up shops and bakeries. Just six blocks from the old steel foundry, in the south end of Dearborn, Arabic is the primary language. In fact, as of 2000, southeast Dearborn was 90 percent Arab American, with recent immigrants from Lebanon, Palestine, and Yemen constituting the majority of the population. Mosques are everywhere in Dearborn, with the National Islamic Temple slated to open in 2004. Given this reality, Ford Motor has sponsored "Islam 101" courses hoping to avert a post-9/11 backlash against workers of Arab descent. The company has also embraced the Arab Community Center for Economic and Social Services. Television news shows like CBS's *60 Minutes* and MSNBC's *America with Ashleigh Banfield* did post-9/11 specials about how the FBI was concerned that terrorist cells existed in the Dearborn area. Among Dearborn's Arab and Chaldean workers, Henry Ford is respected as a great historical figure because of his initiation of the $5 Day, his nondiscrimination policies, and for some, because of his sponsorship of the *Protocols of the Elders of Zion*. "I've always had respect for Henry Ford and his philosophy," one longtime Chaldean employee mused as the company approached its centennial. "When you think about it, Henry Ford hired all the minorities, and they worked so hard. . . . Ford Motor Company is part of our lives."[5] (In a biting article in the August 20, 2002, *Fort Worth Star-Telegram,* reporter Ed Wallace correctly wrote that Henry Ford's anti-Semitism was the "achievement Ford Motor wants to forget" on the eve of its centennial.)[6]

Visitors are not allowed inside the River Rouge plant in Dearborn without a prearranged escort. (Public tours, however, are slated to begin in spring 2004.) Just wandering around the outskirts of the complex affords visitors mixed feelings of shame and wonder. From the right vista you can see the same industrial monuments that Charles Sheeler sketched, Diego Rivera painted, and Robert Frank photographed. You can start at Gate 4 and imagine the scene in 1932 when the Hunger Marchers paraded into Dearborn. You can also visit the graves of the four martyrs at nearby Woodmere Cemetery. UAW Local 600, located just down the road from the Rouge on Dix Avenue, is still the most powerful local union in America. Since most steel is imported into the United States today, it's amazing that Rouge Steel, now an independent company with a special purchasing agreement with Ford, is still in operation. There are, however, fewer employees working the Rouge than during the heyday of Henry Ford. At its peak 101,000 people worked on the complex; today, due to downsizing and automation, only 16,000 work the lines. Amazingly, many of the original buildings have escaped the wrecking ball. Building "B," the original Eagle boat facility, is now Dearborn Assembly, home of the Mustang since 1964. But the old tool-and-die shop, Dearborn Stamping, and the glass and tire factories are all gone. What is most surprising about the Rouge's survival is that the huge freighters still pull up next to the factory just as Henry Ford envisioned them. Beginning in 2004, the Ford F-150 pickup will be built at a new Dearborn Truck Plant at the Ford Rouge Center.[7]

Without question transforming the Rouge into a profitable monument to the so-called clean revolution is a pet project of Bill Ford Jr. "Everybody in the plant will have direct sunlight," he enthused. "They'll be breathing fresh air, nobody will be wearing masks, our productivity will go up 24 percent in the new building—we can measure it. And these concepts are not only not crazy, but they'll be terrific for morale because people will love working here." In all of that, Bill Jr. sounds just like Henry Ford, speaking with pride of the cleanliness of the factories when they were his to run.[8]

While the Rouge (and the internal combustion engine) lives on, the concept of Fordism does not, at least not in its original vertical-integration form. As Barry Lynn wrote in his seminal June 2002 *Harper's* magazine essay, "Unmade in America: The True Cost of a Global Assembly Line," the entire industrial concept of gathering in one place everything needed to manufacture an automobile has become antiquated. Today, to paraphrase Lynn, a single semiconductor might be cut from a wafer in Hong Kong, assembled in China, tested in Seoul, fit into a subcomponent in Thailand, plugged into a component in Argentina, and loaded with a program designed in Singapore.[9] (You can change cities and countries around any way you like.) A Ford car or truck, in other words, is filled with components made all over the world. The problem with this is that if China, for example, broke off trade relations with the United States, the Big Three would be economically devastated—at least temporarily. Yet while Fordism is a nearly extinct concept, globalization is not. One could argue, in fact, that Henry Ford's concept of a "United States of the World" has become the global governing ethos. Economic integration intensifies on a weekly basis. "Globalization is reality," Peter Pestillo, CEO of Visteon, noted, echoing Barry Lynn's essay, "but Fordism is no longer relevant. The auto is now highly integrated—component parts are made all over the world and shipped to assembly plants. Manufacturing doesn't really have boundaries. Anything that is made can be made anywhere in the world."[10]

Recognizing the need to look to the future, Ford Motor Company, following the lead of Toyota and Honda, is also on the verge of creating a revolutionizing new flexible vehicle assembly system for its North American operations. "Henry Ford put the world on wheels with the moving assembly line, and now the company's new flexible assembly system marks a new level of innovation and leadership in the auto industry," Roman Krygier, group vice president of Ford Global Manufacturing and Quality, notes. "Not only is the system the next step forward in flexibility, it'll also cost far less than competing systems."[11] Equipment changeovers that once took months are being accomplished in days. The new flexible assembly line will be extremely cost-effective. Its four main points, according to a Ford Motor Company public affairs bulletin, are these:

- Instead of paying a higher price for flexibility as is usual in the industry, the Ford system will cost 10 to 15 percent less than even traditional, non-flexible systems, with a 50 percent savings in changeover costs. Over the next decade, Ford expects to save $1.5 to 2 billion with this all-new system.
- The body shop employs an industry-first system of standardized cells or modules, all built from a select group of components. Only product-specific tooling needs to be changed or computers and robots reprogrammed to launch new products.
- Each flexible plant will be capable of producing two different platforms with four different models of each platform.
- By mid-decade in North America, about half of Ford's body shops, trim, and final assembly operations will be flexible. That number rises to 75 percent by the end of the decade.[12]

Talking to Bill Ford Jr. about his company's future, I was struck by how much he had changed since we first met in 1997. No longer did he seem unencumbered—and for good reason. He now had the entire responsibility for a great company on his shoulders. His idealism, at least temporarily, had taken a backseat to the reality of saving Ford Motor Company from its downward spiral. "You know," he said to me, his bright blue eyes bulging to add emphasis, "Henry Ford didn't dwell much on the past, no matter what you encounter at Greenfield Village. Even till his last days, after World War II, he was fiddling around with new things, new ideas, asking new questions—I think that's remarkable. He never found a comfort zone, and certainly most people would have expected that. And I kind of hope to never find a comfort zone."

Then he paused, the eyes receded, and he asked me a simple question: "Did I tell you about our new Mustang?"[13]

ACKNOWLEDGMENTS

As noted in the introduction, Julie Fenster was my indispensable associate in writing *Wheels for the World*. Besides being a smart, hardworking, and savvy historian she is unflappable—a quality that always boosted my morale. Together we owe a debt to a number of people and institutions. First among these is my staff at the Eisenhower Center for American Studies at the University of New Orleans (UNO). When one is writing a book of this magnitude it's important to have somebody in charge of manuscript preparation. That person, in this case, was Lisa Weisdorffer. I first met Lisa when she was a student in my "U.S. and the Cold War" class at UNO. Upon graduation she worked for American Classic Voyages and the Neal Auction Company. I was lucky to steal her away to work for me. She spent untold hours helping whip this manuscript into shape. The Eisenhower Center also commissioned Shelby Sadler to proofread and line edit sections of the manuscript. She is a superb editor, and over the years I've learned to trust her literary instinct.

My associate director, Kevin Willey, ran the center when I spent long spells doing research in Michigan. Without complaint he tracked down obscure books and set up my interview schedule. His dedication to the Eisenhower Center is unremitting. While working on *Wheels for the World*, I was able to entrust my center's World War II collection to Michael Edwards, a walking encyclopedia on U.S. military history. My three bosses at UNO—Chancellor Gregory O'Brien, Provost Lou Paradise, and Dean Robert DuPont—supported this book from the start, reducing my teaching load so I could spend time in Dearborn and Detroit. They are all first-rate administrators who love American history and literature. Our UNO team was rounded out by Andrew Travers, a brilliant student worker on loan from Tulane University, who transcribed my interviews with everybody from John Kenneth Galbraith to Chuck Berry and Jack Telnack.

Which brings me to thanking all the former and current employees at Ford

Motor who helped me better understand the company. As noted earlier, Bill Ford Jr. was a tremendous help, as was his staff. While I know they strongly disagree with a number of my interpretations of the company, they always understood it was my book, not theirs. A special salute is owed to the former chiefs of Ford Motor Company who all graciously granted me interviews: Lee Iacocca, Robert McNamara, Don Petersen, Philip Caldwell, and Red Poling. Besides answering a barrage of questions, they unhesitatingly allowed me to telephone them at their homes for follow-up questions. It was quite a chore to track them down and get on their busy calendars but it was worth the effort. Henry Ford II's daughter Anne, who lives in New York, was likewise invaluable in helping me better understand her colorful father. And two members of the Henry Ford Heritage Association—Dick Folson and Mike Skinner—not only proofread large chunks of my manuscript but took me around metropolitan Detroit on an "automobile heritage history tour." Their commitment to preserving the life and legacy of the original Henry Ford is unsurpassed.

While I was writing this book, Ford Motor Company archivists Greta Krapac (who commutes to Dearborn from Windsor, Canada), Cynthia Korolov (a Syracuse, New York, native who has worked for the company for a decade), and Elizabeth Adkins (a top-notch archival manager who recently received a fellowship from the Society of American Archivists) always came to my aid. They all work in Dearborn and dedicate their lives to helping scholars better understand Ford Motor Company. Greta, in particular, worked with me to collect photographs, wade through files, and search for pertinent documents. Cynthia was like a detective, tracking down source materials that other researchers would have missed. At the Henry Ford Museum and Library I want to thank Steve Hamp, Terry Hoover, and Bob Casey for answering queries and offering sound counsel. Likewise, the team at Walter Reuther Library at Wayne State University was extremely helpful in pointing me to important primary and secondary sources related to the UAW.

Although various documents housed at the Henry Ford Museum and Library are cited in the text, I would like to bring special attention to the massive, unpublished history that Charles C. LaCroix wrote about Willow Run. One day in 1942 Henry Ford asked LaCroix, a heritage guide at Greenfield Village, to write a sprawling history of Ford Motor and World War II. "Write me something I'll enjoy reading, not just a lot of statistics," Ford instructed him. Working with the patriotic dedication of a soldier in battle, LaCroix ended up compiling fifty-five large volumes full of prose, complemented with 25,000 photographs. Recently made available to scholars, the unpublished LaCroix volumes, "Ford and the War Effort," constitute the finest, most detailed record available about the U.S. industrial mobilization "miracle" of

World War II. The volumes are a national treasure and should be published at once by a major university press.

To better understand Ford Motor in a global context I visited various industrial facilities around the world. It was amazing to tour the new Ford factory outside of St. Petersburg, Russia, watch Aston Martins being hand-crafted in Newport Parnell, England, see the original home of Jaguar in Coventry, England, and talk with Mazda assembly-line workers in Tokyo. My travels allowed me to grasp the global implications of the automobile industry.

Although I was four months late in delivering the manuscript, my friends at Viking never lost faith in this project. My original editor was Jane von Mehren, editor in chief of Penguin Books. For years she followed my progress with monthly fellowship and unwavering devotion. Then, shortly after I submitted the first half of the manuscript, Jane announced she was pregnant and was taking a leave of absence. We raced to see who would give birth first. She beat me by bringing Lucas Geoffrey Diamond into the world a couple of months before *Wheels for the World* was completed. (Throughout those years her assistant, Brett Kelly, was also always cheerful and helpful.)

At that juncture Molly Stern, senior editor at Viking, stepped into the void. More than any other person she is responsible for marshaling this manuscript into the production stage. It was a joy working with somebody who exudes an undaunted professionalism in every aspect of her job. Her assistant, Jennifer Jackson, also entered the fray with bedrock competence and incessant good cheer. And then there is Michelle Ishay, who designed the dust jacket. With no instruction from me, except to make sure the cover didn't look like a corporate history book, she came up with the simple and elegant photograph of the blue 1949 Ford on a forlorn American road. I liked it at first glance. Carla Bolte receives my gratitude for designing the interior of *Wheels for the World,* while Trent Duffy dutifully copyedited my text. During the final days of the project, Bruce Giffords, production editor, did a sterling job of perfecting the book in myriad ways. His effort was exemplary. Throughout the process Clare Ferraro, president of Viking, and Susan Petersen Kennedy, president of Penguin Group (USA) Inc., supported me in every way imaginable. It was an honor to work for their company.

Lisa Bankoff, my longtime agent at International Creative Management, deserves a special line. Here it is: she is simply the best in the business.

Sadly, while I was writing *Wheels for the World,* my colleague Stephen E. Ambrose died. He had encouraged me to write about Ford Motor Company, convinced it was *the* best way to tell the story of America in the twentieth century. While struggling for his life against cancer, he took the time to read my two chapters pertaining to World War II. He offered some suggestions and gave a big thumbs-up. A few weeks later he was gone. I miss his gruff voice and larger-than-life presence and unfailing comradeship. All I can say to him now is the salutation he always offered his fans at book signings: "Happy Trails!"

I also decided to dedicate *Wheels for the World* to Ford R. Bryan, who proofread chapters and offered wise advice. He knows more about Henry Ford than any person alive. The book also goes to my old Ohio State University teacher Warren Van Tine, whose life has been devoted to studying U.S. labor history. All three men are role models in living the unselfish scholarly life.

Finally, a special thanks is due to my wife, Anne, who stood by me throughout the arduous process of writing *Wheels for the World*. Without her love and support, the book would not have been possible.

New Orleans

NOTES

Unless otherwise noted, the oral reminiscences are from the collection in the Benson Ford Research Center, Henry Ford Museum & Greenfield Village, Dearborn, Michigan.

INTRODUCTION

1. Margaret Ford Ruddiman, "Reminiscences" (oral history project), p. 16, Henry Ford Museum and Library, Dearborn, Michigan.
2. Booton Herndon, *Ford: An Unconventional Biography of the Men and Their Times* (New York: Weybright and Talley, 1969), p. 113, citing Samuel S. Marquis, *Henry Ford: An Interpretation* (Boston: Little, Brown, 1923).
3. W. C. Cowling, "Reminiscences," p. 7.
4. Mike Tressler, "A Unique Relationship Between Henry Ford and Wilbur Donaldson," *Toledo Blade,* August 12, 1973.
5. William and Marjorie McNairn, *Quotations from the Unusual Henry Ford* (Norwalk, Calif.: Stockton Trade Press, 1978), pp. 64, 96.
6. Cowling, "Reminiscences," p. 7.
7. John Kenneth Galbraith, *The Liberal Hour* (Boston: Houghton Mifflin, 1960), p. 163; and Keith Sward, *The Legend of Henry Ford* (New York: Rinehart, 1948), p. 3.
8. Walt Whitman, *Leaves of Grass.*
9. Richard S. Tedlow, *Giants of Enterprise: Seven Business Innovators and the Empires They Built* (New York: HarperBusiness, 2002), p. 122.
10. Dixon Wecter, *The Hero in America* (New York: Charles Scribner's Sons, 1941), p. 415.
11. Author interview with William C. Ford Jr., December 1997, Dearborn, Michigan.
12. Ibid.
13. Centennial Memo, Ford Motor Company, 2002.
14. Jack Beatty, "The Twenties," in *Colossus: How the Corporation Changed America,* ed. Jack Beatty (New York: Broadway Books, 2001), p. 257.
15. Thomas A. Stewart, Alex Taylor III, Peter Petre, and Brent Schlender, "The Businessmen of the Century," *Fortune,* November 22, 1999, pp. 111–12; and Lee Iacocca, "Driving Force: Henry Ford," *Time,* December 7, 1998.
16. Peter Collier and David Horowitz, *The Fords: An American Epic* (New York: Summit Books, 1987), p. 13.
17. Catherine Drinker Bower, *Yankee from Olympus* (Boston: Atlantic/Little Brown, 1944), p. 67.

CHAPTER ONE: ORIGINS

1. Bruce Catton, *Michigan: A History* (New York: W. W. Norton, 1984), p. 184.
2. Willis F. Dunbar, *Michigan: A History of the Wolverine State,* rev. ed. (Grand Rapids, Mich.: William B. Eerdmans, 1980), pp. 1–19.

3. Alexis de Tocqueville, *Journey to America* (New Haven: Yale University Press, 1960), pp. 335–64.

4. Roger Burlingame, *Henry Ford* (New York: Quadrangle, 1970), pp. 17–32.

5. Sidney Olson, *Young Henry Ford: A Picture History of the First Forty Years,* rev. ed. (Detroit: Wayne State University Press, 1997), p. 6.

6. Allan Nevins and Frank Ernest Hill, *Ford,* vol. 1, *The Times, the Man, the Company* (New York: Charles Scribner's Sons, 1954), p. 43, citing Margaret Ford Ruddiman, "Reminiscences" (oral history project), p. 166, Henry Ford Museum and Library, Dearborn, Michigan.

7. Robert Lacey, *Ford: The Men and the Machine* (Boston: Little, Brown, 1986), p. 6.

8. Ford R. Bryan, *Clara: Mrs. Henry Ford* (Dearborn, Mich.: Ford Books, 2001), p. 19.

9. Ford R. Bryan, *The Fords of Dearborn: An Illustrated History,* rev. ed. (Detroit: Harlo Press, 1989), pp. 94–95.

10. Peter Collier and David Horowitz, *The Fords: An American Epic* (New York: Summit Books, 1987), p. 16.

11. Nevins and Hill, *The Times, the Man, the Company,* p. 32.

12. Bryan, *Clara,* p. 336; Bryan, *The Fords of Dearborn,* p. 95; and Carol Gelderman, *Henry Ford: The Wayward Capitalist* (New York: Dial, 1981), p. 5.

13. Bryan, *The Fords of Dearborn,* p. 97.

14. Ibid., p. 120.

15. Margaret Ford Ruddiman, "Memories of My Brother Henry Ford," *Michigan History,* September 1953, p. 227.

16. Collier and Horowitz, *The Fords: An American Epic,* p. 19.

17. Bryan, *The Fords of Dearborn,* p. 117.

18. Ibid., p. 96; and Nevins and Hill, *The Times, the Man, the Company,* pp. 641–42.

19. Collier and Horowitz, *The Fords: An American Epic,* p. 17.

20. Bryan, *The Fords of Dearborn,* p. 96.

21. Collier and Horowitz, *The Fords: An American Epic,* pp. 17–18.

22. Bryan, *The Fords of Dearborn,* p. 97; also in Nevins and Hill, *The Times, the Man, the Company,* pp. 39–41.

23. Olson, *Young Henry Ford,* rev. ed., p. 12.

24. Collier and Horowitz, *The Fords: An American Epic,* p. 18.

25. Bryan, *The Fords of Dearborn,* p. 123.

26. Olson, *Young Henry Ford,* rev. ed., p. 11; and Bryan, *The Fords of Dearborn,* pp. 97–98, 121.

27. Bryan, *The Fords of Dearborn,* p. 97.

28. Lacey, *Ford: The Men and the Machine,* p. 6; and Gelderman, *Henry Ford: The Wayward Capitalist,* p. 6.

29. Olson, *Young Henry Ford,* rev. ed., p. 22.

30. Roger Burlingame, *Henry Ford* (New York: Alfred A. Knopf, 1955), p. 19.

31. James J. Flink, *The Automobile Age* (Cambridge, Mass.: MIT Press, 1988), p. 3.

32. Collier and Horowitz, *The Fords: An American Epic,* p. 19.

33. Ruddiman, "Reminiscences," p. 16.

34. A. M. Smith, "Reminiscences," p. 18.

35. Lacey, *Ford: The Men and the Machine,* p. 11; also Nevins and Hill, *The Times, the Man, the Company,* p. 48, citing Ruddiman, "Reminiscences," pp. 243–44.

36. Edgar A. Guest, "Henry Ford Talks About His Mother," *American Magazine,* July 1923, pp. 11–15, 116–20; also cited in Nevins and Hill, *The Times, the Man, the Company,* pp. 49–50.

37. Lacey, *Ford: The Men and the Machine,* p. 8; also Nevins and Hill, *The Times, the Man, the Company,* p. 49.

38. Allan L. Benson, *The New Henry Ford* (New York: Funk & Wagnalls, 1923), p. 19.

39. Collier and Horowitz, *The Fords: An American Epic,* p. 20.

40. Lacey, *Ford: The Men and the Machine,* p. 12; also Olson, *Young Henry Ford,* p. 18; cited from Nevins and Hill, *The Times, the Man, the Company,* p. 51.

41. Lacey, *Ford: The Men and the Machine,* pp. 6–7.

42. Olson, *Young Henry Ford,* rev. ed., pp. 14, 16–17. Olson remarks of Ford's "jotbooks" that "in over thirty-odd years of jotting down 'Tales from the Vienna Woods' he never spelled the title [of the Johann Strauss waltz] the same twice, and never once correctly."

43. Guest, "Henry Ford Talks About His Mother"; also in Lacey, *Ford: The Men and the Ma-*

chine, p. 11; and Sidney Olson, *Young Henry Ford: A Picture History of the First Forty Years,* 1st ed. (Detroit: Wayne State University Press, 1963), p. 18.

44. Ford R. Bryan, *Friends, Families and Forays: Scenes from the Life and Times of Henry Ford* (Dearborn, Mich.: Ford Books, 2002), pp. 70–75.
45. Bryan, *The Fords of Dearborn,* p. 99.
46. Ruddiman, "Reminiscences," p. 16.
47. Bryan, *Clara,* p. 22.
48. Henry Ford with Samuel Crowther, *My Life and Work* (Garden City, N.Y.: Doubleday, 1923), pp. 22–24.
49. Ruddiman, "Reminiscences," p. 41.
50. Unlike most Irish immigrants, the Fords were Protestant, descended from one of the English families Queen Elizabeth I had resettled in an effort to pacify Ireland toward the end of the sixteenth century. Allan Nevins and Frank Ernest Hill detail this aspect of the Ford genealogy in *The Times, the Man, the Company,* pp. 23–24.
51. Edward F. Monnier, "Reminiscences," pp. 1–9.
52. Ruddiman, "Reminiscences," p. 39; also Bryan, *Clara,* p. 27.
53. E. Monnier, "Reminiscences," p. 39.
54. Ruddiman, "Reminiscences," p. 38.
55. Neil Baldwin, *Henry Ford and the Jews* (New York: Public Affairs, 2001), pp. 2–5.
56. Ruddiman, "Reminiscences," p. 21.
57. Cited from an interview with Edgar A. Guest in David E. Nye, *Henry Ford, Ignorant Idealist* (Port Washington, N.Y.: Kennikat Press, 1979), p. 97.
58. Bryan, *The Fords of Dearborn,* pp. 98–99.
59. Olson, *Young Henry Ford,* rev. ed., p. 22.
60. Ruddiman, "Reminiscences," p. 166.
61. Lacey, *Ford: The Men and the Machine,* p. 15.
62. Bryan, *The Fords of Dearborn,* pp. 99–101.
63. Ruddiman, "Reminiscences," p. 166.
64. Gelderman, *Henry Ford: The Wayward Capitalist,* p. 7.
65. Ford with Crowther, *My Life and Work,* p. 22.
66. Lacey, *Ford: The Men and the Machine,* pp. 12–14, citing Ford with Crowther, *My Life and Work,* pp. 22–23.
67. Bryan, *The Fords of Dearborn,* p. 106.
68. Olson, *Young Henry Ford,* rev. ed., p. 26.
69. Nevins and Hill, *The Times, the Man, the Company,* p. 120, citing *Compendium of the Eleventh Census: 1890, Part II,* pp. 802–4; also in Keith Sward, *The Legend of Henry Ford* (New York: Rinehart, 1948), pp. 9–10.
70. Lacey, *Ford: The Men and the Machine,* pp. 22–23.
71. Bryan, *Clara,* p. 22.
72. Olson, *Young Henry Ford,* rev. ed., p. 26; also Nevins and Hill, *The Times, the Man, the Company,* p. 80.
73. Frederick Strauss, "Reminiscences," p. 3.
74. Bryan, *Clara,* p. 22.
75. Gelderman, *Henry Ford: The Wayward Capitalist,* p. 9.
76. Strauss, "Reminiscences," pp. 4–5.
77. Olson, *Young Henry Ford,* rev. ed., p. 27.
78. Lacey, *Ford: The Men and the Machine,* p. 669.
79. Sward, *The Legend of Henry Ford,* p. 10.
80. Strauss, "Reminiscences," pp. 9–10.
81. Olson, *Young Henry Ford,* rev. ed., p. 30.
82. Strauss, "Reminiscences," p. 36.
83. E. Monnier, "Reminiscences," p. 6.
84. Nevins and Hill, *The Times, the Man, the Company,* p. 87.
85. Olson, *Young Henry Ford,* 1st ed., p. 63.
86. Gelderman, *Henry Ford: The Wayward Capitalist,* p. 10.
87. Bryan, *Clara,* p. 23.
88. Olson, *Young Henry Ford,* rev. ed., p. 15.

89. Ibid., p. 34.
90. Ibid., pp. 34–35.
91. Alfred Monnier, "Reminiscences," p. 11.
92. Matthew Josephson, *Edison: A Biography* (New York: McGraw-Hill, 1959), p. 404.
93. "History of the Bicycle," Automotive Hall of Fame, Dearborn, Michigan.
94. Bryan, *Clara,* p. 23; also Collier and Horowitz, *The Fords: An American Epic,* pp. 25–26.
95. Flink, *The Automobile Age,* p. 5.
96. E. Monnier, "Reminiscences," p. 5.
97. Bryan, *Clara,* p. 15.
98. Collier and Horowitz, *The Fords: An American Epic,* p. 26; Bryan, *Clara,* pp. 15–16; and Louise B. Clancy and Florence Davies, *The Believer: The Life Story of Mrs. Henry Ford* (New York: Coward-McCann, 1960), p. 20.
99. E. Monnier, "Reminiscences," p. 6.
100. Ruddiman, "Reminiscences," p. 59.
101. Collier and Horowitz, *The Fords: An American Epic,* pp. 27–28.
102. Bryan, *The Fords of Dearborn,* pp. 102–3.
103. Bryan, *Clara,* p. 27.
104. William Adams Simonds, *Henry Ford: His Life, His Work, His Genius* (Indianapolis: Bobbs-Merrill, 1943), p. 40.
105. Bryan, *Clara,* pp. 20–30.
106. Bryan, *The Fords of Dearborn,* p. 104.
107. Lacey, *Ford: The Men and the Machine,* pp. 34–36.
108. Bryan, *Clara,* p. 31.
109. Ruddiman, "Reminiscences," p. 87.
110. Bryan, *Clara,* p. 31.
111. Bryan, *The Fords of Dearborn,* p. 183.
112. Gelderman, *Henry Ford: The Wayward Capitalist,* p. 13.
113. Bryan, *Clara,* pp. 29–31; Sward, *The Legacy of Henry Ford,* pp. 10–11; and Collier and Horowitz, *The Fords: An American Epic,* pp. 29–31.
114. Bryan, *Clara,* p. 34.
115. Collier and Horowitz, *The Fords: An American Epic,* p. 31.
116. Bryan, *Clara,* p. 29.
117. Gelderman, *Henry Ford: The Wayward Capitalist,* pp. 9–10; Lacey, *Ford: The Men and the Machine,* pp. 34–37; and Booton Herndon, *Ford: An Unconventional Biography of the Men and Their Times* (New York: Weybright and Talley, 1969), p. 61.
118. Gelderman, *Henry Ford: The Wayward Capitalist,* p. 17; also Lacey, *Ford: The Men and the Machine,* p. 38.
119. Herndon, *Ford: An Unconventional Biography of the Men and Their Times,* p. 61.
120. Bryan, *Clara,* pp. 39–54.
121. Ibid., pp. 37–40.
122. Lee Curson, "Reminiscences," p. 2.
123. Lacey, *Ford: The Men and the Machine,* pp. 41–42.
124. Olson, *Young Henry Ford,* pp. 71–132; also Sward, *The Legend of Henry Ford,* p. 11.
125. Olson, *Young Henry Ford,* p. 72.
126. Oliver Barthel, "Reminiscences," p. 7.
127. Sward, *The Legend of Henry Ford,* p. 11.
128. Olson, *Young Henry Ford,* p. 72.
129. Strauss, "Reminiscences," p. 18; also in Olson, *Young Henry Ford,* p. 61.
130. David M. Bell, "Reminiscences," pp. 3–6.
131. Gelderman, *Henry Ford: The Wayward Capitalist,* p. 18.
132. Norman Rockwell's painting is reprinted in James M. Flammang, David L. Lewis, and the Auto Editors of Consumers Guide, eds., *Ford Chronicle: A Pictorial History from 1893* (Lincolnwood, Ill.: Publications International Ltd., 1997), p. 8.
133. Nevins and Hill, *The Times, the Man, the Company,* p. 152, citing Ford with Crowther, *My Life and Work,* p. 30.
134. James W. Bishop, "The First Ford Car," memo for the record, October 11, 1948, Henry Ford Museum and Library, Dearborn, Michigan.

135. Simonds, *Henry Ford: His Life, His Work, His Genius,* p. 52.
136. Collier and Horowitz, *The Fords: An American Epic,* p. 9.
137. Alva Johnson, "Hero for Business Reasons, Glenn Martin," *The New Yorker,* November 28, 1942, p. 26.
138. Nevins and Hill, *The Times, the Man, the Company,* p. 156; Simonds, *Henry Ford: His Life, His Work, His Genius,* p. 52; and Collier and Horrowitz, *The Fords: An American Epic,* p. 9.
139. Bishop, "The First Ford Car."
140. Simonds, *Henry Ford: His Life, His Work, His Genius,* p. 53; Olson, *Young Henry Ford,* p. 77; and Nevins and Hill, *The Times, the Man, the Company,* p. 157.
141. Collier and Horowitz, *The Fords: An American Epic,* p. 10; also Olson, *Young Henry Ford,* p. 75; Gelderman, *Henry Ford: The Wayward Capitalist,* p. 19; and Lacey, *Ford: The Men and the Machine,* p. 44.
142. Herndon, *Ford: An Unconventional Biography of the Men and Their Times,* p. 62; also Flammang et al., *Ford Chronicle,* p. 9.
143. Bryan, *Clara,* p. 41; also Sward, *The Legend of Henry Ford,* p. 12.

CHAPTER TWO: STARTING UP

1. Allan Nevins and Frank Ernest Hill, *Ford,* vol. 1, *The Times, the Man, the Company* (New York: Charles Scribner's Sons, 1954), p. 166; also Peter Collier and David Horowitz, *The Fords: An American Epic* (New York: Summit Books, 1987), pp. 33–34.
2. Stacey Bredhoff, *American Originals* (Seattle: University of Washington Press, 2001), p. 62.
3. Sidney Olson, *Young Henry Ford: A Picture History of the First Forty Years,* rev. ed. (Detroit: Wayne State University Press, 1997), pp. 84–85. On display at the Henry Ford Museum and Library in Dearborn is the "Programme of Proceedings of the Seventeenth Convention of the Association of Edison Illuminating Companies." Also see Matthew Josephson, *Edison: A Biography* (New York: McGraw-Hill, 1959).
4. Dixon Wecter, *The Hero in America* (New York: Charles Scribner's Sons, 1941), pp. 418–21.
5. M. A. Rosanoff's 1903 quote in *Harper's Monthly,* September 1932, p. 24. See also J. G. Crowther, *Famous American Men of Science* (London: Pelican, 1944), pp. 17–39.
6. John Schwartz, "Living on Internet Time, in Another Age," *New York Times,* April 4, 2002, p. E1.
7. Henry Ford with Samuel Crowther, "Habits Which Make Edison the Greatest American," *Cosmopolitan,* September 1930, p. 54; and Henry Ford, *Edison as I Know Him* (New York: Cosmopolitan Book Corporation, 1930), p. 14.
8. Richard S. Tedlow, "Ford vs. GM," in *Colossus: How the Corporation Changed America,* ed. Jack Beatty (New York: Broadway Books, 2001), p. 257.
9. Ford, *Edison,* pp. 1–16.
10. Olson, *Young Henry Ford,* p. 85. Dow's quote is given slightly differently in Nevins and Hill, *The Times, the Man, the Company,* p. 167: "There's a young fellow who's made a gas car."
11. Ford, *Edison,* p. 5.
12. Ford R. Bryan, *Clara: Mrs. Henry Ford* (Dearborn, Mich.: Ford Books, 2001), p. 44; also Olson, *Young Henry Ford,* p. 91.
13. Robert Lacey, *Ford: The Men and the Machine* (Boston: Little, Brown, 1986), p. 67, citing Charles K. Hyde, *Detroit: An Industrial History Guide* (Detroit: Detroit Historical Society, 1980), p. 10.
14. David Lee Poremba, *Detroit: A Motor City History* (Charleston, S.C.: Arcadia Publishing, 2001), pp. 93–98.
15. Richard Bak, *A Place for Summer: A Narrative History of Tiger Stadium* (Detroit: Wayne State University Press, 1998), pp. 96–97.
16. Keith Sward, *The Legend of Henry Ford* (New York: Rinehart, 1948), pp. 6–7; also Poremba, *Detroit,* pp. 93–98.
17. H. C. Needham, "Reminiscences" (oral history project), pp. 2–3, Henry Ford Museum and Library, Dearborn, Michigan.
18. Allan and Chester Gray, "Reminiscences," p. 2.
19. Olson, *Young Henry Ford,* p. 115.
20. Ibid.; also Nevins and Hill, *The Times, the Man, the Company,* p. 161.

21. Bryan, *Clara*, p. 49.
22. Ibid.
23. Ibid., citing Frederick Strauss, "Reminiscences," pp. 3–7.
24. Lacey, *Ford: The Men and the Machine*, p. 45.
25. Olson, *Young Henry Ford*, p. 103.
26. Bellamy Partridge, *Fill'er Up* (New York: McGraw-Hill, 1952), p. 58.
27. Michael Brian Schiffer, *Taking Charge: The Electric Automobile in America* (Washington, D.C.: Smithsonian Institution Press, 1994), p. 75.
28. Daniel Yergin, *The Prize: The Epic Quest for Oil, Money and Power* (New York: Simon & Schuster, 1991), p. 79.
29. "Rockefeller Riding Again," *New York Times*, June 6, 1910, p. 1.
30. Clifton Fadiman, ed., *The Little, Brown Book of Anecdotes* (Boston: Little, Brown, 1985), p. 472.
31. Olson, *Young Henry Ford*, p. 103, states that Henry Ford applied for his first U.S. patent on April 7, 1897; upon winning it he assigned it to William C. Maybury, on August 30, 1898. Olson also reports that Ford applied for his second patent on December 8, 1898, this one for a "reach-rod construction covering the steering." Also see Bryan, *Clara*, pp. 49–51.
32. Lacey, *Ford: The Men and the Machine*, pp. 44–45.
33. Olson, *Young Henry Ford*, p. 103.
34. Ibid.; also Nevins and Hill, *The Times, the Man, the Company*, pp. 171–72, which states that Ford and his four investors would jointly own any patents arising from the "motorwagon" the engineer signed on to develop.
35. Strauss, "Reminiscences," p. 17.
36. Ibid., pp. 45–46.
37. Olson, *Young Henry Ford*, pp. 101–2.
38. Prescott Hulbert, "Reminiscences," pp. 7–8.
39. Nevins and Hill, *The Times, the Man, the Company*, pp. 172–74.
40. Olson, *Young Henry Ford*, p. 105.
41. Oliver Barthel, "Reminiscences," pp. 22–23.
42. Lacey, *Ford: The Men and the Machine*, p. 46, citing *Detroit Journal*, August 5, 1899; also Nevins and Hill, *The Times, the Man, the Company*, p. 175.
43. Lacey, *Ford: The Men and the Machine*, pp. 46–47; also Nevins and Hill, *The Times, the Man, the Company*, p. 175.
44. Nevins and Hill, *The Times, the Man, the Company*, p. 175.
45. Lacey, *Ford: The Men and the Machine*, p. 46.
46. Nevins and Hill, *The Times, the Man, the Company*, p. 175.
47. Bryan, *Clara*, pp. 58–59; also Collier and Horowitz, *The Fords: An American Epic*, p. 35; Olson, *Young Henry Ford*, p. 104; and Nevins and Hill, *The Times, the Man, the Company*, p. 176.
48. Allan L. Benson, *The New Henry Ford* (New York: Funk & Wagnalls, 1923), p. 69.
49. Lacey, *Ford: The Men and the Machine*, p. 47, citing Strauss, "Reminiscences," p. 53.
50. Nevins and Hill, *The Times, the Man, the Company*, p. 178.
51. Lacey, *Ford: The Men and the Machine*, p. 47.
52. Olson, *Young Henry Ford*, p. 119, citing *Detroit News-Tribune*, February 4, 1900; also Nevins and Hill, *The Times, the Man, the Company*, p. 180.
53. Lacey, *Ford: The Men and the Machine*, pp. 47–48, citing *Detroit News-Tribune*, February 4, 1900; also Nevins and Hill, *The Times, the Man, the Company*, p. 182.
54. Bryan, *Clara*, p. 59.
55. Nevins and Hill, *The Times, the Man, the Company*, pp. 193–94, citing *Census of Manufactures: 1905. Automobiles and Bicycles and Tricycles. U.S. Bureau of the Census, Bulletin 66* (Washington, D.C.: U.S. Government Printing Office, 1907), which states that of the approximately 4,000 American cars manufactured in 1900, more than three fourths were propelled by steam or electric engines.
56. Lacey, *Ford: The Men and the Machine*, p. 48.
57. Nevins and Hill, *The Times, the Man, the Company*, p. 178.
58. Beverly Rae Kimes, "Young Henry Ford," *Automobile Quarterly* 10, no. 2, p. 205.
59. Bryan, *Clara*, p. 59.

60. Beverly Rae Kimes, ed., *Packard: A History of the Motor Car and the Company* (Princeton, N.J.: Automobile Quarterly, 1978), p. 806.
61. Lacey, *Ford: The Men and the Machine*, p. 66.
62. Nevins and Hill, *The Times, the Man, the Company*, p. 191.
63. Hulbert, "Reminiscences," pp. 11–12.
64. Carol Gelderman, *Henry Ford: The Wayward Capitalist* (New York: Dial, 1981), p. 19, citing George S. May, *A Most Unique Machine* (Grand Rapids, Mich.: William B. Eerdmans, 1975), p. 101.
65. Hulbert, "Reminiscences," pp. 11–12.
66. Lacey, *Ford: The Men and the Machine*, p. 48.
67. Bryan, *Clara*, p. 60; also Olson, *Young Henry Ford*, p. 125.
68. Olson, *Young Henry Ford*, p. 103; also Nevins and Hill, *The Times, the Man, the Company*, p. 190, citing Arthur Pound's authorized history of the first twenty-five years of the General Motors Corporation, *The Turning Wheel* (Garden City, N.Y.: Doubleday, 1934), p. 54.
69. Olson, *Young Henry Ford*, p. 121.
70. Lacey, *Ford: The Men and the Machine*, p. 49.
71. Strauss, "Reminiscences," p. 53.
72. Ibid.
73. Olson, *Young Henry Ford*, p. 123; also Lacey, *Ford: The Men and the Machine*, pp. 49–50.
74. Sward, *The Legend of Henry Ford*, p. 14.
75. Lacey, *Ford: The Men and the Machine*, p. 49, citing Henry Ford with Samuel Crowther, *My Life and Work* (Garden City, N.Y.: Doubleday, 1923), p. 36.
76. Lacey, *Ford: The Men and the Machine*, p. 50.
77. Olson, *Young Henry Ford*, pp. 127–28.
78. Lacey, *Ford: The Men and the Machine*, p. 50.
79. Olson, *Young Henry Ford*, p. 135.
80. Ibid., p. 125.
81. Nevins and Hill, *The Times, the Man, the Company*, p. 214.
82. Olson, *Young Henry Ford*, p. 132.
83. Lacey, *Ford: The Men and the Machine*, p. 53.
84. Booton Herndon, *Ford: An Unconventional Biography of the Men and Their Times* (New York: Weybright and Talley, 1969), p. 64; also Olson, *Young Henry Ford*, p. 135; and Lacey, *Ford: The Men and the Machine*, p. 53.
85. Olson, *Young Henry Ford*, pp. 93–94.
86. Fadiman, *The Little, Brown Book of Anecdotes*, p. 213.
87. Nevins and Hill, *The Times, the Man, the Company*, p. 215, citing Alfred P. Sloan Jr., *My Years with General Motors*, eds. John McDonald and Catharine Stevens (Garden City, N.Y.: Doubleday, 1964), pp. 27–30, and Alfred P. Sloan Jr. with Boyden Sparkes, *Adventures of a White-Collar Man* (New York: Doubleday, Doran, 1941), pp. 73–74.
88. Olson, *Young Henry Ford*, p. 135.
89. Ibid., pp. 138–41.
90. Lacey, *Ford: The Men and the Machine*, p. 52.
91. Bryan, *Clara*, pp. 340–44.
92. Nevins and Hill, *The Times, the Man, the Company*, p. 208.
93. Olson, *Young Henry Ford*, p. 150.
94. *Entertainment Weekly*, June 29–July 6, 2001, p. 134.
95. Olson, *Young Henry Ford*, p. 125.
96. Nevins and Hill, *The Times, the Man, the Company*, p. 202, citing William Adams Simonds, *Henry Ford: His Life, His Work, His Genius* (Indianapolis: Bobbs-Merrill, 1943), p. 69.
97. Olson, *Young Henry Ford*, pp. 143–45.
98. Nevins and Hill, *The Times, the Man, the Company*, p. 203.
99. Lacey, *Ford: The Men and the Machine*, p. 54.
100. Collier and Horowitz, *The Fords: An American Epic*, p. 40; also Nevins and Hill, *The Times, the Man, the Company*, p. 203, citing an article in the *Detroit Free Press*, October 6, 1901.
101. Bryan, *Clara*, p. 65; also Lacey, *Ford: The Men and the Machine*, p. 56.
102. Olson, *Young Henry Ford*, p. 145.
103. Bryan, *Clara*, p. 64.

104. Herndon, *Ford: An Unconventional Biography of the Men and Their Times*, p. 65.
105. Nevins and Hill, *The Times, the Man, the Company*, p. 204; also Olson, *Young Henry Ford*, p. 146.
106. Olson, *Young Henry Ford*, p. 146; also cited in Simonds, *Henry Ford: His Life, His Work, His Genius*, p. 71; and Nevins and Hill, *The Times, the Man, the Company*, p. 205.
107. Herndon, *Ford: An Unconventional Biography of the Men and Their Times*, p. 65.
108. Needham, "Reminiscences," p. 10.
109. Bryan, *Clara*, p. 65.
110. Sward, *The Legend of Henry Ford*, p. 15.
111. Quoted in Olson, *Young Henry Ford*, p. 141.
112. Bryan, *Clara*, p. 66; also Nevins and Hill, *The Times, the Man, the Company*, p. 207.
113. Collier and Horowitz, *The Fords: An American Epic*, p. 41.
114. Nevins and Hill, *The Times, the Man, the Company*, p. 206.
115. Olson, *Young Henry Ford*, p. 147; also Nevins and Hill, *The Times, the Man, the Company*, p. 206.
116. Lacey, *Ford: The Men and the Machine*, p. 59.
117. Bryan, *Clara*, p. 69.
118. Lacey, *Ford: The Men and the Machine*, p. 60; citing Barthel, "Reminiscences," p. 28.
119. Henry Ford to Milton Bryant, January 6, 1902, Henry Ford Museum and Library.
120. John B. Rae, *The American Automobile* (Chicago: University of Chicago Press, 1965), p. 59.
121. Olson, *Young Henry Ford*, pp. 125–26; also Lacey, *Ford: The Men and the Machine*, p. 63.
122. Olson, *Young Henry Ford*, p. 154.
123. Nevins and Hill, *The Times, the Man, the Company*, p. 211, citing Ford with Crowther, *My Life and Work*, p. 36.
124. John B. Rae, ed., *Great Lives Observed: Henry Ford* (Englewood Cliffs, N.J.: Prentice-Hall, 1969), p. 1; also David A. Hounshell, *From the American System to Mass Production, 1800–1932* (Baltimore: Johns Hopkins University Press, 1984), p. 11.
125. Collier and Horowitz, *The Fords: An American Epic*, p. 42; also Olson, *Young Henry Ford*, p. 154, and Nevins and Hill, *The Times, the Man, the Company*, pp. 212, 212n. Nevins and Hill report that Henry M. Leland's son, Wilfred C. Leland, told them that Brown and Sharpe once attained the remarkable tolerance of 1/270,000 of an inch.
126. Sward, *The Legend of Henry Ford*, p. 8.
127. Ibid., p. 7.
128. Louis William Steinwedel, "The Two Henrys and the Lincoln Legend," *Saturday Evening Post*, November 1975, pp. 52–53.
129. Lacey, *Ford: The Men and the Machine*, p. 61, citing John B. Rae, *American Automobile Manufacturers: The First Forty Years* (Philadelphia: Chilton Press, 1959), p. 31.
130. Sward, *The Legend of Henry Ford*, p. 14; also Olson, *Young Henry Ford*, p. 153.
131. Collier and Horowitz, *The Fords: An American Epic*, p. 42.
132. Olson, *Young Henry Ford*, p. 154.
133. Gelderman, *Henry Ford: The Wayward Capitalist*, p. 22; also Olson, *Young Henry Ford*, p. 154.
134. Lacey, *Ford: The Men and the Machine*, p. 61.
135. Nevins and Hill, *The Times, the Man, the Company*, p. 205.
136. Olson, *Young Henry Ford*, pp. 111–12.
137. Bryan, *Clara*, pp. 72–73; also Olson, *Young Henry Ford*, p. 154.
138. Olson, *Young Henry Ford*, p. 147.
139. Herndon, *Ford: An Unconventional Biography of the Men and Their Times*, p. 65.
140. Bryan, *Clara*, p. 75.
141. Collier and Horowitz, *The Fords: An American Epic*, p. 42.
142. Lacey, *Ford: The Men and the Machine*, p. 63, citing Ford with Crowther, *My Life and Work*, p. 50; also Olson, *Young Henry Ford*, p. 154; and Nevins and Hill, *The Times, the Man, the Company*, p. 215.
143. William F. Noonan, *Barney Oldfield* (New York: G.P. Putnam's Sons, 1962).
144. Nevins and Hill, *The Times, the Man, the Company*, p. 217.
145. Bryan, *Clara*, p. 75.
146. Herndon, *Ford: An Unconventional Biography of the Men and Their Times*, p. 66.

147. Olson, *Young Henry Ford,* p. 147; also Lacey, *Ford: The Men and the Machine,* p. 64, who also cites Simonds, *Henry Ford: His Life, His Work, His Genius,* p. 76, giving Oldfield's quote as ending, "But I did much the best job of it."

148. Lacey, *Ford: The Men and the Machine,* p. 64.

149. Collier and Horowitz, *The Fords: An American Epic,* p. 45.

150. Nevins and Hill, *The Times, the Man, the Company,* pp. 198–99, citing Barthel, "Reminiscences," pp. 3–7.

151. Lacey, *Ford: The Men and the Machine,* p. 69; also Nevins and Hill, *The Times, the Man, the Company,* p. 225.

152. Nevins and Hill, *The Times, the Man, the Company,* p. 225.

153. Gelderman, *Henry Ford: The Wayward Capitalist,* p. 23; also Nevins and Hill, *The Times, the Man, the Company,* p. 225.

154. Lacey, *Ford: The Men and the Machine,* p. 67.

155. Olson, *Young Henry Ford,* p. 160, citing *Detroit Tribune,* April 1, 1903.

156. Lacey, *Ford: The Men and the Machine,* p. 68, citing Nevins and Hill, *The Times, the Man, the Company,* p. 233.

157. Collier and Horowitz, *The Fords: An American Epic,* p. 43.

158. Lacey, *Ford: The Men and the Machine,* p. 68; also Nevins and Hill, *The Times, the Man, the Company,* p. 226.

159. Olson, *Young Henry Ford,* p. 163.

160. Bryan, *Clara,* p. 74; also Nevins and Hill, *The Times, the Man, the Company,* p. 226.

161. Sward, *The Legend of Henry Ford,* p. 16.

162. Ibid., p. 17.

163. Nevins and Hill, *The Times, the Man, the Company,* pp. 225n, 225–26.

164. William and Marjorie McNairn, *Quotations from the Unusual Henry Ford* (Norfolk, Calif.: Stockton Trade Press, 1978), p. 52.

165. Bryan, *Clara,* p. 77.

166. Collier and Horowitz, *The Fords: An American Epic,* p. 45; also Olson, *Young Henry Ford,* p. 164; and Nevins and Hill, *The Times, the Man, the Company,* p. 226, citing Simonds, *Henry Ford: His Life, His Work, His Genius,* pp. 77–78.

167. Nevins and Hill, *The Times, the Man, the Company,* p. 229.

CHAPTER THREE: FOUNDING FORD

1. Charles H. Bennett, "Reminiscences" (oral history project), p. 17, Henry Ford Museum and Library, Dearborn, Michigan.

2. Robert Lacey, *Ford: The Men and the Machine* (Boston: Little, Brown, 1986), p. 68.

3. Bennett, "Reminiscences," p. 22.

4. Lacey, *Ford: The Men and the Machine,* p. 68.

5. Sidney Olson, *Young Henry Ford: A Picture History of the First Forty Years,* rev. ed. (Detroit: Wayne State University Press, 1997), p. 163.

6. Harry Barnard, "James Couzens of Detroit" (typescript), p. 33, Henry Ford Museum and Library.

7. Ford R. Bryan, *Henry's Lieutenants* (Detroit: Wayne State University Press, 1993), p. 67.

8. Allan Nevins and Frank Ernest Hill, *Ford,* vol. 1, *The Times, the Man, the Company* (New York: Charles Scribner's Sons, 1954), p. 243.

9. Bryan, *Henry's Lieutenants,* p. 67.

10. Harry Barnard, "James Couzens of Detroit," pp. 13–14.

11. Olson, *Young Henry Ford,* p. 163.

12. Bryan, *Henry's Lieutenants,* p. 68.

13. Lacey, *Ford: The Men and the Machine,* p. 69.

14. Barnard, "James Couzens of Detroit," p. 24.

15. Nevins and Hill, *The Times, the Man, the Company,* p. 244; also Bryan, *Henry's Lieutenants,* p. 68.

16. Lacey, *Ford: The Men and the Machine,* p. 69.

17. Barnard, "James Couzens of Detroit," p. 40.

18. John Wandersee, "Reminiscences," p. 36.
19. Bennett, "Reminiscences," p. 16.
20. Lacey, *Ford: The Men and the Machine*, p. 70.
21. Stan Grayson, "The Brothers Dodge," *Automobile Quarterly* 17, no. 1 (Spring 1979), p. 10.
22. Walter G. Griffith, "Reminiscences," pp. 1–2; also Bryan, *Henry's Lieutenants*, p. 307.
23. Griffith, "Reminiscences," p. 2.
24. Ibid., p. 4.
25. Nevins and Hill, *The Times, the Man, the Company*, p. 238.
26. William Adams Simonds, *Henry Ford: His Life, His Work, His Genius* (Indianapolis: Bobbs-Merrill, 1943), p. 79.
27. Lacey, *Ford: The Men and the Machine*, p. 72.
28. Simonds, *Henry Ford: His Life, His Work, His Genius*, pp. 78, 80, 86.
29. John W. Anderson, letter to his father, June 4, 1903, Henry Ford Museum and Library.
30. Lacey, *Ford: The Men and the Machine*, p. 72.
31. Barnard, "James Couzens of Detroit," p. 39.
32. Oliver Barthel, "Reminiscences," p. 23.
33. Barnard, "James Couzens of Detroit," p. 39.
34. Olson, *Young Henry Ford*, p. 177.
35. Lacey, *Ford: The Men and the Machine*, p. 72.
36. Bennett, "Reminiscences," pp. 3–14.
37. Fred L. Black, "History and the Growth of Public Relations in America," *Michigan Business Review,* May 1954, p. 1. Also quoted in David L. Lewis, *The Public Image of Henry Ford: An American Folk Hero and His Company* (Detroit: Wayne State University Press, 1976), p. 15.
38. Ron Chernow, *Titan: The Life of John D. Rockefeller Sr.* (New York: Random House, 1998), pp. 611–12.
39. Henry B. Lent, *The Automobile-U.S.A.: Its Impact on People's Lives and the National Economy* (New York: E.P. Dutton, 1968), pp. 15–16.
40. David Halberstam, *The Reckoning* (New York: William Morrow, 1986), pp. 83–84.
41. Bennett, "Reminiscences," p. 25.
42. Peter Collier and David Horowitz, *The Fords: An American Epic* (New York: Summit Books, 1987), p. 42.
43. Dennis Casteele, *The Cars of Oldsmobile* (Osceola, Wis.: Motorbooks International, 1992), p. 15.
44. Bennett, "Reminiscences," p. 14.
45. Olson, *Young Henry Ford*, p. 177.
46. George H. Dammann, *Ninety Years of Ford*, 2d ed. (Osceola, Wis.: Motorbooks International, 1993), p. 13.
47. Bennett, "Reminiscences," p. 16.
48. Olson, *Young Henry Ford*, p. 177.
49. Bennett, "Reminiscences," p. 16.
50. Ibid., p. 18; also Barnard, "James Couzens of Detroit," p. 36.
51. Collier and Horowitz, *The Fords: An American Epic*, p. 43.
52. Nevins and Hill, *The Times, the Man, the Company*, p. 235.
53. Olson, *Young Henry Ford*, pp. 177–78.
54. Lacey, *Ford: The Men and the Machine*, p. 75.
55. Wandersee, "Reminiscences," p. 4.
56. David M. Bell, "Reminiscences," p. 11.
57. Simonds, *Henry Ford: His Life, His Work, His Genius*, p. 85.
58. Barnard, "James Couzens of Detroit," p. 37.
59. Ibid., p. 40.
60. *Detroit News,* June 16, 1903.
61. Creation of Ford Motor file, Accession 85, box 1—Corporate Minutes, Henry Ford Museum and Library.
62. Creation of Ford Motor file, Accession 122, box 1, Henry Ford Museum and Library.
63. Creation of Ford Motor file, Articles of Association, box 1, Henry Ford Museum and Library.
64. Cited in David L. Lewis, *Ford Country*, 2d ed. (Sidney, Ohio: Amos Press, 1999), p. 69.

65. Olson, *Young Henry Ford*, p. 157.
66. Lewis, *Ford Country*, p. 118.
67. Collier and Horowitz, *The Fords: An American Epic*, p. 46.
68. Ford R. Bryan, *Clara: Mrs. Henry Ford* (Dearborn, Mich.: Ford Books, 2001), pp. 80–81.
69. Bryan, *Henry's Lieutenants*, p. 68.
70. Wandersee, "Reminiscences," p. 34.
71. Collier and Horowitz, *The Fords: An American Epic*, p. 44.
72. Bryan, *Clara*, p. 83.
73. Janet Freeborn, "Torch Still Burns Brightly at Nation's Oldest Family-Owned Ford Dealership," *Automotive News*, January 27, 1997.
74. Bellamy Partridge, *Fill'er Up* (New York: McGraw-Hill, 1952), p. 40.
75. Collier and Horowitz, *The Fords: An American Epic*, p. 46.
76. Barthel, "Reminiscences," p. 80.
77. Frederick Strauss, "Reminiscences," p. 84.
78. Maurice D. Hendry, "Childe Harold Wills: A Career in Cars," *Automobile Quarterly* 5, no. 2, p. 136.
79. Wandersee, "Reminiscences," p. 4.
80. Bryan, *Henry's Lieutenants*, p. 290.
81. Lewis, *Ford Country*, p. 79.
82. Hendry, "Childe Harold Wills," p. 137.
83. Collier and Horowitz, *The Fords: An American Epic*, pp. 43–44.
84. Wandersee, "Reminiscences," p. 34.
85. Lewis, *Ford Country*, p. 117; also Nevins and Hill, *The Times, the Man, the Company*, p. 227.
86. Lewis, *Ford Country*, p. 127.
87. David Burgess-Wise, *The History of the Automobile* (London: W.H. Smith, 1985), p. 33.
88. Ibid., pp. 32–33.
89. Lewis, *Ford Country*, p. 127.
90. Ralph H. Graves, *The Triumph of an Idea: The Story of Henry Ford* (Garden City, N.Y.: Doubleday, Doran, 1935), p. 33; also Nevins and Hill, *The Times, the Man, the Company*, p. 241; and Bryan, *Clara*, p. 83.
91. Bryan, *Clara*, p. 83.
92. Nevins and Hill, *The Times, the Man, the Company*, p. 240; also Barnard, "James Couzens of Detroit," p. 45.
93. Collier and Horowitz, *The Fords: An American Epic*, pp. 46–47, citing Keith Sward, *The Legend of Henry Ford* (New York: Rinehart, 1948), p. 20.
94. Lewis, *Ford Country*, p. 127.
95. Barnard, "James Couzens of Detroit," p. 45.
96. Ibid.
97. George Brown, "Reminiscences," vol. 1, pp. 22–23.
98. Lewis, *Ford Country*, p. 68.
99. Collier and Horowitz, *The Fords: An American Epic*, p. 42.
100. Lewis, *Ford Country*, p. 127.
101. Barnard, "James Couzens of Detroit," p. 46.
102. Dammann, *Ninety Years of Ford*, p. 16.
103. Ford Motor Company advertisement, *Automobile Review*, October 2, 1904.
104. Collier and Horowitz, *The Fords: An American Epic*, p. 47; and Bryan, *Clara*, pp. 84–86.
105. Collier and Horowitz, *The Fords: An American Epic*, p. 48; also Bryan, *Clara*, pp. 85–87.
106. Beverly Rae Kimes, "The Young Henry Ford," *Automobile Quarterly* 10, no. 2, p. 214.
107. Lewis, *Ford Country*, p. 98.
108. Nevins and Hill, *The Times, the Man, the Company*, p. 272.
109. Piquette Plant Preservation Project Archive, Fact Sheet File, Henry Ford Heritage Association, Dearborn, Michigan; also Steve Ford, "Model T Factory, Near Doom," *Detroit News*, September 9, 1998; and Nevins and Hill, *The Times, the Man, the Company*, pp. 247, 266n.
110. Bryan, *Clara*, p. 89.
111. Kimes, "The Young Henry Ford," p. 213.
112. Brown, "Reminiscences," p. 19.
113. Lacey, *Ford: The Men and the Machine*, pp. 80–81.

114. Barnard, "James Couzens of Detroit," p. 67.
115. Bryan, *Clara*, p. 90.
116. Nevins and Hill, *The Times, the Man, the Company*, pp. 279–80.
117. Lacey, *Ford: The Men and the Machine*, pp. 81–82.
118. Barnard, "James Couzens of Detroit," p. 69.
119. Bennett, "Reminiscences," p. 25.
120. Ibid.
121. Barnard, "James Couzens of Detroit," p. 69.
122. Bennett, "Reminiscences," p. 26.
123. Sward, *The Legend of Henry Ford*, p. 22.

CHAPTER FOUR: GROWING SUCCESSES

1. Henry Ford File, Automotive Hall of Fame, Dearborn, Michigan.
2. Richard S. Tedlow, *Giants of Enterprise: Seven Business Innovators and the Empires They Built* (New York: HarperBusiness, 2001), pp. 125–26.
3. Keith Sward, *The Legend of Henry Ford* (New York: Atheneum, 1968), pp. 4–49.
4. David L. Lewis, *The Public Image of Henry Ford: An American Folk Hero and His Company* (1976; reprint, Detroit: Wayne State University Press, 1987), p. 11.
5. Ford R. Bryan, *Henry's Lieutenants* (Detroit: Wayne State University Press, 1993), p. 11.
6. Ottilie M. Leland with Minnie Dubbs Millbrook, *Master of Precision: Henry M. Leland*, 2d ed. (Detroit: Wayne State University Press, 1996), p. 69.
7. Louis William Steinwedel, "The Two Henrys and the Lincoln Legend," *Saturday Evening Post*, November 1975, p. 53.
8. Paul Richard, "From the Collection: Washington's Prize Possessions," *Washington Post*, September 2, 2001, p. G5.
9. William H. Harbaugh, *Power and Responsibility: The Life and Times of Theodore Roosevelt* (New York: Farrar Straus Cudahy, 1961), pp. 164–252; also George E. Mowry, *The Era of Theodore Roosevelt and the Birth of Modern America, 1900–1912* (New York: Harper & Brothers, 1958).
10. Edmund Morris, *Theodore Rex* (New York: Random House, 2001), p. 436.
11. *National Edition of the Works of Theodore Roosevelt*, vol. 16 (New York: Charles Scribner's Sons, 1926), p. 59.
12. *Ford Times* 1, no. 6 (1908), p. 8.
13. Bryan, *Henry's Lieutenants*, pp. 267–68.
14. Charles H. Bennett, "Reminiscences" (oral history project), pp. 39–40, Henry Ford Museum and Library.
15. Ibid., p. 39
16. Floyd Clymer, *Henry's Wonderful Model T* (New York: Bonanza Books, 1955), p. 16.
17. *The Story of the New York to Paris Race* (1908; reprint, Detroit: Clymer Publications, 1952), p. 3.
18. Clymer, *Henry's Wonderful Model T*, p. 14.
19. Robert Lacey, *Ford: The Men and the Machine* (Boston: Little, Brown, 1986), p. 76.
20. Henry Ford with Samuel Crowther, *My Life and Work* (Garden City, N.Y.: Doubleday, 1923), pp. 59–60.
21. David A. Hounshell, *From the American System to Mass Production, 1800–1932* (Baltimore: Johns Hopkins University Press, 1984), p. 39.
22. Lewis, *The Public Image of Henry Ford*, p. 39.
23. Harry Barnard, *Independent Man: The Life of Senator James Couzens* (New York: Charles Scribner's Sons, 1958), p. 50.
24. James Couzens, sales directives, Couzens files, Henry Ford Museum and Library.
25. Ray Miller and Bruce McCalley, *From Here to Obscurity: An Illustrated History of the Model T Ford, 1909–1927* (Avalon, Calif.: Evergreen Press, 1971), p. 14.
26. Lewis, *The Public Image of Henry Ford*, p. 20.
27. Bruce W. McCalley, *Model T Ford: The Car That Changed the World* (Iola, Wis.: Krause Publications, 1994), pp. 7–8.

28. Lacey, *Ford: The Men and the Machine*, p. 62, citing Allan Nevins and Frank Ernest Hill, *Ford*, vol. 1, *The Times, the Man, the Company* (New York: Charles Scribner's Sons, 1954), p. 234.
29. William Greenleaf, *Monopoly on Wheels: Henry Ford and the Selden Automobile Patent* (Detroit: Wayne State University Press, 1961), p. 53.
30. L. Scott Bailey, *The American Car Since 1775* (New York: E.P. Dutton, 1971), pp. 232–372.
31. Carol Gelderman, *Henry Ford: The Wayward Capitalist* (New York: Dial, 1981), p. 28.
32. Lewis, *The Public Image of Henry Ford*, p. 16.
33. Bernie Weis, "Pierce: Early Success," *Automobile Quarterly* 28, no. 4 (1990), pp. 15–16.
34. Lacey, *Ford: The Men and the Machine*, p. 23.
35. "Dr. Day Denounces Autos," *New York Times*, June 6, 1910, p. 5.
36. Alfred P. Sloan Jr. with Boyden Sparkes, *Adventures of a White-Collar Man* (New York: Doubleday, Doran, 1941), pp. 33–36.
37. Ibid.
38. Leland with Millbrook, *Master of Precision*, p. 69.
39. Sloan with Sparkes, *Adventures of a White-Collar Man*, pp. 41–42.
40. Gelderman, *Henry Ford: The Wayward Capitalist*, p. 30.
41. Nevins and Hill, *The Times, the Man, the Company*, p. 600n, citing "Will Be Leaders," *Motor World*, no. 2, May 2, 1901, p. 95.
42. Nevins and Hill, *The Times, the Man, the Company*, p. 116.
43. Beverly Rae Kimes, "A Family in Kenosha: The Story of the Rambler and the Jeffery," *Automobile Quarterly* 16, no. 2 (1978), pp. 130–42.
44. Leland with Millbrook, *Master of Precision*, p. 74.
45. George H. Dammann, *Ninety Years of Ford*, 2d ed. (Osceola, Wis.: Motorbooks International, 1993), pp. 21–22.
46. Harry Barnard, "James Couzens of Detroit" (typescript), p. 47, Henry Ford Museum and Library.
47. Miller and McCalley, *From Here to Obscurity*, p. 15.
48. Dammann, *Ninety Years of Ford*, pp. 24–25.
49. Bellamy Partridge, *Fill'er Up* (New York: McGraw-Hill, 1952), pp. 144–45.
50. Bailey, *The American Car Since 1775*, pp. 138–39.
51. Ford R. Bryan, *Beyond the Model T: The Other Ventures of Henry Ford*, rev. ed. (Detroit: Wayne State University Press, 1997), p. 151.
52. David L. Lewis, *Ford Country*, 2d ed. (Sidney, Ohio: Amos Press, 1999), p. 25.
53. Modern output is described as brake horsepower (bhp), normally a much higher figure than the old-style engine horsepower (hp) under discussion here.
54. Leslie R. Henry, *Henry's Fabulous Model A* (Los Angeles: Clymer Publications, 1959), p. 21.
55. Ibid., p. 18.
56. Miller and McCalley, *From Here to Obscurity*, p. 15.
57. Henry, *Henry's Fabulous Model A*, p. 18.
58. Miller and McCalley, *From Here to Obscurity*, p. 15.

CHAPTER FIVE: GROWING PAINS

1. Louis J. Kinietz, "Reminiscences" (oral history project), p. 7, Henry Ford Museum and Library, Dearborn, Michigan.
2. David L. Lewis, *The Public Image of Henry Ford: An American Folk Hero and His Company* (Detroit: Wayne State University Press, 1976), p. 20.
3. Carol Gelderman, *Henry Ford: The Wayward Capitalist* (New York: Dial, 1981), p. 26.
4. Ford R. Bryan, *Henry's Lieutenants* (Detroit: Wayne State University Press, 1993), p. 69.
5. Charles Dickens's 1853 novel *Bleak House* centers around the Jarndyce family's ruinous, decades-long legal battles over an inheritance.
6. Gelderman, *Henry Ford: The Wayward Capitalist*, p. 26.
7. Richard S. Tedlow, *Giants of Enterprise: Seven Business Innovators and the Empires They Built* (New York: HarperBusiness, 2001), p. 84.

8. Robert Lacey, *Ford: The Men and the Machine* (Boston: Little, Brown, 1986), p. 99.

9. William Greenleaf, *Monopoly on Wheels: Henry Ford and the Selden Automobile Patent* (Detroit: Wayne State University Press, 1961), p. 43.

10. Michael S. Malone, "The Smother of Invention," *Forbes ASAP,* June 24, 2002, pp. 33–40.

11. Gary L. Reback, "Patently Absurd," *Forbes ASAP,* June 24, 2002, pp. 45–48.

12. Lewis, *The Public Image of Henry Ford,* p. 20; and Tedlow, *Giants of Enterprise,* p. 84.

13. Tedlow, *Giants of Enterprise,* p. 86.

14. Gelderman, *Henry Ford: The Wayward Capitalist,* p. 28.

15. Lewis, *The Public Image of Henry Ford,* pp. 20–21.

16. Gelderman, *Henry Ford: The Wayward Capitalist,* p. 29.

17. Ibid., p. 30.

18. H. H. Franklin, September 29, 1903, letter to editor, *Cycle and Automobile Trade Journal,* November 1, 1903, p. 19, reprinted in Greenleaf, *Monopoly on Wheels,* p. 102.

19. Leslie R. Henry, *Henry's Fabulous Model A Ford* (Los Angeles: Clymer Publications, 1959), p. 15.

20. Lewis, *The Public Image of Henry Ford,* p. 21, citing Allan Nevins and Frank Ernest Hill, *Ford,* vol. 1, *The Times, the Man, the Company* (New York: Charles Scribner's Sons, 1954), pp. 295–96.

21. Theodore F. McManus and Norman Beasley, *Men, Money and Motors: A Drama of the Automobile* (New York: Harper & Brothers, 1929), p. 56.

22. Gelderman, *Henry Ford: The Wayward Capitalist,* pp. 26–27, citing Harry Barnard, *Independent Man: The Life of James Couzens* (New York: Charles Scribner's Sons, 1958), p. 54.

23. Lewis, *The Public Image of Henry Ford,* p. 21, citing Nevins and Hill, *The Times, the Man, the Company,* p. 298.

24. Gelderman, *Henry Ford: The Wayward Capitalist,* pp. 32–33; also Henry, *Henry's Fabulous Model A Ford,* p. 18.

25. Nevins and Hill, *The Times, the Man, the Company,* p. 298, citing *Detroit Free Press,* July 28, 1903.

26. Gelderman, *Henry Ford: The Wayward Capitalist,* pp. 33–34, citing Greenleaf, *Monopoly on Wheels,* pp. 120–21.

27. Lewis, *The Public Image of Henry Ford,* p. 20.

28. "Will Fight Selden Patent," *New York Times,* February 13, 1910, sec. 4, p. 4.

29. Henry, *Henry's Fabulous Model A Ford,* p. 18.

30. Gelderman, *Henry Ford: The Wayward Capitalist,* p. 36; also Nevins and Hill, *The Times, the Man, the Company,* pp. 293–322.

31. Oliver Barthel, "Reminiscences," pp. 74, 46.

32. George Brown, "Reminiscences," vol.1, p. 24.

33. Sidney Olson, *Young Henry Ford: A Picture History of the First Forty Years,* rev. ed. (Detroit: Wayne State University Press, 1997), p. 182.

34. Nevins and Hill, *The Times, the Man, the Company,* pp. 342–45.

35. W. Ernest Grimshaw, "Reminiscences," p. 6.

36. Joseph A. Galamb, "Reminiscences," pp. 3–7.

37. Henry Ford, letter to the editor, *The Automobile,* January 11, 1906, p. 107.

38. John Wandersee, "Reminiscences," p. 20.

39. Charles J. "Jimmy" Smith, "Reminiscences," p. 3.

40. Ford, letter to the editor, *The Automobile,* January 11, 1906, p. 107.

41. Wandersee, "Reminiscences," p. 20.

42. Ibid.; also Bryan, *Henry's Lieutenants,* p. 319.

43. Charles H. Bennett, "Reminiscences," p. 47.

44. Bryan, *Henry's Lieutenants,* pp. 123–28; also Lacey, *Ford: The Men and the Machines,* p. 53.

45. James O'Connor, "Reminiscences," pp. 12–13.

46. Richard Kroll, "Reminiscences," p. 10.

47. "Ford Finds $68,000 Check in His Pocket," *New York Times,* December 18, 1910, p. 1.

48. Lewis, *The Public Image of Henry Ford,* pp. 64–65.

49. Brown, "Reminiscences," vol. 1, p. 46.

50. O'Connor, "Reminiscences," p. 43.

51. Ibid.

52. Grimshaw, "Reminiscences," p. 7.
53. Ford, letter to the editor, *The Automobile,* January 11, 1906, p. 107.
54. Norman Beasley, *Knudsen: A Biography* (New York: Whittlesey House, 1947), p. 41.
55. Brown, "Reminiscences," vol. 1, p. 62.
56. Stan Grayson, "The Brothers Dodge," *Automobile Quarterly* 17, no. 1 (Spring 1979), p. 10.
57. Jean Maddern Pitrone, *Tangled Web: The Legacy of Auto Pioneer John F. Dodge* (Hamtramck, Mich.: Avenue Publishing, 1989), p. 54.
58. Ibid., p. 53.
59. O'Connor, "Reminiscences," p. 13.
60. Kinietz, "Reminiscences," p. 8.
61. Nevins and Hill, *The Times, the Man, the Company,* p. 401.
62. "Cheapness Finds a Defender," *New York Times,* January 14, 1909, p. 6.
63. Ford Motor Company advertisement, "A Dollar's Worth of Car for Two Half Dollars," *New York Times,* January 13, 1909, sec. 4, p. 4.

CHAPTER SIX: MODEL T MANIA

1. Garet Garrett, "The World That Henry Ford Made," *Look,* March 25, 1952, p. 35; the exact date when Henry Ford made this famous utterance is not known. The June 1913 (tenth-anniversary issue) *Ford Times* (vol. 6, no. 9), p. 366, uses the quotation saying that it was first made around 1903, when Ford Motor Company was founded.
2. Will Rogers, *Wit and Philosophy from Radio Talks of Will Rogers* (New York: E. R. Squibb and Sons, 1930), p. 33.
3. X, "An Appeal to Our Millionaires," *North American Review,* June 1906, pp. 807–8.
4. Reynold M. Wik, *Henry Ford and Grass-roots America* (Ann Arbor, Mich.: University of Michigan Press, 1972), p. 17.
5. Ibid., p. 15, citing *Breeder's Gazette,* August 24, 1904, p. 290.
6. Ibid., citing X, "An Appeal to Our Millionaires," p. 807.
7. Booth Tarkington, *The Magnificent Ambersons* (Garden City, N.Y.: Doubleday, Page, 1918), pp. 142–44.
8. Roger Butterfield, "Henry Ford's Three Great Revolutions Are Still Going On" (n.d.), clipping file, Henry Ford Museum and Library.
9. "Wilson Blames Speeders," *New York Times,* February 28, 1906, p. 2.
10. Carol Gelderman, *Henry Ford: The Wayward Capitalist* (New York: Dial, 1981), p. 37.
11. Roscoe Sheller, *Me and the Model T* (Portland, Ore.: Binford & Mort, 1965), p. 1.
12. Philip Van Doren Stern, *Tin Lizzie: The Story of the Fabulous Model T Ford* (New York: Simon & Schuster, 1955), pp. 64–68.
13. David L. Lewis, *The Public Image of Henry Ford: An American Folk Hero and His Company* (Detroit: Wayne State University Press, 1976), p. 44.
14. Wik, *Henry Ford and Grass-roots America,* p. 40.
15. Stern, *Tin Lizzie,* pp. 64–68.
16. Ibid., p. 16.
17. Ibid., pp. 16–17.
18. "Cars Registered in the U.S., 1900–98," *The World Almanac and Book of Facts 2001* (Mahwah, N.J.: World Almanac Books, 2001), p. 226.
19. Douglas Brinkley, Introduction to *A Hoosier Holiday,* by Theodore Dreiser (Bloomington, Ind.: University of Indiana Press, 1999), pp. 3–11.
20. Wik, *Henry Ford and Grass-roots America,* p. 1.
21. David L. Lewis, *Ford Country,* 2d ed. (Sidney, Ohio: Amos Press, 1999), p. 128.
22. "The Woman and the Ford" (Detroit: Ford Motor Company, 1910), pp. 1–7.
23. "Ford Simplicity Saves Passengers," *Ford Times* 8, no. 8 (June 1913), p. 394.
24. "Lady Tourists!—Why Not?," *Ford Times* 6, no. 2 (November 1912), pp. 78–79.
25. Virginia Scharff, *Taking the Wheel: Women and the Coming of the Motor Age* (New York: Free Press, 1991), pp. 15–66.
26. Edith Wharton, *A Motor-Flight Through France* (New York: Charles Scribner's Sons, 1908), p. 1.
27. Robert Lacey, *Ford: The Men and the Machine* (Boston: Little, Brown, 1986), p. 92.

28. Stern, *Tin Lizzie,* p. 26.
29. Richard F. Snow, "A Man of the Century," *American Heritage,* July–August 2000, p. 7.
30. Sinclair Lewis, *Babbitt* (New York: Harcourt Brace, 1922), p. 3.
31. Charles Bukowski, *Ham on Rye* (Santa Rosa, Calif.: Black Sparrow Press, 2000), p. 15.
32. Ibid.
33. Sheller, *Me and the Model T,* pp. 59–60.
34. Ibid.
35. "Are Automobiles Expensive?," *New York Times,* February 12, 1909, V, p. 12.
36. "Cheaper to Run a Ford than to Buy Shoe Leather," *Ford Times* 5, no. 6 (March 1912), p. 197.
37. Model T Songs List, AR-98-213579. Henry Ford Museum and Library, Dearborn, Michigan.
38. Wik, *Henry Ford and Grass-roots America,* p. 1, citing Grace Hegger Lewis, *With Love from Gracie: Sinclair Lewis, 1912–1925* (New York: Harcourt Brace, 1955), p. 108.
39. Sinclair Lewis, *Free Air* (Lincoln: University of Nebraska Press, 1993), p. 99.
40. Lewis, *Ford Country,* p. 133.
41. Charles A. Lindbergh, *Boyhood on the Upper Mississippi: A Reminiscent Letter* (St. Paul: Minnesota Historical Society, 1972), p. 25.
42. Ibid., p. 25.
43. Ibid., pp. 25–27.
44. "Two Weeks of Solid Pleasure," *Ford Times* 6, no. 3 (December 1912), p. 127.
45. "A Model T's Journey Across the Truckee Summit, California," *Ford Times* 5, no. 9 (July 1912), p. 325.
46. John Burroughs, *Under the Maples* (Boston: Houghton Mifflin, 1921), p. 44.
47. David L. Lewis, *The Public Image of Henry Ford* (Detroit: Wayne State University Press, 1987), p. 223; and Henry Ford with Samuel Crowther, *My Life and Work* (Garden City, N.Y.: Doubleday, 1923).
48. Norman Brauer, *There to Breathe the Beauty* (Dalton, Pa.: Norman Brauer Publications, 1995).
49. Lewis, *The Public Image of Henry Ford,* p. 223, citing Charles E. Sorensen with Samuel T. Williamson, *My Forty Years with Ford* (New York: W.W. Norton, 1956), p. 18.
50. William Clay Ford Jr., narrator, "Discovery," Ford Motor Company "No Boundaries" Ad Campaign Transcripts (press release), February 19, 2002, p. 2.
51. "Completes Long Journey," *Ford Times* 5, no. 6 (April–May 1912), p. 236.
52. "The Model T's Trip Through the Wilds," *Ford Times* 3, no. 15 (May 1910), p. 332.
53. "Traveling Under Difficulty," *Ford Times* 5, no. 6 (April–May 1912), p. 197.
54. "World's Oldest Owner Buys a Model T," *Ford Times* 5, no. 6 (April–May 1912), p. 196.
55. Edsel Ford, "The Cruise of the Runabout," *Ford Times* 6, no. 12 (August 1913), pp. 336–38.
56. Ibid.
57. "Ford Leads in Minnesota," *Ford Times* 5, no. 6 (April–May 1912), p. 237.
58. Ford with Crowther, *My Life and Work,* p. 200.
59. Wik, *Henry Ford and Grass-roots America,* pp. 32–33.
60. "And This Little Ford Went to Market," *Ford Times* 8, no. 9 (June 1915), pp. 391–94.
61. "A Traveling Food Emporium," *Ford Times* 6, no. 2 (November 1912), pp. 76–102.
62. "Auto-Polo, the Latest in the World of Sport," *Ford Times* 6, no. 3 (December 1912), p. 100.
63. Robert H. Ferrell, ed., *Dear Bess: Letters from Harry to Bess Truman, 1910–1959* (New York: W.W. Norton, 1983), p. 177.
64. "Appealing to a Mass Market," *Nation's Business,* July 1968, p. 73.
65. Ray Miller and Bruce McCalley, *From Here to Obscurity: An Illustrated History of the Model T Ford, 1909–1927* (Avalon, Calif.: Evergreen Press, 1971), p. 15.
66. *Jokes and Jests About the Ford,* vol. 1 (Pittsburgh: Lewis Publishing, 1919), p. 5.
67. Ibid., p. 23.
68. *Funny Stories About the Ford* (Hamilton, Ohio: Presto Publishing, 1915), p. 22; also Accession 233, box 1, Henry Ford Museum and Library.
69. J. M. Fenster, "How General Motors Beat Ford," *Audacity,* Fall 1992, p. 51.
70. *Funny Stories About the Ford,* p. 26.
71. Michael Gladstone White, *Faces of Ford: The Windsor Years* (Windsor, Ont.: Red Oak Press, 1993), pp. 19–22.

72. "Autos Left on the Dock," *New York Times,* January 9, 1912, p. 15.
73. Quoted in Stern, *Tin Lizzie,* p. 97.
74. Wik, *Henry Ford and Grass-roots America,* p. 241.
75. Stern, *Tin Lizzie,* p. 111.
76. Ibid.
77. "Ford Representative in Russia Visits the Home Plant," *Ford Times* 6, no. 2 (November 1912), p. 68.
78. "Ford Wins Recommendation of Russian War Department," *Ford Times* 6, no. 3 (December 1912), pp. 117–19.
79. Wik, *Henry Ford and Grass-roots America,* p. 4.
80. P. H. Leader, letter to the editor, *Ford Times* 6, no. 5 (February 1913), p. 218.
81. Alex Gray, letter to the editor, *Ford Times* 6, no. 5 (February 1913), pp. 221–22.
82. Edward R. Gilman, letter to the editor, *Ford Times* 3, no. 7 (January 1909), p. 26.

CHAPTER SEVEN: FORDISM

1. Writers' Program of the Works Progress Administration, *Michigan: A Guide to the Wolverine State* (New York: Oxford University Press, 1941), p. 290.
2. Roger Burlingame, *Henry Ford* (New York: Alfred A. Knopf, 1955), pp. 64–65.
3. Arthur M. Schlesinger Jr., *The Crisis of the Old Order, 1919–1939* (Boston: Houghton Mifflin, 1957), p. 73.
4. David A. Hounshell, *From the American System to Mass Production, 1800–1932* (Baltimore: Johns Hopkins University Press, 1984), p. 11.
5. Joe Sherman, "Like the Factories He Designed, Albert Kahn Lived to Work," *Smithsonian,* November 1994, p. 54.
6. Paul Cret, eulogy, 1943, quoted in Grant Hildebrand, *Designing for Industry: The Architecture of Albert Kahn* (Cambridge, Mass.: MIT Press, 1974), pp. 1–28.
7. Ibid.
8. Albert Kahn File, Henry Ford Heritage Association, Dearborn, Michigan.
9. Neil Baldwin, *Henry Ford and the Jews* (New York: Public Affairs, 2001), p. 197.
10. Hildebrand, *Designing for Industry,* p. 28.
11. *The Legacy of Albert Kahn* (Detroit: Detroit Institute of Arts, 1970), p. 11.
12. Sherman, "Like the Factories," p. 49.
13. Baldwin, *Henry Ford and the Jews,* p. 198.
14. Dick Skinner Collection, Henry Ford Heritage Association (copy). The original photograph is owned by Wayne State University.
15. Hildebrand, *Designing for Industry,* p. 52.
16. "The New Factory," *Ford Times* 1, no. 6 (July 1, 1908), p. 3.
17. Sean Ulmer, *Albert Kahn Catalog* (Ann Arbor, Mich.: University of Michigan Press, 2001), pp. 2–8.
18. Henry Ford, "The Automobile, Past, Present and Future," *Detroit Saturday Night*; reprinted in *Ford News* 3, no. 15 (May 1910), p. 178.
19. "1903—Eight Years of Ford Progress—1911," *Ford News* 4, no. 10 (June 1911), p. 265.
20. Allan Nevins and Frank Ernest Hill, *Ford,* vol. 1, *The Times, the Man, the Company* (New York: Charles Scribner's Sons, 1954), p. 454.
21. Clarence Hooker, *Life in the Shadow of the Crystal Palace, 1910–1927: Ford Workers in the Model T Era* (Bowling Green, Ohio: Bowling Green State University Popular Press, 1997), p. 28.
22. David L. Lewis, *The Public Image of Henry Ford: An American Folk Hero and His Company* (Detroit: Wayne State University Press, 1976), p. 54.
23. Robert Kanigel, *The One Best Way: Frederick Winslow Taylor and the Enigma of Efficiency* (New York: Viking, 1997), p. 1.
24. John Dos Passos, *The Big Money* (Boston: Houghton Mifflin, 1946), pp. 21–26.
25. David Montgomery, *The Fall of the House of Labor: The Workplace, the State, and American Labor, 1865–1925* (Cambridge: Cambridge University Press, 1987), p. 233.
26. Peter Drucker, *The Practice of Management* (New York: Harper & Brothers, 1954), p. 280.

27. Kanigel, *The One Best Way*, p. 496.
28. Ernest A. Pedersen Sr., "Reminiscences" (oral history project), p. 8, Henry Ford Museum and Library, Dearborn, Michigan.
29. Hooker, *Life in the Shadow of the Crystal Palace*, p. 29.
30. "Motor Car Patents Upheld by Court," *New York Times*, September 16, 1909, p. 5.
31. Ibid.
32. Ford Motor Company advertisement, "This Advertisement Is Published for the Protection of Automobile Buyers," *New York Times*, February 13, 1910, sec. 4, p. 4.
33. Henry Ford with Samuel Crowther, *My Life and Work* (Garden City, N.Y.: Doubleday, 1923), p. 63.
34. "Did Not Infringe on Selden Suit," *New York Times*, January 10, 1911, p. 5.
35. Ibid.
36. "Won't Contest Decision," *New York Times*, January 13, 1911, p. 12.
37. Ford with Crowther, *My Life and Work*, p. 63.
38. Writers' Program, *Michigan*, p. 231.
39. Ibid.
40. Accession 37.102, Detroit Publishing Company, box 12, folder Architecture—Michigan—Detroit (Hotels and Apartments), Henry Ford Museum and Library.
41. Alfred P. Sloan Jr. with Boyden Sparkes, *Adventures of a White-Collar Man* (New York: Doubleday, Doran, 1941), pp. 38–52.
42. George W. Stark, *City of Destiny* (Detroit: Arnold-Powers, 1943), p. 77.
43. "An Emphatic Anniversary," *Ford Times* 4, no. 10 (June 1911), p. 261.
44. Carol Gelderman, *Henry Ford: The Wayward Capitalist* (New York: Dial, 1981), pp. 333–39.
45. John Kenneth Galbraith, "The Mystery of Henry Ford," *Atlantic Monthly*, March 1958, p. 45.
46. "An Emphatic Anniversary," p. 257.
47. Norman Beasley, *Knudsen: A Biography* (New York: Whittlesey House, 1947), p. 10.
48. Ford R. Bryan, *Friends, Families, and Forays: Scenes from the Life and Times of Henry Ford* (Dearborn, Mich.: Ford Books, 2002), p. 276.
49. Alex Lumsden, "Reminiscences," pp. 17–18.
50. William Knudsen, Business File, Automotive Hall of Fame, Dearborn, Michigan.
51. Ford R. Bryan, *Henry's Lieutenants* (Detroit: Wayne State University Press, 1993), p. 155.
52. Beasley, *Knudsen*, pp. 55–56.
53. Logan Miller, "Reminiscences," p. 16.
54. Beasley, *Knudsen*, p. 52.
55. George Brown, "Reminiscences," vol. 1, p. 75.
56. James O'Connor, "Reminiscences," p. 59.
57. Robert A. Shaw, "Reminiscences," pp. 13–14.
58. Henry Ford, "System, the Secret of Ford's Success," *New York Times*, January 3, 1909, sec. 4, p. 7.
59. Miller, "Reminiscences," p. 13.
60. *Life's Picture History of Western Man* (New York: Time, Inc., 1951), p. 107.
61. Kanigel, *The One Best Way*, p. 495.
62. William C. Klann, "Reminiscences," pp. 22–23.
63. Beasley, *Knudsen*, p. 60.
64. Ralph Graves, *The Triumph of an Idea* (Garden City, N.Y.: Doubleday, Doran, 1935), p. 57.
65. Klann, "Reminiscences," pp. 29–30.
66. Ibid.
67. Julian Street, *Abroad at Home* (New York: Century, 1914), pp. 93–94.
68. Klann, "Reminiscences," p. 31.
69. Charles E. Sorensen with Samuel T. Williamson, *My Forty Years with Ford* (New York: W.W. Norton, 1956), p. 142.
70. John R. Lee, "The So-Called Profit Sharing System in the Ford Plant," *Annals of the American Academy of Political and Social Science* 65, no. 154, p. 299.
71. Stephen Meyer III, *The Five Dollar Day* (Albany, N.Y.: State University of New York Press, 1981), p. 72.
72. Ibid., p. 75.

73. Isaac A. Hourwich, "Annual Average Immigration from Germany, 1875–1910," chart in *Immigration and Labor: The Economic Aspects of European Immigrations to the United States* (New York: B.W. Huebsch, 1922), p. 192.

74. Herrmann Losch, "Wanderrungsstatistik," *Die Statistik in Deutschland nach ihrem heutigen Stand* (I Band, 1911), p. 485, quoted in Hourwich, "Annual Average Immigration," p. 180.

75. Niles Carpenter, *Immigrants and Their Children, 1920,* Census Monographs VII, U.S. Bureau of the Census (Washington, D.C.: U.S. Government Printing Office, 1927), p. 62.

76. *Statistical Abstract of the United States, 1950,* U.S. Bureau of the Census (Washington, D.C.: U.S. Government Printing Office, 1950), p. 97.

77. Victor L. Berger, speech, June 14, 1911, cited in *Congressional Record,* pp. 2026–27.

78. Lee, "So-Called Profit Sharing System," p. 305.

79. Meyer, *The Five Dollar Day,* p. 77.

80. Writers' Program, *Michigan,* p. 290.

81. See Oliver Zunz, *The Changing Face of Inequality: Urbanization, Industrial Development and Immigrants in Detroit, 1880–1920* (Chicago: University of Chicago Press, 1982); and Nabeel Abraham and Andrew Shryock, eds., *Arab Detroit: From Margin to Mainstreams* (Detroit: Wayne State University Press, 2000).

82. "Nationality" roster, Ford Sociological Department, Henry Ford Museum and Library.

83. Chuck Shamey, oral history, quoted in 1999 press release "Ford Motor Company Key Factor in Arab and Chaldean Migration to Metro Detroit," Henry Ford Museum and Library.

84. Klann, "Reminiscences," vol. 2, p. 18.

85. Ford with Crowther, *My Life and Work,* p. 103.

86. Hounshell, *From the American System to Mass Production,* p. 257.

87. Keith Sward, *The Legend of Henry Ford* (New York: Rinehart, 1948), p. 49, citing *Automotive Industries,* March 14, 1918, pp. 539–41.

88. Ford with Crowther, *My Life and Work,* p. 265.

CHAPTER EIGHT: THE $5 DAY

1. Howard Zinn, *A People's History of the United States* (New York: Harper & Row, 1980), p. 330.

2. From *The Workers' World at Hagley,* cited in Hank Stuever, "Just One Word: Plastic," *Washington Post Magazine,* June 16, 2002, p. 17.

3. Jack London, *The Iron Heel* (New York: Sagamore Press, 1957), pp. 74–75.

4. Peter F. Drucker, *Management: Tasks, Responsibilities, Practices* (New York: Harper & Row, 1974).

5. James O'Connor, "Reminiscences" (oral history project), p. 27, Henry Ford Museum and Library, Dearborn, Michigan.

6. Garet Garrett, "Henry Ford's Experiment in Good-Will," *Everybody's* 30, no. 4 (April 1914), p. 463.

7. "Ford Labor Policies, $5 Day," press release (retyped from original), January 5, 1914, Fair Lane Papers, Accession 940, box 16, Ford Motor Co. folder, Henry Ford Museum and Library.

8. Logan Miller, "Reminiscences," p. 4.

9. Zinn, *A People's History of the United States,* p. 328.

10. Carl Sandburg, "The People, Yes," *The People, Yes* (Fort Washington, Pa.: Harvest Books, 1990).

11. George Brown, "Reminiscences," p. 82.

12. Charles E. Sorensen with Samuel T. Williamson, *My Forty Years with Ford* (New York: W.W. Norton, 1956), p. 141.

13. George M. Verity, "The Exceptional Position of Mr. Ford's Factory," *Current Opinion* 56, no. 5 (May 1914), pp. 387–88.

14. Gerald Stanley Lee, "Is Ford an Inspired Millionaire?," *Harper's Weekly* 58, March 14, 1914, p. 10.

15. Peter Collier and David Horowitz, *The Fords: An American Epic* (New York: Summit Books, 1987), p. 67.

16. Roger Burlingame, *Henry Ford* (New York: Alfred A. Knopf, 1955), pp. 181–82.

17. Thomas A. Edison, letter to Henry Ford, April 26, 1914, Henry Ford Museum and Library.
18. Burlingame, *Henry Ford*, p. 177.
19. Charles E. Sorensen, "Reminiscences," pp. 28–29.
20. Ida Tarbell, notes, quoted in Harry Barnard, "James Couzens of Detroit" (typescript), p. 115, Henry Ford Museum and Library.
21. Allan Nevins and Frank Ernest Hill, *Ford*, vol. 1, *The Times, the Man, the Company* (New York: Charles Scribner's Sons, 1954), p. 446.
22. Writers' Program of the Works Progress Administration, *Michigan: A Guide to the Wolverine State* (New York: Oxford University Press, 1941), pp. 240–41.
23. Barnard, "James Couzens of Detroit," p. 113.
24. David L. Lewis, *The Public Image of Henry Ford: An American Folk Hero and His Company* (Detroit: Wayne State University Press, 1976), p. 72.
25. John R. Lee, "The So-Called Profit Sharing System in the Ford Plant," *Annals of the American Academy of Political and Social Science* 65, no. 154.
26. Sorensen with Williamson, *My Forty Years with Ford,* pp. 137–38.
27. Barnard, "James Couzens of Detroit," p. 115.
28. Brown, "Reminiscences," vol. 1, p. 76.
29. Garrett, "Henry Ford's Experiment in Good-Will," p. 466.
30. Charles C. Krueger, "Reminiscences," p. 60.
31. Norman Beasley, *Knudsen: A Biography* (New York: Whittlesey House, 1947), p. 65.
32. Brown, "Reminiscences," pp. 8–85.
33. Ibid., p. 82.
34. Reynold M. Wik, *Henry Ford and Grass-roots America* (Ann Arbor, Mich.: University of Michigan Press, 1972), p. 212.
35. LeRoi Jones, *Blues People: Negro Music in White America* (New York: William Morrow, 1983), pp. 97–98.
36. Peter Gavrilovich and Bill McGraw (eds.), *The Detroit Almanac: 300 Years of Life in the Motor City* (Detroit: Detroit Free Press, 2000), p. 389.
37. Jones, *Blues People,* pp. 97–98.
38. Miller, "Reminiscences," p. 4.
39. Lee, "The So-Called Profit Sharing System in the Ford Plant," p. 302.
40. C. G. Milner, "Reminiscences," p. 3.
41. William F. Pioch, "Reminiscences," p. 6.
42. General letter, Ford Motor Company, January 17, 1914, Accession 683, box 1, Henry Ford Museum and Library.
43. Pioch, "Reminiscences," p. 6.
44. Lee, "The So-Called Profit Sharing System in the Ford Plant," p. 305.
45. Garrett, "Henry Ford's Experiment in Good-Will," pp. 471–72.
46. Roderick Nash, *The Nervous Generation: American Thought, 1917–1930* (Chicago: Ivan R. Dee, Inc., 1970), p. 155.
47. Krueger, "Reminiscences," pp. 60–61.

CHAPTER NINE: ALONE AT THE TOP

1. Stephen Meyer III, *The Five Dollar Day: Labor Management and Social Control in the Ford Motor Company 1908–1921* (Albany: State University of New York Press, 1981), pp. 74–75.
2. Charles C. Krueger, "Reminiscences" (oral history project), p. 60, Henry Ford Museum and Library, Dearborn, Michigan.
3. George Brown, "Reminiscences," vol. 1, p. 85.
4. Stanley C. Hollander and Gary A. Marple, *Henry Ford: Inventor of the Supermarket?* (East Lansing, Mich.: Michigan State University Press, 1960), p. 2.
5. Ibid., pp. 1–2.
6. Henry Ford with Samuel Crowther, *My Life and Work* (Garden City, N.Y.: Doubleday, 1923), p. 115.
7. Clifton Fadiman and Andréa Bernard (eds.), *Bartlett's Book of Anecdotes* (Boston: Little, Brown, 2000), p. 211.

8. Peter Furtado, *The New Century: A Changing World, 1900–1914* (London: Chancellor Press, 1993), pp. 14, 86.
9. L. Scott Bailey, *The American Car Since 1775* (New York: E.P. Dutton, 1971), p. 138.
10. "A Question of Color," *Ford Times* 2, no. 17 (Nov. 1909), p. 10.
11. George H. Dammann, *Ninety Years of Ford,* 2d ed. (Osceola, Wis.: Motorbooks International, 1993), p. 59.
12. Harry Barnard, "James Couzens of Detroit" (typescript), p. 131, Henry Ford Museum and Library.
13. Clifton Fadiman, ed., *The Little, Brown Book of Anecdotes* (Boston: Little, Brown, 1985), p. 21.
14. Henry Ford, interviewed by Fay Leone Faurote, *My Philosophy of Industry* (New York: Coward-McCann, 1929), p. 75.
15. David L. Lewis, *The Public Image of Henry Ford: An American Folk Hero and His Company* (Detroit: Wayne State University Press, 1976), p. 216.
16. Ford and Faurote, *My Philosophy of Industry,* p. 75.
17. Jean Maddern Pitrone, *Tangled Web: The Legacy of Auto Pioneer John F. Dodge* (Hamtramck, Mich.: Avenue Publishing, 1989), p. 44.
18. Keith Sward, *The Legend of Henry Ford* (New York: Rinehart, 1948), p. 66.
19. *The Legacy of Albert Kahn* (Detroit: Detroit Institute of Arts, 1970), p. 13.
20. Stan Grayson, "The Brothers Dodge," *Automobile Quarterly,* 17, no. 1 (Spring 1979), p. 7.
21. Pitrone, *Tangled Web,* p. 54.
22. Sward, *The Legend of Henry Ford,* p. 45.
23. Steven W. Sears, "The Five Dollar Day," *Audacity,* Summer 1997, pp. 16–22.
24. Dammann, *Ninety Years of Ford,* pp. 51, 56.
25. Clarence Barron, *They Told Barron* (New York: Harper, 1930), p. 98.
26. *Automobile Topics,* [n.d.] 1914, clipping, Henry Ford Museum and Library.
27. Pitrone, *Tangled Web,* p. 56.
28. "Mr. Ford Doesn't Care," *Fortune,* December 1933, p. 65.
29. Louis J. Kinietz, "Reminiscences," p. 9.
30. *Factory Firsts from Ford* (Detroit: Ford Motor Company, 1915), pp. 9–11.
31. Ibid., p. 13.
32. Ford with Crowther, *My Life and Work,* p. 114.
33. Furtado, *The New Century: A Changing World,* p. 91.
34. E. G. Pipp, *Henry Ford, Both Sides of Him* (Detroit: 1926), p. 100.
35. Douglas Brinkley, *American Heritage History of the United States* (New York: Viking, 1998), pp. 437–38.
36. Theodore Roosevelt, "Righteous Peace Through National Preparedness," speech, Detroit, Michigan, May 19, 1916. Excerpted in Albert B. Hart and Herbert R. Ferleger, *Theodore Roosevelt Cyclopaedia* (New York: Roosevelt Memorial Assoc., 1941), p. 184.
37. Lewis, *The Public Image of Henry Ford,* p. 78.
38. Brown, "Reminiscences," p. 62.
39. Barnard, "James Couzens of Detroit," p. 134.
40. Herman M. Reinhold, "Reminiscences," p. 24.
41. Harry Barnard, *Independent Man: The Life of Senator James Couzens* (New York: Charles Scribner's Sons, 1958), p. 99.
42. Allan Nevins and Frank Ernest Hill, *Ford,* vol. 2, *Expansion and Challenge, 1915–1933* (New York: Charles Scribner's Sons, 1957), pp. 23–24.
43. "Angered by Peace Talk, Associate Quits Mr. Ford," *New York Herald,* October 16, 1915.
44. Writers' Program of the Works Progress Administration, *Michigan: A Guide to the Wolverine State* (New York: Oxford University Press, 1941), pp. 240–41.
45. *Ford News,* December 1915, p. 28.
46. Barbara S. Kraft, *The Peace Ship* (New York: Macmillan, 1978), pp. 9–11.
47. Louis P. Lochner, *America's Don Quixote* (London: Kegan Paul, Trench, Trubner, 1924), p. 17.
48. Ibid., p. 20.
49. Carol Gelderman, *Henry Ford: The Wayward Capitalist* (New York: Dial, 1981), p. 8.

50. Oswald Garrison Villard, *Fighting Years* (New York: Harcourt, Brace, 1939), pp. 301–3.
51. Lochner, *America's Don Quixote,* p. 27.
52. Nevins and Hill, *Expansion and Challenge,* pp. 45–46.
53. Catherine Drinker Bowen, *Yankee from Olympus* (Boston: Atlantic/Little, Brown, 1944), p. 79–80.

CHAPTER TEN: MAKING AN IMPACT

1. Robert Lacey, *Ford: The Men and the Machine* (Boston: Little, Brown, 1986), p. 134.
2. John Aloysius Farrell, *Tip O'Neill and the Democratic Century* (Boston: Little, Brown, 2001), pp. 14–15.
3. *New York Tribune,* January 3, 1916.
4. William Pennypacker Young, *A Ford Dealer's Twenty-Year Ride with the Old and New Model Ford Policies* (Pottstown, Pa., and Hempstead, N.Y.: Lotta L. Young, 1932), p. 54.
5. Ibid., p. 49.
6. Ibid., pp. 20–21.
7. Clement Hirtzel, "Survival of the Fittest," *Ford Times* 8, no. 1 (October 1914), pp. 35, 37.
8. Allan Nevins and Frank Ernest Hill, *Ford,* vol. 1, *The Times, the Man, the Company* (New York: Charles Scribner's Sons, 1954), pp. 354–58.
9. Charles E. Sorensen, "Reminiscences" (oral history project), p. 9, Henry Ford Museum and Library, Dearborn, Michigan.
10. Mira Wilkins and Frank Ernest Hill, *American Business Abroad: Ford on Six Continents* (Detroit: Wayne State University Press, 1964), p. 57.
11. Ibid., p. 92.
12. David Burgess-Wise, "Perry, Percival Lea Dewhurst—Lord Perry of Stock Harvard," file, Henry Ford Museum and Library; also Ford R. Bryan, *Henry's Lieutenants* (Detroit: Wayne State University Press, 1993), pp. 232–33.
13. P. L. D. Perry, "The Ford in England," *Ford Times* 7, no. 7 (April 1914), p. 293.
14. Bryan, *Henry's Lieutenants,* p. 229.
15. Charles E. Sorensen with Samuel T. Williamson, *My Forty Years with Ford* (New York: W.W. Norton, 1956), p. 12.
16. Perry, "The Ford in England," p. 293.
17. Bryan, *Henry's Lieutenants,* pp. 227–33.
18. "Lord Churchill's Trip to Balmoral," *Ford Times* 7, no. 7 (April 1914), p. 297.
19. Allan Nevins and Frank Ernest Hill, *Ford,* vol. 2, *Expansion and Challenge, 1915–1933* (New York: Charles Scribner's Sons, 1957), p. 21, citing Henry Ford with Samuel Crowther, *My Life and Work* (Garden City, N.Y.: Doubleday, 1923), pp. 26, 25.
20. Bryan, *Henry's Lieutenants,* p. 107.
21. Bryan, *Henry's Lieutenants,* pp. 105–7, citing "Farkas and the Fordson," *Ford Life,* May–June 1971.
22. Joseph A. Galamb, "Reminiscences," pp. 7–10.
23. Eugene J. Farkas, "Reminiscences," p. 64.
24. Benjamin B. Lovett, *Good Morning* (Dearborn, Mich.: Dearborn Publishing, 1926); and Eva O'Neal, *Henry Ford and Benjamin B. Lovett: The Dancing Billionaire and the Dancing Master* (Detroit: Harlo Press, 1992).
25. Eugene Farkas quoted in Bryan, *Henry's Lieutenants,* p. 105.
26. Nevins and Hill, *Expansion and Challenge,* p. 58.
27. Wilkins and Hill, *American Business Abroad,* p. 71.
28. Sorensen with Williamson, *My Forty Years with Ford,* p. 238.
29. Nevins and Hill, *Expansion and Challenge,* p. 61; also David L. Lewis, *The Public Image of Henry Ford: An American Folk Hero and His Company* (Detroit: Wayne State University Press, 1976), p. 180.
30. Nevins and Hill, *Expansion and Challenge,* pp. 60, 630, citing Articles of Association, and Minute Book, Henry Ford & Son Company, Henry Ford Museum and Library.
31. Nevins and Hill, *Expansion and Challenge,* p. 63.
32. Ibid., pp. 23, 626.
33. Alex Lumsden, "Reminiscences," p. 26.

34. William F. Pioch, "Reminiscences," p. 18.
35. Lumsden, "Reminiscences," p. 27.
36. Nevins and Hill, *Expansion and Challenge,* p. 66.
37. Ernest Grimshaw, "Reminiscences," p. 16.
38. Timothy J. O'Callaghan, *The Aviation of Henry and Edsel Ford* (Ann Arbor, Mich.: Proctor Publishing, 2000), p. 3.
39. Ibid., pp. 1–12.
40. Tom Crouch, *The Bishop's Boys: A Life of Wilbur and Orville Wright* (New York: W.W. Norton, 1989), p. 462.
41. Seth Shulman, *Unlocking the Sky: Glenn Hammond Curtiss and the Race to Invent the Airplane* (New York: HarperCollins, 2002), p. 68.
42. Lewis, *The Public Image of Henry Ford,* p. 92, citing *Detroit News,* February 5, 1917.
43. Oswald Garrison Villard, *Fighting Years* (New York: Harcourt, Brace, 1939), p. 305.
44. William C. Klann, "Reminiscences," p. 124.
45. Stan Grayson, "In the Cause of Liberty," in *Packard: A History of the Motor Car and the Company* (Princeton, N.J.: Princeton Publishing, 1978), p. 185.
46. Klann, "Reminiscences," pp. 124–27.
47. Nevins and Hill, *Expansion and Challenge,* p. 68n.
48. George Brown, "Reminiscences," vol. 2, p. 118.
49. Jonathan Daniels, *The End of Innocence* (New York: Lippincott, 1954), p. 176.
50. Robert Lacey, *Ford: The Man and the Machine,* p. 157, citing Nevins and Hill, *Expansion and Challenge,* p. 71.
51. Brown, "Reminiscences," p. 121.
52. Nevins and Hill, *Expansion and Challenge,* p. 74.
53. Peter Collier and David Horowitz, *The Fords: An American Epic* (New York: Summit Books, 1987), pp. 70–72.
54. *Henry Ford Estate: National Historic Landmark* (guidebook published by University of Michigan), p. 30.
55. Clipping File (display), Fair Lane Archive, University of Michigan—Dearborn.
56. Robert Grese and Jens Jensen, *Making Natural Parks and Gardens* (Baltimore: Johns Hopkins University Press, 1992); and Ford Bryan, *Clara: Mrs. Henry Ford* (Dearborn, Mich.: Ford Books, 2001).
57. W. Griffith, "Reminiscences," pp. 20–31.
58. Donn P. Werling, "Jens Jensen and Henry Ford: The Landscape Artist and the Entrepreneur," pamphlet, Fair Lane Archive, Dearborn, Michigan.
59. Bryan, *Henry's Lieutenants,* p. 229.
60. Ibid.
61. *Detroit News,* July 12, 1916.
62. Ibid.
63. Ford R. Bryan, *Friends, Families, and Forays: Scenes from the Life and Times of Henry Ford* (Dearborn, Mich.: Ford Books, 2002), pp. 297–303.
64. Bryan, *Henry's Lieutenants,* p. 114.
65. Nevins and Hill, *Expansion and Challenge,* p. 75.
66. Charles Voorhees, "Reminiscences," vol. 1, p.47.
67. A. J. Lepine, "Reminiscences," p. 64.
68. Bryan, *Henry's Lieutenants,* pp. 114–15.
69. Harold Hicks, "Reminiscences," p. 152.
70. Keith Sward, *The Legend of Henry Ford* (New York: Rinehart, 1948), pp. 94–95, citing *New York Times,* November 7, 1922.
71. Sward, *The Legend of Henry Ford,* p. 94.
72. Nevins and Hill, *Expansion and Challenge,* p. 78.

CHAPTER ELEVEN: CHALLENGING EVERY FOE

1. *Facts from Ford* (Highland Park, Mich.: Ford Motor Company, 1920), pp. 56, 58, 60.
2. W. Ernest Grimshaw, "Reminiscences" (oral history project), pp. 17–18, Henry Ford Museum and Library, Dearborn, Michigan.

3. Ernest G. Liebold, "Reminiscences," pp. 23–41.

4. William C. Klann, "Reminiscences," vol. 2, p. 124.

5. "Ford Is an Anarchist" (editorial), *Chicago Tribune,* June 23, 1916.

6. Reynold M. Wik, *Henry Ford and Grass-roots America* (Ann Arbor, Mich.: University of Michigan Press, 1973), p. 52.

7. Richard Norton Smith, *The Colonel: The Life and Legend of Robert R. McCormick* (Boston: Houghton Mifflin, 1997), p. 231.

8. Merlo J. Pusey, *Charles Evans Hughes,* vol. 1 (New York: Columbia University Press, 1973), p. 389; and Beverly Rose Kines (ed.), *Packard: A History of the Motor Car and the Company* (Princeton, N.J.: Princeton Publishing, 1978), pp. 172–85.

9. Klann, "Reminiscences," vol. 2, p. 124.

10. Allan Nevins and Frank Ernest Hill, *Ford,* vol. 2, *Expansion and Challenge, 1915–1933* (New York: Charles Scribner's Sons, 1957).

11. William F. Pioch, "Reminiscences," pp. 17–18.

12. Keith Sward, *The Legend of Henry Ford* (New York: Rinehart, 1948), p. 118.

13. Nevins and Hill, *Expansion and Challenge,* p. 79.

14. Spenser Ervin, *Henry Ford vs. Truman H. Newberry: The Famous Senate Election Contest* (New York: Richard R. Smith, 1935).

15. Sward, *The Legend of Henry Ford,* p. 116, citing *Detroit News,* September 20, 1918.

16. Nevins and Hill, *Expansion and Challenge,* p. 119.

17. Ibid., p. 116.

18. "Ford Fight Nonpartisan," *New York Times,* October 2, 1918, p. 13.

19. David L. Lewis, *The Public Image of Henry Ford: An American Folk Hero and His Company* (Detroit: Wayne State University Press, 1976), p. 121.

20. "The Newberry Conviction," *Literary Digest,* April 3, 1920, p. 23.

21. Sward, *The Legend of Henry Ford,* p. 118, citing *Detroit News,* February 5 and February 6, 1919.

22. "Taft and Roosevelt Support Newberry," *New York Times,* October 23, 1918, p. 10.

23. Carol Gelderman, *Henry Ford: The Wayward Capitalist* (New York: Dial, 1981), pp. 145–46, citing *Detroit Saturday Night,* October 26, 1918.

24. Sward, *The Legend of Henry Ford,* p. 116.

25. "Ford Wants to Aid Wilson's Policies," *New York Times,* October 17, 1918, p. 15.

26. Nevins and Hill, *Ford: Expansion and Challenge, 1915–1933,* pp. 114–24.

27. *Chicago Tribune,* May 25, 1916.

28. Walter Lippmann, "A Little Child Shall Lead Them," December 4, 1915, collected in Walter Lippmann, *Early Writings* (New York: Liveright, 1970); also Mary Moline, comp., *The Best of Ford* (Van Nuys, Calif.: Rumbleseat Press, 1973), pp. 86–89.

29. "Sherman Attacks Ford and His Car," *New York Times,* February 20, 1920, p. 17.

30. Lewis, *The Public Image of Henry Ford,* p. 48, citing *New York Times,* June 17, 1918.

31. Lewis, *The Public Image of Henry Ford,* p. 99.

32. "Ford Says $176,000 Beat Him at Polls," *New York Times,* November 16, 1918, p. 9.

33. Sward, *The Legend of Henry Ford,* p. 120, citing *Pipp's Weekly,* September 17, 1921.

34. Lewis, *The Public Image of Henry Ford,* p. 44.

35. David A. Hounshell, *From American System to Mass Production, 1800–1932* (Baltimore: Johns Hopkins University Press, 1984), p. 261, citing Reginald McIntosh Cleveland, "How Many Automobiles Can America Buy?" *World's Work* 27 (1914), pp. 679–89.

36. Nevins and Hill, *Expansion and Challenge,* p. 91.

37. Ray Miller and Bruce McCalley, *From Here to Obscurity: An Illustrated History of the Model T Ford, 1909–1927* (Avalon, Calif.: Evergreen Press, 1971), p. 181.

38. Robert Lacey, *Ford: The Men and the Machine* (Boston: Little, Brown, 1986), p. 168, citing "Dodges Due to Get $2,300,000 from Ford," *Detroit Journal,* November 1, 1917.

39. Nevins and Hill, *Expansion and Challenge,* p. 91.

40. "Hints Ford Plans Win Approval," *Detroit Evening News,* June 6, 1917.

41. Sward, *The Legend of Henry Ford,* p. 72.

42. "Henry Ford Retires as Motor Plant's Head," *New York Times,* November 23, 1918, p. 13.

43. Upton Sinclair, *The Flivver King* (New York: Phaedra, 1969), p. 56.

44. "Ford Loses Dividend Suit," *New York Times,* February 8, 1919, p. 15.

45. Sinclair, *Flivver King,* pp. 56–57.

46. "New Ford Co. Facing a Fight," *New York Times,* March 11, 1919, p. 15.
47. Bernard A. Weisberger, *The Dream Maker: William C. Durant, Founder of General Motors* (Boston: Little, Brown, 1979), p. 138.
48. "Fords Acquire Stock Control in Their Company," *New York Times,* July 12, 1919, p. 1.
49. Nevins and Hill, *Expansion and Challenge,* p. 111.
50. "Plan to Finance $75,000,000 Credit," *New York Times,* July 12, 1919, p. 4.
51. George Brown, "Reminiscences," vol. 2, pp. 107–11.
52. Sward, *The Legend of Henry Ford,* p. 190.
53. John Wandersee, "Reminiscences," p. 42.
54. Charles E. Sorensen with Samuel T. Williamson, *My Forty Years with Ford* (New York: W.W. Norton, 1956), p. 235.
55. Wandersee, "Reminiscences," p. 42.
56. "Henry Ford Still Thinks Soldiers Are Murderers," *New York Times,* July 16, 1919, p. 2.
57. Lewis, *The Public Image of Henry Ford,* p. 78.
58. *Chicago Tribune,* May 25, 1916.
59. "Henry Ford's Six-Cent Verdict," *Literary Digest,* August 30, 1919, p. 20
60. George F. Will, "Celebrating an Intellectual Dynamo," *Washington Post,* July 14, 2002, p. B7.

CHAPTER TWELVE: WITHSTANDING THE DOWNTURN

1. "Otto Kahn Speaks at Founder's Day Celebration of Carnegie Institute," *New York Times,* April 25, 1919, p. 12.
2. Mary Moline, comp., *The Best of Ford* (Van Nuys, Calif.: Rumbleseat Press, 1973), pp. 338–41.
3. Catherine Gourley, *Wheels of Time* (Brookfield, Conn.: Millbrook Press, 1997), p. 38.
4. Moline, *The Best of Ford,* p. 348.
5. "Ford People Say France Won't Resell Cars at Big Profit nor Let Them Import Metals," *New York Times,* February 5, 1919, p. 1.
6. *Fortune,* December 1933, p. 128.
7. James B. Ross, letter to *Popular Science,* July 30, 1953, Accession 233, box 1, Henry Ford Museum and Library, Dearborn, Michigan.
8. Letter (anonymous) to *Popular Science,* undated, clipping in ibid.
9. George H. Dammann, *Ninety Years of Ford,* 2d ed. (Osceola, Wis.: Motorbooks International, 1993), p. 81.
10. Thomas P. Hughes, *American Genesis: A History of the American Genius for Invention* (New York: Penguin, 1989), p. 208.
11. Garet Garrett, *The Wild Wheel* (New York: Pantheon, 1952), p. 108.
12. David A. Hounshell, *From the American System to Mass Production, 1800–1932* (Baltimore: Johns Hopkins University Press, 1984), p. 267.
13. Hughes, *American Genesis,* p. 208, citing Allan Nevins and Frank Ernest Hill, *Ford,* vol. 2, *Expansion and Challenge, 1915–1933* (New York: Charles Scribner's Sons, 1957), pp. 206–7; also Grant Hildebrand, *Designing for Industry: The Architecture of Albert Kahn* (Cambridge, Mass.: MIT Press, 1974), p. 121.
14. Walter G. Griffith, "Reminiscences" (oral history project), p. 19, Henry Ford Museum and Library.
15. Harold M. Cordell, "Reminiscences," p. 39.
16. Louis P. Lochner, *America's Don Quixote: Henry Ford's Attempt to Save Europe* (London: Kegan Paul, Trench, Trubner, 1924), p. 18.
17. See James M. Miller, *The Amazing Story of Henry Ford* (privately published, 1922); and Henry Ford with Samuel Crowther, *My Life and Work* (Garden City, N.Y.: Doubleday, 1923).
18. Richard Hofstadter, *The Age of Reform: From Bryan to F.D.R.* (New York: Alfred A. Knopf, 1955), pp. 80–81.
19. Ibid.
20. Norman Hapgood, "Henry Ford," *Hearst's International,* June 1922, p. 14.
21. Ibid.
22. Robert Lacey, *Ford: The Men and the Machine* (Boston: Little, Brown, 1986), p. 207.
23. Ernest Liebold, "Reminiscences," p. 458.

24. Ford R. Bryan, *Beyond the Model T: The Other Ventures of Henry Ford,* rev. ed. (Detroit: Wayne State University Press, 1997), p. 104.
25. Liebold, "Reminiscences," p. 447; also Bryan, *Beyond the Model T,* p. 103.
26. Bryan, *Beyond the Model T,* p. 178.
27. "Taft Flays Story of Zion Protocols," *New York Times,* December 24, 1920, p. 4.
28. Bryan, *Beyond the Model T,* p. 103, citing Circulation Reports, Dearborn Publishing Company, Accession 62-2, box 52, Henry Ford Museum and Library.
29. "Topics in Brief," *Literary Digest,* August 30, 1919, p. 20.
30. Alex Groner, *The American Heritage History of Business and Industry* (New York: American Heritage, 1972), p. 273.
31. "Ford Tells How He Foiled Wall Street," *New York Times,* July 23, 1921, p. 2.
32. "Ford Cuts Cars to Pre-War Prices," *New York Times,* September 22, 1920, p. 9.
33. "Downward Rush of Motor Car Prices," *New York Times,* September 26, 1920, sec. 7, p. 2.
34. C. G. Milner, "Reminiscences," pp. 4–5.
35. William Pennypacker Young, *A Ford Dealer's Twenty Year Ride with the Old and New Model Ford Policies* (Pottstown, Pa., and Hempstead, N.Y.: Lotta L. Young, 1932), pp. 121–22.
36. John Emerson Roberts, *Henry Ford's Attack on the Jew* (Kansas City, Mo.: J. E. Roberts, n.d.), p. 10. At New York Public Library, Humanities—Jewish Division.
37. Nevins and Hill, *Expansion and Challenge,* p. 168.
38. Ford R. Bryan, *Henry's Lieutenants* (Detroit: Wayne State University Press, 1993), p. 155.
39. George Brown, "Reminiscences," vol. 2, p. 137.
40. "Ford Tells How He Foiled Wall Street," p. 23.
41. Harold Hicks, "Reminiscences," p. 53.
42. "Financiers Loud in Praise of Ford," *New York Times,* July 24, 1921, p. 2.
43. L. E. Briggs, "Reminiscences."
44. Norman J. Ahrens, "Reminiscences," p. 8.
45. Henry Ford, "Ford Tells How He Fooled Wall Street," *New York Times,* January 23, 1921, p. 2. For more information on the D. T. & I. railroad, see Henry Ford, *Today and Tomorrow* (Garden City, N.Y.: Doubleday, Page & Co., 1926), pp. 196–205.
46. Ford, *Today and Tomorrow,* pp. 196–205.
47. Sir Isaiah Berlin, *The Hedgehog and the Fox* (New York: Simon & Schuster, 1953), pp. 1–4. Berlin's actual, often cited quote reads: "There exists a great chasm between those, on one side, who relate everything to a single central vision . . . and, on the other side, those who pursue many ends, often unrelated and even contradictory. . . . The first kind of intellectual and artistic personality belongs to the hedgehogs, the second to the foxes."
48. Ralph Graves, *The Triumph of an Idea* (Garden City, N.Y.: Doubleday, Doran, 1935), pp. 82, 88.
49. *Lincoln Library* (Buffalo: Frontier Press, 1928), p. 1352.
50. The Lincoln Highway was conceived in 1913 by land-use planner Carl Fisher, who would go on to turn some tracts of southern Florida swampland into today's Miami Beach.
51. "Ford Car No. 10,000,000 Starts on Its Career," *New York Times,* July 13, 1924, sec. 8, p. 2; also *Ford News,* June 22, 1924, p. 1.
52. David L. Lewis, *The Public Image of Henry Ford: An American Folk Hero and His Company* (Detroit: Wayne State University Press, 1976), pp. 52–53.
53. Dammann, *Ninety Years of Ford,* p. 110.
54. *Ford News,* March 1, 1922, p. 1.

CHAPTER THIRTEEN: THE ROUGE

1. Luke McLuke, "Phord Philosophy," in *Funny Stories About the Ford* (Hamilton, Ohio: Presto Publishing, 1915), vol. 2, p. 42.
2. "More Than One Million Cars and Trucks Is Production Mark of 1921," *Ford News* 1, no. 12 (January 22, 1922), p. 1.
3. Arthur Pound, "The Ford Myth," *Atlantic Monthly,* January 1924, p. 42.
4. Ford R. Bryan, *Clara: Mrs. Henry Ford* (Dearborn, Mich.: Ford Books, 2001), p. 144.
5. "Human Interest Story Number Five," A. C. Tait, Accession 940, box 17, Sociological Department (1) Human Interest Stories, Henry Ford Museum and Library, Dearborn, Michigan.

6. James O'Connor, "Reminiscences" (oral history project), p. 31, Henry Ford Museum and Library.
7. *Helpful Hints and Advice to Employees* (Detroit: Ford Motor Company, 1915), p. 26.
8. "Human Interest Story Number Nine," F. W. Andrews, Accession 940, box 17, Sociological Department (1) Human Interest Stories, Henry Ford Museum and Library.
9. William C. Klann, "Reminiscences," vol. 2, p. 142.
10. Thomas Williams, "Reminiscences," p. 3.
11. *Facts from Ford* (Highland Park, Mich.: Ford Motor Company, 1920), p. 57.
12. Allan Nevins and Frank Ernest Hill, *Ford,* vol. 2, *Expansion and Challenge, 1915–1933* (New York: Charles Scribner's Sons, 1957), p. 339.
13. H. S. Ablewhite, "Reminiscences," p. 11.
14. "Henry Ford Seen Through a Reducing Glass," *Current Opinion,* September 1923, p. 290.
15. Bryan, *Clara,* p. 144.
16. "Why Prentiss Bid for Ford Plant," *New York Times,* February 13, 1927, sec. 13, p. 11.
17. Pound, "The Ford Myth," p. 42.
18. C. G. Milner, "Reminiscences," pp. 5–6.
19. "Mr. Ford's Five-Day Week," *Literary Digest,* April 29, 1922, p. 8.
20. Alex Lumsden, "Reminiscences," p. 53.
21. Ibid., p. 52.
22. Anthony Harff, "Reminiscences," p. 19.
23. Ernest Grimshaw, "Reminiscences," p. 23.
24. Logan Miller, "Reminiscences," p. 13.
25. Garet Garrett, *The Wild Wheel* (New York: Pantheon, 1952), p. 101.
26. Harff, "Reminiscences," p. 1.
27. William Pioch, "Reminiscences," p. 65.
28. A. M. Wibel, "Reminiscences," pp. 1–7.
29. Carol Gelderman, *Henry Ford: The Wayward Capitalist* (New York: Dial, 1981), p. 270.
30. John H. Van Deventer, "Ford Principles and Practice at River Rouge," *Industrial Management,* September 1922, p. 131.
31. "Leaders of Industry See Big Future for Dearborn," *Detroit Times,* September 7, 1924.
32. "Four Units of the Huge West Side Plant of the Ford Motor Company on Rouge River," *Detroit News,* August 24, 1924.
33. "First European Freighter at Rouge," *Ford News* 5, no. 18 (July 15, 1925), p. 1.
34. Gelderman, *Henry Ford: The Wayward Capitalist,* pp. 268–69.
35. Van Deventer, "Ford Principles and Practice at River Rouge," p. 194.
36. "Open Hearth Next to Start," *Ford News* 6, no. 1 (March 22, 1926), p. 1.
37. "Cement Plant Doubles Output in Three Years," *Ford News* 3, no. 20 (August 15, 1927), p. 4.
38. "20,000,000 Pounds of Fertilizer Made Yearly at Rouge," *Ford News* 4, no. 8 (February 15, 1924), p. 3.
39. "New Paper Mill Gives Value to Waste," *Ford News* 4, no. 12 (April 15, 1924), p. 1.
40. "By-Products Sale 11 Million in '25," *Ford News* 6, no. 1 (March 22, 1926), p. 1.
41. John H. Van Deventer, "Machine Operations on Ford Cylinders and Fordson Pistons," *Industrial Management,* March 1923, p. 359.
42. Pioch, "Reminiscences," p. 27.
43. Miller, "Reminiscences," pp. 18–19.
44. Lumsden, "Reminiscences," p. 54.
45. T. F. Stebbins Jr. and N. Keys Jr., *Charles Sheeler: The Photographs* (Boston: Museum of Fine Arts, 1987), pp. 25–27.
46. Mary Jane Jacob, *The Rouge: The Image of Industry in the Art of Charles Sheeler and Diego Rivera* (Detroit: Detroit Institute of Arts, 1978), pp. 2–11.
47. Ibid., pp. 9–11.
48. *Vanity Fair,* February 1928; also Jacob, *The Rouge,* p. 14.
49. Nelson Lichtenstein, *The Most Dangerous Man in Detroit: Walter Reuther and the Fate of American Labor* (New York: Basic Books, 1995), pp. 14–27.
50. Jack London, *The Iron Heel* (New York: Sagamore Press, 1957), p. 114.
51. Lichtenstein, *The Most Dangerous Man in Detroit,* pp. 20–22.

CHAPTER FOURTEEN: LINCOLN MOTOR

1. "Ford Defends Business," *New York Times,* May 14, 1925, p. 2.
2. Ralph C. Epstein, "The Rise and Fall of Firms in the Automobile Industry," *Harvard Business Review* 5, no. 2 (January 1927).
3. Norman Beasley, *Knudsen: A Biography* (New York: Whittlesey House, 1947), p. 111.
4. Walter Wagner, "Reminiscences" (oral history project), p. 19, Henry Ford Museum and Library, Dearborn, Michigan.
5. Thomas E. Bonsall, *Seventy-five Years of Lincoln* (Baltimore: Turning Point Publishing, 1995), p. 23.
6. James D. Bell, "The Cadillac Standard," *Automobile Quarterly* 3, no. 3 (Fall 1964), p. 293.
7. Maurice Hendry, *Lincoln: America's Car of State* (New York: Ballantine Books, 1971), pp. 19–36.
8. Bonsall, *Seventy-five Years of Lincoln,* pp. 24–25.
9. Alfred P. Sloan Jr., *My Years with General Motors,* eds. John MacDonald and Catharine Stevens (Garden City, N.Y.: Doubleday, 1964), p. 20.
10. Ibid., p. 26.
11. Keith Sward, *The Legend of Henry Ford* (New York: Rinehart, 1948), p. 28.
12. Ottilie M. Leland with Minnie Dubbs Millbrook, *Master of Precision: Henry M. Leland,* 2d ed. (Detroit: Wayne State University Press, 1996), pp. 100, 112–15.
13. James J. Flink, *The Automobile Age* (Cambridge, Mass.: MIT Press, 1988), pp. 66–69.
14. Thomas E. Bonsall, *The Lincoln Motorcar: The Complete History of an American Classic* (Baltimore: Stony Run Press, 1980), pp. 9–10.
15. Wagner, "Reminiscences," pp. 25–26.
16. Ferry W. Hawkins, *The Buildings of Detroit: A History* (Detroit: Wayne State University Press, 1980), p. 337.
17. Wagner, "Reminiscences," p. 27.
18. Bonsall, *Seventy-five Years of Lincoln,* p. 28.
19. Ibid.
20. Ralph C. Getsinger, "Reminiscences," p. 17.
21. Allan Nevins and Frank Ernest Hill, *Ford,* vol. 2, *Expansion and Challenge, 1915–1933* (New York: Charles Scribner's Sons, 1957), p. 64.
22. Maurice Hendry, *Lincoln: America's Car of State* (New York: Ballantine, 1971), pp. 39–46. See also Leland with Millbrook, *Master of Precision,* p. 196.
23. "The Lincoln Motor Failure," *New York Times,* November 10, 1921, p. 29.
24. "Threat to Impeach Daugherty in House," *New York Times,* April 12, 1922, p. 2.
25. Ford L. Bryan, *Clara: Mrs. Henry Ford* (Dearborn, Mich.: Ford Books, 2001), p. 183.
26. *Best Ford Jokes* (New York: Haldeman-Julius Company, 1927), p. 39.
27. "Offer $8,000,000 for Lincoln Motors," *New York Times,* January 1, 1922, p. 16.
28. Leland with Millbrook, *Master of Precision,* pp. 223–36.
29. Bonsall, *Seventy-five Years of Lincoln,* p. 36.
30. Ibid., p. 15.
31. Bernard A. Weisberger, *The Dream Maker: William C. Durant, Founder of General Motors* (Boston: Little, Brown, 1979), pp. 203–74.
32. Ibid., pp. 318–40.
33. "Ford Plans to Buy Lincoln Motor Company," *New York Times,* January 12, 1922, p. 19.
34. *Detroit News,* February 5, 1922.
35. Bonsall, *Seventy-five Years of Lincoln,* p. 4.
36. "Fords Pay $8,000,000 for Lincoln Motors," *New York Times,* February 5, 1922, p. 5.
37. Nevins and Hill, *Expansion and Challenge,* p. 172.
38. Leland with Millbrook, *Master of Precision,* pp. 252–65.
39. "Ford 'Plays Square' at $4,000,000 Cost," *New York Times,* March 10, 1923, p. 15.
40. Getsinger, "Reminiscences," pp. 43–44.
41. Wagner, "Reminiscences," pp. 44, 50.
42. Hendry, *Lincoln: America's Car of State,* p. 31.
43. Getsinger, "Reminiscences," p. 21.

44. *New Zealand Fordist,* October 1922, pp. 3–4.
45. Hendry, *Lincoln: America's Car of State,* pp. 30–47.
46. Ibid., pp. 34–36.
47. "Babe Ruth's 1940 Lincoln Zephyr Convertible to Be Offered at Arizona-Biltmore Auction," *Public Relations Newswire,* October 28, 2000.
48. Kenneth N. Metcalf, "Biography of a Chair," *Lincoln Herald* (Winter 1961), p. 201; and "Lincoln's Chair to Be Auctioned," *Detroit Free Press,* November 24, 1929.
49. Hendry, *Lincoln: America's Car of State,* p. 139.

CHAPTER FIFTEEN: FORD AVIATION

1. Timothy J. O'Callaghan, *The Aviation Legacy of Henry and Edsel Ford* (Ann Arbor, Mich.: Proctor Publications, 2000), p. 6.
2. William B. Harwood, *Raise Heaven and Earth: The Story of Martin Marietta People and Their Pioneering Achievements* (New York: Simon & Schuster, 1993), pp. 108–9.
3. O'Callaghan, *The Aviation Legacy,* pp. 23–24.
4. Eugene Rodgers, *Flying High: The Story of Boeing and the Rise of the Jetliner Industry* (New York: Atlantic Monthly Press, 1996), p. 37.
5. Ken McGregor, "Beam Dream," in *Saga of the U.S. Air Mail Service,* ed. Dale Nielsen (Washington: Air Mail Pioneers, 1962), p. x.
6. O'Callaghan, *The Aviation Legacy,* p. 39.
7. Richard Hallon, *Legacy of Flight: The Guggenheim Contribution to American Aviation* (Seattle: University of Washington Press, 1977), p. 17.
8. T. A. Heppenheimer, *Turbulent Skies: The History of Commercial Aviation* (New York: John Wiley & Sons, 1995), p. 5.
9. O'Callaghan, *The Aviation Legacy,* p. 8.
10. Ibid, p. 10.
11. William Stout, "Reminiscences" (oral history project), p. 72, Henry Ford Museum and Library, Dearborn, Michigan.
12. W. M. Nelson, "Duralumin and Its Corrosion," *Aviation,* November 1, 1923, pp. 738–40.
13. Glenn Hoppin, "Reminiscences," p. 73.
14. Ibid., p. 69.
15. Allan Nevins and Frank Ernest Hill, *Ford,* vol. 2, *Expansion and Challenge, 1915–1933* (New York: Charles Scribner's Sons, 1957), p. 340.
16. *New York World,* August 7, 1925.
17. Stout, "Reminiscences," p. 73.
18. "First Plane Made in Ford Airport," *New York Times,* March 19, 1925, p. 13.
19. O'Callaghan, *The Aviation Legacy,* p. 143.
20. Rodgers, *Flying High,* p. 39.
21. Jacob A. Vander Meulen, *The Politics of Aircraft: Building an American Military Industry* (Lawrence, Kan.: University Press of Kansas, 1991), pp. 3–17.
22. Stout, "Reminiscences," p. 87.
23. "Fords Interested in Making Airplanes," *New York Times,* April 14, 1925, p. 2.
24. "Unique Mooring Device Features Airship Tower Under Construction at Dearborn," *Ford Times* 5, no. 16 (June 15, 1925), p. 1.
25. John Toland, *The Great Dirigibles* (New York: Dover, 1972), p. 102.
26. Stout, "Reminiscences," pp. 91–92.
27. Hoppin, "Reminiscences," pp. 87–88.
28. Nevins and Hill, *Expansion and Challenge,* p. 239.
29. *Literary Digest,* August 1926.
30. O'Callaghan, *The Aviation Legacy,* p. 58.
31. "Fords Plan to Cut Cost of Airplanes," *New York Times,* July 29, 1926, p. 1.
32. Harold Hicks, "Reminiscences," vol. 2, p. 70.
33. Ibid., p. 72.
34. "Ford Company Buys Airplane Concern," *New York Times,* August 7, 1925, p. 8; and O'Callaghan, *The Aviation Legacy,* p. 11.

35. O'Callaghan, *The Aviation Legacy*, p. 54.
36. H. I. Block, "Ford's Air Liners Run Like Scheduled Trains," *New York Times*, November 14, 1926, sec. 9, p. 8.
37. Al Esper, "Reminiscences," p. 37.
38. O'Callaghan, *The Aviation Legacy*, pp. 42–47.
39. Ibid.
40. Hicks, "Reminiscences," p. 75.
41. Stout, "Reminiscences," p. 108.
42. William Moffett to Henry Ford, March 1925, Henry Ford Library and Museum.
43. Commander Richard E. Byrd to Edsel Ford, February 2, 1926, Papers of Admiral Richard E. Byrd, RG 56.1, folder 4471, Ohio State University Byrd Polar Research Center Archival Program, Columbus, Ohio.
44. Edsel Ford to Commander Richard E. Byrd, February 2, 1929, ibid.
45. Commander Richard E. Byrd to Edsel Ford, April 4, 1926, ibid.
46. Commander Richard E. Byrd to Edsel Ford, July 25, 1927, ibid.
47. O'Callaghan, *The Aviation Legacy*, pp. 98–103.
48. Edsel Ford to Commander Richard E. Byrd, October 17, 1927, Papers of Admiral Richard E. Byrd, RG 56.1, folder 4471, Byrd Polar Research Center Archival Program.
49. Esper, "Reminiscences," p. 49.
50. "Lindbergh at Ford Airport," *Ford News* 7, no. 21 (September 1, 1927), p. 8.
51. David L. Lewis, *Ford Country: The Family, the Company, the Cars* (Sidney, Ohio: Amos Press, 1990), p. 26.
52. Ibid., p. 25.
53. Ford R. Bryan, *Henry's Lieutenants* (Detroit: Wayne State University Press, 1993); and Automobile Hall of Fame, Dearborn, Michigan, pp. 275–79.

CHAPTER SIXTEEN: GOOD-BYE, MODEL T; HELLO, MODEL A

1. John Keats, *The Insolent Chariots* (Philadelphia: J.B. Lippincott, 1958), p. 6.
2. John B. Rae, *The American Automobile Industry* (Boston: G.K. Hall, 1984), p. 8.
3. Pete Davies, *American Road* (New York: Henry Holt, 2002), p. 2.
4. Peter Jennings and Todd Brewster, *The Century* (New York: Doubleday, 1998), p. 103; and David L. Lewis, "Sex and the Automobile: From Rumble Seats to Rockin' Vans," in *The Automobile and American Culture,* eds. David L. Lewis and Laurence Goldstein (Ann Arbor, Mich.: University of Michigan Press, 1980), p. 129.
5. Folke T. Kihlstedt, "The Automobile and the Transformation of the American House, 1910–1935" in Lewis and Goldstein, *The Automobile and American Culture*, p. 160.
6. Robert S. Lynd and Helen M. Lynd, *Middletown: A Study in Contemporary American Culture* (New York: Harcourt Brace, 1929), pp. 253–60.
7. William Clay Ford, video interview, Ford Motor Company Centennial, 2002, Dearborn, Michigan.
8. Louis Haber, *Black Pioneers of Science and Invention* (New York: Harcourt Brace, 1992).
9. Norman Beasley, *Knudsen: A Biography* (New York: Whittlesey House, 1947), p. 109, citing Malcolm W. Bingley, *Detroit Is My Home Town.*
10. Dennis Hackett, *The Big Idea: The Story of Ford in Europe* (Nottingham, England: Thomas Forman & Sons, 1978), pp. 21–34.
11. Beasley, *Knudsen*, p. 111.
12. Henry Ford with Samuel Crowther, *My Life and Work* (Garden City, N.Y.: Doubleday, 1923), p. 93.
13. *Detroit News*, November 24, 1922.
14. Alfred P. Sloan Jr., *My Years with General Motors*, eds. John McDonald and Catharine Stevens (Garden City, N.Y.: Doubleday, 1964), p. 69.
15. "Think General Motors Will War upon Ford," *New York Times*, February 11, 1922, p. 3.
16. Sloan, *My Years with General Motors*, p. 149.
17. Henry Ford, *My Life at Work* (Garden City, NY: Garden City Publishing Co., 1922), pp. 67–71.
18. Sloan, *My Years with General Motors*, p. 152.

19. Beverly Rae Kimes, "Copper-Cooled Debacle to First-Place Victory," *Automobile Quarterly* 18, no. 4 (Winter 1980), p. 440.
20. Beasley, *Knudsen,* p. 132.
21. William Pennypacker Young, *A Ford Dealer's Twenty Year Ride with the Old and New Model Ford Policies* (Pottstown, Pa., and Hempstead, N.Y.: Lotta L. Young, 1932), p. 65.
22. Beasley, *Knudsen,* p. 129.
23. George Brown, "Reminiscences" (oral history project), vol. 2, pp. 155–56, Henry Ford Museum and Library, Dearborn, Michigan.
24. Alex Lumsden, "Reminiscences," pp. 53–54.
25. P. E. Haglund, "Reminiscences," p. 59.
26. Logan Miller, "Reminiscences," p. 19.
27. Charles Sorensen, "Reminiscences," p. 66.
28. Ernest Kanzler to Henry Ford, January 26, 1926, Accession 1, box 180, folder 2, Henry Ford Museum and Library.
29. Haglund, "Reminiscences," p. 61.
30. Albert Smith, "Reminiscences," p. 42.
31. James O'Connor, "Reminiscences," p. 41.
32. David L. Lewis, "Henry Ford's Anti-Semitism and Its Repercussions," *Michigan Jewish History,* January 1984, pp. 3–10.
33. Christopher Hitchens, "Jewish Power, Jewish Peril," *Vanity Fair,* September 2002, pp. 196–98.
34. James C. Young, *New York Times,* December 26, 1926.
35. "The New Motor Sensation," *Boston News Bureau,* May 18, 1927.
36. Harold Hicks, "Reminiscences," pp. 140–41.
37. "New Ford Car Announced; Details Forthcoming Soon," *Ford News* 7, no. 15 (June 1, 1927), p. 6.
38. Bill Gates, *Business at the Speed of Thought: Using a Digital Nervous System* (New York: Warner, 1999), p. 180.
39. Lee Strout White, "Farewell, My Lovely," *The New Yorker,* May 16, 1936.
40. John Steinbeck, *Cannery Row* (New York: Penguin Books, 1994), pp. 62–63.
41. John Steinbeck, "A Model T Named 'IT,'" *Ford Times* 45, no. 7 (July 1953), pp. 34–35.
42. Ibid., p. 39.
43. Morris Buske, "Dad Are We There Yet?," *Michigan History* 83, no. 2 (March/April 1999), pp. 17–24.
44. Leicester Hemingway, *My Brother Ernest Hemingway* (Sarasota, FL: Pineapple Press, 1996), p. 105.
45. Trevor & Morris File (including sales receipt), Henry Ford Museum and Library.
46. Ralph H. Graves, *The Triumph of an Idea: The Story of Henry Ford* (Garden City, N.Y.: Doubleday, Doran, 1934), p. 91.
47. Sloan, *My Years with General Motors,* p. 169.
48. Allan Nevins and Frank Ernest Hill, *Ford,* vol. 2, *Expansion and Challenge, 1915–1933* (New York: Charles Scribner's Sons, 1957), p. 440.
49. "Auto Buyers Holding Back; Ford Statement Awaited," *New York Post,* April 30, 1927.
50. William F. Pioch, "Reminiscences," pp. 42–43.
51. "Personal Glimpses," *Literary Digest,* December 3, 1927, p. 54.

CHAPTER SEVENTEEN: MODEL A AND TRADE ABROAD

1. Lois Gordon and Alan Gordon, *American Chronicle: Six Decades in American Life* (New York: Atheneum, 1987), pp. 69–77.
2. "Sees New Ford Car as Dominating Business Factor," *Michigan Manufacturer and Financial Record,* October 15, 1927.
3. Advertisement, *Valdosta Times,* November 28, 1927.
4. "Ford Car Photos Taken as Editor 'Scoops' Nation," *New York Evening Post,* November 14, 1927, p. 1.
5. James M. Flammang, David L. Lewis, and the Auto Editors of Consumers Guide, eds., *Ford Chronicle: A Pictoral History from 1893* (Lincolnwood, Ill.: Publications International Ltd., 1997), pp. 60–62.

6. "Ten Percent of U.S. Population Sees New Ford First Day of Show," *Ford News* 8, no. 4 (December 15, 1927), p. 1.
7. Thomas Edison to Henry Ford, n.d. (received December 15, 1927), Accession 1630, box 3, folder 14, Henry Ford Museum and Library, Dearborn, Michigan.
8. "Personal Glimpses," *Literary Digest*, December 3, 1927, p. 54.
9. "Seized as Speeder in New Ford; Only in Second, Driver Says," *New York Times*, January 11, 1928, p. 1.
10. *New York Evening Post*, December 14, 1927.
11. "New Offices for Ford Son," *Ford News*, January 8, 1927, pp. 1–4.
12. Allan Nevins and Frank Ernest Hill, *Ford*, vol. 2, *Expansion and Challenge, 1915–1933* (New York: Charles Scribner's Sons, 1957), p. 456.
13. Peter Winnewisser, *The Legendary Model A Ford* (Iola, Wis.: Krause, 1999), p. 28.
14. "Couzens Wants First 'A' Sold in Washington," *Philadelphia Inquirer*, December 3, 1927, p. 2.
15. "Mirrors of Motordom," *Iron Trade Review*, October 10, 1927.
16. "Asserts Chevrolet Will Outsell Ford," *New York Times*, January 12, 1928, p. 22.
17. "Ford's Output 1,200 to 1,500 Daily," *New York Times*, March 23, 1928, p. 26.
18. "Ford Law Force Ousted," *New York Times*, January 30, 1929, p. 18.
19. William and Marjorie McNairn, *Quotations from the Unusual Henry Ford* (Norwalk, Calif.: Stockton Trade Press, 1978), p. 26.
20. "Ford Undersells Germans," *New York Times*, March 31, 1924, p. 27.
21. Will Rogers, "The Grand Champion," *American Magazine*, December 1929, pp. 34–37.
22. Ben Yagoda, *Will Rogers: A Biography* (New York: Alfred A. Knopf, 1993), pp. 251–52.
23. McNairn and McNairn, *Quotations*, p. 101.
24. Garet Garrett, *The Wild Wheel* (New York: Pantheon, 1952), p. 14.
25. Henry Ford, "If My Business Were Small," *System* 43, no. 6 (June 1928), p. 735.
26. Henry Ford, "Why I Believe in Progress" (interview with Fay Leone Faurote), *The Forum*, November 1928, p. 682.
27. Samuel Crowther files, Accession 285, boxes 38–50, Henry Ford Museum and Library. These files are filled with Crowther's correspondence with E. G. Liebold.
28. Matthew Josephson, *Edison: A Biography* (New York: McGraw-Hill, 1959), p. 457.
29. Thomas Edison musing on Henry Ford, n.d., Accession 1630, box 3, folder 46, Henry Ford Museum and Library.
30. Actors and Actresses, Accession 1660, box 1, Henry Ford Museum and Library; also Ford Motor Company Archives, Dearborn, Michigan.
31. "Ford Against Execution," *New York Times*, August 10, 1927, p. 4.
32. "Ford Sees Hoover the Next President," *New York Times*, January 10, 1928, p. 18.
33. Delancey Ferguson, "An Evening with Henry Ford," *The New Yorker*, February 13, 1954, p. 78.
34. S. N. Behrman, *Duveen* (New York: Random House, 1951).
35. Ford R. Bryan, *Friends, Families, and Forays: Scenes from the Life and Times of Henry Ford* (Dearborn, Mich.: Ford Books, 2002), pp. 59–61.
36. Jerome Davis, "Henry Ford, Educator," *Atlantic Monthly*, June 1927, p. 803.
37. B. C. Forbes, "Twenty Reasons Why Ford Reached the Top," *Forbes*, April 1, 1925, p. 840; and David L. Lewis, *Ford Country*, 2d ed. (Sidney, Ohio: Amos Press, 1999), p. 78. The Couzens gift was given in 1929.
38. Mary Moline, comp., *The Best of Ford* (Van Nuys, Calif.: Rumbleseat Press, 1973), p. 340.
39. Ford R. Bryan, *Friends, Families, and Forays*, pp. 283–88.
40. Ibid.
41. Robert Lacey, *Ford: The Men and the Machine* (Boston: Little, Brown, 1986); various Berry College newspaper clippings, Berry College, Georgia.
42. Lewis, *Ford Country*, pp. 35–36.
43. Charles Hillinger, "Broadening the Mind on a 28,000 Acre Campus," *Los Angeles Times*, December 4, 1988.
44. "American Capital Motorizing Europe," *Literary Digest*, May 4, 1929, p. 80.
45. "Motor Vehicles Registration According to Population," 1926 record, Automobile Hall of Fame, Dearborn, Michigan.
46. L. E. Briggs, "Reminiscences" (oral history project), p. 38, Henry Ford Museum and Library.
47. Ibid., p. 41.

48. Lewis, *Ford Country*, p. 94.
49. Ibid., p. 95.
50. McNairn and McNairn, *Quotations*, p. 47.
51. "Says, in Article in *Nation's Business*, That Soviets' Desire to Become Independent Is His Reason for Giving Aid," *New York Times*, June 20, 1930, p. 7.
52. "Ford Sells $30,000,000 in Cars to Russia . . ." *New York Times*, May 31, 1929, p. 1.
53. Mira Wilkins and Frank Ernest Hill, *American Business Abroad: Ford on Six Continents* (Detroit: Wayne State University, 1964), p. 226
54. Ibid., pp. 226–27.
55. Josef Stalin to Mr. Lambe, Washington, D.C., September 21, 1944, Accession 23, box 38, Henry Ford Museum and Library.
56. Wilkins and Hill, *American Business Abroad*, pp. 226–29.

CHAPTER EIGHTEEN: COPING WITH THE GREAT DEPRESSION

1. Henry Ford in collaboration with Fay Leone Faurote, *My Philosophy of Industry* (New York: Coward-McCann, 1929), pp. 18–19.
2. Matthew Josephson, *Edison: A Biography* (New York: McGraw-Hill, 1959), p. 479, citing E. G. Liebold, "Reminiscences" (oral history project), p. 693, Henry Ford Museum and Library, Dearborn, Michigan.
3. Ron Chernow, *The House of Morgan: An American Banking Dynasty and the Rise of Modern Finance* (New York: Atlantic Monthly Press, 1990), pp. 314–15.
4. Ford R. Bryan, *Friends, Families, and Forays* (Dearborn, Mich.: Ford Books, 2002), pp. 31–32.
5. David Kennedy, *Freedom from Fear: The American People in Depression and War, 1929–1945* (New York: Oxford University Press, 1999), pp. 22–23.
6. Kevin Phillips, *Wealth and Democracy: A Political History of the American Rich* (New York: Broadway Books, 2002), p. 275.
7. Maury Klein, *Rainbow's End: The Crash of 1929* (New York: Oxford University Press, 2002), p. xiii.
8. Robert Sobel, *The Age of Giant Corporations: A Microeconomic History of American Business, 1914–1984* (Westport, Conn.: Greenwood Press, 1984), pp. 52–75.
9. For how Edsel Ford coped with the Great Depression, see Henry Dominguez, *Edsel: The Story of Henry Ford's Forgotten Son* (Warrendale, Pa.: Society of Automotive Engineers, 2002), pp. 119–34.
10. Klein, *Rainbow's End*, p. 242.
11. "More Money to Spend," *Outlook* 152, December 18, 1929, p. 617.
12. *New York Times*, November 25, 1929.
13. "Ford Output Gains 138%," *New York Times*, January 8, 1930, p. 20.
14. "Ford Dealers Rebel; Many Leave Ranks," *Business Week*, April 2, 1930, p. 9.
15. "Some Say Ford Can't Cut Price; Some Say He Shouldn't: He Does," *Business Week*, June 11, 1930, p. 7.
16. "Ford Explains Policy of Letting Out Work," *New York Times*, March 24, 1930, p. 2.
17. Peter Gavrilovich and Bill McGraw, eds., *The Detroit Almanac: 300 Years of Life in the Motor City* (Detroit: Detroit Free Press, 2000), pp. 45–46.
18. Edmund Wilson, "The Despot of Dearborn," *Scribner's*, July 1931, p. 26.
19. "Ford Chief Alters Statement on Reds," *New York Times*, July 27, 1930, p. 22.
20. David L. Lewis, "Harry Bennett, Ford's Tough Guy, Breaks Thirty Years of Silence and Tells His Side of the Story," *Detroit Free Press*, January 20, 1974; and "Harry Bennett's Story of His Ford Years," *Detroit Free Press*, January 27, 1974.
21. John McCarter, "The Little Man in Henry Ford's Basement," *The American Mercury* 50, no. 197 (May 1940), p. 7.
22. William C. Klann, "Reminiscences," vol. 3, p. 287.
23. Logan Miller, "Reminiscences," p. 43.
24. Omar Martineau, "Reminiscences," pp. 7–11.
25. Ford R. Bryan, *Henry's Lieutenants* (Detroit: Wayne State University Press, 1993), p. 31.
26. August Meier and Elliott Rudwick, *Black Detroit and the Rise of the U.A.W.* (New York: Oxford University Press, 1979), pp. 10–11.

27. Keith Sward, *The Legend of Henry Ford* (New York: Rinehart, 1948), pp. 329–37.
28. "Detroit Sees Future Ruled by New Ford," *New York Times,* March 6, 1932, sec. 3, p. 6.
29. "Edsel Ford for Shorter Week to Absorb Labor Surplus," *New York Times,* March 3, 1931, p. 6.
30. "Ford Plans to Offer All-Year-Round Jobs," *New York Times,* April 1, 1931, p. 60.
31. "Standard of Living of Employees of Ford Motor Co. in Detroit," *U.S. Bureau of Labor Statistics Monthly Review* 30, no. 6 (June 1930), pp. 1209–51.
32. Charles R. Walker, "Down and Out in Detroit," *Forum,* September 1931, pp. 129–30.
33. Letter from Edsel Ford, n.d., 1931, Henry Ford Museum and Library.
34. Henry Dominguez, *Edsel: The Story of Henry Ford's Forgotten Son* (Warrendale, Pa.: Society of Automotive Engineers, 2002), pp. 119–34.
35. Andre Millard, *Edison and the Business of Innovation* (Baltimore: Johns Hopkins University Press, 1990), p. 320.
36. Wyn Wachhorst, *Thomas Alva Edison: An American Myth* (Cambridge, Mass.: MIT Press, 1981), p. 164.
37. Paul Israel, *Edison: A Life of Invention* (New York: John Wiley & Sons, 1998), pp. 461–62.
38. "Ford Reveals Plan for Great Output," *New York Times,* February 28, 1932, p. 19.
39. Sward, *The Legend of Henry Ford,* p. 231.
40. Maurice Sugar, "Bullets—Not Food—for Ford Workers," *The Nation,* March 23, 1932, p. 333.
41. *Detroit Free Press,* March 8, 1932.
42. Oakley Johnson, "After the Dearborn Massacre," *The New Republic,* March 30, 1932, pp. 173–74.
43. *Detroit News,* March 9, 1932.
44. T. H. Watkins, *The Great Depression: America in the 1930s* (Boston: Little, Brown, 1993), pp. 94–98.
45. Quoted in Sward, *The Legend of Henry Ford,* p. 236.
46. *New York Times,* March 9, 1932.
47. Upton Sinclair, *The Flivver King: A Story of Ford-America* (Chicago: Charles H. Kerr, 1937), p. 88.
48. John Dos Passos, *The Big Money* (Boston: Mariner Books/Houghton Mifflin, 2000), pp. 44–45.
49. *Detroit Times,* March 9, 1932.

CHAPTER NINETEEN: MODEL Y: THE FORD AMERICANS NEVER KNEW

1. June Derry, "Technology and Gender in Aldous Huxley's Alternative Worlds," in *Critical Essays on Aldous Huxley,* ed. Jerome Meckier (New York: G.K. Hall, 1996), pp. 103–4.
2. Aldous Huxley, *Brave New World* (1932; reprint, New York: Penguin, 1971), pp. 32–34.
3. Sybille Bedford, *Aldous Huxley: A Biography* (New York: Random House, 1974) pp. 250–65; and Jerome Meckier, *Aldous Huxley: Satire and Structure* (London: Chatto & Windus, 1969) p. 48.
4. Grover Smith, ed., *Letters of Aldous Huxley* (London: Chatto & Windus, 1969), p. 653.
5. Louis-Ferdinand Céline, *Journey to the End of the Night* (New York: New Directions, 1983), pp. 192–201.
6. Ibid.
7. Edsel Ford to Percival Perry, October 22, 1930, Ford Motor Co. Ltd. Subsidiary—London, Henry Ford Museum and Library, Dearborn, Michigan.
8. "Ford Motor Company" company meeting, reprinted from *The Times* (London), March 8, 1930, Accession 6, box 256, subject files July–Dec. 1929, Ford Motor Co. Ltd., p. 2, ibid.
9. Quoted in Mira Wilkins and Frank Ernest Hill, *American Business Abroad: Ford on Six Continents* (Detroit: Wayne State University Press, 1964) p. 236.
10. Andrew Whyte, *Jaguar: The History of a Great British Car,* foreword by Sir William Lyons (Cambridge, England: Patrick Stephens, 1980), pp. 12–67.
11. Wilkins and Hill, *American Business Abroad,* p. 239.
12. Henry Dominguez, *Edsel Ford and E. T. Gregorie* (Warrendale, Pa.: Society of Automotive Engineers, 1999), p. 57.

13. Harold Hicks, "Reminiscences" (oral history project), vol. 2, p. 175, Henry Ford Museum and Library.
14. A. R. Smith, "Reminiscences," Henry Ford Museum and Library.
15. Alfred P. Sloan Jr., *My Years with General Motors*, eds. John McDonald and Catharine Stevens (Garden City, N.Y.: Doubleday, 1964), p. 273.
16. David L. Lewis, "Edsel Ford: The Gentle Businessman," Edsel Ford Centennial Lecture, November 11, 1993, p. 12, Edsel and Eleanor Ford House Archives, Grosse Pointe Shores, Michigan.
17. A. J. Lepine, "Reminiscences," pp. 62, 63, 64.
18. Eugene W. Lewis, *Motor Memories* (Detroit: Alved Publishers, 1947), pp. 113–20.
19. Lewis, "Edsel Ford," p. 9.
20. Richard Bak, "The Edsel Enigma," *Hour,* December 1997–January 1998, p. 63.
21. Thomas E. Bonsall, "Edsel: The Forgotten Ford," *Automobile Quarterly* 29, no. 3 (Fall 1991), p. 21.
22. Ford R. Bryan, *Clara: Mrs. Henry Ford* (Dearborn, Mich.: Ford Books, 2001), pp. 203–4.
23. Mrs. Stanley Ruddiman, "Reminiscences," p. 97.
24. Patrick Marnham, *Dreaming with His Eyes Open: A Life of Diego Rivera* (New York: Alfred A. Knopf, 1998), pp. 239–41.
25. Diego Rivera, *My Art, My Life* (New York: Citadel Press, 1960), p. 111.
26. Bertram D. Wolfe, *Diego Rivera: His Life and Times* (New York: Alfred A. Knopf, 1963) p. 249.
27. Rivera, *My Art, My Life,* p. 115.
28. Marnham, *Dreaming with His Eyes Open,* pp. 244–45.
29. Andrea Kettenman, *Rivera* (Cologne: Taschen, 2000), pp. 48–52.
30. Bak, "The Edsel Enigma," p. 70.
31. Emil Zoerlein, "Reminiscences," vol. 1, p. 73.
32. Stanley Ruddiman, "Reminiscences," p. 30.
33. L. E. Briggs, "Reminiscences," p. 60.
34. Dominguez, *Edsel Ford and E. T. Gregorie,* p. 51.
35. Griffith Borgeson, "Fords for Over There," *Automobile Quarterly* 25, no. 2, p. 137.
36. Ford R. Bryan, *Henry's Lieutenants* (Detroit: Wayne State University Press, 1993), pp. 232–33.
37. Nelson Lichtenstein, *The Most Dangerous Man in Detroit: Walter Reuther and the Fate of American Labor* (New York: Basic Books, 1995), p. 18.
38. Ibid, p. 12.
39. Frank Cormier and William J. Eaton, *Reuther* (Englewood Cliffs, N.J.: Prentice-Hall, 1970), p. 20.
40. Irving Bluestone, "Working Class Hero: Walter Reuther," *Time,* December 6, 1998, p. 158.
41. Victor Reuther, *The Brothers Reuther and the Story of the UAW* (Boston: Houghton Mifflin, 1976), p. 70.
42. V. Y. Tallberg, "Reminiscences," p. 48.
43. Prince Louis Ferdinand, letter January 3, 1935, Accession 6, box 292, subject files 1935, Ford Motor Company Subsidiary—Cologne, Henry Ford Museum and Library.
44. "Extract of Mr. Hitler's Speech at the Opening of the International Automobile Show," February 1936, Accession 6, box 297, subject files 1936, FMC Ltd. Subsidiary—Cologne, ibid.
45. Tallberg, "Reminiscences," p. 49.
46. "Appendix G, Ford-Werke Results of Operations, 1933–1953," *Research Findings About Ford-Werke Under the Nazi Regime* (Dearborn, Mich.: Ford Motor Company, 2001), pp. 135–36.
47. Ibid., p. 8, n. 35.
48. Tallberg, "Reminiscences," pp. 51–52.
49. Sir Percival Perry to Edsel Ford, January 25, 1932, Accession 6, box 274, subject files 1932, Ford Motor Co. Ltd. Subsidiary—Cologne, Henry Ford Museum and Library.
50. Correspondence and minutes, Accession 6, boxes 324–25, ibid.
51. Quoted in Wilkins and Hill, *American Business Abroad,* pp. 273–74.

52. "Statement Re: Negotiations with the appointee of the Chancellor . . . ," Accession 6, box 287, subject files 1934, Ford Motor Co. Ltd. Subsidiary—Dagenham, Henry Ford Museum and Library.

53. Heinrich Albert, memorandum, September 4, 1934, Accession 6, box 287, subject files 1934, Ford Motor Co. Ltd. Subsidiary—Dagenham, ibid.

54. Tallberg, "Reminiscences," pp. 81–82.

55. Prince Louis-Ferdinand, letter of January 3, 1935, Accession 6, box 292, subject files 1935, Ford Motor Company Subsidiary—Cologne, Henry Ford Museum and Library.

56. Heinrich Albert, letter of August 17, 1936, Accession 6, box 297, subject files 1936, Ford Motor Company Ltd. Subsidiary—Cologne, ibid.

57. Russell Roberge, "Reminiscences," pp. 2–7.

58. Charles Sorensen, letter to Dr. Albert, September 18, 1935, Accession AR-98-213541, box 131, file: Ford Cologne 1930s—Nazi influence, Henry Ford Museum and Library.

CHAPTER TWENTY: FOR BETTER AND FOR WORSE IN DEARBORN

1. James Newton, *Uncommon Friends: Life with Thomas Edison, Henry Ford, Harvey Firestone, Alexis Carrel, and Charles Lindbergh* (San Diego: Harcourt Brace Jovanovich, 1987), pp. 100–101.

2. Allan Nevins and Ernest Frank Hill, *Ford: Expansion and Challenge, 1915–1933* (New York: Charles Scribner's Sons, 1957), pp. 570–621.

3. Nelson Lichtenstein, *The Most Dangerous Man in Detroit: Walter Reuther and the Fate of American Labor* (New York: Basic Books, 1995), p. 18.

4. Alan Brinkley, *Voices of Protest: Huey Long, Father Coughlin and the Great Depression* (New York: Alfred A. Knopf, 1982), p. 102.

5. Dan B. Miller, *Erskine Caldwell: The Journey from Tobacco Road* (New York: Alfred A. Knopf, 1994), pp. 223–26.

6. Emil Zoerlein, "Reminiscences" (oral history project), vol. 2, p. 97, Henry Ford Museum and Library, Dearborn, Michigan.

7. Charles J. "Jimmy" Smith, "Reminiscences," p. 28.

8. Clem Davis, "Reminiscences," p. 28.

9. Zoerlein, "Reminiscences," vol. 2, p. 97.

10. Davis, "Reminiscences," p. 44.

11. Ibid., p. 35.

12. Henry Dominguez, *Edsel Ford and E. T. Gregorie* (Warrendale, Pa.: Society of Automotive Engineers, 1999), p. 65.

13. Keith Sward, *The Legend of Henry Ford* (New York: Rinehart, 1948), p. 207.

14. Frank Ransome Jr., "A Lament for the Model A," *Popular Science,* September 1954.

15. John Dillinger to Henry Ford, May 16, 1934, Accession 1, box 181, Henry Ford Museum and Library.

16. Clyde Barrow to Henry Ford, April 10, 1934, Accession 285, box 1524, Henry Ford Museum and Library.

17. Vincent Curcio, *Chrysler: The Life and Times of an Automotive Genius* (New York: Oxford University Press, 2000), pp. 361–99.

18. *Fortune,* December 1933, pp. 63–65.

19. Victor Reuther, *The Brothers Reuther and the Story of the UAW* (Boston: Houghton Mifflin, 1976), p. 82.

20. Frank Cormier and William J. Eaton, *Reuther* (Englewood Cliffs, N.J.: Prentice-Hall, 1970), p. 32.

21. Piers Brendon, *The Dark Valley: A Panorama of the 1930's* (New York: Alfred A. Knopf, 2000), pp. 266–67.

22. John Barnard, *Walter Reuther and the Rise of the Auto Workers* (Boston: Little, Brown, 1983), p. 40.

23. Harvey Firestone file, Accession 285, box 372, Henry Ford Museum and Library. Also see Harvey S. Firestone with Samuel Crowther, *Men and Rubber: The Story of Business* (Garden City, N.Y.: Doubleday, Page, 1926).

24. Cormier and Eaton, *Reuther,* p. 98.

25. Zoerlein, "Reminiscences," vol. 3, p. 233.
26. Al Esper, "Reminiscences," p. 88.
27. Cormier and Eaton, *Reuther,* p. 198.
28. H. S. Abelwhite, "Reminiscences," p. 64.
29. W. Griffith, "Reminiscences," p. 32.
30. Abelwhite, "Reminiscences," p. 40.
31. Ibid., p. 69.
32. Griffith, "Reminiscences," p. 32.
33. Anthony Harff, "Reminiscences," p. 32.
34. Ibid., p. 83.
35. Zoerlein, "Reminiscences," vol. 3, p. 236.
36. Lichtenstein, *The Most Dangerous Man in Detroit,* pp. 81–82.
37. Ford Bryan, *Clara: Mrs. Henry Ford* (Dearborn, Mich.: Ford Books, 2001), p. 238.
38. Keith Sward, *The Legend of Henry Ford,* pp. 370–75.
39. Reuther, *The Brothers Reuther,* p. 183.
40. *UAW—Ford: Sixty Years of Progress 1941–2001* (Detroit: UAW/Ford National Programs Center, 2001), p. 33.
41. Lichtenstein, *The Most Dangerous Man in Detroit,* pp. 178–79.
42. Keith Sward, *The Legend of Henry Ford,* pp. 370–420.
43. Lichtenstein, *The Most Dangerous Man in Detroit,* pp. 178–79.
44. "New Strike Battles Bring Threat of Federal Action," *Life,* April 14, 1941, p. 31.
45. Cy Rubin and Eric Newton, eds. *The Pulitzer Prize Photographs* (Arlington, Va.: Freedom Forum Newseum, 2000), p. 9.
46. Lichtenstein, *The Most Dangerous Man in Detroit.* Also August Meier and Elliott Rudwick, *Black Detroit and the Rise of the U.A.W.* (New York: Oxford University Press, 1979), pp. 3–107.
47. Ford Bryan, *Clara,* p. 275.
48. Cormier and Eaton, *Reuther,* p. 162.
49. *UAW—Ford,* p. 34.
50. William C. Richards, *The Last Billionaire* (New York: Bantam Books, 1951), pp. 285–86.

CHAPTER TWENTY-ONE: MERCURY

1. Edward Cray, *Chrome Colossus: General Motors and Its Times* (New York: McGraw-Hill, 1980), pp. 264–85.
2. Vincent Curcio, *Chrysler: The Life and Times of an Automotive Genius* (New York: Oxford University Press, 2000), p. 618.
3. Richard Bak, "The Edsel Enigma," *Hour,* December 1997–January 1998, p. 59.
4. Peter Collier and David Horowitz, *The Fords: An American Epic* (New York: Summit Books, 1987), p. 144.
5. Ibid., p. 254.
6. Fred Roe, *Duesenberg: The Pursuit of Perfection* (London: Dalton Watson, 1982), pp. 125–86.
7. Julie M. Fenster, "World's Fair '33," *Automobile Quarterly* 25, no. 1 (Spring 1987), p. 54.
8. Beverly Rae Kimes, *The Classic Era* (Des Plaines, Ill.: Classic Car Club of America, 2001), pp. 313–15.
9. Maurice Hendry, *Lincoln: America's Car of State* (New York: Ballantine, 1971), p. 90.
10. Henry Dominguez, *Edsel Ford and E. T. Gregorie* (Warrendale, Pa.: Society of Automotive Engineers, 1999), p. 76.
11. E. T. Gregorie, Design Oral History Project, Edsel B. Ford Design History Center, Dearborn, Michigan, p. 53.
12. Author interview with E. T. Gregorie, September 2002, St. Augustine, Florida.
13. Dominguez, *Edsel Ford and E. T. Gregorie,* p. 91.
14. G. Eugene "Bud" Adams, Design Oral History Project, p. 51.
15. John A. Gunnell, *Fifty-five Years of Mercury: The Complete History of the Big "M"* (Iola, Wis.: Krause Publications, 1994), p. 7.
16. Author interview with Gregorie.
17. Michael Lamm and David Lewis, "The First Mercury," *Special Interest Automobiles,* no. 23 (July–August 1974), p. 18.

18. Gunnell, *Fifty-five Years of Mercury*, p. 9.
19. Collier and Horowitz, *The Fords: An American Epic*, p. 159.
20. Gregorie, Design Oral History Project, p. 45.
21. Michael Lamm and David Lewis, "The Mercury Renaissance," *Automobile Quarterly* 8, no. 2 (Fall 1969), p. 152.
22. Gregorie, Design Oral History Project, p. 45.
23. Author interview with Gregorie.
24. Gregorie, Design Oral History Project, p. 53.
25. Ibid., p. 79
26. Ibid., p. 53.
27. Lamm and Lewis, "The First Mercury," p. 21
28. "Ford Liberalizes Dealer Agreements," clipping books, unidentified newspaper, n.d., Henry Ford Museum and Library, Dearborn, Michigan.
29. "Almost Sells '39 Model to Edsel Ford," *Detroit Times*, November 18, 1938.
30. Gunnell, *Fifty-five Years of Mercury*, p. 17.
31. "Henry Ford and the Beanstalk," press release, Ford Motor 75th anniversary, May 1, 1978.
32. "Experimenting with the Soybean," *Ford News*, March 1933.
33. Ford R. Bryan, *Friends, Families and Forays: Scenes from the Life and Times of Henry Ford* (Dearborn, Mich.: Ford Books, 2002), p. 60.
34. "Mr. Ford Doesn't Care," *Fortune* 8, December 1933, pp. 65–134.
35. "Henry Ford and the Beanstalk."
36. Ford R. Bryan, *Friends, Families and Forays*, pp. 60–61.
37. Linda O. McMurry, *George Washington Carver: Scientist and Symbol* (New York: Oxford University Press, 1981), pp. 1–110.
38. Ford R. Bryan, *Friends, Families and Forays*, p. 61.
39. George Washington Carver to H. O. Abbott, April 25, 1940, box 48, George Washington Carver Papers, Tuskegee Institute Archives, Tuskegee, Alabama.
40. Linda O. McMurry, *George Washington Carver*, p. 387.
41. Ford R. Bryan, *Friends, Families and Forays*, pp. 68–69.
42. "200 Editors See New Ford Models," *Boston Globe*, October 25, 1938.
43. Author interview with Gregorie.
44. Dominguez, *Edsel Ford and E. T. Gregorie*, p. 156.
45. Edsel Ford memo to Lincoln (production manager), Accession 6, box 2387, Henry Ford Museum and Library.

CHAPTER TWENTY-TWO: BUILDING UP TO WAR

1. Robert Lacey, *Ford: The Men and the Machine* (Boston: Little, Brown, 1986), p. 390.
2. Keith Sward, *The Legend of Henry Ford* (New York: Rinehart, 1948), pp. 450–55.
3. Neil Baldwin, *Henry Ford and the Jews* (New York: Public Affairs, 2001), pp. 281–92.
4. *Research Findings About Ford-Werke Under the Nazi Regime* (Dearborn, Mich.: Ford Motor Company, 2001), p. 27.
5. Ken Silverstein, "Ford and the Fuehrer," *The Nation*, January 24, 2000, pp. 11–16.
6. "Ford Favors Admitting Jewish Refugees," *Flint Journal*, [c. December 3, 1938], clipping file, Henry Ford Museum and Library, Dearborn, Michigan.
7. William and Marjorie McNairn, *Quotations from the Unusual Henry Ford* (Norwalk, Calif.: Stockton Trade Press, 1978), p. 106.
8. Wayne Cole, *Roosevelt and the Isolationists* (Lincoln: University of Nebraska Press, 1983), pp. 310–528.
9. A. Scott Berg, *Lindbergh* (New York: Putnam, 1998), pp. 411–43.
10. Wayne S. Cole, *Charles A. Lindbergh and the Battle Against American Intervention in World War II* (New York: Harcourt Brace Jovanovich, 1974), p. 119.
11. Allan Nevins and Frank Ernest Hill, *Ford*, vol. 3, *Decline and Rebirth, 1933–1962* (New York: Charles Scribner's Sons, 1963), p. 181.
12. "Battle of Detroit," *Time*, March 23, 1942, p. 13.
13. Wayne S. Cole, *America First* (Madison, Wis.: University of Wisconsin Press, 1953), pp. 132–33.
14. Lacey, *Ford: The Men and the Machine*, pp. 384–85.

15. Edward Cray, *Chrome Colossus: General Motors and Its Times* (New York: McGraw-Hill, 1980), p. 315.
16. Norman Beasley, *Knudsen: A Biography* (New York: Whittlesey House, 1947), p. 230.
17. Ibid., p. 235.
18. Frank Cormier and William J. Eaton, *Reuther* (Englewood Cliffs, N.J.: Prentice-Hall, 1970), p. 191.
19. Beasley, *Knudsen,* p. 264.
20. "Willow Run Airplane Plant," Accession 435, box 46, folder: Willow Run Ceremony, p. 5, Henry Ford Museum and Library.
21. Mira Wilkins and Frank Ernest Hill, *American Business Abroad: Ford on Six Continents* (Detroit: Wayne State University Press, 1964), pp. 316–17.
22. Timothy O'Callaghan, letter to the author, September 2, 2002.
23. Nelson Lichtenstein, *The Most Dangerous Man in Detroit: Walter Reuther and the Fate of American Labor* (New York: Basic Books, 1995), p. 162.
24. Ibid., pp. 162–78.
25. Clinton B. F. Macauley, "Where the Auto-Makers Stand," *Aviation,* November 1941, p. 150.
26. Nevins and Hill, *Decline and Rebirth,* p. 178.
27. "Sorensen of the Rouge," *Fortune,* April 1942, p. 114.
28. "Battle of Detroit," p. 12.
29. Author interview with Philip Caldwell, October 2002, Stamford, Connecticut.
30. "The Airplane to Be Built" (typescript), Accession 435, box 40, folder: Willow Run Bomber Plant, Henry Ford Museum and Library; also, "28 Tons of Aerial Might," publicity material, Accession 629, box A1, folder: Defense—Willow Run Plant, p. 2, ibid.
31. Charles E. Sorensen with Samuel T. Williamson, *My Forty Years with Ford* (New York: W.W. Norton, 1956), pp. 279–86.
32. Don Sherman, "Willow Run," *Air and Space,* August–September 1992, p. 77.
33. "Ford Speeds Plan to Build Army Bombers," press release, Accession 629, box A1, folder: Defense—Willow Run Plant, Henry Ford Museum and Library.
34. F. W. Loskowske, "Reminiscences" (oral history project), pp. 93–94, Henry Ford Museum and Library.
35. Sherman, "Willow Run," p. 77.
36. "Ford's Warbird Hatchery!," *Detroit Free Press,* March 5, 1941, p. 11.
37. Cray, *Chrome Colossus,* p. 317.
38. "Ford to Build Bombers in This Huge $47,000,000 Plant," press release with timeline, Accession 629, box A1, folder: Defense—Willow Run Plant, Henry Ford Museum and Library.
39. Raymond Moley, "Ford Does It Again," *Newsweek,* May 25, 1942.
40. "60 Firms Share Job of Tooling Ford Bomber Plant," press release, Accession 629, box A1, folder: Defense—Willow Run Plant, Henry Ford Museum and Library.
41. Radio broadcast (transcript), Accession 285, box 2673—Willow Run General 1943, p. 1, ibid.
42. "Detroit's War Load," *Business Week,* January 17, 1942, pp. 16–20.
43. "Gandhi's Spinning Wheel," ACC-292147, Henry Ford Museum and Library.
44. "India: Background of Ford Participation in Indian Market," AR-65-1 5:1, ibid.; also Wilkins and Hill, *American Business Abroad,* p. 300.
45. Henry Ford to Mahatma Gandhi, July 25, 1941, ACC-292147, Henry Ford Museum and Library.
46. T. A. Raman, "Story of the Spinning Wheel: From Mahatma Gandhi to Henry Ford" (memo for the record), December 12, 1942, ACC-292147, ibid.
47. Ibid.
48. Ibid.; also see Mahatma Gandhi to Henry Ford, April 16, 1942, ACC-191147, Henry Ford Museum and Library.
49. E. N. Hurley to Henry Ford, June 12, 1942, Accession 1630, box 2, folder 59, ibid.
50. Thomas Edison to E. N. Hurley Sr., [c. 1916], Accession 1630, box 2, folder 59, ibid.

CHAPTER TWENTY-THREE: WILLOW RUN AND THE B-24 LIBERATORS

1. Hickman Powell, "Look Out, Hitler, Here Comes the Flood!" *Popular Science,* May 1943, p. 78.
2. Robert Lacey, *Ford: The Men and the Machine* (Boston: Little, Brown, 1986), pp. 392–93.

3. Powell, "Look Out, Hitler," p. 78.
4. David L. Lewis, *The Public Image of Henry Ford: An American Folk Hero and Company* (Detroit: Wayne State University Press, 1976), p. 350.
5. "War Is Horsepower," *Fortune,* November 1941, p. 66.
6. William Knudsen (Willow Run) clipping file, Henry Ford Museum and Library.
7. Mike Smith and Thomas Featherstone, *Labor in Detroit* (Chicago: Arcadia Publishing, 2001), p. 8.
8. *Detroit Free Press,* February 1, 1942.
9. Charles C. LaCroix, "Ford and the War Effort" (fifty-five unpublished volumes), Accession 435, shelf locations 108-E1, 108-F2, and 108-F4, Henry Ford Museum and Library.
10. *New York Times,* December 5, 1942.
11. Clem Davis, "Reminiscences" (oral history project), pp. 43–44, Henry Ford Museum and Library, Dearborn, Michigan.
12. Anthony Harff, "Reminiscences," p. 72.
13. Ibid., p. 71.
14. Clarence Gabrielson to Henry Ford, October 23, 1942, Accession 285, box 2491, folder: Willow Run—General, Henry Ford Museum and Library.
15. Charles C. LaCroix, "Ford and the War Effort."
16. Charles Sorensen, "Reminiscences," p. 194; also p. 138.
17. David Kennedy, *Freedom from Fear: The American People in Depression and War, 1929–1945* (New York: Oxford University Press, 1999), p. 653.
18. Allan Nevins and Frank Ernest Hill, *Ford,* vol. 3, *Decline and Rebirth: 1933–1962* (New York: Charles Scribner's Sons 1963), pp. 197–251.
19. Charles A. Lindbergh, *The Wartime Journals of Charles A. Lindbergh* (New York: Harcourt Brace, 1970), p. 613.
20. A. Scott Berg, *Lindbergh* (New York: Putnam, 1998), p. 440.
21. Ibid.
22. Wayne S. Cole, *Roosevelt and the Isolationists, 1932–45* (Lincoln, Neb.: University of Nebraska Press, 1983), p. 513.
23. *Ford News,* October 1942, p. 258.
24. Sorensen, "Reminiscences," p. 45.
25. Ford File, Franklin D. Roosevelt Library, Hyde Park, New York.
26. "Speeding the Auto Conversion," *Business Week,* January 31, 1942, p. 15.
27. Dr. G. Bronn, memo to the author, September 24, 2002.
28. H. S. Abelwhite, "Reminiscences" (oral history project), p. 63, Henry Ford Museum and Library, Dearborn, Michigan.
29. James Swinehart, "Willow Run," *Detroit News,* May 8–9, 1942.
30. Logan Miller, "Reminiscences," p. 59.
31. Sorensen,"Reminiscences," p. 147.
32. Berg, *Lindbergh,* pp. 446–47.
33. Miller, "Reminiscences," p. 65.
34. L. E. Briggs, "Reminiscences," p. 65.
35. Charles Voorhess, "Reminiscences," p. 28.
36. Harff, "Reminiscences," pp. 73–74.
37. Briggs, "Reminiscences," p. 62.
38. Sorensen, "Reminiscences," pp. 201–4.
39. Voorhess, "Reminiscences," p. 188.
40. Mrs. Stanley Ruddiman, "Reminiscences," p. 90.
41. "Housing Muddle," *Business Week,* March 13, 1943, p. 75.
42. Charles E. Sorensen with Samuel T. Williamson, *My Forty Years with Ford* (New York: W.W. Norton, 1956), pp. 281–300.
43. Miller, "Reminiscences," pp. 70–71.
44. Charles E. Sorensen with Samuel T. Williamson, *My Forty Years with Ford* (New York: W.W. Norton, 1956), p. 305.
45. Harff, "Reminiscences," p. 74.
46. "All Quiet on the River Rouge," *Business Week,* June 24, 1944, p. 21.

47. Radio broadcast (typescript), Accession 285, box 2673, folder: Willow Run General—1943, Henry Ford Museum and Library.
48. Dan Richards, "Bomber Plant Tales to Roll," *Ann Arbor News,* July 26, 1972.
49. "Yellow Easy," Willow Run Plant Data, vol. 3, no. 8, Accession 285, box 2830, folder: Willow Run Plant Data, Henry Ford Museum and Library.
50. David L. Lewis, *Ford Country* (Sidney, Ohio: Amos Press, 1999), pp. 214–215.
51. The Curtiss-Wright report is part of LaCroix, "Ford and the War Effort."
52. Stephen E. Ambrose, *Wild Blue: The Men and Boys Who Flew the B-24s over Germany* (New York: Simon & Schuster, 2001), pp. 21–27.
53. Michael Sherry, *The Rise of American Air Power: The Creation of Armageddon* (New Haven: Yale University Press, 1987), p. 135.
54. Tony Marcano, "Famed Riveter in War Effort, Rose Monroe Dies at 77," *New York Times,* June 2, 1997.
55. "Rockwell's Rosie the Riveter Painting Sold for $4.9 Million," Associated Press, May 22, 2002; also Sothebys.com (April 2002).
56. Marcano, "Rose Monroe."
57. Author interview with Vicki Jarvis, May 2002.
58. Ibid.
59. Tom Brokaw, *The Greatest Generation* (New York: Random House, 1998), pp. 96–97.
60. Dave Elsila, "Little People with Big Jobs," *Solidarity,* October 1997.
61. Douglas Brinkley, *American Heritage History of the United States* (New York: Viking, 1998), pp. 442–43.
62. *Detroit News,* October 14, 1943.
63. August Meier and Elliott Rudwick, *Black Detroit and the Rise of the U.A.W.* (New York: Oxford University Press, 1979), p. 14.
64. I. F. Stone, "Behind the Ford Contract," *PM,* December 14, 1940.
65. Herbert R. Rifkind, "The Jeep—Its Development and Procurement Under the Quartermaster Corps, 1940–1942" (typescript), p. 106, Historical Section, Office of the Quartermaster General, Washington, D.C.
66. Major E. P. Hogan, "The Jeep in Action," *Army Ordnance,* September–October 1944, p. 271.
67. Robert Sherrod, *Tarawa: The Story of a Battle* (New York: Bantam Books, 1993), p. 71.
68. Wesley Frank Craven and James Lea Cate, eds., *The Army Air Forces in World War II,* vol. 6 (Chicago: University of Chicago Press, 1955), p. 329.
69. Henry Ford II, Press release on the retirement of Mead Bricker, May 4, 1950, Ford Motor Company Archives, Dearborn, Michigan.
70. Allan Nevins and Frank Ernest Hill, *Ford,* vol. 3, *Decline and Rebirth, 1933–1962* (New York: Charles Scribner's Sons, 1963), p. 226.
71. Lewis, *The Public Image of Henry Ford,* p. 362.
72. Thomas E. Bonsall, *The Lincoln Motorcar: The Complete History of an American Classic* (Baltimore: Stony Run Press, 1980), p. 116.
73. "Notice of Termination," April 27, 1945, Willow Run Plant Data, vol. 3, no. 16, Accession 285, box 2830, folder: Willow Run Plant Data, Henry Ford Museum and Library.
74. Timothy J. O'Callaghan, *The Aviation Legacy of Henry and Edsel Ford* (Ann Arbor, Mich.: Proctor Publications, 2000), pp. 175–76.
75. Stephen B. Adams, *Mr. Kaiser Goes to Washington: The Rise of a Government Entrepreneur* (Chapel Hill, N.C.: University of North Carolina Press, 1997), p. 217.

CHAPTER TWENTY-FOUR: PEACEFUL REVOLUTION

1. Gilbert Burck, "Henry Ford II," *Life,* October 1, 1945, p. 109.
2. Ford R. Bryan, *Clara: Mrs. Henry Ford* (Dearborn, Mich.: Ford Books, 2001), p. 248.
3. Henry Ford II, interviews with David L. Lewis, April 14, 1980; March 3, 1982; Ford Motor Company Archives, Dearborn, Michigan.
4. Walter Hayes, *Henry: A Life of Henry Ford II* (New York: Grove Weidenfeld, 1990), p. 7.
5. "Young Henry Takes a Risk," *Time,* February 4, 1946, p. 76.
6. Hayes, *Henry: A Life of Henry Ford II,* p. 9.

7. Ibid., p. 7.
8. "Who's News," *Newark* [N.J.] *News,* August 16, 1943, in clipbook 31, Henry Ford Museum and Library.
9. Allan Nevins and Frank Ernest Hill, *Ford,* vol. 3, *Decline and Rebirth, 1933–1962* (New York: Charles Scribner's Sons, 1963) p. 184.
10. Burck, "Henry Ford II," pp. 109–11.
11. Ibid., pp. 114–17; and Nevins and Hill, *Decline and Rebirth,* p. 184.
12. A. J. Lepine, "Reminiscences" (oral history project), p. 84, Henry Ford Museum and Library.
13. Burck, "Henry Ford II," p. 117.
14. Burck, "Henry Ford II," p. 118.
15. Hayes: *Henry: A Life of Henry Ford II,* p. 13.
16. Charles E. Sorensen with Samuel T. Williamson, *My Forty Years with Ford* (New York: W.W. Norton, 1956), p. 306.
17. Harry Bennett, *We Never Called Him Henry* (New York: Fawcett, 1951), pp. 170–80.
18. Charles Voorhess, "Reminiscences," p. 190.
19. Ibid., p. 189.
20. Rufus Wilson, "Reminiscences," p. 35.
21. Jon Pepper, "Ford Tapes," *Detroit News,* September 19, 1994, p. 1.
22. Booten Herndon, *Ford: The Men and Their Times* (New York: Weybright and Talley, 1969), p. 182.
23. André Fontaine, "Revolution on the Rouge," *Collier's,* November 15, 1947, p. 58.
24. Nevins and Hill, *Decline and Rebirth,* p. 294.
25. "Ford Becomes a Matriarchy," *Business Week,* April 26, 1947, pp. 93–94.
26. Jon Pepper, "'Scared' Ford Sought to Control Company," *Detroit News,* September 19, 1994.
27. "Henry Ford Resigns," *Detroit Times,* September 22, 1945, p. 1.
28. Bennett, *We Never Called Him Henry,* pp. 178–80.
29. Pepper, "'Scared' Ford Sought to Control Company."
30. Harry Bennett, *We Never Called Him Henry,* p. 179.
31. "The Little Giant Goes," *Time,* October 8, 1945, p. 81.
32. Emil Zoerlein, "Reminiscences," vol. 2, p. 239.
33. "Ford President Brings More Than a Name to His Job," *Business Week,* September 29, 1945, p. 18.
34. Bob Finlay, "Men of Achievement," *Forbes,* December 1, 1947, p. 12.
35. "Production During the Military Operation, 10.3," *Research Findings About Ford-Werke Under the Nazi Regime* (Dearborn, Mich.: Ford Motor Company, 2001), p. 96.
36. David Burgess-Wise, *Complete Catalogue of Ford Cars in Britain* (Devon, England: Bay View Books, 1991), p. 18.
37. Lawrence J. White, *The Automobile Industry Since 1945* (Cambridge. Mass.: Harvard University, 1971), p. 12.
38. Genat, *The American Dealership* (Osceola, Wis.: MBI Publishing, 1999), p. 27.
39. "War Tasks Are Seen Hitting Auto Output Plans," *Journal of Commerce,* December 7, 1944, Accession 23, box 14, folder: Henry Ford II press conference December 6, 1944, clippings, Henry Ford Museum and Library.
40. Burck, "Henry Ford II," p. 118.
41. Genat, *The American Dealership,* pp. 27–28.
42. Henry Miller, *The Air-Conditioned Nightmare* (New York: New Directions, 1970), pp. 41–42.
43. "Young Henry Takes a Risk," p. 76.
44. "Ford Runs Ford," *Business Week,* October 6, 1945.
45. Logan Miller, "Reminiscences," p. 75.
46. Harold Hicks, "Reminiscences," p. 211.
47. Burck, "Henry Ford II," p. 109.
48. Anthony Harff, "Reminiscences," p. 83.
49. Ford R. Bryan, "My Ten Years at River Rouge" (typescript), pp. 16–17, Henry Ford Museum and Library.
50. Norman Beasley, "'Young Henry' Is on His Own," *Redbook,* June 1946, p. 108.
51. David Halberstam, *The Best and the Brightest* (New York: Random House, 1972), pp. 226–27.
52. John A. Bryne, *The Whiz Kids* (New York: Doubleday, 1993), p. 82.

53. Ibid., p. 104.
54. Author interview with Philip Caldwell, October 2002, Stamford, Connecticut.
55. Halberstam, *The Best and the Brightest,* p. 229.
56. J. Mel Hickerson, *Ernie Breech* (New York: Meredith Press, 1968), p. 37.
57. Ibid.
58. Alfred P. Sloan Jr., *My Years with General Motors,* eds. John McDonald and Catharine Stevens (Garden City, N.Y.: Doubleday, 1964), p. 367.
59. Hickerson, *Ernie Breech,* p. 130.
60. Henry Ford II, interviews.

CHAPTER TWENTY-FIVE: DEATH IN DEARBORN

1. Robert Rankin, "Reminiscences" (oral history project), pp. 12–15, Henry Ford Museum and Library, Dearborn, Michigan.
2. Ibid., p. 35.
3. Walter Hayes, *Henry: A Life of Henry Ford II* (New York: Grove Weidenfeld, 1990), pp. 13–15.
4. Clara Snow, "Reminiscences," pp. 20–21.
5. Rankin, "Reminiscences," p. 36.
6. *Detroit Free Press,* May 28, 1944.
7. Ford R. Bryan, *Henry's Lieutenants* (Detroit: Wayne State University Press, 1993), p. 89.
8. Carol Gelderman, *Henry Ford: The Wayward Capitalist* (New York: Dial, 1981), p. 288.
9. Author interview with Jack Telnack, September 2002.
10. Ford R. Bryan, *Friends, Families and Forays: Scenes from the Life and Times of Henry Ford* (Dearborn, Mich.: Ford Books, 2002), pp. 317–25.
11. Ernest G. Liebold, "Reminiscences," pp. 135–39.
12. James Newton, *Uncommon Friends: Life with Thomas Edison, Henry Ford, Harvey Firestone, Alexis Carrel, and Charles Lindbergh* (San Diego: Harcourt Brace Jovanovich, 1987), p. 98.
13. Ibid., p. 99.
14. Ibid., pp. 99–102.
15. Henry Ford, "The Only Real Security: An Interview with Samuel Crowther," *Saturday Evening Post,* February 1, 1936.
16. David L. Lewis, "Henry Ford: Legend and Legacy," *The Ford Legend,* Spring 1999, p. 8.
17. Harry Bennett, *We Never Called Him Henry* (New York: Fawcett, 1951), p. 180.
18. Snow, "Reminiscences," p. 23.
19. Frank Morris, "Henry Ford Dies Suddenly in Dearborn at 83," *Detroit Times,* April 8, 1947, p. 2.
20. Peter Collier and David Horowitz, *The Fords: An American Epic* (New York: Summit Books, 1987), pp. 225–26.
21. Rankin, "Reminiscences," p. 66.
22. Charles Voorhess, "Reminiscences," vol. 2, p. 191.
23. John McIntyre, "Reminiscences," p. 33.
24. Collier and Horowitz, *The Fords: An American Epic,* p. 226.
25. "Ford Hailed by President," *Detroit News,* April 9, 1947, p. 4.
26. Don Lochbiler, "Body Lies in State at Village," *Detroit News,* April 9, 1947, p. 1.
27. Ibid.
28. "Thousands File Past Bier . . ." *Detroit News,* April 9, 1947, p. 4.
29. "The Father of the Automobile Dies," *Life,* April 21, 1947, pp. 33–38.
30. Author interview with Robert McNamara, June 2002, Washington, D.C.
31. Richard S. Tedlow, *Giants of Industry: Seven Business Innovators and the Empires They Built* (New York: Harper Business, 2001), p. 177.
32. *Time,* April 21, 1947, p. 28.
33. Arthur Pound, "The Ford Myth," *Atlantic Monthly,* January 1924, p. 41.
34. John Kenneth Galbraith, *The Liberal Hour* (Boston: Houghton Mifflin, 1960), pp. 141–49.
35. Ibid.
36. Ibid.
37. *Detroit News,* November 10, 1911.
38. Ibid., p. 57.

39. Ibid., p. 28.
40. Henry Ford "Celebrity" File, Photographic Department, Ford Motor Company, Dearborn, Michigan.
41. Henry Ford to Thomas Edison, June 27, 1929, Accession 1630, box 3, folder 36, Henry Ford Museum and Library.
42. Author interview with Philip Caldwell, October 2002, Stamford, Connecticut.
43. *Ford News,* February 1937, p. 1.

CHAPTER TWENTY-SIX: HUMAN ENGINEERING

1. Henry Ford II, interviews with David Lewis, April 14, 1980; March 3, 1982; Ford Motor Company Archives, Dearborn, Michigan.
2. J. Mel Hickerson, *Ernie Breech* (New York: Meredith Press, 1968), p. 130.
3. Ernest Breech, "Decentralization—What It Is and How It Works," *The Decentralization Story* (company publication), Accession 881, box 5, folder: FMC Organization and Administration—Reorganization, p. 2, Henry Ford Museum and Library.
4. L. E. Briggs, "Reminiscences" (oral history project), p. 66, Henry Ford Museum and Library, Dearborn, Michigan.
5. Ibid., p. 68.
6. Author interview with John Kenneth Galbraith, September 2002, Cambridge, Massachusetts.
7. Henry Ford II, interview with David Lewis.
8. Author interview with Robert McNamara, June 2002, Washington, D.C.
9. Griffith Borgeson, "Lincoln Today," *Motor Trend,* July 1952, pp. 48–53.
10. "The Lincoln Continental," *Fortune,* March 1952, p. 99.
11. "Lincoln-Mercury Moves Up," *Fortune,* March 1952, p. 97.
12. "Ford Reshapes His Empire," *Business Week,* August 27, 1949, p. 20.
13. Mira Wilkins and Frank Ernest Hill, *American Business Abroad: Ford on Six Continents* (Detroit: Wayne State University Press, 1964), p. 362.
14. Peter F. Drucker, *Adventures of a Bystander* (New York: Harper & Row, 1979), p. 292.
15. Ibid.
16. André Fontaine, "Revolution on the Rouge," *Collier's,* November 15, 1947, p. 20.
17. "The Rebirth of Ford," *Fortune,* May 1947, p. 82.
18. Peter Collier and David Horowitz, *The Fords: An American Epic* (New York: Summit Books, 1987), pp. 195–320.
19. "Goodwill Builders," *Business Week,* July 30, 1949, p. 58.
20. Author interview with Peter Pestillo, September 2002, Dearborn, Michigan.
21. Nelson Lichtenstein, *The Most Dangerous Man in the World: Walter Reuther and the Fate of American Labor* (New York: Basic Books, 1995), pp. 271–72.
22. Ibid.
23. Frank Cormier and William J. Eaton, *Reuther* (Englewood Cliffs, N.J.: Prentice-Hall, 1970), p. 275.
24. Henry Ford II, "The Challenge of Human Engineering," speech, January 9, 1946 (and brochure), Accession 536, box 1, Henry Ford II—speeches, Henry Ford Museum and Library.
25. "Turning Point," *Fortune,* April 1949, p. 189.
26. Cormier and Eaton, *Reuther,* p. 295.
27. "Ford Peace—But Will It Last?," *Business Week,* June 4, 1949, p. 92.
28. "Ford Plan: Pattern on Pensions?," *U.S. News & World Report,* October 7, 1949, p. 42.
29. "Plant Transfers Irk Unions," *Business Week,* December 1, 1951, p. 36.
30. Breech, "Decentralization—What It Is and How It Works," p. 1.
31. "'Human Engineering' Program Pays Off for Ford," *Business Week,* October 30, 1948, pp. 88–95.
32. "Turning Point," p. 191.
33. David Halberstam, *The Reckoning* (New York: William Morrow, 1986), p. 202.
34. John A. Gunnell, *Fifty-five Years of Mercury: The Complete History of the Big "M"* (Iola, Wis.: Krause Publications, 1994), p. 56.

35. William L. O'Neil, *American High: The Years of Confidence, 1945–1960* (New York: Free Press, 1986), p. 30.
36. Lorin Sorensen, *Ford's Golden Fifties* (St. Helena, Calif.: Silverado Publishing, 1997), p. 11.
37. Ibid., pp. 12–13.
38. "Ford Puts on a Big Show," *Business Week,* June 19, 1948, p. 54.
39. Strother MacMinn, "Fifties Finest," *Automobile Quarterly* 25, no. 1 (1987), p. 77.
40. Christopher Finch, *Highways to Heaven: The Auto Biography of America* (New York: HarperCollins, 1992), pp. 185–87.
41. Jack Kerouac, unpublished journal, 1948–1949, Berg Collection, New York Public Library, New York.
42. Author interview with Chuck Berry, May 2001, St. Louis, Missouri.
43. Chuck Berry, *Autobiography* (New York: Harmony Books, 1987), pp. 97–103.
44. Michael Lyndon, *Folk Rock,* (New York: Delta, 1971), p. 11.
45. Warren Belasco, "Motivation, with Chuck Berry and Fredrick Jackson Turner" in David L. Lewis and Laurence Goldstein, eds., *The Automobile and American Culture* (Ann Arbor, Mich.: University of Michigan Press, 1980), pp. 262–70.
46. United Foundation Campaign Headquarters, press release, October 24, 1949, Ford Motor Company Archives, Dearborn, Michigan.
47. "Detroit's Torch Lights the Way," *Life,* November 14, 1949, p. 73.
48. "U.S. Spotlight on City as Torch Drive Opens," *Detroit Free Press,* October 19, 1949, p. 1.
49. *Newsweek,* November 21, 1949, p. 25.
50. *Rouge News,* August 26, 1949.

CHAPTER TWENTY-SEVEN: FIFTY YEARS OLD AND STILL GROWING UP

1. "What Ford Is Getting for $1.4 Billion," *Business Week,* October 17, 1953, p. 134.
2. Studs Terkel, *"The Good War": An Oral History of World War Two* (New York: Pantheon, 1984), p. 573.
3. "Impact of the War on Communications," *Research Findings About Ford-Werke Under the Nazi Regime* (Dearborn, Mich.: Ford Motor Company, 2001), pp. 87, 92.
4. Sir Percival Perry, report, September 19, 1946, AR-98-213541, box 131, Henry Ford Museum and Library, Dearborn, Michigan.
5. Ken Silverstein, "Ford and the Fuehrer," *Nation,* January 24, 2000, p. 16.
6. "Financial Overview of Ford-Werke," *Research Findings About Ford-Werke,* pp. 67–69.
7. Silverstein, "Ford and the Fuehrer," pp. 11–16.
8. "Simon Reich Commentary," *Research Findings About Ford-Werke,* p. 7.
9. Letter to author from Elizabeth Adkins, Ford Motor Company archivist, January 7, 2003.
10. Alfred P. Sloan Jr., *My Years with General Motors,* ed. John McDonald with Catharine Stevens (Garden City, N.Y.: Doubleday, 1964), p. 332.
11. Heinrich Albert, to Edsel Ford, July 1, 1941, Accession 6, box 329, subject file 1941, FMC Subsidiary—Cologne, Henry Ford Museum and Library.
12. "Ford-Werke A/G Cologne" (report), June 12, 1946, Accession 880, box 7, postwar, ibid.
13. Mira Wilkins and Frank Ernest Hill, *American Business Abroad: Ford on Six Continents* (Detroit: Wayne State University Press, 1964), p. 367.
14. "End-of-War and Postwar Military Government Supervision," *Research Findings About Ford-Werke,* p. 102.
15. Phil Patton, *Bug: The Strange Mutations of the World's Most Famous Automobile* (New York: Simon & Schuster, 2002), p. 82.
16. Wilkins and Hill, *American Business Abroad,* p. 343.
17. David Burgess-Wise, *Complete Catalogue of Ford Cars in Britain* (Devon, England: Bay View Books, 1991), p. 13.
18. R. Perry Zavitz, *Monarch Meteor* (Bothwell, Ont.: Quad Printing, 1993), p. 7.
19. "Ford of Canada Spreads Out," *Business Week,* May 16, 1953, p. 92.
20. William McGinnis, "Reminiscences" (oral history project), February 17, 1989, pp. 50–51, Ford Motor Company Archives, Dearborn, Michigan.

21. J. Mel Nickerson, *Ernie Breech* (New York: Meredith Press, 1968), pp. 145–46.
22. Sloan, *My Years with General Motors,* p. 318.
23. Henry Ford II, interview with David Lewis, March 3, 1982, p. 32, Henry Ford Museum and Library.
24. Ford R. Bryan, *Friends, Families and Forays: Scenes from the Life and Times of Henry Ford* (Dearborn, Mich.: Ford Books, 2002), p. 270.
25. Robert L. Heilbroner, "The Fabulous Ford Foundation," *Harper's,* December 1951, p. 27.
26. "Ford Foundation," *Fortune,* December 1951, p. 116.
27. Heilbroner, "The Fabulous Ford Foundation," p. 30.
28. Paul F. Douglas, *Six upon the World* (Boston: Little, Brown, 1954), p. 44.
29. "Paul G. Hoffman Is Dead at 83," *New York Times,* October 9, 1974, p. 1.
30. Heilbroner, "The Fabulous Ford Foundation," p. 26.
31. Alan R. Raucher, *Paul G. Hoffman: Architect of Foreign Aid* (Lexington, Ky.: University Press of Kentucky, 1985), p. 83.
32. John A. Gunnell, *Fifty-five Years of Mercury* (Iola, Wis.: Krause Publications, 1994), p. 56.
33. Lorin Sorensen, *Ford's Golden Fifties* (St. Helena, Calif.: Silverado Publishing, 1997), p. 37, citing "1950 Presidential Lincoln," *Lincoln-Mercury News Bureau,* June 12, 1950.
34. "Lincoln-Mercury Moves Up," *Fortune,* March 1952, p. 178.
35. Maurice Hendry, *Lincoln: America's Car of State* (New York: Ballantine, 1971), p. 111.
36. *Ford at Fifty* (New York: Simon & Schuster, 1953), p. 90.
37. Henry Ford II, address to National Security Industrial Association, Rotunda Theater, May 17, 1951, Accession 536, box Ford, Henry II (speeches), Henry Ford Museum and Library.
38. *Ford at Fifty,* p. 91.
39. Griffin Farielle, *Red Scare: Memories of the American Inquisition* (New York: W.W. Norton, 1995), p. 325.
40. Henry Ford II, address, Day with Ford Engineers, Dearborn, Michigan, January 10, 1952, Accession 536, box Ford, Henry II (press conferences), Henry Ford Museum and Library.
41. "Ford Looks to Outsell Chevrolet," *Business Week,* June 13, 1953, p. 102.
42. Sorensen, *Ford's Golden Fifties,* p. 69.
43. The Rotunda File, Ford Motor Company Archives, Dearborn, Michigan.
44. Michael Parris, *Fords of the Fifties* (Tucson, Ariz.: California Bill's, 2000), p. 107.
45. "The Ford Illustrations of Norman Rockwell," *Life,* January–February 1972; and Mary Moline, comp., *The Best of Ford* (Van Nuys, Calif.: Rumbleseat Press, 1973), pp. 284–91.
46. Walter Hopps, *Robert Rauschenberg: The Early 1950s* (Houston: The Menil Collection and Houston Fine Arts Press, 1991), pp. 3–17.

CHAPTER TWENTY-EIGHT: GRAND THUNDERBIRDS, TOUGH TRUCKS, AND THE EDSEL FLOP

1. Albert Bochroch, "Ferrari in America," in *Ferrari: The Man, the Machines,* ed. Stan Grayson (Princeton, N.J.: Princeton Publishing, 1975), pp. 179–82.
2. *Corvette: Thirty Years of Great Advertising* (Princeton, N.J.: Princeton Publishing, 1983), p. 16.
3. "The Rouge and the Black," *Time,* May 18, 1953, pp. 102–6.
4. Franklin Q. Hershey, "Glory Days! My 35 Years as an Automobile Designer," *Automobile Quarterly* 27, no. 1 (1989), p. 31.
5. John F. Katz, *Soaring Spirit* (Kutztown, Pa.: Automobile Quarterly, 1989), p. 10.
6. Ford Product Planning Committee, letter of February 9, 1953, cited in Alan Tast, *Thunderbird 1955–1966* (Osceola, Wis.: Motorbooks International, 1996), p. 14.
7. "Ford Thunderbird: An American Legend" (typescript), p. 4, Henry Ford Museum and Library, Dearborn, Michigan.
8. Katz, *Soaring Spirit,* p. 11.
9. Richard M. Langworth, *The Complete Book of Corvette* (Skokie, Ill.: Publications International Ltd., 1987), p. 45.
10. "Background Data on Thunderbird," September 23, 1954, Henry Ford Museum and Library.
11. *The Corvette Black Book* (Powell, Ohio: Michael Bruce Associates, 1984).
12. Karl Ludvigsen, "The Short, Happy Flight of the Early Bird," *Automobile Quarterly* 9, no. 1 (Fall 1970), p. 94.

13. "1964 Thunderbird," www.automotivemileposts.com.
14. Roger Ebert, "American Graffiti," www.univie.ac.atanglistik/easyrider/data/American.
15. Charlotte W. Craig and Ted Evanoff, "New T-Bird's Takeoff Cheered," *Detroit Free Press,* January 4, 1999.
16. Paul A. Eisenstein, "2002 Ford Thunderbird: And We'll Have Fun, Fun, Fun," May 28, 2001, www.thecarconnection.com.
17. Eric Larrabee, "The Edsel and How It Got That Way," *Harper's,* September 1957, p. 71.
18. Joyce Carol Oates, *We Were the Mulvaneys* (New York: Plume, 1997), p. 138.
19. John A. Gunnell, ed., *Standard Catalogue of American Light-Duty Trucks* (Iola, Wis.: Krause Publications, 1993), p. 308.
20. Don Bunn, *Classic Ford F-Series Pickup Trucks, 1948–1956* (Osceola, Wis.: MBI, 1998), p. 65.
21. "Benson Ford Dies," *Detroit News,* July 27, 1978.
22. Maurice D. Hendry, *Lincoln: America's Car of State* (New York: Ballantine, 1971), pp. 113–14.
23. Tim Howley, "Quality, Performance and Style," *Automobile Quarterly* 17, no. 2 (Spring 1979), p. 200.
24. "The Rouge and the Black," p. 102.
25. Hendry, *Lincoln: America's Car of State,* p. 119.
26. "Here's the Ford Plan to Sell Stock," *U.S. News & World Report,* March 18, 1955, p. 29.
27. "When Ford Takes in Partners," *U.S. News & World Report,* November 18, 1955, p. 44.
28. "Here's the Ford Plan to Sell Stock," p. 30.
29. "Ford Goes into New Era with Stock Sale in 1956," *Business Week,* November 12, 1955, p. 168.
30. "The Ford Family Sells," *Time,* November 14, 1955, p. 104.
31. John Brooks, "This Way to Sign Up for Ford, Boys!," *The New Yorker,* February 11, 1956, p. 43.
32. "History's Biggest Issue," *Life,* January 30, 1956, pp. 37–38.
33. "The Fading of a Dream," *Business Week,* January 18, 1958, p. 67.
34. "Behind the Scenes," *Newsweek,* January 2, 1956, p. 47.
35. Brooks, "This Way to Sign Up for Ford, Boys!," p. 40.
36. "A Comeback for Ford," *Business Week,* January 26, 1957, p. 116.
37. Richard M. Langworth, "Continental Mark II," *Automobile Quarterly* 12, no. 1 (Spring 1974), p. 98.
38. Ibid., p. 102.
39. Ibid.
40. "Selling Like Hotcakes," *Business Week,* November 26, 1955, pp. 28–30.
41. Richard Austin Smith, "The Solid Gold Continental," *Fortune,* December 1955, p. 134.
42. "How to Build a Dealer Empire," *Business Week,* June 22, 1957, p. 52.
43. Larrabee, "The Edsel and How It Got That Way," p. 72.
44. John Brooks, "The Edsel," *The New Yorker,* November 26, 1960, p. 76.
45. David Wallace, "Naming the Edsel," *Automobile Quarterly* 13, no. 2 (Spring 1975), p. 184.
46. Ibid., p. 186.
47. Thomas E. Bonsall, *Disaster in Dearborn: The Story of the Edsel* (Stanford, Calif.: Stanford University Press, 2002), p. 115.
48. Wallace, "Naming the Edsel," p. 190.
49. Ibid.
50. Bonsall, *Disaster in Dearborn,* pp. 116–22.
51. John Perrault, "The Edsel Generation and the Generation Gap," *Ford Buyer's Guide* (1989), p. 94.
52. Bonsall, *Disaster in Dearborn,* p. 1.
53. Ibid., p. 190.
54. Brooks, "The Edsel," p. 224.
55. Roy Brown, "Reminiscences," Ford Motor Company Archives.
56. Edsel Owners Club, Inc., file, Ford Motor Company Archives, Dearborn, Michigan; and author interview with Edsel Henry Ford, July 2002.
57. Author interview with Thomas Rugg, July 2002, Rancho Cordova, California.
58. David McCumber, letter to the author, May 23, 2002.

CHAPTER TWENTY-NINE: A WHOLE NEW BUSINESS

1. Henry Kaiser oral history interview, May 16, 1955, Eisenhower Center, University of New Orleans, Louisiana.
2. James J. Flink, *The Automobile Age* (Cambridge, Mass.: MIT Press, 1988), p. 278.
3. James M. Rubenstein, *Making and Selling Cars: Innovation and Change in the U.S. Automotive Industry* (Baltimore: Johns Hopkins University Press, 2001), p. 215.
4. Maryann Keller, *Rude Awakening: The Rise, Fall, and Struggle for Recovery of General Motors* (New York: William Morrow, 1993), p. 47.
5. George David Smith, *From Monopoly to Competition, the Transformation of Alcoa, 1888–1986* (Cambridge: Cambridge University Press, 1988), p. 209.
6. William Rodgers, *Think: A Biography of the Watsons and IBM* (New York: Stein and Day, 1969), pp. 211–13.
7. Thomas Watson Jr., *Father, Son & Co.: My Life at IBM and Beyond* (New York: Bantam, 1990), pp. 215–16, 267–70.
8. Alfred P. Sloan Jr., *My Years with General Motors*, ed. John McDonald with Catharine Stevens (Garden City, N.Y.: Doubleday, 1964), p. 298.
9. John D. Morris, "Inquiry Damage to G.M. Doubted," *New York Times*, November 13, 1955, p. 79.
10. "Ford Says Its New Dealer Agreement . . . ," *New York Times*, April 5, 1957; and "New Auto Sales Pact," *New York Times*, April 16, 1957.
11. "Foreign Cars Line Up for Hotter U.S. Race," *Business Week*, April 11, 1959, p. 24; "An Historic Turnabout," *Business Week*, March 15, 1958, p. 74; and "Imported Cars Slow Down," *Business Week*, September 9, 1961, p. 68.
12. "The Arabian Bazaar," *Time*, March 24, 1961, p. 78.
13. "New Autos Make a Poor Start," *Business Week*, November 30, 1957, pp. 30–33.
14. Phil Patton, *Bug: The Strange Mutations of the World's Most Famous Automobile* (New York: Simon & Schuster, 2002), p. 91.
15. Flink, *The Automobile Age*, p. 16.
16. Patton, *Bug*, p. 203.
17. "In the Lead," *The Economist*, November 1, 1958, p. 447.
18. "The British Are Here," *Sales Management*, January 1958, p. 77.
19. Rubenstein, *Making and Selling Cars*, p. 33.
20. "Seeking a Place on U.S. Roads," *Business Week*, August 2, 1958, p. 68.
21. Stanley Seneker, "Reminiscences" (oral history project), p. 21, Henry Ford Museum and Library, Dearborn, Michigan.
22. "Exploring the 1958 Auto Market," *Conference Board Business Record*, August 1958, p. 306.
23. "Who Owns the Foreign Cars?," *Business Week*, May 23, 1959, p. 36.
24. Tom Mahoney, *The Story of George Romney* (New York: Harper, 1960), p. 122.
25. *UAW–Ford: Sixty Years of Progress 1941–2001* (Detroit: UAW-Ford National Programs Center, 2001), p. 49.
26. Berry Gordy, *To Be Loved: The Music, the Magic, the Memories of Motown* (New York: Warner Books, 1994), p. 68.
27. Ibid., pp. 69–81.
28. Author interview with Larry Rivers, May 1997, New York.
29. Jack Kerouac, "Introduction" to Robert Frank, *The Americans* (New York: Grove Press, 1959), p. 9.
30. Robert Frank to Mary Frank, July 1955, Robert Frank Collection, National Archives, Washington, D.C.
31. A. W. Tucker and P. Brookman, eds., *Robert Frank* (Houston: Museum of Fine Arts, and New York: New York Graphic Society, 1986), p. 22.
32. Robert Frank, *Flowers Is . . .* (Tokyo, 1987), p. 1.
33. Nancy Watson Barr, *Truth, Memory, and the American Working-Class City: Robert Frank in Detroit and at the Rouge* (Detroit: Bulletin of the Detroit Institute of Arts, 2002), p. 72.
34. "The 40s for the 60s," *Newsweek*, November 21, 1960, p. 88.
35. Henry Ford II, interview with David Lewis, April 18, 1980, p. 57, Henry Ford Museum and Library.

36. George Brown, "Reminiscences," pp. 47–49.
37. "Birth Pangs at Detroit for a New Economy Car," *Life,* September 14, 1959, p. 157.
38. "Road Test: Ford Falcon," *Road & Track,* November 1959.
39. "Birth Pangs at Detroit for a New Economy Car," p. 158.
40. "New Engineering, Sales Features of the Big Three's Little Three," *Business Week,* October 3, 1959, p. 106.
41. Robert Sheehan, "It's a New Kind of Ford Motor Co.," *Fortune,* February 1962, p. 117.
42. Harold Sperlich, "Reminiscences," pp. 17–18.
43. "Small-Car Push," *Time,* March 23, 1959.
44. J. Mel Hickerson, *Ernie Breech* (New York: Meredith, 1968), p. 167.
45. Edmund Baumgartner, "Reminiscences," pp. 8–9.
46. "Preliminary Road Test: Ford Falcon," *Car and Driver,* November 1959.
47. "Road Test: Ford Falcon."
48. George H. Dammann, *Ninety Years of Ford,* 2d ed. (Osceola, Wis.: Motorbooks International, 1993), p. 311.
49. "Strong Hand at Ford's Wheel," *Forbes,* November 15, 1961, p. 20.
50. "The 40s for the 60s," p. 88.
51. David Halberstam, *The Best and the Brightest* (New York: Random House, 1972), pp. 232–40.
52. Sheehan, "It's a New Kind of Ford Motor Co.," p. 204.
53. "Strong Hand at Ford's Wheel," p. 21.
54. Sheehan, "It's a New Kind of Ford Motor Co.," p. 114.
55. Mira Wilkins and Frank Ernest Hill, *American Business Abroad: Ford on Six Continents* (Detroit: Wayne State University Press, 1964), p. 413.
56. Ibid., p. 407.
57. "Ford Offer Stirs British Ire," *Business Week,* November 19, 1960, p. 50.
58. "Watching the Fords . . . ," *Newsweek,* November 28, 1960, p. 74.
59. Wilkins and Hill, *American Business Abroad,* p. 423.
60. Ibid., p. 410.
61. Henry Ford II, interview with Lewis, p. 57.
62. Robert S. McNamara, "Reminiscences," pp. 14–15.

CHAPTER THIRTY: MUSTANG GENERATION

1. "Catching the Customers at the Most Critical Age," *Business Week,* October 26, 1957, p. 84.
2. William Clay Ford Sr., "Reminiscences" (oral history project), May 21, 1990, pp. 49–50, Ford Motor Company Archives, Dearborn, Michigan.
3. Lee Iacocca with William Novak, *Iacocca* (New York: Bantam Books, 1984), p. 4.
4. Author interview with Lee Iacocca, November 2002, Bel Air, California.
5. Iacocca with Novak, *Iacocca,* p. 24.
6. William Clay Ford Sr., "Reminiscences," pp. 49–50.
7. Randy Leffingwell, *Mustang* (Osceola, Wis.: Motorbooks International, 1995), p. 15.
8. Interview with Iacocca, November 2002.
9. "The Mustang—A New Breed Out of Detroit," *Newsweek,* April 20, 1964, p. 98.
10. Judith Goldman, *James Rosenquist: The Early Pictures, 1961–1964* (New York: Rizzoli International, 1985), p. 89.
11. Constance W. Glenn, *Time Dust: James Rosenquist, Complete Graphics, 1962–1992* (New York: Rizzoli International, 1993), p. 18.
12. "The Careful Breeding of a Mustang," *Sales and Management,* January 1, 1965, pp. 3–7.
13. Lee Iacocca, speech, April 6, 1965, Accession AR-98-213542, box 45, Henry Ford Museum and Library, Dearborn, Michigan.
14. Donald N. Frey, "Reminiscences," June 8, 1989, p. 33, Ford Motor Company Archives.
15. Joe McCarthy, *Mustang* (New York: Sports Car Press, 1973), p. 17.
16. Jack Telnack, "Reminiscences," August 14, 1989, pp. 20–21, Ford Motor Company Archives.
17. McCarthy, *Mustang,* p. 17.
18. Frey, "Reminiscences," p. 35.
19. "The Careful Breeding of a Mustang," pp. 3–7.
20. Iacocca, speech, April 6, 1965.

21. McCarthy, *Mustang*, p. 19.
22. Ibid., p. 69.
23. Iacocca with Novak, *Iacocca*, p. 43.
24. Arjay Miller, "Reminiscences," March 14, 1988, p. 43, Ford Motor Company Archives.
25. Berkeley Pop Culture Project, *The Whole Pop Catalog* (New York: Avon Books, 1991), p. 125.
26. Ford Division, press release, February 6, 1964, Accession AR-98-213542, box 45, Henry Ford Museum and Library.
27. "Ford's Pet Pony," *Ford Science Front* (clipping), May 1964.
28. "The Mustang—A New Breed Out of Detroit," p. 100.
29. Joel Makower, *Boom! Talkin' About Our Generation* (Chicago: Contemporary Books, 1985), p. 188.
30. "Mustang Gallops March 9 at River Rouge Assembly Plant," *Rouge News*, February 28, 1964, p. 8.
31. "Advertising: A Campaign of Another Color," *New York Times*, January 18, 1965.
32. "'Mustang' Heads Stable of World's Fair Cars," Ford Motor Company press release, April 1964, Accession AR-74-18056, Henry Ford Museum and Library.
33. Interview with Iacocca, November 2002.
34. Ibid.
35. Iacocca with Novak, *Iacocca*, p. 72, citing *Time*, April 20, 1964.
36. Lou Slawson, "Reminiscences," June 24, 1987, p. 22, Ford Motor Company Archives.
37. "All-New Mustang Kicks Up Heels," *Rouge News*, April 24, 1964, p. 1.
38. McCarthy, *Mustang*, pp. 25–26.
39. "The Careful Breeding of a Mustang," pp. 3–7.
40. "The Mustang—A New Breed Out of Detroit," p. 100.
41. "New Mustang Operation," *New York Times*, January 29, 1965.
42. "Mustang Production," *Dearborn Press*, April 22, 1965.
43. "Notebook," *Printer's Ink*, November 1965.
44. Iacocca, speech, April 6, 1965.
45. W. S. Walla, "Reminiscences," June 29, 1987, p. 35, Ford Motor Company Archives.
46. McCarthy, *Mustang*, p. 33.
47. Ford Division, press release, April 15, 1965, Accession AR-97-213543, box 7, Henry Ford Museum and Library.
48. "Ford Plans for Mustang's Birthday," *Steel*, April 5, 1965.
49. Suzanne E. Smith, *Dancing in the Street: Motown and the Cultural Politics of Detroit* (Cambridge, Mass.: Harvard University Press, 1999), p. 127.
50. Joe Whitburn, *The Billboard Book of Top 40 Hits*, 3d ed. (New York: Billboard Publications, 1987), p. 195.
51. Martha Reeves with Mark Bega, *Dancing in the Street: Confessions of a Motown Diva* (New York: Hyperion, 1994), pp. 123, 260.
52. Smith, *Dancing in the Street*, p. 130.
53. Interview with Iacocca, November 2002.
54. Mack Rice, "Mustang Sally," as found on www.mylyricarchive.com/mustang.htm.
55. Steve Parker, "2002 Mustang Bullitt," *Desert Sun*, August 12, 2001.
56. William Clay Ford Jr., "WCF Mustang" television commercial, first aired February 25, 2002.
57. George Barris and David Fetherstone, *Barris: TV and Movie Cars* (Osceola, Wis.: Motorbooks International, 1996), pp. 20–23.
58. Ibid., p. 6.
59. Ibid., pp. 70–76.
60. Ibid., pp. 94–96.
61. McCarthy, *Mustang*, p. 37.
62. Author interview with William Clay Ford Jr., May 2002.

CHAPTER THIRTY-ONE: JET SET

1. Author interview with Robert McNamara, June 2002, Washington, D.C.
2. Peter Collier and David Horowitz, *The Fords: An American Epic* (New York: Summit Books, 1987), p. 296.

3. Walter Hayes, *Henry: A Life of Henry Ford II* (New York: Grove Weidenfeld, 1990), p. 95.
4. Ibid., p. 83.
5. Alex Gabbard, *Ford Total Performance* (New York: HP Books, 2000), p. 127.
6. Bob Ottum, ". . . Ford Came Flying," *Sports Illustrated,* December 25, 1967, p. 29.
7. Joseph C. Ingraham, "Racing Triumphs Spur Ford Sales," *New York Times,* September 7, 1963.
8. Dr. John Craft, *Ford, Lincoln, and Mercury Stock Cars* (Osceola, Wis.: Motorbooks International, 1999), p. 32.
9. "Ford Deserts Pact to Base Ads on Racing," *Chicago Tribune,* March 6, 1963.
10. Dick Griffin, "Ford Gets Blame on Racing Ads," *Chicago Daily News,* March 9, 1963.
11. Ingraham, "Racing Triumphs Spur Ford Sales."
12. Ottum, ". . . Ford Came Flying," p. 31.
13. Bob Latshaw, "Bully, Jim; Thanks, Henry," *Detroit Free Press,* June 3, 1965.
14. Leo Levine, "Clark Breezes to Record Indianapolis Victory," *New York Herald-Tribune,* June 1, 1965.
15. William Dillman, "Racing Fans Are Car Buyers," *Chicago Sun-Times,* June 6, 1965.
16. Fred Olmstead, "Ford Tells Why It Races," *Chicago Tribune,* November 8, 1963.
17. Dillman, "Racing Fans Are Car Buyers," citing "Race on Sunday, Sell on Monday," Ford brochure.
18. Ottum, ". . . Ford Came Flying," p. 30.
19. Ford Motor Company, press release, July 5, 1966, AR-74-18056, p. 4, Henry Ford Museum and Library, Dearborn, Michigan.
20. Jan B. Norbye, "Ford Is Back and Ferrari's Quaking," *Popular Science,* June 1967.
21. "Three of a Kind," *Newsweek,* February 20, 1967.
22. "Ford Wins Sports Car Manufacturers Championship," Ford of England press release, June 13, 1966, AR-74-18056, Henry Ford Museum and Library.
23. "U.S. 'Steamroller' Too Much for Ferrari Cars to Battle," *New York Herald-Tribune,* March 24, 1966.
24. "Spotlight on Detroit," *Motor Trend,* January 1966.
25. Pete Waldmeir, "The Man Behind Ford's Venture into Auto Racing Circles," *Detroit News,* June 15, 1965.
26. Murray Forsvall, "Shelby Plus Ford Equals Big," *Dallas Times Herald,* February 11, 1965.
27. Gabbard, *Ford Total Performance,* p. 96.
28. Joe Dowdall, "Racing Has a Fringe Benefit," *Detroit News,* August 31, 1968.
29. "Torque of the Town," *A Century of Winning* (Middlesex, England: Haymarket Autosport, 2001), p. 26.
30. "Le Mans Adds Fuel to Ford's Future," *Business Week,* June 25, 1966, p. 36.
31. Jack B. Weiner, "Ford's Road Ahead," *Dun's Review,* August 1965, p. 70.
32. "Cortina Takes the Crown," *Time,* October 6, 1967, p. 109.
33. David Burgess-Wise, *Complete Catalogue of Ford Cars in Britain* (Devon, England: Bay View Books, 1991), p. 45.
34. "Ford Charts Two-Prong Attack in Europe," *International Management,* April 1969, p. 27.
35. "Going Multinational," *Time,* June 30, 1967, p. 69.
36. "You Don't Get Much Sloan Feedback Here," *Forbes,* July 1, 1966, p. 38.
37. "Ford Charts Two-Prong Attack in Europe," p. 26.
38. Dan Cordtz, "Henry Ford, Superstar," *Fortune,* May 1973, pp. 288–89.
39. Ibid., p. 289.
40. Ibid., p. 289.
41. ". . . And in the Catbird Seat," *Business Week,* September 30, 1969, p. 139.
42. Arjay Miller, interview with David Lewis, March 14, 1988, p. 110, Ford Motor Company Archives, Dearborn, Michigan.
43. Ibid., p. 41.
44. "A Famed GM Name Now Drives Ford," *Business Week,* February 10, 1968, p. 114.
45. "Why Knudsen Was Fired," *Time,* September 19, 1969, p. 88.
46. Miller, interview with Lewis, p. 30.
47. "Behind the Palace Revolt at Ford," *Business Week,* September 20, 1969, p. 140.
48. Miller, interview with Lewis, p. 41.

49. "Behind the Palace Revolt at Ford," p. 138.
50. Miller, interview with Lewis, p. 101.
51. Ibid., p. 77.
52. "Why Knudsen Was Fired," p. 90.

CHAPTER THIRTY-TWO: TROUBLE ALL AROUND

1. Walter Henry Nelson, *Small Wonder: The Amazing Story of the Volkswagen* (Boston: Little, Brown, 1967), p. 278.
2. Lewis Mumford, quoted in "Love (Hate) That Automobile," *Forbes,* July 1, 1966, p. 32.
3. Alvin Toffler, *Future Shock* (New York: Random House, 1970), p. 429.
4. James J. Flink, *The Automobile Age* (Cambridge, Mass.: MIT Press, 1988), pp. 388–89.
5. Joyce Carol Oates, "Ford," *The Iowa Review* 9, no. 3 (Summer 1978).
6. Author interview with John Sinclair, January 2002, New Orleans, Louisiana.
7. "$25,000 to the People's Community Civic League of Detroit," Ford Motor Company press release, June 26, 1967, AR-74-18056, Henry Ford Museum and Library, Dearborn, Michigan.
8. "The Fire This Time," *Time,* August 8, 1967.
9. "A Solid Step to Save Detroit," *Fortune,* January 1972, p. 33.
10. Richard Bok, *A Palace for the Summer: A Narrative History of Tigers Stadium* (Detroit: Wayne State University Press, 1998), pp. 301–5.
11. Douglas Brinkley, *Rosa Parks* (New York: Viking, 2000), pp. 202–4.
12. Jeffrey Eugenides, *Middlesex* (New York: Farrar Straus Giroux, 2002).
13. Wayne S. Doran, interview with David L. Lewis, August 1, 1989, p. 3, Ford Motor Company Archives, Dearborn, Michigan.
14. "Ford Sets Up Urban Affairs Department," *Detroit News,* August 4, 1967.
15. "Ford Meets Urban Crisis," *Steel,* August 8, 1967.
16. "How Detroit Gropes Toward Racial Peace," *Business Week,* November 11, 1967.
17. "Inner City Recruitment Program," Ford Motor Company press release, November 1967, AR-74-18056, Henry Ford Museum and Library.
18. Henry Ford II, speech, August 24, 1967, AR-74-18056, p. 1, ibid.
19. "Inner City Recruitment Program—First Anniversary and the 5,000th Employee," Ford Motor Company press release, October 28, 1968, AR-74-18056, ibid.
20. Joy Bennett Kinnon, "Factory Worker Gives $700,000 to Charity," *Ebony,* October 1996, p. 63.
21. Author interview with Mat Dawson Jr., May 2000, Shreveport, Louisiana.
22. "Forklift Philanthropist Gives Again," *USA Today,* April 14, 1999, p. 7A.
23. Richard Feldman and Michael Betzold, *End of the Line: Autoworkers and the American Dream* (New York: Weidenfeld & Getty, 1988), p. 265.
24. Henry Ford II, speech, November 17, 1967, AR-74-18056, p. 1, Henry Ford Museum and Library.
25. Doran, interview with Lewis, p. 51.
26. Henry Ford II, interview with David Lewis, April 6, 1985, p. 26, Ford Motor Company Archives.
27. Henry Ford II, speech, March 26, 1968, AR-74-18056, p. 1, Henry Ford Museum and Library.
28. Ibid.
29. Henry Ford II, speech, April 5, 1968, AR-74-18056, p. 1, Henry Ford Museum and Library.
30. Henry Ford II, letter to employees, January 17, 1968, AR-74-18056, p. 1, ibid.
31. Photography Research Department, microfilm publicity files, Ford Motor Company Archives.
32. Elmore Leonard, *52 Pick-Up* (New York: Avon, 1982) and *City Primeval: High Noon in Detroit* (New York: Avon, 1982).
33. Kai Bird, *The Color of Truth: McGeorge Bundy and William Bundy, Brothers in Arms* (New York: Simon & Schuster, 1998), pp. 392–93.
34. Walter Hayes, *Henry: A Life of Henry Ford II* (New York: Grove Weidenfeld, 1990).
35. Ibid.
36. "The Making of the Maverick," *Time,* March 21, 1969, p. 88.
37. John Naughton, "Reflections on Ford Motor Company," n.d., Ford Motor Company Archives, Dearborn, Michigan.

38. Anthony Fredo, interview with David Lewis, April 13, 1989, pp. 2–3, Ford Motor Company Archives.
39. "The 'Blue Denim' Boom," *Time,* July 3, 1972, p. 38.
40. George H. Dammann, *Ninety Years of Ford,* 2d ed. (Osceola, Wis.: Motorbooks International, 1993), p. 430.
41. *Moody's Handbook* (New York: Moody's, 1971), p. 363.
42. "Better Outlook for Ford," *Financial World,* September 15, 1971, p. 5.
43. Lee Iacocca with William Novak, *Iacocca* (New York: Bantam Books, 1984), p. 92.
44. "Better Outlook for Ford," p. 5.
45. *Moody's Handbook,* p. 363.
46. Douglas Brinkley, *The Majic Bus: An American Odyssey* (New York: Harcourt Brace, 1993), p. 71.
47. Thomas Pynchon, *V* (Philadelphia: Lippincott, 1963), pp. 28–29.
48. Iacocca with Novak, *Iacocca,* p. 90.
49. "Mustang: Back to the Old Corral," *Nation's Business,* September 1973, pp. 26–27.
50. "Can Detroit Sustain Its Breakneck Pace?" *Business Week,* April 7, 1973, p. 26.
51. "Straining to Keep Up with Soaring Sales," *Business Week,* February 10, 1973, p. 25.
52. Frank Cormier and William J. Eaton, *Reuther* (Englewood Cliffs, N.J.: Prentice-Hall, 1970), p. 422.
53. Nelson Lichtenstein, *The Most Dangerous Man in Detroit: Walter Reuther and the Fate of American Labor* (New York: Basic Books, 1995), pp. 437–38.
54. "Dying Detroit," *The Wall Street Journal,* December 20, 1971.
55. Robert A. Popa, "Ford's Plan for Riverfront Excites Gribbs, Council," *Detroit News,* November 25, 1971.
56. Doran, interview with Lewis, p. 3.
57. Robert A. Popa, "Ford Bids for Riverfront Property," *Detroit News,* October 8, 1971.
58. Popa, "Ford's Plan for Riverfront Excites Gribbs, Council."
59. Henry Ford II, interviews with Lewis, April 14, 1980; April 18, 1980; March 3, 1982.
60. Bill Black, "Henry Ford, the Riverfront, and Life at 'Plantation North,'" *Michigan Chronicle,* December 18, 1971.
61. Remer Tyson, "Ford's Architect Shares Dream of a Vibrant Detroit," *Detroit Free Press,* December 5, 1971.
62. *Moody's Handbook,* p. 363.
63. "'I Hope to Hell New York Goes Dark for a Week,'" *Fortune,* May 1973, p. 191.
64. Jean Herschaft, "The Social Calendar," *Jerusalem Post,* May 30, 1980.
65. Ford Motor Public Statements on the Arab Boycott, AR-86-56512, folder: Mideast and Africa, Ford Motor Company Archives.
66. James Graham, "Energy-Saving Advice Abounds in City," *Detroit News,* November 11, 1973.
67. Christopher Finch, *Highways to Heaven: The Auto Biography of America* (New York: Harper-Collins, 1992), p. 291.
68. "Waiting for a Small Car?," *U.S. News & World Report,* January 28, 1974, p. 35.
69. "The Painful Change to Thinking Small," *Time,* December 31, 1973, p. 19.

CHAPTER THIRTY-THREE: FINANCIAL CRISIS

1. Max Jurosek, interview with David L. Lewis, August 15, 1989, Ford Motor Company Archives, Dearborn, Michigan.
2. John Updike, *Rabbit Is Rich* (New York: Alfred A. Knopf, 1981), p. 3.
3. David Halberstam, *The Reckoning* (New York: William Morrow, 1986), p. 479.
4. Ibid.
5. Francis T. Cullen, William J. Maakestad, and Gray Cavender, *Corporate Crime Under Attack* (Cincinnati: Anderson, 1987), pp. 156–58, citing "Part of a Conversation Among President Nixon, Henry Ford II, Lido Anthony Iacocca, and John D. Ehrlichman in the Oval Office on April 27, 1971, Between 11:08 and 11:43," National Archives, Watergate transcripts.
6. "A Sculptor on Wheels," *Newsweek,* October 23, 1978, p. 80.

7. Michael Thoryn, "Automobiles: Regulatory Hazards on the Road Ahead," *Nation's Business,* October 1978, p. 64.
8. Walter Guzzardi Jr., "The Mindless Pursuit of Safety," *Fortune,* April 9, 1979, p. 54.
9. Jean A. Briggs, "Detroit and Congress, Eyeball to Eyeball," *Forbes,* February 15, 1977, p. 34.
10. Ibid., p. 35.
11. Ibid., p. 34.
12. Lee Iacocca, speech, December 6, 1972, AR-98-213543, box 21, folder: Energy Crisis, p. 4, Henry Ford Museum and Library, Dearborn, Michigan.
13. Douglas Edwards, speech, Anti-Defamation League dinner, May 14, 1980, AR-97-213543, box 26, p. 5, ibid.
14. Kathleen K. Wiegner, "Detroit Fights Back," *Forbes,* July 15, 1977, p. 37.
15. "How the Japanese Blitzed the California Auto Market," *Forbes,* September 15, 1971, p. 29.
16. Bennett Bidwell, interview with David Lewis, April 8, 1988, p. 17, Henry Ford Museum and Library.
17. Arthur Connors, interview with David Lewis, September 16, 1989, pp. 25–26, ibid.
18. "Too Small, Too Soon," *Time,* April 5, 1976, p. 65.
19. Dan Cordtz, "What Lies Ahead Down Small Car Lane," *Fortune,* July 1974, p. 80.
20. "Big Cars Boom—Is It the Last Gasp?," *U.S. News & World Report,* February 14, 1977, p. 51.
21. Wiegner, "Detroit Fights Back," p. 36.
22. "When Better Cars Are Built, Will Detroit Build Them?," *Consumer Reports,* April 1977, p. 187.
23. Lee Iacocca with Sonny Kleinfield, *Talking Straight* (New York: Bantam Books, 1988), pp. 148–51.
24. Author interview with Lee Iacocca, December 2002, Beverly Hills, California.
25. Iacocca with Kleinfield, *Talking Straight,* pp. 86–89.
26. "Future Shock in Detroit," *Newsweek,* August 8, 1977, p. 68.
27. Henry Ford II, interview with David Lewis, March 3, 1982, p. 22, Henry Ford Museum and Library.
28. Robert Alexander, interview with David Halberstam, p. 3, Halberstam papers, Boston University, Boston, Massachusetts.
29. Henry Ford II, interview with Lewis, p. 50.
30. "Final Test Report," October 2, 1970, Product Development Engineering Office, Ford Motor Company, reprinted in facsimile in Lee Patrick Strobel, *Reckless Homicide* (South Bend, Ind.: End Books, 1980), p. 276.
31. "Rear End Crash Test Results, 1971–1972 Pinto Car at Fixed Barrier," Ford Motor Company document, reprinted in facsimile in ibid.
32. Product Review Meeting, April 22, 1971, original Ford Motor Company document, reprinted in facsimile in ibid.
33. Mark Dowie, "Pinto Madness," *Mother Jones,* September–October 1977, p. 21.
34. Quoted in Strobel, *Reckless Homicide,* p. 170.
35. "Three Cheers in Dearborn," *Time,* March 24, 1980, p. 24.
36. Cullen, Maakestad, and Cavender, *Corporate Crime Under Attack,* p. 165.
37. Francis T. Cullen, William J. Maakestad, and Gray Cavender, "The Ford Pinto Case and Beyond," in *Corporations as Criminals,* ed. Ellen Hochstedler (Beverly Hills, Calif.: Sage Publications, 1984), p. 116.
38. William Lowther, "Blessed Be the Name of Ford," *MacLean's,* March 24, 1980, p. 30.
39. Cullen, Maakestad, and Cavender, *Corporate Crime Under Attack,* p. 164.
40. Gillian Mackay, "Another Reverse for Ford," *MacLean's,* June 23, 1980, p. 39; and "The Massive Recall That Ford Faces," *Business Week,* December 8, 1980, p. 32.
41. "Ford Transmissions," *Consumer Research,* March 1981, p. 4.
42. Halberstam, *The Reckoning,* p. 375.
43. Henry Ford II, interview with Lewis, p. 85.
44. Lee Iacocca with William Novak, *Iacocca* (New York: Bantam Books, 1984), p. 108.
45. "'Somebody Called Ford,'" *Fortune,* August 14, 1978, p. 13.
46. Halberstam, *The Reckoning,* p. 543.
47. Reginald Stuart, "Iacocca Relieved of Duties at Ford," *New York Times,* July 18, 1978, p. D5.

48. Halberstam, *The Reckoning*, p. 542.
49. Robert Alexander, interview with Halberstam, p. 2.
50. "Ford to Chrysler: No Thanks," *Newsweek*, April 20, 1981, p. 84.

CHAPTER THIRTY-FOUR: THE QUALITY CRISIS

1. Author interview with Lee Iacocca, November 2002, Bel Air, California.
2. "Henry Ford II: A Tribute," *Detroit News*, September 30, 1987.
3. Curt Schleier, "Give Yourself a Green Light," *Investor's Business Daily*, September 27, 2002.
4. Paul H. Weaver, *The Suicidal Corporation* (New York: Simon & Schuster, 1988), p. 29.
5. Donald L. Petersen and John Hillkirk, *A Better Idea* (Boston: Houghton Mifflin, 1991), p. 94.
6. Author interview with Harold "Red" Poling, November 2002, Bloomfield Hills, Michigan.
7. Jeremy Main, "Ford's Drive for Quality," *Fortune*, April 18, 1983, p. 62.
8. Robert L. Shook, *Turnaround* (New York: Prentice-Hall, 1990), p. 13.
9. Weaver, *The Suicidal Corporation*, pp. 54–60.
10. Petersen and Hillkirk, *A Better Idea*, p. 5.
11. David Halberstam, *The Reckoning* (New York: William Morrow, 1986), p. 517.
12. Schleier, "Give Yourself a Green Light," p. 1.
13. Author interview with Peter Pestillo, October 2002, Dearborn, Michigan.
14. Robert Metz, "Sizing Up Cash-Rich Ford," *New York Times*, November 24, 1978, p. D4.
15. Petersen and Hillkirk, *A Better Idea*, p. 56.
16. "Ford's $3 Billion Gamble," *Newsweek*, October 25, 1982, p. 132.
17. Jean Lindamood, "Jack Telnack and His Better Ideas," *Car and Driver*, March 1981, p. 40.
18. Harold Poling, interview with David Lewis, January 26, 1989, p. 17, Henry Ford Museum and Library, Dearborn, Michigan.
19. Henry Ford II, interview with David Lewis, March 3, 1982, ibid.
20. Shook, *Turnaround*, p. 65.
21. Petersen and Hillkirk, *A Better Idea*, p. 20.
22. Ibid., p. 21.
23. Poling, interview with Lewis, p. 12.
24. Richard Feldman and Michael Betzold, eds., *End of the Line: Autoworkers and the American Dream* (New York: Weidenfeld & Getty, 1988), p. 20.
25. Jerry Flint, "A Million Jobs to Go," *Forbes*, November 23, 1981, p. 40.
26. Ibid.
27. Interview with Pestillo, October 2002.
28. Feldman and Betzold, *End of the Line*, p. 66.
29. Main, "Ford's Drive for Quality," p. 62.
30. "UAW-Ford Agreement," *Monthly Labor Review*, April 1982, p. 62.
31. "Detroit's New Balance of Power," *Business Week*, March 1, 1982, p. 90.
32. "Detroit Gets a Break from UAW," *Business Week*, November 30, 1982, p. 94.
33. Poling, interview with Lewis, pp. 10–11.
34. "What's Creating an 'Industrial Miracle' at Ford," *Business Week*, July 30, 1984, p. 80.
35. William Serrin, "Giving Workers a Voice of Their Own," *New York Times*, December 2, 1984, p. 131.
36. Joseph M. Callahan, "Sharonville—An Inspiration for America," *Automotive Industries*, April 1987, p. 16.
37. Main, "Ford's Drive for Quality," p. 64.
38. "What's Creating an 'Industrial Miracle' at Ford," p. 80.
39. Feldman and Betzold, *End of the Line*, p. 89.
40. Ibid., p. 19.
41. Petersen and Hillkirk, *A Better Idea*, pp. 99–100.
42. Henry Ford II, interview with Lewis, p. 15.
43. Jill Bettner, "Hot Wheels," *Forbes*, April 3, 1984, p. 135.
44. John S. Dorfman, "Make or Break," *Fortune*, April 1983, p. 98.
45. "Ford Zooms into the Fast Lane," *Time*, July 18, 1983, p. 43.
46. "Ford's $3 Billion Gamble," p. 132.
47. Patrick Bedard, "On the Right Track," *Car and Driver*, August 1985, p. 136.

CHAPTER THIRTY-FIVE: TEAM TAURUS

1. Author interview with Donald Petersen, October 2002, Montecito, California.
2. Author interview with Philip Caldwell, October 2002, Stamford, Connecticut.
3. *Consumer Reports,* May 1986, p. 8.
4. Author interview with Jack Telnack, September 2002.
5. John McElroy, "Jack Telnack: 1989 Man of the Year," *Automotive Industries,* February 1989, p. 54.
6. Jean Lindamood, "Ford Fights Back," *Car and Driver,* March 1985, p. 48.
7. Gary Witzenburg, "The Art of Automaking Redefined," *Automobile Quarterly* 25, no. 1, p. 99.
8. Mary Walton, *Car: A Drama of the American Workplace* (New York: W.W. Norton, 1997), pp. 10–11.
9. Witzenburg, "The Art of Automaking Redefined," p. 99.
10. Lindamood, "Ford Fights Back," p. 48.
11. McElroy, "Jack Telnack: 1989 Man of the Year," p. 54.
12. Joseph M. Callahan, "How Team Taurus Got the Goodies," *Automotive Industries,* August 1985, p. 44.
13. Russell Mitchell, "How Ford Hit the Bull's Eye with Taurus," *Business Week,* June 30, 1986, p. 69.
14. Joseph M. Callahan, "Ford Finds 400 Ways to Say Quality," *Automotive Industries,* January 1986, pp. 44–45.
15. William Jeanes, "The Ford That Wasn't a Ford," *Car and Driver,* October 1985, p. 44.
16. Callahan, "How Team Taurus Got the Goodies," p. 44.
17. Francis J. Gawronski, "Designed for Easy Service," *Automotive News,* February 18, 1985, p. 24.
18. Lance Ealey, "Ford's Lewis Veraldi: Man of the Year," *Automotive Industries,* February 1987, p. 64.
19. Mitchell, "How Ford Hit the Bull's Eye with Taurus," p. 69.
20. Callahan, "How Team Taurus Got the Goodies," p. 44.
21. Mimi Vandermolen, "Shifting the Corporate Culture," *Working Woman,* November 1992, p. 25.
22. Katrina Onstad, "Just Drive, She Said," *Canadian Business,* Spring 1997, p. 54.
23. Gretchen Worth, "Driving Force," *Working Woman,* March 1986, p. 58.
24. Author interview with Harold "Red" Poling, November 2002, Bloomfield Hills, Michigan.
25. Witzenburg, "The Art of Automaking Redefined," p. 100.
26. William D. Marbach, "Cars of the Future," *Newsweek,* October 28, 1985, p. 85.
27. Helen Kahn, "GM and Ford to Miss CAFE Figure," *Automotive News,* January 7, 1985, p. 1.
28. Patrick Bedard, "Ford Taurus LX," *Car and Driver,* October 1985, p. 46.
29. Interview with Poling, November 2002.
30. Interview with Petersen, October 2002.
31. Alex Taylor III, "The Stylist Who Put Ford Out in Front," *Fortune,* January 5, 1987, p. 82.
32. Interview with Telnack, September 2002.
33. "Ford's Mr. Turnaround," *Fortune,* March 4, 1985, p. 84.
34. Interview with Petersen, October 2002.
35. Al Fleming, "Red Poling," *Automotive News,* August 4, 1987, p. D4.
36. Richard Johnson, "103,000 Orders for Taurus/Sable," *Automotive News,* December 9, 1985, p. 52.
37. Bedard, "Ford Taurus LX," pp. 42, 46–47.
38. Bruce Nussbaum, "Smart Design: Quality Is the New Style," *Business Week,* April 11, 1988.
39. Russell Mitchell, "Taurus and Sable Are Blasting Off for Ford," *Business Week,* March 3, 1986, p. 39.
40. "Taurus-Sable Styling a Problem for GM10," *Automotive News,* December 30, 1985, pp. 1–2.
41. Author interview with Gil Trainor, September 2002, Harvey, Louisiana.
42. Author interview with Jim Click, September 2002, Tucson, Arizona.
43. Robert Shook, *Turnaround* (New York: Prentice-Hall, 1990), p. 163.
44. Eric Taub, *Taurus* (New York: Dutton, 1991), p. 253.

45. Harold "Red" Poling, interview with David L. Lewis, January 26, 1989, Ford Motor Company Archives, Dearborn, Michigan.
46. Interview with Caldwell, October 2002.
47. Interview with Petersen, October 2002.
48. Ronald Reagan, remarks at the Ford Claycomo Assembly Plant in Kansas City, Missouri, April 11, 1984, presidential speech files, Ronald Reagan Library, Simi Valley, California.
49. David L. Lewis, *Ford Country* (Sidney, Ohio: Amos Press, 1987), p. 11.
50. Interview with Caldwell, October 2002.
51. James M. Callahan, "Surrendering the Helm in Style," *Automotive Industries*, February 1985, p. 40.
52. Interview with Caldwell, October 2002.
53. Author interview with Peter Pestillo, October 2002, Dearborn, Michigan.
54. Anti-Defamation League of B'nai B'rith press release, April 15, 1980, AR-86-100123-11, Ford Motor Company Archives.
55. Al Stark, "Atonement for the Sins of His Grandfather," *Detroit News*, September 30, 1987.
56. Dwight E. M. Angell and Kathleen Bohland, "Legionnaires' Bout Set Off Ford's Illness," *Detroit News*, September 30, 1987, p. 1.
57. Patricia Montemurri, Charlotte Craig, and William J. Mitchell, "Detroit Loses a Legend," *Detroit Free Press*, September 30, 1987.
58. Ibid.
59. Ibid.
60. James V. Higgins, "Will Fords Retain Power?," *Detroit News*, September 30, 1987.
61. "*Newsweek*'s Jim Jones Remembers Henry Ford II," *Ward's Auto World*, October 1987, p. 19.
62. Author interview with Anne Ford, November 2002, New York.
63. "Expressions of Sympathy Flow from Around the World," *Automotive News*, October 5, 1987, p. 76.
64. *Detroit News*, September 30, 1987.
65. Ibid.
66. Jack Beatty, ed., *Colossus: How the Corporation Changed America* (New York: Broadway Books, 2001), p. 223.
67. Lewis, *Ford Country*, p. 103.
68. David Halberstam, "Industrial Prince Played as Jester, Too," *Detroit Free Press*, September 30, 1987.
69. Henry Ford II, interviews with David L. Lewis, April 14, 1980; April 18, 1980; March 3, 1982, Henry Ford Museum and Library, Dearborn, Michigan.
70. Paul Lienert, "Is There a Ford in Company's Future?," *Detroit Free Press*, September 30, 1987.
71. Ibid.
72. Author interview with William Clay Ford Jr., December 1999, Dearborn, Michigan.
73. William Clay Ford Jr., "Henry Ford and Labor: A Reappraisal" (senior thesis, Firestone Library, Princeton University, Princeton, New Jersey, 1979).
74. Interview with William Ford Jr., December 1999.
75. Ibid.
76. Interview with Petersen, October 2002.
77. Ibid.

CHAPTER THIRTY-SIX: NEW HORSES

1. Alex Taylor III, "The Odd Eclipse of a Star CEO," *Fortune*, February 11, 1991, p. 86.
2. Michelle Krebs and David Versical, "Chevy Boss Says Ford Will Win Again in '89," *Automotive News*, January 16, 1989, p. 1.
3. Jim Harbour, "What Is Ford's Secret?," *Automotive Industries*, January 1989, p. 7.
4. Jim Harbour, "Ford, Where Quality Is Job 1," *Automotive Industries*, September 1986, p. 17.
5. Alton F. Doody and Ron Bingaman, *Reinventing the Wheels: Ford's Spectacular Comeback* (New York: Harper & Row, 1990), p. 120.
6. Author interview with Philip Caldwell, October 2002, Stamford, Connecticut.
7. Doody and Bingaman, *Reinventing the Wheels*.

8. "Ford 'Victory' Stuns McNamara," *Automotive News*, February 23, 1987, p. 58.
9. "The Ford Dilemma: Go for the Glory?," *Forbes*, December 28, 1987, p. 35.
10. Author interview with Donald Petersen, October 2002, Montecito, California.
11. Alex Taylor III, "Ford's Really Big Leap at the Future," *Fortune*, September 18, 1995, p. 134.
12. Interview with Petersen, October 2002.
13. Interview with Caldwell, October 2002.
14. Harold "Red" Poling, interview with David L. Lewis, January 26, 1989, Ford Motor Company Archives, Dearborn, Michigan.
15. David Landis, "Racing for Power at Ford," *USA Today*, January 18, 1989, p. 1B.
16. James B. Treece, "Ford's Bruce Blythe Has a Big Blank Check—and a Mission," *Business Week*, December 21, 1987, p. 79.
17. Laura Landro and Bradley A. Stertz, "Ford to Buy Associates Corp. . . . ," *Wall Street Journal*, July 28, 1989, p. 1.
18. Ibid.
19. Interview with Petersen, October 2002.
20. J. Mel Hickerson, *Ernie Breech* (New York: Meredith Press, 1968), p. 55.
21. Richard Johnson and Giancarlo Perini, "Ford, Fiat Contend for Hand of Alfa . . . ," *Automotive News*, September 22, 1986, p. 1.
22. Richard Johnson, "Fiat to Buy Alfa; Ford Bid Spurned," *Automotive News*, November 10, 1986, p. 1.
23. Paul Ingrassia, "Ford to Buy Aston, Following Two Rivals in Prestige Market," *Wall Street Journal*, September 8, 1987, p. 1.
24. Dan Neil, "The Name Is Martin, Aston Martin," *Worth*, October 2002, pp. 82–83.
25. Author interview with David Kitchener, July 2002, Newport Pagnell, England.
26. Ibid.
27. Aston Martin clipping file, Ford Motor Company Archives, Dearborn, Michigan.
28. Author interview with Donald Petersen, November 2002, Montecito, California.
29. Julie Fenster, "British Wheels," *New York Times*, July 31, 1988.
30. Dan Fisher, "Detroit Stalking Jaguar; Last of Its Breed," *Los Angeles Times*, October 15, 1989, p. D1.
31. Annual Report, Ford Motor Company, 1989.
32. James Risen, "Ford Paying Dearly to Catch Up with the Japanese," *Los Angeles Times*, November 3, 1989, p. D1.
33. Jerry Flint, "Back on the Road: Ford's Got Jaguar Back in the Black . . . ," *Forbes*, June 5, 1995, p. 100.
34. Risen, "Ford Paying Dearly," p. D1.
35. Laurie Laird, "Jaguar Chairman and CEO Nicholas Scheele . . . ," *Europe*, March 1993, p. 12.
36. Interview with Petersen, October 2002.
37. Robert Sobel, *Car Wars* (New York: E.P. Dutton, 1984), p. 322.
38. Charles Thomas, Francis J. Gawronski, and Al Fleming, "Flying: Ford's Financial Fortunes Skyrocket . . . ," *Automotive News*, May 4, 1987, p. 62.
39. Interview with Petersen, October 2002.
40. Hilary E. MacGregor, "Ford Gains Foothold in Once Impenetrable Market," *Los Angeles Times*, April 13, 1996, p. D1.
41. Earle Eldridge, "Volvo, BMW Stocks Rise on Rumors," *USA Today*, September 24, 1998, p. 3B.
42. Edmund Sanders and Marjorie Miller, "Ford to Buy Land Rover from BMW," *Los Angeles Times*, March 17, 2000, p. C1.
43. Scott Miller, "Ford to Add Land Rover to Luxury Group," *Wall Street Journal*, March 20, 2000, p. A26.
44. "Land Rover Joins Ford's Luxury Vehicles Group," *Mergers and Acquisitions*, May 2000, p. 15.
45. Author interview with Bob Dover, July 2002, Graydon, England.
46. Taylor, "Ford's Really Big Leap at the Future," p. 134.
47. Annual Report, Ford Motor Company, 1995.
48. Annual Report, Ford Motor Company, 1993.
49. Annual Report, Ford Motor Company, 1995.

50. Earle Eldridge, "Honda Claims the Title for Accord," *USA Today,* March 11, 1996, p. 4B.
51. *The World Almanac and Book of Facts 2002,* p. 227.
52. Jacqueline Mitchell, "Autos: Luxury Cars Go Unsold as Buyers Opt for Jeep-like Look," *Wall Street Journal,* May 9, 1994, p. B1.
53. Author interview with Lee Iacocca, November 2002, Bel Air, California.
54. Ken Gross, "Sales Stealers," *Automotive Industries,* October 1992, p. 16.
55. Alan Adler, "Red Hot Wheels: Truck Makers Struggle to Build Enough as Orders Pick Up," *New Orleans Times-Picayune,* July 31, 1993, p. C2.
56. John McElroy, "1991 Ford Explorer: Ford Aims to Dominate the Sport Utility Segment," *Automotive Industries,* February 1990, p. 93.
57. Adler, "Red Hot Wheels," p. C2.
58. "Lincoln-Mercury Opens New World Headquarters," press release, July 14, 1998, Ford Motor Company Archives.
59. Danny Hakim, "Lincoln-Mercury Unit Will Return to Michigan," *New York Times,* November 9, 2002, p. B4.

CHAPTER THIRTY-SEVEN: MOMENTUM

1. Jamie Butlers, "Too Many Plants Making Too Many Vehicles," *Detroit Free Press,* January 12, 2002.
2. Author interview with William Clay Ford Jr., August 2002, Dearborn, Michigan.
3. Author interview with Lee Iacocca, October 2002, Bel Air, California.
4. "Edsel Ford II to Retire from Credit Unit," *Los Angeles Times,* April 10, 1998, p. 4.
5. Keith Naughton, "Ford: The Man, His Roots, His Role, His Priorities," *Business Week,* September 28, 1998.
6. Author interview with William Clay Ford Jr., March 2002, Dearborn, Michigan.
7. Betsy Morris, "Can Ford Save Ford?," *Fortune,* November 18, 2002, p. 54.
8. Author interview with Anne Ford, November 2002, New York.
9. Ron Stodghill II, "The Ford in Ford's Future," *Time,* December 8, 1997, p. 76.
10. "Bill Ford Will Succeed Trotman," *Ward's Auto World,* December 1997, p. 10.
11. Judith VendeWater, "Longest Serving Barkeep Gets Bravos from Busches," *St. Louis Post-Dispatch,* July 1, 2002, p. B2.
12. Doris Hajewski, "Johnson's Mistakes a Lesson for All," *Milwaukee Journal Sentinel,* August 26, 2001, p. 1D.
13. "Ford Great-Grandson Will Run Automaker," *Houston Chronicle,* September 12, 1998, p. 2.
14. Author interview with William Clay Ford Jr., August 2002.
15. David Sedgwick, "Fire-Tested Ford Executive Directs Historic Reorganization," *Detroit News,* August 21, 1994.
16. Marjorie Sorge, "1999 Executive of the Year," *Automotive Industries,* February 1999, p. 59.
17. "Jacques Knifed: Shake-up at Ford," *The Economist,* November 3, 2001.
18. Michael Lewis, *The New New Thing: A Silicon Valley Story* (New York: W.W. Norton, 1999).
19. Kathleen Kerwin, "Remaking Ford," *Business Week,* October 11, 1999, p. 17.
20. Ford's interactive websites are DealerConnection.com, BuyerConnection.com, and OwnerConnection.com.
21. "Ford's E-Business News Timeline," press release, February 3, 2000, Ford Motor Company.
22. Author interview with William Clay Ford Jr., December 1999.
23. Joseph Cabadas, "Jac Nasser Looks at Industry Future," *U.S. Auto Scene,* February 7, 2000, p. 4.
24. William J. Holstein, "The Dot Com Within Ford," *U.S. News & World Report,* February 7, 2000.
25. Author interview with William Clay Ford Jr., December 7, 1999.
26. Kerwin, "Remaking Ford," p. 18.
27. Visteon file, information sheets, Ford Motor Company Archives, Dearborn, Michigan.
28. Robyn Meredith, "Ford Is Getting Its Ducks in a Row for Divestiture of Its Parts Unit," *New York Times,* November 11, 1999, p. C1.
29. Author interview with Peter Pestillo, October 2002, Dearborn, Michigan.

30. Norihiko Shirouzu, "Ford Sets Distribution for Visteon Spinoff," *Wall Street Journal,* June 5, 2000, p. A4.
31. Jacques Nasser, "Let's Chat About the Business" (memo), June 30, 2000, Ford Motor Company Archives.
32. Jeremy Cato, "Ford's New Mission," *Vancouver Sun,* November 30, 2001, p. D3.
33. Charlotte W. Craig, "The Bottom 10 Percent Will Go Empty-handed," *Detroit Free Press,* December 23, 1999.
34. James R. Healey, "Image Woes Helped Lead to Ouster," *USA Today,* October 31, 2001, p. 6B.
35. Mary Connelly, "Ford Eyes 8–10 New Markets for Dealer Consolidation," *Automotive News,* June 14, 1999, p. 51.
36. Doron Levin, "Stock Is a Shaky Meal Ticket for Ford Family," *Pittsburgh Post-Gazette,* August 24, 2001, p. C14.
37. John McElroy, "1991 Ford Explorer," *Automotive Industries,* February 1990.
38. Ford R. Bryan, *Friends, Families, and Forays* (Dearborn, Mich.: Ford Books, 2002), pp. 34–43.
39. "Key Dates in the Firestone Tire Case," Associated Press, May 21, 2001.
40. "Tyre Straights," *The Economist,* September 2, 2000, p. 57.
41. Chuck Seilnacht, memo, March 12, 1999, Ford Motor Company Archives, Dearborn, Michigan.
42. "Firestone's Rough Road," *Time,* September 18, 2000, p. 40.
43. Mary Connelly, "Job One at Ford, Ease Fears About Explorer," *Automotive News,* August 14, 2000, p. 47.
44. "Firestone's Rough Road," p. 40.
45. James B. Arndorfer, "Ford's Fallout Hits Dealers, Suppliers," *Crain's Chicago Business,* September 18, 2000, p. 4.
46. "Jac Nasser, President and CEO, Ford Motor Company (NYSE:F), Television Commercial Addressed Efforts to Replace Recalled Bridgestone/Firestone," press release, August 29, 2000, Ford Motor Company.
47. "Customers Will Really Decide What Tires They Want in the Longer Term" (transcript of Jacques Nasser appearance on CNBC), December 7, 2000, CNBC press release.
48. Jim Suhr, "Corporate Image Experts: Ford, Firestone Feud Has No Winner," Associated Press, May 22, 2001.
49. "Ford Adds Tires to Vehicle Warranty Coverage," Reuters, January 2, 2001.
50. Keith Naughton and Mark Hosenball, "Facing Falling Sales and Legal Jeopardy, Ford Splits with Firestone," *Newsweek,* June 4, 2001, p. 38.
51. Ibid.
52. Harry Stoffer, "Wanted: Ford, Firestone Referee," *Automotive News,* June 4, 2001, p. 32.
53. Ed Garsten, "Ford Replacing Firestone Tires at a Cost of $2.1 Billion," Associated Press, May 23, 2001.
54. Danny Hakim, "Safety Agency Rejects Request to Investigate Ford Explorer," *New York Times,* February 13, 2002, p. C11.
55. Jeffrey McCracken and Alejandro Bodipo-Memba, "Ford's Quality Slipped with Morale, Seniority," *Detroit Free Press,* November 17, 2001.
56. Matthew L. Wald, "America's Tires: Worn Down, Overlooked and Underinflated," *New York Times,* October 14, 2001, p. F1.
57. *Fortune,* April 15, 2002, pp. F1–2.
58. "Two American Legends Since 1903: Authentic American Muscle," press release, November 22, 1999, Ford Motor Company.
59. Laura Ricks, "One Tough Truck," *New Orleans Times-Picayune,* p. F1.
60. Ibid.
61. Ford Motor Company, F-150 Heritage and Market Trends file, Ford Motor Company Archives, Dearborn, Michigan.
62. Danny Hakim, "Will Soft Touches Mean Softer Sales for the Mighty F-150?," *New York Times,* January 5, 2003, section 3, p. 1.
63. Laura Ricks, "The Fabulous Thunderbirds," *New Orleans Times-Picayune,* March 29, 2002, p. F2.

64. Mark Truby, "Resilient Explorer Rides Again," *Detroit News,* September 5, 2002.
65. Ibid.
66. "Ford's Troubled Firestone Tires Headed for Football Field," *New York Times,* March 9, 2002, p. C4. Also see R. J. King, "Ford Field to Feature Fantastic Trimmings," *Detroit News,* March 10, 2002, p. B1.
67. Keith Naughton, "Growing a Green Plant," *Newsweek,* November 13, 2000, p. 58.
68. Author interview with William McDonough, March 2000, Dearborn, Michigan.
69. Ibid.
70. Keith Schneider, "Ford Gives River Rouge a Green Coat," *New York Times,* October 23, 2002.
71. William McDonough and Michael Braungart, "The *Next* Industrial Revolution," *Atlantic Monthly,* October 1998. For good profiles of McDonough, see Roger Rosenblatt, "The Man Who Wants Building to Love Kids," *Time,* February 22, 1999, pp. 70–73; and Andrea Truppin, "1999 Designer of the Year," *Interior,* January 1999.
72. Author interview with Lee Iacocca, November 2002.
73. "Ford Debuts Escape HEV Concept Car at Los Angeles Auto Show," press release, January 4, 2001, Ford Motor Company.
74. Derrick Z. Jackson, "Can a Green Ford Save the Earth . . . ," *Cleveland Plain Dealer,* November 6, 2001.
75. Author interview with Daniel Becker, November 2002, Washington, D.C.
76. Author interview with William Clay Ford Jr., August 2002.
77. Christopher Whalen, "A Ford in Ford's Future," *Insight on the News,* December 17, 2001, p. 22.
78. Interview with William Clay Ford Jr., August 2002.
79. David Bjerklie, "In Brief: Family Is Job One," *Time,* May 28, 2001, p. 92.
80. Jeffrey McCracken, "Great-Grandson of Founder Takes Over Ford," *Detroit Free Press,* October 31, 2001.
81. Interview with Anne Ford, November 2002.
82. Daniel Howes, "After Performance at Ford, Nasser Would Be Better Off Staying in Shadows," *Detroit News,* November 14, 2002.
83. Danny Hakim, "Ford's Ex-Chief Hired to Rebuild Polaroid," *New York Times,* November 12, 2002.
84. Claudia H. Deutsch, "Fiscal and Technical Advice for Ex-Ford Chief as He Arrives at Polaroid," *New York Times,* November 18, 2002, p. C4.
85. Nicholas Scheele, interview with Paul Kangas and Susie Gharib, October 30, 2001, *Nightly Business Report,* Community Television Foundation.
86. Interview with William Clay Ford Jr., August 2002.
87. Jennifer Dixon, "Plant Closings, Slowdowns Will Wound Entire Cities," *Detroit Free Press,* January 12, 2002.
88. Interview with William Clay Ford Jr., August 2002.
89. *UAW—Ford: Sixty Years of Progress 1941–2001* (Detroit: UAW-Ford National Programs Center, 2001), p. 82.
90. Mike Hudson, "Unions Fight to Maintain Relevance," *Detroit News and Free Press,* September 1, 2002.
91. "Ford Paid Former CEO Nasser $17.8 Million," *USA Today,* April 10, 2002.
92. Danny Hakim, "Ford to Cut 35,000 Employees and Shut Five Plants," *New York Times,* January 14, 2002.
93. Jeffrey Ball, "Sierra Club Ads Challenge Ford CEO," *Wall Street Journal,* June 13, 2002.
94. "A Cherished Piece of History Rides Again," Ford Motor Company National Park Files, Ford Motor Company Archives.
95. Eric Mitchel, "Explorer Passes a Milestone," *Ford World,* October 2002, p. 3.
96. Danny Hakim, "Lincoln-Mercury Unit Will Return to Michigan," *New York Times,* November 9, 2002.
97. Robin Sidel and Joseph B. White, "Ford Motor's Bonds Suffer Another Hit," *Wall Street Journal,* October 9, 2002, p. C1.
98. Danny Hakim, "A Low Cost Model Is a Big Headache for Ford," *New York Times,* November 6, 2002, p. C1.
99. Interview with Iacocca, November 2002.

100. Allan Gilmour, interview with Mike O'Neil, Ford Motor Company Archives, Dearborn, Michigan.
101. Norihiko Shirouzu, "Ford Posts Loss of $800 Million, but Plans to Increase Output," *Wall Street Journal,* April 18, 2002, p. A2.
102. Jeffrey McCracken and Alejandro Bodipo-Memba, "Ford Boss Takes Centre Stage to Rev GT40 Sales," *Edmonton Journal,* February 26, 2002, p. H30.
103. Danny Hakim, "The Next Spokesman to Put a Human Face on Ford," *New York Times,* February 20, 2002, p. C8.
104. Interview with William Clay Ford Jr., August 2002.
105. Ford Motor Company, "No Boundaries," press release, ad campaign transcripts, March 13, 2002, Ford Motor Company Archives.
106. Ford Motor Company, full-page magazine advertisement, *Entertainment Weekly,* August 24–31, 2001, p. 105.
107. Russ Devault, "Roush Mustang Pulls Out the Stops," *New York Post,* October 3, 2002, p. 55.
108. Ford Motor Company, full-page newspaper advertisement, *USA Today,* October 12, 2002, p. 5C.
109. Greg Schneider, "Ford Invents the Model Two: The Firm That Got America Rolling Was Desperate for Customers," *Washington Post,* October 27, 2002.
110. Ibid.
111. "Vegas Dealers Flip for Ford Freestyle," press release, October 8, 2002, Ford Motor Company, Ford Motor Company Archives.
112. Author interview with William Clay Ford Jr., July 2002, Dearborn, Michigan.

EPILOGUE

1. Author interview with William Clay Ford Jr., July 2002, Dearborn, Michigan.
2. Bill McGraw, "A Model Vehicle," *Detroit Free Press,* May 7, 2001.
3. Interview with William Clay Ford Jr., July 2002.
4. Ibid.
5. Ford Motor Company and Arab Americans file (quotes from workers), Ford Motor Company Archives, Dearborn, Michigan.
6. Ed Wallace, "The Achievement Ford Wants to Forget," *Fort Worth Star-Telegram,* August 20, 2002.
7. "2005 Ford F-150 to Be Built at New Dearborn Truck Plant," press release, November 8, 2002, Ford Motor Company.
8. Interview with William Clay Ford Jr., July 2002.
9. Barry Lynn, "Unmade in America: The True Cost of a Global Assembly Line," *Harper's,* June 2002, pp. 33–40.
10. Author interview with Peter Pestillo, October 2002, Dearborn, Michigan.
11. Roman Krygier, "Manufacturing Flexibility" (memo), November 18, 2002, Ford Motor Company.
12. "Ford Implements All-New, Next Generation Flexible Vehicle Assembly" (internal memo), Ford Motor Company Archives, Dearborn, Michigan.
13. Interview with William Clay Ford Jr., July 2002.

SELECTED BIBLIOGRAPHY

When I first submitted the bibliography of *Wheels for the World* to Viking it was nearly one hundred pages long. Predictably my editor, Molly Stern, squawked. After all, our goal was to tell the history of Ford Motor Company in a single, reader-friendly volume, and the bibliography would have pushed our page count perilously close to the one-thousand page mark—the point where reviewers deem the book a "tome" and make doorstop jokes. Instead, I offer this brief suggested reading list, along with a breakdown of the major archival collections consulted in writing *Wheels for the World,* with the understanding that specific textural references can best be found in the endnotes. Once again, it's worth mentioning that the "Reminiscences" housed at the Henry Ford Museum and Library and the more recent "Oral Histories" maintained at Ford Motor Company Archives (both in Dearborn, Michigan) proved to be my most indispensable primary source material. And the *Detroit News* and *Free Press* must also be mentioned. Over the decades the reporters of these venerable institutions have covered the automobile industry with determined vigilance. Constantly, I've relied on their sterling newspaper coverage to better comprehend the Big Three.

ARCHIVES

Automotive Hall of Fame, Dearborn, Michigan
Benson Ford Research Center, Henry Ford Museum & Greenfield Village, Dearborn, Michigan
Bentley Historical Library of the University of Michigan, Ann Arbor, Michigan
Burton Historical Collection of the Detroit Public Library
Dick Skinner Collection, Henry Ford Heritage Collection, Dearborn, Michigan
Edsel and Eleanor Ford Archives, Grosse Pointe Shores, Michigan
Edsel B. Ford Design History Center, Dearborn, Michigan
Fair Lane Archives, Dearborn, Michigan
Ford Motor Company Archives, Dearborn, Michigan
Franklin D. Roosevelt Library, Hyde Park, New York
Henry Ford "Celebrity" File, Photographic Department, Ford Motor Company, Dearborn, Michigan
Papers of Admiral Richard E. Byrd, The Ohio State University Byrd Polar Research Center Archival Program, Columbus, Ohio
Piquette Plant Preservation Project Archive, Henry Ford Heritage Association, Dearborn, Michigan
Robert Frank Collection, National Archives, Washington, D.C.
Ronald Reagan Library, Simi Valley, California
The Rotunda File, Ford Corporate Archives, Dearborn, Michigan
Tuskegee Institute Archives, Tuskegee, Alabama
Walter Reuther Library, Wayne State University, Dearborn, Michigan

BOOKS

Abraham, Nabeel, and Andrew Shryock, eds. *Arab Detroit: From Margin to Mainstreams.* Detroit: Wayne State University Press, 2000.

Ambrose, Stephen E. *Wild Blue: The Men and Boys Who Flew the B-24s over Germany.* New York: Simon & Schuster, 2001.

Bailey, L. Scott. *The American Car Since 1775.* New York: E.P. Dutton, 1971.

Barnard, Harry. *Independent Man: The Life of James Couzens.* New York: Charles Scribner's Sons, 1958.

Barnard, John. *Walter Reuther and the Rise of the Auto Workers.* Boston: Little, Brown, 1983.

Barr, Nancy Watson. *Truth, Memory, and the American Working-Class City: Robert Frank in Detroit and at the Rouge.* Detroit: Bulletin of the Detroit Institute of Arts, 2002.

Barris, George, and David Fetherstone. *Barris: TV and Movie Cars.* Osceola, Wis.: Motorbooks International, 1996.

Beasley, Norman. *Knudsen: A Biography.* New York: Whittlesey House, 1947.

Bennett, Harry. *We Never Called Him Henry.* New York: Fawcett, 1951.

Benson, Allan L. *The New Henry Ford.* New York: Funk & Wagnalls, 1923.

Berg, A. Scott. *Lindbergh.* New York: Putnam, 1998.

Best Ford Jokes. New York: Haldeman-Julius Company, 1927.

Bonsall, Thomas E. *Disaster in Dearborn: The Story of the Edsel.* Stanford, Calif.: Stanford University Press, 2002.

———. *The Lincoln Motorcar: The Complete History of an American Classic.* Baltimore: Stony Run Press, 1980.

———. *Lincoln: Seventy Years of Fine Car Heritage.* Baltimore: Stony Run Press, 1992.

———. *Seventy-five Years of Lincoln.* Baltimore: Turning Point Publishing, 1995.

Brauer, Norman. *There to Breathe the Beauty.* Dalton, Pa.: Norman Brauer Publications, 1995.

Bryan, Ford R. *Beyond the Model T: The Other Ventures of Henry Ford.* Rev. ed. Detroit: Wayne State University Press, 1997.

———. *Clara: Mrs. Henry Ford.* Dearborn, Mich.: Ford Books, 2001.

———. *Forays and Foibles.* Detroit: Wayne State University Press, 2002.

———. *The Fords of Dearborn: An Illustrated History.* Rev. ed. Detroit: Harlo Press, 1989.

———. *Henry's Attic: Some Fascinating Gifts to Henry Ford and His Museum.* Dearborn, Mich.: Ford Books, 1995.

———. *Henry's Lieutenants.* Detroit: Wayne State University Press, 1993.

Bryne, John A. *The Whiz Kids.* New York: Doubleday, 1993.

Bunn, Don. *Classic Ford F-Series Pickup Trucks,1948–1956.* Osceola, Wis.: Motorbooks International, 1998.

Burgess-Wise, David. *Complete Catalogue of Ford Cars in Britain.* Devon, England: Bay View Books, 1991.

———. *The History of the Automobile.* London: W.H. Smith, 1985.

Burlingame, Roger. *Henry Ford.* New York: Alfred A. Knopf, 1955.

Catton, Bruce. *Michigan: A History.* New York: W.W. Norton, 1984.

Chandler, Alfred D., Jr., and Herman Daems, eds. *Managerial Hierarchies: Comparative Perspectives on the Rise of Modern Industrial Enterprise.* Cambridge, Mass.: Harvard University Press, 1980.

Collier, Peter, and David Horowitz. *The Fords: An American Epic.* New York: Summit Books, 1987.

Conot, Robert. *American Odyssey.* New York: William Morrow, 1974.

Cray, Edward. *Chrome Colossus: General Motors and Its Times.* New York: McGraw-Hill, 1980.

Curcio, Vincent. *Chrysler: The Life and Times of an Automotive Genius.* New York: Oxford University Press, 2000.

Dominguez, Henry. *Edsel Ford and E. T. Gregorie.* Warrendale, Pa.: Society of Automotive Engineers, 1999.

Drucker, Peter F. *Adventures of a Bystander.* New York: Harper & Row, 1979.

———. *Management: Tasks, Responsibilities, Practices.* New York: Harper & Row, 1974.

———. *The Practice of Management.* New York: Harper Brothers, 1954.

Ervin, Spenser. *Henry Ford vs. Truman H. Newberry: The Famous Senate Election Contest.* New York: Richard R. Smith, 1935.

Factory Firsts from Ford. Detroit: Ford Motor Company, 1915.

Facts from Ford. Highland Park, Mich.: Ford Motor Company, 1920.

Flink, James J. *The Automobile Age.* Cambridge, Mass.: MIT Press, 1988.

Ford at Fifty. New York: Simon & Schuster, 1953.

Ford, Henry. *Edison as I Know Him.* New York: Cosmopolitan Book Corporation, 1930.

Ford, Henry, with Samuel Crowther. *My Life and Work.* Garden City, N.Y.: Doubleday, 1923.

———. *Today and Tomorrow.* Garden City, N.Y.: Doubleday, Page and Company, 1926.

Ford, Henry, interviewed by Fay Leone Faurote. *My Philosophy of Industry.* New York: Coward-McCann, 1929.

Funny Stories About the Ford. 2 vols. Hamilton, Ohio: Presto Publishing, 1915.

Galbraith, John Kenneth. *The Liberal Hour.* Boston: Houghton-Mifflin, 1960.

Gelderman, Carol. *Henry Ford: The Wayward Capitalist.* New York: Dial, 1981.

Graves, Ralph H. *The Triumph of an Idea: The Story of Henry Ford.* Garden City, N.Y.: Doubleday, Doran, 1935.

Greenleaf, William. *From These Beginnings: The Early Philanthropies of Henry and Edsel Ford, 1911–1936.* Detroit: Wayne State University Press, 1964.

———. *Monopoly on Wheels: Henry Ford and the Selden Automobile Patent.* Detroit: Wayne State University Press, 1961.

Halberstam, David. *The Best and the Brightest.* New York: Random House, 1972.

———. *The Reckoning.* New York: William Morrow, 1986.

Hawkins, Ferry W. *The Buildings of Detroit: A History.* Detroit: Wayne State University Press, 1980.

Hayes, Walter. *Henry: A Life of Henry Ford II.* New York: Grove Weidenfeld, 1990.

Hendry, Maurice. *Lincoln: America's Car of State.* New York: Ballantine, 1971.

Henry, Leslie R. *Henry's Fabulous Model A.* Los Angeles: Clymer Publications, 1959.

Hildebrand, Grant. *Designing for Industry: The Architecture of Albert Kahn.* Cambridge, Mass.: MIT Press, 1974.

Hofstadter, Richard. *The Age of Reform: From Bryan to F.D.R.* New York: Alfred A. Knopf, 1955.

Iacocca, Lee, with Sonny Kleinfield. *Talking Straight.* New York: Bantam Books, 1988.

Iacocca, Lee, with William Novak. *Iacocca.* New York: Bantam Books, 1984.

Israel, Paul. *Edison: A Life of Invention.* New York: John Wiley & Sons, 1998.

Josephson, Matthew. *Edison: A Biography.* New York: McGraw-Hill, 1959.

Kanigel, Robert. *The One Best Way: Frederick Winslow Taylor and the Enigma of Efficiency.* New York: Viking, 1997.

Keats, John. *The Insolent Chariots.* Philadelphia: J.B. Lippincott, 1958.

Keller, Maryann. *Rude Awakening: The Rise, Fall, and Struggle to Recovery for General Motors.* New York: William Morrow, 1993.

Kennedy, David. *Freedom from Fear: The American People in Depression and War, 1929–1945.* New York: Oxford University Press, 1999.

Klein, Maury. *Rainbow's End: The Crash of 1929.* New York: Oxford University Press, 2002.

Lacey, Robert. *Ford: The Men and the Machine.* Boston: Little, Brown, 1986.

Leland, Ottilie M., with Minnie Dubbs Millbrook. *Master of Precision: Henry M. Leland.* 2d ed. Detroit: Wayne State University Press, 1996.

Lewis, David L. *Ford Country.* 2d ed. Sidney, Ohio: Amos Press, 1999.

———. *The Public Image of Henry Ford: An American Folk Hero and His Company.* Detroit: Wayne State University Press, 1976. Reprint, 1987.

Lewis, David L., and Lawrence Goldstein, eds. *The Automobile and American Culture.* Ann Arbor, Mich.: University of Michigan Press, 1980.

Marnham, Patrick. *Dreaming with His Eyes Open: A Life of Diego Rivera.* New York: Alfred A. Knopf, 1998.

Marquis, Samuel S. *Henry Ford: An Interpretation.* Boston: Little, Brown, 1923.

McCalley, Bruce W. *Model T Ford: The Car That Changed the World.* Iola, Wis.: Krause Publications, 1994.

McManus, Theodore F., and Norman Beasley. *Men, Money and Motors: A Drama of the Automobile.* New York: Harper Brothers, 1929.

McMurry, Linda O. *George Washington Carver: Scientist and Symbol.* New York: Oxford University Press, 1981.

McNairn, William, and Marjorie McNairn. *Quotations from the Unusual Henry Ford.* Norwalk, Calif.: Stockton Trade Press, 1978.

Meier, August, and Elliott Rudwick. *Black Detroit and the Rise of the U.A.W.* New York: Oxford University Press, 1979.

Meyer, Stephen, III. *The Five Dollar Day.* Albany, N.Y.: State University of New York Press, 1981.

Miller, Ray, and Bruce McCalley. *From Here to Obscurity: An Illustrated History of the Model T Ford, 1909–1927.* Avalon, Calif.: Evergreen Press, 1971.

Montgomery, Davis. *The Fall of the House of Labor: The Workplace, the State, and American Labor, 1865–1925.* Cambridge: Cambridge University Press, 1987.

Nevins, Allan, and Frank Ernest Hill. *Ford.* 3 vols. New York: Charles Scribner's Sons, 1954–1962.

Parris, Michael. *Fords of the Fifties.* Tucson, Ariz.: California Bill's, 2000.

Patton, Phil. *Bug: The Strange Mutations of the World's Most Famous Automobile.* New York: Simon & Schuster, 2002.

Pitrone, Jean Maddern. *Tangled Web: The Legacy of Auto Pioneer John F. Dodge.* Hamtramck, Mich.: Avenue Publishing, 1989.

Rae, John B. *The American Automobile.* Chicago: University of Chicago Press, 1965.

———. *The American Automobile Industry.* Boston: G.K. Hall, 1984.

Rivera, Diego. *My Art, My Life.* New York: Citadel Press, 1960.

Scharff, Virginia. *Taking the Wheel: Women and the Coming of the Motor Age.* New York: Free Press, 1991.

Sheller, Roscoe. *Me and the Model T.* Portland, Ore.: Binford & Mort, 1965.

Sinclair, Upton. *The Flivver King: A Story of Ford-America.* New York: Phaedra, 1969.

Sloan, Alfred P., Jr. *My Years with General Motors.* Edited by John McDonald and Catherine Stevens. Garden City, N.Y.: Doubleday, 1964.

Sloan, Alfred P., Jr., with Boyden Sparkes. *Adventures of a White-Collar Man.* Garden City, N.Y.: Doubleday, Doran, 1941.

Sorensen, Charles E., with Samuel T. Williamson. *My Forty Years with Ford.* New York: W.W. Norton, 1956.

Sward, Keith. *The Legend of Henry Ford.* New York: Rinehart, 1948.

Tedlow, Richard S. *Giants of Enterprise: Seven Business Innovators and the Empires They Built.* New York: HarperBusiness, 2001.

UAW—Ford: Sixty Years of Progress 1941–2001. Detroit: UAW-Ford National Programs Center, 2001.

Walton, Mary. *Car: A Drama of the American Workplace.* New York: W.W. Norton, 1997.

Weisberger, Bernard A. *The Dream Maker: William C. Durant, Founder of General Motors.* Boston: Little, Brown, 1979.

Whyte, Andrew. *Jaguar.* Cambridge: Patrick Stephens, 1980.

Wik, Reynold M. *Henry Ford and Grass-roots America.* Ann Arbor, Mich.: University of Michigan Press, 1972.

Wilkins, Mira, and Frank Ernest Hill. *American Business Abroad: Ford on Six Continents.* Detroit: Wayne State University Press, 1964.

Winnewisser, Peter. *The Legendary Model A Ford.* Iola, Wis.: Krause Publications, 1999.

Yergin, Daniel. *The Prize: The Epic Quest for Oil, Money and Power.* New York: Simon & Schuster, 1991.

Zinn, Howard. *A People's History of the United States.* New York: Harper & Row, 1980.

NEWSPAPERS AND PERIODICALS

Air and Space; American Quarterly; American Magazine; The American Mercury; Annals of the American Academy of Political and Social Science; Army Ordnance; Atlantic Monthly; Audacity; The Automobile; Automobile Quarterly; Automobile Review; Automobile Topics; Automotive Industries; Automotive News; Aviation; Boston Globe; Boston News Bureau; Business Week; Canadian Business; Car and Driver; Chicago Daily News; Chicago Sun-Times; Chicago Tribune; Cleveland

Plain Dealer; Collier's; Consumer Research; Cosmopolitan; Current Opinion; Cycle and Automobile Trade Journal; Dallas Times-Herald; Dearborn Press; Desert Sun; Detroit Evening News; Detroit Free Press; Detroit Journal; Detroit News; Detroit Saturday Night; Detroit Times; Don's Review; Ebony; Edmonton Journal; Entertainment Weekly; Europe; Everybody's; Financial World; Flint Journal; Forbes; Forbes ASAP; Ford Buyer's Guide; The Ford Legend; Ford Life; Ford News; Ford Science Front; Ford Times; Fortune; The Forum; Forward; Harper's; Harvard Business Review; Hearst's International; Hour; Industrial Management Magazine; Insight on the News; Investor's Business; Iowa Review; Iron Trade Review; Jerusalem Post; Life; Lincoln Herald; Lincoln-Mercury News Bureau; Literary Digest; Look; Los Angeles Times; MacLean's; Mergers and Acquisitions; Michigan Business Review; Michigan Chronicle; Michigan History; Michigan Jewish History; Michigan Manufacturer and Financial Record; Milwaukee Journal-Sentinel; Motor Trend; The Nation; Nation's Business; Newark News; New Orleans Times-Picayune; The New Republic; Newsweek; The New Yorker; New York Evening Post; New York Post; New York Review of Books; New York Times; New York Herald-Tribune; New Zealand Fordist; North American Review; Outlook; Parade; Philadelphia Inquirer; Pittsburgh Post-Gazette; Popular Science; Printer's Ink; Public Relations Newswire; Redbook; Road & Track; Rouge News; Sales Management; St. Louis Post-Dispatch; Saturday Evening Post; Scribner's; Smithsonian; Solidarity; Special Interest Automobile; Sports Illustrated; Steel; System; Time; The Times (London); U.S.A. Today; U.S. Auto Scene; U.S. Bureau of Labor Statistics Monthly Review; U.S. News & World Report; Valdosta (Ga.) Times; Vancouver Sun; Vanity Fair; Wall Street Journal; Washington Post; Washington Post Magazine; Working Woman; World's Work; Worth.

INDEX